Criminal Psychology
Nature, Nurture, Culture

ABOUT THE AUTHOR

Laurence Miller, Ph.D. is a psychologist in Boca Raton, Florida, specializing in clinical psychology, neuropsychology, forensic psychology, police psychology, and business psychology. In addition to maintaining a full-time psychotherapy practice, Dr. Miller is a consulting psychologist for the West Palm Beach Police Department, the Palm Beach County Sheriff's Office, and Troop L of the Florida Highway Patrol. Dr. Miller also consults with local, regional, and national law enforcement agencies on cases involving law enforcement stress, officer misconduct, fitness for duty, work-related disability, psychological services for police officers and their families, and law enforcement management and administration.

Dr. Miller is a court-appointed forensic psychological examiner for the Palm Beach County Criminal, Juvenile, and Family Court, and he serves as an independent expert witness in civil and criminal cases involving brain injury, traumatic stress syndromes, psychological disorders, civil and criminal competencies, criminal culpability, workplace violence and harassment, workplace stress, psychological disability, fitness for duty, and personal injury.

Dr. Miller is an adjunct professor at Florida Atlantic University and at Palm Beach State College, where he teaches courses in abnormal psychology, neuropsychology, forensic psychology, criminal psychology, police psychology, business psychology, and clinical psychology. He is also an adjunct instructor at the Criminal Justice Institute-Police Academy of Palm Beach County, where he has taught courses in law enforcement stress management and law enforcement crisis intervention. In addition, Dr. Miller conducts training seminars and continuing education programs regionally and nationally on topics pertaining to the brain, health, law, psychology, and organizational management.

Dr. Miller is the author of over 300 publications, including books, book chapters, professional journal articles, popular publications, and online resources. He is the editor of the *International Journal of Emergency Mental Health* and serves as a peer reviewer for several other professional journals. He is a frequent guest on regional, national, and international radio and television, and serves as a script and media consultant to television shows and movies. Dr. Miller writes the *Practical Police Psychology* column (policeone.com/columnists/laurence-miller/) on the <u>PoliceOne.com</u> website. He is also a musician and performs at local venues as time allows.

Dr. Miller can be reached at 561-392-8881 or at docmilphd@aol.com.

Books by Laurence Miller, Ph.D.

Inner Natures: Brain, Self, and Personality. St. Martin's Press, 1990.
Freud's Brain: Neuropsychodynamic Foundations of Psychoanalysis. Guilford, 1991.
Psychotherapy of the Brain-Injured Patient: Reclaiming the Shattered Self. Norton, 1993.
Shocks to the System: Psychotherapy of Traumatic Disability Syndromes. Norton, 1998.
Practical Police Psychology: Stress Management and Crisis Intervention for Law Enforcement. Charles C Thomas, 2006.
METTLE: Mental Toughness Training for Law Enforcement. Looseleaf Law Publications, 2008.
Counseling Crime Victims: Practical Strategies for Mental Health Professionals. Springer, 2008.
From Difficult to Disturbed: Understanding and Managing Dysfunctional Employees. Amacom, 2008.

CRIMINAL PSYCHOLOGY

NATURE, NURTURE, CULTURE

A Textbook and Practical Reference Guide for Students and
Working Professionals in the Fields of Law Enforcement,
Criminal Justice, Mental Health, and Forensic Psychology

By

LAURENCE MILLER, PH.D.

CHARLES C THOMAS • PUBLISHER, LTD.
Springfield • Illinois • U.S.A.

Published and Distributed Throughout the World by

CHARLES C THOMAS • PUBLISHER, LTD.
2600 South First Street
Springfield, Illinois 62704

© 2012 by CHARLES C THOMAS • PUBLISHER, LTD.

ISBN 978-0-398-08715-9 (hard)
ISBN 978-0-398-08716-6 (ebook)

Library of Congress Catalog Card Number: 2011036337

With THOMAS BOOKS *careful attention is given to all details of manufacturing
and design. It is the Publisher's desire to present books that are satisfactory as to their
physical qualities and artistic possibilities and appropriate for their particular use.*
THOMAS BOOKS *will be true to those laws of quality that assure a good name
and good will.*

Printed in China
MM-R-3

Library of Congress Cataloging-in-Publication Data

Miller, Laurence, 1951–
 Criminal psychology : nature, nurture, culture : a textbook and practical referene guide for students and working professionals in the fields
of law enforcement, criminal justice, mental health, and forensic
psychology / Laurence Miller.
 p. cm.
 Includes bibliographical references and index.
 ISBN 978-0-398-08715-9 (hard) -- ISBN 978-0-398-08716-6 (ebook)
 1. Criminal psychology. 2. Criminal psychology--Textbooks. 3.
Criminal psychology--United States. I. Title.

 HV6080.M55 2012
 364.3--dc23
                                          2011036337

To
My colleagues, students,
friends, and family

Preface

Imagine two twins, separated at birth, pursuing independent but parallel educations and careers, only to discover in middle age that they've been working side-by-side in adjoining offices their whole lives, toiling over the same project, occasionally exchanging a few words and ideas, but never realizing their common bond or their full potential for productive collaboration. This pretty much describes the current relationship between the fields of psychology and criminal justice. Both twins are preoccupied with the nuances of human thought, emotion, intention, volition, behavioral expression, and self-control. Both of these siblings recognize that a deep understanding of human motivation as it applies to health and disease, crime and justice, individuals and societies, is essential in order to formulate accurate theoretical models of the human mind because these often have immediate and important consequences for real people's lives.

Criminal Psychology: Nature, Nurture, Culture endeavors to arrange a family reunion by introducing readers to the foundations of criminal psychology as it is understood and practiced from the research lab and classroom to the police beat and courtroom. This text offers a comprehensive, yet assimilable, review of the field of criminal psychology and, at the same time, can serve as a practical reference guide for working professionals in the fields of law enforcement, criminal justice, mental health, and forensic psychology. The title, *Criminal Psychology* is chosen quite purposefully: to make a full contribution to the broad field of criminal justice, psychology must go beyond dry, superficial descriptions of criminal behavior, in order to seek an understanding of the complex causal biopsychosocial dynamics of crime, because only in this way can our civilization develop the tools and strategies to control it.

Recent years have seen an explosion of interest among students in the field of forensic science, including behavioral forensic science. Movies, television shows, books, CDs, DVDs, and Internet websites present a constant stream of information on criminal profiling, special victims units, serial homicide, sex offenders, terrorism, hate crimes, and mass violence. In addition, attorneys, judges, mental health professionals, and forensic examiners are looking for authoritative, yet practical, information that can guide their work with the more common cases of robbery, assault, family violence, child abuse, sex offenses, and juvenile crime that comprise their caseloads. Thus far, academia is struggling to keep up; in fact, my own experience has been that the student demand for quality training in these areas far exceeds the supply.

For many years, I've taught undergraduate and graduate courses in Abnormal Psychology, Neuropsychology, Business Psychology, and Clinical Psychology. In these courses, I've often introduced forensic applications of these topics, and found that this invariably whetted students' appetites for broader and deeper knowledge in this area. Several years ago, I developed and began teaching several new courses at Florida Atlantic University and Palm Beach State College, one in Police Psychology, another in Criminal Psychology, and a third in Forensic Psychology. My dilemma was to find appropriate texts for these courses.

In the case of Police Psychology, I solved the problem by writing my own text. *Practical Police Psychology: Stress Management and Crisis Intervention for Law Enforcement* began as a manual for law enforcement personnel, but quickly expanded from materials I had been using to teach this class at the Palm Beach County Police Academy to an academic textbook accessible to students and practitioners in psychology, law enforcement, criminal justice, and public safety. For the Forensic Psychology course, there appear to already exist a few workmanlike texts to choose from, but my own contribution is a possible project for the future. As for the Criminal Psychology course, there are a few existing texts on "Criminal Behavior" on the market, but I've found them unsatisfying in terms of their organization and coverage of topics–at least with respect to how I want to teach this subject.

Criminal Psychology: Nature, Nurture, Culture is a comprehensive integration of psychology and criminal justice than can be utilized for graduate and advanced undergraduate courses in Criminal Psychology, Forensic Psychology, Abnormal Psychology, and Criminal Justice. It can also be used as a handbook and reference source for clinical and forensic psychologists, mental health practitioners, attorneys, judges, law enforcement, and military personnel.

This book is predicated on two fundamental concepts. First, to understand any kind of human phenomena, it is essential to go beyond observable behavior to study the way people actually think and feel, to understand what drives those inner mental states, and to be able to discern what consequences they have for the persons themselves and those around them. Indeed, the crucial legal questions that both psychology and criminology attempt to address–competency to stand trial, sanity or insanity at the time of the offense, prediction of future dangerousness, among others–all rely on a precise understanding of the biological, psychological, and social forces affecting a given defendant, not simply a description of his or her behavior.

Second, any theory or model that explains abnormal behavior–including criminal behavior–must be able to explain normal behavior. That is, a cardiologist diagnoses low blood pressure or hypertension because she knows the scientifically established reference ranges for normal blood pressure. A psychologist makes an assessment of mental retardation or giftedness because he knows where on the scientifically validated bell-curve of intelligence this particular subject falls. Similarly, when we ask why a given person's behavior is sufficiently impulsive, aggressive, psychotic, deceptive, predatory, manipulative, callous, nonreflective, and/or violent to be called "criminal," we must understand what are the normal reference ranges of these traits that keep most of us out of trouble. Thus, continuity between the normal and abnormal is a fundamental basis for understanding any natural phenomenon, including human behavior.

As an instructional text, this book is organized around the way I teach my courses. First, I believe that knowledge–any knowledge–that has practical, real-world applications and that affects the lives of real people, must be based on the highest standards of authoritative research and scholarship. In their daily practice, forensic psychologists will be asked to conceptualize why a given defendant is or is not competent to stand trial, how the standards of the insanity defense may or may not apply to another defendant, or whether a third defendant is or is not sufficiently dangerous to warrant early parole or involuntary civil commitment. They may also be asked if the unique configuration of elements at a crime scene can contribute to developing a psychological profile of a sexual homicide perpetrator, or whether an existing institutional policy is sufficient to prevent, respond, and recover from an incident of school violence, workplace violence, or terrorist attack. This cannot be done without a solid foundation of scientific knowledge. Therefore, this text is built on psychological and criminological sources that have been researched and validated as thoroughly as possible.

Second, whether trying to learn a new subject myself or encouraging students to absorb, retain, understand, and master a new domain of knowledge, I have always found it especially effective to present the material from more than one perspective. Done right, this kind of 360-degree learning model yields not redundancy, but integration and consolidation of knowledge. Thus, this book is organized into five sections. Part I examines the nature and origins of criminal behavior. These chapters outline the role of psychology in the criminal justice system, and review the biology, psychology, and sociology of crime to develop a naturalistic model of criminal behavior in the context of past and contemporary human societies. Then the practical applications of this model to forensic psychology, mental health treatment, law enforcement, and criminal justice are outlined, setting the stage for the more detailed discussions in the chapters to follow.

Part II examines the major classes of mental disorder that may be associated with criminal behavior. The structure of each chapter consists of a description of the syndrome, followed by applications to law enforcement, criminal justice, and forensic mental health. This includes initial law enforcement contact, criminal competencies, insanity defense and mitigation, adjudication in the criminal justice system, sentencing and corrections, and mental health treatment options. Topics covered include organic brain syndromes, psychoses and schizophrenia, anxiety and mood disorders, personality disorders, and a special consideration of antisocial personality disorder and the psychopath.

Part III deals with death. The topics include homicide, multiple homicide, serial homicide, and mass homicide, including serial killing, workplace and school violence, and terrorism. Part IV covers sexual offenses and crimes within the family, including rape and sexual assault, sex crimes against children, family violence, child battery, domestic violence, and family homicide. In Part V, the psychological perspective on a variety of crimes is considered, including stalking and harassment, theft and robbery, gang violence, organized crime, arson, hate crimes, and the psychology of corrections and the death penalty.

Sidebars, or Boxes, within each chapter illustrate that chapter's topics with examples from the media, or explore in-depth applications of, or controversies surrounding, particular topics in criminal psychology, e.g., whether juveniles should be tried as adults, the validity and practicality of crime scene offender profiling, or the use of "designer defenses" in arguing cases. In some chapters, certain material is organized into Tables for easy reference. Throughout each chapter, case examples from the professional literature, the news media, and the author's own clinical and forensic psychology practice are used to illustrate the concepts and applications discussed in this book.

Most students quickly come to realize that, once you've penetrated the subject of any domain of knowledge, you begin to understand how much more there is to learn about the topic. Indeed, each of this book's chapters–indeed, each subtopic–could easily be expanded to a text of its own. My deep hope is that students utilizing this text in an undergraduate or graduate Criminal Psychology, Forensic Psychology, Abnormal Psychology, Criminal Justice, or similar course will be stimulated and energized to go beyond the material offered here, to research further details and develop their own ideas. To facilitate further exploration, **terms** and **phrases** of unique or important interest appear in **boldface** throughout the text. Additionally, extended research will be aided by this volume's extensive bibliography. Only by building on what we know and expanding it will knowledge advance in the twin fields of Psychology and Criminal Justice–knowledge that directly impacts the lives of real people every single day.

So many roads and signposts have guided this project toward its final destination that I can only summarize the acknowledgments here. Some of the material for this book was initially developed in the pages of many journals and publications, and in Internet web columns, particularly the *International Journal of Emergency Mental Health, Journal of Offender Therapy and Comparative Criminology,* and the *Practical Police Psychology* web column on the PoliceOne.com website. Additionally, a good deal of this volume's content has been "field tested" in multiple classrooms and courses at Florida Atlantic University and Palm Beach State College. Sharp students continue to keep me on my toes with regard to accuracy and usefulness of course content, as well as clarity and comprehensibility of teaching style.

My work with the men and women of the West Palm Beach Police Department, Palm Beach County Sheriff's Office, and Troop L of the Florida Highway Patrol has given me a street-level perspective on the daily practice of law enforcement and criminal justice. Similarly, working on cases with the attorneys and judges at the 15th Judicial Circuit Palm Beach County Court allows me to appreciate how fundamental issues of normal and abnormal psychology inform the criminal justice system every day.

I want to thank Mike Thomas, editor-in-chief of Charles C Thomas Publisher, for quickly adopting this project, which had its origins elsewhere, and for competently, courteously, and professionally expediting its publication. A special "Purple Heart" for copyediting goes to Claire Slagle, who stalwartly navigated the punishing terrain of this book's bibliography to assure that every single reference was accurate and properly placed. And, assuring that this volume is as esthetically pleasing to behold as it will hopefully prove edifying to read, my thanks to graphic designer Trevor Ollech for a cover design that evokes the deep historical, natural, and cultural themes that comprise the essence of this work. As always, the Thomas people are a pleasure to work with.

Finally, thanks once again to my family for their patience and support as I continue to spend innumerable hours sequestered in my grotto, constructing brick by brick yet another grand project. It is their foundation that allows these edifices to rise confidently and stand securely.

L.M.

Contents

xiii

PART III

THE HOMICIDES

PART IV

SEX CRIMES AND FAMILY CRIMES

PART V

OTHER CRIMES AND PUNISHMENTS

Criminal Psychology
Nature, Nurture, Culture

Part **I**

The Nature and Origins of Criminal Behavior

Why do people commit crimes? Why do some of these people commit so many crimes and seem to make a lifestyle of it? Professionals in all fields tend to view things from the perspective of their own familiar, comfortable domains of expertise. To the biochemist, a misbehaving human being is a bag of twisted molecules. To the sociologist, he is the product of group dynamics. The psychologist sees him as having been shaped by the events of his life, while the theologian worries about his unsaved soul. And, as the criminologist ponders how to punish and deter his wrongdoing, the dramatist enlists him as a metaphor for the injustices and hypocrisies of modern society. Accordingly, the theories and models of criminal behavior presented in Chapters 1–3 outline the role of psychology in the criminal justice system, and review the biology, psychology, and sociology of crime to develop a naturalistic model of criminal behavior in the context of past and contemporary human societies. We all come into this world hardwired with certain traits and dispositions. However, how these are expressed in our outward behavior is a product of a complex interaction among our genes, brains, families, and the cultures and societies we live in.

Chapter **1**

Psychology in the Criminal Justice System

The real significance of crime is in its being
a breach of faith with the community of
mankind.

– Joseph Conrad

WHAT IS CRIMINAL PSYCHOLOGY?

Criminal psychology is the application of the principles of normal and
abnormal psychology to the understanding, prediction, and control of
criminal behavior. It is a branch of **forensic psychology**, which is the theory and practice of psychology in matters pertaining to the law. Forensic psychology, in turn, is divided into **civil forensic psychology** and **criminal
forensic psychology**, paralleling the binary court structure in the **adversarial justice system** of the United States and other countries.

Civil courts deal with matters between citizens: contracts and wills,
divorce and custody, compensation claims and personal injury. In civil cases,
one party, the **plaintiff**, files a **lawsuit** against a second party, the **defendant**. The standard of proof in most civil cases is **preponderance of the
evidence**, that is, the jury deciding the case must only be more certain than
not about their verdict, which is generally interpreted as "just over 50 percent sure." The jury may find for the plaintiff or for the defendant; in many
jurisdictions, the losing side is responsible for paying court costs and other
fees.

In **criminal courts**, it is the state or the federal government who brings
a **criminal charge** against a citizen or organization for violating the law. The
accused party is still called the **defendant**, but the side bringing the charge
is the prosecution, whose legal representative is the **prosecutor**, **state attorney**, **district attorney**, or **federal attorney**. The standard of proof in most
criminal cases is **beyond a reasonable doubt**, which is usually interpreted
to mean "at least 90–95 percent sure." If the jury finds for the prosecution's
side, the defendant is **convicted**. If they find for the defendant, he or she is

acquitted. In some cases where the victim or his/her family has suffered some compensable damage or loss, a civil suit will be filed following, or along with, the criminal charge (this process was made famous by the O.J. Simpson case).

In its practical applications, criminal psychology draws on **academic and experimental psychology** for the rich empirical database pertaining to mind, brain, law, and society. It also utilizes the principles of **clinical psychology** to develop improved models of diagnostic classification and treatment modalities for at-risk offenders. Also subsumed within, or connected to, the field of criminal psychology are the areas of **police psychology** and **law enforcement behavioral science** which apply principles of criminal psychology to interview and interrogation, crime scene analysis, and offender profiling. Finally, **criminology** is the branch of sociology that studies the causes and effects of crime in different societies and communities.

ICD, DSM and CCM

Clinicians of all specialties understand that, without a reliable and valid methodology and terminology of diagnosis, it becomes impossible for professionals to communicate meaningfully with one another and to render appropriate treatment. In medicine, the standard diagnostic handbook is the *International Statistical Classification of Diseases and Related Health Problems,* now in its 10th edition, known to medical personnel as *ICD-10.* In psychiatry and psychology, it is the *Diagnostic and Statistical Manual of Mental Disorders,* which has gone through many editions since its first publication in 1952, and now in its 6th edition, *DSM-IV-TR* (for "text revision," meaning no new classifications were added or deleted to the latest edition, only the wording of some diagnostic criteria have been changed; APA, 2000). *DSM-V* is scheduled for publication in 2013. A major conceptual and textual revision occurred in the 1980 *DSM-III,* with the introduction of **multiaxial diagnosis**, allowing clinicians to organize psychiatric assessment into five dimensions, or **axes**, with the intent of permitting a much more refined and comprehensive clinical picture (Table 1.1).

Partly in response to the mental health community's drive toward standardizing and regularizing psychological assessment and psychiatric diagnosis, the **Federal Bureau of Investigation (FBI)** began a 10-year project to similarly standardize classification of violent crimes, culminating in the 1992 *Crime Classification Manual: A Standard System for Investigating and Classifying Violent Crimes* (Douglas et al., 1992), or *CCM*. Again, not without controversy, this volume provides a common terminological and conceptual language for criminal investigators and criminal justice professionals

TABLE 1.1.
DSM-IV-TR MULTIAXIAL DIAGNOSTIC SYSTEM

Axis I: **Major mental disorders and clinical syndromes**, such as childhood disorders, organic brain syndromes, substance abuse disorders, psychotic disorders, mood disorders, anxiety disorders, impulse control disorders, somatoform disorders, psychophysiological disorders, sleep, eating, and sexual disorders, and others. *[handwritten: physical symptoms w/ unknown cause]*

Axis II: **Personality disorders and mental retardation**. A separate axis is devoted to these two classes of syndromes because they are believed to represent more stable, ingrained features of the person than the disorders on Axis I, although this conceptual distinction continues to be controversial.

Axis III: **Medical conditions and physical disorders** that may affect the conditions diagnosed on Axes I and II (e.g., hypertension and cardiovascular disease associated with multi-infarct dementia) or that may be unrelated to them (e.g., diabetes or arthritis co-existing with bipolar disorder).

Axis IV: **Psychosocial and environmental factors** contributing to the severity or expression of the disorder, or to the individual's overall coping abilities, including health problems, legal problems, educational and employment issues, or family problems.

Axis V: **Global Assessment of Functioning**, which is a numerical rating scale, from 0 to 100, for assessing how well the individual is handling the demands of everyday life presently and within the past year. Generally, most reasonably well-functioning people would score between 65 and 80, while a score below 55 is considered to represent significant difficulty in maintaining a functional lifestyle, and an even lower might indicate the effects of severe psychopathology.

to utilize in order to enhance the investigation and prosecution of violent criminals.

In fact, the present textbook generally follows the *DSM* and the *CCM*. The first half of the text describes clinical syndromes associated with criminal behavior, and the second half flips the perspective to discuss categories of crime in the context of both normal psychology and psychopathology. Two basic tenets of the present text are:

Any theory that explains *abnormal* behavior must be able to explain *normal* behavior. Just as an understanding of heart disease is predicated on first understanding how the normal cardiovascular system works, so do the principles of normal cognitive, clinical, and neuropsychology enable us to make sense of syndromes of abnormal thinking and behavior, including those that lead to those actions society labels as criminal behavior.

The presence or absence of a diagnosable mental condition does not by itself make a legal determination. Forensic psychological analysis involves much more than simply making a diagnosis–that's what a clini-

[handwritten left margin: In order to be abnormal, normality needs to be defined]

[handwritten bottom right: less about a diagnosis, more about understanding brain space]

cal psychologist does, and it is only the first step in answering a legal question. The crucial second step entails making the <u>connection between the mental disorder or condition in question and the legal issue being considered.</u> Did the subject with schizophrenia kill his workmate because of a psychotic delusion or because he was mad at him for stealing his promotion? Is the mentally retarded and learning disabled defendant automatically incompetent to stand trial or can she understand the relevant legal criteria and assist in her own defense? Does the brutal nature of the defendant's single crime indicate that he is a poor risk for conditional early release or should we remand him to outpatient treatment and give him a second chance in life? These are all issues that can only be addressed by experts with knowledge of *both* psychology and the law.

[handwritten margin note: Does psychology play into the crime?]

THE CRIMINAL JUSTICE SYSTEM

Psychological principles and practices have applications at several stages in the criminal justice process, as illustrated by the following summarized walk through the criminal justice system (Kitaeff, 2010; Melton et al., 1997; Roesch et al., 2011; Schmalleger, 2007; Wrightsman, 2001).

Arrest

Arrest is the entry point into the criminal justice system. An arrest can be made at the scene of a crime that is observed by a law enforcement officer, or based on a crime reported by a victim or other complainant, if there is sufficient evidence that the crime has taken place. In many cases, arrest is a discretionary decision by a police officer, although there are some crimes, such as domestic assault and battery (Chapter 17), where mandatory arrest laws apply. In some cases, usually involving minor crimes, police can issue a **Notice to Appear (NTA)**, sometimes called a **"summons,"** which orders the suspect to show up for a hearing. An arrest can also be made following an **investigation**, which may include interview and interrogation of a suspect and/or collection of other evidence. If the suspect is not already in custody, a **warrant** may be issued for his or her arrest. Arrest can occur peacefully or by force.

Miranda rights. Also referred to as the **Miranda warning**, this is familiar to everyone who watches TV cop and courtroom shows. It is named after the case of *Miranda v. Arizona,* where, in 1963, Ernesto Miranda was accused of kidnapping and rape, and confessed to the crime without being told that he did not have to speak or that he was entitled to have a lawyer present. At trial, Miranda's lawyer failed to get the confession thrown out, but in 1966

TABLE 1.2.
THE MIRANDA RIGHTS

You have the right to remain silent.

If you give up this right, anything you say can and will be used against you in a court of law.

You have the right to have an attorney present during questioning.

If you cannot afford an attorney, one will be provided for you free of charge.

If you choose to answer questions, you have the right to stop answering at any time.

Do you understand the rights I have just explained to you?

Do you wish to answer questions?

Do you want an attorney?

---

the Supreme ruled that the statements made to the police could not be used as evidence because Miranda had not been advised of his rights. Since then, before any questioning of a suspect by police, he or she must be "Mirandized," or "read his/her rights" (Table 1.2).

Miranda rights need only be read if the police want to question the suspect. In many cases, the arresting officers may clearly have observed the crime and arrested the suspect and have no need to ask any questions, in which case the Miranda rights may not have been read at all.

BOX 1.1. WHAT TO DO IF YOU'RE STOPPED BY THE POLICE

It's happened to me and it's happened to you: You're tooling down the road, pedal to the metal, when you see them—those swirling blue lights in your rearview mirror. So you pull over and wait for the officer to sidle up to your drivers' side window. If there is something suspicious about your car or your license plate, he/she may call for back-up. Whether confronted by the entire municipal police force or just your local neighborhood patrol cop, law enforcement officials, criminal justice experts, and criminal defense attorneys all agree on a few basic rules of engagement for citizens to make the encounter go as smoothly as possible.

Stay calm in your words and actions. Most police officers live and work by the dictum, "Safety first." Keep your hands visible, empty, and out of your pockets. Move slowly and try not to make any sudden gestures. Never attempt to touch a police officer—even a friendly shoulder pat can be interpreted as "assault on a LEO" (law enforcement officer). Calm, cool, and collected should be your guidelines for the encounter.

continued

BOX 1.1.—*Continued*

Be polite and respectful. Basic respect doesn't mean you have to fawn and grovel; just maintain the same demeanor of speech and action you would with a new neighbor or business partner—polite, civil, and dignified. This also doesn't mean you can't express your opinion about the encounter ("But officer, I really did see the light as yellow, not red, when I passed through it"), just watch your tone of voice to keep the situation from escalating.

Give only the information required. Typically, this consists of your name and address which, in a traffic stop, will come from your license and registration. Many officers will ask pedestrians or motorists, "Where are you going?" because a citizen who stumbles over the answer may be up to no good. Technically, you have the right to say, "I'm afraid that's none of your business, officer," but, especially if you've got nothing to hide, use your judgment and simply tell the officer that you're going to work, or headed home, or on your way to your kid's soccer game, and get it over with.

To search your person or your vehicle the police must have a warrant, or have probable cause that you committed a crime, or obtain your permission to do so. The officer will typically run your plates, to determine if you have any outstanding warrants. If not, he or she may do a walk around your vehicle and peer intently into your car's interior, looking for any suspicious evidence to create **probable cause** for a search. Failing that, if he's still not convinced you're a solid citizen, he may ask your permission to search you or your vehicle. It's up to you to either good-naturedly agree to this unwanted intrusion on your time and personal space or to respectfully decline, but the suspicion this engenders may lead the officer to give you and your vehicle one last once-over to see if there's *anything* he can pin on you. In most cases, this will be the end of it and you'll be on your way. Remember that if you *do* give the officer permission for a search and he *does* turn up something illegal, you can't argue later that the search was illegitimate. So use your judgment.

Two special considerations involve **firearms** and **medications**. First, in some jurisdictions it is perfectly legal to carry a handgun in your vehicle as long as you keep it concealed from open view; in other areas, a **concealed weapon license** is required. In either case, if you allow the officer to search you or your vehicle, let him know you have the weapon in the car *before* he finds it. Second, if you're carrying a legitimately prescribed narcotic medication on your person or in your vehicle, make sure it's in the prescription bottle with the label on it, or carry a copy of the prescription label with you to avoid being arrested for **possession of a controlled substance**.

If you feel the officer is abusing you, don't resist, but do remember. That doesn't mean don't question or don't object. You can ask why the officer is asking a particular question or why he is conducting some action: "Officer, is it necessary to throw around the stuff in my back seat like that?" "Do I have to stand out here in the rain?" But if you're being physically restrained or abused, don't physically resist, which will only result in an escalation of the unwanted contact. Instead, keep your wits about you and try to observe and remember as much as you can about what's going on, including the officer's physical description, name tag, badge number, police car number, and so on. As soon as you're able to do so safely, write this information down to help you retain and recall it. In general, the chances of overt abuse by officers, especially on traffic stops, is far less than it used to be because, increasingly, such police encounters are audio- or video-recorded, which most officers actually appreciate because it protects them against false accusations of police misconduct.

Keep your friends out of it. Advise any friends present that the best thing they can do for you is to stay silent and act as extra sets of eyes and ears. Remember that the officers don't know who anybody is, and the more potential trouble they detect, the more officers are likely to respond to the scene. So everybody stay calm, keep it simple, and don't give anybody a reason to overreact.

If you sustain injuries, record them. In the event that you actually suffer physical injuries at the hands of a police officer, and you have not been taken into custody, seek medical attention immediately to document the injuries and request that photographs be taken. If for some reason the medical staff won't do this, wait till you are able to, and take the pictures yourself. Also, this is where your Good Samaritan friends can help out, too—have them witness the injuries and/or take the pictures for you.

File a written complaint. If you feel your rights have been violated, file a written complaint with the police agency. Because most police departments depend in part on the cooperation and good will of the public in order to effectively do their jobs, they usually take these matters very seriously. Keep a copy of the complaint, and make sure a family member or close friend has a copy.

If you are arrested. Do not resist; if you do, then in addition to any other charges will be added **resisting arrest with violence** if you physically struggle or attack an officer, or **resisting arrest without violence** if you ignore or refuse to obey a command or passively resist by remaining immobile when ordered to move. You may be read your **Miranda rights** (Table 1.2) if the officer wants to question you. In general, it's better to invoke your right to remain silent and request a lawyer before any questioning in order to avoid inadvertently incriminating yourself. You will probably be handcuffed, searched, and taken to the police station or local jail for processing. This is *not* the time to threaten to sue or to file a complaint, or to tell the officers that your brother-in-law is on the City Council. At this point, *cooperation without self-incrimination* is your best policy. Get a lawyer and defend yourself.

Booking

After the arrest, the suspect is taken to the local police station or similar facility, where photos are taken (the **mug shot**) and the suspect is **fingerprinted**. Personal identifying data are recorded and the details of the charges are read to the suspect. The suspect is again advised of his rights and signs a form acknowledging this. An administrative record of the arrest is made, and the arresting officers prepare an **arrest report**. This document describes in detail what took place before, during, and after the arrest.

Initial Appearance

Within several hours the suspect is brought before a magistrate who reads the charges, again advises the suspect of his rights, and provides the opportunity for **setting bail**, or **posting bond**. This is a sum of money put in escrow by the court, which will be forfeited if the suspect flees or fails to appear for trial. There are two other possibilities: If the crime is not serious and the suspect is deemed to pose little risk of failing to show up for trial, he may be **released on his own recognizance** (**ROR**), that is, he remains free until he is summoned to appear for his trial. At the other extreme, the suspect may be **remanded to custody** if the magistrate believes that he is so great a flight risk that no sum of forfeited money will induce him to stick around for trial, or if the suspect simply lacks the funds to make bail (in most cases, the court will allow the suspect to actually put up 10% of the total bail amount, with the understanding that the remainder will be collected if the suspect **fails to appear**, or "**skips**").

Present at the initial appearance are usually the **prosecutor** or **district attorney** (**DA**) and the suspect's lawyer. If the defendant does not have a private lawyer (as many do not), it is at this point that a court-appointed defense attorney is assigned to the suspect. These **public defenders** (**PDs**) are attorneys, usually at the start of their careers, who are either employed by the court, or are outside contractors who are recruited from a roster of local attorneys who represent criminal cases.

Preliminary Hearing

This is the forum in which it is determined whether sufficient evidence exists to continue the criminal justice process for this case; that is, whether an actual crime has been committed and whether there is evidence that this defendant committed it. In some cases, this is done by the prosecutor filing an **information**, which is a document that outlines the legal and factual reasons why the DA thinks the case should proceed to trial. In other cases, the case is argued before a **grand jury**, which is a jury specifically convened to assess evidence concerning whether sufficient grounds exist to bring the case to trial (because it usually contains fewer members than the grand jury, the jury that actually tries the case is technically called the **petit jury**). If the grand jury believes the evidence is sufficient, it will issue an **indictment**.

Arraignment

This is the first appearance of the subject, now called a **defendant**, before the court that has the authority to conduct a trial. At the arraignment, the judge reads the indictment, again informs the defendant of his rights, and asks the defendant to enter a **plea**. The plea can be either **guilty**, **not guilty**, or **no contest** (**nolo contendre**), the latter meaning that the defendant does not admit guilt, but does not contest the charges against him. The judge has discretion to accept or reject any of these pleas, if he or she feels there is a compelling reason to do so. For most major crimes, somewhere between the arraignment and the trial, prosecutors and attorneys engage in the process of **plea bargaining**, in which the defendant may agree to plead guilty to a lesser but related charge carrying a reduced penalty, in exchange for sparing the court the effort and expense of a trial. Since a trial is the most time-consuming and labor-intensive activity within the criminal justice system, if the majority of cases were not plea-bargained, the criminal justice system would collapse under its own weight. Many factors go into the determination of the plea's details, including prior criminal history, assessments of future dangerousness, and the defendant's mental status and psychiatric history.

Adjudication

This is the trial itself. The 6th Amendment of the U.S. Constitution gives its citizens the right to a **trial by a jury of their peers**, with a few exceptions, including: (1) where the crime is a minor one in which the maximum sentence upon conviction would be less than 6 months; (2) where the defendant chooses to waive his right to a jury trial because he believes it would be in his interest to have the judge hear and decide the case–called a **bench trial** (because judges are spoken of as "sitting on the bench")–usually in cases where there are a lot of technical details or where the defense attorney believes it would be difficult to empanel a fair, impartial, or sympathetic jury; or (3) in juvenile court, which are almost always bench trials (see below).

Sentencing

In some jurisdictions, sentences are set by legal statute and judges have little to do but apply the law. In other jurisdictions, judges have discretion as to the nature and severity of sentences; even in these cases, there is a finite range of penalties that can be applied. A **suspended sentence** may be given for the first offense of a less serious crime, often when there is some mitigating circumstance, and usually with the condition that the convictee do something to address the problem that contributed to the crime, such as entering a drug treatment program, or to "pay society back" by performing some form of **community service**. In **probation**, a sentence is passed but some or all of the sentence may not actually be imposed, usually with strict conditions with regard to daily activities, such as travel, alcohol and drug use, etc. This is enforced by regular contact with a **probation officer** (**PO**), who monitors the convictee's conduct by regular face-to-face meetings, and, increasingly, by the use of electronic tracking devices (e.g., "ankle bracelets"). Confinement to local facility for a period of less than a year and a day is referred to as being sentenced to **jail**, while a **prison** sentence usually involves confinement at a state facility for longer periods of time, from several years up to life imprisonment. The ultimate penalty, in jurisdictions where this is applied, is **death**.

At the conclusion of a trial in which the jury has found the defendant guilty, the judge sets a date for the **sentencing hearing**. In some jurisdictions, the jury who decided on the defendant's guilt also deliberates and determines the sentence. In other jurisdictions, the judge determines the sentence and outlines his or her reasoning in a **sentencing report** that summarizes the facts of the case and provides the rationale for his or her decision. In cases where there is judicial discretion, the sentencing hearing is the forum in which third parties can present evidence or personal appeals intended to influence the sentencing decision in a stricter or more lenient direction. **Aggravating factors**, typically presented by the prosecution's side, may include the defendant's past criminal history, the particularly cruel and callous manner in which the crime was committed, the lack of a stable family or social structure that the defendant can return to, and so on. **Mitigating factors**, typically presented by the defense side, seek to portray the defendant as overall less malevolent and dangerous: he was influenced by bad peers, his mind was addled by drugs or alcohol, he didn't cause unnecessary harm or injury during the crime, and so on.

One type of aggravating circumstance that may be presented occurs in the form of a **victim impact statement**. Here, the actual victim(s) of the crime, or if the victim is deceased or incapacitated, his or her relatives and close friends, are permitted to tell the court about the impact the crime has had upon their lives. These are often emotional proceedings, as victims and their associates try to impress upon the judge the harm that has been done beyond the formal charges and beyond what has been presented as dry evidence during the trial. Conversely, one type of potential mitigating factor occurs in the context of **diminished capacity**, that is, that the defendant's mental state at the time of the crime was sufficiently impaired as to lessen his overall culpability for the criminal act. Typically, the same kind of evidence is presented that may have been insufficient to form grounds for an **insanity defense**, that is, a mental disorder that is not severe enough to have precluded the defendant from knowing what he was doing (see below), but of sufficient magnitude to at least cloud his judgment or hobble his volition, rendering his criminal act just a little less blameworthy. It is here that all the standard and creative arguments for an abusive family upbringing, bad peers, and history of mental illness are made, sometimes successfully, sometimes not.

Corrections

If the defendant is sentenced to prison, he may be placed in a **minimum**, **medium**, or **maximum security prison**, based upon the seriousness of the crime and how much of a disciplinary risk he is judged to be. Most offenders do not serve their entire sentences, and are granted **parole** after some portion of their sentence has been served, especially if they have managed to stay out of trouble while incarcerated. Similar to probation, the parolee is subject to a range of conditions and restrictions and is assigned a **parole officer** (**PO**) who makes sure he follows the rules.

In cases of the **death penalty**, there are usually numerous **appeals**, and it is not uncommon for convictees to remain on **death row** for one or two decades before the sentence is either overturned, carried out, the defendant is granted a new trial, or the defendant dies.

The Juvenile Justice System

There are several differences between the juvenile justice system and the adult justice system (see also Chapter 19). **Juvenile courts** typically have jurisdiction over matters concerning children and adolescents, including adoption, abuse and neglect, and criminal activity by juveniles ("**juvenile delinquency**"). They also handle what are called **status offenses**, i.e., acts that would be legal if committed by adults, but are crimes only because of the age status of juveniles. These include such things as curfew violations, driving restrictions, truancy, sexual activities, and alcohol consumption. Most cases in adult court come from arrests of the subject by law enforcement officers, while in juvenile court, subjects may be referred by school officials, social service agencies, parents and other family members, or even neighbors, in addition to more common police arrests. More commonly than for adults, juveniles are likely to be given Notices to Appear (see above), especially for less serious status crimes such as underage drinking.

Around the time of arrest, a decision is made either to pursue the case within the criminal justice system or to subject the case to **diversion** into an alternative program, most commonly a mental health or substance abuse treatment facility or program. In making such a determination, the court may hold an **adjudicatory hearing**, in which it hears arguments for and against diversion, one of the factors usually being the subject's mental competency to stand trial (see discussion below).

Another form of diversion that may be considered is whether to try the case in juvenile court or in adult court (see also Chapter 19). Some states statutorily exclude some very serious crimes from the jurisdiction of the juvenile court, trying these defendants as adults, regardless of age. In other states and in the federal government, prosecutors are given the discretion of pursuing the case in juvenile court or diverting it to adult criminal court. If tried in juvenile court, the defendant retains most of the rights and **due-process safeguards** that exist in adult criminal court. Most juvenile courts are tried by a judge, while a few states make provisions for a jury trial in some juvenile court cases. If the juvenile defendant is tried in adult court, it will be a jury trial, just as in any other adult case.

Juvenile courts have more options in adjudicating cases than do adult courts. Like adult courts, judges in juvenile court can sentence defendants to **incarceration** (usually for far less time than would be given an adult for the same crime), **restitution** or **fines** (usually paid by the parents or guardians, or deducted from any work salary the juvenile defendant may be earning), or **commitment to a residential mental health or substance abuse treatment facility**. Additional options in juvenile court include the power to order children to be removed from their homes and placed in **foster care**, and to order juveniles into treatment or into participation in special anti-crime, substance abuse counseling, anger management, or driver education classes.

If sentenced to incarceration, upon release the juvenile may be ordered to a period of **aftercare** which is similar to parole supervision of adult offenders. If they violate the terms of aftercare, they may be placed in a locked facility. Once under juvenile court jurisdiction, juveniles remain so until they reach legal adulthood, which in most states is age 21. In some jurisdictions, juvenile offenders may be classified as **youthful offenders** or **sex offenders** (see also Chapters 14, 15), which may lead to extended confinement or extended probation.

Mental Health Courts

According to a 2009 report from the Council of State Governments Justice Center, about 17 percent of people who enter the criminal justice system have some form of serious mental illness. In 2000 the U.S. Congress passed the **America's Law Enforcement and Mental Health Project Act**, allocating federal funds to local jurisdictions for the establishment or expansion of mental health specialty courts and diversion programs. Today, there are approximately 250 of these **mental health courts** around the country (Kitaeff, 2011; Schwartz, 2008; Steadman et al., 2001, 2010).

The basic philosophy of the mental health court system is that, if some forms or instances of criminal behavior are clearly related to a subject's mental illness, then prosecuting these crimes through the usual legal channels is senseless because it will only result in the proverbial "revolving door," whereby punishment is unlikely to have a deterrent effect on behavior that is driven by illness. Therefore, these courts have the power to order such defendants into specialized treatment programs that target the mental illness, hoping thereby to reduce the overall rate of recidivism.

While laudable in intent, mental health courts have not proven to be a panacea. Recent studies show that participation in the mental health court system reduces subsequent incarceration days by somewhat less than 10 percent. In addition, following participation, subjects with schizophrenia and unipolar depression are more likely to be rearrested than subjects with bipolar disorder. On the other hand, even a small reduction in recidivism rate can have a significant impact on public safety and allocation of law enforcement and criminal justice resources. The mental health court system is clearly a work in progress and will doubtless benefit from increased attention to the types of defendants served and the types of treatment modalities utilized (Kitaeff, 2011; Schwartz, 2008; Steadman et al., 2001, 2010).

PSYCHOLOGY IN THE CRIMINAL JUSTICE SYSTEM

Although there are a broad range of **criminal competencies**, the majority of psychological evaluations for the criminal court will involve three main areas: (1) competency to stand trial; (2) mental status at time of offense ("insanity" evaluation); and (3) prediction of future dangerousness. The following are a few critical points of understanding that are often overlooked by clinical and judicial professionals alike.

First, as noted above, the **mere presence or absence of a diagnosable mental condition does not by itself make a legal determination**. That is, just because a young adult defendant suffers from a long history of schizophrenia doesn't *automatically* mean she is incompetent to stand trial as long as she can be shown to appreciate the nature of the charges and possible penalties and assist in her own defense (Chapter 5). Just because an elderly defendant has no mental health history doesn't *automatically* mean that we should ignore elements of his confused behavior and speech that might point to signs of a beginning dementia (Chapter 4). The presence of a young woman's bipolar-manic command hallucinations does not *automatically* constitute the affirmative defense that she was legally insane at the time she murdered her infant child (Chapter 16). The absence of any prior mental health treatment history does not *automatically* invalidate the claim that the military veteran man stabbed his neighbor because he believed he was being attacked by enemies during a PTSD flashback (Chapter 6). In all such cases, it is the examining expert's responsibility to assert or refute the clinical-forensic connection between the defendant's mental state and the relevant legal question.

Second, **any conclusions about the relevance of the defendant's mental state to the legal question at issue must consider the point in time of that issue's relevance**. For example, competency to stand trial examinations are typically conducted within several weeks of an upcoming trial; consequently, the court is interested in what the defendant's mental state is now, not several months ago or longer, when the crime was actually committed. Conversely, an insanity evaluation concerns itself with the defendant's mental state at the time the crime was committed; what his or her condition is right now may be relevant for current competency, but not for the insanity defense itself, because that is a **retrospective diagnosis** (see discussion below).

In one of the examples above, because schizophrenia tends to follow an exacerbating-remitting course, and is also frequently affected by the level of the subject's medication compliance, the young mother may have been psychotically delusional and have believed that the hallucinated voice was God telling her to send her child to Him at the time she killed him; thus, at that time, she may have met the formal criteria for insanity. But now, 12 months later, she has been taking her medication and is no longer delusional and, although hardly a paragon of mental health, is sufficiently intact to meet the formal criteria for competency to stand trial. Meanwhile, our elderly defendant, despite a few problems with memory and speech, may have been mentally clear enough to be responsible for his actions 18 months ago when he attacked his neighbor, but now his cognitive capacities have worsened to the point that he can no longer productively assist in his own defense. Therefore, although for most defendants there is likely to be a rough equivalence in mental status from one point in time to another, this cannot be merely assumed, and must be carefully assessed.

The time factor also affects the evaluative process itself. For competency to stand trial, the examiner is making diagnostic and forensic conclusions based on a defendant's condition that he can currently observe. However, insanity evaluations–mental status at the time of the offense–means that, necessarily, this is a **retrospective diagnosis**, that is, the examiner is making conclusions about the defendant's mental state at a particular point–often a *particular moment*–in the past that the examiner has not personally observed. In this, the examiner must rely on careful review of records of the event, as well as often interviewing witnesses to the event. Sometimes, this can truly be a case of psychological detective work. More generally, clinicians do this all the time, as when a family therapist relies on a parent's or spouse's report of the behavior of another family member during an incident at home. However, whereas the therapist will have several sessions to clarify the correct chain of events and the causes behind them, in the forensic arena the examiner may only have one evaluation opportunity to get it right, often requiring a considerable amount of background research in addition to direct examination of the defendant (see discussion below).

Finally, for **prediction of future dangerousness** or **risk of future offending**, the psychological examiner must maneuver a veritable clinical-forensic time machine back and forth between past mental status, current functional level–which, in cases of parole hearings, may be years or decades after the criminal act–and predicted mental state and behavior in the future. Once again, this may not be qualitatively different than what clinical evaluators and therapists do in making recommendations for future treatment, education planning, occupational rehabilitation, vocational adjustment, and so on. However, in making dangerousness predictions, the examiner and the court have the responsibility of weighing the defendant's rights against the safety of the public.

BOX 1.2. HOW TO CONDUCT A FORENSIC PSYCHOLOGICAL EXAMINATION

You've been ordered by the court to conduct a forensic psychological examination. What does that mean, exactly? How is that different from any other kind of psychological examination?

continued

BOX 1.2.—*Continued*

To begin with, there are a few major differences between a forensic exam for legal purposes and a clinical exam for treatment purposes. If a patient voluntarily goes to a psychologist for help, the **fiduciary relationship** that exists is between doctor and patient and the purpose of any formal evaluation is to diagnose and effectively treat the patient's disorder or to help them with their problem. The content of the examination and any additional treatment records are confidential, and the patient is free to terminate the evaluation or treatment process at any time.

In the forensic setting, the fiduciary relationship exists between the psychologist and the court and/or the attorneys involved in the case. The purpose of the exam is to assess the aspects of the defendant's mental status that are relevant to the legal issue in question, not necessarily to treat their disorder, although the examining psychologist may make treatment recommendations as part of his or her conclusions. The results of the exam will typically go to the court or to the attorney who ordered it, although the defendant's attorney will probably get a copy of the report and he or she may then share the findings with the defendant. In many cases, it will be the defendant's own attorney who requests the evaluation in order to document some mental condition that he or she feels will affect the case, e.g., competency to stand trial or an insanity defense. The defendant is still free to refuse or terminate the examination, but there will likely be legal consequences for doing so. In some cases, either the defense or prosecuting attorney (or both) may arrange for the forensic psychological examination to be transcribed and/or videotaped.

In a few cases, if the defendant has been seeing a psychotherapist in treatment, or has undergone mental health treatment in the past, those records may be **subpoenaed** by the prosecution if the defendant puts his or her own mental status at issue as part of his or her case, e.g., claiming incompetency, insanity, or diminished capacity. In such cases, in the **discovery** part of the legal process, all parties have a right to review any relevant factors that might affect the defendant's mental status. In rare cases, the treating clinician may even be called to testify, although courts are generally reluctant to violate doctor-patient confidentiality, except in extreme and compelling circumstances.

The exact procedures and measures utilized in the psychological exam will depend of the specific referral question. Virtually all forensic psychological exams begin with the doctor **reviewing relevant records** of the case, to provide a background for the examination. A good portion of the exam will involve a face-to-face **clinical interview**, in which the psychologist asks the defendant to explain his account of events, typically followed-up by a series of clinical and case-relevant questions. These include the defendant's ability to provide a coherent narrative, his understanding of relevant legal criteria, his medical, academic, and employment history, any current signs and symptoms he may be experiencing, and a set of **mental status exam questions** to assess the defendant's orientation, memory, reasoning, and emotional state.

Depending on the nature of the exam, the psychologist may choose to administer several **psychological tests** to the defendant, some requiring direct interaction with the examiner, others consisting of questionnaires and checklists. This can range from only a few standardized measures in an uncomplicated case, to an extensive, hours-long battery of neuropsychological and personality tests in cases involving possible brain damage, severe psychopathology, or atypical syndromes. The complete examination may therefore take only an hour or two, or may extend over days. When the examination is complete, the psychologist will analyze the result and issue a **report** to the court.

The best advice to prospective examinees is to *be honest* because nothing poisons a case and casts doubt on the defendant's credibility more than the confirmation or even suspicion that he or she may be lying, malingering, or trying to manipulate the findings. Finally, even in an adversarial forensic setting, each defendant has the right to be treated with reasonable respect and courtesy. No psychological examination should ever be conducted in a needlessly hostile or confrontational atmosphere. Defendants who feel they have been treated abusively should report this to their attorney, as it may affect the interpretation of the examination results.

CRIMINAL COMPETENCIES: PSYCHOLOGICAL AND LEGAL FACTORS

In the criminal justice system, there are actually a whole range of **criminal competencies**, covering every step of the legal process, from the point of arrest to carrying out the sentence. A defendant must be competent to: be arrested, waive Miranda rights, consent to search, enter a pleas, stand trial, be sentenced, and be executed, among others. Collectively, these are sometimes referred to as **competency to proceed** with the legal matters pending in the case. However, in actual practice, psychologists will perform the overwhelming majority of competency evaluations for **competency to stand trial**.

Milton Dusky was a 33-year-old man who was convicted of kidnapping and rape of an underage girl. On review of the case, the U.S. Supreme Court issued the decision, known as ***Dusky v. United States (1960)***, or simply the ***Dusky* decision**, in which the Court ruled that, in order to be **competent to stand trial**, a defendant must have a **sufficient present ability to consult with his lawyer with a reasonable degree of rational understanding and a rational as well as factual understanding of the proceedings against him**. Essentially, the defendant must be able to understand the charges against him, appreciate the range of possible penalties, and be able to assist in his own defense.

While the precise interpretation of these criminal competency standards varies from jurisdiction to jurisdiction, certain commonalities exist with respect to the basic mental capacities required for an individual to constructively participate in his or her own defense. Note that defendants need not be able to provide detailed, nuanced, and legalistic interpretations of the law; they only need to have a sufficient basic level of understanding to enable them to participate productively in their own defense. In addition, simple ignorance of the legal system does not equate with incompetency: if the defendant possesses the cognitive capacity to learn and profit from instruction, he or she meets competency requirements. Often this can be assessed right in the examination session by explaining the relevant legal concept to the defendant and asking him to relate it back in his own words later. Thus, to be competent to stand trial, a defendant must:

Have an appreciation of the charges against him/her. He need not know the precise legal terminology, but must have some understanding of what he's being charged with. "They say I used a gun to hold up the liquor store."

Have an appreciation of the range and nature of possible penalties. Again, this need not be a legalistic disquisition, but the defendant needs to know that he's not going to get a fine and community service for a mass murder, or be electrocuted for shoplifting a candy bar. "I might have gotten probation on the robbery or up to five years, but it's another mandatory five for the gun."

Appreciate the adversarial nature of the legal process. This means the defendant understands the roles of the key players in the legal process–judge, jury, and especially his defense attorney and the prosecution's attorney. "The DA is trying to put me in jail; my lawyer's trying to prove I didn't do it."

Have the capacity to disclose to his/her attorney pertinent facts associated with the alleged offenses. Note that the defendant's account of these "facts" need not be entirely accurate; in fact, they may be completely untrue and at variance with the testimony of multiple witnesses–after all, the defendant is bound to tell his version of the story in trying to beat the charge. His account may even be frankly delusional ("angels from another dimension told me to do it"). What matters for this criterion is whether or not he can clearly and consistently articulate and communicate to his attorney his own version of events in a coherent and understandable way.

Have the capacity to manifest appropriate courtroom behavior. A defendant who is inattentive, disruptive, combative, or otherwise behaviorally inappropriate will not be able to benefit from a court trial. The likelihood of these behaviors often can be inferred from the defendant's behavior during the competency examination, as well as reports from witnesses who have had the opportunity to observe him prior to the trial. For example, a defendant who continuously dozes off, frequently jumps up from his seat, constantly interrupts the examiner, or repetitively spews foul language during the examination may be likely to do these things in court.

Have the capacity to testify relevantly. Again, the defendant has the right to give whatever idiosyncratic version of events he can cook up (however, if he knowingly lies under oath, that's **perjury**, which is a crime), as long as it will be understandable to the trier of fact (jury, or judge in a bench trial).

Clearly, a wide variety of everyday cognitive, temperamental, and behavioral skills are required to retain competency, including attention, concentration, memory, expressive and receptive language, reasoning, judgment, frustration-tolerance, and self-control. Many of these features can be discerned within the interaction between the examiner and defendant, while others are revealed upon specific questioning, and still others come to light as the result of specialized psychological and neuropsychological tests and measures. It is important to realize that the standards of criminal competency do not require the defendant to be a rocket scientist or paragon of mental health, otherwise no one would ever proceed through the legal system. Indeed, in delineating the criteria above, the law sets a relatively high bar for being considered incompetent: despite the particular diagnosis, the defendant must be unable to understand the legal process or make legal decisions on his own behalf. This accounts for those cases in the media where apparently "crazy" defendants are allowed to proceed to trial, or even proceed **pro se** (on their own behalf, not represented by counsel). But recall that "craziness" in and of itself does not vitiate criminal competency unless it significantly affects the above criteria.

Following a competency examination, a defendant may be found:

Competent to proceed, in which case the defendant moves to the next step in the legal process, usually the trial.

Incompetent to proceed, with recommendations for measures that will restore competency. Recall that mere ignorance of the workings of the legal system is not incompetency; if the defendant can profit from simple instruction, even during the context of the examination ("No, the judge doesn't decide guilt or innocence, that's the jury's job"), and if the defendant can remember this information and articulate it later, competency is not violated. Many jurisdictions have defendants attend an actual legal mini-seminar, or **competency education class**, that acquaints them with the relevant rules of procedure for conducting a trial. More commonly, competency restoration involves therapeutic measures, typically medication, to stabilize the cognitive, emotional, and behavioral status of mentally ill defendants to the point where they meet the criteria for competency. An ongoing area of controversy is to what extent defendants can be treated against their will (i.e., violating a patient's **right to refuse treatment**) solely for purposes of criminal competency restoration, and judicial rulings and case law continue to evolve.

Permanently incompetent to proceed. This will likely be the case where the failure to meet competency criteria stems from a stable, permanent condition (e.g., moderate-severe mental retardation), one that is likely to only worsen over time (e.g., Alzheimer's dementia), or one in which all standard forms of treatment have proven ineffective (severe psychotic illness, refractory to all medications). In such cases, the defendant may be released or, far more commonly, civilly committed.

THE INSANITY DEFENSE AND DIMINISHED CAPACITY

First, I'll ask *you* a question: In what percentage of felony criminal cases do you think accused offenders beat the rap using the insanity defense?

If you're like most ordinary citizens surveyed following John Hinckley's acquittal by reason of insanity for shooting President Reagan in 1981, you probably guessed a figure of little more than 50 percent. In informal surveys of my college classes, the estimated figure usually hovers around 5 to 20 percent. In reality, **not guilty by reason of insanity** (**NRGI**), or **not guilty by reason of mental disease or defect**, or simply the **insanity defense**, is raised as an affirmative defense in about one out of every 100 felony cases. In about half of these, the defendant is so obviously disturbed that both prosecution and defense agree to adjudicate the case as NGRI without trial. In another quarter of these cases, the two sides come to an agreement during the trial, and so in only *one-quarter of one percent* of felony cases, i.e., one in 400, does a TV-style "battle of the experts" ensue–hardly an epidemic. That's because, as in the case of criminal competencies, a relatively high bar is set with regard to a person's **criminal responsibility**.

Insanity Defense Standards

As an American citizen above the age of 18, you have a plethora of legal rights, including the right to buy and sell property, to enter into contracts, to marry and divorce, to consent to or refuse medical treatment, to make medical, educational, and legal decisions for your minor children, to decide what to do with your assets when you die, to have a fair trial if accused of a crime, and so on. In all of these, the law confers upon you a **presumption of competency**, that is, you are considered by default to be mentally competent to do all these things unless someone objects and can rigorously prove otherwise. This accounts for the occasional sticky cases where a family tries to have an elderly parent or brain-injured spouse declared incompetent so they can take over his medical care and, more controversially, control his finances against his expressed wishes.

But it works the other way, too. As jealously as the law guards your legal presumption of competency in the service of maintaining your rights and freedoms, it also insists upon your legal responsibility to obey the local, state, and federal laws of your area of residence, and if you break these laws, there is a presumption of criminal responsibility for your actions unless you or someone else at your behest can rigorously prove otherwise.

A basic tenet of the American legal system is that, to be justly punished for a crime, a defendant must be proven to: (1) have actually committed the offense in question (**actus reus**) and to (2) have had the mental capacity to have committed the act consciously, knowingly, and purposefully (**mens rea**). Note that not guilty by reason of insanity is not an excusatory or mitigatory factor; it is a verdict of *not guilty,* just as "not guilty" as if the defendant didn't do it at all. That's because the law recognizes a subtle but crucial psychological and philosophical principle of human nature: for an act to be committed consciously (I *know* I'm doing it) and purposefully (I *decide* to do it) requires the presence of **identity** (it is *"I"* who am doing it) and agency (it is my *free choice* to do it, not otherwise compelled). This principle, tacitly or overtly, underlies the two major NGRI standards of the United States and most Western societies.

The two major principles that guide insanity evaluations in the United States are the **M'Naughten test** and the **American Law Institute** (**ALI**) **test**; different states employ one or the other standard. The first goes back to the 1843 case of Daniel M'Naughten, who was acquitted by reason of insanity for killing the British prime minister's secretary while attempting to assassinate the PM himself. Queen Victoria was not amused at this verdict and ordered the House of Lords to come up with a more rigorous standard, which ultimately became the one that bears the defendant's name.

According to M'Naughten, in order to establish a defense on the grounds of insanity: "It must be clearly proved that, at the **time of committing an act** [at that specific time, no matter what the mental state may have been prior or subsequent to the act], the party accused was laboring under such a **defect of reason** [his powers of perception and/or cognition were severely impaired], from **disease of the mind** [there must be an identifiable, diagnosable syndrome, recognized by the medical community to account for the mental disturbance], as to **not know the nature and quality of the act he was doing** [he literally did not know what he was doing], or if he did know it, that he **did not know he was doing wrong** [he literally could not tell right from wrong based on the prevailing laws and moral standards of his culture]."

In 1962, the **American Law Institute** drafted the **Model Penal Code test**, which came to be known as the **ALI test**: "A person is not responsible for criminal conduct if at the time of such conduct, as a result of **mental disease or defect** [same as M'Naughten], he lacks **substantial capacity** [may not be totally lacking in capacity, but enough to impair his judgment and/or self-control] either to **appreciate the criminality (wrongfulness) of his conduct** [same as M'Naughten] or to **conform his conduct to the requirements of the law** [even if he understands that what he is doing is wrong, he is substantially powerless to control it]."

The chief differences between the standards is that M'Naughten is a purely **cognitive test**, according to which the defendant either literally didn't know what he was doing during the commission of the crime ("I thought the waiter holding the teapot in the Chinese restaurant was an enemy Vietcong soldier about to throw a bomb when I stabbed him"), or else he could not distinguish right from wrong ("I didn't know it was against the law to force someone at gunpoint to have sex with me against her will if she teased me all night at the bar"). ALI preserves the right-wrong standard but provides a **volitional prong** ("The brain tumor pressing on my client's amygdala produced a rage attack that he couldn't control;" "My client was powerless to resist the command hallucinations caused by his paranoid schizophrenia"). What both standards share is a fairly strict set of exclusion criteria to invoke a NGRI defense. Both insanity standards (unlike the competency criteria discussed earlier) require the presence of a diagnosable medical, neurological, or psychiatric disorder, an identifiable and medically recognized clinical syndrome, i.e., a "mental disease or defect." But this is not in itself sufficient: the symptoms of that disorder must so impair the defendant's mental functioning that he literally does not know what he is doing or does not know right from wrong at the time of the offense (M'Naughten), or make it impossible for him to control his actions (ALI).

Clinically, there are very few mental disorders whose symptoms are sufficiently profound to produce such a level of impairment. Most qualifying syndromes would fall into the category of severe psychosis or some type of organic brain syndrome. Implicitly, the law seems to insist that if it strives to preserve your autonomy as a human being through its vigorous defense of your legal rights and competencies, then it expects you to curb the mundane and sundry irritations and temptations that are part of general human nature or your own unique personality and developmental history. Just as your right to make a will or decide whether to take a medication isn't instantly whisked away the moment you undergo a bout of depression or get stressed out after a car accident, so your responsibility to obey the laws of the land doesn't automatically evaporate under the influence of a crappy day or a pitiable childhood. As a citizen in a free society, you are expected to exert reasonable control of your actions; beings who cannot do that, such as small children or pets, are not punished like adult humans for their harmful actions, but neither are they afforded legal rights.

The obvious question: What about intoxication? As anyone who has attended a New Year's Eve celebration or college frat party will attest, over-enthusiastic enjoyment of alcohol or any number of substances can and does frequently result in states of dramatically impaired consciousness that could probably easily sail past the strict criteria of M'Naughten or ALI. So, it is precisely the ubiquity of such inebriations that impels the law to arbitrarily and purposefully exclude **voluntary intoxication** as an affirmative NGRI defense. Otherwise, how easy would it be to get mad at someone, tank out at home or at your local tavern, stagger over to your adversary, pound him, stab him, or blow him away, and then later claim you were just too spit-faced to know what you were doing? Nice try but no deal. But if you're enjoying a harmless aperitif at your local establishment, and some miscreant slips a rufie or other illegal adulterant into your drink, and this sends you into a mindless paroxysm of destruction, then the fact that this was an **involuntary intoxication** may be grounds for a legitimate NGRI defense, as long as no witnesses testify that you did it to yourself.

Diminished Capacity

One area where even voluntary intoxication may be raised as a mitigating factor is in a plea of **diminished capacity**, which is distinct from NGRI, and which is usually raised at the time of sentencing for a crime for which the defendant has already been found guilty. Since the purpose at this stage is not to determine legal guilt or innocence, as in an insanity defense, issues of mitigation due to diminshed capacity typically require a less severe degree of impairment than NGRI. Although invoking substance abuse is rare, and could easily have the opposite effect on a judge's sentencing decision (not only did the defendant commit the assault and robbery, but he's a drunk and a druggie), more commonly, the standard types of clinically relevant, but not necessarily directly determinative, psychological factors are invoked. These may include: history of early childhood abuse; dysfunctional family of origin; susceptibility to undue influence by antisocial peers; limited intellectual capacity; or any number of medical or mental disorders sufficient to affect one's actions, but not severe enough to meet the NGRI standard.

If there has been any kind of abuse of the insanity defense by mental health experts, we partly have ourselves to blame. Too often, I've listened to testimony or read the transcripts of clinicians arguing for NGRI on the basis of a diagnosed mental disorder alone. The part of the fault that lies with the lawyers is not rigorously holding those clinicians to the strict M'Naughten or ALI standards. Most of us would argue that a civilized society depends on the proper mixture of discipline and compassion, and adjudicating a defendant whose compromised mental state may have had an appreciable effect on his or her criminal behavior is almost always a delicate process.

PREDICTING FUTURE DANGEROUSNESS AND RISK FACTORS FOR FUTURE OFFENDING

One theme that will emerge throughout this text is that not everyone is equally likely to commit crimes, even given equivalent circumstances. In fact, research consistently shows that the most seriously violent 5 percent of the population commit almost 50 percent of violent crimes, the so-called **5/50 rule**. In different geographical locations and with different demographic groups, this may vary somewhat (some places it may be 6/60 or 7/70), but the fact remains that, across cultures, ethnicities, and nationalities, a small proportion of persistently antisocial offenders is committing up to ten times the rate of crime as their fellow citizens. Thus, one important role for forensic psychological examiners is to help the courts decide who is more or less likely to reoffend upon release. This question has important implications for **probation**, **parole**, and **civil commitment** decisions.

Risk status for future offending can be divided into several dimensions (Douglas & Skeem, 2005; Douglas & Kropp, 2002; Douglas et al., 1999; Kraemer et al., 1997; Monahan et al., 2001; Mulvey et al., 1996; Skeem & Mulvey, 2000, 2002; Skeem et al., 2004; Webster et al., 2000). As can be seen, these dimensions will frequently form an overlapping and intersecting matrix in the determination of risk assessments.

Static risk factors are relatively stable or permanent characteristics of the person or situation that are not likely to change over time. Most biological factors or events in the past would fall into this category, such as a defendant's genetic history, his family upbringing, and any deficiencies in adaption or coping he may have, such as a developmental disorder or learning disability. **Dynamic factors** are those that are subject to change, depending on the circumstances. Example: a young man with poor frustration-tolerance and a family history of violence (static risk factor = psychobiological predisposition to violence) is angered by a family member and explodes into rage, intending to kill her, but remembers he lent his guns to his cousin for a hunting trip, so he kicks the TV and storms off to get drunk (dynamic risk factor = availability vs. unavailability of weapons).

Acute risk factors are those that are immediately extant in the situation, e.g., an irritating provocation, state of intoxication of the subject, availability of means of escape, goading peers, absence of credible deterrents, etc. **Short-term risk factors** generally operate over periods of hours to days to weeks, e.g., developing problems at work or at home, coping with an illness, worsening financial difficulties, and so on. **Long-term risk factors** operate over spans or weeks to months to years, and include many of the static risk factors discussed above, as well as several dynamic risk factors, such as the subject's socioeconomic status, the general economic climate, his general state of physical and mental health, etc. These long-term factors *may* change, but are not likely to any time soon, since they tend to form a network of entrenched variables surrounding the subject.

Direct risk factors are often considered to be such things as substance abuse, abusive childhood, low educational level, joblessness and poverty, bad peers, and living in a hostile community environment, subject to frequent provocations. But, upon closer study, many of these same variables are seen to represent **proxy risk factors** for criminal violence; that is, they are correlated with other risk factors, without necessarily being causal, and in many cases, the relationship is bidirectional. For example, there is a well-known correlation between substance use and aggression, and it is true that substance intoxication generally lowers the threshold for an impulsive, violent response to a challenge or frustration. But it is also true that people who are impulsive, frustration-intolerant, and gratuitously violent also seek out substances of abuse as part of their irresponsible, sensation-seeking lifestyle.

Similarly, many criminals have been abused as children and now abuse their own offspring. But did they learn to do this from their parents or did they inherit the genetic predisposition to violent behavior that impels them to aggress against people generally? Poor education and inconsistent unemployment are certainly associated with criminal behavior, but do these social conditions force desperately broke citizens to turn to crime to survive or do those with the poorest academic potential, the least stable temperament, and the weakest sense of personal responsibility and goal-directedness more often find themselves in the lowest socioeconomic echelons of society?

In attempting to untangle these complex factors, criminal psychologists have fairly consistently identified a set of risk factors for criminal behavior that appear to apply across localities and points of time (Andrews & Bonta, 1994, 2006; Appelbaum et al., 1999, 2000; Barratt, 1994; Beyers & Loeber, 2003; Caprara et al., 1996; Charles et al., 2001; Dodge et al., 1990; Douglas

& Skeem, 2005; Douglas & Webster, 1999; Eronen et al., 1996; Harmon-Jones, 2000; Link & Stueve, 1994; Lipsey et al., 1997a, 1997b; McCarthy et al., 2002; McNiel et al., 2003; Monahan et al., 2001; Novaco, 1994; Schwartz et al., 1998; Skeem et al., 2005; Swanson et al., 1990, 1996; Webster & Jackson, 1997; Webster et al., 1997).

Impulsivity. This is the tendency to respond to situations without sufficient reflection or consideration of consequences. It is also associated with poor frustration-tolerance and weak self-control. These are individuals with a "hair-trigger" temper, who "leap before they look." They will often endorse and self-justify these actions, seemingly heedless of their own role in their interpersonal and legal difficulties ("The whole system is rigged to keep me down"), or in some cases actually self-applauding their wanton spontaneity, despite the destructive effects on their lives and those around them ("Planning is for chumps: I do what I want when I want it").

Negative emotionality. Many offenders have a characteristically dour, edgy, anxious, agitated, pessimistic, suspicious, and hostile attitude that makes them highly prone to overreacting to the slightest provocation. They tend to attribute malign motives to others and to react accordingly. Consequently, they often find themselves in conflict with multiple people, and will frequently complain that they can't trust anybody.

Antisocial attitudes. Many chronic offenders take great pride in their badass status and do their best to advertise it to the world. They often see themselves as noble warriors in a hostile environment, deserving of praise (and the status, money, and women that go with it), for being clever enough and strong enough to outwit or pound down rivals and take what they want. Characteristics of criminal thinking are explored further in Chapters 3 and 21.

Alcohol and substance abuse. As noted above, this can be a direct or proxy factor for criminal violence. So well-associated is the connection between alcohol and criminal behavior that virtually all probation and parole agreements mandate abstention from substances and avoidance of establishments where alcohol is served or of persons who are associated with drug use.

Unstable interpersonal relationships. Again, this may represent a case of bidirectional influence. Impulsive, violent, and unstable people are less likely to enter and remain in long-term relationships and, at the same time, the absence of those relationships may deprive them of one last buffer against violent behavior ("Okay, for the sake of my wife and kids, I won't do this crime and risk going back to jail").

Psychosis. As discussed in Chapter 5, psychosis by itself is a weak predictor of criminal violence, but when associated with paranoia, delusions of thought control, and command hallucinations (the so-called **threat/control-**

override syndrome; see Chapter 5), this can represent a very dangerous situation.

Poor treatment compliance. For those at-risk offenders who have been assigned to, or have been receiving, treatment, failure to adhere to clinical recommendations or to follow through with treatment is a strong risk factor for recidivistic criminal behavior.

BOX 1.3. MAY IT PLEASE THE COURT: TESTIFYING TIPS FOR EXPERT WITNESSES

You've completed your forensic psychological evaluation and submitted your report (Box 1.2). In some of these cases, you may be subpoenaed to testify about your findings and conclusions in court. Your task now becomes to ensure that the facts and interpretations you present tell the complete story and that your delivery of these facts makes your testimony clear, credible, and convincing. Here are some practical recommendations for testifying in court based on a survey of the literature, the insights of some of my professional colleagues, and my own experience as an expert witness in forensic psychology (Barton, 1990; Miller, 2006e, 2009d; Mogil, 1989; Posey & Wrightsman, 2005; Simon, 1995; Taylor, 1997; Vinson & Davis, 1993).

TYPES OF WITNESSES AND TESTIMONY

A **fact witness** is someone who has personal knowledge of events pertaining to the case and can only testify as to things he or she has personally observed ("I saw Fred arguing with his supervisor in the break room"). Fact witnesses may not offer **opinions**, which are interpretations and extrapolations of the available facts ("Fred looked mad and this kind of hothead is likely to fly off the handle and attack someone"). These opinions are the province of the **expert witness**, who, in a criminal case is likely to be appointed by the court, although either prosecution or defense (more likely the latter) may retain an independent expert witness. In presenting their opinions, expert witnesses may make statements about aspects of the case that they have not personally observed but in which they have specialized knowledge and training in fields such as medicine, psychology, or economics, that can assist the **factfinders** (judge or jury) in rendering their decision. Although experts are typically allowed more leeway than fact witnesses, the content of their testimony may be carefully vetted by the court for **admissibility**.

PREPARING FOR TESTIMONY

Review your notes on the case as many times as necessary; there's no such thing as too much preparation. The more thoroughly you know your facts and the-

continued

BOX 1.3.—*Continued*

ories about the case, the easier it will be to answer questions thrown at you from "left field" because you won't be relying on rote memorization of individual answers to different questions; instead, your knowledge and recollection will be an organic, holistic, automatic process that's hard to trip up by clever cross-examination. In most cases, you'll probably have one or more meetings, or at least a conference call, with the attorney who retained you to go over your testimony for purposes of clarification and narrative flow, and to get a sense of what you'll be asked by both sides. Use role-play and rehearsal—many attorneys do it—to make yourself comfortable with verbally articulating your points.

ON THE STAND

To the average juror, a doctor or other professional conveys an air of authority and respect, so use this to your advantage. An important part of trial testimony is the impression you make on the jury by your demeanor, language, and grace under pressure. Therefore, in the witness box, your general attitude should be one of confidence, not cockiness. Maintain composure and dignity at all times and act like the professional you are. Remember, no matter how nasty the cross-examination, you are not the one on trial here, so avoid either being cowed into submission or baited into an angry overreaction. Also remember that it's not you who will ultimately decide the case for the prosecution or defense; your responsibility is to clearly present the facts, your conclusions, and the evidence that supports them to the factfinders, and then let them do their job.

Body language is important. Sit up straight and try not to slouch or fidget. If there's a microphone in front of you, sit close enough so that you don't have to lean over every time you speak. If you're in a swivel chair, try to avoid twisting and spinning; make a conscious effort to plant your feet firmly on the floor while speaking. Keep your presentation materials neatly organized in front of you, so you can find documents and exhibits when you need them.

While testifying, look at the attorney while he or she is questioning you, then switch your eye contact to the jury while answering the question; it's them you have to establish a connection with, and jurors tend to find witnesses more credible when they "looked straight at us." Be neither overly detached nor overly intense. *Open, friendly,* and *dignified* are the attitudinal words to remember. Speak as clearly, slowly, and concisely as possible to be understood. Keep sentences short and to the point. Maintain a steady voice volume and use a normal conversational tone. Your general attitude toward the jury should convey a sense of collegial respect, that is, you are there to present the facts as you know them to a group of mature adults who you are confident will make the right decision.

CROSS-EXAMINATION TRICKS AND TRAPS

Listen carefully to each of the cross-examining attorney's questions before you respond. If you don't fully understand the question, ask the attorney to repeat or rephrase it. Don't be baited into giving a quick answer; if you need a couple of seconds to compose your thoughts, take them. Speak as clearly and concisely as possible. Answer each question completely, but don't overelaborate or ramble. If you don't know the answer to the question, state plainly, "I don't know." Don't try to bluff your way out of a tricky question. Don't become defensive. Above all, be honest. If anyone in the courtroom detects even a whiff of deliberate BS, especially from a doctor or other professional they're supposed to be able to trust, it will befoul the remainder of your entire testimony.

Attorneys will often phrase questions in a way that constrains your answers in the direction they want you to go. If you feel you cannot honestly answer the question by a simple yes-or-no answer, say so: "Sir, if I limit my answer to yes or no, I will not be able to give factual testimony. Is that what you wish me to do?" Sometimes, the attorney will voluntarily reword the question. If he or she presses for a yes-or-no answer, at that point either your attorney will probably pop up to voice an objection or the judge will usually intervene. The latter may instruct the cross-examining attorney to allow you more leeway in responding, or to rephrase his or her question, or the judge may simply order you to answer the question as it has been asked, in which case that's what you do—with a resigned look on your face.

Another attorney ploy is to phrase questions in such a way as to force you to respond in an ambiguous manner by prefacing your answer with such phrases, as "I believe," "I estimate," "To the best of my recollection," and so on. If the facts warrant it, be as definite about your answers as possible; if they don't, honestly state that this particular piece of your testimony may not lend itself to precise quantification or may not be a clear perception or recollection, but be firm about what you *are* sure about. In general, give as accurate and thorough an answer as you can, but try not to answer beyond the question, which may only provide more ammunition for the cross-examining attorney. Again, if you don't know the answer to a question, just say you don't know. Jurors will respect and appreciate honest ignorance of a few details far more than a disingenuous attempt to make everything "fit" with your testimony.

Finally, remember that most citizens, which includes most jurors, want to believe that the people they place their trust in—doctors, police officers, and others—have their best welfare in mind. This means that they will mentally bend over backward to give you the benefit of the doubt if you can give them a credible reason to do so. It also means that if you betray them through dishonesty or flagrant disrespect, they may come down on you especially hard for violating that trust. Prepare carefully for your case, be clear and honest in your testimony, maintain dignity and decorum, and, in at least some cases, you'll walk out of court with a smile on your face for a job well done.

SUMMARY AND CONCLUSIONS

Criminal psychology is the application of the principles of normal and abnormal psychology to the understanding, prediction, and control of criminal behavior. It is related to the fields of clinical and forensic psychology, criminology, and criminal justice. In the United States, the justice system is divided into the **civil court** and **criminal court** systems, each with somewhat different rules and procedures, but both relying on the **adversarial system of justice**. The standard manual of psychological and psychiatric diagnosis is the ***Diagnostic and Statistical Manual of Mental Disorders,*** now in its 4th edition. A widely used manual for classifying violent crimes is the FBI's ***Crime Classification Manual***. The criminal justice process typically consists of **arrest, booking, initial appearance, preliminary hearing, arraignment, trial, sentencing, and corrections**. Crimes committed by children are adjudicated in **juvenile court**. Special **mental health courts** may handle cases in which mental illness is a primary factor. Forensic psychological evaluations for criminal court are most likely to fall into the categories of (1) **competency to stand trial**; (2) **mental state at time of offense**, or **not guilty by reason of insanity**; (3) **risk assessment**, or **prediction of dangerousness**. In addition to conducting **forensic psychological evaluations**, an important role of the forensic psychologist is **testifying in court**.

Chapter 2

Biological Theories
of Criminal Behavior

To the man with a hammer,
Everything looks like a nail.
– Mark Twain

Professionals in all fields tend to view things from the perspective of their own familiar, comfortable domains of expertise. To the biochemist, a misbehaving human being is a bag of twisted molecules. To the sociologist, he is the product of group dynamics. The psychologist sees him as having been shaped by the events of his early life, while the theologian frets about his unsaved soul. And, as the criminologist ponders how to punish and deter his wrongdoing, the dramatist enlists him as a metaphor for the injustices and hypocrisies of modern society.

Accordingly, the theories and models of criminal behavior presented in this and the next chapter should be viewed not as dueling paradigms, but as diverse vantage points fixed upon a common question: What makes a small subset of all societies consistently violate its laws and norms of behavior and how can this understanding help us reduce the impact of crime on our civilization? Invoking the dictum from Chapter 1 that *any theory that explains deviant behavior must explain normal behavior,* this chapter considers biologically-based conceptualizations of criminal behavior, while the next chapter discusses psychosocial models.

GENETICS AND CRIME

Winthorpe is a very steady young man.
    We're lucky to have him managing our firm.
        Oh, hogwash. Exeter, Harvard–
        He's the product of good environment.
        It's got nothing to do with environment.
        With his genes, you could put him
        anywhere and he'd come out on top.
        Breeding, same as in race horses–it's in the blood.
    Trading Places, 1983

How Heredity Works

Most of us remember the basics of heredity from high school Bio. The genetic configuration of any given individual is the **genotype**, while the final result, expressed in the physical structure and behavioral characteristics of the individual is the **phenotype**. Sexually reproducing organisms like humans receive half of their genetic complement from dad, the other half from mom. **Genes** are laid out in complex patterns along **chromosomes**, and determine the composition of **proteins**, either: (1) **structural proteins** that form the physical substrate of bone, muscle, blood, skin, and internal organs; or (2) **enzymes** which facilitate the myriad ongoing chemical reactions of the body that are essential to life. Both of these are important for creating and maintaining the structure and function of the **nervous system** which, in turn, is responsible for mediating behavior. For example, in the nervous system, genes encode proteins called **peptides**, which are the building blocks of the many kinds of **neurotransmitters** used by specific neural pathways (Anderson, 2007; Malmquist, 1996).

Genetic Transmission of Criminal Behavior: Family Studies

Virtually no serious behavioral scientist disputes that some form of genetic predisposition underlies all forms of behavior, including antisocial and criminal behavior. This research has been repeated and replicated in many countries, with ethnically and culturally diverse subject groups, and over various historical time periods. There is actually far more evidence for heritability of petty property crime than for serious violent crime, probably because violent crimes for most people are rare events and therefore difficult to analyze statistically and because property theft is likely to be a far more common and "normal" part of a particular offender's daily lifestyle (Anderson, 2007; Volavka, 1995, 2002).

The two main methods of studying the genetics of crime are **adoption studies** and **twin studies**. In the first, behavioral scientists analyze the influence on offspring from high-crime families who are adopted away shortly after birth and raised in more stable, law-abiding households, or (far less commonly) vice versa. In the second methodology, identical twins, who share a common genetic heritage but are serendipitously raised apart, are identified and the influence of different family factors on the same biological substrate can thereby be studied. Theoretically, the more like the biological parents the behavior of these children turns out to be, the stronger the case for genetic factors, relatively uninfluenced by environmental forces.

Converging findings from adoption studies have shown a slight increase in the crime rate of adopted offspring of noncriminal biological parents who are raised by adoptive criminal parents. When offspring of criminal biological parents are raised by adoptive noncriminal parents, the crime rate of the offspring is higher. The highest rates of offspring offending occur where children of biological criminal parents are raised by those same parents or in households with other criminal parents. Heritability rates for criminal behavior seem to go hand-in-hand with rates of alcoholism and antisocial personality disorder or its childhood version, conduct disorder (Chapter 19), as well as with borderline personality disorders and personality disorders in general (Chapters 7, 8). When these correlations are strong, the criminal activity tends to be more violent, rather than the petty criminality found among those without a serious alcohol abuse history. It may be that a tendency toward substance abuse is associated with greater intensity of thrill-seeking antisocial behavior in general (Chapter 8).

Interestingly, the relationship between offspring criminality and biological criminal parents is stronger when the biological criminal parent is the mother. This may be because, since males are more predisposed to criminal behavior than females, females need to have a higher "dose" of genetic criminal predisposition in order to pass it on to their biological offspring. Biological parents' socioeconomic status has more effect on their offspring's criminality than the adoptive parents' status, probably because the social and economic status of the biological parents is related to their heritable cognitive and emotional status; that is, the more unstable and impulsive biological criminal parents are less likely to have achieved an appreciable level of economic success (Anderson, 2007; Bohman, 1996; Brennan et al., 1996; Cloninger et al., 1981; Coolidge et al., 2001; Mednick et al., 1984, 1987; Slutske et al., 1997; Wolfgang et al., 1972).

Finally, quality of parenting, family environment, and social factors do play a role in either aggravating or mitigating criminal behavior in the offspring of both biologically criminal and noncriminal parents; that is, genetic and family environment interact. For example, several studies show that a genetic predisposition to crime can be ameliorated by a stable, happy home life for many at-risk children (Anderson, 2007; Caspi et al., 2002; Kagan, 2010; Kim-Cohen et al., 2004). Children with a specific genotype resulting in low levels of the neurotransmitter **monoamine oxidase-A** (**MAOA**) are more likely than other children to develop conduct disorder, but only when combined with a history of parental maltreatment. Children who are maltreated but lack the genotype for low MAOA also show higher rates of conduct disorder than controls, but not as high as those with that specific genotype. In other words, the highest rates of antisocial behavior in children, and later, adults, occurs when parental maltreatment combines with a specific genotypic vulnerability factor (Caspi et al., 2002; Foley et al., 2001, 2004; Jaffee et al., 2004; Rusk & Rusk, 2007; Tancredi, 2005).

Indeed, this should not be surprising, according to the **stress-diathesis model**, initially proposed for schizophrenia and mood disorders (Caspi & Moffit, 2006; Caspi et al., 2003; Monroe & Simons, 1991; Sher et al., 2005; Zubin & Spring, 1977), but later applied to a wide variety of psychological disorders and syndromes. In this model, environmental influences, the **stressors**, evoke, reinforce, suppress, or redirect the genetic predisposition, or **diathesis** (from the Greek, "to set, place, or arrange"), to determine the ultimate form of expression of any given trait or disorder. This is also often expressed as the **nature-nurture** question. Thus, subjects who would develop severe psychotic or mood symptoms in a maximally stressful rearing environment might show a much milder clinical profile under optimum child-rearing conditions. By extension, the same should apply to criminal behavior, which is what the family studies cited above seem to suggest.

Gene-Environment Correlations

But are people simply passive recipients of environmental events, genetic cake mixes waiting to be stirred, kneaded, and baked into our final form in the capricious kilns of our upbringing? Actually, there are at least three ways that heredity ("diathesis") and environment ("stress") can mutually influence behavior, including criminal behavior (Kagan, 2010; Kendler et al., 2007; Lykken, 1995; Plomin et al., 1977; Scarr & McCartney, 1983).

Passive gene-environment correlation occurs when the actions of the environment, for example, the behavior of a child's parents or the influence of his peers, prods a dormant genetic predisposition into life. Thus, a somewhat spirited but so-far self-controlled child is spurred to flagrantly aggressive behavior at home by frequent parental abuse, or goaded into fights with schoolmates by living in a rough neighborhood, and this becomes his stable pattern of dealing with interpersonal situations.

In **reactive gene-environment correlation**, the genetically primed behavior actually provokes the environmental response, which further reinforces the behavior; a classic vicious cycle. For example, a child's inherited chronically hyperactive, oppositional, and disruptive behavior causes his mother to withdraw from him, his father to beat him, his teachers to neglect him, and his peers to attack him. This only hardens him further and leads to continued and escalating attempts to get his way by being a badass.

Active gene environmental correlation occurs when the heritable trait impels the subject to purposefully seek out environments that reinforce it and to avoid those that tend to mitigate it. So, the kid who loves to read finds his way to the neighborhood library, the budding young ballplayer seeks out other junior athletes to spend his time on the field with, the musically talented child saves money for a guitar and forms a band, and the aspiring punk ferrets out likeminded delinquents to hang out with and terrorize the neighborhood.

Thus, for example, it is not just "bad peer influence" that deterministically channels the behavior of some youths toward delinquency, but that children with an impulsive, egocentric, and power-oriented temperament and cognitive style may seek out like-minded compatriots, who will then reinforce each other's antisocial behavior. This has been referred to as the **shopping-model effect** whereby children, and later adults, actively seek out peers who are most like them—something all of us do to one extent or another. This relationship has been confirmed for such behaviors as smoking, alcohol use, and conduct disorder (Jacobson et al., 2002; Lyons et al., 1995; Rose et al., 2001; White et al., 2003).

BOX 2.1. "MY CHROMOSOMES MADE ME DO IT"
THE XYY SUPERMALE CRIMINAL

You probably learned that each of us inherits one sex chromosome from each parent. If you receive an XX configuration, you become a girl; an XY configuration makes you a boy. Later in life, these chromosomes determine our respective female and male traits, such as size, strength, aggressiveness, and so on. Since the mid-20th century, geneticists have been able to identify the sex chromosome pattern of individuals. If the Y chromosome is associated with all things "male," what would happen if a particular guy happened to get a double dose? Would he be excessively aggressive? Have scientists discovered a "crime chromosome"?

The first **XYY man** was identified in 1961 and was not inordinately aggressive, being regarded at the time simply as an interesting genetic anomaly associated with such unimposing "hypermaleness" traits as increased height and weight, lower intelligence, and bad acne (Horgan, 1993; Hoffman, 1977; Sherman, 1961; Witken et al., 1976). Subsequent research showed this genetic variant to be found in about one in every 700-1000 males, and that these subjects showed a slightly higher incidence of violence than males in general. The problem is that almost all of these studies were done not on the general population, but on subjects confined to prisons and mental hospitals precisely because of their criminal behavior and/or psychopathology, thus skewing the sample. Larger studies of XYY males in the general community have failed to confirm that XYY males have a significantly higher rate of most crimes; however, they may be at higher risk for spouse

continued

BOX 2.1.—*Continued*

abuse (Owen, 1972; Volavka, 1995; Witkin et al., 1976). Overall, most authorities agree that XYY "maleness" is a notable, albeit minor, independent risk factor for violent crime in general (Anderson, 2007).

That, however, didn't stop the media from fanning the flames of moral panic by characterizing XYY males as hulking brutes, battering a destructive swath through helpless communities, killing, ravaging, and plundering all in their path. Criminal defense attorneys lost no time in utilizing XYY status as an affirmative defense in those rare cases where the genetic test turned up positive. These were rarely successful for the simple fact that XYY evidence failed to meet the existing legal standards of scientific certainty regarding the precise link between the XYY trait and criteria for insanity or diminished capacity (Denno, 1988). In recent years, despite improvements in genetic technology, the controversy seems to have died down.

THE NEUROCHEMISTRY OF VIOLENCE

One of the things that genes encode for are the enzymatic proteins that comprise **neurotransmitters**, chemical messengers that enable brain cells, or **neurons**, to communicate with one another. Each neuron releases a specific type of neurotransmitter into the small space between neurons, called a **synapse**. The neurotransmitter molecules bind to special **receptor proteins** on the **postsynaptic membrane** of the next neuron and cause a tiny change in the electrical potential of that cell. The summation of thousands of both excitatory and inhibitory synaptic inputs on any given neuron at any given time determines that neuron's firing pattern, which in turn sends a message to the next neuron in the sequence (along with all the other thousands of inputs to that next neuron), influencing its firing pattern, and so on. Take thousands of possible synaptic patterns for any particular neuron at any particular moment and multiply that by up to 100 billion neurons in the brain, and you get a sense of the complexity of neural processing.

While numerous chemical substances that have potential neurotransmitter properties have been identified in the human organism, the main types of neurotransmitter that have been well-studies in connection with violence and criminal behavior are: **dopamine**, **norepinephrine**, and **serotonin**.

Dopamine

Dopamine is the key neurotransmitter of the brain's reward system. Basically, if something feels good, gets you pumped, and you want to do it more, dopamine is involved. These activities include eating, sex, athletics, power-oriented conflict, and the use of substances that produce a pleasurable high. Some researchers have hypothesized that addictions represent a **"reward deficiency syndrome"** linked to disturbances in the dopamine system which makes some people less responsive to the rewards of everyday life, impelling them to seek greater degrees of stimulation from external chemicals. In fact, heightened vulnerability to alcoholism has been found to be associated with a particular variant of the gene that codes for the dopamine receptor molecule, called **DRD2**. Increased dopamine is also associated with **hypermotivational syndromes** such as aggression, mania, obsessive-compulsive disorder, and psychosis. Medications that reduce dopamine levels, (**antipsychotic drugs**), ameliorate these conditions, while drugs that enhance dopamine levels (**stimulants** like amphetamine and cocaine) worsen them (see also Chapter 4). But remember that complex behaviors (and even many seemingly simple ones) are rarely accounted for by a single gene or neurotransmitter system, and dopamine levels in the brain are mediated by other neurotransmitters, such as serotonin and norepinephrine. Too little dopamine renders a person unfocused, unmotivated, impulsive, and distractible, which is what is experienced by many children and adults with **attention deficit hyperactivity disorder**, or **ADHD** (Chapters 4, 19) (Anderson, 2007; Blum et al., 1995, 2000; Coccaro & Kavoussi, 1996; Comings & Blum, 2000; Thanos et al., 2004; Volkow et al., 2003).

Norepinephrine

Norepinephrine is synthesized from dopamine, and is associated more with a wary, irritable, anxious, hypervigilant, and sometimes paranoid type of arousal. In states of bipolar mania (Chapter 6), subjects typically cycle through a primarily dopaminergic stage of expansive grandiosity, then to a more dysphoric and agitated norepinephrinergic stage, before finally crashing into the depressed phase, in which both neurotransmitters are temporarily depleted. Both animal and human studies have confirmed a relationship between elevated levels of norepinephrine and heightened aggression. For example, medications such as the **tricyclic antidepressants** that increase net levels of norepinephrine in the nervous system increase aggressive behavior in patients with agitated forms of depression (Anderson, 2007; Coccaro & Kavoussi, 1996; Raine, 1993).

Serotonin

The newest class of mood stabilizing medications target the serotonin system. **Serotonin** normally functions as a behavioral moderator, balancing out the actions of other neurotransmitters, and serving to inhibit impulsive-aggressive behavior. Low or unbalanced levels of serotonin are associated with irritability, depressed-agitated mood, hostility, suicidality, and impulsive aggression, including assault, homicide, and firesetting. There appear to be two **alleles**, or variants of the serotonin gene, a short version and a long version. The short version makes a person more vulnerable to stress, causing the individual to react with impulsive emotionality, either depression or aggression, or both, while the long version appears to bolster stress resilience (Anderson, 2007; Caspi et al., 2003; Coccaro, 1989; Coccaro & Kavoussi, 1996; Linnoila et al., 1983; Raine, 1993; Raine et al., 1995; Soderstrom et al., 2003; Virkkunen et al., 1996a, 1996b; Volavka, 1995, 1999).

Serotonin appears to have another intriguing connection with an aggressive predisposition. There is a general correlation between body size and aggressiveness, such that larger individuals tend to be overall somewhat more aggressive than smaller ones. Serotonin levels are controlled by a peptide called **somatostatin**, which is produced by both the brain and the gut, and is responsible for releasing serotonin into the body. Thus, low levels of somatostatin mean low levels of serotonin, which is associated with dysphoric mood and impulsive aggression. But somatostatin also mediates the control of **growth hormone** in the other direction: high somatostatin inhibits growth hormone secretion, resulting in smaller stature. Therefore, individuals who are genetically predisposed to have low somatostatin levels will have lower serotonin and higher growth hormone levels, resulting in a person who is physically larger and more impulsively aggressive. Of course, both serotonin level and growth hormone secretion are affected by a number of other factors, but the somatostatin connection may be one reason why bigger is often badder (Anderson, 2007; Raine, 1993).

BOX 2.2. "MY MOLECULES MADE ME DO IT"

With widespread information about serotonin's role in regulating mood and influencing behavior being disseminated through pharmaceutical advertising and the popular media over the last several decades, it was only a matter of time until criminal defense attorneys latched onto this latest field of neurobiological information to fashion new and improved grounds for NGRI or diminished capacity defenses in capital murder cases. All major attempts to do this utilized expert testimony from qualified medical mental health professionals—and all were unsuccessful (Anderson, 2007; Bernet et al., 2006).

In *State v. Payne* (2003) a capital murder death penalty sentence was appealed on the grounds that the defendant was unable to control his impulses or form the necessary *mens rea* to commit capital murder due to low serotonin levels. The prosecution pointed out that, since the crime was planned and pre-meditated, the defendant's alleged state of impulse control was irrelevant, and the sentence was upheld. In *Hill v. Ozmint* (2003), defense experts opined that the defendant's murderous behavior was due to a genetically-based serotonin defi-ciency which, moreover, could be treated with medication, which meant he would no longer be a danger. The appellate court was not impressed, and Mr. Hill was executed by lethal injection. Serotonin deficiency impairing criminal responsibility was invoked once again in the murder conviction appeal of *Hall v. State* (2005), and once again the appellate court rejected the defendant's appeal and confirmed the sentence.

Like many brain-based criminal defenses, courts appear very reluctant to set precedents that will open the floodgates of this kind of neurotransmitter defense. As with many conditions, the conclusion seems to be that mere presence of a bio-logical predisposition does not automatically obliterate a person's ability to choose and direct his or her actions. In fact, the State of Michigan procedurally excludes the presentation of a biological condition as an affirmative rebuttal of *mens rea* (*People v. Uncapher*, 2004). The bar remains, as in most cases it should be, a high one.

Monoamine Oxidase

Monoamine oxidase (**MAO**) is not a neurotransmitter itself but an en-zyme that breaks down several other neurotransmitters, including dopamine, norepinephrine, and serotonin. Antidepressant drugs that slow this process (called **MAO Inhibitors**, or **MAOIs**) have the net effect of making more of the neurotransmitter molecules available within brain synapses at any given time. There are two versions of MAO, the A and B form, produced by two different genes. As noted earlier, children with the **MAOA variant** are much more likely to develop mood disorders and conduct disorder, but only if they also experience significant degrees of abuse and neglect. Those children with the same MAOA gene who are raised in stable, supportive families show lit-tle or no higher rates of these disorders, demonstrating, in this case at least, a clear protective effect of stable upbringing on a genetic propensity to anti-social behavior (Anderson, 2007; Beitchman et al., 2004; Brunner, 1996; Foley et al., 2004; Kagan, 2010; Lykken, 1995).

HORMONES

Besides the nervous system, the other main communication conduit of the body is the **endocrine system**, whose chemical communicators are called **hormones**. These are secreted into the general circulatory system to reach their **target cells**. Hormones may also be produced by special **neurosecretory cells** within the nervous system. The level of a particular hormone at any given time is determined by a delicate feedback system, in which falling levels of a hormone in the blood are detected by the **hypothalamus** in the brain, which then sends a message to the **pituitary gland** to stimulate the particular endocrine organ (thyroid, gonads, adrenals) to release greater amounts of its particular hormone. Conversely, rising hormone levels cause the hypothalamus to turn down the signal to the pituitary, which in turn results in a lowered level of that endocrine gland's activity. Beginning in the womb, hormones interact with the nervous system to determine the substrates of individual behavior and, like the nervous system, the reactivity of the hormonal system is influenced by early and later life experiences. Several hormones have been implicated in aggressive and antisocial behavior (Anderson, 2007; Campbell, 1996; Malmquist, 1996; Volavka, 1995, 1999).

Testosterone

Because of its association with "maleness," **testosterone** has received most of the attention with regard to its relationship with aggression. Indeed, long before the advent of modern physiology, people have always recognized the association of the male testes with sexual prowess and interpersonal boldness. For example, neutering domestic animals has long been known to "take the fight out of them," making them overall more docile and controllable. Even today, our colloquial language reflects this association, as when we chide a timorous colleague to "grow a pair." The well-known **age-crime curve** (Chapters 8, 19), in which the number of offenses committed by young males rises sharply in early adolescence, peaks in late adolescence and early adulthood, and drops off significantly by age 30, closely tracks the age-related level of circulating testosterone. Both males and females have testosterone (produced by the ovaries and adrenal glands in females), but the levels are significantly higher in males (Boyd, 2000; Anderson, 2007; Quinsey et al., 2004).

Testosterone has been implicated in aggression, but its effects, particularly in primates and humans, interact with social factors, the relationship typically being reciprocal. That is, higher levels of testosterone lead to more assertive dominance-seeking which, if successful, results in even greater elevations of testosterone secretion, leading to enhanced dominance seeking, and so on. The effect of social factors, particularly in terms of hierarchical status, appears to have a greater impact on circulating testosterone levels in more sociable animals, including rodents, primates and humans (Anderson, 2007; Brain, 1993; Volavka, 1995, 1999).

In prison settings, higher testosterone levels have been found to be correlated with conviction for more violent crimes, rule violations in prison, fighting and interpersonal aggression, and parole board violations, as well as life history factors of childhood delinquency, substance abuse, sexual promiscuity, and repeated conflicts with authority. Conviction for homicide, rape, assault, and domestic violence is associated with higher testosterone levels than conviction for property or narcotics crimes. Furthermore, murderers with higher testosterone levels tend to kill people they know and to plan the killing ahead of time, i.e., they are more "cold-blooded" and ruthless than homicide convictees who have killed impulsively. Although women overall produce much less testosterone than men, the correlation between testosterone levels and aggression holds for women as well: in female prison samples, testosterone level is correlated with severity of violent crime conviction and with level of disruptive, aggressive, and confrontational behavior while incarcerated (Anderson, 2007; Dabbs & Hargrove, 1997; Dabbs & Morris, 1990; Dabbs et al., 1987, 1988; Soler et al., 2000).

While high levels of testosterone have reliably been shown to correlate with higher levels of aggressive activity, this does not necessarily mean overtly antisocial activity. Rather, the behavior that testosterone mediates can be best described as **assertive dominance**—the kind of personality and behavior seen in professional athletes, military leaders, successful entrepreneurs, and so on. These are people who know what they want and have the resolve and determination to get it, despite obstacles. In the presence of an otherwise nonpathological personality makeup, these are simply the successful, go-getting persons we all admire. For example, winners of wrestling, boxing, and judo bouts show sharp rises in testosterone levels, but these are relatively transient. It doesn't even have to be physical competition: winners of chess games and simple coin tosses experience a rise in testosterone. Trial attorneys who "battle it out" in court have higher testosterone levels than corporate attorneys who do mainly desk work and, again, this relationship holds for both men and women. Venture capitalist entrepreneurs show higher testosterone levels than investors in safer securities. Direct participation is not necessary, either: fans of soccer matches or other team sports experience a rise in testosterone when exulting over their team's win. Partly through its effect on increasing dopamine levels, testosterone may be the hormone associated with assertive self-confidence that facilitates an aggressive response to challenge and thereby confers an adaptive evolutionary advantage in maintaining status within social groups (Anderson, 2007; Archer, 1991; Bernhardt et al., 1997; Boyd, 2000; Mazur et al., 1992; McCaul et al., 1992; Salvador et al., 1985, 1999; White et al., 2006).

Thus it may be that, only when coupled with excessive impulsivity and/or overly dysphoric mood, does high testosterone lead to frankly "antisocial" behavior from the standpoint of that group's cultural norms. In fact, the overly violent, antisocial behavior that is called "criminal" in most societies seems to most closely relate biochemically to a combination of high testosterone and low serotonin. This association has, for example, been identified in rapists (Giotakos et al., 2003). Testosterone, then, may be more related to dominance than to aggression per se. Recognizing that there is a potential cost in injury to any unnecessary physical confrontation, an otherwise normal male will attempt to achieve dominance by reputation enhancement and intimidation, and any actual fighting will be limited to that which is seen as absolutely necessary to preserve his hierarchical status. In modern humans, social dominance can, for example, be achieved by success in sports, entrepreneurial wealth-accumulation, earning of professional degrees, or celebrity status, none of which need involve physical confrontation. However, combined with low serotonin, this balance is disrupted and the individual may then show the indiscriminate and criminal violence of the bully or predator, which, in most societies, is not condoned or tolerated (Bernhardt, 1997; Higley et al., 1996; Mazur, 1985; Mazur & Booth, 1998; et al., 1992; McCaul et al., 1992). Finally, overuse of exogenous testosterone, or **anabolic steroids** by bodybuilders and other athletes can enhance aggression and lead to the development of an aggressive steroid psychosis, or **'roid rage**, which in some cases has been associated with acts of extreme violence (see Chapter 4).

Premenstrual Syndrome

"Don't bother me, I'm PMS," is a refrain often heard from women who are feeling particularly irritable at a certain time of the month. About midway through a woman's monthly cycle, the levels of **estrogen** and **progesterone** rise during ovulation, followed by a sharp drop in progesterone a few days prior to menstruation. In some women, this is associated with **premenstrual syndrome** (**PMS**), characterized by impaired concentration, increased irritability, mood swings, depression, and occasionally aggression. A few cases have occurred of violent crimes committed by women during this phase, leading to the hypothesis that PMS may be a risk factor for violence and even the basis for a legal claim of diminished capacity. However, as with any of the other biological and psychosocial factors we've considered, hormonal status alone is unlikely to explain the entire basis for violence. And again, as with most of the other factors described herein, it appears that only a small subset of women are particularly prone to commit violent acts during the premenstrual phase of their cycle (Anderson, 2007; Fishbein, 1992; Raine, 1993; Volavka, 1995).

Growth Hormone

Growth hormone is secreted by the pituitary gland and plays a crucial role in determining body size and stature. As noted earlier, aggression is correlated with body size for the simple reason that if someone is going to be a basher and a brawler, they're likely to be better at it if they're bigger and stronger (Raine, 1993). High levels of growth hormone are also associated with low serotonin levels, due to the mediating effect of **somatostatin** which enhances growth and inhibits serotonin (see above). And **human growth hormone** has been abused, along with testosterone, as a growth and performance enhancer by athletes and other "macho" types.

Cortisol

Cortisol is secreted by the **adrenal cortex** in response to physical and psychological stress. It mobilizes blood sugar, suppresses inflammation, and aids in fat, protein, and carbohydrate metabolism. Individuals who are especially responsive to stress and challenge show heightened cortisol levels along with increases in other indices of physiological arousal, while the opposite is seen in relatively stress-resilient persons. Individuals who are diagnosed with conduct disorder in childhood (Chapter 19) and as antisocial personalities in adulthood (Chapter 8) tend to show unusually low cortisol levels, along with low readings on other physiological arousal measures. That is, some forms of persistent aggression often occur in the context of relative physiological underarousal, boredom-proneness, fearlessness, and imperviousness to punishment, all of which may be adaptive if the individual is to be a successful hunter or warrior, but may border on recklessness if it leads to unwise confrontations resulting in death or serious injury. Low cortisol levels have been found in aggressive children and in habitually violent adolescent and adult offenders, and is correlated with substance abuse. There also seems to be a reciprocal relationship among cortisol, testosterone, and serotonin levels in habitually violent individuals (Anderson, 2007; Dabbs et al., 1991; Kagan et al., 1988; King et al., 1990; Lahey et al., 1990; McBurnett et al., 1996; Raine, 1993; Susman et al., 2006; Tennes & Krey, 1985; Van Praag, 1996; Virkkunen, 1985; Volavka, 1995).

Thyroid Hormones

The **pituitary gland** stimulates the **thyroid gland** to produce a number of **thyroid hormones** which are necessary to control bodily metabolism: too little thyroid hormone, and metabolism abnormally slows (**hyperthyroidism** or **Cushing's syndrome**); too much, and it speeds up excessively (**hyperthyroidism** or **Graves' disease**). Attempts to link either high or low thyroid hormone levels directly to aggression have been inconclusive, but correlations have been reported with juvenile delinquency and adult criminality, probably secondarily associated with the known connection between thyroid hormone status and mood disorders, borderline personality disorder, and attention deficit hyperactivity disorder, which can all be risk factors for aggression, especially when combined with other risk variables (Alm et al., 1996; Anderson, 2007; Stalenheim et al., 1998; Stein et al., 1995; Volavka, 1995).

TOXIC-METABOLIC FACTORS

A host of toxic and medical conditions can cause changes in mental status, some of which may be associated with aggressive, violent, or other impulsive behavior.

Hypoglycemia

Sudden drops in blood sugar can lead to a variety of disordered mental states, usually involving faintness, impaired concentration, and in some cases unconsciousness. A few cases of violent behavior associated with **hypoglycemia** have been reported, but these are difficult to disentangle from other coexisting factors, such as alcohol use (which is known to affect blood glucose levels, as well as having its own disinhibiting actions), access to a healthy diet, and comorbid personality disorder and/or mental illness (Anderson, 2007; Rumsey & Rapoport, 1983; Volavka, 1995).

Encephalitis

Infections of the brain may occasionally be associated with violent behavior, both during the acute stage of infection and as a long-term sequel. **Herpes simplex encephalitis** is caused by a virus with a special affinity for the emotion-mediating **limbic system** of the brain, and can result in impulsive aggressive behavior, but usually in the context of a severe dementia that clearly identifies itself as an organic brain syndrome. More difficult to reconcile are brain infections that affect behavior in the presence of otherwise apparently normal cognitive functioning. The syndrome of **encephalitis lethargica** was first described as a sequel of the great influenza pandemic of 1919. Many children who survived the initial infection later displayed impulsive, aggressive behavior and many ultimately committed serious violent offenses such as murder and robbery. The cause was hypothesized to relate to damage to **frontal lobe** and **limbic system** brain structures. Sporadic cases of marked antisocial behavior change following childhood illnesses are cited today, but the precise connection is often difficult to establish (Anderson, 2007; Greenebaum & Lurie, 1948; Levy, 1959; Lishman, 1978; Tardiff, 1998; Volavka, 1995).

Metallic Toxins

Overexposure to certain **heavy metals** can damage the brain and may be associated with aggressive behavior. The most frequent culprit in this category is **lead toxicity**, which occurs most commonly in industrial exposures, as a consequence of eating lead paint, or from breathing fumes of lead-based gasoline, all of which are now becoming increasingly rare in modern industrialized societies. Lead is a neurotoxin that is known to cause brain damage at certain levels of exposure. Experimentally, lead has been shown to impair certain brain receptors that are important to learning. In general, a modest association has been found between lead exposure and antisocial behavior. For example, lead levels have been found to be correlated with disciplinary problems in school, delinquency in childhood, and later arrests as adolescents and adults. Homicide rates have been found to be significantly higher in neighborhoods with the highest air lead concentrations than in those with the lowest concentrations. Causal relationships are difficult to disentangle, however, because lead paint exposure is most likely to occur in older, run-down neighborhoods, populated by residents of low socioeconomic status who may already possess additional risk factors for criminal behavior, such as unstable family, child abuse or neglect, substance abuse, poor diet, limited education, and genetic vulnerabilities (Anderson, 2007; Denno, 1990; Dietrich et al., 2001; Fulton et al., 1987; Marlowe et al., 1985; Nihei et al., 2000; Pihl & Ervin, 1990; Stretesky & Lynch, 2001; Volavka, 1995).

In addition to lead, exposure to other metals, such as **cadmium** and **manganese**, has been cited as a risk factor for criminal behavior, but these associations remain unproven. In the past, **industrial manganism** was a cause of a Parkinson-like disorder of movement, cognition, and behavior, including learning disabilities and impulsive behavior. Later studies from hair analysis suggested that some children with ADHD had higher levels of manganese in their bodies. In animal studies, exposure to manganese is associated with a significant reduction in dopamine in brain areas important for planning, directing, goal-orienting, and impulse control. At the present time, the role of heavy metal exposure, aside from lead, as an independent risk factor for violent crime remains suggestive, but unverified (Anderson, 2007; Marlowe & Bliss, 1993; Marlowe et al., 1985; Masters et al., 1998; Pihl & Ervin, 1990; Tran et al., 2002).

PSYCHOPHYSIOLOGY

For historical purposes, the term **psychophysiology** has come to mean the study of the electrical activity of the brain, and the two most common psychophysiological research clinical diagnostic methodologies are the **electroencephalogram** (**EEG**), which measures the brain's ongoing activity, and the **evoked potential** (**EP**), which measures how the nervous system processes perceptual stimuli.

One of the most frequently observed EEG abnormalities associated with violence consists of excessive **alpha wave** and **theta wave** activity, an abnormality consistent with the **underarousal theory** of psychopathy and habitual criminality (see also Chapter 8). This theory posits that some individuals seek excessive stimulation through antisocial behavior to compensate for their constitutionally low levels of physiological arousal. In fact, habitually violent offenders are often found to be low on most indices of physiological arousal, such as heart rate, skin conductance (sweat gland activity), and muscle tension. The behavioral consequence of such underarousal and overfiltering would be relative stimulus deprivation and chronically low levels of arousal–these individuals have nervous systems that are prone to boredom with the mundane activities of ordinary life. To compensate, they seek out and create situations that are of stimulating interest, such as involvement in exciting sports or other entertaining activities, but which often also involve significant drama and conflict–a trait that has been termed **sensation-seeking** (Zuckerman, 1979, 1990). Especially for sensation seekers with the shriveled consciences associated with antisocial personality and psychopathy (Chapter 8), their lives become centered around exciting, thrill-enhancing activities, regardless of the suffering they cause to others. For many of these individuals, this means using drugs, being sexually promiscuous, driving fast, getting into fights, and so on. For those whose need for power, control, and dominance are especially high, this may express itself in impulsive or sadistic violence (see also Chapter 8, 10) (Driver et al., 1974; Fenton et al., 1974; Forssman & Frey, 1953; Hill & Pond, 1952; Krynicki, 1978; Mednick et al.,

1987, 1982; Okasha et al., 1975; Petersen et al., 1982; Raine et al., 1990, 1995; Riley, 1979; Sayed et al., 1969; Volavka, 1995; Williams, 1969).

One early study (Raine et al., 1990) seemed to support the idea that underarousal may be critically involved in the development of antisocial and criminal behavior. The investigators measured resting skin conductance, heart rate, and EEG activity in 101 15-year-old schoolboys, which were then related to criminality status as assessed 9 years later at age 24. Criminals were found to have significantly lower resting heart rate, reduced skin conductance activity, and more slow-frequency EEG theta activity than noncriminals at both points in time. This study also found long latency **brainstem averaged evoked responses (BAERs)**, which psychologically can be interpreted as indicating reduced arousal and excessively high filtering of environmental stimuli.

NEUROPSYCHOLOGY

Neuropsychology is the field of psychology concerned with the relationship between the various structures and systems of the brain and their role in cognition, emotion, and behavior. Methods of both clinical and research study include the clinical interview, observation, and examination of subjects; administration of specialized tests and measures; and use of ancillary technologies, such as neuroimaging studies. Disease or injury to different structures and pathways in the brain produce different syndromes of impairment. As a simplified summary, disorders of the **brainstem** may be associated with disturbances in consciousness and awareness. Injury to the cortical and subcortical **sensorimotor pathways** may result in impaired vision, hearing, body sense, or movement. Disease or damage to the **limbic system** often results in disorders of emotion and motivation. In humans, the **cerebral cortex** comprises the largest volume of brain tissue, and is divided into two hemispheres and four lobes. Damage to the **occipital lobe** causes disturbances of vision. **Parietal lobe** damage results in disorders of bodily sensation, mathematical and spatial reasoning, and sense of direction. Injury to the temporal lobe impairs hearing, memory, language, and emotional processing. **Frontal lobe** damage is frequently associated with disorders of complex movement and purposeful activity, as well as impaired abstract reasoning, impulse-control, goal-following, and behavioral self-regulation. For most people, dysfunction of the **left hemisphere** of the cerebral cortex affects primarily verbal skills, while **right hemisphere** damage impairs mainly visuospatial functions. Three main systems that have been implicated in the understanding criminal behavior are as follows.

The Subcortex and Limbic System

The **limbic system** consists of the septal area, hippocampus, amygdala, head of the caudate nucleus, thalamus, ventromedial and posterior hypothalamic nuclei, midbrain tegmentum, pons, and the fastigial nuclei and anterior lobe of the cerebellum. Normally, the orbitofrontal cortex (see below) modulates limbic control of aggression, but this inhibitory control is susceptible to breakdown or override caused by overwhelming internal drive states or excessive outside provocation, even in healthy individuals–e.g., getting mad and "losing it." Infections or tumors of the limbic system have also been associated with aggressive behavior, although the more common response to limbic damage is overall flattening and blunting of emotion and behavior. Violent behavior, when it does occur, usually consists of short, impulsive outbursts that are spontaneous or provoked by some immediately irritating circumstance. Planned, premeditated criminal activity is highly unlikely to represent an organic limbic system pathology as the major cause (Elliott, 1992; Hall, 1993; Volavka, 1995).

Much of the attention paid to the limbic system's role in criminal violence has been focused on the **amygdala**, a bilateral structure that sits within the anterior tip of the temporal lobes. It is thought that the amygdala serves to assign emotional importance to incoming stimuli, with the **hippocampus**, which sits adjacent to it in the brain, determining whether that data will be consolidated into long-term memory. Bilateral surgical removal of both amygdalas in monkeys produces the famous **Kluver-Bucy syndrome** (Bucy & Kluver, 1955), consisting of emotional blunting, psychic blindness (inability to recognize objects and especially faces, despite intact vision), and hyperorality (putting everything in one's mouth). A few human cases of Kluver-Bucy syndrome have been reported, usually caused by bilateral temporal lobe encephalitis or bilateral surgical extirpation of the anterior temporal lobes to treat intractable epilepsy. Such persons usually require some degree of supervision or custodial care.

In cases where no actual physical brain damage has been identified, researchers have attempted to discover whether habitually aggressive individuals may have some kind of innate deficiency in amygdala processing. Some studies have shown subjects with aggressive histories to have poorer recognition of facial expression (Adolphs et al., 2005; Weiss et al., 2006), while other studies have linked structural changes and hyperactivity of the amygdala's threat-recognition mechanism with the low expression of X-linked MAOA found in children with low serotonin levels who are especially vulnerable to the behavioral effects of early child abuse (Caspi et al., 2002; Meyer-Lindenberg et al., 2006; see above). Still other studies have supported a connection between abnormally low amygdala reactivity to threat stimuli and the reduced physiological reactivity found in habitually antisocial or psychopathic subjects who are prone to sensation-seeking, resistant to fear-conditioning, and deficient in empathy and remorse (Birbaumer et al., 2005; Coricelli et al., 2005; Dolan, 2002; Gordon et al., 2004; Kiehl et al., 2001; LeDoux, 1996; Mobbs et al., 2007; Takahashi et al., 2004). However, it is not clear if these brain anomalies are specific to persons with antisocial behavior or what exact role they may play in that behavior.

The Frontal Lobes

The frontal lobes are considered to be the seat of the so-called **executive functions** of the brain. This is the largest portion of the cerebral cortex (one-third of the entire cortical volume in man) that enables us to reason, anticipate, plan, sustain goals, imagine possibilities, restrain impulses for a deferred benefit, carry out complex activities, and communicate effectively with others–in short, what makes us human (Luria, 1980; Mattson & Levin, 1990; Nauta, 1971; Stuss & Benson, 1984). Neuropsychologists distinguish among three different functional areas within the so-called **prefrontal cortex** (the "thinking" portion of the frontal lobe that sits anterior to the frontal motor areas) to specify the location, direction, and function of each region. The dorsolateral prefrontal cortex is found in the lateral part of the prefrontal area and is connected with the orbitofrontal cortex. The **dorsolateral prefrontal cortex** is thought to be responsible for behavioral inhibition, for cognitive control, for information-processing skills, and for working memory. The **orbitofrontal cortex** is found directly above the eyes and is interconnected with the amygdala and several other areas of the brain. Its task is primarily to modulate emotions, to help maintain goal-oriented activity, and to regulate complex decision-making processes. Finally, the **medial prefrontal cortex** is located deep within the brain and is connected with the dorsolateral prefrontal cortex, with the hypothalamus, and with the amygdala. The medial prefrontal cortex allows for the completion of tasks that demand a significant amount of focused attention and emotional regulation (Beaver et al., 2007; Bechara et al., 2000; Ishikawa & Raine, 2003; MacDonald et al., 2000; Schoenbaum et al., 1998). Essentially, what your frontal lobes enable you to do is to use all your other brain capacities in a coordinated, planful manner in order to fulfill the immediate and long-term goals that are important to you.

Interestingly, psychometrically assessed tests of intelligence, memory, and other isolated cognitive skills may be relatively unaffected by brain damage confined to the frontal lobes, as many routine skills and items of previously acquired knowledge are largely retained; test scores on many cognitive and intellectual measures may be within normal limits. What is more commonly seen in such frontal lobe cases are less-easily quantifiable disturbances of attention, planning, judgment, self-monitoring, self-control, and initiating and carrying through activities in the real world, especially in complex, non-routine situations where greater degrees of cognitive flexibility and novel problem-solving are called for (Lezak, 2004; McFie, 1975; Miller, 1986d, 1990c, 1993d; Rosenthal, 1987; Stuss & Benson, 1984).

For example, on neuropsychological testing, adjudicated male delinquents have been found to be impaired in their ability to comprehend, manipulate, and utilize conceptual material (Berman & Siegal, 1976). Violent male penitentiary prisoners are more impaired than nonviolent prisoners on measures of cognitive, language, perceptual, and psychomotor abilities (Spellacy, 1978), and assaultive delinquents have a greater number of EEG abnormalities, poorer verbal memory, and increased perseveration, as compared with nonassaultive delinquents (Krynicki, 1978), supporting the hypothesis that many antisocial individuals have particular problems in planning their actions, perceiving the consequences of those actions, and altering those actions in the face of changing circumstances (Yeudall et al., 1982).

More impulsive, assaultive subjects in an adult, male prison population have been found to show significant impairment, compared to less violent prisoners, on tasks requiring complex integration of information from the visual, auditory, and somesthetic processing systems, as well as impaired ability to create, plan, organize, and execute goal-directed behaviors and to sustain attention and concentration, similar to findings with frontal lobe patients (Bryant et al., 1984). This work has been replicated in a nonprison population, showing that psychopathic inpatients at a Veterans Administration alcohol and drug treatment program performed more poorly than nonpsychopathic inpatients on a variety of measures sensitive to frontal lobe impairment, even when overall IQ was controlled for (Sutker & Allain, 1987). Overall replication of this neuropsychological research has not been unanimous (Hare, 1984, 1986), but the bulk of the neuropsychological findings, partially supported more recently by neuroimaging data (see Chapter 8), support the hypothesis of predominant left hemisphere and frontal lobe neuropsychological impairment in nonbrain-injured, but impulsively antisocial populations (Blair, 2005; Glenn & Raine, 2008; Goodman et al., 2007; Miller, 1987, 1988c, 1990b, 1990c, 1998a; Palermo, 2009; Raine et al., 1998).

From a social and interpersonal perspective, the frontal lobes, particularly the orbitomedial frontal areas, are involved in the inhibitory control of maladaptive and inappropriate behaviors. Patients with orbitomedial frontal injury may become irritable, short-tempered, hostile, selfish, immature, and impulsive (Heinrichs, 1989; Pontius & Yudowitz, 1980; Raine, 1993; Thompson, 1970; Volavka, 1995; Volkow & Tancredi, 1987; Williams, 1969; Yeudall, 1977; Yeudall & Fromm-Auch, 1979; Yeudall et al., 1982). If violence occurs, it is rarely in the form of a planned attack. Rather, frontal-lobe aggression seems to represent an "escape," "release," or "misdirection" of aggression due to the brain's impaired ability to maintain emotional equilibrium or to control the behavioral expression of changes in mood. It is because of this disinhibition factor that frontal lobe patients egocentrically or "childishly" overreact to minor provocations or frustrations.

In its most usual clinical presentation, an external irritant or frustration–a thwarted goal, an annoying person–provokes an emotional response from the frontal lobe subject, which quickly escalates beyond what most people would regard as appropriate for the degree of provocation. Once started, the subject seems to have little or no control over the behavior. Serious sustained violence and destructiveness are seldom seen in frontal lobe outbursts; rather, shouting, crying, cursing, fist-pounding on furniture, and throwing of reachable objects are the most common manifestations, the overall impression being more of a tantrum than a concerted aggressive attack, although extreme physical violence, characterized by disinhibited "overkill," occasionally occurs. Insight into, and remorse over, the outburst is rare, and the patient's labile emotional state can often easily switch from rage to sadness to mirth with the right kind of prodding and cajoling (Miller, 1990b, 1990c, 1993d, 1998a).

Historical and contextual factors are important, as serious violent crime rarely emerges in previously nonaggressive persons following an acquired lesion (stroke, brain tumor, head injury) limited to the frontal lobes (Volavka, 1995). Additionally, although frontal lobe dysfunction is suggested by neuropsychological testing in many persons characterized by criminal or violent behavior, many of these tests are not specific for frontal lobe dysfunction and may suggest longstanding developmental cognitive impairment related to several brain regions and systems, including the ones that may underlie Gottfredson & Hirschi's (1990) **self-control theory of crime** (Chapter 3). And even if one accepts that these tests accurately assess impaired frontal lobe functioning, this by itself would be insufficient to prove a causal connection between such localized impairment per se and criminal violence. Finally, it may be that aggression following frontal lobe damage occurs only or mainly when other areas, such as the limbic system, are injured as well. Again, great care must be taken in clinical evaluation and forensic case formulation when applying neuropsychological techniques, concepts, and arguments to issues of complex behavior, such as violent criminal activity (Anderson, 2007; Miller, 1986e, 1987, 1990c; Volavka, 1995, 1999). In fact, neuropsychological tests of frontal lobe functioning have not by themselves been found to be generally effective in rendering determinations about criminal competency and responsibility (Reid-Proctor et al., 2001).

BOX 2.3. "MY FRONTAL LOBES MADE ME DO IT"

As with any brain variable, correlations with particular forms of behavior—constructive or maladaptive—are hardly one-to-one. Nevertheless, some criminal attorneys have used a "**frontal lobe defense**" for purposes of arguing absence of criminal responsibility or mitigation. These have often been based on reports of significantly disordered, seemingly compulsively disinhibited behavior that appears to be out-of-character for patients discovered to have frontal lobe pathology.

For example, one 40-year-old man with no prior legal or psychiatric history, began visiting prostitutes, spending hours with pornography, and attempted to molest his 12-year-old stepdaughter. He was arrested, convicted, and given the choice of attending a sexual addiction program or going to prison. Even with this sentence looming before him, he was unable to restrain his sexual impulses. Subsequent neurodiagnostic work-up revealed a large tumor impinging on his right orbitofrontal cortex. The tumor was removed and, with it apparently went the sexually impulsive behavior; however, the sexual activity soon began again and a brain scan showed the tumor had regrown. A second surgery again eliminated the behavior, presumably by again removing the pressure from this man's frontal lobes (Burns & Swerdlow, 2003; Swerdlow & Burns, 2002). What is not explained in this narrative is why the disinhibited, impulsive behavior was sexual in nature and not, for example, aggressive. Was the nature of the acts determined by other brain variables, e.g., proximity of the tumor to the limbic system, or did the brain pathology simply disinhibit a latent tendency toward sexual acting-out that would otherwise have been well-controlled in this seemingly otherwise law-abiding man? We'll never know that for sure.

A more explicit use of the "frontal lobe defense" occurred in the well-known case of Kip Kinkel, one of the rampage school shooters at Springfield, Oregon in 1998 (see Chapter 12). Kinkel's attorneys entered a not-guilty-by-reason-of-insanity (NGRI) plea based on the presence of what were described as "small cavities" observed in the frontal lobes on scans of Kinkel's brain. However, they failed to demonstrate that these purported lesions bore any causal connection to the acts of violence, and Kinkel was convicted and sentenced to 111 years in prison (Mobbs et al., 2007).

Probably the most famous frontal lobe case in neuropsychology goes back to 1848 and involves a 25-year-old foreman of a construction crew working on America's cross-continental railroad, which often involved blasting through solid rock with dynamite. Phineas Gage was a hard worker, a sober, diligent, and respected supervisor who was not afraid to roll up his sleeves and get down in the work pits with his men. On one occasion, he was packing gunpowder into a rock with a tamping iron when a stray spark prematurely ignited the charge, blasting the 3½-foot, 1¼-inch, 13-pound iron projectile up through Gage's left cheek and out the top of his skull. Amazingly, he survived this explosive missile injury, but much of his left frontal lobe was destroyed. He recovered physically and his memory and general intellect did not appear to be appreciably impaired, but according to his family and friends, he was "no longer Gage," that is, his personality had dramatically altered. He had previously been a dignified, soft-spoken, polite, and considerate young man. After the accident, he became profane, irritable, and violent—in short, a different person. He eventually tried to go back to work, but was unable to keep any employment for more than a few weeks. Although he had retained the knowledge and technical skills to perform his various jobs, he had lost his social graces and his ability to work with others, and eventually made his living exhibiting himself (and his ever-present tamping iron) in various shows and exhibitions (Anderson, 2007; Blake et al., 1995; Stuss et al., 1992).

One of my own cases of this type began with a call from a local criminal defense attorney who'd gotten my name from another lawyer I had worked with on a civil personal injury case. His 23-year-old client, he said, was "clearly impaired by brain damage" during the commission of his offense (armed robbery and assault) because he had been in numerous fights in the past, had gotten knocked out many times, and on one admission to a hospital following one of these melees, a brain scan indicated a left frontal subdural hematoma (bleeding in the brain), which resolved over time. That was over three years ago. Since then, the client had been arrested several times, mostly for drug possession and petty theft, but this time, he and two accomplices robbed a convenience store and pistol-whipped the owner (resulting, paradoxically, in serious brain damage to the victim). The attorney assured me that my job would be easy because "everybody knows that frontal lobe damage makes you unable to control your behavior—I just need an expert to say so."

Upon reviewing the records, I contacted the attorney and informed him that I was not that expert. That is, I could not make a credible case for frontal lobe damage as a mitigating factor in this case because: (1) the defendant's criminal record far predated the index injury; (2) there was no evidence of persisting lesions in the brain on follow-up scans; (3) even if there were, there was no evidence that the defendant's behavior changed significantly from before the injury to after (in fact, he had been involved in several fights since the index injury); and (4) his overall behavior was inconsistent with someone who is significantly "brain-damaged." The attorney sulked away and I have no idea how the case was resolved.

The Cerebral Hemispheres

The brain is a bilateral structure. For most people, language functions are mediated primarily by the left hemisphere, while visuospatial functions are handled mainly by the right hemisphere; this relationship is slightly weaker for left-handers and for women. Concerning the neuropsychology of violence, a number of studies have observed that neuropsychological deficits in groups of violent offenders tend to involve primarily left hemisphere functions of verbal comprehension and expressive speech articulation. This is consistent with a large number of studies on delinquent and conduct disordered children that suggest that lowered IQ in these groups is primarily a function of lowered verbal (left hemisphere) IQ, as opposed to lowered performance, or spatial (right hemisphere) IQ (Brickman et al., 1984; Flor-Henry, 1976; Gabrielli & Mednick, 1980; Miller, 1984b, 1986c, 1986e, 1988a; Mungas, 1988; Nachson, 1988; Serafetinides, 1965; Tarter et al., 1984; Moffitt, 1990a, 1990b; Raine et al., 1995; Yeudall, 1977; Yeudall & Fromm-Auch, 1979).

Neuropsychological Integration

An attempt to bring together many of the neuropsychological and psychobiological data of the preceding decades was formulated into a neurodevelopmental theory by Geschwind & Galaburda (1985). The theory begins with a few well-validated observations: (1) left-handedness is more common in men than women; (2) many developmental disorders of language, speech, thought, and emotion, such as stuttering, dyslexia, and autism, are strongly male-predominant; (3) women are on average superior in verbal ability, while men tend to have better spatial skills; (4) for both sexes, people who are left-handed or who have learning disabilities (the two are frequently seen together) often exhibit a superiority in right-hemisphere functions such as art or spatial reasoning; (5) left-handedness and ambidexterity occur more frequently in the various developmental disorders of childhood, such as dyslexia and attention deficit disorder; (6) certain disorders are more common in left-handers and are frequently seen in combination, for example, migraine headaches, nearsightedness, dyslexia, disorders of pigmentation, skeletal anomalies, allergies, and other immune system disorders.

Recall the above discussion about the role of the male hormone testosterone in human behavior. We know that, even in the womb, the male gonads begin secreting this hormone into the intrauterine environment in greater amounts than by females. Thus, the gestating male brain is exposed to higher concentrations of testosterone, which has the effect of delaying maturation and cell migration to the left hemisphere more than the right. With more neuronal binding sites available in the right hemisphere, more neuronal connections occur there than on the left and, by the time the left hemisphere catches up, it has already lagged behind in terms of interneuronal connectivity. This, according to the theory, accounts for the average superiority of males in spatial cognitive abilities and more action-oriented responding, and the average superiority of females in more verbal-reflective cognition and controlled responding. Since life is a series of overlapping bell curves, you will still see thoughtful, verbally bright males and impulsive, spatially adept females, but the ratios will be somewhat smaller. Hence the neuropsychobiological profile of the child at risk for criminal behavior–low verbal IQ, poor academic functioning, impulsive response style, egocentric orientation, high aggressiveness, and poor emotional and behavioral self-control–may be something that begins before birth. This trait complex may be genetically programmed at the front end, and either reinforced or mitigated environmentally at the back end, but in between, in the womb, the brain's wiring may well be tuned in part by the same hormonal forces that evoke and reinforce many of these traits later in life.

Note that only a minority of these children and adults will pursue a relentlessly persistent criminal lifestyle per se. Most will simply amble through life, trying to get by with limited education and employment skills, perhaps capitalizing on their good mechanical aptitude and avoiding trouble when they can, but at times succumbing to temptation to follow their characteristically impulsive, nonreflective instincts, which may result in decisions that blow up in their faces. Perhaps only when combined with the extreme lack of empathy and remorselessness of the psychopath (Chapter 8) and/or the extreme emotional dysregulation of a mood disorder (Chapter 6) do these biobehavioral ingredients combine to produce the perfect recipe for the "born criminal."

BOX 2.4. DESIGNER DEFENSES I (BIOLOGICAL): THE TWINKIE DEFENSE

As we saw in Chapter 1, both major versions of the **insanity defense** (M'Naughten and ALI) require that the defendant's cognitive and/or volitional impairment be severe and that it be caused by a recognized diagnostic syndrome. This is usually taken to mean one of the diagnoses in the DSM-IV-TR or its predecessors. Defenses of **diminished capacity** typically require less proof of total cognitive or volitional impairment, but also commonly cite some known diagnostic entity. Yet, over the years, creative defense attorneys—and sometimes defendants themselves—have tried to apply novel defenses based on syndromes that heretofore have not existed in the psychiatric and psychological literature. In this chapter and the next one, I present three examples of what have come to be called **designer defenses**, one based on the biological model described in this

continued

BOX 2.4.—*Continued*

chapter, and two based on the psychological and sociological models discussed in Chapter 3. We'll start with biology.

On November 27, 1978, Dan White, a clean-cut, conservative, but disgruntled San Francisco city employee, showed up at City Hall for a meeting to negotiate the terms under which he might be rehired for the job he'd petulantly quit earlier that month. Instead, White pulled a gun and shot to death San Francisco Mayor George Moscone along with City Supervisor and flamboyant gay activist Harvey Milk. He attempted to flee the scene but was captured a short time later.

At his trial, one of his defense attorneys asserted that White had been depressed at the time of the crime, as evidenced by radical changes in his life-style, including quitting his job, conflicts with his wife, and deterioration in his daily grooming and health habits. Much was made of the fact that White had been a diet and fitness fanatic, but since his purported psychological decline, he had been consuming junk foods and soft drinks, cited as further evidence of how hopeless and helpless he felt. As an element of his testimony, the psychiatrist for the defense cited the controversial evidence that excessive sugar intake could adversely affect brain metabolism and worsen mood disorders, especially bipolar mood swings. Another psychiatrist testified that White had killed the two men in a fit of explosive rage while on "automatic pilot."

Based on this testimony, White's defense attorney was able to persuade the jury that his client's capacity for rational thought was diminished at the time of the crime. Although White was not acquitted on the grounds of insanity, the jury found that his mental state was sufficiently impaired to preclude the deliberative pre-meditation required for first degree murder conviction (despite the fact that White had smuggled in a gun and had planned out his escape route), and convicted him of voluntary manslaughter instead. White served 5 years of a 7-year sentence and was released in 1984. In 1986 he committed suicide by carbon monoxide.

Although the particular pastry, Hostess Twinkies (a popular sugar-coated spongecake with vanilla crème filling), was never mentioned by name, one enter-prising reporter, Paul Krassner, coined the term "Twinkie defense" and later went on to write a book about the case called Sex, Drugs and the Twinkie Murders. But to fully appreciate the impact this case has had on public's impression of scientif-ic testimony, it is important understand the confluence of historical and cultural factors operating at the time.

In 1978, the country was still recoiling from the countercultural revolution of the 1960s which, for many conservative-minded Americans, was challenging their established world views on politics, values, and social mores. At that time, such cultural phenomena as the sex and drug-fueled disco scene and the rise of the new gay rights movement were viewed by many as palpable threats to the moral, religious, and cultural foundations of American life. Along comes a clean-cut, con-servative, health-conscious man, who has been forced out of his job (so he believes) by unfair treatment at the hands of his unethical (and, at least in one case, sexually perverse) bosses, has been driven to a life of demoralized personal dissolution, seething in his room while cramming down spongecake, who, one day, in a fit of righteous vengeance, blows away his perceived malfeasors. Now he pleads exoneration because his brain was addled by sugary junk food at the time of the crime. The media could not have found a more mouth-watering confection of events and terminology: disgruntled conservative employee Dan *White* shoots to death gay activist Harvey *Milk* and claims, "the *Twinkies* made me do it." *Twinkies killed the twink! Twinkies and Milk!* Even in the days before the Internet, the story received international attention. But there was a second important reason this case got traction, one that has been less well recognized.

Remember the basic defense: sugary snack foods exacerbated Whlte's mood disorder to the point where he was no longer fully responsible for his actions. Forgetting for a moment that, other than based on his own self-report, nobody would have been able to verify just how much oversweetened junk White had allegedly been scarfing down, what on earth could snack foods have to do with murder? It turns out that just several years before, parents of children with learning disorders and then-termed "hyperactivity" or "minimal brain dysfunction" (later to be termed Attention Deficit Hyperactivity Disorder in DSM-III; see Chapter 19) began being drawn to claims that excessive glucose ingestion (along with a host of other dyes, preservatives, and additives ordinarily found in processed snack foods) could worsen symptoms of inattention, distractibility, impulsivity, and hyperactivity, and that by restricting or eliminating refined sugar and other additives from their diets, these kids could lead normal lives, succeed in school, and generally not be such pains in the butt to parents and teachers. Further, in some circles, these claims expanded to include the assertion that at least some of these clinical cases were *caused* by the malevolent foodstuffs.

Followers of dietary restriction therapies soon coalesced into a cult-like movement and, despite scientific evidence that is no less shaky today than 30 years ago, this advocacy group has only grown, as many well-intentioned but desperate parents continue to seek solutions to their kids' behavior problems. If anything, the broader suspicion that we are being poisoned by a host of unseen contaminants—pollution, toxic mold, radon, power lines—has increased as our technology-driven lives become more complex, confusing, and intimidating.

Thus, by 1978, the zeitgeist was set for someone to introduce the idea that the overconsumption of junk food could have far more sinister effects than simply causing some 4th-grader to throw a tantrum over his homework. Without this prevailing cultural climate, would 12 Jurors have taken seriously the idea that a snack food could make a man sufficiently lose his reason to commit murder without compunction? As noted in Chapter 1, the insanity defense is invoked infrequently and is even more rarely successful. Dietary designer defenses such as those in the Twinkie category have seldomly been preferred in the last three decades (the snack food and soft drink companies are no doubt relieved). But the idea that exogenously introduced chemicals of all types can affect our behavior stubbornly persists. Ironically, numerous people who are panicked over yellow dye in their corn flakes will still smoke, drink alcohol excessively, and fail to use seat belts while driving, because human nature programs us to take more caution with

continued

BOX 2.4.—*Continued*

seemingly uncontrollable threats (I don't make the corn flakes) than those which at least appear to be within our control (I can decide whether or not to light up or buckle up).

SUMMARY AND CONCLUSIONS

As much as we must respect the physical side of human nature, biological theories of criminal behavior should be viewed as complementary to the psychosocial models presented in the next chapter. **Genes** predispose each person to a particular set of traits, but these are evoked, expressed, and reinforced in the context of our environments. **Neurotransmitters** are the chemical communicators of the nervous system and certain neurotransmitters have been associated with certain types of thought, feeling, and behavior which, in turn, provide the substrate for both normal and antisocial behavior. This is further influenced by the action of **hormones**, some of whose effects may begin before we are born, and other which are triggered at certain development periods in life. For example, the male hormone **testosterone** is associated with assertive dominance and status-seeking, but does not necessarily presage violent criminal behavior unless linked with certain other disturbances, such as neurotransmitter imbalances and neuropsychological patterns.

A variety of **toxic-metabolic factors** can influence behavior, but not always in a consistent direction. Many habitual criminals seem to show a general **psychophysiological underarousal** of their nervous systems which may impel them to crave and seek stimulation. **Neuropsychological studies** suggest that anomalies in the brain's **frontal lobes** impair the ability to reason, plan, tolerate frustration, restrain impulses, and maintain goals, and that this may be associated with the impulsive, egocentric, irresponsible, exploitive, and predatory behavior shown by many habitual criminals. Problems with **left-hemisphere** language processing may account for the relative inability to conceptualize reflective and adaptive solutions to problems, as well as being associated with a number of verbal learning disorders that stunt educational achievement and employment opportunities, further reducing the range of constructive life options. Biological conceptualizations may be misused in the form of **designer defenses** that appeal to pseudoscientific causal explanations for criminal behavior.

Chapter **3**

Psychosocial Theories
of Criminal Behavior

> In my opinion, this child does not need to have
> his head shrunk at all. Juvenile delinquency is
> purely a social disease.
> — "Officer Krupke," *West Side Story,* 1957

As important as biology and neuroscience may be for understanding the physical substrates of criminal behavior, brains and bodies do not function in a vacuum. In fact, the cycles of biological vs. psychological vs. sociological theories of crime seem to rise and fall in waves, according to the prevailing political and economic climate of the times. Under conservative administrations, the predominant attitude seems to be that people are responsible for their own behavior, so that when winners win it is to their credit, and when losers lose, it's their own fault. Accordingly, attributing the behavior of people to "social forces" would dilute these internal attributions of responsibility, so that "bad people" must have "bad brains" and/or willfully "bad behavior" and therefore there is little the well-off can do to help these hopeless miscreants—other than keep them away from the "good" people. In more liberal political climes, we are more likely to regard ourselves as our brothers' keepers, and believe that how we structure the social and economic hierarchy can influence the actions of our fellow citizens for good or for ill.

PSYCHOLOGICAL THEORIES OF CRIME

Psychodynamic Theories

Psychodynamic, or **psychoanalytic**, models of the mind stem from the work of Sigmund Freud and his followers. A basic assumption of psychodynamic theory is that a large portion of human motivation and mental life is unconscious. We may think we are behaving for self-chosen, rational reasons, but much of the true motivation for what we do is kept out of consciousness. This material remains below the surface because it would be too disturbing

63

for us to acknowledge, as it consists largely of sexual and aggressive instincts, whose expression has been thinly restrained by the demands of civilized living. In this model, human personality is formed in childhood as the result of how successfully each child negotiates the conflicts around sex and aggression that arise in a largely invariant set of developmental stages. Failure to work through these conflicts between instinctual drives and parental controls, and later, the demands of society, leads to repression of these conflicts and the development of various kinds of personality disorder and psychopathology. On a day-to-day level, repressed instinctual sexual energy (**libido**) could also push unconscious material to leak out in disguised form through the "big three" expressive modalities of psychoanalytic theory: **symptoms**, **dreams**, and **parapraxes** ("Freudian slips").

Freud developed several paradigms of the mind to encompass his theories, but the final model he endorsed, and the one most recognized today, was a tripartite model consisting of the id, ego, and superego. The **id** is the repository of instinctual drives and urges, a seething mental cauldron of unthinkable secret desires that would be too disturbing for the individual to acknowledge. Through development, the individual learns how to satisfy his or her needs by dealing constructively with reality, the task of the **ego**, which employs the cognitive functions–reason, reflection, memory, planning, organization, and task-persistence–that enable the person to get what he or she needs in an appropriate manner, e.g., buying a meal at a restaurant instead of stealing someone else's sandwich; bringing flowers and going on a date instead of committing rape.

But whereas the ego knows *how* to negotiate the demands of the real world to get the person's needs satisfied, it doesn't necessarily know *when* it's appropriate to do so; the ego is practical but amoral. As part of the process of learning the rules for being a socialized, civilized human being, the developing child internalizes the societal rules, demands, strictures, and punishments, as expressed by the first "law" he or she ever knows, the parents, and later reinforced by the formal laws and conventional rules of school life, work life, and society in general. Out of this develops each individual's **superego**, the codex of morality that governs our law-abiding behavior–what most people would call a conscience. In the best case, the child successfully assimilates reasonable parental rules, which are modified as appropriate to the child's age and growing responsibility, until a confident, independent, and well-socialized adolescent and young adult emerges. However, overly lax, excessively harsh, or confusingly inconsistent parental caretaking and discipline can warp the superego's development in unhealthy directions. Children with weak superegos fail to develop internalized restraints and therefore spend their lives attempting to gratify their impulses at the expense of others, unmindful and uncaring of the harm they cause. Overly harsh and punitive superegos bind the individual in anxiety and social inhibition, and lead the person to become self-doubting, self-loathing, obsessive-compulsive, and paranoid. In these cases, internalized anger at oneself may be expressed as anger at others, leading to the paradox that both too-weak and too-harsh superegos may be associated with aggressive, antisocial behavior.

To keep unwanted thoughts and urges and painful truths about oneself out of conscious awareness, the ego utilizes a number of **defense mechanisms**. In moderation, these are adaptive because they allow us to maintain a reasonable degree of self-esteem and productive motivation in daily life. Used excessively, however, defense mechanisms throttle self-insight and reduce us to reactive automatons, buffeted to and fro by our repressed desires, but remaining enigmas to ourselves (even if our motives are often transparently obvious to others). The major classes of defense mechanism are as follows:

Repression. This is the basic defense mechanism that underlies all the others. It is an automatic, unconscious process that the ego uses to keep unwanted mental matter from awareness, i.e., not thinking about it without being aware that you're not thinking about it.

Suppression. A conscious, purposeful effort by the person to keep painful information out of awareness, i.e., deliberately *forcing yourself* not to think about it: "I know this is bad, but I just won't dwell on it." This is often aided by distraction: "I'll just think about something else."

Denial. The person deliberately refuses to recognize a painful truth that is otherwise objectively obvious: "Oh, no, that college did *not* just send me that rejection letter; I *can't* not go to that school; I don't believe it!"

Rationalization. Coming up with a superficially logical or laudable reason for something that is irrationally or malevolently motivated: "I did you a favor by stealing your boyfriend because everyone knows he's a jerk and I was just protecting you from getting hurt."

Displacement. You want to express an emotion against one person, but it's not safe to do so (usually because they're an authority figure and have some power over you), so you take it out on someone more familiar or safer. For example, your boss or teacher ticks you off, so you come home and explode on your family for some minor irritation.

Projection. Repudiating your own wishes, feelings, and motives by attributing them to someone else: "You hate me, you just want me to fail so that you'll look good at my expense" (when it's really you that harbors the resentment against the other's success). Projection is a fundamental defense mechanism underlying some forms of paranoia (Chapters 5, 7).

Reaction formation. Purposefully acting in just the opposite way to how you really feel, but being unaware that you're doing so, fooling yourself into believing that's how you really feel. For example, you lather syrupy praise on someone you actually loathe, or you join a celibate cult in response to your own uncontrollable sexual urges.

Acting out. Sometimes considered a combined subform of projection and reaction formation, the individual repudiates pain, shame, hurt, vulnerability, and weakness by aggressive displays that highlight strength and rebellion. This is often imputed by criminal psychologists to some adolescents who "act out" the pain of their abusive upbringing by engaging in delinquent acts.

Sublimation. Considered the healthiest of the defense mechanisms, this turns a potential negative into an adaptive positive by channeling dark urges into socially constructive activity. For example, a boy who likes to cut up animals becomes a respected surgeon instead of a serial killer; another adolescent who finds himself attracted to child pornography becomes a sex crimes investigator instead of a pedophile; a third young man who is large, aggressive and likes to be on top becomes a star athlete instead of a street thug.

While psychodynamic theory has remained largely within the realm of clinical diagnosis and treatment, a few psychoanalysts have attempted to apply these concepts directly to criminology. Freud himself always emphasized the role of sexuality (**eros**) in human development and only later in his career (Freud, 1915, 1930, 1933) came to acknowledge the role of aggression in human personality, after the ravages of the First World War made this dark side of human nature unavoidable. Even then, Freud seemed to have trouble accepting human aggression on its own terms and relegated it to the role of an artifact of a quasi-scientific, metaphysical death instinct (**thanatos**), whereby all life sought to regain its original state of inorganic stasis.

Nevertheless, some of Freud's followers recognized the independent role of aggression in human mental life. One of Freud's early followers, Alfred Adler (1917) talked about the **striving for superiority** and the **will to power** that drove different forms of human behavior, including criminal behavior. Karl Menninger (1938, 1963) chronicled the ways in which the aggressive instinct manifested itself in both individual psychopathology and societal disruption. Many of the so-called **neoFreudians**, such as George S. Klein (1954), Heinz Hartmann (1958), and Riley Gardner (1959) placed greater emphasis on the cognitive functions of the ego and discussed how the ego could mold the aggressive instinct into something positive and productively forceful, or allow it to assume a malevolently destructive shape.

More recently, Menninger (2007) has used psychoanalytic theory to explain the dynamics underlying mass violence such as school shootings (Chapter 12), which he conceives of as being triggered by **uncontained rage**. The initial stimulus is the perception of some (real or imagined) shame-producing injury, insult, disappointment, or frustration that is regarded as being profoundly unfair, producing what is called a **narcissistic wound**. This outrage is experienced as intolerable and cries out for some kind of response. Assuming the individual has the weaponry to take action, he lashes out destructively. Theorists from the earliest days of psychoanalysis have pointed out how the gun is not simply a mechanism for killing, but represents, in shape and function, the ultimate symbol of male potency and power (men who are feeling disempowered in life frequently report dreams of firing a gun at an adversary, only to have the bullets dribble languidly to the ground a few feet away).

As a psychological treatment modality, psychoanalysis requires a considerable dedication of time, and effort, and finances, involving regular and frequent therapeutic sessions, often spanning years, in order to help the patient break through his resistances to recognizing and overcoming the defense mechanisms that keep him from bringing unconscious conflicts to awareness and working them through. Even then, as Freud himself stated, the best that can be hoped for is to "transform neurotic misery into ordinary unhappiness." Certainly, as a way of counteracting criminal behavior, the enormous expenditure of clinical resources necessary to treat each individual offender would be impractical. Yet, psychoanalysis survives today, less as a recognized treatment modality, as much as a source of ideas and concepts that still hold fundamental validity, for example, the fact that many of us harbor impulses, fears, and wishes we are partly or wholly unaware of, and the importance of early social relationships in forming character. If anything, most people are actually pleased by the idea of having levels, depths, dimensions, and potentialities to their personality that may remain untapped and yet to be explored.

Behaviorism and Social Learning Theories

Whereas psychoanalysis emerged from the field of clinical psychiatry and medicine, **behaviorism** developed out of academic and experimental psychology, through the works of Edward L. Thorndike, Ivan Pavlov, John B. Watson, and B.F. Skinner. The central empiricist premises of behaviorism are that all behavior is shaped and maintained by its consequences, and that what happens to an organism and what it actually does is all we can objectively observe and study—no inferred mental models or arcane psychodynamics tolerated here. In the behaviorist view, there are no guaranteed innate traits or instinctual forces that differentiate one human being from another, and each individual can learn to be a sinner or a saint, depending on the complex network of rewards and punishment he or she is exposed to, what behaviorists call **contingencies of reinforcement**. Language and higher thinking, although unique to man, nevertheless represent just more complex forms of behavior. For the behaviorist, what the Freudians would call the "unconscious" is comprised of contingencies of reinforcement that the person has never become aware of, or that he or she has been reinforced for keeping out of conscious awareness. In fact, consciousness itself is the ability to describe and manipulate one's own contingencies of reinforcement.

Applied to the field of sociology in general, and criminology in particular, behaviorism finds expression in **social learning theory** (Bandura, 1973, 1977), which recognizes that humans learn by observing others, as well as from their own experiences. Thus, in shaping our socialization within a given community, we can see what kinds of rewards and punishments happen to other people whose behavior we might wish to emulate. In some communities, if good things tend to happen to good people, that's the direction we're likely to go in; in other communities, if being the baddest punk on the block is what garners respect and material rewards, we'll be swayed in that direction.

At the end of the 1938 film, *Boys Town,* Father Flanagan, played by Spencer Tracy, fixes his gaze heavenward and intones, "There are no 'bad' boys." The good father could have been describing **differential association theory** (Matsueda, 1988; Silver, 2000a, 2006; Silver et al., 2002; Sutherland, 1929, 1932, 1934; Sutherland & Cressey, 1974), developed within that same time period, which posits that, like all behavior, criminal behavior is learned and that there are no innately "bad" children, no predestined "born criminals." Young criminals-to-be learn two things from the families, social groups, and communities they grow up in. First, they master the specific techniques and methodologies of crime, such as picking locks, using a firearm, or buying and selling drugs. Second, more broadly, they learn to assimilate the identity of a criminal, gleaned from their own needs and values and those of their compatriots, because this identity gives them a sense of meaning unavailable through any other life activity. Then, to reinforce this meaning-providing identity, they limit their associations to like-minded fellows, further cementing their criminal identity, leading to more such differential associations, and so on, in a cycle of mutual reinforcement. Alert readers will note that this is similar to the concept of **active gene-environment correlation** discussed in Chapter 2, except that differential association theory rejects a primary role for biological predispositions to criminal behavior.

Bloodlessly robotic as it is sometimes made to sound, behaviorism is potentially far more optimistic than the psychodynamic theories which posit churning instinctual conflicts formed during fixed developmental stages as the origins of personality and behavior. In the behaviorist model, all we need do to improve the individual or the whole society is discover the countercondi-tioning programs that will unlearn the bad behavior and teach more socially adaptive behavior. Or better yet, find out what is the "best" method of parenting and community socialization, and then apply this to communities across the country, sort of like a vast behavioral immunization program, to prevent children from going down the wrong path to begin with. Albeit, such an ambitious social engineering project would be more complicated than it sounds, but the behavioral approach at least offers an aspirational model that could, if the basic theory is correct, one day improve the health and safety of societies worldwide (indeed, such a behavioristic Utopia was set out in novelistic form back in 1948 by none other than B. F. Skinner himself, in *Walden Two*). However, most people have a hard time accepting that the sum total of their lives can be articulated as a set of contingencies of reinforcement.

EARLY CRIMINAL PSYCHOLOGICAL TYPOLOGIES

Given its disruptive effects on societies around the world, and in all historic eras, people have always attempted to account for criminal behavior since the beginning of civilization. In 1907, the psychiatrist Havelock Ellis proposed a division of criminals into three major types:

Instinctive criminal. This is the "born criminal" popular in many descriptions. This individual is an impulsive, uncontrolled predator, whose criminality is so much a part of his personality and identity as to be virtually immune to correction or change, what Ellis characterized as a "moral monster." Ellis observed that this kind of dangerous, habitual offender is, thankfully, relatively rare. More modern depictions of the psychopath (Chapter 8) seem to echo this description.

Occasional criminal. More common is the individual that, ordinarily law-abiding, succumbs to the temptation to commit crimes out of economic necessity, social pressure, or other situationally motivating factors. However, with repeated acts, and especially with the reinforcement of criminal peers, the occasional criminal might evolve into the next type.

Habitual criminal. This person has come to adopt crime as a way of life. While usually not as violent and dangerous as the instinctive criminal, the habitual criminal engages in a string of petty and occasionally major crimes until he is caught.

Taking an explicitly psychological approach, derived partly from psychodynamic theory, Abrahamsen (1952) categorized criminal offenders into four categories:

Monetary offenders are motivated by practical, materialistic needs; they steal for money or other valuables, or commit violence to maintain gang territories or for revenge.

Neurotic offenders are impelled by unresolved unconscious conflicts, which give their crimes a seemingly "senseless" character, such as in kleptomania or firesetting (Chapter 20).

Unconscious guilt drives some offenders, with the primary motivation being to place themselves at risk of being caught and punished; this subtype may overlap with the neurotic offender above.

Character disorder underlies the criminal activity of those offenders described as pathological liars and cheaters, swindlers and con-men, alcoholics and drug addicts, nymphomaniacs and pedophiliacs, rapists and murderers.

Guttmacher (1972) divided criminals into four groups, including:

Normal criminals. What is "normal" about these offenders is simply that they are the most common type, typically raised in dysfunctional families, associating with like-minded criminal peers, and generally engaging in a pattern of repetitive, petty, and mostly nonviolent crime.

Accidental or occasional criminals. Those in this small group, are ordinarily law-abiding, but are lured or pressured into an isolated act of crime by particular circumstances.

Organically or constitutionally predisposed criminals. These are criminals whose mental retardation, dementia, epilepsy, or other organic brain syndrome renders them especially susceptible to impulsive criminal behavior or to being influenced by others to commit illegal acts.

Psychopathic or sociopathic criminals. This is the hard-core group of dangerous, violent repeat offenders who exploit and injure other people seemingly without compunction or restraint.

Common elements across these typologies seem to identify: (1) a mostly law-abiding citizen that is occasionally tempted or goaded into committing an isolated crime; (2) a more habitual criminal who makes a lifestyle out of mostly petty offenses, but occasionally may commit a major crime; (3) a hard-core predator who regularly commits serious offenses; and (4) a disturbed offender who, out of neurosis, psychosis, or organic brain syndrome is either driven, or cannot stop himself, from committing crimes, many of which may have a bizarre or seemingly senseless pattern. As subsequent chapters will illustrate, these primary types do account for a substantial proportion of criminal offenders.

SELF-CONTROL THEORY OF CRIME

It seems intuitively obvious that many crimes at least partially result from a person's failure–due either to inability or unwillingness–to control his or her impulses. The question is whether this is a generalized trait that can explain criminal behavior.

Gottfredson & Hirschi (1990) developed their **self-control theory of crime** to explain why some people are more at risk for criminal behavior than others. A great deal of criminological and psychological research supports the idea that individuals characterized by low self-control are highly impulsive, egocentric, action-oriented, thrill-seeking, frustration-intolerant, easily-irritated, risk-taking, and irresponsible to the obligations of school, work, and family commitments. They are frequently involved in deviant, maladaptive, self-defeating, aggressive, and criminal behavior. A number of studies have supported the role of low self-control in various crimes, including street robbery, bank robbery, narcotics offenses, and white-collar crimes, and in generally recidivistic criminal behavior (Arneklev et al., 1999; Benson & Moore, 1992; Britt & Gottfredson, 2003; Cretacci, 2008; DeLisi, 2001, 2005, 2008; DeLisi et al., 2003; Evans et al., 1997; Gibson & Wright, 2001; Higgins, 2004, 2005; Hochstetler & DeLisi, 2005; Longshore et al., 2004; McGloin et al., 2004; Paternoster & Brame, 1997, 2000; Piquero et al., 2005; Pratt & Cullen, 2000; Schultz, 2004; Stewart et al., 2004; Tremblay & Pare, 2003; Unnever et al., 2003; Wiebe, 2003; Winfree et al., 2006).

Many of the preceding descriptors sound like the traits associated with frontal lobe impairment (Chapter 2) which underlie many neuropsychological theories of criminal behavior. However, self-control theory's pointed repudiation of any biological explanatory framework unfortunately limits what could certainly be a fruitful area of collaborative research into the cognitive neuropsychology of crime.

CRIME AND HUMAN NATURE

Attempting a grand synthesis of biology, psychology, sociology, economics, and politics, James Q. Wilson & Richard J. Herrnstein published their best-selling and now-classic volume, *Crime and Human Nature,* in 1985. They conceptualized criminal behavior as a combination of the following factors, which coalesce and reinforce one another:

Innate traits, such as impulsivity, low frustration tolerance, preference for short-term gains rather than long-term goals, and low IQ, especially low verbal IQ.

Family environment, including abusive or neglectful parenting and failure to teach self-control and socialization skills.

Subcultural factors, including association with delinquent peers and membership in gangs that endorse predatory criminal behavior as a mark of status.

Schools, which influence the propensity toward criminal behavior in two ways: first, by the quality of education they provide as a means of personal betterment within the legitimate societal workforce, and second, by the values they inculcate as representatives of mainstream society.

Economics, which may lower or raise the tendency toward criminal behavior, depending on the way in which good or hard times influence the opportunities people have to legitimately earn what they want or turn to underground criminal economies, such as robbery or drug dealing.

Mass media, which have a twofold effect: first, by setting up expectations of what constitutes the "good life," and second, by legitimizing and glorifying aggressive behavior through TV, movies, and sensationalistic journalism.

CRIMINAL THINKING

In the traditional psychodynamic model, much attention is paid to unconscious emotional motivators or behavioral influencers. However, consistent with the work of the later neo-Freudian **ego psychologists**, and paralleling the so-called **cognitive revolution** in psychology in general, there has been a recent trend to analyze how criminals actually *think* to see if their mental processes are in fact different from that of the noncriminal population (Andrews & Bonta, 1998; Yochelson & Samenow, 1976a,b, 1977; Samenow, 1984; Wellman, 1990). Accordingly, a number of typologies of criminal thinking have been developed.

Criminal Thinking Styles

One of the first systematic explorations of criminal cognition came from the work of Yochelson & Samenow (1976a,b) who emphasized a qualitative difference between the way career criminals conceptualize the world and the rest of us do. For example, the authors described three cognitive processes, spanning different time periods in the commission of a crime, that enable a criminal to commit the act:

Corrosion. This is a process of rationalization and justification that allows the criminal to erode the psychological impediments prior to committing a criminal act: "I deserve what they all have"; "It's a dog-eat-dog world"; "Everybody does it"; "He/she [the victim] deserves it."

Cutoff. At the time of the crime, any last qualms about committing the deed are banished by a rapid cognitive device, often accompanied by an internal verbal cue, sometimes expressed aloud: "Screw it"; "Let's rock"; "Just freakin' do it."

Power thrust. After the fact, the criminal continues to justify his actions, and to bolster his self-image as a tough taker of what he wants: "I'm the man"; "No one messes with me"; "There are wolves and there are sheep in this world, and I'm a wolf."

Criminal Cognitive Patterns

Walters (1990, 1995, 2002) has adapted Yochelson & Samenow's (1976a, 1976b) conceptualization to elaborate eight cognitive patterns that he believes characterize criminal thinking:

Mollification. Rationalizing criminal behavior by blaming external forces: "The deck is stacked against me: I have no choice but to steal;" "He disrespected me: I have no choice but to smack him down so I don't look like a punk."

Cutoff. Quickly squelching thoughts that would deter a criminal act: "Just do it"; "Don't wuss out."

Entitlement. Feeling that one is special and has the right to commit the crime: "I'm smarter/stronger than him, so I deserve to take what he's got"; "I bought her dinner, so she better have sex with me."

Power orientation. Having a need to be in control at all times: "They better know they can't mess with me"; "You gotta crack a few heads so they'll respect you."

Sentimentality. In some cases, the criminal tries to offset the perceived wrongfulness of his acts by invoking thoughts of the good things he's done: "Sure, I rob people–you gotta do that to survive. But at least I give some of that money to my old lady and her kids; I know plenty of guys who blow it all on drugs."

Cognitive indolence. Using mental shortcuts instead of trying to figure out complex problems: "I don't have time to think about all that crap, I'll just do what I need to do and worry about it later."

Discontinuity. There is a lack of stability, reliability, and perseverance to the criminal's overall behavior and lifestyle; behavior is propelled impulsively, rather than being guided reflectively: "Hey, why waste brain cells thinking about it–just friggin' do it!"

Hostile Attribution Bias

Hostile attribution bias is the predisposition to interpret the otherwise harmless or neutral words and actions of others as having malicious intent: "The world is a mean place and people will always try to get you if you don't get them first." These are children, adolescents, or adults who always seem to be "looking for trouble," and this may overlap with the clinical syndrome of paranoid personality disorder (Chapter 7). Vicious cycles usually arise when other people become irritated at the constant suspicion, even direct attacks, on the part of the subject, and so come to really shun or revile him or her, which only fuels the hostile attribution bias still further, in an escalating vicious cycle (Graham & Hudley, 1994; Matthews & Norris, 2002; Nasby et al., 1980; Quiggle et al., 1992; Tiedens, 2001; Zelli et al., 1995).

Culture of Honor

To explain the increased rate of violence in males of the Southeastern United States, as well as of African-American males in northern cities whose predecessors migrated from the culture of the American South, some theorists have evoked the concept of **honor-related schemata** (a **schema** is a mental framework which helps organize and explain a set of observations) which cohere around the preservation of an honorable self-image: "Don't mess with me—I'm a man to be reckoned with." In naturalistic research studies, Southern men have been observed to be significantly more likely to resort to violent retaliation than northern men when insulted or challenged by an adversary or bystander (Cohen et al., 1996; Nisbett, 1993).

Me vs. Them

From detailed study of seriously violent inmates and parolees, Toch (1992) observed that these subjects harbor two main cognitive schemata that heighten their risk for violent behavior. **Self-preserving strategies** consolidate and enhance one's own view of oneself as powerful, entitled, and deserving of respect and high status: "I'm big, I'm bad, so do what I say or stay out of my way." **Dehumanization of others** mentally reduces other people to inconsequential worms who deserve to be exploited or defeated in order to enhance the subject's own status: "Who cares what they think—I'm the boss."

Criminal Cognitive and Personality Traits

From an analysis of FBI files utilized in criminal profiling (also see Chapter 10), Palermo & Kocsis (2005) have derived a set of cognitive and personality traits that they believe to underlie the thinking of habitual criminal offenders:

Egocentricity. The criminal believes that the world revolves around him and that other people's stuff—property, sex, status—are just there for the taking.

Impulsivity. Emotionally shallow, rapid, nonreflective responding is his style, with little regard for the consequences or long-range implications of his actions.

Frustration. The downside of habitually leaping before you look is that many of your decisions will be dead wrong and very often you will not get what you want—or will get the opposite. Consequently, many offenders often feel powerless, overwhelmed and unable to handle the normal demands and responsibilities of life. This chronic frustration and self-loathing commonly manifests itself in anger which is projected outward on others: obviously, the criminal tells himself, it must be everybody else's fault except mine that I'm always screwing up.

Narcissism. The outward projection of blame is abetted by the characteristic egocentricity, grandiosity, sense of entitlement, and hypersensitivity to criticism that is a core narcissistic component the criminal thinking style (see also Chapter 7). For many criminals, failure to get the admiration and deference they think they deserve, leads to the aggressive acting-out of malignant narcissism (Kernberg, 1975), in which case the subject can go from seductively charming to violently dangerous in the blink of an eye.

Obsessive-compulsiveness. Some criminals compensate for the impulsive, frustrated directionlessness of their lives by developing a rigid, opinionated, and stereotyped style of thinking and behavior; in essence, they veer back and forth between impulsive and compulsive, but virtually never attain that middle point of being adaptively reflective (Miller, 1988b, 1989b). Thus, their overall behavioral pattern shows a labile, inconsistent quality to it, often veering from a compulsive lack of flexibility at one point in time, to impulsive aimlessness at another, in both cases perpetuating the sense of frustration noted earlier. Obsessive rigidity may be seen in the ritualistic behavior of some **organized serial killers** (Chapter 10).

Paranoia. It was David Shapiro (1965) who first delineated the continuities between the obsessive-compulsive and paranoid cognitive styles, both involving a rigid, strereotyped way of viewing the world and the actions of the people in it. Many criminals carry around a major chip on their shoulder, mistrusting the motives of others and viewing every human interaction with suspicion. Being generally dishonest and deceptive themselves, they use the defense mechanism of **projection** (see above and Chapter 7) to attribute these qualities to others, often provoking confrontations that only further confirm and entrench their jaded view.

Sadism. The essence of sadism is power, which is enjoyed through the infliction of pain and humiliation against a helpless victim. This feeling of control and dominance is something the sadistic criminal craves, which explains why many crimes are committed with gratuitous violence beyond that necessary to accomplish the goal (e.g., pistol-whipping or sexually molesting store clerks and customers in robbery). This sense of power offers a powerful antidote to the feelings of frustration and failure periodically experienced by many criminals, and may be a key component of the motivation of some types of serial offenders (Chapters 10, 14).

Aggressivity. This is the obvious tendency of many criminals to use force as a means of getting what they want, but it also refers to a general orientation toward interpersonal interactions, that talking and negotiating is for chumps, and that power and dominance represent "the only language people listen to."

Ambivalence. Inconsistent in most things, this also applies to many criminals' relationships with other people, often showing conflicting feelings of love and hate toward mates, friends, and family members. In part, this is aggravated by the criminal's own lack of a stable sense of self, which makes it hard to form stable relationships with others, a key feature of the borderline personality and others (Chapter 7), and is also fueled by his characteristic suspiciousness and mistrust of others around him.

Maladaptive Criminal Thinking Patterns

Recently, Mandracchia et al. (2007) have studied the thinking patterns of 435 convicted offenders, and have derived a total of 77 "**thinking errors**" that they factor-analyze into three main categories:

Control. Criminals are into power in all aspects of their lives, and shun any trace of weakness: it's all-or-nothing. To keep this inflatedly invulnerable self-perception going, criminals attempt to control, manipulate, and intimidate others, while banishing any thoughts or feelings of anxiety or sentimentality from their consciousness.

Cognitive immaturity. In ironic contrast to their tough-guy image, many of these offenders are characterized by a childlike self-pitying attitude and a set of immature cognitive patterns by which they interpret the world and make decisions to act. They react impulsively, rather than think about consequences. They plan poorly and fail to follow-up on commitments. They overuse generalization and intuition to the neglect of analysis and reflection. They have a black-and-white view of other people as either allies, enemies, or victims to be exploited, and these perceptions can change sporadically. They externalize blame and self-justify all of their actions.

Egocentrism. It's all about me, me, me, and what I can do—and what others are supposed to do—to make me feel good about myself. Criminals assume the world is supposed to revolve around them. They consider themselves special and entitled. They avoid any activity which they cannot excel at quickly and easily. They assume people are always talking about them, and this may acquire a paranoid quality, impelling them to retaliate for perceived slights and confrontations.

Implicit Theories and Criminal Cognitive Schemata

Whereas some theorists attribute criminal behavior to blind, irrational psychodynamic forces or the conditioning effect of social rewards and punishments, others, as we've just seen, focus on how criminals actually think about their choices and behaviors, how they make the decision to commit crimes or not. In one view, we all harbor **implicit theories** (Polaschek et al., 2009; Polaschek & Collie, 2004) about our lives and the world we live in. Implicit theories are composed of structured interconnected networks of beliefs, organized around a dominant theme or narrative that explains how the world works. An implicit theory provides an explanatory scaffolding to our identity, by which we justify our own actions and explain the actions of others. As guardians of identity, implicit theories are very resistant to revision and we tend to skew our interpretations of events in the direction of our implicit theories, which explains why ingrained beliefs and behaviors are so hard to change. Influenced by a combination of our genetic heritage, family upbringing, and experiences within our communities, our implicit theories may be cynical and malevolent or benign and accepting. Law-abiding citizens have their implicit theories and criminals have theirs. Implicit theories typically express themselves in a series of **cognitive schemata** by which we recurrently interpret and direct our behavior in given situations.

Recently, Polaschek et al. (2009) has described five types of cognitive schemata that he has identified in his study of violent prisoners:

Beat or be beaten. If you don't make the first move to establish your status, then others will take you for a punk. Usually this means that, on the slightest pretext of challenge or confrontation, the subject had better beat down his opponent decisively so there's no mistake about who's on top. Of course, this means that inevitably, the defeated party will be obligated to retaliate to reaffirm his own status in the power hierarchy.

Self-enhancement. Far from being a threat or a burden, many of these men welcome aggressive challenges precisely in order to give them the opportunity to display their prowess and dominance. In this way, they are constantly enhancing their own image as powerful and may actively seek out confrontations to keep proving this. The downside is that any form of defeat is intolerable and will impel the burning urge for retaliation, so essentially, the person is never finished fighting.

Self-preservation. Some of these men justify their badass reputation and behavior by convincing themselves that they have no choice: the world they live in is a cold, mean, predatory place and it's eat or be eaten. In some settings, such as a prison community or gang-ridden neighborhood, this may not be far from the truth. Sometimes, however, this paranoid attitude may generalize to people who would otherwise be considered harmless or even friendly, such as family members and romantic partners.

I am the law. Another kind of self-justification relates to a sense of inflated self-importance in which many of these men feel morally superior and entitled, even obligated, to "discipline" others when they believe the situation calls for it, all in the service of keeping the peace or protecting those things and people important to them, thus elevating their violent activities to a noble purpose. Naturally, they expect the recipients of this tough love peace-keeping effort to be grateful and, when this is not forthcoming, these erst-while protectors may turn on their reluctant charges and punish them for their ingratitude and betrayal.

I get out of control. Heightening their sense of unpredictable and uncontrollable dangerousness, these men revel in their reputations as loose cannons or "crazy motherf-'s" because it imparts a force-of-nature invincibility to their reputations. It also provides an excuse for the overkill response that many of these men show in their rageful attacks: "If he didn't want his head beat in, he shouldn't have messed with me–everybody knows that once I get going, I can't stop till it's over." Interestingly, loss of control is rarely attributed to the effect of drugs or alcohol, which would impart an outside cause to it and thereby dilute its dangerously unpredictable impact; after all, if I'm only a potential monster when I'm drunk or high, does that mean you can mess with me when I'm straight? In fact, many of these men pride themselves in being able to "hold my juice" without getting overwhelmed by substance effects, and have utter contempt for those who become careless and sloppy when intoxicated or who let their lives be controlled by addiction.

Commonalities in Criminal Thinking Typologies

Across the various typologies reviewed above, certain consistencies about the "criminal mind" seem to emerge. The habitual criminal is egocentric and narcissistic, and sees everything and everyone in terms of how they can benefit him. He is extremely invested in status, dominance, and power, and pursues these through a combination of cunning manipulation and explosive combativeness. He is rigid and inflexible in his thinking and sees everything from a me-versus-them perspective. He accepts little responsibility for his actions and justifies everything he does in an inconsistent and self-serving way. He eschews sentimentality, but may become agitated and depressed when he fails to get what he wants. His relationships are characterized by mistrust, hostility, exploitiveness, shallow emotionality, and instability. He lives in a cold, cruel world partly of his own making because he acts coldly and cruelly toward others, and partly because he surrounds himself with others like himself who mutually reinforce one another's adversarial worldview.

BOX 3.1. DESIGNER DEFENSES II (PSYCHOLOGICAL): BATTERED WOMAN SYNDROME

It's one thing to utilize established psychological syndromes and diagnostic categories as the basis for an affirmative NGRI defense, but just how "established" do these clinical entities have to be? On September 26, 2008, April Moylan, a 41-year-old Port St. Lucie, Florida woman accused of trying to kill her husband, Michael, by shooting him in the head, was released from jail after her defense attorney and prosecutors brokered a plea deal based on the **Battered Spouse Syndrome Defense**. In July of 2007, Michael Moylan appeared at a local hospital Emergency Room bleeding behind the ear and complaining of a headache. Doctors quickly determined that he had been shot in the head with a .32-caliber revolver, and he was treated and survived his injuries. April subsequently admitted to shooting her husband from beneath her pillow, at first claiming it was an accident. She was arrested on the charge of possession of a firearm by a convicted felon, but when evidence pointed to a deliberate attack, she was later rearrested on attempted murder charges.

April Moylan subsequently changed her plea to a Battered Spouse Syndrome defense, and her attorney retained Dr. Lenore Walker a psychologist at Nova Southeastern University, to examine her. It was Dr. Walker who opined that the defendant was suffering from Battered Spouse Syndrome at the time of the shooting. April Moylan has Dr. Walker to thank in another, more fundamental, way as well. In 1984, Walker published the first edition of her book, *The Battered Woman Syndrome*. Although the term **battered woman** had been used before, Walker's treatise was the first major attempt to describe and define this pattern of domestic violence as a distinct psychological syndrome, comparable to **posttraumatic stress disorder** (Chapter 6), that could be used as an affirmative defense in criminal cases. The book described the escalating cycle of violence often seen in domestic battery cases (see also Chapter 17) and the sense of helplessless that characterizes women who feel psychologically demoralized and trapped and so come to regard killing their abuser as the only way out.

Coincidentally, in the same year, the TV movie, *The Burning Bed* was broadcast on national television. This biopic starred Farah Fawcett as the real-life character, Francine Hughes, a woman who, by all accounts, had been severely physically and psychologically brutalized by her husband, Mickey Hughes, for 14 years. On March 9, 1977, after one of his many beatings, and, as she would later report, believing she had no other option, she doused her sleeping spouse with gasoline as he lay in a drunken stupor on his bed, and set him ablaze. The 10-woman, 2-man jury found that, in response to her feeling of imminent threat to her

continued

BOX 3.1.—*Continued*

life, Hughes had suffered "temporary insanity" during the commission of her crime and she was acquitted on the grounds of NGRI.

Coming at the height of the Women's Movement of the 1970s, the well-publicized trial attracted both professional and media pundit opinions with regard to whether "women's rights" included the entitlement to summarily execute abusive husbands. Should women be a "protected class" afforded special consideration in the criminal justice system? What about men who feel threatened and kill their wives? Partially in response to the wave of approval that greeted attempts by persecuted wives to strike back at their tormenters, and now given a clinical-scientific rationale by scholars like Walker, the Florida State Supreme Court ruled in 1999 that victims of marital violence can use Battered Spouse Syndrome as an affirmative defense in the charge of spousal murder or assault; this is now the case in 14 other states. In still other states, domestic battery (see Chapter 17) can be used as grounds for mitigation based on diminished capacity. It was this Florida decision that enabled April Moylan, nine years later, to go free.

For the present purposes, the main objection to Battered Woman Syndrome (or its newer, more egalitarian incarnation, **Battered Spouse Syndrome**) is one that applies to all such **designer defenses** (see also Boxes 2.2 and 3.2): it subverts the primary purposes of diagnosis, which is for classification, explanation, and treatment. If a woman is suffering from a recognized diagnostic syndrome, such as Brief Psychotic Disorder with Marked Stressors—the closest clinical correlate to the legal concept of "temporary insanity"—then this may legitimately be used as an affirmative NGRI defense or factor in mitigation. But to simply make up syndromes that apply to specific events (killing one's abusive spouse) or specific classes of persons (battered spouses) risks opening the floodgates to a torrent of designer defenses for exculpation of major crimes, including murder: Abused Child Syndrome, Bullied Student Syndrome, Mistreated Employee Syndrome, and so on.

This concern, however, may be misplaced. Juries are notoriously hard-nosed when it comes to even mainstream psychological defenses like bipolar psychosis or PTSD, so it is not surprising that Battered Woman (or Spouse) Syndrome is rarely successful as a sole NGRI defense, although, as noted above, many states permit it to be considered as a mitigating factor at sentencing. Other designer defenses would probably fare accordingly.

SOCIOLOGICAL THEORIES OF CRIME

Sociological theories of criminal behavior recognize that it is individuals who commit crimes, but emphasize the role of social, cultural, and political factors in shaping and influencing a person's probability of acting antisocially (Akers, 1985; Silver, 2006).

Differential Association Theory

Discussed earlier in connection with social learning theories, this is the "birds-of-a-feather" conceptualization that individuals who share proximity, common interests, and personality styles will imitate and reinforce one another's behavior as a way of forming and maintaining both an individual and group identity. Just as persons with particular academic, or athletic, or musical interests will find one another and prefer one another's company, so will those whose avocation is crime and deviance. This theory was discussed above in the context of behavioral and social learning models of crime.

Strain Theory

Another intuitive observation is that hard times often bring out the worst in people—but perhaps only in certain kinds of people. **General strain theory** (Agnew, 1992, 2004) posits that individuals under stress, defined here as loss of valuable resources or infliction of physical, emotional, or economic pain, will naturally experience heightened levels of frustration, anger, and fear. This impels them to "do something," or to take what the theory calls **corrective action**, which may include violence if this is seen as a viable "corrective" measure to deal with the problem, in the form of coercion, retaliation, or general aggression. Individuals with a mental disorder may be at greater risk because their coping abilities are already weakened and because they are much more likely to lack such practical stress-reducing resources as adequate food, shelter, money, or a supportive family. Additionally, their unusual behavior is alienating to many people, increasing their stigmatization, further reducing potential sources of social bonding and support, and further preventing them from seeking help in negotiating important life transitions. Finally, when impacted by the mental health or criminal justice system, they may feel manipulated, restrained, or coerced, and may use violence to "defend" themselves (Agnew, 2004; Elbogen et al., 2005; Estroff et al., 1991; Felson, 1992; Hiday, 1997; Hirschi, 1969; Laub et al., 1998; Link et al., 1999; Sampson & Laub, 1993; Silver, 2002, 2006; Silver & Teasdale, 2005).

Rational Choice Theory

Do some people just choose to be criminals? They do if they have a good enough reason, according to **rational choice theory**, which assumes that criminal behavior, like all behavior, is never purposeless, but always has some goal. In this view, people are not blindly driven by unconscious animal forces or behaviorally programmed like tinker-toy automatons, but make conscious, rational, deliberative decisions about their actions, based on their analysis of costs vs. benefits. Thus, if violence will net someone a tangible gain (money, property, status) that outweighs the costs (injury, incarceration, social ostracism), then that's what he or she will use (Felson & Steadman, 2004; Silver, 2006; Tedeschi & Felson, 1994). In the rational choice model, four main incentives appear to motivate violence (Black, 1983; Felson, 2004; Katz, 1988; Toch, 1980):

Getting one's way. Violence is used to intimidate, threaten, coerce, or compel someone to do something they would not otherwise not do, or to dissuade them from doing something they want to do. Examples include robbery, exploitive or predatory sex, witness tampering, or murder (the ultimate dissuader).

Getting justice. "Justice," here, is from the perspective of the perpetrator, as a justified response to being wronged in some way. From the victim's point of view, of course, the act probably represents unjustified revenge or gratuitous violence.

Display of power. Every schoolkid is familiar with the bully (Chapter 12) who uses aggression to maintain the obedience of his subjects, persecute his victims, and intimidate his rivals. Violence as a power display ranges from the second grade to international relations.

Thrill-seeking. For some people, it's just so cool to squish someone and see them squirm. Frequently connected with power displays, violence for the fun of it is often just an extension of socially acceptable forms of aggressive thrill-seeking, such as contact sports (what do you think "contact" means in football or boxing?) or financial competition.

In the rational choice model, mental illness may affect the process by which people choose certain actions, but only in the most severe cases does it entirely strip away a person's rational faculties to the extent that they are not making choices for themselves (Silver, 2006). Indeed, as reviewed in Chapter 1, the statutes concerned with criminal competencies and criminal responsibilities rely on this principle.

Social Disorganization Theory

Crime rates are typically found to be higher in areas where social organization is more fragmented, but is this cause or effect? **Social disorganization theory** focuses on the neighborhood environment in which the violence occurs. Studies from around the world seem to converge on the conclusion that a major correlate of violence in a given community is **neighborhood disadvantage,** a concept that includes the proportion of residents who are poor, unemployed, living in single-family households, and receiving public assistance. Mental illness may contribute to this by being a risk factor for unemployment and/or unstable family relationships, and communities with sparse resources are less likely to allocate an appreciable percentage of those resources to mental health services. In addition, mentally ill residents of disadvantaged neighborhoods are more likely to commit violence than those living in better areas (Bursik & Grasmick, 1993; Kubrin & Weitzer, 2003; Sampson et al., 1997; Shaw & McKay, 1942; Silver, 2000a, 2000b, 2006; Silver & Miller, 2004; Wacholtz & Mullaly, 1993).

Subcultural Theories

Much of criminal psychology and sociology starts with the premise that crime is, by definition, a "deviant" act, that is, something that most people wouldn't do to meet their respective needs. This probably has a lot to do with the fact that criminological theories are generally developed by academic researchers with middle-class values who identify with a civilized culture. But what if there are certain subcultures where wrong is right and being a law-abiding citizen is maladaptive, even suicidal? **Subcultural theories** emphasize that the norms of behavior in certain communities reinforce aggression as the preferred method of getting what you want. Typically, these involve economically depressed urban or rural communities where young males are socialized to be tough. Some theorists have attempted to put a political cast on this behavior, characterizing it as a form of rebellion against a hostile dominant culture by young people who have been in the marginalized and disenfranchised for ethnic or economic reasons (Arrigo, 2006; Bernard et al., 2010; Schmalleger, 2007). The theory does not explain, however, how these subcultures form in the first place or why everyone in that subgroup does not show equal amounts of criminal behavior.

Economic Theories

True to their name, economic theories take a more overtly materialistic view, i.e., that economic deprivation makes crime a necessity to provide basic material needs for the perpetrator and his family (Arrigo, 2006; Bernard et al., 2010; Schmalleger, 2007). This kind of "I-stole-a-loaf-of-bread-to-feed-my-starving-kids" explanation was probably far more valid during the Great Depression of the 1930s than it is today. In modern times, "necessities" frequently include social necessities, such as nice clothes, a flashy car, even jewelry in order for the subject to keep up with his or her peers. This may lead to grand theft or drug trafficking to make the necessary money. The implication is that if these economically-driven criminals had access to "straight jobs" that could garner them equivalent income, they would take the legitimate route. But it is unlikely that individuals who know they can make a big score in one drug sale or armed robbery are going to plod away at a dull, low-status job where it will take months to earn an equivalent sum. This theory also fails to explain why some criminals seem to commit violence for its own sake, such as assault, rape, and murder, with no identifiable material payoff, other than self-gratification or enhanced peer status (although one could argue that enhanced status is typically associated with more material goods; e.g., we frequently speak of the "rich and famous" or the "rich and powerful"). It also doesn't explain why, in economically deprived areas and eras, *most* people do not become criminals, but continue, for the most part, to grumblingly but lawfully eke out their livelihoods.

Ideological Theories

> *Q:* What's a Conservative?
> *A:* A Liberal who got mugged.
> *Q:* What's a Liberal?
> *A:* A Conservative who got arrested.

Ideological theories are social models of crime that posit some political or religious (often combined) ideological basis for behavior that the surrounding community labels as criminal (Arrigo, 2006; Bernard et al., 2010; Schmalleger, 2007). For example, liberal economic and political theorists, expressed in its most extreme form in Marxist theory, would argue that crime is inevitable in a capitalist society because the nature of capitalism is to exploit the working class and to create gaping disparities in income and material lifestyle between rich and poor. Therefore, the only way the disenfranchised poor can fight back against such an inequitable system is through what the ruling rich call "crime," but what is really a combination of survival skills and social protest–a version of the subcultural and economic theories described above.

Conversely, economic and socially conservative theorists see the world in terms of a "just deserts" viewpoint. Those who enjoy the finer things in life have worked hard and diligently (or their forebears have) to earn them, have saved frugally and restrained their impulse to spend more than they can afford, have obeyed the law and followed the rules of society, have established stable families, and afforded their children adequate health, education, and preparation for a career and livelihood. By contrast, those who lack these bounties have only themselves to blame for being lazy, irresponsible, and unwilling to defer gratification, for taking unnecessary risks and squandering their resources, for failing to follow society's laws and frequently finding themselves in trouble, for having multiple, superficial sexual relationships with little stable family life, and for abusing, neglecting, or otherwise ill-treating and ill-preparing their children for the demands of adult life.

Ideological theories can also take on a religious tone and these can sometimes be intertwined with the political. Failure to follow the will of God as laid out in one's religious tradition leads to poor self-control and a cavalier "anything-goes" attitude toward morality, say the religious conservatives. People need the paternal oversight of a benevolent God—and, by extension, His representative clergy here on earth. No surprise, then, that the poor and the violent attend religious services less often than the successful and the law-abiding.

Easy for you to say and pray, retort the religiously liberal. You have all the material comforts you've accrued by wheeling and dealing and using the advantages your parents gave you. Now you try to keep us in servitude and exploit us as workers and consumers by claiming that your way is God's will, when it is the repressive strictures of organized religion and the imbalanced society it represents that are themselves responsible for making us feel like busting out and enjoying life while we can.

Note how these social theories of crime are really statements about human nature. Conservative ideological theories view the vast masses of humanity as dull, wayward children who require the constant monitoring and control by the few enlightened, militarily and economically powerful elites in order to keep the brutish instincts of the lower classes in check by focus on hard work and discipline. Liberal ideological theorists see human nature as basically benevolent and mutually cooperative, given a nonrepressive social and economic climate in which to germinate and flourish. Like cognitive styles, these "ideological styles" may relate strongly to an individual's core personality and the tendency of people with particular cognitive, temperamental, social, political, and religious orientations to differentially associate with one another, creating entrenched ideological subgroups, each of whose members are convinced of the absolute correctness of their positions and beliefs, and amazed and outraged that their view isn't strikingly obvious to everyone else (DeHart-Davis, 2007; Harris, 2010; Kagan, 2010; Lakoff, 2008).

BOX 3.2. DESIGNER DEFENSES III (SOCIOLOGICAL): BLACK RAGE

On December 7, 1993, Colin Ferguson, a 36-year-old Jamaican immigrant, boarded a crowded Long Island Railroad train filled with rush hour commuters on their way home from work, and opened fire with a large-capacity handgun, killing 6 and wounding 19. When arrested, police found notes in his pockets declaring his hatred for White people, Asians, and "Uncle Tom Negroes." This was hardly Ferguson's first act of racial animosity, although it was his deadliest.

Colin Ferguson was born in Kingston, Jamaica to a wealthy family and came to the United States on a visa in 1982. Unable to find work in this country other than menial jobs, he reportedly attributed this to the rabid racism of American society, a theme that would define his life. Over the ensuing years, he was married and divorced, was fired from several jobs, and, despite being an academically bright student, was dismissed from two universities due to continual classroom disruptions and heated confrontations with students and faculty, often punctuating his diatribes with the exclamation, "Black rage will get you!" After his college experience, he continued to get into numerous disputes with neighbors and local businesses, and persistently harassed his ex-wife and local citizens, leading to run-ins with the police, which Ferguson always claimed to be the result of racially-tinged animosity. His landlord and neighbors noted Ferguson's growing obsession with an impending racial apocalypse in which Black people would kill White people in revenge for their oppression.

Finally, on December 7, 1993, Ferguson boarded the Long Island Railroad train and began walking down the aisle, repeating over and over, "I'm going to get you," as he methodically fired his gun left and right at seated Caucasian and Asian passengers. He paused to reload his 15-round magazine, then continued his grim gauntlet through the car. When he paused to reload a second time, he was overpowered by passengers and handcuffed by an off-duty police officer. Upon questioning by detectives, he was reported to be oriented and lucid and to show no remorse.

At his trial, Ferguson's lawyers, William Kunstler and Ronald Kuby, fashioned an innovative designer insanity defense, cobbled together from elements of post-traumatic stress disorder, child abuse, and Battered Woman's Syndrome (see Box 3.1). They appealed to a 1968 study by African-American psychiatrists William Grier and Price Cobbs, notably titled, "Black Rage," which argued that the constant pressure of racial discrimination and oppression experienced by most American Blacks inevitably leads to a state of angry mistrust of White people that smolders in the psyches of Black Americans and that, given sufficient provocation, may sometimes erupt in paroxysms of uncontrollable rage. This, fueled by Ferguson's obvious mental instability, argued his attorneys, rendered him not responsible for his actions at the time of the shootings, i.e., "social oppression made him do it."

But the jury never got to hear about the **Black Rage Defense**. Becoming more delusional with time, Ferguson subsequently fired his attorneys and rejected an insanity defense, claiming instead that it wasn't really him that shot all those people, but an unknown gunman who grabbed his weapon while Ferguson fell asleep on the train. He also proclaimed that he was receiving messages from God that various people and organizations were trying to kill him. In spite of all this, prosecutors took pains to prove his competency to stand trial so that he would not get off too lightly. But in determining that he met the minimum competency requirements, they were forced to concede his legal right to proceed **pro se**, i.e., on his own behalf, without an attorney. The trial became a televised media circus, with Ferguson's rambling questions and courtroom rants filling the nightly news slots. But the jury was hardly amused: Ferguson was convicted of multiple counts of murder and attempted murder, and sentenced to 315 years and 8 months to life in prison. He will be eligible for parole on August 6, 2309.

Legal and practical problems plagued the Black Rage Defense from the start. To begin with, Battered Woman's Syndrome, to which it was compared, refers to a specific victim of a specific tormentor retaliating directly against her abuser because of her fear for her life, based on her experience with this particular person. The perpetrator of a Black Rage attack targets nonspecific White and Asian people with whom he has no personal connection or experience. Add to this the fact that the Black Rage theory itself emphasizes the corrosive effects of enculturated racism that American Blacks experience from early childhood onward— yet Colin Ferguson grew up in the racially homogeneous African-Caribbean nation of Jamaica and came to the U.S. when he was 24 years old. In addition, his generally paranoid and confrontational personality virtually assured that even the most innocuous of encounters would be interpreted as acts of malignant bias.

Aside from these logical and conceptual issues, the prospect of using a sociological theory like Black Rage as a characterological descriptor of an entire class of people carries with it some dire unintended consequences. What if the defense had prevailed and Ferguson was acquitted by reason of insanity, creating a legal precedent? Let's say Drs. Grier and Cobb are right that most Black Americans carry around a hair-triggered powder keg of anger, ready to blow at the slightest racial provocation. Since some people naturally have better control of their impulses than others, how can the rest of us tell which Black people are the potential time bombs and which are "safe"? To protect ourselves, do we just assume that *all* Black Americans are unpredictably dangerous, because we can't discern if the otherwise harmless-looking citizen who approaches us to ask for directions is about to explode if we give the wrong answer? Do we err on the side of caution and just avoid Black people altogether out of a justified sense of self-protection? And if I shoot my Black neighbor over an argument about my dog pooping in his yard, do I claim at my trial that I had no choice but to protect my home and my family, because the court in the Ferguson trial ruled that Black people have Black Rage, and I was just engaging in proactive self-defense?

Any legal theory that paints American Blacks as extraordinarily dangerous creates other legal problems as well. If I hire a Black waiter, or Black airline pilot, or Black nurse, or Black teacher, or Black sales representative, and one of these

continued

BOX 3.2.—*Continued*

people injures a customer, passenger, patient, student, client, or coworker, can I be sued for negligent hiring in the same way as if I failed to do a background check and hired an employee with a criminal or mental illness history? Shouldn't society do its best to keep inherently dangerous people out of professions where they have contact with the public? Shouldn't they be monitored and quarantined to protect the rest of us? See where this is going?

We know that some people are more prone to antisocial behavior than others for a variety of factors that have to do with biology, psychology, and sociology. But statements that subsume a whole class of people—even if benignly intended—end up providing a pretext for the worst kind of stereotyping, profiling, discrimination, and ultimately persecution. One of the tenets of American justice is that each individual is judged by the merits of his or her individual case. If Colin Ferguson's, or anyone else's, personal history of racial discrimination contributes to their mental state at the time of a crime, that can be taken into consideration, but according to the law, people are treated as individuals not "types," and carelessly concocted designer sociological defenses carry no more weight than biological or psychological defenses.

EVOLUTIONARY CRIMINAL PSYCHOLOGY

Oh well I'm the type of guy who will never settle down,
Where pretty girls are well, you know that I'm around.
– Dion, *The Wanderer,* 1961

Now listen people what I'm telling you,
A-keep away from-a Runaround Sue.
– Dion, *Runaround Sue,* 1961

Yes, the rules *are* different for men and women, and have been for millions of species for millions of years. Endeavoring to pull together brain, mind, and society, the past two decades have seen the burgeoning of the field of **evolutionary psychology** (Buss, 2008; Gaulin & McBurney, 2003), which seeks to apply the principles of Darwinian evolution by natural selection to complex human behavioral traits and behaviors, including criminal behavior (Duntley & Shackleford, 2008; Walsh & Beaver, 2008). As such, evolutionary psychology is a blend of biological and psychosocial theorizing that seeks to explain how human personalities and psychopathologies, mediated by the human brain, have evolved.

In **Darwinian evolutionary theory** (Darwin, 1959, 1871), all traits–physical or behavioral–survive within a population of organisms if they have individual or collective survival value with regard to the surrounding physical and social environments. In one example, as vegetation becomes sparse and remaining foliage hangs higher and higher on treetops, giraffes with slightly longer necks are more likely to reach the food that will enable them to survive to reproductive age in order to produce copies of themselves that, in turn, possess the longer-necked trait, until after many generations, all giraffes in a population have longer necks than their forebears. In another example, as access to food or mates becomes scarce and primates must employ increasingly clever strategies to obtain these goods, those with somewhat more complex brains are likely to survive to reproduce bigger-brained offspring, until all such group members are busily outsmarting one another. Note that modern evolutionary theory is **nonteleological**, that is, giraffes don't grow longer necks *in order* to reach higher foliage, and primates don't expand their cerebral cortexes *in order* to catch bigger prey or outmaneuver rivals. Rather, simply as a matter of random selection, those individuals who happen to have these traits in even slightly greater abundance are overall more likely to leave more offspring behind. Not always, but often enough that over thousands of generations, the physical and psychological configuration of the species changes.

Summarizing a vast literature (Buss, 2008; Cochran & Harpending, 2009; Duntley & Shackleford, 2006; Shackelford & Duntley, 2008; Walsh & Beaver, 2008), we can boil down the major principles of evolutionary psychology as they apply to normal and abnormal, criminal and noncriminal, behavior:

Many organisms, including humans, are social organisms. From bacterial swarms, to ant colonies, to wolf packs, to baboon troops, to tribal villages, to megametropolises, living creatures of many kinds have evolved to live in interdependent social groups because, whether for purposes of hunting, defense, or child-rearing, group-living organisms are more likely to survive and reproduce than single organisms.

Successful group living involves a balance of cooperation and competition. Many activities, such as foraging, hunting, tool and shelter building, defense against rival groups, and so on, depend on the cooperative efforts of many group members: all participate, all get a portion of the spoils. In other circumstances, however, there may not be sufficient food, tools, shelter, or mates to go around and members of the very same group may now find themselves competing for these very resources. Thus, at any given time, group members may be collaborating on a hunt or in building a shelter, but at the same time, competing as rivals over the best hut, the sharpest weapons, or the most desirable mating partners. Thus, group-living humans had to evolve the traits of compromise and deal-making, along with the traits of deceit and self-interest.

Males and females have different reproductive strategies. The grossly disparate investment that each sex makes to perpetuating the species is apparent to most people by the time they reach fifth grade. Generally, because the effort involved is minimal, males seek to maximize the dissemination of their DNA by coupling with as many females as possible; therefore they tend to be relatively indiscriminate in their mating escapades. Females, however, must invest a tremendous amount of time, energy, and material resources to conceive, carry, bear, and raise a child; therefore, they tend to be far more choosy about whom they pair up with–they want to pick someone with the strength and status to be a good provider, while at the same time, being as sure as possible of his fidelity, so they aren't quickly abandoned when the next pretty, young paleolithic hottie comes along.

Females utilize and enhance their physical attractiveness because, for most of human history and prehistory, this was their currency for survival. In the preindustrial natural world that ancestral humans evolved in, once having left her family of origin, a mateless female might be unable to provide for her own physical needs, much less for a baby she is carrying or children she is raising. Having a male mate who is able and willing to provide resources for his family could literally be a matter of life and death, which explains why, even today, the beauty industry is recession-proof. At all ages, most human females pay very close attention to the way they look; even if happily mated, there is a chance their mate might die or leave, so they continue to advertise their attractiveness, albeit more subtly, to other men in the social group–"just in case."

For their part, males seek to maximize their image of strength and status in order to attract the "sexiest" (i.e., seemingly most reproductively fit) females, and to intimidate other males from mate-poaching. This is because, when a male decides to settle down and devote himself to his family, he wants to be sure it's *his* family, and the only way to guarantee this is to protect his mate from potential cuckolders, either by intimidation of his rivals or sequestration of his mate–keeping her in the cave or covering her in loose bearskins when she goes out.

Both sexes cheat on their mates, but males do it more often than females because, from the gritty logic of evolutionary reproductive fitness, it pays for any particular man to be both a **cad** and a **dad** (Cashdan, 1993)–investing in the next generation at home, while trying to sneak a little of thy DNA into thy neighbor's wife, so the hapless stooge ends up unwittingly raising the cheater's offspring. For similar reasons, although less frequently, women cheat, especially with a higher-status male than their present mate, because they essentially get their dad-man to support the cad-man's offspring who may be stronger and healthier, and thereby have a greater chance of surviving to reproductive age and having caddish offspring of their own. Women who are promiscuous, i.e., mating with many different males, are playing a tricky survival game. On the one hand, none of these men knows if the baby she ultimately carries is theirs, so each man might be inclined to make some minimal investment in resources, or "token gifts," to ensure the survival of (maybe) his DNA. On the other hand, no one man is going to bet all he has on the off-possibility that the child is exclusively his. Thus, the woman takes the chance that she'll be able to summate the numerous smaller gifts into a livable income and rely on some of these men for nominal services ("Move that rock for me, will you, sweetie?") from time to time.

Again, consistent with the nonteleologism of natural selection, note that even we modern cogitating humans don't sit around making mental calculations of our chances of reproductive success. Men just "know" that it "feels good" to be boffing around and often brag about it to their friends. Women just "know" that men are a bunch of two-timing cads and search for their one true knight in shining loincloth who possesses the prized combination of strength and fidelity. These behavioral traits have survived not through conscious calculation, but because humans who possessed them were most likely to propagate themselves.

Sex and aggression are powerful motivating forces in human societies. Here, Darwin could easily agree with Freud or Adler. In small, interdependent tribal societies, males compete for the best females, i.e., those whose health and reproductive fitness are signaled by physical beauty and behavioral charm. Likewise, females compete for access to physically powerful and high-status males, because these mates are more likely to father healthy offspring and to be able to provide for them and their mother. Most social organisms live in hierarchically organized groups, some genetically programmed, as in an ant colony, many others, especially in higher species, flexibly formed and rearranged by continual competition and jockeying for position by group members, usually males. Those at the top typically enjoy access to all the goods that maximize personal and reproductive survival: the best food, the most lavish cave or hut, healthier and more numerous mates, and so on. Social hierarchies give the group a certain day-to-day stability, but the order may be periodically challenged by rivals.

"Survival of the fittest" applies to groups as well as individuals. There are several species of birds that, when the flock is threatened by a predator, an individual member feigns a broken wing, luring the predator toward the "easy" target, and allowing the other birds to escape. At the last moment, the voluntary decoy gives up his ruse and takes flight, but in at least a proportion of cases, the avian Good Samaritan miscalculates and becomes the predator's meal. What accounts for this "altruistic" behavior in animals that presumably do not live their lives by any explicit moral code?

The answer is that the code is implicit, embedded in the DNA of that species, and it is guided by two evolutionary principles, the first known as **inclusive fitness**. In virtually all close-knit social groups, individual members will be bonded by varying degrees of genetic relationship: mothers and fathers, sisters and brothers, aunts, uncles, cousins, and so forth. So by risking oneself for the good of the group, there is an excellent chance that, among the saved, there will be some genetic relative of the volunteer. Note that the bird doesn't volitionally "plan" this decoy behavior. Rather, birds whose cousins occasionally sacrifice themselves for the good of the group will have genetic relatives who probably share those same traits and will pass them down to their offspring, perpetuating the cycle. Similarly, members of a human tribal family group who throw themselves at a predator or hostile warrior are instinctively saving a little piece of themselves to carry on.

But what if there really are no blood relatives in the group—why then risk one's life or share one's resources, instead of maximizing one's own reproductive fitness by keeping it all to oneself and never sticking one's neck out for anyone else? Because, as the song goes, "we need each other." This is the second relevant evolutionary behavioral concept, **reciprocal altruism**: you scratch my back and I'll scratch yours; you share your food when I'm hungry and I'll keep you from starving when you can't hunt or work; you stay away from my mate when I'm out of town, and I won't poach your cave-babe when your back is turned. Group cohesion and reciprocal altruism are thus powerful forces for mutual survival and perpetuation of social organisms, which accounts for their presence in myriad species, including humans (see also Chapter 13).

Diversity contributes to overall group fitness. We all know that people are different. But unlike social insects, where queen, worker, and drone classes are genetically preprogrammed, in higher animals group members are not genetic cookie-cutter copies of one another. In humans, personality and behavioral diversity (Chapter 7) contribute to overall inclusive fitness by providing a range of talents for natural selection to operate on, thus giving a psychologically diverse group more flexibility in meeting environmental challenges. In the multigenerational life cycle of the tribe, there will be times when fighting is more adaptive than flirting, when generosity trumps greed, when quick, bold action is needed, while at other times, reflective deliberation will prevent rash and impulsive group decisions. Not all group members can carry out these interpersonal skills equally, that's why it's important to have different kinds of people in your community (a similar principle is advocated in the business psychology literature under the rubric of "work-team diversity"). Thus, groups which contain members with a varied palette of personalities and cognitive styles will be better able to meet an overall wider variety of challenges.

Persistence of psychopathology. However, some personality and be-havioral traits, especially those that shade over into what we call psycho-pathology or mental illness, may seem too extreme to have any appreciable adaptive value. For example, traits like severe aggressiveness, psychosis, de-pression, selfishness, and so on would seem to be maladaptive in most social groups and lead to ostracism, diminished mating opportunities, and the eventual extinction of these traits in the human population. Yet they persist in a small segment of almost any society. Why? It's because most such traits and characteristics are not all-or-nothing entities, i.e., it's not a matter of either you have psychosis, antisociality, mood instability or you don't. In-stead, within a given genetic family line, traits are expressed in greater or lesser degrees of severity across different members of a family, and traits that are adaptively detrimental in their extreme form may be a survival plus in more moderate doses. Thus, one family member may be delusional, while others are simply creative thinkers and imaginative inventors. One group member may be destructively impulsive and violent, getting into fights with fellow tribe-mates, while his brother and cousins are fearless and bold, and make good soldiers and defenders of the group. Another member is obses-sively gloomy, while her aunt is the meticulous, hard-nosed realist who helps the group look before they leap into dangerous decisions. Since carriers of the more mild-moderate versions of the trait may occasionally have offspring in which the trait is abnormally concentrated, the severely afflicted individ-ual need not mate him- or herself to assure a small but steady supply of such individuals in any particular population. The extreme forms of the trait are the societal "side effects" of the more moderate and adaptive forms, and that's why they will always be with us.

Criminal behavior as an adaptive strategy. Criminal behavior may seem like a form of extreme maladaptive behavior, but in certain contexts, it can be the preferred survival and reproductive strategy. Egocentric, aggres-sive, and remorseless individuals who are **resource poachers** and **repro-ductive cheaters** sacrifice a certain degree of solidarity and support from their communities and may risk censure, punishment, banishment, or even death for their actions, but enough of them will survive long enough to dis-seminate their DNA and thus ensure the persistence of a small, but perni-ciously energetic subset of the breeding population. Indeed, all the things that most of us consider fun in moderation–"sex, drugs, and rock & roll"–are in some respect connected with reproductive fitness, e.g., getting a pumped-up high to dance all night at a singles club and eventually score for the evening. But for the hard-core criminal cheater, these are not recreations that punctuate stable periods of productive work; they are his whole lifestyle. And since he devotes so much extra time and effort to filching, fighting, and fornicating, he is, paradoxically, likely to survive, for a time at least, on the backs of us solid citizens and to leave copies of himself behind to perpetuate the cycle.

SUMMARY AND CONCLUSIONS

Psychosocial models of crime should be seen as complementary to, not competitive with, the biological explanations discussed in Chapter 2. **Psychodynamic theories** of crime view deviant behavior as an expression of unresolved unconscious conflicts that drive antisocial acting-out through a series of defense mechanisms. **Behavioral and social learning theories** attribute all behavior, including antisocial behavior, to differential learning experiences that occur in different environments. Historically, early theories of crime focused on the identification of a set of "**criminal types**," while more recent conceptualizations focus on temperamental and cognitive features of habitual criminals, such as levels of **self-control**, and **criminal thinking styles**. Modern theories also attempt to integrate finding from diverse fields, such as biology, psychology, sociology, economics, and criminology. **Sociological theories** of crime approach the role of the larger community in shaping, reinforcing, or mitigating criminal behavior from the perspective of economics, political or religious ideology, or subcultural factors in crime. **Evolutionary psychology** attempts perhaps the broadest integration of human criminal behavior into the realm of normative adaptive behavior of people in the past and present, and, indeed, within the natural world as a whole. While some of these conceptualizations have been twisted into **designer psychological defenses** and **designer sociological defenses**, as yet I know of no cases where evolutionary psychology has been invoked as an exculpatory factor, but perhaps it's only a matter of time until a defendant argues that "Darwin made me do it."

Part **II**

Personality, Psychopathology, and Crime

Crime is not a disease, so it can't be cured like a bladder infection or reset like a broken leg. But, while most mentally disordered persons are not criminals, criminal behavior does often occur in the context of a variety of psychological disorders and syndromes, and Chapers 4–8 examine the major classes of psychopathology that may be associated with criminal behavior. Organic brain syndromes may impair judgment and increase the risk of impulsive action. Subjects with schizophrenia and other psychotic disorders may commit violent acts in response to command hallucinations or delusions of persecution. Anxiety and mood disorders can fracture the emotional gyroscope that normally keeps extreme emotional fluctuations in check. And the egocentricity, nonreflective cognition, and behavioral impulsivity seen in many of the personality disorders render these subjects highly susceptible to aggressive overreactions to seemingly trivial provocations. Finally, the cold-blooded predatory mindset of the psychopath virtually guarantees that he will spend his life violating the rights of others to get what he wants, thereby perennially running afoul of the law and mostly loving every minute of it.

Chapter 4

Brain Syndromes
and Substance Abuse

BRAIN SYNDROMES AND CRIMINAL BEHAVIOR

In a general sense, virtually any kind of brain impairment can be associated with heightened risk for impulsive, antisocial behavior in both adults and children. As noted in Chapter 2, impulsive criminality seems to be most associated with damage to the brain's left hemisphere and/or frontal lobes which mediate the "executive functions" of planning, organizing, anticipating, directing, controlling, and self-correcting behavior, as observed in the histories of these subjects and as measured by neuropsychological tests (Brower & Price, 2001a, 2001b; Cohen et al., 2003; Morgan & Lilienfeld, 2002; Paschall & Fishbein, 2002; Wood & Liossi, 2006). However, most brain-injured people do not commit crimes, so is there an additional factor that puts some of these cognitively impaired individuals at special risk? And can particular brain syndromes be offered as affirmative defenses to argue for NGRI or mitigation?

DEMENTIA

Dementia: Symptoms and Syndromes

The term **dementia** refers to an organic brain syndrome that impairs perception, thinking, language, memory, and behavior. As the American population continues to age, the criminal justice system can expect to have to deal with an increasing number of such individuals. The main causes of dementia in the elderly are Alzheimer's disease, Parkinson's disease, and stroke. In younger subjects, dementia may occur as the result of AIDS, toxic-metabolic and medical syndromes such as kidney or liver disease, or from heavy drug use or overdose.

Symptoms of dementia include **disorientation** to **time** ("What day is this? What year are we in?"), **place** ("What street are we on? Do you know what city we're in? Where do you live?"), and **person** ("What's your name? Where were you born?"). **Aphasia** is a disturbance of language and can involve the comprehension of speech, the production of speech, or both. **Aprosodia** is a flattening of the emotional expressiveness of speech. **Agnosia** is impaired perceptual recognition, and **apraxia** is a disturbance of complex movement. Other signs and symptoms of dementia include general agitation and **sundowing**, which is a tendency to become more active and agitated at night. This makes it more likely that these individuals will wander out of their homes at night, especially since the rest of the family may be asleep.

Typically, the behavior of subjects with dementia will be relatively peaceful, albeit confused; however, they may become defensively aggressive if they feel threatened. Most cases of law enforcement contact with these individuals will involve: (1) trespassing, where they simply wander onto private property; (2) theft or shoplifting where they pick up a store item because they think it's theirs or just because it's there; (3) assault related to defensively lashing out when they feel threatened, such as when confronted by an irate shopkeeper; or more rarely, (4) sexual offenses based on inappropriate comments or physical contact with others which is related to disinhibition of behavior or impaired judgment due to neuropsychological decline.

Senior citizens charged with crimes may not have full-blown dementia: the condition may not be sufficiently advanced to affect adjudication, or the defendant's mental status may fluctuate over time For example, in the case of Alzheimer's dementia, the most common form, the disease progresses slowly, in stages. A defendant therefore may have been sufficiently cognitively intact to form a *mens rea* at the time of the offense, but be found not competent to stand trial many months later when the case comes to court. To complicate matters, in the early stages of the disease, concurrent factors, such as fatigue, an infectious illness, medication effects, and so on, may interact with the dementia-related cognitive impairment so that the individual is cognitively better on some days than others, even though the overall trajectory of the syndrome is downward. In such cases, the subject may still be restored to competency if the superimposed factor can be effectively treated; how long he or she remains competent will be affected by the continued progression of the dementia. If a defendant is declared unrestorably incompetent to stand trial, the judicial process ceases and the individual can either be released to the community, which usually means either the family or a long-term care facility, or, if he or she is declared to be dangerous, involuntarily civilly committed to a psychiatric hospital (Frierson et al., 2002; Heck & Herrick, 2007; Morris & Parker, 2009).

BOX 4.1. NOT MELLOWED WITH AGE

In what worshippers first feared was a terrorist attack, shots rang out in front of a Boca Raton, Florida synagogue during a Rosh Hashanah service on October 4, 2005. The truth turned out to be even more bizarre. One of the congregants, Marc Beneyer, age 79, had been dating a woman 27 years his junior, until the woman became disturbed by his increasingly paranoid, controlling, and abusive behavior, and decided to break off the relationship. When the older man refused to be deterred, and persisted in stalking and harassing her (Chapter 18), she obtained a restraining order against him with the help of her long-time employer, who was also a congregant of that temple. On that particular holiday, the woman, her 15-year-old daughter, her new boyfriend, and her employer were all attending holiday services, when Beneyer appeared at the temple, sat down some distance away, and proceeded to glare at the woman and her daughter who, feeling extremely uncomfortable, left the sanctuary.

A short time later, Beneyer asked the employer if he could have a word with him outside, and the younger man agreed. Beneyer excused himself for a moment "to get something from my car" and returned with a handgun. The employer turned to flee back into the synagogue and Beneyer shot him twice in the back, then continued to fire into the temple, barely missing a group of children. Police quickly arrested the gunman, who at first declared, "I didn't want to shoot him— I'm possessed." The victim survived the shooting and was hospitalized, expected to recover from his wounds.

Beneyer was evaluated for competency to stand trial, and all but one of the examiners found him competent. Any mental disorder he had seemed more related to narcissism and paranoia (Chapter 7) than to an organic dementia per se. Two twists on this story were, first, while in prison, Beneyer was charged with conspiring to have his own attorney killed because he believed he was not working his case adequately. And second, many months after the shooting, the victim died abruptly: apparently, one of the bullets had lodged too close to his heart to be safely operable, so it was left in place, presumed to pose no danger. However, the metal shifted, causing the victim's heart to fail and conferring a murder charge on Beneyer, who will spend the rest of his remaining life in prison.

EPILEPSY AND SEIZURE-LIKE DISORDERS

The syndrome of **epilepsy** subsumes a group of disorders characterized by the presence of recurring **seizures**, which are abrupt, paroxysmal electrophysiological discharges in the brain that produce a variety of behavioral and experiential symptoms, depending on which parts of the brain are affected. Most seizures are fairly unmistakable while they are occurring; however, there are a number of seizure types that produce disturbances primarily in thought, consciousness, and complex behavior, which may not be readily identifiable as manifestation of a medical disorder. In addition, epilepsy may be comorbid with a variety of other medical and mental disorders, including substance abuse, which can exacerbate it, or traumatic brain injury, which can precipitate it (Miller, 1994d, 1994e).

Epilepsy: Seizure Types

Epileptic seizures are classified into several main subtypes. **Grand mal seizures** conform to most people's conceptualization of a seizure: an abrupt whole-body extensor spasm that causes the subject to lose consciousness and fall to the ground, followed by several seconds of whole-body flexor-extensor muscular contractions that gradually abate and leave the subject mentally confused and physically exhausted when he regains consciousness. **Focal seizures** involve only a portion of the body or one side of the body, usually the arm or leg, and are characterized by a few seconds of rapid, involuntary, stereotyped contractions, for which the subject typically remains conscious. In **petit mal seizures**, most common in children, there is a very brief loss of consciousness for perhaps a few seconds, but no significant disturbance of posture or muscle tone: the individual may be observed to "blink out" for a brief spell. The subject may experience anywhere from a few to several hundred such spells in the course of a day, which can disrupt the continuity of perception, learning, and memory. Many children with petit mal seizures outgrow them by adolescence or early adulthood, or they may transform into another seizure type.

Temporal Lobe Epilepsy

The type of epilepsy most often associated with behavioral disturbances that may lead to conflict with the law is **psychomotor epilepsy**, also known as **temporal lobe epilepsy**, or **TLE**, because the electrophysiological disturbance most commonly originates from the brain's **temporal lobes**, a region containing several limbic system structures that are associated with emotion, motivation, and memory (Chapter 2). During a temporal lobe seizure, awareness of the person's surroundings may be severely disturbed, and his behavior may not appear to be under his control. The seizure has an abrupt onset and gradual recovery, and can last for several minutes.

Subjects describe all manner of sensory, perceptual, cognitive, and emotional alterations heralding the onset of a TLE seizure, ranging from shapes and colors; strange sounds; religious visions and voices; sudden fear, sadness, or elation; sudden memories from the past; feelings of great profundity and mystical clarity; stomach flutters and other physical sensations. A common TLE experience is **deja vu**, or false familiarity, the feeling that "I've been here or done this before." A dreamy, partial-consciousness state of disorientation often prevails during the seizure, during which the subject may be nonresponsive or only minimally responsive to others' questioning or commands. After the seizure passes, the subject may have spotty recall or no memory at all for the event.

One type of TLE symptom that might get a subject in trouble are collectively known as **automatisms**, which are stereotyped, repetitive actions that, in themselves, are normal in the proper contexts, but occur during the seizure in an inappropriate form or circumstance. These include wandering around; dressing and undressing; sexual and bathroom behavior; picking up and carrying off objects; and approaching others with short, repeated vocalizations. One of my patients had several arrests for indecent exposure for taking off his clothes and walking around a supermarket and wandering down a street. Another patient was arrested for gathering up objects in a barbershop while waiting for a haircut.

In between seizures, some TLE patients display what clinicians call the **interictal TLE personality**, with a characteristic set of symptoms, including emotional intensity; interpersonal clinginess (**viscosity**); obsessive-compulsive preoccupations and behavior; excessive writing and note-taking (**hypergraphia**); and sometimes bizarre sexual interests (**fetishisms**). It is thought that this personality style develops from the frequent and repeated abnormal excitation of the brain's temporal lobe limbic system by frequent TLE seizures that begin in childhood or just prior to adolescence.

Finally, patients with TLE, as well as other forms of epilepsy, are likely to be treated with a range of **antiseizure medications**, many of which have strong sedating, disinhibiting, and cognitively confusing effects of their own. Unsupervised patients can miss doses or take overdoses because of memory problems, or may simply choose to misuse their medication if these are not controlled by a responsible third party.

There has been a longstanding debate about the relationship of epilepsy in general, and TLE in particular, to violent behavior. It is now generally agreed that, like organic conditions generally, most aggressive activity in TLE is related to defensiveness out of a feeling of fear, or to combativeness upon being restrained while in a state of confusion. Aggressive behavior can also occur in the postictal period, while the subject is still in a confusional state. Although prisoners have higher rates of seizure disorders of all types than the general population, inmates with epilepsy do not commit more violent crimes than those without (Alberto-Tassinari et al., 2005; Delgado-

Escueta et al., 1981; Elliott, 1982, 1984, 1992; Gerard et al., 1998; Gunn, 1978; Gunn & Fenton, 1971; Ito et al., 2007; Kanemoto et al., 1999; King & Ajmone-Marsan, 1977; Lewis et al., 1982; Logsdail & Toone, 1988; Mark & Ervin, 1970; Marsh & Krause, 2000; Miller, 1994d, 1994e; Monroe, 1982; Pincus & Tucker, 1978; Ramani & Gummit, 1981; Rodin, 1973; Savard et al., 1991; Sumer et al., 2007; Williams, 1969; Wood, 1987). Nevertheless, epilepsy has been used as a criminal defense in at least a few cases (Beresford, 1988; Pollack, 1984; Volavka, 1995).

Episodic Dyscontrol Syndrome, or Intermittent Explosive Disorder

In a rare condition called **episodic dyscontrol syndrome (EDS)**, or **intermittent explosive disorder (IED)** in *DSM-IV-R* (APA, 2000), severe aggressive behavior can appear as a sudden, often unprovoked, "storm-like" outburst that is primitive and poorly organized, that usually consists of flailing, spitting, scratching, punching, or throwing, and that is usually directed at the nearest available person or object. The act itself can be quite destructive to furniture, pets, or people who happen to get in the way, but serious injury to bystanders is usually the result of misguided efforts by observers to subdue the patient during an episode. In such cases, the wild thrashing that inflicts the injurious blows probably represents a desperate attempt to escape restraint, rather than a directed assault against a particular individual–although sudden, directed, but usually unsustained, attacks may occur as well. EDS/IED has been associated with cases of impulsive, unpremeditated homicide, "senseless" attacks on strangers, spouse battery, child abuse, criminally aggressive driving, destruction of property, and even attacks on animals and inanimate objects (Elliott, 1990, 1992).

More complex, better-organized outbursts are typically short-lived and may be followed by feelings of regret and remorse when the individual becomes aware of what he has done. Murder carried out in such states may be characterized by **overkill**, such as an assailant beating or stabbing his victim dozens or hundreds of times, often in what witnesses describe as a "frenzy." Such uncontrolled violence is likely to be further fueled by alcohol or drugs. Indeed, in some subjects, EDS can often be triggered by even small amounts of these substances, producing the syndrome of **pathological intoxication**, which is characterized by uncontrolled violence following seemingly trivial drug or alcohol ingestion. Although these violent behavioral states have been shown to be associated with distinct electrophysiological brain changes, it is still unclear whether they represent true seizures per se (Elliott, 1992; Miller, 1987, Pincus & Tucker, 1978).

Planned, purposeful homicide is almost never a seizure phenomenon, because it requires complex preparation and action sequences that are beyond the mental capability and time frame of a typical seizure or seizure-like episode. Even in the case of sudden, impulsive violence, it is a fact that many people with a characteristically "short fuse" simply fly into a rage and commit murder without any particular brain syndrome being the cause (Miller, 1998a; Volavka, 1995). In such cases it may be difficult to differentiate this kind of distinct "brain syndrome" from the type of aggressive response familiar in individuals known for having just such a hair-trigger emotional ignition system, that is, subjects for whom it takes less than the usual degree of irritation, frustration, or provocation to elicit a violent response. Observers in these cases may agree that there appears to be some connection with the eliciting confrontation ("the other guy was really trying to tick him off"), but the reaction appears both premature and excessive for the relatively mild nature of the provocation ("but then, he like, just exploded and pounded the crap out of the guy"). In such cases, the behavior, while extreme, may appear to be more in control, more organized, and more clearly directed against the source of the antagonism than would occur in a typical seizure or seizure-like episode.

During an EDS/IED attack, self-awareness of the actual period of violent behavior varies from patient to patient, usually in association with the severity of the dyscontrol episode itself. Some patients claim total amnesia for the episode, while others report a vague, fugue-like recollection. Still others maintain clear awareness of the outburst, but report being powerless to stop it (a classic "irresistible impulse" defense); these are often the patients who express the greatest remorse after the attack. In many cases, the individual may retain sufficient control to momentarily suspend or redirect the violence–to "take the fight outside"–or switch the target of the attack from a spouse or child to a chair or wall (Miller, 1990b, 1990c, 1998a).

EDS/IED cuts across several diagnostic classifications, such as psychoses, personality disorders, especially antisocial, narcissistic, and borderline personality disorder (Chapter 7), epilepsy, mental retardation, toxic-metabolic disorders, attention deficit hyperactivity disorder, and conduct disorder in children, and may occur without a prior history of traumatic injury or other acquired brain damage. When episodic rage does follow a brain injury, a particularly common site of damage is the medial portion of the temporal lobes which contain many of the limbic structures that modulate emotion and motivation (Chapter 2). However, while the neuropathology in some cases of organic aggression can be documented by radiological or EEG abnormalities, many cases lack objective neurologic signs or positive findings on neuropsychological testing (Bach-y-Rita & Veno, 1974; Bach-y-Rita et al.,

1970, 1971; Elliott, 1982, 1984; Mark & Ervin, 1970; Miller, 1990b, 1990c, 1998a; Malmquist, 1996; Monroe, 1978, 1982; Pincus & Tucker, 1978; Williams, 1969; Wood, 1987).

The relationship between episodic dyscontrol and paroxysmal electrophysiological disorders such as epilepsy is not yet entirely clear, but probably reflects a midpoint on a continuum between normal behavior with normal EEG findings on one end, and frank seizures with clearly epileptiform EEG patterns on the other. In fact, EEG patterns of patients with EDS/IED often show this "in-between" pattern of electrophysiological irregularities (Adamec & Stark-Adamec, 1983; Mark & Ervin, 1970; Miller, 1997c, 1998a; Pincus & Tucker, 1978; Racine, 1978). Offenders diagnosed with EDS/IED have been found to have low serotonin levels (Linnoila et al., 1983), itself a risk factor for impulsive violent behavior (Chapter 2).

IED has been used as a defense for the charge of second degree murder in at least one case; the jury found the defendant guilty and he was sentenced to 25 years in prison (Bernet et al., 2006).

Limbic Psychotic Trigger Reaction

The **limbic psychotic trigger reaction (LPTR)** has been described largely through the work of Dr. Anneliese Pontius (1981, 1984, 1987, 1996, 1997, Pontius & Yudowitz, 1980), and is characterized by bursts of violent behavior that occur in response to repeated mild or moderate stress, which most people cope with by constructive activity or seeking social support. But in some individuals, typically young males described as "shy loners," the stress-related memories reverberate and increase in intensity in the brain's limbic system, which is involved in both memory and emotion. In response to some actual or symbolic trigger, these individuals may attack total strangers without an apparent plan or motive.

Certain features of LPTR seem to place it in a category somewhere between posttraumatic stress disorder (PTSD; see Chapter 6), IED, and a temporal lobe seizure. When these subjects encounter a trigger, there are often several minutes of confusion and disorientation, which may include an **aura**, such as sounds, flashing lights, or strange body sensations. The next phase includes hallucinations, delusions of grandeur, and out-of-character acts, including robbery, sexual assault, or murder. These paroxysmal episodes may last up to 20 minutes, longer than most seizures, and may include dizziness, nausea, sweating, cold sensations, and uncontrolled urination, erection, or ejaculation. These symptoms, along with the violent act itself, occur seemingly without emotion, but are well-remembered, which further distinguishes them from most seizure-like phenomena. Most subjects are frightened and remorseful about what they've done.

Although the term "limbic psychotic trigger reaction" implies some documentable dysfunction of the limbic system, there is no specific brain abnormality that has been identified to explain this syndrome. Abnormalities in brain functioning are found in about half of these subjects, but there appears to be no common pattern to them. The "psychotic" component relates to the fact that there is a delusional and hallucinatory quality to the episodes, but between episodes, these subjects do not resemble patients with schizophrenia or other psychotic disorders (Chapter 5). The "trigger" part refers to the fact that each subject has very individualized eliciting experiences and each trigger is very specific. Most triggers are found to relate to prior traumatic experiences in the subject's life that had been repressed. Similar to a PTSD flashback (Chapter 6), the trigger evokes a reliving of the traumatic experience, from which the subject attempts to defend himself with a violent reaction.

LPTR is a rare syndrome, and Pontius (1987, 1996, 1997) provides detailed differential diagnostic criteria to distinguish it from other neurological and psychiatric disorders. For example, in conducting court-appointed psychiatric examinations of some 200 men charged with homicide and other felonies over two decades, Pontius has found only 18 cases that she believes to be true LPTR.

TRAUMATIC BRAIN INJURY

In the United States, an estimated 400,000 people are admitted to civilian hospitals with TBI's every year, and about one million suffer from head injury effects at any given time; with returning military veterans from the Iraq and Afghanistan theaters, this number is likely to swell (Slagle, 1990; French et al., 2010). The constellation of somatic, cognitive, and behavioral symptoms seen after TBI was first termed the **postconcussion syndrome** by Strauss and Savitsky (1934), and many of the symptoms described in that original report are psychological in nature: irritability, poor concentration, loss of confidence, anxiety, depression, and hypersensitivity to light and noise. Today, the postconcussion syndrome describes a cluster of symptoms that occur following a closed head injury–sometimes a seemingly "mild" head injury–and it continues to be a source of clinical and forensic controversy (Dinn et al., 2009; Evans, 1992; Levin, 1990).

Commonly reported postconcussive symptoms include headache, dizziness, fatigue, slowness and inefficiency of thought and action, impaired attention, concentration and memory, irritability, anxiety, depression, impaired sleep patterns, nightmares, heightened somatic concern, hypersensitivity to noise and light, blurred or double vision, concrete thinking, cognitive inflexibility, problems in judgment, impulsivity, poor organization and planning, impaired problem solving, lack of self-control, irritability, emotional lability, problems in sustaining motivation, egocentricity, lack of empathy, unawareness of personal impact on others, and general socially inappropriate behavior. Many of these symptoms may be confused with psychological stress reactions or other psychopathology, and in fact may be comorbid with these. Many of these symptoms have been associated with injury to the frontal lobes of the brain, but are not specific to this etiology (Eslinger, 1998; Miller, 1989a, 1990b, 1991a, 1992a, 1993c, 1993d, 1996, 1998c, 1999a, 1999b, 1999c; Parker, 1990; Stuss & Benson, 1984).

Perhaps the single most vexing clinical and theoretical issue with brain-injured patients is the relationship between impulsive, sometimes violent, behavior, acquired brain damage, and premorbid personality and cognitive style. Several studies have reported an association between traumatic brain injuries with loss of consciousness and the subsequent manifestation of antisocial and frankly criminal behavior, including threats of violence, recidivistic violence, family violence, and murder (Blake et al., 1995; Brooks et al., 1986; Eslinger et al., 1995; Felthous, 1980a, 1980b; Grafman et al., 1996; Greve et al., 2001; Lewis & Shanok, 1977; Lewis et al., 1986, 1988; McKinlay et al., 1981; Rosenbaum & Hoge, 1989; Rosenbaum et al., 1994; Shallice & Burgess, 1991; Slaughter et al., 2003; Small, 1966; Wood, 1987; Wood & Rutherford, 2004; Wood & Liossi, 2006). Military service members who sustain a traumatic brain injury with unconsciousness are more likely to be discharged due to behavior problems, substance abuse, and/or criminal charges than other military personnel (Grafman et al., 1996; Ommaya et al., 1996). Brain injuries in childhood have been correlated with later development of pedophilia, schizophrenia, and violent behavior as adults (Abdel-Malik et al., 2003; Blanchard et al., 2002; Leon-Carrion & Ramos, 2003; Max et al., 2001).

Most etiological theories of post-brain injury antisocial behavior specify impairment of the self-regulating functions of the frontal lobes and the verbal self-monitoring functions of the left hemisphere, purported to result in a disinhibition of impulsive, limbic system-mediated behavior, although involvement of the temporal lobes has been implicated as well (Barker et al., 2007; Dinn et al., 2009; Grafman et al., 1996; Koechlin et al., 1999; McAllister, 1992; Miller, 1987, 1988a, 1988b; Mobbs et al., 2007; Morgan & Lilienfeld, 2002; Petrides, 1995; Raine et al., 1997; 2000; Ruff et al., 2003; Seidenwurm et al., 1997; Soderstrom et al., 2000; Tateno et al., 2003; Tonkonogy, 1991; Volkow et al., 1995; Wong et al., 1994; Wood & Liossi, 2006).

While, especially for forensic purposes, it is tempting to attribute a deleterious behavior change to an external injury, clinicians have long recognized that these impulsive, egocentric, and sometimes aggressive behavioral tendencies and personality characteristics may in fact have predated the brain injury and perhaps contributed to it, inasmuch as those who pursue a thrill-seeking, aggressive, and risky lifestyle are more likely to find themselves in situations where they could be injured, such as in car crashes and fights (Bond, 1984; Miller, 1989a, 1992b, 1994b, 1998a). In such cases, postinjury frontal lobe disinhibition may merely worsen a dysfunctional behavioral pattern that has already existed for some time. Demographic data suggest a high incidence of impulsive, even criminal, behavior in this demographic group prior to injury, and many of these same supposedly "organic" traits are found in groups of uninjured individuals clinically identified as psychopaths or antisocial personalities, in whom there is, in turn, an associated high rate of substance abuse and other impulse-control disorders (Begun, 1976; Cleckley, 1982; Cloninger, 1987; Craig, 1982; Miller, 1985b, 1987, 1988c, 1989a, 1992b, 1994b, 1998a; Millon, 1981; Sperry, 1995; see Chapter 8). For example, recent research suggests that much of the correlation between violence and brain injury can be explained by comorbid substance abuse (Dinn et al., 2009), which may either be a direct factor or a proxy variable associated with antisocial personality disorder. A similar relationship may exist among schizophrenia, substance abuse, and crime (Chapter 5).

Accordingly, many of the observed neuropsychological and personality patterns seen in some brain-injured patients may reflect this premorbidly impulsive, stimulation-seeking, emotionally and behaviorally labile, and antisocial cognitive style, as opposed to being solely or mainly attributable to the effects of brain damage itself. Premorbid deficits in frontal lobe "executive control," therefore, may characterize the thought and behavior of those individuals most likely to incur a traumatic brain injury in the first place, and in fact may be a common risk factor for incurring traumatic injuries of all types (Miller, 1989a, 1992b, 1994b, 1998a;). Nevertheless, there is probably a subset of subjects who's impulsive antisocial behavior is a more-or-less direct product of the brain injury itself, and we do see these cases in clinical practice (Miller, 1991a, 1993d, 1998c).

SLEEP DISORDERS

BOX 4.2. TEEN FACING SEX CHARGES SAYS HE WAS SLEEPWALKING
South Florida Sun-Sentinel, Saturday, August 28, 2010, p. 3B:

A 17-year-old boy accused of fondling and having sexual relations with a 13-year-old girl is blaming his sleepwalking habit for the charges he's facing, which
continued

BOX 4.2.—*Continued*

include lewd and lascivious battery and lewd and lascivious molestation on a person younger than 16. The suspect told police he must have a "mental problem" because he "does not care about sex," but reported that he woke up around 2:00 or 3:00 am and realized he was fondling the young girl. He denied recalling sexual acts with the girl, but admitted it could be a "possibility" because of his sleepwalking condition. For her part, the girl reported that, two weeks after the fondling incident, he came into her room around 4:00 a.m. and forced her to have sex, according to her police statement. The suspect told police that he has a problem with sleepwalking, and that he "knew the incidents would come out."

There's an old saying about people who are chronic disturbers and annoyers of those around them: "What trouble can he get into while he's asleep?" It turns out that, for a few people, the answer is: plenty.

Far from being a state of uniform quiescence, sleep is actually an active and varied state of consciousness. During every nightly sleep cycle, most healthy individuals go through three or four sleep cycles, each lasting about 60–90 minutes. Each cycle is composed of five basic sleep stages, ranging from the light, twilight state when we are just dozing off (stage 1 sleep), through two more stages of progressively deeper sleep (stages 2 and 3), and finally to stage 4, called **slow-wave sleep** (**SWS**), or **delta sleep**, for the slow traces (delta waves) seen on an EEG. Following SWS, however, there occurs a sleep stage whose brain waves resemble that of an awake person—yet the person is still fast asleep. This is called **rapid eye movement sleep**, or **REM sleep**, named for the observation that the sleeper's eyeballs seem to be moving rapidly beneath his or her eyelids. It is during REM sleep that most dreaming occurs, including disturbing nightmares, and there is a complex neurophysiological network in the brainstem that is responsible for keeping the sleeper immobile and unable to act out the dream in real life (**REM paralysis**). During SWS, a limited form of dreaming may occur, called **night terrors**, in which the sleeper experiences heightened physiological arousal, but usually recalls very little dreamlike content.

A class of syndromes called **disorders of arousal** involve a pathological disinhibition of movement during REM or SWS, that allows the dreamer to act out the content of his or her dreams. In most instances, the consequences are innocuous, if embarrassing. However, in a few cases, they have led to criminal violence and even homicide.

REM Sleep Behavior Disorder

REM Sleep Behavior Disorder (**RSBD**) is characterized by the malfunctioning of the normal REM sleep paralysis brainstem mechanism, permitting the sleeper to literally act out his or her dreams (Schenck & Mahowald, 1995; Schenck et al., 1986, 2009). As with most REM sleep, during a RSBD episode, the dreamer's eyes are usually closed, and the eyes under the lids appear to be following some observed activity. Most violent activity tends to occur in response to a bedmate trying to rouse the sleeper, although spontaneous acts of aggression may occur, as when the sleeper is dreaming of being attacked and grabs the spouse, thinking he or she is the attacker. In such cases, bedmates have reported tremendous strength on the part of the dreamer. Documented acts committed during RSBD episodes have included choking or headlocking the bed partner, jumping from the bed into a wall or furniture, or throwing the bed partner out of a window.

RSBD behaviors tend to be quick and brief, and the sleeper is usually fully alert and oriented upon awakening, usually able to recall the content or "story" of the dream related to his or her behavior, although not the real-life behavior itself. Although RSBD subjects tend to report more aggressive dreams that nonaffected subjects, they are no more likely to be aggressive in their daily waking lives, and their nighttime violence is usually confined to the bedroom.

Slow-Wave Sleep (SWS) Disorders of Arousal

Slow-Wave Sleep (**SWS**) **disorders of arousal** do not involve the acting-out of a dream. As the name implies, they occur during slow-wave sleep, not REM sleep, but they share the feature of disinhibition of movement that characterizes both disorders (Cartwright, 2004; Guilleminault et al., 1995; Pressman, 2007). SWS disorders of arousal include sleepwalking, confusional arousals, and night terrors. In most cases, the acts committed during these episodes are noncriminal and nonaggressive, but in a small proportion of cases, extreme violence has been documented, including assault and murder. In **sleepwalking**, the individual gets out of bed and may wander just a few feet or several miles, either meandering slowing or running agitatedly. The eyes may be open and there is often an automatistic and confused aspect to the subject's behavior. Violent or sexual acts have been documented to occur in a small proportion of cases during these episodes, the former usually triggered by attempts to arouse the sleepwalker, the latter often having no clear precipitant other than opportunity. Arousal from the SWS state is more gradual than from REM, and the subject does not remember his or her behavior during the episode. It has been theorized that these episodes represent a dis-

connection of frontal lobe volitional control of action from the more stereotyped and automatic action sequences that mediate most routine behaviors.

Confusional arousals involve the same brain mechanisms and disturbances in consciousness as sleepwalking, except that the sleeper does not
leave the bed. In cases of violence, the only ones at risk are usually those
who share the bed. **Night terrors** that occur during SWS are distinguished
from REM nightmares by the former's predominance of physiological fear
arousal (shaking, sweating, heart palpitations, screaming), and paucity of
dream content: the subject is typically unable to recount what he appeared
so agitated about in his sleep. Fragments of frightening visual imagery may
occur during night terrors, impelling the sleeper to try to escape or to defend
himself violently, which may result in a confusional arousal or sleepwalking
episode. In a few cases, SWS phenomena have been successfully used as a
defense of diminished capacity.

DEVELOPMENTAL DISORDERS

These are disorders that usually begin in childhood and have no discernable external cause, such as a traumatic brain injury or cerebral infection.
That is, they are assumed to be **development disorders** that are present at
birth or appear spontaneously at a young age, and then either remain stable
or progress over time. The main syndromes in this category include mental
retardation, autism, Asperger's disorder, and the interrelated syndromes of
attention deficit hyperactivity disorder, oppositional defiant disorder, and
conduct disorder; the latter three are considered in Chapter 19.

Mental Retardation

Mental retardation (MR) is defined as: (1) measured intelligence quo-
tient (IQ) below 70; (2) deficits in adaptive behavior and social functioning;
and (3) onset before the age of 18 (APA, 2000). MR is usually classified as
mild, moderate, or severe. Individuals with moderate to severe MR typically require full-time supervision or custodial care. But those with milder forms
of MR may live in the community or in group work and residential settings
where they may get into legal trouble. MR offenders comprise about 5–10
percent of the convicted prison population. In residential settings, such as
boarding schools, low frustration tolerance may lead to interpersonal squab-
bles that turn into serious fights, although many persons with MR characteristically show a placid, nonconfrontational demeanor. In some settings, theft
is a problem, as some MR subjects may regard taking another's property as

one of the few forms of power and control available to them.

In the community, their often childlike impulsivity may make them prone to misdemeanor crimes, such as shoplifting or public nuisance. When confused or frightened, they may easily become silent and withdrawn or, less commonly, defensively aggressive. MR is frequently comorbid with other mental disorders, so it is possible to see mood disorders, anxiety disorders, or psychotic disorders coexisting with intellectual deficiency, which may further increase the risk for impulsive behavior. These individuals are also not immune to alcohol and drug abuse, and this may render their behavior even more unpredictable. Ordinarily, they tend to be quite compliant and trusting, and thereby make perfect patsies for other criminals to use as drug couriers or stashers of stolen goods (Day, 1988; Hodgins, 1992; Holland et al., 2002; Jones, 2007; Murphy et al., 1995; Noble & Conley, 1992; Thompson & Brown, 1997; Winter et al., 2004).

BOX 4.3. POLICE RESPONSE TO MENTALLY RETARDED CITIZENS

When confronted by police officers, most MR citizens encountered by police officers on street patrol will not be committing a serious crime, but are more likely to be lost and confused, or to have just committed an act of shoplifting or public nuisance about which someone has made a complaint. In most cases, a brief interaction will be sufficient to determine that something is atypical about this person's thought, speech, and behavior. Officers should pay attention to missing, excessive, or disheveled clothing or other unusual styles of dress. There may be peculiarities in the subject's gait and movement, as many mentally retarded individuals also have mild-moderate disturbances in motor coordination. The subject's speech may have a simplistic, childlike quality, it may be characterized by various speech disorders, such as lisps, stutters or variations of volume and pitch, or it may sound relatively normal. When confronted by authorities, such as the police, MR subjects are likely to become afraid or confused, or to be overcompliant and dependent.

If it is unclear as to whether the subject is mentally retarded or suffering from some other form of disorder, officers may utilize a few curbside tests of cognitive and intellectual functioning. Can the subject identify their name and residence? Can they give coherent directions to where they live or where they're going? Can they repeat a question in their own words? Can they write their names clearly? Can they recognize coins and make change? Tell time? Use a telephone? When questioning MR subjects, officers should begin by using simple, open-ended questions, rather than yes-or-no questions, because MR subjects tend to be overcompliant and will often answer a question based on what they believe will please the questioner, especially an authority figure like a police officer. However, if they

continued

BOX 4.3.—*Continued*

don't understand a more complex query, simple yes-or-no questions may be necessary.

When coming across the scene of a crime or other disturbance involving a MR subject and other people, it may not be immediately clear who is the suspect, victim, witnesses, or bystanders. The MR subject may be intimidated and be silent while the others do the talking and make their own cases. Officers should be careful to question everyone present very carefully, and document these interviews. If officers must arrest the MR subject, they should ensure that Miranda rights are understood, for example, by asking the suspect to rephrase them in his own words. Interviews and interrogations may yield unnatural compliance and false confessions due to the pliability and suggestibility of MR subjects, or they may be met by confused silence. If a mentally retarded suspect has to be criminally detained, all care should be taken not to house him with the general population, where he may be abused. Of course, this will depend on the realities of the situation and available facilities. In criminal trials, mental retardation may be raised as an issue of competency to stand trial and/or as an exculpatory or mitigating factor in the commission of the crime (Bowker, 1994; Clare & Gudjonsson, 1993; Clare et al., 1998; Jones, 2007; Miller, 2006f).

Autism and Asperger Syndrome

Autism, or **autistic disorder** (APA, 2000) is a neurodevelopmental disorder of early onset, characterized by restricted speech, stereotyped patterns of behavior, obsessive need for order, stability, and routine, and impaired interpersonal communication, sometimes accompanied by bizarre and/or self-injurious behavior. **Asperger syndrome** (**AS**) appears to be a milder form of the disorder, lacking the severe impairment in communication, but showing heightened impulsivity, lack of empathy, restricted social contact, formalistic speech patterns, intensive preoccupation with unique or unusual subjects, need for motoric stimulation (spinning on chairs, fast carnival rides) alternating with hypersensitivity and aversion to certain types of sensory stimulation (lights, sounds, or tactile stimulation such as clothing or showers), and motor coordination problems (Asperger, 1944; Kanner, 1943, 1949; Katz & Zemishlany, 2006, in press; Mouridsen et al., 2008; Wing, 1981; see also Chapter 19).

Most subjects with moderate to severe autism will be living at home or in custodial care, limiting their opportunity for aggressive interactions with others; in addition, they typically prefer to avoid human contact, so these individuals have a much lower frequency of interpersonal violence than the general population (Mouridsen et al., 2008). When autistic subjects do show aggressive behavior, it is commonly in connection with disruption of a routine or intrusion upon some stereotyped activity, which causes the subject to panic and lash out defensively, often combining self-harm with outer-directed aggression (Baron-Cohen, 1988; Chen et al., 2003; Howlin, 1997; Mawson et al., 1995; Mouridsen et al., 2008; Palermo, 2004; Wing, 1986).

Subjects with AS are generally more out there in the world, yet may lack the interpersonal empathy that ordinarily lets people intuit what effects their words or behavior will have on other people. While the overall rate of criminal behavior in AS subjects is low, they have been documented to commit a broad range of criminal acts as adolescents and adults, which are often carried out in a bizarre and idiosyncratic way. These include physical and sexual assault, stalking and harassment, theft and burglary, vandalism and arson, murder and attempted murder, and attacks on family members. In many cases, these acts are triggered by violations of personal space or deliberate or unintentional body intrusion (e.g., touching an AS subject who has tactile hypersensitivity), disruption of a routine or activity (interrupting reading or TV watching to get ready for bed or to undergo a clinical evaluation), misinterpretation of others' statements or activities (the subject is asked a question and thinks it's an insult or attack) or unempathic satisfaction of needs (sexual assault of another person because the subject feels it's okay). In some cases, the motives are the same as in any other person, e.g., jealousy or revenge (Bankier et al., 1999; Baron-Cohen, 1988; Barry-Walsh & Mullen, 2004; Bjorkly, 2009; Chen et al., 2003; Chesterman & Rutter, 1993; Everall & LeCouteur, 1990; Ghaziuddin et al., 1991; Hall & Bernall, 1995; Katz & Zemishlany, 1986, in press; Kohn et al., 1998; Mawson et al., 1985; Milton et al., 2002; Murrie et al., 2002; Raja & Azzoni, 2001; Schwartz-Watts, 2005; Scragg & Shah, 1994; Silva et al., 2002; Siponmaa et al., 2001; Wing, 1977, 1981). Some authorities believe that the relative inability to understand the interpersonal consequences of their actions lends a diagnosis of AS to a defense of diminished capacity (Freckelton & List, 2009; Symblett & Wilson, 1993; Barry-Walsh & Mullen, 2004).

Fetal Alcohol Syndrome

A mother's lifestyle before and during her pregnancy can exert a powerful effect on her offspring's physical and mental health, as well as his or her later involvement with the criminal justice system.

Fetal alcohol syndrome (FAS) was first identified and described in 1968. It consists of a set of physical, neurological, and psychological abnormalities, including small head and body size, delayed development, a distinct facial appearance, perceptual and motor deficits, mental retardation, learning disabilities, hyperactivity, and impulsivity. It ranges in severity from mild to severe and is caused specifically by maternal ingestion of alcohol during pregnancy, making it an entirely preventable form of childhood disorder. There may be a dose-response relationship, in that the higher the alcohol intake during gestation, the more severe the abnormalities, but there is also evidence that different mothers show genetic variability in their ability to metabolize alcohol that affects their risk. Children with moderate-to-severe forms of FAS usually are serious management problems at home and at school and, in adolescence and adulthood, their poor judgment and impulsivity account for a host of medical, psychiatric, and legal problems (Agarwal & Goedde, 1992; Anderson, 2007; Chen & West, 1999; Jones et al., 1973; Kaemingk & Paquette, 1999; Mattson & Riley, 1998; Shaywitz et al., 1980; Streissguth et al., 1991; Young, 1997).

Since no "safe" dose of alcohol during gestation has been identified, the general advice of clinicians for mothers has been zero intake. However, excessive alcohol use as a risk factor rarely occurs in isolation, and is typically correlated with other substance misuse (see below), as well as with tobacco smoking during gestation, which has been independently linked to attentional problems, hyperactivity, aggressive behavior, and subsequent criminal activity in the offspring (Biederman, 2005; Brennan et al., 2002; Fergusson et al., 1998; Fried et al., 1998; Orlebeke et al., 1997). Even here, the relationship is not clear because alcohol, drug use, and smoking are highly correlated with parental impulsivity, poor self-control, and low socioeconomic status, which raises the question of which behavioral traits are genetically transmitted to offspring, and which are the result of external risk factors like smoking and substance use. Parental impulsivity and substance use are also associated with earlier onset of sexual activity and earlier age of pregnancy, which are themselves independently correlated with a higher rate of behavioral problems in offspring, partially related to higher prenatal exposure to testosterone in younger mothers, and partly to impulsivity and behavioral problems in the biological fathers (Anderson, 2007). Thus, both clinicians and forensic specialists need to exert care and diligence in teasing out the causal psycholegal matrix in any given case.

ALCOHOL, DRUG ABUSE, AND CRIME

In my classes, I often open the topic of alcohol and drug abuse by posing the rhetorical question: "Why do people use drugs and alcohol?" The students are reluctant to respond, thinking I'm expecting some profound,

TABLE 4.1.
BRAIN SYNDROMES THAT MAY BE
ASSOCIATED WITH CRIMINAL BEHAVIOR

Dementia: Organic illness of the brain. May be associated with trespassing, confusional shoplifting (they think the item is really theirs), defensive aggression, or sexual offenses due to impaired perception, judgment, or impulse control.

Temporal Lobe Epilepsy (TLE): Seizure disorder characterized by disturbed perception, consciousness, and behavior, including repetitive, stereotypic **automatisms**. May be associated with inappropriate public undressing, sexual and bathroom behavior, inappropriate touching, or defensive aggression. Seizures typically persist for only a few seconds to minutes.

Intermittent Explosive Disorder (IED)/Episodic Dyscontrol Syndrome (EDS): Seizure-like disorder characterized by paroxysmal attacks of extreme violent rage, with features of overkill, diminished awareness of surroundings or actions, poor recall of the event and remorse for the seemingly uncharacteristic action.

Pathological Intoxication: Paroxysmal IED/EDS-like rage attacks triggered by small amounts of alcohol.

Limbic Psychotic Trigger Reaction (LPTR): Paroxysmal episodes of defensive violence, triggered by a person or circumstance that evokes a traumatic memory.

Traumatic Brain Injury/Postconcussion Syndrome: Results from a blow to the head which may or may not cause unconsciousness. May result in impaired judgment and self-control, irritability, mood swings, egocentricity, lack of empathy, impulsivity, and heightened susceptibility to aggressive behavior due to impairment of the brain's frontal lobes. May also be facilitated by premorbid impulsivity and thrill-seeking behavior, leading to risky activities like fighting or unsafe driving that in turn result in accidents or assaults producing brain injury–a vicious cycle.

REM Sleep Behavior Disorder (RSBD): Malfunction of brainstem mechanisms normally inhibiting movement during REM sleep results in subjects literally acting out their dreams. Usually nonviolent, but may cause inadvertent injury to bed partner or self (e.g., kicking, running, colliding with furniture); subject may occasionally directly assault bed partner in the context of a defensive or aggressive dream.

Night Terrors: Extreme fear experienced during non-REM sleep may cause subject to defensively lash out in bed.

Confusional Arousals: Subject moves about in bed during non-REM sleep, may occasionally assault bed partner.

Somnambulism: Sleepwalking. Subject gets out of bed and may engage in complex behavior, occasionally including violent behavior.

Mental Retardation: Intellectual limitations may be associated with impaired judgment, poor frustration tolerance, and impaired self-control. May lead to stealing or fighting.

continued

TABLE 4.1.–*Continued*

__Autism:__ Neurodevelopmental disorder of early onset, characterized by restricted speech, stereotyped patterns of behavior, obsessive need for order, stability, and routine, and impaired interpersonal communication, sometimes accompanied by bizarre and/or self-injurious behavior. Rarely overtly aggressive, but may become defensively violent if frightened or frustrated.

__Asperger's Syndrome:__ Impaired empathy, poor understanding of social cues, and need for structure and sameness may result in defensive aggression when personal boundaries are violated. Also may be susceptible to inappropriate behavior, e.g., staring at people, blunt comments, or inappropriate touching.

__Fetal Alcohol Syndrome (FAS):__ Multiple developmental musculoskeletal and nervous system disorders due to maternal use of alcohol during pregnancy. Usually associated with mental retardation or cognitive impairment, hyperactivity, impulsivity, poor judgment, and under-controlled aggressive behavior.

nuanced theoretical explanation. Then I write on the board: BIFGS. What's that? Dramatic pause. Next board entry: *Because It Feels Good, Stupid.* Bottom line: People use and abuse substances because, in one form or another, they replicate, magnify, and enhance sensations, perceptions, and actions that are naturally reinforcing–i.e., they make us feel good. Too much of a good thing, however, and we may find ourselves in trouble (Miller, 1985a, 1985b, 1986a, 1989a, 1990a, 1990c, 1991b, 1992b).

There are several ways alcohol and drugs can be associated with criminal behavior. First, alcohol and drug intoxication may dilute inhibitions to impulsive, antisocial, and frankly criminal behavior. Second, activities related to the purchase, sale, and trafficking in illegal substances may lead to crimes of robbery and murder. Third, the mere possession of many substances constitutes a crime in itself. Note that, in most cases, the law specifically excludes **voluntary intoxication** as an affirmative NGRI defense; otherwise, it would be only too easy to get oneself drunk or high, go out and commit a crime, and then claim lack of responsibility for one's actions based on that self-induced state of intoxication. However, if it can be proved that the state of impairment was not voluntary (e.g., someone slipped a powerful drug into the defendant's drink without his knowledge), then this factor could conceivably be raised as a defense, considering the totality of the circumstances.

Intoxication and Withdrawal: Signs, Symptoms, and Syndromes

Signs of **alcohol intoxication** are familiar to anyone who has ever been at a New Year's Eve party: slurred speech, impaired coordination, silly behavior, and so on. It is possible, however, for many drinkers who are legally intoxicated to act relatively normally, especially if they have been long-term and experienced alcohol users. Alcohol has varying effects, depending on the particular drinker, with some inebriated individuals becoming mellow and tractable, others angry and agitated. In general, alcohol and most other drugs lower inhibitions and self-control, which no doubt accounts for their popularity.

Less common, but potentially more serious, are signs and symptoms of **alcohol withdrawal** in subjects who are physiologically dependent on alcohol. This usually presents as an agitated state with tremors ("the shakes"). In severe cases, this can be accompanied by hallucinations and/or seizures. A distinctive state of agitated delirium, characterized by intense fear and tactile and visual hallucinations of vermin crawling on or under one's skin, is called **delirium tremens ("the DTs")**. Typically, such individuals will be so clearly impaired that the need for immediate medical attention is obvious. Years of long-term heavy abuse of alcohol can also lead to **alcoholic dementia**, but these subjects are likely to be confined to home or institutions and are not typically encountered in the community, although some old-timers in low-demand, routine jobs who are nearing retirement may skirt through their workday in a cognitively impaired state (Miller, 2008c).

An even rarer, but more dangerous, syndrome is **pathological intoxication** (thought to have afflicted the author Edgar Allen Poe), in which small amounts of alcohol trigger violent rages in susceptible individuals. This is thought to be due to an electrophysiological disturbance in sensitive limbic areas of the brain, and the episode appears to resemble states of episodic dyscontrol syndrome or intermittent explosive disorder (see above). Witnesses will describe an explosion of rage in which the subject appears to be "on automatic" or "like a runaway train," fueled by adrenalin and capable of inflicting severe damage to anyone who gets in his way. These episodes typically last only a few seconds to minutes, and are sometimes characterized by "overkill" (multiple blows and extreme violence). During these brief episodes, it is useless to try to talk the subject out of his aggressive actions. The only effective strategy is to call for help and to employ appropriate physical restraint to keep the subject from harming others. Certain individuals may be especially at risk, such as those with antisocial personality disorder (Chapter 8), schizophrenia (Chapter 5), and mood disorders (Chapter 6) (Elliott, 1992; Langevin et al., 1987; Miller, 1985b, 1989a, 1991b, 1992b, 1997c; Pincus & Tucker, 1978; Volavka, 1995; Yesavage & Zarcone, 1983).

Other substances of abuse have different effects on behavior, depending on their biochemical action within the user's brain. **Stimulants** ("uppers"), such as cocaine and amphetamine, produce a racing kind of high, with rapid thought and speech, erratic and impulsive behavior, and a ramped-up energy level. Such individuals may occasionally become violent, but more commonly, they will present as simply annoying and raucous, quite similar to the manic state described in Chapter 6; in fact, many manic subjects deliberately use stimulants to enhance and extend their natural high. Danger may arise when their overconfidence and impulsivity lead to temper flare-ups provoked by confrontations with other people.

Central nervous system **depressants**, or **sedative-hypnotics** ("downers"), such as barbiturates (e.g., Quaaludes) or benzodiazepines (e.g., Xanax, Valium), have effects similar to alcohol, which include a calming effect and loosening of inhibitions, which may lead to impulsive and dangerous actions. Alternatively, these subjects may become so drowsy and out-of-it that they pose a danger while driving or operating machinery.

The effects of **hallucinogens**, such as marijuana, LSD, or angel dust, may range from mellow goofiness to violent delirium. **Organic hydrocarbons**, such as the glue and paint thinner enjoyed by sniffers or "huffers," tend

TABLE 4.2.
SUBSTANCE USE EFFECTS ON BRAIN AND BEHAVIOR

Alcohol: Intoxication may impair judgment and lower inhibitions to aggressive and sexual behavior. **Pathological intoxication** involves extreme violence triggered by small amounts of alcohol in susceptible persons (Table 4.1). Withdrawal after heavy alcohol dependence may be associated with heightened irritability and, in severe cases, may result in **delirium tremens** (**DTs**). After years of heavy alcohol abuse, **alcoholic dementia** can result in impaired judgment and disinhibited behavior.

Sedative-Hypnotics: Barbiturates and benzodiazepines. Have effects similar to alcohol. Intoxication produces sedation and disinhibition, with greater risk of impulsive behavior.

Stimulants: Cocaine, amphetamines. Intoxication increases arousal, energy level, impulsivity, and aggressiveness, and may impair judgment and self-control. Withdrawal produces an irritable-dysphoric state in which the subject may be easily provoked.

Hallucinogens: LSD, PCP, marijuana. Depending on the dose, usually produces a dreamy, perceptually altered state. Not usually associated with antisocial behavior, but persons with a predisposition to aggression may act out this way under the influence. "Bad trips" may result in defensive aggression. Certain substances, such as PCP, can produce an agitated delirium.

Organic Hydrocarbons: Glue, paint thinner, cleaning products. Produce a toxic delirium, the effects ranging from somnolence to violent agitation.

Anabolic steroids: Testosterone or testosterone analogs. In high doses may produce a manic-like aggressive psychosis (**'roid rage**). In lower doses, may heighten susceptibility to aggressive reaction to minor challenges.

to produce a toxic delirious state; these latter substances are also extremely injurious to nervous tissue and can produce brain damage causing persisting cognitive impairment.

Anabolic steroids are drugs which replicate the effects of the male sex hormones testosterone and dihydrotestosterone to increase protein synthesis within cells, especially skeletal muscle cells, and have generally virilizing properties, such as increased hair growth and deepening of the voice. Consequently, they are frequently used by bodybuilders and other athletes to pack on muscle and increase strength and endurance. Psychologically, they can produce a state of pumped enthusiasm and overconfidence, and may have addictive potential through their effects on the neurotransmitter dopamine (Chapter 2). Overuse of anabolic steroids has been associated with states of aggressive hypomania, called **'roid rage**, which have resulted in acts of violence, and the probability of criminal behavior under the influence of these drugs is probably higher for those already possessing other risk factors for violence (Chapters 2, 3, and 8). Side effects of anabolic steroid abuse include acne, increased cholesterol levels, hypertension, heart and liver damage, testicular atrophy, and gynecomastia (male breast development).

SUMMARY AND CONCLUSIONS

Although less commonly encountered in the criminal justice system than other mental disorders, brain syndromes can present important forensic challenges, as they may affect many aspects of emotion, cognition, and behavioral self-control. **Dementia** can impair judgment and disinhibit aggressive behavior. **Temporal lobe epilepsy** may occasionally be associated with combative violence during a confusional state, but more intense, directed aggression may be seen in seizure-like violent episodes characterizing **episodic dyscontrol syndrome/intermittent explosive disorder** or **limbic psychotic trigger reaction**. There is a complex causal interrelationship between **traumatic brain injur**y and impulsive violence, in that impulsive people are more at risk for any kind of injury, and traumatic damage to the brain's frontal lobes can further disinhibit egocentric, antisocial behavior in susceptible individuals. Various sleep disorders may be associated with violence, including **REM sleep behavior disorder**, **confusional arousals**, and **somnambulism**. A number of developmental disorders such as **mental retardation, autism, Asperger's syndrome**, or **fetal alcohol syndrome** can include aggressive or other criminal behavior as part of the symptom spectrum. Finally, **alcohol and drug abuse** can disinhibit antisocial behavior, especially in individuals already at risk.

In evaluating the clinical effects and forensic implications of brain syndromes and substance abuse, it is important to be cognizant of the complex web of factors that may contribute to criminal behavior in these cases. Many people use substances without becoming violent or engaging in criminal activity. Characterologically impulsive and violent people usually don't need to be impaired or intoxicated to commit their crimes, although brain dysfunction and/or chemical abuse may lower the threshold. Factors associated with higher risk for criminal behavior—low SES, low educational level, underemployment, poor verbal IQ, impulsivity, history of head injuries, and inconsistent parenting (Chapters 2 and 3)—are also independently associated with alcohol and drug abuse, without one necessarily causing the other. This type of clinical-forensic integrative thinking is essential for the valid assessment of real-life cases.

Chapter **5**

Schizophrenia and
Psychotic Disorders

Psychotic disorders comprise a group of syndromes, whose common feature is a significant break with reality, characterized by severe disturbances of mood, thought, and goal-directed action. They encompass the diagnoses of schizophrenia, schizoaffective disorder, delusional disorder, and other psychotic disorders (Table 5.1).

SCHIZOPHRENIA: CLINCAL FEATURES

The most commonly diagnosed form of psychotic disorder is **schizophrenia**, which is a progressive syndrome, usually first presenting in adolescence or early adulthood (although childhood forms occur), and characterized by **delusions** (false beliefs) and **hallucinations** (false perceptions). The latter are typically auditory (hearing voices), and more rarely, visual (seeing things) or tactile (strange sensations). Untreated schizophrenics may suffer episodic bouts of delusional and hallucinatory psychosis, between which they may appear simply odd or weird, unable to maintain any consistent work or other activity. Associated features include **alogia** (poverty of speech), **anhedonia** (deficient ability to experience pleasure), **avolition** (lack of motivation and goal-directed behavior), **asociality** (isolation and withdrawal from human interaction), and **blunted affect** (a flat, unresponsive emotional style and facial expression).

Although diagnostic overlap is common, schizophrenia may be primarily of the **paranoid** type, characterized mainly by delusions of persecution and accusatory hallucinations; the **disorganized** type, characterized by general aimlessness and lack of contact with reality; the **catatonic** type, which is more commonly seen in institutional settings because of their near-immobility; or the **undifferentiated** type, which may comprise features of the other three classifications or show additional symptoms.

121

TABLE 5.1.
PSYCHOTIC DISORDERS

Schizophrenia: Serious disorder of thought, mood, speech, and/or behavior, and disruption of contact with reality. Characterized by the presence of **delusions** (disturbances of belief) and **hallucinations** (disturbances of perception).

Paranoid Type: Predominance of persecutory delusions and hallucinations, may include **command hallucinations**. Typically, the most cognitively and behaviorally intact of the schizophrenias. May commit crimes in response to delusions of persecution or command hallucinations telling the subject to defend himself or retaliate.

Disorganized Type: Disorganization of speech and behavior, lack of goal-directedness, flat or inappropriate emotion, "weird" behavior, social isolativeness, fragmented and themeless delusions and hallucinations. Usually associated with misdemeanor crimes such as public disturbance or petty theft, but occasional impulsively violent acts may be seen. May be complicated by substance abuse.

Catatonic Type: Characterized mainly by abnormal movement, ranging from immobility to bizarre limb and facial posturing, to idiosyncratic mannerisms, to excessive stereotyped or aimless activity. No special association with criminal behavior.

Undifferentiated Type: Presence of delusions, hallucinations, and/or disturbed thought, mood, speech, or behavior, but not meeting the criteria for the above categories or representing a combination of types. No special association with criminal behavior.

Residual Type: Presence of disturbed thought, mood, speech, and/or behavior, but without the presence of prominent delusions or hallucinations. No special association with criminal behavior.

Schizoaffective Disorder: Presence of symptoms of a unipolar or bipolar mood disorder (Chapter 6) along with symptoms of a psychotic disorder. May commit criminal behavior as part of a manic episode or in response to delusional or hallucinatory content.

Delusional Disorder: Characterized by the presence of one or more nonbizarre delusions (i.e., they could be plausible if you accept the premise) that persist for at least one month, without prominent hallucinations. Daily behavioral functioning is typically less disturbed than in schizophrenia. Delusions may be classified as **erotomanic** (another person–either someone I know or a celebrity–is in love with me), **jealous** (my mate is being unfaithful), **grandiose** (I'm special and superior), **persecutory** (which is why they all resent me and are out to get me), or **somatic** (and why they secretly infected me with an experimental virus that is discoloring my skin and causing me to emit a foul odor). Criminal acts may be committed in response to grandiose, persecutory, or jealous delusions. Erotomanic delusions may lead to criminal stalking behavior (Chapter 18).

Shared Psychotic Disorder: A delusion that develops in an individual involved in a close relationship with someone already suffering from a delusional psychotic disorder, sometimes referred to as **folie a deux**. For example, the wife of a man who thinks he is a king develops the delusion that she is the queen. Criminal acts may be committed in tandem by couples who share grandiose or persecutory delusions.

Schizophreniform Disorder: Presence of psychotic symptoms for a period between one month and six months, without prominent deterioration of thought, mood, speech, or behavior during the psychotic episodes, and with relatively normal functioning between episodes. Criminal acts may be committed during psychotic episodes.

Brief Psychotic Disorder: Presence of psychotic symptoms for a period between one day and one month, with delusions, hallucinations, and/or prominent deterioration of thought, mood, speech, or behavior during the psychotic episodes, but with relatively normal functioning between episodes. Criminal acts may be committed during psychotic episodes. Closest clinical correlate to the legal concept of "**temporary insanity**."

Psychotic Disorder due to a General Medical Condition: The psychotic disorder develops as the direct result of a neurological or medical syndrome, e.g., brain injury, epilepsy, liver or kidney disease, diabetic hypoglycemia, brain infection, brain tumor, etc. Although rare, impulsive criminal behavior may occur during organic psychotic episodes.

Substance-Induced Psychotic Disorder: The psychotic disorder develops as the direct result of an intoxicating substance, e.g., cocaine or methamphetamine psychosis, bad LSD trip, sedative or alcohol withdrawal, etc. Criminal acts may be committed during chemically-induced psychotic episodes. Must be distinguished from the effects of the substances themselves, i.e., voluntary intoxication (not an affirmative defense) or substance-induced psychosis (possibly an affirmative defense).

SCHIZOPHRENIA, MENTAL ILLNESS, AND CRIMINAL BEHAVIOR

Psychological and criminological thinking about the relationship of crime to mental illness in general, and schizophrenia in particular, has gone through several cycles over the past decades. Perhaps in a well-meaning attempt to not overly stigmatize the mentally ill, research and clinical reports emerging in the 1960s and 1970s largely asserted that the mentally ill were no more likely to be violent than anyone else. Since 1980, well-controlled studies have concluded that, although the majority of mentally ill citizens are not violent, and such individuals are far more likely to be the victims of violence than its perpetrators, serious mental illness, particularly schizophrenia, does confer an elevated risk for commission of violence and other criminal behavior, compared with other citizens. The rate of self-reported violence is five times higher among schizophrenic subjects, and the prevalence of schizophrenia is three times higher in prisons than in the general population, although differences in arrest rates and quality of legal representation associated with poverty and untreated illness may also influence this disparity (Arboleda-Florez et al., 1998; Arsenault et al., 2000a; Barrowcliff & Haddock, 2006; Belfrage, 1998; Brennan et al., 2000; Brinded et al., 1999; Brink et al., 2001; Caldwell & Gottesmann, 1990; Erb et al., 2001; Fazel & Grann,

2004; Gunn, 2000; Hodgins et al., 1996; Hodelet, 2001; Lindqvist, 1986; Lindquivt & Allebeck, 1990; Link & Stueve, 1995; Malmquist, 1996; Monahan, 1992, 2002; Mullen et al., 2000; Mulvey, 1994; Naudts & Hodgins, 2006a, 2006b; Silver, 2006; Silver et al., 2008; Swanson et al., 1990; Taylor & Gunn, 1999; Tengstrom et al., 2004; Tiinhonen et al., 1997; Wallace et al., 2004; Walsh et al., 2001; Wessely & Taylor, 1991; Wessely et al., 1994; Yesavage, 1983).

The question is why. We know that not all clinical types and patterns of schizophrenia pose equal risk factors for criminal behavior. For example, there appear to be two separate developmental trajectories for schizophrenic subjects who commit crimes (Naudts & Hodgins, 2006a; Tengstrom et al., 2001, 2004). The first group, which has been labeled **late starters**, shows no antisocial or criminal behavior prior to the onset of their schizophrenic syndrome, which is usually in their teens or early twenties. The criminal offending of these subjects is likely to be associated with psychotic episodes and to involve random and bizarre acts of violence, often in defense against delusions and hallucinations of being threatened. **Early starters**, by contrast, have typically shown a pattern of repeated antisocial behavior since early childhood, chronic delinquency during adolescence, and persistent criminality in adulthood, when their schizophrenia is most likely to be diagnosed. Their crimes are more likely to resemble crimes of nonschizophrenic citizens (shoplifting, robbery, sexual assault, physical battery), although there may be delusional aspects as well. Early starters are also more likely to begin alcohol and drug use at an earlier age.

In fact, there is a distinct parallel between late and early starting antisocial schizophrenia and Moffitt's (1993) distinction between **adolescent-limited** and **life-course persistent delinquents** (Chapter 19), and early starters are many times more likely than late starters to meet diagnostic criteria for antisocial personality disorder (Hodgins et al., 1996; Tengstrom et al., 2001). It appears, then, that comorbid antisocial personality disorder may explain most of the elevated criminal behavior seen in some schizophrenics. A person may be unlucky enough to have both syndromes, but it is the antisocial personality that generates the criminal behavior, while the schizophrenia may be responsible for the delusional quality of some violent acts, and also impairs the individual's overall ability to develop and maintain more socially adaptive patterns of behavior.

Schizophrenia and Substance Abuse

Substance abuse is more prevalent among the schizophrenic population than among the general population, with rates as high as 20–50 percent

(Allebeck et al., 1993; Arndt et al., 1992; Blanchard et al., 2000; Rice & Harris, 1995; RachBeisel et al., 1999; Smith & Hucker, 1994). In addition, mental illness, violence and substance abuse share many of the same risk factors, including gender, age, ethnicity, individual and neighborhood socioeconomic status, family history of physical and sexual abuse, stressful life events, and poor access to social support services (Aneshensel, 1992; Hiday, 2006; Hiday et al., 1999, 2001; Silver, 2000a, 2000b, 2006; Silver & Teasdale, 2005; Swanson, 1993; Swanson et al., 1990).

In subjects with schizophrenia, substance abuse is consistently found to be a risk factor for violent offending (Appelbaum et al., 2000; Cuffel et al., 1994; Modestin & Ammann, 1995; Monahan et al., 2000; Rasanen et al., 1998; Tengstrom et al., 2000, 2004), and we know that a high rate of substance abuse is common among individuals with antisocial personality disorder (Chapter 8) (Hemphill et al., 1994; Smith & Newman, 1990; Windle, 1999). Early onset of substance abuse has been found to be a risk factor for criminality and violence in adulthood among persons with or without comorbid major mental illness (Fulwiler & Ruthazer, 1999; Fulwiler et al., 1997; Hodgins, 1992; Mueser et al., 1997).

For schizophrenics, then, substance abuse by itself may no more be a risk factor for violence than it is for most people. However, a high rate of substance abuse from an early age is a marker for child and adolescent conduct disorder that becomes antisocial personality disorder in adulthood (Chapters 8, 19). Individuals with comorbid schizophrenia and antisocial personality disorder may display a higher rate of substance abuse and criminal behavior, not because the alcohol or drugs are making them commit crimes, but because the substance abuse is a proxy risk factor (Chapter 1) associated with antisocial personality (Tengstrom et al., 2004).

Thus, when subjects with severe mental illness in general, and schizophrenia in particular, become violent, this is almost always associated with two main factors, either: (1) schizophrenic subjects with comorbid antisocial personality disorder and substance abuse, for whom impulsive and predatory aggression would be a way of life, whether psychotic or not; or (2) schizophrenic subjects in the throes of a paranoid delusional psychosis who are attempting to protect themselves or retaliate for perceived threats (Buchanan & Leese, 2001; Hiday, 2006; Link & Stueve, 1994; Link et al., 1992; MacCulloch et al., 1993; Monahan, 2001; Monahan & Steadman, 1983; Rasanen et al., 1998; Silver, 2006; Silver & Teasdale, 2005; Silver et al., 2008; Swanson et al., 1990; Tiihonen, 2001; Tiihonen et al., 1996; Vartianinen & Ryynanen,1996; Webster et al., 1997). To complicate matters, rather than destigmatizing the mentally ill, the **deinstitutionalization movement** of the 1960s and 1970s may have had the opposite effect on public perception of mental

illness and crime. By resulting in more visible members of this group among
the ranks of the homeless street people, average citizens have become more
frightened from their increased encounters with them (Lamb, 1984; Malmquist, 1996).

Delusions, Command Hallucinations and Violence

In light of the above, it would be useful to identify a particular pattern of
psychotic thinking that is linked to violent behavior. Paranoid schizophrenic
subjects may be an especially dangerous group, since they are most likely to
be experiencing delusions of persecution, and are the most cognitively intact
subgroup of schizophrenics, allowing some degree of planning and plotting
in their attacks. A review of records of paranoid schizophrenic psychiatric
patients who had attempted to gain access to the U.S. President or other high
government officials found that one in seven had been arrested for murder
or aggravated assault during the 9 to 12 years following their discharge from
mental hospitals where they had been committed (Shore et al., 1985, 1988).

In subjects with schizophrenia, particularly paranoid schizophrenia, the
presence of persecutory delusions may impel them to lash out as a way of
protecting themselves, i.e., to launch a "preemptive strike." Also, **command
hallucinations** may order the subject to utilize offensive or defensive aggression to ward off or retaliate for an imagined attack. The phenomenon of
command hallucinations has special implications for forensic psychology because it is in these cases, where an internal voice has "commanded" the subject to commit an violent act, that issues of free will and criminal responsibility are most likely to be raised in the context of a NGRI defense.

In this regard, auditory command hallucinations are common among
schizophrenic subjects, up to 50 percent of whom report such phenomena
(Barrowcliff & Haddock, 2006; Hellerstein et al., 1987; Hersh & Borum,
1998; Rogers et al., 1990, 2002). Command hallucinations are associated
with a range of dangerous behaviors toward self and others, including self-
inflicted eye injuries, swallowing of foreign objects, self-mutilation of the
hands or genitals, suicide attempts, physical assault, sexual assault, and murder (Hall et al., 1981; Jones et al., 1992; Karp et al., 1991; Rowan & Malone,
1997).

However, as common as command hallucinations may be, the available
evidence suggests that most subjects who experience them do not automatically comply (Barrowcliff & Haddock, 2006; Breier & Astrachan, 1984;
Goodwin et al., 1971; Shore et al., 1989; Thompson et al., 1992). Far from the
common stereotype of schizophrenic subjects slavishly obeying hallucinated
commands to hurt or kill others or themselves, most subjects attempt to resist

these commands, at least initially. Often the hallucinated commands occur in the form of hostile voices condemning the subject for unspeakable sins, for which the ordered actions constitute a form of atonement. The subject is typically in a frightened, agitated state during the hallucinatory episode, which may last for days. He or she may attempt to mask the voices with music or other loud sounds, to drown them out with alcohol or drugs, or to scream back at them. When the subject complies with the hallucination, it is usually not willingly, but out of desperation to end the persecution. In a few cases, however, some subjects, most commonly paranoid schizophrenics, will describe command hallucinations that are congruent with, and reinforce, their conspiratorial delusional system, and in these cases, compliance may be more voluntary.

A consistently cited direct risk factor for violence among schizophrenic offenders is the **threat/control override syndrome** (Link & Stueve, 1994; Link et al., 1992, 1998; Swanson et al., 1996), which consists of: (1) delusions of persecution; (2) delusions of thought control; and (3) command hallucinations. The key element here is that the subject believes that his very thoughts are being manipulated and that the only way to regain his autonomy and free will is to attack the malevolent force that is trying to control his mind and make him think and do horrible things; the voices then command him who to attack and sometimes how to do it. Under these circumstances, the subject may be especially dangerous because he feels he "has no choice," therefore, the threat of mind control overrides his resistance to the violent act.

Further study (Chadwick & Birchwood, 1994) has shown that auditory command hallucinations can vary within and between subjects with respect to: (1) how benevolent or evil the voice is regarded to be and how important or authoritative is the perceived source; (2) the directed intensity or severity of the command (spitting and cursing at someone vs. beating and stabbing them); (3) the expected consequences of disobeying the command (be arrested, go to Hell); (4) the subject's current state of mood (despondent, agitated) and/or degree of fatigue from struggling with the voices; leading to (5) the actual level of compliance with the command (refusal, partial compliance, or full compliance). In this regard, a schizophrenic subject's range of responses to a hallucinated command is similar to that of a nonpsychotic individual who may be ordered to do something by an actual person.

For example, in Chadwick & Birchwood's (1994) study, when the source of the command was perceived as benevolent and the severity of the ordered act was mild, all subjects complied fully. Where a mild act was commanded by a hostile voice, compliance dipped slightly to 83 percent. A severe command generated by a malevolent voice was resisted by all but one subject, indicating that schizophrenic subjects are ordinarily no more likely to obey a homicidal order from a hostile hallucinated voice than you or I would be to kill someone just because a real person told us to. Interestingly, however, the majority of the schizophrenic recipients of severe commands from hostile voices had also received mild commands from the same source and had decided to comply with the latter. In some of these cases, it seemed as if the subjects were attempting to "bargain" with the voices by offering to comply with a less severe command in order to be let off the hook about the more severe one (Chadwick & Birchwood, 1994). Thus, far from the stereotype of blind obedience to hallucinated voices, schizophrenic subjects show a range of judgment and decision-making with regard to their hallucinations, in many ways comparable to the responses of healthy people to real-life interactions (Beck-Sander et al., 1997).

Barrowcliff & Haddock (2006) have adapted this research into a set of practical investigatory queries to use when evaluating defendants claiming NGRI on the basis of supposedly irresistible command hallucinations. The forensic psychological examiner should clarify the specific source, content, and direction of the commands, i.e., who does the subject think is making the command, what is the voice telling them to do, and to whom are they to do it? Is the voice benevolent or malevolent? Do they believe the voice is more authoritative or powerful than themselves? Is the voice justified in issuing the command; do they agree with the command? What do they think will happen to them (or other people) if they refuse or resist?

Developmental and Biological Features of Schizophrenia and Crime

Recently, Naudts & Hodgins (2006a, 2006b) have reviewed the research comparing neurological symptoms, neuropsychological test performance, and structural brain imaging of persons with schizophrenia, with and without a history of violence. Findings suggest that among men with schizophrenia, those who have displayed a stable pattern of antisocial and aggressive behavior since childhood, as compared with those with no such history, perform better on neuropsychological tests tapping specific executive functions and more poorly on assessments of orbitofrontal functions, show fewer neurological signs and symptoms, and display larger reductions in volume of the amydala, more structural abnormalities of the orbitofrontal system, and smaller reductions in volumes of the hippocampus. In fact, evidence suggests that among men with schizophrenia, better cognitive and psychosocial functioning is associated with substance misuse and with antisocial behavior (Foley et al., 2005; Horn et al., 2003; Joyal et al., 2003; Krakowski et al., 1989; Lafayette et al., 2003; Lapierre et al., 1995; Miller, 1984b: Rasmussen et al., 1995; Ridderinkhof et al., 2004; Salyers & Mueser, 2001; Schanda et al., 1992; Stirling et al., 2005). Why should this be? Part of the reason may relate to the diagnostic category. In the studies reviewed by Naudts & Hodgins' (2006a), most subjects had a diagnosis of paranoid schizophrenia, which, as noted above, is associated with higher Verbal IQ scores and better overall cognitive functioning, as compared with other schizophrenic subtypes (Seltzer et al., 1997).

BOX 5.1. POLICE RESPONSE TO SEVERELY MENTALLY ILL CITIZENS

Dealing with mentally disordered citizens is an important part of patrol policing (Miller, 2006d). Many departments have Crisis Response Teams (CRTs) for handling such situations, but in most cases, it will be up to the individual officer to stabilize the scene where no specialized team exists, or at least until such a team can arrive. Thus, officers who encounter a psychotic individual should observe a few basic rules of engagement (Mohandie & Duffy, 1999).

First, if possible, assess the nature of the subject's psychotic state and overall behavior and approach the subject as slowly and as nonthreateningly as possible. Remember that the predominant emotions of most schizophrenic subjects in a psychotic crisis are fear, paranoia, and defensiveness. If more than one officer is present, keep the sensory overload to a minimum by having only one officer speak at a time. Try to determine if the subject can be verbally engaged. Always speak and act slowly, firmly, and deliberatively.

If the subject is willing to talk, encourage venting, but not ranting. If the subject expresses delusional ideas and beliefs, neither argue nor agree with the delusions. Through their painful life experiences, most schizophrenic citizens have learned that other people don't believe their delusional ideas, so pretending to do so may serve only to further alienate or enrage an already-disturbed psychotic subject. Conversely, it is highly unlikely that trying to "talk sense" into a delusional subject is going to make him suddenly see things more rationally.

A more effective strategy is to utilize active listening skills (Miller, 2006f) to let the subject know you're trying to understand him. Then, acknowledge the content of the delusion and try to ally yourself with the subject's perspective and perception of the situation, while keeping the focus on present reality. That is, commiserate with the distress the subject is obviously feeling, but don't dismiss or talk down to him. This may sometimes be a challenge due to the natural tendency most people have of treating a "crazy person" like a child, which will usually only further infuriate a fearful and delusional subject.

Wrong: "C'mon now, nobody's after you, it's just your imagination. Why don't you be a good boy and come with us."
Better: "I'm not sure I understand the whole situation, but I can see this is really upsetting you. Anything we can do to help?"

continued

BOX 5.1.—*Continued*

While speaking to the subject, utilize appropriate proxemics (personal space) and body language, as well as verbal and nonverbal calming techniques. Remember that fearful, suspicious, delusional subjects may be exquisitely sensitive about physical boundaries and proximity—they're always on the alert for the next attack. Unless and until physical restraint becomes necessary, keep a reasonable distance and inform the subject of what you are about to do: "Sir, I'm going to reach into my pocket to take out a pen and a pad, so I can write down some notes, okay? It's just a pen and pad." Then move slowly. Always use caution, however, because the subject may become panicked and turn violent in a flash.

If physical restraint or arrest is required, utilize appropriate back-up and safe takedown procedures. If the subject appears to be cooperating, try to allow for some degree of dignity and self-respect to be preserved, again remembering that he or she can be extremely volatile. If an arrest is not made, transport the subject to an appropriate medical or psychiatric receiving facility. Unfortunately, many mentally ill subjects who would best be served by medical-psychiatric treatment are nevertheless turned away from such facilities due to lack of space or the facility's refusal to accept intoxicated or potentially violent patients. In such cases, officers often have no choice but to arrest the subject on a misdemeanor charge in order to transport him to jail for his own and others' safety.

DELUSIONAL DISORDERS

Delusional disorders are distinguished clinically from schizophrenia by the fact that the affected individuals may function adequately in most life areas, despite the presence of isolated, fixed ideas, which are themselves sufficiently out of sync with reality to qualify as delusions. Delusional disorders are further classified into several subtypes.

Clinical Features of Delusional Disorder

Erotomanic delusional disorder involves the belief that someone is in love with the subject, or should be because it is fated that they be together. For example, a movie fan is convinced that a singer or starlet is in love with him because of the "secret, private code messages" she sends out through her song lyrics, films, or TV appearances.

Jealous delusional disorder is more than just jealousy per se, as it involves a suspicion beyond what most people would consider reasonable, as in the person who is absolutely convinced that his or her mate is cheating on them and who, despite no hard evidence, interprets every action as a confirmation of that.

Grandiose delusional disorder involves the belief that one has special powers of perception, insight, and knowledge and that one ought to be accorded special status as a result: "I have the one true secret for world peace, if only I could get before the UN General Assembly and tell everyone."

Persecutory delusional disorder characterizes the individual who believes that "they" (whoever they are) are after him—often for the purpose of stealing or silencing his grandiose idea, which is why grandiose and persecutory delusions are frequently found together.

Somatic delusional disorder involves some perceived disturbance or distortion of the body, as in the person who is convinced that his body is decaying from within, shrinking or expanding, or that radio waves are changing his skin color or brain patterns.

Criminal Aspects of Delusional Disorder

In terms of percentages, **paranoid** or **persecutory delusions** are the most common types found among subjects with these disorders, an observation that seems to hold true across diverse cultures, although complex conspiracy theories involving large numbers of people in intricate, technologically sophisticated plots are naturally more common in industrialized Western societies (Bentall & Taylor, 2006; Harper, 1994; Stompe et al., 1999). According to one account (Trower & Chadwick, 1995), paranoid delusions may be divided into two categories: (1) **poor-me paranoia**, in which the individual believes himself to be the innocent victim of unwarranted persecution; and (2) **bad-me paranoia**, where it is the subject's own evil deeds or intent that have earned him the persecution and punishment of some other entity or group. These categories are fluid, however, and a given subject may vacillate between varying levels of deservingness of his or her persecution, being more likely to show comorbid depression during the bad-me phase. Also, many have noted clinically that paranoia may be tinged with narcissism, in what we might call **superior-me paranoia**, in which the subject believes he or she is being pursued out of envy or competition to squelch the subject's grandiose idea or intended action (Miller, 1986b, 2008c).

Also, as noted above, although the term delusion implies that the belief is one that is false or exaggerated, a number of paranoid delusions may contain kernels of truth, and this may lead to the development of vicious cycles. For example, a characteristically suspicious person so irritates and alienates those around him that eventually they really do come to thoroughly dislike him and avoid him, which he picks up and takes as confirmatory evidence of their animosity all along. Some research supports this stress-diathesis model of paranoid delusional ideation. That is, discriminatory treatment may make an otherwise healthy person angry or depressed, but their interpretation of events will be roughly within the bounds of reality. However, someone with a predisposition toward delusional thinking will overinterpret these events and elaborate them into a full-blown paranoid conspiracy theory (Bentall & Taylor, 2006; Day et al., 1987; Janssen et al., 2003).

With relevance to criminal behavior, a delusion, especially a paranoid delusion, only becomes dangerous if the person decides to act on it and, understandably, it is the more violent act-outs that come to both clinical and legal attention. Only two studies have specifically addressed the phenomenology of acting on delusions (Buchanan et al., 1993; Wessely et al., 1993), concluding that 60 percent of delusional patients report acting upon their beliefs. However, the range of severity of these actions is quite wide, most involving attempts to escape or seek protection against the supposed persecution, or channeling of activities in the form of lawsuits or other actions, with a minority involving physical harm directed against others.

Vexatious Litigants

And speaking of lawsuits . . . a commonly encountered subtype of delusional disorder, with features of paranoia and narcissism, is described as **querulous paranoia** by Mullen & Lester (2006), often manifesting itself in the form of the so-called **vexatious litigant**. This describes the individual whose life becomes consumed by the pursuit of a personal grievance to the point where it crowds out his other daily activities and disrupts the functioning of the courts or other agencies attempting to resolve the claims. Note that the single-minded pursuit of a cause believed to be just, even an unpopular cause, may hardly be a sign of psychopathology, and may represent a healthy sense of forthright social or political activism. It is only when there is a striking imbalance between the extreme lengths the pursuer goes to in relation to the gains made that we suspect an underlying delusional or overvalued motive as the root of this obsession.

Mullen & Lester (2006) divide this syndrome into three subtypes; however, in actual practice, the categories can overlap and individuals can fulfill more than one role.

Unusually persistent complainants. These individuals generally pursue their grievances through established government or corporate agencies, such as Workers Compensation, Social Security, Veterans Administration, etc. It is not the merits of the case that suggest a pathological basis for this preoccupation, but rather the grossly inordinate amount of time and resources spent in pursuit of what most people would regard as a trivial complaint, as if the fate of the world rested on having this particular claim settled (Lester et al., 2004; Mullen & Lester, 2006).

Vexatious litigants. Some complainants choose to pursue their cause through the courts. They will file endless lawsuits and charges and clog up the court system with their appeals. Many litigants will first retain attorneys to handle their cases, but most of these eventually drop out, either due to exhaustion of their client's funds or the attorneys' own frustration at having their time monopolized by these clients, for whom nothing is ever done fast enough or right enough, and who act as if they are the lawyer's only client. Or these litigants may cycle through several lawyers, each one eventually being dismissed for presumed incompetence, until eventually, they come to represent themselves in court, where their lack of knowledge of court protocol and inappropriate behavior further gum up the works. Their often irritable, entitled attitude may sometimes result in inappropriate comments and actions in the court, resulting in contempt charges by the judge. Nevertheless, they are ingenious in accessing information about the workings of the legal system and using this to full advantage to pursue their claims (Freckelton, 1988; Goldstein, 1995; Mullen & Lester, 2006; Rowlands, 1988).

Unusually persistent petitioners. Here, the complainant has decided to "take it to the top" by directly petitioning prominent people, usually local politicians, but sometimes national political figures or prominent news media celebrities. They will send voluminous and repeated communications setting out their case and pleading for help from the important figure who they "know will understand." They fully expect this figure, once he or she has learned of the righteousness of the petitioner's cause, to take up the banner and make it a top priority. When the persistent communication fails to evoke the expected crusade on his behalf, the querulous individual may shift from requests to demands, from demands to recriminations, and from recriminations to threats, occasionally attempting to make direct contact with the public figure upon whom they have become fixated, thereby creating a stalking scenario (Chapter 18). During the course of these transitions, they may come to the realization that their hero is really not the savior they had built him or her up to be in their mind and, indeed, may flip over to the idea that maybe this figure was part of the evil plot all along and is only standing in their way–how else to explain the figure's repeated failure to act on a cause that is so obviously just? It is here that the persistent petitioner may become dangerous, as they now feel that they have "no choice" but attack the public figure–and others connected with the perfidious plot–either out of revenge or as a last desperate bid to dramatize the seriousness of their complaint.

What all three subgroups of vexatious litigants share in common is a total and relentless focus on their quest for vindication and justice to which all else is subordinated. By the time they come to the attention of clinical or criminal justice professionals, they have usually expended all available resources and alienated every potential source of support. They are desperate for the "really big win" that will vindicate, validate, and compensate them for the years, sometimes decades, they have spent in their crusade. Indeed, the more time and resources they've expended, the more they feel they deserve the ultimate victory. Any compromise is considered a humiliating defeat, and anyone who fails to spring into action to help them must be part of the obstructionist opposition. In many cases, this escalates to the point of delusional paranoia, at which point, they may become dangerous (Mullen & Lester, 2006).

SUMMARY AND CONCLUSIONS

Citizens with **schizophrenia** are far more likely to be the victims of crime than its perpetrators; nevertheless, there is a somewhat elevated risk for the commission of violence in these subjects. Much of this can be attributed to two main factors: (1) a comorbidity of schizophrenia and antisocial personality disorder in the same subject, in which case the aggressive behavior, along with comorbid substance abuse, is probably more related to the antisociality than to the psychotic disorder; and (2) the **threat/control override syndrome**, in which persecutory delusions of thought control, combined with command hallucinations to defend oneself, may lead to a violent response. In fact, most schizophrenic subjects with violence-related command hallucinations attempt to resist them. **Delusional disorders** don't involve the serious deterioration in daily functioning seen in schizophrenia, but these subjects can become quite fixed on their **erotomanic, jealous, grandiose**, or **persecutory** delusions, and some may become **querulous complainants** and **vexatious litigants**, consumed with a quixotic mission to prevail in their self-perceived and self-created cosmic struggle.

Chapter 6

Anxiety and
Mood Disorders

For most people, our normal mood at any given time is neither especially happy or sad, angry or loving, agitated or calm, but just a steady sense of what I call **provisional well-being**: the overall feeling that life has its ups and downs but everything is basically okay for the moment and we hope for better days. It's like the feeling between meals when we are neither hungry nor full, when, in fact, we're too preoccupied with what we're presently doing to pay conscious attention to our gastronomical–or emotional–states at all. All healthy people show a range of moods, getting periodically happier, sadder, angrier, calmer, and so on, in response to various life circumstances, and some otherwise normal people seem to be dispositionally predisposed to either the cheerier or more dour side of the mood spectrum. Like any trait or syndrome, it is the *extremes* of mood that characterize a disorder, especially when these mood disturbances impair healthy life functioning or produce unreasonable conflict with others.

Mood disorders generally fall into the two broad categories of anxiety disorders and depressive disorders, although the symptoms often overlap.

ANXIETY DISORDERS

Anxiety disorders are characterized by heightened worry, fear, and arousal. **Generalized anxiety disorder** (**GAD**) involves a pervasive feeling of anxiety that is not necessarily tied to any specific event or circumstance, sometimes referred to as "free-floating anxiety." These individuals are always anxious about something, although the level of anxiety may wax and wane in response to different circumstances. Others may perceive these individuals as never being able to relax or be at peace.

Some individuals, with or without GAD, may suffer from **panic disorder**, which involves brief episodes of extremely elevated physiological arousal and fear. The affected individual may experience a racing, pounding heart, profuse sweating, rapid, shallow breathing, numbness and tingling in the face and extremities, and faintness or lightheadedness–all the hallmarks

TABLE 6.1.
ANXIETY DISORDERS

Generalized Anxiety Disorder: Persistent and excessive anxiety and worry, not necessarily associated with any particular event or circumstance. Not typically associated with aggressive criminal behavior, but subjects may abuse illegally-obtained drugs to control symptoms.

Panic Disorder: Recurrent and unexpected **panic attacks**, which may occur spontaneously or be triggered by specific events or circumstances. May occur **with agoraphobia**: triggered by fear of being exposed and vulnerable; or **without agoraphobia**: occurring spontaneously or triggered by other events or circumstances. As above, most crimes will involve illicit drug possession and use to control symptoms.

Specific Phobia: Excessive fear or anxiety triggered by one or more specific objects, events, or circumstances (e.g., insects, bodies of water, confined spaces, heights), often leading to avoidance of circumstances that could risk an exposure. In rare cases, subjects may commit traffic violations or trespassing to avoid a feared route, but otherwise this syndrome is not typically associated with criminal behavior.

Social Phobia: Excessive fear or anxiety evoked by exposure to social situations, especially where some form of performance or social interaction is required (e.g., giving a presentation, attending a party), often leading to avoidance of social situations. Not typically associated with criminal behavior.

Obsessive-Compulsive Disorder: Characterized by **obsessions** (fear of dirt, preoccupation with safety) which cause excessive anxiety, which in turn may be partially relieved by **compulsions** (repeated hand-washing, repeated checking of locked doors). Not typically associated with criminal behavior.

Acute Stress Disorder: Experiencing of a traumatic event causes short-term (less than one month) arousal, intrusive symptoms, and avoidance behaviors. Not typically associated with criminal behavior.

Posttraumatic Stress Disorder: Experiencing of a traumatic event causes longer-term (greater than one month) arousal, intrusive symptoms, and avoidance behaviors (see Table 6.2). Defensive violent behavior may occur during a dissociative flashback. Comorbid substance abuse is also a risk factor.

Anxiety Disorder due to a General Medical Condition: The anxiety is caused by a medical syndrome or condition, e.g., adrenal tumor, hypoglycemia, brain injury, etc. May lead to criminal behavior if the medical condition increases agitation and impulsivity.

Substance-Induced Anxiety Disorder: The anxiety is caused by the direct effect of a substance, e.g., amphetamine, cocaine, or caffeine overdose, alcohol or sedative withdrawal. May lead to criminal behavior if the substance increases agitation and impulsivity (stimulants) or decreases inhibitions (alcohol, sedatives).

of sheer terror. Many subjects fear they will pass out during an attack, although this is actually extremely rare. The attacks may occur in response to certain events, or they may happen randomly "out of the blue." Panic attacks are also likely to occur in the context of depression, often in response to perceived abandonment or loss of support.

If the anxiety and panic are associated with particular places or situations, the individual may develop one or more **phobias**, which are irrational extreme fears of particular persons, places, or things. Note that these are not delusions, because the person recognizes that the fear is not rational, yet he or she feels powerless to control it and must avoid the feared situation to forestall panic. Thus, sufferers often feel demoralized and out of control at not being able to will themselves out of these irrational fears. Phobias may be generalized, involving fears of a wide variety of people, places, or things that are usually related or have some elements in common; or they may be quite specific, e.g., to a particular locale, class of objects, or type of animal.

Individuals with severe anxiety disorders are unlikely to pursue a dangerous criminal lifestyle, although noncontact crimes, such as economic and computer crimes may be more common. Often, anxious individuals become dependent on alcohol or on prescription or nonprescription drugs to quell their symptoms and may engage in criminal behavior around illegal drug possession or sale to make money to buy more drugs.

POSTTRAUMATIC STRESS DISORDER

Posttraumatic stress disorder (**PTSD**) is a syndrome of emotional and behavioral disturbance that follows exposure to a traumatic stressor or set of traumatically stressful experiences that are typically outside the range of normal, everyday experience for that person, and which produce a reaction of fear, shock or horror.

Demographics of PTSD

The estimated lifetime prevalence of PTSD in the American population is 7.8 percent, with women more than twice as likely as men to receive a diagnosis of PTSD (10.4% vs. 5.0%) over their lifetime. The lifetime prevalence of having at least one diagnosable traumatic event is over 60 percent for men and over 50 percent for women. Men are more likely to report experiencing combat trauma, physical attacks, and being threatened or kidnapped, while women more often report exposure to rape, sexual molestation, neglect, and abuse in childhood. Higher rates of traumatic events and subsequent devel-

TABLE 6.2.
POSTTRAUMATIC STRESS DISORDER (PTSD)

<u>**Criterion A–Precipitating Traumatic Stressor:**</u> The person has been exposed to a traumatic event in which he/she was confronted with death or injury to self or others and which involved the experience of intense fear, helplessness, or horror.

<u>**Criterion B–Persistent Reexperiencing Symptoms:**</u> The person persistently or repeatedly re-experiences the traumatic event through waking recollections, disturbing dreams, dissociative reliving experiences ("flashbacks"), and/or psychological or physiological hyperreactivity to stimuli that directly or symbolically resemble the traumatic experience.

<u>**Criterion C–Persistent Avoidance Symptoms:**</u> The person: (1) behaviorally avoids a range of situations which remind, resemble, or symbolically represent the traumatic event, leading to a constriction of social activity; and/or (2) experiences a psychological numbing to outside stimuli which constricts his/her emotional responsivity and interpersonal interaction.

<u>**Criterion D–Persistent Arousal Symptoms:**</u> The person experiences increased anxiety, hypervigilance, irritability and anger, exaggerated startle response, difficulty sleeping, and/or impaired attention, concentration, and/or memory.

Onset of PTSD may be **acute** (duration less than 3 months), **chronic** (duration more than 3 months), or **delayed** (onset is 6 months or more following the traumatic stressor).

opment of PTSD are found in those with major mental illness and severe personality disorders, and multiple lifetime traumas and child sexual abuse (Chapter 15) have been found to be most predictive of PTSD. The lifetime prevalence of PTSD amongst Vietnam War veterans is estimated to be 30.9 percent for men and 26.9 percent for women. It is possible that the rate will be equivalent or higher for veterans returning from the recent Iraq and Afghanistan theaters (Friel et al., 2008; Kessler et al., 1995; Kulka et al., 1990b; Mueser et al., 1998; Nash, 2007).

Acute Stress Disorder (ASD) was introduced as a diagnostic category in the *DSM-IV* (APA, 1994) primarily to help identify those at risk of developing later PTSD. ASD is defined as a reaction to the traumatic stressor that occurs within four weeks after the index trauma. Although ASD focuses more on dissociative symptoms than PTSD, it also includes symptoms of reexperiencing, avoidance, and hyperarousal. Preliminary prospective studies suggest that between 60 percent and 80 percent of individuals meeting criteria for ASD following a traumatic event will meet criteria for PTSD up to two years later. The ASD diagnosis has been criticized as pathologizing common, if not universal psychological distress reactions to traumatic events (Koch et al., 2006). However, the diagnosis recognizes that some subjects may show traumatic reactions close in time to the injurious event, and it reinforces the importance of early treatment where this is clinically indicated to forestall the development of more long-lasting posttraumatic syndromes.

PTSD Signs and Symptoms

PTSD is associated with a characteristic pattern of signs and symptoms (APA, 2000; Meek, 1990; Merskey, 1992; Miller, 1993c, 1994c, 1998c, 1999d, 1999e, 1999f, 2000a, 2002b, 2006d, 2007c, 2007d, 2008b, 2010; Modlin, 1983; Parker, 1990; Weiner, 1992). In *DSM-IV TR,* the diagnosis requires the presence of: (1) a precipitating traumatic stressor; (2) physiological hyperarousal; (3) intrusive symptomatology, such as obsessive rumination, flashbacks, or nightmares; and (4) numbing/withdrawal symptoms, such as isolation, dissociation, or impaired memory (see Table 6.2). In the full spectrum of PTSD symptomatology, any of the following may be seen:

Anxiety. The subject describes a continual state of free-floating anxiety or nervousness. There is a constant gnawing apprehension that something terrible is about to happen. He or she maintains an intensive hypervigilance, scanning the environment for the least hint of impending threat or danger. Panic attacks may be occasional or frequent.

Physiological Arousal. The subject's autonomic nervous system is always on red alert. He or she experiences increased bodily tension in the form of muscle tightness or "knots," tremors, or shakiness, restlessness, fatigue, heart palpitations, breathing difficulties, dizziness, headaches, stomach and bowel disturbances, urinary frequency, or menstrual disturbances. About one-half of PTSD subjects show a classic startle reaction: surprised by an unexpected door slam, telephone ring, sneeze, or even just hearing their name called, the subject may literally jump out of his seat and then spend the next few minutes recoiling from anxiety.

Irritability. There may be a pervasive chip-on-the-shoulder edginess, impatience, loss of humor, and quick anger over seemingly trivial matters. Friends may get annoyed, coworkers may avoid the subject, and family members may feel abused and alienated. A particularly common complaint is the patient's increased sensitivity to children's noisiness or the family's bothering questions.

Avoidance and denial. The subject tries to blot out the event from his or her mind. He avoids thinking about the traumatic event and shuns news articles, radio programs, or TV shows that remind him of the incident. "I just don't want to talk about it," is the standard refrain, and the subject may claim to have forgotten important aspects of the event. Some of this is a deliberate, conscious effort to avoid trauma-reminders, while part of it also involves an involuntary psychic numbing that blunts most incoming threatening stimuli.

The emotional coloring of this denial may range from indifference to anxiety to anger.

Intrusion. Despite the subject's best efforts to keep the traumatic event out of his or her mind, the disturbing incident pushes its way into consciousness, often rudely and abruptly in the form of intrusive images of the event by day and frightening dreams at night. In the most extreme cases, the subject may experience **flashbacks** in which he seems to be mentally transported back to the traumatic scene in all its sensory and emotional vividness, sometimes losing touch with current reality, but often experiencing these dissociative hallucinatory experiences in relatively clear consciousness, which makes them seem even more "crazy." More commonly, the intrusive recollection is described as a persistent psychological memory-demon that "won't let me forget" the terrifying events surrounding the trauma.

Repetitive nightmares. Even sleep offers little respite. Sometimes the subject's nightmares replay the actual traumatic event; more commonly, the dreams echo the general theme of the trauma, but miss the mark in terms of specific content. For example, a subject traumatized in an auto accident may dream of falling off a cliff or having a wall collapse on him. Or a sexual assault victim may dream of being attacked by vicious dogs or drowning in a muddy pool. The emotional intensity of the original traumatic experience is retained but the dream partially disguises the event itself. This symbolic reconfiguration of dream material is, of course, one of the main pillars of Freudian psychoanalytic theory (Chapter 2; see also Miller, 1986f, 1989c, 1991d, 1993b, 1997a).

Impaired concentration and memory. The subject complains of having gotten "spacey," "fuzzy," or "ditsy." He has trouble remembering names, tends to misplace objects, loses the train of conversations, or can't keep his mind focused on work, reading material, family activities, etc. He may worry that he has brain damage or that "I'm losing my mind." In fact, given the comorbidity of PTSD and traumatic brain injury (Chapter 4), seen with increasing frequency among both civilian accident victims and returning military veterans (Miller, 1994c, 1998c, 2008d; Vasterling et al., 2010), a careful differential diagnosis is often required to tease apart the manifestations of these overlapping syndromes in order to provide the best treatment for each.

Sexual inhibition. Over 90 percent of PTSD subjects report decreased sexual activity and interest; this may further strain an already struggling marital relationship. In some cases, complete impotence or frigidity may occur, especially in cases where the traumatic event involved sexual assault.

Withdrawal and isolation. The subject shuns friends, neighbors, and family members and just wants to be left alone. He has no patience for the petty, trivial concerns of everyday life–bills, gossip, news events–and gets annoyed at being bothered with these piddles. The hurt feelings this engenders in those he rebuffs may spur retaliatory avoidance, leading to a vicious cycle of rejection and recrimination.

Impulsivity and instability. More rarely, the trauma survivor may take sudden trips, move from place to place, walk off his job, disappear from his family for prolonged periods, uncharacteristically engage in drunken binges, gambling sprees, or romantic trysts, make excessive purchases, or take dangerous physical or legal risks. It is as if the trauma has goaded the subject into a "what-the-hell-life-is-short" attitude that overcomes his usual good judgment and common sense. Obviously, not every instance of irresponsible behavior can be blamed on trauma, but a connection may be suspected when this kind of activity is definitely out of character for that person and follows an identifiable traumatic event. Far from taking such walks on the wild side, however, the majority of trauma survivors continue to suffer in numbed and shattered silence.

Evolution of the Trauma Response

But the phenomenology of ASD and PTSD consists of more than a tabulation of index symptoms, and the reaction to a traumatic event can begin within the first few moments of the crisis. Hollywood portrayals to the contrary, during the immediate crisis, most people don't become overwhelmed or paralyzed by intense fear or shock; in the breach, many behave quite adaptively (Aldwin, 1994; Weiner, 1992; Miller, 1994c, 1998c, 2010). Assault victims calculate their avenues of escape; passengers purposefully unstrap their seat belts and climb out of the window of their burning plane or submerging automobile; office workers find the exit and file down the stairwell of the bombed building, even helping others in the process. In many cases, the entire organism seems to go on automatic and is directed toward survival. A certain degree of adaptive depersonalization or dissociation may take place, an unnatural mental detachment from the surrounding events that enables the person to deal with the practical survival needs of the situation; this is often described in retrospect as "like being in a dream" or "happening in slow motion." Cinematic wild-eyed panic is extremely rare and disaster management experts frequently note how difficult it is to overcome inertia and get people to move at all during an emergency (Miller, 1998c).

After the event, the numbing depersonalization may continue for some time, the survivor feeling confused and bewildered. It's as if the psychoanesthetic freeze elicited during the trauma incident needs time to thaw out in the more temperate affective climate of real life. Unfortunately, though, "real life" doesn't last very long, as the intrusive recollective and emotional winds rush in at the weak chinks that begin to form in the crumbling psychic armor. Thus begins the wrenching emotional seesaw of painful intrusion alternating with numbing denial, along with many of the other posttraumatic stress symptoms that define this syndrome.

In the best cases, the major symptoms and disturbances diminish in the course of weeks to months as the event becomes integrated into the life narrative and personal history of the individual. A more realistic awareness of individual vulnerability is built up, so that basic feelings of security and confidence are restored. However, in some cases, a number of mental roadblocks may stand in the way of the trauma survivor's making peace with himself and the world (Everstine & Everstine, 1993; Matsakis, 1994; McCann & Pearlman, 1990; Miller 1994c, 1998c, 1999f, 2007c, 2007d).

One of these involves guilt and stigma. Many trauma survivors believe that they could have somehow prevented the traumatic event from occurring. Others interpret the event as a kind of hard knocks wake-up call for their poor judgment, or as cosmic punishment for past misdeeds. Many survivors feel "marked by fate," especially if this is not their first traumatic experience (there is at least one documented case of a man who survived both the 1993 and 2011 World Trade Center terrorist attacks). Still others experience a violation of their bodily and territorial integrity; they feel fragmented and scattered, and the slightest upset makes them irritable and isolative. They may literally wince when touched or when others encroach upon their personal space, and they become panicky in rooms or in crowds where they are unable to negotiate a clear route of escape.

The traumatic event and its aftermath can deal a shattering existential blow. The trauma survivor is starkly confronted with his or her own vulnerability and mortality in a way that most people manage to avoid by using the normal, adaptive denials of everyday life. The victim's existential violation may be all the more painful if the trauma took place at the hands of another person; worse still if the actions of the malfeasor were maliciously intentional or uncaringly negligent. And even more devastating may be traumas perpetrated by a known and heretofore trusted person, such as a family member, friend, workmate, neighbor, doctor, or clergy member (see Chapter 15).

Being in a trauma mode is difficult to stop, hard to let go of. Many trauma survivors generalize the helplessness of the cognitive survival state to other aspects of their lives, now feeling powerless to control even their own behavior or to influence the actions of others. Or they may impute domineering or retaliatory motives to anyone who tries to exert even the normal, socially appropriate influence or control over them, e.g., bosses, doctors, parents, or spouses. In some cases, outright paranoia and hostility may develop.

Even after things seem to have calmed down, when the trauma survivor has achieved some measure of delicate equilibrium, the stresses or returning to the normal routines of work and family life may trigger PTSD reactions. Also, delayed PTSD reactions may crop-up years or even decades after the event, as illness or the aging process begin to deplete the individual's adaptive reserves (Bonwick & Morris, 1996; Lipton & Schaffer, 1986; Miller, 1998c, 1999e; Nichols & Czirr, 1986; Potts, 1994; Robinson et al., 1994).

PTSD and Violent Crime

A few incidents of flashback-associated violence by individuals with military-related PTSD, almost all of the Vietnam era, and often intertwined with media accounts of "going postal" (see Chapter 11), may have led to the popular perception of traumatized military veterans as walking powder kegs, ready to explode at the slightest provocation. However, even without the presence of dissociative flashbacks, the general emotional lability and irritability of some individuals with PTSD may lower the threshold to violent behavior if they also possess some of the other risk factors, including personality disorder, substance abuse, or mood disorder. In rare cases, PTSD can overlap with and interact with neuropsychiatric syndromes, such as intermittent explosive disorder or limbic psychotic trigger reaction (Chapter 4).

Recently, a typology of PTSD-related violence has been proposed by Friel et al. (2008):

Military combat PTSD. This is the "classic" group of PTSD subjects. Controlling for standard risk factors for violence, such as antisocial personality, substance abuse, and sociodemographic features, some studies have supported an independent etiological role for PTSD in an increased rate of overall violent behavior, including firearm-related violence, although the precise nature of this relationship is not clear (Collins & Bailey, 1990; Freeman & Roca, 2001; Shaw et al., 1987).

Flashback-associated violence. Aside from the general lowering of the threshold to violence by PTSD symptoms, many experts have cited **dissociative flashbacks**, in which the subject loses orientation for present reality and believes he is under attack, prompting a response of defensive violence. In most of these reported cases, the victim of the attack is misidentified as a former enemy who is perceived to be threatening the subject during the dissociative flashback which may be perceived to replicate the original traumatic situation, such as a war zone or scene of a criminal attack. Amnesia may be reported for the dissociative episode, although it is not clear how much of this is self-serving when criminal charges are pending, inasmuch as many other subjects with noncriminal-related flashbacks can clearly recall the episodes (Moskowitz, 2004; Silva et al., 1998, 2001).

Sleep disturbance-associated violence. As discussed in Chapter 4, violent behavior can be seen as a component of a variety of **parasomnias**, and disturbed sleep and nightmares are common symptoms of PTSD. Much PTSD-related sleep-associated violence appears to consist of acting out an attack dream (Silva et al., 2001), similar to the phenomena described for **REM-sleep behavior disorder**; in fact, it is possible that traumatic act-out dreams may represent a situationally-induced form of RSBD.

Mood disorder-associated violence. Mood disturbance is a common, if nonspecific, symptom of PTSD, so it would not be surprising if the irritability and emotional lability of PTSD subjects caused them to have a hair-trigger reaction to provocation; no doubt this will be exacerbated in those who have had a long-standing angry, hostile, and impulsive temperament to begin with (Chemtob et al., 1994; Lasko et al., 1994; Silva et al., 2001). Again, depending on the nature of the violent act, this could overlap with IED or LPTR, as described in Chapter 4.

Combat Addiction

Recently, Grossman & Christensen (2007) have described a phenomenon whereby certain military veterans become "addicted" to the violence they experienced and perpetrated in wartime and find it hard to leave the aggressive mindset behind when they return to the civilian world. Individuals affected by this **combat addiction** will seek out or create circumstances where they can reexperience the dangerous thrill of previous combat experiences by engaging in a repeated pattern of aggressive behavior. Preoccupation with weapons, fighting, and sexual offending are typical expressions of this kind of "living on the edge." The heightened excitement of violence is typically followed by a "down" period in between, similar to the cyclical build-up and discharge of tension described for many rapists and serial homicide offenders (Chapters 10 and 14). While some of these individuals may be trying to master traumatic memories by acting them out, most will describe a never-ending quest to recapitulate the "rush" they felt in combat, and most realize that their antisocial behavior can get them into trouble, but report nevertheless being driven to engage in it (Friel et al., 2008; Grossman & Christensen, 2007; Solursh et al., 1991), which is not really the definition of PTSD per se. In addition, one must be cautious of the self-serving rationalization of a characterologically sadistic psychopath who uses "combat stress" as an excuse to perpetrate acts of violence that he would have gleefully engaged in anyway.

Noncombat Trauma

Aside from war, transportation accidents, natural and man-made disasters, crime victimization, mass violence, and terrorism can all constitute traumatic stressors (Miller, 1994d, 1998c, 2007c, 2007d). Increases in fights, assaults, aggressive driving, attempted homicides, and suicide attempts have been reported after a café fire (Reijneveld et al., 2003), earthquake (Goenjian, 1993), and school shootings (Cullen, 2009; Johnson, 2000). Again, the question remains as to who is predisposed to act out their trauma by way of violence rather than by some other kind of painful expression.

Active Shooter PTSD

Although it may be hard to generate much sympathy for the perpetrator of a violent crime, victims may not be the only ones to suffer trauma, and some criminals report being traumatized by their own actions, especially where such behavior is unusual and uncharacteristic of that person. Even where the act of **killing is socially sanctioned**, as in law enforcement and the military, soldiers and police officers often go through a series of stages following the service-related taking of a human life (Campsie et al., 2006; Grossman, 1996; Miller, 2006d, 2008d; Nielsen, 1991; Williams, 1999).

The first phase occurs prior to the shooting itself and consists of **concern about being actually able to pull the trigger** when the time comes, of not freezing up and letting one's comrades down. The second phase is the **actual killing experience**, which is often done reflexively, with the solider describing him/herself as "going on automatic." Elated at having survived the deadly encounter, and having proven to himself that he can do the deed, there is a third stage of **exhilaration** that comes from having "popped my cherry" and from having been able to put one's training into action. This exhilaration, fueled by adrenalin, can create a high or rush, which in some cases can give rise to combat addiction, noted above. Rodgers (2006) describes the kind of "adrenalin overdosing" that can lead to the type of combat addiction described earlier.

Remorse and nausea, the fourth phase—or what police psychologists (Nielsen, 1991; Williams, 1999) have called the **recoil and remorse** phase—follows the rush of exhilaration and is often associated with a close-range kill; this may be the more common type of response experienced by police officers who tend to confront their adversaries in close quarters, than by many soldiers who often fire from a distance. A sense of identification and empathy for the victim sets in, especially if the slain combatant was a fellow enemy soldier "just doing his job like I was," as opposed to an insurgent bomber or assassin, for whom there will be far less sympathy or identification. The service member may be creeped-out by his own initial response: "I enjoyed killing that guy too much—is there something wrong with me?"

For police officers, feelings of guilt or self-recrimination may be especially likely in cases where the decision to shoot was less than clear-cut or where the suspect's actions essentially forced the hand of the officer into using deadly force, such as in botched robberies, domestic disputes, or suicide-by-cop scenarios (Kennedy et al., 1998; Lindsay & Dickson, 2004; Miller, 2000a, 2006c, 2006d, 2006f; Perrou & Farrell, 2004; Pinizzotto et al., 2005). Military service members may be able to feel more justification in killing on a traditional battlefield, but may experience many of the same kinds of self-recriminations in the nontraditional fighting arenas that have characterized most wars since the Vietnam era, in which targets are often elusive and ambiguous, with blurred lines between combatants and civilians.

During this recoil/remorse phase, the military or law enforcement service member may seem detached and preoccupied, spacily going through the motions of his job duties, and operating on behavioral autopilot. He may be sensitive and prickly to even well-meaning probing and congratulations by his peers ("How close was the enemy?" "Way to go, killer—you got the bad guy"), and especially to accusatory-like interrogation and second-guessing from official investigators or the media: "Officer Jackson, did you really believe you were in fear for your life from a confused teenager?" "Sergeant, did you really believe that civilian family was hiding a group of insurgents?"

Also, during this recoil phase, a variety of posttraumatic symptoms may be seen, most of which will resolve in the next few days or weeks (Anderson et al., 1995; Blum, 2000; Cohen, 1980; Geller, 1982; Honig & Sultan, 2004; Russell & Beigel, 1990; Williams, 1999). Physical symptoms may include headaches, stomach upset, nausea, weakness and fatigue, muscle tension, and changes in appetite and sexual functioning. Sleep is typically impaired, with nightmares and frequent awakenings. Typical posttraumatic reactions of intrusive imagery and flashbacks may occur, along with premonitions, distorted memories, and feelings of déjà vu. Some degree of anxiety and depression is common, often accompanied by panic attacks. There may be unnatural and disorienting feelings of helplessness, fearfulness, and vulnerability, along with self-second-guessing and guilt feelings. Substance abuse may be a risk.

The final phase, **rationalization and acceptance**, can be a long process and many military veterans wrestle with their war experiences for a lifetime. Similarly, in law enforcement (Miller, 2006d, 2008d; Nielsen, 1991; Williams, 1999), as the officer begins to come to terms with the shooting episode, a similar resolution or acceptance phase may ensue, wherein he or she assimilates the fact that the use-of-force action was necessary and justified in this particular instance of the battle for survival that often characterizes law enforcement deadly encounters. Even under the best of circumstances, resolution may be partial rather than total, and psychological remnants of the experience may continue to haunt the officer periodically, especially during future times of crisis. But overall, he or she is eventually able to return to work with a reasonable sense of confidence.

In the worst case, adequate resolution may never occur, and the police officer or soldier enters into a prolonged posttraumatic phase, which may effectively end his or her law enforcement or military career. In less severe cases, a period of temporary stress disability allows the service member to seek treatment, to eventually regain his or her emotional and professional bearings, and to ultimately return to the job. Still other service members return to work right away, but continue to perform marginally or dysfunctionally until their actions are brought to the attention of superiors (Bender et al., 2005; Campsie et al., 2006; Miller, 2006f, 2007e; Rudofossi, 2007).

In the criminal justice arena, some murderers and other offenders have been described as showing symptoms of PTSD following their violent crimes, as well as from the stress of arrest and incarceration. Inasmuch as perpetrators with true antisocial personality disorder (Chapter 8) are unlikely to feel much anxiety or remorse over their aggressive actions (other than at having gotten caught), they are unlikely to develop **perpetrator PTSD** (although they may try to fake it). The crimes of those who do develop this syndrome tend to be impulsive, unplanned "crimes of passion" in subjects with a controlled-inhibited type of aggression, and they tend to occur in response to a clear provocation; hence the violence is out of character for the perpetrator, which contributes to its traumatizing effect. A number of these perpetrators will be willing to plea-bargain rather than face further traumatization by reliving the crime at trial (Byrne, 2003; Friel et al., 2008; Grey et al., 2003; Harry & Resnick, 1986; Papanastassiou et al., 2004; Pollock, 1999).

PTSD, the Insanity Defense, and Diminished Capacity

As discussed in Chapter 1, in the United States, UK, and several other countries, grounds for not guilty by reason of insanity are established when it can be demonstrated that the defendant is either unable to understand the nature and quality of his act or know right from wrong (M'Naughten), or be able to control his actions (ALI). In those rare cases where a murder defendant claims NGRI due to PTSD, the only PTSD component that might meet this high bar would be a dissociative flashback in which the defendant literally believed he was experiencing the original trauma and genuinely felt in fear for his life, causing him to defensively retaliate by killing the victim (Friel et al., 2008; Packer, 1983; Sparr, 1996); essentially, this would be equivalent to a severe delusional psychosis. The presence of other PTSD symptoms, such as anxiety, irritability, nondissociative flashbacks, nightmares, and hyperarousal, would not in themselves create grounds for an insanity defense, any more than a mood disorder, anxiety disorder, personality disorder, or any other psychiatric condition. The level of traumatization, i.e., how severe the original ordeal the defendant went through or the symptoms he suffered afterwards, would be irrelevant, as being in severe emotional pain is not in itself grounds for insanity, any more than would be suffering from a severe toothache.

Probably for this reason, PTSD is very infrequently raised as an insanity defense, somewhat more commonly in the United States than in the UK, probably because of this country's Vietnam legacy (Mackay & Kearns, 1999). Of the four PTSD/NGRI/murder cases that I have been consulted on by defense counsel over the years, one defendant was grossly malingering, two did indeed suffer PTSD (one military, one civilian law enforcement-related), but showed no evidence of dissociative flashback phenomena during the crime (one involved a bar fight, the other a domestic battery that turned deadly, both involving alcohol), and the fourth was observed by witnesses to commit the murder in what appeared to be a rageful frenzy, but there was no evidence of impaired mental status other than extreme anger, and there had been a long prior history of bad blood between the defendant and the victim related to workplace disputes. In all cases, I informed the respective defense attorneys that I could not credibly make a case for PTSD-related NGRI. One attorney suspected as much and was actually relieved to be off the hook. Another was summarily fired by his client for sending him to a quack (me), and the two others went off to seek further opinions.

If not sufficient for an insanity defense per se, PTSD, like many other psychopathological syndromes, may be used to argue for diminished capacity as a mitigating factor at sentencing. One might even expect defendants with this diagnosis to receive greater sympathy than those with other syndromes, especially if the defendant suffered his or her trauma in the course of "his service to his community or country," (police officer or military veteran), or at least was an innocent victim (criminal assault victim)–unlike the defendant who appeals for mercy on the basis of having been in the throes of a substance addiction, which is far less likely to garner sympathy. In a few cases of military PTSD, defense counsel may attempt to use the combat addiction phenomena discussed above as a mitigating factor, although this is not an actual diagnostic category (Silva et al., 2001) and might qualify as a designer defense (Chapters 2, 3).

Whatever legal purposes a diagnosis of PTSD may be put to in mitigating responsibility for a crime, it is vital that a defense psychological expert witness be able to credibly draw a clear, bright line connecting the effects of the disorder and the criminal behavior in question (Appelbaum et al., 1993; Friel et al., 2008; Sparr, 1996; Sparr et al., 1987). For example, assault or murder committed during a fearful, dissociative flashback, absent any evidence of premeditation or prior relationship between perpetrator or victim, might qualify as an NGRI defense, but probably not where there was a history of animosity between the parties, or where the defendant was heard making threats to or about the victim. A PTSD-afflicted military veteran's extreme irritability, hair-trigger temper, sleeplessness, and attempts to self-medicate with alcohol might be grounds for mitigation at sentencing on an assault or murder conviction, but not if witnesses have attested to the fact that he was pretty much an angry, drinking, trouble-making bad boy long before his military service. As in every aspect of a forensic psychological evaluation, adequate attention to all details of the case is essential.

MOOD DISORDERS

Mood disorders are generally classified into unipolar and bipolar types, depending on whether the extreme changes in mood are in one direction (down-depressed) or both directions (down-depressed and up-elated or up-angry).

Major Depressive Disorder

Major depressive disorder is characterized by episodes of depressed mood that may last for weeks or months at a time. In severe cases, the individual may be virtually immobilized. More characteristically, subjects feel dejected, demoralized, helpless, and hopeless. Sleep and appetite may be impaired; alternatively, some individuals become hypersomnic (sleep virtually all the time) or may binge-eat. Concentration and memory may be affected to the point where the individual feels he or she is becoming demented. Gone is any motivation or enthusiasm for work, play, or family activities. Accompanying emotions may include anxiety, panic, irritability, or anger. The disorder usually recurs in cycles over the lifespan, and, in most cases, is very responsive to proper treatment, which optimally consists of some combination of mood-stabilizing medication and psychotherapy. The greatest risk in depression is **suicide** (Box 6.1).

TABLE 6.3.
MOOD DISORDERS

Major Depressive Disorder: Characterized by episodes of depression, sufficiently severe to impair normal life activities, and persisting for weeks or months. Suicidal subjects may kill others to spare them the pain of being alone (usually family members), or to obtain final revenge for causing their plight (workplace and school violence; see Chapters 11, 12).

Dysthymic Disorder: Persistent depressed mood for most of the day for a duration of at least 2 years, but usually with preserved ability to carry out most essential life tasks (school, work, family), although typically with diminished efficiency and enjoyment. Not usually associated with criminal behavior.

Bipolar I Disorder: Characterized by cycles of **mania** (elevated or agitated mood with delusional features) or **hypomania** (elevated or agitated mood without delusional features), alternating with **depression**, over a time scale usually involving days or weeks. In between episodes, some patients may experience a normal mood, others not. Criminal behavior may occur during the impulsive, delusional manic phase, or as part of a suicidal crisis in the depressed phase.

Bipolar II Disorder: Characterized by cycles of depression, sometimes alternating with hypomania, but not mania. Same risk for criminal behavior as above, but less commonly.

Cyclothymic Disorder: Alternating cycles of hypomanic and depressed mood persisting for at least 2 years duration, but usually with preserved ability to carry out most essential life tasks (school, work, family), although typically with diminished efficiency and enjoyment. Not typically associated with criminal behavior, although angry irritability during the hypomanic phase can lead to confrontations.

Mood Disorder due to a General Medical Condition: Mood disorder that is the direct result of a medical syndrome or condition, e.g., depression due to a brain tumor or hypothyroidism, or hypomania due to toxic brain effects of liver disease. Criminal behavior may occur as part of the medically-induced syndrome.

Substance-Induced Mood Disorder: The mood disorder is caused by the direct effect of a substance, e.g., psychostimulant drugs producing mania, or sedative-hypnotic drugs or stimulant withdrawal producing depression. Criminal behavior may occur as part of the substance-induced syndrome.

BOX 6.1. SUICIDE: "MYTHS" AND REALITIES

Many people, and even a fair number of medical and mental health professionals, are misinformed about the nature of suicide. But even the blanket term "myths" may be misleading, which is why this box's title has the word in quotes. That's because some common suppositions and misconceptions about suicide may indeed contain kernels of truth. Accordingly, this box covers some facts and stats about suicide in general (Baechler, 1979; Baker & Baker, 1996; Bongar, 2002).

Myth 1: Those who threaten suicide don't really do it. Many disturbed people use suicidal threats as an attention-seeking or manipulative ploy or as a cry for help, and the number of suicidal threats is far greater than the number of suicidal acts. However, like most chest pains that turn out to be false alarms, yet are treated seriously when they occur, suicidal threats or gestures may be potentially lethal and should never be ignored. Responding in a forthright way demonstrates both concern for the subject and the fact that there are real consequences (e.g., temporary involuntary commitment, a permanent mental health record) for "playing games." Therefore, all suicidal threats should be taken seriously.

Myth 2: Discussing suicide will impel the person to do it. Think about it: could someone talk you into killing yourself if you really don't want to? Well-meaning friends, family members, first responders, and even some clinicians may avoid asking a subject about suicidal ideation for fear of "putting ideas in her head." In fact, just the opposite is almost always true. Most depressed persons have already thought of suicide, indeed, they may be currently ruminating about it but reluctant to bring it up for fear of being seen as crazy or of having restrictive action taken. Yet most are actually relieved to have another person question them about their suicidal thoughts because it gives them the opportunity to discuss their fears and concerns. If someone has actually not been considering suicide, or wants to conceal it, usually the only consequence of your raising the issue will be the person's disavowing it. But better to have as much information as possible, rather than too little.

Myth 3: Suicide is always an irrational act. It is difficult for most people to relate to the excruciating mental pain that would drive a person to end his or her life. But remember that the hallmarks of depression are helplessness and hopelessness: if everything in life is pain and nothing is pleasure, and it's never going to end, then what's the point of going on? Under these perceived circumstances, ending one's life may seem like the only rational thing to do.

Myth 4: Suicide is always an impulsive act. It sometimes is, in which case there is not much one can do to intervene because the person completes the act with little or no warning. In many other cases, however, the individual will express

continued

BOX 6.1.—*Continued*

his or her suicidal ideation to someone: family member, friend, clergy, clinician, or 911 operator. In such cases, the person is at least somewhat ambivalent about taking his or her own life and this leaves room for intervention.

Myth 5: Individuals who commit suicide are mentally ill. In most cases, suicide does not occur in an emotional vacuum, but takes place in the context of a history of mood disturbances, life disruption, and erratic behavior. Most suicidal individuals are clinically depressed, and a few may be struggling with some form of persecutory delusion, sometimes in combination. While a subject doesn't have to be obviously "crazy" to consider taking his or her own life, knowing the subject's mental health history is important mainly for predicting what kind of post-crisis life this person will be going back to, and thereby formulating an intervention strategy that realistically takes these life circumstances into account.

Myth 6: Suicide runs in families. Yes and no. Mood disorders like depression and bipolar disorder usually have a genetic-familial component and suicide is an additional risk factor in these syndromes, so, in that sense, suicide can be said to run in families. This does not mean, however, that someone with a family history of depression and suicide is predestined to take their own life, only that the risk is somewhat greater than in others without such a legacy. As with many other family medical and mental health risks (hypertension, diabetes, obesity, or depression), proper treatment can help many individuals "beat the odds" of their family history.

Myth 7: Once suicidal, always suicidal. Again, partly true. Since, as a general rule, the best predictor of future behavior is past behavior, a person who has attempted suicide once is at greater risk of attempting it again under conditions of stress that precipitate a depressive episode. The goal of any effective treatment is to give the person the coping skills necessary to reduce the frequency and intensity of these crises, and thereby make suicidality less of an automatic, reflexive choice.

Myth 8: Once the suicidal crisis has passed or the person's mood has improved, the danger is over. It may be over for that moment, but without follow-up treatment, there is increased risk of future crises. This highlights the need for follow-up treatment after the immediate crisis has been resolved.

Dysthymic disorder is a more persistent, but less severe, mood disorder. Such individuals mentally limp through their daily activities, able to function sufficiently to get by at work or at home, but experience little pleasure or excitement from life–the "walking wounded," leading drab, joyless existences. Many of these individuals will deny being depressed per se, but report that they've never really known what it feels like to be happy, or even "normal," although they know that other people experience these states. Some individuals with major depressive disorder will recover from their severe episodes, but only to a bland baseline state of dysthymia, rarely experiencing anything that could be called a happy or even normal mood—sometimes referred to as **double depression**.

Most individuals with major depressive disorder will lack the motivation or stamina to engage in any effortful behavior, much less homicide. And most depressed people are far more a danger to themselves than others (Box 6.1). However, the delusions of some patients suffering from depression with psychotic features may include ideas of reference, suspiciousness, and delusions with nihilistic and/or persecutory themes; these may or may not be accompanied by auditory and sometimes visual and olfactory hallucinations. Compulsive rumination is also a common feature of depression (Coryell & Zimmerman, 1986; Lyukouras et al., 1987; Malmquist, 1996). All these factors may combine to predispose the depressed subject to commit an aggressive act for perceived self-protection or retaliation. Acts of criminal violence where some significant degree of depression plays a role, sometimes accompanied by psychotic features, include workplace or school mass violence (Chapters 11, 12), some types of relationship violence (Chapter 17), familicide, psychotic filicide (Chapter 16), and suicide-by-cop but, interestingly, not usually suicide terrorism (Chapter 13).

Psychodynamically, violence in psychotic depression may in some cases represent a mobilization, externalization, and projection of anger that has remained previously unexpressed through the course of the depressive state. This is usually comingled with a pervasive hopelessness at resolving the situation in any way but a violent one, which is why suicide is a common accompaniment of such violent acts, as in the case of mass homicide or suicide-by-cop. The suicidal perpetrator both internalizes the perceived negative attributions of others toward himself, and at the same time projects his self-perceived badness and unworthiness onto others, so that, in essence, all must be punished by death (Malmquist, 1981, 1996).

Postpartum Syndromes

Postpartum depression is a fairly common complication of childbirth, occurring in 13 percent of women within the first 4 to 8 weeks after delivery, and lasting an average of 7 to 8 months, although 20 percent of these mothers experience a chronic course, persisting 2 years or longer. About half of these women will experience a recurrence following a subsequent delivery, and a significant proportion of women have had a history of depression that predates their first delivery, as well as a family history of mood disorder. In women at risk for this syndrome, postpartum depression appears to be triggered by the steep decline in reproductive hormones that occurs following delivery.

Postpartum depression is distinguished from the much rarer **postpartum psychosis**, which occurs in less than 1 in 500 deliveries, has a fairly rapid onset following delivery, lasts only a few days, and may be associated with bipolar disorder. Active harm to the child is more likely to be associated with postpartum psychosis, while the mother with postpartum depression may simply be apathetic and unmotivated and may therefore neglect her infant (Bloch et al., 2005; Friedman et al., 2005; Krischer et al., 2007; O'Hara & Swain, 1996; Rush, 2007).

Bipolar Disorder

Bipolar disorder, also known as **manic-depressive illness** is characterized by extreme shifts in mood, from elation to depression, usually with an absence of normal mood in between: for such individuals, there are only highs and lows. The **hypomanic** phase typically begins with the individual feeling energized and overconfident–"pumped." He becomes hyperactive and grandiose, spinning all kinds of half-baked unrealistic plans, but being increasingly impulsive and distractible. Thinking and speech become rapid and forced. Need for sleep decreases and the individual may become hypersexual; all appetites are on sensory overdrive. The overall impression is of someone on stimulant drugs, and indeed, such individuals may abuse amphetamines, cocaine, or alcohol to enhance the natural high and try to keep it going. In severe cases, the subject becomes delusional and develops hallucinations, in which case the episode is diagnosed as full-blown **mania**.

At the beginning of the hypomanic phase, the individual may appear quite engaging and entertaining in a kind of gonzo-comic way, but as the manic phase progresses, he becomes increasingly short-tempered, irritable, anxious, and paranoid. Inevitably, the crash comes as the subject cycles into the depressed phase. At this point, he may increase his use of stimulants to try to prolong the high, but eventually even this isn't enough to stave off the depressive avalanche. Suicide is a distinct risk at this stage. In other bipolar patients, the manic episodes do not involve much elation at all, but are characterized mainly by irritability, anger and paranoia, and may be misdiagnosed as schizophrenia. Subjects with **Bipolar I** disorder experience both manic and depressed phases, whereas those diagnosed with **Bipolar II** swing only into the depressed phase, recovering to their characteristc emotional baseline (which may be normal mood or dysthymia) between episodes, with some patients occasionally cycling into a mild version of the hypomanic phase.

The high emotionality, pressured speech and behavior, impulsivity, impaired judgment, and sometimes delusional psychosis of mania would seem to implicate this phase of bipolar disorder in a high risk for criminal behavior. The prevalence of Bipolar I disorder is 6 times higher in prison populations than in the general community, although still relatively low (6% versus 1%). Mania is also significantly higher in incarcerated juveniles than in juvenile community samples (22% vs. 1%). Over a quarter of men diagnosed with bipolar disorder have a history of arrest. Men with bipolar disorder have a higher arrest rate than those with unipolar depression, and the number of lifetime manic episodes and psychiatric hospitalizations correlates with number of lifetime arrests Most bipolar arrestees show symptoms of mania with psychosis at the time of their arrest, and many are arrested within a short period of time after being released from a psychiatric facility (Barzman et al., 2007; Calabrese et al., 2003; Dean et al., 2007; Graz et al., 2009; Lewinsohn et al., 1995; Modestin et al., 1997; Pliszka et al., 2000; Quanbeck et al., 2004, 2005b; Solomon & Draine, 1999).

Not surprisingly, there is a strong association between bipolar disorder and substance abuse, with rates of comorbidity ranging from 60 percent to 90 percent. Manic subjects often use substances to keep their racing, high thoughts and behavior going as long as possible and to forestall the inevitable depressive crash. The comorbidity of bipolar mania and substance abuse is the highest of any set of psychiatric risk factors for criminal arrest, and comorbid bipolar-substance abuse patients are hospitalized twice as often as those with bipolar disorder alone. In addition, these dual diagnosis patients remain in treatment for shorter periods of time. There also appears to be a comorbidity between childhood bipolar disorder and conduct disorder (Cassidy et al., 2001; Graz, 2009; Kemp et al., 2008; Kovacs & Pollock, 1995; Kutcher et al., 1989; Quanbeck et al., 2005a, 2005b; Regier et al., 1990; Sonne et al., 1994; Verduin et al., 2005; Wozniak et al., 1995; see also Chapter 19).

The types of crimes that bipolar arrestees are most commonly charged with include violent crimes, such as assault and battery, as well as property crimes, such as breaking and entering, vandalism, theft, and arson. Interestingly, despite the aggressive nature of these crimes, the mood state most associated with their commission is typically not the irritable, suspicious manic phase, but the euphoric, grandiose, expansive phase. Impulsivity and psychosis, especially paranoid delusions and hallucinations, appear to be the most common driving force for these interpersonally violent or property-destructive crimes. Unlike the demographic breakdown for most types of

violent crime, male and female manic subjects are equally likely to be arrested for a violent crime, and substance abuse heightens the risk of violence for
both sexes (Asnis et al., 1997; Barratt et al., 1995; Friedman et al., 2005; Link
et al., 1995; Monahan, 1992; Quanbeck et al., 2004, 2005b; Sallom et al.,
2002; Swann et al., 2004; Swanson et al., 1990; Wulach, 1983).

BOX 6.2. POLICE RESPONSE TO CITIZENS WITH MOOD DISORDERS

The most frequent law enforcement crisis intervention context for an anxious
or depressed subject is potential suicide, although depressed subjects are frequently seen in correctional and other institutional settings, as well as on daily
street patrol (Miller, 2006f).

The first priority is safety. Assess for suicidality and emphasize the subject's
well-being, especially since the police response is often associated with a confrontation: "I'm officer Smith and this is officer Jones. We're here to make sure
you're okay and to get you any help you need right now."

Violence against others is rare in unipolar depression, although it may occur
as part of a "suicide pact" with another person, usually an elderly couple with a
serious illness or disability, or a delusional psychosis in a filicidal mother (Chapter
16). Violence is a more likely risk for bipolar manic individuals who may be angry
and delusional.

Move slowly and take your time, avoiding any unnecessary intimidation. Use
verbal and nonverbal calming techniques, and employ cautious physical restraint
where necessary. Subjects in a manic state may not initially intend to attack you,
but may be subject to explosions of anger upon hair-trigger provocation. And if they
do get physical, you'll be dealing with a huge adrenalin factor and it's going to take
a lot of force to keep this person under control, so injuries on all sides are a distinct risk. Especially in these cases, your judicious use of verbal and nonverbal de-
escalation techniques can make the difference between a subject who gets talked-
down and psychiatrically treated and one who gets restrained and arrested for
assaulting an officer. Assuming no arrest is called for, if the subject requires further
disposition, transport him or her to an appropriate receiving facility.

Legal Aspects of Mood Disorders

Occasionally, depression, or more commonly bipolar disorder, often
combined with substance abuse, may be offered as a mitigating factor in
some nonviolent crimes, such as financial embezzlement or child molestation. In these defenses, the idea will be proferred that the mood disorder
clouded the perpetrator's judgment so that he felt he "had nothing to lose"
by committing the crime.

Suicide by Cop

The idea that a suspect would deliberately expose himself to police gunfire in order to effect his own demise has long been familiar to law enforcement officers, but the phenomenon was first explicitly articulated by Wolfgang in 1959 and the actual term, **suicide-by-cop** (**SBC**) was coined by police officer and psychologist Karl Harris in 1983.

It is estimated that approximately 10 percent of the approximately 600 police shootings a year in the United States are provoked SBC incidents. Most involve uniformed officers who are on duty at the time of the shooting, and the greatest number of SBC incidents occur in the context of a police response to an armed robbery, the next most common situation being a domestic disturbance call. While some SBC incidents arise spontaneously out of the anger and panic of these situations, a good number of them appear to be planned, as shown by the fact that, in nearly a third of SBC cases, investigators find a suicide note which apologizes to the police for deliberately drawing their fire. Officers involved in SBC incidents often feel a sense of powerlessness and manipulation, which is why SBC is reported to be an especially stressful and demoralizing form of shooting trauma (Allen, 2004; Feuer, 1998; Homant et al., 2000; Kennedy et al., 1998; Miller, 2006c, 2006f; Pinizzotto et al., 2005; Van Zandt, 1993; Wilson et al., 1998).

The typical SBC subject is a white male in his mid-20s with a history of drug and alcohol abuse. He has had prior contact with the law but usually for minor offenses, although this may have given him some familiarity with how police operate and with their responses to critical incidents. Aside from substance abuse, he has probably had a history of other psychological disorders, the most common diagnosis being schizophrenia or bipolar disorder, although there is at least one report of attempted SBC following a traumatic brain injury (Bresler et al., 2003).

The crisis episode is commonly precipitated by the rupture of some important relationship in connection with the subject's self-esteem or social support, such as a family or job crisis, which leads to feelings of hopelessness, anger, and despair. Almost half of SBC subjects have attempted suicide previously and almost half are intoxicated at the time of the present SBC crisis. Many SBC attempts begin as self-suicide crises, but when law enforcement arrives on the scene, some subjects appear to delegate the lethal job to the officers. Up to two-thirds of SBC subjects take hostages, and SBC incidents that emerge from hostage-barricade incidents are more likely to involve a seriously mentally disordered subject. In all reported cases, subjects resisted arrest or orders by police to surrender and all possessed a firearm or other lethal weapon that they used to threaten others (Feuer, 1998; Kennedy et al.,

1998; Lord, 2000; Miller, 2006a, 2006d; Perrou & Farrell, 2004; Wilson et al., 1998).

Why would someone try to get themselves killed by a police officer? Mohandie & Meloy (2000) have delineated a range of motivations for SBC, which in fact can be applied to most kinds of suicide. Feelings of hopelessness, desperation, rage, and/or revenge usually occur in some combination in persons who attempt suicide. For such individuals, there appears "no way out," other than to die. What may be unique to SBC cases, however, is how these feelings are acted out. Many suicidal persons are concerned about what others will think of them after their death. If the suicide attempter believes that taking one's own life bespeaks weakness or cowardice, what better face-saving way to go out than in a hail of gunfire, brought down by overwhelming force of arms during one last act of defiant resistance (Hafenback & Nasiripour, 2005; Homant et al., 2000; Miller, 2006c, 2006f)?

Another related source of motivational confusion relates to religious prohibitions against suicide: the person may no longer want to live in this cruel, painful world, but he doesn't want to go to Hell, either. With a SBC, he can essentially tell God that it's not his fault the police killed him. In many cases, the decision to have the police serve as executioners is made impulsively and, in some cases, the subject just as abruptly changes his mind and surrenders (Pinizzotto et al., 2005).

Practical considerations may also underlie the wish to die but not to appear to have killed oneself, such as exclusion clauses for suicide on life insurance policies or lessening the shame to one's family. Also, a person who wants to die may fear the physical pain and distress involved in actually taking his or her own life (cutting, suffocating), or may be afraid of chickening out at the last moment or botching the job which would only leave him a cripple or a vegetable. In this regard, SBC makes grim sense in terms of its finality: being gunned down by multiple police bullets is an efficiently lethal way to die (Allen, 2004; Clagett, 2004; Homant et al., 2000; Praet, 2002; Van Zandt, 1993).

Still other cases might be called **suicide in front of cop**. Here, the subject summons police to the scene, or they happen to arrive as part of a general callout, and the subject makes a point of killing himself in full view of the officers (or within earshot, if by phone). This gesture may be performed out of sheer despair, or the subject may want the officers–iconic symbols of societal authority–to bear witness to his act of desperate martyrdom. Alternatively, he may be trying to exert a different form of manipulative control, not by actually inducing the cops to shoot him, but by forcing them to witness his death as a way of highlighting their impotence to talk him down.

Indeed, it is this issue of *control* that seems to be most disturbing to the responding officers. Police officers hate to feel that they've failed, especially when that failure occurs in the context of being baited and manipulated into a deadly force confrontation that has none of the heroic earmarks of an armed standoff with a "real" felon. Moreover, the idea of "giving up" is fundamentally distasteful to the warrior mindset of most cops who, by dint of temperament and training, characteristically adopt a suck-it-up-and-do-it-anyway attitude. Thus, being guiled into becoming the instrument of another person's easy-way-out may be all the more disturbing (Blum, 2000; Doss, 2007; Duran, 1999; Duran & Nasci, 2000; Miller, 2006c, 2006d, 2008f).

SUMMARY AND CONCLUSIONS

While highly **anxious** or severely **depressed** individuals would hardly seem to constitute the "criminal type," anxiety and mood disorders may occasionally be associated with criminal activity, as when subjects self-medicate with illegal drugs, or when they ally themselves with more powerful partners to achieve a sense of security, only to discover that these new mates or pals want them to abet illegal acts. Extreme violence may occasionally be committed during the course of a **dissociative flashback** associated with **PTSD**, but a careful analysis of both the defendant and the situation is essential for making a causal connection between this syndrome and any legal considerations of exculpation or mitigation.

Depressed and despondent subjects, especially when combined with anger and paranoia, may become both suicidal and homicidal, and decide to take others to the grave with them. Some may commit mass violence (Chapters 11 and 12) or provoke **suicide by cop** scenarios as a grand gesture of suicidal rebellion. Subjects in a state of **bipolar hypomania** may commit impulsive acts of violence if they feel thwarted in some grandiose goal, while the delusions and hallucinations of the more severe **manic state** may impel violent responses to paranoid misperceptions or hallucinatory commands. **Postpartum psychosis** may be associated with killing of one's infant (**filicide**), but such episodes typically last only a few days, while **postpartum depression** may persist far longer, but is more likely to be associated with apathy and neglect, rather than violence per se. A despondent individual may bait police officers to kill him in a **suicide by cop** scenario. Finally, anxiety and mood disorders are among the most successfully treatable of mental disorders, and all efforts should be made to address legitimate treatment issues in the context of criminal justice adjudication.

Chapter 7

Personality Disorders

PERSONALITY: TRAITS, TYPES, AND DISORDERS

We all have personality *traits*. Some of us are outgoing and gregarious, others keep to themselves. Some people are orderly and meticulous and never seem to have an unplanned moment, while others enjoy life spontaneously, but seem to have trouble finding their shoes. Some are open, trusting souls who love not wisely but too well, while others never trust anyone farther than they can throw them.

But when these quirks of personal color begin to grate harmfully on others or significantly derail the success of the persons themselves, psychologists regard them not just a personality traits, but as personality *disorders*. The official definition (APA, 2000) of a **personality disorder** is "an enduring pattern of inner experience and behavior that deviates markedly from the expectations of the individual's culture, is pervasive and inflexible, has an onset in adolescence or early adulthood, is stable over time, and leads to distress or impairment" (p. 629).

Generally, a personality disorder represents a characteristic style of maladaptive interactions with other people that persists across situations and is stubbornly resistant to change. Personality-disordered individuals typically have little insight into their own behavior or understanding of the adverse impact they have on themselves and others. Alternatively, they justify their self-defeating or offensive behavior as being due to unfair fate or the fault of someone else. Some personalities are characteristically egocentric, seeing things only from their own perspective, and they often lack impulse control, these traits combining to focus their efforts on always trying to meet their own needs, often at the expense of others. Other personalities may be self-deprecating to a fault, never seeming to be able to assert themselves or stand up for their rights. It is the extremes of their self-perception and conduct toward others that distinguish personality disordered individuals from those with mere traits. Many such individuals appear to lack a core stable sense of self, so they are always searching for something external to ground their sense of identity. In personal relationships and in workplace settings, people with personality disorders can cause considerable difficulty for both others and themselves (Lowman, 1993; Miller, 1992a, 2003c, 2003d, 2008c; Millon & Davis, 2000; Palermo, 2009; Sperry, 1995; Stone, 2007).

Personality disorders are classified on Axis II of the *DSM-IV-TR* (APA, 2000) because, along with mental retardation (the only other Axis II classification), they are thought to be enduring and stable parts of an individual's psyche, as opposed to the myriad disorders on Axis I which are conceptualized as more akin to "diseases" in the medical sense. Personality disorders are grouped into what are called **clusters**. **Cluster A** (the "**odd cluster**") includes the Paranoid, Schizoid, and Schizotypal Personality Disorders. Individuals with these disorders often appear odd, aloof, or eccentric. **Cluster B** (the "**dramatic cluster**") includes the Antisocial, Borderline, Histrionic, and Narcissistic Personality Disorders, and these individuals typically appear dramatic, emotional, and erratic. Finally, **Cluster C** (the "**anxious cluster**") includes the Avoidant, Dependant, and Obsessive-Compulsive Personality Disorders, who characteristically come across as anxious, reserved, and withdrawn (APA, 1994; Millon & Davis, 2000; Sperry, 1995). Mixed personality types or disorders, as noted above, generally stay within a cluster, but cross-cluster combinations are not uncommon (see Table 7.1).

Personality Disorders and Criminal Behavior

In essence, the majority of persons who commit serious crimes, especially on a habitual basis, could probably be diagnosed as having a personality disorder or, more commonly, a blend of personality traits and disorders. The impulsivity, egocentricity, nonreflectivity, cognitive rigidity, insecurity, suspiciousness, hypersensitivity to criticism and humiliation, feelings of powerlessness, poor social skills, restlessness, negative emotionality, all-or-nothing thinking, and disordered volition that characterize most individuals with personality disorders makes them more prone to react with aggression than deliberation when faced with an interpersonal challenge. Often a violent act is perceived as the "only way out" of a dilemma that other people might find a range of options to deal with (Kalis et al., 2008; Palermo, 2007a, 2009; Palermo & Kocsis, 2005; Stone, 2007).

This chapter will discuss the types of personality disorder that have been associated with criminal behavior. Antisocial personality disorder will be considered separately in Chapter 8.

TABLE 7.1.
PERSONALITY DISORDERS

Cluster A–The "Odd" Cluster:

Paranoid Personality Disorder: Pervasive distrust and suspiciousness, bias toward interpreting others' motives as deceptive and persecutory. Subject may overreact to perceived offenses and attacks with retaliatory behavior.

Schizoid Personality Disorder: Detachment from social relationships and restricted range of interpersonal emotional expression. Impaired empathy may lead to impulsively aggressive overreaction in uncomfortable social situations.

Schizotypal Personality Disorder: Deficient interpersonal relationships accompanied by cognitive and perceptual distortions and behavioral eccentricities. Aggressive or other criminal behavior may occur as part of the delusional system. Also susceptible to substance abuse.

Cluster B–The "Dramatic" Cluster:

Histrionic Personality Disorder: Excessive and shallow emotionality, dramatic attention-seeking behavior, and impressionistic, suggestible cognitive style. Dramatic criminal displays may occur as a way of seeking attention.

Borderline Personality Disorder: Fragile self-image and identity, unstable interpersonal relationships, behavioral impulsivity, self-harm, fear of abandonment, alternating idealization and devaluation in relationships. Extreme anger and violence may occur in response to the perception of abandonment or betrayal.

Narcissistic Personality Disorder: Pervasive pattern of grandiosity, need for admiration, sense of entitlement, and lack of empathy. Sense of entitlement may lead to the manipulation and exploitation of others, often seen in financial crimes. Physical violence may be seen in the course of **narcissistic rage**, when the subject's grandiosity and specialness are challenged.

Antisocial Personality Disorder: Disregard for and violation of the rights of others, failure to conform to social norms, deceitfulness, exploitiveness, manipulativeness, impulsivity, recklessness, irresponsibility, and lack of remorse. Typically associated with a persistent criminal lifestyle (see Chapter 8).

Cluster C–The "Anxious" Cluster:

Avoidant Personality Disorder: Social inhibition, feelings of inadequacy, and hypersensitivity to criticism. Not usually associated with criminal behavior, but may abuse illegal drugs to control anxiety.

Dependent Personality Disorder: Submissive and clinging behavior stemming from an excessive need to be taken care of, difficulty making decisions without guidance or support. Not usually associated with criminal behavior, but fear of separation may lead the subject to carry out certain behind-the-scenes criminal activities under the influence of a more manipulative personality type.

Obsessive-Compulsive Disorder: Preoccupation with orderliness, perfectionism, and/or cleanliness, often accompanied by obsessive thoughts and compulsive, ritualistic behavior, to the detriment of openness and spontaneity in human relationships. Not usually associated with criminal behavior, but may perform many of the bookkeeping, organizing, and managerial functions of complex criminal organizations.

HISTRIONIC PERSONALITY DISORDER

Histrionic Personality Disorder is a pattern of excessive emotionality, attention-seeking, need for excitement, flamboyant theatricality in speech and behavior, a nonlogical and impressionistic cognitive style, and the use of exaggeration to maintain largely superficial relationships for the purpose of getting emotional needs met by being cared for by others. When such needs are not met, the histrionic personality may become petulant, angry, depressed, and/or develop a wide range of psychosomatic ailments and symptoms.

Clinical and Developmental Features

Commonly diagnosed in women, when she is in her "up" mood, the histrionic personality will be delightful and entertaining to be with, bubbly, flirty, the life of the party. In fact, histrionic personalities naturally gravitate to careers that put them in front of crowds: acting, politics, teaching, sales, and so on. These are the "people persons" *par excellence.*

Unlike the overly intense, needy, and edgy persona of the borderline (see below), histrionic personalities typically present themselves as interpersonally engaged and genuinely likeable. Even when snubbed and rejected, they are less likely to nurse a grudge because anger and gloom are downer emotions, and these individuals will rationalize or compartmentalize almost any bad feelings in order to just feel good again. With their quick wit and engaging "touchy-feely" interpersonal style, histrionic personalities tend to form great first impressions because, for them, this is not an act. They genuinely love getting attention from people and actively seek out such positive interactions.

The problem comes in the follow-through. The histrionic personality is characterized by what has been described as an **impressionistic cognitive style** (Gardner et al., 1959; Shapiro, 1965). Decisions tend to be formed on the basis of impressions and intuitions, with rational analysis of facts and stats regarded as an intrusive annoyance: "If it feels right, it must be true; don't bother me with piddling details." In some contexts, this gut-instinct type of decision making may lead to flashes of insight and spontaneous creativity, but without careful follow-up organization and planning, the plan or project often disintegrates into a million directionless pieces.

Worse, without grounding in logic and reason, impressionistically formed opinions and decisions tend to shift abruptly: what feels right and is therefore absolutely true today is completely different than what felt right and was absolutely true yesterday; same for tomorrow. Additionally, in their desire to please and be liked by everyone, histrionics may often change their story to suit what they believe this particular listener wants to hear. This is usually not deliberate deception, but a mostly unconscious and instinctive attempt to do anything to put themselves in the best possible light and get people to like them. Not surprisingly, then, these individuals can be extremely frustrating to deal with in both business and personal relationships because those who interact with them never really know who the "real" person is (Miller, 2003c, 2008c).

Criminal Aspects of Histrionic Personality Disorder

While rarely in the class of hard-core criminals, the histrionic personality's hypersensitivity to criticism and tendency to decompensate when feeling unloved and rejected, may make him or her prone to emotional and behavioral outbursts that can include suicidal gestures or attacks of rageful violence (Beck & Freeman, 1990; Cloninger, 1987; Tardiff, 2001). Unlike the long-smoldering anger of the Borderline or Paranoid personality, the histrionic's outburst is more likely to be in the nature of an abrupt and short-lived temper tantrum which, like a suicidal gesture–and the two may take place in close propinquity–is focused on garnering maximal attention: "Look what you've driven me to!" However, because histrionic personality disorder can sometimes be comorbid with serious mood disorders, true suicidality is a distinct risk factor.

BORDERLINE PERSONALITY DISORDER

Borderline Personality Disorder is a pattern of instability in interpersonal relationships, fragile self-image, and wild emotional swings. Manic highs of boundless optimism may lead to rash, impulsive actions, which are later regretted with depressive self-loathing, sometimes to the point of suicidal gestures; not surprisingly, bipolar disorder (Chapter 6) is a frequently accompanying syndrome and the two conditions may in fact be expressions of a common disorder.

Clinical and Developmental Features

Like the histrionic personality, borderline personality disorder is more commonly diagnosed in women. At extremes, borderline personalities seem to be out of touch with reality: whatever they feel or believe at the moment is the absolute truth, which may then abruptly shift 180 degrees if a different mood or thought strikes them. This can give their behavior and relationships a mercurial Jekyll-and-Hyde quality. They are prone to **minipsychotic episodes** in which their thought, speech, and behavior temporarily take on a near-delusional quality and they may seem to be out of touch with reality, yet able to maintain a façade of normality, and "switch gears" when the situation demands. Indeed, it is this frequently-traversed psychological border between psychosis and neurosis that gives the borderline syndrome its name.

Their changeability may sometimes be mistaken for phoniness, but unlike the antisocial or paranoid personalities, the borderline is not necessarily consciously lying or manipulating. Like the histrionic personality, with which it may overlap, the borderline sincerely believes in whatever version of the truth she is telling at the moment, and if she changes her story, she expects you to happily go along with the new version—and will get angry if you don't. At other times, however, she may quite deliberately lie and make up whatever story she thinks will get people to do what she wants; she feels entitled to manipulate people in this way because she feels there's no other way to get them to like her and meet her needs. Again, the problem is that even the lies aren't consistent; the story versions keep changing and her audience gets sick and tired of trying to keep up.

This changeability also affects personal and business relationships, a phenomenon known as **alternating idealization and devaluation**. There are no gray areas in borderline personalities' estimation of other people; individuals are either loved or hated, and the feelings may swing from one extreme to the other with equal intensity. This mental absolutism is facilitated by a process called **splitting**: people are not seen as having textured and complex characters; they're either all good or all bad—again, often the same people at different times. The result is maddeningly unpredictable behavior because you never know from one encounter to the next how your borderline workmate or family member will react. History means nothing, context means nothing; whatever the dominant emotion is at the moment colors the borderline's feelings about and interactions with the other person, no matter what the objective reality may be. Borderline personalities make excessive use of the defense mechanism of **projective identification**, in which they take an internally intolerable feeling, thought, or impulse, and attribute it to someone else, e.g., they believe their own inner feelings of isolation, rage, and self-loathing are being directed against them by another person with whom the borderline subject has a relationship.

Part of the reason for this dizzying alternation between rigidity and fluidity relates to the core problem of **identity diffusion** with borderline personalities: with their weak egos and porous self-other boundaries, they just don't feel like whole, substantial people, so they rely on others to mold and support their own self-identities. This accounts for their characteristic fear of abandonment and dread of being alone. Without external social support, they are unable to modulate their own feelings of emptiness and disintegration, and may resort to substance abuse, marathon sex, binge eating, or self-injury to provide some kind of external stimulation, some bodily anchor to temporarily stabilize the drifting vessel of their psyche.

Anger is another core feature of the borderline personality. Frequently capable of superficial cordiality and charm, borderlines may fly into rages–privately smoldering or openly aflame–that seem inextinguishably all-consuming. In personal relationships, this anger usually relates to the fear of being abandoned by overly idealized others: "I loved you, I trusted you! How dare you not fulfill my each and every emotional need: I hate you, I'll kill you!" As employees, they may overidentify with their work role or supervisors to the extent that threatened job loss is equated with death of self. Except perhaps for paranoid personalities, borderlines are the types most likely to hold a grudge. They can be destructively vindictive and relentlessly stalk their targets (Chapter 18), or they can bide their time and wait for the right moment to strike back. Outward-directed anger may alternate with inward-directed self-loathing in the form of suicidal gestures. On a less extreme level, borderlines are often the classic "injustice collectors" who always seem to carry around a voluminously catalogued and cross-referenced mental file of hurts, slights, and betrayals that they can flawlessly recall and recount at a moment's notice. Nothing is ever forgotten or "got past," and there is no "closure" on any issue (Blackburn & Coid, 1999; Coid, 1992; Grinker et al., 1968; Gunderson, 2001; Gunderson & Singer, 1975; Hurt & Clarkin, 1990; Kernberg, 1975; Jordan et al., 1996; Malmquist, 1996; Millon & Davis, 2000; Palermo, 2009; Perry & Herman, 1993; Pope et al., 1983; Skodol et al., 2002; Sperry, 1995; Zanarini et al., 1998; Zimmerman & Coryell, 1989).

Classic psychodynamic theories of borderline personality disorder relate the characteristic weak ego and primitive defense mechanisms to being raised in a family setting where the primary caretaker, usually the mother, has a cold and/or hostile attachment style to the developing infant and child. The child defends itself from the fear of losing attachment to its mother by introjecting a grandiose idealization of the mother, which turns into a tendency to idealize others as all-benevolent and devoted nurturers and protectors. When these others ultimately fail to satisfy the borderline's quenchless need for support and nurturance, this can switch to devaluation, representing the internalization of, and projective identification with, the image of the angry "bad parent." Some authorities cite a high rate of physical and sexual abuse in the childhood histories of borderline patients, although this is controversial (Gunderson & Singer, 1975; Kernberg, 1992; Kohut, 1971; Perry & Hermann, 1993; Tardiff, 2001; Widom, 1989a, 1989b).

Neuropsychological theories of borderline personality disorder have focused on findings that appear to implicate disordered frontal lobe-limbic connectivity, including volume reduction in the right anterior cingulate cortex and dorsolateral prefrontal cortex, putatively supporting a hyperarousal-dyscontrol model of borderline aggression and emotional lability (Goodman et al., 2007; Palermo, 2009). Of course, it is not clear whether these findings, even if replicable, relate to emotional dyscontrol in general or the borderline syndrome per se. Also, such neuroimaging findings are reported as well for patients with other syndromes, such as schizophrenia. Indeed, as seen in Chapters 2 and 4, frontal lobe disinhibition syndromes appear to be ubiquitous across neuropsychiatry.

Criminal Aspects of Borderline Personality Disorder

Unstable moods, impulsivity, fragile dependency needs, and externalization of blame are potent risk factors for violence. In a typical borderline cycle, perceived rejection or abandonment precipitates identity diffusion, triggering extreme panic, which quickly turns to rage. At first, similar to the histrionic personality, the borderline may attempt to manipulate the other person into reestablishing a supportive connection through seduction, deception, somatization ("playing sick"), or threats. Once it is clear that the other person cannot be cajoled or intimidated back, the borderline's white-hot hatred erases any caution or judgment, and "payback" becomes an all-consuming, self-righteous, self-vindicating moral imperative. This accounts for the sheer relentlessness with which borderlines pursue their victims, sometimes becoming stalkers (Chapter 18), and tirelessly ferreting out information on their quarry: rifling through pockets or drawers, checking cell phone logs, hacking into computer files, making unexpected phone calls and unannounced visits, and so on. They may attack the other person physically and even lethally.

They are also skilled at manipulating others to do their dirty work for them or, if necessary, hiring a contract killer or arsonist to do the job. When they do commit direct violence, it is often in a dissociative state or during a minipsychotic episode, and the crime is often characterized by extreme savagery or overkill. The emotional instability of borderlines also means that murder-suicides are not uncommon. Less violent assaults, even verbal ones, may nevertheless be characterized by an almost delusional lack of decorum and social boundaries, as borderline mates may assail their partners during business meetings, childrens' school events, and other grossly inappropriate venues (Malmquist, 1996; Palermo, 2009; Palermo & Kocsis, 2005).

When convinced of his or her own self-righteousness or entitlement, the egocentricity and violence of the borderline subject can rival that of the psychopath (Chapter 8), as in the case of women who have killed their husbands in order to be with a new lover, killed their children to free themselves for a new relationship, or, in one case, killed a pregnant woman, stole her fetus, and used it to try to manipulate her boyfriend into marrying her by claiming it was her own (Hughes, 1992; Stone, 2007). Some women who have a serial pattern of killing older men (see also Chapter 10) might be committing symbolic revenge against male relatives who had sexually abused them in childhood (Harter, 1990), although obvious financial motives must be considered as well; in the latter case, it may be an example of a female psychopath (Chapter 8). When apprehended for their crimes, borderline subjects often state that they committed these acts because they felt they "had no choice"; unlike the cold, remorseless predation of the psychopath, the borderline is driven primarily by emotion and is truly convinced in the justifiability of his or her actions.

In fact, next to antisocial personality disorder, the borderline may be the most common personality type associated with violent crime, as indicated by the finding that nearly 30 percent of male and female offenders in one prison sample met diagnostic criteria for borderline personality disorder, and more than 90 percent had at least one self-reported borderline symptom, which included (in order of frequency) impulsivity, anger, unstable mood, suicidal thoughts or behaviors, and paranoid ideation. As in the general population, the rate for borderline personality disorder was higher among women than among men, although a significant number of male prisoners received this diagnosis. Again, as in the general population, prisoners with borderline personality disorder showed high rates of comorbid psychiatric disorders, including anxiety, mood disorder, eating disorders, and substance abuse (Black et al., 2007).

In the criminal forensic setting, the inconsistent, deceitful, confabulatory, and sometimes frankly delusional quality of some borderline defendants' thought and speech may raise questions about their competency to stand trial, including being able to understand the charges against them and participate in their own defense. Less commonly, the minipsychotic episodes of the borderline defendant may be used to present an insanity defense; indeed, these time-limited episodes of impaired cognition, emotional agitation, and behavioral dyscontrol are probably closer to most people's conception of "temporary insanity" than many other syndromes. Additional defenses that involve borderline dissociative states, but may not be identified as such, include premenstrual syndrome (Chapter 6) or battered women's syndrome (Chapters 3, 17).

In many criminal cases, the borderline defendant's attitude of self-righteous indignation—that she is the injured party, not the victim, and that the victim absolutely deserved what he or she got, if not worse—works against the defendant, as juries during the trial, and the judge at sentencing, view the defendant as "unrepentant," which, in fact, she is. Other borderline defendants, especially those with a strong streak of histrionic personality, may tearfully feign remorse, sometimes quite convincingly, other times so dramatically as to strain credulity (Malmquist, 1996). In general, the impulsivity, acting-out, and less severe forms of dissociation would not qualify as mitigating criminal responsibility, while more severe dissociative symptoms or minipsychotic episodes might create grounds for a NGRI defense or mitigation at time of sentencing (Bray, 2003).

NARCISSISTIC PERSONALITY DISORDER

Narcissistic personality disorder is a pattern of grandiosity, sense of entitlement, arrogance, need for admiration, and lack of empathy for others' feelings or opinions.

Clinical and Developmental Features

More commonly diagnosed in males, individuals with this pattern typically get in trouble because they believe rules are for other people and that they are allowed to bend the law because of their special entitlement and powers of perception, insight, and judgment. They expect others to appreciate, admire, and defer to them, and will become irritated or rageful when they don't get the respect they feel they naturally deserve. In other words, these are the classic "egotists" who are largely indifferent to the feelings and reactions of others and expect unearned high praise regardless of their actual effort or accomplishment. With their sense of entitlement and grandiosity, narcissistic personalities may not get it that others don't share their own inflated view of their competencies and worth, or the narcissist may simply not care about the meaningless opinions of inferior beings. In mild cases, the narcissist may perceive that others don't fully appreciate his importance, but may "forgive" them because, after all, how can such puny underlings possibly hope to understand his greatness. In more severe cases, the narcissist may have difficulty differentiating self from other and wish from reality, and so may idiosyncratically construe events on the basis of his own desired outcomes rather than on actual reality or sensitivity to the feelings and reactions of others. In such cases, this personality style may blend into the paranoid one.

Many narcissists are into thrills that make them feel good about themselves, so risky and potentially criminal behavior associated with such personalities may include substance abuse, pathological gambling, sexual exploits, and other high-adrenalin adventures. In such cases, narcissistic personality disorder often shades into and is commingled with elements of the antisocial pattern.

Yet under the surface of many narcissists' superficially impervious egos lies a core of fragile self-esteem and intense feelings of shame and inadequacy. In such cases, the expansive, handshaking, backslapping narcissist who's getting the adulation he thinks he deserves may abruptly flip over into a sullen, nasty, and vengeful enemy when the thin skin of his good fellowship is scratched by a stray critique, jibe, or embarrassing question. In these cases, one observes elements of the borderline personality and, indeed, historically, early psychoanalytic writers considered these two to be related pathologies. In other cases, the narcissistic hide is so thick and tough that even the worst fusillade hurled at him hardly makes a dimple—he *knows* that others merely resent him for his greatness and, like an elephant scoffing at a gnat before flicking it aside, he indulgently takes their petulant pewlings in stride.

Also like the paranoid and antisocial personalities, all blame and responsibility for the narcissistic person's problems are typically externalized, or, alternatively, the narcissist may retain insight into the responsibility for his behavior, but feel it is "justified" based on his superior ability or entitlement: it would be wrong for anyone else to take that money because that would be stealing, but if I do it, it's justified because I really earned it and deserve it, even if no one else thinks so. Narcissists' extreme sensitivity leads them to overinterpret rejections or disappointments. Some narcissists are possessed of a self-righteous morality that makes them contemptible of lesser beings who fail to live up to their lofty standards. In many cases, their zeal to "reform" others only thinly masks an overweening need for power and authority by being the top dog (Malmquist, 1996; Millon & Davis, 2000; Palermo, 2009; Sperry, 1995).

Criminal Aspects of Narcissistic Personality Disorder

Despite being full of themselves, many individuals with narcissistic personality disorder do possess genuine talents and abilities and do manage to achieve success in various endeavors in work and life, which at least partly satisfies their craving for adulation and superiority. However, having done well in some areas, they cannot seem to accept that they can hardly excel and be deferred to in every aspect of life. Additionally, they rarely feel that they have risen high enough and it is always the lack of appreciation for their greatness—or worse, direct obfuscation by jealously resentful rivals—that keeps them from their rightful pinnacle. Although they are capable of great deliberation and planning, many decisions are made impulsively, as this personality disorder, like the borderline, is frequently comorbid with bipolar disorder. In these cases, the narcissistic individual may find himself in a perennial spiral of personal, vocational, and legal hasssles (Malmquist, 1996). Many white-collar criminals (Leap, 2007) probably have pathologically narcissistic individuals in their ranks. Indeed, when these corporate crimes are finally unearthed, observers may be surprised at the paltry gains for which the perpetrator has been willing to put his entire career, family, fortune, and freedom at risk. "Why did you do it?" someone will inevitably ask, and the answer is often some version of, "Because I could." The same probably describes many politicians and other people in power who engage in an escalating spiral of financial or sexual malfeasance until their activities are revealed.

Some crimes of violence by such individuals may be committed in a state of **narcissistic rage**. This is likely to occur when the ego-defenses of the narcissist are eroded or overwhelmed. The individual's superiority at work or control over his family are challenged, or, more commonly, several assaults to his specialness and entitlement occur simultaneously, summating into the feeling that his brittle, fragile self-esteem is about to be shattered. As with the case of other Cluster B personality disorders, this tends to elicit an all-or-nothing response: "If I'm not the boss, then I'm a punk," and the normal smooth façade of the narcissist can flash over into a spasm of rage, not unlike the rage response of the borderline personality. The outburst need not be physically aggressive and may limit itself to a verbal tirade or destruction or sabotage of the offending entity's (person's or organization's) property or work.

When the response is an overtly violent one, how it is carried out will be determined by the relationship between the narcissist and the target. In personal relationships, such as cases of domestic violence (Chapter 17), the goal will be to reestablish dominance and control, and the level of violence may be only that which is necessary to show the partner "who's boss." In workplace disputes (Chapter 11), the disaffected narcissist may at first file griev-ances and threaten or take legal action, but if this fails to achieve vindication, more overt sabotage, destruction, or violence may occur, again to reestablish a dominant position. In extreme cases, where the narcissist believes he is truly losing control (his mate is finally leaving him; he's being demoted or fired at work), the rage may reach its boiling point, with the goal now being to obliterate and expunge the source of his humiliation. Murder, often char-acterized by overkill in personal relationships (Chapter 17) or mass violence in organizational disputes (Chapter 11), may then be the outcome, because the narcissist believes that his ego has been so irreparably shattered that no-thing can restore it, so he has "nothing to lose" (Malmquist, 1996; Palermo, 2009; Palermo & Kocsis, 2005; Stone, 2007; Tardiff, 2001).

An especially dangerous species of narcissism has been referred to as **malignant narcissism** (Beck & Freeman, 1990; Kernberg, 1989; Stone, 1989b; Tardiff, 2001), which may contain elements of the antisocial and para-noid styles as well. The sense of entitlement of this subject leads him to relentlessly exploit and subdue others for his own purposes, albeit sometimes with a veneer of an ostensibly lofty goal. This pattern may characterize the ruthless cult leader or political dictator (Chapter 13), or underlie the relent-less and remorseless predatory acts of the serial killer (Chapter 10).

PARANOID PERSONALITY DISORDER

Paranoid personality disorder is a pattern of pervasive distrust and suspiciousness, so that others' actions and motives are invariably interpreted as deceptive, persecutory, or malevolent.

Clinical and Developmental Features

More often diagnosed in males, the paranoid radar is supersensitive in picking up verbal and nonverbal cues of duplicity, hostility, and betrayal. Actually, the perceptions may be quite accurate; it's the interpretations that are skewed. Like skilled psychologists, paranoid personalities often show keen insight into human motives and actions, but unlike trained profession-als who recognize a range of motivations for people's behavior, the paranoid personality has only one all-fitting interpretation, i.e., people are mean, du-plicitous, selfish creatures who will smile in your face and then turn around and screw you behind your back the first chance they get.

This, in fact, pretty much describes the paranoid personality himself, since **projection**—the attributing to others of internal motives most distasteful to oneself (Chapter 3)—is the primary psychological defense mechanism of the paranoid personality. These individuals can't help being suspicious and always having to keep their guard up: what else can they do, surrounded by a sea of enemies? In addition to projection, paranoid personalities tend to externalize blame generally; nothing is ever their fault. And why should it be, since underlying the paranoid cognitive style is often a sense of narcissistic grandiosity: they're so talented and special that people naturally hate them and want to take them down a peg. Of course, this is typically their own projected view of others in positions of authority, whose power and status they bitterly envy and covet.

Other paranoid personality traits include pathological jealousy, extreme litigiousness, and under stress, they many become clearly delusional. Some, having a fragile ego structure, may react to stress in a catastrophic manner. Others are more self-assured and imperturbable, showing a general detachment and aloofness in interpersonal relationships. In their daily lives, most paranoid personalities are rigid, tense, and unable to relax, always searching the environment for clues or hints from others that they misinterpret as being directed at undermining them. In essence, the basic problem with their thinking is that they interpret the actions or demeanor of others as invariably threatening, exploitive, or harmful to themselves. They even mistrust family members, friends, and associates.

In their egocentricity and attitude of unerring infallibility, there are similarities between the paranoid and narcissistic personalities. But whereas the narcissist might self-servingly accept certain sycophants into his inner circle of trusted admirers, the paranoid trusts no one. When your willingness to serve has reached its limit and you want to leave or rebel, the narcissist will merely discard you, but the paranoid will hunt you down and punish you for your betrayal. In this, the paranoid resembles the borderline personality. But the latter's shifting moods and malleable perceptions leave room for possible eventual exculpation of your sins and mitigation of your sentence—if you can somehow earn your way back into her good graces. The paranoid's vendettas, however, are carved in stone: once on the hit list, your fate is sealed.

Because paranoid personalities frequently have a talent for technical details and are able to channel considerable energy in pursuing their goals, they may actually achieve considerable success at work. Thus, in highly competitive industries and jobs that call for complex strategic combativeness against well-defined corporate enemies, paranoid personalities may be quite successful and may even emerge as leaders. However, a war-room mentality that is not kept in check, or outward-directed suspicion that is blown back toward friends, family members, or coworkers, can result in an excess of negative fallout. Thus emerges a vicious cycle of mistrust and hostility as coworkers

come to shun their persistently obnoxious paranoid associate, only confirming his suspicions of plots and intrigue, leading to more outright avoidance
and hostility and perhaps even preemptively defensive moves on the part of
others. Eventually, as the saying goes, "just because you're paranoid, it does-
n't mean they're *not* out to get you" (Malmquist, 1996; Miller, 2003c, 2008c;
Palermo, 2009; Palermo & Kocsis, 2005; Stone, 2007; Tardiff, 2001).

Criminal Aspects of Paranoid Personality Disorder

Most forms of aggression by paranoid subjects will be perceived by the
perpetrator himself as either a defensive preemptive strike or justified retaliation for some purported outrage committed against him. Like the antisocial
personality (Chapter 8), the paranoid individual feels entitled to attack his
target, but not because he's simply tougher or cleverer than the victim, but
because he's *earned* the payback and victim *deserves* it. Paranoia may figure
prominently in many of the cases of workplace violence and other mass
homicides reported in the past several decades (Chapter 11), particularly the
"commando-style" attack of the "disgruntled worker" (Boxer, 1993; Miller,
1998c, 1999g, 2002a, 2007b; Stone, 2007; Tardiff, 2001). In interpersonal
relationships, this may be seen in those types of intimate partner violence
that involve "pathological jealousy," as opposed to the narcissistic domestic
batterer who is driven by control, or the antisocial batterer who's motive is
power and dominance, or the borderline batterer who's pathological dependency makes him explode at any threat of abandonment (see Chapter 17).

DEPENDENT PERSONALITY DISORDER

Dependent personality disorder is a pattern of submissive and clinging behavior stemming from an excessive craving for care and nurturance:
"neediness" is the word here.

Clinical and Developmental Features

Dependent personalities live in fear of rejection or withdrawal of support
by significant others. They look to others to provide guidance and direction
and are ready-made followers. Sometimes hidden behind a façade of independence and genuine real-world accomplishment, they look for other people to validate their essential worthiness as human beings. Even neutral interactions, such as workplace communications, are apt to be taken more personally than would be by others, and, as such, their feelings are easily hurt,
even by seemingly neutral or innocuous comments or actions, although they

are far less likely to nurse a grudge than the narcissistic, paranoid, or borderline personality (Malmquist, 1996; Miller, 2003c, 2008c; Palermo, 2009; Palermo & Kocsis, 2005; Stone, 2007; Tardiff, 2001).

Criminal Aspects of Dependent Personality Disorder

However, like the borderline, any kind of violent response from a dependent subject is likely to be precipitated by a destabilizing relationship disruption. At first, like borderline and histrionic personalities, some dependent subjects may attempt to assuage their panic with drugs or alcohol or they may develop a range of psychosomatic symptoms to curry sympathy with the other person. Alternatively or concurrently, they may beg, plead, or become overly ingratiating in an attempt to persuade the other person to stay. However, when they have exhausted all their options, a few dependent individuals may resort to violence and even murder, all the more paradoxical in a person who has always seemed so meek and accommodating all along. There may be several factors to account for this (Malmquist, 1996).

First, many dependent subjects respond to a loss of a loved one, job, or other relationship by becoming ill, abusing substances, sinking into depression, or even becoming suicidal, but their intense pain is largely internalized. But for a small number, probably where there are features of borderline and narcissistic personality as well, their total inability to cope with the rupture fills them with murderous rage: "How dare he/she leave me–don't they know how much I need them? How could they do this to me?" Dependent subjects may be especially prone to carry out murder-suicides, less so as an act of vengeance, as with the borderline, but more often out of the desire to "spend eternity together" with the separated loved one, whether they believe that this actually involves a supernatural afterlife or not: "If we can't be together in life, we'll be together in death."

In some cases, however, desire for revenge at the deserter for "destroying" the dependent subject may fuel the homicide, with the suicidal component reflecting the utter loneliness and hopelessness of the dependent person that he or she will ever be loved and cared for again. In some cases, as with other personalities, the anger of the dependent personality may be displaced onto others, such as psychotherapists ("that quack talked my wife into leaving me") or divorce attorneys ("that shylock is helping my husband dump me for that bimbo"). Occasionally, these others may be harassed, stalked, sued or attacked. Indeed, in those divorce cases which seem to drag on endlessly with incessant delays and new demands, there is often one party with strong dependency traits who will do anything, even risk financial ruin, to keep the relationship going any way they can.

SCHIZOID AND SCHIZOTYPAL PERSONALITY DISORDER

The central characteristics of both schizoid and schizotypal personality disorder include avoidance of others, severe deficiencies in social skills, generalized withdrawal from life, and sometimes impairment in perceptual and cognitive capacities.

Clinical and Developmental Features

Schizoid personality disorder is a pattern of aloof detachment from social interaction, with a restricted range of emotional expression. These are people who don't need people, and are perfectly happy being left to themselves. **Schizotypal personality disorder** involves more serious disturbances of thinking, more bizarre behavior, and possibly delusions. It is thought that these two personality disorders really represent points on a continuum from schizoid to schizotypal to outright schizophrenia, the latter characterized by severe distortions of thought, perception, and action, including delusions and hallucinations (Chapter 5). In fact, schizoid and schizotypal personality disorders may episodically deteriorate into psychotic states, especially under conditions of stress (Loza & Hanna, 2006; Palermo, 2009). Kinship with schizophrenia is further suggested by neuroimaging findings that are similar between the two syndromes, including larger volume of the cerebral ventricles and atypical neuroanatomy of the hippocampus and caudate nucleus, suggesting problems in memory and programming of activity (Goodman et al., 2007; Palermo, 2009).

Schizoid and schizotypal personalities show a lifelong pattern of social withdrawal. Their range of affect is constricted, and they isolate themselves because of the general discomfort they feel in social interactions. They appear cold, aloof, distant, unsociable, unemotional, uninvolved, and generally odd to those who interact with them. They frequently hold solitary noncompetitive occupations and lack an intimate life. They have difficulty expressing anger. They often involve themselves with astronomy, philosophy, mathematics, dietary health fads, and other arcane interests. They may display magical thinking, ideas of reference, suspiciousness or paranoid ideation, and may experience depersonalization and derealization. Although generally not frankly psychotic, they spend a great deal of time in fantasy (Millon et al., 2000; Palermo, 2009; Sperry, 1995).

Criminal Aspects of Schizoid/Schizotypal Personality Disorder

The cold aloofness and complete lack of sympathy for the suffering of others that characterizes the personality and behavior of many serial killers

(Chapter 10) has suggested that many of these predators have a schizoid component to their personality structure, along with narcissistic and psychopathic traits. Indeed, research has found that 50 percent of male perpetrators of serial sexual homicide self-report traits consistent with schizoid personality disorder, admixed with psychopathic and sadistic tendencies. The rate of schizoid personality disorder in this admittedly small sample is fifty times greater than in the general population (Stone, 2001, 2007). Other cases of violence associated with schizoid personality disorder include spousal homicide (Loza & Hanna, 2006). However, although the majority of subjects with schizoid/schizotypal personalities may appear weird and off-putting, most are not overtly dangerous. This applies to most other personality disorders as well, except for the antisocial personality (Chapter 8).

BOX 7.1. POLICE RESPONSE TO CITIZENS
WITH PERSONALITY DISORDERS

Because personality disorders are ubiquitous, police officers will encounter these individuals in virtually every service call they undertake, including traffic stops, domestic disturbance calls, or questioning crime victims or witnesses (Miller, 2006f).

Histrionic Personality Disorder

These will be the overemotional citizens that police encounter, and the ones who may try to ingratiate themselves with local officers by virtue of their wit and charm. They crave attention, and officers who are able to project an attitude of empathic concern will probably find these subjects more than willing to cooperate. However, they may often change their story to suit what they believe you want to hear, not necessarily as a deliberate deception, but a virtually unconscious attempt to do anything to put themselves in the best possible light and get you to like them. Careful, gentle probing of inconsistencies may be necessary to get at the facts.

Borderline Personality Disorder

Officers most commonly encounter these individuals on domestic disturbance calls or in workplace disputes, since their most intense conflicts involve those with whom they've had some kind of previous relationship. Extremely sensitive to rejection or betrayal, they may respond with intense anger, which may escalate to violence. In such cases, be sure to separate the disputing parties and use calming techniques and active listening to convey a sense of sincere concern, backed

continued

BOX 7.1.—*Continued*

by no-nonsense resoluteness that violence won't be tolerated. Stay away from discussing issues, which may only further inflame the borderline subject, and focus concretely on what you want the subject to do.

Narcissistic Personality Disorder

Expect two kinds of reactions from narcissistic subjects. The first is an over-familiar, back-slapping camaraderie that implies that he and you are really of equal status or have a common bond: "It's okay, officer, I understand what you're trying to do—my uncle's a cop in Atlanta and I used to work security over at the stadium." You can use this to your advantage by allowing the subject to "take your side" and emphasize how what you're asking him to do is of mutual benefit: "I'm glad you have an understanding of law enforcement protocol, sir. That's why I know you'll appreciate the need to move your vehicle to make it easier for us to do our job here."

The other reaction (sometimes after the first reaction fails to get the antici-pated collegial response) is outrage at not being respected as a special case: "I'm an important man in this community—you can't treat me like a common criminal!" In these situations, verbally disarm the subject by being somewhat deferential, but at the same time, maintaining the need for your actions: "We understand, sir, but it's necessary for the thoroughness of our investigation that we ask these ques-tions of anyone. We do appreciate your patience and cooperation."

Dependent Personality Disorder

Citizens with dependent personalities will respond well to a supportive, col-laborative approach to questioning. The caution is that, like the histrionic person-ality, in their eagerness to please, dependent subjects may be apt to tell you what they think you want to hear, not necessarily what is actually the case, so follow up your open-ended questions with a few close-ended queries to nail down the de-tails. Be careful, however, not to give the impression that you don't trust the sub-ject, which he or she will take as a stinging rebuke, and which may then close off any further productive communication.

Schizoid Personality Disorder

The main interactive feature of interest to patrol officers is that these subjects may seem detached and disinterested during an encounter, not because they're ignoring or disrespecting you, but because they may be internally preoccupied or because human interaction is of little interest to them to begin with. In most cases, their blank, far-away facial expression and attitude will be quite noticeable. Even where they do communicate, the sometimes bizarre and delusional nature of the information they provide may compromise its validity and usefulness. Encouraging a free narrative will likely yield either an incoherently rambling stream-of-consciousness oration, or a rigidly obsessive reiteration of key ideas or phrases. Instead, it will be more effective to use a firm and directive approach to focus the schizoid subject's attention on simple, precise questions. These queries should be designed to yield specific, tangible bits of information that can then be painstakingly fitted together to create a coherent narrative of useful information.

SUMMARY AND CONCLUSIONS

We all have personalities, but they are regarded as **personality disorders** when they significantly interfere with our own or others' functioning. The emotional lability, sensitivity to rejection, and either-or cognitive style of the **histrionic, dependent**, and **borderline** personalities may lead to criminal aggression and violence when they believe they have been abandoned, insulted, or betrayed. **Paranoid** personalities may retaliate for perceived injustices against them, while **narcissistic** personalities may fume with outrage at the failure of underlings to afford them proper deference and respect. The odd appearance and behavior of **schizoid** and **schizotypal** personalities may result in conflicts with workmates or family members. Any of the personality disorders may be complicated by comorbid psychotic, mood, or substance abuse disorders, creating a vicious cycle. Finally, it is unlikely that personality disorders alone will create grounds for legal incompetency or impaired criminal responsibility, although in rare instances, an episode of **borderline minipsychotic episode** or **narcissistic rage** might be presented by a particularly creative defense attorney as an exculpatory or mitigating factor.

Chapter **8**

Antisocial Personality Disorder and the Psychopath

There are no bad boys.
> – Spencer Tracy as Father Flanagan
> in *Boys Town,* 1938

Bad men do what good men dream.
> – Forensic psychiatrist
> Robert Simon, 1996

ANTISOCIAL PERSONALITY DISORDER AND PSYCHOPATHY: CONTINUITY OR SEPARATE CATEGORIES?

I have devoted a separate chapter to this personality type because subjects with **antisocial personality disorder** are probably more frequently encountered in law enforcement and criminal justice settings than any other type; indeed, this is as close as one gets to a quintessential "criminal personality." Alternatively known as **psychopaths**, these individuals are characterized by a completely egocentric world view, lack of empathy for others, craving for immediate gratification, poor frustration tolerance, excessive need for stimulation and excitement, poor planning and goal-direction, an impulsive and nonreflective cognitive style, relative imperviousness to punishment, poor performance in academics and employment, the use of cunning, conning, and intimidation to get what they want from people, and complete lack of remorse or compassion. In short, these are individuals who seem to have been born without a conscience.

HISTORY OF THE ANTISOCIAL PERSONALITY/PSYCHOPATH CONSTRUCT

As discussed in Chapter 7, a number of personality disorders may be associated with impulsive, vengeful, aggressive, exploitive, predatory, and violent acts, but the antisocial personality is the only type that is literally defined by these acts because he makes them his basis for existence. Hence, many of us are alternately repelled and fascinated by that small group of people who live a remorselessly exploitive and predatory existence and are proud of it. Accordingly, throughout history, clinicians, criminal justice experts, and philosophers have struggled to explain this unique and disturbing breed of human being (Arrigo & Shipley, 2001; Bernard et al., 2010; Lalumiere et al., 2008; Lykken, 1995; Palermo, 2009; Palermo & Kocsis, 2005; Stoudemire, 1994; Stout, 2005; Vien & Beech, 2006; Vitacco et al., 2008; Zavaliy, 2008).

It was Aristotle who identified a category of citizen whose evil intent and wicked actions seemed to far surpass the ordinary bad acts of otherwise normal community dwellers. He saw these special cases as lying somewhere between man and beast, and characterized them as "brutes." As we'll see, this atavistic conception of antisocial personalities and habitual criminals—that they represent a form of "throwback," a more primitive form of proto-human—is a theme that emerges again and again in the history of psychology, anthropology, and sociology. Indeed, biological criminologists of the nineteenth century urged law enforcement investigators to look for the "beetling brows" of the Neanderthal to help identify this criminal type.

Calling it by different names, diverse cultures recognize the existence of a subset of lawless individuals among their respective communities. For example, **kunlangeta** is an Eskimo word used to describe a man "whose mind knows what to do but he does not do it;" that is, the term recognizes that it is not ignorance of rules that drives this individual, but a deliberate flouting of those rules. The kunlangeta repeatedly lies, cheats, steals, refuses to do his share of the hunting and other work of the village, and sexually preys on other men's wives. Half a world away, the Yorubas of Nigeria use the term **arankan** to describe a person "who always goes his own way regardless of others, who is uncooperative, full of malice, and bullheaded." The common themes of these two concepts, as well as of the Western concept of the psychopath/antisocial personality, is a person, usually male, who is selfish, impulsive, lazy, angry, stubborn, exploitive, predatory, and remorseless.

The French physician, Philipe Pinel (1801), the "father of modern psychiatry," noted for his advocacy of humane treatment of the mentally ill, was struck by the fact that certain patients who habitually got in trouble with the law seemed to be relatively nonpsychotic and cognitively intact, yet appeared to completely lack a moral sense, suffering from what he termed a **manie sans delire**, or madness without confusion. Benjamin Rush (1812), the so-called father of American psychiatry, believed that there was an "innate preternatural moral depravity" in habitual criminals that had a biological basis. Indeed, so alien to most people's (including most doctors') moral sense was the conscienceless predatory lifestyle of the psychopath, that clinicians groped for some biological quirk or neural deformity to explain it. The English physician James C. Pritchard (1835) used the term **moral insanity** to describe this syndrome, which he hypothesized to be due to a detachment of the individual's "feelings and attitudes" from the "higher mental faculties," foreshadowing modern frontal lobe-limbic disconnection theories (see below).

Later in the nineteenth century, Cesare Lombroso (1889) revived the **atavism** concept of criminality (Chapter 2), positing that certain chronic offenders were developmentally and evolutionarily primitive "born criminals." Relatedly, Richard von Krafft-Ebing (1869, 1922), despite his pioneering research and advocacy of humane treatment for patients with sexual disorders, displayed no such clinical compassion for remorseless psychopaths, who he referred to as "savages," and advocated locking them away in mental asylums for their own and society's safety.

Although commonly attributed to Cleckley (1955), it was Julius Koch (1891) who first used the term **psychopathic** to refer to a diverse group of syndromes that would today be classed as personality disorders. One subcatetory, the **psychopathic inferior**, was characterized by emotional, behavioral, and moral aberrations, and was believed to be a hereditary disease. The psychopath was a **moral imbecile**, according to Maudsley (1898) who, like many of his colleagues, attributed the behavior to a perturbation of brain functioning. Presaging the more modern accounts of Cleckley and Hare (see discussion below), Kraepelin (1915) described what he termed the **psychopathic personality** as a glib, charming liar and manipulator, who could nevertheless turn violent in a flash. Reflecting the rising influence of sociological criminology in Western, and especially American, psychiatry at the beginning of the twentieth century, Partridge (1930) introduced the term **sociopath** to describe people with a habitual pattern of violating social norms.

In the latter half of the twentieth century, Macdonald (1961) emphasized the psychopath's self-centeredness, impulsivity, immaturity, callousness, and striking absence of empathy and, indeed, of most emotions, except for anger. He also noted, however, that far from being atavistic brutes, many psychopaths were clever enough to reach positions of power and success by virtue of some combination of ruthlessness and cunning. Halleck (1967) used the curious term **activist** to refer to the psychopath's relentless efforts to bend the world to his own needs, often by flouting or manipulating the law.

It was work of Hervey Cleckley (1941, 1955, 1976, 1982), however, that planted the psychopath firmly on the psychiatric map, with his treatise on the subject, *The Mask of Sanity,* first appearing in 1941. This classic book, filled with both detailed clinical descriptions and colorful case histories, emerged in several editions over time and continues to be used as a reference today. Cleckley's psychopath was, as in earlier descriptions, grandiose, arrogant, callous, superficial, exploitive, and manipulative. And like earlier writers, Cleckley was struck by the seeming incongruity between the relatively intact cognitive faculties of language, perception, communication, and reasoning, as opposed to the impulsive lack of judgment and completely self-centered thinking that characterized these individuals. Indeed, the title of his tract came from the idea that, although the psychopath maintains a mask of sanity in the superficial sense, i.e., not frankly psychotic and possessed of adequate and sometimes keen superficial intelligence, his stunted emotional empathy, childish immaturity and impulsivity, shallow and superficial "pseudoemotions," impaired reflective thinking but heavy reliance on rationalization, relentless persistence of self-gratifying antisocial behavior, seeming imperviousness to punishment, inability or unwillingness to learn from his mistakes, capacity for both impulsive and coldblooded aggression, and complete lack of remorse for his actions indicated that his seeming sanity was merely a "mask" covering an extremely distorted perception of reality and extremely disturbed ability to function in it. In fact, Cleckley described how, under some conditions, the psychopath might regress to a near-psychotic state, which might involve extreme violence.

Cleckley enumerated a set of clinical descriptive and diagnostic criteria for identifying the psychopath, including superficial charm and good intelligence; absence of delusions and other signs of irrational thinking; absence of nervousness or other neurotic manifestations; unreliability, untruthfulness and insincerity; lack of shame or remorse; inadequately motivated antisocial behavior (e.g., taking great risks for seemingly paltry rewards); poor judgment and failure to learn from experience; pathological impulsivity and incapacity for love; general poverty in major affective reactions; specific loss of insight; unresponsiveness in interpersonal relations; fantastic and uninviting behavior; suicide rarely carried out; sex life impersonal; and failure to follow any life plan (Table 8.2).

In recent decades, Cleckley's mantle has been picked up by Robert Hare (1970, 1991, 1996, 2003) who has refined both the clinical and empirical study of the psychopath, and developed Cleckley's clinical diagnostic criteria for psychopathy into a psychometric instrument, the ***Psychopathy Checklist*** and ***Psychopathy Checklist-Revised***, or PCL-R (Hare, 2003; see Table 8.2). Hare has also described the activities of relatively high-functioning psychopaths in the broader social and business worlds (Babiak & Hare, 2007). Meanwhile, a related diagnosis, the **antisocial personality disorder** was included on Axis II in the 1980 edition of *DSM-III* (Table 8.1). Although the two clinical constructs share similarities, they are not identical, which will be discussed further below.

CLINICAL-DESCRIPTIVE FEATURES OF ANTISOCIAL PERSONALITY DISORDER/PSYCHOPATHY

Subjects with **antisocial personality disorder** are characterized by a completely self-centered world view, lack of empathy for others, and a craving for immediate gratification, with little or no frustration tolerance. They have an excessive need for stimulation and excitement, and their behavior is impulsive, erratic, and characterized by difficulty in sustaining long-term goal-directed behavior. More so than other offenders, punishment seems to have little effect on them, a feature that has both been noted behaviorally and documented neurophysiologically. Commonly, there is a long history of substance abuse and criminal activity, dating from childhood, at which ages (below 18) the syndrome is known as **conduct disorder** (APA, 2000) (see also Chapter 19).

In their youth, antisocial personalities typically have done poorly in academics, especially verbal subjects, although they may possess contrastingly high mechanical skill and athletic prowess. They were probably bullies since grade school. When older, they tend to be unreliable workers. They usually perform poorly on IQ tests, again especially in the verbal areas, yet they typ-

TABLE 8.1.
DSM-IV-TR DIAGNOSTIC CRITERIA FOR
ANTISOCIAL PERSONALITY DISORDER

A. Pervasive pattern of disregard for and violation of the rights of others occurring since age 15 years, as indicated by three or more of the following:

1. Repeated failure to conform to social norms and lawful conduct, often resulting in confrontations with the criminal justice system.
2. Deceitfulness, lying, conning, and manipulation of others for profit or personal gratification.
3. Impulsivity, failure to plan, and little regard for consequences.
4. Irritability and aggressiveness, hypersentivity to challenge, with frequent physical fights and assaults.
5. Reckless disregard for the safety of self or others.
6. Consistent irresponsibility, failure to sustain financial, social, or work obligations.
7. Lack of remorse, indifference to, or rationalization of, the harm caused to others.

B. The individual is at least age 18 years.

C. There is evidence of conduct disorder with onset before age 15 years.

D. The occurrence of antisocial behavior is not exclusively during the course of schizophrenia or a manic episode.

ically possess a very keen social intelligence that they use to "psych out" others in order to exploit them for their own ends. They can be glibly persuasive, seductive, sympathetic, intimidating, or threatening with facile ease, often in the same conversation. They are the classic con artists who can turn on the charm or flare into fury if that's what it takes to get what they want from others. Human beings, in their minds, are just objects to use and throw away, and there is no true sense of loyalty or friendship. People who value such human traits as love, honesty, commitment, or honor are seen by antisocial personalities as fools and suckers who deserve to be exploited.

Some authorities make a point of distinguishing "true" Cleckleyian or PCL-R psychopathy from *DSM* antisocial personality disorder. True to the atheoretical and descriptive orientation of *DSM-IV-TR*, the diagnostic criteria for ASPD are mostly objective and behavioral, such as impulsivity, exploitive behavior, substance abuse, and so on. Derived more from traditional clinical study, the psychopathy concept includes additional inferred intrapsychic components, such as lack of remorse, callousness and coldness of emotion. While some antisocial personalities would not necessarily meet full Cleckleyian criteria for psychopathy, there is great overlap between the two concepts and the terms are often used interchangeably. Many authorities have commented on the core feature of pathological egocentricity or malignant narcissism (Kernberg, 1992) that underlies psychopathy—the belief that if I want something, I am automatically entitled to take it. Psychopathy is present in approximately 15 percent to 20 percent of criminal offenders and is one of the strongest predictors of violent recidivism in prisoners (de Barros & de Padua-Serafim; 2008; Blair, 2001, 2003; Glenn & Raine, 2008; Hare, 1991, 1993, 2003; Hart & Hare, 1996; Lykken, 1995; Martens, 2000; Palermo & Farkas, 2001, Palermo & Kocsis, 2005; Raine et al., 1997; Robins, 1966; Robins & Price, 1991; Stout, 2005; Zavaliy, 2008).

Although antisocial personality disorder is most often diagnosed in men, this syndrome is also identified in a subset of female offenders. Like their male counterparts, antisocial women tend to have lower educational levels, high rates of unemployment, greater use of alcohol and drugs, and lower socioeconomic status. Compared with nonantisocial women, they tend to become single mothers and to have their children earlier. Unlike antisocial males, however, antisocial women show a significantly increased rate of medical symptoms, health problems, psychiatric diagnoses and suicide attempts. Many suffer from depression, psychotic disorders, and posttraumatic stress disorder, and many of these women also show features of borderline and histrionic personality disorder. Their antisocial acts tend to less overly violent and more manipulative, exploitive, and deceptive (Bardone et al., 1996; 1998; Climent et al., 1973; Lewis et al., 1991; Pajer, 1998; Pajer et al., 2006;

Robertson et al., 1987; Robins, 1966; Robins & Price, 1991; Storm-Mathisen & Vaghum, 1994; Teplin et al., 1996; Zoccolillo & Rogers, 1991). In addition, earlier studies documented an apparent pattern of assortive mating in families which contained high rates of antisocial personality disorder in males and depression and somatoform disorders in females–the so-called "St. Louis triad," named for the location where the study was carried out.

SUBTYPES OF ANTISOCIAL PERSONALITY DISORDER/PSYCHOPATHY

Part of the antisocial-psychopathy overlap may relate to different dimensions of exploitive vs. predatory vs. aggressive antisocial behavior. One dimension appears to be mostly objective and behavioral, such as impulsivity,

TABLE 8.2.
CLECKLEY-HARE DIAGNOSTIC CRITERIA FOR PSYCHOPATHY (PCL-R)

Factor 1: Aggressive Narcissism

1. Glibness and superficial charm
2. Grandiose sense of self-worth
3. Pathological lying
4. Cunning/conning manipulativeness
5. Lack of guilt or remorse
6. Emotional shallowness
7. Callousness and lack of empathy
8. Failure to accept responsibility for own actions

Factor 2: Socially Deviant Lifestyle

1. Proneness to boredom and need for stimulation
2. Exploitive and parasitic lifestyle
3. Poor behavioral control
4. Promiscuous sexual behavior
5. Lack of realistic, long-term goals
6. Impulsivity
7. Irresponsibility
8. History of juvenile delinquency
9. Early behavioral problems
10. Revocation of conditional release due to violation of probation

Traits Not Correlated with Either Factor

1. Many short-term marital relationships
2. Criminal versatility

exploitive behavior, substance abuse, and involvement in criminal activity. The other dimension appears more intrapsychic and trait-derived, such as lack of remorse, callousness, coldness of emotion, and glib manipulativeness.

Hare (1991, 2003) makes this distinction explicit in the two factors of the **Psychopathy Checklist-Revised (PCL-R)**:

Factor 1 is called **aggressive narcissism** and includes glibness and superficial charm; grandiose sense of self-worth; pathological lying; cunning and manipulativeness; lack of remorse or guilt; shallow affect; callousness and lack of empathy; and failure to accept responsibility for one's own actions.

Factor 2, **socially deviant lifestyle**, more closely tracks the *DSM-IV* diagnostic criteria for antisocial personality disorder, and includes proneness to boredom and need for stimulation; parasitic lifestyle; poor behavioral control; promiscuous sexual behavior; lack of realistic long-term goals; impulsivity; and irresponsibility. Finally, two traits that do not load heavily on either factor are many short-term marital relationships and criminal versatility.

Similarly, Lykken (1995) describes a spectrum of **antisocial personalities**, and distinguishes between two groups of subjects showing antisocial behavior. In this classification, the **primary psychopath** resembles the profile outlined by Cleckley (1982) and describes the subject whose antisocial tendencies and activities result largely from heritable differences in temperament and brain function, making it unusually difficult to socialize this individual as he grows up. However, most crime is not committed by these individuals, but rather by **sociopaths**, individuals with essentially normal temperament who have failed to acquire adequate socialization, not by reason of any significant temperamental-neurobiological abnormality, but through failure of the usual civilizing agents of parents and community.

Another framework, using similar terminology but with different meanings, has been preferred by Wilkowski & Robinson (2008), citing literature identifying what they call **primary psychopathy**, encompassing the traits of emotional callousness and a lack of empathy, guilt, and remorse. These individuals lack the emotions that deter most people from habitually committing antisocial acts. **Secondary psychopathy** consists primarily of impulsivity and low frustration tolerance. These individuals lack the restraint and behavioral control to inhibit self-gratifying illicit actions (Blair et al., 2005; Colledge & Blair, 2001; Fowles & Dindo, 2006; Frick, 1995; Harpur et al., 1988; Levenson et al., 1995; Lynam et al., 1999; Morgan & Lilienfeld, 2000).

In this model, two temperamental-cognitive factors underlie the formation of the psychopathic personality. **Fearfulness** is a key temperamental element in the development of a conscience, as young children initially learn the rules of society based on a system of rewards and punishments. Deficient fearfulness makes it harder to reinforce codes of normative and law-abiding behavior because there is very little to deter impulsive, self-gratifying actions. The cognitive trait of **effortful control** refers to the ability to override a dominant, self-gratifying response, even when the person is motivated to do so. It is one of the so-called executive functions mediated by the frontal lobes of the brain (Chapter 2). The combination of moderate fearfulness and adequate effortful control allows most children to learn and eventually internalize the rules, regulations, and standards of conduct for their particular societies; they comprise the emotional-cognitive recipe for a conscience. When either or both of these ingredients are deficient, the individual is at risk for psychopathic personality and antisocial behavior (Blair et al., 2005; Fowles & Dindo, 2006; Frick & Marsee, 2006; Kochanska & Askan, 2006; Kochanska et al., 1996; Rueda et al., 2004; Wilkowski & Robinson, 2008).

Although often associated with violent criminality (the "brute" model), there are many ways of being antisocial without being overtly violent. Indeed, the cunning-conning feature of psychopathy implies that deception, seduction, and exploitation figure prominently among the ways these subjects take advantage of others. Burt (2009) cites research supporting a distinction between what he calls **physically aggressive** (**AGG**) and **nonaggressive rule-breaking** (**RB**) forms of antisocial behavior, with separate etiological and developmental pathways (Frick et al., 1993; Loeber & Schmaling, 1985).

AGG antisocial behavior appears to be a relatively stable trait, occurring in about 5% of children, mostly boys, and continuing into adult life, whereas RB behavior contains more females (although still male-predominant), increases steadily through adolescence to a plateau, and is less stable over time (Moffitt, 2003; Tremblay, 2003). The AGG pattern, much more so than the RB pattern, seems to be linked to abnormal neurophysiological markers of emotional and cognitive functioning, such as low autonomic arousal and brain wave potentiation associated with deficient fear conditioning, and impaired hypothalamic-pituitary-adrenal axis functioning mediating the stress response (Burt & Donnellan, 2008; Burt & Larson, 2007; Cohen & Strayer, 1996; Fahey et al., 1993; Krueger et al., 2005; McBurnett et al., 2000; Pardini et al., 2003; Raine, 2002a, 2002b; Ramirez, 2003). Finally, AGG seems to be more highly heritable than RB; the latter appears to be more influenced by the family setting and environmental factors, although some degree of genetic predisposition is likely to exist for the RB syndrome as well (Barr & Quinsey, 2004; Deater-Deckerd & Plomin, 1999; Eley et al., 1999, 2003; Hudziak et al., 2003; Larsson et al., 2006; Tackett et al., 2005; van der Valk et al., 1998. Overall, the AGG pattern appears to be associated with innate deficiencies in both empathy and self-control to a greater extent than the RB pattern (Burt, 2009).

What all of these models seem to indicate is that much antisocial behavior is sporadic, limited, and committed by individuals who seem to have evaded or avoided adequate socialization as children; in this sense, it is at least *potentially* correctable or preventable. This, however, is contrasted with a small, hard core of seemingly incorrigible antisocial individuals, who commit a disproportionately high rate of criminal acts, and who seem to innately lack the very capacity for normal civilized existence—as close to the model of the "born criminal" that modern behavioral science can describe.

DEVELOPMENT OF PSYCHOPATHY

Subjects who will become adult psychopaths or be diagnosed with antisocial personality disorder can be identified as early as age 3. There is remarkable consistency in antisocial behavior from childhood, through adolescence, and into adulthood. In childhood, the syndrome is called **conduct disorder** (Chapter 19), with the diagnosis changing to **antisocial personality disorder** at the arbitrary cutoff age of 18. Some children are aggressively exploitive from early on, while others show a milder form of disrespect and rule-breaking, called **oppositional defiant disorder**. Some of these children remain at this level, while others progress to conduct disorder and later antisocial personality disorder. **Attention deficit hyperactivity disorder** (**ADHD**) is frequently comorbid with either syndrome. High levels of **trait callousness** in adolescence seem to be especially associated with significant psychopathy in adulthood. Standard demographic risk factors, such as family dysfunction, crime-ridden neighborhood, delinquent peers, and poverty may somewhat affect the trajectory of antisocial development, but do not significantly alter its course, especially for boys showing strong antisocial traits by age 13 (Frick et al., 1994; Glenn & Raine, 2008; Glenn et al., 2007; Loeber et al., 2002; Loney et al., 2003; Lykken, 1995; Lynam & Gudonis, 2005; Lyman et al., 2008; Palermo & Kocsis, 2005; Salekin & Lochman, 2008; Wootton et al., 1997).

Many of the above findings are consistent with Moffit's (1993) theory of **life-course-persistent vs. adolescent-limited delinquency** (Chapters 3 and 19). The former category closely tracks the continuity of antisocial behavior through the life span, albeit with changing forms of that behavior, reflecting the underlying antisocial disposition; for example, hitting, biting, and stealing toys at age 4, shoplifting, bullying, and truancy by age 10, drug dealing, mugging, and car theft at age 16, robbery and rape at age 22, and fraud and child abuse at age 30. Again, while optimum environmental influences may have a moderating effect on these behaviors, they are unlikely to alter the basic underlying antisocial predisposition (Lykken, 1995; Lytton, 1990; Vien & Beech, 2006).

Protective Factors

Nevertheless, certain factors have been found to reduce the risk that antisocial children and adolescents will progress to full-blown antisocial personality disorder or psychopathy in later life. The question that must be asked about all these protective factors, however, is to what extent they are they characteristics external to the person that moderate the existing risk factors and deflect the antisocial trajectory, versus core dispositional traits that make it unlikely that the individual would have developed full-blown antisocial personality disorder or psychopathy in the first place. We know that higher overall IQ, better verbal communicative skills, and higher academic functioning are all related to reduced probability of antisocial outcome, as are a supportive, nurturing relationship with at least one adult caregiver or mentor and regular interaction with a prosocial peer group (Cohen et al., 2003; Fergusson & Lynskey, 1996; Lynam et al., 2008; Moffitt, 1990a; Quinton & Rutter, 1988; Werner & Smith, 1992). But are these the children who were cognitively, temperamentally, and psychosocially "at risk" to begin with?

For example, the "protective" effect of nurturing, supportive parents and a prosocial peer group appear to have its greatest effect on children who are diagnosed with oppositional defiant disorder (the rebellious, but less severely antisocial variant), as opposed to conduct disorder (which includes the antisocial traits of emotional callousness and behavioral exploitation and aggression). Protective environmental effects, especially parental or other mature adult influences, are also most effective when they are operative before age 5–6, and their influence decreases if they are applied at later ages (Carlo et al., 1999; Fowles & Kochanska, 2000; Gershoff, 2002; Hastings et al., 2000; Kochanska, 1997; Kochanska & Murray, 2000; Laible & Thompson, 2002; Lykken, 1995; Pardini & Loeber, 2007; Salekin & Lochman, 2008). Thus, the mitigatatory external circumstances appear to make the most difference to the least severely antisocial children and only if applied relatively early; the implication is that older, hard-case antisocial youth will be relatively impervious to these protective factors. Interestingly, these studies do not address whether the effects of more internal protective factors, such as high IQ and good academic performance, differ between conduct disordered vs. oppositional youth.

TABLE 8.3.
RISK AND PROTECTIVE FACTORS FOR ANTISOCIAL BEHAVIOR

Risk Factors:

Male sex
Low IQ, especially verbal IQ
Underaroused temperament and need for stimulation
ADHD, Learning Disorders, Oppositional Defiant Disorder, and/or Conduct Disorder in childhood
Poor academic functioning
Early onset of antisocial behavior, especially aggressive behavior, by age 13
Multiple episodes of antisocial behavior before age 13
Early association with antisocial peers
Poor parenting
Poor relationship with adults
Crime-ridden environment

Protective Factors:

Higher IQ, especially verbal IQ
Normal temperament
Absence of diagnosed childhood behavioral disorders
Absence of frequent and/or serious antisocial behavior before age 13
Good academic functioning
Good communication skills
Good relationship with adults
Establishment of relationship with mature adult mentor
Engagement in constructive activities, even within a distressed neighborhood

The Older Psychopath

Can a person stay antisocial forever? In their efforts to finds clues to prevention, researchers typically give most of their attention to risk and protective factors in childhood and adolescence. Frequently overlooked is what happens to antisocial individuals at the other end of the age spectrum, in middle and late adulthood. Until recently, most of the existing literature consisted of decades-old writings which generally concluded that the relative absence of older seriously antisocial perpetrators meant that a kind of "psychopathic burnout" or "mellowing" took place in later life. Largely ignored was the possibility that the impulsive, risky, and confrontational style of these subjects meant that by middle and older age, most were either dead or incarcerated.

The sparse literature on this subject has yielded only two empirical studies to date. A longitudinal study by Black et al. (1995) examined 71 men over the age of 60 who had been confined to a psychiatric hospital between 1945 and 1970 on the basis of a diagnosis of antisocial personality disorder. About a quarter of these men showed a sustained decrease in antisocial behavior over time, while a little less than a third showed some improvement, but repeatedly relapsed into an antisocial pattern. More than 40 percent of these older men showed no decrease in antisocial behavior. In other words, about three-fourths of men who had been antisocial in their youth and early-middle adulthood remained either steadily or episodically antisocial into later age.

Van Alphen et al. (2007) studied a sample of elderly offenders in the Dutch corrections system who had been diagnosed with antisocial personality disorder. The three most frequently cited crimes of the elderly subjects in this sample were sexual offenses, fraud, and assault, with lesser rates of homicide, theft, burglary, illegal drug use or drug dealing, vandalism, arson, and traffic offenses. Traits and behaviors characterizing these elderly offenders included lack of empathy, externalization of responsibility, egocentric behavior, lying, and making threats. Less than a third of the sample reported any "mellowing" of antisocial behavior with time, and almost half insisted that age had no mitigating effect on their criminal behavior. For those whose antisocial behavior was slowed by age, about a third of these cited some disabling medical condition as the reason, a quarter noted social factors, and another quarter cited a general psychological mellowing over time. Thus, for most subjects with ASPD or psychopathy, both the traits and behaviors appear to continue as long as the individual is physically able to keep getting himself into trouble.

COGNITIVE-EMOTIONAL FEATURES OF PSYCHOPATHY

A number of psychological traits and characteristics have been cited to be associated with persistent psychopathy and antisocial personality disorder.

Intelligence

Decades of research have documented that male juvenile delinquents and adult habitual criminals obtain mean IQ scores approximately 10 points lower than the general population (a mean of about 90 in comparison to the national mean of 100). Furthermore, most of the decrement appears to involve Verbal IQ, with Performance IQ (visuospatial and mechanical skills) frequently found to be in the normal range or even above-average; indeed, significant VIQ<PIQ discrepancies are common findings on psychological

testing of delinquent and criminal groups (Heilbrun, 1982; Heilbrun & Heilbrun, 1985; Miller, 1987, 1988c; Wilson & Herrnstein, 1985). But it is less clear if the relationship applies specifically to those subjects who meet strict Cleckleyian criteria for psychopathy, with a number of findings suggesting normal or even higher intelligence among "pure" psychopaths (Hare, 2003; Walsh et al., 2004), perhaps reflecting the cunning-conning dimension of this syndrome. Indeed, intelligence per se would appear to be a morally neutral cognitive trait that can be used for good or ill, depending on the person and the circumstances.

For example, for most people, higher intelligence is a protective factor against the development of criminality and antisocial behavior, presumably through its internal association with improved reflectivity and self-control, as well as its external relationship to higher education and economic attainment (deWit et al., 2007; Harris et al., 2001; Miller, 1998d; Miller et al., 2003; Wilson & Herrnstein, 1985). Yet, for individuals diagnosed as psychopaths, higher intelligence has been correlated with an earlier onset of criminal behavior (Johansson & Kerr, 2005), although this finding has not been universally replicated (Walsh et al., 2004). Perhaps the keen manipulative intelligence of at least some budding psychopaths facilitates the early start of their exploitive, parasitic, and predatory lifestyle. The finding that low IQ seems to be linked specifically to the callousness and lack of empathy dimension of psychopathy (Vitacco et al., 2008) suggests that psychopaths who, conversely, *are* more interpersonally intuitive and nuanced in their emotional perception and expression, may be the very geniuses of deception that become the classic manipulators and con artists.

However, IQ is only one aspect of reasoning in general, and moral reasoning in particular. As noted above, the idea that psychopaths have defective moral reasoning dates back to Pritchard's (1835) concept of "**moral insanity**." Cleckley (1941) considered the distortedly egocentric thinking of psychopaths to be a masked psychosis, and the frequent use of language for deflection, obfuscation, and manipulation–as opposed to true communication–to be a form of "**semantic dementia**." For example, a number of authors have commented on how some incarcerated prisoners seem unable to grasp the connection between their crime and their incarceration, steadfastly clinging to the narcissistic notion that they should have somehow been "entitled" to get away with it (Cleckley, 1982; Correia, 2009; Zavaliy, 2008; see also Chapter 21).

Temperamental Traits

Temperament refers to the general style of thinking, behaving, and reacting that is characteristic of a particular person, and numerous studies have examined temperamental traits in delinquent children and antisocial adults, including some labeled psychopaths (Glueck & Glueck, 1950; Lykken, 1995; Reiss & Roth, 1993; Sampson & Laub, 1993), with the following temperamental traits emerging most commonly.

Fearlessness. From an early age, many of these individuals appear to be virtually immune to pain and punishment, which often gives their behavior an impulsive, daring quality. These are not the children who are going to be easy to socialize through the usual set of rewards and punishments because the more risks they take and survive (injuries are, not surprisingly, common), the more their risk-tolerance is reinforced, and the more reckless they become (Farrington, 1986b; Kagan, 1994; Lykken, 1995).

However, Samenow (2004; Yochelson & Samenow, 1976a, 1976b) believes that the apparent boldness of psychopaths is not due to a natural absence of fear and anxiety, but that these subjects are especially adept at suppressing their fear and masking it with a persona of aggressive invulnerability in order not to betray softness or weakness of any kind. Similarly, Cardasis et al. (2008) views subjects with antisocial personality disorder as defending against painful emotions by utilizing defense mechanisms such as acting-out, denial of anxiety, isolation, displacement, projection, and rationalization (see Chapter 3). In this view, failure to develop mature ego functions is associated with inadequate or pathological attachments early in life and results in disturbed ego identity and object relations in adulthood (Kernberg, 1976). This, for example, may explain the propensity of individuals with ASPD to overutilize outward physical body markings, such as piercings and tattoos, as a method of grafting on an identity where there has been failure to internalize one, an **"exoskeletal defense"** (Demello, 1993; Fisher, 1963; Grumet, 1983; Manuel & Retzlaff, 2002; Popplestone, 1963). However, while these kinds of overcompensation theories may apply to many criminals who commit antisocial behavior, and to some individuals who meet the *DSM-IV-TR* diagnostic criteria for antisocial personality disorder, whether they describe the true psychopath is questionable.

Impulsiveness and sensation-seeking. The tendency to crave excitement and to take risks in order to achieve this stimulation is a temperamental trait that is widely recognized within psychology (Krueger et al., 2007), including the constructs of **disinhibition** (Clark & Watson, 1999; Gorenstein & Newman, 1980), **impulsivity** (Barratt, 1994; Dickman, 1990; Whiteside & Lynam, 2001), **ego control** (Block & Block, 1980), **constraint** (Tellegen,

1985), **sensation seeking** (Zuckerman & Kuhlman, 2000), **novelty seeking** (Cloninger et al., 1993), and **effortful control** (Rothbart et al., 2000). Naturally, impulsivity and sensation seeking are abetted by fearlessness, as the individual progressively seeks out more and more exciting experiences through sex, drugs, and, eventually, crime. Indeed, antisocial personalities are the most likely criminals to identify the "thrill" or "rush" of committing the offense as one of the primary motivators. Comorbidities among conduct disorder and ADHD in youth may represent the synergistic reinforcement of stimulus-craving to counteract inattention, distraction, and boredom (Biederman et al., 1992; Gottesman & Goldsmith, 1994; Lykken; 1995).

Aggressiveness. Verbal and physical aggressiveness are stable traits of the antisocial personality from early childhood, well into adulthood. Impulsivity no doubt contributes to these individuals' gaining a reputation for having a "hair-trigger" temper, and their associated fearlessness and love of a thrill makes them much more likely to initiate a confrontation and fight to the bitter end (Eron & Huesmann, 1984, 1990; Farrington, 1991; Huesman et al., 1984; Lykken, 1995; Olweus, 1979; Reiss & Roth, 1993).

BOX 8.1. POLICE RESPONSE TO CITIZENS WITH ANTISOCIAL PERSONALITY DISORDER/PSYCHOPATHY

Because of their frequent contact with the criminal justice system, citizens with antisocial personality disorder/psychopathy are more likely than those with other personality disorders to be encountered by law enforcement during their patrols or in response to calls for service. In these situations, officers may have to question these subjects or simply resolve low-level street disputes to keep them from flaring over into an arrestable offense (Miller, 2006f).

The first guideline for law enforcement interaction with these individuals relates to the subject's penchant for manipulation and exploitation of any encounter. Officers should be alert to the cunning-conning dimension of the glib psychopath, especially when they feel themselves "liking this guy too much." But these characters can turn abruptly violent if they don't think they're getting their way, so officers should never let down their guard.

The best approach is the most direct. If an arrestable offense has not yet occurred, clearly and firmly explain to the subject what he has to gain from cooperating with you and what he has to lose if he doesn't. Don't get into a discussion about reasons and explanations, as antisocial personalities are experts at using vague or confusing language to manipulate the conversation. Your attitude should be authoritative: not abrasive, but not too "officer friendly," either of which will invariably be seized upon as a weakness to exploit. Remember, the one thing antisocial personalities do respect is power, and if you firmly present yourself as

continued

BOX 8.1.—*Continued*

a reasonable, but no-nonsense officer, while providing the subject with a face-saving way of complying with your request without looking like a chump, he may eventually, if grudgingly, comply—often with a big grin, like the solution was all *his* idea:

> *Officer:* Look, you may have your reasons for waiting here, but I need you to move off this street corner right now. If you leave now, our business is done. If you continue to give me a hard time, I *will* arrest you for loitering and take you in. Please make your decision now so we can get on with our day.

> *Subject:* [after a tense moment, seeming to be deciding what to do, lets out a big laugh] Sure, officer, whatever you say—always want to be a good citizen who helps out the police any way I can. Catch you later, brother. [Saunters away, laughing.]

BAD BRAINS?
THE NEUROBIOLOGY OF ANTISOCIAL
PERSONALITY DISORDER/PSYCHOPATHY

When considering the relentlessly exploitive, predatory, and remorseless life histories of subjects with antisocial personality disorder/psychopathy, a common plaint is, "Why do they do it?" Recalling the dictum from Chapter 1 that any theory that explains abnormal behavior must be able to explain normal behavior, this section will endeavor to put this lifestyle pattern into a naturalistic biopsychosocial context.

Genetics

As discussed in Chapter 2, the question of behavioral genetics hinges on just what is inherited. Unlike cystic fibrosis or Huntington's disease, criminality per se is not inherited, yet the innate biological predisposition that makes a particular child more or less difficult to socialize does have strong heritable component, what Lykken (1995) has referred to as the **nature via nurture** perspective. For example, the average heritability of psychological traits is approximately 70 percent upon repeated measurement, and a highly consistent and stable trait like IQ has a heritability of up to 85 percent when corrected for instability. As discussed earlier, IQ, especially verbal IQ, is reliably found to be lower in subjects characterized by antisocial behavior and criminality. Temperamental and physical traits correlated with antisocial personality disorder and psychopathy, such as fearlessness, impulsivity, thrill-seeking, and aggressiveness, have heritability estimates between 50 percent and 70 percent (Lykken, 1995; Robins, 1966, 1978; Wilson & Herrnstein, 1985).

In some instances, the penetrance of the antisocial genetic trait complex is so robust that these children become delinquent, no matter what circumstances they are raised in. In many other cases, however, the strength of the antisocial trait complex is mediated by the effects of early family and social environment (Mishra & Lalumiere, 2008). In some cases, these gene-environmental relationships can be quite specific. For example, a genetic polymorphism on the X chromosome associated with the monoamine oxidase-A enzyme (which breaks down some catecholamine neurotransmitters; see Chapter 2) moderates the relationship between gene and environment (Caspi et al., 2002). That is, abused and maltreated children with a genotype associated with low expression of the gene (i.e., they break down these transmitters more slowly and incompletely) are significantly more likely to engage in antisocial behavior as adults than abused and maltreated individuals with a genotype associated with high expression of the gene (i.e., rapid and efficient neurotransmitter breakdown). Other gene-environment interactions have been demonstrated for the serotonin transporter gene and its effect on risk for adult mood disorder (Caspi et al., 2003). Thus, for a few "bad" children, a "good" environment won't make much of a dent in their later criminal behavior, while for a few "good" children, being raised in a "bad" environment does not necessarily doom them to a life of crime.

Neurochemistry

Clinical research into the neurobiololgy of violence typically focuses on the brain's phylogenetically older **limbic system** that mediates the basic experience and expression of emotion, motivation, and physiological arousal. The limbic structures that modulate aggression include the lateral septum, raphe nuclei, olfactory bulbs, amygdala, and parts of the hypothalamus. Serotonin is the neurotransmitter most clearly implicated in the inhibitory control of aggression. Potentiation of GABA activity also inhibits aggression. Dopamine and norepinephrine generally enhance aggression, and it is possible that the noradrenergic system modulates the relationship between serotonin and aggression by raising the preparedness of the organism to react aggressively. Strong evidence for the inhibitory role of serotonin on aggression comes from neuropharmacological studies of killing behavior in rats. In general, results from animal studies indicate that manipulations which elevate levels of brain serotonin inhibit aggressive behavior, whereas procedures that lower brain serotonin levels induce or increase aggression (Raine, 1993; Raine et al., 1995; Volavka, 1995, 1999).

Neuroendocrinology

As discussed in Chapter 2, **testosterone**, the male sex hormone, has been reliably associated with dominance and aggressive behavior, although not necessarily criminal violence. It appears to be the interaction of high testosterone (high dominance-seeking) and other factors, such as low serotonin (impaired mood stability and impulse control) that account for what we call criminal behavior, that is, what distinguishes the successful soldier, football player, or business entrepreneur from the mugger, rapist, or murderer (Birger et al., 2003; Glenn & Raine, 2008; Higley et al., 1996).

In many species, especially primates, including humans, testosterone levels interact with social factors. Individuals with a history of violent behavior often have slight elevations in testosterone, but the elevation may be a consequence of the behavior or its antecedent. That is, the influence is two-way: social factors influence levels of neurotransmitters and hormones; these substances in turn affect the animal's behavior and thus its social standing. Higher testosterone levels impel the individual to compete harder and winning the competition further increases testosterone levels. In anatomically intact animals not treated with drugs or other substances, social factors such as dominance appear to be more important than biological factors in regulating aggression, and the preponderance of social factors is more apparent in primates than in lower species (Volavka, 1995, 1999).

Some subjects with psychopathy or antisocial personality disorder show an imbalance between testosterone and cortisol, a hormone secreted by the adrenal cortex and regulated by the pituitary gland, by way of the hypothalamus, i.e., the **hypothalamo-pituitary-adrenal axis**, or **HPA** (Glenn & Raine, 2008; Van Honk & Schutter, 2006). Cortisol is released in increased amounts under conditions of stress to help mobilize the body's resources, provide energy, and reduce inflammation (Chapter 2). Psychobiologically, cortisol potentiates the fear response, sensitivity to punishment, and withdrawal behavior, rendering the organism more likely to take self-protective action. In contrast, testosterone is a product of the **hypothalamic-pituitary-gonadal (HPG) axis** and is associated with approach-related behavior, reward-sensitivity, and fear reduction. Thus, testosterone and cortisol have mutually antagonistic properties, cortisol suppressing the activity of the HPG axis, diminishing testosterone production and inhibiting its effects, while testosterone, in turn, inhibits activity of the HPA axis. The precise ratio of these hormones at any given time will be determined by the nature of the environmental stressor (dominance challenge versus imminent danger) and by the psychobiological makeup of the individuals involved.

For example, overall higher testosterone-to-cortisol ratios are generally found in antisocial and aggressive boys and girls, and these biochemical findings are associated with a variety of antisocial behaviors including employment difficulty, chronic lawbreaking, marriage failure, drug and alcohol abuse, and violent behavior. Whether this hormonal relationship is specific to those with a diagnosis of psychopathy or antisocial personality disorder, however, remains unclear (Glenn & Raine, 2008).

Psychophysiology

Hare's (1970) original **underarousal theory of psychopathy** postulated that psychopaths have a pathologically low level of endogenous autonomic and cortical arousal, which impels them toward sensation-seeking behavior, including antisocial behavior, to compensate; that is, they are driven to seek or create their own thrills to keep themselves sufficiently aroused and amused. Since then, this finding has been largely confirmed by other researchers (Lykken, 1995; Raine, 1990, 1993; Vien & Beech, 2006). The two most common psychophysiological research methods are the **electroencephalogram** (**EEG**), which measures the brain's ongoing electrical activity, and the **evoked potential** (**EP**) which measures how the nervous system processes perceptual stimuli.

One of the most frequently observed EEG abnormalities associated with violence consists of excessive slow-wave **theta** activity, an abnormality consistent with the underarousal theory of psychopathy (Hare, 1970; Raine et al., 1995; Williams, 1969). One early prospective study (Raine et al., 1990) measured resting skin conductance, heart rate, EP, and EEG activity (all indices of psychophysiological arousal) in 101 15-year-old schoolboys. Nine years later, at age 24, those boys who had the lowest measures of arousal had become criminal men and continued to show significantly lower resting heart rate, reduced skin conductance activity, and more slow-frequency EEG theta activity than noncriminals. They also showed longer-latency EP responses, indicating a higher-set filtering mechanism for environmental stimuli, again consistent with endogenous low arousal and a tendency to compensate by increased sensation-seeking behavior (Raine et al., 1990; Zuckerman, 1979, 1990).

Neuropsychological Studies

An indirect behavior measure of brain functioning comes from analyzing a subject's performance on specialized **neuropsychological tests**, which assess attention, concentration, memory, language skills, spatial reasoning, sensorimotor functioning, cognitive processing speed, abstract conceptualization, and problem-solving skills. These tests are not just used for research, but are commonly utilized in the clinical assessment of patients with neurological or neuropsychiatric disorders. Many of these measures were developed and used before the advent of sophisticated neuroimaging technologies.

A number of such studies have observed that neuropsychological deficits in violently antisocial offenders tend to involve primarily left hemisphere functions of language, verbal comprehension, verbal reasoning, and expressive speech articulation. This is consistent with a large number of early and more recent studies on delinquent and conduct disordered children which suggest that the observed lowered IQ in these groups is primarily a function of lowered Verbal (left hemisphere) IQ, as opposed to lowered performance, or spatial (right hemisphere) IQ (Brickman et al., 1984; Hart, 1987; Mungas, 1988; Tarter et al., 1984; Moffitt, 1990a; Raine et al., 1995).

For example, on neuropsychological testing, adjudicated male delinquents were found to be impaired in their ability to comprehend, manipulate, and utilize conceptual material (Berman & Seigal, 1976). Violent male penitentiary prisoners were more impaired than nonviolent prisoners on measures of cognitive, language, perceptual, and psychomotor abilities (Spellacy, 1978), and assaultive delinquents had a greater number of EEG abnormalities, poorer verbal memory, and increased perseveration, as compared with nonassaultive delinquents (Krynicki, 1978). The significant finding of frontal-like impairment in another series of delinquents led to the hypothesis that antisocial individuals have particular problems in planning their actions, perceiving the consequences of those actions, and altering those actions in the face of changing circumstances (Yeudall et al., 1982). The presence of frontal-like deficits was further established in a group of adult psychopaths, using a variety of neuropsychological measures (Gorenstein, 1982).

More impulsive, assaultive subjects in an adult, male prison population showed significant impairment, compared to less violent prisoners, on tasks requiring complex integration of information from the visual, auditory, and somatosensory processing systems, as well as impaired ability to create, plan, organize, and execute goal-directed behaviors and to sustain attention and concentration, similar to findings with organic frontal lobe patients (Bryant et al., 1984). This work was replicated in a nonprison population, showing that diagnosed psychopathic inpatients at a Veterans Administration alcohol and drug treatment program performed more poorly than nonpsychopathic inpatients on a variety of measures sensitive to frontal lobe impairment, even when overall IQ was controlled for (Sutker & Allain, 1987). Overall replication of this neuropsychological research has not been unanimous (Hare, 1984, 1986), but the bulk of the data support the hypothesis of predominant

left hemisphere and **frontal lobe** neuropsychological impairment in non-brain injured, but impulsively antisocial populations (Miller, 1987, 1988c, 1990a,b, 1998a). The question is whether this applies to the more cognitively intact Clecklyian psychopath.

In conceptualizing these findings, most researchers do not assert that characterologically impulsive, antisocial individuals have injured frontal lobes in the same pathophysiological sense as a stroke, gunshot, or head trauma concussion victim (although they may be at risk for, and have sustained, actual brain injuries due to their risky, confrontational lifestyle). Rather, chronically antisocial subjects most likely possess a particular constitutional neuropsychodynamic organization underlying their impulsive cognitive style, one important component of which is an underdevelopment of, or deficiency in, frontal lobe control over behavior. To the extent that this neuropsychodynamic pattern affects test performance, we may see frontal-like deficits on some neuropsychological measures, as well as in their general behavior. Further exogenous damage to the brain, especially to orbitofrontal and ventral-prefrontal brain regions, through fights and risk-taking accidents would only worsen this disinhibitory condition, a circumstance further aggravated by the well-known tendency of antisocial/psychopathic subjects to abuse drugs and alcohol (Baker et al., 1997; Dinn et al., 2009; Fulwiler & Ruthazer, 1999; Fulwiler et al., 1997, 2005; Gorenstein & Newman, 1990; Kreutzer et al., 1995; Miller, 1987, 1988c, 1989a, 1990a,b,c, 1992b; Moffitt & Henry, 1991; Mungas, 1983; Northoff et al., 2000; O'Doherty et al., 2001; Rolls, 1995, 1998; Rosenbaum & Hoge, 1989; Wildgruber et al., 2004).

Structural and Functional Neuroimaging

As we've seen, much of the discussion about the neuropsychology of the psychopath relates to its similarities and differences vis-à-vis antisocial personality disorder. The impulsivity trait of psychopathy would seem to imply a decrement in frontal lobe functions of anticipating, planning, sustaining, and inhibiting behavior, commonly observed in antisocial subjects with multiple offenses. However, the cunning-conning dimension of psychopathy would almost seem to imply the opposite: frontal lobes that are working only too well, albeit in the service of deception and manipulation (see also Chapter 10). To complicate matters further, many neuropsychological studies conflate the concepts and terminology of psychopathy and antisocial personality disorder, so the study subjects probably include individuals from both categories. The final question is: "So, what?" which is a conundrum that applies to all brain studies of psychopathological syndromes. That is, the mere presence of abnormal findings–in the brain or anywhere else–does not by itself explain the phenomenology of the behavior without a clear conceptual framework to give those findings a clinical and forensic context. Nevertheless, neuropsychological and neuroimaging studies have yielded some intriguing clues.

Brain imaging research that utilizes such techniques as **computerized tomography (CT)**, **magnetic resonance imaging (MRI)**, **regional cerebral blood flow (rCBF)**, **positron emission tomography (PET)**, and **functional magnetic resonance imaging (fMRI)** allows direct assessment of structural and functional brain abnormalities, and thereby provides an additional methodology for studying neurobiological factors that predispose to violent and aggressive behavior (Raine et al., 1995).

As noted above and in Chapter 2, neuropsychological research has shown that the **frontal lobes** of the brain are crucially involved in behavioral self-awareness and self-control, while the **temporal lobes** contain many of the limbic structures that mediate emotional and motivation states such as sexuality and aggression (Miller, 1987, 1994b; Volavka, 1995, 1999). Mills & Raine (1994) reviewed 20 brain imaging studies using CT, MRI, rCBF, and PET, in the study of violent and sexual offending. Based on these findings, the authors concluded that: (1) there is a tendency for frontal lobe dysfunction to be associated with violent offending such as murder; (2) temporal lobe dysfunction may be more associated with nonviolent sexual offending including nonforced incest and pedophilia; and (3) frontotemporal dysfunction may be associated with combined violent and sexual offending, such as forcible rape.

The authors hypothesize the existence of a continuum, with frontal dysfunction and violence at one end, and temporal dysfunction and sexual offending at the other. The middle of this continuum may involve some degree of both temporal and frontal dysfunction, and a mix of both sexual and violent behavior. Subsequent study has shown both violent and sexual samples to have frontotemporal dysfunction, including one study which used a sample made up almost evenly of rapists and incest offenders/pedophiles (Wright et al., 1990). Another study (Volkow & Tancredi, 1987) revealed frontal dysfunction in violent individuals who had no remorse for their actions, a prominent personality trait of psychopaths, which suggests that psychopathy may also be represented at the frontal end of the continuum (Mills & Raine, 1994).

The neuroethologically-based categorization of aggressive acts into predatory vs. affective (also see below) was studied in human murderers by Raine et al. (1998) who assessed glucose metabolism (a measure of regional brain activity) using PET in 15 predatory murderers, nine affective murderers, and 41 controls in left and right hemisphere prefrontal (medial and lateral) and subcortical (amygdala, midbrain, hippocampus, and thalamus) regions. The key findings in this study were: (1) **affective murderers** had lower prefrontal activity and higher subcortical activity than comparison groups; (2) **predatory murderers** had prefrontal activity levels similar to comparisons, but excessive subcortical activity; and (3) the excessive subcortical activity in both affective and predatory murderers was restricted to the right hemisphere (Raine et al., 1998).

The results support the hypothesis that emotional, impulsive murderers are less able to regulate and control aggressive impulses generated from subcortical limbic structures due to deficient frontal lobe regulation. The authors hypothesize that excessive subcortical activity predisposes to aggressive behavior, but that affective and predatory murderers differ in terms of the regulatory cortical control they exert over aggressive impulses. While the predatory violent offenders have sufficient left frontal lobe functioning to modulate such aggressive behavior so as to intimidate, deceive, and manipulate others to achieve desired goals, affectively violent offenders lack this prefrontal modulatory control over their impulses, resulting in more unbridled, dysregulated, aggressive outbursts (Raine et al., 1998).

More recent neuroimaging and functional metabolic studies of antisocial/psychopathic subjects have found a number of brain regions to show abnormalities, including the the orbitomedial, basolateral, posteromedial, and dorsolateral prefrontal cortex, anterior and posterior cingulate cortex, the amygdala, hippocampal formation, parahippocampal gyrus, ventral striatum, reticular activating system, septum, dorsomedial and anterior thalamic nuclei, and ventromedial hypothalamus (Blair, 2005; Glenn & Raine, 2008; Goodman et al., 2007; Hall, 1993; Kiehl, 2006; Palermo, 2009; Raine et al., 2004; Volavka, 1995). Again, with such a mounting catalog of affected brain regions, the "so, what?" question needs to be addressed.

Theoretically, it has been postulated that impaired **amygdala** functioning might disrupt the ability to form stimulus-reinforcement associations, impairing the ability to connect one's harmful actions with the victim's pain and distress and to attend to emotional stimuli, which underlies empathy for victims. For example, amygdala dysfunction has been associated with deficits in aversive conditioning, recognition of fearful facial expression, passive avoidance learning, and augmentation of the startle reflex by visual threat primes (Blair, 2006; Glenn & Raine, 2008). However, far from being emotionally clueless (perhaps more characteristic of subjects with schizoid personality disorder; see Chapter 7), many psychopaths are exquisitely attuned to others' emotional states, which they use to manipulate and torment their victims, either because they don't care or they sadistically enjoy the infliction of pain.

The **hippocampi** are involved in the learning and consolidation of information. The finding of asymmetries within the hippocampus in "unsuccessful," i.e., caught and convicted, psychopaths leads Raine et al. (2004) to postulate that hippocampal dysfunction may result in affect dysregulation, poor contextual fear conditioning, and insensitivity to the cues that might have allowed the subject to anticipate and evade capture.

Integration and Theory

Some researchers have attempted to tie together the diverse threads of evidence from psychobiological studies of antisocial behavior. For example, Elliott (1992) delineates the neuropsychological substrate of aggressive psychopathy as consisting of nonspecific EEG abnormalities, resistance to aversive conditioning, low levels of serotonin metabolites in the cerebrospinal fluid of adult psychopaths, low levels of serotonin in the platelets of children with aggressive conduct disorder, the presence of minor neurologic abnormalities, or "soft signs," and impairment on neuropsychological testing.

Van Honk & Schutter (2006) propose that higher levels of cortisol enhance communication between subcortical and cortical brain regions and strengthen cortical control over subcortical drives. In contrast, higher levels of testosterone inhibit this kind subcortical-cortical cross-talk. Thus, the lower-than-normal cortisol levels and higher-than-normal testosterone levels found in many antisocial/psychopaths may underlie a decoupling of cortical control over subcortically-mediated drives, resulting in higher rates of impulsive antisocial behavior. Again, this emphasis on the impulsivity dimension fails to explain why many psychopaths can bide their time until the moment arrives when they can exact their "cold-blooded" predation or revenge, and also overlooks the fact that the sadistic infliction of pain is precisely the motive of many antisocial criminal acts.

EVOLUTIONARY PSYCHOLOGY OF ANTISOCIAL PERSONALITY DISORDER/PSYCHOPATHY

Aggression: Affective and Predatory

As noted above and in Chapters 2 and 10, in the ethological and neuropsychological literature on aggression, one of the most widely validated behavioral and psychobiological distinctions is that between **affective aggression** and **predatory aggression** (Eichelman, 1992; Eichelman et al., 1993; Meloy, 1997b; Volavka, 1995). Affective aggression involves high states of emotional and physiological arousal and typically occurs in ritualized intraspecies fighting for food, territory, mates, and social status. Since the usual purpose of affective aggression is to intimidate and dominate within an established social structure, serious physical injury usually does not occur, and actual death of one of the combatants is rare and probably accidental. Predatory violence is more "cold-blooded," involves low emotional and physiological arousal, usually requires some degree of preparatory stalking, and typically occurs across species, usually between hunter and prey, with the goal clearly being to kill and consume the prey animal for sustenance, not out of hatred or revenge. In humans, affective and predatory aggression can be admixed, with the additional enhancement of more complex planning and socialization.

A long tradition of experimental brain research on cats (the quintessential lone predator) has demonstrated separate neurophysiological pathways mediating predatory versus affective aggression (Siegel & Pott, 1988). In human children, "**reactive aggressives**" were found to be much more likely to have a history of physical abuse and social information processing deficits than "**proactive aggressives**" (Dodge et al., 1997). Adult criminals diagnosed as psychopaths are more likely to engage in predatory aggression than nonpsychopathic criminals, who commit more affectively violent acts (Meloy, 1992, 1997b; Serin, 1991; Williamson et al., 1987). Neurophysiologically, human affective-impulsive violent offenders differ from controls on electrophysiological and neuropsychological test measures of impaired information processing (Barratt et al., 1997) and in having lower levels of serotonin and monoamine oxidase A (Coccaro et al., 1996; Virkunnen et al., 1995; Volavka, 1999).

Recall that neither affective-impulsive nor predatory forms of aggression are "pathological" in animal species; on the contrary, such creatures couldn't survive without these traits. Even in humans, normal ranges of these traits have been documented. Barratt et al. (1999) asked a group of 216 college students to assess their own aggressive acts using a specially designed anonymous self-report questionnaire. The results identified four factors associated with aggressive behavior: (1) impulsive aggression; (2) mood on the day the act occurred; (3) premeditated aggression; and (4) agitation. Thus, impulsive and premeditated (i.e., affective and predatory) aggression were found to be independent constructs that exist in varying degrees among these otherwise normal college students. In this study, impulsive aggression was characterized in part by feelings of remorse following the acts and by thought confusion. Premeditated aggression was related to more purposeful social gain and dominance.

According to the principles of **evolutionary psychology** (Lykken, 1995; Mishra & Lalumiere, 2008), just as our human species evolved an innate readiness for learning language, so we evolved a predisposition for learning and obeying basic social rules, for nurturing our children and helping our neighbors, and for making a contribution to the group effort for survival. But, like the ability to acquire language, our innate readiness to become socialized in these ways must be elicited, developed, and practiced during childhood, within the context of our families and communities. Further, like language, these influences probably have their greatest effect during certain early **critical periods** in development.

In the resource-scarce world in which ancestral human evolved, access to food, mates, tools, shelter, and other resources necessary for survival and procreation necessitated a cyclical combination of cooperation and competition within small, close-knit tribal and family groups. As today, individuals differed in regard to their innate and acquired propensities for cooperation versus competition. Children who were adequately socialized grew up to be balanced adults–willing to cooperate with others in hunting, defense, or equitable resource-sharing, but able to stand up for themselves in response to efforts to cheat or exploit them. Some individuals may have been unusually accommodating; these group members were unlikely to provoke aggression on the part of their tribe-mates, but might be easy targets for exploitation by others. At the other end of the personality spectrum, certain tough or selfish characters seemed to only be out for themselves and to be willing to cajole, manipulate, exploit, or physically attack others in order to get their way. Some of these individuals may have been born with difficult-to-socialize temperaments, showing all the risk factors for antisocial behavior described above; today, we would call these individuals **psychopaths**. Others may have started out with relatively normal temperaments, but were raised under neglectful or abusive conditions and therefore never acquired the adequate socialization to make them functional members of the group; these individuals might better be characterized as **sociopaths** (Lykken, 1995; Mishra & Lalumiere, 2008).

We know that the peak age for young males to engage in risky and aggressive behavior is18 to 24 because that is the age range when these young men are most likely to be consolidating their identity and status within their particular community or subculture and most likely to be competing for mates and other resources (Chapters 3 and 19). Young males compete not only with each other but also with older males who have had more time to accumulate skills, resources, and status, which are features important to female mate choice. The costs of failing to confront other males and to take risks in the service of status-consolidation may be dire, as in most preindustrial societies there is a very finite amount of these resources. Risky and aggressive behavior by young males may thus serve as a signal of qualities desirable to females, such as health, attractiveness, and ability to extract resources from the environment, and may intimidate other males from challenging one's status. In these cases, the behavior is not so much "anti-" social as it is a matter of taking advantage of the social milieu to get oneself situated at a comfortable status rank. It is only when one's self-centered exploitation and/or aggression outweighs one's relative contribution to the group's welfare that this behavior becomes truly antisocial (Hill & Chow, 2002; Lalumiere & Quincy, 2000; Mishra & Lalumiere, 2008; Wilson & Daly, 1985).

Some modern-day statistics support this evolutionary conceptualization (Fagot et al., 1998; Gray et al., 2002; Mishra & Lalumiere, 2008; Quinsey et al., 2001; Serbin et al., 1998; Stouthamer-Loeber & Wei, 1998). In many studies, age at first intercourse is strongly related to indicators of antisocial tendencies. For example, teenage fathers (i.e., precociously reproductive young males) are more likely to be characterized by low socioeconomic status and parental antisociality, and to have committed serious crimes by a relatively young age. For females, early childhood aggression predicts early age of pregnancy and motherhood. Antisocial men are more likely to utilize sexual coercion, aggression, or deception in the pursuit of mating opportunities. Gang leaders and other dominant males enjoy increased access to sexual partners, and young males are more likely to engage in risky behavior when in the presence of peers. In later adulthood, the adaptive imperative shifts from competing for mates to raising offspring, associated, for most males, with a decline in criminal and risky behavior (**"cad versus dad"**). However, for the true psychopath, antisocial behavior may persist for a lifetime because it is, in fact, a lifestyle. As long as these individuals can force or wheedle out of others what they need to survive and reproduce, there will always be some of their number among the more socialized majority of society's members.

BOX 8.2. THE "SUCCESSFUL PSYCHOPATH"

Although we may hate to admit it, many people get a vicarious thrill through identifying with the kind of conscienceless power that the psychopath projects, even if we could never bring ourselves to perpetrate some of more odious acts of these characters. Why do you think gangster shows and movies are such a hit, and how else do you explain the morbid fascination with serial killers and sex offenders (see Chapters 10, 14, 15)? But even staying within the law, colorful fictional or true-life depictions of clever psychopaths who manipulate the rules, game the system, and get away with it, are often the subject of guilty envy and admiration (Hall & Benning, 2005). One thinks of Gordon Gekko in *Wall Street,* J.R. Ewing in *Dallas,* Detective Vic Mackey of *The Shield,* and of course, Don Corleone and his son Michael of *The Godfather* fame.

Indeed, not all psychopaths are violent and incarcerated criminals. Some are untrustworthy and unreliable employees or unscrupulous and predatory busi-

continued

BOX 8.2.—*Continued*

nessmen, corrupt politicians, "white-collar" criminals, unethical or immoral doctors, lawyers, clergypersons, or law enforcement officers, who victimize their patients, clients, parishioners, and the general public. These are the "successful
psychopaths," i.e., those who exemplify the essential personality characteristics
of psychopathy, but who manage to skirt the edges of serious antisocial behavior
and legal trouble—until they're caught (Babiak, 1995; Hall & Benning, 2005; Hare,
2003; Leap, 2007; Smith, 1978; Vien & Beech, 2006; Widom, 1977).

In his iconic volume, Cleckley (1941, 1988) presented several case histories
of prominent members of society, including physicians, businessmen, and political figures who managed to cheat, plagiarize, and manipulate themselves into
positions of wealth and authority. These accounts of the "successful psychopath"
have been followed by more recent examples, all of whom have displayed the
hallmarks of the Cleckley-Hare psychopath: superficial charm, egocentricity, manipulativeness, parasitic lifestyle, irresponsibility, and lack of remorse (Babiak,
1995; Hall & Benning, 2005).

The following example of a high-functioning psychopath is a composite of
several cases I have evaluated in the context of both criminal and civil trials
(Miller, 2008c).

The Case of the Dastardly Doctor

You don't get to the top of the medical management game by being a wuss,
Carl told himself. Like any business, it was eat or be eaten. He always knew he
was a smart operator: he had brains and knew how to use them to get ahead. He
sailed through college and medical school—partly because of his native intelligence, partly because of devising new and cleverer ways to cheat on exams.

In medical school, he was almost expelled twice for cheating, but managed to
fast-talk his way out of the jams. While in med school, he ran an online travel
agency and some other businesses that were eventually shut down by authorities.
Although bright, he was involved in so many outside activities that he graduated
med school with only average grades. He took his residency in orthopedics,
already with an eye to setting up a chain of rehab clinics.

He opened his first clinic with a bank loan and, with his charm and enthusiasm, was soon attracting a steady stream of patients, many from attorneys representing Workers Comp and other insurance cases who were seeking quick disability determinations for their clients so they could collect cash settlements. This
quickly evolved into an illegal kickback scheme with several disreputable attorneys, generating fraudulent disability reports for insurance collections.

The money was pouring in, and Carl soon opened a second, then a third clinic, expanding his insurance fraud operation, even while doing a fair share of legitimate, good-quality rehabilitation, largely through the efforts of his dedicated
physical therapy staff. Cracks in the operation started appearing when Carl told
his staff that he expected their clinical notes to be written so as to highlight dis-

ability, whether present or not. Staff who balked at this record-tampering scheme were either bribed to comply or forced to resign.

But why stop with insurance profits? Medication management is an important part of rehabilitation, and Carl soon had a lucrative side-business as a narcotic pill-pushing "candyman" to a steady stream of selectively referred chronic pain patients. This expanded with the opening of several more pill-mill operations, with customers streaming in from across the state and around the country. With all his profits, licit and illicit, Carl invested in real estate and securities and was quickly becoming a wealthy man. He was poised to open several more clinics, when the hammer fell.

One of his pain-pill patients died of an overdose and the family sued. One investigation led to another, and within a matter of months, Carl was the subject of numerous criminal charges and additional civil lawsuits. With characteristic cunning and aplomb, Carl and his lawyers managed to work out a deal whereby he would avoid jail time and pay a combined settlement in exchange for surrendering his state medical license and divesting his stake in his clinics, which were sold off to a huge national medical management chain.

Which gave Carl another idea: even without a medical license, he still understood the business end of health care and, through a combination of intelligence and guile, quickly fast-tracked himself an online Master of Healthcare Business Administration degree. He then pitched himself to the board of another major medical management company, a rival of the firm that had bought his clinics. He got himself hired as a district manager, and it wasn't long before he rose to the rank of executive vice president of the corporation. He proved to be especially good at acquiring and expanding existing facilities and opening up new ones. The awards, bonuses, and accolades poured in, and Carl was soon the wealthy hero of the organization.

What his back-slapping corporate comrades didn't know, however, was that Carl was operating another string of insurance scams and pill-pushing clinics under a pseudonymous company name in another state. When this latest deception was discovered, it all came crashing down. Carl had simply spread himself too thin and no amount of cleverness or money could get him out of this one. Carl is now serving a prison term and, not surprisingly, continues to operate several, albeit more modest, businesses from his new address.

CRIMINAL JUSTICE ISSUES OF ANTISOCIAL PERSONALITY DISORDER/PSYCHOPATHY

As with other personality disorders (Chapter 7), a diagnosis of psychopathy or antisocial personality disorder is virtually never successfully invoked as an affirmative insanity defense or grounds for diminished capacity. If anything, depictions of the heartless, ruthless, predatory, and sadistic behavior of such a defendant is far more likely to be considered an aggra-vating factor at sentencing, seen as rendering the defendant impervious to rehabilitation and at especially high risk for reoffending (Palermo, 2009). However, for most noncapital crimes, these individuals will eventually be released from incarceration, and most will fairly quickly pick up their anti-social activities where they left off, with nothing for law enforcement and criminal justice authorities to do but wait to catch them next time.

Some dissenting voices (Morse, 2008; Zavaliy, 2008) have recommend-ed utilizing the weight of genetic and psychobiological data as evidence that psychopaths are truly incapable of controlling their behavior or understand-ing the true nature and quality of their actions, and are thus essentially "incurable." Far from resulting in their release, however, these authors rec-ommend using that information as grounds for indefinite preventive deten-tion, as with some dangerous offenders, sex offenders, and drug addicts (*Foucha v. Louisiana,* 1992; *Jones v. United States,* 1983; *Kansas v. Crane,* 2002; *Kansas v. Hendricks,* 1997). To date, this argument has yet to be presented in an actual court case, but it would be fascinating to hear the court's ruling on such a matter, as it would open up an entire new universe of implications and complications for the "bad brain" defense (see also Chapters 2 and 4).

SUMMARY AND CONCLUSIONS

There have always been a small subset of incorrigibly exploitive and predatory members of every human society. **Antisocial personality disor-der** and **psychopathy** appear to be overlapping clinical concepts, with some distinctions, largely in the areas of impulsivity and social deviance charac-terizing the DSM-4-TR antisocial personality disorder, with callous grandios-ity and glib manipulativeness more associated with the Cleckleyian psy-chopath. The antisocial/psychopath pattern begins in childhood as **conduct disorder**, reaches a peak of offending in adolescence and early adulthood, and in the majority of cases, persists throughout the lifespan into old age.

Antisocial/psychopathic subjects are characterized by a completely self-centered world view, lack of empathy for others, and a craving for immedi-ate gratification, with little or no frustration tolerance. They have an exces-sive need for stimulation and excitement, a seeming imperviousness to pun-ishment, and their behavior is impulsive, erratic, and characterized by diffi-culty in sustaining any long-term goal-directed behavior. Antisocial behavior runs in families and is associated with a number of genetic, neurochemical, electrophysiological, and neuropsychological markers, but, as yet, no distinct psychobiological "antisocial fingerprint." Their deficiencies in verbal intelligence and problem-solving skills seemingly implicates left hemisphere and frontal lobe dysfunction, but this may be more the case for antisocial personality disorder than for the classic Cleckleyian psychopath, whose keen cunning and conning seem to suggest especially good cognitive skills, at least in some areas.

Antisocial behavior persists within human populations because, in less severe forms, it may be associated with boldness, assertiveness, and aggressive extraction of resources from the environment, leading to high reproductive success, the latter characterizing even otherwise dysfunctional antisocial/psychopathic subjects (i.e., there's "one thing" they know how to do right). Some psychopaths are "successful" in terms of using their aggressive cleverness to amass great wealth and power, often brought down, however, by their impulsive thrill-seeking or narcissistic overreaching.

Given the relentless intractability of antisocial behavior in these subjects, some authorities have recommended civil commitment of psychopathic/antisocial offenders, similar to that with sex offenders or other "incurable criminals." The challenge of early identification and management of such individuals is often stymied by a lingering sociological mythology that all children are the same and that anyone can be salvaged from a life of crime, which all evidence suggests is not the case. There are indeed bad boys (and a few girls) who become bad men (and a few women), and we have not as a society formulated a coherent policy to deal with them.

Part III

The Homicides

Chapters 9–13 deal with death. Homicide is perhaps the quintessential crime because it involves depriving a person of his or her very existence. Even more tragic is that most people will be killed by a person they know, and the trigger is typically a petty argument or dispute that escalates out control and that is rendered lethal by the availability of modern weapons. Serial and mass homicides, however, are typically crimes against strangers. The perpetrator of serial sexual homicide kills to achieve maximal sexual gratification from stalking, capturing, torturing, mutilating, and murdering another human being. Those who commit mass murder in schools and workplaces may know some of their victims, but don't care if strangers die, as long as the body count is high. While these individuals typically feel justified in meting out payback for real or imagined offenses against them, terrorists go a step further and invoke some ideological mandate for their violence, a psychological rationalization that allows them to feel righteous in the act of shedding blood. At least the serial killer doesn't pretend to have any deeper motive or higher purpose for his atrocities; he simply feels narcissistically entitled to torture and kill people because it makes him feel good.

Chapter 9

Homicide

Hell of a thing, killing a man; taking away
everything he has or ever will have.
       – Clint Eastwood as William Munny
        in *Unforgiven,* 1992

This section of the text starts with homicide because the willful and illegitimate taking of another person's life is regarded by most members of the public as the quintessential crime–just check out the TV crime shows. Tens of thousands of people are murdered in the United States annually, and the crime of murder is most often perpetrated by offenders using firearms. Murder victims and offenders come from all walks of life, but certain groups and individuals are at higher risk for involvement than others, such as family members, intimates, youth gang members, work associates, minorities, and those residing in high crime areas (Flowers, 2002a,b,c; Kitaeff, 2011).

DEFINITIONS OF HOMICIDE

Homicide is not necessarily against the law. The term **homicide** originated sometime in the fourteenth century from the Latin *homicidium,* a word composed of *homo,* meaning man, and *cidium* deriving from the verb *caedo,* which means to cut or to kill. The term **murder** originated earlier, sometime before the twelfth century, in part from the Middle English *murther* which means to kill someone without justification or reason. Although the terms homicide and murder are commonly conflated in both professional discourse and popular discussion, homicide is defined simply as the killing of one human being by another, without any particular attribution of blame or motive, whereas murder is the crime of *unlawfully* killing a person, especially with malice aforethought (Flowers, 2002c; Palermo & Kocsis, 2005).

In fact, the law recognizes a variety of categories of homicide, each with their own attribution of psychological motive and responsibility, and each having a distinct legal definition with respect to adjudication and punishment (Flowers, 2002c; Kitaeff, 2011). What is intriguing about these categories is how closely criminal justice concepts track the cognitive psychology of motivation and intent.

Homicide is the killing of one human being by another. Being killed by an animal, machine (unless directed by another person), disease, or act of nature, no matter how gruesome or tragic, is not homicide. Homicide may or may not constitute a crime, depending on the circumstances.

Prosecutable Homicides

Murder: the unlawful killing of one human being by another. There are two basic types of murder in law.

First-degree murder: killing that is willful, deliberate, and premeditated. The killer plans to commit the unlawful homicide (**malice aforethought**) and carries it out with full knowledge and intention of the act. *Example:* a cheated-upon husband lies in wait for his wife and her lover to return home, then leaps from the closet and stabs them both to death.

Second-degree murder: killing that is malicious and/or reckless without premeditation or necessarily with intent to kill. *Example:* a robber holds up a convenience store, grapples with the counter clerk, and in the struggle, shoots the clerk to death, later claiming "I didn't mean to hurt anybody, he just should have given me the money."

Manslaughter: the unlawful killing of a human being without express or implied malice. There are two types of manslaughter.

Voluntary manslaughter: killing that takes place in the heat of anger and is not premeditated or committed with malice–the classic "crime of passion." The killing occurs impulsively and spontaneously, but is still seen to have been within the free will of the killer. *Example:* during a domestic argument, the wife says something that is perceived as insulting to the husband, and he flies into a rage, picks up a lamp and strikes her in the head, killing her.

Involuntary manslaughter: killing due to negligence, defined as failure to perform a legal duty expressly required or requested to safeguard human life, from the commission of an unlawful act not considered a felony, or from the commission of a lawful act in a negligent or improper manner. *Example:* To cut overhead costs, a restaurant manager knowingly fails to follow industry standards for cleaning and sterilizing cooking and serving utensils, and several customers contract hepatitis B, one dying of the disease.

Vehicular homicide: the killing of one person by another through criminal negligence during the operation of a motor vehicle. *Example:* Racing home from a party, a woman tries to beat a red light at an intersection and runs over an elderly pedestrian, killing him. Note that there is no intention to kill or harm anyone with the vehicle; if the woman had been deliberately trying to run down her hated mother-in-law with the car, the crime would be classified as murder (Flowers, 2002c).

Nonprosecutable Homicides

Justifiable homicide: killing that has legal justification. *Example:* After giving fair warning to back off and leave, a homeowner uses a lawfully owned firearm to shoot an intruder who persists in threatening the home owner's family.

Excusable homicide: a completely accidental or unintentional killing without blame or fault on the part of the killer. *Example:* Despite clearly posted warning signs and barriers, some truant school kids manage to scale a fence and trespass onto a construction site, and one of them is electrocuted by an exposed cable.

Victim Subtyping of Homicides

Familicide: killing of all or most of a person's family or close relatives.
Filicide: killing of one's own child by a parent.
Feticide: killing of an unborn fetus.
Infanticide: killing of infant, usually by a parent.
Parricide: killing of one's parent.
Patricide: killing of one's father.
Matricide: killing of one's mother.
Fratricide: killing of one's brother.
Sororicide: killing of one's sister.
Uxoricide: killing of a wife by her husband.
Mariticide: killing of a husband by his wife.
Multicide: killing of two or more people.
Serial homicide: killing of at least three people over an extended period of time, with a cooling-off period between the homicides.
Mass homicide: killing of four or more victims at a single time and place.
Suicide: killing oneself. In many jurisdictions, this is still technically considered a crime (Flowers, 2002c).

SINGLE, MULTIPLE, SERIAL, AND MASS HOMICIDES

The majority of murders can be classified into two distinct types: **single homicides** and **multiple homicides**, the latter including three subgroups:

serial killers, mass killers, and spree killers (Chaiken et al, 1994; Douglas et al, 1992; Ferguson et al, 2003; Fox & Levin, 2003; Hickey, 2003; La Brode, 2007). The essential differences between these classifications pertain to the time course of the killings and the time lag (or cooling-off period) between them. Although frightening, multiple homicides comprise only 3 percent to 4 percent of total homicides in the United States (Fox & Zawitz, 2003).

Single Homicides

The majority of homicides are spontaneous acts, usually between family members, friends, and acquaintances, triggered by quarrels and other stress-ful events and often associated with substance abuse (Flowers, 2002c; Palermo & Kocsis, 2005; Schlesinger & Miller, 2003). In fact, homicide in general is not typically a repeat crime because the vast majority of murders occur under a unique set of precipitating and triggering circumstances unlikely to be duplicated (Revitch & Schlesinger, 1981a). The single homi-cide offender is usually more of an emotional reactor, and his offense is more likely to be the outcome of a loss of control under the effect of interpersonal conflict and strong emotion. The average age of the homicide offender varies from 14 to 34. He is often married or lives at home with his parents, and is more socially involved than the serial offender (Flowers, 2002c; Palermo & Kocsis, 2005).

Serial Homicide

Serial killers murder at least three victims during an extended period of time, spanning years to decades, with cooling-off periods between the mur-ders, indicating premeditation of each killing. There may be extended breaks of months or years between spates of frequent killing. The murders usually are done alone, although some serial killers use an accomplice, and there have been several cases of serial killer couples or teams (Chapter 10).

Spree Killers

Spree killers murder their victims at two or more locations, spanning a shorter period of time, usually involving hours to days to weeks, and in con-cert with other criminal activity, such as "Bonnie and Clyde"-type crime sprees.

Mass Murderers

Mass murderers kill four or more victims at a single time and place. Examples include most workplace and school violence incidents (Chapters 11 and 12). The fantasies and plots of mass murderers tend to involve revenge against actual or imagined persecutors. Whereas the torture and murder activities of serial killers tend to be slow and close-up, involving low-tech weapons that gouge, flay, or strangle, the typical goal of mass murderers is to kill many as many victims as possible, quickly, efficiently, and at once, using the highest level of lethal technology available to them to do the most damage–handguns, assault weapons, explosives, arson, etc. Although mass murders account for only a relatively small number of homicides in the United States, their psychological effects on the surrounding communities can be devastating (Dietz, 1986; Gore-Felton et al, 1999; Johnson et al, 2002; Meloy, 1997; North et al, 1994; Palermo, 1997; Simon, 1996).

Types of mass murderers. According to Holmes & Holmes (1992), there are five types of mass murderers:

Disciples commit mass murder after being ordered to kill by a persuasive, dominating leader. Many acts of terroristic violence fall into this category (Chapter 13).

Family annihilators murder most or all of their family. They are often the family patriarch or oldest son with a history of depression and substance abuse (Chapter 16).

Pseudocommandos are usually single assailants who stockpile weapons of mass murder, then target a particular place to carry out a military-style assault.

Disgruntled employees target a current or former place of work and commit mass murder against a supervisor and other employees they may hold a grudge against, while also killing others randomly or as "collateral damage" (Chapter 11).

Set-and-run mass killers use a remote weapon such as a bomb or poison gas to inflict maximum casualties, while observing the events that take place from a vantage point out of harm's way.

The deadliness of mass homicide incidents increases where the perpetrator has shown a past history of paranoid thinking, violent behavior, and an interest in guns (Lester et al., 2005).

Characteristics of mass murderers. Psychological and criminological analysis of mass murderers in Western societies (Cantor et al, 2000; Delisi & Scherer, 2006; Fox & Levin, 1998, 2003; Hempel et al, 1999; Lester, 2002; Lester et al, 2005; Malmquist, 1996; Mullen, 2004; Palermo, 1997; Petee et al, 1997) has yielded a fairly consistent set of defining characteristics.

Motives and circumstances. Despite the workplace or school violence events that make the headlines (Chapters 11 and 12), the majority of mass killings occur in the context of domestic or family disputes, fueled by anger, jealousy, and/or depression, with drug and alcohol abuse a frequent precipitating or aggravating factor. In both domestic and workplace mass murder scenarios, the event has often been preceded by a major life setback such as a romantic separation or job loss.

Perpetrator characteristics. Mass killers are often middle-aged, single or divorced, socially isolated males who have had difficulty establishing themselves in mature adult work and family roles. As children, many have been bullied or rejected by peers and, as they grew up, displayed a morbid fascination with weapons and violence through books, magazines, movies, and video games.

Personality and psychopathology. Their personalities are often characterized by obsessive, rigid, and moralistic thinking, grandiose narcissism, and delusional persecutory ideation—the hallmarks of the Axis II, Cluster B personality disorders discussed in Chapter 7. Less commonly, they show frankly antisocial or psychopathic traits, or significant criminal or substance abuse histories, and are rarely suffering from major psychoses, although they may be depressed and delusional at the time of their murders (Chapter 5, 6). Those mass killers diagnosed as schizophrenic are less likely to commit suicide during their rampage and more likely to be captured.

Attack patterns. The mass murder is often precipitated by a major loss related to employment or a relationship. A "warrior mentality" suffuses the planning and attack behavior of the subject, and greater death tolls and higher casualty rates are significantly more likely if the perpetrator is psychotic at the time of the offense. Alcohol typically plays a minor role during the actual attack. A large proportion of subjects express their central message or motivation for the attack in what Hempel et al. (1999) call a **psychological abstract**, a phrase uttered with great emotion at the beginning of the mass murder, e.g., "God hates liberals," "This will show my damn boss!" In other cases, notebooks, letters, or computer records are later found in the perpetrator's home. However, only 20 percent of these murderers directly threaten their intended victims before the attack. Death by suicide or at the hands of others is the usual outcome for the killer. This homicidal subtype seems to characterize many cases of workplace, school, and other institutional mass violence (Dewan, 2008; Miller, 1999g, 2007a; Neuman & Baron, 1998; see Chapters 11, 12).

DEMOGRAPHICS OF HOMICIDE

Psychological, criminological, and sociological research has established certain facts and principles about homicide in the modern world (Duntley & Buss, 2008; Flowers, 2002b,c; Malmquist, 1996; Overpeck et al., 2002; United Nations, 1998; U.S. Dept. of Justice, 1998a,b).

Place and Time

From the point of view of not being a murder victim, it seems we live in the best of times. Excluding deaths due to warfare or genocide, the overall homicide rate among modern industrialized societies is the lowest it has been in history, with the United States showing the highest murder rate among industrialized nations, and Japan and Austria having the lowest. But even the U.S. rate is far lower than most preindustrial cultures and developing nations around the world.

According to the U.S. Department of Justice, the overall homicide rate in this country has been declining over the past two decades, with the greatest decline seen in the largest metropolitan areas. This has been due in part to a drop in youth violence, tighter gun control laws, better economic conditions during the 1990s, and a drop in violent crime in general. For example, the U.S. homicide rate in 2006 was 5.7 per 100,000 people that year (U.S. Department of Justice, 2007), which translates into approximately a one in 225 lifetime risk of being a victim of homicide in this country. Nevertheless, this has also been the era of sensationalized episodes of mass violence, including workplace violence, school violence, and terrorism.

Moreover, even the official homicide rate may represent an underestimation of the overall level of violence in the United States and other industrialized societies. The homicide rates in many nations would actually be much higher were it not for emergency medical interventions that were not available to our ancestors for most of our evolutionary history and, indeed, even as recently as a few decades ago. Faster ambulance response times and better emergency room care, much of it developed by military doctors during the 1990–1991 Gulf War, may be responsible for what would have been up to 50,000 additional homicides now becoming assaults and other crimes because the victim survived what would have been fatal gunshot and stab wounds a generation ago (Duntley & Buss, 2008; Harris et al., 2002).

Homicide rates peak in the summer months and in December, periods of time when more people congregate, travel, and spend time with family, increasing the probability of interpersonal contact and interpersonal conflict (Chertwood, 1988). Murder is most likely to occur on Saturday night and early Sunday morning (Hagedorn, 1994), no doubt reflecting the fact that this is the prime weekly recreational time slot for most Americans, typified by the risk factors of intermale conflict and alcohol intoxication. At least one study (Lieber, 1978) has documented a correlation between a full moon and murder rates, but the theoretical significance of this finding–not to mention any practical applications–remain uncertain.

Individual Factors

Homicide is largely a crime between men (Batton, 2004; Fox & Zawitz, 2006; Roberts, 2009; Silverman & Kennedy, 1987; Wolfgang, 1967; Zahn & Sagi, 1987). Men perpetuate 7 out of 8 homicides and are the victims in 3 out of 4 homicides. The homicide victimization rate was more than 3 times higher for men (8.7 per 100,000) than for women (2.4 per 100,000) in 2004, and more than 65 percent of all male-perpetrated homicides also had a male victim during this time period (Fox & Zawitz, 2006). The smallest homicide category is that of female-on-female homicides, which account for only 2.4 percentof all homicides in the U.S. (Fox & Zawitz, 2006; Glass et al., 2004). However, more than 30 percent of homicides committed by women have an intimate partner as victim (Jensen, 2001; see also Chapter 17).

If you make it through the first day of your life, the worst is over; if you live to see your first birthday, you can relax again. That's because you are ten times more likely to be murdered on the day you are born than at any other time during your life. After that, your risk of being murdered drops precipitously but is still higher during your first year of life than at any other age. Your murder risk then declines throughout early and middle childhood, with another moderate spike in adolescence and young adulthood, when you're likely to be at your friskiest and riskiest. After that, your risk dips again and becomes largely determined by other factors such as personality, family, occupation, ethnicity, and socioeconomic status.

You are far more likely to be killed by someone you know than by a stranger; homicide is typically intrafamilial and intraracial. For example, infanticide is primarily committed by parents. Blacks are seven times as likely as Whites to commit murders and six times as likely to be victims. The most frequent precipitant to murder involves an argument between people who know each other, often friends or family members, with alcohol use heightening the risk. The highest proportion of murders taking place during the commission of a felony involves elderly victims. Despite the public's fascination with serial and mass murders, most homicides are one-time events, involving a single killer and a single victim (Flowers, 2002c).

While the National Rifle Association's claim that "guns don't kill people, people kill people," may be logically correct, in two-thirds of the murders taking place every year in the United States, when people kill people, they use guns. The reason is obvious: it is stunningly simple to take someone's life with a firearm. In days past, it took a lot of skill and effort to kill someone with a stick, rock, blade, garrote, club, or bare hands. You had to stalk, surprise, or confront your adversary, and they usually fought back–often with the same types of weapons you had. The contest typically involved a lot of prolonged grappling and maneuvering, and was a tremendous expenditure of energy, even for the victor. Typically, the physically stronger contestant would win. And even if you succeeded in killing your opponent, chances are you would have sustained wounds that might later prove fatal or disabling. Thus, it is not surprising that the forces of natural selection have consigned most intraspecies (usually intermale) fighting to ritualized forms of combat which result in few serious injuries–otherwise, there may not have been enough members of the group left to propagate the next generation.

But long-range killing changes the equation. Even "primitive" ballistic weapons, such as archery, spears, slingshots, and catapults multiply the killing potential of a single user. These weapons may have initially been developed for hunting, but their users quickly recognized their potential for getting even with rivals or plundering resources from other tribes. Even here, however, it takes a certain degree of athletic prowess, practice, and energy to wield a lance or crossbow effectively and the stronger or more adept opponent retains the advantage. Firearms level the playing field. A physically much weaker individual can dispatch a much larger and stronger opponent, or even a group of them, literally by a twitch of his finger. In such circumstances, the natural precautions that might make a hostile rival, pillaging raider, or jealous mate think twice before engaging an adversary in hand-to-hand combat are swept away by the sheer ease and simplicity of pulling a trigger, often from some distance away. Add to this the concealability of modern handguns, and it is apparent why these firearms are the weapons of choice for most murders, including individual homicides as well as gang homicides, drug-related murders, and mass murders. Recent gun control legislation has helped make a dent in firearm-related lethal violence; however use of these weapons continues to have the strongest cause and effect relationship to murder (Flowers, 2002c).

BOX 9.1. LAW ENFORCEMENT LINE-OF-DUTY HOMICIDES

One sad exception to the current downward trend in homicides is the killing of law enforcement officers in the line of duty—**line-of-duty-deaths**, or **LODDs**—which has recently been on the rise in the beginning of the twenty-first century, after a steady downward trend from the 1970s through the 1990s.

When people think of mass casualties of police officers and other emergency service workers, they tend to evoke the September 11, 2001 terrorist attacks on the World Trade Center in New York. This was, indeed, the single deadliest day in the history of U.S. law enforcement, with 72 police officers killed that day. But almost as many law enforcement personnel were slain by ordinary criminals around the country in 2001, which represented a four-year high in murders of police officers. Every year, at least 52 police officers are killed in the line of duty, and 26,000 others are injured in service-related assaults. Overall, since 1960, this translates into a total of 2,219 police officers killed in the line of duty, and 328,000 more that have been injured in assaults. Law enforcement's dirty little secret is that a high proportion of officers (43% in one study) are killed or nonfatally shot by their own gun or a fellow officer's weapon. Nevertheless, fewer officers are dying in the line of duty today as there were back in the bad old days of the 1970s, which is largely attributable to better officer training, more cops on the street, better use of protective gear, and improved firepower of officers relative to the criminals they confront.

Police are most likely to be slain with a handgun, followed by rifle and shotgun deaths. Two-thirds of assailants have prior criminal records. Most homicides of police officers occur at night, with Friday being the most dangerous day, Sunday the least dangerous. Most officer deaths occur in the course of a traffic stop or making an arrest; the next highest category is during workplace or domestic disturbance calls. The South is the most dangerous part of the U.S. for police officers, with more than twice the number of LODDs occurring there than in any other region. A sizable number of officers also die in job-related accidents, which is a line-of-duty death that does not often get the same attention as deaths at the hands of criminals. Most of these involve automobile and motorcycle crashes (Anderson, 2002; Flowers, 2002b,c; Geller, 1993; Haddix, 1999; Miller, 2006f; US Department of Justice, 2003; Violanti, 1999).

THEORIES OF HOMICIDE

Many of the theoretical formulations discussed for crime in general in Chapters 2 and 3 can be applied to the explanation of homicide. The difference is that while severe in nature, murder is a low-frequency event, even among habitual criminals and certainly among ordinary citizens who may be driven to a single, isolated act of extreme violence under extraordinary provocation. Thus, the same types of biological, psychological, and socio-cultural dynamics that underlie more common forms of criminal behavior may not apply to murder. Nevertheless, this section will review the main features of theories that attempt to explain criminal homicide.

Biological and Neuropsychological Theories

As for violent crime in general, to understand the roots of homicide we need to distinguish biological theories that purport to explain outbursts of violence attributable to a brain disorder or disease vs. theories that posit a stable, if developmentally aberrant, neuropsychological configuration in criminals who adopt violence, including murder, as part of their lifestyle.

As to the first category, all of the genetic and neuropsychological disorders that predispose to violence in general can occasionally lead to violence that proves lethal, either as a specific impulse to kill or as an unintended consequence of the violent outburst itself. These would include chromosomal disorders, mental retardation, seizure disorders, intermittent explosive disorder, pathological intoxication, sleep disorders, brain injury, endocrine disorders, hormonal imbalances, toxic-metabolic disorders, nutritional deficiencies, and all of the other medical and neuropsychiatric disorders discussed in Chapter 2.

The second category of developmental neuropsychological disorders would include cerebral hemispheric asymmetry, frontal lobe dysfunction, dopamine metabolism anomalies, attention deficit hyperactivity disorder spectrum disturbances, and genetic family loading for criminal behavior—factors that would not likely be considered "diseases" per se, but genetically-predisposed and environmentally-reinforced traits that occur at the extreme edges of the bell curve of developmental socialization.

Psychological and Sociocultural Theories

Once again, the psychological theories utilized to explain criminal violence in general (Chapter 3) can be applied to homicide as a specific category. These include the **criminal personality theory** of Samenow (1984, 2002, 2007) and Yochelson & Samenow, 1976a,b), which posits that criminals actively seek excitement from the boredom of life, rejecting the stimulations and satisfactions of normal family and career pursuits in favor of illicit thrills involving fighting, stealing, drug use and—either deliberately or inadvertently—homicide.

As noted in Chapter 3, such individual psychology theories leave unexplained just why certain individuals have this type of cognitive style, while most thankfully do not. A neurobiological theorist would appeal to genetics and brain structure to explain the differences, while **social learning theorists** would cite the common observation that people learn from experience and that young people come to imitate and emulate what they experience in their early family life and, later, in the culture around them. If certain violent behaviors, including homicide, are seen as reinforced responses to social confrontations, then these may be imitated and emulated by the members of that cultural group, which, in the purest form of social learning theory, may also explain gender differences in violent behavior (Bandura, 1973; Berkowitz, 1993; Daly & Wilson, 1989; Eagly, 1995; Hoyenga & Hoyenga, 1993; Sutherland & Cressey, 1974).

Relatedly, sociocultural theories such as **strain theory** (Merton, 1938) hypothesize that certain individuals in society who are frustrated by lack of resources, overwhelmed by the stresses of survival, and barred from ascending the socioeconomic ladder through legitimate means by discrimination or economic disenfranchisement, may then resort to criminal behavior as an adaptive strategy. If robbery and murder are seen as the only way to obtain goods, these crimes may be committed and accepted within that social group as "the price of doing business" (Arrigo, 2006; Bernard et al., 2010; Duntley & Buss, 2008; Kitaeff, 2011; Malmquist, 1996). Again, however, these theories fail to account for why only a small proportion of such stressed and strained citizens–a percentage that is remarkably consistent from population to population–resort to homicide to redress the social imbalances they experience.

Other sociocultural theories of violence and homicide focus more specifically on certain group motivations for violence. The **subcultures of violence theory** (Wolfgang & Ferracuti, 1967) is basically a social learning theory of violence as applied to whole subpopulations of society. This model posits that violence becomes normalized within cultures whose members are regularly exposed to it in their families and neighborhoods. The theory leaves unexplained, however, just how this vicious cycle gets going: do otherwise nonviolent people learn to use violence by observing it all around them or do inherently violent people gravitate to communities where this strategy will be effective?

Similarly, the **culture of honor theory** (Nisbett, 1993) has been used to explain the high rate of violence and homicide, often taking place over issues of group status, "respect," and seemingly inconsequential interpersonal disputes, that plagues many economically deprived African-American communities (the "inner cities") of the United States. This stems, the theory posits, from the fact that many African-Americans are descended from ancestors who spent many generations in the American South, where they were steeped in a medieval-like jousting culture of preserving one's honor through confrontation and battle. This, in turn, is related to another medieval feature of early Southern American society: the feudal nature of the slave-based plantation system and, post-emancipation, the sharecropper system that supplanted it, essentially preserving the feudal society in the agrarian South, as opposed to the more industrialized North. Also, as noted in Chapter 20, in any society or subculture in which one's status or very survival may depend on not being seen as an exploitable "chump," risking one's life and taking another's life may be a grimly practical means of establishing one's rung on the rough cultural hierarchy one finds oneself in.

Evolutionary Psychology Theories

As reviewed in Chapter 2, it was the Italian physician Cesare Lombroso (1876) who introduced his **theory of atavism** to explain the bioevolutionary basis of criminal behavior. Informed by the works of Charles Darwin, Lombroso regarded criminals, including murderers, as **atavisms**, or throwbacks to earlier developmental forms of human beings (Bernard, 2010; Flowers, 2002c). This, of course, affirmed the separation maintained in the minds of polite Victorian society between the more refined (and, according to the theory, therefore more evolved) social aristocracy and the brutish "lower classes," many of whom could now be viewed as essentially cavemen in modern clothing (the first Neanderthal skull was unearthed in 1856), whose animalistic natures were evidenced by their lust for violence.

Absent the insights of modern paleoanthropology, it was expectable that nineteenth century theorists would regard such primitive human societies and subcultures as analogous to the primates they observed in their zoos and read about in the "jungle adventure" stories of the day. Violence and murder would thereby be only natural to these brutes. As such, Lombroso opined that these atavistic criminals could be identified (today, we'd say profiled) by distinct physical characteristics, such as stance, gait, limb length, cranial shape, and "beetling brows."

Over a century of research and theory in anthropology, psychology, criminology, and evolutionary theory has resulted in a more refined evolutionary model of human interaction, of both the amicable and aggressive types, and including crimes such as murder (Duntley & Buss, 2008). As discussed in Chapter 3, most primate species, including humans, are social creatures, and for most of human evolutionary history, our ancestors lived in groups of between roughly 50 and 150 individuals, depending on a complex matrix of family and social relationships to survive and procreate.

According to **homicide adaptation theory** (Buss & Duntley, 2003, 2004; Duntley & Buss, 2008), the killing of one individual by another within in a small interdependent tribal clan would have had a potentially powerful destabilizing effect on group cohesion and therefore on the survival of a widening circle of group members. Rival families would become embroiled in a vicious cycle of destructive blood feuds. Hunting, foraging, and tool-making would grind to a halt, and fractured group cohesion would make the clan more vulnerable to hostile groups, while fewer resources would be available to raise offspring. Powerful social forces, then, would have evolved to discourage frequent lethal combat within a clan, since groups that permitted such violent free-for-alls were less likely to survive and pass on their genes.

Therefore, according to homicide adaptation theory, the rare circumstances in which killing a member of your own clan, tribe, village, or community would be evolutionarily adaptive would be where the benefits of risking censure, ostracism, and revenge clearly outweighed the risks, that is, where killing your neighbor, or even a family member, was "worth it." According to the theory, these circumstances would include:

Defensive or preemptive strike. Homicide to stop or prevent the killing, rape, injury, or exploitation of self, kin, mates, or coalitional allies, either now or in the future. Premeditated murder depends on the ability to plan ahead, which is a cognitive skill most highly developed in humans, but also seen more rudimentarily in many predatory species who stalk and hunt for a living.

Resource protection. Killing to preserve the essential survival and procreative resources of food, clothing, tools, weapons, shelter, and mates from being robbed or pilfered by another group member. Naturally, this would be expected to vary according to the relative abundance or scarcity of such resources at any given time.

Reputation management. Killing to prevent having to continuously fend off rivals by "making an example" of one prominent adversary to establish your status. Such a spectacle would hopefully discourage future offenses against you and yours by showing the clan that you're no cavechump. Even today, homicide-related reputational enhancement—and with it, higher social status and greater mating opportunities—are seen in groups as diverse as the forest-dwelling Yanomamo of Venezuela (Chagon, 1988) and the urban-dwelling gang members of New York and Los Angeles (Alvarez & Bachman, 2002; Ghiglieri, 1999; Vigil, 2003).

Reproductive primacy. Stepchildren would have been at increased risk of neglect, abuse, and murder by any new male mate of their mother, since this man would have had a genetic investment in maximizing the survival success of his own offspring. In good times, these stepchildren may have been tolerated or even welcomed as members of the male's new extended family, but in leaner times, they may well have been seen as expendable burdens. Even in modern societies, stepchildren are still at heightened risk for abuse and homicide (Chapter 16).

Quality control. In the grim calculus of ancestral human survival, preservation of your family or the group as a whole, especially in tough times, may have depended on eliminating "dead weight," i.e., group members who couldn't or wouldn't fend for themselves or contribute to the group's living activities. This might include genetically impaired children, infirm elderly members, or disabled adults. As in preindustrial societies today, ancestral humans probably did not make these decisions lightly, and these sacrificial acts would not likely be regarded as murder, unless there was some intragroup political dispute over who should go and who gets to stay.

Duntley & Buss (2008) cite numerous examples of similar homicidal and infanticidal behavior across diverse species of social animals, including lions, wolves, hyenas, cougars, cheetahs, monkeys, chimpanzees, and gorillas (Crocket & Sekulic, 1984; Fossey, 1984; Ghiglieri, 1999; Wrangham & Peterson, 1996). In most of these species, infanticide of another male's offspring to induce estrus and sexual receptivity in the female is the primary motive, with intraspecific aggression between males typically being limited to ritualized combat displays or nonlethal injury. Primates, however, especially chimpanzees, the hominoid apes most closely related to us genetically, have been observed to form coalitions to attack, murder, and often cannibalize rival group members or even unpopular members of their own group.

Applied to modern criminal law, homicide adaptation theory—and evolutionary psychology generally—may provide some insight into why human societies divide homicides into the variety of legal categories discussed above. According to the present theory, for a murder to be accepted without severe consequences within a small interdependent community, it had better have occurred for a legitimate or understandable reason. Killing another person to obtain more resources when you already had enough would likely not be tolerated in almost any society. Even when some justification could be understood for your actions, such as clubbing a man to death upon discovering him in your cavebed with your wife (resulting, perhaps, in your killing her, too), this might be viewed more leniently when occurring as a "crime of passion" than where you plan, stalk, lie in wait, ambush, and kill your rival (murder in the first degree).

Nevertheless, like all theories, homicide adaptation theory and others which appeal to evolutionary psychology still must explain why some members of a group are more susceptible to aggression and homicide as an adaptational strategy than others. Indeed, as noted in Chapter 7, there must be a reason why diversity of human personality has persisted in the human race, indeed, in most social creatures, or we'd all have long ago become the same—or extinct.

PERSONALITY, PSYCHOPATHOLOGY, AND HOMICIDE

Using the knowledge and insights from previous chapters, we can now summarize the primary psychological dynamics that underlie homicidal behavior in different perpetrators.

Personality Disorders

Antisocial personality disorder is a pattern of consistent disregard for, and violation of, the rights of others. It is typically associated with impulsivity, criminal behavior, sexual promiscuity, substance abuse, and a lack of empathy and conscience leading to an exploitive, parasitic, and/or predatory lifestyle (Chapter 8). These individuals will do whatever it takes to get what they want, including murder, and they may be among the most remorseless and "cold-blooded" of killers. At the same time, their hedonistic-utilitarian mindset means that they are less likely to be goaded into an emotional reaction that does not involve them personally, but they are very sensitive to slights and insults and may respond impulsively and explosively if challenged.

Narcissistic personality disorder is a pattern of grandiosity, sense of entitlement, arrogance, and need for admiration (Chapter 7). As long as these individuals feel they are getting the respect and adulation they deserve, they may be condescendingly congenial. If others fail to appreciate them sufficiently, most narcissists will usually just snub the ingrates and move on to more worshipful acolytes. However, those with **brittle narcissism** may react in an explosive fashion if their thin skin is even slightly pricked, and may then respond with violence to expunge their assailant. In a related pattern, **malignant narcissism** describes an extreme sense of entitled exploitiveness that overlaps somewhat with elements of the antisocial and paranoid personalities. When these individuals don't get what they feel they deserve, they may have no compunctions about squashing the insignificant bugs who dare to thwart their grandiose plans, and murder, planned or impulsive, may be one result.

Borderline personality disorder is a pattern of erratic and intense relationships, alternating between over-idealization and devaluation of others, self-damaging impulsiveness, emotional instability and mood swings, a chronic feeling of emptiness, persistent identity disturbance, and impaired interpersonal relationships (Chapter 7). This is the personality disorder most likely to commit murder as a "crime of passion" or sometimes planned to redress the abominable betrayal they feel at the hands of a lover, friend, workmate, or family member. These crimes may be committed impulsively and explosively during a minipsychotic episode, or the killer may coldly and patiently stalk the victim until the time to strike is right. In either case, the murder will entail white-hot righteous justification on the killer's part.

Paranoid personality disorder is a pattern of pervasive distrust and suspiciousness, so that others' actions and motives are invariably interpreted as deceptive, persecutory, or malevolent (Chapter 7). This is the personality type that is most likely to carry out a preemptive strike on a perceived enemy. If the purported threat is seen as severe enough, this might spur the person to murder as the "only way out."

Dependent personality disorder is a pattern of obedient and clinging behavior stemming from an excessive need for care and nurturance (Chapter 7). The rare murders committed by these individuals are typically acts of desperation, carried out when all attempts to thwart a feared separation have failed: "If I can't have you, no one can." In many of these cases, the homicide may be accompanied by suicide.

Histrionic personality disorder is a pattern of excessive emotionality, attention-seeking, need for excitement, flamboyant theatricality in speech and behavior, and an impressionistic and impulsive cognitive style (Chapter 7). Many of these homicides may be accidental, the perpetrator only "trying to scare" the victim into giving her the attention she craves. In other cases, the perpetrator may commit murder as part of a "show-off crime," in the context of a gang initiation or to impress his friends, family members, or potential mates.

Schizoid personality disorder is a pattern of aloof detachment, witdrawal from others, and a restricted range of emotional expression. **Schizotypal personality disorder** additionally includes more serious delusional thinking and more bizarre behavior (Chapter 7). Their unempathic detachment from human feelings and bizarre interpretation of situations make a few of these individual prone to impulsive violence when they perceive any threat to their delusionally ordered world view, or when they feel pressured to do anything that is outside their comfort zone. Murder, however, is relatively rare.

Mental Disorders

Schizophrenia comprises a group of serious mental disorders characterized by severe disturbances of mood, thought, and goal-directed action, including delusions (disturbances of belief) and hallucinations (disturbances of perception). Of the several subtypes, it is **paranoid schizophrenia**, characterized by delusions of persecution and accusatory hallucinations, that is at the most risk for violence, including possibly homicide. As noted in Chapter

5, the most dangerous psychological configuration has been termed the **threat-control-override syndrome**, characterized by persecutory delusions and command hallucination. Still, most persecutory delusions and hallucinations induce fear, not rage, in schizophrenic subjects, and **disorganized** and **undifferentiated schizophrenic** types may lash out defensively, but rarely deliberately attack another person with intent to kill. However, the presence of comorbid substance abuse and antisocial personality disorder heighten the risk for violence, including homicide.

Delusional disorders are distinguished clinically from schizophrenia by the fact that the affected individuals may function adequately in most life areas, despite the presence of isolated, fixed ideas that are sufficiently out of sync with reality to qualify as delusions. If these delusions are primarily persecutory, the perpetrator may carry out a preemptive strike in a manner similar to the paranoid personality disorder or paranoid schizophrenic. More commonly, these individuals may become **querulous complainants** or **stalkers** (Chapters 5, 18).

Bipolar disorder is characterized by extreme shifts in mood, from elation to depression, usually with an absence of normal mood in between. Impulsive violence is usually seen in the manic phase when the mood is cycling from grandiose and expansive to agitated and irritable, or in those cases characterized mainly by "**mean mania**" (Chapter 6). In such cases, homicide is typically the accidental byproduct of extreme impulsive violence, usually in response to some perceived threat to the individual's safety or ego stability.

Major depressive disorder is characterized by episodes of depressed mood that may last for days, weeks, or months at a time (Chapter 6). Homicide may occur in two contexts here. In the first, as the depression begins to lift, the repressed anger that may have undergirded it is released and the individual decides to take decisive action against the person who has wronged him. In the second, homicide occurs as part of a **homicide-suicide**, as in cases of family homicide and filicide (Chapter 16).

Posttraumatic stress disorder (**PTSD**) is a distinct syndrome of emotional and behavioral disturbances following exposure to a traumatic stressor that injures or threatens self or others, and that involves the experience of intense fear, helplessness, or horror (Chapter 6). Symptoms include: (1) a heightened state of physiological arousal; (2) pervasive anxiety and hypervigilance; (3) intrusive thoughts and images about the traumatic event, alternating with (4) numbing and avoidance to blot out reminders of the trauma; (5) repetitive nightmares; (6) irritability, impatience, and loss of humor; (7) impaired concentration and memory; and (8) general restriction and avoidance of life activities. When it occurs, homicidal violence is usually seen in the context of an extreme dissociative flashback in which the individual believes he is back in the threatening situation and attempts to defend himself by aggressing against the perceived attacker.

Brain Syndromes

Most **seizure disorders** rarely cause violence, but individuals with **temporal lobe epilepsy** may lash out defensively in the throes of a psychomotor seizure, and individuals with **intermittent explosive disorder**, or **episodic dyscontrol syndrome** may commit acts of extreme homicidal violence during an episode, including **overkill**.

Traumatic brain injury can result in deficits in impulse control, frustration tolerance, judgment, and behavioral control, especially when the brain's frontal and temporal lobes are involved in the injury. As noted in Chapter 2, however, those individuals most prone to aggressive, antisocial behavior postinjury are usually the ones most likely to show signs of such behavior preinjury, and their aggressive, impulsive lifestyle (often including substance abuse) may be one important factor that puts them at greater risk of injury in the first place.

Dementia refers to a group of progressive, degenerative brain syndromes, such as Alzheimer's disease, that typically occur later in life and impair perception, thinking, language, memory, and behavior. Most violence committed by dementia sufferers is due to confusion and defensiveness in response to feeling threatened. Homicide, when it occurs, is typically accidental, most commonly vehicular homicide from inability to control a vehicle when driving.

At the other end of the age spectrum, **developmental disorders**, such as **attention deficit hyperactivity disorder** (**ADHD**) and **conduct disorder**, are frequently comorbid disorders first diagnosed in childhood (Chapter 4, 19). Conduct disorder, the childhood version of antisocial personality disorder, usually accounts for the child's propensity to commit violence, while ADHD may impair judgment and impulse control and thereby contribute to impulsive actions that can result in aggression. Although not common, sensationalized accounts of children committing murder have appeared in every era (Chapter 19).

Alcohol and drug abuse can lower the threshold to violence, including homicidal violence, by diminishing inhibitions generally. Certain substances, such as hallucinogens and psychostimulants, may be especially prone to heighten arousal and physiological reactivity, while other substances, such as alcohol and sedative drugs, increase violence risk by lowering inhibitions. In certain predisposed individuals, even small amounts of alcohol can trigger

pathological intoxication, characterized by episodes of extreme violence that may include homicide.

"**Rational" murder** describes homicides that are committed for some utilitarian purpose, such as to acquire money, mates, or other resources. Even in these cases, the ability to coolly take the life of another innocent human being probably implies some antisocial component to the personality structure. However, it should be noted that when a homicide victim is conceptualized as being outside the bounds of "our" society, killing may not be stigmatized, and may involve no mental disorder at all, but be applauded as a necessary and courageous act, as when soldiers kill the "enemy" in battle (Schlesinger & Miller, 2003).

BOX 9.2. DEATH NOTIFICATION AND BODY IDENTIFICATION

A frequently neglected topic in both the criminal justice and mental health treatment systems is the nature of proper notification of family members that a loved one has been killed or that the body of a missing relative has been located and identified. Family survivors require the utmost sensitivity when faced with their loved one's violent death (Miller, 2008a). In some cases, the family member may have actually witnessed the death. Other times, the murder has taken place outside the family's awareness, and it now becomes someone's job to inform them and, in some cases, to help them identify the remains of their loved one.

Death Notification

Over the last several years, several practical death notification protocols have been developed, some specifically for the families of murder victims, others for different kinds of bereavement, such as motor vehicle fatalities, military deaths, or acts of terrorism (Boss, 1999, 2002; Collins, 1989; Dias et al, 2003; Eberwein, 2006; Miller, 2004, 2008b, 2009a, 2009b; Nardi & Keefe-Cooperman, 2006; Parrish et al, 1987; Ptacek & Eberhardt, 1996; Spungen, 1998; Stewart, 1999; Von Bloch, 1996; Wells, 1993), which I have integrated into the following set of recommendations.

Preparation. Preparation includes pre-visit clarification of the correct name and address of the family, as well as basic facts of who the survivors are: spouse, parents, children, and others. It also includes a basic run-through of what is to be said and anticipating any reactions and the appropriate responses to them.

Initial contact. Whenever possible, go in person. Go in pairs or in a small group, and decide who will be the lead person whose job it will be to actually say the words and give the bad news. The other team members provide backup support, monitor the survivors for adverse reactions, and provide temporary supervision of young children during the notification, if needed. If no one is home when you get there, wait a reasonable amount of time, then leave a card with a note and a number to call. When the call comes, return to the family's home to make the notification.

Presenting the information. When you do arrive, ask for permission to enter. Suggest that family members sit down face-to-face with you. Ask if there are any other family members in the house that need to hear this information. Conversely, ascertain if some family members (e.g., young children, frail elderly) may be better off not being present during the notification. Prepare the family that bad news is coming, get to the point quickly, and state the information simply and directly. Use the deceased's name or his/her relationship to the family member being informed:

> "We're sorry to have to bring you this terrible news, Mrs. Jones. Your daughter, Helen, was killed in a store robbery by a suspect who the police are actively trying to apprehend. Helen and her personal effects are at Municipal Hospital."

Allow time for the news to sink in. It may be necessary to repeat the message several times in increasingly clear and explicit terms. Tolerate silence and be prepared for the calm to be broken by sudden eruptions of grief and rage. Answer all questions tactfully and truthfully, but don't reveal more information than is necessary at that time. Repeat answers to questions as many times as it takes for the family to understand them. Try to be as calm and supportive, comforting and empathic, as possible.

Practical assistance. Offer to make phone calls to family, friends, neighbors, employers, clergy, doctors, and so on. Respect the family's privacy, but don't leave a family member alone if you suspect they might not be safe. Provide family members in writing with the names and telephone numbers of a victim advocate, prosecutor, medical examiner, social service agency, and/or hospital. Explain to family members what will happen next, e.g., body identification, police investigation, and criminal justice procedures. Give family members as much information as they ask for, without overwhelming them. Determine if the family members require some means of traveling to and from the medical examiner's office, hospital, or police station, and enlist the aid of police or social services in doing so.

Body Identification

If physical remains have been located, the next step for families is often the identification of their deceased loved one. The finality of identifying the deceased's body can have a paradoxically dual effect. On the one hand, there is the confrontation with the victim's remains and the final shattering of any hope that he or she may still be alive. On the other hand, the actual sight of the deceased relieves the bereaved of **ambiguous loss** and often provides a strange sort of reassuring confirmation that the victim's suffering is finally over (Boss,

continued

BOX 9.2.—*Continued*

2002; Rynearson, 1988, 1994, 1996; Rynearson & McCreery, 1993; Sprang & McNeil, 1995).

A number of authorities (Ahrens et al., 1997; Collins, 1989; Eberwein, 2006; Nardi & Keefe-Cooperman, 2006; Stewart, 1999; Spungen, 1998; Von Bloch, 1996; Wells, 1993) have provided useful guidelines for helping survivors through the process of body identification.

Family choice. Unless there is a legal requirement, let survivors make the decision as to whether they want to view their loved one's remains. In cases where it is forensically necessary to involve the family in the identification process, as when the victim has been missing for a long time, be sure to provide appropriate support.

Physical contact. Family members may want to touch the deceased, grasp the loved one's hand, or hold a deceased child as a way of beginning to accept the reality of the death and saying goodbye. Be prepared to give the bereaved a reasonable amount of time. In some cases, where evidence is still being collected and law enforcement may not want the body moved or touched, inform the family of this and arrange for another viewing, if they choose, when all the forensic examinations have been completed. If the victim's body is significantly mutilated, dismembered, burned, decomposed, or disintegrated, identification may have to be made through dental records, personal effects, and so on. Explain to the family members why this is necessary and give them the choice of whether or not to view or touch the remains. If they choose to do so, try to arrange to have the viewing area as clean as possible. Understand, however, that law enforcement may insist on keeping the body as it was found if evidence is yet to be collected, so inform the family of that. As always, provide the appropriate support.

No remains. Where no body has been recovered, state this plainly. If there is hope that remains may yet be found, state this too, but try to be as realistic as possible about the chances. Notify the family of whatever identification procedures may be occurring, such as DNA-matching, and direct them to the proper authorities. Also, if artifacts from the victim are found at the scene, such as a pair of glasses, a piece of jewelry, or a child's toy, these might be in police custody for use as evidence in later prosecution. Let the family know this and explain to them the procedures for reclaiming these heirlooms, should they wish to do so. When no definitive remains are found, "symbolic remains" may serve as a surrogate. For example, following 9/11, an urn of ashes from Ground Zero was offered by the City of New York to each family of a missing person (Boss, 2002). Be sensitive to the family's needs.

Death Notification and Body Identification with Child Victims

Although loss of any family member is wrenching, special sensitivity is needed when the victim is a young child. Ahrens et al. (1997) surveyed parents of children who died or who were dead on arrival at a hospital emergency department. When the death notification was carried out in a sensitive, respectful, and empathic manner, this had a powerful, immediate, and long-term positive effect on the family's ability to cope with their child's death. Most parents found it reassuring and comforting to hold their dead child. Almost all the parents wanted some physical memento of the child, such as a lock of hair or a mold of the hand. Notifiers should do whatever they can to afford parents and other caretakers as much support and comfort as the situation allows.

SUMMARY AND CONCLUSIONS

Homicide is often seen as the ultimate crime because it places us at the intersection of power and vulnerability, malevolence and mortality. With exquisite precision, the law parses homicide into carefully articulated categories, each tracking a separate psychological state of motivation and intent. The causes of homicide, as with all of the criminal behavior described in this text, reflect a combination of biological, psychological, and social dynamics, shaped by the evolution of human beings within interdependent family groups and societies. Certain psychopathologies and personality disorders may be associated with homicidal behavior for different reasons, but it is still only a small proportion of even the most seriously disturbed, under the most strained circumstances, who go so far as to take another's life.

Chapter 10

Serial Homicide

In the United States, homicide accounts for approximately 20,000 deaths annually (Chapter 9). In ordinary civilian life, most people do not kill, but we may enjoy watching others do it on television and at the movies, or reading about it in books or on websites. We also like to study murder and other crimes, which is one of the reasons you're reading this book. Perhaps some of us have secret fantasies that resemble those of the murderer, yet we retain control of our behavior and remain law-abiding members of society. For serial murderers, however, such fantasies lose their vicarious function and become a cognitive staging ground for the actual commission of their crimes (Hickey, 1997; Simon, 1996).

The serial killer watches the same spy movies and police programs we do, shows where detectives or glamorous international agents doggedly and cleverly pursue malfeasors (the lead character of one such popular 1980s TV detective series was actually named "Hunter"), ostensibly for the good of society. The nascent killer absorbs society's fascination with media portrayals of criminals and others who "don't play by the rules" and he feels the same tingle of exhilaration at the opportunity to vicariously track down and destroy those who "have it coming."

But whereas our involvement in such mayhem begins and ends at the level of fantasy, the perpetrator of **serial killing**, or **serial murder**, or **serial homicide** (the most common terms) goes further. For most of us, dramatized portrayals of violence are entertaining, perhaps even cathartic, as the ancient Greeks suggested. But for the serial killer, such fantasies are the first step, not the last. His fantasies build, along with a neuropsychodynamically driven hunger that only the orgiastic release of torturing and murdering another human being will provide. What for most humans (typically males) constitutes a momentary journey into cruelty during the "heat of battle," as, for example, in military service, becomes for the serial killer his life's guiding purpose and mission. That is why he is so relentless. That is why he will always continue to kill until he is dead or securely confined.

HISTORY AND CONCEPT OF SERIAL KILLING

Schlesinger (2000a,b) provides an insightful historical review of attempts to understand serial homicide, which will be summarized here. Ancient Roman emperors, such as Caligula, indulged their sadistic inclinations at will, as no doubt did many a despot with a cruel streak, who could exert state-sanctioned power over other people.

In the 1400s, French nobleman Gilles de Rais raped, tortured, and killed several hundred children, reportedly deriving more pleasure from their agonies—which included dismemberment, neck-breaking, and decapitation—than from having sex with them (Benedetti, 1972). In sixteenth century Europe, the brutal mutilations inflicted on some serial homicide victims led to the deaths being blamed on werewolves, since only a supernaturally and bestially malevolent being could possibly be responsible for killings of this degree of savagery.

In 1866, Richard von Krafft-Ebing published his classic text, *Psychopathia Sexualis* ("Sexual Psychopathology"), which contained the first comprehensive tract on serial sexual homicide in the modern era, and which presents a careful description of many of the characteristics that serial homicide investigators still use today to profile these crimes. These include the tendency to lie and manipulate, take souvenirs from the crime scene, use ligatures, prolong torture for increased sexual arousal and pleasure, engage in an escalation of sadistic behavior, use pornography, humiliate and degrade victims, and carefully plan the murders to avoid detection. von Krafft-Ebing noted also that these offenders often displayed no obvious signs of psychopathology. Finally, he described "signature" aspects of the crime, which represent the killer's idiosyncratic touches on the crime scene believed to reflect his personality and psychopathology, and which is often used as a key datum in profiling (see Box 10.2).

Probably the most famous serial murderer of all time, Jack the Ripper, terrorized Victorian England in the late 1800s (Begg et al., 1991). Like many modern serial killers, Jack specialized in murdering prostitutes, stabbing, disemboweling, sexually mutilating the victims and, in some cases, carefully removing their internal organs and arranging them around the victim or taking them from the crime scene. The surgical precision with which these eviscerations were performed led to speculation that Jack may have been a practicing surgeon at one of the local hospitals in the Whitechapel district of London; such a "double life" is not uncommon in the histories of many serial killers today. A further similarity to some modern cases was Jack's proclivity for sending taunting letters to the press, threatening to continue and escalate his actions. As with many modern unclosed files, the Ripper case remains unsolved to this day; Jack's killing spree apparently ended as abruptly as it began and his identity was never discovered.

Resembling more a milquetoast than a monster, Albert Fish was a bow-tied sadist, masochist, pedophile, serial murderer, and cannibal who operated from the 1920s to the 1930s in New York (Schecter, 1990). In one instance, he abducted a schoolgirl under the guise of taking her to a birthday party, strangled her, cut up her body, made a stew of her corpse (complete with potatoes and vegetables), and consumed this dish over the next several days. As a final sadistic touch, six years after the murder, Fish sent a letter to the child's mother, detailing how he had killed and eaten her daughter. This led to his arrest shortly after the letter was traced to his home. In addition to serial murder, Fish engaged in a variety of sadomasochistic behaviors, including eating his own excrement, inserting rose stems in his penis, and inserting 29 sewing needles into his groin, clearly visible on X-ray years later. The Albert Fish case illustrates the heterogeneity and versatility of sadomasochistic behaviors that appear to involve the common phylogenetic features of sex, death, and eating.

One of the more famous serial killers of modern times is Albert DeSalvo, commonly known as the Boston Strangler, who killed 13 women over an 18-month period in the early 1960s (Rae, 1967). DeSalvo displayed the kind of escalation in violence often seen in serial homicide careers, first as a voyeur, then progressing to burglary, later becoming a rapist, and finally a serial murderer. Also typical of many serial killers was his penchant for using charming seduction to gain entry to his victims' homes, often posing as a repairman or a scout for a modeling agency. The victims were strangled and stabbed, and broomsticks and other objects were inserted into their vaginas. His signature behavior often consisted of placing a bow made from the victims' stockings around their necks.

The term **serial murderer** was coined by FBI Special Agent Robert Ressler during the "Son of Sam" killings (which were actually shootings, not sexual homicides) in New York City in the 1970s. Up to that time, there were probably less than ten serial murderers identified in the United States. By the 1980s, the FBI calculated that approximately 35 serial killers were active in the United States, and in recent years that estimate has swelled to between 200 and 500, accounting for 2000 to 3500 murders a year, more than 10 percent of all murders in the United States In fact, with only 5 percent of the world's population, the United States may have up to 75 percent of the world's serial killers, perhaps due to the open, mobile nature of American society. The increase in the number of serial killers captured and recorded may be due an actual surge in the rate of this crime or to better profiling and crime-solving techniques (Box 10.3). Despite the singular successes glorified in the popular media, the **case clearance rate** (proportion of crimes that are solved) of serial murders is fairly low. Thus, serial killers are precisely so dangerous and frightening because they rarely stop killing unless they die or are apprehended (Bureau of Justice Statistics, 2003; Chan & Heide, 2009; Flowers, 2002c; Hickey, 1997; Holmes 1989; Holmes & Holmes, 1994, 1996; Johnson & Becker, 1997; Miller, 2000c; Palermo & Kocsis, 2005; Simon, 1996; Volavka, 1999).

Since the late 1970s, the media and the public have become increasingly fascinated by serial killers (Table 10.1). But because human nature and behavior are relatively stable across times and places, virtually all of the contemporary offenders chronicled in modern clinical case histories and media accounts could find a home within the pages of Krafft-Ebing's 1866 treatise. For example, prostitutes continue to be a favored target of serial killers, either because of psychodynamic preoccupations with the sins of tainted womanhood, or because they are simply convenient disenfranchised victims who are easy to find, isolate, and kill without arousing too much of a public outcry–as opposed, for example, to preppie college students.

Also recently seen are cases of vampirism and cannibalism: Jeffrey Dahmer could trade recipes with Albert Fish on their mutual taste for **anthrophagy** (see below). Children also continue to be victimized: John Wayne Gacy would feel right at home in the 1400s with Gille de Rais. Many contemporary offenders are highly intelligent and outwardly charming, often with histories of fire-setting and animal cruelty, and some still send taunting letters to the press. In the popular imagination, extraterrestrial aliens have now replaced werewolves as suspects in particularly gruesome livestock mutilations which may in reality represent training exercises for a few disturbed individuals who may later go on to carve up humans. And like their predecessors, many modern serial murderers have had seemingly stable relationships with girlfriends and wives, many of whom claim ignorance when their mate's double life is exposed.

Indeed, so great is the public's fascination with the kind of conscience-less power embodied by the serial killer, so great is the thrill that many people get from momentary vicarious identification with such pure remorselessness, that some serial killers–much like gangsters–have achieved the status of criminal rock stars, appearing in numerous crime anthologies, on T-shirts, in movies, and in song lyrics. Real-life serial killers have even worked their way into Hollywood. Ed Gein wore the skin of his victims during his autoerotic transvestite rituals: this became the inspiration for the "Buffalo Bill" character in *Silence of the Lambs* (LaBrode, 2007).

But at the same time we're enthralled by the serial killer, we're also afraid of him. Surveys have shown that the public puts their fear of serial killers second only to the fear of terrorist bombings (Schlesinger, 2000b). Again, this reflects the fact that one's idiosyncratic notions of "good" and "bad" human behavior are often determined by individual circumstances, ideology, and culture (see also Chapter 13). Vegetarians think meat-eaters are barbarians. Steak-lovers chomp on their juicy morsels with gusto, but would retch at the thought of eating the flesh of another human being. Fore Islanders of New Guinea eat the brains of their recently deceased relatives as a religious ritual and would regard as profoundly disrespectful any family member who declined. The patriarchs of the Old Testament routinely practiced animal sacrifice as a devotion to God, but regarded as demonic the child sacrifice practiced by contemporaneous worshippers of Baal. Eating one's enemy to assimilate his strength and power, or the taking of body parts as trophies, has characterized victorious warriors in every age; as recently as September 2010, U.S. Army soldiers were charged with keeping leg bones, finger bones, and teeth from slain Afghanis. Thus, the study of serial killers–by whom we are simultaneously fascinated and repelled–must be interpreted in the context of our own clinical and cultural environment.

TABLE 10.1.
SOME FAMOUS AMERICAN SERIAL KILLERS

Albert Fish: Active 1928–1935. Kidnapped, tortured, mutilated, and ate children. Claimed he was ordered by God to commit at least some of his crimes. Also self-mutilated and ate human feces. In one case, he sent a detailed letter to a murdered little girl's parents, describing in sadistic detail what he did to the child; this, fortunately, led to his capture.

Henry Lee Lucas: Active 1960–1983. Initially boasting of mutilating and killing up to 500 people, he later recanted many of these and was convicted of murdering 11 victims.

Albert DeSalvo: Active 1962–1964. The "Boston Strangler" sexually assaulted and strangled women from 19 of 85 years of age. Once of the first "celebrity serial killers," he was referred to in the 1969 Rolling Stones' song, *Midnight Rambler.*

John Wayne Gacy: Active 1972–1978. Posed as a police officer, detained boys and young men at his home, sexually assaulted them, strangled them, and buried their bodies under his house.

Arthur Shawcross: Active 1972–1990. Strangled or beat to death young women, mainly prostitutes, and dumped their bodies along a river in upstate New York.

Ted Bundy: Active 1974–1982. Charming and seductive, he raped, killed, and mutilated his female victims, displaying trophies, including severed heads, in his apartment. Unsuccessfully tried to fake multiple personality disorder as an insanity defense.

David Berkowitz: Active 1976–1977. Terrorized the New York City area as the "Son of Sam," based on his letters to the press claiming to receive demonic messages and commands from his neighbor's dog. Stalked young, long-haired women and shot them to death with a handgun, leading to another moniker, the "44-Caliber Killer."

Dennis Rader: Active 1976–1986. Called himself the "BTK Killer" for "Bind-Torture-Kill." Tortured and murdered his victims and sent letters and packages to the media. Disappeared for 18 years, then reemerged, with new messages for the media, which led to his arrest.

Wayne Williams: Active 1979–1982. Convicted of murdering 21 African-American children in the Atlanta area. At the time, black serial killers were thought to be a rarity; subsequent research has shown this not to be the case.

Jeffrey Dahmer: Active 1987–1991. Lured boys and young men to his apartment, drugged them, had sex with them, murdered them, mutilated them, and cannibalized them, storing multiple body parts around his home. Also experimented with making "sex slave zombies" out of some of his victims by performing crude lobotomies on them.

Aileen Wuornos: Active 1989–1991. A rare female serial killer, she shot seven men to death, claiming they had tried to rape her while she was working as a prostitute. The movie about her was titled, *Monster,* although it could be argued that her crimes were considerably less monstrous than those of many of the male serial killers described here.

John Allen Muhammad: Active 2002. Along with a young protégé, Lee Boyd Malvo, the "Beltway Snipers" paralyzed the Washington, DC area, which was still reeling from the 9/11 terrorist attacks (Chapter 13), killing a total of 10 people with a single hunting rifle from the trunk of an old car, and leading pundits to speculate what kind of havoc could be wrought if a dozen or a hundred dedicated snipers were to coordinate such attacks around the country.

CHARACTERISTICS OF SERIAL KILLERS

Although heterogeneity exists within any psychological or criminological category, certain common features characterize serial killers.

Demographic and Descriptive Features

The typical serial murderer is a white male in his 20s to 40s, although older cases are seen, especially for killers who have escaped detection for many years, and minority groups are becoming increasingly represented. This individual is often a loner, though many are married or live in relatively stable relationships. He may appear to others as intelligent and charming. He may be stably employed or subject to frequent changes in jobs and living locales (Chan & Heide, 2009; Fox & Levin, 2003; Hazelwood et al., 1992; Holmes & DeBurger, 1985; Lester, 1995; Rappaport, 1988).

Criminal History

Although many serial killers, when apprehended, are found to have no prior criminal record, other studies have found that more than half of serial killers and other multiple homicide offenders have a past criminal history, and a few have shown a lifelong, often escalating, pattern of antisocial and criminal behavior (DeLisi, 2001, 2003, 2005; Delisi & Scherer, 2006; Farrington, 2000; Fox & Levin, 2003; Harbort & Mokros, 2001; Nagin & Farrington, 1992; Piquero et al., 2003).

A frequent association appears between serial homicide and two other crimes: burglary and rape (Delisi & Scherer, 2006; Douglas & Olshaker, 1998; Hazelwood & Douglas, 1980; Prentky et al., 1989; Ressler et al., 1983, 1986a, 1986b). While the reasons for this particular association are not settled, it might be speculated that both of these crimes involve the willful violation of another person's intimate self, either their home or their physical body. Burglaries and rapes are, in essence, both *invasions* of another person who has been dehumanized, much as past and present armies of conquest have engaged in rape and pillage of a conquered enemy's home territory, and robbery is used by street criminals to demoralize rival gangs (Chapter 20). It should not be surprising, therefore, that this pattern of behavior may frequently escalate to the ultimate violation of a person's body, murder.

Characteristics of the Crime

The victims of serial murder are predominantly female, white, and young adults, although same-sex murders are not uncommon, and some serial killers target children (see below). The majority of crimes are intraracial in nature, although a few serial killers have targeted ethnic groups different from themselves. As a notable exception to the general rule that we are most likely to be killed by someone we know, serial sexual homicides are twice as likely as homicides in general to involve strangers (Flowers, 2001; Schlesinger, 2004, 2007; U.S. Dept. of Justice, 1997a).

Many serial killers collect **trophies** from the crime scene that they keep as mementos of the kill. These can range from articles of jewelry or clothing to internal organs or other body parts. Other serial killers engage in **necrophilia**, having sex with the dead body, some even preserving the body, or parts of it, for later use, or returning to the hidden crime scene to have repeated sexual contact with the decomposing corpse (La Brode, 2007; Schlesinger, 2000b; Schlesinger & Miller, 2003).

A significant number of serial killers engage in some form of postmortem manipulation, mutilation, and/or cannibalism of their victims, some drinking the blood or eating parts of their victims at the crime scene or later, a practice called **anthropophagy**. Albert Fish made stew from at least one of his victims. Jeffrey Dahmer cannibalized several of his victims, storing the remains in his freezer like cuts of meat from the grocery. He described the experience of eating his victims as sexually exhilarating (Ressler & Schachtman, 1997).

In **Reinfield's syndrome**, also known as **clinical vampirism**, the killer feels a compulsion to drink the victim's blood. A number of researchers have commented on the similarity of these behaviors to the activities of predatory animals, including the common house cat, as well as to the customs of primitive human societies, where drinking the blood or eating a body part (e.g., the heart) of a slain adversary is believed to convey the dead foe's power to the victor and to protect the warrior from vengeance by the victim's spirit. Examples include Maori warriors who taste the blood of their slaughtered enemies and executioners in Niger who lick the blood of their victims from the knife (Reiwald, 1950).

Indeed, this fusion of killing, sex, and eating highlights the primal interaction of these life and death forces in the phylogenetic world of natural survival. In this sense, the serial killer frightens us all the more because his behavior strips away the veneer of civilized behavior and starkly illustrates the dark places our human natures can go.

When serial killers are identified, it is often because, in acting out their fantasies, they leave their characteristic **signature** on the victims' bodies or at the crime scene. These are unique traces of behavior that are often used as clues in profiling serial crimes, for example: (1) patterns of attack, forms of bondage and torture, e.g., **piquerism** (intense, focused injury to the breasts of the victim); (2) type of killing, postmortem body positioning, dress or undress, postmortem mutilation or dismemberment (**necrosadism**), and trophy-taking. Serial murderers act out an intense fantasy relationship with their victims, and thereby require the victims to be essentially anonymous props on whom they can inflict torment and death to achieve the exhilaration of sexual gratification. In this interpretation, the selection, stalking, and capturing of their victims are essentially their version of foreplay, with the torture and killing culminating in the orgasmic climax (Arrigo & Purcell, 2001; Chan & Heide, 2009; Hickey, 2003; Holmes & Holmes, 2001a, 2001b; Johnson & Becker, 1997; Geberth & Turco, 1997; La Brode, 2007; Langevin, 2003; Malmquist, 1996; Purcell & Arrigo, 2006; Simon, 1996; Starr et al., 1984).

Some of the signature behaviors may involve one or more **paraphilias**, such as **fetishism** (sexual preoccupation with body parts, inanimate objects, or bizarre activities); **transvestism** (dressing in the opposite sex's clothing); **exhibitionism** (public sexual displays), and **voyeurism** (surrepetitious watching of others' sexual activity).

One common fetish is the tendency for many serial killers to blindfold their victims (Holmes, 1989). This probably has little to do with fear of identification, since the perpetrator intends to kill his victim eventually. More commonly, the motive involves injecting yet more terror into the victim who cannot see what is happening to her, as well as effecting a further dehumanization of the victim by avoiding her gaze; for similar reasons, **enucleation** (gouging out of the eyes) is a common signature practice of serial killers, premortem or postmortem. Some authorities (e.g., Malmquist, 1996) also believe that blotting out the victim's eye contact is a means of counteracting the shame that may occasionally try to break through the serial killer's defenses, although the general consensus seems to be that most of these perpetrators have far too little conscience for this to be a significant factor.

The serial killer devotes a tremendous amount energy and intelligence to the planning and execution of his attacks, becoming more proficient each time he kills. Many serial killers are fascinated by police and detective work, and educate themselves in police procedures by reading books, taking courses, watching detective shows, and speaking with local police officers. Some have impersonated police officers, and in some cases, even inserted themselves into the investigations of the very crimes they have committed. John Wayne Gacy kept a police radio in his home; Wayne Williams photographed crime scenes; Ted Bundy once worked for the King County Crime Commission; Dennis Nilssen served a year on the London Police Force; and Edmund Kemper hung out at a bar near police headquarters, pestering off-duty officers with questions about the very murders he had committed (Simon, 1996; Starr et al., 1984).

TYPOLOGIES OF SERIAL KILLERS

Considering the amount of clinical and criminological attention that has been devoted to serial killers, it should not be surprising that a plethora of typologies has been developed to classify different types of perpetrators. The more well-known typologies are described below to illustrate the commonalities in observations among different researchers studying the same phenomenon.

Deitz Typology

Deitz (1986, 1987) has proposed a typology that divides multiple murderers into five categories:

Psychopathic sexual sadists kill for the sheer pleasure of torturing and murdering their victims in a sexual way. This has also been termed **lust murder** or **erotophonophilia** (Hickey, 2003; Schlesinger, 2004). This is probably closest to the classic serial killer that is the subject of most descriptions. Examples include Ted Bundy and John Wayne Gacy.

Crime spree killers embark on one or more jaunts of murder, usually in association with other crimes, most commonly robbery, but they also derive a thrill from the power and flaunting of authority their acts entail. An historical example would be Bonnie and Clyde; a fictionalized cinematic portrayal appears in the 1994 film, *Natural Born Killers*.

Organized crime functionaries consist of professional or semiprofessional "hit men," individuals who kill primarily for money, although they almost certainly enjoy a sense of power and control from being in this line of work. Other examples would include political assassins and territorial dispute killings by rival criminal gangs (Schlesinger & Miller, 2003; also see Chapter 20).

Custodial killers describe murder by those who care for vulnerable victims. The most common examples include "angel of death" cases involving nurses in hospitals or nursing homes who surreptitiously murder ill or elderly patients, usually by asphyxiation or medication overdose.

Psychotic killers murder under the influence of some form of delusion, such as defending themselves against malevolent pursuers (persecutory delusion) or receiving a divine command to rid the world of certain types of people (grandiose delusion).

Holmes Typology

Another widely-used typology of serial killers (Holmes & DeBurger, 1985, 1988; Holmes & Holmes, 1996) uses the following descriptors:

Spatial mobility killer. This typology maintains a clinical and forensic distinction between **geographically stable** serial murderers who live in one area and kill in that same or a nearby area, and **geographically transient** murderers who travel to other locales to commit their crimes.

Visionary serial killer. This type of killer is induced to murder by delusions and/or command hallucinations which impel him to do so. His victims are typically strangers, and his psychotic state at the time of his crimes sometimes results in the invocation of an insanity defense. This type appears closest to one variety of Dietz's (1986, 1987) psychotic killer, discussed above.

Mission serial killer. This may represent another type of Dietz's psychotic killer, who is following a religious or political imperative to eradicate a certain group of people. In the Holmes classification, the mission killer need not be grossly psychotic, but simply affected by what would be described as a delusional disorder in *DSM-IV-TR* (Chapter 5), or he may have no mental health diagnosis at all and simply be acting on an extreme ideological belief that it is necessary to eliminate some identifiable class of people.

Comfort-oriented serial killer. This killer's motive for murder contains at least some utilitarian purpose. It may include the hired assassin who kills purely for profit or the individual who murders family members for financial gain, in which case the profit motive may be admixed with feelings of hatred and revenge.

Hedonistic serial killer. This is the type of serial murderer who derives sexual pleasure from the act of killing, which is usually prolonged and contains acts of mutilation, torture, dismemberment, domination, or necrophilia. This is probably closest to Dietz's psychopathic sexual sadist, as well as to the classic serial killer description.

Power/control serial killer. Similar to the above type, this murderer derives pleasure from the prolonged torture and killing of another human being, but here the emphasis is more on the control and domination aspects of the killing than the sexual component per se. Of course, there is likely to be a great deal of overlap between these two categories.

A empirical study of the Holmes serial murderer typology was carried out by Canter & Wentink (2004), based on an analysis of crime scene evidence from 100 U.S. serial murders. They found limited support for aspects of the lust, thrill, and mission serial killer categories, and features of the power/control serial killer were found to generalize to serial killers as a whole, rather than forming a distinct type. The findings suggested that more attention should be paid to styles of interactions with victims (e.g., restraints, torture, mutilation, theft of property, etc.), rather than just inferring the motivations of individual offenders.

Rappaport Typology

Rappaport's (1988) typology describes five types of serial killers:

Spree killers kill a series of victims during a continuous span of murder and are basically similar to Dietz's and others' descriptions of the crime spree killer.

Functionaries of organized criminality are the contact killers, assassins, and hit men familiar from previous descriptions.

Custodial killers are medical personnel, foster parents of disabled children, or other caretakers who poison or asphyxiate victims for financial gain, revenge, ideology, or twisted altruism ("angels of mercy/angels of death").

Psychotic killers murder under the influence of delusions and/or hallucinations, familiar from above descriptions.

Sexually sadistic killers are murderers who derive sexual pleasure through inflicting pain on their victims, which describes both Dietz's psychopathic sexual sadist and Holmes' hedonistic serial killer.

Serial Killer Typologies: Conceptual Commonalities

The commonalities of typological descriptions coming from different observers in different times and places speaks for a certain construct validity of the categories described by each. These appear to boil down to a basic set of common serial or multiple murderer subtypes:

Sexual sadists who kill for the intense pleasure derived from the domination, control, torture, humiliation, and murder of another human being.

Delusional killers on a mission, either frankly psychotic or more ideologically-driven, to rid the world of persons they consider undesirable.

Custodial killers who murder helpless or dependent persons under their care. Note that this group may overlap with the above, e.g., the health care worker who believes that society should not waste resources on sick or disabled people or that God has commanded that it would be more merciful to put them out of their misery.

Utilitarian killers whose motive at least partly involves some practical financial or other material gain, although the motive may be mixed with anger or revenge, as in the aggrieved spouse who wants to put a final end to the wrangling over a bitter divorce.

Organized-Disorganized Dichotomy

Probably, the best-known, and increasingly controversial, classification scheme of serial killers is the one developed by the FBI's Behavioral Science Unit, which divides serial killers into organized vs. disorganized categories (Geberth, 1990; Geberth & Turco, 1997; Hazelwood & Douglas, 1980; Hickey, 1997; Palermo & Kocsis, 2005; Ressler et al., 1986a, 1988).

Organized serial killer. This perpetrator is above average in intelligence and considers himself superior to other people. He is organized in most aspects of his life and takes great care with personal appearance, grooming, and belongings. His crime is well-thought-out and carefully planned. The crime is usually committed away from his area of residence or work and the killer is quite mobile, often traveling many miles to commit his murders. Fantasy and ritual are important to the organized killer, and he selects a victim, typically a stranger, whom he considers the "right" type in terms of age, physical appearance, behavior, and other qualities. The killer typically carries a carefully prepared **torture kit** containing his preferred implements of bondage and mutilation. He may follow and stalk this victim for hours or days, and he may take great pride in verbally manipulating his target into a position of vulnerability. His capture and control of the victim are calculated to afford him maximum power over his hapless prey. Alcohol is often used during the murder. He often takes a souvenir or trophy from his victim that he may later use to relive the event or enhance his fantasies surrounding the killing. He is often familiar with police procedures and takes pride in thwarting investigations and taunting law enforcement officials by the careful placement or concealment of evidence. In some cases, he is currently or has formerly worked in some branch of law enforcement or security, or aspired to do so. He may be a "student" of previous or contemporaneous serial killers, reading up on their exploits and even corresponding with them in prison. He typically learns from each of his own crimes and becomes increasingly sophisticated in his predatory and elusive tactics. Although casual observers may describe some serial killers as solitary and strange in their daily behavior, just as commonly he may appear normal and a "regular guy" to coworkers, family, and neighbors.

Disorganized serial killer. This killer is average or below average in intelligence. He is often a loner and a recluse. He is typically an underachiever, feels sexually and interpersonally inadequate, has a poor self-image, and is considered weird or odd by acquaintances. He typically engages in such sexual activities as voyeurism, exhibitionism, lingerie thefts, and fetish burglaries, and uses sadistic and fetishistic fantasy pornography in autoerotic activities. He is less careful about planning, and his crime scenes typically display more haphazard behavior. The violent offense is more impulsive and spontaneous, and the victim is often a target of opportunity. The disorganized killer's crimes lack the manipulation and cunning of the organized killer, and typically consist of **blitz attacks** that are intended to silence the victim quickly through blunt force trauma. After the sudden sexual and physical violence to the victim, death usually follows quickly. The attack may be characterized by **overkill**, with multiple stabs and blows. Postmortem activities with the corpse may include biting, exploratory dissection, mutilation, insertion of foreign objects, or masturbation onto the body; there may or may not be actual penile penetration of the body. As the name implies, the crime scene is sloppy and disorganized, with little or no effort to conceal the evidence. Trophies are less frequently taken, but there may be a secondary robbery of opportunity.

As with most classificatory systems, intermediate types are frequently found, and sometimes a crime scene has elements of both organized and disorganized categories, in which case it is called **mixed** (Geberth, 1990; Geberth & Turco, 1997; Hickey, 1997; Ressler et al., 1986a, 1988). And, as with most psychological and criminological descriptors that deal with the untidy realities of human nature, authorities are coming to agree that the organized-disorganized system should be thought of more as a continuum than as a rigid dichotomy, and that this information should be utilized as one set of data, along with the other information collected in the course of the investigation (Box 10.2).

BOX 10.2. HOW TO INVESTIGATE A SERIAL HOMICIDE

A body has been discovered in your precinct. As an experienced homicide investigator, you understand that a murder or suspicious death necessitates an established protocol to assure the preservation of the crime scene and the integrity of the evidence (Geberth, 2006; Rossmo, 2009). If you were the homicide investigator assigned to the case, here's what you would do.

THE CRIME SCENE

Much of the useful information you will obtain about the serial homicide case will be gathered at the crime scene (Geberth, 1990, 2006; Rossmo, 2009; Turvey, 1999), which is why it is vitally important that this be done correctly.

continued

BOX 10.2.—*Continued*

Preliminary Steps

Working a crime scene begins even before you get there. You will probably get the call by radio or phone from an officer who has discovered the crime scene or been led to it by a citizen. Instruct the officer(s) on duty to preserve the crime scene, to hold any witnesses or suspects for questioning, and to begin initiating a log or timeline, accounting for all activities at the scene and the people and vehicles who have had access to the scene.

Initial Procedures

Don't just barrel into the crime scene. As you approach, observe the area as a whole—neighborhood, roadways, pedestrian pathways—before focusing on the crime scene itself and securing the location. For an indoor crime scene, this may be as simple as closing a door or blocking off a hallway. If the crime scene is outdoors, a wide area surrounding the body should be cordoned off; here, the biggest problem is often keeping unauthorized people away from the scene.

When you arrive, confer with the on-scene officer and have him or her escort you on an initial "**walk-through**" of the scene, while mentally absorbing the crime scene and starting to develop a preliminary mental image of plausible events. At the same time, begin taking photos, ascertain if there is any fragile or perishable evidence that needs to be collected right away, and maintain a running time line of events by use of notes or a recorder.

Describing the Scene

A complete description of the victim should include sex, age, build, hair color, clothing or missing clothing, positioning of the body, evidence of premortem injury or postmortem mutilation, and any evidence that could yield clues as to cause of death. Describe the immediate surroundings as well as the location and position of the body in relation to objects and furnishings in an indoor setting or items or landmarks at an outdoor scene.

Note the presence of any obvious weapons in the vicinity, including firearms, blades, bludgeons, garrotes, etc. Equally important, be alert for common or unusual objects that could be used as potential weapons, such as workshop tools, cooking utensils, electrical cords, heavy furnishings, and so on. If a weapon is nearby, take detailed notes but don't yet handle it. Look for obvious signs of violence such as bullet holes, shell casings, blood stains, or the presence of vials, bottles, or syringes. Do not collect evidence at this stage of the investigation, but observe and document anything of relevance on the scene. In major cases, in larger agencies, personnel from the evidence lab will arrive to implement collection procedures. In smaller departments, you may have to do this yourself.

An important aspect of on-scene investigation of serial homicide is an analysis of **crime scene staging**, in which the offender manipulates the crime scene in an attempt to confuse or misdirect law enforcement investigators from the true cause of death or motive for the killing (Hazelwood & Napier, 2004). Common scenarios include homicides staged to look like suicides or accidents, or domestic homicides staged to look like robbery (Adair & Doberson, 1999; Geberth, 1996; Imajo, 1983; Meloy, 2000). In serial homicides, the perpetrator is more apt to stage murder scenes precisely to shock and/or taunt police and the media. Thus, when examining a murder scene, consider who would benefit from the scene being staged as it is found (Hazelwood & Napier, 2004).

Preliminary Interviews

Obtain a detailed account of what the on-scene officer(s) have seen and done. Record these observations and opinions, and use them to guide—but not bias—your own observations and opinions of the case. Although all fields of expertise rely on quick, heurisitically-driven recognition of patterns (Klein, 1998), each homicide case is unique and may require a fresh approach or perspective, so keep an open mind. Also remember, however, that crime scene investigation is always a team effort, so take information where you can get it and discuss it with whoever might provide useful insight.

Any potential witnesses should be interviewed at the scene to take advantage of their fresh observations and recollections and the opportunity for witnesses to guide investigators to evidence that might otherwise be overlooked or destroyed. Some witnesses may be transported to the department for further questioning.

VICTIMOLOGY

Not just for serial homicides, but even for single murders, when there are no viable suspects, when witnesses cannot provide productive leads, and when the crime scene yields too few clues to make a definitive determination, sometimes the only way to get a grasp on the causes and circumstances of the homicide is to develop a thorough understanding of the victim, a process known as **victimology** (Joyce, 2006; La Brode, 2007).

Purposes of Victimology

A thorough understanding of who the victim is, where she lived and worked, her background and social relationships may the vital first step in ascertaining why she was victimized, who the killer was, and what may be his preferred type of victim (Napier & Baker, 2002; Napier & Hazelwood, 2003). Aside from investigative considerations, victim identification also allows the victim's family to obtain closure on the fate of their missing loved one (see Box 9.2, Chapter 9).

continued

BOX 10.2.—*Continued*

Victim Data Collection

In rare cases, clues are as obvious as finding the victim's wallet or some other form of identification at the crime scene. Most commonly, obtaining clues to the victim's identity will involve good old-fashioned gumshoe work—taking photos of the victim's face and then canvassing the area to see if residents or merchants recognize her. An accurate description of clothing and any other personal effects at the scene is also essential. Try to obtain viable fingerprints. If the body is autopsied, the medical examiner will document any distinguishing features, marks, scars, tattoos, piercings, and so on. All of this information will prove useful in checking against computerized **Missing Person/Unidentified Body Reports**. But remember that any high-tech computer search and cross-matching is only as good as the data put into it, and this data will come from a careful analysis of the crime scene.

Evidence Collected

The following pieces of data are important in developing a comprehensive **victimology profile** (Joyce, 2006).

Injuries sustained. Actually, this information will overlap with general crime scene data collected. In an indirect way, the pattern of injuries may yield clues to the motives and identity of the killer which may, in turn, offer clues to his relationship with the victim and, thereby, to the victim's identity. For example, a level of extreme violence usually indicates that the perpetrator purposefully wanted to make sure the victim was dead; alternatively, it may indicate someone prone to go into an explosive psychotic rage.

Location. Many homicides, including serial homicides, occur because a particular victim was at the wrong place at the wrong time. Thus, once investigators have gotten a sense of the demographics of the victim, and possibly previous victims, an important part of victimology is assessing whether the victim belongs where the body was found. What was the premed honors student doing in the seedy bar district? Was she trying to buy drugs? Why was the usually workaholic business manager not in her office, but at home in her apartment at 3:30 in the afternoon? Was she meeting someone? Who?

Since many homicides occur inside a car, the location where the car is found may be an important piece of data, along with whether that type of vehicle fits that type of neighborhood. For homicides that occur inside a private residence, look for evidence of forced entry, lack of which may indicate that the victim knew her killer or that the perpetrator used deception to gain entry (e.g., posing as a repairman or police officer); alternatively, it may have involved a domestic quarrel between the woman and a current or former lover. When commercial locations are the homicide site, robbery, drug deals, or worker-manager disputes are usually the main factors to consider.

In many cases of serial homicide, the victim's body is deposited many miles from the location where she was abducted or killed. Such scenarios, indecorously termed "**dump jobs**," are notoriously difficult cases to solve because it is almost impossible to trace the victim's last steps.

Occupation. What did the victim do for a living and what kinds of people would she be likely to come in contact with in the course of her work and social life? This in turn might yield clues as to important characteristics of her killer. For example, a college professor or corporate office manager is likely to deal with and socialize with men of a more upscale demographic than would a cocktail waitress or hotel housekeeping worker. The key is to look both for patterns that make sense and for those that don't fit.

Family and friends. Interviewing these collaterals is important for two reasons. First, as noted in previous chapters, most interpersonal violence, including murder, occurs between people who know each other. Thus, speaking with friends and relatives may well uncover clues to the perpetrator's identity. Serial homicide, however, tends to be a crime committed against strangers, so ruling out familiar suspects may point to a killer who was heretofore unknown to the victim. Second, the victim may have confided in close friends or relatives and this may give investigators a clue to her whereabouts shortly before she was killed. In some cases, the victim may have been engaged in a "secret life" that put her at risk for victimization and she may have told only a few close confidantes about this.

Legal history. Again, don't overlook the obvious. Check computer databases to see if any victim features match subjects in the database with a criminal or civil litigation history.

THE VICTIM PROFILE AND IDENTIFYING THE OFFENDER

Now, you'll use your training, experience, intuition, and powers of logical analysis to put the data together to form a victim profile (Douglas et al., 1986; Geberth, 1990; 2006; Palermo & Kocsis, 2005; Rossmo, 2009). Especially in serial homicide investigations, knowing who the victims are is often a vital first step in apprehending their killer.

Developing the Victim Profile

Begin with the information you've painstaking gathered at the crime scene through your notes and photos, including information about the general location, traffic patterns, and ease of access for various types of individuals. Your data will also include all physical evidence gathered at the crime scene, such as footprints, blood spatters, and objects possibly used as weapons or bindings. An autopsy of the victim will usually provide clues in reconstructing the sequence of the crime, method of death, and injuries sustained while alive. This is also where your victim profile comes in, allowing you to put together characteristics of the victim that

continued

BOX 10.2.—*Continued*

match the killer's **modus operandi**, or **MO**, i.e., his particular methodology of committing crimes that may contain commonalities which offer clues to his identification. (This is distinguished from the **signature**, which reflects the offender's deliberate individualistic manipulation of certain elements of the crime scene).

Developing the Offender Profile

The construction of an **offender profile** generally involves a standard procedure (Annon, 1995; Ault & Reese, 1980; Douglas et al., 1986; Homant & Kennedy, 1998; Snook et al., 2007). Crime scene data are collected by investigators and forwarded to the profiler who analyzes the data and provides predictions about the likely characteristics of the offender. The FBI's Crime Scene Analysis breaks the process down further into six steps:

- **Profiling Inputs**. All potentially relevant evidence is collected from the crime scene, including physical evidence, photos, investigator notes, and reports of witness interviews.
- **Decision Process Models**. Evidence is organized, studied, and analyzed to discern patterns and commonalities that can link the crime to others and yield clues to offender detection.
- **Crime Assessment**. From this pattern analysis, investigators attempt to reconstruct the crime scene, including a timeline of events and the role each person present, whether perpetrator, victim, or bystander.
- **Criminal Profile**. Steps 1–3 are combined to create a criminal profile incorporating the motives, physical qualities, personality, and behavioral tendencies of the perpetrator. This profile is also used to guide interview strategies for different types of suspects.
- **Investigation**. The working profile is distributed to active investigators on the case and to any other individuals and organizations that may have databases or information pertinent to identifying the suspect. If few useful leads are turned up, new incoming information may be used to revise and update the profile.
- **Apprehension**. If and when a suspect is identified (in about 50% of cases), he is interviewed, investigated, and compared with the profile. If a reasonable suspicion exists that the subject could be the perpetrator, a warrant is issued for his arrest. At trial, the careful presentation of evidence by law enforcement agents, forensic laboratory analysts, forensic psychologists, and others is what often proves critical in making the case against the offender.

In creating your offender profile, try to give as complete a description of the perpetrator as possible, including gender, age, race or ethnicity, intelligence level, education, military service, job status, living circumstances, nature of interpersonal relationships, and business and social contacts. Regard these descriptive statements as hypotheses that you will test against accumulating information. Many of these hypotheses will simply be generalizations based on your training and experience, while others may be more intuitively arrived at by mentally playing out the crime in different scenarios and imagining what sort of person would be involved. Then, match these alternatives to your local and regional criminal databases to see if any further identifying leads come up. Depending on the volume of the data and nature of the case, your final written profile may range from a few paragraphs to multiple pages. Finally, disseminate your profile to investigators and local law enforcement agencies. If no useful leads or clues develop, update and revise the profile as new data come in.

DEVELOPMENTAL HISTORIES AND DYNAMICS OF SERIAL KILLING

For the past several decades, law enforcement investigators and behavioral scientists have utilized a standard developmental profile of serial killers that has consisted of the following basic developmental and clinical features (Arrigo & Purcell, 2001; Briken et al., 2006; Brittain, 1970; Burgess et al., 1986; Canter et al., 1996; Chan & Heide, 2009; DeLisi & Scherer, 2006; Dietz et al., 1990; Egger, 2002; Flowers, 2002a,c, 2006; Gee et al., 2003; Folino, 2000; Grubin, 1994a,b; Harbort & Mokros, 2001; Hazelwood et al., 1992; Holmes & Holmes, 2001; Langevin, 2003; Langevin et al., 1988; Lester, 1995; MacCulloch et al., 1983; Malmquist, 1996; Marshall & Barbaree, 1990; McKenzie, 1995; Meloy, 2000; Meloy et al., 1994; Myers et al., 1998, 2003; Palermo, 2004; Palermo & Kocsis, 2005; Prentky et al., 1989; Proulx et al., 1996, 2007; Purcell & Arrigo, 2006; Oliver et al., 2007; Ressler & Schachtman, 1992; Ressler et al., 1988, 1996; Sears, 1991; Simon, 1996).

Childhood characteristics. Although serial killers typically reach the peak of their activity in their early 20s to mid-30s, their fantasized fusing of cruelty with sexuality usually begins in adolescence, sometimes in childhood, and develops over the lifespan. A number of serial killers have been illegitimate or adopted children and several were sons of prostitutes. Many were severely abused physically and sexually as children, and a number have had intensely ambivalent, smothering relationships with their mothers that were characterized by both maternal abuse and sexual attraction to the mother. There was often a strong family history of psychiatric, substance abuse, and/or legal problems. However, the upbringing and family life of a number of other serial killers could not be characterized as pathological in any major sense; these children grew up in relatively stable homes with both parents present and did not describe any abuse history.

The play of children who would become serial killers commonly has a repetitive, stereotyped, aggressive pattern. They often lie, steal, destroy property, set fires, and are cruel and callous to other children. Many have shown the triad of bedwetting, firesetting, and cruelty to animals that predicts antisocial behavior in later years (Chapter 8). In particular, many have especially enjoyed torturing animals from an early age. Most have grown up shy, lonely, highly sensitive, with feelings of being rejected, unloved, and neglected, and harboring a baseline hostility toward specific persons and/or the world at large. A few, however, have reportedly been gregarious, extroverted conversationalists. In such cases, their outward behavior is incongruous with their basic inner feelings; they have learned to "play the game." Most would meet some or all criteria for conduct disorder as children (Chapters 8 and 19), and for antisocial, narcissistic, and/or schizoid personality disorder as adults (Chapers 7 and 8). Many have records of previous arrests and convictions for a wide variety of crimes, while others remain under the legal radar until their serial killings are discovered.

Adolescence and early adulthood. Odd and isolated since childhood, the future serial killer turns inward and nurtures sadistic sexual fantasies, often accompanied by masturbation, transvestism, voyeurism, exhibitionism, and other fetishes, usually involving violent pornography. The early fantasies may consist of elaborations on certain actual experiences or may be stimulated by "experiments" conceived in various types of movies, magazines, video games, Internet porn, combat websites, and so on. Some of this material may be integrated into actual sexual experiences or into masturbatory fantasies. At some point, the individual begins to incorporate actual people into his sexually murderous fantasies and begins to mentally rehearse more realistic scenarios for stalking, abducting, and torturing victims to death. In these developing fantasies, as in the later actual killings, the victims become depersonalized, reduced to contemptible objects that exist solely for the gratification of the perpetrator.

As adolescents and young adults, these subjects' criminal careers often begin with assault and escalate to battery, arson, rape, and eventually murder. Once they have fully acted out and gotten away with their sexually violent fantasies, they feel increasingly empowered. The killings feed their fantasies of invincibility which spur further killings. Over time, the abduction, torture, and murder sequences become more ritualized and more refined, and the killers learn from their near-miss mistakes, becoming increasingly efficient in their killings and evasion of capture. Even at this stage, fantasies may still be employed because, unlike reality, the fantasied scenario can always be "perfect."

Consistent with Simon's (1996) contention that "bad men do what good men dream," many people have sexual fantasies, even sadistic sexual fantasies, as any stroll through the innumerable Internet websites serving this interest will confirm. However, only a tiny proportion of those individuals have either the desire or wherewithal to cross the line into actual physical violence against real human beings. For example, long before widespread use of the Internet, Crepault & Couture (1980) studied a sample of 94 "normal" men (i.e., having no legal or mental health histories) and found that 66 percent of them engaged in regular sexual fantasies of any type, with a smaller but significant proportion reporting that they enjoyed fantasies of bondage (39%), rape (33%), other sexual aggression (27%), and humiliation (15%). Experts from the time of Kraft-Ebing (1898/1965) to the present (Chan & Heide, 2009) have recognized that it is a singular lack of conscience combined with an inflated sense of entitlement that characterizes those sadistic criminals that cross over into actual predation on other people.

One representative clinical investigation of the historical psychological dynamics of future serial sexual murderers comes from an in-depth study of adolescents by Johnson & Becker (1997), who present the detailed case histories of nine 14- to 18-year-old males who had expressed a desire to perpetrate serial killings and were referred to the authors for a forensic evaluation after having committed some nonsexual but violent legal offense.

These adolescents reported repetitive and explicit fantasies of sexual torture, mutilation, and murder, dating from an early age, and increasing over time. The sexually violent fantasies were described as arousing and exciting by these youths; in fact, the types of sexual fantasies reported by these adolescents were strikingly similar to those described by established serial killers who have been apprehended and interviewed. Some of these boys had already begun to practice their sadistic craft on pets and other animals. This study confirmed that the evolving nature of the sexually sadistic fantasy life seen in nascent serial killers often begins in adolescence and is a key factor in identifying youth who are at risk for becoming sexually sadistic serial murderers.

In a more recent study of 61 convicted serial killers, Harbort & Mokros (2001) found that they were most likely to be of average intelligence, and only three (5.2% of the sample) reported having been sexually abused as children. Psychological descriptors used to characterize these murderers included lack of empathy, hostile emotional state, emotional instability, egocentricity, lack of responsibility, low frustration tolerance, poor impulse control, and low self-confidence. Except for the last descriptor, the rest are all hallmark traits of narcissistic and antisocial personalities (Chapters 7 and 8).

SPECIAL POPULATIONS OF SERIAL KILLERS

As we've seen, most serial killers are heterosexual males; however, like any generalization about human nature, there are exceptions, and this section will consider some atypical varieties of serial killers and multiple homicide offenders.

Sadist-Masochist Serial Killers

For a subset of serial killers, sadism is suffused with masochism, and these individuals derive pleasure from both giving and receiving pain (Hill et al., 2006; Knoll, 2009; Myers et al., 2008), often involving acts of self-mutilation, genital self-torture, or **autoerotic asphyxiation** (choking oneself almost to the point of unconsciousness; Everitt, 1999; Newton, 1990). Theories to explain the origin of these **sadist-masochist serial offenders** include: (1) identification with an earlier parental figure who has been both an aggressor and a victim (Macgregor, 1991; Stein, 2004); (2) being raised by a sexually provocative and punitive mother (Meloy, 2000; Fox & Levin, 1994); (3) becoming a "substitute victim" to vicariously experience the victims' pain, so as to heighten his enjoyment of inflicting further pain ("Wow–if this is what it feels like, she must really be suffering . . .") (Knoll, 2009); and (4) the **grandiose sadism theory**, in which the serial offender assumes the very identity of the victim (e.g., wearing her clothes, her scalp as a wig, or even her skin as a jacket or shawl) in order to extend his control over the victim beyond her death (Knoll, 2009; Warren et al., 1996).

Female Serial Killers

As with violent crimes generally, male serial killers far outnumber female serial killers; however, about 15 percent of multiple homicide offenders spanning the past two centuries have been women (Hickey, 1997; Kelleher & Kelleher, 1998; Malmquist, 1996; Perri & Lichtenwald, 2010). There are several features of female serial killers that distinguish them from their male counterparts (Arrigo & Shipley, 2001; Flowers, 2002b, 2002c; Flowers & Flowers, 2001; Kelleher & Kelleher, 1998; Palermo & Kocsis, 2005; Seagrave, 1992).

Unlike most male offenders, who kill out of compulsive rage and/or predatory lust, the motives behind serial homicides committed by women tend more toward monetary gain or histrionic attention-seeking. One exception may have been Eileen Wournos, who appears to have killed men out of pathological revenge and control-seeking. Female killers tend to start somewhat later than males, usually around age 30. With regard to methodology, males use more brute force, and are more likely to shoot, strangle, suffocate, stab, or bludgeon their victims, who are usually strangers. Female serial killers are more likely to use poison as a lethal tool and to kill people they know, including family members, spouses (**"black widow"** cases), or dependent persons under their care (**"angel of death"** cases). Female serial homicides rarely require the kind of behavioral profiling applied to more traditional male cases (Box 10.3).

Holmes & Holmes (1994) have elaborated a typology of female serial killers that parallels their typology for men:

Visionary serial killers: women who murder in response to directives to kill from voices in their head or visions. These women often suffer from a severe psychotic illness or mood disorder.

Comfort-oriented serial killers: females who murder for financial or material benefit. These are the "black widows" who may be highly mobile and skilled at changing their identities to lure unsuspecting victims in diverse locations over time, thereby racking up a string of wealthy (and soon deceased) husbands, before being apprehended.

Power-seeking serial killers: females who kill for the thrill and power gained through having full control over life and death of the victim. These include the "angel of death" cases that occur in health care facilities, although the killer may also target disabled family members.

Hedonistic serial killers: women who kill for sexual gratification. Unlike the prominence of this type for men, this is probably rare as a primary motive in female serial killers. However, many of these women may derive gratification through their association with a male serial killer (see below).

Disciple serial killers: women who kill under the command of a charismatic leader. Also rare, this may occur in a religious cult, more commonly as part of her personal allegiance to a charismatic male. The women who participated in the Tate-LaBianca murders in 1969 were under the thrall of Charles Manson, who remains in prison for the crimes.

Couple Serial Killers

Although rare, in some cases, two people with similar homicidal urges find each other. Cinematically dramatized in the 1994 film, *Natural Born Killers,* these **couple killers, partner killers, team killers**, or **tandem killers**, as they are variously called, commit their murders as a duo, one member typically baiting, befriending, or seducing the victim into a position of submission, with the other member then perpetrating or joining in the killing. The motives may range from pure robbery-murder for profit to prolonged torture-murder for sexual gratification, with various gradations in between (Flowers, 2002c; Flowers & Flowers, 2001; Owen, 2004).

Jenkins (1990) has described four types of partner or group serial killer:

Dominant-submissive pairs. In this group, one member, usually the male, is the dominant partner. The women participate in the murders mostly to please the man and often act as the bait to lure victims. They may or may not participate in the actual torture and murder of the victim, but may observe it. These women may later describe themselves as reluctantly willing participants, but more commonly claim that they were "brainwashed" by the man.

Equally dominant teams. Here, both members of the couple derive satisfaction from the killings, and both members are willing participants in the crime. The woman may participate in the capture and binding of the victim, more rarely in the torture and murder itself. She may enjoy witnessing the crime. The couple may subsequently use their recollections of the crime, aided by photographs, videos, and even objects or body-part trophies, to enhance their sexual activity.

Extended family or group. These may range from actual biological families who collaborate in serial murder to cult-families, such as the original Charles Manson group in the 1960s, in which unrelated people come together to form a small commune or tribal group that participates in homicide, typically for reasons ranging from robbery to sexual gratification to loosely-articulated philosophical/ideological reasons, sometimes with all of these motives combined.

Organized or ceremonial social groups. Here, the ideological or political aspect has become more crystallized and systematic. These are often quasi-religious cults who commit mass murder, as in the 1995 Aum Shin-rykio sarin gas attack on the Tokyo subway, but in some cases, individual victims may be targeted as well. Sexual motives are far less common in these groups.

Mention should also be made of couples in which the woman may not actually participate in the crimes, but may herself be subjected to physical and sexual torture by her mate, as part of a **consensual sadomasochistic relationship** (Knoll, 2009; Warren & Hazelwood, 2002). In some of these cases, the man has been a violent sexual offender outside of the relationship, including serial sexual homicide. The women may or may not have known about their mates' crimes, reminiscences of which were sometimes overtly or surreptitiously used to enhance the sexual pleasure of the man or both partners during their own sexual activities.

Homosexual Serial Killers

Another minority group in the serial killer universe consists of men who kill men. To date, there have been two main typologies developed to characterize this subgroup.

Geberth (1996b) has offered a six-fold typology of homosexual serial homicide:

Interpersonal violence-oriented disputes. These are essentially "lover's quarrels" between homosexual partners or ex-partners that escalate to violence and murder. Unless they occur in a repeated pattern, it is unlikely that these acts meet the definition of serial homicides, per se.

Forced sodomy. Here the gratification occurs through the act of sexual domination; death in these cases is usually accidental from excessive force used to brutalize or restrain the victim, most often either blunt force trauma or asphyxiation. Again, unless repeated, whether this satisfies the definition of serial homicide is questionable.

Lust murder. This homosexual serial killing pattern probably comes closest to its heterosexual correlate described in the literature. In these crimes, the act is carefully premeditated and reinforced by sadistic fantasies. A certain type of victim may be stalked and seduced or overpowered into submission. Death is sadistically prolonged by torture and genital mutilation, trophies may be taken, and there may be concealment or staging of the body.

Power murder. This is similar to the above category (and the two may well overlap), except that here, the sexual motivation is thought to be secondary to the thrill of power and domination. The victims are likely to be chosen for their physical vulnerability or social marginality, such as children, teens, or prostitutes. Although torture may be a feature of these killings, mutilation and dismemberment are just as likely to occur postmortem to create "shock value" for whoever discovers the body. Anger, more than lust, appears to drive this kind of homosexual serial homicide.

Robbery-homicide. Here, the offender cruises the gay scene, often posing as a prostitute, looking for vulnerable victims to rob. Either deliberately as part of the plan, or inadvertently, some of these robberies end in murder.

Homophobic murder. Episodes of gay-bashing may escalate to murder, again, either deliberately or accidently. The offenders may be self-repudiating homosexuals or homophobic heterosexual males.

More recently, Beauregard & Proulx (2007) have proferred a typology of homosexual serial homicide consisting of three categories.

Avenger. These individuals can be found among the ranks of homosexual, heterosexual, or bisexual prostitutes, whose lifestyles often revolve around drug and alcohol consumption. Many have criminal records, including property crimes and violence. Psychological, physical, and/or sexual abuse during childhood appear to form the core dynamic of this pattern. The victim is often an older man (parental figure?). When a particular sex act is requested by this partner, pickup, or prostitution patron, it purportedly triggers a traumatic memory and violence erupts, which may eventuate in murder. Essentially, the offender violently avenges himself on the hapless sex partner for the grievances and abuses he's suffered at the hands of others. The murder scene is characterized by signs of intense rage and death usually occurs by strangulation or by use of a weapon of opportunity (sharp utensil, heavy object, belt or cord).

Sexual predator. This is the homosexual lust murderer, motivated by sadistic sexual fantasies, and on the prowl for vulnerable victims, often children or adolescents, who may be homosexual or not. There is often a prior criminal history. The killing is premeditated, the victim is stalked and abducted, and acts of torture, sodomy, and mutilation are typically performed in the course of the sadistically prolonged murder. This type most closely resembles the classic heterosexual serial killer.

Nonsexual predator. This type of murderer is not motivated by anger or by sadistic sexual fantasies, and the homicide is usually accidental or impulsive, occurring in the course of a robbery which is the primary motive for the encounter. Often, the offender chooses his victim at a gay cruising venue, gains access to the victim's residence under the guise of intending to have sex with him, attempts to rob the place, and when confronted by the victim, feels compelled to overpower him, killing him in the process. The attempted robbery may also occur in an alleyway, car, or other secluded locale. Sex may occur prior to the crime to pacify the victim, but the motive for the encounter is not primarily sexual. The offender may act alone or with an accomplice, and alcohol or drugs are frequently involved. The perpetrator usually has a varied criminal history with an emphasis on property crimes.

Homosexual Serial Killer Typologies: Conceptual Commonalities

The commonalities between these typologies appear to involve the following basic subtypes, which may sometimes overlap:

Profit. Homosexual serial murderers whose motives are primarily to rob the victim.

Sadistic sexual gratification. Like many heterosexual sadistic sexual homicide perpetrators, the homosexual serial killer derives intense pleasure from the torture and murder of another human being.

Power. The sexual component is ancillary to the sense of power and domination.

Homophobia. The killer destroys that which he is most afraid of or disturbed by.

Professional Serial Killers

Some people make their living by killing other people. Their crimes can be said to be "serial" in the sense that these assassinations and contract killings are repeated, in the same way as anyone's job activities occur on a regular basis; however, they may be far removed psychologically from the type of sexually sadistic serial killer usually associated with this term. Schlesinger & Miller (2003) have explored the characteristics and psychological dynamics of what they term **contract murderers**, which they classify into three types:

Amateur. These actually comprise the majority of murderers for hire, largely because of their low cost and relatively easy availability within the criminal subculture. This subject frequently has a history of petty crimes and of addiction, psychopathology, and a marginal lifestyle. The most common scenario involves a small-time crook who is hired by an associate to eliminate a no-longer-wanted spouse or lover for purposes of jealousy, money, or revenge. Although initially motivated by cash, many of these minor-league hitmen actually come to enjoy the thrill and power associated with taking another person's life.

Semiprofessional. The semiprofessional contract murderer is more technically sophisticated and has had more on-the-job training than the amateur. His criminal history is longer and has involved more serious crimes, and he may have served stretches in prison. Semiprofessionals are less likely to show major psychopathology, but frequently display traits of antisocial personality and have histories of violence in their background. The semiprofessionals plan their contract murders with a higher level of sophistication and attention to detail than amateurs. The typical target of a semiprofessional contract murderer is a business associate or rival criminal, but in some cases, the semiprofessional is hired to eliminate a spouse or other family member. Because he is more expensive than the amateur, the clientele of the semiprofessional tend to stably employed or otherwise financially comfortable individuals with something substantial to gain from the target's elimination.

Professional. As the name implies, the professional contract murderer takes his vocation seriously, actually studying and training himself in the art and science of killing. He may be a former military, law enforcement, or security personnel and carries his lethal skills over into his criminal trade. Most of these professional assassins are on retainer with organized crime cartels, although some freelance their services to various criminal and political organizations as needed, commanding stiff fees for a professional job which typically includes the efficient elimination of the target and cleaning up of evidence that could tie the crime to either the assassin or the hirer. The target is usually a prominent functionary in a rival criminal organization or a political figure. The job may also involve multiple targets, in which case, bombing or arson may be involved. In some cases, "legitimate" government agencies may retain this person's service when they want to carry out a military or political assassination that cannot be traced back to them.

Serious psychopathology is uncommon in these individuals and, indeed, the best of them must possess keen intelligence and the ability to restrain impulsive action. While contract killers by definition could be said to harbor antisocial personality traits, many of these individuals rationalize their actions as being on a par with paramilitary mercenary soldiers and, as noted above, some of them may actually have this experience. However, it is not unreasonable to speculate that some degree of narcissistic power thrill underlies these assassins' motivation for continuing in this line of work.

NEUROPSYCHOLOGICAL CONCEPTS OF SERIAL KILLING

Much evidence points to neurological and neuropsychological factors in criminal aggression in general and sadistic serial killing in particular (Pallone & Hennessy, 1996). One problem has been that most current neuropsychological theories tend to be too narrowly localizationistic, prompting the need to look for a more integrative psychological/neurobehavioral/ethological theory that blends brain, mind, individual development, phylogenesis, and situational factors. This represents a move away from a reductionistic approach, and encourages a more systemic and interactive understanding of the brain's role in violent behavior (Martell, 1996; Miller, 1987, 1990, 1998a).

Aggression: Impulsive and Predatory

As we saw in Chapter 2, in the animal ethological and neuropsychological literature on aggression, one of the most widely validated behavioral and neuropharmacological distinctions is between affective or impulsive aggression, and predatory aggression (Eichelman, 1992; Eichelman et al., 1993; Kitaeff, 2011; Meloy, 1997b; Volavka, 1995).

Affective aggression involves high states of emotional and physiological arousal and typically occurs in ritualized intraspecies fighting for food, territory, mates, and social status. One thinks of two wolves in a pack battling over top-dog rank, or two rival human gang members signifying, cursing, or threatening each other with gestures, fists, or weapons. In natural environments, the usual purpose of affective aggression is to intimidate and dominate rivals within an established social structure, so serious physical injury usually does not occur. Actual death of one of the combatants is rare and probably accidental, although for modern humans, access to technologically lethal weapons makes death more likely.

Predatory aggression is more "cold-blooded," involves low emotional and physiological arousal, usually requires some degree of preparatory stalking, and typically occurs across species, especially between hunter and prey, with the goal clearly being to kill and consume the prey animal for sustenance, not out hatred or revenge; in a very real sense, "it's business, not personal." One thinks of a leopard quietly and patiently stalking a gazelle, before rushing in for the kill, which usually involves a single, efficient bite to the throat, or a professional hit man stalking his target for days or weeks, before quietly and efficiently dispatching him with a garrote, blade, or bullet. In many species, including humans, affective and predatory aggression can be mixed, and in higher animals, primates, and especially man, this includes the additional cognitive feature of more complex planning and socialization.

The meticulous stalking of his victim by the organized serial killer would appear to represent a clear expression of predatory aggression. In addition, some types of mass murder can be characterized as a predatory mode of violence–planned, purposeful, emotionless, consistent with the "warrior mentality" (Hempel et al., 1999; Meloy, 1997b, 1999; see Chapters 11 and 12). Recall that both affective-impulsive and predatory forms of aggression are not "pathological" in animal species; on the contrary, such creatures couldn't survive without these traits and, under certain circumstances, the same may be true for humans.

For example, Barratt et al. (1999) had a group of 216 college students assess their own aggressive acts using a specially designed self-report questionnaire. The results found impulsive and premeditated aggression to be separate reasons that students gave for acting aggressively. In particular, impulsive aggression was frequently followed by feelings of remorse for the acts and by internal confusion over the motives. On the other hand, premeditated aggression was related to more purposeful social gain and dominance, replicating the hierarchical structure seen in many species who live in interdependent social groups.

Neurochemistry of Violence

Recall from Chapter 2 that serotonin is the neurotransmitter most clearly implicated in the inhibitory control of aggression within the brain's limbic system. Potentiation of GABA activity also inhibits aggression. Dopamine and norepinephrine generally enhance aggression, and it is possible that the noradrenergic system modulates the relationship between serotonin and aggression by raising the preparedness of the organism to react aggressively. High testosterone, the male sex hormone, is clearly associated with aggression, especially when paired with low serotonin, but its effects, particularly in primates and humans, interact with social factors. In addition, hormones of the hypothalamic-pituitary-adrenal axis, such as cortisol, involved in the stress response to threatening situations, also play an intricate role in the regulation of aggression (Anderson, 2007; Raine, 1993; Raine et al., 1995; Volavka, 1995, 1999).

Psychophysiology of Violence

One of the most frequently observed EEG abnormalities associated with violence consists of excessive **theta** activity, an abnormality consistent with the **underarousal theory of psychopathy** (Chapter 8) which posits that psychopaths seek excessive stimulation through antisocial behavior to compensate for their constitutionally low levels of physiological arousal; that is they are **sensation-seekers** (Raine et al., 1990, 1995; Williams, 1969; Zuckerman, 1979, 1990). Additional psychophysiological evidence for underarousal includes long latency **brainstem averaged evoked responses (BAERs)**, significantly lower resting heart rates, and reduced skin conductance activity. Yet, psychopathic subjects also show enhanced **P300** amplitudes, indicating increased attention to stimuli of interest. If serial killers are indeed a particularly lethal subspecies of psychopath, this would explain their relentless focus on stalking their quarry (Chapter 18), as well as the orgiastic pleasure from torture and murder that their sensation-craving brains cannot obtain in any other way.

Neuroimaging Studies

Recall from Chapter 2 that the frontal lobes of the brain are crucially involved in behavioral self-awareness and self-control, while the temporal lobes contain many of the limbic structures that mediate emotional and motivation states such as sexuality and aggression (Miller, 1987, 1993d, 1998a; Volavka, 1995, 1999). Mills & Raine (1994) reviewed 20 brain imaging studies of violent and sexual offenders, using CT, MRI, rCBF, and PET technologies. The authors concluded that frontal lobe dysfunction was more associated with violent offending, such as murder, while temporal lobe dysfunction was associated with less violent sexual offending, such as incest and pedophilia. Dysfunction that involved both regions of the brain was associated with offending that combined sexual and violent elements, such as rape. Another study (Volkow & Tancredi, 1987) revealed frontal dysfunction in violent individuals who had no remorse for their actions, a prominent personality trait of psychopaths (Miller, 1987, 1989b).

The neuroethologically-based categorization of aggressive acts into predatory vs. affective was studied by Raine et al. (1998) using PET scans with 15 predatory murderers, nine affective murderers, and 41 nonviolent controls. The results indicated that, while both affective and predatory murderers showed heightened activity in subcortical limbic brain regions, only affective murderers showed impaired frontal lobe functioning. Thus, affective murderers appear to be deficient in their ability to regulate and control aggressive impulses generated from subcortical limbic structures due to impaired frontal lobe regulation. Predatory murderers, however, retain the frontal lobe ability to direct, control, and modulate their activity, but they do so in the service of their limbically-driven compulsion for sex and dominance. Again, although this was not studied directly, there is an intriguing potential correlation between these findings and the organized-disorganized dichotomy of serial killers discussed above.

Cravings, Compulsions, and Kindling

The sudden, explosive, paroxysmal nature of some forms of violence has led to the idea that they may represent a variant of seizure disorder, such as **psychomotor** or **temporal lobe seizures** (Money, 1990; see Chapter 2). However, paroxysmal brain activity need not represent frank seizures per se. Research has identified an electrophysiological process that investigators have named **kindling**, by analogy to easily combustible material (e.g., dry leaves or twigs) that must be heated to a certain temperature before igniting and then going on to facilitate the combustion of the main fuel pile (e.g., fireplace branches and logs). In experimental research, repeated stimulation of temporal lobe limbic structures, particularly the **amygdala**, produces a cumulative increase in excitability and a lowering of the seizure threshold. That is, each stimulus makes the brain more sensitive, until finally, a subsequent minor stimulus that would have been insufficient in itself to evoke a seizure-like response if given the first few times, now incites the already-primed brain into paroxysmal activity with correspondingly uncontrolled behavior. Kindling has been used as a model for the slow, progressive build-up of angry or dysphoric feelings in humans that eventually flashes over into full blown violence or depression (Adamec, 1990; Adamec & Stark-Adamec, 1983; Goddard, 1967; Miller, 1997c, 2000b; Post, 1980; Racine, 1978).

Several researchers have proposed kindling as a neurophysiological model for predatory violence (Niehoff, 1999). Simon (1996) believes that kindling may have specific applicability to serial sexual murderers because of the escalating pattern of killings, the build-up of dysphoric tension prior to each killing, and the relief felt after the killings. It may be that serial killers have an unrecognized, aberrant, or atypical form of mood disorder, so that torturing helpless victims to death literally affords them an exhilarating, if perverse, antidepressant high.

This compulsive aspect of serial killing may actually represent an extreme subtype of a more general typology of cravings, addictions, compulsions, and so-called "irresistible impulses" (Soutullo et al., 1998). In *DSM-IV-TR* (APA, 2000), the essential feature of an **impulse control disorder** is the failure to resist an impulse, drive, or temptation to perform an act that is harmful to the person or to others. *DSM-IV-TR* further stipulates that for the diagnosis of an impulse control disorder, the individual must feel an increasing sense of tension or arousal before committing the act and then experience pleasure, gratification (the "rush"), and relief in the commission of the act. Behaviors included in this class of disorders are as diverse as **kleptomania** (compulsive stealing), **pyromania** (compulsive fire-setting; Chapter 20), **pathological gambling**, **trichotillomania** (compulsive hair-pulling), and **intermittent explosive disorder** (Chapter 2). It has been hypothesized that serotonergic abnormalities underlie some of the impulsive and/or compulsive features of impulse control disorders, noradrenergic or dopaminergic abnormalities underlie their pleasurable or euphoric features, and abnormalities in all three systems underlie the affective dysregulation of these disorders (Simon, 1996; Soutullo et al., 1998; Stein et al., 1993).

On this dimension, we might situate serial killers not on the extreme impulsive end, because unlike the "pure" psychopath who's numerous and varied antisocial acts are impelled by the whims of the moment, many serial killers seem locked in to a particular form of violent expression: they can't adequately release their tension in any way *but* the sadistic act. However, the "compulsive" quality of their murderous behavior lacks the overly self-reflective, ego-dystonic, anhedonic quality of true obsessive-compulsives: serial killers may say they are "driven" to kill, but they certainly enjoy doing it, feel entitled to do it, and rarely regret it.

PSYCHOLOGICAL THEORIES OF SERIAL KILLING

A dramatic crime like serial homicide might be expected to generate a plethora of psychological theories, spanning centuries. Here we will consider a few of the more well-known representative modern conceptualizations.

Psychodynamics

Simon's (1996) approach places the underlying psychology of the serial killer not primarily in antisocial predation and narcissistic entitlement, but fundamentally in a core of self-loathing, from which he briefly relieves himself in the actions of controlling, torturing, and killing a victim. In this view, only the most intensely violent, sexually sadistic exploitation of his victims brings the serial sexual killer out of an emotional deadness to life, temporarily enabling him to feel calm and relaxed. As noted above, many serial killers report a profound sense of relief after carrying out a torture and murder episode, stating that this act is the only way they can feel "normal"–at least until the urge builds toward another murder. Similarly, Malmquist (1996) highlights the profound depression and despair reported by many serial killers just prior to their next murderous act, with the subjugation, degradation, and slow destruction of a helpless human being acting as a mood-elevating tonic for these murderers–the kind of perverse antidepressant function of serial killing noted earlier. However, many serial killers report no such dysphoric feelings and give every impression of killing simply because they revel in the control and power of their acts.

For all their individual permutations, Schlesinger (2000) maintains that the fundamental psychological dynamics of all true serial homicides can be distilled down to three core components: (1) sexual sadism, (2) intense fantasy, and (3) a compulsion to act out that fantasy. In any given serial murder case, all three components will be present, but the proportion and intensity of each will differ from killer to killer.

Sadism. This is defined as sexual arousal derived from the physical suffering, humiliation, domination, and control of the victim, and is at the core of serial homicide: these individuals kill sadistically because nothing else gives them the same kind of thrilling stimulation.

Fantasy. As noted above, in the early development of the serial killer, fantasies of domination, control, and sexual aggression initially serve as mental rehearsal for the behavior and are later used to relive and reinforce the pattern of killings once they have begun.

Compulsion to kill. Many offenders describe a state of mounting inner tension, precipitated and maintained by fantasy, that builds over time into an almost unbearable state, the only relief for which is obtained by the act of sexually sadistic murder. Once the homicide is carried out, the tension is discharged, and the offender feels a sense of relief and satisfaction–until the cycle begins again.

Schlesinger (2000) points out that, powerful though this compulsion may be, it does not constitute an "irresistible impulse" in the legal sense. Moreover, various descriptions by the offender of "another personality taking over" are not indications of multiple personality disorder or dissociation. The serial offender knows exactly what he is doing and he technically has volitional control over his actions but chooses to kill because he seeks the thrill and relief from his state of inner tension, much in the same way as a drug addict compulsively seeks his high, but can volitionally abstain if the stakes are high enough (e.g., violating parole and going back to prison).

Cognitive Style and Cognitive Distortions

The previous point is a crucial one for understanding the behavior not just of serial killers but of most "crimes of passion," be it rape, assault, or murder. Many people *feel* compelled to take some kind of violent action, but most of us don't, even though we understand how good it might feel to "let it all out." This may be because the act in question would violate our own personal moral code or it may simply be because we don't want to get caught and sent to jail by the cops or be consigned to Hell by God. But, either way, we *stop ourselves,* while the serial killer does not. In Chapter 3, we reviewed the ideas of some criminal psychologists, such as Samenow (1984, 2002, 2007), that most criminals *choose* to commit their crimes because they "think differently" than the rest of us. So it is legitimate to explore just what patterns of thinking might be involved in giving oneself license to brutally destroy another human being for one's own gratification.

Palermo & Kocsis (2005) describe serial killers as having a particular **cognitive map**. They view the world as hostile and are correspondingly unable or unwilling to properly interact with other people. Their thinking is trapped in a circuitously narcissistic, isolative, and self-referencing cycle, which revolves around fulfilling their need for perverse stimulation to reduce their state of inner tension. The commission of their crime represents an act of narcissistic grandiosity, reinforcing their sense of entitlement to use other people for their own gratification and, with each act, reestablishes a certain degree of inner psychological homeostasis until the next time.

Research with rapists and other sexual offenders (Malamuth & Brown, 1994; Polaschek & Gannon, 2004; Polachek & Ward, 2002; Scully & Marolla, 1984, 1985; Ward & Keenan, 1999) has established that many of these perpetrators possess particular attitudes and cognitive styles, which the researchers call **implicit theories**, or **ITs** (see also Chapter 14). These are basic views of the world and of themselves that allow the offenders to rationalize and justify their sexually predatory actions.

Beech et al. (2005) carried out a systematic study of the cognitive styles of two groups of offenders: rapists and sexual murderers. The researchers found no significant differences in the kinds of ITs manifested by the two groups, but the ITs themselves fell into several categories:

Dangerous world. "The bitch deserves it–they all deserve it." This was the most common IT found in sexual murderers and consisted of viewing other people, especially other women, as being unreliable, unfair, and abusive, thereby reinforcing feelings of anger and resentment against those perceived to have wronged the subject. This then often spurs a retaliatory response, either against a woman who was perceived to have offended the subject, or to a target of convenience that resembled the alleged betrayer in some way.

Male sex drive is uncontrollable. "We're guys: we're gonna do what we're gonna do." Three basic versions of this IT were disclosed: (1) general feelings of powerlessness that shaded over into perceived inability to control their sexual behavior; (2) being overwhelmed by aggressive emotions that were externalized as an irresistible force; or (3) being overwhelmed by sadistic sexual fantasies and compulsive urges that were perceived as taking on a life of their own, making it "only a matter of time" until the crime erupted.

Women as sex objects. "They're women, sex is what they're for." This mindset views women as existing primarily to be at the sexual beck and call of men, not considered autonomous human beings with choices and priorities of their own.

Entitlement. "I take what I want." Related to the above IT, this mindset harbors the internal message that the offender deserves sex because he has been aroused by a particular woman ("If she didn't want it, she wouldn't be dressed like that") or were just entitled to take sex if they wanted to simply because they were powerful males ("Hey, if you date a tiger, you're gonna get bit").

Women are unknowable. "No one knows what women want." This IT was relatively rare in the study and was only noted in a few cases. Here, women are viewed as objects of inscrutable mystery and hence suspicion, exacerbating latent feelings of insecurity and inadequacy in these men, which often resulted in them regarding all women as uniformly deceptive and manipulative. This frustration and confusion would then lead to aggression to reassert control and "teach her a lesson" or "show her who's boss." Interestingly, the most common means of murder in this group was strangulation, which is a method of killing where the perpetrator has complete domination over the life of the victim to the point where he can literally control her every breath and prolong or shorten the time to death at will.

SOCIOCULTURAL THEORIES OF SERIAL KILLING

As discussed in Chapters 2 and 3, predisposition is not predestination, and a person's innate biological temperament and individual upbringing are always played out against the local and national culture in which he or she resides. Culture reinforces adaptively prosocial or antisocial behavioral tendencies which then, in turn, contribute to the interpersonal climate of that very culture, in a cyclical fashion.

That the influence of the surrounding society cannot be discounted is evidenced by the differing prevalence rates in serial homicide in different regions of the United States (DeFronzo et al., 2007), with California and Florida having between 3–5 times the rate of New York, Illinois, Ohio, and Pennsylvania. Something in the social and cultural environments of these different regions, then, may be contributing to so great a difference in the number of serial killings. Or, perhaps, milder weather in the two high-rate states means that more people are out and about, increasing the potential pool of victims. Related to climate, both states have large tourist industries, with greater numbers of transient workers and residents than in the more demographically stable Northeast and Middle America states, facilitating the comings and goings of geographically mobile criminals. More basic to sociocultural dynamics per se, a number of theories have been offered to explain these sociocultural factors (see Chapter 3), the most prominent of which will be reviewed here.

Trauma Control Model

Hickey's (1997) **trauma control model** starts by considering the traditional biological, developmental, demographic, and familial factors, including childhood trauma, that contribute to criminality in general and serial homicide in particular. But in this model, the potentiality for a sadistic sexual compulsion to become a series of homicidal acts must be disinhibited and activated by **sociocultural facilitators**, which inhere in the values and customs of the surrounding society. For example, an adolescent's aggressive and sexual urges might be sublimated into some form of productive activity in a closely-knit, values-oriented culture, while these urges may only be inflamed and encouraged in a society which glorifies violence and objectifies women through sexually violent videogames and easily available Internet pornography.

Once again, all the rough porno in the world, titillating to the curious adolescent mind as it may be, is not automatically going to turn an otherwise well-socialized young man into a sadistic serial killer. But for a youth already harboring these dark urges, the cultural facilitators can easily be seen as giving "permission" to engage in the violent act: "It can't be that bad if I played in on my X-Box."

Holmes et al. (1999) suggest that the contributory role of trauma in the development of budding serial killers need not occur in the remote childhood past of these subjects, but may take place more contemporaneously in the lives of adolescents. In fact, certain segments of the population, such as residents of crime-ridden and economically depressed inner-city neighborhoods, may be exposed to traumatically stressful events on a fairly regular basis. Breslau & Davis (1992) and Breslau et al. (1991) found that a high proportion of young adults from an economically depressed and crime-ridden inner-city neighborhood showed classic signs and symptoms of posttraumatic stress disorder (PTSD). Precipitating events included sudden injuries, serious accidents, physical assaults, rape or attempted rape, threats to one's life, narrowly escaping injury in an assault or accident, and receiving news of the death or serious injury of a close friend or relative. For someone with an innate tendency to externalize traumatic events into sexually aggressive action, these types of experiences might well light the fuse that sparks intermittent explosions of violence.

Finally, as with innate predispositions to violence in general (Chapter 2), it is probably the case that the influence of developmental trauma and the facilitation of sociocultural variables occurs on a continuum, ranging from subjects who would only be spurred to violence by the most adverse and/or permissive circumstances, to those whose sexually sadistic urges are so strong that they will inevitably be acted out, no matter what the personal history and surrounding circumstances may be.

Subcultural Theory

Indeed, a number of sociocultural theories of serial killing largely dispense with internal psychological factors and focus more exclusively on the role of the social and physical environment. **Subcultural theory** (Wolfgang & Ferracuti, 1967) proposes that exposure to violent influences in the surrounding subculture may facilitate the transition from violent sexual urges to elaborated fantasies and finally to violent sexual behavior. For example, today's adolescent who harbors sexually sadistic fantasies will quickly discover a smorgasbord of appetizing fantasy material just a few computer clicks away. Again, by itself, no book, no movie, no website, no video game ever turned a boy scout into a murderer (see also Chapter 19), but the narcissistically psychopathic sexual sadist-to-be may be able to nurture his torture fantasies and more rigorously study the craft of homicide in a culture that demeans human beings in general and women in particular, and that provides the technological means to spend hours a day steeping oneself in violent fantasy material.

Routine Activity Theory

Routine activity theory (Cohen & Felson, 1979) focuses specifically on the physical, structural, and social influences that influence a killer's opportunity to commit crimes, including serial murder. These include such factors as:

Availability of appropriate victims: e.g., a college town filled with young women versus a middle-class bedroom community inhabited mostly by families and retirees.

Number of places for concealment: either of the perpetrator himself or the victim's body, e.g., a wooded rural area vs. a busy urban shopping district.

Population density: large urban areas may provide the advantage of more anonymous victims to choose from, while less populated areas may afford greater mobility and concealability of crimes and victims (e.g., a "torture shack" set deep in the woods).

Population characteristics: Larger, transient neighborhoods may afford the killer greater anonymity and opportunity to evade detection than smaller, more settled, closely-knit communities where everyone knows everybody else.

Population demographics: The opportunity for serial murder is generally higher in locales with more divorced women, single mothers, and unemployed women because these are potentially more vulnerable targets due to their being home alone much of the time, or without other adults present for protection. Unemployment also means they are less likely to be afforded the insulation of a populated workplace and, if they do go to work, are more likely to depend on potentially less safe public transportation than the relative security of a private vehicle (Maume, 1989). Single women are also more likely to be relegated to job positions that involve off-hours, relative isolation, and poor security (see Chapter 11), all of which increase their potential as targets.

DeFronzo et al. (2007) systematically applied routine activity theory to the study of serial homicide rates and found that the interstate variation in the incidence of male serial killers noted earlier could be at least partially explained by three variables: (1) the percentage of the population living in urban areas; (2) the percentage of divorced people in the state; and (3) the percentage of single-person households. Thus, the common factor in accounting for higher serial murder rates in states like Florida and California appears to be the greater availability of suitable victims. The lesson for both psychology and criminology is to be careful not to allow attention to psychobiological and individual developmental and familial factors blind us to the role of practical issues such as demography, sociology, and culture, precisely because it is upon these latter factors that social policies can have the greatest day-to-day control—we can improve lighting, make changes in zoning, and provide more police security far more easily than we can change human nature. Accordingly, efforts at crime prevention should target not just interdiction of offenders, but preventive efforts to increase the safety of potential victims.

BOX 10.2. CRIMINAL PROFILING: ART, SCIENCE, OR FALLACY?

The term **criminal profiling**, **behavioral profiling**, or the current official FBI term, **criminal investigative analysis**, refers to "a technique for identifying the major personality and behavioral characteristics of an individual based upon an analysis of the crimes he or she has committed" (Douglas et al., 1986, p. 405). Information from books, TV shows, movies, true and fictionalized accounts, and the media's general fascination with the dark side of human behavior have all combined to produce an explosion of interest in the field of criminal profiling over the past number of years. In academia, too, behavioral profiling research is being accepted for publication in prominent psychology and criminal justice journals, and there is even a new journal devoted entirely to this subject: the *Journal of Investigative Psychology and Offender Profiling* (Douglas & Olshaker, 1995, 1998; Dowden et al., 2007; Hazelwood & Michaud, 1999, Innes, 2003; McCrary & Ramsland, 2003; Michaud & Hazelwood, 1999; Ressler & Schactman, 1992, 1997; Vorpagel & Harrington, 1998). However, a growing number of critics have expressed concern that the popularity and enthusiastic application of this technique have far exceeded any evidence for its scientific validity (Dowden et al., 2007; Hicks & Sales, 2006; McCann, 1992; Muller, 2000; Palermo & Kocsis, 2005).

continued

BOX 10.3.—*Continued*

ORIGINS AND PROCESS OF CRIMINAL PROFILING

Some form of profiling has always been a part of law enforcement criminal investigation, however efforts by the FBI to develop and implement a formal and systematic process for crime scene profiling only began as recently as 1978, with the formation of the FBI's **Behavioral Science Unit**, or **BSU**, which evolved into the **Profiling and Behavioral Assessment Unit** (Annon, 1995; Douglas et al., 1986; Geberth, 1990; Hickey, 1997; Homant & Kennedy, 1998; McCann, 1992; Pinizzotto, 1984; Ressler et al., 1988). The process was developed specifically to deal with cases of serial homicide and/or serial rape. The FBI currently has 12 full-time profilers who collectively are involved in about 1000 cases per year. In addition, many state and local police, often FBI-trained, apply profiling to an unknown number of additional cases. With some slight differences in approach, profiling has also become popular in Canada, Great Britain, and the Netherlands (Dowden et al., 2007; Palermo & Kocsis, 2005; Turvey, 1999; Wikin, 1996). Despite the emphasis on psychology, however, profilers as a group have not articulated a uniform theory of human behavior that guides their investigations, and it is often unclear as to whether they are trying to reconstruct the personality of a given offender or merely generate a loosely connected series of psychologically descriptive statements concerning the interpersonal style and the underlying motives of the suspect (Dowden et al., 2007).

PROFILING: ART OR SCIENCE?
THE VALIDITY AND USEFULNESS OF CRIMINAL PROFILING

It has been estimated that about 50 percent of serial homicide cases are solved with the help of behavioral profiling techniques (Holmes, 1989)—and even this may be an overly optimistic estimate. In spite of a few well-publicized successes, there have been quite a number of cases where such profiles have proven to be inaccurate, unhelpful, or misleading in solving crimes (Innes, 2003, Jeffers, 1992; Muller, 2000; Wilson & Soothill, 1996). This has led the pendulum of opinion to swing in the other direction, with some critics asserting that behavioral profiling is little better than astrology (Ainsworth, 2001), while others take a more middle ground in the debate over whether profiling is mainly a highly skilled art (Douglas & Burgess, 1986; Rossi, 1982; Turvey, 1999; Vorpagel, 1982; Vorpagel & Harrington, 1998) or should aspire to be a replicable, scientific technique (Canter, 1994; Kocsis, 2003a,b; Palermo & Kocsis, 2005; Rossmo, 2009).

In one study, (Pinnizzotto, 1984) less than half of a sample of law enforcement officers considered offender profiles to be significantly helpful in solving their cases, and in only 17 percent of cases did the profiles lead to the actual identification of a suspect. A subsequent study (Pinizzotto & Finkel, 1990) compared the skill and accuracy of five different groups in evaluating a previously solved murder and rape case: (1) "expert profilers"—instructors in the FBI's BSU, (2) "trained profilers"—police personnel who had undergone training from the BSU, (3) police detectives with no formal training in profiling, (4) licensed psychologists, and (5) university students. The expert and trained profilers wrote longer and more detailed offender profiles and their profiles were ranked higher in overall usefulness by an independent panel of detectives. However, the profiles of the expert and trained profilers were actually the *least* useful in predicting the actual characteristics of the murderer, although they did somewhat better than the other groups in predicting the rapist's characteristics.

What do psychologists think about psychological profiling? Bartol (1996) found that 70 percent of a group of 152 police psychologists seriously questioned the validity and usefulness of the profiling process. But are they any good at it? Kocsis et al. (2000) directly compared the profiling skills of psychologists to that of police officers, and found that the only significant differences were that psychologists more accurately predicted the offender's physical features and offense behaviors—nothing particularly "psychological" about that. A recent meta-analysis (Snook et al., 2007) found that self-described expert psychological profilers were little better than comparison groups at predicting offender physical attributes, cognitive processes, social history, and offense characteristics. Such findings have led critics to categorically assert that psychologists have no special insight into the criminal mind nor any special skills with regard to criminal profiling (Bennell et al., 2006).

At present, the evidence for the overall validity of criminal profiles in solving serial homicides appears far weaker than at first suggested by the initial flush of enthusiasm (Hicks & Sales, 2006; Homant & Kennedy, 1998; Palermo & Kocsis, 2005; Snook et al., 2007). Probably, this represents expectable growing pains in the maturation of any field of behavioral research and practice, and criminal behavioral profiling will no doubt ultimately be found to occupy a middle ground somewhere between hard science and psychobabble. Certainly, in the investigation of crimes of all types, psychological profiling should never be relied on to the exclusion of traditional procedures of evidence collection and analysis, and should be regarded as one ancillary piece of the investigatory puzzle that can occasionally yield useful information. Again, the tension between art and science in all fields of applied human behavior is one that must be dealt with forthrightly if our credibility is to be maintained (Miller, 1990c, 1991d, 1998c, 2006f, 2008b, 2008c).

SUMMARY AND CONCLUSIONS

Serial sexual homicide may be viewed as a nonsocialized and consensually criminalized form of solitary human predation that occurs out of context of, and without the communal validation of, the individual's social group as an acceptable, temporary extension of combat or other socialized aggres-

sion against an out-group. In essence, like a star football player who is expelled from the team for repeatedly tackling fans, or the rogue cop who
habitually and gratuitously brutalizes innocent civilians, the predatory serial
killer "doesn't play by the rules." He stalks and kills the wrong people and
doesn't get our permission first. So we stalk and pursue him and try to appre-
hend him, as part of our law enforcement "manhunt."

The neuropsychodynamics of serial killing depend upon the subtype.
Impulsive, violent, **disorganized** murders probably involve sudden
episodes of disinhibition related to weakened frontal lobe control over lim-
bically-evoked violence or the ability to postpone it, deflect it, or conceal the
crime afterwards. Personality correlates would probably involve some per-
mutation of antisocial and schizoid dynamics.

But the planning and calculating capacities of the frontal lobes appear to
work only too well in the cunningly efficient **organized** subtype of predatory serial killer, who shows, if anything, uncommon cleverness in stalking victims and eluding capture. Here, hyperactive temporal lobe-limbic mechanisms may give the behavior its stereotypical, repeated, and driven quality.
By this account, the predatory serial killer is literally a limbically-kindled
engine of destruction. He won't stop and doesn't want to because nothing in
life could possibly replace the thrill of dominating and destroying another
human being. His intact cognitive planning skills are utilized in the service
of his well-honed murderous craft, which he justifies to himself by his sense
of superiority and by his disdain and hateful contempt for his inferior victims. His personality correlates probably involve combinations of narcissistic, psychopathic, and schizoid traits; he is the lone killer who is more clever
than all of us; he is "entitled" to kill, and, aside from his penchant for a specific type of brutal murder, he may or may not fit the classical pattern of antisocial personality.

The sexual element of serial killing derives from the limbic fusion of sex
and aggression that occurs commonly in many forms of normal sexual play,
that becomes magnified during the rape frenzies of warfare or individual sex
crimes, that may become permanently warped by an abusive but hypersex-
ualized maternal upbringing, and that remain a stable feature in the neuropsychodynamics of the serial killer. Sexuality entails vulnerability, and that
vulnerability can either be shared for the purposes of enhanced human intimacy, or exploited for the infliction of human cruelty and horror (see also
Chapter 14).

Finally, sociocultural factors provide the soil in which the developing serial killer germinates his sadistic fantasies and cultivates the means to carry
them out. Large populations containing many anonymous, vulnerable, and
marginalized victims, steeped in a cultural ethos that glorifies power and vio-

lence, especially sexual violence, will have higher rates of serial homicide than more closely-knit, values-oriented societies due to a combination of moral training and sheer availability of victims. It must be recognized, however, that even the most morally Edenic society will always contain a few members whose selfish pursuit of their own satisfaction will eventually lead them to prey on others.

Thus, when we study serial killers, that very twinge of mixed fascination and revulsion we feel should remind us that the human capacity for empathic attunement to others is precisely what allows the police detective or FBI agent to kiss his wife and kids goodbye, and then go off to work where he will try to "think like a criminal" in order to heighten the chance of capturing and removing those true predators who's own sadistic pleasure is their only imperative.

Chapter **11**

Mass Homicide I: Workplace Violence

A disgruntled [pick one: postal worker, law
client, insurance claimant, store customer,
hospital patient, factory worker] stormed into
his place of business yesterday, killing six
people before turning the gun on himself.
Film at 11:00.

We've all heard this kind of TV news headline all-too commonly in recent years. Often the lead story is followed by interviews with coworkers or associates whose comments almost invariably follow one of two main
themes:

"He was always a little strange, you know, quiet. Kept to himself a lot,
didn't get along with too many people, but came in, did his job, and
never caused any real trouble. Certainly, nobody figured him for a stone
killer. Man, we didn't see this one coming."

Or:

"Dammit, I knew it was just a matter of time till something like this
happened. This guy was bad news, a ticking bomb, and we all knew it.
But there were no precautions or any real kind of discipline at all. We
tried to tell management, but they just got annoyed, said there was nothing they could do, and told us not to stir up trouble. When he finally
snapped, we were sitting ducks."

For most people, the prospect of a violent incident happening at their
workplace is too frightening to contemplate. This is precisely why most employees and managers find it temporarily more comfortable to hide their
heads in the sand and pretend that "this kind of thing doesn't happen here."
When an incident does erupt, the affected organization is then faced with

medical and mental health care costs, lost business, a frightened and alienated workforce, employee and community lawsuits, and possible criminal charges.

To illustrate the combination of fear and denial that surrounds this topic, data from the Census of Fatal Occupational Injuries indicates that workplace homicides in the United States actually decreased 48 percent from their peak in 1994 (total of 1080) to 2005 (total of 564). Nevertheless, most people believe that such events are on the increase, and a survey of employers taken two years after the attacks on September 11, 2001 found that workplace violence, not terrorism, was ranked as the leading security concern (Schouten, 2006). Certainly, although the incidence of workplace violence may have trended down over the past decade, the overall number of these events is still higher than that of a generation ago.

Most of the types of criminal violence described in this book impact their victims suddenly and with little warning or control; correspondingly, the clinical, law enforcement, and administrative emphasis is usually on investigating and prosecuting the offenders, as well as treating victims, survivors, their families, and other stakeholders *after the fact.* However, unlike almost every other type of criminal violence discussed in this book, workplace violence is the one area where people can take concrete steps *ahead of time* to minimize the chances of serious violence occurring at their place of business and to put in place policies and procedures that will enable the company to recover and move on; the same principle applies to school violence (Chapter 12).

In fact, employee surveys show that one of the things valued most by members of any organization is the effort their company makes to keep them safe. And employees who feel that their organizations are looking out for them are generally more loyal, more productive, have less turnover, and are less likely to file grievances and disability claims (Albrecht, 1996; Denenberg & Braverman, 1999; Flannery, 1995; Mantell & Albrecht, 1994; Schouten, 2006). So maintaining a safe workplace and a secure workforce is also a good way of doing business

The subject of workplace violence also highlights the intersection and mutual influences of biological, psychological, and sociocultural factors in producing violent criminal behavior, insofar as every workplace is a village whose standards and ethos reflect the larger cultural environment and, at the same time, contain elements that are unique to each organization (Miller, 2008c).

WORKPLACE VIOLENCE: DEMOGRAPHICS AND STATISTICS

Several decades of research and practical experience (Albrecht, 1996, 1997; Barling et al., 2009; Blount, 2003; Bulatao & Vandenbos, 1996; Denenberg & Braverman, 1999; Flannery, 1995; Johnson & Indvik, 2000; Kinney, 1995; Labig, 1995; LeBlanc & Kelloway, 2002; LeBlanc et al., 2005; Mantell & Albrecht, 1994; Miller, 1997b, 1998c; 1999g, 2001a, 2001b, 2002a, 2007b, 2008c; Mitroff, 2001; Namie & Namie, 2000; Neuman & Baron, 2005; Potter-Efron, 1998; Schaner, 1996; Schneid, 1999; Schouten, 2006; Shapiro et al., 2005; Simon, 1996; Spector et al., 2007; Vega & Comer, 2005) have established some facts about violence in the workplace.

Homicide is the number one killer of women and the third leading cause of workplace death for men, after motor vehicle accidents and machine-related fatalities. A worker is about twice as likely to be murdered at his or her job than to die in a fall, four times more likely than to be accidentally electrocuted, five time more likely than to go down in a plane crash, and dozens of times more likely than to be killed in a terrorist attack. The majority of workplace homicides are committed by firearms. Most violence is perpetrated by people outside the company, but intracompany violence by employees or ex-employees is not rare, and most people find the prospect of being harmed by a coworker far more frightening than by an outsider, probably because most of us feel that we ought to be safe with the people we work with. The riskiest occupations for all different forms of physical injury are recreational workers, bartenders, liquor store salespersons, taxicab drivers, retail sales clerks, food service workers, police officers, parking attendants, gas station attendants, auto mechanics, security guards, social workers, grocery store and jewelry store cashiers, bus drivers, firefighters, and service station attendants. Service and sales workers have the most work-related homicides, especially if they work alone and/or at night, followed by executives, administrators, and managers.

Workplace violence costs American businesses approximately $4.2 billion a year. This translates into about $250,000–$500,000 per incident, in terms of lost work time, employee medical benefits, decreased productivity, diversion of management resources from other productive business, increased insurance premiums, increased security costs, bad publicity, lost business, and expensive litigation costs. In terms of the human cost, most workers polled after an incident say that they are psychologically traumatized by the threat of future workplace violence, and a sizable proportion lose work time due to stress disability. For every actual workplace killing, there occur over one hundred acts of sublethal violence, including fistfights, nonfatal shootings, stabbings, sexual assaults, vandalism, sabotage, bombings, and arson.

Although entirely unexpected episodes of explosive violence do occasionally occur, in most cases the warning signs are present but often overlooked and ignored. Perpetrators who turn deadly frequently engage in threats and harassing behaviors before their actions escalate to physical attacks and killing, and this kind of verbal abuse and harassment can have an equal or greater destructive impact on employee morale and productivity than physical assault. Ironically, employees who resort to fisticuffs create an obvious disturbance, cause potentially costly injury, and are an embarrassment to the company; consequently, they are most likely to be assertively disciplined. But "mere" verbal threats, curses, racist or sexist remarks and innuendos, and personal property sabotage typically aren't taken as seriously, since they seem to affect few employees or stakeholders outside the direct targets of the abuse and therefore often remain under the radar. In fact, complaints about antisocial workplace behavior are commonly downplayed by management or treated as nuisances that get in the way of doing business and are thus dismissed with comments like, "Grow up," "Deal with it," "Work it out yourselves," or, "Don't make a big deal about it and it'll go away." Alternatively, the persecuted victim, rebuffed by management, feels he has no choice but to take matters into his own hands and retaliates explosively, becoming himself a perpetrator of workplace violence, a dynamic very similar to that noted in many school shootings over the past decades (Chapter 12).

WORKPLACE VIOLENCE: REASONS AND MOTIVES

A number of studies and reviews have attempted to account for the motives and reasons behind episodes of workplace violence, using reports of victims, perpetrators, and coworkers (Barling et al., 2009; Hoobler & Swanberg, 2006; Labig, 1995; Rugala & Isaacs, 2004; Simon, 1996). Typical motives identified among workplace violence perpetrators include: (1) being dissatisfied with customer service; (2) interpersonal conflicts with coworkers; (3) perceived racial or other prejudice; (4) disputes or gripes about disciplinary procedures; (5) being fired, laid off, or downsized; (6) marital, family, or other personal problems; (7) drug or alcohol abuse; (8) current or prior criminal history; or (9) nonspecific "stress." A sizable proportion of incidents have unknown or unclear causes, indicating that many violent incidents at work have no easily identifiable or comprehensible reason, at least at the time they occur.

The average working person, who would never resort to violence him- or herself, might nevertheless understand or even empathize with someone who has exhausted all legitimate channels of grievance, and flies off the handle after suffering blatantly unfair treatment or discrimination at the hands of a coworker or supervisor. But while workplace abuses and humiliations are common, acts of violence are rare, indicating that personality and psychopathology factors play a prominent role in determining who simply stews and grumbles about an actual or perceived workplace offense and who resolves to take matters into their own hands (Silver, 2008; Swanson et al., 2006).

THE WORKPLACE VIOLENCE CYCLE

Even accounting for individual variations in personality and psychopathology (see below), there appears to be a common, predictable pattern in the evolution of many workplace violence incidents, especially those that are perpetrated by current or former employees (Kinney, 1995; Labig, 1995; Miller, 1997b, 1998c; 1999g, 2001a, 2001b, 2002a, 2007b, 2008c). The cycle typically begins when the individual encounters a situation, actual or perceived, that he experiences as antagonistic or stressful. This may be a single overwhelming incident or a capping event to a cumulative series of stressors–the "straw that breaks the camel's back." The subject reacts to this event cognitively and emotionally, based on his predisposing personality, current psychopathology, and life experiences. For the typical workplace violence perpetrator, this reaction often involves some toxic combination of persecutory ideation, projection of blame, and violent revenge fantasies.

As these thoughts and emotions continue to percolate, the individual increasingly isolates himself from the input of others and enters an insular mode of self-protection and self-justification in which a violent act may come to be perceived as "the only way out." Once the decision to commit violence has been made, the only thing left to determine is the actual means of attack. The operational plan may be executed impulsively and at once, or may undergo numerous revisions. The violent act may occur any time from hours to days to weeks to months to years following the final perceived injustice. In a number of cases, the violent plan may be sidelined as the worker obtains new employment and/or other things in his life begin to improve. Months or years may go by, and the worker may cycle in and out of several life crises and recoveries. At some point, the accumulation of stressors becomes too great and he decides to seek vengeance against those that have wronged him. If he construes the source of all his problems to be the company that fired him several years ago, or if this is simply the most accessible target of opportunity, he may direct his anger at his former organization, surprising the people who now work there, many of whom had forgotten about him or never knew him because they came on long after he had been fired. Thus, innocent people may lose their lives in this type of delayed-reaction attack (Kinney, 1995; Labig, 1995; Miller, 1998c 1999g, 2007b, 2008c).

CAUSES OF WORKPLACE VIOLENCE

Although each workplace violence perpetrator brings his own personality to the event (see below), certain common psychological, social, and cultural factors appear to underlie this type of crime.

Changed Workplace and Work Ethic

Changes in the American workplace over the past decades have created fertile ground for cultivating employee discontent that can lead to potential violence. Survivors of downsized, outsourced, or off-shored companies are forced to take on extra work and fill multiple jobs, increasing work stress and heightening insecurity about the future. For those terminated, anger and hopelessness mount at the inability to replace lost jobs with new positions that afford equal pay and benefits. The sense of long-term common organizational purpose that may once have existed between managers and rank-and-file employees has largely evaporated as companies are seen as being concerned only for the bottom line and workers are treated as disposable commodities. A young workforce is emerging that may be less equipped for the world of new work technology, work culture, and work ethic than in the past. Most teenagers and young adults are introduced to work in low-skill jobs with minimal mentoring at the same time as there is a developing culture of resentment and entitlement in the workplace and elsewhere. High turnover encouraged by poor management reinforces the impression that everyday work is for chumps and further denigrates legitimate authority. Managers and supervisors, themselves often young, inexperienced, and poorly trained, are increasingly unable or unwilling to use effective discipline. This environment creates the perfect breeding ground for psychologically "sick workplaces" (Barling, 2009; Denenberg & Braverman, 1999; Flannery, 1995; Johnson & Indvik, 2000; Kinney, 1995; Hoobler & Swanberg, 2006; Labig, 1995; Mantell & Albrecht, 1994; Neuman & Baron, 1997, 2005; Rugala & Isaacs, 2004; Schouten, 2006; Shapiro et al., 2005; Simon, 1996; Spector et al., 2007; Vega & Comer, 2005).

News and Entertainment Media

Glamorized violence continues to be a staple of news, entertainment, and "reality" media, which commonly misinterpret and misrepresent reported workplace violence events and the reasons behind them. In straining for simple conclusions or lurid angles, the media typically talk with a perpetrator's friends or co-workers, who may sympathize with his agenda or may spin their own bizarre interpretations of what happened and why. The all-too common conclusion of this sound-bite journalism is that the lethal perpetrator is either a "nut case" or, alternatively, is engaged in a crusade of righteous retribution against an unfair or darkly conspiratorial employer or governmental agency. By itself, no television program or Internet blog or zine entry will automatically make a basically stable person run out and shoot up an office or factory. But overhyped media coverage, while constituting mere infotainment for most people, may lead a few disturbed viewers to justify their own future acts of violence, especially if they suffer from one or more forms of personality disorder or psychopathology considered below.

Work, Identity, and the Meaning of Life

Satisfying work affords more than an income; for most of us, it provides stability, direction, security, a sense of achievement, self-worth, camaraderie, and a feeling of belonging to a common family or tribe (Miller, 2008c; Simon, 1996). Positive identification with one's vocational role is a normal, even healthy trait, as part of the matrix of overlapping identity systems that include family, friends, religious beliefs, and other roles. But some people's entire identity and sense of self-worth are inextricably and unhealthily tied up with their jobs.

For most individuals, losing a job is a traumatic event, akin to being cast out of one's community, but for most, it is also a survivable event. As with any crisis or traumatic bereavement, after an appropriate period of mourning and anguish, most people pick up the pieces, go forward, and search for new opportunities. But for a small minority of vulnerable personalities, job loss—especially if perceived as unfair—is a devastating blow to the psyche, a mortal ego wound. For such individuals, job loss becomes a devastating personal failure rather than a disappointing but survivable event. Such a blow is all the more acute when an overemphasis on work has crowded out relationships and other resources that might have been called upon to support the employee through the crisis.

For some of these marginally stable people, the loss of a job reverberates with hidden vulnerabilities rooted in their past. Fueled by such a history of narcissistic wounds, job loss may trigger an overwhelming rage that seems out of proportion to the current loss. Blame is externalized and vengeance brews as the worker begins to think, "I'll show them they can't ruin my life and get away with it." For some, the intolerability of the job loss leads to hopeless suicidality with a retaliatory tinge: "If they can screw me, I can screw them back–bigtime. Why should other people go on having what they want and enjoying themselves, when I can't? I may be going out, but I'm not going out alone."

The idea brews in the perpetrator's mind that after he's gone, his Rambo-like exploits will be reported to millions of people around the world; his name will be a household word. Far from meekly slinking away, our hero will leave this world in a blaze of glory–just like in the movies (Flannery, 1995; Kinney, 1995; Labig, 1995; Mantell & Albrecht, 1994; Simon, 1996).

WORKPLACE VIOLENCE PERPETRATORS

A number of researchers (Rugala & Isaacs, 2004; Schouten, 2006) have divided acts of workplace aggression into four types, which reflect the generally established demographics (Flannery, 1995; Labig, 1995) of workplace violence.

Categories of Workplace Violence

Type I: Criminal activity. This is violence that results from associated criminal activity, such as robbery or sexual assault. Here, the primary goal may not be aggressive behavior per se but, if necessary, the perpetrator will use whatever it takes to achieve his objective. As noted earlier, the majority of murders on the job are committed by strangers and strangers also commit most workplace robberies, although sometimes these criminals have a particular grudge against the targeted business, in which case this act may overlap with one or more of the other three categories. Certain job-related factors that increase the risk of an employee being killed by a robber include exchanging money with the public, guarding valuable property, working late night or early morning hours, working in high-crime areas, or working in community settings, such as government offices or health care facilities.

Type II: Customer/client violence. Violence perpetrated by customers or clients can be spontaneous events, such as a customer who becomes frustrated during a retail transaction or an emergency room patient who becomes agitated when he doesn't receive the drugs he wants (LeBlanc & Kelloway, 2002; Scalora et al., 2003; Yagil, 2008). Customer-perpetrated violence can also be delayed, as in acts of vengeance against a business, clinic, or government office for perceived wrongs done to the perpetrator (Flannery, 1995; Kinney, 1995). In medical and mental health settings, "customers" also mean current and former patients (see Box 11.2).

Type III: Coworker violence. Unlike acts by strangers, most workers feel that violence by people they know and work with ought to be more predictable and preventable. Violence committed by coworkers or former coworkers comprise the classic perpetrator of workplace violence, the one that makes the headlines when the event is dramatic or unexpected, often referred to in the media as a "disgruntled employee." However, as Flannery (1995) points out, the term *disgruntled* typically connotes mere ill-humor or discontent that fails to adequately describe the state of rage and psychological disorganization that characterizes most perpetrators of serious workplace violence.

The typical disgruntled employee is less likely to be terminated for being incompetent to do his duties than for being unable to get along with other people on the job. He usually has particular problems with supervisors. Often, the employee's colleagues have an intuitive sense that this person is dangerous, or just unstable. In many cases, there is a spectrum of disgruntled worker actions, ranging from passive-aggressive behavior, incivility, harassment, and sabotage to lethal violence. Often, early levels of acting-out are tolerated or ignored by coworkers or management, which only serves to encourage the escalation of intimidation and aggression (Flannery, 1995; Greenberg, 2010).

Type IV: Domestic Violence spillover. Violence may be committed on the job by spouses and lovers involved in domestic disputes. Or those infatuated with a particular employee may stalk or harass her at work (Labig, 1995; Meloy, 1997a). This is discussed further below and in Chapters 17 and 18.

Workplace Violence Perpetrator Types

In addition to the typology described above, workplace violence in all four categories also varies along an intensity continuum, ranging from threatening looks and gestures, to acts of sabotage and property destruction, to actual physical assaults that may result in injury or death. Mantell & Albrecht (1994) have developed a specific typology of coworker workplace violence perpetrators:

The **covert employee** engages in silent, hidden, or behind-the-scenes activities that serve to disrupt the workplace, including small-scale sabotage, vandalism, anonymous and/or threatening faxes or e-mails, and suspicious phone messages. At this level, the threats tend to be indirect, anonymous, and verbal; any physical damage is usually mild and aimed at inanimate objects. The worker at this stage is satisfied to be a silent saboteur.

The **fence-sitter** straddles the border between covert sabotage and overt confrontation. At this level, the threats are more verbally direct and the damage is more intrusive and destructive to office equipment or other employees' personal property. The perpetrator may target someone in the company for special verbal abuse or property vandalism, but physical attacks against persons have not yet occurred.

The **overt employee** escalates the aggressive activity so that the risk of this subject's attacking other workers is now high. Activities at this stage may include injurious physical assaults, as well as extreme forms of sabotage and vandalism, often aimed at some tangible symbol of the target company.

The **dangerous employee** is potentially homicidal and may be psychotic and armed. Activities include direct threats, confrontations, and aggression, often involving firearms. The signs of impending escalation have usually been apparent well in advance of the overt acts.

A given employee may remain at any one of these levels or escalate up the violence ladder to whatever level he feels comfortable with. He may also move up and down between levels as circumstances change. As a rule, the fewer forthright disciplinary measures are taken at lower levels, the more likely is the worker to feel emboldened to escalate the level of violence.

MENTAL DISORDER AND WORKPLACE VIOLENCE

Research and clinical experience indicate that mental disorder must be considered a risk factor for workplace violence, as it is for violence in general (Brennan et al., 2000; Corrigan & Watson, 2005; Flannery, 1995; Mantell & Albrecht, 1994; Miller, 1990a,c, 1998c, 2008c; Silver et al., 2008; Simon, 1996; Swanson et al., 2006; see Chapter 5), and this category of perpetrator often overlaps with the disgruntled employee category. Most commonly, the psychopathology seen in this type of individual represents a combination of paranoid ideation (Chapters 5, 7), Cluster B personality disorder (Chapters 7, 8), and mood disorder (Chapter 6).

Paranoid Workers

Workers with **paranoid personality disorder** are characterized by a longstanding pattern of misinterpreting the words, actions, and motives of others as threatening, demeaning, or exploitive. They may be quite outspoken in their complaints, often filing numerous grievances and lawsuits before resorting to violence.

Workers with **delusional paranoid disorders** (now referred to as **delusional disorder, persecutory type**) may be excellent, punctual, reliable workers, and have few if any performance or conduct problems, as long as work does not involve their systematized delusions. These are the so-called "silent paranoids." However, their inner mental life is typically a swirl of hyperlogical intrigues and conspiracy theories, and they are always plotting and outthinking their "enemies," careful, however, not to tip their hand until some crisis forces the delusional system out into the open. Then, they proceed to irritate and alienate supervisors and coworkers with their weird and obnoxious behavior, until these compatriots actually do come to shun and revile the pest, which fuels the paranoia still further: "See how they're acting? I knew it was just a matter of time till they showed their true colors." Eventually, as the saying goes, "just because you're paranoid, it doesn't mean they're *not* out to get you."

Paranoid schizophrenics are severely disturbed and show a range of psychotic symptoms during the active phase of their illness, including disorganized thinking and hallucinations. Indeed, their sheer level of pathology may make them relatively easy to spot and many of them do not last long in conventional work situations.

Personality-Disordered Workers

Workers with **antisocial personality disorder** are likely to have left a long wake of employment, financial, legal, and personal troubles behind them. They are motivated exclusively by self-interest and will qualmlessly utilize any means necessary, including cunning and conning, violence or intimidation, to get what they want. Many are also often quite impulsive and nonreflective and may thus compound their workplace troubles through poor judgment and thoughtless actions. Their work behavior thus seems to be an expression of their overall exploitive interactions with people in general. A recent study (Roberts et al., 2007) showed that a diagnosis of **conduct disorder** in childhood and adolescence reliably predicted increased proneness as adult employees to engage in **counterproductive work behaviors** (Ones, 2002; Robinson & O'Leary, 1998) that include theft, embezzlement, tardiness, absenteeism, substance abuse problems, disciplinary actions, accidents, sabotage, violence, and sexual harassment.

Workers with **borderline personality disorder** typically experience drastic mood swings, unstable personal and professional attachments, and extremely intense emotional reactions. Having idealized a particular job setting, supervisor, or workmate, the borderline employee may be plunged into rageful despair by a subsequent rebuff or disappointment, real or imagined.

Their thirst for vindication and restoration of self-worth becomes an all-consuming passion and may include destructive or violent acts.

Avoidant-dependent employees are characteristically shy and socially anxious, and therefore hardly the type to be seen as potentially violent, but if they have made work their whole life and then experience rejection or separation from that role, then a violent act may seem the only way to "make my point."

Workers with Anxiety and Mood Disorders

Borderline, avoidant-dependent, and other personality-disordered employees often suffer varying degrees of **depression**. Impulsive violence against others and against the self often go together, and the sense of hopelessness that is part of the depressed state may facilitate aggressive acting-out if the demoralized worker feels he has "nothing to lose" and decides to take others to the grave with him. Indeed, the most common psychological recipe for workplace violence, or mass violence of any type, consists of the "fatal formula" of *anger x paranoia x depression*.

Workers who have themselves been victims of violence or other trauma may be experiencing **posttraumatic stress disorder** (**PTSD**). They bring their hypersensitivity and hair-trigger reactivity to the jobsite, where seemingly minor jibes and hassles may "set them off," although, as noted in Chapter 6, violence as the direct result of such PTSD flashbacks is difficult to prove.

Workers with Organic Brain Syndromes or Substance Abuse

Although relatively rare in a typical employment setting, organic brain impairment due to brain injury, strokes, epilepsy, dementia, or substance abuse (Chapter 4) may be associated with violent outbursts and may be preceded by impairment in memory, concentration, reasoning, or planning that affects job performance.

Workers with **temporal lobe epilepsy** occasionally show aggressive outbursts associated with seizure activity. These tend to be short and circumscribed and to occur in a state of relative disorientation and unawareness, followed by partial or total amnesia for the event.

Intermittent explosive disorder is characterized by sudden outbursts of rage upon minimal provocation and may be associated with subclinical abnormal brain wave activity. The rage attacks are typically impulsive and unplanned and are perceived by the perpetrator himself as uncontrollable, although consciousness is retained, memory for the event is variable, and personal remorse is often expressed at "losing control." These are probably more likely to occur off-work or at the office Christmas party, in circumstances where alcohol is involved, sometimes evoking the syndrome of **pathological intoxication** (Chapter 4). Aside from this, **alcohol and drug abuse** can potentiate violence from almost any other cause, and many employees' under-the-radar substance habits may go undetected and unaddressed for long periods of time.

RISK AND PROTECTIVE FACTORS FOR WORKPLACE VIOLENCE

One of the roles of mental health professionals who work in the field of **management psychology** or **industrial/organizational (I/O) psychology** is to assist executives, managers, and supervisors in identifying risk and protective factors in the hiring process of employees and in later coaching, counseling, and disciplinary actions that may be necessary (Borum et al., 1999; Dupre & Barling, 2006; Fein & Vossekuil, 1998; Kinney, 1995; Labig, 1995; LeBlanc & Kelloway, 2002; Mantell & Albrecht, 1994; Miller, 2008c; Schouten, 2006; Simon, 1996). Note that risk factors and protective factors may be either static or dynamic (Douglas & Skeem, 2005; Mills, 2005; Philipse et al., 2006; see Chapter 1).

Static risk/protective factors are those that are immutable or at least relatively stable, such as individual genetic background, demographic background, and personality type that the employee brings to the workplace.

Dynamic risk/protective factors are those that fluctuate over time and can either increase or decrease the level of risk or protection. These include workplace climate, situational stressors, and interpersonal resources. Of course, static and dynamic factors may interact, e.g., a worker with a narcissistic-paranoid personality style who alienates potential sources of support may thereby put greater stress on himself, which he deals with by abusing alcohol.

Risk Factors for Workplace Violence

As noted earlier, many of the risk factors for workplace violence are the same as for violence in general, and include the following (Anderson & Bushman, 2002; Barling et al., 2009; Baron et al., 1999; Blount, 2003; Dill et al., 1997; Douglas & Martinko, 2001; Glomb & Liao, 2003; Greenberg & Barling, 1999; Haines et al., 2006; Harvey & Keashley, 2003; Hepworth & Towler, 2004; Herschcovis et al., 2007; Inness et al., 2005; Johnson & Indvik, 2000; Judge et al., 2006; Lipsey et al., 1997; McFarlin et al., 2001; Neuman

& Baron, 2005; Parkins et al., 2006; Penney & Spector, 2002; Schaner, 1996; Schneid, 1999; Schouten, 2006; Shapiro et al., 2005; Skarlicki et al., 1997; Vega & Connor, 2005):

Demographic risk factors include male sex, young age (under 40), low socioeconomic status, and unmarried status.

Personal risk factors include past history of assaultive or other violent behavior, consistent with the general principle that the most reliable risk factor for future violence is past violence. This includes nonwork violence (domestic violence, military misconduct). It also includes verbal threats; in fact, the combination of current threats and past violence history is an especially ominous sign. If the present employment setting is similar to past environments where violence has occurred, the chances of imminent danger increase dramatically. Workers at risk for violence often have a history of other employment problems, such as unstable or migratory job history, multiple complaints filed about work stress and working conditions, frequent overreaction to changes of policy or personnel, chronic labor-management disputes, and often a string of prior unresolved physical and emotional injury claims.

High-risk workers often single out certain coworkers or supervisors as their special agents of persecution, and these may later become the targets of harassment or violence. There may be a specific motive and plan behind the aggression, and this may have been communicated in gripe sessions to other workers or kept a tightly guarded secret. High-risk workers also frequently possess the practical means and methods for violent actions, such as firearms and other weapons. They are often fascinated with military or law enforcement culture and paraphernalia (cop shows, gun magazines) and show excessive interest in media reports of violence (news clippings, scrapbooks), especially accounts of past episodes of workplace violence.

Psychological risk factors for workplace violence include low intelligence and poor conceptual reasoning ability; an impulsive and nonrational cognitive style; high trait anger and/or poor control of anger and temper; few if any healthy outlets for frustration and nervous energy; low self-esteem or pathologically high narcissistic self-esteem; a rigid all-or-nothing tendency to completely disown or endorse violent or other socially unacceptable feelings; a tendency to externalize blame for all the bad things that happen to them ("It's not my fault, they set me up again"); one or more diagnosable medical or neurological disorders; one or more diagnosable psychiatric syndromes or personality disorders; a history of childhood physical abuse or witnessing family violence; current alcohol or drug problems; current unstable family life (which can be a source of stress, as well as indicating a volatile temperament); and subtle or overt pleas for help of some kind.

While some workers with stable personality disorders may be able to maintain acceptable work records for years, such an employee undergoing an acute crisis will usually not be able to keep his distress secret for very long, and coworkers and supervisors will notice something is wrong. The relationship between psychological disturbance and work disruption often occurs in a vicious cycle, where declining performance brings managerial criticism, which provokes further anger and deterioration in work, alienation of coworker support ("Those suckups—now they're *all* out to get me") and so on. If the opportunity to intervene administratively or clinically is lost, the downward spiral may continue until violence is seen as "the only way out" (Labig, 1995; Mantell & Albrecht, 1994; Simon, 1996).

Organizational risk factors. While the focus of behavioral researchers tends to be on individual risk factors for violence, this book's theme is that violence always takes place in a psychosocial context: acts of targeted violence arise from an interaction among the potential perpetrator, past stressful events, situational factors, and the potential target. Accordingly, a number of organizational risk factors for workplace aggression have been identified. These include pay cuts and freezes, especially when considered arbitrary and unfair, as when managers get their raises but rank-and-file employees are asked to "sacrifice;" generally perceived unfair procedures with respect to hiring, firing, promotions, and discipline; abusive supervision or discipline; conversely, failure to adequately discipline or control aggressive or disruptive coworkers, leading employees to feel that the company is not committed to their safety at work; generally poor leadership causing ambiguity and confusion about job roles; clumsily executed changes in management, especially when the new management is relatively clueless about the organizational culture they are inheriting; and poor and confusing leadership (Allen & Lucero, 1998; Anderson & Pearson, 1999; Barling et al., 2009; Baron & Neuman, 1996; Berry et al., 2007; Borum et al., 1999; Bowling & Beehr, 2006; Chen & Spector, 1992; Dupre & Barling, 2006; Greenberg & Barling, 1999; Hershcovis et al., 2007; Hoobler & Swanberg, 2006; Inness et al., 2005; Neuman & Baron, 1998; Skarlicki & Folger, 1997).

Where the violence is targeted to a specific person or persons, characteristics of the potential subject of the attack must be examined, insofar as much ill will may be generated by an abusive or obnoxious manager or coworker. Even though that does not justify violence by the attacker, it represents a powerful, and potentially correctible, situational factor that, if handled properly, might deter a tragedy (see Box 11.1).

Protective Factors

Just as important as risk factors, but frequently overlooked, are a number of **protective factors** that may inhibit violent acting-out in workers under stress (Berry et al., 2007; Kinney, 1995; Labig, 1995; Roberts et al., 2007; Robinson & O'Leary-Kelly, 1998). These include a rational, reflective, future-oriented cognitive style; an emotionally stable personality; a repertoire of good coping skills; a history of handling adversity in an adaptive way; no significant violent or antisocial history, especially recent history; no significant alcohol or drug abuse problems; good overall work history; feeling that the job provides some degree of autonomy and satisfaction; no major financial difficulties; a stable and secure family life; varied outside interests in hobbies, friendships, religious and community groups; and high scores on measures of agreeableness, conscientiousness, and constraint. Note that many of these traits describe the adaptive personality and cognitive style that has been associated with optimal frontal lobe functioning, as discussed in Chapter 2.

BOX 11.1. DOES YOUR ORGANIZATION HAVE A WORKPLACE VIOLENCE PROGRAM?

For many organizations, workplace violence today is where domestic violence (Chapter 17) was a decade or so ago: they respond to the most egregious episodes, but still prefer to handle lower-level violations as an "internal" matter, much as domestic violence was once considered a private "family" matter (Rugala & Isaacs, 2004). However, recognizing the impact a workplace violence incident can have for their businesses, many public agencies and private industries are considering it part of the standard of care to implement **workplace violence prevention and response programs**. Sometimes this is done because the organization really is concerned about the health, safety, and morale of its people. Other times, the motive may be more legalistic and practical, to avoid criminal charges and/or civil claims of **negligent hiring**, **negligent retention**, **negligent training**, **negligent supervision**, **negligent firing**, and **negligent security**, as well as claims for **intentional infliction of emotional distress** (Kennedy & Homant, 1997; Neuman & Baron, 1998; Petty & Kosch, 2001; Schneid, 1999). While not every contingency can be planned for, the following is a model program (Miller, 1999g, 2008c) that has broad applicability to organizations of many types.

WORKPLACE VIOLENCE PREVENTION

"The best form of crisis intervention is crisis prevention" (Miller, 2006d, 2008b, 2008c), therefore, emphasis is given to the strategic and systemic factors that

continued

BOX 11.1.—*Continued*

make workplaces more congenial and less adversarial places to be. These include the following.

Clear Policies

Companies with few or no workplace violence incidents, and a low level of workplace conflict overall, usually share several common features:

- Clear, strong, fair, and consistent written policies against violence and harassment
- Effective grievance procedures
- Reliable security programs
- A supportive work environment
- Open channels of communication
- Training in resolving conflicts through team building and negotiation skills

Organizations should have a clearly understood and articulated policy of **zero tolerance for violence**. This should be conceptualized as a safety issue, the same as with rules about fire prevention, storm preparation, bomb scares, and other emergency drills. Plans should be in place that specify how threats are reported and to whom, as well as a protocol for investigating threats. Other policy and procedure items include security measures, disciplinary and grievance procedures, and services available for dispute mediation, conflict resolution, stress management, safety training, and other administrative and mental health services (Albrecht, 1996, 1997; Crawley, 1992; Flannery, 1995; Kinney, 1995; Labig, 1995; Neal & Griffin, 2004; O'Brien, 1992; Potter-Efron, 1998; Slaiku, 1996; Spector et al., 2007; Thilmany, 2007; Yandrick, 1996).

Safe Hiring

As deceptively simple as it sounds, the best way to avoid workplace violence is not to hire violent workers in the first place. While there are no 100 percent infallible strategies for weeding out future troublemakers, productive efforts in this regard include **application review** and **background checks**, careful **interviewing** of prospective employees, and administration of psychometric tests and other fair and appropriate **psychological screening** measures (Albrecht, 1997; Kinney, 1995; Labig, 1995; Mantell & Albrecht, 1994; Miller, 2003c, 2008c). Usually, the more complex, sensitive, and responsible the job position, the more rigorous the screening protocol.

Safe Discipline

When employees commit a correctible infraction, the ideal goal of any disciplinary program is to strike a balance between a too heavy-handed vs. an overly lax approach. One model of **corporate discipline** (Grote, 1995; Mantell & Albrecht, 1994) relies on a collaborative approach. By identifying areas of agreement and disagreement, looking for alternatives, thinking creatively, and eventually finding solutions that have the support and commitment of all parties, a manager is more likely to be able to defuse the tension that may spark workplace violence. Discipline should occur in stages, with a clear policy and rationale (Grote, 1995; Grote & Harvey, 1983). When an employee's questionable work behavior is suspected to be caused or exacerbated by a mental disorder, he or she should be referred for a **psychological fitness-for-duty (FFD) evaluation**, and the results and recommendations should be carefully documented and implemented (Miller, 2006f, 2007e; Rostow & Davis, 2002, 2004; Stone, 1995, 2000).

Safe Termination

Not every employee can be salvaged. As with discipline, necessary termination can be clear and firm, without being inhumane. A termination should include a systematic process of documentation. The key to effective termination is to make it as clear as possible to the employee that this action is for a specific job-related reason, rather than for general "attitude" or personal issues. The employee should be treated with reasonable respect, but should understand that the termination action is final and will be backed up. Fired employees should be informed of any counseling or other services offered by the company for the transition period (Grote, 1995; Flannery, 1995; Labich, 1996; Labig, 1995; Mantell & Albrecht, 1994; Robbins, 2001; Root & Ziska, 1996).

RESPONSE TO WORKPLACE VIOLENCE EMERGENCIES

Sometimes, despite the best efforts at prevention, a dangerous situation begins to brew and a violent incident becomes a looming possibility. Or the incident just erupts explosively and personnel have to respond immediately. The nature of the response—and the subsequent psychological effects and legal ramifications—will depend on how thorough the preincident violent response plan and training have been (Bush & O'Shea, 1996; Mack et al., 1998; Schneid, 1999; Yandrick, 1996).

Warning Signs of Impending Violence

Warning signs may be observed hours, days, and sometimes weeks prior to a violent incident (Albrecht, 1997; Flannery, 1995; Mantell & Albrecht, 1994). Signals that an employee may be on the verge of losing control include:

- Disorganized physical appearance or dress
- Increased agitation
- Tense body language
- Evidence of alcohol or substance abuse

continued

BOX 11.1.—*Continued*

- Increased general verbal argumentativeness
- Direct or veiled verbal threats, especially to specific persons
- Preoccupation with violent events in the media
- Carrying weapons

Defusing Potentially Dangerous Situations

Plans and training for defusing violent episodes must be developed, put in place, and reviewed periodically (Bolz et al., 1996; Caraulia & Steiger, 1997; Dubin, 1995; Gilliland & James, 1993; Labig, 1995; McMains & Mullins, 1996; Miller, 2008c; Rogan et al., 1997; Schaner, 1996). These include:

- Initial actions to take when a violent episode appears to be threatening
- Codes and signals for summoning help
- Chain of command for handling emergencies
- Training in appropriate use of verbal control tactics and body language to deescalate dangerous situations
- Scene control and bystander containment
- Strategies for dealing with weapons and armed perpetrators
- Protocols for resolving hostage situations

RECOVERING FROM WORKPLACE VIOLENCE

The crisis is not over when the police and paramedics leave. People may have been killed, others wounded, some held hostage, and many psychologically traumatized. Plans and policies for dealing with the aftermath of workplace violence are just as important as planning for the incident itself, and both may come under sharp scrutiny in later investigations and litigation.

Plans, Policies, and Procedures

Companies should proactively set up policies and procedures for responding to the aftermath of a workplace violence incident (Albrecht, 1996, 1997; Braverman, 1999; Caponigro, 1999; Dattilio & Freeman, 2000; Flannery, 1995; Gilliland & James, 1993; Kennedy & Homant, 1997; Kinney, 1995; Mantell & Albrecht, 1994; Schneid, 1999; Susskind & Field, 1996). The plan should include the following elements.

- **Mental health mobilization** includes a prearranged plan for company representatives to contact their mental health professionals immediately, arrange for the clinicians to meet first at the top levels of the organization for executive and/or managerial briefings, set up **critical incident stress debriefings** or other interventions for affected employees and stakeholders, and arrange a follow-up schedule for mental health clinicians to return for further psychological services as needed.

- **Media and public relations measures** include a specially designated media spokesperson to brief the media and shepherd them away from grieving employees, family members, and eyewitnesses. A firm, forthright, proactive, and sincere approach is preferable, from someone in a high position within the organization. The key question to be answered will be, "What is this company doing for the survivors and stakeholders?"

- **Employee and family interventions** include a designated person to notify the victims' families of the incident, and to be ready to offer them immediate support, counseling, and stress debriefing services. Personnel managers should arrange time off for grieving and traumatized employees as appropriate. After the initial stages of the incident have passed, mental health clinicians should help managers and supervisors find ways for the employees to memorialize the victims.

- **Law enforcement, physical security, and cleanup measures** include a designated staff member or team to immediately check, protect, or restore the integrity of the company's data systems, computers, and files. A company representative should be designated to work with local law enforcement. The crime scene should be kept intact until law enforcement has gone over the area. A cleanup crew for the site of the incident should be available, pending approval from law enforcement investigators, and such cleanup operations should be conducted in as respectful a manner as possible.

- **Legal measures** include notifying in-house legal counsel or the company's outside law firm, and they should be asked to respond to the scene, if necessary.

- **Post-incident investigations** include questions about the nature of the perpetrator; his relationship to the organization; his relationship to coworkers and supervisors; his history of disciplinary action or termination; the actions that led to his dissatisfaction or disgruntlement; any restraining orders and their enforcement; the workplace stressors that may have been involved; financial pressures, drugs, or alcohol, mental illness or personality disorders; any warning signs that should have been heeded; and the company's overall security and threat assessment procedures. The goal is to use what has been learned from the tragedy to ensure, as much as is ever possible, that something like this won't happen again.

VIOLENCE IN HEALTH CARE FACILITIES

A hospital or treatment center ought to be the one place you feel safe as you check in, or are brought in, to recover from an illness or injury. Yet, even these institutions of healing are not immune from criminal violence.

General Hospital Violence

Health care workers rank among the groups with the highest rates of workplace-related violence (Beech & Leather, 2006; Hahn et al., 2008; Wells & Bowers, 2002). For one thing, hospitals and treatment centers are often located in downtown urban areas with high crime rates in the surrounding community. Many emergency room patients may be in various states of confusion and agitation, especially in major urban medical centers and hospitals that handle a large volume of gunshot and other assault wound cases (Olshaker et al., 2001), or have psychiatric units. Most violent attacks are carried out by patients, long-term care residents, or visitors.

For example, up to half of health care workers have been subjected to verbal abuse by patients or visitors, and about a quarter have been physically assaulted. Patients are more likely to be verbally or physically aggressive than visitors. Among staff, nurses carry the highest risk, probably because they are typically on the front lines of direct patient care in most facilities. Younger, less experienced staff are at higher risk than those with more time on the job. Factors contributing to the potential for violence include clinical and cognitive status of the patient, tone of interaction between hospital staff, patients, and visitors, and general organization and running of the facility. Illness is a high-stress event, and patients who are confused, frightened, frustrated, in pain, or feel they are not being taken seriously are more likely to become aggressive. Similarly, visitors who feel like they are being ignored, dismissed, or disrespected are more likely to erupt (Beech & Leather, 2006; Hahn et al., 2008; Hinson & Shapiro, 2003; Wells & Bowers, 2002; Winstanley, 2005).

Violence in Mental Health Care Settings

It seems intuitively obvious that patients with mental health problems would be more volatile and dangerous than general medical patients, and there appears to be some evidence for this. Especially at risk for attack are health care providers who treat serious mental illnesses, and emergency mental health services personnel who provide assistance during disasters. In recent years, disgruntled patients who have failed to find relief for their mental and physical pain or who think they have been badly treated by the medical or mental health care system have come back to kill and injure emergency room and mental health clinic personnel (Flannery, 1995; Simon, 1996; see Box 11.2).

According to an American Psychiatric Association Task Force report and other studies, 40–50 percent of psychiatrists are assaulted by patients one or more times during their careers. Psychiatrists appear to be at higher risk than psychologists or social workers in inpatient institutional settings, but not in outpatient office settings. Nearly three-quarters of attacks against psychiatrists occur during the first meeting of the doctor and patient (Binder, 1995; Flannery, 1995; Miller, 1997b, 1998c, 1998e, 2008c; Simon, 1996; Tardiff, 1995; see Box 11.2).

Violence in Long-Term Care Facilities

Most people chuckle when they hear stories of aggression or sexual activity in long-term care facilities such as nursing homes for the elderly. After all, "what kind of trouble could grandma and grandpa get into?" But consider that nursing homes contain a large number of residents who may be physically intact, but cognitively impaired, rendering them more impulsive and less restrained than others of the same age, as well as being congregated together in situations that may lead to conflict over food or services. In addition, violence also may occur in group homes for mentally handicapped younger adults.

Risk factors for such **resident-to-resident aggression** in long-term care facilities include male gender; tendency to wander; moderate functional dependency; cognitive impairment; depressive symptoms; delusions and hallucinations; and constipation (which is probably a physically irritating factor, and also may necessitate very intrusive nursing interventions). Long-term care facilities may also contain high numbers of convicted felons and registered sex offenders. Both assailants and victims tend to be relatively intact physically, but cognitively impaired. Injuries usually consist of bruises, lacerations, and fractures. Residents are most likely to be assaulted by their peers in either their own or the assailant's room, but attacks also occur in hallways, dining rooms, and other common areas. A typical precipitant is one resident's intrusion into another's personal space, which is more common in less spacious facilities. Not infrequently, police are summoned to investigate or intervene in resident-to-resident violence (Bridges-Parlet et al., 1994; Lachs et al., 2007; Morgan & Stewart, 1998; Ng et al., 2001; Nijman & Rector, 1999; Rudman et al., 1994; Ryden et al., 1991; Rosen et al., 2008; Shinoda-Tagawa et al., 2004).

In the other direction, abuse of elders with dementia and other forms of cognitive impairment may also occur at the hands of caregivers, either family members or nursing home staff. Common predisposing and precipitating factors for **caregiver aggression** are the resident's disturbing and disruptive behavior, and frustration in trying to meet the resident's needs, such as feeding, toileting, bathing, dressing, and medical care (Lachs & Pillemer, 1995; Lachs et al., 1997; Pillemer & Moore, 1989; Pillemer & Suitor, 1992).

BOX 11.2. ARE MENTAL HEALTH CARE WORKERS
AT SPECIAL RISK? WHAT CAN THEY DO?

Hospitals and clinics, especially in some geographic areas, are known to be high-risk environments for violence against health care workers. While some of the hostility comes from the patients themselves, friends or relatives may also become aggressive toward health care staff. The most dangerous health care settings are emergency rooms, acute crisis care centers, and psychiatric units (Binder, 1995; Flannery, 1995; Miller, 1997b, 1998c, 1998e; Rugala & Isaacs, 2004; Simon, 1996; Tardiff, 1995).

Risks for Mental Health Care Workers

While a good deal of traditional psychotherapy and other mental health services still take place in outpatient, private office-based settings, mental health services, especially for poorer, underinsured patients, are increasingly being provided in institutional settings, ranging from public hospitals, to walk-in clinics, to correctional facilities. Much of this involves crisis intervention and emergency mental health services with seriously disturbed patients. This type of mental health practice is tough, demanding work that can take an exhausting toll on practitioners. As the demographics of 21st century mental health practice continue to shift, more seriously disordered patients are also turning up in routine medical and mental health clinics and office settings, many with inadequate insurance coverage to properly treat their problems (Albrecht, 1997).

To make matters worse, an increasing number of these seriously mentally ill patients are being released prematurely from hospitals, with little or no follow-up care. By law, these patients have the right to refuse medication or involuntary hospitalization unless they pose a clear and immediate threat to themselves or others. Thus, by the time they are brought to a receiving facility, they are usually in a severely disturbed and agitated state, putting health and mental health care workers at heightened risk for assault (Rugala & Isaacs, 2004). Therapists and mental health care professionals are often threatened, sometimes stalked, and occasionally assaulted. Some are seriously injured, and a few of our colleagues have been killed (Miller, 1998c, 1998e).

High-Risk Patients and High-Risk Mental Health Care Workers

High-risk factors for violence in institutional settings by mentally-disordered patients parallel the risk factors for violence found generally among psychiatric populations. Male gender, young age, the presence of severe personality disorder and/or psychosis, brain syndromes, substance abuse, and prior history of violence perpetration and/or victimization pose the greatest individual risk factors. The most common form of attack is being struck by a fist or kicked (Bjorkly, 1999; Blair, 1991; Fink, 1995; Flannery, 1995, 2005; Flannery et al., 2006; Hansen, 1996).

In institutional medical settings, nurses experience the greatest number of physical assaults and verbal threats, but physicians, medical technicians, nurse's aides, social workers, paramedics, and others also experience their fair share of violence. In institutional mental health care settings, psychiatrists and nurses appear to be at higher risk than psychologists or social workers, but not necessarily in outpatient settings. More than three-fourths of assaults against mental health care workers occur during the first meeting between the clinician and a previously unknown patient, and relatively younger, less experienced clinicians are more likely to be attacked. The most common reasons given by patients for assaulting mental health staff include rude, irritable, impatient, dismissive, disrespectful, and/or confrontational behavior by the clinician, as well as sensory overload, causing the patient to feel frightened, threatened, and/or overwhelmed. The most common reasons given by clinicians for why they were assaulted include refusing to meet a patient's request, setting a limit, failing to set a limit, making an unfavorable comment to a patient, provocation by other staff or patients, the patient being in an acutely psychotic state, or trying to compel a patient to take unwanted medication (Binder, 1995; Daffern & Howells, 2002; Fink, 1995; Flannery, 1995, 2005; Flannery et al., 2006; Krakowski & Czbor, 2004; Mellesdal, 2003; Miller, 1997b, 1998e; Albrecht, 1997; Rugala & Isaacs, 2004; Simon, 1996; Tardiff, 1995).

Assaulted Staff Action Program (ASAP)

Building on the work of Mitchell & Everly (1996) in the field of **critical incident stress management** (**CISM**), Flannery and colleagues (Flannery, 1995; Flannery et al., 1991, 1996, 1998, 2006) have designed a comprehensive, voluntary, peer-help, systems approach, called the **assaulted staff action program** (**ASAP**), for health care staff who are assaulted by patients at work. The program provides a range of services, including:

- Individual critical incident stress debriefings of assaulted staff members
- Debriefings of entire hospital units, if necessary
- A staff victims' support group
- Employee-victim family debriefing and counseling
- Referrals for follow-up psychotherapy, as necessary

The ASAP team structure is comprised of 15 direct-care staff volunteers. Doctors and health care workers are often themselves the last persons to seek or accept mental health treatment. Therefore, to depathologize the process and maximize its appeal, the approach is conceptualized as psychoeducational, rather than as formal clinical counseling or psychotherapy per se. The ASAP has three supervisors, and the ASAP team director is responsible for administering the entire program and for ensuring the quality of the services.

When combined with pre-incident training and stress management, the ASAP program has reportedly proven effective in ameliorating the psychological impact of patient assaults on employees and in significantly reducing the overall level of

continued

BOX 11.2.—*Continued*

institutional violence. In facilities where it has been applied, the program has proven to be cost-effective in terms of reduced staff turnover, less use of sick leave, fewer industrial accident claims, and less medical expense as overall assault rates have declined. Indeed, the authors make the practical, bottom-line point that the costs associated with the entire program are far less than that of one successful lawsuit.

WORKPLACE VIOLENCE AND WOMEN

As more women join the workforce, they increasingly become the targets of violence. Accordingly, certain special considerations affecting women on the job warrant special attention.

Demographics

Homicide is the number one cause of death for women in the workplace. Although the leading instrument of death on the job is some kind of firearm, women are six times more likely than men to be strangled to death at work. In the United States, while only one out of five people murdered at work is a woman, 40 percent of women who die on the job will die from homicide, compared to 10 percent of men. In other words, while men are more likely to die from falls, electrocution, or other industrial accidents, women are more likely to die from workplace violence (Kinney, 1995; Rugala & Isaacs, 2004; Simon, 1996).

Types of Workplace Violence Against Women

Women are targets of many different forms of workplace violence, including homicide, rape, sexual abuse and harassment, gunshot wounds, stabbing, strangulation, physical beatings, verbal abuse, and psychological trauma. Both the number and the percentage of women who work outside the home have increased steadily throughout the twentieth and early twenty-first centuries. At the same time, divorce rates are high and single motherhood continues to increase. Women in the workforce may be victimized because they appear more vulnerable or weaker than men. For example, many women are relegated to low-wage and low-status service or clerical jobs that place them on the front lines as cashiers, waitresses, and other positions where workplace security measures are often meager or nonexistent. Employees in such low-status positions are less likely to have the clout to persuade employers to take threats seriously. In some cases, workers who "make trouble" are simply fired so that the boss doesn't have to deal with the aggravation.

When women do try to move up and break into the preserves of "man's work," from police and firefighting to executive management positions, this may engender emotionally emasculating resentment in insecure men, who may feel that their jobs or promotions have been unfairly "stolen" by women. When violence at work does strike women, the repercussions are likely to impair both the financial and emotional well-being of their families. This is especially the case for women who are the breadwinners in single-parent households (Kinney, 1995; Simon, 1996).

Sexual Harassment and Domestic Violence

Sexual harassment has become perhaps the quintessential form of interpersonal workplace problem experienced by women, and severe forms of sexual harassment can be regarded as a form of workplace violence. Even verbal intimidation or harassment can inflict acute and longstanding psychological and emotional harm. In addition, sexual harassment is often a precursor of more overt forms of physical violence, such as assault, rape, or murder in the workplace (Berdahl & Aquino, 2009; Kinney, 1995; Pierce et al., 2008; Schouten, 1996).

Domestic disputes have become the third major source of conflict leading to homicide in the workplace for a number of reasons (Barling et al., 2009; Brownell, 1996; Friedman, 1996; Hamberger & Holtzworth-Munroe, 1994; Hoffman & Baron, 2001; Kinney, 1995; Labig, 1995; Meloy, 1997a; Swanberg et al., 2006; Walker, 1984). A sagging economy usually brings an increase in domestic violence as unemployed husbands or boyfriends come to resent their wives or partners who work and threaten their authority at home. Rejection of on-the-job Romeos or confrontation of workplace sexual harassers often places these women at increased risk of violence at the hands of the spurned and the jilted. When romances outside the workplace sour, the rejected male abuser may become a stalker (Chapter 18), who usually knows where the woman works and generally has ready access to her place of employment. A common response of employers who are fed up with all the drama is simply to fire the woman.

Protective and Preventive Measures

With regard to domestic violence spillover, sometimes court **restraining orders** or **orders of protection** work, and sometimes they just make matters worse. Much depends on the ability and willingness of local police to enforce them. Many **domestic violence** cases involve a victim who is struggling back-and-forth to let go of the abuser (see also Chapter 17), which can prove to be quite frustrating for bosses and coworkers who are trying to be helpful, because their well-intentioned suggestions may be rejected or misinterpreted by the ambivalent or frightened employee. People's privacy at work should of course be respected, but if they are going through messy domestic battles or, for that matter, other personal crises that affect their jobs and their lives, they need to know that it is all right to confide in the right persons at work and that the proper protective or other assistive measures will be taken. Along with this, they may also need to be reminded of their responsibility to deal constructively with personal problems that impair their job functioning and potentially put other employees at risk (Hoffman & Baron, 2001; Labig, 1995; Pierce & Aguinis, 1997; Pierce et al., 2008).

Companies can take several steps to protect employees from **stalkers** (Flannery, 1995; Hoffman & Baron, 2001; Kinney, 1995; Meloy, 1997a; Pierce & Aguinis, 1997). The first step is the establishment of a policy providing protective services to threatened employees. If possible, the threatened employee's office or work station should be relocated to a place unknown to the stalker, and her work schedule altered to confuse the stalker. Descriptions or photographs of the stalker should be provided to receptionists, security officers, and other relevant personnel. Law enforcement can be encouraged to enforce restraining orders by forging links between company security and local police. If the threat is acute, the employee at risk should be given time off. Silent alarms or buzzers should be placed at the threatened employee's work station and security cameras should be deployed near entrances to her work area; ideally, these measures should be implemented at all vulnerable locations. Such security measures work best when they are planned, coordinated, and integrated with other safety plans on the job site (see also Chapter 18).

With regard to **sexual harassment**, companies can take several effective measures (Kinney, 1995; Pierce & Aguinis, 1997; Pierce et al., 2008; Schouten, 1996). A serious sexual harassment policy should describe the specific conduct that constitutes harassment and state that such conduct is tolerated neither by the company nor by state or federal law. The policy should explain the employee's right to report sexual harassment without fear of retaliation and without having to directly confront the harasser, at least at the time of the initial complaint. The policy should have a grievance procedure that the harassed employee can follow, as well as sexual harassment hotlines for emergency situations; such hotlines are now required by law in at least 30 states.

SUMMARY AND CONCLUSIONS

Although overall rates of workplace violence have been declining over the past decade, the prospect of being killed or injured where one goes daily to earn their living is still a frightening prospect to most employees. The most frequent types of workplace violence incidents are those perpetrated by persons outside the organization, such as robbers. The most common profile of the current or former employee who commits violence in the workplace is a young or middle-aged male with a combination of anger, paranoid ideation, and depression. A variety of diagnostic syndromes can be associated with workplace violence, but none are specific to it.

Organizational factors related to how employees are treated can reduce or heighten the risk for workplace violence. Companies that have strong workplace violence and misconduct policies and procedures are better able to prevent such incidents and recover from them faster. Violence at work may be a special problem for women because it often intersects with domestic violence and other aspects of a woman's personal life. Protecting women employees should be part of a company's overall workplace violence prevention program.

Chapter **12**

Mass Homicide II: School Violence

In Chapter 11, we discussed how most working adults have a reasonable expectation of safety at their jobsites. Children's "job" is to go to school—shouldn't they have the same expectation? Whereas most workplace violence is committed by outsiders, violence by coworkers may be more traumatizing. But for children at school, is precisely their schoolmates that are most likely be responsible for targeting them, either through everyday bullying and harassment, or in rare but lethal mass violence attacks. Thus, the school environment exerts a powerful impact on the cognitive, emotional, and behavioral development of children (Bluestein, 2001).

BULLYING AND PEER VICTIMIZATION

Peer victimization is the experience of being the target of aggressive behavior by other students or other children who are not siblings and not necessarily age-mates (Hawker & Boulton, 2000; Olweus, 1993a; Ross, 1996).

Bullying can be defined as the illegitimate use of sadistic and/or coercive power by children or adults against another person. Bullying is defined as a specific type of aggression in which: (1) the behavior is intended to harm or disturb; (2) the behavior is repeated over time; and (3) there is an imbalance of power, with a more powerful person or group attacking a less powerful one (Farrington, 1993; Nansel et al., 2001; Rigby, 2002; Smith & Sharp, 1994). Bullying can include physical abuse (hitting, kicking, tackling, tripping, destruction of property), verbal abuse (mocking, taunting, spreading rumors), or social exclusion (Lagerspetz et al., 1988; Monks et al., 2009).

Punking is a relatively new term that describes the practice of verbal and physical violence, humiliation, and shaming usually done in public by males to other males. Punking is commonly used by adolescent boys and is often described interchangeably with bullying (Phillips, 2007).

LEGAL ASPECTS OF BULLYING

Historically, the practice of peer victimization among children has often been delegitimized and rationalized as "roughhousing" or "boys will be boys" horseplay (Phillips, 2007). The kinds of intimidation and harassment that would get an employee fired at almost any job are routinely tolerated by school authorities when they occur between students. In many of the cases of school violence that have been closely studied, the perpetrators had been harassed or persecuted in some way by other students for years and their efforts to have their plights resolved by school authorities had been rebuffed or ignored. An even greater number of bullied students suffer in silence.

In addition to the human costs, school violence of any kind, like workplace violence (Chapter 11), can have legal repercussions. *Stoneking v. Bradford Area School District, 1988* found that if a school is aware of dangerous and unlawful activities on its premises and takes insufficient action to address them, it may be held liable because of students' rights to liberty under the 14th Amendment. However, school officials may be protected from liability if they can demonstrate "due diligence" in preventing crime on their campuses, which provides a powerful incentive for schools to take proactive measures.

As bullying began to be increasingly regarded as unacceptable among children as well as adults, federal and state governments moved to prohibit it on school campuses, using *Title IX of the 1972 Federal Education Amendment,* which prohibits harassing behavior in schools and school-sponsored contexts. Under Title IX, harassment includes a pattern of behavior or a single incident, perpetrated by anyone, that creates an intimidating or hostile environment in which the targeted person cannot work or learn. Additionally, the *Equal Protection Clause of the 14th Amendment* of the United States Constitution has been used to protect against bullying, stating that schools are responsible for equally protecting all students and that all citizens are due equal protection under the law. Lastly, states such as Washington have instituted their own antibullying statutes that are enforced statewide in schools (Phillips, 2007).

Ironically, although more stringent legislative regulation exists for school safety than workplace safety, the latter have been much more proactive than the former in developing antiviolence programs (see Box 11.1), and acts of aggression among children are still tolerated far more than those among adults. Perhaps this disparity exists because, in most corporate settings, a fistfight between two employees can affect production and the bottom line to a far greater extent than a similar scuffle between two public school students. In addition, as noted above, there is still a widespread attitude that, while any kind of violence between adults at a jobsite is unacceptable, some degree of aggression among children at school is normative and therefore tolerable.

TYPES OF SCHOOL BULLYING AND HARASSMENT

Although stories of adults abusing children are more likely to make the headlines (Chapter 16), bullying and related peer-to-peer abuse are probably far more common than adult-to-child abuse (Ambert, 1994). According to the School Crime Supplement to the National Crime Victimization Survey, 14 percent of teens between the ages of 12 and 18 disclosed being bullied in the past 6 months (DeVoe et al., 2005). Nansel et al. (2001) studied 15,686 U.S. youths in grades 6 though 10 and found that 26 percent of the boys reported bullying others up to once a week, whereas 21 percent of boys reported being bullied regularly; other studies have found bullying rates to vary from 2–20 percent and victim rates to vary from 5–20 percent of grade school and high school students (Smith et al., 1999). These statistics translate into millions of children, mostly boys, being involved in bullying either as a bully, a victim, or both. In addition to this direct participation, millions of youths and adults participate by witnessing these behaviors.

Although bullying typically begins to occur in the upper grade school environment, young children have been observed to display aggressor, victim, and defender roles as early as age 4 or 5 (Monks et al., 2009), confirming the early development of personality traits that lead to later patterns of behavior. Self-reported bullying victimization rates appear to climb after age 8 and reach a peak around the middle school or junior high school years (grades 6–8, ages 11–14), declining after age 16. Interestingly, self-reports of bullying others show no such decline; however, with increasing age, bullying tends to shift more toward verbal and relational types (Monks et al., 2009; Olweus et al., 1993b,c; Smith et al., 1999), probably reflecting the fact that older children and adolescents are likely to get in more serious trouble for physical aggression than younger children.

Some experts in school violence have classified bullying and harassment into several overlapping categories, the most common of which will be reviewed here (Bjorkvist, 1994; Crick et al., 1999; Hawker & Boulton, 2000; Olweus, 1993a; Ross, 1996; Smith et al., 2008).

Individual bullying involves one-on-one aggression, usually when one student singles another out for special persecution. This is probably the most common kind of bullying that occurs in schools and neighborhoods.

Group bullying is also relatively common and involves a bunch of kids ganging up on the victim; the phenomenon is known as **mobbing** in the

European literature. Often, only one member of this gang may actually commit an aggressive act, with the rest of the cohort cheering him on. On other occasions, however, several members of the group may join in the violence. In such cases, there is always the danger that the aggression will escalate to serious injury or even death of the victim.

Direct bullying involves the direct aggression of one child against another. Examples include hitting, kicking, shoving, tripping, and destruction of the victim's property.

Indirect bullying is carried out through a third party or in some way that conceals the identity of the aggressor. This may include secret sabotage of the victim's belongings, homework assignments, reputation, and so on, most recently including **cyberbullying** (see below).

Relational bullying is behavior that damages peer relationships and acceptance within the social group. This is the preferred method of girls who bully and, in many cases, can be as psychologically devastating to the ostracized victim as physical injury. A related and more general concept is **verbal victimization**, in which the student's status is attacked or threatened with words, and which can be exceedingly vicious and damaging to a student's psyche and self-image. This, too, is a favorite bullying tactic of girls.

Bias bullying occurs where the target is singled out primarily because of his or her special status, such as race, religion, sexual orientation, disability, and so on (Carter & Forsyth, 2009; Graves et al., 2010; Mishna, 2003; Monks et al., 2008; Wainscot et al., 2008). In many cases, it can be difficult to disentangle which aspects of bullying are related to the group identity of the victim and what proportion has to do with the individual him- or herself.

Cyberbullying involves the use of computers and mobile phones and can include abusive e-mails, text messages, and images. Modern camera-phones allow students to take embarrassing candid shots of other students, and then circulate them on the Internet; this also includes so-called **sexting** which involves the sending of nude or sexually explicit photos or film clips of oneself or others, which in many jurisdictions can be prosecuted as a sex crime (Chapter 15). Cyberbullying may also involve **cyberstalking**, which is discussed in Chapter 18.

Sibling bullying occurs between brothers and sisters, and can include physical, verbal, relational, or sexual abuse; the latter may be properly called bullying when the primary motive is aggression and intimidation, rather than sexual gratification per se, however this may be difficult to distinguish in individual cases. Within families, the bully is typically about twice as old as the sibling victim, and the most common pattern is brother-sister bullying, followed by brother-brother and sister-sister bullying. Stepsiblings are especially at risk for all types of bullying, including sexual abuse (Adler & Schultz,

1995; Becker et al., 1986; De Jong, 1989; Gilbert, 1992; Johnson, 1988; La-viola, 1992; Monks et al., 2009; Pierce & Pierce, 1987; Smith & Israel, 1987).

Institutional bullying takes place within the confines of institutions where people are retained for any length of time, such as prisons, youth detention centers, or long-term inpatient psychiatric facilities. In these settings, social hierarchies, or pecking orders, are sure to develop, with winners, losers, and those in the middle. For example, up to half the children in residential youth homes report either being bullied or bullying others, and much of this abuse goes undetected by institutional authorities. In some cases, bullying may reflect institutional gang-related activity. Children under age 12 are particularly susceptible to this abuse (Farmer & Pollock, 1998; Freundlich et al., 2007; Sinclair & Gibbs, 1998). Another example is the adult prison population. Interestingly, indirect and relational bullying in prison may be more common than direct aggression because the latter is understood to have severe consequences, including lengthening of sentence, if discovered (Bjorkqvist, 1994; Ireland, 1999; Ireland & Monaghan, 2006; Ireland et al., 2007; see Chapter 21). Finally, bullying and harassment at work has been covered in Chapter 11: again, for much the same reasons as in other adult populations, workplace bullying is far more likely to be nonphysical so as to stay "under the radar." It is also more likely than other forms of bullying to involve abuse of authority when perpetrated by bosses on hapless employees, although much peer-to-peer bullying occurs in the workplace as well.

TYPES OF BULLIES

A combination of research (Barter et al., 2004; Coloroso, 2003; Shafii & Shafii, 2001) and practical experience has produced a general consensus as to a typology of bullies.

Antisocial bully. This is the bully on a power trip. Clinical correlates typically involve features of conduct disorder (Mandel, 1997), which is the childhood precursor of adult antisocial personality disorder (Chapters 8 and 19). These are the children and adolescents, almost always boys, who simply enjoy dominating and controlling others. They are not the "troubled kids" of the classic psychosocial literature; in fact, they show a distinct lack of care or conscience about anything but their own gratification. Many display a variety of antisocial behaviors including sexually coercive and victimizing behavior (Basile et al., 2009). Many of these kids can be quite charming and crafty, and able to play innocent with adults, and they may show a keen interpersonal perceptiveness that they utilize to manipulate others (Sutton et al., 1999). Because of their charismatic power, they often attract followers and wannabes who then become the bully's cheering section, encouraging his aggressive actions for the vicarious power rush it gives them. In fact, in many school and neighborhood settings, bullying and intimidating behavior, including violence, may be an effective strategy for some children to climb the social dominance hierarchy at the expense of other children (Hawley, 2007; Olweus, 1993a, 1995; Pellegrini, 2007). This may work against the efforts of many of the increasingly popular antibullying programs (Box 12.1).

Distressed bully. This type of bully most closely fits the stereotype of the "troubled kid." There is typically an edgy, dysphoric quality to this child's personality: he may suffer from a mood disorder, ADHD, or borderline, schizoid, or paranoid personality disorder. He is less likely than the antisocial bully to go looking for trouble, but his irritable, mistrustful attitude and impulsive, hair-trigger temper may cause him to lash out at anyone he suspects of disrespecting him, persecuting him, harassing him, or otherwise getting on his case. He may feel remorse after such an outburst or he may attempt to justify it. This type of bully is sometimes called the **bully-victim** because he is likely to assume both roles at different times and with different students. He is also more likely to suffer multiple types of abuse in school, at home, and in the community (Holt et al., 2007).

Situational bully. Most of the time, this child will keep to himself, but when stressed, he tends to project his anger at a target of convenience. Diagnoses may include ADHD, Asperger's syndrome, childhood bipolar disorder, or schizoid personality disorder. The sheer unpredictability of his behavior may make him even more shunned by his peers because they never know when he's going to be a nice guy and when he's going to "go off."

TYPES OF VICTIMS

Consistent with the observation that there are not always pure victims and pure villains, a general victim typology has emerged from research on bullying (Coloroso, 2003; Shafii & Shafii, 2001) and from practical experience.

Anxious/depressed victim. This is the marginalized student, often known to his peers as the nerd or geek, who is usually at the bottom of the social pecking order and is often a prime target for bullies, first, because of his weakness and submissiveness and, secondly, because he typically has few buddies who will stand up for him. This victim spends an inordinate amount of time just trying to stay out of the bully's way. Often these victims suffer in silence for years and may develop a variety of serious physical and psychological disorders.

Martyring/rescuing victim. These victims seem to wear their victim-hood like a badge of honor and derive a grim sort of satisfaction from gar-nering sympathetic attention to their plight. Often, they overlap with the vic-tim-bystander type discussed below or the bully-victim described above. They seem to be on a mission to highlight the bully's aggression and are less like-ly to run and hide than the anxious-depressed victim.

Provocative victim. An extension of the above, this is the victim that seems to be "asking for it." In a roundabout, passive-aggressive way, this vic-tim achieves a kind of victory over the bully by showing that he can "take it" and can bounce back and ask for more. Furthermore, his ability to manipu-latively evoke an aggressive response gives this student a paradoxical form of control over the behavior of a physically stronger person. In many cases, other students don't know what to make of this kid. On the one hand, he seems crazy by acting like a glutton for punishment; on the other hand, he accrues a kind of grudging respect for standing up to the bully, even without directly retaliating. Because of the low payoff in terms of stoking their own sense of power and control, bullies often come to avoid this victim ("I'm not wasting any time on this nut case") and gravitate toward someone else who presents a less willing, but more reactive victim.

TYPES OF BYSTANDERS AND WITNESSES

In many cases, the power rush that bullies get from their aggression re-quires an audience, some members of which who are willing, others con-scripted or coerced, and still others who are gawkers of opportunity. Ac-cordingly, there has evolved a typology of bystanders (Coloroso, 2003; Shafii & Shafii, 2001).

Victim-type bystander. Bullies often have more than one chosen vic-tim; in fact, there may be a hierarchy of victims, with members of this reluc-tant fraternity changing rank order at the bully's whim. Some in the group standing around and witnessing the confrontation, may be former or current victims themselves and are only too glad to have someone else take the heat for now, even if they feel a little guilty about it. Others who have thus far es-caped the bully's depredations may feel it's only a matter of time till his at-tention turns to them.

Bully-type bystander. This is the wannabe bully, the kid who may not be bad enough or tough enough to be a schoolyard thug himself, so he sat-isfies himself by allying himself to, and thereby identifying with, the alpha aggressor. He'll be in the crowd, cheering the primary bully on, or at least encouraging him by his presence. Some of these kids retain their sidekick role, while others eventually graduate to full bully status themselves.

Avoidant bystander. This is the bystander who makes every effort to distance himself from the disturbance because he just doesn't want the hassle. This type often overlaps with the victim-type bystander, except that the avoidant bystander has so far managed to stay under the bully's radar and wants to keep it that way.

Chameleon-type bystander. This student will do whatever it takes to avoid being a victim himself. If the bully needs a cheerleader, he'll cheer. If he can get away with ducking out, he'll flee. If there's a school-sponsored anti-bully coalition forming and he thinks it will be better for him to be in their camp, he'll switch sides. He has learned to adapt and survive by morphing his behavior into whatever form the situation requires.

FACTORS CONTRIBUTING TO SCHOOL BULLYING

There's an old saying: "Life is a fifth-grade class." Most social animals, from fish to birds to mammals to primates to people, have hierarchies and pecking orders, and this is exemplified in the schoolyard relationship dynamics among bullies, victims, and bystanders (Cillessen & Mayeux, 2007; Coloroso, 2003; Galloway & Roland, 2004; Phillips, 2007; Shafii & Shafii, 2001; Vaughn & Santos, 2007). Several factors play a role.

Individual factors include biological traits of temperament, personality, and psychopathology. They also include factors of resilience and self-confidence to assertively stand up to aggression while not unnecessarily making oneself a target. Research has shown that certain types of maladjustment, such as loneliness, depression, anxiety, and low self-esteem, are positively associated with such peer relationship difficulties as submissiveness, social withdrawal, and unpopularity with peers. These peer relationship difficulties are themselves risk factors for continued peer victimization (Hawker & Boulton, 2000).

School factors include the formal policies and programs that are in place for dealing with bullying, harassment and peer violence (Box 12.1, 12.2), as well as the general atmosphere of the school administration with regard to supporting student disclosure and standing behind students who are being victimized, as opposed to taking a hands-off, "let-them-work-it-out" attitude.

Cultural factors denote the fact that schools are often a reflection of their communities and the larger surrounding society, and the behavioral climate at school will be influenced by the religious, social, and family values of the surrounding community which, in turn, contribute to school spirit, community connectedness, and morale. For example, a school climate that

encourages and supports an ideal norm of masculinity as a Hollywood cari-
cature of macho strength, power, and control, often via the emphasis on the
school's sports team performance, can expect a heightened incidence of students solving problems through physical aggression (Gilligan, 1997; Farmer,
2007; Kimmel, 1996; Phillips, 2007).

EFFECTS OF BULLYING

Studies have shown that school victimization exerts a variety of harmful
effects on students' physical and mental health (Carney & Merrell, 2001;
Dawkins, 1995; DeVoe et al., 2005; Hawker & Boulton, 2000; Haynie et al.,
2001; Holt et al., 2007; Johnson, 1989; Miller, 2002b, 2007a, 2008b; Nansel
et al., 2001, 2003; Olweus, 1993b,c; O'Moore, 2000; Pitcher & Poland, 1992;
Rigby, 2003), including lowered self-esteem; increased loneliness and isolation; anxiety and panic attacks; depression and suicidal thoughts; posttraumatic stress disorder; greater use of tobacco and alcohol; psychosomatic
symptoms and stress-related illnesses; increased number of doctor visits; negative perceptions of their school; reduced school attendance; impaired academic performance and grade deterioration; and greater likelihood of carrying weapons to school for defense, heightening the odds of a lethal confrontation.

Most bullied students don't ask school authorities for help: they mainly
try to stay out of the bully's way and cope on their own (Kochenderfer &
Ladd, 1997; Naylor et al., 2001). Only rarely, do disturbed, desperate students resort to violence themselves (see below) but, when they do, it often
highlights systemic problems that have occurred for a long time—a strong
parallel with workplace violence (Chapter 11).

THEORIES OF BULLYING

As we've seen throughout this text, a variety of theoretical formulations
have been offered to explain most types of violent and criminal behavior.
The following summarizes the main theoretical formulations that have been
applied to bullying behavior.

Attachment Theory

Attachment theory posits that children build an internal working model
of healthy or unhealthy relationships based on the quality of attachment they

receive from caregivers early in life. These working mental models then influence how they relate to others which, in turn, affects how others treat them, in an ongoing cycle. An individual with an **insecure attachment style** may respond to others with high levels of defensive hostility and aggression, and such early insecure attachment may account for bullying behavior in some students, young offenders, and adult prisoners (Ireland & Power, 2004; Miller et al., 2010; Monks, 2009; Monks et al., 2003; Troy & Sroufe, 1987).

Social Learning Theory

According to **social learning theory**, children learn what they observe, and if they grow up in a family with high levels of interpersonal hostility, aggression, manipulation, and intimidation, they will model these behaviors in their subsequent dealings with peers in school and elsewhere (Baldry, 2003b; Farrington, 1993; Twemlow & Fonagy, 2005; see also Chapter 3). In the school setting, children who bully may be further reinforced by the attainment of power and status in their respective peer groups (Batsche & Knoff, 1994; Cillessen & Mayeux, 2007; Pellegrini, 2007).

A variant of this theory, the **social information processing model** (Crick & Dodge, 1994, 1999) proposes that such a dysfunctional early history leads to cognitive distortions which bias thinking and responding in the direction of hostility. Indeed, studies show that children who become bullies typically grow up in families characterized by little warmth and closeness, frequent violence, and either inconsistent or overly harsh discipline–sometimes a combination of both (Farrington, 1993; Olweus, 1993b; Schwartz et al., 1997). This may lead to the development of aggression-supporting beliefs that further prompt aggressive responding (Slaby & Guerra, 1988). Of course, these are general family risk factors for antisocial behavior in general.

Sociocultural Theories

As noted in Chapter 3 and throughout this book, individuals always behave within a particular context, and **sociocultural theories** seek to understand the situational forces that influence a given individual to behave prosocially or aggressively. As in the case of workplace violence (Chapter 11), all organizations, whether they are a school, workplace, healthcare or penal institution, have an **organizational culture** that reinforces some behaviors and discourages others. In the case of school bullying, educational institutions that rely on rigid authoritarian rule enforcement, that discourage help-seeking by victims, and that either overtly or implicitly reinforce aggressive goal-seeking (e.g., by glorification of sports team winnings to the neglect of academic achievement) will tend to have a higher rate of bullying and other forms of inter-peer aggression than schools with a more reflective, communicative, problem-solving orientation (Leymann, 1996; Roland & Galloway, 2002; Salmivalli et al., 1996).

Evolutionary Psychology of Bullying

Also noted throughout this text, **dominance hierarchies** are a common feature of social species, from fish to primates, and one of the functions of such formalized pecking orders is to reduce the overall level of harmful conflict within a group by each member more or less knowing and keeping his or her place. In most such groups, including human ones, males typically compete for dominance by displays of physical prowess and, uniquely in humans, by verbal sparring and jousting, while female status accrues by virtue of physical attractiveness, attachment to a high-status male, and symbolic representations of family resources, such as jewelry and property. As the reciprocal to dominance, a set of **submission behaviors** have also evolved that enable lower-status members to avoid serious injury by such signaling behaviors as crouching, bowing, smiling, whimpering, and averting gaze (Bernstein, 1970; Eibl-Eibelsfeldt, 1971; Farmer & Caldwallader, 2000; Hinde, 1979; Mazur, 1994; Morris, 1977; Olweus, 1993a; Sagan & Druyan, 1992; Vaughn & Santos, 2007).

Recall the discussion in Chapter 2 concerning the role of **testosterone** in aggression and dominance behavior, a relationship that has been well-documented in animals and adult humans. A number of studies have found such a correlation in children as well: those children most prone to use aggression as a serious social manipulation tool have higher testosterone levels than nonaggressive children or children who engage in relatively noncompetitive "playful aggression" only (Olweus, 1988; Olweus et al., 1980; Sanchez-Martin et al., 2000). But by adolescence, testosterone levels appear to correlate not with aggression per se, but with **social dominance**. In fact, adolescent boys with the highest testosterone levels were found to be those who were rated by their peers as being higher in social status but without being overly aggressive (Schaal et al. 1996). Their stable dominance pattern seemed to be related to a confident social adroitness which sent the message that they took no crap and meant business, but didn't have to posture, bellow, and pounce to command respect.

Indeed, the deference and admiration bestowed on the alpha males in many older adolescent groups appears to depend less on aggression-based dominance and more on what has been characterized as **competence-based eminence** (Erchul, 2001; French & Raven, 1959; Kemper, 1990; Keverne, 1979; Kolbert & Crothers, 2003; Olweus, 1993b). This is the quality that signals an individual's ability to generate concrete accomplishments—athletic, academic, economic, or otherwise—which makes subordinates want to emulate and identify with him. In working clinically with adolescents, I often discuss the street concept of "respect" that many of them have, which is typically associated with aggressive dominance. I point out to these tough guys (and tough guy wannabes) that when a person does what you want just to avoid a beat-down, that's not respect, but "fear." They'll comply and defer to you, but just until somebody bigger and stronger than you tells them otherwise, or until your reign of terror is overthrown. True respect is when someone will go along with what you want because they have confidence that you know what the right thing to do is—or at least, they'll comply with you because they admire you, want to be like you, and want to be liked by you, not just because they're afraid of you.

Some of what we usually define as bullying, therefore, may be a mechanism of social dominance used by adolescent males to enforce a social hierarchy within a school system or elsewhere, in the same way as many social species (birds, wolves, primates) form hierarchies, as ancestral humans forged hierarchies within their tribal family groups and, indeed, the way many societies, from simple to complex, are stratified today. Whereas some bullies are overly aggressive and are feared by their constituents, others, who wield their power in a more controlled but effective fashion, are rated as popular by their peers, are often admired by teachers and other adults, have above-average confidence and self-esteem, and are often able to expand their spheres of influence within their particular environment, e.g., the school or neighborhood (Adler & Adler, 1996; Farmer & Cadwallader, 2000; Kolbert & Crothers, 2003; Orecklin, 2000). In these cases, of course, they would no longer fit the standard definition of a bully as one who uses unnecessary aggression and coercive control solely or mainly for his own sadistic gratification.

As discussed in Chapters 13 and 20, many criminal organizations, from street gangs to multinational crime cartels to terrorist organizations, show a hierarchical structure. Whereas males typically compete over social status and access to females (or the resources that will attract females), females fight over sexual reputation and access to resource-rich ("blingworthy") males, characteristically using more indirect and relationship-based dominance strategies than males (Campbell, 1995; Cillessen & Mayeux, 2007; Crick et al., 1999; Hawley, 2007; Kolbert & Crothers, 2003; Olweus, 1993a; Vaughn & Santos, 2007).

In nature, one of the main functions of dominance hierarchies among social creatures is to minimize fighting and maintain group stability, so that the group as a whole can focus their efforts on basic survival functions like obtaining food and defending against enemies, which require some measure of group cooperation. Accordingly, most social creatures are hardwired to display characteristic submission behaviors that allow the loser of a conflict to literally or symbolically "cry uncle" before he is seriously hurt, and losers of dominance contests, across species, show measurable reductions in testosterone levels following their loss of status (Booth et al., 1989; Eibl-Eiblsfeldt, 1971; Elias, 1981; Gladue et al., 1989; Mazur & Lamb, 1980; Mazur et al., 1992; Rejeski et al., 1989; Rose et al., 1975). In humans, the social withdrawal that characterizes some types of clinical depression (often associated with a drop in testosterone) has been conceptualized as such a self-protective insulation following a confrontation that could result in serious injury if pursued as a "lost cause" (Hodges et al., 1997; Kemper, 1990; Price, 1988). These evolutionary psychology conceptualizations of bullying may have important implications for intervention, as discussed in Box 12.1.

Conceptual Integration

Because of human psychological diversity, some youths may be predisposed to being either bullies or victims by virtue of their individual biological temperaments and cognitive styles, which are further reinforced by early family upbringing and social learning. Aggressively dominant parents are likely to bequeath this trait to their offspring and further inculcate this behavioral pattern by overly harsh and/or inconsistent discipline, as well as by dysfunctional caretaking, leading the child to form an insecure attachment style that leads to other relationship difficulties. One element of this may be a social information processing style biased toward an inflexible dominant-submissive view of human relationships: "You're either on top or at the bottom—there's nothing in between." Students with this orientation will attempt to fight their way to the top of the schoolyard hierarchy, which maintains a fragile stability, to the detriment of those at the bottom of the pecking order. School environments that endorse a hands-off, "boys-will-be-boys" attitude toward peer aggression tacitly condone and encourage such behavior.

Remember, however, that stable social hierarchies can exist without violence or intimidation. In fact, most productive organizations have some kind of hierarchy, some based on jockeying for position, but most relying on earned merit and competence as the route to advancement—the concept of **eminence vs. dominance** described above. This is what effective school-based anti-bullying programs should try to build on (Box 12.1).

BOX 12.1. SCHOOL ANTI-BULLYING PROGRAMS: WHAT ARE THEY? DO THEY WORK?

Over the past decade, many schools have implemented **bullying prevention programs** of one type or another. However, until recently, very little research has been done to determine if they are acrtually effective (Farrell et al., 2001; Ferguson et al., 2007).

ANTI-BULLYING: WHO ARE WE TARGETING?

One key problem concerns the target of the intervention. Drawing from the model of anger-management and domestic batterer programs (Chapter 17), many school anti-bullying programs focus on the motivation and behavior of the perpetrator himself. However, as we've seen throughout this book, human behavior retains a remarkable consistency and is very difficult to change. For example, the literature on bullying suggests that bullies are aggressive, impulsive, power-seeking, and skillfully manipulative, an exaggerated form of dominant alpha-maleness and ruthless self-centeredness (Bollmer et al., 2006; Gini, 2006; Hawley, 2007; Heydenberk et al., 2006; Jolliffe & Farrington, 2006; Kolbert & Crothers, 2003; Olweus, 1995; Pellegrini, 2007; Phillips, 2007).

Thus, programs that focus on the cognitive and emotional dimensions of bullying and that attempt to inculcate a sense of moral sensitivity and appropriate empathic reactivity in these students may be facing an insurmountable challenge. In the communal social setting that schoolchildren live in, bullying and violent behavior may, in fact, be a very effective strategy for some children to climb the social dominance hierarchy at the expense of other children (Ferguson et al., 2007; Hawley, 2007). What possible incentive would a bully have to follow a program precisely designed to reduce his status? When students are forced to participate in such programs as a group, the already-nonviolent children who initially approach the project with enthusiasm may quickly become frustrated and disillusioned when they see the bullies either disingenuously "playing the game" for the adults or openly flouting the whole enterprise. This only serves to erode overall respect for school programs and policies in general (Kolbert & Crothers, 2003).

A SCHOOL PROGRAM FOR MANAGEMENT OF BULLYING: THE *P.A.S.S.* MODEL

The problem, then, is that most bullies enjoy their role and will not voluntarily give it up. Accordingly, to be effective, anti-bullying programs must refocus their efforts and emphasize what other students can do to keep themselves from being victims. From a review of the literature (Bender & McLaughlin, 1997; Coloroso, 2003; Farmer et al., 2007; Hawker & Boulton, 2000; Kolbert & Crothers, 2003; Pitcher & Poland, 1992; Ross, 1996; Shafii & Shafii, 2001) and my own professional experience (Miller, 2007a, 2008b), I have developed a model program for

continued

BOX 12.1.—*Continued*

combating bullying, harassment, and peer aggression in schools, that I have termed the *P.A.S.S.* **model**.

P = POLICY. This consists of educational programs and written policies regarding bullying, harassment, and peer victimization. As with workplace violence and workplace safety (Chapter 11), a structured program is essential in order to achieve student, faculty, family, and community buy-in for the concept and practice of school safety.

A = ACTION. This is the practical application of the policy-and-procedures phase above. These measures include a structured program for reporting and investigating threats and incidents, training in peer mediation and conflict resolution, and, where necessary, direct intervention with students, parents, and law enforcement.

S = SUPPORT. This assures needed back-up services such as mentoring and extracurricular activities, as well as mental health referral and consultation.

S = SUPERVISION. This provides oversight to the program in the form of periodic review of program effectiveness, with recommended modifications, as well as periodic monitoring of individual students who may be at high risk for being either bullies or victims.

STUDENT STRATEGIES FOR HANDLING SCHOOL BULLYING: THE *D.I.C.E.* MODEL

Again, from a review of the literature (Bender & McLaughlin, 1997; Coloroso, 2003; Farmer et al., 2007; Hawker & Boulton, 2000; Hawley, 2007; Johnson, 2000; Pitcher & Poland, 1992; Ross, 1996; Shafii & Shafii, 2001) and my own experience in working with schools and counseling individual students (Miller, 2007a, 2008b), I have developed a model protocol that educators and counselors can teach students to use, with proper training and practice, to combat bullying, harassment, and peer aggression in schools, that I have termed the *D.I.C.E.* **model**.

D = DOCUMENT incidents of bullying and harassment. Note the date, time, location, and people involved, including the bully(ies), victim(s), bystanders, and other people around. Be as detailed as possible, but be unobtrusive about doing it. Even the mere fact of recording this information often gives these kids a modicum of empowerment and control.

I = INFORM teachers, family, friends, or anyone you trust. This is often the trickiest part because many victims may fear the stigma of being labeled a snitch far more than they fear the bully's depredations. For many kids, this is a personal decision and teachers, parents, and counselors cannot force a child to divulge being the victim of a bully unless there is an issue of direct child endangerment, in which case it may become a matter of **mandated reporting of abuse** to law enforcement by teachers or clinicians. A key element is for some adults and/or peers to serve as safe havens where the bullied kids can go without fear of retaliation.

C = CONFRONT bullies and bystanders in a constructive way. The operative word here is "constructive" which I define as any strategy that will reduce the frequency and/or intensity of interpersonal aggression. Many of these are detailed in the references above.

E = EMPOWER yourself with pride-building activities and peer support. Victimization feeds off low self-esteem and powerlessness. Find things you're good at. Find people who like you and will support you. Develop a crew, a set of friends you can count on. Of course, for many children, especially in smaller schools and communities, this may be a daunting task.

SCHOOL MASS VIOLENCE

Jonesboro. Columbine. Virginia Tech.

School violence is not really *back* in the news because it never really left. Eclipsed by the national preoccupation with terrorism (Chapter 13), recent campus mass violence incidents remind us that most killers of Americans are still our own citizens and that many of these murders take place where we least expect them–in our schools. The U.S. Secret Service and Department of Education use the term **targeted school violence** to describe violence that occurs in schools or at school functions in which the perpetrator(s) and victim(s) are known or identifiable prior to the intended violence. In essence, the attacker has preselected his targets–typically other students, but sometimes faculty or administrators–for destruction (Reddy et al., 2001; Vossekuil et al., 2002).

DEMOGRAPHICS AND CLINICAL
EFFECTS OF SCHOOL VIOLENCE

Although there has been an overall decline in rates of juvenile violent crime since the mid-1990s, according to the National School Safety Center (Bender & McLaughlin, 1997), the Federal Bureau of Investigation (FBI, 2004) and other sources (Cornell, 2006; Devoe et al., 2005), school violence continues to pose a significant problem for society. Incidents of mass violence, involving high-powered weaponry and multiple casualties, are still rare events on school campuses, with less than 1 percent of youth homicides occurring in schools. However, almost three million crimes of every type are committed on or near a school campus each year, comprising 11 percent of all reported crimes in America. These include rape, sexual assault, robbery, aggravated assault, and simple assault. In general, youths under age 18 account for approximately 16 percent of violent crimes in the United States.

The number of children who carry guns to school on a daily basis is estimated to range from 135,000 to 200,000. The *incidence,* or frequency, of youth
violence as a whole has been decreasing since the 1970s; however, during the
same period, the *severity* of juvenile violence has dramatically increased,
including a greater number of homicides, involving more potent weapons. In
addition, students are committing violence at increasingly younger ages.

IMPACT OF SCHOOL VIOLENCE

The psychological ripple effects of school violence extend far beyond the
incidents themselves. For example, in the first year following the Columbine
High School shooting, there were a disproportionately high number of vehicular accidents, suicide attempts, assaults, and several student deaths (Cullen,
2009; Johnson, 2000). A study of children's acute responses to a sniper attack
on an elementary school playground showed that the children exhibited
traumatic responses similar to those of adults. One hundred and fifty-nine
school-age children were interviewed approximately one month after the
event. Children with less severe degrees of exposure (i.e., who were not in
the playground at the time of the attack) rarely evidenced acute posttraumatic symptoms as compared to greater incidence of PTSD among highly
exposed children (Pynoos et al., 1987). Posttraumatic symptoms can also affect teachers and other school personnel (Ardis, 2004; Daniels et al., 2007;
Dworkin et al., 1988; Newman et al., 2004; Nims, 2000).

SCHOOL VIOLENCE PERPETRATORS
AND THE SCHOOL VIOLENCE CYCLE

For all the media attention given to school violence, very little empirical
work has been done regarding the psychology of this kind of youthful mass
murder. Accordingly, much of what we know about school violence perpetrators has been extrapolated from studies of other types of mass murder,
especially adult perpetrators of workplace violence (Chapter 11), who have
been studied for several decades, as opposed to school shootings, which are
a more recent societal phenomenon (Johnson, 2000; Miller, 2002b, 2007a,
2008b; Pitcher & Poland, 1992).

As noted previously, high-profile multiple murders on school campuses,
horrific though they may be, are still relatively low-frequency events; much
more common are the everyday instances of bullying, harassment, and nonlethal violence that occur on school campuses across the nation and the

world. These, too, can be psychologically traumatizing and may set the stage for episodes of explosive retaliatory violence.

Indeed, analysis of the mass school shootings of the past decade highlight the close association that often exists between bullying and harassment (see previous section) and school mass violence. In these events, the cycle of violence typically begins when the student undergoes a physical or verbal humiliation that he perceives as the "last straw" in a cumulative series of abuses. Based on his predisposing personality and psychological dynamics, his reaction will consist of some combination of persecutory ideation, projection of blame, and violent revenge fantasies. As thoughts and emotions stew, the student may isolate himself from the input of others or he may seek out and commiserate with like-minded schoolmates who have gone through the same ordeal. Either together or alone, he may plot a violent revenge scenario.

Most often, even the other kids who have endured similar abuses and sympathize with the student's plight—and may even gleefully share his revenge fantasies—will stop short of actually turning those fantasies into reality: "Whoa, man, you don't mean you're actually thinking of *doing* it?" Sometimes, these erstwhile compatriots may report the impending plot to school authorities; in other cases, they decline to participate, but maintain the code of silence, typically rationalizing that "he's just talking crap—he'd never really do something like that." In a few malevolent cases, the silent partners may achieve a grim satisfaction from letting the angry student to the dirty work while they sit back and enjoy the carnage.

Easy access to weapons or materials to make explosive or incendiary devices provide the means to carry out the revenge plot. As with workplace violence, the actual commando-style mission may be executed impulsively and all at once, or it may undergo numerous revisions and months of planning. In most cases, as with other types of mass violence, the episodes end with the death of the perpetrators, either by their own hand or by responding law enforcement authorities.

BOX 12.2. DO VIDEOGAMES CAUSE MASS MURDER?

Following a number of well-publicized school rampage shootings, media pundits have characteristically fallen all over themselves, loudly groping for answers and reasons for such a tragedy. A common target of scorn is the video game industry, especially violent video games like *Grand Theft Auto* and *Doom*. The latter figured prominently in headlines surrounding the 1999 Columbine shooting, where the perpetrators, Eric Harris and Dylan Klebold were found to have been

continued

BOX 12.2.—*Continued*

enthusiastic devotees of the game (Anderson & Dill, 2000). Constant immersion in graphic role-plays of death and destruction, so the reasoning goes, steeps young brains in a conscience-numbing culture of glorified violence, making it only a matter of time until some of these youths cross the line between fantasy and reality and become the next mass murderers. This is usually accompanied by clarion calls for the abolition of such video games and for a more general "return to morals" as an antidote to runaway youth corruption and mayhem.

For example, following the 2007 Virginia Tech rampage, the deadliest campus massacre to date, multiple media commentators, including "Dr. Phil" McGraw, were quick to draw a straight line between violent video games and violent youth behavior. Imagine these experts' surprise when investigators concluded that the shooter, Seung-Hui Cho, had little or no experience with, or interest in, video games.

That wouldn't have made much difference to them, according to a recent review by Ferguson (2008), as these types of **moral panics** (Cohen, 1972) typically take on a life of their own, regardless of any supporting or disconfirming data. Indeed, recent evidence suggests that blaming video games—even gross, gory, and disturbing ones—for causing murderous behavior may be case of the tail wagging the dog (Ferguson, 2007a, 2007b, 2008; Savage, 2008; Sherry, 2007). Millions of kids, mostly boys, play these games on a regular basis, and the overwhelming majority seem to be able to recognize the difference between blowing someone's head off on a screen and doing so in their classroom.

In fact, when you look at the statistics, it seems that the relation between video game use and violence may even be a negative one. Whereas over 90 percent of law-abiding males play violent video games (Griffiths & Hunt, 1995; Olson et al., 2007), a recent study by the U.S. Secret Service and Department of Education (2002) found that only 59% of school shooters had demonstrated significant interest or involvement with violent media of any kind. Should we interpret this data to argue that violent video games are a protective factor against violence, and that we should be handing out copies of *Grand Theft Auto* at every schoolyard to avert the next tragedy?

Of course, the empirical reality is somewhat more complex. Younger readers of this text can ask their parents about the hue and cry that went up in the early days of television when a previous generation of pundits breathlessly drew a connection between that era's wave of juvenile delinquency and exposure to TV violence in cop shows and Westerns, typically featuring fistfights and gun battles that, by today's standards, would be considered laughably tame.

The seemingly paradoxical finding of a lower incidence of violent video game use among the most violent youths may relate to the **threshold factor** discussed elsewhere in this text. That is, for individuals with an especially strong innate predisposition to violence, it takes far less external prompting to bring this aggression out. Preoccupied with their own bloody fantasies, perhaps abetted by specialized Internet material more inflammatory than that found in any commercial game, students contemplating mass murder just don't need *Doom* to teach them how to kill or to supply the requisite motivation or encouragement. They may also quickly become bored with the score-counting aspect of these games, preferring to concentrate on garish images and narratives that can be found elsewhere or conjured up from their own bloody fantasies.

One reason why something like a video game is so easy to blame for youth violence relates to the old story of the man searching for his keys, not where he knows he dropped them, but down the street under the lamppost because that's where the light is. The causes of school mass violence and youth crime in particular are complex and involve thorny questions of biogenetic predisposition, family environment, socioeconomic forces, access to medical and mental health care, and, of course, the easy accessibility of lethal firearms. According to the moral panic concept, blaming one particular "evil thing," like a video game, is simple and allows politicians, social scientists, media commentators, and ordinary citizens to convince themselves they're actually doing something by targeting these playthings, instead of committing themselves to a far more difficult—but ultimately more effective—course of action in combating the real factors that lead to risk of violence (Burns & Crawford, 1999; Ferguson, 2008; Kutner & Olson, 2008; Lawrence & Mueller, 2003; Sternheimer, 2007; Surette, 2006; Trend, 2007). Many of these games may indeed be odious, and perhaps some controls should be sought on their general availability. But just as pornography is not solely to blame for all sex crimes (Chapters 14, 15), turning video games into the new bogeyman for school violence deflects attention away from more important factors.

Yet there may be one area in which video games do contribute to the lethality of modern-day rampage shootings. Grossman & Christensen (2007) point out that the newer games that involve simulated shooting scenarios are almost identical to the combat simulators used by law enforcement and the military to train their personnel. As police officers and soldiers have spent increasing amounts of time practicing in both simulated and real-life shooting scenarios, their accuracy has increased over the successive wars the United States has been involved in since the middle of the twentieth century. Thus, soldiers in Vietnam had a significantly higher **kill ratio** than those in World War II, and this ratio climbed further in the first Gulf War. Better firearms practice, aided by high-tech simulations, has increased the deadly accuracy of the average soldier or law officer.

And kids, too. Racking up thousands of hours of simulated shooting in video game scenarios, Grossman & Christensen (2007) contend, accounts for the uncanny accuracy and resulting high kill ratio observed in many school rampage shootings. Typically, these kids didn't just burst into a room firing wildly; in many cases, surviving witnesses recounted how the shooters calmly and methodically walked through the classroom, picking off individual students with one or two shots at close or medium range. They rarely missed. Only a few of the rampage shooters had much time practicing with real weapons. Thus, Grossman & Christensen (2007) believe that the video game industry is inadvertently training a generation of potentially deadly assassins. That so very few (thankfully) choose to utilize these gaming skills to murder their peers, however, suggests that heritable trait factors, family training, and cultural influences combine in a uniquely toxic way in those rare children who become mass murderers.

SCHOOL SHOOTER TYPOLOGIES

In the past decade, a number of studies of students characterized as **rampage school shooters** or **classroom avengers** have been undertaken by the FBI (O'Toole, 2000), the U.S. Secret Service, Department of Education (Vosskuil et al., 2002), and other agencies (Leary et al., 2003; McGee & DeBernardo, 1999; Meloy, 2001a; Newman et al., 2004; Verlinden et al., 2000). Common school shooter traits and characteristics identified across these studies include clinical signs of depression, suicidality, mood swings, low self-esteem, and personality disorders, especially paranoid, narcissistic, and antisocial traits. These students display a fascination with violence in the form of videogames and websites, and are often irritable, angry, and aggressive, yet few have histories of violent criminal behavior prior to their rampage. They have often been bullied, and they feel rejected, isolated, and persecuted, hanging out with a few chosen friends who share their interests or social circumstances. Although they may be occasional or chronic users of marijuana, serious drug abuse is uncommon and overt psychosis is rarely a feature (Langman, 2009a,b).

Recently, Langman (2009a) undertook an in-depth analysis of 10 school rampage shooters (9 high school and one college) and developed a psychological typology that focuses not just on their commonalities, but on the distinguishing features that can hopefully be used for accurate profiling, prediction, and prevention of future tragedies. The categories are as follows:

Traumatized Shooters

The shooters in this category are Mitchell Johnson, 13 (Jonesboro, Arkansas, 03/23/98); Evan Ramsey, 16 (Bethel, Alaska, 02/19/97); and Jeffrey Weise, 16 (Red Lake, Minnesota, 03/21/05). All three came from broken homes and suffered physical and sexual abuse as children. Each had at least one parent with a substance abuse problem and at least one parent with a criminal history. In particular, each had a father or father-figure whose criminal history involved the use of firearms. Mitchell Johnson's stepfather had been incarcerated for drug and weapons violations. The fathers of both Jeffrey Weise and Evan Ramsey had engaged in armed stand-offs with the police, and Weise's father committed suicide during his confrontation. None of the school shooters in the other two categories had parents with such a criminal history.

The traumatized shooters all had substantial peer influence to carry out their attacks. Mitchell Johnson was recruited by the younger Andrew Golden to commit the Jonesboro massacre. Jeffrey Weise's cousin egged him on to

TABLE 12.1.
SOME FAMOUS AMERICAN SCHOOL VIOLENCE INCIDENTS

<u>Bethel, Alaska, 02/19/97</u>: **Evan Ramsey**, age 16, entered the Bethel Regional High School and opened fire with a shotgun, killing the school principal and a classmate, and wounding two other people.

<u>West Paducah, Kentucky, 12/01/97</u>: During a prayer meeting, **Michael Carneal**, age 14, opened fire on a group of students at Heath High School, killing three and injuring five.

<u>Jonesboro, Arkansas, 03/24/98</u>: After triggering the fire alarm at the Westside Middle School, Andrew Golden, age 11 and Mitchell Johnson, age 13, disguised in camouflage fatigues, shot at classmates exiting the building from a nearby woods. Four students and one teacher were killed and nine students and one teacher were injured.

<u>Edinboro, Pennsylvania, 04/24/98</u>: At an 8th-grade graduation dance at an off-campus restaurant, **Andrew Jerome Wurst**, age 14, shot and killed a teacher and wounded a second teacher and two students.

<u>Springfield, Oregon, 05/20/98</u>: After murdering both his parents, **Kipland Philip ("Kip")** **Kinkel**, age 15, went to Thurston High School where he killed two students and wounded 22 others.

<u>Littleton, Colorado, 04/20/99</u>: Its name now iconic in the annals of school violence, Columbine High School came under a virtual military-style assault by **Eric Harris**, age 18, and **Dylan Klebold**, age 17, who murdered 12 students and one teacher, and wounded 24 other people, before killing themselves.

<u>Red Lake, Minnesota, 03/21/05</u>: On the Red Lake Indian Reservation, **Jeffrey Weise**, age 16, murdered his grandfather and his grandfather's girlfriend, then drove the older man's police car to the Red Lake Senior High School, where he shot and killed five students, one teacher, and one unarmed security guard, subsequently committing suicide.

<u>Blacksburg, Virginia, 04/16/07</u>: The deadliest school shooting to date took place not at a high school but at a college, Virginia Polytechnical Institute and State University ("Virginia Tech"). **Seung-Hui Cho**, a South Korean English major, with a history of psychiatric problems, killed 33 people and wounded many others in two separate attacks on the campus, before turning the gun on himself.

carry out the Red Lake shooting. Evan Ramsey had contemplated suicide until his friends convinced him to go out in a blaze of murder in Bethel.

Psychotic Shooters

The largest category includes Michael Carneal, 14 (West Paducah, Kentucky, 12/01/97); Seung Hui Cho, 23 (Blacksburg, Virginia, 04/16/07); Kip Kinkel, 15 (Springfield, Oregon, 05/21/98); Dylan Klebold, 17 (Littleton,

Colorado, 04/20/99); and Andrew Wurst, 14 (04/24/98, Edinboro, Pennsylvania). These shooters all displayed symptoms of schizophrenia or schizotypal personality disorder, with prominent paranoid delusions, and auditory hallucinations.

Perhaps surprisingly, all of the psychotic shooters came from intact, reasonably stable families with no history of abuse, parental drug problems, or parental criminal history. However, all five were the youngest siblings in their families, and all had older siblings who showed no psychotic symptoms and were far more successful academically and socially. This appeared to engender a great deal of bitterness and resentment on the part of the shooters, who felt like outcasts and rejects in their own families as well as at school. These feelings were no doubt amplified in the context of their paranoid delusional systems.

Psychopathic Shooters

These were Andrew Golden, 11 (Jonesboro, Arkansas, 03/24/98) and Eric Harris, 18 (Columbine, Colorado, 04/20/99), both of whom also apparently came from intact, nondysfunctional families. Indeed, their immediate and extended families included many members with histories of law-abiding familiarity with firearms in the military and law enforcement fields, and both boys grew up in households where hunting and competitive shooting were common recreations. Yet, these boys seemed to show a fascination with weapons that went far beyond professional or recreational use.

As the name suggests, both of the psychopathic shooters demonstrated clear signs of narcissism, impaired empathy and conscience, and prominent sadistic tendencies. They were also the group that actively recruited and encouraged other students to join them in their rampages. Illustrating the fact that serious antisocial behavior can often be observed quite early, Andrew Golden was only 11 when he utilized his psychopathic manipulative skills to convince the older, but traumatically disturbed, Mitchell Johnson to join him in the Jonesboro attack. Likewise, the psychopathic Eric Harris was able to talk the psychotic Dylan Klebold into being an accomplice in the Colombine massacre.

While examining common factors in the causation of any type of crime is important, Langman's (2009a) typology reminds us how crucial it is to complement that approach with an analysis of how individual differences impact the expression of these general factors. Bad peers, violent video games, crazy families, and relentless bullies are common facts of life among almost any school-age student population, yet violent rampages are the overwhelming exception, hardly the inevitable response. Only a few types of students react to these circumstances with mass murder. Accordingly, as with workplace violence, the preferred approach to school violence is identification of both individual and situational risk factors as a key to prevention and effective response (Box 12.2).

BOX 12.3. WHAT DO THEY KNOW?
ENLISTING STUDENT HELP TO AVERT THE NEXT MASSACRE

After every one of the school mass violence incidents that makes the headlines, people ask, "What could we have done to prevent this?" and "What can we do to avert a similar tragedy next time?" Many of the recommendations for preventing and responding to school violence have important parallels to measures successfully implemented for dealing with workplace violence (Chapter 11, Box 11.1, 11.2) and therefore many of the same principles and practices apply to schools, with a few unique variations.

SCHOOL VIOLENCE PREVENTION:
THE ROLE OF TRUST AND COMMUNICATION

Unlike the case with most workplace violence episodes, which are typically committed by lone plotters who keep their plans to themselves, in virtually all of the major school violence incidents, subsequent investigation has found that at least some of the killer's peers had an inkling that something bad was about to go down and, in a few cases, the killers' intentions had been plastered for months across the Internet and swirled through the school rumor mill. Students interviewed after the fact have reported that they failed to inform adults in authority because they didn't think they would be believed, they didn't want to be a snitch, and because they didn't think the perpetrator "would really do it."

Thus, vitally important to school violence prevention is the presence of a supportive faculty with open channels of communication (Daniels et al., 2007; Davis et al., 2007). Supportive faculty members and administrators create a safe, comfortable environment and indicate their availability by being a visible presence on school property. Lines of communication are kept open and students are encouraged to consult faculty with problems, discouraging the code of silence (O'Toole, 2000) that often lets plots fester secretly until they explode into violence. Studies have found that positive student behavior in general is more likely to occur when students perceive faculty as supportive, helpful, willing to make time for students, helping students organize and complete their work, providing enjoyable classes, and taking a personal interest in students (Brand et al., 2003).

Modeling similar programs in the workplace, many schools have assertively and well-intendedly implemented policies of **zero tolerance for violence**. The challenge, however, is to maintain a sense of proportion and balance, because not all threats are equally serious (APA Zero Tolerance Task Force, 2008; Daniels

continued

BOX 12.3.—*Continued*

et al., 2007; Murakami et al., 2006; O'Toole, 2000; Skiba & Knesting, 2002). For example, a study of 188 threats over an academic year (Cornell et al., 2004) found that 70 percent of these could be classified as "transient" or "low-level" threats, which were quickly resolved by school administrators. The remaining 30 percent of threats were classified as "substantial," requiring greater evaluation and intervention. Out of the 188 cases, only three resulted in a student getting expelled; however, under a strict zero-tolerance policy, all 188 students would have been thrown out of school. Judgment and common sense should prevail.

WARNING SIGNALS OF IMPENDING VIOLENCE

Here is where student cooperation is crucial in preventing a tragedy. As noted above, in the workplace, it is less common to encounter the kind of code of silence found among students in a school. Workers that feel threatened in any way will be more likely to report their concerns, as long as they feel there is some reasonable chance that something constructive will be done about it. But, in most school settings, for a student to violate the code of silence and report a threat means that the student must be convinced that something *really* bad is about to go down, and school officials should therefore respond appropriately.

In fact, the U.S. Secret Service's threat assessment approach specifically encourages soliciting information from fellow students (Murakami et al., 2006; Vossekuil, 2002). Daniels et al. (2007) conducted a content analysis of news reports of school rampages that were prevented or interrupted before lethal violence could occur. Half the plots involved solitary students, while half involved two or more coconspirators. The most common motive for plotting a school rampage was to retaliate for being bullied, and victims of bullying were more likely to carry weapons with them on school grounds than nonvictims (Carney & Merrell, 2001). In the majority of cases, the plotters informed others of their plans through conversation or e-mails, sometimes describing in detail the guns, explosives, and other weapons they planned to use, and often trying to recruit others to join the plot.

In Daniels et al.'s (2007) analysis, the most common way rampage plans were discovered was by other students coming forward and reporting their concerns to school administrators or the police. In a few cases, alert school officials discovered the plots on their own. Communication and connectedness between students and faculty were felt to be important factors in students coming forward (Karcher, 2004), in that trusting student-faculty relationships encouraged students to report impending plots of violence by their peers.

DEFUSING POTENTIALLY VIOLENT SITUATIONS

Plans and training for defusing violent episodes should be developed, put in place, and reviewed periodically. These include initial actions to take when a violent episode appears to be escalating, codes and signals for summoning help, chain of command for handling emergencies, appropriate use of verbal control tactics and body language, scene control and bystander containment, measures for dealing with weapons, and procedures for resolving hostage situations.

But the groundwork for successful resolution of crises is laid long before the crisis develops and it inheres in the culture of the school environment. In three schools that had been involved in armed hostage-barricade situations that were safely resolved, the key factor turned out to be the prior development of an open, trusting relationship with every student in the school, which provided the emotional leverage to resolve crises successfully (Davis et al., 2007). During the hostage-barricade crisis itself, a trusted faculty member was able to capitalize on the pre-existing relationship to effectively talk down the disturbed student hostage taker and prevent serious violence. Overall, it was easier for negotiators to remain calm and to induce correspondingly calm behavior in the perpetrators when such a preexisting relationship existed.

SUMMARY AND CONCLUSIONS

Creating safe schools requires an understanding of the types of bullies, victims, and bystanders that exist among the student population. It necessitates a credible system for reporting bullying and harassment and a program for intervening. Inasmuch as many instances of school mass violence are related to desperate retaliation by persecuted students, an effective anti-bullying program is the first important step to preventing mass violence. Additional measures include a prepared, coordinated, and practiced program for preventing, responding to, and recovering from school violence. Students, parents, and faculty should understand that mass violence on school campuses, like plane crashes, are exceedingly horrible events, but they are also exceedingly rare.

Chapter **13**

Mass Homicide III: Terrorism and Political Violence

The word **terrorism** derives from the Latin, *terrere,* which means "to frighten," and the first recorded use of the term as it is currently understood derives from the "Reign of Terror" in the 1890s associated with the French Revolution–perhaps the first modern example of state-sponsored terrorism. Although we may think of it as a recent crisis in this country, terrorism has existed ever since combatants discovered that they could intimidate a larger population by targeting a smaller group. However, terrorism has achieved special prominence in the modern technological era, beginning in the 1970s as international terrorism, continuing in the 1980s and 1990s as American domestic terrorism (e.g., Oklahoma City in 1995), and apparently coming full circle in the twenty-first century with mass terror attacks on United States soil by foreign nationals (e.g., New York and Washington, DC in 2001).

From a criminological and public safety perspective, terrorism combines features of a mass murder attack, political action, and a disaster scenario (Miller, 1998c, 2003a, 2003b, 2004, 2005, 2006a, 2006b). Some experts believe that current intervention efforts will prevent future attacks, while others believe that the worst is yet to come (Bolz et al., 1996; Keller, 2002; McCauley, 2007; Savitch, 2003; Schmid, 2000).

THE NATURE AND PURPOSES OF TERRORISM

The Federal Bureau of Investigation (FBI) defines **terrorism** as "the unlawful use of force or violence against persons or property to intimidate or coerce a government, the civilian population, or any segment thereof, in furtherance of political or social objectives." According to the U.S. Department of Defense, "terrorism is the calculated use of violence or threat of violence to instill fear, intended to coerce or try to intimidate governments or societies in the pursuit of goals that are generally political, religious, or ideological"

(Seger, 2003). The key terms in both of these definitions are coercion and intimidation, as well as the ability to convert weakness of numbers into strength of impact.

Psychologically, terrorism can be viewed from several perspectives. On the one hand, almost all conventional warfare contains a terroristic element. Why threaten war at all, unless the goal is to intimidate your enemy into complying with your demands? And if they resist, a common military strategy is to instill as much fear as possible, in order to increase the likelihood of their surrender with minimal casualties on the attacker's part. Technological advances in weaponry in any war, in any era, have often initially been referred to as "terror weapons," including the iron blade, crossbow, mounted cavalry, long-range cannon, poison gas, machine gun, blitzkrieg armored assault, napalm, atomic bomb, and anthrax (Cromartie & Duma, 2009). In many cases, the psychological intimidation effect of many of these weapons far exceeds their actual casualty rate.

On the other hand, where one side's conventional battlefield armies are deficient, terrorism puts disproportionate psychological power into the hands of small groups of ideologues or opportunists. Historically, a terrorist act is rarely an end in itself, but is rather designed to instill fear in whole populations by targeting a small, representative group (Laquer, 1987; Loza, 2007)—Mao Zedong spoke of "killing one to move a thousand." However, this may be changing. A major characteristic of mass terrorism like the World Trade Center attack and the much-feared potential nuclear-biological-chemical (NBC) terrorism of the future (Cromartie & Duma, 2009; Romano & King, 2002) is the terrorists' apparent desire to wreak maximum destruction as an end in itself, going far beyond the symbolic value of the act and turning terrorism into a veritable war of annihilation.

Overall, most terrorist acts have one or more goals (Thackrah, 2004): (1) to disrupt routine activities, or "business as usual," in the target population; (2) to inflict as much damage as possible, although in some cases restraint may be used if "surgical" attacks against precise targets are desired; (3) to create physical pain and psychological disorientation in the target population; and (4) to undermine the target population's confidence in its own leadership or government.

Butler (2002) divides terrorism into two broad categories: **Instrumental terrorism** describes terrorist acts carried out to coerce a group into taking some action or complying with a demand. The perpetrators are usually political terrorists who want to effect a tangible result, such as driving out an occupying force from their land or manipulating a government to comply with their demands. Theoretically, at least, the terror will end if and when the demands are met or a compromise is forged.

Retributive terrorism involves acts that are primarily intended to destroy, not influence, the designated enemy. Here, there is little that the targets can do to appease their attackers because they are hated, not for any particular actions on their part, but for the very fact that they exist; therefore, nothing less than their complete eradication will suffice. Radical religious terrorists and racial supremacists usually fit this definition. Often, instrumental- and retributive-type terrorist groups are mixed and ill-defined even among themselves, which further complicates negotiations and compromises.

Several elements appear almost universally in modern terrorist activities (Bolz et al., 1996; Burleigh, 2009; Laquer, 1987; Loza, 2007; Thackrah, 2004):

Use of violence as a primary methodology of influence, persuasion, or intimidation. In this case, the true "target" of the terrorist act extends far beyond those directly affected. A federal building is bombed to make a point about government intrusion into citizens' private affairs. A coffee shop is blown up to effect withdrawal of unwanted settlements in disputed territories. Foreign military troops are ambushed to drive unbelievers from holy sites. The goal of these activities is to use threats, harassment, and violence to create an atmosphere of fear that will eventually lead to some desired behavior on the part of the larger target population or government. This is what Butler (2002) means by instrumental terrorism, above.

Selection of victims for maximum propaganda value. To influence as many people as possible, terrorists typically act to ensure a high degree of media coverage. A great deal of thought may go into the symbolic value of the attacks, or the victims may simply be targets of opportunity. This approach may backfire if the goal is to garner public sympathy and noninvolved innocents, especially children, are killed along with the symbolic targets (Silke, 2005). Alternatively, if the aim to inflict as much pain and panic as possible, then indiscriminate slaughter may serve just that purpose: the target population had better comply because now they know that the terrorists "are desperate enough to do anything." Traditionally, the aim of most terrorist acts has been to achieve maximum publicity at minimum risk, yet such phenomena as suicide bombings show that ideological zeal will often overrule self-preservation; indeed, it is this lack of restraint even in the guarding of one's own life that makes suicide terrorism so frightening (see below).

Use of unconventional military tactics. These often revolve around secrecy and surprise, as well as the targeting of civilians, including women and children. This is a commonly cited distinction between a terrorist and a soldier, the latter fighting "fair" by observing consensual rules of combat engagement. Again, if the goal is to inflict maximum horror, then it makes sense to choose locations that contain the largest number of victims from all walks of life. Everyone is a target. No one is safe. These types of glaring acts are also the most likely to garner media attention.

For example, Nacos (2003) points out that the September 11th terrorists calculated their acts precisely to achieve the maximum amount of publicity. She quotes an Afghan Jihad terror manual as advising holy warriors to target "sentimental landmarks" such as the Statue of Liberty in New York, the Big Ben clock tower in London, and the Eiffel Tower in Paris because their destruction would "generate intense publicity." Moreover, according to this account, terrorists hope to highlight the hypocrisy of Western civil libertarian values by forcing democratic governments to defensively adopt a variety of harshly repressive anti-terrorism measures. Case in point is the controversy that has surrounded the political, social, and humanitarian ramifications of using enhanced interrogation methods–the "torture debate"–or the use of unmanned drone attacks to take out terrorist leaders, which may involve collateral civilian casualties.

Intense and absolutist loyalty to the cause. Although there are exceptions, most of the membership of ideologically-driven terrorist organizations are not part-timers or mercenaries. In general, the ability to commit otherwise unspeakable acts–not to mention give one's own life–necessitates an unshakable belief that these acts are somehow in the cause of some absolutely right and worthy purpose.

CHANGING DEMOGRAPHICS OF INTERNATIONAL TERRORISM

Most of the international terrorist groups of the 1960s and 70s consisted of well-educated, well-trained, well-traveled, multilingual, and reasonably sophisticated middle-class men and women–the Hollywood stereotype of the urbane revolutionary: cigarette dangling archly from his mouth, submachine gun cloaked under his Armani jacket. This individual tended to be intelligent, disciplined, and sufficiently resourceful to deal with unforseen circumstances or last-minute changes in plans in order to successfully complete his mission–a veritable James Bond of terrorists. New members were typically recruited from among the ranks of university students or within urban cultural centers (Strentz, 1988).

In the 1980s, 1990s, and 2000s, the prototypical terrorist who commits act of violence in his home country is likely to be a poorly educated, unemployed, and ill-trained male refugee of Middle Eastern or South Asian origin. These are teenagers or young men who have grown up as members of street gangs, although not necessarily criminal per se, and any formal education they have received has been steeped in extreme religious and political doctrine. They have been taught to hate Western society, America in particular, and they especially resent those who have been able to escape their drab life and make successes of themselves, often in the very America that they are supposed to loathe. Psychologically, this is a defensive reaction formation against the despair of ever being able to partake of the bounties they may secretly envy–so these are now viewed as evil temptations, unholy excesses of Western decadence, to be expunged and destroyed. A smaller group of terrorists may attain a certain degree of educational status and cosmopolitanism, often by having been educated in Western countries, but have come to find the clash of values threatening to their religious and cultural self-identity (Gibbs, 2005; Loza, 2007; Sageman, 2004; Strentz, 1988; Thackrah, 2004).

Another difference between 30 years ago and today is that the regional and international support structure of today's terrorist is not nearly as extensive as it was in the past. Despite the current politicized fears about conspiratorial funding and logistical support of worldwide networks of terrorist cells sponsored by powerful rogue nations, the more common trend today is for local terrorist groups to act in relative isolation or with only loose coordination. Their successes depend not so much on paramilitary precision as in their focus on relatively unprotected targets, taking advantage of weaknesses in the targets' security systems and exploiting the element of surprise.

Today's terrorists actually spend less time and money on training than in the past. Popular media and Hollywood accounts often portray battalions of terrorist recruits receiving the equivalent of a graduate university education in terror technology at secret training centers hidden in deserts or jungles. While a few scattered facilities of this type may exist, today's terrorists typically do not receive the type of broad paramilitary training that is geared for a wide range of tactics, strategies, and contingencies. More commonly, they narrowly prepare for a specific mission, the approach being to train fast and hit hard (Strentz, 1988). One reason for this is simply the plentiful availability and expendability of young terrorist recruits. Especially for those missions that involve suicide–whether a lone backpacker blowing up a bus, or a hijack team turning a plane into a bomb–there is obviously no need to train the perpetrators beyond the operation itself because nobody's coming back.

VARIETIES OF DOMESTIC TERRORISM

While today's headlines concentrate on terror from abroad, we may forget our somewhat less recent concern with a feared wave of domestic terrorism surrounding the Oklahoma City Federal Building bombing in 1995. But just because we are currently preoccupied with threats from outside the United States does not mean that the homegrown terrorist organizations have all packed up and moved away (Scoville, 2003). One of the most comprehensive studies of domestic terrorism (Smith, 1994), conducted in the pre-Oklahoma City period spanning the 1960s to the early 1990s, identified two main groups of American terrorists based on political philosophy, described as **left-wing** vs. **right-wing**, and characterized along several dimensions:

Ideologically, left-wing terrorists tend to have an economic and political focus, typically socialistic or Marxist, emphasizing economic equality and social justice. They are thus expansive and inclusive. Right-wing terrorists tend to have a religious, mystical, self-aggrandizing, and racial exclusionary focus. They are typically strongly anti-communist, and espouse a strong Protestant work ethic, swift and severe justice, and emphasis on social order.

Demographically, left-wing terrorists tend to be somewhat younger than right-wing terrorists. While the average age of arrest of both groups is about the same (35 for left-wings, 39, for right-wings), fewer left-wings are over age 40, compared to larger numbers of older right-wings. Both forms of terrorism are overwhelmingly male preserves, but more so for right-wings than left-wings who include more women in both their leadership and rank and file. The major demographic difference is in race, with almost all of right-wing terrorists identified as white, compared to less than a third of left-wings. Another significant difference, but in the opposite direction, is in education: more than half of left-wing terrorists have college degrees, compared to little over a tenth of right-wings. A similar breakdown affects occupation, the left-wing group comprised of significantly more professionals–physicians, attorneys, teachers, social workers–than right-wings, who attract more blue collar, unemployed, or so-called "impoverished self-employed" workers. Left-wing terrorists tend to come from urban places of residence, while right-wings are predominantly from rural backgrounds.

Strategically and tactically, left-wing terrorists favor an urban base of operations, employ a cellular organizational structure to guard against infiltration, and utilize safe-houses. Right-wing terrorists emphasize rural bases of operation, often in the form of geographically isolated paramilitary camps and compounds, and favor national networking, relying on strict ethnic exclusionism to guard against infiltration by outsiders. In their terroristic activities, left-wings tend to target seats of government or capitalist institutions, while right-wings focus on federal law enforcement agencies or opposing racial or religious groups.

The fortunes of extreme right-wing domestic political organizations have waxed and waned over the past three decades (Pitcavage, 2003). Currently, the extreme right is comprised of two major groups: (1) those which are primarily *antigovernment*, such as the so-called **militia movement**, which advocates separation and autonomy from governmental control; and (2) those which are primarily *hate-oriented* in nature, targeting certain racial or religious groups as befouling the larger society and impeding the development of a racially pure utopia. Overall, at the beginning of the twenty-first century, the militia movement appears to be on the decline, while white supremacist groups seem to be retaining their numbers, although shake-ups in leadership may be fragmenting their ranks.

TERRORIST TYPOLOGIES

Even though what we can call the "modern" literature on terrorism is barely three decades old, the sheer number of attempts to ideologically, politically, and sociologically classify and categorize terrorist subtypes far exceeds the scope of this chapter. Accordingly, this section will summarize a few of the representative taxonomies that have the greatest bearing on our attempts to understand the terrorist mind.

"Crusaders, Criminals, and Crazies"

As in any complex organization, different roles are filled by different members of terrorist and other extremist groups, each with their own individual contributions to the goals and strategies of the organization (Horgan & Taylor, 2001; Pitcavage, 2003). One early classification system (Hacker, 1976) divided terrorists into three groups:

Crusaders are the most ideologically driven of terrorists, motivated by their devotion to their cause. These individuals serve as the focal points of the group, rallying the group's commitment and planning strategic operations against the group's enemies, however those are defined.

Criminals are essentially violent individuals in search of an excuse to act out their antisocial impulses through an ostensibly acceptable and noble cause. They are typically the least ideologically committed to the group, and may easily change venues under the lure of new and better opportunities to practice their aggressive and sadistic craft. These are the odious, if necessary, thugs of the group who carry out the organization's dirty work, largely because they are good at it and enjoy it.

Crazies are seen as having some form of mental disorder, which may either rivet their loyalty to the group or result in dangerous instability in terms of their commitment and behavior. Rootless or disgruntled individuals of this type are commonly attracted to the religious or philosophical certitude of many extremist groups and, if their psychopathology can be channeled for the group's purposes, they may play useful roles within the terrorist organizational structure.

American and International Terrorists

Another prominent classification of terrorist group members grew out of Strentz's (1988) study of the highly-motivated and well-trained American and international terrorist organizations that emerged in the late 1960s and 1970s. For certain groups of modern terrorists, the substance of this analysis still applies today:

The **leader** of a terrorist group usually exhibits an egocentric slant on reality, which may extend to the level of paranoia. He tends to see the world as a web of plots and conspiracies, especially by inferior cultures or religious infidels who are polluting and poisoning the purity of the self-defined chosen group. Not overtly psychotic, his characterological paranoia may be well-hidden to the outside world, cloaked by the superficial persona of charismatic self-confidence and commanding presence–thus his emergence as a messianic leader.

The **activist-operator** typically has an antisocial or psychopathic personality structure. This type is frequently a former or current mercenary soldier or ex-convict with a long and varied criminal history. He may have been recruited from a prison population by the terrorist leader, who then allows the opportunist to take the spotlight, while the leader remains behind the scenes as the "brains" of the organization. For his part, the activist-operator exploits this opportunity to lead a thrillingly violent and hedonistic lifestyle with the tactical support and doctrinal blessing of the leader and the organization. However, the activist-operator is rarely truly committed ideologically to the group's mission, and may secretly harbor contempt for the abstract philosophies and lofty goals of the leader and his organization. Yet he stays in for the rush and the power trip he gets from his role as organizational "muscle."

The **idealist** may be genuinely dedicated to a better world, is willing to give his all, and is therefore eagerly co-opted by the terrorist organization for its own ends. Ever the faithful servant, the idealist is often initially assigned routine maintenance and support duties until he or she (this category is more likely than others to include some women) proves worthy of more sophisticated and dangerous operations. These are often desperate, dependent young people who are seeking truth and philosophical guidance and have fallen victim to the leader's rhetoric and the opportunist's deceit.

Secret Service Profiles of Terrorists

While the above analyses may appear overly theoretical and academic, another terrorist typology is based on the practical profiling needs of U.S. Secret Service agents and executive protection specialists who are charged with the daily task of guarding political, corporate, and media figures (June, 1999):

Crusading terrorists are ideologically motivated by their religious or political convictions.

Ultraconservative political terrorists espouse a firm belief in individual rights over the intrusive strictures of a repressive, ultraliberal government. These groups are characterized by an ultraconservative, right-wing political orientation, and an authoritarian, quasi-military organization, often involving an independent militia.

The **political anarchist** has an ultraleftist orientation, which may paradoxically reject the intrusion of government as strongly as the ultrarightest, but for opposite reasons: that the government is racist, elitist, and economically oppressive.

Religious terrorists believe they are accountable to no one but God, and therefore justify killing in His name and for His purposes. These are also the most likely types to sacrifice their own lives to earn their places in Paradise.

The **criminal terrorist** is more an opportunist than an idealist, and commits terrorist acts for personal gain or sadistic gratification rather than for a cause.

Terrorist Subtypes: Commonalities

What all these typologies appear to concur on is the identification of certain common subsets of terrorist group members, including: (1) an ideologically-driven **charismatic leader**; (2) **supportive followers** who are drawn to the group's goals and ideals and who carry out the routine duties of the organization; and (3) one or more **violent operatives** who are likely to be in it for the thrill, the profit, or some combination of less-idealistic personal motives.

Terrorism, Fanaticism, and Destructive Cults

Indeed, insular organizations of many types seem to harbor many of the same characters, whether they explicitly espouse violent terrorism or not. For example, in their core features of ideological certitude, charismatic leadership, and thorough indoctrination of members, terrorist groups share many of the features that are known to characterize **cults**. Bohm & Alison (2001) analyzed the characteristics of various cult groups and identified several features that marked what the researchers call **destructive cults**, that is, cults that are willing and able to commit violence, including murder:

Destructive cults typically follow a charismatic leader who may claim to be specially chosen or uniquely qualified to lead the group to glory; he (less commonly, she) may even claim to be an incarnation of a religious or historically significant figure. The leader and his lieutenants commonly enforce loyalty by severe discipline and by physically preventing members from leaving the group. The destructive cult has a well-spun persecutory conspiracy theory and a siege mentality, typically stockpiling weapons, building defensive barricades, and carrying out regular "doomsday drills." The cult may openly or tacitly endorse individual killings or mass murder; the latter may be accompanied by mass suicide, either as a further symbolic instrument of their cause or, more commonly, as what they perceive to be justified self-defense, a last resort when the hostile world starts closing in and the leader's authority is threatened.

This is also very similar to Lifton's (2000) concept of **apocalyptic groups**. These groups typically view the world in terms of a hypermoralistic black and white, good and evil dichotomy. Their mission is either to await the destruction of the corrupt world, or hasten it through their acts of subversion, sabotage, and/or violent attacks. Individually and collectively, they use the defense mechanisms of denial, numbing, rationalization, and isolation to justify their actions. Groups of this kind may have either a political or a religious ideology, often some combination of both (Divine & Rafalko, 1982; Victoroff, 2005).

BECOMING A TERRORIST

As noted throughout this text, many individuals impulsively commit acts of violence for a variety of reasons. But the conscious, deliberate decision to commit oneself to a way of life that includes violence as an instrument of policy or ideology typically represents the culmination of a succession of life events and periods of reflection and interpretation, however one-sided. And while individual motivations for becoming a terrorist may vary, certain common psychological factors appear to contribute to the decision to join this fraternity of violence (Borum, 2004; Crenshaw, 2000; Friedman, 2002; Gibbs, 2005; Gilligan, 2000; Horgan, 2003a; Kennedy, 2007; Merari, 2007; Moghaddam, 2007; Silke, 2003a; Stern, 2003).

Terrorism, Ideology, and Identity

The first issue concerns viewing terrorism as something one does, as opposed to something one is, which relates to the psychology of **personal and group identity**. According to this model, what we believe and what we do comprise the individual elements of our self-definition that together form the broad structure of our identity. Different identity components will exist in different proportions for each person, depending on our upbringing and life experiences. For some people, their vocation may be the most important element ("I'm a doctor; I'm a teacher"), for others, their politics ("I'm a Republican; I'm a Socialist") or religion ("I'm a Protestant; I'm a Muslim"). For most of us in Western, free-market, democratic societies, our identity is composed of a range of elements ("I'm a Republican, Episcopalian, music-loving, family-oriented, tennis-playing, stamp-collecting American"). Most citizens of the Western world are able to enjoy such a richly textured identity because our economy and culture give us a wide range of choices.

But for most of the less-advantaged peoples of the world, menial work gives little satisfaction, political freedom is sparse or nonexistent, avenues of recreational escapism are few, and social mobility and hope for a better life is little more than a fantasy. From such an existence, these people struggle to create a meaning-system that is firm and irrefutable in order to ease the instability and uncertainty of their daily lives. For such individuals, **"ideologies are the guardians of identity"** (Crenshaw, 2000; Gibbs, 2005; Kruglanski et al., 2009; McCauley, 2007; Moghaddam, 2007; Victoroff, 2005).

By this account, if a person already has very little, the one thing that can't be taken away is his religious or political or philosophical belief, especially if that belief tells him that his privations and deferred dreams actually serve some loftier spiritual or social purpose, that there will come a time of eternal redemption following an apocalyptic crisis. If doubts arise, or circumstances occur to challenge these beliefs, he will fight to preserve the fabric of identity that keeps his world view from unraveling. Add to this the fact that adolescence and young adulthood are the critical periods for identity formation, and it becomes understandable that most terrorists come from the ranks of the young and disaffected (Crenshaw, 1986; Post et al., 2003; Taylor & Quayle, 1994; Victoroff, 2005).

But identity is always personal, not just social and ideological, and a common factor in the history of many would-be terrorists is the combination of frustrated social aspirations and individual humiliations (Ezekiel, 1995; Fanon, 1965; McCauley, 2007; Staub, 2003a; Taylor & Quayle, 1994). In fact, as discussed in Chapters 2 and 3, social forces almost always combine with individual predispositions to influence a person's propensity toward violent behavior. A gang member just trying to get over in a crumbling Detroit ghetto, a jobless Ohio high school dropout floundering in a rust-belt economy, or a Middle Eastern youth leading a hardscrabble existence in an economically depressed dictatorship could all commiserate on their shared lack of opportunities, almost daily put-downs at the hands of hostile authorities, and the limited chances for a better life through little or no fault of their own—all the while watching others, who they believe are no more deserving than themselves, getting a far better opportunity to enjoy life.

In areas where this deprivation is combined with overt political persecution, there often develops a collective sense of injustice. Combine this with the typical period of adolescent angst, adrenalin, and testosterone, and embed it in an eye-for-an-eye religious culture, and terrorism or some other extreme action may be seen as a perfectly legitimate means of "striking back." What better way to defuse one's desires for the comforts of the material life than to sublimate those yearnings into 180-degree antipathy, to brand that subconsciously coveted life as categorically evil and try to destroy it? And far better than eruptions of individual rebellion that may be condemned as mere street crime, political or religiously-guided terrorism has the added benefit of receiving the sacred seal of approval from a respected community, if not by the society as a whole. The budding terrorist thereby focuses his frustration, channels his aggression, and gains respect at the same time (Crayton, 1983; Juergensmeyer, 2000; Loza, 2007, Sageman, 2004; Stern, 2003; Thackrah, 2004; Victoroff, 2005; Volkan, 1997).

The Terrorist Decision-Making Process: A Representative Model

While the causes and motivations for terrorism are individual and complex, and there is no set formula for creating a terrorist member or group, certain regularities in the psychological and sociopolitical dynamics of such groups have been identified. In one representative model (Borum, 2003), the evolution of the terrorist mindset is divided into four stages:

Stage 1 ("**It's not right**") begins with an individual or group identifying some set of conditions in their life that is unpleasant, undesirable, or unacceptable. This can be poverty, political repression, erosion of moral values, or anything else that produces confusion, discomfort, or distress.

Stage 2 ("**It's not fair**") involves a basis of comparison. Not only does the disadvantaged group—through no fault of their own—have it bad, others—through no credit of theirs—have it better. This breeds resentment and a desire to find a "cause" of this gross injustice, which leads to:

Stage 3 ("**It's your fault**"), in which the cause of the injustice is projected onto a reviled out-group, alien culture, or corrupt regime. All the sociopolitical complexities of the situation are homogenized and distilled into a single, all-purpose explanation for the in-group's problems: "they" are against "us." In this thinking, if your group or society or way of life is persecuting us, tormenting us, keeping us down, and laughing in our faces, then:

Stage 4 ("**You're evil**") is the logical next step of the process, in which the purported exploiters and tormenters are dehumanized and demonized. By this logic, any aggressive action on the part of the in-group is justified and elevated to the status of noble resistance and freedom-fighting. That is, if you're evil and I'm good, then I'm entitled—indeed, obligated—to destroy you in the name of righteousness, to make the ends justify the means, and to dismiss as collateral damage any innocent bystanders who happen to get in the way.

Of course, not everyone who has been victimized becomes a terrorist. As originally noted by Crozier (1960), "men do not necessarily rebel merely because their conditions of life are intolerable: it takes a rebel to rebel" (p. 9). That is, many people who have been neglected, abused, persecuted, even tortured or seen their communities subjected to genocide, do not allow themselves to become poisoned by the lust for revenge. Instead, such individuals may transmute their pain into a devotion to helping others, what Staub (2003a, 2003b) calls **altruism born of suffering**. This, unfortunately, gets far less attention than the more violent responses. The vast majority of victims, however, become neither violent revolutionaries nor crusading altruists; they either anonymously continue to eke out their livelihoods or at best covertly encourage and abet the more direct activities of social-change groups—becoming the "silent partners" of mainstream or extremist organizations.

Terrorist Recruitment and Selection

Assuming one makes the decision to become a terrorist, how does one start? Much depends on the nature of the political or religious organization one wishes to join (Argo, 2006; Kassim, 2008; Kennedy, 2007; Sageman, 2005; Silke, 2003a; Taylor & Ryan, 1988; Weinberg & Eubank, 1994; Victoroff, 2005).

Some terrorist organizations are entities unto themselves, while others exist as splinter groups of larger, more mainstream political organizations. Some groups will be eager to attract new members, while others will screen prospective applicants carefully. In some communities, terrorist group members may be well-known to the general populace; in others, the neighbors may be genuinely surprised when the "double life" is eventually revealed.

Typically, the would-be terrorist approaches some larger legitimate group associated with the extremist cause, starts working with it, and may eventually express an interest in, or be selected for, more dangerous work. The recruit may be subjected to tests of loyalty and commitment, having to prove himself through successively more dangerous acts. Some individuals join mainstream organizations just to do conventional work, but are eventually socialized into the more radical aspects of the group's activities. Most modern authorities stress the far greater importance of interpersonal relationships and social bonds in cementing the new member's loyalty to the group, than any particular religious or political ideology, per se, although the importance of the latter may grow as the new member becomes enculturated to the group's values.

In still other cases, native or visiting members of the population, often itinerant workers, come into contact with political group members, and are befriended by them. The subject is typically not at first aware that his new compatriots have any association with an extremist organization. A soft-pedal approach to recruitment then ensues, by way of discussions and commiseration with their mutual plight. When the subject expresses a strong desire and willingness to "do something," the new friends then decide that the time is right to make the appropriate introductions and suggest to the subject that there is indeed a way to put his beliefs into more direct action.

THE PSYCHOLOGY AND POLITICS OF TERRORISM

Surprisingly, until quite recently, psychological factors have not figured prominently in most terrorist analyses (Borum, 2003; Silke, 2003). Aside from such dismissive expletives as "they must be crazy," or "they're evil," traditional terrorist typologies have focused less on individual psychology, and more on social, cultural, and demographic factors. Much of this research emerged from the 1960s–70s social science approach that viewed human behavior as largely shaped by societal and cultural forces, particularly those of economic inequality and political oppression (see Chapter 3). But obviously, violent extremism is not the inevitable natural consequence of imposed injustice. In fact, as noted above, many such individuals devote themselves to peaceful and constructive forms of social change, while the overwhelming majority pursue the more modest goal of working to improve their own lot, simply struggling along and praying for better days. Something, then, beyond mere adversity, turns a person into a terrorist, which is why the study of individual psychological factors becomes important.

TERRORISTS AND PSYCHOPATHOLOGY

"Bad enough that they throw their own lives away, but don't they care that they're killing innocent people? That proves that only a crazy or evil person would do such a thing."

Killing the Innocent: Strategies and Rationalizations

As a counterpoint to our reflexive revulsion at the seeming inhumanity of killing innocent civilians, there are three basic forms of rationalization that the terrorist mindset employs (Butler, 2002):

Target population is not innocent. In this extreme view, no member of the target population is entirely blameless because they are all evil by association with the enemy group, or because their own evil acts have targeted innocents as well. Thus, bus bombings of out-group women and children are only playing tit-for-tat with killings of in-group civilians that occur during military raids by the other side. In the terrorists' mindset, the noncombatants at these sites are not innocent because they represent and support, whether directly or remotely, the goals and priorities of the hated target group.

Collateral damage. In this case, some victims, for example, children, may in fact be innocent in the direct sense, but in all noble struggles there is always the possibility of collateral damage. This was the rationalization literally expressed by Timothy McVeigh to justify the Oklahoma City bombing in 1995 in which many children at a daycare center in the targeted Murrah Building were killed, and this is generally the attitude of conventional military personnel who are assigned to pacify hostile civilian populations. This is also clearly the position of paramilitary assassination teams who seek to eliminate hostile terrorist leaders to prevent further violence–they are not targeting civilians per se, but if civilians are in the vicinity, then they die with the terrorists simply by virtue of unlucky proximity.

It's called terrorism for a reason. In a grotesquely practical sense, if pure coercive terror is the goal, then the greater the number of innocents slain, the better. In fact, sophisticated terrorists know that responsibility for tragedy tends to affix itself to targets of immediacy and opportunity, and populations will ultimately blame their own leaders for not protecting them if terrorist strikes continue to occur. Thus, in this latter mindset, targeting innocents is not a side-effect or a regrettable necessity, but a deliberate strategic goal to destabilize the target society's will to resist and to foment unrest and hostility toward its own leadership.

Terrorists: Sick or Evil?

As for the issue of mental illness, it is tempting to view wicked behavior as crazy because doing so helps take some of the frighteningly malevolent sting out of it (Baumeister, 1991; Martin, 2006; Slobogin, 2007). If someone commits a horrid, atrocious act out of pathology or insanity, the intentionality of the act is diluted–on some level, we say the person is "driven to it" or "can't control it," which is a less scary prospect than the idea that the person just chose to perpetrate the atrocity. As we've seen throughout this text, such explanations are routinely proffered for the causes of street crime, serial killings, workplace violence, and school violence (Chapters 9, 10, 11, 12, 20). Reducing something to an anomalous scientific curiosity, no matter how perverse, gives us some intellectualized control over it. Detached clinical analysis inserts a psychological barrier between our rational knowledge of the brutal act and the uncomfortable feelings such knowledge provokes. It also gives us a motivational escape clause: if only we can determine the "causes" of these pathologies, we can potentially eliminate the danger–some day, at least.

Finally, pathologizing a violent act committed against us delegitimizes any traces of justification we may sneakingly suspect underlies the act. If they're just crazy, then they would have attacked us no matter what we did, and nothing we could have done to address their alleged grievances would have dissuaded these delusional killers. But if it's not a sickness, if someone could coldly, rationally, and with full intention and self-justification, commit such horrendous acts, then the acts and their perpetrators are all the more frightening because maybe something we did or failed to do is partially responsible for our fate. Rather than accept any degree of responsibility, it's better to just regard them as a bunch of evil psychos.

Diagnosing Terrorists

In recent years, there has been an uptick in research, reflection, and speculation on the mental status of terrorists, unavoidably complicated by the fact that: (1) there are many different forms of terrorism, with many different underlying motives and ideologies; and (2) even within a specific group, the natural diversity of human personality ensures that different members will be involved in the group's activity for different reasons. A review of the recent literature (Heskin, 1984; Jueregenmeyer, 2000; Knutson, 1981; Lester, 2003; Loza, 2007; Meloy et al., 2001; Orbach, 2001; Pearlstein, 1991; Pedhahzur, 2005; Post, 1986; Ruby, 2002; Sageman, 2004; Silke, 1998; Stern, 2003; Thackrah, 2004; Victoroff, 2005) yields the following summary of descriptors of terrorists and their leaders, which I have grouped into the following categories.

Cognitive factors include: (1) rigid, primitive, nonanalytic, and unsophisticated thinking; (2) oversimplification of complex issues; (3) subjective interpretation of the world, rather than objective analysis; (4) extreme all-or-nothing thinking, i.e., ideas and people are either right or wrong, good or evil; (5) nonrelativistic, absolutist thinking, i.e., rules and principles are for all people at all times; (6) educational system based on memorization and indoctrination; (7) nonconsideration of alternative viewpoints–in fact, imposition of one's own political and/or religious world view on others occurs in their sphere of influence, along with labeling of all nonbelievers as traitors and/or infidels; (8) utopian world view, i.e., the rightness of their cause will ultimately be revealed and save the world; (9) unbelievers should and will be destroyed.

Emotional factors include: (1) disappointment, disillusionment, frustration, fear, disgust, anger, and hatred toward all other faiths and ideologies; (2) need for thrills, excitement, and adventure; (3) feeling of competence, potency, and power; (4) immortality power. i.e., being a part of something greater than oneself; (5) feeling of belonging to a supportive and purposeful social group with like-minded friends and colleagues.

Personal and demographic factors include: (1) financial pressures; (2) unemployment, inability to find work, or unwillingness to take on ordinary work; (3) marriage and family stresses, parent-child problems, childlessness, infidelity; (4) military experience, or lack of opportunity for formal military service, or failed attempt at military service; (5) addiction or history of petty criminality; (6) failure to adjust to modernity.

Personality and psychopathology factors include: (1) personality traits of authoritarianism, envy, dependency, omnipotence, entitlement, emotional detachment, inferiority complex, disempowerment, low self-esteem, and feelings of humiliation; (2) personality disorders, including antisocial, borderline, dependent, narcissistic, and paranoid (also see below); (3) identity disturbance, role confusion; (4) altered or dissociative states, which permit them to suspend conscious critical faculties and reality orientation.

Studying the "Positive Psychology" of Terrorists

Others have argued that although terrorist actions may seem irrational or delusional to society in general, terrorists in fact act rationally within their own frame of reference, and there is no evidence to indicate that they are significantly mentally disordered or otherwise psychologically abnormal (Crenshaw, 1992; Horgan, 2003a; Kassim, 2008; Laqueur, 1987; Sageman, 2004; Silke, 1998; Thackrah, 2004; Victoroff, 2005; Wilson, 2000). In this view, most terrorists emerge out of a normal psychology of emotional commitment to their cause and comrades. Their involvement in religiously- or ideologically-driven terrorist activities provides them with a sense of self-actualization, power, and social status within a valued group, a way out of their routine life, and a highly honored glorious name and camaraderie that would be otherwise impossible.

For example, a few studies have explicitly compared politically-motivated terrorists with common street criminals whose motives were largely for personal gain (Lyons & Harbison, 1986). The activities of both groups had included various forms of violence, including murder. The political subjects ranged from Irish Republican Army (IRA) members to Italian left- and right-wing terrorists. In general, while the psychological profiles of the ordinary criminals tended to resemble those reported in the general criminal psychology literature—low verbal IQ, impulsivity, poor planning and self-control, exploitive interpersonal relationships, and alcohol and drug habits (see Chapters 2 and 3)—the political criminals tended to be of at least normal intelligence, and free of serious mental disorder or substance abuse.

These political terrorists did not show the early developmental antisocial pattern characterizing many chronic offenders, nor any significant history of lawlessness prior to their involvement in violent political activity. They were overall better educated and capable of cooperative and collaborative decision-making, organization, and action. They did not believe themselves to be mentally ill or to require psychiatric attention, yet they generally complied with the forensic examinations. When confronted with the human consequences of their acts, the political convicts showed steely reserve, but unlike the coldblooded remorselessness of the true psychopath, these political terrorists seemed to be able to rationalize and compartmentalize their violent activities, believing that these were necessary actions in fighting for their greater cause—the "collateral damage" rationalization noted above.

In an examination of 384 psychological profiles of suicide bombers, Pape (2005) was unable to identify a single case that would meet diagnostic criteria for a major mental disorder such as psychosis or depression. Additionally, there was no evidence for significant sexual or lifestyle problems or past suicide attempts. Similarly, Sageman's (2004) analysis of over 400 biographies of terrorists from around the globe found that over 90 percent of them grew up in intact, stable families, and three-fourths were married with children at the time of their terrorist involvement. Three-fourths of the sample came from upper- or middle-class backgrounds, and two-thirds had at least some college education. Aside from chronic feelings of isolation and alienation, there was no evidence of significant psychopathology in this group. One percent of the sample showed evidence of a formal psychotic thought disorder, which is actually below the base rate for this symptom in the general population.

In this interpretation, then, relative psychological strength, not weakness, may underlie the characters of a subset of the most effective terrorists. A certain psychological resilience and philosophical resolve may be required for becoming a successful career political activist, whether this involves terror or nonviolent resistance. For example, nonviolent political activists who have been physically tortured by their regimes have been found to show milder posttraumatic psychological disturbance following their ordeals than ordinary civilians who were merely rounded up for routine questioning (Basoglu et al., 1997). Indeed, because of their rebel status, the known activists typically underwent more prolonged and more brutal interrogation than the civilians, yet showed less severe reactions. One reason is an obvious selection factor: only those with a certain innate mental toughness and sense of loyalty are likely to opt for, and stick with, a lifestyle that offers few tangible rewards and many dangers. Yet it works the other way, too: an intense religious, philosophical, or political belief in what one is fighting for enables that person to fight all the more ferociously and resist interrogation and counterindoctrination more stubbornly.

Thus, being a successful career terrorist seems to require a combination of several "positive" psychological qualities (Horgan, 2003b; Victoroff, 2005). Terrorist members must be reliable, trustworthy, and loyal to the ideals of the group and to the directives of its leaders. They must cope with the pressures of living an underground or double life, and must forswear gratification of normal human desires for material comfort, family, friendships, and all the other taken-for-granted benefits of an ordinary life. They may have to withstand imprisonment, interrogation, and torture–or the temptation of a substantial bribe–without betraying the group. Ultimately, they may have to give their lives.

In this view, full-time ideological terrorists therefore share many of the characteristics of undercover police officers, government secret agents, organized crime operatives, witness protection program clients, and others who spend some or all of their lives in the shadows. It is their ideologies and methods that differ. It may well be that the "**successful terrorist**" possesses many of the disordered traits reviewed above, but their perseverance at their task may require a certain additional trait of adaptive toughness that pulls together the other elements of their personality and enables them to maintain focus on their goals. It may also be that diagnosable mental disorder is a feature of more short-term, unstably committed terrorists who are utilized for a single operation, whereas more stable, long-term commitment to the group's ideology and goals, however odious we may regard them, requires a more stable and resilient personality structure.

TERRORIST PERSONALITIES: TRAITS, TYPES, AND DISORDERS

As discussed above, it is probably a mistake to attribute all or most terrorist acts–no matter how horrifying–to severe psychopathology, and being a career terrorist may require a certain degree of mental toughness and resilience, but that does not mean that terrorists are paragons of mental health. In fact, most behavioral interviews with captured terrorists are typically conducted by intelligence or law enforcement personnel, not psychologists, so less florid signs and symptoms of personality disorder and other more subtle psychopathology might be missed (Merari, 2007).

In this section, I present a terrorist typology based on current personality theory (Miller, 2006a, 2006b). As discussed in Chapter 7, when features of character become more than minor variations on the human theme, psychologists regard them not just as personality traits, but as **personality disorders**. The official definition of a personality disorder is "an enduring pattern of inner experience and behavior that deviates markedly from the expectations of the individual's culture, is pervasive and inflexible, has an onset in adolescence or early adulthood, is stable over time, and leads to distress or impairment" (APA, 2000). It is thus the *extremes* of their self-perception and conduct toward others that distinguish personality disordered individuals from those with milder traits (Millon & Davis, 2000; Sperry, 1995).

Terrorist Leaders: Narcissistic and Paranoid Personalities

Narcissistic personality is a pattern of grandiosity, sense of entitlement, arrogance, need for admiration, and lack of empathy for others' feelings or opinions. These are the classic cultic terrorist leaders, convinced of their own authority and infallibility, who regard themselves as "above the law" because of their special powers of perception, insight, and judgment in matters of absolute truth and justice. They are often quite engagingly charismatic, can be quite erudite and knowledgeable, and are able to ensnare impressionable devotees with their unshakable certitude, conviction of infallibility, and infectious zeal for the cause. These are the leaders who give the orders and expect the followers to obey without question. In general, leaders tend to be more than a decade older than the rank and file members they command (Loza, 2007).

Paranoid personality is a pattern of pervasive distrust and suspiciousness, so that others' actions and motives are almost invariably interpreted as deceptive, persecutory, or malevolent. Aside from the narcissistic personality style, these are the other main group of quintessential cult leaders, and indeed, it is not uncommon for such leaders to combine various proportions of narcissistic and paranoid traits in their personalities. Less an inviting charmer than the pure narcissist, the paranoid leader's philosophy is more likely to have a racial or religious exclusionary focus as well as a darkly conspiratorial tinge, in contrast to the expansive narcissist's more universalist philosophy. However, narcissistic terrorists may become dangerous when their competence or authority is challenged, resulting in **narcissistic injury**, which may spark **narcissistic rage** (Akhtar, 1999; Crayton, 1983; Kohut, 1972, 1978; Morf, 1970), the object of which is to repudiate the induced sense of weakness and helplessness by destroying the perceived source of that psychological wound (see Chapter 7).

Over the long term, however, the paranoid may be the most dangerous type of terrorist leader because perceived external threats and the group's holy mission justify committing any kind of violent act on a regular basis to further his absolutist religious or political agenda (Bohm & Alison, 2001). Thus, terrorist acts against religious infidels, political rivals, or racial inferiors are justified as perfectly legitimate defenses of the faith, social structure, or ethnic purity. As such violent acts continue, the world actually does come to hate the terrorist group and everyone connected with it, thus confirming the paranoid conspiracy theory in a vicious cycle—hence the adage: "Just because you're paranoid, it doesn't mean they're *not* out to get you."

The combined narcissistic-paranoid type seems to correspond to Strentz's (1988) **leader** definition, and may be exemplified in religious terrorist or cult leaders who believe that they are manifestly chosen to lead the masses to their own versions of salvation and spiritual perfection, which in turn, may necessitate the annihilation of their enemies in the name of absolute religious or political truth. These are also the leaders who, when threatened, are most likely to lead their followers to mass suicide, believing that without their own divine guidance, the underlings literally have no further reason to exist. However, leaders in general are less likely to sacrifice their own lives than to encourage others to do so for the cause (Loza, 2007).

True Believers and Unstable Deceivers: Borderline and Antisocial Personalities

Borderline personality is a pattern of erratic and intense relationships, alternating between overidealization and devaluation of others; self-damaging impulsiveness; emotional instability, including inappropriately intense anger and/or depressive mood swings and suicidality; persistent identity disturbance in self-image and interpersonal relationships; and a chronic feeling of emptiness that may lead to the quest for stimulation through provocation or escalation of conflict. Initially, borderlines may form intensely powerful allegiances to group leaders and ideologies. Even though the characteristic changeability of their attachments makes them unreliable long-term loyalists, their intervals of intense idealistic devotion and their willingness to take great risks in its service may make them useful–and expendable–functionaries for dangerous terrorist missions.

Antisocial personality is a pattern of consistent disregard for, and violation of, the rights of others. It is typically associated with impulsivity, criminal behavior, sexual promiscuity, substance abuse, and an exploitive, parasitic, and/or predatory lifestyle. While possessed of similar traits of entitlement and self-importance as the narcissist, antisocial personalities are distinguished by their complete lack of empathy and conscience, which allows them to treat other people solely as sources of their own gratification. Inasmuch as self-sacrifice to any cause will be alien to their personalities (McCauley, 2007), they typically become part of terrorist organizations as profiteers or for the sheer thrill of being able to wreak destruction on inferior, helpless citizens, and are often the skilled assassins or bombers of the group (Meloy & McEllistrem, 1998). They can also be quite shrewd in a cunning-conning type of way, and the more intelligent among these types may accumulate considerable fiefdoms of wealth and power, or rise to positions of great authority within the terrorist organization (Martens, 2004). This personality type seems to most closely parallel Strenz's (1988) cynical and hedonistic **activist-operator** terrorist subtype.

Good Soldiers and Worker Bees: Avoidant and Dependent Personalities

Avoidant personality is a pattern of social inhibition, feelings of inadequacy, and hypersensitivity to criticism. While it is unlikely that many individuals with these traits would choose a murderous vocation like terrorism, a few members may have initially been attracted to the helping and social justice aspects of some religious and political movements as a form of self-therapy, or to garner good will and admiration from citizens and camaraderie from fellow group members. Indeed, the structure, order, predictability, and ideological certainty offered by many terrorist political and religious organizations are sublimely comforting to avoidant personalities, affording them respite from the moral ambiguities of the outside world, while allowing them to perform an ostensibly useful function within a group of supportive comrades. Only later may they realize that these seductively benevolent organizations have a more violent side. In such groups, avoidant members are unlikely to be on the front-lines, but may provide valuable assistance in support and supply roles that do not require physical confrontation.

Dependent personality is a pattern of submissive and clinging behavior stemming from an excessive need for care and nurturance. Whereas avoidant subjects fear people and prefer to be away from them, dependent personalities desperately need people and fear only their rejection or flagging support. Dependent personalities cling to others to provide guidance and direction, and a charismatic cult leader is the perfect object of this attachment. Dependent members of terrorist groups may actually be dedicated functionaries, so long as independent decision-making is kept to a minimum. Interactions with colleagues or leaders are apt to be taken more personally than with other group members, as dependents are always hungry for validation of their usefulness and worthiness. This need can be exploited to great effect by group leaders because, while the daringness of dependents will not likely be as great as with borderline or antisocial members, dependent personalities' loyalty and perseverance will likely be more dogged and persistent.

Avoidant and dependant personalities, along with borderlines, probably define the ranks of many of the **idealist** terrorist subtypes in Strentz's (1988) classification. The political or religious group provides them with meaning and validation, and they will be fiercely loyal to that group unless and until some different group can provide a new focus for their dependant allegiance.

Limelight Seekers and Loose Cannons: Histrionic and Schizoid-Schizotypal Personalities

Histrionic personality is a pattern of excessive emotionality, attention-seeking, need for excitement, flamboyant theatricality in speech and behavior, an impressionistic and impulsive cognitive style, and the use of exaggeration to maintain largely superficial relationships for the purpose of getting emotional needs met by being admired and cared for by others. These are the "showboats" of any organization who enjoy being at the center of attention. Although less strong on discipline or willing to get their hands dirty than other types, terrorist organizations may nevertheless solicit these individuals as front-men or -women in the legitimate areas of entertainment, the media, or politics to take their case to the larger world stage or to infiltrate mainstream organizations. The risk is that the histrionic member's hunger for recognition may eclipse his or her loyalty to the group, in which case the member may draw too much attention to the group's activities and thus become an expendable liability.

Schizoid personality is a pattern of aloof detachment from social interaction, with a restricted range of emotional expression. These are people who don't need people, and are perfectly happy being left to themselves.

Schizotypal personality additionally includes more serious disturbances of thinking and more bizarre behavior. The central characteristics of both schizoid and schizotypal personalities include avoidance of other people, severe deficits in social skills, generalized withdrawal from life, and sometimes impairment in perceptual and cognitive skills. It is thought that these two personality disorders really represent points on a continuum from schizoid to schizotypal to outright schizophrenia, the latter characterized by severe distortions of thought, perception, and action, including delusions and hallucinations (Chapters 5, 7). In fact, schizoid and schizotypal personality disorders may episodically deteriorate into psychotic states, especially under conditions of stress.

While such individuals are typically not joiners, the unstable identity structure of many schizoid and schizotypal personalities may lead them on philosophical and spiritual quests that end up at the door of social and religious movements with terrorist ties. They will be the "oddballs" of the group who mainly keep to themselves, but may show fierce commitment if the movement's philosophy appeals to their idiosyncratic world view. However, they may have a tendency to decompensate and become delusional under prolonged, intense stress, and are then more likely to become an expendable liability to the group.

BOX 13.1. COULD YOU PROFILE A TERRORIST?

One of the results of the recent "war on terror" is that government and law enforcement authorities have urged all citizens to be vigilant about suspicious activity that could potentially signal the next terror attack. Military, police, and security personnel are encouraged to monitor critical infrastructure and potential target sites for evidence of terrorist activity in general, as well as indicators of the presence of a suicide bomber in particular. But are there reliable ways for ordinary citizens to detect terrorist activities before they explode into violence? And can we profile suspected terrorists with any degree of accuracy? A recent review (Kennedy, 2007) provides some practical insights into the stages of planning and preparation that precede a terror attack. Because military and law enforcement personnel cannot be everywhere, regular citizens may often serve as the eyes and ears of antiterror efforts. Here are some suggestions for how to do this.

Preventing an Attack

To begin with, terrorists typically conduct protracted surveillance on a given target in order to determine target strengths and weaknesses as well as the

continued

BOX 13.1.—*Continued*

behavior of first responders such as police and paramedics. Therefore, be alert for anyone recording or monitoring pedestrian traffic, photographing the site, drawing sketches, or making notations on maps. Terrorists may also attempt to elicit information about a place, person, or operation simply by asking about it, so note if anyone seems a little too curious about the goings-on at a government facility or private corporation, especially if these queries involve security measures and points of entry and exit. They may also attempt to place key people in sensitive work locations in order to gather this information.

Terrorists often try test the security of a target simply by their presence. That is, they move into a neighborhood surrounding a sensitive facility and ascertain police or security responses to these habitations. Another common ploy is to actually get operatives employed at the facility, so they can more directly observe daily protocols and test security systems. At this point, there may be little to distinguish the would-be saboteurs from ordinary tourists or new neighbors or workmates. More obvious signs frequently cited by law enforcement include unusual purchases, thefts, or discovered caches of weapons, explosives, ammunition, chemicals, uniforms, technical manuals, police equipment, medical supplies, or counterfeit identification. The key here is incongruity: a farmer buying several hundred pounds of fertilizer may not be a big deal; an urbanite office worker doing the same thing should arouse suspicion.

Usually following a period of surveillance and intelligence gathering, terrorists may carry out several practice exercises or "dry runs" before the final assault. For example, they may try to drive a lunch van through a checkpoint containing—this time—a load of sandwiches and cupcakes and, if successful, on a subsequent trip the menu may consist of C4 and gasoline drums. Therefore, keen observation by authorities or citizens may be the most important key to interdicting an actual attack. Various preincident indicators may come days, weeks, or months apart, so be careful to document and report each instance of suspicious activity, even though it may appear to be an isolated or inconsequential act. The final point of interdiction is when the terrorists deploy for their actual strike. Many tragedies have no doubt been averted even at this late stage by the careful vigilance of watchful citizens.

Terrorist Profiling

The capabilities and limitation of behavioral profiling in general have been discussed in Chapter 10. But whereas offender profiling in a serial homicide case is intended to yield clues to the killer's identity *after* the crime has been committed, in the case of terrorist profiling, the goal is to identify the perpetrator(s) *before* the attack takes place. In this sense, the process is more akin to the kind of behavioral profiling discussed in connection with workplace violence (Chapter 11).

As the present chapter makes clear, "terrorists" comprise a heterogeneous group, spanning multiple nationalities, cultures, and ethnicities. However, since

September 11, 2001, of most concern to citizens of the United States and other Western countries is the identification of radical Islamic terrorists; consequently, most of the attention has been devoted to this group. Of course, no single profile has proven applicable to all acts of terrorism, and some terrorist acts have been carried out by atypical perpetrators, e.g., women, children, and nonethnic-specific individuals. However, as a further reinforcement of the idea of human behavioral consistency, a fair number of suicide terrorists have actually been intercepted based on the following set of physical and behavioral clues (Kennedy, 2007):

Ethnic profile:
- Young, Middle-Eastern-appearing males, traveling alone and dressed in loose or bulky clothing, perhaps inappropriate for the current weather.
- Lower part of their faces may seem paler from having recently shaved off a beard.
- Alternatively, use of disguises that seem oddly out of place.
- Perspiring or exuding a flowery scent from freshly applied body oils.

Behavioral profile:
- Appearing nervous or under the influence of some sort of drug.
- Appearing overly serious and determined.
- Unresponsive to salutations or voice commands, seeming to be single-mindedly focused on their route of travel.
- Alternatively, they may be smiling, humming, or chanting due to the joy they anticipate at becoming martyrs.
- Tightly gripping a backpack or other luggage that contains explosives.
- Midsections may appear stiff from bomb packet attached to their bodies.
- Avoiding eye contact, staying away from security personnel, and attempting to position themselves near a crowd of people.

In general, behavioral profiling of terrorist activity has proven to be far more productive in interdicting terrorist incidents than ethnic or racial profiling; this probably applies to all kinds of criminal and behavioral profiling. Aside from the important issue of false-positives—unjustly stigmatizing many innocent people just for the way they look—this distinction has practical implications, because as suicide terrorism and other forms of terrorism evolve, more Western, female, prison recruits, and second-generation citizens of non-Islamic nations, may become involved in this form of terror, erasing any usefulness of ethnic profiling. However, human behavior remains remarkably stable and skilled behavioral observations will remain the key element in identifying threats and preventing attacks.

SUICIDE TERRORISTS

What's worth giving up your life? That may depend on what you think your life is worth. By definition, a suicide attack in one that is operationally dependent on the death of the perpetrator (Ganor, 2000), that is, the mission cannot be successfully completed without the actor dying in the process–to penetrate the enemy's defenses, they can't just throw the bomb, they must *be* the bomb. For some individuals, death in the name of a noble cause may be the one act that gives life its ultimate meaning–a paradox that most people in Western cultures have difficulty comprehending.

Suicide Terrorism: Facts and Demographics

Suicide terrorism is an age-old phenomenon (Kassim, 2008). In the ancient Roman empire, revolutionary Jewish groups called Zealots and Sicaris sacrificed themselves to battle the occupying Roman forces. The small Muslim sect of Ismaili Muslims in the eleventh and twelfth centuries sent Hashshashin (from which we get the word **assassin**) on suicide missions against the occupying Sunni Muslim Empire and later the Christian Crusaders.

However, whereas dedicated fighters have always been willing to risk or sacrifice their lives for a cause they believe in by throwing themselves at overwhelmingly superior forces, the goal itself was usually not purposefully to die. Hence, some authorities believe that true suicide terrorism, in which the attackers purposefully kill themselves as a necessary operational means of killing others, may be a phenomenon unique to the twentieth and twenty-first centuries, when advances in weapons technology have enabled one or a few people to instantaneously kill dozens, hundreds, or thousands. Precisely for that reason, suicide terrorist attacks have generally been more lethal than other forms of terrorism (Ganor, 2000; Kennedy, 2007).

For example, the Japanese kamizakee pilots of World War II, who crashed their explosive-laden planes into American battleships, knew that there was no way to cause an equivalent degree of damage other than directing the planes themselves. More recently, the October 1985 suicide bombing attack by Hezbollah that killed 241 American Marines and 58 French troops depended on a terrorist purposefully driving an explosive-laden vehicle into the compound. Of course, the most iconic example of targeting a vehicle to cause destruction was the September 11, 2001 al-Qaeda use of commercial planes to kill thousands of Americans in New York City and Washington, DC. By contrast, the 1995 Oklahoma City bombing, the 2004 Madrid railway bombings, and the 2005 London bus bombings, all involved explosives that were planted in or near these "soft" targets and therefore did not require the active suicide of a human actor to carry out the plan.

The number of suicide attacks has been increasing around the world: three-fourths of the 583 documented suicide attacks that have been carried out since 1981 have occurred between 2000 and 2004. At the same time, the locales at which these attacks have occurred remain extremely focused. Although suicide attacks have taken place in 30 countries, 88 percent of all such attacks have occurred in only six countries: Lebanon, Turkey, Russia, Israel, Iraq, and Sri Lanka; three-fourths of all suicide terrorist attacks have occurred in the last three countries alone. Thus, although the number of such attacks is increasing, there is hardly an "epidemic" of suicide terrorism spreading across the globe, certainly not in Europe or America (Merari, 2007).

Suicide: Culture and Belief Systems

In conceptualizing suicide terrorism psychologically, the first problem concerns the term "suicide" itself. In the Western mind, suicide is invariably associated with despair, with capitulation, with depression, with a disordered mind—what sane person wants to kill themselves? Western religions generally discourage purposeless suicide, and are not entirely comfortable even with the idea of giving one's life as an affirmative act of faith. We in the West tend to take religion as one component of a full life, not the end-all and be-all of life itself, and we recoil at the idea of willingly giving our lives for a religious principle, even if history has shown zealots of all stripes to have far less compunction about killing others for their religious ideals. But we often look upon people who choose to be suicide bombers with a sense of bemused but itchy revulsion: we just don't get it.

This kind of understanding requires an appreciation of the role death plays in many cultures' conception of living. For most religions, or even secular mass political movements, death may be the entree into one or another form of eternal life. Becker (1973, 1975) pointed out how annealing oneself to something that transcends one's own life can give a person what he called **immortality power**. Religion is the most obvious expression of this, since most faiths promise an afterlife of some sort. Whether you accept this literally as playing a harp on a cloud, or more metaphorically as a melding with some universal cosmic consciousness, it boils down to the essential reassurance that when you die, you *don't really have to die.* Somehow, in some form, you defeat physical death by continuing on as part of something greater than yourself.

But immortality power is not denied to the secularist or atheist, either (Sprinzak, 2001). Indeed, the messianic zeal that has characterized proponents of socialism, fascism, humanism, or any of the sweeping sociopolitical movements of the past century illustrates their power to grant their adherents at least historical and philosophical immortality (Abramson, 2009). Any member of these groups may be the smallest cog in the grand engine of historical destiny, but he is nevertheless part of the whole machine and thereby derives both limitless power and eternal existence through his connection with it. The reason that religion and politics are such loaded topics for discussion is precisely because to challenge someone's belief system is to threaten not just their life's meaning, but their very life itself.

Add to this the millennia of human evolution within close-knit, intradependent, insular tribal clans, each guided by its own totemic deities, and it's easy to see why we quite naturally gravitate to the beliefs of our in-group, and why, especially under conditions of stress, scarce resources, and conflict, my in-group will be elevated to absolute righteous goodness, and your out-group will be loathed and demonized. This conceptualization explains the paradoxical acts of altruism that seem to fly in the face of self-preservation, acts that are familiar to every war-movie fan who has gotten choked up at the brave soldier who throws himself on the grenade to save his buddies. He willingly dies so that his companions might live. Why?

In Becker's (1973, 1975) interpretation, what the soldier is really saving is his transcendent alliance with his warrior clan, and by extension, the survival and immortality of his nation and cultural heritage. He physically dies, but his people live on, and, by association, so does he. It certainly helps to know that God is on his side, too, as this gives him the added bonus of "real" immortality and honor in Heaven. But even this spiritual perk may not be necessary, as history has shown millions willing to sacrifice themselves, or at least risk their safety, for the sake of political beliefs or even the chance of personal wealth, honor, or power—yet another species of immortality (Becker, 1973, 1975; Shermer, 2004; Wilson, 1993; Yalom, 1980).

Accordingly, it makes sense that suicide attacks seem to spring most readily from cultures that condone and encourage self-sacrifice, especially in the context of long-running conflicts that have endured extensive and repeated casualties on both sides (Silke, 2003b). Suicide attacks, in this view, may emerge from a sense of desperation, but not despair or depression (Borum, 2003). Suicide attackers are not killing themselves as a way of "going out and taking as many of you as I can" in the kind of final exit that marks the suicidal workplace or school violence perpetrator (Chapters 11 and 12). This is not reckless and hopeless self-destruction, but a forthright noble act, the ultimate sacrifice–gift, even–that the suicide attacker can give for his cause and his people.

The Psychology and Pragmatics of Suicide Terrorism

The few psychological analyses that have been carried out on this subject have found that Middle Eastern suicide terrorists are rarely the severely mentally disturbed fanatics caricatured in the Western media (Attran, 2004; Borum, 2003; Kennedy, 2007; Silke, 1998, 2003b). Rather, they are typically young men in their late teens and early 20s who have been generally well-behaved youth in their communities, good students, and regarded as helpful and generous. They come from relatively stable, religious homes, often with large extended families. But, like many terrorists, at least part of their decision to sacrifice themselves comes from the rage and resentment at what they perceive to be an endless onslaught of unjust persecutions and humiliations at the hands of the out-group. Thus, it is not depression and despair that fuels their self-sacrificial impulse, but the assertive, energetic desire to fuse themselves with something greater and stronger, to become one with an eternal and omnipotent vindicating force (Pape, 2005; Merari, 2007; Sageman, 2004; Silke, 2003b).

Probably the most systematic and comprehensive study of suicide terrorists from around the globe since 1983 has been carried out by Merari (1990, 2007), including interviews with suicide terrorists who survived or were stopped in their attacks, as well as the findings of a psychological autopsy of 34 Palestinian terrorists from 1993 to 1998. In this group, the average age of the would-be suicide attackers was in the mid-20s and most were unmarried men living in refugee camps. Socioeconomically, they represented a cross-section of Palestinian society, yet their education tended to be somewhat higher than the norm. In fact, Bergen & Pandrey (2006) found that more than half of their sample of 79 terrorists held university degrees—a slightly higher ratio than the general American population. Relatedly, in Merari's (1990, 2007) study, retribution for personal suffering did not seem to be a prime motivating factor in this group. While many of these subjects had suffered what they regarded to be abuses at the hands of authorities, most of them had already committed themselves to the cause by the time these indignities had occurred, although no doubt any further perceived abuse only bolstered their hatred and resolve. In other cases, the commitment to the cause appeared to be more abstract and ideological in nature.

In contrast to the popular Western notion that all Mideast terrorism is motivated by religious fanaticism, nearly two-thirds of the suicide attacks in Merari's (1990, 2007) study were carried out by secular groups. These conclusions are further reinforced by Pape's (2005) comprehensive analysis of 315 suicide attacks that occurred around the world from 1980 to 2003. Of these, all but 14 were carried out with the purpose of manipulating or coercing what were believed to be militarily or governmentally oppressing forces. Even when carried out by groups like Hezbollah and al-Qaeda, the motivations for the suicide terrorist attacks were primarily strategic and political, not religious. Furthermore, fully 57 percent of the terrorists profiled in this study were identified as secular in orientation, not religious. Of course, as discussed above, it is difficult to disentangle the relationship between religion and politics in any absolutist ideological system: an American soldier may choose to give his life for "God and country" as sincerely and fervently as any member of al-Qaeda, but in both cases, the sacrifice involves not just the actor's death itself, but some practical strategic purpose, in addition to tying the actor to some higher cause.

Consistent with the earlier discussion in this chapter, in Merari's (1990, 2007) sample of suicide terrorists, no evidence was found in any of the subjects for significant psychopathology, either through school or medical records, in interviews with friends or relatives, or in direct interviews with would-be or thwarted terrorists themselves. In particular, there was no evidence for the standard clinical risk factors for suicide and there was no set "terrorist personality" type that characterized all the subjects. Most of the subjects regarded their planned suicide as a proactive projection of power in the cause of a struggle they believed in, rather than as an escape from responsibility or giving up on life.

Azam (2005) invokes the evolutionary psychology concept of **kin selection** to account for some forms of suicide terrorism. As noted in Chapter 3, just as some birds will sacrifice themselves to distract a predator from their genetically related kin, so may some suicide terrorists sacrifice themselves to commit what they believe to be self-protective (albeit outwardly destructive) acts in order to preserve those group members with whom they share familial, ethnic, religious, and/or ideological kinship. This is, of course, Durkheim's (1897) original sociological concept of **altruistic suicide**, which is similar to the Islamic religious concept of **istishad**, or selfless death in the service of Allah (Pedahzur et al., 2003; Post et al., 2003; Sageman, 2004).

A further indication that suicide terrorism is typically not the purposeless throwing away of lives is further illustrated by the simple pragmatic fact that, culture notwithstanding, the utility of suicide missions is often dictated by the numbers (Pape, 2003). Considering the sacrifice involved, terrorist organizations seek to maximize the deadly payoff, and suicide bombings that kill only one or two other persons represent a poor return on their investment. In the Middle East, terrorists typically try to glean a respectable margin on their bombings, favoring targets that concentrate their victims tightly, such as loaded buses or markets; for example, the average ratio for this region is 7 dead, 30 injured per bombing. By contrast, the Kurdistan Workers' Party eventually abandoned suicide bombings because they failed to get their kill ratio above a mere 1 to 1 (Silke, 2003b).

In addition to return on investment, suicide bombing is efficient in another way: it is relatively easy. A certain level of training, preparation, and precision timing is required to execute an attack if the aim is to complete the mission and then escape to fight another day. Hijackings and hostage-takings require a lot of planning and pinpoint coordination among many players to carry out successfully. By contrast, in many cases all the suicide bomber usually has to do is literally show up and pull a cord or press a cell phone button.

Not that suicide attacks take place without planning, but much of the preparatory work is typically done by others behind the scenes, leaving the suicide attacker's mind clear to pray and reflect on the greater purpose of his mission. In fact, the **preparation, planning, and execution of a Middle Eastern suicide attack** has by now become almost a standard sequence of operations (Seger, 2003):

First, a target is selected, usually fairly easily if it is going to be a civilian "soft target." Intelligence is gathered to determine the feasibility of the attack and to develop the best plan of approach. Recruitment, screening, and selection of appropriate mission candidates takes place, and the bomber-to-be undergoes appropriate tactical training and spiritual indoctrination. The explosive packet is prepared and the attacker is then transported to the scene of his martyrdom, where the attack is carried out. As one former terrorist leader is quoted as saying, all one needs to qualify as a suicide bomber is "a moment of courage" (Van Natta, 2003).

Courage, however, may sometimes need a little outside help, so many terrorist organizations build into the process a number of fail-safe measures to ensure that the suicide mission is completed. For one thing, emphasizing indoctrination of the subject and leaving the tactical details to others limits the number of psychological junctures at which doubts or wavering motivation might intrude. As part of the rigorous indoctrination process, there occur a number of "point-of-no-return rituals" to ensure compliance (Merari, 2007; Seger, 2003). These include having subjects write last letters to friends and relatives, videorecording a goodbye narrative, and saying final prayers. Once a person has pledged himself to a suicide mission, religious groups cement that commitment by thenceforth referring to the subject as "the living martyr." In essence, the person has already left the physical world and exists in a temporary corporeal state solely to carry out his last mission on earth.

Even so, there are a few isolated cases where suicide attackers have changed their minds and opted out at the last minute. As a final safeguard against such last-moment derelictions, some groups take the decision out of the bomber's hands by arranging for remote control detonation (Silke, 2003b). In some cases, this is part of the indoctrination ritual: like any successful operation, the fewer surprises, the better.

LEAVING TERRORISM

It has generally been assumed that, like the Mafia, the only way out of a terrorist organization is feet first. The terrorist lifestyle is not an easy one, and although most members stay committed, some actually do leave (Brockner & Rubin, 1985; Crenshaw, 1986; Horgan, 2003b). The motivations for quitting may vary, depending on the personality of the terrorist and the nature of the organization. Some terrorist group members may reconsider their commitment upon surviving or being deterred from a suicide mission, as noted above. Others may just become quietly disillusioned and drift away. The ability to do this may depend on the type of relationship the member has had with the group.

A number of terrorist organizations rely on a kind of freelance subcontractor system involving operatives who perform a specific task, then drop out of sight until needed next time. The advantage for the organization is that this looseness makes the connection hard to trace. The drawback is lack of control, putting the organization at the mercy of even one blabbermouth or loose cannon. At the other extreme are terrorist organizations that utilize only a select cadre of dedicated operatives, carefully selected, screened, and indoctrinated, who have earned the right to carry out missions through a hierarchical progression of skill and loyalty tests. Different gradations of commitment may be seen across various extremist groups.

In some cases, once the member is in, there is only one terminal opt-out policy. In others, members who don't wish to carry out violent missions may be assigned intelligence, technical, and other support roles. In the latter case, the member's distaste for personally carrying out violence does not diminish his commitment to the broader goals of the group. In still other cases, the roles are fluid, and members are cross-trained, alternating between direct attack and behind-the-scenes support operations from mission to mission.

Kernels of doubt about one's commitment to the cause per se may sprout from the realization that the noble ideals and personal aspirations that led to joining the group in the first place are strikingly removed from the day-to-day realities of the member's role in the organization. Even if the idealism remains, it may become apparent that there is no quick-fix justice, no immediate gratification of the desire for glory, and that the group is in it for the long haul, which may involve a seemingly endless cycle of successes and set-backs. The member may also come to regret giving up the things that, in the beginning, seemed small sacrifices to make for the cause of a better world–love, family, friends, children, or just the opportunity to walk the streets without looking over one's shoulder, or sleep through the night without keeping one eye open. Maybe the member thought he would eventually have these things in the "new paradise," but now realizes it will be a long time coming, perhaps not in his lifetime–although for religious adherents, it may be enough that true paradise awaits in the next world. Like many a disenchant-ed radical, the disaffected member's original naive self-deception may be projected onto the group itself, as the member suspects that he was tricked and misled from the start. In some cases this may actually have been true.

Yet, it is difficult for a person to just quit something to which they have devoted their life, heart, and soul for any length of time, for which they have made sacrifices and burned bridges. The theory of **cognitive dissonance** states that, when confronted with information that disconfirms someone's beliefs or devalues their actions, the first impulse is to dig in their heels and cling ever more desperately to the crumbling ideological structure. No one wants to leave their immortality project flapping in the wind. People want to be existentially consistent and will struggle and fight to retain this consisten-cy in their beliefs. Only when overwhelmed by the sheer volume of contrary evidence does the belief system begin to topple. In what Horgan (2003b) calls the **spiraling of commitment**, the individual may then attempt to squeeze out one desperate last act of violent activity to try to convince him-self of the rightness of his cause, before then being emotionally and philo-sophically jerked 180 degrees and coming to revile the very group for which he once was willing to give his life. Alternatively, he may react to this shat-tering of his world view by simply slinking away in a state of burned-out apa-thy.

That is, of course, assuming that any form of elective retirement is even an option. While giving one's notice may not automatically be fatal, the deci-sion to leave a terrorist organization is rarely as simple as a goodbye and a handshake. The organization may have a lot invested in the terrorist mem-ber in terms of time and training. There is always the security issue, and sometimes vows to keep silent are not enough. Again, as with some orga-nized crime groups, withdrawal of membership may simply be out of the question. This is especially true where political and criminal groups overlap, like some of the drug cartels in Latin America or bank-robbing white su-premacist groups in the United States (Scoville, 2003). In religious groups, there may be a great deal of social stigma and ostracism by the supporting community for betraying the ideals of one's faith.

As noted above, security is always an issue. Once having left the group, any protection from rival groups, law enforcement, or government agencies is gone: "Once you're out, you're on your own." This, plus the reactive hostility the former member may now feel for his former comrades, makes him a prime security risk. Of even more concern to extremist organizations is the ex-member using the colors and mantle of former membership to carry out personal crimes, thereby tarnishing the group's purist political or religious image. Such unapproved activities are almost guaranteed to land the expatriate on the group's hit list.

Some ex-members of terrorist organizations do parlay their lethal skills into frankly criminal activity, alone or as part of a newly joined or organized crime group. In fact, if sufficient numbers of political or religious group members become disaffected in this way, the whole nature of the group may morph from a social change organization to a criminal gang. Again, as noted above, there is sometimes no clear dividing line, and mixed "Robin Hood" groups of this type may develop and proliferate in crisis-affected regions, much as with the current kidnap-for-ransom gangs in parts of Africa, Latin America, and the Middle East. In other cases, as increasing numbers of moderate members leave, the toxic ideological extremism of the remaining members becomes more concentrated and the focus of the group's activities becomes increasingly violent (Staub, 2003a).

Even ex-members who achieve a relatively safe state of security, who just try to keep a low profile and stay off the grid, may come to loathe their unbearable isolation and alienation, leading to depression, substance abuse, and reckless actions. Much like informers sequestered in federal witness protection programs, such social isolation and demoralization may increase the risk of blowing their cover and thereby become targets for elimination.

The good news for the rest of us is that even a few exceptions to the once-a-terrorist-always-a-terrorist rule may provide insights and tools for deterring terrorism. If we can learn more about what makes terrorists give up the life, perhaps we can encourage more of them to seek alternatives to destruction for expressing their concerns, whatever we may think of the merits of their cause. But inasmuch as the best intervention is prevention, far better still would be to work the path backward to the causes of terrorism, to find a way to pull the fuse from the bomb before it is lit.

STOPPING TERRORISM

Currently, the conventional anti-terrorism methodology used by Western governments and throughout most of the world consists of a surgical version of "shock and awe." According to this strategy, after identifying the perpetrators of a terrorist attack, the aim is to hit them soon, hit them hard, and thereby teach a lesson to any other malfeasors who may be thinking of hatching similar plots. However, systematic analysis has shown that the standard retaliatory approach to terrorism not only fails to deter and discourage it, but in fact actually increases the violence by encouraging further retribution (Brophy-Baermann & Conybeare, 1994; Silke, 2003c). This leads to more counterattacks, and counter-counterattacks, resulting in the oft-cited **cycle of violence**."

Habituation and Sensitization

This seeming paradox can actually be explained by a very elemental principle in psychophysiology: **habituation**. Application of a novel aversive stimulus elicits a marked response from the nervous system the first few times it occurs. Repeated application of the stimulus results in a lessening of the response; in essence, the nervous system adaptively tones down the impact of the stimulus so that the organism can go about its business. Think of getting used to a tight pair of shoes, or an annoying sound in the room, or splinter in your finger. Until you can actually do something about it, you just "put it out of your mind," and keep going. The exception occurs with especially painful or severe stimuli which threaten the life and safety of the organism; then, the nervous system may actually become *more,* not less, responsive to repeated application of the stimulus or similar ones, a phenomenon called **sensitization** (a variant of this is discussed in Chapter 10 under the concept of neurophysiological kindling). In humans, sensitization can lead to post-traumatic stress disorder and other traumatic disability syndromes (Miller, 1997c, 1998c, 2000b, 2008b).

The problem with most military reactions to terrorist attacks is that they rarely are the total, all-cleansing, scorched-earth campaigns that military forces intend them to be—and sometimes they are not intended to be that at all. In fact, part of the standard doctrine of retaliation consists of a proportional, or step-wise, approach, as if terrorist acts were equivalent to workplace rule infractions or schoolyard hijinks. A graded response defeats the whole purpose of deterrence completely: if you want to create habituation, what better way to do it than administer carefully incremented doses of punishment, progressively inoculating your enemy against further retaliation, and thus emboldening him by your perceived lack of resolve.

Indeed, factions at war seem to engage in a strange kind of mutual mislogic (Silke, 2003c) that goes something like this: If they kill our people, this shows just how evil they are, and their aggression will only stiffen our devotion to our righteous cause and motivate us to fight to the bitter end. On the other hand, if we kill their people, that will show them we mean business, teach them a lesson, and they will melt into submission at our mighty force. The result? Escalating violence on both sides. Perhaps unwilling to be seen as utter barbarians, the stronger side fails to wage a war of total destruction, thereby diluting the effect of whatever half-hearted retaliation it applies and thereby achieving not subjugation, but further rebellion.

Carrots and Sticks

So why do these ineffectual actions continue? One reason is that they make good press for politicians and generals who generally prefer doing something to doing nothing. Even if total victory is elusive, who in power wants to be the one that backs down a step, who calls a truce, who searches for dialogue? What leader wants to be seen as "soft on terror"? In fact, public opinion consistently shows that, in the face of attack, populations of even the most civilized Western democracies generally view negotiations and diplomacy as hapless dithering and prefer their leaders to act forthrightly and aggressively, especially when dealing with foreign enemies.

For example, Silke (2003c) documents that American support for the use of capital punishment for ordinary criminals has normally fluctuated between 59 and 75 percent, far lower than poll percentages for the use of deadly force against terrorists. The author finds it intriguing that there is less public support for the killing of offenders whose guilt has been established beyond a reasonable doubt in a court of law than there is for the swift call for retribution when the perpetrators are outsiders with even a suspicion of evil intent against "us" (Butler, 2002; Ruth & Reitz, 2003).

On a larger scale, to the extent that terrorism is at least partly motivated by legitimate social and political grievances of the host population, any comprehensive antiterrorism approach must inevitably deal with these factors (Burleigh, 2009; Staub, 2003a; Zakaria, 2003). Unfortunately, this is often misinterpreted as "coddling terrorists." But engagement is not the same thing as surrender, and many an adversary has been defanged by giving him the courtesy of just being heard. A key principle of all forms of **active listening**–whether in criminal interrogation, business negotiation, or psychological crisis intervention–is to engage your opponent by taking the time to hear his point of view, demonstrate that you have done your best to understand it, and then present your own side of the case (McMains, 2002; Noeser & Webster, 1997). You don't have to agree on the issue. You may even go to war over it later. But once you have established a dialogue on a subject, it is hard to completely forget or discount it, and the possibility of further communication will hang over the smoke of battle, even as the conflict rages on.

An application of this approach to deterring some domestic extremists in the U.S. and Europe has been to simply meet with them (Silke, 2003c). Law enforcement officers visit the group members at their homes and encourage them to discuss their concerns and views. The officers try to be as nonjudgmental as possible, refraining from arguing or attempting to change the views expressed. At the meeting's conclusion, the officers provide the extremists with a business card and encourage them to call with any additional concerns. The aim is to provide a human face to the featureless governmental visage the extremists have confronted in the past. Supposedly, this removes some of the paranoia that law enforcement is simply out to get the extremists because of their views, but an ulterior motive may also be to send the not-so-subtle message that "we're on to you." The problem is that, while this may be intended to insert both a dialog factor and an intimidation factor, causing the group to think twice about their next action, it also carries the risk of driving the group further underground.

This kind of reaching out to as-yet peaceful extremists works best if it is coupled with an aggressive response to actual terrorist violence. The basic logic of this "velvet glove-iron fist," "carrot and stick," or "good cop-bad cop" approach goes like this: Treat people with basic respect and decency, give them the benefit of the doubt when appropriate, avoid unnecessarily demeaning or humiliating acts on the host population, conduct yourself professionally, but if the group crosses the line and commits unwarranted terror, don't vacillate—apply commensurately forceful and targeted punishment so that they understand the price to be paid for unconstructive violence. Indeed, this is precisely the philosophy behind the move toward **community policing** in neighborhoods across the United States (Miller, 2006f; Peak, 2003; Toch & Grant, 2005). Whether domestic or foreign, the goal is for the authorities to be seen not just as an intractable army of occupation, but as dealing with the population fairly, yet responding forthrightly when necessary. As noted above, the challenge is to determine what is the appropriate and effective dose of both carrot and stick in each situation.

Talking won't stop all terrorists, of course. Where terrorism represents an act of desperation to achieve otherwise legitimate rights and freedoms by a marginalized, disenfranchised, or persecuted group, the ruling power's willingness to put at least some issues on the table might well be effective in stemming further terrorist acts, because the subgroup now feels it has something to gain from pursuing the dialog, at least for now. But with many domestic or international extremists, fueled by religious or racial fanaticism and programmed to destroy their enemy at all costs, no amount of either accommodation or forceful counterreaction is likely to deter them (Silke, 2003c;

Staub, 2003a). They want to kill us because they hate us, period. Indeed, habituation can also occur to well-meaning measures, as when small concessions are mocked and reviled as being too little too late, mere window dressing or cosmetic changes, or worse, being taken as signs of weakness to be exploited. Just as the doctrine of proportional, step-by-step aggressive retaliatory response to terrorism must be carefully rethought, so must the form and amount of agreement and concessions, so that making peace is not mistaken for giving in or selling out.

Finally, for peace to truly work, justice must be provided for the innocent victims of terror (Staub, 2003b). It is not enough to declare that the war is over, now everybody go home and forget about it. As the South African Truth and Reconciliation Commission and the so-called Restorative Justice Movement in the United States (Chapter 21) illustrate, evildoers–whatever their original motivation and rationalization–must undergo some societally sanctioned consequences for their actions: mere expressions of repentance, however sincere, may not be enough.

Also, formal social arrangements must be made that acknowledge and validate the unacceptable suffering that was imposed on **victims**, and that also makes future harmdoing less likely. Simply arresting and releasing violent terrorists as political bargaining chips sends a corrosive message to victims and to society that we don't really take this seriously, that it's all a game. In our fascination with the psychology of terrorists, we must not overlook or abandon the victims of terror.

GENOCIDE AND POLITICAL VIOLENCE

Despite the fact that they involve some of the most heinous acts that human beings can commit against one another–murder, rape, torture, looting and destruction of property, kidnapping and enslavement, and atrocities against children–the systematic study of these so-called **crimes against humanity** have been largely neglected by the fields of psychology and criminology, left almost entirely to the domains of sociology and political science (Brannigan, 1998; Gibbons, 1997; Maier-Katin et al., 2009).

Human Rights and Crimes Against Humanity

A concept that most of us take for granted–that people have basic rights as citizens and human beings–is a relatively new one, historically, emerging in the Western political philosophy of the Enlightenment, beginning only several hundred years ago (Radzincwicz, 1996). Even more recently, under the principle of ***nullum crimen sine lege*** (no crimes without law), it could be argued that the commission of a given atrocity, horrible though it may have been, actually was not a criminal act per se, since it did not violate any specific laws present at that time and in that country. Hence, the Nazis on trial at Nuremberg could unblinkingly assert that, since elimination of Jews and other undesirables was indeed the law of the land at that time, those who carried out the Holocaust were, in a formal legalistic sense, guilty of nothing.

Largely for reasons such as these, the concepts of **universal human rights** and **crimes against humanity** were elaborated. In 1949, the Universal Declaration of Human Rights established criminal court jurisdiction over genocidal acts, and subsequently, the International Criminal Court was established (to which the United States is not a signatory). The list of actions qualifying as crimes against humanity in the original Nuremburg Tribunals established after World War II by the Allied Control Council (1945), as well as the most recent formulation of the Rome Statute of the International Criminal Court (2002), include murder, extermination, enslavement, imprisonment, deportation, torture, rape, forced prostitution, forced pregnancy, forced sterilization, and other nonmilitary "inhumane acts intentionally causing great suffering or serious injury." Clearly, this list encompasses many of the violent actions that, when committed by individuals, are considered crimes in almost every modern society.

THEORIES OF GENOCIDAL CRIME

As with terrorism, serial killing, mass homicide, and other crimes of violence that shock us with their sheer cruelty, behavioral and social scientists have struggled for explanations for genocidal acts. Several of the more prominent theories are presented below.

Banality of Evil/Ordinary People Theory

Much of the early research on genocidal crimes focused on the Nazi genocide during World War II. The sociological and historical question was: how could so many German citizens participate in, comply with, or at least passively condone the persecution and genocidal murder of millions of Jews and other undesirables? Weren't such crimes the acts of monsters? Postwar theories focused on how a small but powerful group of ideological gangsters essentially hijacked the military and political systems, then supposedly either brainwashed or strongarmed the citizenry to go along with their dastardly plot. Based on the work of Hannah Arendt (1963) and Stanley Milgram

(1974), this theory posited that the capacity to perpetrate extreme evil exists in all of us, but is normally suppressed by the inhibitions of conscience, learned from family upbringing and cultural norms. But, placed in unusual and stressful personal, economic, and political circumstances, anyone can be led to commit the worst kinds of terror against their fellow human beings, even people who had been their neighbors for years. Similar explanations have been offered for massacres that occurred in ancient and modern times, including such recent incidents as took place in Cambodia, Rwanda, Yugoslavia, and even the lynchings that occurred in Southern American towns during the nineteenth and twentieth centuries (Browning, 1992; Chalk & Jonassohn, 1990; Gellately & Kiernan, 2003; Glover, 1999, Hilberg, 1992; Koonz, 2003; Mamdani, 2001; Midgley, 1984; Tolnay & Beck, 1992).

For example, Arendt (1963) followed the trials of Nazi war criminals and concluded that most of them were neither ideological zealots nor sadistic psychopaths, but simply bureaucrats who, over time, came to carry out the organization and perpetration of mass murder with the same bland detachment as that of an office executive or farm manager (Adolf Eichmann had, in fact, been a chicken farmer before the war) who goes to work every day, does his job, and comes home to eat dinner with his family. This, then, was the so-called **banality of evil**.

Milgram (1974) carried out a series of now-famous **obedience to authority experiments** (one can only imagine trying to get such a study past an academic review board today), in which volunteers were asked to administer electric shocks of increasing voltage to a co-volunteer (who was actually a shill for the experimenters and who's wiring was hooked up to an inert box) upon each wrong answer on a cognitive task. At some point in the experiment, the sham co-volunteer would appear to exhibit pain, mild at first, but later conveying dire agony, and in some cases would appear to lose consciousness, yet a high proportion of volunteers continued pushing buttons of increasing voltage when encouraged or, in some cases, ordered to do so by an officious-looking, white-coated, professorial scientist-type with a clipboard in his hand. The message seemed to be that ordinary people will persist with actions that they believe are torturing, and possibly killing, someone else, as long an authority figure tells them it's okay.

That this kind of behavior may reflect traits a bit more sinister than mere sheep-like obedience, however, emerged from another research program conducted around the same time, the so-called **prisonerization study** (Haney et al., 1973; Zimbardo, et al., 1973). Here, volunteers, often ordinary college students, agreed to participate in what they thought was research on the effects of institutionalization. One group of students was randomly assigned to the "guard" category and another randomly picked to be the "inmates," and they were told to act, over the next several weeks, like whatever they thought guards and inmates should act like. In this study, all the subjects knew that all the others were volunteers like themselves, there were no shills or actors, and no higher authority figure either ordered or deterred any particular behavior. Yet, over the course of several days, the "guards" increasingly got into their roles, in some cases abusing the "inmates" to the point where the experiment had to be stopped. The disturbing conclusion was that all it takes for ordinary people to become power-mad sadists is to put them in a position of control over another human being in the presence of mutual encouragement by like-minded comrades. In such cases, it seemed, we can all become monsters; nobody has to tell us to do it (Zimbardo, 2000; Zimbardo et al., 2007). A very real modern example of this psychological dynamic is the prisoner abuse episode that occurred at the Abu Ghraib prison during the Iraq War, in which rank-and-file soldiers were accused of brutalizing prisoners and taking souvenir photos of their activities.

The banality of evil/ordinary people theme has been further elaborated by such researchers as Browning (1992) and Goldhagen (1997) who have meticulously chronicled a number of incidents during the Nazi Holocaust in which common citizens were observed to willingly, enthusiastically, and even gleefully participate in rape, torture, and mass murder of their neighbors, once these others had been branded as undesirables by virtue of race or religion. In many of these cases, they had the tacit approval of the occupying German forces, but in many such instances, the ordinary townsfolk went "above and beyond" in their brutality, surprising even the Nazi troops with their zeal for murder. These authors and others (Brannigan, 1998; Glover, 1999; Kressel, 1996; Maier-Katin et al., 2009; Midgley, 1984) have compared the genocidal events taking place during World War II with similar episodes of contemporary mass violence occurring around the world–Bosnia, Rwanda, and so on–in which a veritable carnival atmosphere seems to prevail, further stoking the orgies of torture, murder, rape, and mutilation that ordinary people seem capable of when sectarian hatreds are unleashed by wars and other social upheavals and the perpetrators can justify their cruel actions as self-protective in some way, or by appealing to a higher cause (Ridley, 1996). Certainly, there is nothing "banal" about these events for either the perpetrators or the victims.

Psychosocial Theories

As we've seen in Chapter 3, there are a variety of psychosocial theories that have been offered to explain the motivations behind individual crimes. Surprisingly, much less attention has been devoted to the psychological study of genocidal violence. **Social learning theory** (Bandura, 1973, 1998) posits that all behavior, including aggressive behavior, is learned, shaped, and maintained through reinforcement from families and societies in which the individual develops. However, Maier-Katin (2009) points out that this cannot account for the seemingly spontaneous and out-of-character outbursts of genocidal violence that erupt episodically in the "ordinary people" described above—unless, of course, what has been inculcated through social learning is not necessarily the violent action itself, but the underlying prejudices and hatreds that the individual has learned to suppress under the normal conditions of society. Thus, when war and social upheaval peel away this thin veneer of civilization, the well-learned animosities are primed to erupt in expressions of violence.

Brannigan & Hardwick (2003) have attempted to use Gottfredson & Hirschi's (1990) **general theory of crime** (Chapter 3) to elaborate a model of genocide based on the **theory of low self-control**. According to this concept, genocidal violence and crimes against humanity reflect the same kinds of impulsive, risky, thrill-seeking behavior that characterizes individual acts of violence. Yet, as pointed out by Maier-Katin et al. (2009), this would appear to fly in the face of observations that the overwhelming majority of those "ordinary people" who commit isolated acts of genocidal violence don't seem to have shown especially weak self-control in other significant areas of their lives. In addition, the kind of meticulous planning and organization that goes into perpetrating genocide on the scale of thousands or millions is thoroughly inconsistent with aimless, reckless impulsivity. Like the slow, patient, but sadistic serial killer, the planner of mass extermination uses his keen executive planning and organizing skills for evil ends.

Evolutionary Psychology of Genocide

Brannigan (1998) has elaborated an evolutionary psychology theory of genocide that begins with the observation that tribal clan solidarity and xenophobia for out-groups is a universal phenomenon in social species from fish to birds to mammals to humans. Brannigan draws on the research of Holloway (1974), Ridley (1996), and others who have shown that nonhuman primates, such as chimpanzees, will form military coalitions and attack non-group members, and that male members of primate groups will engage in raids on other groups to obtain females. As with humans, the precise structure of these social coalitions can be quite fluid, and those who are members of the inner circle one day may be ostracized and marginalized on another. So it may be that an ethnically different family that has been your peaceful neighbor for years suddenly becomes cast into the role of enemy when hard times force a competition for resources, with the accompanying breakdown in social restraints. In such cases, we may have to grope for rationalizations to figure out why we didn't see the "danger" in these outsiders for all these years, but now they suddenly have become threats to be expunged. In our minds, the outsiders have "changed sides" and we may respond with hostility, aggression, and genocide.

Theory of Social Conformity and Crimes Against Humanity

Based on their review of the history, sociology, and psychology of genocidal violence, Maier-Katin et al. (2009) propose a theory of crimes against humanity that attempts to bring this phenomena within the scope of criminology. According to this model, the precondition for genocidal criminality is intense and widely prevalent societal strain caused by military, economic, or political disruption that makes citizens feel endangered and insecure about the future. This heightens the overall level of suspicion and paranoia within a small community or larger society (Bernard, 1990; Griffin & Bernard, 2003; Ogle et al., 1995).

As this mass paranoia grows, a widening group of "others" begin to take on characteristics of the enemy: the disease-spreaders, the job-stealers, the crime-committers, the economic exploiters, the infidels, and so on. This tribalistic us-versus-them mindset morphs into a witch hunt mentality, as the evil others are further marginalized and dehumanized. All that remains is for someone to tell the group how to focus their panicked outrage and fearful hatred, typically against a target of convenience rather than the true source of the upheaval. This provides fertile ground for the rise of demagogues–charismatic leaders that can galvanize the populace to take out their rage on the "deserving" targets. Further, these violent actions can be couched in noble terms and appeals to higher values: "preserving the world for [fill in the blanks] by ridding it of [fill in the blanks]." This not infrequently incorporates clinical metaphors to further delegitimize and dehumanize the victims and elevate the atrocity to a veritable medical necessity, as when perpetrators speak of "cutting out the cancer" or "disinfecting the social body," leading to euphemisms like "ethnic cleansing" or the "final solution." The witch hunt becomes a lynch mob, albeit one that can be well-organized and can take place on a large scale over distance and time.

In the context of the "ordinary people" approach, Maier et al. (2009) appeal to the universal malleability of human nature to support their theory that virtually anyone can become a villain–or hero, for that matter–given the proper set of circumstances. However, as we've seen throughout this text, all persons are *not* equal in their propensity for individual or mass criminal violence. Presented with the same set of circumstances involving resource scarcity, economic upheaval, and military occupation, the psychopath will still act cruelly and self-servingly but will be even freer to harm and exploit others in the absence of normal social controls. The paranoid and dependent personalities will cling to conspiracy theories and attach themselves to charismatic leaders, willing to commit any atrocity to preserve both their bodily and psychological integrity. The schizophrenic citizen may become even more delusional, and those with anxiety disorders, mood disorders, or avoidant personalities may quickly succumb to the stress of societal disruption and flee or become victims themselves. All of these individual reaction tendencies will be overlaid by the instinctive tribalism that adaptive evolution has programmed into our brains to help us "circle the wagons" and assume a defensive survival mode to keep the in-group intact. To counteract this powerful force, efforts must focus on universalizing those aspects of humanity that can be generalized among cultures and peoples, while learning to acknowledge, adapt to, accommodate, and not be threatened by the real differences among us that give humans their diversity.

SUMMARY AND CONCLUSIONS

Just as there is no one type of person, there is no one type of terrorist or genocidal criminal. Some are purely evil, most are not. Some are seriously mentally ill, most are not. Many are religiously or politically committed, some waver. The psychology of terrorism and political violence can best be understood by considering: (1) ideological motivation; (2) individual personality and psychopathology: (3) societal sanctions and support for terrorist activities: and (4) response to anti-terror efforts. One of the more exciting prospects in this field is the use of psychological knowledge to devise more effective investigative strategies and means for deterring terrorism by appealing to the specific personalities and ideological structures of individual terrorists and extremist organizations. Behavioral science may also be useful in devising more psychologically effective antiterrorist responses, whether these be military or political. Finally, the psychological study of genocide may yield its most productive fruit in enabling us to deflect mass fanatical violence-prone movements from fomenting in the first place.

Part IV

Sex Crimes and Family Crimes

Chapters 14–17 cover sexual offenses and crimes within the family. Rape distorts and perverts what should be among the most tender and intimate of human experiences by turning it into a weapon of violation. Sexual or physical abuse of children uniquely outrages us because it involves predatory adults taking advantage of innocent victims. Domestic battery and family violence illustrate the sad reality that people do often hurt the ones they claim to love.

Chapter 14

Sex Crimes I: Rape and Sexual Assault

In the criminal justice system, sexually based
offenses are considered especially heinous . . .

Thus intones the introductory voice-over of TV's long-running series, *Law
and Order: Special Victims Unit.* But why are these crimes more "heinous"
than others, and why are their victims so "special?"

SEXUAL ASSAULT: A SPECIAL KIND OF CRIME?

Sexual assault may be special for several reasons. First, although it can
theoretically happen to either sex, women are disproportionately represented among its victims, so one-half of the human population is overwhelmingly impacted by the danger of this kind of crime.

Second, unlike almost any other kind of violence, sexual assault corrupts
what in other contexts ought to be the most intimate and tender of human
encounters. The same act can be a gift of love or a weapon of violation, depending on the circumstances and the relationship between the parties. No
other physical encounter between human beings carries such a disparate
potential for good or evil.

Finally, it's *sex*–and human beings are just naturally intrigued and titil-
lated by this singularly visceral yet sublime function that plays such a powerful role in all human societies, whether flaunted or suppressed, bestowed or
exploited, sacralized or profaned. Sex has also always been inextricably entwined with other vital survival activites, such as pair-bonding, child-rearing,
clan affiliation, and community cohesion.

RAPE: DEFINITIONS AND DEMOGRAPHICS

The word **rape** derives from the Latin *rapere,* which means to "seize
quickly," (Palermo & Kocsis, 2005), forming the basis of such words as *rapi-*

er (dueling sword), *raptor* (swift bird of prey), and *rapacious* (predatorily greedy).

The U.S. Department of Justice (1998a) describes several classifications of rape, supplemented by terminology from other sources.

Forcible rape: Sexual relations with a female forcibly and against her will. This is what most people understand to be rape.

Statutory rape: Sexual relations with a female under the statutory age, with or without her consent. Technically, a minor under the statutory age is legally unable to give consent. The age of consent may vary from place to place.

Rape by fraud: Sexual relations with a consenting adult female under fraudulent conditions. For example, a doctor has sex with a patient under the guise of "treatment."

Date rape: Nonconsensual sexual relations within the context of a dating relationship.

Marital, or intimate partner rape: Nonconsensual sexual relations within a marital or other intimate relationship.

Rape appears to be a universal phenomenon across cultures. In most Western countries, rape is defined as forcible penetration without consent. However, the source of penetration (penis, other body part, or foreign object), target of penetration (vaginal, anal, or oral), gender and age of perpetrator and victim, and definition of consent vary greatly across nations and localities (Koss, 1992; Gannon et al., 2008; Polaschek et al. 1997). In the United States, each state holds its own legal definition of rape. Across studies, approximately 75 percent of rapes are vaginal, and in 25 percent of cases, the rapist also demands oral sex; in 10 percent of cases, he demands both oral and anal sex. Six percent of cases involve anal sex only, with the remaining 4 percent classified as "other" (Broude & Greene, 1978; Gannon et al., 2008; McKibbin et al., 2008; Rozee, 1993; Sanday, 1981).

Although the documented prevalence estimates of rape or attempted rape in the United States are as high as 15 percent (Kilpatrick et al., 1992; Resnick et al., 1993; Tjaden & Thoennes, 2000a), the true prevalence rate is probably even higher because many rapes are never reported and many unwanted sexual advances may not be regarded as rape per se. One-fourth of college women report being the victim of sexual assault or attempted sexual assault. In 83 percent of cases, this involves someone they know. The majority of these assaults happen in the freshman year (McKibbin et al., 2008; Muehlenhard et al., 1992; Russell, 1984).

Rape is primarily a crime against the young. Only 13 percent of rape victims are over age 25, 22 percent are 18–24, 32% are 11–17, and 29 percent are under age 11, meaning that a clear majority of female rape victims are legal minors. Among sexual assault victims, 24 percent of the attackers are strangers, 42 percent involve current or ex-husbands or boyfriends, 10 percent involve relatives, and 15 percent involve others, such as family friends, neighbors, or casual dates. Clearly, the overwhelming majority of sexual assaults take place at the hands of someone the victim knows. The most common locale for a date rape is the victim's own residence, followed by the perpetrator's residence (Gannon et al., 2008; Malamuth et al., 2005; McKibbin et al., 2008).

About 25 percent of rape victims sustain physical injury serious enough to require hospitalization or other medical attention, but only 5 percent sustain what could be regarded as severe physical injury. The most common methods of force or coercion involve verbal threats or intimidation or the use of alcohol or drugs, followed by physical overpowering. Weapons are used in a minority of cases (Malamuth et al., 2005; McKibbin et al., 2008; Olshaker et al., 2001).

Apparently, some men are not shy about forcing themselves on unwilling partners. Approximately 6–8 percent of men in large samples from such countries as the United States, New Zealand, and South Africa admit to having perpetrated acts that could be considered rape or attempted rape, and up to 25 percent of these men admit to perpetrating some form of sexual aggression (Collings, 1994; Gavey, 1991; Koss et al., 1987; Muehlenhard & Linton, 1987). At least one-third of men sampled admit they would rape under certain conditions, and a large number of men report coercive sexual fantasies (Malamuth et al., 2005; McKibbin et al., 2008). In many such cases, the male perpetrator justifies his actions by saying he feels "entitled" to sex because of the expenditure of a date and/or because the woman was "teasing" him or "led him on."

CHARACTERISTICS OF RAPISTS

As with many of the criminal classifications described in this text, the risk factors and accompanying psychosocial characteristics of rapists are a combination of several generic descriptors of defendants in the criminal justice system and a few features that may be specific to perpetrators in this crime category. General risk factors and characteristics include: male predominance, young adult age, low socioeconomic status, low educational level, unstable employment history at unskilled jobs, prior criminal history, and disproportionately non-European ethnicity. Approximately half of incarcerated rapists are rearrested within three years for a sexual offense or other crime (Ahlmeyer et al., 2003; Amir, 1971; Bard et al., 1987; Craissati, 2005;

Crowell & Burgess, 1996; Dickey et al., 2002; Gannon et al., 2008; Grubin & Gunn, 1990; Polaschek et al., 1997; Scully, 1990; Segal & Marshall, 1985; Stermac & Quinsey, 1986; Walters, 1987).

Although not as young as their victims, rape, like most crimes, is an offense largely committed by young males, with 46 percent of rapists under age 25, 17 percent under age 18, and 15 percent under age 15. In other words, almost a third of rapes in the United States are committed by juveniles (Gannon et al., 2008).

Characteristics more specific to rapists and other sexually aggressive and/or coercive perpetrators as a group include: endorsement of traditional male-female sex roles, hostile or competitive attitudes toward women, endorsement of **rape myths** ("No means yes;" "They all really want it"), acceptance of the use of violence towards women, higher masculinity scores on psychometric assessment instruments, earlier age of first sexual experience, greater number of sexual experiences, and low satisfaction with conventional sexual experiences (Berkowitz, 1992; Burt, 1980; Craig, 1990; Koss et al., 1985; Malamuth, 1986; Mosher & Anderson, 1986; Muehlenhard & Linton, 1987; Polaschek et al., 1997; Scully, 1990).

The question is often raised, "Is rape a crime of sex or a crime of violence?" Clearly, it's both, inasmuch as the act of sex is used as an instrument of violence. Or is it that violent people tend to be violent in most of their interactions, including sex? In fact, research shows that, in their criminal histories and general behavior, rapists far more resemble other types of violent offenders than they do perpetrators of nonviolent sex crimes, such as child molesters (Chapter 15). The criminal history of rapists tends to be diverse and generalized, and includes theft, burglary, assault, and drug-related offenses. When they recidivate, rapists are just as likely to reoffend violently as sexually. It appears that for most rapists, their violent sexuality is a feature of their overall violent antisocial lifestyle (Elliott, 1994; Gannon et al., 2008; Hanson & Bussiere, 1998; Hunter et al., 2000; Lalumiere et al., 2005; Looman et al., 2004; Quinsey et al., 1995; Simon, 2000; Smallbone et al., 2003).

RAPISTS: PSYCHOLOGY AND PSYCHOPATHOLOGY

As discussed in Chapters 10 and 13, one way to deal with our fear and revulsion at atrocious human behavior, such as terrorism or serial killing, is to objectify it by turning it into a sterilized clinical category: if someone horribly hurts another person, we feel less uncomfortable calling the perpetrator or the behavior "sick" instead of "evil." The danger is that by overpathologizing unwanted behavior, such as rape, we risk removing the actor's responsibility for that behavior, and we limit our efforts to understand the full range of normal and abnormal behavior that can lead to sexual crimes.

Rapist Diagnostic Categories

Note that rape itself is not a diagnosis, it is a crime. The *DSM-IV-TR* diagnostic category of **sexual sadism** might describe rapists who enjoy hurting and humiliating their victims, but the sadism diagnosis could apply in consensual sadomasochistic sex play as well. Historically, a separate diagnostic category of "rape paraphilic disorder" was rejected by the DSM Committee precisely on the forensic-political grounds that it might constitute an easy defense for rapists who wish to pathologize their behavior as grounds for exculpation or mitigation. A similar rationale was responsible for the jettisoning of "sadistic personality disorder" that appeared in *DSM-III-R* (APA, 1987) from the subsequent *DSM-IV* (APA, 1994). In the case of sex offenders generally and rapists specifically, the consensus seems to be that the incidence and severity of general psychiatric diagnoses do not exceed those of other offender populations and that there is no diagnostic category that is specific to sex offenders (Grubin & Gunn, 1990; Herman, 1990; Hillbrand et al., 1990; Monahan, 1992; Polaschek et al., 1997; Scully & Marolla, 1985; Seghorn et al., 1987).

As noted earlier, in studies of sex offenders, rapists are often contrasted with child molesters because the former are thought to combine sex and violence, while the latter represent a control group of "pure" (i.e., not combined with violence) sexual offending. To examine this dichotomy, a Swedish study (Langstrom et al., 2004) compared retrospective psychiatric diagnoses for prisoners convicted of sex crimes. Prisoners in this group who met the formal diagnostic criteria for any psychiatric diagnosis were surprisingly rare. The most prevalent diagnoses for rapists were alcohol abuse or dependence (9.3%), drug abuse (3.9%), personality disorder (2.6%), and psychosis (1.7%), with even lower rates of these diagnoses for child molesters.

Probably the most common diagnosis in violent sex offenders such as rapists is antisocial personality disorder or psychopathy (Gannon et al., 2008), and most researchers support the conclusion that rapists have significantly higher rates of psychopathy than child molesters (Abracen et al., 2006; Firestone et al., 2000; Porter et al., 2000; Serin et al., 1994; Vess et al., 2004), with estimates of psychopathy in the rapist group as high as 40–50 percent compared with a 10–15 percent prevalence rate for child molesters (Hare, 1991, 1999, 2003).

Rapists' Psychological Dynamics

Aside from diagnostic classification, another way to approach the psychology of rape is by understanding the psychological history, development, and dynamics of individuals who become rapists. As with all psychopathology and crime categories, the challenge is to discriminate between generic developmental factors for antisocial behavior versus specific causal or contributory factors for particular behavioral categories. For example, several studies have shown that rapists' early histories are characterized by relatively high rates of physical and sexual abuse, and unstable or dysfunctional family relations, all of which could adversely impact their ability to form secure attachments during childhood, which in turn would impair their ability to function normally in mature adult relationships (Ainsworth, 1989; Beech & Mitchell, 2005; Bowlby, 1969, 1973; Dhawan & Marshall, 1996; Gannon et al., 2008; Haapasalo & Kankkonen, 1997; Lisak & Roth, 1990; Marshall & Barbaree, 1989; Ward et al., 1996). However, there is nothing specific to future rapists about this developmental profile, and most people who endure and survive hellish families of origin don't displace their pain and rage onto others; they either suffer in silence or try to work through what they can.

More pointedly, the rapists studied by Smallbone & Dadds (1998) reported more dysfunctional *paternal* attachments characterized by abuse, violence, and lack of care and sympathy, whereas intrafamilial child molesters reported more dysfunctional *maternal* attachments, leading the authors to hypothesize that this may lead to an aloof and insensitive interpersonal style in rapists' adult relationships. However, the same pattern was also found in nonsexual offenders convicted of property crimes, confounding the specificity hypothesis.

Sexual Sadism

The term **sexual sadism** denotes forms of sexual conduct that extract pleasure from inflicting pain, humiliation, domination, and suffering upon another human being, typically involving the fusion of sexual arousal and aggression, and often characterized by sadistic fantasy preceding the commission of sexually sadistic act (Brittain, 1970; Groth et al., 1977; MacCulloch et al., 1983; Nitschke et al., 2009). Diagnostically, this would coincide with the **sexual sadism** diagnosis in the **paraphilias** section of *DSM-IV-TR* (APA, 2000), which involves the repeated experience of strong sexual urges and fantasies, and/or commission acts that involve infliction of psychological or physical suffering on others. The diagnostic criteria require that the symptoms be present for at least six months and produce significant distress or significantly impair the individual's functioning. But what if the individual is not distressed because he likes it?

Consistent with the reality that it is rare to find a "pure" example of any diagnostic or criminal classification category, research and clinical studies show that a sizable minority of sexual sadists also engage in **masochistic fantasies and behavior**, **exhibitionism** (displaying sexual activity to others), **voyeurism** (observing sexual activity of others), **fetishism** (excessive sexual preoccupation with a particular body part, inanimate object or unusual activity), **frotteurism** (poking or rubbing one's exposed or covered penis against another person, often in a public place), **pedophilia** (sexual acts with, or interest in, children, and **forcible sexual assault** (Abel et al., 1988; Hill et al., 2006; Hucker, 1997; Marshall et al., 2005; Nitschke et al., 2009). There is some evidence that the risk of reoffending following incarceration and/or treatment is highest among those sexually sadistic rapists who show the greatest number and variety of paraphilias (Berner et al., 2003; Hanson & Bussiere, 1998; Hanson & Morton-Bourgon, 2005; Nitschke et al., 2009).

The question naturally arises: what about consensual sadomasochistic sex play? The answer hinges on the word "consensual." Rape implies force or coercion that violates the will of the victim, whereas when the recipient consents to the act, he or she is still the subject of the sadistic act, but not a victim per se (Nitschke et al., 2009). The other question relates to the "distress" or "dysfunction" criterion. How would we classify the serial rapist who feels compelled to inflict sexual pain upon his victims, but feels no distress at all about it—in fact, he enjoys it intensely, which is why he keeps doing it.

Recently, Nitschke et al. (2009) have asserted that sexual sadism is an underdiagnosed disorder in sexual offenders. However, it is unclear if this classification category adds anything new to the criminal category of rape, which already implies a certain degree of malicious intent, or to the diagnostic categories of Sexual Sadism and Antisocial Personality Disorder, which would be expected to be common comorbid Axis I and Axis II disorders. Still, there may be special forensic and risk factors that apply to individuals with extreme sexual sadism, for example, differences in recidivism rate (Berner et al., 2003) that have implications for treatment and adjudication.

Rape and Substance Abuse

Alcohol and drugs are clearly implicated in many rapes and sexual assaults, but not necessarily for the reasons people think. Far more important than the mental status of the rapist is the state of intoxication of the victim, a situation that reverses the usual relationship of substance abuse to criminal behavior. Because of its frequent association with socializing, alcohol has been the most studied substance, and alcohol has always been seen as the route to sexual success in otherwise ambiguous mating situations. In general, the more the intended rape victim is incapacitated through intoxication, the less physical force and restraint the sexual assaulter has to use, and thereby the more he can rationalize that the sexual encounter was consensual and not forced. For the sexually sadistic rapist, however, a too-impaired conscious state of the victim is counterproductive because he wants her mentally aware enough to experience the suffering he inflicts. In these cases, the alcohol is simply a tool to get her in a vulnerable state.

Research shows that where the victim and offender are partners or ex-partners, alcohol is less frequently involved than in rapes where the two parties are casual friends or strangers (Abbey et al., 1996; 2003; Hall & Moore, 2008; Horvath & Brown, 2006; Kanin, 1985; Ullman et al., 1999a, 1999b). This may be because the perpetrator, by virtue of an ongoing or prior intimate relationship, feels "entitled" to have sex with his victim and therefore sees no need to loosen her up with alcohol. On the other hand, two people who meet at a singles bar, or two workmates who are flirting at the office Christmas party, may use alcohol to lubricate their socialization, with the perpetrator now perceiving the victim as an easier target, and the victim unwittingly dulling her vigilance and judgment until it is too late.

Drug-facilitated sexual assault, or **DFSA** (Hall & Moore, 2008; Hurley et al., 2006) has been defined as a category of offenses in which victims are subjected to nonconsensual sexual acts, while they are incapacitated or unconscious due to the effects of alcohol and/or drugs and are therefore unable to resist or to give consent. These scenarios are commonly described as **date rapes**. There are three basic ways in which DFSA can take place (Lebeau & Moyazari, 2001). First, the victim can voluntarily ingest the intoxicating substance: e.g., after a grueling week at work, a woman goes to a club and parties hard, going over her usual limit, and meets a man who then takes advantage of her impaired mental state. Second, the victim can voluntarily and involuntarily ingest intoxicating substances: e.g., her new paramour urges her to have "just one more" drink and/or invites her out to the parking lot to smoke a joint with him. Third, the victim can involuntarily ingest an intoxicating substance: e.g., the new friend slips a barbiturate or hallucinogen into her drink while she's in the ladies room, or the marijuana cigarette is laced with PCP.

Indeed, if one were to design or select the ideal intoxicating substance for purposes of date-rape, it would be colorless, odorless, and tasteless, would act rapidly to relax the body, disinhibit impulses, and evoke a positive mood, and, as an added bonus, would induce amnesia for the unconsented sexual encounter (Schwartz et al., 2000). Although alcohol is by far the commonest substance associated with sexual assault (mainly because it is legally available almost everywhere), a wide variety of other substances have been associated with sexual encounters of this kind (Elsohly & Salamone, 1999; Hall & Moore, 2008; Hindmarch et al., 2001; Slaughter, 2000), including marijuana, cocaine, benzodiazepines, barbiturates, amphetamines, opiates, hallucinogens, anticholinergics, beta-blockers, antidepressants, and other psychotropic medications, often used in combination with alcohol. In many cases, the rape victim fails to report concomitant drug and alcohol use, either out of embarrassment or because some of the substances are illegal.

Substance intoxication of the victim has implications for the severity of the rape (Abbey et al., 1996; Hall & Moore, 2008; Rickert & Wiemann, 1998; Testa et al., 2004; Ullman & Brecklin, 2000; Ullman & Knight, 1999a, 1999b). Significant intoxication is associated with a higher chance of sexual assault by a stranger, reduced ability to ward off an attacker, greater likelihood of rape completion with penetration, and more severe physical injury. Use of alcohol by the would-be rapist may cause him to misinterpret friendly cues or signals of mild interest as overt sexual invitations, while the potential victim's intoxication may induce her to relax her normal defensive vigilance and thereby underestimate signs of danger.

THEORIES OF RAPE

Rape: Neuropsychological Features

As noted in Chapter 2, advances in neuroimaging and neurophysiological techniques have enabled behavioral scientists to examine brain correlates of a variety of psychological states and psychopathological syndromes. As always, one must carefully examine exactly what it is those brain states are correlating with before making conclusions about their role in criminal or other behavior. For example, neuroimaging studies have reported structural abnormalities in the temporal lobes of sadistic rapists (Aigner et al., 2000; Gannon et al., 2008; Hucker, et al., 1988; Langevin et al., 1989; Wright et al., 1990), although it is unclear as to what exactly the correlation is with brain activity in those areas.

In the now classic report by Mills & Raine (1994), reviewed in Chapter 10, the authors analyzed 20 brain imaging studies of violent and sexual offenders, using CT, MRI, rCBF, and PET technologies. They concluded that nonsexual violent offending, such as murder, was more often associated with frontal lobe dysfunction, while nonviolent sexual offending, such as incest and pedophilia, was more often associated with temporal lobe dysfunction.

Offending that combined both elements, i.e., sexual violence such as rape, was associated with dysfunction in both brain regions.

Using an extensive neuropsychological test battery, Joyal et al. (2007) compared the response patterns of rapists and pedophiles. The results showed both groups of sex offenders to be impaired on tasks sensitive to verbal skills, attentional control, and behavioral inhibition, suggestive of basal frontotemporal brain dysfunction, while performing normally on tests of reasoning and visuospatial processing, suggesting preserved posterior parietal lobe functioning. Interestingly, however, pedophiles appeared more deficient in the affected abilities than did the rapists, a finding that has been found by others (Lalumiere et al., 2005).

Rape: Psychological Theories

Psychodynamic theories. As a sexual crime, rape would seem an apt candidate for psychodynamic theories that postulate a relationship between psychosexual development and later character disorder and deviant sexual behavior (Gannon et al., 2008; Polaschek et al., 1997). In Freud's (1905/1953) original theory, deviant sexual behavior of all types had its origin in unresolved infantile sexual urges that persisted in distorted form into adulthood and was very resistant to treatment (Chapter 3). More recently, feelings of sexual or personal inadequacy, repressed homosexual urges, and hostility toward women as a reaction formation against unresolved Oedipal conflicts have been posited (Cohen et al., 1971; Groth et al., 1977). Based mostly on individual case analyses, these psychodynamic inferences are difficult to develop into a general theory of sexual deviance in general or rape in particular.

Behavioral theories. Classical conditioning theories of rape highlight the pairing of sexual arousal with aggression and dominance cues, while theories that incorporate operant conditioning principles emphasize the reinforcement of deviant sexual behavior by pleasure, status, or power (Abel et al., 1977; Amir, 1971; Hall & Hirschman, 1991; Malamuth, 1986; Marshall & Barbaree, 1990; Quinsey et al., 1984). But these theories fail to explain how and why such conditioned responses occur and why these connections do not inevitably form for all individuals exposed to them.

Social cognitive theories. Emphasizing cognitive processes more than emotional or behavioral forces, these theories focus on distortions of perception and interpretation of their own and their victims' sexual desires and behaviors as the primary factor influencing the rapist's mindset (Cleary, 1988; Lipton et al., 1987; Marshall & Barbaree, 1989; Scully, 1988; Stermac & Segal, 1989). Examples of such cognitive distortions include overinterpreting victim seductiveness ("She crossed her legs and smiled at me, so she must want it"), mistaking fearful passivity with consent or enjoyment ("She didn't yell or fight or anything, so she must have liked it"), or general self-serving cognitive distortions about female sexuality ("'No' means 'try harder'—some women just want you to work for it," or, "Some women don't know what they want until you show them"). One problem with social cognitive theories is the implicit assumption that all that is necessary for rapists' to renounce their urge to inflict sexual pain and dominance is to show them the error of their misconceptions. Unfortunately, it is typically the powerful sexually aggressive motivation that drives the biased thinking, not the other way around.

Rape: Feminist Theories

Beginning with the **Women's Movement** in 1971, a somewhat radical set of feminist theories, pioneered by Brownmiller (1975), asserted that rape constitutes a deliberate instrument of male dominance and supremacy, and thus represents one of a variety of strategies used by men to subjugate and control women and to intimidate them into remaining in a subservient role in a male-dominated society. By this account, rape and other social control tactics are supported politically, religiously, and culturally, for example, by demeaning media portrayals of women, especially pornography (Baron & Straus, 1987; Ellis, 1989; Gannon et al., 2008; Herman, 1990; Jozsa & Jozsa, 1980; McKibbin et al., 2008; Murnen et al., 2002; Polaschek et al., 1997; Russell, 1988).

Why would half the human population put up with this type of discrimination and abuse? Feminist theory asserts that these sex-role attitudes and relationships result from the socialization processes of young males in most societies, attitudes that encourage the view of women as subservient to men. Such **rape-prone cultures** are characterized by greater gender segregation, higher acceptance of traditional male ("macho") attitudes, and general endorsement of attitudes supporting male entitlement and supremacy relative to women (Burt, 1980, 1984; Herman, 1990; Reiss, 1986; Sanday, 1981; Ward, 1995).

While one can empathize with the feeling of exploitation and disenfranchisement experienced by many women, it is clearly a case of theoretical overreaching to ascribe a sexual crime committed by a minority of men to a deliberate social control mechanism planned and perpetrated by all men in a given society. Most rapists need no such societal sanction to inflict unwanted sex upon their victims; indeed, many of these individuals get their thrills precisely from flouting the laws and mores of the square culture around them. Moreover, attributing rape to a deliberate social control mechanism may have the unintended consequence of effectively "normalizing" it: if rape dominance is just an automatically encultured male trait, how can it be a crime? Also, where do all these men learn to dominate women? From their mothers? Their fathers? Television and video games? Religious institutions? And if sexual suppression of women is such a universal phenomenon, why don't all women feel the same way? Clearly, any credible theory has to account for the range of motivations and personalities that characterize individual members of any society.

Rape: Evolutionary Theories

Recall from Chapter 3 that evolutionary psychology posits a continuum from so-called normal to abnormal behavior, in that many of the behaviors considered pathological by mental health clinicians, and criminal by law enforcement authorities, in fact represent extreme versions of behavioral adaptations that were selected for their survival value among ancestral humans. According to the evolutionary psychology of sex, men's reproductive prime directive is to insert their DNA into as many females as possible. The more aggressive a man is in doing this, the more likely he will leave offspring behind that show the same aggressive reproductive behavioral pattern. In this model, rape would represent an extreme variant of copulatory maximization, leading to enhanced reproductive fitness (Buss, 1994a, 1994b, 2004; Ellis, 1989, 1991, 1993; Gannon et al., 2008; Malamuth & Heilman, 1998; McKibbin et al., 2008; Quinsey & Lalumiere, 1995; Shields & Shields, 1983; Symons, 1979; Thornhill & Palmer, 2000; Thornhill & Thornhill, 1992).

From this perspective, it makes adaptive sense that women at the peak of their fertility would be preferential targets of rape and, as noted above, numerous studies have documented that young, attractive women are most often victimized by rapists (Ghiglieri, 1999; Greenfield, 1997; Kilpatrick et al., 1992; Shields & Shields, 1983; Thornhill & Palmer, 2000; Thornhill & Thornhill, 1983). Indeed, rape is by no means just a human phenomenon; forced copulation is seen in a wide variety of animal species (Ellis, 1989; Galdikas, 2005; Gannon et al., 2008; McKibbin et al., 2008; McKinney et al., 1984; Schurmann & van Hooff, 1986; Thornhill, 1980).

But if that's the case, then why are all men not rapists? Because there's a catch. First of all, many of these women have family members or rival mates to ward off or punish such unwanted intrusions, so there's always some personal risk involved in carrying out these sexual depredations. In addition, reproductive fitness also requires a certain degree of parental investment to ensure that the offspring sired by this frenzy of copulation actually have a chance of surviving to reproductive age themselves. This usually means supporting the mother in bearing and raising these children by providing a steady supply of resources and protection, in which case evolution will also favor traits of stability and commitment to family on the part of some fathers, and these traits will be passed on to surviving offspring as well.

Recalling the principle of human psychological diversity (Chapter 3), any sizable community will probably contain a range of personalities in their men, from impulsive, sexually aggressive males to stable, caretaking fathers— the **cad versus dad** dichotomy spoken about by evolutionary psychologists (Palmer, 1991; Thornhill, 1980; Thornhill & Palmer, 2000; Thornhill & Thornhill, 1983). In addition, as noted above, most male members of the community will not look favorably on their wives and daughters being targets of sexual predation and will consequently elaborate a set of legal and religious censures to discourage reproductive exploitation on the part of a few scalawags.

Thus, in the resource-scarce environments in which most ancestral humans evolved and lived, and which characterize many societies in the present day, rapists and other reproductive cheaters may spread a disproportionate amount of DNA around, but only a small lucky bit of it will go on to replicate itself. Thus has evolved the balance in most societies wherein the majority of males reproduce in the context of family and community, yet a few rapists and other reproductive cheaters pop up in every generation.

The evolutionary psychology theory of rape does not explicitly account for the diversity of rape motivations as specified in different rape typologies (Darke, 1990; Groth & Birnbaum, 1979; Knight & Prentky, 1990; Polaschek et al., 1997; Scully & Marolla, 1985; see discussion below). For example, what would be the evolutionary advantage of brutal, sadistic rape behavior that injures the female being impregnated over merely coercive rape that allows her to walk away and subsequently bear her child? However, as noted in Chapters 2 and 3, just as the psychology of any one human being is a mélange of inherited and learned traits and characteristics, some in concert with one another, others in conflict, so does evolution involve working with complex interactions of physical and psychological traits (Palmer, 1991; Thornhill & Palmer, 2000). Many human physical traits that would seem to be adaptive liabilities (thin skull vulnerable to fractures and upright gait susceptible to back injuries) possess adaptive value in other contexts that, in sum, allow their persistence over generations (large head allows for bigger brain, walking upright means freeing hands for tool use). Similarly, a violent, sexually sadistic male who relishes the prospect of rape and pillaging may prove valuable as a warrior against a hostile tribe, but you wouldn't want this guy around your sister or daughter. Different evolutionary trade-offs in different human societies, in response to different environmental and social selection factors, means that each society will have a somewhat different ratio of personality types, including (from our modern, civilized perspective) some "psychopathological" and "criminal" types.

RAPIST TYPOLOGIES

Recognizing the heterogeneity of both personality type and criminal classification, several efforts have been made to classify and categorize different types of rape perpetrators. The basic clinical and conceptual similarities among typologies bespeaks a certain degree of interobserver reliability and consistency across different populations at different times: apparently, these observers are chronicling the same types of behavior in their separate samples. The two "classic" rape typologies are the Groth power-anger rape typology and the Massachusetts Treatment Center (MTC) typology.

Power-Anger Rape Typology

Groth and his colleagues (Groth & Birnbaum, 1979; Groth & Burgess, 1970, 1978; Groth & Oliveri, 1989; Groth et al., 1977) derived a typology from their study of rapists that was based on the perpetrator's purported psychodynamics and motivation. In fact, a large proportion of the work produced on serial rape profiling by the FBI (Hazelwood; Hazelwood & Douglas, 1980), including incorporation into the FBI's *Crime Classification Manual* (Douglas et al., 1992) was strongly influenced by the Groth typology (Palermo & Kocsis, 2005). The categories include:

Anger-retaliatory rapist. This rapist wants to punish women. He uses excessive force and engages in degradation and humiliation of his victim, often involving profane language on his part and forcing the victim to "talk dirty" to him. For this perpetrator, sex is viewed as filthy and disgusting, and he expresses his anger and contempt for women by sexually degrading them. He usually attacks strangers, but the victims typically resemble a female from the perpetrator's past or present, with whom he has had an unpleasant or conflicted relationship. Thus, the anger-retaliatory rapist is driven by symbolic revenge on his female victims, and his overall behavior may reflect anger at women in other ways, such as domestic violence (Keppel & Walker, 1999; see also Chapter 17).

Power-assertive rapist. This rapist wants to dominate women. The main motivation for this offender is power and control, a sexual conquest displaying his authority, potency, mastery, and domination. He is typically a hypermasculine "macho" type, often a bodybuilder (Keppel & Walker,

1999). He will use the amount of force necessary to subdue his victim, to "show her who's boss." If the victim meekly submits, very little aggression or injury may occur, but if she vigorously resists, he is prepared to get as brutal as necessary to control her. Often, he will question his victim: "How do you like it?" In some cases, the victim may be kidnapped and held captive, with repeated sexual assaults occurring throughout the abduction. As the experience becomes less and less gratifying for the rapist, the victim may be let go, she may be killed, or she may escape by feigning compliance.

Sadistic-hedonistic rapist. This rapist enjoys hurting women. For him, aggression has become eroticized, and his acts may involve extreme forms of bondage and torture, including genital mutilation. Sexual sadism seems to be higher in anal rapists than in vaginal rapists (Neuwirth & Eher, 2003). He often targets "bad" women, such as strippers and prostitutes, possibly because they remind him of the general wickedness of sex, or because he can more easily justify abusing women who seem to be "asking for it," or just because they are targets of opportunity. His crimes may involve stalking, abduction, and sometimes murder, in which case he has transmogrified into the sexual serial killer (Chapter 10).

Massachusetts Treatment Center Rape Typology

The work of Knight and his colleagues (Knight, 1999; Knight & Prentky, 1987, 1990) at the Massachusetts Treatment Center (MTC) has resulted in what is commonly referred to as the "MTC typology."

Displaced aggression rapist. This violent and aggressive offender wants to harm, humiliate and degrade women, combining features of the anger rapist and power rapist in the Groth typology. He may engage in physically injurious acts like biting, cutting, or tearing to further punish his victims, who are usually strangers, although they may possess certain characteristics in common, perhaps reminiscent of females who have incurred his wrath in the past or more recently. Indeed, the term "displaced aggression" denotes the idea that the rage the rapist is taking out on his hapless victim actually has its origin elsewhere. The rapist often demands oral sex in order to become stimulated and because it is seen as a form of dominance. Often these perpetrators are found to be hypermasculine, "macho" types.

Sexually sadistic rapist. This type most closely tracks Groth's sadistic rapist whose internal fusion of sex and aggression results in an intense sexual excitement associated with the infliction of pain. He may tell himself that women enjoy being dominated and is likely to be one of the offenders who believes that "no means yes." He is more likely than other types to engage in marital/intimate partner rape and domestic violence. His approach to the victim often begins with charm and seduction. During the rape, the violence may escalate beyond that necessary to subjugate and torture the victim, resulting in her death. Like Groth's sadistic rapist, the sexually sadistic rapist in this typology most closely resembles the serial killer and, in fact, one may morph into the other.

Compensatory rapist. Also called the **power-reassurance rapist**, this is typically a passive, withdrawn, and socially inept male who is making a desperate attempt to prove his sexual prowess and adequacy by "sweeping away" the object of his affections by dogged persistence. He often lives in a fantasy world, fueled by pornography and by mainstream romantic movies in which the protagonist gets the girl only after going to extraordinary lengths to pursue and win her, behaviors that in the real world would be classified as stalking (Chapter 18). But he has convinced himself that if he can only overpower her just this once, she will be so impressed by his ardor that she will beg for more. He will usually be the least violent type of rapist, but may become enraged if his efforts are vigorously rebuffed, especially if the rejection is seen as particularly humiliating.

Opportunistic rapist. Sometimes referred to as the **impulsive rapist** or **exploitive rapist**, this offender takes his sex where he can get it. He is less likely to go hunting for victims, per se, but a sexual assault may occur in the context of another crime, such as a store robbery or home burglary. During the assault, he is likely to use only the amount of force necessary to restrain and subdue the victim, and is not usually interested in inflicting pain for its own sake, although he may strike the victim if she resists violently or insults him. This offender is usually characterized by a long and varied history of antisocial and criminal behavior.

What the Groth and MTC typologies seem to share in common is their division of rapists into categories which reflect motives of: (1) anger, dominance, and control; (2) sadistic infliction of pain as eroticized violence; (3) compensatory forceful seduction; and (4) sex crime of opportunity.

Quadripartite Model of Sexual Aggression

The Groth and MTC models of rape ascribe different motives to the different behaviors of the rapists in each of their overlapping classifications. A typology that seems to classify rapist behaviors according to completely different psychological forces is Hall & Hirschman's (1991) **quadripartite model of sexual aggression**. The four factors described by this model are physiological sexual arousal, cognitive distortions, affective dyscontrol, and personality traits, and the four rapist types defined by this model are as follows.

Physiologically driven rapist. This may be the rapist most likely to be described as being "driven by his hormones." He often works himself up in a sexually aroused state using sexually aggressive pornography and then feels a compulsion to commit the act in real life.

Cognitively driven rapist. This rapist mentally calculates the likelihood of a successful sexual conquest, based upon what he interprets as rape-justifying cues (e.g., the potential victim dresses or acts provocatively) and low risks for apprehension and failure (e.g., low-traffic area, victim is alone or drunk). Although his cognitions are likely to be biased and self-serving, this rapist at least thinks about what he is planning to do.

Affectively driven rapist. No such deliberations get between the impulse and the act in this category of rapist. His sexual aggression occurs abruptly and angrily at any target of opportunity. Such offenders are generally impaired in emotional and behavioral self-regulation, and are likely to show dysfunctional patterns in wide areas of their lives.

Personality driven rapist. Personality disorders, most commonly antisocial personality disorder (Chapter 8), characterize this rapist, whose sexual offending is part of a larger pattern of impaired interpersonal attachment and dysfunctionally antisocial behavior dating back to childhood.

Behavioral Thematic Rape Typology

Canter (1994; Canter et al., 2003) proposes that rapist behavior can be defined in terms of the predominant theme or role (person, victim, or vehicle) that the victim plays for the rapist, as well as by the type and severity of victim violation, leading to five categories:

Hostility. The offender uses sexual violence to demean and humiliate the victim.

Control. The offender uses physical restraint and other controlling behaviors to immobilize the victim.

Theft. The offender combines the sexual assault with robbery of money or property.

Involvement. The offender attempts some form of pseudointimacy with the victim.

Mixed. Approximately one-quarter of the sexual offenders could not be classified in any of the above categories or showed features of several categories.

Implicit Theories Rape Typology

While earlier typologies have focused on the motivations and resultant behaviors of rape offenders, more recent classifications have taken a more cognitive approach in exploring how rapists think. One conceptualization (Gannon, 2008; Polaschek & Gannon, 2004; Polaschek & Ward, 2002; Ward, 2000a) relies on a theoretical framework, termed **implicit theories**, to ex plain the cognitive mindset that underlies the rapist's behavior. Accordingly to this model, rapists hold offense-supportive schemata, or implicit theories, about women's beliefs, desires, and future intentions that make it easier for these men to alienate and objectify them as objects of rape. Note that this conceptualization does not posit separate subtypes of rapists per se, but proposes that any given rapist may hold any combination of the following major implicit schemata:

Women are sexual objects. Women (whether they admit it or not) are sexually preoccupied and receptive to sexual invitations. "They all want it."

Women are dangerous. Women are malevolent, deceptive, and highly unpredictable. "Don't trust 'em, just screw 'em."

Men are entitled. Men are the bosses in society and should get what they want. "Well, I take whatever I want, and baby, I want you" (lyric from *Can't Get Enough* by Bad Company, 1974).

Men are uncontrollable. The sex drive of men is so powerful that, once aroused, it cannot be contained. "When I get going, I can't stop."

According to this theory, rape-supportive implicit schemata develop during childhood and are well entrenched and resistant to change by the teen years and young adulthood. However, it is not clear why simply harboring one or more of these schemata would necessarily impel a young man to commit rape. Surely, the vast majority of men who happen to regard women as dangerous, deceitful, lust-provoking sex objects don't go around raping them. Their beliefs may account for a lot of unhappy, dysfunctional relationships, but in order to cross the line into committing a violent sex crime like rape, there must be something additional operating in the offender's character structure, such as severe narcissism and/or antisocial personality disorder.

Evolutionary Psychology Rapist Typology

As noted earlier, evolutionary psychological theories of rape generally appeal to the concept of reproductive cheating whereby some men attempt to maximally disseminate their DNA, while avoiding investment in family caretaking (Buss, 1994a, 1994b, 2004; Ellis, 1989, 1991, 1993; Quinsey & Lalumiere, 1995; Thornhill & Palmer, 2000; Thornhill & Thornhill, 1992).

Forensic evolutionary psychology has apparently advanced conceptually to the point where it can offer its own nuanced typology, such as the one proposed by McKibbin et al. (2008). These authors hypothesize that different forms of rape represent extreme variants of the general male mating strategy, as influenced by differences in personality and situational factors. This leads the delineation of five types of rape strategy:

Disadvantaged rapist. This is the poor, desperate guy who can't get a date any other way, either because of low status, poverty of resources, or physical unattractiveness. He is thus driven to secure copulations any way he can, including force, if necessary (Kalichman et al., 1998; Lalumiere et al., 1996).

Opportunistic rapist. While it is not clear how this differs fundamentally from the preceding category, except perhaps by having more material resources, this man is described as being generally glad to mate with women who will have him, but if unable to find a willing partner, he may resort to coercion and rape, especially if the risks are low, as, for example, when men are acting in groups or during wartime (Gottschall, 2004; Palmer, 1989; Thornhill & Palmer, 2000).

Specialized rapist. Men in this group are quickly aroused by violent sexual stimuli. As discussed earlier, in most societies, rape carries the risk of censure, banishment, retaliation by the victim's family, or other punishment if confronted. The adaptive advantage to quicker arousal and ejaculation is to allow the rapist to sneak in, do the deed, and be gone in a hurry (Thornhill & Palmer, 2000). It is known that sperm count in male ejaculate rises in response to competition by other males (Baker & Bellis, 1989, 1993), and rape has been estimated to result in pregnancy twice as often (6% of matings) as does consensual sex (3% of matings) (Gottschall & Gottschall, 2003). The hit-and-run mating tactic of rape may therefore have survived because in some circumstances, despite the risks, it is an especially effective reproductive strategy.

High mating-effort rapist. This is the aggressive, dominant, confident, and sexually promiscuous "macho man" who typically prefers to rack up his sexual conquests by seduction, but will have no compunction about using force to get what he wants. He is often the perpetrator of acquaintance rape or date-rape. His callous exploitation of other people, including women, would probably net him a diagnosis of psychopathy (Lalumiere & Quinsey, 1996; Lalumiere et al., 2005; Muehlenhard & Linton, 1987).

Partner rapist. This is the husband, boyfriend, or other intimate partner who demands increased sexual activity from his mate in response to perceived competition by other males, and will take it by force if she refuses, For some men, the impetus may be a suspicion of his mate's infidelity; for others, the mere expression of interest in his mate by other males may trigger a violently jealous sexual assault against the woman (Thornhill & Thornhill, 1992). As will be discussed further below, **intimate partner rapes** account for between 10 percent and 20 percent of all rapes (Finkelhor & Yllo, 1985; Hadi, 2000; Russell, 1990). Women are particularly likely to be raped by their partner during a breakup, especially one which was precipitated by suspicions of infidelity (Thornhill & Palmer, 2000).

Comparing Typologies

There appears to be no end of theoretical typologies of rape, but are any of these systems actually useful in aiding investigators to behaviorally profile potential suspects? Recently, Goodwill et al. (2009) used logical regression analysis to compare three of the above typologies, the Power-Anger model, the MTC typology, and the Behavioral Thematic typology with respect to their ability to predict an offender's previous convictions from crime scene data. The order of effectiveness was Power-Anger, MTC, and Behavioral Thematic, respectively. However, none of the models was as effective in prediction as a more comprehensive multivariate approach that analyzed a wide range of crime scene behaviors. Thus, while many of these typologies speak to the motives and psychodynamics of different kinds of rapists, a less theoretical, and more empirical and practical approach might be best for real-life investigations of the perpetrators.

SERIAL RAPISTS

As discussed in Chapter 10, while murder is usually a single event for any given perpetrator, certain individuals refine and extend the act of homicide into a lifestyle pattern of sadistic serial killing. Similarly, a subset of nonlethal sexual offenders make serial rape their life's preoccupation. Behaviorally and psychologically, the **serial rapist** is closer in kind to the serial killer than he is to the sporadic violent rapist (Palermo & Kocsis, 2005). For example, both serial killers and serial rapists are characterized by a type of ruthless and remorseless psychopathy that infuses them with a sense of narcissist omnipotence, entitling them to use other human beings simply as objects for their own gratification. Like the serial killer, the serial rapist also fuels his sexual acts through intensive sadistic sexual fantasy, often abetted by print or online sadomasochistic pornography, except that in the rapist's case, the act of domination and humiliation, and the prospect of infecting his victim with a tormenting future memory is more gratifying than killing her (Graney & Arrigo,

2002). However, the victim's death may occur inadvertently, either because she is not strong enough to survive the attack, or because she attempts to vigorously resist, inducing heightened rage and violence in the attacker, which turns lethal.

Characteristic Serial Rapist Behaviors

The sporadic, opportunistic rapist, who takes his victim where he finds her, doesn't usually prepare for any particular encounter. Therefore, he may not attempt to conceal his identity or may employ pseudoconcealment tactics on the spot, e.g., making his victim look the other way, or covering his face with an object found at the scene. In contrast, for the serial rapist, this is a carefully thought-out mission, and he comes prepared with concealment for himself (e.g., ski mask) or means to prevent the victims from identifying him (e.g., blindfold). Many serial rapists take additional precautions, such as using gloves and condoms to avoid leaving DNA, shaving their body hair, disguising their voice, or threatening the victim that he will come back and kill her if she tells the police. Although he tries to avoid leaving clues that could lead to his arrest, like the serial killer, the serial rapist revels in the notoriety generated by his crimes. Some offenders, however, take almost no measures to avoid concealing their identity, relying instead on victim intimidation to ensure her silence. About one-third of all offenders are consuming alcohol at the time of their offenses, and a smaller proportion use drugs (Palermo & Kocsis, 2005).

Victims are usually alone when attacked. A preferred locale for serial rapes is a college campus, probably due to the abundance of young females in addition to relatively light law enforcement presence. On interviews, offenders themselves cite victim availability as a key factor in choosing a target. Other rapists may stake out private homes to see where single women live and determine their habits, then gain access to their homes, either by burglary, home invasion, or impersonation, and commit the rape there, often accompanied by a **fetish burglary**, i.e., stealing of an intimate or personal item as a souvenir. Vehicles are frequently used in the commission of the rapes but, unlike in many other crimes, the vehicle is typically not stolen and belongs to the perpetrator (Hazelwood & Burgess's, 1987a,b; Palermo & Kocsis, 2005; Schlesinger & Revitch, 1999).

Three main types of approaches characterize the serial rapist assault (Hazelwood & Burgess, 1987; Palermo & Kocsis, 2005). The **con approach** relies primarily on seduction. The rapist openly approaches the victim to request information ("I'm new in town, can you tell me how to get to the mall?"), ask for assistance ("This must be a new type of ATM, do you know how it works?"), or offer help ("Let me try to get your car started for you, I used to have one these models"), or just strike up a conversation. Once the victim's guard has been lowered and the physical environment offers some concealment, the offender quickly turns aggressive and subdues his prey.

In the **surprise approach**, the rapist preselects his quarry and stalks her surreptitiously, waiting for his opportunity to strike. He may have covertly surveilled her walking route to and from the bus stop and waits till she gets within the narrow space between two buildings. Or he may wait patiently outside her home until an hour or so after the lights go out so he can break in and catch her sleeping. Finally, the **blitz approach** involves a sudden full-scale assault to overwhelm and subdue the victim by physical force, often using binding devices and/or chemicals to impair consciousness. Sometimes the offender is carrying these in preparation for the attack as part of a **rape kit**; other times, he utilizes makeshift binding devices found at the scene (extension cord, pantyhose).

Once the assault is in progress, offenders maintain control of the victim by physical intimidation, verbal threats, or display of a weapon. Bladed weapons are used far more often than firearms, probably because they are much easier to obtain and conceal and because they can be used as a further fear-inducing device by threatening injury and mutilation. Surprisingly, the majority of serial rapists use little or no physical force during their assault, apparently taking pride in their ability to verbally dominate and intimidate the victim into doing what they want. Those who do employ some degree of violence do not seem to escalate the level of violence with each successive attack, as is often the case with serial killers (Chapter 10).

The most common sexual act committed during the rape is vaginal intercourse, followed in frequency by oral sex, kissing, and fondling. Anal intercourse and foreign object penetration are committed less often. According to victim reports, approximately, 40 percent of offenders experience some form of sexual dysfunction during the assault.

Serial Rapist Personal and Psychological Characteristics

Typically, the serial rapist is intelligent, employed, well-groomed and tends to blend unobtrusively into the community (Hazelwood & Burgess, 1987a,b; Hazelwood & Warren, 1993; Palermo & Kocsis, 2005). At the time of their apprehension, most serial rapists are between 23 and 55 years old, with a mean age of 35.2 years. A little over half have been raised in socioeconomically average or only moderately disadvantaged households; only a minority could be described as having grown up poor. About a third report having been abused as children, and over one-third report prior or co-occuring fetishism or paraphilic behavior. Most report a heterosexual orientation. Over half have had military service and over half have had at least one psychiatric hospitalization. Most are married or have been married at least once and many live in a single-family home with parents, spouses, and/or children.

MARITAL-INTIMATE PARTNER RAPE

As recently as 1970, in all 50 states of the United States, a husband could legally have sex with his wife against her will and not be charged with rape. By 1994, all states had criminalized **marital rape**, although the exact terms and definitions differ from state to state. Still, rates of marital and nonmarital intimate partner rape continue to range from 10 percent to 26 percent (Abrahams et al., 2004; Finkelhor & Yllo, 1985; Hadi, 2000; Kilpatrick et al., 1992; Russell, 1982, 1990; Watts et al., 1998). In one recent study (Goetz & Shackelford, 2006) which surveyed the prevalence of intimate partner rape in independent groups of young men and women in committed relationships, 7.3 percent of men admitted to raping their current partner at least once and 9.1 percent of women admitted that they had experienced at least one rape by their current partner. However, such statistics should be interpreted with caution since many victims of what would legally constitute marital rape may not always identify themselves as victims (Martin, 2007). Women are particularly likely to be raped by their partner during a breakup instigated by men's concerns about their partner's infidelity (Thornhill & Palmer, 2000).

Not all marital rape victims choose to resist, many finding it more expedient to go along with the unwanted sex, perhaps convincing themselves that nonconsensual sex within a marriage is not really rape, or that it constitutes "wifely duty," or that "he's a good guy in other ways," which may in fact be true. Other women may fear alienating the affection or good will of their partners, or simply fear losing their financial support. Still others acquiesce because they are simply too physically weak to resist and don't want to be injured. When it occurs, resistance is more likely to be verbal than physical, such as distracting the perpetrator or trying to talk him out of it. Even physical resistance can involve nonforceful measures such as avoiding the perpetrator, running away when he makes an advance, or covering and shielding oneself from the advance. More forceful forms of resistance include hitting, kicking, or pushing the perpetrator away (Martin, 2007).

Marital-Intimate Partner Rape: Descriptive and Clinical Features

The major question for such studies is: what constitutes a definition of rape? In or out of a committed relationship, rape by physical force is just one form of sexual coercion that can occur within an intimate relationship (Koss & Oros, 1982; Weis & Borges, 1973). Other pressures include threats of violence, verbal intimidation, intoxication, and more subtle tactics of behavioral and emotional manipulation (Shackelford & Goetz, 2004).

Martin (2007) describes **threatened or forced sex** as occurring when the woman is physically coerced into having sex against her will. She cites Finkelhor & Yllo's (1985) study of 326 women living in the Boston area, which classified forced sex in marriage into three categories:

Battering rape was the most common form of marital rape in the sample. In these cases, marital rape was not necessarily sexually motivated per se, but was an extension of general violence in the relationship.

Force-only rape was the second most common form or marital rape. These marriages were characterized by continuous disagreements over sexual preferences and activities, but otherwise contained a minimal degree of violence. Perpetrators of this form of marital rape only employed enough physical force to achieve their desired sexual act.

Obsessive rape, the least common form of marital rape in this sample, was characterized by unusual sexual activities such as bondage and the use of pornography.

Nonphysical sexual coercion occurred when a husband used his resources or power in the relationship to cow his wife into complying with his sexual demands. This type of interpersonal coercion actually takes place far more often than physical threats or use of force. Here, the woman acquiesces to unwanted sex largely out of her fear of the nonphysical repercussions—emotional, financial, or otherwise—of resisting.

Risk Factors for Marital Rape

Although a variety of characteristics of both men and women have been hypothesized as risk factors for marital rape, very few have been rigorously studied. Not surprisingly, many of the risk factors for male violence in general apply to a propensity to commit marital rape, such as personal and family history of violence, unemployment, hypermasculine orientation, alcohol and drug use, and the presence of sexually coercive fantasies. Risk factors for being victims of marital rape include being younger, having experienced rape previously outside marriage, and being currently divorced or separated from one's husband (Delosi & Margolin, 2004; Martin, 2007).

Beyond that, a fairly well-agreed upon predictor of marital rape is the overall quality of the marriage as a whole (Martin, 2007)–although it might be hard to separate the quality of any relationship from the personal characteristics of the members of that relationship. Relationship characteristics associated with an increased risk for marital rape include non-sexual marital aggression, low marital quality, status disparities between the partners, and continuous disagreements over finances, alcohol or drug use, and sex. These factors seem to have an additive effect, so that the more of these factors exist in the marriage, the more likely the risk for marital rape.

Research has shown that victims of marital rape suffer from a variety of psychological disorders, most commonly depression and PTSD symptomatology, and victims are at higher risk for suicide. Marital rape victims also report a high rate of physical health effects, such as physical injuries, gynecological problems, and chronic illnesses (Martin, 2007). Although less common, marital rape victims occasionally kill or seriously injure their partners (Chapter 3).

RAPE VICTIMS

Psychological Effects of Sexual Assault

Sexual assault affects one-fourth of women and up to 7 percent of men and is associated with significantly increased risk of anxiety, depression, substance abuse, PTSD, dissociative disorders, and suicide risk (Breitenbecher, 2001; Classen et al., 2005; Desai et al., 2002; Elliott et al., 2004; Kushner et al., 1993; Macy, 2007; Maker et al., 2001; Messman & Long, 1996; Resick, 1993).

The relationship between sexual violence and health has been described as the **radiating impact of violent victimization** (Macy, 2007; Riger et al., 2002), in which violence immediately and directly influences women's physical and mental health, and then spreads out to affect careers, friendships, families, and whole communities. Despite this impact, a surprisingly small number of sexual assault victims seek mental health services for problems related to their assault (George et al., 1992; Golding et al., 1989; Ullman, 2007).

Neuropsychological Effects

Sexual assault may have effects on the brain. Examining neuropsychological functioning among rape survivors with PTSD, Jenkins et al. (2000) found their performance to be significantly worse than that of other groups on measures of sustained and divided attention. Although the attentional dysfunction reported in this study was mild, the affected women reported that it significantly impaired their handling of day-to-day tasks. The authors posit that PTSD victims sleep poorly, are easily startled by extraneous stimuli, and spend considerable energy trying to avoid intrusive thoughts. Each of these factors could impair performance on tests of sustained attention. Alternatively, dissociation is a common feature in PTSD victims, and this would also be expected to significantly interfere with one's ability to concentrate and sustain attention.

A third possibility is that impaired attention in PTSD may also be the result of brain dysfunction. As discussed in Chapter 2, possible substrata include alterations in noradrenergic function (Bremmer et al., 1995) and damage to limbic structures produced by stress-induced elevations in glucocorticoid levels (Sapolsky et al., 1990). It is also quite possible that some rape victims may have sustained traumatic brain injuries during a violent sexual assault (Miller, 1993c, 1993d), although this factor was supposedly controlled for in the present study.

Women's Defenses Against Rape

McKibbin et al. (2008) have elaborated a unique evolutionary theory of women's adaptations against the threat of rape which is applicable to the present day. Despite the demographic fact that most rapists are known to the victim (Kilpatrick et al., 1992; Resnick et al., 1993), studies demonstrate that women have a far greater fear of being raped by a stranger (Thornhill & Thornhill, 1990a, 1990b), which suggests that for ancestral humans, any intrusions into the tribe by rival groups constituted a more acute danger to group survival than intragroup aggression (McKibbin et al., 2008). Within the community, women may form alliances with one another or try to pair up with physically intimidating and/or socially dominant men (Smuts, 1992; Wilson & Mesnick, 1997). Women also tend to perform fewer socially risky behaviors when they are fertile, while engaging in more consensual sex (Morris & Udry, 1982). Thus, coerced sexual behavior, in the context of what would be an otherwise reasonably safe and secure family and social environment that provides basic material needs and protection from outsiders, may be a trade-off that many women have been—and continue to be—willing to make.

Rape in the Military

A sad concomitant of the increase in female military members is the rise in reported rapes during these women's service (Zinzow et al., 2007). The true number of sexual assaults in the military is unknown because many of these go unreported. Part of the problem may relate to bringing bad habits and risky behaviors from home. A substantial proportion of women join the military to escape violent or unstable family and neighborhood environments (Sadler et al., 2004). Studies suggest that more than half of female veterans have experienced physical or sexual abuse prior to joining the military (Engel et al., 1993; Sadler et al., 2004), and prior trauma exposure is known to predict future trauma exposure.

Thus, without seeming to blame the victims, military mental health interventions might try to find ways to help these women reduce behavioral risk factors that predispose them to sexual assault and abuse during their service (Zinzow et al., 2007). These skills might carry over productively to their civilian lives as well. This won't solve all military sexual abuse, however, and the service branches must be proactive in encouraging women to come forward and aggressively pursue valid cases.

Sexual Revictimization

The above point about pre- and post-military sexual assault risk factors also applies more generally. Throughout this text, we've referred to the **consistency principle**, the well-validated observation that the best predictor of future behavior is past behavior. As applied to sexual victimization, the evidence shows that women who experience sexual violence once or more in their lives are at increased risk for subsequent revictimization (Eby et al., 1995; McFarlane et al., 2005; Resick, 1993). Repeated experiences of violent victimization can cumulatively impair a woman's psychological health and coping resources, and thus increase her subsequent risk of revictimization, in an escalating vicious cycle (Arata, 2002; Casey & Nurius, 2005; Miller et al., 2008b). This is why clinical and judicial intervention is so important.

Treatment of Rape Victims

While detailed clinical treatment recommendations are beyond the scope of this text (see Miller, 2008b), the overall consensus in this field seems to be that psychological treatment modalities, particularly support and cognitive-behavioral therapies enable about two-thirds of rape-traumatized women to recover sufficiently to move on with their lives (Miller, 2008b; Vickerman & Margolin, 2009).

BOX 14.1. PSYCHOLOGICAL TREATMENT OF RAPE VICTIMS: DEALING WITH SELF-BLAME

One of the increasingly popular and effective psychotherapeutic strategies for helping victims of trauma work through and recover from their ordeal is **cognitive-behavioral therapy**, particularly a strategy called **cognitive restructuring**. The rationale of cognitive restructuring is to counteract irrational catastrophizing beliefs and replace them with more rational, realistic, and adaptive beliefs and attitudes. For example, a victim who was assaulted in a parking garage is helped to realize that all enclosed spaces need not harbor danger, as long as reasonable precautions are taken. The goal is laudable: by allowing herself to engage in a wider range of activities, she forestalls a behaviorally crippling constriction of her lifestyle.

However, how do you define "irrational"? And who defines it? The victim? The therapist? As Muran & DiGuseppe (2000) point out, what determines an irrationally catastrophizing mindset, as opposed to one which is adaptively vigilant to further danger, often boils down to a clinical judgment, and in some cases, a value judgment. Telling a traumatized rape victim that her ruminative thought of, "This was a terrible thing that happened to me—what if I get raped again?" is *irrational* will likely be perceived as insensitive and invalidating, and may strain therapeutic credibility, as the patient thinks (or, more rarely, tells the therapist directly): "Easy for you to say, sitting there in your nice, safe, comfortable chair. You're not the one who was choking on your own pantyhose while some monster was poking your genitals with a knife." Better to validate the horror of the experience itself and focus the cognitive restructuring strategies on more appropriate dysfunctional beliefs, such as self-blame or the belief that the patient has become "damaged goods."

Even here, caution is advised. Work with trauma victims (Miller, 1998c, 2008b) shows that seemingly maladaptive self-blame may be the patient's only antidote to the far more disturbing belief that fate is random, her actions are meaningless, the world is unpredictably dangerous, and she is helpless and powerless to prevent something like this from happening again. If something I did caused or contributed to the rape last time, this reasoning goes, then if I do something *different* next time, maybe I won't ever get raped again. This is, paradoxically, self-protection by self-blaming, and therapists must be careful that, if they strive to peel this tattered emotional field dressing from the raw emotional wound, they'd better have a clean, fresh, soothing psychic bandage to take its place.

Still, the concept of causality need not be entirely eliminated, but can be productively redirected by taking thoughts that attribute the traumatic event to fixed, immutable qualities of character ("I'm a stupid slut for going to that bar") and restructuring them in terms of potentially changeable behaviors ("I should never have gotten in a car with someone I just met in a bar"). This retains credibility by refusing to facilely dismiss or sugar-coat what the patient did that may have set her up for the assault, but realistically offers a behavioral and existential escape clause by empowering her to do something different, should the situation ever arise again (Janoff-Bulman, 1979; Meyer & Taylor, 1986). It also makes therapeutic change more palatable because it doesn't insist that the patient alter her entire lifestyle. For example, she may have no intention of discontinuing her visits to singles bars because that may be her only practicable venue for socializing, but at least she can learn how to protect herself from the same kind of bad experience happening again, without totally turning her life inside out and becoming a recluse. Some examples of typical maladaptive self-statements following a sexual assault that are cited by Muran & DiGuseppe (2000) as targets for therapeutic cognitive restructuring are noted below, along with my own (Miller, 2008b) comments and caveats:

"**I'm damaged goods now. No one will want me.**" Ascertain if this has a basis in reality. For example, although it may not be true that "no one" will want her; this won't be very reassuring if the rape victim is reeling from rejection by the boyfriend or husband who has been the primary partner in her life.

"**I deserved this because it was my fault**." Try to reconceptualize *fault* as *causation* that can be altered.

"**I'm scarred for life; I'll never be the same again**." It's true that a severe trauma will probably change the victim in some way, and trying to deny this may be unrealistic and countertherapeutic. But there is a difference between a small, barely perceptible scar—physical or psychological—and a huge gash that assaults the victim's senses every time she looks at—or thinks about—herself. Set realistic goals and work toward them.

"**This has to be a secret. Nobody can ever know that I was raped.**" Typically, this means that the victim wants to keep this a secret from certain people—usually romantic partners, relatives, or friends—because she fears rupture of these relationships or just doesn't want to be endlessly interrogated and embarrassed. Whenever possible, this should be respected. In fact, some overly voluble victims may need special guidance in how to clam up or at least pick appropriate people to share their experience with, and who to keep out of the loop because it's none of their business.

"**If I was aroused during the assault, I must be a slut or a sicko.**" In many cases, simple education about the facts of sexual physiology may disabuse the victim of this belief. But sometimes, a sexual encounter that began pleasantly enough turns sour in the course of the act itself. Or the patient may have had a few nice dates with the same man in the past and had gotten used to being pleasantly aroused. This time, however, it was a coerced situation, but the old sexual feelings came back automatically as a form of Pavlovian conditioning. Explain this to the victim in terminology she can relate to ("Even if someone forces you to drink alcohol, you still get drunk.").

"**I shouldn't cry this much. I should be getting over this by now. Most normal people wouldn't react this way**." Experienced clinicians know that "normal" includes a wide range of reactions to trauma, in both intensity and type, based on the nature of the event and the patient's baseline personality. Unless clearly dangerous or pathological, patients' reactions should be tolerated and vali-

continued

BOX 14.1.—*Continued*

dated, and practical strategies should be offered for dealing with extreme reactions.

 "I'll never trust anyone again." In a well-meaning attempt to give the patient hope, many clinicians try to dismiss this notion as quickly as possible: "Of course, you'll trust again; just give it a little time." But, especially early in the recovery process, this may ignore the self-protective function of taking such a seemingly pessimistic stance: now she just doesn't trust herself, so by foreswearing future relationships, she is temporarily able to reassure herself that she'll never be duped and preyed upon again. Later in the treatment process, when some degree of self-confidence has been regained, this issue can be revisited. Also, problems with trust may have predated the sexual assault for some patients and have been exacerbated by, even if not entirely caused by, the recent assault. As always, knowledge-based clinical experience, sound judgment, and common sense should guide the treatment process (Miller, 1998c, 2008b).

SUMMARY AND CONCLUSIONS

Rape and sexual assault may strike us as especially offensive because they purposefully pervert what should ordinarily be among the most intimate forms of human communication. Those who rape do so for a number of reasons, but they basically involve the motives of anger, power, eroticized cruelty, and opportunistic mating. As a reproductive strategy, rape has certain risks as well as benefits, which probably accounts for its persistence in human populations as a minority mating tactic. Although most women fear rape by strangers, they are far more likely to be sexually assaulted by someone they know, especially their own mate. Rape can take both a physical and psychological toll on its victims, and clinicians continue to explore more effective ways to treat rape survivors and to develop proactive strategies to prevent revictimization.

Chapter 15

Sex Crimes II: Sexual Offenses Against Children

In addition to sexual assault of adults, (Chapter 14), sex crimes can involve children as victims–and sometimes as perpetrators–as well as other vulnerable members of society. Indeed, we feel a special revulsion for crimes perpetrated on those least able to defend themselves.

PARAPHILIAS

Sex crimes against children are often placed in the broader context of behavior that is considered sexually deviant according to the clinical criteria and cultural norms of a given society. The *DSM-IV-TR* (APA, 2000) divides sexual disorders into three groups: the **Sexual Dysfunctions**, characterized by inhibitions in sexual desire or dysfunction of sexual response; the **Paraphilias**, characterized by arousal in response to sexual objects or situations not part of "normal" arousal-activity patterns, and which may interfere with normal sexual behavior; and the **Gender Identity Disorders**, characterized by consistent psychological identification with the opposite sex and persistent discomfort with one's own (Aggrawal, 2009b).

Paraphilias, according to the *DSM-IV-TR,* are diagnosed by two criteria. Criterion A requires the presence of recurrent, intense sexually arousing fantasies, sexual urges, or behaviors generally involving nonhuman objects, the suffering or humiliation of oneself or one's partner, and/or involvement of children or other vulnerable and nonconsenting persons, that occur over a period of at least 6 months and are not secondarily associated with another disorder. For some individuals, paraphilic fantasies or stimuli are necessary for sexual arousal and are always included in sexual activity, while for others, the paraphilic stimuli are used optionally or sporadically, and the individual can, at least sometimes, engage in sexual activity without them. Criterion B requires that the sexual urges, fantasies, and/or resultant behavior cause clinically significant distress or impairment in social, occupational, or other important areas of functioning (Aggrawal, 2009b).

The paraphilias listed in *DSM-IV-TR* include the following.

Exhibitionism: Persistent and intense sexual feelings and urges to expose one's genitals to unsuspecting strangers. Note that explicit genital displays are common social signaling mechanisms among males and females of many species, to attract mates, as well as to intimidate rivals. In humans, this is often done symbolically, as in "giving the finger" or the famous pop entertainer's "crotch-grab."

Voyeurism: Sexual excitement attained from the act of observing another person who is naked, or disrobing, or engaging in sexual activity. As primates with a powerfully developed visual sense, human beings naturally employ "looking" as an adjunct to sexual activity, or there would be no pornography industry. In normal sexual encounters, looking is typically the prelude to doing. This is only diagnosed as a paraphilia if watching another engage in sex is the sole or preferred sexual activity, with actual sex secondary.

Fetishism: Persistent, intense sexual fantasies, urges, and behavior connected with the fondling of, or sexual play with, inanimate objects or isolated body parts. Where the object, whether a specialized sex toy or creatively improvised household item, is used in the course of regular sexual activity, it would not necessarily be considered a fetish object unless sex could not be enjoyed without it, or it–not a person–was the sole object of sexual activity. This also does not include cases where the object is used as a "second choice" to compensate for the absence of a preferred human partner (e.g., Internet pornography, phone sex service, vibrator, inflatable doll). Note that most fetishistic objects involve sexually-related items, such as undergarments, rather than ordinary or unusual objects. These souvenirs represent concrete reminders or symbolizations of a desired human partner that the user can fondle or smell to evoke a mental image of the person and thereby achieve arousal. Also note that fetish souvenirs are commonly taken from crime scenes by serial rapists and killers (Chapters 10, 14).

Transvestic fetishism: Sexual excitement derived from wearing the clothes of the other gender. This can range from individual, relatively unobtrusive items of clothing, such as shoes or undergarments, to full **cross-dressing**, involving clothes, hairstyle, and makeup. This can occur in both men and women, and is not necessarily associated with either homosexuality or gender identity disorder, although the incidence of transvestic fetishism is probably somewhat higher in these groups.

Frotteurism: Sexual excitement induced by touching and rubbing against another person without their consent. This most commonly occurs in crowded areas, such as busy train stations or supermarket checkout lines, where the "accidental" abutment of one person against another can be more easily explained away.

Sexual masochism: Sexually arousing fantasies, urges, or behavior involving the act of being humiliated, physically punished, or otherwise made to suffer.

Sexual sadism: Sexual excitement derived from inflicting physical and/or psychological suffering upon another.

Pedophilia: The desire, urge, or use of children for sexual excitement and gratification, involving children of either sex. If this behavior occurs within a family, it is commonly termed **incest**. This will be discussed further below.

Paraphilia not otherwise specified (NOS): This is sometimes wryly referred to as the "whatever-floats-your-boat" category, and technically describes other sexual preferences that don't meet the criteria for the above syndromes. Although the *DSM-IV-TR* authors are unclear about why some acts make the diagnostic "A-list" and some do not, they cite the following as examples (which they stress is not an exhaustive list) of the NOS category: **telephone scatalogia** (making obscene phone calls or "dirty talk" over the phone—today, this might also include emailing and texting); **necrophilia** (sex with corpses—note that this is a common activity for serial killers; see Chapter 10); **tyndarianism** (mate-swapping), **triolism** (sexual arousal by watching one's mate having sex with another person); **partialism** (exclusive focus on one part of the body for sexual stimulation and activity, e.g., the famous "foot fetish"); **zoophilia** (sex with animals); **urophilia** (sex involving urine or urination); **coprophila** (sex involving feces or defecation); **klismaphilia** (sex involving the giving or receiving of enemas). Note that in many species, elimination activities are regularly part of mating behavior, no doubt due to the anatomical proximity and shared neural innervations of the genital and excretory organs. And even ordinary human sexual play often incorporates activity involving body parts not solely structured for procreation.

Clearly, a number of the paraphilias listed in *DSM-IV-TR* could be considered harmless indulgences, either because they don't affect other people (object fetishism, transvestic cross-dressing) or because their activities involve a consenting adult partner (sadomasochism, elimination). Indeed, for most of these activities, what distinguishes them as being play, as opposed to prosecutable crimes, is not their inherent bizarreness, but whether or not the other individuals involved do or do not consent. For example, the relatively nonviolent acts of dropping your trousers in public, rubbing up against someone in a shopping mall, or spying on your lovemaking neighbors through their window are all crimes that can get you arrested and prosecuted. However, the infliction of relatively intense binding, spanking, and sexual thrusting, if done as part of a mutually agreed-upon S&M rape fantasy by consenting adults, is totally within the law. Conversely, while internally fantasizing about sex with children may be diagnosed as pedophilia and is otherwise nobody's business, acting upon these fantasies with a real child constitutes the prosecutable crime of sexual assault on a minor, no matter how "willing" that minor may be claimed to have been.

It is also important to understand that almost all of these activities, while considered paraphilias by their exclusivity, commonly form components of normal sex play. In addition, most people engage in at least some whacky fantasies that they keep to themselves and would never consider crossing the line and actually carrying out–again explaining why depictions of an almost unbelievably vast range of sexual practices are so widely available on the Internet and elsewhere.

In fact, you're not even safe in church. Aggrawal (2009a) undertook a comprehensive sexual content analysis of the Judeo-Christian Bible and found examples of the following behaviors described therein, some of which would be diagnosed as paraphilias today, and most of which would be considered crimes. These include: adultery, incest, sexual harassment, drug facilitated sexual assault, individual rape, gang rape, homosexuality, transvestism, voyeurism, bestiality, exhibitionism, and necrophilia. Apparently, some Bible characters never heard of "Thou shalt not."

NEUROPSYCHOLOGY OF SEXUAL DEVIANCE

As with many of the syndromes described in this text, psychologists and criminologists continue to search for neurobiological clues to deviant sexuality, the major problem, of course, hinging on the definition of "deviance."

Following a brain injury, the most common complaint about sexuality is a marked reduction in sex drive and sexual activity that accompanies a more general deterioration in motivation and cognition (Joyal et al., 2007; Miller, 1993c,d, 1994f; Toone et al., 1989; Zasler, 1994). Less commonly, brain injury which produces an **irritative lesion**, i.e., a damaged area that abnormally disinhibits or stimulates surrounding tissue, has been reported to be associated with abnormal sexuality, as are some cases of frontal and temporal lobe damage, especially when the impairment involves subcortical structures in the limbic system of the brain, as often occurs with temporal lobe epilepsy. The resulting symptoms and behaviors have included hypersexuality, fetishism, and transvestism (Absher et al., 2000; Cummings & Mendez, 1984; Davies & Morgenstern, 1960; Dewhurst et al., 1970; Epstein, 1961; Ghika-Schmid et al., 1995; Gorman & Cummings, 1992; Hoenig & Kenna, 1979; Hunter et al., 1963; Kolarsky et al., 1967; Lang, 1993; Marlowe et al.,

1975; Mendez et al., 2000; Mendez et al., 2004; Miller, 1993c,d, 1994; Mitchell et al., 1954; Walinder, 1965).

However, complicating these interpretations is the specificity problem. How do we know that the sexual disorders seen following a brain injury were not there previously, albeit perhaps in milder form? And even if we can establish the onset of the disturbed sexuality to the time of injury, how do we know that hypersexuality represents a sexual disorder per se, as opposed to being attributable to the generalized impulsivity, impaired behavioral self-regulation, and general increase in antisocial behavior reported following some brain injuries, especially those which involves the frontal lobes and their subcortical connections (Joyal et al., 2007; Lang, 1993; Mega & Cummings, 1994; Miller, 1990b, 1994b, 1993d, 1998a; Volavka, 2002)?

This problem is even more acute when we attempt to correlate specific cognitive and behavioral findings in sex offenders with specific systems of the brain. For example, a number of neuropsychological studies of sex offenders have found performance patterns involving impaired verbal processing, cognitive inflexibility, and impaired behavioral control, implicating left-hemisphere frontal and temporal lobe dysfunction (Flor-Henry, 1987; Galski et al., 1990; Lang, 1993; Raine et al., 1998; Stuss & Knight, 2002). But we know that this is a common pattern for antisocial criminals in general, who tend to be characterized by histories of ADHD, learning disorder, conduct disorder, history of fights and brain injuries, and low socioeconomic status.

An additional problem is that many of these studies, probably out of a need for large enough subject pools to run statistical analyses, lump together diverse types of sexual offenders, e.g., exhibitionists, fetishists, pedophiles, incest perpetrators, and rapists as an experimentally homogeneous group, and compare them to nonoffender control groups. But the psychological characteristics and behavior patterns—and their associated neuropsychological profiles—are likely to be different for, say, a violently sadistic rapist versus a nonviolent child molester, muddying any interpretation of the neuropsychology of "sexual deviance" as a whole.

A somewhat better-controlled set of studies of the neuropsychology of sexual deviance has recently been carried out by Spinella et al. (2006) and Joyal et al. (2007). These results generally support previous findings, that is, impairment in verbal processing, verbal memory, response inhibition, and sustained attention among sexual offenders, along with normal set shifting, cognitive flexibility, and visuospatial processing, implicating left frontotemporal regions of the brain. In particular, the findings pointed specifically to basal frontotemporal brain regions that have been associated specifically with behavioral self-regulation.

Finally, why does distorted sexuality have to be associated with a disordered brain? It is quite possible that the genetic-development factors that influence a person's extreme sexual preferences are no more related to "brain damage" than the factors that determine extreme tastes in food or music. What the neuropsychological research may be identifying is a behavioral pattern of impulsivity, egocentricity, impaired judgment, deficient empathy, and discounting of consequences that makes some people more likely than others to act on urges that most would suppress. So, whereas most people who find themselves sexually attracted to children or who harbor hatred against women might seek nonaggressive and nonexploitive ways of working these impulses out (through fantasy or pornography, for example), or might try to suppress and sublimate the urges themselves, the narcissistic psychopath or simply impulsive egotist may "turn off the brakes" and indulge his desire. As Simon (1996) states, "Bad men do what good men dream."

BOX 15.1. HAPPY BIRTHDAY, PERVERT

Unrepentant Child Molester, 100, Freed, South Florida SunSentinel, December 11, 2009, p. 2A.

New York's oldest registered sex offender is scheduled to move by week's end out of a Buffalo halfway house for released inmates and into a place of his own, after completing his latest terms in state prison for molesting young girls. Retired telephone company worker and great-grandfather, Theodore Sypnier, celebrated his 100th birthday in the Groveland Correctional Facility, where he was serving a 10-year sentence for raping and sodomizing two sisters, aged 4 and 7. He was released on parole in 2007, but was reincarcerated after failing to attend sex offender counseling. According to investigators and prosecutors, Sypnier has been using his grandfatherly charm to snare his young victims for at least 60 years, and has expressed no remorse for his crimes. He will be on parole until 2012, when, authorities fear, he will continue his depredations till the day he dies—whenever that is.

PEDOPHILIA AND CHILD SEXUAL ABUSE

When we think of sex offenders, the group that almost always earns special revulsion are those offenders that take advantage of children. There seems to be a natural protective instinct in most people when it comes to insulating the innocent, which is why the penalties for child sex offending are generally the harshest among all types of sex offenses. This, however, can sometimes lead to excesses of panic and hysteria that work against the overall purposes of justice (Box 15.3).

Pedophilia: Description and Demographics

Approximately one-fifth to one-third of female children in the United States experience some form of sexual abuse, and this rate may be even higher in the early histories of patients referred for mental health treatment (Elliott & Briere, 1995; Finkelhor, 1994; Finkelhor et al., 1990; Jacobsen & Herald, 1990; Walsh et al., 2010). Much of this abuse takes place in the child's home, perpetrated by adult relatives and/or caretakers who may not be strict pedophiles per se.

Pedophilia is defined as a persistent sexual interest in prepubescent children, as reflected by one's sexual fantasies, urges, thoughts, arousal patterns, or behavior. **Hebephilia** refers a sexual interest in young postpubescent children, while **ephebophilia** denotes an interest in children in the mid- to late-adolescent age range. Recent evidence (Seto, 2009) suggests that hebephilia and ephebophilia may be distinct from pedophilia, as individuals who report being preferentially attracted to adolescents show different sexual arousal patterns than do individuals who prefer prepubescent children. Nevertheless, the term **pedophilia** is most frequently used to stand for a sexual interest in children generally.

In the real clinical and forensic world, however, these preferences often form a spectrum. Some pedophiles exclusively prefer children, having no interest in adolescents or adults. Others are attracted to the full younger age spectrum, from preschoolers to high schoolers. The age preference of some pedophiles can be quite narrow, while others have a wider range. Some may prefer children, but will have adult sexual relationships when their preferred object is unavailable. Other men who prefer adults will have sex with children if adult partners are unavailable; these individuals would not necessarily be classified as pedophiles per se, but are willing to use children as sexual objects of opportunity. Still others enjoy fantasies and/or acts of sex equally with children, adolescents, and adults; some of these individuals may have families and a few actually manage to insinuate themselves into fields related to childcare, education, or even child protective services.

Overall, pedophilic men report fewer adult sexual partners than nonpedophilic men, pursue fewer romantic relationships with age peers, and those relationships tend to be generally more lonely and isolative, less emotionally and sexually satisfying (Blanchard et al., 2001; Lang et al., 1990; Seto, 2009). Generalized hypersexuality, substance use, psychosis or other severe mental disorder, some brain syndromes, or revenge against an adult partner are other causes and motives for sex with children. (Seto, 2002, 2008, 2009; Seto & Lalumiere, 2001). Although pedophilia is a male-predominant syndrome, female pedophilia is being increasingly recognized (Denov, 2003; also see below).

Pedophilia: Psychodynamics and Cognitive Styles

While most psychological studies of pedophiles focus on descriptive diagnostic features, very few have attempted to gain a deeper understanding of the psychological dynamics and defense mechanisms that underlie this behavior, that enable an adult to sexually exploit a child. As discussed in Chapter 3, **defense mechanisms** are cognitive strategies that individuals use, often unconsciously, to minimize inner conflict by changing the perception and interpretation of external events and internal motivations (Vaillant, 1994). As noted earlier, a higher rate of antisocial personality is found among sex offenders as a whole, and this subpopulation will typically feel no compunction about exploiting other people, including children, because they have no conscience whose pangs they need to quell. But it is hardly the case that all sex offenders are psychopaths, and many of these latter offenders must attempt to justify their activities to themselves in some way.

Drapeau et al. (2008) undertook such a psychological analysis of men convicted of nonviolent child sexual abuse and found that these subjects tended to utilize less mature defense mechanisms than those used by a control group. They found, for example, that child abusers use less **intellectualization** which employs abstract reasoning to objectify and distance emotionally disturbing thoughts or impulses. They also rely less on **rationalization**, which involves devising plausible-sounding reasons and self-serving excuses for potentially unpleasant motives, feeling, and urges.

These child sex abusers instead tended to utilize more immature defense mechanisms such as **dissociation**, in which the unwanted thought, impulse or feeling is split off and quarantined from consciousness (Perry, 1990): "I didn't know what I was doing." For example, some of the child abusers in the Drapeau et al. (2008) study described how the sexual impulse just came over them, and some described committing the act as if in a kind of trance or dream state. Other abusers relied on **denial** which involves mentally discounting the act itself or at least any negative effects thereof: "I didn't really hurt him; he seemed fine about it."

In other cases, the abuse activity itself represented a form of **displacement**, in which a consciously disavowed feeling or impulse toward one person is unconsciously redirected toward someone else, usually a physically or psychologically safer target (Johnston & Johnston, 1997). One expression of this in Drapeau et al.'s (2008) sample involved a subject reacting to a conflict with an authority figure from his past or present by "taking it out on" a child in a sexually exploitive way. In other cases, the offenders used their sexual relationship with a child more generally to bolster their own sense of control, power, self-worth, and mastery. Still other offenders were seeking love, intimacy, or recognition from a child that they were unable to obtain from adult relationships.

Fantasy was another prominent defense mechanism utilized by this group of child abusers, although, as discussed previously, an active fantasy life is a common feature of almost all sex offenders and a component of healthy sexuality as well. Fantasy is a convenient mental strategy for substitute gratification because the daydreamer can make the story come out any way he likes. In the present sample, this typically involved fantasies in which the abuser's sexual interaction with a child was a means of helping that child awaken their youthful sexuality in a glorious way—a fantasy which obviously contained a great deal of denial and rationalization as well.

A number of Drapeau et al.'s (2008) child sex offenders, as well as in previous studies (Prodgers, 1984; Brennan et al., 1990), employed **splitting**, which involves the mental segmentation of oneself or other people into an all good–all bad dichotomy, instead of seeing people as complex blendings of traits and characteristics; as discussed in Chapter 7, splitting is a prominent feature of certain syndromes, such as borderline personality disorder. Some child abusers who use this defense might describe their victims as pure and perfect works of art whose inner and outer beauty could only be appreciated in the abusers sexual interaction with the child. Alternatively, some abusers might describe their victims as precocious juvenile tempters who malevolently seduced the abuser into having sex with them.

Projective identification involves taking one's own repudiated thoughts, feelings, or impulses and mentally pinning them on someone else as if it were really that person's idea all along. Then, the projector can tell himself that his own behavior is really just a response to that other person (Drapeau et al., 2004a, 2004b, 2008). An adult who is sexually attracted to a child, for example, might tell himself that the child is acting seductively, that the child really wants to have sex with an adult, and that the offender is thus only giving the child what he or she wants.

Finally, some sex abusers in this sample utilized the primitive defense of **acting-out**, which entails giving full vent to one's feelings and impulses, rather than making any attempts at restraint, sometimes even at great risk to the perpetrator. Sometimes, this may involve elements of denial and rationalization as well: "She gave me a hug and started rubbing against me and the next thing I know, we had our clothes off and were doing it; I didn't even have time to think about it."

Evolutionary Theory of Pedophilia

As discussed in Chapter 3, in evolutionary terms, males are naturally pre-disposed to prefer younger females because younger women are more likely to be healthy and they are also more likely not to have borne or to be carrying another male's offspring. Inasmuch as virginity guarantees paternity, the younger the girl, the more likely she is to be the exclusive carrier of the prospective husband's genes; hence the preference for child brides and the numerous rituals surrounding virginity on one's wedding night that are still active in many cultures up to the present day.

This might be a satisfactory explanation in cases of hebephelia (preference for young postpubescent girls), but what about men who are attracted to 7-year-olds? Recall that for most ancestral humans, and even in many societies around the world today, polygamy and child marriage are still the norm. That is, especially in societies where women are considered men's property, or at least subservient to them, daughters are valuable commodities that can be bartered for other goods or privileges within the community, or across communities to cement treaties and alliances or further trade and commerce. Insofar as every community will contain a spectrum of personalities, some men will prefer mostly older or same-age women, most men will be flexible and accept whatever mate they can get, and a few will have a natural predilection for the youngest girls. Since the age of consent is an arbitrary social convention, what might legally be considered child sexual abuse or statutory rape (Chapter 14) in one society might be perfectly legitimate mating in another.

Pedophile Typologies

Recognizing that heterogeneity applies to all criminal classifications, including pedophilic sex offending, a number of typologies in this category have been developed based on clinical and forensic study of different pedophile types.

Holmes & Holmes (1996) developed a typology of what they called **child molesters**, based on the work of Burgess et al. (1978), as well as their own observations.

Situational child molester. This offender does not have a preferential interest in children per se, but will molest them as targets of opportunity if other sexual outlets are unavailable. This offender will also target the elderly, the disabled, and other available victims as the situation allows. The situational child molester is further divided into four subtypes. The **regressed pedophile** can engage in sex with adults, but many molest children, usually females, in response to some ego-threatening situation in which he is likely to regard the child as a "pseudoadult." The **morally indiscriminate pedophile** also has sex with adults, but may forcefully or coercively abuse children as a way of getting his thrills by controlling helpless victims, which he fantasizes about with the aid of bondage-related pornography. The **sexually indiscriminate molester** also has no particular preference for children but abuses them, often including his own children or stepchildren, as part of a more generally sexually omnivorous pattern involving a wide variety of common and unusual sexual practices and partners. The **naïve/inadequate child molester** suffers from some form of brain syndrome, intellectual deficiency, or mental disorder that makes him unable to understand the wrongfulness of his actions and/or control his impulses, and he will abuse children because he is regarded as too weird or undesirable by peers to obtain sex through the usual social channels.

Preferential child molester. This offender does prefer children to adults as sexual objects, and this category is divided into three subtypes. The **seductive molester** courts and "grooms" his young victims with gifts and attention. He is likely to rationalize that he and the child have a special relationship based on mutual affection. He may be concurrently molesting several children, and is the least likely of the three subtypes to use violence. The **fixated molester** gets his name from the concept that his sexuality has been fixated at a primitive stage of psychosexual development where he finds children sexually attractive because he is, psychosexually, essentially a child himself, often appearing emotionally immature, and socially inept. He, too, is not likely to physically harm his victims, but slowly wins them over by a gradual process of seduction; often, physical affection and intimacy with these children is as important to him as actual sex. He also may be abusing a number of children at the same time, and often makes a project of this, moving around to obtain victims and utilizing the Internet to contact others.

The **sadistic pedophile** is the most violent and dangerous type of child molester because, much like the adult serial rapist (Chapter 14) or serial killer (Chapter 10), his erotic gratification is based on the fusion of sexual arousal and sadistic aggression. This offender's crimes are premeditated and ritualized, and he may have a varied criminal record involving other types of violent crimes. Typically preferring young boys, he will stalk and abduct them, then enjoy torturing, sexually assaulting, and mutilating the children, taking maximal pleasure from the fear, pain, and horror of his young victims. To heighten the torment, he may tell the children that their parents hate them and ordered this punishment. Typically, the child dies as a result of the abuse, but in some cases may be left alive, often with some degree of mutilation or permanent disability. This offender typically moves from place to place to perpetrate his crimes. Essentially, this is a serial rapist or serial killer with children as the victims, and thus truly represents every parent's worst nightmare.

While the categories in Holmes & Holmes' (1996) child molester typology may seem overly partialized and overlapping, they seem to boil down to three basic conceptual types: (1) the sexual omnivore who will have sex with anyone he can, adult or child; (2) the preferential child molester who fancies some kind of special relationship with each of the children he has sex with, often "grooming" them over time; (3) the predatory sadistic child abuser who enjoys carrying out acts of sexual violence on children, often eventuating in their death: essentially a serial rapist/serial killer of children.

Pedophiles, Child Pornography, and Offender Risk

In the United States, the **Prosecutorial Remedies and Other Tools to end the Exploitation of Children Today (PROTECT) Act of 2003** makes it a crime to possess, manufacture or distribute pornography containing visual depictions of sexual acts engaged in either by real children or computer generated images that are indistinguishable from real children (Beech et al., 2008). In addition, individual states have their own anti-child pornography laws.

BOX 15.2. TEXTUAL HARASSMENT
High Schoolers Accused of Sending Naked Pictures to Each Other

Greensburg, PA:
    Three teenage girls who allegedly sent nude or semi-nude cell phone pictures of themselves, and three male classmates in a Greensburg Salem High School who received them, are charged with child pornography . . ."It's very dangerous," said [an investigator]. "Once it's on a cell phone, that image can be put on the Internet where everyone in the world can get access to that juvenile's picture. You don't realize what you are doing until it's already done."

Nevertheless, advances in Internet technology, including high-speed access, digital audiovisual recording, and mobile phone technology, has opened a whole new world for pedophiles and purveyors of **child pornography** (Beech et al., 2008; O'Connell, 2001). Sex offenders can use the Internet to receive and transmit images for personal use or sale, to set up or join existing virtual networks and clubs of like-minded individuals with a sexual interest in children, and to troll for young victims via legitimate social networking groups (e.g., Facebook) or Internet chat rooms (Durkin, 1997). As part of the grooming process, pedophiles often use downloaded pornographic images to desensitize and normalize the intended sexual behavior: "See, plenty of kids do it" (Lanning, 2001).

Sexually oriented images of children freely available on the Internet range from commercial ads for children's clothing, to "child modeling" sites depicting children in underwear or swimwear, to "child erotica" images of nude but not sexually posed children, to grossly explicit sex acts involving "virtual children," i.e., drawn or computer-generated images of children–all legal in many jurisdictions. Less commonly available child pornographic images may include depictions of sexually posed nude children, sexual touching or simulated sex between clothed or naked children, sex acts including sexual intercourse with children by other children or adults, or sadistic sex acts with actual children–all illegal in most jurisdictions. Victims can vary in age from toddlers to teenagers. In prosecuting such **kiddie porn** cases, it is sometimes a judgment call as to what kinds of images qualify as illegal child pornography. Child pornography collections can run into the hundreds or thousands of images and videos, often organized, categorized, and cross-referenced by the collector (Beech et al., 2008; Taylor, 2003).

One important question concerns the relationship of Internet child pornography use to actual assaults on children. Does repeated exposure to sexualized child images prime the abuser to go out and find a living victim, or do practicing pedophiles reinforce their desires and habits by viewing these images in between acts of abuse? We know, for example, that many individuals arrested for sexual abuse of children have extensive child pornography collections (Dobson, 2003; Wellard, 2001), and some of these individuals use these images in preparation for, or during, the commission of their acts (Condron & Nutter, 1988; Nutter & Kearns, 1993). However, since this is, by nature, a secretive and insular group, we have no way of knowing how many individuals quietly and regularly use Internet and other child pornography and never assault a living child (Sullivan & Beech, 2004), although evidence suggests that masturbatory sex with child porn images is a prelude to active exploitation of children (Calder, 2004), just as masturbatory fantasy often precedes sex crimes of many types.

Recall that, technically, pedophilia is a diagnosis, not a crime, and as a psychological diagnosis it refers to fantasies as well as actions. According to

DSM-IV-TR, pedophilia can be diagnosed from information regarding the subject's sexual thoughts, fantasies, urges, or arousal patterns, with or without actual behavior (Seto, 2008, 2009). In fact, criminal activity by pedophiles is most likely to involve possession of illegal child pornography, and one study found that more than half of these offenders had no known physical contact with children (Seto, 2006). In fact, there is some evidence that greater collection and use of child pornography is a better indicator of pedophilic preference than number of actual sexual contacts with children (Riegel, 2004; Seto et al., 2006).

As with the relationship of violent video games to school violence (Chapter 12) or that of sexually sadistic adult pornography to serial rape and murder (Chapters 10 and 14), no doubt far more individuals utilize child pornography in their sexual fantasies and autoerotic behavior than actually go out and assault real children. The issue is complicated, however, by the fact that whereas most adult sadistic and violent entertainment is legal to own and use privately, the possession of explicit child pornography is a crime in itself. Thus, men with pedophilic urges who might be content to satisfy themselves in front of their computer screen and never accost a living child could nevertheless be prosecuted as criminals for simply possessing their illegal images. In other cases, pedophiles avail themselves of technically legal soft-core Internet child images, or may even utilize commercially available images from clothing ads and children's magazines.

Although the risk posed by pedophiles with no known history of sexual contacts with children is unknown, Seto (2009) hypothesizes that child pornography offenders with a greater number of images, a higher ratio of child to adult images, images depicting younger children, and images including both male and female children are more likely to be at risk for seeking live sexual contact with children. One might additionally hypothesize a relationship between explicitness of images (child nudity versus actual sex acts with children) and risk for live sex offending, but this has not been addressed in research.

In fact, the risk for criminal offending against children may be related more to general propensity to antisocial behavior than it is to sexual proclivity per se. Note from Chapter 14 that studies wishing to compare violent vs. nonviolent sex offenders will typically put rapists in the first group and so-called "child molesters" in the second, assuming a generally low rate of violence in the latter group. Yet, in terms of recidivism, pedophilic sex offenders are more likely to sexually reoffend than are nonpedophilic rapists (Seto, 2009). In one study (Seto & Eke, 2005), child pornography offenders with a prior criminal history of any kind were more likely to commit a contact sexual offense, or any offense, during the follow-up period. This suggests that it is those pedophiles who, in addition to their sexual preference, are more impulsive, callous, risk-taking, substance-using, and disregarding of laws and social conventions who pose the greatest risk of sexually contacting real children. That is, antisocial personality is a risk factor for crossing the line from a pornographic image to the actual sexual abuse of a child (Harris et al., 2003; Seto, 2008; Seto et al., 2004), consistent with the general finding in the psychological and criminological literature that mental disorders per se have a weak relationship with criminal behavior unless associated with a psychopathic or antisocial personality (Chapters 5, 8).

The issue is further complicated by the fact that some pedophiles press their computers into double-duty: accessing child pornographic images and also searching for young victims through Internet chat rooms and social networking sites. Many of these offenders engage in a protracted grooming process online, much as they would with face-to-face victims, where the chat becomes more and more explicit, pornographic and personal images may be exchanged, and the perpetrator tries to win over the confidence of his young target until, finally, a meeting can be arranged. Sometimes, but not always, the offender will disguise his identifying demographics, but usually he will present himself pretty much as he is (e.g., paunchy, balding, middle-aged "father figure"), if only to prevent shock and disappointment on the part of the target at their anticipated first meeting. However, the victims of this kind of online recruitment tend to be somewhat older, typically adolescents, because these subjects are more likely to have unmonitored access to computers (now, also cell phones), and are more likely to be inherently sexually curious than prepubescent children (Wang et al., 2005; Wolak et al., 2004, 2008).

Like most paraphilias, however, the neurodevelopmental sexual nature of pedophilia makes it especially resistant to change. Under legal duress, pedophiles can control their *behavior*–i.e., not approach children and not download illegal images–but their *preferences* are unlikely to change (Cantor et al., 2008, Seto, 2008, 2009). Thus, the goals of intervention with identified pedophiles are typically to prevent access to victims by restricting their residence and movement, to try to reduce sexual urges through chemical means, and to encourage or mandate them to attend specially designed abstinence support programs similar to the ones used by substance abusers (see Box 15.3).

Child Pornography Collector Typologies

Even before the age of the Internet, Hartman et al. (1984) classified collectors of sexualized child images (mostly photographs, videotapes, or drawn images at that time) into four types, which can be easily applied to online collectors today. **Closet collectors** are secretive about their collection and are usually not interested in abusing actual children. **Isolated collectors** accumulate images that impel and reinforce their sexual contact with real children. Some of these images (photos, videos) may involve their own sexual activities with the children, as souvenirs to fantasize over. **Cottage collectors** belong to pedophile clubs or file-sharing networks whose members trade and share their collections, partly to obtain new images and partly for the appearance of validation and normalization it gives their activities ("If so many people do it, how bad can it be?"). **Commercial collectors** turn their hobby into a business; they have seen the financial benefits of their collection and exploit those benefits for profit.

A more recent typology of Internet child porn users by Sullivan & Beech (2004) distinguishes between three types. **Type 1 offenders** collect images as part of a larger pattern of sexual offending, which includes contact with actual children. **Type 2 offenders** collect images to satisfy a growing sexual interest in children, which may cross over to actual physical contact with children. **Type 3 offenders** access images out of curiosity or to gratify a full or partial interest in children, but these individuals refrain from attempting to make physical contact.

A third typology is Alexy et al.'s (2005) categorization of Internet child pornography users into three types. **Traders** are hobbyists or business people who trade or sell images online and thereby feed the market for Internet child porn. **Travelers** use the Internet to identify potential child victims and lure them into meeting them for sexual activity. **Trader-travelers** essentially play both roles, trafficking in pornographic images and using the Internet to snare young victims.

Overall, these typologies appear to broadly categorize Internet child pornography offenders into three main groups: (1) those who access child porn images out of curiosity or as part of their typically broader web search for images, including adults and adolescents. Some of these web surfers may prefer child images, but are least likely to cross the line into committing contact offenses with real children; (2) those who do victimize children and use child porn images to fuel their pre-abuse fantasy and/or to locate and seduce potential victims; and (3) those who traffic in child porn images for profit, including those who make their own images and videos using children. Note that these groups can overlap, e.g., the porn trader and collector who sells some of his images and keeps others for his own use.

FEMALE CHILD SEX OFFENDERS

Description and Demographics

As noted above, sexual abuse of children is mostly a man's crime; men commit 95 percent of all sex crimes in the United States (Finkelhor et al., 1990). Although cases of sexual abuse of children by women have been documented since the 1930s (Bender & Blau, 1937), cultural resistance has accounted for this crime being largely neglected and overlooked (Denov, 2001). It is only in the last few decades that the phenomenon of **female child sex offenders,** or **FCSOs,** has been more widely acknowledged and studied within psychology and criminology (Gannon & Rose, 2008; Strickland, 2008).

The true prevalence of female sexual abuse of children is unknown (Strickland, 2008). What we do know is that, although the average age of female child sex abusers appears to be in the range of 26–36 years, women of all ages may sexually abuse children. Younger women, some who may scarcely be more than children themselves, and older women ("auntie" or "grandma" types) may be overlooked as suspects or treated outside the criminal justice system when detected (Vandiver & Walker, 2002). Victims range in age from infants to adolescents (Briggs & Hawkins, 1995; Ogilvie & Daniluk, 1995).

There appears to be no consensus as to whether male or female children are more vulnerable to sexual abuse by adult women (Gannon & Rose, 2008). However, in one study of adults who had been sexually abused as children (Finkelhor et al., 1990), 17 percent of the male victims in the sample reported having been abused as a child by a woman and 1 percent of the female victims reported being abused by a female perpetrator, suggesting that adult female abuse of male children is far more common.

Like their male counterparts, female child sex offenders may pick victims of convenience or opportunity, may be family caregivers, or may take jobs that involve spending time with children, such as teachers or day care center workers. In the latter cases, many female abusers are known to their victims (Faller, 1987, 1995; Finkelhor & Russell, 1984; Finkelhor & Williams, 1988; Fromuth & Conn, 1997; Gannon & Rose, 2008; Grayston & DeLuca, 1999; Hunter et al., 1993; Kaufman et al., 1995; Kercher & McShane, 1984; Lewis & Stanley, 2000; Moulden et al., 2007; Vandiver & Walker, 2002). However, unlike male sex offenders, who usually operate secretively and alone, female abusers are far more likely to commit their abuse in the company of a male co-perpetrator (Grayston & De Luca, 1999; Green & Kaplan, 1994; Kaplan & Green, 1995; Nathan & Ward, 2001; Vandiver, 2006; Vandiver & Walker, 2002). In general, female sex offenders tend to use less physical force and rely more on seduction or coercion, compared to male sex offenders, and they are also less likely than males to use alcohol or drugs at the time of their offense (Gannon & Rose, 2008; Kubik et al., 2002; Lewis & Stanley, 2000).

Developmental Factors

Developmentally, female sex offenders tend to come from more deprived backgrounds than nonsexual female offenders, having often been subject to poor living conditions, food deprivation, and lack of medical care. They frequently have suffered extreme emotional, verbal, physical, and sexual abuse within their own families of origin (Fromuth & Conn, 1997; Gannon & Rose, 2008; Green & Kaplan, 1994; Lewis & Stanley, 2000; McCarty, 1986; Nathan & Ward, 2001; Strickland, 2008).

Psychological traits, disorders, and developmental dynamics associated with female child sex offenders include: emotional immaturity and dependency; low self-esteem; physical and/or psychological abuse as children and/or adults, including domestic violence (Chapter 17): social isolation and impaired intimacy; sexual dysfunction; deficient or confused interpersonal boundaries; suppressed needs and repressed anger; and substance abuse. Female child sexual offenders express greater feelings of being victimized and mistreated throughout life and view themselves as powerless to change their lives. A combination of these factors may have the effect of stunting the normal developmental pathways needed to build appropriate coping and social skills, healthy personality organization, communication skills, social relationships, and feelings of self-worth. Such low self-esteem and emotional isolation may especially characterize female child sex offenders who co-perpetrate with men, many of whom report enhanced closeness with their male partner gained from "sharing" the experience of child sex abuse. In general, the sexually abusive behavior may represent an attempt to gain some power and control and/or receive affection and acceptance not available elsewhere (Ford, 2006; Gannon & Rose, 2008; Green & Kaplan, 1994; Hunter & Matthews, 1997; Matthews, 1993; McCarty, 1986; Miccio-Fonseca, 2000; Nathan & Ward, 2002; O'Connor, 1987; Saradjian, 1996; Strickland, 2008; Travin et al., 1990).

Although, as noted in other chapters, childhood physical and sexual abuse are common and nonspecific factors in the histories of many types of criminals, there may be some specific ways this history affects a woman's propensity to become a sex offender herself. For example, sexual abuse of females may impair self-worth and contribute to adult role confusion, relationship difficulties, and sexual dysfunction. Many women who have been abused in childhood later exhibit emotional role-reversal behavior with their children, in which they depend on their children to meet their emotional needs (Gelinas, 1983; Laumann et al., 1999; Maltz, 2003; Strickland, 2008).

Personality and Psychopathology

Diagnostically, features of borderline and paranoid personality characterize many female sexual offenders, as they do with offenders of many types. Avoidant personality is found in some samples, but not others. Surprisingly, little evidence for psychopathy or antisocial personality has been found in samples of female sex offenders, despite this being a common feature of male sex offenders. This suggests that the psychodynamics of at least some female sex abusers of children are different from that of many males. However, female child sex offenders may share with their male counterparts a tendency toward impulsivity and impaired emotional self-regulation, which are key features of both borderline and antisocial personality disorder. They also are as likely as men to rationalize that the child really seduced them and/or to minimize any harmful effects to the child, for example, asserting that it made the child more "mature," or regarding lack of penetration as "not really sex" (Gannon & Plascheck, 2006; Gannon & Rose, 2008; Green & Kaplan, 1994; Nathan & Ward, 2001; Quinsey et al., 1995; Strickland, 2008).Ward, 2000; Ward & Keenan, 1996; Ward et al., 1998).

Unlike their male counterparts, however, pedophilia, in the sense of deviant sexual interests and urges per se, appears to be far less frequently found in female child sex abusers, as compared to males; for females, intimacy, boundary, and self-worth issues seem to predominate as motives for their offending (Gannon & Rose, 2008; Grayston & De Luca, 1999; Nathan & Ward, 2001, 2002). Finally, brain injury, mental retardation, and/or other type of cognitive impairment may sometimes further compromise these women's emotional stability, coping skills, and self-control (Faller, 1987, 1995).

Female Child Sex Offender Typologies

As with other diagnostic and criminological classifications, a number of typologies of female child sex offenders have been offered. Matthews et al. (1991) propose three main categories, with a fourth added by Gannon & Rose (2008).

Predisposed (intergenerational) female child sex offender. This offender perpetuates the cycle of abuse from her own childhood by inflicting it on other children, often members of her own family or even her own children. Her own abuse as a child seems to have reinforced an eroticized relationship between sex and adult-child affection or, alternatively, this offender may have at least partially inherited her pedophilic urges from the abusing parent.

Teacher/lover female child sex offender. This adult female offender typically initiates sexual conduct with an adolescent boy, often a student in her high school class. She is the most likely offender to rationalize that the boy enjoys the contact and that he in fact may have initiated it, and to regard it more along the lines of an adult "affair." This type of female offender does not usually report a personal history of sexual victimization; rather the motivation appears to center around her own youthful desirability and her power over male sexuality.

Male-coerced female child sex offender. This woman commits her sexual abuse of a child under the influence, intimidation, or force of a male partner. Her traits of passivity, dependence, low self-worth, and feelings of powerlessness make her especially susceptible to the influence of a dominant male. The question, of course, is what degree of coercion is necessary to compel this woman to commit the acts and if these really are done against her will or at least without enjoyment.

Psychologically disturbed female child sex offender. This woman carries out her abuse under the influence of, or at least in the presence of, some form of organic brain syndrome or severe mental disorder. However, this says nothing about the specific motives that may drive the offending.

Vandiver & Kercher (2004) propose a typology of female child sex offenders with six categories:

Heterosexual nurturer. These female sex offenders average 30 years of age and tend to victimize young adolescent boys. These are similar to the teacher/lover category in the previous typology. These women romanticize their relationship with the boy, regarding it as an adult love affair, and are usually motivated by a desire for intimacy and to feel attractive, sometimes in response to unmet sexual and emotional needs in their adult relationships.

Noncriminal homosexual offender. These women initiate sexual relations with young adolescent girls, sometimes acting with a male accomplice, sometimes on their own. It is termed "noncriminal" because the perpetrator's motive is primarily romantic, not exploitive, however, the act will be illegal if the younger partner is underage.

Homosexual criminal offender. This abuser victimizes teenage girls for primarily economic reasons, i.e., pornography and/or prostitution. They may or may not work with one or more male and female accomplices and their offending is part of a general pattern of criminal activity.

Female sexual predator. These women are often under age 30 and have committed a relatively high number of sexual offenses against mainly young adolescent boys, and their sexual abuse occurs in the context of a wide range of other exploitive and criminal behavior.

Young adult child exploiter. These women are somewhat younger than those in the other categories, typically in their mid-twenties, and tend to victimize male or female younger, prepubescent children of grade school age, often including members of their own families.

Aggressive homosexual offender. These women primarily victimize adolescent females and may also be likely to commit a sexual assault against an adult.

What these typologies seem to be describing in common are categories of female child sex offenders that include: (1) true sexual predators of young adolescents; (2) a romanticized relationship with a young teen to compensate for unmet needs for intimacy and approval; (3) career criminals who exploit children and adolescents for profit; (4) mentally disordered offenders; and (5) female sex offender under the influence or coercion of a male partner.

BOX 15.3. SEXUAL PREDATOR LAWS AND SEX OFFENDER REGISTRIES: PROTECTING THE INNOCENT OR MORAL PANIC?

Beginning in the early 1990s with Washington and Minnesota, 16 states now have **sexually violent predator (SVP) laws**, and these are currently being considered in the legislatures of several more states. Through the process of **civil commitment**, SVP laws allow the continued incarceration of sex offenders beyond the expiration of their criminal sentences if they are judged to be mentally disordered and to constitute a danger to the public. SVP laws require four basic criteria for committing a sexual offender to additional confinement: (1) the presence of a mental disorder; (2) an elevated risk of future sexual offending; (3) a causal connection between the mental disorder and the sexual misconduct; and (4) the commitment is for purposes of treatment (Prentky et al., 2006).

In general, the law allows for civil commitment of offenders deemed to be dangerous to self or others, for the protection of its citizens and even from oneself. However, as Prentky et al. (2006) point out, in most standard commitment proceedings, the legal actions occur within a short time interval of the most recent dangerous act, typically a matter of hours or days, e.g., the police pick up a psychotic homeless person who is threatening passersby and bring him to a hospital. In the case of SVP commitment, determinations are being made about the imminent future sexual dangerousness of a person who may have been incarcerated for decades and therefore whose last actual criminal act is in the remote past. Mental health professionals have long lamented the weak predictive power of clinical dangerousness assessment over more than a few months' time, yet decisions are being made to continue to lock up offenders who haven't offended in years.

continued

BOX 15.3.—*Continued*

Another problem is the requirement of a diagnosis of mental disorder that is causally connected to the putative risk of future offending. As with assessments for criminal competency and insanity evaluations (Chapter 1), the mere presence of a mental disorder is not sufficient: there must be a direct connection between the malady and the malfeasance. This often results in clinical-forensic gymnastics as mental health professionals scramble to connect the evidentiary dots. Syndromes that have been cited as grounds for continued confinement under SVP laws include paraphilias, impulse control disorders, ADHD, conduct disorder, antisocial personality disorder, other personality disorders; sexual dysfunction disorders, and mood disorders (Abracen & Looman, 2006; Ahlmeyer et al., 2003; Becker et al., 2003; Dunsieth et al., 2004; Grant, 2005; Jackson et al., 2004; Kafka, 2003; Kafka & Hennen, 2002; Kafka & Prentky, 1998; Kavoussi et al., 1988; Levenson, 2004; Zander, 2005; O'Connor et al., 1998; O'Donohue et al., 2000; Quinsey et al., 1981; Raymond et al., 1999). Since most individuals with these disorders do not commit crimes, the burden should be on the state to prove that these diagnoses—even if valid—would directly cause this offender, at this point in time, to go out and commit future sex crimes.

Yet, states rarely have difficulty meeting sufficient evidentiary requirements to continue an offender's incarceration under the SVP laws. Part of this may relate to the understanding and clinical experience that certain types of offenders are indeed driven by a powerful impulse to commit their acts of choice, no matter how much time has passed (Chapters 8, 10, 18). According to Douard (2007), however, many of these decisions may be less a matter of valid clinical-forensic predictive correlations than due to the visceral sense of revulsion that average citizens—and many mental health and criminal justice professionals—have toward those who commit sex crimes, especially crimes against children. In this view, SVP statutes are essentially punitive expressions of societal disgust and fear of contamination by offenders who force us to confront the darkest regions of our collective sexual natures. By medicalizing the sin, we give ourselves justification for hating the sinner and expunging him from our presence. Even the term *predator* connotes a certain relentless animality, further reducing the human status of the offender to a kind of sexually rapacious werewolf, fit only to live in a cage.

Many would argue that, as unjust as it might seem to indiscriminately lock sex offenders up and throw away the key, certainly, we shouldn't just hand that key over to a clearly dangerous predator and let him stroll out the door to offend anew. In addition to extended incarceration, many countries, including the U.S. maintain **sex offender registries** in which released felons who have been convicted of sex crimes, especially crimes against children, remain in a data base that tracks their whereabouts and severely limits where they can live and who they can associate with. While the rationale for this is, again, protection of a vulnerable citizenry, what happens when these statutes are applied to the very persons they were designed to protect, i.e., children? As we've seen, something as hormonally knuckleheaded as sending a phone image of your own pubes to one of your 10th grade friends can get you arrested and prosecuted for child pornography.

But juveniles who commit isolated instances of sex offenses, even ones far more serious than sexting, may not, according to Chaffin (2008), be at any increased risk for persistent lifelong sex crime careers, and we may be prematurely damning these kids to an unfairly truncated life. Indeed, the law's response to juvenile sex offenders seems exactly opposite of that to other forms of juvenile crime, where every effort is made not to stigmatize and harshly punish acts that would be major crimes if committed by adults, but are given the benefit of the doubt as immature indiscretions when committed by children. The rationale of the juvenile justice system as a whole (Chapters 1, 19) is that youthful behavior patterns are typically more fluid and malleable than those of adults, more amenable to treatment, and that, therefore, many of these youngsters are worthy of a second chance.

In fact, the available psychological and criminological evidence suggests that young adolescents with sexual behavior problems pose no special risk for future sex offending, especially if they are afforded proper treatment (Alexander, 1999; Caldwell, 2002; Carpentier et al., 2006; Jones, 2007). The chief risk factor for any kind of repeat sex offending, child or adult, appears to be a history of any kind of chronic, persistent antisocial behavior, as it is with most types of criminal offending (Chapters 3, 8, 19), and in one large-scale study (Caldwell, 2007), 85 percent of all future sex crimes committed by the entire released juvenile delinquent population were committed by former *nonsexual* delinquents, including all 3 sexual homicides as well as all 54 nonsexual homicides.

Thus, in this view, what drives the get-tough policies on youthful sex offenders, is, again, the sense of **moral panic**: if we don't "crack down" on these precocious perverts, they'll grow into unstoppable sexual monsters who prey on us all. As with most criminal behavior, there is probably a particularly antisocial subset of youthful sex offenders who, if undeterred, will grow into adult persistent predators, but the evidence so far seems to be that most kids who commit isolated sexual offenses are best served by a moderate dose of criminal justice (i.e., not "coddled" or "let get away with it"), coupled with adequate treatment. For the worst of the worst—repeat offenders, especially of brutal crimes—special measures may apply, including stiffer penalties, extended civil commitment, and sex offender registries. Indeed, why is there no "persistent (nonsexual) violent offender" registry for armed robbers or gangbangers?

CHILD CARE PROVIDER SEX OFFENDERS

As noted earlier, one efficient way for a child sex abuser to gain access to victims is to secure the kind of employment that involves children, and research shows that many of these offenses occur in the context of these positions (Colton & Vanstone, 1998; Fehrenbach et al., 1986; Margolin, 1991; Moulden et al., 2007; Sullivan & Beech, 2002; Wasserman et al., 1986).

For example, one large-scale study of high-profile child sex abuse cases in schools and daycare facilities in the United States (Finkelhor & Williams, 1988) found that facility directors, teachers, nonprofessional staff such as teaching aides and volunteers, as well as family members or friends of the employees, accounted for the majority of the abuse. Most of these employees were female and about half acted in collaboration with another perpetrator. Female abusers tended to have higher education, greater social stability, and less history of other deviant behavior than male perpetrators. There were slightly more boy than girl victims and these children were quite young, in the range of 3 and 4 years old, as is typical for daycare settings of this type.

Most offenses took place in private and secluded areas of the facility, such as bathrooms and offices, and were most likely to occur during nap times or during other times of the day when staff presence was low or there were few other children around. The most typical sexual acts perpetrated were fondling and touching, although a number of children experienced oral-genital contact, penetration, or were forced to have sex with other children (Finkelhor & Williams, 1988). Other studies have found that the younger the offender, the more violent the sexual abuse, with adolescent caretakers committing the most serious abuse. Despite the predominance of female caretakers in child day care centers, males still commit a disproportionate number of sexual victimizations in these settings (Finkelhor & Russell, 1984; Margolin, 1991; Margolin & Craft, 1989, 1990; Mouldin et al., 2007).

The most common circumstance surrounding caretaker child sexual abuse appears to involve the child's regular babysitter, who typically is trusted and being paid by the parents. The perpetrators tend to be high school-age teens and the victims preschoolers or kindergarteners. One-third of the abusers are women, who offend against both boys and girls, as compared to men who target mainly girls. The second most common scenario involves a friend, partner, or family member of the regular caretaker who is filling in while the regular caretaker is out. Other situations involve live-in caretakers, friends of the child's family, abuse that takes place during sleepovers at another child's house, and when the regular caretaker is unavailable and the parent leaves the child with a relatively unfamiliar substitute. Most of the offenders in these groups are male and many are found to have had prior sexual abuse histories (Margolin, 1991; Moulden et al., 2007).

Unlike many other child sex abusers, who use charm, seduction, bribery and other grooming techniques to lure their victims into sex, caretaker offenders tend to be more authoritarian and controlling and to use their familiarity with the child to emotionally manipulate and entrap the victim. Also, unlike most child molesters who operate alone, caretaker offenders are more likely to work with one or more accomplices in planning and carrying out the sexual abuse; this is especially the case with female abusers, who often work with a male partner (Faller, 1995; Finkelhor & Russell, 1984; Finkelhor & Williams, 1988; Gallagher, 1999; Kaufman et al., 1995; Moulden et al., 2007; Sloan, 1988).

Siblings, other family members, or teenage family friends are often employed as babysitters, and studies estimate that about a third of child sexual abuse in caretaker settings is perpetrated by juveniles (Davis & Leitenberg, 1987; Johnson, 1989; Moulden et al., 2007). Most perpetrators are male, and many come from dysfunctional families, characterized by substance abuse, sexualized behavior in caregivers, emotionally distant or intrusive relationships with parents, and physical, emotional, and/or sexual abuse. Many abusers are psychosocially inept or uncomfortable with same-aged peers and gravitate toward younger children, first as playmates, but later crossing the line into sexual abuse as the boundaries between friendship and a sexualized relationship begin to blur (Becker, 1998; Moulden et al., 2007; O'Brien & Bera, 1986).

SEX ABUSE BY CLERGY

It is especially tragic when one comes to feel betrayed by the very person who is supposed to represent one's entire body of faith and worldview. During the past several decades, the Roman Catholic Church has been shaken by a series of scandals involving apparently widespread sexual abuse committed by clergy in many countries, but focusing on the United States. In addition, other religious denominations are not immune (Neustein, 2009; Plante, 2004; Plante & Aldridge, 2005; White & Terry, 2008).

Description and Demographics

In the United States, it is estimated that 4 percent of the total number of Catholic priests, over four thousand in all, may have sexually victimized over ten thousand children during the past 52 years, with the majority of the abuse reaching a peak in the 1970s and declining over the succeeding decades (John Jay College of Criminal Justice, 2004). The majority of the abuse consists of the touching and fondling of teenage boys. This report does not address the unknown number of cases of sexual exploitation of adults by clergy. Finally, sexual abuse of parishioners appears to be a widespread phenomenon across religious denominations, including Protestant, Jewish, Muslim, and Buddhist clergy (Disch & Avery, 2001; Fogler et al., 2008; Francis & Turner, 1995; Friedman, 2009; Neustein, 2009; Plante, 1999; Plante & Daniels,

2004; Richards, 2004; Ruzicka, 1997; Silberg & Dallam, 2009; Young & Griffith, 1995).

Psychology of Clergy Child Sex Abusers

Despite the preferential abuse of adolescent boys found in this population, less than half of Catholic priests and seminarians self-identify as homosexual in confidential surveys (Cozzens, 2002; Wills, 2000), and, in general, there is no evidence to suggest that homosexual men are more likely to commit sexual crimes with minors than heterosexual men (Plante & Daniels, 2004). With regard to victim age, approximately 2 percent of priests could be described as pedophiles, i.e., have a sexual interest in prepubescent children, with an additional 4 percent regarded as ephebophiles, i.e., sexual interest in adolescents (Sipe, 1990, 1995). Whereas some of these priests report being equally attracted to children or adults, others exclusively prefer children (Groth & Oliveri, 1989). Some authorities (Plante & Daniels, 2004; Sipe, 1990) believe that the Catholic Church's decades-long "don't ask, don't tell" policy has led to the creation of a quiet gay subculture in the priesthood.

Psychological studies of priests who sexually abuse children have found elevated indices of depression, low energy, addiction problems, constricted range of emotions, overcontrolled hostility, difficulties with authority, defensive coping, repressive cognitive style, and, in some cases, neuropsychological signs of cognitive dysfunction. These abusers tend to be mistrustful, isolative, angry, and resentful, yet they repress, deny, or minimize their hostility. They often feel misunderstood, impatient with others, burdened by responsibility, and show little regard for the values and attitudes of other people. Developmentally, these men often report chaotic family backgrounds and disturbed preordainment personal histories, including physical or sexual abuse and/or psychiatric diagnoses involving themselves and/or family members (Blanchard, 1991; Haywood et al., 1996; Lothstein et al., 1999; Plante & Aldridge, 2005; Plante et al., 1996; Robinson et al., 1994). None of these features is specific to any particular group, but may suggest a chronic sense of narcissistic entitlement and failure to get their needs for admiration met through their clerical positions, which may be expressed in inappropriately intimate and exploitive relationships with youthful parishioners.

In an interesting interpretation, White & Terry (2008) have compared the priestly subculture of the Roman Catholic Church with that of many police departments, including features of frequent isolated working conditions, division of labor with specialized units, and limited career mobility, along with the valuing of such traits as autonomy, integrity, duty, virtue, and confidentiality. Both groups are expected to behave as models of honor and righteousness that people can look up to, and to put aside personal problems to protect and serve their respective constituents. Thus, the pressure to be near-perfect may build in some vulnerable individuals to the point where they either "crack" and develop some form of mental disorder, or project their frustrations outward in the form of financial or sexual abuse of certain members of the very flock they are supposed to protect. This may be why "bad priests" inspire the same mix of anger, revulsion, and betrayal as "bad cops" (Miller, 2006d).

BOX 15.4. HOW TO PREVENT INSTITUTIONAL CHILD SEX ABUSE

The clergy, day care center, and other child sex abuse scandals of recent years have prompted calls for measures to prevent these offenses from occurring in the future. What can institutions do to minimize the risk of victimization of children by those very persons entrusted with their care? A useful set of recommendations comes from the work of Carcara (2009), who notes that sexual predators naturally gravitate to employment settings where fewer child protective measures are in place. Organizations such as the 4-H Club and Boys and Girls Clubs of America have already developed policies and programs to counteract the perception of children as "soft targets." Unfortunately, many religious institutions are still lagging behind. The following are benchmark policies and procedures that organizations can adopt and adapt to their own individual settings.

- Establish a standardized application and hiring process for all clergy, heath care workers, educators, institutional employees, and volunteers, including thorough background checks, waiting periods, and probationary periods.
- Establish a mechanism for oversight and accountability, including a designated safety-management officer or similar position with the authority to enforce policies.
- Institute training for all personnel in safety-related precautions and procedures, including identification standards, drop-off and pick-up procedures, bathroom protocols, and chaperones for away trips and overnight events.
- Restrict access of unauthorized persons to children, including nonsanctioned workers, noncustodial parents, older youth or other volunteers in the children's ministry, or any other strangers.
- Enhance visibility of activities through environmental design (windowed rooms, intercom systems) and/or physical presence (employee monitoring, unannounced drop-ins).
- Encourage staff awareness of signs of abuse or other unwarranted activity.
- Encourage confidential reporting of abuse by concerned employees or others, and follow up with a fair but rigorous investigation of all complaints.

SUMMARY AND CONCLUSIONS

The sexual exploitation and abuse of children is driven by the same type of powerful compulsive urges that motivate many other acts of sex and violence. Human sexuality is astoundingly diverse, expressed clinically in the psychological cataloguing of various types of **paraphilias**. One of these, **pedophilia**, a sexual interest in children, is technically not illegal if limited to fantasy, but is a prosecutable crime if carried out with real minors. Even within this group, there are different types of pedophiles with different underlying psychodynamics, motives, and behavior patterns. Evidence of brain impairment has been found in some child sex offenders, but the patterns identified are not specific to this syndrome. **Child pornography** by itself never turned a nonpedophile into a child predator, but child sex offenders frequently use such images to fuel and reinforce their activities, although there is a subset of noncontact pedophiles who are content to limit their abuse to their laptops. The Internet may also be used to troll for victims, but these are unlikely to be young children and more often involve teenage victims. Although less common than male perpetrators, females sexually abuse children, but the patterns and motives may differ somewhat from their male counterparts. Clergy members, day care workers, educators, and others who work with children in high-trust settings continue to be studied with regard to their propensity for child sexual abuse. As with many of the crimes that take place in institutional settings (Chapters 11, 12, 19, 21), proper policies and protocols can prevent and limit the harm of a substantial proportion of these offenses that might otherwise go undetected and undeterred.

Chapter **16**

Family Crime I: Child Abuse and Family Violence

BOX 16.1. COLD CASE

Three Dead Infants Found in Family Freezer in Germany,
South Florida SunSentinel, May 6, 2008

A 44-year-old woman was arrested on suspicion of killing three of her babies after their bodies were discovered in the family freezer by her grown children looking for pizza, police said. The three infants are believed to have been born alive, but authorities were awaiting autopsy results to determine how they died. The woman's 18-year-old son and his sister had been looking for a frozen pizza and came across a cache of expired food, so they decided to clean out the freezer. The son then found three identical packets on the bottom of the freezer. Upon opening one, he saw the head and arm of an infant that was wrapped in a hand towel. The overweight mother apparently had concealed the three pregnancies, thought to have been in the 1980s, from friends, neighbors, and her own family.

This was only the latest in a string of similar cases in Germany. In one case, a woman was convicted of manslaughter in 2006 for killing eight of her newborn babies and burying them in flower pots and a fish tank in the garden of her parents' home. In another case, a 28-year-old woman was charged with manslaughter after the remains of three babies were discovered in her house and the home of a relative. She has denied killing these children.

Y ou are more likely to be killed on the day you were born than at any subsequent time in your life, and your killer is most likely to be your parent or other close caretaker. If you survive day one, your chances of being murdered drop tenfold, but until the middle grade school years, you are still at far greater risk of being killed or physically abused by a close family member than by a stranger. Adults often wistfully recall the supposed halcyon days of their early youth, but ask anyone who's currently a kid, and you'll get a different answer.

441

CHILD BATTERY

Parents physically abuse their children for a variety of reasons and occasionally kill them, either intentionally or, more commonly, as an accidental consequence of severe abuse. Historically, **corporal punishment** was common as a means of controlling and disciplining children. Today, although constraints on child punishment exist in all Western societies, it is still legal and socially acceptable to use some degree of physical punishment to maintain control within the home; except for the police and military, no other person or institution has the legal right to use physical force to control another person's behavior (Shilling, 2003; West & Lichtenstein, 2006; Williams, 1976).

Characteristics of **battering parents** (Lesnik-Oberstein et al., 1995; Marks, 2001; Steele, 1978, 1987) include: high levels of hostility with low levels of inhibition; history of abuse or neglect in the parent's own early life; lack of attachment to, or empathy for the child, involving low awareness of or interest in the child's physical and emotional state and needs; very high expectations of the child, expecting the child to act like an adult; a belief that abusive behavior is justified if the child didn't meet expectations, for example, if the child's appearance or behavior is seen as disobedient or "defective;" displacement of interparental or other adult-focused aggression onto the child.

FILICIDE: KILLING OF A CHILD

History of Filicide

Historically, **filicide**, the killing of children, has been a fairly normal part of human communal life since ancient times. Caananite worshipers of Baal and the ancient Greeks ritually sacrificed children to their gods. In the Bible, Abraham almost sacrificed Isaac, but was stopped by the same God who originally commanded it. More prosaically, in ancient times, parents, especially fathers, could dispatch their children for reasons of scarce resources or for population control. In 374 AD, Roman law formally criminalized infant-killings as murder, but filicide remained a common practice. During the Middle Ages, physical deformity or supposed demonic possession were the main reasons parents killed their children. Most Western countries had criminalized filicide by the end of the eighteenth century, but mothers who killed their children were often treated more leniently than other murderers. By the beginning of the twentieth century, filicide had become a crime under the category of manslaughter in England, based on the assumption that a mother who would kill her own child must be mentally ill. By contrast, in the United States, maternal filicide remained a crime involving a charge of first-degree murder, placing the burden of proving a mental illness on the defendant (Dobson & Sales, 2000; Gauthier et al., 2003; McKee & Shea, 1998; Montag & Montag, 1979; Moseley, 1986; Palermo, 2002; Shilling, 2003; West & Lichtenstein, 2006; West et al., 2009; Williams, 1976).

Filicide: Description and Demographics

The term **filicide** refers to the murder of a child aged 1 to 18 by his or her parent or primary caretaker. **Infanticide** is the murder of a child up to one year old, while **neonaticide** describes the killing of a child within 24 hours of delivery. **Active neonaticide** is the killing of a newborn by direct violent action, usually shaking, beating, or suffocating, while **passive neonaticide** involves letting the newborn die of negligence or neglect, usually by failing to feed it or leaving it exposed to the elements. The first day of life represents the window of highest risk, followed by the first year of life, during which the risk is four times greater than that of the general population, after which the likelihood of being killed by a parent slowly and steadily declines with the child's age. In 20 percent of filicides, the offending parent subsequently commits suicide (Bourget et al., 2007b; Browne & Lynch, 1995; Crittenden & Craig, 1990; Deadman, 1964; Flowers, 2002c; Grimmins et al., 1997; Marks, 2001; Palermo, 2002; Resnick, 1969, 1970; Rodenburg, 1971; Schloesser et al., 1992; West & Lichtenstein, 2006).

Tragic and repellent as such a crime may seem, filicide is a relatively rare event. When it does occur, mothers and fathers are both equally likely to be perpetrators, albeit for different reasons. The younger the child, the more likely is the mother to be the murderer, especially during the first week of life. After that, fathers are the more common filicidal killers, from several weeks after birth up through middle and late childhood. The younger the child, the more the death is likely to result from inaction or neglect, as opposed to direct violence (Bourget & Gagne, 2005; Brewster et al., 1998; Greighton, 1995; Jason et al. 1983; Kunz & Bahr, 1996; Lucas et al., 2002; Marks, 2001; Marks & Kumar, 1993; Resnick, 1970; Sorenson & Peterson, 1994).

Neonaticides involve an equal number of male and female victims. After that, mothers are somewhat more likely to kill girls and fathers are more likely to kill boys. Younger victims are more likely to have been physically abused by the parent prior to the killing. With older infants and children, males are somewhat more likely to be killed. For children aged 1 to 5 years, the most likely perpetrator is a parent; however, with increasing age, children are more likely to be killed by someone other than the parent, since they spend more time out of the home. Children aged 1 to 5 may also be at increased risk of harm from stepparents compared to biological parents. Several studies have reported that victims of filicide are more often first-born children, although this is not settled (Anderson et al., 1983; Bourget et al., 2007b; Crittenden & Craig, 1990; Cummings & Mueller, 1994; Daly & Wilson, 1988; Jason et al., 1983; Kunz & Bahr, 1996; Lucas et al., 2002; Marks, 2001; Marks & Kumar, 1993; Myers, 1970).

Filicide Typologies

Resnick (1969) reviewed 131 cases of child murder reported in the literature and classified filicides according to their apparent motive, as follows.

Altruistic filicide. The parent is planning suicide, but does not want to leave the child behind to suffer without the parent's care, so she believes it is more merciful to end the child's life. In some cases, the suicidal parent believes she and the child will be united in Heaven; in other cases, there is no such religious theme and the parent is just sparing the child a life of loneliness and neglect at the hands of uncaring strangers. Alternatively, a nonsuicidal parent, sometimes the caretaker of a handicapped child, makes the decision to "put the child out of his/her misery" to spare the child further real or imagined suffering. This was the most common category in Resnick's (1969) sample.

Acutely psychotic filicide. The parent delusionally believes that there is some rationale for killing her child. In some cases, this may overlap with the above category, as where she hears the voice of God telling her to send her child to a "better place." In other cases, she may believe that the child is evil or possessed and must be destroyed. These delusions may be accompanied by command hallucinations to kill the child. This is the next most common category.

Unwanted child filicide. The child is a burden to the parent or an impediment to a desired relationship, so she purposefully sets about to get rid of the problem. There may be a rationalization that overlaps the altruistic theme ("everyone will be better off this way"), or the parent may coldly and calculatingly plan to eliminate the child.

Accidental filicide. The child's death was the unintended consequence of severe battering, usually occurring in the context of a history of such abuse. This was the least common category.

Spousal revenge. This may be more common with fathers, but can occur with either parent, where the parent or stepparent deliberately kills the child to get back at the other parent.

Scott (1973a) ostensibly based his own filicide typology on the "source of the impulse to kill," that is the stimulating conditions or circumstance, rather than on the perpetrator's motivation, however, his categories seem similar to that of Resnick (1969). Scott's (1973a) classification includes:

Victim constitutes the stimulus. Something the child does triggers the filicidal response in the parent. This may involve an extremely exasperating child, or just normal kid behavior that is disturbing to an unstable, immature, and impulsive parent.

Stimulus arises outside the victim. Usually, this means it comes from inside the perpetrator, in the form of displaced anger, resentment of the child, revenge against the other parent, or other perpetrator-based motive.

Perpetrator's mental illness. This is a more specific subcategory of the above. Here, the parent suffers from some form of mental disorder, usually a severe mood disorder or schizophrenia, that lowers the threshold to a murderous response to the child.

Elimination of unwanted child. The parent does not want to care for the child anymore and so eliminates the problem by killing him/her.

Mercy killing. The parent "altruistically" kills the child to spare him/her the future pain of loneliness if the parent is contemplating suicide, or to "put him out of his misery" if the child is disabled or is an excessive behavior problem. As noted above, this filicide category may overlap with the mental illness category (delusions and command hallucinations telling the parent to kill the child) and/or with the unwanted child category (how convenient that the voices are telling the parent to send the high-maintenance child to Heaven where the angels will assume his eternal caretaking needs).

D'Orban (1979) reconfirmed the basic categories of the Scott (1973b) typology, but added another category, **neonaticide**, to separate out parents who kill their children shortly after birth. D'Orban's (1979) study of 89 filicidal women found that the most frequent filicide scenario involved a frustrated, angry mother who had lost her temper at some aspects of the child's behavior (crying, feeding, eliminating, etc.), and/or displaced her aggression from other sources onto the child, and battered the child until he or she died, whether the death was intentional or not. Maternal psychosis at the time of the child's murder was the least common scenario and usually occurred in the course of a severe depression or psychotic decompensation. Unwanted children died either of passive neglect or direct aggression. In d'Orban's (1979) sample, there appeared to be no discernable secondary gain to the mothers who were mercy killers; instead, all of these cases seemed to involve the child truly suffering from some condition. A subsequent analysis of this data pool (Marks, 2001; Marks & Kumar, 1995) revealed that younger infants (under 6 months) were more likely to be killed by battering mothers, whereas older children were most likely to be killed when the mother was psychotic.

While not presented as a formal typology per se, Wilkey et al. (1982) identified seven categories of filicide which are more descriptive than motivational:

Neonaticide: killing of an infant within 24 hours of birth.

Infanticide: killing of an infant under 12 months old; in this sample, postpartum psychosis was the most common cause.

Euthanasia: killing of an ill, disabled, or otherwise abnormal child.

Accident: the unintended death of a child resulting from an intentional beating.

Neglect: death of a child from starvation, deprivation, or lack of care.

Murder-suicide: A parent kills a child and possibly other family members, and then commits suicide.

Murder: A parent kills a child for no discernable reason.

Consistent with other reports (Copeland, 1985; Marks, 2001), the largest category of filicides in Wilkey et al.'s (1982) sample consisted of accidental deaths due to child battery. These studies have also found that younger children and male children are more likely to be killed in the course of battering.

Returning to the issue of motive, Bourget & Bradford (1990) proposed five major categories of filicide:

Pathological filicide involves a parent with a major mental illness, and also includes altruistic motives and may involve a murder-suicide scenario.

Accidental filicide includes death due to various forms of child abuse, such as child battery and **Munchausen syndrome by proxy** (see below).

Retaliating filicide is the murder of a child to punish the spouse or partner.

Neonaticide is usually committed by unmarried young mothers to dispose of the results of an unwanted pregnancy.

Paternal filicide emphasizes the significance of gender as a filicidal category in and of itself.

Bourget & Gagne (2002) developed a classification system that places clinical and demographic correlates of filicide into a binary framework involving the presence or absence of a conscious intention to kill the child:

Mentally ill filicide occurs in association with a major mental disorder in the parent, such as psychosis, major depressive disorder, or postpartum illness when the infant is very young. Intentionality may be present, as in the case of command hallucinations or delusions of altruism, but the perpetrator is clearly in a mentally compromised state at the time the child is killed.

Fatal abuse filicide includes cases of child neglect, child battery, and **shaken-baby syndrome**. Typically, no major mental illness is present and the intention is usually to quiet the child or punish it, but not necessarily to kill it.

Retaliating filicide does involve the specific intent to kill the child, with anger or revenge as the motive.

Mercy filicide is also specifically intentional, but here the motive is to end the life of a child with a severe disabling condition. The classification does not specify whether the motive is more altruistic, i.e., to spare the child suffering, self-interested, i.e., to relieve the caregiver of an unwanted burden, or a mix of motives.

Other/unknown filicide subsumes cases that do not fit into the other categories or that include overlapping categories.

Friedman et al. (2005) based their typology on a critical analysis of the literature on maternal filicide, dividing filicidal mothers into three groups or "populations."

General population. These women typically serve as their child's primary caregiver, have experienced a personal history of abuse, and are having financial difficulties. While some of these mothers are abusive and/or neglectful, others may try to be decent parents, but suffer from mental illness.

Psychiatric population. Mothers in this category suffer from major mental illness, including psychosis, depression, and suicidal ideation. They typically have undergone one or more psychiatric hospitalizations. They tend to be married, unemployed, users of alcohol, and have a history of being physically abused themselves.

Correctional population. These women have been convicted and incarcerated for killing their children. Prior to their filicidal crime, they typically have been unemployed, unmarried, with little social support, limited education, and a history of substance use. Some also suffer from a major mental disorder.

Commonalities in Filicide Typologies

A number of common filicidal perpetrator categories emerge across the typologies reviewed above. One is the mother with serious **mental illness** who kills her child in a psychotically depressed and/or delusional state. This may overlap with the **altruistic filicide** category which seems to include two subclassifications, first, the suicidal mother who believes her child will be unable to survive without her and, second, the mother who intends to survive (perhaps to care for other children), but carries out a mercy killing on a seriously ill or disabled child whom she sees as "putting out of his misery."

This latter subcategory, in turn may overlap with the **unwanted child fili-cide**, in which the child has become too much of a burden for the caretak-ing parent; she may then rationalize the killing as being for the child's own good or, alternatively, merely dispatch the child out of a more utilitarian motive of wanting to find or keep a mate, or ease a financial burden. A sec-ond type of unwanted child filicide involves a young, unwed mother who has denied her pregnancy and seeks to get rid of her infant immediately after it is born; this will be discussed further below.

No such noble or sympathetic motives characterize the **revenge filicide** perpetrator who kills a child to strike back at that child's other parent. Unlike the other categories, these perpetrators are usually men and may or may not be biologically related to the child, i.e., may be a natural father, stepfather, or live-in boyfriend. Here, the child becomes the scapegoat for the offending adult's anger. Although not typically suffering from major mental disorders, these men probably could be described as immature, impulsive, aggressive, and characterized by one or more personality disorders. In rare cases, a nat-ural mother may kill her own child to get back at the natural father; these wo-men are more likely to be more seriously mentally disturbed. Anger also typ-ifies the child batterer who commits accidental, or **fatal abuse filicide** in the course of physically abusing a child—the intention is not to kill the child, but death may be an unintended consequence.

Finally, some parents commit a kind of **passive filicide** through neglect of the child's needs, and this may co-occur with physical abuse, which in turn may lead to **accidental filicide**. Moreover, where the abused and neglected child is seen as a pest or a burden, this may eventually turn into an **unwant-ed child filicide**.

Filicide: Psychology of Parents

The typologies reviewed above provide some basis for exploring the psy-chological dynamics of parents who kill their children.

In general, psychological motives for maternal filicide appear to vary both by the age of the child and the age of the mother. For example, a sub-stantial body of research has indicated that neonaticide is most often com-mitted by poor, young, single, school-aged mothers who lack resources and family support (Beyer et al., 2008; Dobson & Sales, 2000; Drescher-Burke et al., 2004; Meyer & Oberman, 2001; Miller, 1999a, 1999b; Resnick, 1970). Women who commit neonaticide are less likely to suffer clinical depression, psychotic illness, or to have attempted suicide than mothers who have killed an older child (Bourget & Labelle, 1992; d'Orban, 1979; Haapasalo & Petaja, 1999; Pitt & Bale, 1995).

Note that in many cultures, the religiously-sanctioned shaming and shunning of unwed mothers makes killing an unwanted infant virtually imperative to preserve the honor of the mother's family, aside from other culturally-sanctioned motives, such as infants who are physically deformed or believed to be cursed, or female filicide committed out of a preference for male children (Adinkrah, 2001, 2002; Gupta, 2005; McKee & Shea, 1998; Stanton et al., 2000; West & Lichtenstein, 2006; Wilczynski, 1995).

Multiple psychosocial stressors as motivating factors for maternal filicide have been identified, including being the primary caregiver for at least one child, unemployment and financial problems, history of abuse in the parent's own childhood, ongoing abusive adult relationships, conflict with family members, limited social support, and general social isolation (Bourget & Bradford, 1990; Bourget & Gagne, 2002; d'Orban, 1979; Haapasalo & Petaja, 1999; Lewis & Bunce, 2003; McKee & Shea, 1998; Simpson & Stanton, 2000).

More specific psychological characteristics of the different filicidal subtypes are as follows.

Psychology of Unwanted Child Filicide. Most commonly, this involves a young, unmarried woman in her teens, living at home, who, following an unintended, unwanted, and frequently concealed pregnancy, commits neonaticide to dispose of the newborn baby. This is usually, but not always, the first pregnancy, although recent research indicates that many of these mothers have been pregnant previously, some multiple times, with living children at the time of the index filicide. These young women may be poor and lack access to health and other support resources, or they may come from more upscale, middle-class backgrounds, where they fear stigmatization for becoming pregnant and/or the disruption of life plans that would be associated with having a baby, and may thus avoid medical and psychosocial services that would have been available to them. Many of these young mothers may have had sex impulsively or under pressure from a boyfriend and failed to take contraceptive precautions or to have planned for a pregnancy. The child is most likely to be killed or disposed of within minutes or hours of birth; if it survives beyond the first day of life, its risk of being killed by the mother declines sharply (Beyer et al., 2008; Bourget et al., 2007b; Bourget & Labelle, 1992; Dobson & Sales, 2000; Drescher-Burke et al., 2004; Marks, 2001; Meyer & Oberman, 2001; Miller, 2008b; Pitt & Bale, 1995; Resnick, 1970).

The key feature of unwanted child filicides committed by these young, unattached mothers is that most often the pregnancy has been concealed from others and denied to herself. Although these women are rarely psychotic, this kind of denial involves a particular mental dissociative splitting and compartmentalization. In most cases, the woman intellectually "knows" she is pregnant, but for all intents and purposes acts as if the condition didn't exist, as if by simply not thinking about it, it won't be real—similar to the kind of "knowing denial" many people utilize when confronted with any unbearably unpleasant truth. To bolster the denial, the young mother fails to seek any prenatal care or plan for the delivery. This denial is often abetted by the baby's father, the mother's family, and the extended family and community, in a consensual conspiracy of silence. After the child is born and disposed of, the mother returns to her normal daily life as quickly as possible (Beyer et al., 2008; Brozovsky & Falit, 1971; Dobson & Sales, 2000; Green & Manohar, 1990; Marks, 2001; Meyer & Oberman, 2001; Pitt & Bale, 1995; Spinelli, 2001; Vallone & Hoffman, 2003).

For those mothers in denial, an intriguing mind-body transformation sometimes occurs, where her very physiology appears to collude with her psychological repudiation of the pregnancy. Unlike happily expectant mothers who are proud to display their "bump," in these young pregnancy-denying women, the abdominal contour often remains remarkably flat, despite the presence of a full-term fetus. There are often no symptoms of pregnancy, such as morning sickness or urinary incontinence, and there may even be a continuation of menstrual cycles. In most cases, with or without these atypical bodily changes, the denying mother will conceal her pregnancy with clothing or may diet to lose weight and not appear larger. Interestingly, these women don't usually try to abort the fetus, because attempting to terminate the pregnancy would be an acknowledgement that it actually exists (Marks, 2001).

When labor begins, the contractions and dilation often happen particularly fast and the woman may at first attribute the pain to menstrual cramps or intestinal distress. The labor pains may be interpreted as a need to defecate and the delivery itself as a bowel movement, accounting for those media stories of "baby born in a toilet stall." Also, toilet stalls are one of the few private places the mother can quickly retreat to if labor comes on fast in a public area. Some mothers may simply leave the neonate where it is, walk away, and continue on as if nothing happened, but for most, the arrival of the actual baby is experienced as a traumatic shock that breaks through the dissociative denial and throws the young mother into a state of panic. The only "solution" then becomes to dispose of the evidence, so that the denial can continue, and it is at this point that killing the infant may appear as the only way out. Indeed, the sheer physiological resiliency of these young mothers is impressive: giving birth alone and unassisted, disposing of the neonate, cleaning up the crime scene, all the while remaining undetected by those around her at home, in a hotel room, or public bathroom, and immediately going on with routine activities, such as going back to work or class, or socializing with family or friends (Beyer et al., 2008; Marks, 2001; Meyer & Oberman, 2001).

Efficient in disposal and concealment as many of these women are, others engage in seemingly bizarre behavior surrounding the birth, such as the mother placing the deceased infant's body in a container, driving around with it in the trunk or back seat of her car, keeping it in a backpack or under her clothes, storing the corpse in a desk drawer or file cabinet, returning to bed with the dead or still-living infant, or breastfeeding the infant before discarding it. When the episode is finally over, most of these women experience a tremendous sense of relief at being able to go on with their lives in an unburdened and uninterrupted manner (Beyer et al., 2008; Bradley, 2003; Oberman, 1996; Spinelli, 2001).

Note that all 50 states now have some form of **Safe Haven Infant Protection Act** or **Safe Surrender Law** enabling new mothers to drop off their unwanted infant at a hospital or fire station without penalty. This humane and practical measure unintendedly had tragicomic consequences in 2008, when some parents in Omaha, Nebraska began dropping off their "unwanted" children who ranged in age from 1 to 17. States that had well-meaningly passed such statues quickly realized that some kind of cutoff age was required, and most quickly revised their laws, so that the age of penalty-free drop-off of an infant is now limited to several days after birth in most areas.

Psychology of Fatal Abuse Filicide. The early family life of women who become battering mothers has typically been characterized by large numbers of children in the household, chaotic and violent family backgrounds, separation of parents, financial and housing problems, and family members with criminal histories. When adult, the battering filicidal women are often pregnant or have more than one child and/or children in ill health or with disabilities at the time of the offense, and to be undergoing significant financial and relationship stress. Prenatal care is likely to be minimal or nonexistent. About half of these mothers have a prior history of battering, either of the slain child or other children. Many of these mothers could be described as having personality disorders but not severe depression or psychosis at the time of the filicide, and they are not typically suicidal (Bourget & Gagne, 2002; Bourget et al., 2007b; Brewster et al., 1998; Browne & Lynch, 1995; Cummings & Mueller, 1994; d'Orban, 1979; Haapasalo & Petaja, 1999; Husain & Daniel, 1984; Korbin, 1989; Lewis & Bunce, 2003; Marks, 1996; Scott, 1973a).

Psychology of Retaliating Filicide. Retaliating maternal filicide is rare; most retaliators are fathers (see below). Women who commit retaliating filicide typically have severe personality disorders and a history of frequent suicide attempts. It is not known how many of these retaliating mothers are biological parents or stepparents (Bourget & Bradford, 1990; d'Orban, 1979; Lewis & Bunce, 2003; McKee & Shea, 1998; Resnick, 1969; Scott, 1973a).

Psychology of Altruistic Filicide. This can take several forms. Some mothers suffer delusional guilt or self-persecution about being "bad mothers" and believe that their children would be better off dead than continuing to live with them; the mother's own suicide may or may not be part of the plan. Other mothers may be responding to a delusional belief, sometimes reinforced by command hallucinations, to kill children because they are "evil" or to atone for the mother's own sins (McKee & Shea, 1998; Stanton et al., 2000; West & Lichtenstein, 2006; Wilczynski, 1995).

Psychology of Psychotic Filicide. In the category of mentally ill filicidal mothers, the most common diagnosis is major depressive disorder with psychotic features, with schizophrenic psychoses a close second. Psychotic mothers tend to kill older children, to kill multiple children in a single episode, and to kill more violently, typically using a weapon. These mothers tend to be older themselves and to have more education than nonpsychotic filicidal mothers. They are also more likely to be divorced and unemployed, and to have a history of substance abuse, psychiatric treatment, psychiatric hospitalization, and attempted suicide. They are more likely to commit suicide after killing older children. Parental suicide attempts are uncommon following neonaticide, unwanted child filicide, retaliating filicide, and fatal abuse filicide, presumably because each of these categories of filicidal parents has some reason to go on living. Interestingly, fathers are more often perpetrators of filicide-suicide than mothers. The more depressed the parent is at the time of the killing, the more likely is there to occur a filicide-suicide. Parents who commit filicide during a delusional manic episode usually do so impulsively with little premeditation, while those suffering from major depressive disorder with psychotic features often brood and ruminate about their own and their children's deaths for days or weeks before carrying out the act (Bourget & Bradford, 1990; Bourget & Gagne, 2002, 2005; Bourget & Labelle, 1992; Bourget et al., 2007b; Brewster et al., 1998; Cooper & Eaves, 1996; Crittenden & Graig, 1990; Daly & Wilson, 1988; d'Orban, 1979; Felthous & Hempel, 1995; Gottlieb, 1996; Haapasalo & Petaja, 1999; Harder, 1967; Hatters et al., 2005; Holden et al., 1996; Husain & Daniel, 1984; Lewis & Bunce, 2003; Lewis et al., 1998; Lucas et al., 2002; Marks & Kumar, 1995; Marleau et al., 1999; Marzuk et al., 1992; McKee & Shea, 1998; Myers, 1970; Palermo et al., 1997; Rodenburg, 1971; Resnick, 1969; Scott, 1973a; Silverman & Kennedy, 1987; Somander & Rammer, 1991; Stanton et al., 2000; Tuteur & Gloptzer, 1959).

Postpartum Depression and Psychosis. The question often arises as to what role postpartum depression or postpartum psychosis play in the motivation for filicide. Up to 85 percent of mothers will experience some postpartum psychological disturbance, and about 10% will suffer a serious postpartum mental disorder. About 90 percent of mothers will experience a recurrence. **Postpartum depression** occurs in a minority of women in the first few months following pregnancy. Symptoms include sadness, fatigue, insomnia, appetite changes, reduced sex drive, depression, anxiety, and irritability. The onset is typically gradual and the condition may persist for weeks or months. Clinically, the syndrome resembles major depressive disorder, and violence is a very rare occurrence, although suicidality may be a risk. In **postpartum psychosis**, the onset is more abrupt, and the syndrome evolves over hours, days, or weeks. Clinically, the syndrome resembles bipolar mania (Chapter 6), with euphoria, hyperactivity, decreased sleep, pressured and disorganized speech, flight of ideas, grandiose, paranoid, or religious delusions, behavioral disinhibition, irritability, and sometimes violence. Like bipolar disorder, the postpartum mood change can cycle into a depressive phase, which may include persisting psychotic features. If clinicians or family members observe the woman during this latter phase, they may mistake the syndrome for the postpartum depression described above, leading to the mistaken belief that postpartum depression per se is a major risk factor for violence, including filicide (Bright, 1994; Brockington, 1996; O'Hara, 1995; O'Hara & Swain, 1996; McKee & Shea, 1998; Millis & Kornblith, 1992; Sharma & Mazmanian, 2003; Stanton et al., 2000; Spinelli, 2004; West & Lichtenstein, 2006).

As to the etiology of postpartum depression and psychosis, many of these episodes occur in the context of an already existing mood disorder that may have been treated in the past. Family members of these women frequently have mood disorders as well. Sudden and extreme shifts in hormone levels around the time of delivery may activate these risk factors in susceptible women. Further contributors may include psychosocial stress factors, such as social isolation, dysfunctional marriage, single parenthood, financial difficulty, multiple children, and family pressures. Finally, many women are advised to go off their psychotropic medication during pregnancy, heightening the risk for a psychological rebound of symptoms (Bright, 1994; Connell, 2002; Millis & Kornblith, 1992; Palermo, 2002; Sharma & Mazmanian, 2003; Spinelli, 2004; Stanton et al., 2000; West & Lichtenstein, 2006).

Filicidal Fathers

While parents of either sex may kill their children, certain features distinguish male filicide perpetrators. With fathers, infants and younger children are at greater risk for filicidal death than older children, but paternal neonaticide is rare, probably because at that age, mothers are almost always the primary caretakers. When fathers murder their children, it is typically in the context of a battering episode that turns deadly. Head trauma is a common cause of death. Almost always, the child has done something "wrong" that serves as an pretext for the father's anger, triggering a beating which may prove fatal. Behaviors on the part of the child that prompt the abuse typically include crying excessively, being too noisy, being generally cranky or annoying, refusing to eat or do some chore, wetting or soiling himself, refusing to smile, staring at the father (probably interpreted as a willful challenge), or somehow indicating that the child prefers the other parent. It is often these fathers' generally dysphoric emotional tone, impulsive anger, and feelings of inadequacy masked by easily-bruised compensatory narcissism, that makes them susceptible to overinterpreting the child's behavior as excessively irritating or confrontational. As noted above, some fathers may kill a child to retaliate against the mother or to "punish" her for humiliating him, often by her being the breadwinner while he stays home (see also Chapter 17), or for presumed infidelity (who knows what's happening out there while she's at work?). A significant number of filicides occur during parental separations, and fathers are more likely than mothers to kill their partners in the course of a filicide (Adinkrah, 2001; Bourget & Bradford, 1990; Bourget & Gagne, 2005; Bourget et al., 2007b; Brewster et al., 1998; Campion et al., 1988; Cooper & Eaves, 1996; Fox, 1996; Goetting, 1988; Krugman, 1985; Lucas et al., 2002; Marleau et al., 1999; Marks, 2001; Palermo, 2002; Resnick, 1969; Rodenburg, 1971; West et al., 2009).

More than half of these men are not the biological fathers of the children they kill. Nevertheless, a large proportion of them are unwillingly conscripted into being the main caretakers of these children while the mother works. Although not usually typified by a major mental disorder, the majority of these men have some kind of personality disorder, often in the narcissistic-borderline spectrum, characterized by impulsivity and emotional dyscontrol, and often complicated by substance abuse. A few studies have found some of these fathers to be psychotic. Educational level is typically low, employment is inconsistent, and more than two-thirds of these men have one or more criminal convictions, as well as previous contacts with the mental health system. Most of these men have come from punitive family backgrounds themselves that included parental violence. Fathers are more likely than mothers to attempt or complete suicide following the filicide, and the probability increases with the number of victims slain in a particular incident, particularly where this involves older children (Bourget & Gagne, 2005; Bourget et al., 2007b; Brewster et al., 1998; Cooper & Eaves, 1996; Crittenden & Graig, 1990; D'Orban, 1979; Felthous & Hempel, 1995; Hatters et al., 2005; Krugman, 1985; Lewis & Bunce, 2003; Lucas et al., 2002; Marks, 2001; Marks & Kumar, 1995; Marleau et al., 1999; Scott, 1973b; Somander & Rammer, 1991).

A special kind of family homicide is **familicide**, where the perpetrator, almost always the father, kills all of his children and his spouse. The motivation of this perpetrator, sometimes called the **family annihilator**, appears to fall into two main classes: (1) the **angry father** with longstanding dominance and control issues, who has a grievance against his wife, and who kills to end his marriage and family responsibilities; and (2) the **hopeless father** who kills his family to save them from perceived impending doom; this may be the male equivalent of the maternal altruistic-psychotic filicide described above (West et al., 2009).

Evolutionary theories of paternal filicide emphasize the phenomenon of **kin selection** (Chapter 3). It is known that fathers are more likely to kill their stepchildren than their biological children; in fact, a child under the age of 5 is eight times more likely to be killed by a stepfather than by a biological father. Many if not most men in blended families make an honest effort to incorporate their new mate's children into their hearts and lives, but where paternal risk factors for immature, impulsive, and aggressive behavior already exist, this may not go so smoothly. Similar to males of many species, such human stepfathers have less of a genetically vested interest in maintaining their stepchildren to adulthood. So if the man's initial reasons for investment in his stepchild's welfare—basic paternal decency or the loyalty and devotion of the children's mother—are perceived to be ruptured or threatened, these men may react by neglecting, abusing, and ultimately killing their nonbiological wards (Daly & Wilson, 1988; Hamilton, 1964; Weekes-Shackelford & Shackelford, 2004; West et al., 2009).

Filicide: Legal Aspects

The legal systems of some countries, such as Great Britain, Canada, Austria, Germany, Australia and New Zealand, make a special provision for filicidal women who kill their children in the first year after birth, acknowledging that this is the primary time period for postpartum psychological disorders. Hence, filicidal women who kill during these times are often paroled or sent to psychiatric hospitals rather than to prison. In Britain, in particular, postpartum psychosis can be specifically raised as a mitigating factor in cases where mothers kill their children. In contrast, in the United States, maternal filicide is typically treated as murder, unless the defense can prove impaired *mens rea* due to severe psychiatric disorder, as with any other NGRI murder defense. Even in the United States, however, filicidal fathers are many times more likely to be criminally convicted and sentenced than mothers (Connell, 2002; Dobson & Sales, 2000; Friedman et al., 2005; West & Lichtenstein, 2006).

MUNCHAUSEN'S SYNDROME BY PROXY

Hard as it is to understand how a parent, especially a mother, could harm or kill her children, we might stir up a dollop of empathy for the parent who is so stressed out or grossly psychotic that she beats or kills her offspring in a rageful meltdown or a delusional haze. But how are we to react to a mother who methodically, purposefully, knowingly, and repeatedly harms her growing child, leading to his or her death in some cases, all for the purposes of seeking attention? This is the syndrome that has come to be known as **Munchausen's syndrome by proxy**, or **MSBP**.

MSBP: Description and Demographics

In the eighteenth and nineteenth centuries, European children were entertained by fictional tales of a certain Baron von Munchausen (based on a real historical character) who was fond of regaling his listeners with fantastic stories of flying to the moon, being swallowed by giant sea creatures, and singlehandedly saving whole cities, all these narratives spilling effortlessly from his lips, articulated so confidently and fluidly, the story being changed and embellished with each retelling, that the sheer implausibility of these adventures seemed almost beside the point. In the *DSM-III*, first published in 1980, **Munchausen's Syndrome** was used to describe a disorder in which patients report multiple and shifting physical symptoms, all due to deliberate surreptitious acts of self-injury to make themselves appear sick. In *DSM-IV*, this had become the noneponymously named **factitious disorder**, but the concept, and in some clinical settings, the Munchausen name, remained.

The key to diagnosis hinges on motive. Unlike **somatization disorder**, where nonveridical symptoms are produced unconsciously by the patient as a way of dealing with some intrapsychic conflict or life crisis, and unlike **malingering**, in which the subject deliberately and knowingly fakes illness or impairment for some practical gain (money in a lawsuit, exculpation for a crime), in Munchausen's Syndrome/Factitious Disorder, the patient does consciously and deliberately induce the symptoms and is aware that he or she is doing so, but the primary motive is to assume the **sick role**, with all of the attention, care, and martyrdom that such a designation brings (Miller, 1984a, 2002c). When these subjects choose another person—a proxy—as the vehicle of their subterfuge, it becomes MSBP.

Although it has probably existed since there have been parents and children, MSBP has only been recognized as a phenomenon and described as a clinical syndrome since the 1970s (DiMaio & Berstein, 1974; Meadow, 1977). Since then, there has been an expansion of interest in these parents who induce illness in their children. The term **pediatric condition falsification syndrome** has been adopted by the American Professional Society on the Abuse of Children (Schreier, 2002a), but MSBP remains the most recognizable designation and will be used here. MSBP occurs where a parent, almost always the mother, deliberately fakes or directly induces symptoms of illness in one or more children for the purpose of obtaining attention and admiration for herself as a devoted caretaker and sometimes for the satisfaction derived from deceiving medical experts.

Until the subterfuge is discovered, these mothers are almost always described as exceptionally knowledgeable about their child's illness and lovingly devoted to their care. They often have some training in the medical field, e.g., having worked as a nurse, physical therapist, or medical lab technician, but of course now gladly sacrificing their career to devote their full time to their child's care. These mothers characteristically present themselves as almost unnaturally upbeat, optimistic, cooperative, and pleasant to the treatment staff, yet never seem to leave their child's side, spending a great deal of time alone with the child. Suspicions begin to arise when the child keeps presenting with inconsistent or confusing symptoms or fails to respond to multiple treatments. At this point, the veracity of the illness or the mother's motives may begin to be questioned, in which case she quickly withdraws their child from care and moves on (Awadallah, 2005; Bools et al., 1994; Feldman, 2004; Flowers, 2002c; Marks, 2001; Trimble, 2004).

Common forms of inducing medical symptoms in the children of MSBP mothers include withholding food or medicine, tampering with laboratory specimens or medical equipment, feeding or injecting infectious or toxic substances, using laxatives and tranquilizers, and smothering. Approximately half of confirmed MSBP cases involve illnesses of the central nervous system such as breathing and sleep-related disorders, and cases of MSBP are commonly misdiagnosed as **sudden infant death syndrome** (**SIDS**). While a wide variety of illnesses may be fabricated, more common presentations include recurrent episodes of apnea (interruption of breathing); recurrent vomiting, diarrhea, or other gastrointestinal distress, fevers either due to infection or of unknown origin, pseudoseizures witnessed only by the mother, or real seizures occurring in the presence of physicians, but clandestinely induced by the mother. Up to 10 percent of MSBP cases eventuate in the child's death. About 75 percent of child victims are under 6 years of age, but ages can range from infants to teenagers (Awadallah, 2005; Bools, 1996; Ewing, 1997; Feldman, 2004; Gray & Bentovim, 1996; Marks, 2001; Rosenberg, 1987; Sheridan, 2003).

MSBP Perpetrator Characteristics and Psychology

As noted above, both malingering and factitious disorder involve the conscious and deliberate fabrication or exaggeration of symptoms. However, in malingering there is an identifiable, external, understandable incentive, such as evading culpability or obtaining compensation. In factitious disorder (Munchausen's syndrome), the deliberate symptom production is inferred to be for purposes of obtaining emotional support, attention, and sympathy by assuming the sick role. When the syndrome occurs through the proxy of a child, the mother's motivation is usually to seek attention and admiration for herself, but may also include the satisfaction of deceiving, controlling and manipulating the powerful medical establishment (Feldman, 2004; Flowers, 2002c; Marks, 2001; Schreier, 2002b).

Studies examining the psychological characteristics of MSBP mothers have found their families of origin to have been typified by histories of early abuse. Some, but by no means all, of these mothers may have been MSBP victims themselves. The MSBP mothers show a high prevalence of personality disorder, particularly in the narcissistic, borderline, and antisocial categories, and many have problems in their current adult relationships. Many have their own personal history of factitious disorder, somatoform disorder, or self-injury, and many have worked in the health care or caretaking professions and are familiar with medical procedures and terminology; alternatively, they have self-educated through books or the Internet.

These mothers tend to have an overly close, clinging, smothering relationship, with their child, which they portray as loving care and selfless devotion. For all this dedication, they seem to lack understanding or tolerance for the normal, developmentally appropriate behaviors of childhood, often demanding that their children be polite, submissive, and controlled. Behind the competent, caring façade is often a core of loneliness, inadequacy, poor self-esteem, and desperate need for attention and validation by a powerful authority figure, achieved by playing the martyred caretaker. Husbands of these women (the child victim's father or stepfather) are typically found to be aloof, emotionally distant, and often physically absent parents, with little direct involvement in the children's lives, and who appear to be either genuinely unaware of the mother's victimization of the affected child, or who willfully ignore the incriminating signs in order to maintain peace in the household. Less frequently, the husband will facilitate his wife's actions (e.g., drive the mother and child to doctors' appointments), but without directly participating in the abuse. In less than 10 percent of cases are fathers direct collaborators or the primary MSBP perpetrators.

MSBP mothers often cease the abuse when the child becomes old enough to ask questions, and may then select a younger sibling for the same treatment. However, a good number of such child victims buy into a kind of symbiotic relationship, obtaining emotional sustenance from the mother, and continuing to defend and praise their devoted parent long after they themselves have turned adult and the mother's actions have been medically and legally exposed (Awadallah et al., 2002; Bools et al. 1994; Feldman, 2004; Flowers, 2002c; Marks, 2001; Rand & Feldman, 2001; Rosenberg, 1987, 1995; Samuels et al., 1992; Sanders & Bursch, 2002; Schreier, 1997; Schreier & Libow, 1993; Sheridan, 2003).

BOX 16.2. MUNCHAUSEN'S SYNDROME BY PROXY: CHILD PROTECTION OR WITCH HUNT?

Because of the sophistication with which MSBP mothers carry out their years-long abuse of their children, detection, even by skilled medical professionals, is often evaded or delayed. Most physicians are trained in the philosophy of patient and family advocacy, and many are uncomfortable accusing a seemingly devoted mom of harming her own child. Adding to the confusion is the often incredible persistence of the ruse and outraged denial of wrongdoing even where the mother is presented with incontrovertible evidence (e.g., video recording) of her misdeeds; few mothers confess to their actions. In most cases, these mothers have a keen sense as to when medical suspicions are rising, and most will abruptly check their child out of treatment and disappear when they start to feel the heat, only to show up in another town, often with a new name and identity, to begin the subterfuge anew (Awadallah et al., 2005; Marks, 2001).

As with many initially obscure syndromes, as MSBP has become more well-known, an overcorrective response may lead to **moral panic**. Hence, a less well studied problem than failure to detect cases of MSBP are cases in which otherwise innocent and devoted mothers are branded as medical abusers without sufficient evidence. Some clinicians may now be so attuned to detect "red flags" of MSBP (often out of fear of prosecution or litigation for failure to protect their

continued

BOX 16.2.—*Continued*

patient), that they misinterpret innocent or ambiguous medical and behavioral signs and symptoms as evidence of criminal abuse. Indeed, some of these maternal behavioral "warning signs" are overgeneralized, confusing, and contradictory, and many of the index behaviors are commonly be found in mothers with legitimately ill or disabled children. Thus, physicians are told to suspect MSBP if the mother is too anxious or too calm, if she presents as ingratiating or hostile, if her relationship with her child appears cool and distant or overinvolved and smothering, if she is overcompliant or resistant to medical recommendations, and so on (Morley, 1995; Pankratz, 2006).

Once suspected of being a MSBP mother, now anything she says or does is interpreted as fitting the "profile." The slightest medical discrepancies are now interpreted as "obvious" signs of maternal abuse, including honest errors in judgment, slight inconsistencies in relating medical history, questioning of medical diagnoses and prescriptions, or disagreement with doctors on any matter. The mother may be blamed for botched lab results or perfunctory examinations at busy clinics. For this parent, the label of MSBP has now become a self-fulfilling prophecy, and anything the mother says in her own defense is dismissed as a part of her pattern of lies.

Such suspicions may lead to the child being removed from the home by child protective services, with the burden of proof on the mother to prove that she is worthy of getting her child back. Mothers may be questioned by police, arrested, and many are prosecuted. Worse, many of these mothers are economically strapped single parents, making it especially difficult for them to negotiate the medical system and now the legal system that is questioning their competence. Mothers may feel emotionally crushed or outraged that the doctors they turned to for help have now become their persecutors. If the case goes to court, often direct evidence of malfeasance is equivocal, and prosecutors rely on **syndrome evidence**, i.e., there is no hard data to prove misconduct, but the mother fits the "profile," often opined upon by ideologically driven expert witnesses, in order to justify child protective services or criminal prosecution of the mother (Krener & Adelman, 1988; Pankratz, 2006).

To balance the rights of mothers and protection of children, Pankratz (2006) recommends a graded, rational approach. If MSBP is suspected, the doctor should discuss his or her concerns directly with the mother in order to establish a program to manage the child's condition. Separation of mother and child should be considered only with evidence of imminent danger, as many state laws direct. A determination of MSBP should be made only on the basis of hard evidence of maltreatment, not dubious profiling. While these recommendations seem sensible and well-meaning, the ironic reality is that most true MSBP mothers, when they detect a whiff of suspicion, much less encounter direct confrontation of their actions (no matter how delicately presented), will withdraw their child from treatment and move on. Paradoxically, it may be the innocent mothers, who are genuinely seeking medical care for their child, and who lack the financial resources to go elsewhere, who may stick around long enough to be snagged in the net of suspicion. Scrupulous care, clinical expertise, and rigorous standards of legal and medical evidence-gathering must be applied to these sensitive cases.

PARENT ABUSE

An increasingly common phenomenon I'm seeing in my clinical practice is parents, almost always single mothers, coming in for advice on how to handle their abusive offspring, almost always adolescent sons. Across ethnic, economic, and social lines, the stories are strikingly similar: Mom is a working single parent, split up from the boy's father when the child was in grade school or earlier. There may or may not be other siblings. The ex-mate had been a struggle to live with, and violence, drugs, and cheating had all been part of the equation that led to the parental split, with dad now long out of the picture or inconsistently in and out of the son's life. Beginning around age 13 to 15, but sometimes even earlier, junior begins to neglect school, do drugs, hang out with the local delinquents, and expect his hard-working mother (two jobs are not uncommon) to be a money machine to front these activities. Unmindful and uncaring of the daily struggles of his supporting parent, he may also request other perks, such as having his friends over to the house to smoke dope, or conscripting her as the chauffeur to and from his frequent jaunts.

Should any of these requests be refused, he will take matters into his own hands, stealing cash, checks, or credit cards from his mother, disappearing with the car (often leaving her with no way to get to her job) and, if that doesn't work, intimidating her with violence. This may begin with destruction of property (I've seen more than one photo of a trashed room with holes battered in the walls), and if there is still an insufficient response to his entitled demands, he may feel he "has no choice" but to beat the crap out of her. Sometimes he's sorry later, sometimes he couldn't care less. Many of these mothers have walked into my office or into court (not surprisingly, many of these youths have juvenile court files a foot thick by the time they're 16) in neck braces, arm casts, with canes or walkers, often bruised and cut, with multiple old wounds in various stages of healing, as if these parents had been in a concentration camp, which, in a sense, they have been.

Hardened and realistic, and not expecting any miracles, having already been to every police station and mental health center in their district, what these mothers still hope to extract from me is some special insight or technique that will help them better handle their out-of-control son. In many cases, I've heard almost the same exact words: "Can you just talk to him?"– as if one or two counseling sessions with me are going to effect a radical personality transformation that will turn their child from a thug into an angel. So when I finally ask the seemingly obvious question–"If your son is holding you down and punching you and strangling you, why don't you call 911?"– often, they will look at me in shocked horror and reply: "I can't call the police on him–he's my *son.*"

Bad enough to be afraid of your spouse or intimate partner; how much worse to live in fear of the child you bore and raised, to fear for your safety and survival from the very person who is supposed to represent your future. And while even the most brainwashed battered spouse (Chapter 17) may eventually come to her senses and either leave or turn in her abusive mate, how do you abandon your own offspring? How do you send your baby to jail?

Parent Abuse: Description and Demographics

Parent abuse can be defined as any act perpetrated by a child or adolescent that causes a parent to feel threatened, intimidated, and/or controlled (Kennair & Mellor, 2007; Paterson et al., 2002). As with partner abuse, it can include physical, psychological, and financial abuse. **Physical abuse** includes hitting, punching, kicking, shoving, breaking things, punching holes in the walls, throwing things, and spitting. **Psychological abuse** involves intimidating the parent, making the parent fearful, playing malicious mind games, making unrealistic demands on parents, and/or making manipulative threats, involving either intentions to harm the parent or to hurt themselves or siblings, even pets. In **financial abuse**, the child steals the parent's money, credit cards, or belongings, sells family possessions, destroys the home or parent's belongings or other's property, incurs debts the parents must repay, or simply demands money or intimidates the parent into buying the child items.

Despite the obvious similarities between the behavioral expressions of both parent abuse and intimate partner abuse (Chapter 17), there is an important difference that relates to the unique dynamics of the parent-child relationship. Partners who have the opportunity to leave a clearly abusive relationship may be willing to seize the opportunity if they have reasonable assurances of safety and financial stability. But even the most physically and psychologically brutalized mother will have a hard time abandoning her child, and she frequently engages in ever-expanding rationalizations to maintain the relationship. Even if she wanted such a separation, it's not that easy. The law in most jurisdictions requires parents to provide care for minor children—even 6'5", 250-pound abusive male minor children—and usually the only alternative is to have the child live with another relative, which may not be an option, or to have him arrested, which most parents are loathe to do; even if they do so, he's likely to be back home in a short time, angrier than ever. Parents, especially mothers, may be reluctant to report the abuse for fear of stigmatization as a "bad parent," and many parents internalize this designation and live in shame (Agnew & Huguley, 1989; Charles, 1986; Cottrell, 2001; Edenborough et al., 2008; Harbin & Madden, 1979; Jackson & Mannix, 2004; Kennair & Mellor, 2007; Koniak-Griffin et al., 2006; Paterson et al., 2002).

Paralleling the sex distribution of other aggressive acts, sons are more likely to be physically abusive and daughters are more likely to be emotionally and verbally abusive toward their parents. As they age, sons are less likely to hit their mothers and more likely to hit their fathers (if present in the home), while daughters become increasingly physically abusive to both parents with age. However, parent abuse is more common in single-parent households, probably because most of these are headed by mothers who are generally easier to intimidate than fathers. The abusive behavior appears to be starting at increasingly younger ages, now at around 12–14, as opposed to 15–17 a little over a decade ago, and some children are capable of abusive or manipulative behavior as young as 5 or 6. Some of the discrepancy inheres in what parents, especially mothers, are willing to label "abuse" by their offspring. A parent may rationalize early-onset temper tantrums, destruction of household objects, theft of money or valuables, or grabbing and pushing behavior as mere willfulness or troubled acting-out in her physically smaller, school-aged child. But when her man-sized 16-year-old son finally puts her in the hospital after a severe beating, she may retrospectively recognize the abuse she has suffered over the years and come to label it as such (Agnew & Huguley, 1989; Cottrell, 2001; Cottrell & Monk, 2004; Evans & Warren-Sohlberg, 1988; Kennair & Mellor, 2007; Kumagai, 1981; Livingston, 1986; Nock & Kazdin, 2002).

Parent Abuse: Psychology

A number of psychological factors have been associated with parent abuse, although none are likely to be sufficiently causative in themselves. In research interviews, abusive children and adolescents report a lack of emotional closeness with parents and a reluctance to talk to them about their problems. Abusive kids show lower frustration tolerance and more oppositional, demanding, and aggressive behaviors, which may be one reason why parents find it so hard to be close with these children. Abusive kids are also more likely to be poor students, to be disruptive in school, to hang out with antisocial peers, and to abuse drugs, probably reflecting the ADHD-learning disorder-conduct disorder triad discussed in Chapter 19. Many of the disputes with parents reflect demands for money to buy alcohol or drugs. A significant proportion of abusive children and adolescents have been physically or sexually abused by their parents, usually the father, or have witnessed domestic violence. In some cases, the kids begin abusing the mother soon after the violent father leaves the home, reflecting a swirl of motivations that may include: (1) direct anger at the mother for "making" the father leave; (2) displaced anger at the father's abandonment taken out on the mother; (3) modeling and idealization of the violent father's behavior (identification with the aggressor); and (4) repudiation of dependency needs by attacking the maternal source of nurturance and support. In a few cases, the child may attack one parent to protect the other (Brezina, 1999; Browne & Hamilton, 1998; Busby, 2005; Cornell & Gelles, 1982; Cottrell & Monk, 2004; Evans & Warren-Sohlberg, 1988; Kennair & Mellor, 2007; Livingston, 1986; Micucci, 1995; Miller, 2008b; Nock & Kazdin, 2002; Paulson et al., 1990; Peek et al., 1985; Wells, 1987).

Blame it on the parents! There have been many theories about what kind of parenting styles may serve to discourage or enable abuse by children, or antisocial behavior in general. Some studies have found that children and adolescents are more likely to abuse their parents when those parents are either overly strict or overly permissive. Having inconsistent family rules and consequences is often cited as a predisposing factor in family violence (Agnew & Huguley, 1989; Charles, 1986; Kennair & Mellor, 2007; Micucci, 1995; Paulson et al., 1990); however, it is equally possible that even well-meaningly diligent parents may ultimately give up trying to discipline their obstinately out-of-control children. Or the children may both genetically inherit and behaviorally model one or both parent's impulsive, unstable approach to most of life's responsibilities, including parenting. Abusive kids quickly learn to size up how far they can coerce their parents and what they can get away with, and then go for it. Other kids (usually boys) engage in a kind of role-reversal when one parent (usually the father) leaves the home, overtly or tacitly assuming the dominant male role in the household, which also may include exploiting and abusing the resident female, his mother. In some cases, this represents an internalization of the male parental role to provide a sense of security and control; in other cases, it may simply represent the inherited and/or modeled dominating behavior of the now-absent parent (Cottrell & Monk, 2004; Holtzworth-Munroe & Stuart, 1994; Kennair & Mellor, 2007).

PARRICIDE

As with child abuse, sometimes abuse of a parent inadvertently escalates to homicide. In other cases, however, the murder of a parent is planned and carried out meticulously and cold-bloodedly. Next to parents killing their children, the opposite circumstance is probably one of the most creepily horrifying scenarios that most adults can contemplate: my baby can exterminate me.

Parricide: Description and Demographics

Parricide is defined as the killing of a mother or father by a son or daughter. Each year in the U.S., approximately 300 parents are killed by their children, comprising 12 percent of all intrafamilial homicides. Parricide is typically committed by white, non-Hispanic, older adolescent or adult male offspring of middle- or upper-middle-class background, sometimes as part of a murder-suicide or out of revenge or delusional psychosis associated with paranoid schizophrenia. Parricidal children are typically between 20–30, but about a quarter of them are under 18 at the time they kill, which is more than twice the rate at this age of juvenile homicide perpetrators generally. Parricide victims are typically in their 40s or 50s, with stepparents slightly more likely to be killed at a younger age. Fathers are more likely to be killed than mothers. Male children are more likely to murder their mother or both parents, while female children are more likely to kill their mothers. Younger teens or children who kill a parent are often victims of abuse. Even so, they are often described as dangerously antisocial, and/or to have been abusing drugs or alcohol from an early age. Many cases of juvenile parricide are carried out with the cooperation of siblings, or in some cases, others, such as a boyfriend. The parricidal child typically lives with his or her parents and the killing is most often committed in the victim's home (Bourget et al., 2007a; Campion et al., 1985; d'Orban & O'Connor, 1989; Ewing, 1990a, 1997, 2001; FBI, 1995; Flowers, 2002a, 2002c; Heide, 1995, 1999; Labelle et al., 1991; Meloy, 1992; Millaud et al., 1996; Mones, 1991; Newhill, 1991; O'Connell, 1963; Planasky & Johnson, 1977; Sadoff, 1971; U.S. Bureau of Justice Statistics, 1994; Websdale, 1999).

Parricide: Motives and Psychopathology

Early conceptualizations of parricide emphasized psychodynamics associated with violent repudiation of repressed incestuous or Oedipal desires; more recent accounts have focused on current family dynamics and motives.

From an analysis of the existing literature (Bender & Curran, 1940; Benedek & Cornell, 1989; Bjorkly, 2002a, 2002b; Bluglass, 1979; Bourget & Whitehurst, 2004; Bourget et al., 2007a; Campion et al., 1985; Casu et al., 1994; Chamberlain, 1986; Clark, 1993; Cravens et al., 1985; d'Orban & O'Connor, 1989; Eronen et al., 1996; Ewing, 1990a, 1997, 2001; Flowers, 1986, 2002a, 2002c; Gillies, 1965; Green, 1981; Heide, 1995; Hoptman et al., 2002; Junginger, 1996; Maas et al., 1984; Maloney, 1994; Millaud et al., 1996; Mones, 1991; Newhill, 1991; Planasky & Johnson, 1977; Sadoff, 1971; Silva et al., 1989, 1992; Singhal & Dutta, 1990; Swanson, 1993; Swanson et al., 1990; Tanay, 1976; Virkkunen, 1974; Weisman & Sharma, 1997; Weisman et al., 2002), there appears to emerge a typology of parricide offenders consisting of five major categories, having (as with most typologies) some degree of overlap.

Abuse Parricide. Here, the parricide occurs mainly in response to a history of severe, persistent abuse by the slain parent. The abuse is often characterized by **polyabuse**, including physical beatings, sexual molestation, psychological humiliation, neglect of nutrition and basic needs, etc. In this context, killing the parent is conceptualized as a form of self-defense, to prevent the abuse from continuing. Often, several children in the family have been abused by the same parent, and, in some cases, the killing is done by a sibling of the abused child who has witnessed the abuse of his or her brother or sister. The overall dynamic appears similar to that of **the battered spouse syndrome** discussed in Chapters 3 and 17. The perpetrators of this type of parricide tend to be younger than other types, typically older children or teens. Most perpetrators are boys and firearms are the most commonly used weapon.

Parental discord, spousal violence, and substance abuse often characterize the home life of these abusive families. Many of these adolescents have tried to get help or to escape from their abusive family environment, but have been frustrated in their efforts to do so. Typically, there has been no prior history of antisocial or criminal behavior; indeed, they are often characterized by teachers and other observers as "good kids" who do well in school, generally stay out of trouble, and give little or no evidence of significant psychopathology. Nevertheless, many of these children come to feel increasingly isolated, helpless, and hopeless. In some cases, the killing is described as having occurred in a dissociative state. After the parricide, despite the legal repercussions, there is often a palpable sense of relief that the abusive parent is gone. This sense of "good riddance" may be shared by other members of the family who had been terrorized by the slain parent.

Family Conspiracy Parricide. This may be a subset of the above abuse parricide category, and may also overlap with the antisocial-economic parricide category below. In a family conspiracy parricide, a child kills one parent as either the knowing or unwitting agent of the other parent. In one scenario, the parent subtly and unconsciously incites the child to kill the other parent. In other cases, the parent may subtly convey that he or she will "look the other way" or even cover for the child if he or she decides to take justice into his or her own hands. Or one parent may make overt comments about the abusing parent to the effect that "everyone would be better off if he was dead." In still other cases, the parent blatantly encourages or even bribes the child to kill the abusive parent. Finally, the other parent may not be aware of the child's intent to kill, but helps the child conceal the evidence in the aftermath, out of a protective instinct toward her offspring; this is commonly the case where the child may not be an abuse victim himself, but kills the father (or more commonly, stepfather) to protect his mother who has been the primary abuse victim. Conspiracies may also involve siblings, as in the famous Menendez case, where two teenage brothers murdered both parents, ostensibly to collect their inheritance early, and only when caught, claimed a lifetime of abuse. Thus, in such family conspiracy parricide cases, it is extremely important to discern the veracity of the reported abuse, as many of these cases overlap with the antisocial-economic category below.

Antisocial-Economic Parricide. This type of parricide offender kills a mother or father for selfish reasons, primarily greed, to obtain money or property, or occasionally as revenge for an actual or perceived offense. Often, there has been a long history of antisocial behavior in the young perpetrator, beginning with conduct disorder in childhood, but severe mood or psychotic disorder is absent. **Double parricides**, although a minority of all parricides, may be more common in this more seriously disturbed subset. Not surprisingly, these types of parricides are likely to involve families with some degree of wealth. In many cases, as with the Lyle and Erik Menendez case, the killings seem "senseless," in that the children would someday inherit the money anyway. In these situations, other motivations may play a role, such as resentment of one or both parents for being successful, feelings of personal inadequacy on the part of the parricidal child, or the admixture of other factors, such as an actual or perceived abuse history; indeed, as noted above, a history of such abuse is typically offered after the fact as a justification or exculpatory excuse for the killing.

Mental Illness Parricide. This type of parricide is usually committed by an older adolescent or adult child with a severe psychotic or depressive mental illness that makes him unable to take care of himself and leaves him dependent on his parents. The most common diagnosis in these cases is some form of schizophrenia, and there is typically a long history of psychosocial disturbance making it impossible for the grown child to live independently, and associated in many cases with prior violent acting-out against family members or others. The perpetrator usually commits the parricide during a paranoid psychotic episode with prominent persecutory delusions and possibly command hallucinations. A few cases of parricide committed in the context of **Capgras syndrome** (delusional misidentification) have been described. Schizophrenic offspring are more likely to kill mothers than fathers, perhaps because mothers are typically the primary caretakers, so there may be more conflictual issues in the relationship; or mothers are just more often likely to be home and are therefore more easily available targets of opportunity. In double parricides, fathers are usually killed before mothers, perhaps to remove the more difficult target first. Almost a third of psychotic parricidal killers may be intoxicated at the time of the murder. The parricidal killings by schizophrenic offspring are often characterized by overkill, decapitation, and body mutilation, including genital mutilation. Up to half of perpetrators attempt or complete suicide following the killing.

Accidental Parricide. This occurs in two contexts. In one scenario, a father and his adolescent or adult son, often with a long history of bad blood between them, get into a heated argument in which the son strikes the father, inadvertency killing him. Intoxication and/or mental illness may play a role in up to one-third of these cases.

The other scenario involves a history of elder abuse by an adult child in which the dependent parent is physically battered and/or neglected; there may be economic motives as well, e.g., keeping the parent alive to collect disability or pension payments. Daughters may be equally likely to perpetrate this abuse as sons. At some point, the beatings or starvation or lack of sanitation and medical care result in the inadvertent death of the parent and the abusive child loses his or her "golden goose." He or she may then attempt to conceal the death to keep the checks coming for as long as possible. This category would also overlap with the antisocial-economic parricide classification, and may share features of the accidental filicide category discussed earlier.

Altruistic Parricide. This tends to occur with elderly parents, usually in their 70s and 80s, killed by their middle-aged adult children. The context is usually a severe, painful, and incurable illness or disability in which the child is the overburdened caretaker. This kind of "mercy killing" is almost always nonviolent, via narcotic overdose or carbon monoxide poisoning. Although primarily motivated by compassion for the suffering parent, many of these perpetrators are clinically depressed at the time of the killing. In some cases, they will claim that it was the parent's last wish that they not be allowed to linger. Essentially, this type of parricide is similar to altruistic filicides and altruistic spouse homicides where the primary motive is to spare the victim further suffering.

FRATRICIDE: SIBLING HOMICIDE

Fratricide: Description and Demographics

Although the term **fratricide** literally means murder of a brother, the term also includes **sororicide**, or the killing of a sister. Fratricide is the first crime that occurs in the Bible, committed by Cain against his brother Abel in the Book of Genesis. Today, over 100 people are murdered by siblings in the United States every year. Males are 3–4 times as likely to be both victims and perpetrators of sibling homicide. About three-fourths of sibling homicides involve brothers as victims, and one-quarter involve sisters. In about 70 percent of cases, the perpetrator and victim are of the same sex. Most perpetrators and victims are adults, however, younger siblings are more likely to murder older siblings. Most fratricides occur in a private home. Studies vary as to method of fratricide, estimates of firearm use ranging from 30 percent in Canadian samples to 60 percent in the United States, with most of the remainder involving bladed weapons. Most fratricide perpetrators have no prior criminal record, but alcohol use is involved in about 60 percent of such incidents (Bourget & Gagne, 2006; Daly et al., 2001; Flowers, 2002a; Gebo, 2002; Marleau & Saucier, 1998; Underwood & Patch, 1999).

Fratricide: Perpetrator Characteristics, Motives, and Psychodynamics

As with many homicides generally, most murders of siblings–what can be termed **impulsive fratricides**–typically erupt from family arguments over money or property, often in the context of a pre-existing or ongoing power struggle between the siblings. In many cases, these sibling rivalries may have been festering for years, and the danger is heightened where the adult siblings continue to live in the same residence. Paradoxically, the murderer and his sibling victim may have been "drinking buddies," and many fratricides (as with other family homicides and homicides in general) are fueled by alcohol consumption at the time of the crime in families with a pre-existing high risk for alcohol and substance use. The homicide is often preceded by a physical altercation (pushing, grabbling, punching, grappling), and there may have been few or many such confrontations in the past, but this time, the fight gets out of control and escalates to homicide.

A second, less common type of sibling homicide–which can be called **psychotic fratricide**–involves the intentional and premeditated murder of a brother or sister by a sibling who is psychotic or severely mentally ill at the time of the murder and who usually has a prior history of such illness. In these cases, the fratricide may be part of a broader attempt at **familicide**, or killing the whole family (see below), although in most cases of fratricide, suicide following the event is rare (Bourget & Gagne, 2006; Daly & Wilson, 1988; Daly et al., 2001; Ewing, 1997; Gebo, 2002; Underwood & Patch, 1999).

FAMILICIDE: FAMILY ANNIHILATION

As noted above, some fratricides are committed in an attempt to wipe out the perpetrator's entire family. **Familicide** is the killing of most or all of one's family, and is relatively rare compared to other domestic homicides. The typical perpetrator is a white, male, middle-aged head of the household who is struggling to cope with multiple stresses, and who reacts by killing his wife and children. He will usually attempt to kill all family members, sometimes even including pets. A firearm is typically the weapon of choice. The familicidal act is often followed by suicide, although a few family annihilators apparently change their mind and attempt to flee (Ewing, 1997; Flowers, 2002c).

A common profile of the familicidal perpetrator is a middle-aged man, with prominent depressive and/or paranoid features, who exhibits an obsessive need for complete control over everyone and everything in his life, including work and family members. His control of family members is typically rationalized as "protecting" them. Now, he is experiencing a variety of cumulative stresses, such as employment problems, financial hardship, increasing maturity and independence of his children, strained relationship with his spouse, and especially the threat of separation from his spouse. He feels his hold on life slipping away, begins to decompensate into a state of suicidal hopelessness and helplessness, and decides that killing his family is the only way to "protect" them after he is gone, which is often at least partly a reaction formation against partially repressed anger and resentment of having been put in this situation by his ungrateful family (Ewing, 1997; Flowers, 2002a). In many respects, this motive may be similar to the kind of altruistic filicide committed by mothers, as discussed above, as well as containing features of mass homicide perpetrator psychology, discussed in Chapters 11 and 12. In other cases, the familicide may be motivated by explicit revenge against one or more family members; in these latter cases, the perpetrator is more likely to flee.

As rare as male-perpetrated familicide is, still less common are cases where females murder their entire families. In these cases, despondency over a severed relationship, probably in an individual with a dependent or borderline personality organization on the background of severe depression, is the most common profile. Also rare are juveniles who attempt to annihilate their entire families. Similar to some parricide perpetrators (see above), many of these young killers suffer from a serious psychiatric disorder, often compounded by child abuse (Ewing, 1997; Flowers, 2000).

SUMMARY AND CONCLUSIONS

Is it true that "you always hurt the ones you love"? Well, some of them, anyway. In this chapter we see the varied ways that violence in the family can express itself. Children may be battered and abused by parents and caretakers who, emotionally, are little better than children themselves. Some of these beatings may inadvertently lead to accidental death, but **filicide** may be committed more deliberately by parents who are psychotic, who believe the child's death is "for their own good," who seek revenge against the other parent, or who find the child an intolerable burden. Some young mothers kill and dispose of their newborns as part of a massive denial system regarding the pregnancy itself. Other mothers make a crusade of their martyred devotion to their chronically sick children, whom they harm themselves to garner attention and manipulate authority in **Munchausen's Syndrome by Proxy**. Sometimes the generational tables are turned, and children become abusers of their parents, usually single mothers by teenage sons or elderly parents by middle-aged offspring. **Parricidal** children may kill their own parents and **fratricidal** siblings may kill one another, usually over issues of family status or money. Finally, the **family annihilator** commits **familicide**, usually in a state of either extreme rage or psychotic despair.

Chapter 17

Family Crime II:
Domestic Violence

BOX 17.1. MISSED LUNCH

O.J. Simpson owes me lunch. Let me explain.

On January 24, 1995, the trial opened in which football legend and movie actor O.J. Simpson was accused of murdering his wife, Nicole Brown Simpson, and her friend, Ronald Goldman. As most Americans know, this case became a bellwether for the issue of domestic violence, and one of the local mental health associations in South Florida convened a full-day conference, to be held October 3rd of that year, to address the wide range of social, political, and legal issues related to the topic of domestic violence. To this end, the conference committee enlisted a panel of speakers, including attorneys, judges, social service workers, victim advocates, and a psychologist—guess who. My presentation was scheduled to take place right after lunch, at 1:00 p.m., and was to address the psychological factors, in both victims and perpetrators, that contribute to domestic violence. So far, so good.

Fast-forward to October 3, 1995, the day of the conference. I decided to arrive early so I could have lunch with a few of the other speakers and conferees who were colleagues and friends of mine. I arrived at the conference center at about 11:30 am, only to discover that all the good parking spots were taken up by local news media vehicles, and I was forced to deposit my car on a grassy knoll some distance away. "Cool," I thought to myself, "It's about time the media took mental health issues seriously." Still, I was a little suspicious of all this attention for a local conference.

I walked inside, stopped off at the registration table to get my speaker's ID badge and ribbon, and walked into the main conference area to search for my lunch companions, just around noon. Almost immediately, a camera was poked in my face and a news commentator, who apparently had spied my speaker's badge and rushed over for a sound bite from this local expert, asked me, "What do you think the verdict will be? What impact do you think it will have on women's rights?" Give me credit for one thing: I was able to cough up a reasonably articulate one- or two-liner that seemed to satisfy this newsie before he rushed off to ambush the next presenter. But my erstwhile lunch companions were nowhere to be found. And the general tone of the whole place was something like subdued pandemonium.

Then, one of the conference organizers spotted me and pulled me aside: "Dr. Miller," she said, "there may be a little change in the program; I hope you don't mind." Uh-oh, I'm thinking, now what—are they going to cancel my presentation and assign me to valet parking? She went on to tell me that, earlier this morning, it had been announced that the O.J. verdict would be rendered at precisely—you guessed it—1:00 p.m. today, and would I mind if they played the verdict on TV, and then my presentation could comment on the verdict—as long as, of course, I didn't go too much over my time limit.

Okay, I'm thinking, I'm a sport, and, besides, what better way to get a lunch-addled conference crowd to find their seats on time and actually pay attention to what I'm saying. The conference organizer then showed me the podium where I'd be speaking, which was flanked on either side by two huge wide-angle TV screens, poised to dwarf the puny human figure that would soon be squeaking out his commentary. I was told that we'd wait until the verdict was announced on TV, allow some time for the audience to react, and then I'd go on to present my program. And, oh yes, they had some questions for me and other matters to attend to before the news broadcast, so no time for lunch (okay, a quick bagel and coffee, but that doesn't count).

To my last day, I'll remember the exact time the O.J. verdict was announced—1:12 p.m.—because I was zeroed in on my watch, calculating how much presentation time I'd have to shave off with each passing minute. When the not-guilty verdict finally came forth, the reaction of the conference audience—most of whom were mental health, social service, and criminal justice professionals involved daily in dealing with domestic violence cases, most of whom were women, and many of whom were minorities—replicated the reaction of viewers around the country: some factions gasping in disbelief, others sitting stonily and registering no response at all, a few trying to conceal expressions of satisfied vindication. This was the act I had to follow.

I clambered up onto the podium between the now-blankly looming TV screens which seemed to be mutely glaring down on me, as if to chide: "And after this, what could *you* possibly have to say?"—a sentiment which also seemed to be reflected in the intently skeptical stares of my growingly antsy audience. I began my presentation with a balanced (at least so I thought) review of the risk factors for domestic violence in perpetrators and the characteristics of victims that may place them at risk for abuse, and got about a quarter-way through my speech, when hands started shooting up. If I didn't previously believe in the power of displacement and projection, I certainly did now, because the audience members proceeded to lob a withering fusillade of invective at me for even the mere suggestion that there was anything in a woman's personality or behavior that would "justify" her being abused by her mate.

Which, of course, was not what I was saying, and I tried to explain as much, but the audience was having none of it. I fielded more questions, made some basic points of my presentation, philosophically accepted my conscripted whipping-boy role as evil-male-psychologist-stooge-of-the-masculine-industrial-complex-who's-blaming-the-victim-yet-again by absorbing some of the pain and out-

continued

BOX 17.1.—*Continued*

rage swirling around the room, and basically felt lucky to get out there alive and let the next presenter take over—a female judge. I stuck around in the lobby for about an hour to answer a few stray questions and do one more brief media sound-bite, then high-tailed it back to my office for my afternoon appointments. I never did get lunch. O.J., you owe me.

B ecause it intersects so many areas–psychology, sociology, anthropology, criminal justice, politics, even religion–the topic of **domestic violence** continues to be a volatile and contentious issue. Furthermore, like the discussion of marital rape in Chapter 14, what makes these crimes so vexing is that, on the one hand, they take place in the home, which is the one place most people expect to feel safe, and they are perpetrated by a spouse or other close partner which toxically commingles intimacy and violence. On the other hand, the very familiarity of the persons involved and the home environs in which these acts take place, make the pattern so much harder to break and harder to see danger coming until something irrevocably harmful occurs.

DOMESTIC VIOLENCE:
CLINICAL AND DEMOGRAPHIC FEATURES

Only in the past several decades has **domestic violence (DV)**, or **intimate partner violence (IPV)**, or **domestic battery** received increased national and worldwide attention. Beginning with the Women's Movement of the 1970s, advocacy of this issue led to U.S. Surgeon General C. Everett Koop's designation of domestic violence as a major public health issue in 1985, followed by the 1994 passage of the **Violence Against Women Act** by the U.S. Congress. Domestic violence is generally considered to consist of any physical, sexual, or psychological/emotional abuse toward a current or former intimate partner (e.g., spouse, boyfriend/girlfriend) or close family member (e.g., a parent; see Chapter 16). Although the emphasis has been on physical violence between married or cohabiting intimate partners, psychological abuse can take a toll as well, although rarely does the latter come to the attention of criminal justice authorities (Alpert et al., 1997; Garcia et al., 2007; Haywood & Haile-Mariam, 1999; Sartin et al., 2006; Scott, 1999).

A considerable body of research, clinical, and forensic experience (Aldorondo & Straus, 1994; Appel & Holden, 1998; Arias & Pape, 1999; Browne

& Williams, 1989; Burke, 2007; Campbell, 1992a, 1992b, 1995, 2002; Cascardi et al., 1999; Cavanaugh & Dobash, 2007; Clements & Ogle, 2007; Coker et al., 2002; Crofford, 2007; Farr, 2002; Follingstad et al., 1991; Garcia et al., 2007; Gleason, 1993; Golding, 1994, 1999; Huss & Ralston, 2008; Kellerman, 1992; Kennair & Mellor, 2007; Lesserman & Drossman, 2007; Logan et al., 2002; Mbilinyi et al., 2007; Mercy & Saltzman, 1989; Miller, 2008b; Olshaker et al., 2001; Rennison & Welchans, 2000; Shackleford et al., 2000; Sheridan & Nash, 2007; Simmons & Lehman, 2007; Stark & Flitcraft, 1996; Stover, 2005; Tjaden & Thoennes, 2000c; U.S. Department of Justice, 1994; Vitanza et al. 1995) has established some basic facts about domestic violence:

In the United States, more than one million cases of domestic violence occur every year. Domestic violence accounts for three-quarters of all assaults against women, including nearly one-quarter of the 1.4 million intentional injuries treated in emergency departments. Domestic violence adversely affects approximately 1.7 million women at any given moment. A woman in the United States is beaten by her husband or boyfriend every nine seconds. Over 20 percent of couples in the United States have experienced one or more episodes of partner violence over the previous year. In their lifetime, over 20 percent of women experience physical violence, over 7% are raped by their intimate partner (Chapter 14), and approximately 5 percent are stalked (Chapter 18). While some women exclusively batter men, this is the exception; approximately 85 percent of domestic violence victims are women, although often both partners become embroiled in a fight and injure each other. While cases of child abuse by adults (Chapter 16) are usually considered separate from domestic violence between adults, up to 8 million children have witnessed domestic violence within their household, and up to 75 percent of these children have been abused themselves. In addition, some older and adolescent children abuse one or more parents, usually the mother (Chapter 16).

The most common mechanism of injury in domestic violence is blunt force trauma to the head, face, or body; the next most common injury is strangulation. Children are often injured while trying to protect their mothers from being beaten. Conversely, women may be beaten in the course of trying to prevent their children from being abused. Even pets may be attacked and injured. At least 2000 women are killed each year by a domestic partner; in fact, women are far more likely to be killed by a domestic partner than by a stranger. The risk of lethal violence is increased in cases where the batterer makes frequent threats to kill the victim, uses a weapon against her, chokes her, or commits sexual violence against her.

The aftermath of domestic violence can affect the victim's physical and mental health long after the battering relationship ends, and may include major depression, psychosexual disorders, anxiety, panic disorder, PTSD, substance abuse, headaches, fibromyalgia and other chronic pain syndromes, chronic fatigue syndrome, temporomandibular joint disorders, irritable bowel syndrome, and suicide attempts. These effects are more severe, the greater the intensity and frequency of the violence.

DOMESTIC VIOLENCE PERPETRATOR CHARACTERISTICS

There are a number of individual factors that contribute to domestic violence; typically these factors will have an additive or cumulative effect, each one multiplying and exacerbating the effects of the others. Many of these risk factors are general risk factors for antisocial behavior in general, as discussed throughout this book.

For example, domestic violence perpetrators tend to be young males, to have a history of prior and concurrent antisocial behavior, substance abuse, previous arrests, lower educational and occupational level, dysfunctional families of origin, histories of abuse as a child, and current conflictual relationships at home and in the community (Aldarondo & Sugarman, 1996; Gondolf & White, 2001; Huss & Ralston, 2008; Lee et al., 2004; Sartin et al., 2006).

Some authorities have attempted to categorize domestic batterers based on personality type. In this view, men with **antisocial personality disorder** tend to view their marriage as just another relationship to exploit, so they may quickly resort to violence when they don't get their way. Men with **narcissistic and paranoid personality disorders** tend to have thin and easily bruised egos and may misinterpret innocuous statements and actions by their mates as signs of disrespect and betrayal that warrant retaliation. **Borderline and dependent personality-disordered** batterers are likely to be pathologically enmeshed with their mates, yet conceal it behind a façade of exaggerated independence and violent hypermachoism. Women who are domestic violence perpetrators are also most likely to have a **borderline** personality configuration which puts them at greater risk of perpetrating acts of violence toward their relationship partners, which in turn may spur vicious cycles of retaliation, leading to greater violence, resulting in **dual arrests** (Allen & Farmer, 1996; Dutton, 1995; Weaver & Clum, 1993).

Acquired brain injury and/or developmental brain dysfunction has been posited as a contributing factor in domestic violence. Extrapolating from the general neuropsychology of violence, some authorities point to **frontal and temporal lobe dysfunction** as a substrate of impulsive aggression in the family (Golden et al., 1996; Marsh & Martinovich, 2006). Only a few studies have examined this directly (Cohen et al., 1999, 2003; Marsh & Martinovich, 2006; Rosenbaum & Hoge, 1989; Rosenbaum et al., 1994), generally finding that, overall, about half of convicted male domestic violence perpetrators report a history of traumatic brain injury, with some evidence of lower IQ and impaired executive functioning in the perpetrator group. However, as we've seen throughout this text, this is a nonspecific finding for violent individuals in general.

DOMESTIC VIOLENCE PERPETRATOR TYPOLOGIES

Clinical and Research-Based Batterer Typologies

Some researchers (Johnson, 1995; Leone et al., 2004) have dichotomized domestic violence into two main types: **Intimate terrorism** is characterized by one partner's efforts to exert total control over the other partner, using a variety of coercive strategies, including physical violence. Although spontaneously rageful outbursts may erupt, there is typically a cold and calculated quality to this violence, betraying its primarily manipulative nature. **Situational couple violence**, is less directly coercive, but arises mainly in specific situations where conflict escalates into physical aggression, i.e., the perpetrator "loses it." Alternatively, this classification may represent less of a dichotomy and more of a spectrum that ranges from instances of situational couple violence to more enduring patterns of intimate terrorism (Hughes et al., 2007).

Based on clinical and forensic interviews, Edin et al. (2008) sorts partner-violent men into three categories, based on the latency and impulsivity of their aggression:

"He-man"–attacking man–immediate aggression. This is a traditional "man's man," working at a man's job (usually involving physical labor), and found more commonly in rural than in urban areas. He holds a traditional male authoritarian view of the man as head of the household, and if he feels this status is being threatened, he may defensively and impulsively lash out against any family member, typically the spouse, who directly or implicitly threatens his dominant role.

"Pressure cooker"–exploding man–sudden aggression. This man bottles up his anxieties and insecurities behind an emotionally detached and placid facade because he fears losing control of his aggression if this stolid persona is challenged. He may not respond immediately, but once provoked past the "tipping point," his reaction explodes out of control, and he may be capable of extreme violence.

"Super partner"–persuading man–ultimately aggressor. This is the perfect husband who does everything to meet his partner's and family's needs–working two jobs, fixing up the house, helping with the child care–yet he feels unappreciated and unloved. At first, this spurs him to even more feverishly self-sacrificing efforts, but eventually he gets the message that, no matter what he does, this devotion will never be reciprocated and, worse, he begins to suspect that his mate is casting an eye toward others. Finally, "at the end of his rope," having exhausted all attempts to win her over, he "snaps" and a violent outburst ensues.

Probably the most well-known and influential domestic batterer typology to date is the tripartite model proposed by Holtzworth-Munroe & Stuart (1994):

Relationship/family-only batterers. These are theorized to comprise about 50 percent of identified batterers, have relatively low overall rates of marital violence, and are relatively free of significant substance abuse or psychopathology.

Borderline/dysphoric batterers. Comprising about 25 percent of batterers, these men exhibit moderately high rates of violence in the home, but are relatively nonviolent in other settings. As the name implies, these batterers exhibit personality disorders mainly in the borderline-schizoid spectrum, complicated by anger, depression, and substance abuse.

Generally violent/antisocial batterers. Violence is a way of life for these men, about 25 percent of the total, who engage in high rates of aggression in the home and general antisocial behavior in the community.

In a follow-up validation study with a community sample of men, Holtzworth-Munroe et al. (2000) found support for the existence of their original three groups, as well as for an unanticipated fourth group they labeled the **low-level antisocial batterer**, comprising 33 percent of the total sample. These men generally fell somewhere between the family-only and generally violent batterers in terms of the frequency and severity of their aggressive behavior. A further follow-up study (Holtzworth-Munroe et al., 2003) confirmed that these subtypes continue their behavior over time, with the greatest persistence of antisocial behavior seen in the generally violent group.

The intuitive as well as clinical appeal of the Holtzworth-Munroe & Stuart (1994) batterer typology has led several other researchers to study its applicability to different groups (Capaldi & Kim, 2007; Gottman et al., 1995; Hamberger et al., 1996; Huss & Ralston, 2008; Langhinrichsen-Rohling et al., 2000; Sartin et al., 2006; Tweed & Dutton, 1998). Generally, the results all point to the same three primary clusters of batterers: (1) the otherwise nonpathological perpetrator who occasionally flies off the handle during a family dispute, but is otherwise nonviolent (**family-only batterers**, or **FO**); (2) the edgy, irritable, depressed, immature, and dependent perpetrator whose impulsive battering reflects the presence of a borderline, narcissistic, or other Cluster-B-type personality disorder (**borderline/dysphoric batterers**, or **BD**); and (3) the perpetrator with antisocial personality disorder, whose domestic violence is just part of a more generally manipulative, coercive, and aggressive interpersonal style (**generally violent/antisocial batterers**, or **GVA**). A few studies have found some overlap between the BD and GVA batterer subtypes, consistent with the natural diagnostic overlap of clinical syndromes discussed throughout this book.

Further research (Capaldi & Kim, 2007; Huss & Ralston, 2008; Sartin et al., 2006) has shown that FO batterers are more likely to complete batterer treatment programs than the other two classes, reflecting the often-noted phenomenon that those who need intervention the most are the least likely to seek it and/or complete it. Not surprisingly, GVA batterers have the highest recidivism rate, consistent with their generally aggressive lifestyle, followed by BD and FO batterers, respectively. The few studies that have examined women who are batterers (Babcock et al., 2003; Swan & Snow, 2002) have found them to cluster into GV and FO groups, with no BD group, which seems odd, considering that borderline personality disorder is diagnosed more often in women (Chapter 7).

Batterer Typologies in the Legal System

There have also been some attempts to apply research-based domestic violence typologies to the practical adjudication of family law cases (Jaffee et al., 2008; Johnson, 1995, 2005; Kelly & Johnson, 2008), which has yielded four main groups.

Abusive-controlling violence (ACV). This is an ongoing pattern of using threat, force, emotional abuse, and other coercive means to intimidate and dominate one's partner, with the perpetrator almost always being the male in the relationship.

Conflict-instigated violence (CIV). In these cases, violence is perpetrated by both partners, who have limited skills in resolving conflicts. A fight escalates to violence, police are called to the scene of a domestic violence incident, and in some cases, both partners may be arrested, i.e., a **dual arrest**.

Violent resistance (VR). This essentially involves the victim of a domestic violence attack (typically the woman) defending herself vigorously against the attacker (typically the man). In some cases, this has resulted in the victim killing her attacker, which may either be regarded by the law as self-defense, or may be prosecuted as an unwarranted overreaction to the abuse.

This category may also overlap with the CIV category, as when one of two sparring partners escalates the fight to fatal violence.

Separation-instigated violence (SIV). This represents a rare, out-of-character violent reaction by either a man or woman in response to an ongoing or threatened divorce or other relationship rupture, in the context of a relationship that has not otherwise been characterized by excessive violence or coercive control.

BOX 17.2. DOMESTIC VIOLENCE AND LAW ENFORCEMENT I: POLICE RESPONSE TO A DOMESTIC VIOLENCE CALL

Of all the calls for service that police officers make, the ones they dread the most are domestic disturbance calls, even though these are typically less physically dangerous than some other kinds of calls, such as traffic stops. There seems to be an instinctive reluctance to intrude into the physical and psychological private spaces of a person's homestead, but for police officers to uphold the law and to protect potential victims, this sometimes becomes necessary.

Police Response to Domestic Calls

Danger aside, there are reasons why most police officers disdain intervening in family disputes more than almost any other kind of police work (Balenovich et al., 2008; Blau, 1994; Miller, 2006f; Russell & Beigel, 1990; Sun, 2007). Part of this inheres in the extraordinarily interpersonally demanding aspects of such calls. Even if no arrest is made, sorting out and calming down a domestic dispute, essentially performing crisis intervention, mediation, and arbitration, all in the midst of a chaotic scene that may involve adults, children, intoxicated subjects, and potentially hidden weapons, stretches an officer's communication and diplomacy skills to the limit. If an officer is not already somewhat experienced and comfortable in using these communication and crisis intervention skills, this will prove to be a painfully challenging call. As a self-protective psychological defense, many officers consider domestic calls not to be "real" police work; disparaging them as "social work" or "bullshit calls."

More compellingly, intervening in domestic disputes may resonate with the personal experiences of many officers, whose own family lives may have been, and/or continue to be, far from idyllic (also see Box 17.3). Thus, the personal identification factor is especially strong for this kind of police work.

Not all concerns are psychological, however. Domestic disturbance calls remain the second most physically dangerous police interventions from the perspective of potential officer injury, and about a third of these calls involve a violent crime. People are typically in an extreme emotional state, often intoxicated, rarely rational, and therefore most prone to suspend judgment and caution and assault an officer. The paradox is that, because many officers regard these as b.s. calls, they may be even less likely to take appropriate precautions than they would in responding to a robbery in progress or a suspicious traffic stop. At the same time, potentially aggressive occupants may feel more secure and more justified in attacking the responding officers while on home turf. Finally, a domestic disturbance call can easily escalate to an assault, murder, or **hostage-barricade situation**, thereby posing further danger to officers and civilians.

Overall, the most frequent type of response to domestic disturbance calls is "no action taken," often because the responding officers have been able to resolve the situation before physical violence and an arrestable offense have occurred. Alternatively, the situation has spontaneously cooled or one party has left the scene by the time the officers arrive. Of course, when domestic assault has occurred, officers are mandated to make an arrest. As noted earlier, domestic battery tends to be a repeat crime, and arrest of the perpetrator is what usually has the strongest deterrent effect on recidivism.

In many cases, it is unclear who started the fight, but by the time police arrive, both members of the couple have attacked each other. The use of **mandatory arrest policies** in cases of domestic violence in most jurisdictions has brought growing attention to the role of the female partner in domestic disputes, leading in many cases to the arrest of both parties (Steinmetz & Lucca, 1988). Some victims' advocates have suggested that many of these women are not true aggressors themselves, but rather injured their attackers while defending themselves. However, officers arriving at the scene may not be able to make this distinction and, even if they could, mandatory arrest policies dictate that anyone who has committed an assault—no matter how justified they thought it was at the time—may be subject to arrest, compounding the abuse of at least some of these women who may be busted for protecting themselves (Abel, 2001; Allen et al., 2004; Hirschel & Buzawa, 2002; Hughes et al., 2007; Martin, 1997).

Unfortunately, those batterers most likely to learn their lesson from such an arrest are those least likely to be repeat offenders in the first place. That is, they are ordinarily nonviolent, law-abiding, well-educated, and gainfully employed citizens who have something substantial to lose from being arrested and prosecuted for a crime. Typically, for these men, the domestic assault was a one-time overreaction carried out in a distraught state, not a regular, persistent pattern of behavior—characterized as the **situational** or **family-only batterer** in the Holtzworth-Munroe & Stuart (1994) typology described elsewhere in this chapter. For the chronic repeat offender, however (the **borderline-dysphoric** or **generally violent batterer**), even multiple arrests are not likely to be an effective deterrent; nor will the abuse be stopped by restraining orders or any other measures short of incarceration of the offender or extrication of the spouse from the relationship and having her get as far away as possible.

Citizen Dissatisfaction with Police Domestic Violence Response

As just noted, once a domestic assault has occurred, officers are mandated to take the necessary arrest action. But, as with almost every aspect of patrol

continued

BOX 17.2.—*Continued*

policing (Miller, 2006d; Peak, 2003; Russell & Beigel, 1990), having an interpersonal and communication skill-set to use in family dispute and domestic violence calls can greatly reduce the potential for escalation and the necessity for making arrests or using physical force in a subject's home. As always, **the best form of crisis intervention is crisis prevention** (Miller, 2006f, 2008b). In addition, the tact and sensitivity—or lack of it—with which officers handle domestic dispute calls will resonate within the individual household and with the broader community and will influence citizens' subsequent interactions with the police. Therefore, it would be useful to have some perspective on how citizens perceive local law enforcement responses to their domestic conflict calls.

Just this kind of constructive criticism was actively solicited in a study by Kennedy & Homant (1984), who surveyed the reactions of a group of citizens who had called police to respond to a domestic crisis. The study found that citizen dissatisfaction with officer response to domestic violence calls fell into several categories:

Minimizing the situation. Citizens were distressed when responding officers seemed to downplay the seriousness of the assault or the severity of the injuries: "That just looks like a scratch; it's hardly even bleeding much." "He only hit you once with the plate? Was it a ceramic or a plastic plate?"

Disbelieving the victim. Citizens felt that officers treated them as if they were lying or exaggerating: "You sure that bruise is new? It looks like something you might've bumped into a few days ago. Sometimes you can bang your arm and not even realize it." "Well, if you say he's been beating on you all afternoon, how come you waited till now to call us?"

Uncaring attitude. Victims felt like the officers were "just going through the motions" of taking the report, giving the impression that they had any number of better things to do than to waste their time on this bullshit call. This attitude was conveyed by distracted attention, disinterested or skeptical tone of voice, minimal eye contact, and often cross-talk, knowing glances, and joking with other officers or civilians on the scene, sometimes even including the accused perpetrator in the humor.

Macho cop. Officers sometimes (defensively?) adopted a tough, no-nonsense, "just-the-facts-ma'am" attitude, without showing a trace of concern or consideration for the distraught emotional state of the victim. In fact, these officers seemed to get annoyed when victims broke down with emotion or failed to give an orderly narrative of events that the officer could record.

Little or no practical information provided. Citizens were dismayed that many officers failed to offer practical information or guidance about victims' shelters, legal and financial support services, procedures for filing complaints, obtaining restraining orders, and so on. Often, when victims asked these questions directly, they received disdainful shrugs or don't-know responses, or officers who were persuaded to yield this information gave the impression that this was one more imposition on their time.

The common thread in these officer reactions seems to be a mixture of distaste for the domestic call itself and contemptuous disregard for the victims. One dynamic behind this may be the defensively macho orientation of many cops who regard victims as "losers," no matter where the fault lies, and are thus fearful of their own unconscious identification with the victim. Therefore, they distance themselves psychologically by downplaying the seriousness of the harm and/or denigrating the victim's motives and reactions (Miller, 2006f).

However, the Kennedy & Homant (1984) study did find that some citizens expressed satisfaction at responding officers' actions when these actions could be characterized as **small human acts of caring and consideration**. These included an engaged, interested interpersonal style; waiting for the victim to tell her whole story; questioning the victim to make sure the officer understood what she was saying; providing follow-up information and referrals; offering to call social services for the victim; and even making a follow-up call a few days later to check how the victim was doing. Citizens who got this, unfortunately much rarer, form of police response reported overwhelmingly more positive views of their local law enforcement agency. The general lesson for **community policing** is obvious: treating citizens with respect and consideration pays dividends in terms of both citizen cooperation and police safety.

CAUSAL FACTORS IN DOMESTIC VIOLENCE

Socioeconomic and Cultural Influences

Low socioeconomic status is a risk factor for domestic violence for several reasons. First, individuals with a higher rate of psychopathology, substance abuse, impulsivity, and risk factors for crime and violence in general tend to cluster within this demographic group. Second, economic strain, not to mention increased exposure to crime and poorer access to health care, all put additional psychosocial stress on these families, further reducing frustration tolerance and increasing violence-proneness (Chapter 3). Finally, women in these strata tend to have far fewer employment and family options than middle-class women, and may therefore opt to stay in heavily flawed relationships because, "better a dirty pair of pants to wash than no pants at all." Often it boils down to a paycheck and sheer survival. But nobody likes to feel like they're trapped, so the victim may well rationalize that the man and the overall situation are not really that bad and that "he really loves me" (Miller, 2008b).

Alcohol and Drug Abuse

As discussed elsewhere in this text, no drug "makes" someone commit domestic violence or any other kind of crime, but most substances can weaken already fragile inhibitions and may lower the threshold to impulsive action, including violence. Substance abuse is also a broader risk factor because it both drains money from the household pool and interferes with regular employment, further increasing economic strain. Drug use almost always involves participation, at some level, in the criminal subculture of one's community and, in some neighborhoods, drug dealing is a common and accepted means of supplementing one's income, often to buy more drugs for one's own use. Alcohol or substance use by the wife may also contribute to domestic arguments that flash over into violence, often involving both parties, and is more likely to be a factor where the woman is the aggressor, especially in cases where women have killed their batterers during a fight (Blount et al., 1994; Fagan, 1990; Flowers, 2002c; Jurik & Winn, 1990; Kantor & Jasinski, 1998; Stuart et al., 2004; Welte & Abel, 1989).

Domestic Violence Victims

Unfortunately, the search for contributory victim characteristics and relationship dynamics is often mischaracterized as blaming the victim (Box 17.1). However, these are important data that may be useful for treatment and protection of victims (Aldarondo & Sugarman, 1996; Coolidge & Anderson, 2002; Magdol et al., 1998; Mears et al., 2001; Miller, 2008b; Sartin et al., 2006). For example, higher rates of depression, PTSD, substance abuse, paranoid and dependent personality disorders, and self-defeating patterns of behavior have all been found in women who have been in multiple abusive relationships, and these women are at higher risk for future domestic violence victimization. Not surprisingly, high levels of overall marital conflict constitute a risk factor for partner violence.

Illness, Disability, and Pregnancy

Any factor that puts a strain on the dyadic relationship may constitute a risk factor for domestic violence, especially where individuals are already predisposed. One cruel irony is that women who are ill, disabled, or pregnant are more likely to be targets (Hassouneh-Phillips & Curry, 2002; Sullivan & Knutson, 2003), for varied reasons. First, disabled women may not be able to "pull their weight," economically, domestically, or sexually. Second, such women are likely to need extra care and attention and to be perceived as especially demanding. However, in some cases, the enforced invalidism of the wife is actually welcomed by a male partner who prizes control because, "now she's home where I can keep an eye on her." It is only when the woman recovers and wants to return to a more active lifestyle that trouble may erupt.

The Domestic Violence Cycle

The domestic violence cycle typically begins with the man becoming angry, suspicious, jealous, or resentful about something his wife purportedly has said or done. He attempts to restrict and control his mate who, in turn, may become resentful herself and resort to deception or outright rebellion. This only fuels the man's sense of righteous indignation, which may spark physical violence because "she deserves it" or to "teach her a lesson." In fact, one of the greatest risk factors for lethal domestic violence is the woman's stated intention to leave the relationship (Aldarondo & Straus, 1994; Capaldi & Kim, 2007; Wilson & Daly, 1993a,b). Depending on whether or not the violence is reported, the partner may or may not be arrested. After the storm has passed, many men display superficially sincere signs of remorse, often complete with tears and flowers, asserting some version of: "It's only because I love you so much and can't bear the thought of losing you" that led to the violent loss of control. Many women are so taken in by the next few days' or weeks' worth of lovey-dovey reconciliation that they quickly forget the bruises and scars, so much wanting to believe that "he's changed his ways, it'll be all right now." But soon, the cycle begins again.

Domestic Violence: Treatment and Desistance

As noted earlier, those batterers with the greatest severity and frequency of violence are the least likely to seek, accept, or comply with **court-ordered batterer intervention programs**, and are most likely to persist or resume their aggression, with treatment drop-out rates of approximately 40 percent (Rosenfeld, 1992; Sartin, 2006). For those who manage to complete the programs, post-treatment recidivism rates range from 40 percent to 80 percent (Huss & Ralston, 2008; Stover, 2005). However, inasmuch as even small reductions in the rates of domestic violence can have a substantial impact on thousands of women's lives (Babcock et al., 2003), it is important to understand what factors contribute to desistance or reduction in intimate partner violence.

Using the Holtzworth-Munroe & Stuart (1994) typology discussed above, researchers (Langhinrichsen et al., 2000; Sartin et al., 2006) have found that family-only and borderline-dysphoric batterers are more likely to complete batterer intervention programs than are generally violent batterers, consistent with what we know about the poor treatment record with antisocial personalities in general (Chapter 8). Generally violent batterers are also rated by clinicians as more violent and overall less likeable than other types.

INTIMATE PARTNER HOMICIDE

A victim of an intimate partner violence perpetrator is likely to spend her life with this man in a cycle of torment and dashed hopes. But sometimes, the violence escalates to the point of lethality, in which case it becomes **intimate partner homicide**, or **IPH**.

IPH: Description and Demographics

Women are more than twice as likely to be murdered by a male intimate partner than by any other type of killer. Approximately 15 percent of murders each year in the United States occur between intimate partners, and approximately 33 percent of female homicide victims are killed by their male partners; estimated rates of homicide by females on male intimate partners range widely, from 4 percent to 34 percent. In contrast to rising rates of female crime in other categories (Chapter 1), from the 1970s to the 2000s, the proportion of male homicides by a female intimate partner has decreased, while the percentage of female victims of male intimate partner homicide has increased—so more men are killing their wives and girlfriends, while fewer women are killing their men. Paralleling crime statistics in other categories, IPH is more common in minority couples than white couples. In 2004, more Americans lost their lives at the hands of intimate partners than were killed by enemy forces in Iraq. Up to 90 percent of women have been stalked by their intimate partners prior to being killed (Chapter 18), and a common scenario is for the perpetrator to kill his partner when she returns home to retrieve her belongings. IPH perpetrators are more likely than other kinds of murderers to commit suicide after killing their partner. Firearms are the weapons of choice in IPHs, although a variety of other weapons or objects may be used (Bachman & Saltzman, 1995; Bailey et al., 1997; Browne & Williams, 1989; Bureau of Justice, 1998; Buteau et al., 1993; Campbell et al., 2001; Farmer & Tiefenthaler, 2003; Flowers, 2002c; Fox & Zawitz, 2006; Garcia et al., 2007; Gauthier & Brankston, 2004; Kellerman & Mercy, 1992; Koziol-McLain et al., 2006; McFarlane et al., 1999; Mercy & Saltzman, 1989; Milroy, 1995; Morton et al., 1998; Rennison & Welchans, 2000; Roberts, 2009; Sorenson & Wiebe, 2004; Starzomski & Nussbaum, 2000; Tjaden & Thoennes, 2000a, 2000b, 2000c; U.S. Department of Justice, 1994, 2000; Zahn & Sagi, 1987; Zawitz, 1994; Zepp, 1996).

IPH: Risk Factors

Women who are separated or divorced are especially at risk for being murdered by an ex-intimate partner, especially where the relationship has been characterized by jealousy and the woman leaves the relationship for another man. For women still living in the relationship, the following are identified risk factors for IPH: (1) a past history of intimate partner violence; (2) the abuser is unemployed; (3) the abuser has a criminal history; (4) there are firearms in the home; (5) one or both partners have a history of mental illness (6) one or both partners are abusing substances; (7) one or both partners are socially isolated; (8) the woman is pregnant; (9) the woman is forced to have sex while pregnant; (9) there are one or more children in the home who are not the abuser's biological offspring; (10) the woman is older than age 30; (11) the woman is 15 or more years younger than her partner—in fact, many of these women began their relationships when they were teenagers. Approximately one in five high school girls surveyed report having at one time been physically or sexually abused by an intimate partner. In general, young women, poor women, and minority women are at increased risk for both domestic violence and intimate partner homicide (Bailey et al., 1997; Bourget et al., 2000; Browne, 1987; Bullock & Cubert, 2002; Caetano et al., 2005; Campbell & Soeken, 1999; Campbell et al., 2003a, 2003b; Chang et al., 2005; Decker et al., 2005; Dixon et al., 2008; Flowers, 2002c; Frye, 2001; Gallup-Black, 2005; Garcia et al., 2007; Gauthier & Brankston, 2004; Gazmararian et al., 1995, 1996; Gyimah-Brempong & Racine, 2006; Hiroeh et al., 2001; Jurik & Winn, 1990; Kellerman & Heron, 1999; Krulewitch et al., 2003; Kung et al., 1998; Lewandowski et al., 2004; McFarlane et al., 1996; O'Leary & Schumacher, 2003; Paulozzi et al., 2001; Rennison & Welchans, 2000; Roberts, 2009; Rosenbaum, 1990; Starr et al., 2004; Walsh & Hemensway, 2005; Weinsheimer et al., 2005).

IPH: Motives and Causes

Family History. A number of studies support a relationship between witnessing violence in the home as a child and later perpetration of, as well as victimization by, intimate partner violence, although, as with most family studies, it is difficult to disentangle biological and social learning factors (Bensley et al., 2003; Garcia, 2007; Fagan et al., 1983; Herrenkohl et al., 2004; Kalmuss, 1984; Liebschutz et al., 2002; Rennison & Welchans, 2000; White & Widom, 2003; Whitfield et al., 2003).

Personality and Psychopathology. In the Holtzworth-Munroe typology (Holtzworth-Munroe & Stuart, 1994; Holtzworth-Munroe et al., 2000), borderline/dysphoric and generally violent/antisocial batterers are most likely to commit IPH. The common dynamic seems to be male loss of control over an intimate partner, which triggers murderous rage that may either vengefully smolder or impulsively explode, and is characterized by extreme violence and overkill (Campbell, 1992b; Dixon, 2008; Dobash et al., 1992; Ewing, 1997; Flowers, 2002; Holmes & Holmes, 1994).

Evolutionary Psychology of IPH. The evolutionary psychology model recognizes male sexual jealousy as one of the most frequently cited causes of intimate partner violence, which is seen as a tactic used by men to restrict a partner's sexual behavior. In this hypothesis, men have evolved perceptual and cognitive mechanisms for detecting risk of a partner's sexual infidelity, including assessments of the time spent apart from him, the presence of potential male rivals, and his partner's behavioral indicators of the likelihood of her committing infidelity (e.g., flirting). Since human nature is naturally risk-averse, the male mind evolved to be hypersensitive to cues of a partner's sexual infidelity, generating more false positives than false negatives because the net reproductive benefits of the former outweigh the costs of the latter–that is, better to sometimes unjustly accuse his mate that to let her get away with an occasional dalliance. In some men, this sexual jealousy may reach extreme proportions that we might call pathological. In such cases, jealously-fueled partner violence may escalate to homicide, either by accident during a jealous rage, or deliberately in response to the fear that one's mate is cohabiting with rival males or planning to do so ("If I can't have you, no one can"). The likelihood of such killing will be moderated by contextual factors, such as violation of clan rules, costs to social reputation, presence of his mate's relatives who might retaliate, likelihood of obtaining a replacement mate, and so on (Buss, 2000; Buss & Malamuth, 1996; Daly & Wilson, 1988; Daly et al., 1982; Dobash & Dobash, 1979; Duntley & Buss, 2008; Dutton & Golant, 1995; Figueredo & McClosky, 1993; Frieze, 1983; Gage & Hutchinson, 2006; Goetz & Shackelford, 2006; Haselton & Nettle, 2006; Peters et al., 2002; Russell, 1982; Schmitt & Buss, 2001; Shackelford & Buss, 1997; Shackelford et al., 2002; Symons, 1979; Wilson & Daly, 1993b,c, 1996).

Female IPH Perpetrators

As discussed above, women are at least twice as likely to be killed by a male intimate partner than vice versa, and the patterns tend to differ as well. Generally, men are more likely to kill their partners after an escalation of violence, usually after their partners attempt to leave the relationship, while women tend to kill their partners in self-defense, in defense of others (usually children), or in retaliation for prior abuse. A generalized history of violence is less common in female IPH perpetrators than in males. In most studies of female IPH, the key factors have been found to be a history of repeated physical and psychological abuse and the woman's perception that there were no other viable options to escape the abusive environment for herself and/or her children, i.e., so-called **battered woman syndrome** (Chapter 3) (Bailey et al., 1997; Browne, 1987; Campbell, 1992, 1995; Campbell et al., 2001; Ewing, 1997; Flowers, 2002c; Garcia et al., 2007; Hall-Smith et al., 1998; Kellerman & Heron, 1999; Lee et al., 2002; McFarlane et al., 1999; Mercy & Saltzman, 1989; Moracco et al., 1998; Smith et al., 1998; U.S. Department of Justice, 1998; Walker, 1984).

Nevertheless, there are other reasons why women kill their male partners, including jealousy, substance abuse, mental illness, or financial motivations, i.e., marrying a succession of men for their money and doing away with each of them ("black widows"). In some cases, emotional and financial motives may be mixed, i.e., the abused woman who is tired of the maltreatment and feels that she deserves some "payback," both in blood and money (Flowers, 2002c; Polk & Ransom, 1991).

Same-Sex IPH

Homosexual couples are not immune from domestic violence or IPH; between 15 percent and 20 percent of gay and lesbian couples are affected by either. However, there are more male victims than female victims of same-sex IPH, probably reflecting the greater propensity of males to commit physically violent acts in general. This is supported by the finding that firearms are three times more likely to be used in heterosexual IPHs than in homosexual ones; stabbing is more common in the latter, again reflecting a more "up close and personal" type of violence that occurs between many men (Bell & Villa, 1996; Garcia et al., 2007; Island & Letellier, 1991; Paulozzi et al., 2001; Taff & Boglioli, 1997).

BOX 17.3. DOMESTIC VIOLENCE AND LAW ENFORCEMENT II: DOMESTIC VIOLENCE IN POLICE FAMILIES

At one time, this was law enforcement's dirty little secret. When a domestic batterer is a fellow cop, there is the added complication that an arrest and conviction for domestic violence can mean surrender of his weapon and can effectively end the officer's career (Miller, 2006f).

continued

BOX 17.3.—*Continued*

Police Officer Domestic Violence

Recent studies suggest that the incidence of domestic violence among police officers may exceed that of the general population, and the true rate may be even higher than these studies disclose because of the reluctance of police to report fellow officers. The highest rates occur among narcotics and patrol officers, officers working night shifts, those who work more than 50 hours a week, and those who take an excessive number of sick days. Police family domestic violence is also a risk factor for **police homicide-suicide** (Neidig et al., 1992; Pam, 2001; Violanti, 2007).

Therefore, until recently, many departments have maintained a conspiracy of silence around such occurrences, often persuading the complainant spouse that loss of her husband's job would be financially devastating to the family, and urging the couple to settle things "off the record" (Gallo, 2005; Kruger & Valtos, 2002; Lott, 1999; Sanders, 1997). Many small, medium, and large police agencies still have inadequate policies and programs to deal with the problem (Los Angeles Board of Police Commissioners, 1997; Southwestern Law Enforcement Institute, 1995). Accordingly, the following is an outline of a protocol that addresses the key elements in police officer domestic violence intervention (Gallo, 2005; Kruger & Valltos, 2002; Lott, 1999; Sanders, 1997).

Police Officer Domestic Violence Intervention: Policies and Procedures

As with all departmental programs, success stands or falls with the level of commitment and buy-in by the senior administration. Domestic violence protocols will have little impact if they are not enthusiastically endorsed by the agency's leadership. Police leaders need to demonstrate by both their words and deeds that unwarranted violence by their officers will not be tolerated. Accordingly, departmental policy should spell out as clearly as possible what types of behaviors are not acceptable. To this end, police leaders should have a good understanding of the dynamics of domestic violence and the magnitude of the problem, both within their own department and in their communities. A commitment to addressing the problem forthrightly in their own departments includes the creation of a culture of disapproval among department leaders, and the allocation of time and resources for adequate training and dealing with incidents.

Training. The key to any credible and permanent strategy for preventing domestic violence is adequate and appropriate training. Training for police officers should cover a comprehensive range of topics, including response, tactics, officer safety, verbal crisis intervention, and conflict-resolution skills. In particular, special training must be provided for officers on how to handle domestic violence calls involving other officers.

Problem Recognition. Astute police supervisors may be able to detect signs of impending or ongoing domestic violence in officers within their own department. The legitimate response to: "What happens at home is my business," is:

"No, it's not, because, (a) if it escalates to an arrestable offense, we lose a good officer; (b) there are liability issues for the department of letting a potentially violent situation go unaddressed; and (c) any kind of family stress that affects our personnel concerns us."

Many of the signals that a domestic violence problem may be brewing or has been going on for some time in an officer's family are generic stress-related symptoms, while others are more specific and may include increased isolativeness of the officer; signs of sleeplessness and fatigue; indication of alcohol, illegal drug, or prescription medication abuse; emotional lability or Jekyll-and-Hyde personality changes; increased incidence of excessive force complaints on the job; talking about the spouse in a particularly derogatory way; blaming the spouse for all the officer's problems; and signs of physical injury that are attributed to "accidents," but may represent wounds received in physical altercations with the spouse.

Investigation and Response to Incidents. Police departments should respond to domestic violence incidents with a comprehensive approach. Kruger & Valltos (2002) recommend that the Internal Affairs Department immediately conduct an initial preliminary inquiry to determine the need for a formal internal investigation. The latter would follow the agency's established protocol for criminal misconduct cases, including suspension of the officer's police powers and reclamation of their weapon and police vehicle. Officers should be placed on off-duty status, pending administrative investigation and referral for a **psychological fitness-for-duty evaluation** (Miller, 2006d, 2007e; Rostow & Davis, 2002, 2004).

If the officer is found psychologically fit for duty, administrators might transfer the officer from off-duty to modified-duty, such as noncontact status assignments (the dreaded "desk job"), until the investigation is complete. If the officer has sustained a criminal conviction related to the domestic battery charge, he will usually be terminated from the department. If lesser or suspended charges ensue, the department retains the right to keep the officer or let him go; if he stays, the officer will be expected to comply with any departmental follow-up measures, as well as with any court orders, that arise from the case.

Counseling and Therapy. This resource should be presented as an option, not a requirement or punishment or, worse, a way of deflecting legitimate legal consequences for the officer's actions. Although sometimes a skilled clinician can sufficiently connect with a reluctant, involuntary patient to accomplish some meaningful therapeutic work, in most cases, when people are "forced" to go to counseling or psychotherapy, true progress is rarely made (Miller, 1993a, 1998c, 2006f, 2008b).

DOMESTIC VIOLENCE IN THE WORKPLACE

As noted in Chapter 11, the area of domestic violence at work represents the perfect area of collaboration among clinical mental health practitioners, organizational psychology and management consultants, law enforcement, and public and private industry executives and managers to set up effective programs for prevention, response, and recovery (Miller, 1999g, 2008b, 2008c).

Domestic Violence at Work: Facts and Stats

Research and practical observation in the fields of both management and psychology (Brownell et al., 1996; Brush, 2003; Duhart, 2001; Friedman et al., 1996; Hamberger & Holtzworth-Munroe, 1994; Hensing & Alexanderon, 2000; Hoffman & Baron, 2001; Kinney, 1995; Labig, 1995; Leone et al., 2004; Logan et al., 2007; McFarlane et al., 1999, 2002; Meloy, 1997; Nicastro et al., 2000; Petty & Kosch, 2001; Riger et al., 2000, 2002; Rothman et al., 2007; Simon, 1996; Swanberg & Logan, 2005; Swanberg et al., 2005, 2006a, 2006b, 2007; Tolman, & Raphael, 2000; Tolman & Rosen, 2001; Walker, 1994; Wettersten et al., 2004; Wright et al., 1996) have established a number of facts about domestic violence in the workplace.

Almost half of the U.S. workforce is made up of women. Therefore, spill-over from domestic problems is likely to affect a large number of workplaces across the country. Each year in the United States, an average of 18,700 workers are assaulted by their intimate partners while on the job. Murder is the number one cause of occupational death for women. It is the second leading cause of death for men only because men are more likely to be employed in physically riskier occupations such as construction or emergency services. Women are disproportionately represented in some of the riskiest jobs. Most of the service industry, entertainment industry, small retail, and unprotected office jobs are held by women. Women are less likely than men to be able to choose their work hours and so may find themselves working late at night in relatively isolated surroundings, or conversely, in crowded, noisy environments filled with unsavory characters.

Abusive husbands or partners harass 74 percent of employed battered women at work, and battered women miss an average of three days of work per month due to injuries, embarrassment, depression, or doctor and lawyer appointments. Even women who resolve to get away from the abuser can often change their personal phone numbers and residences far more easily than they can change employment.

At least domestic violence doesn't discriminate: women in middle-status jobs are as likely to be harassed by partners as those in low-status jobs. The risks and costs to businesses of domestic violence spillover in the workplace include lost worker productivity due to absenteeism, physical disability, loss of sleep, fatigue, impaired concentration, anxiety and depression, and disturbed interaction with coworkers and customers. Work schedules may be disrupted due to child care, doctor and lawyer appointments, court appearances, or direct sabotage of work schedules or work products by the abusive partner.

Women in abusive relationships cost employers more in terms of higher health insurance outlays, increased personnel costs for replacement and temporary workers, and increased security and human resource utilization. There may also be increased legal liability to employers for negligent security, failure to protect the harassed employee, failure to protect other workers, sexual harassment and "hostile workplace" claims, and so on. Unfortunately, when domestic violence continues to adversely affect the company's comfort, safety, and/or bottom line, the most expedient response of the employer is often to get rid of the problem by firing the woman.

Recognizing the Warning Signs

Sometimes the signs that domestic violence spillover into the workplace are obvious; other times they may be more subtle (Kinney, 1995; Labig, 1995; Logan et al., 2004; Sullivan et al., 1992, 1994; Swanberg et al. 2007), and may include any of the following.

Spouse or partner makes threats or other harassing communications to the victim. This may be overt or subtle. Typically, the partner will call numerous times during the day, with verbiage and attitudes ranging from sweet and conciliatory to rageful and threatening. Until recently, phone contact was the preferred form of communication; these days, harassers are increasingly likely to use e-mail or text messaging–although many will avoid these media for fear of leaving an electronic trail.

Spouse or partner makes threats or other harassing communications to victim's supervisor, coworkers, or customers. Again this can be overt, as in the irately jealous spouse who calls his wife's boss to tell him, "Do you know you have a slut working for you?" Or it can be more subtle, as in sending coworkers items from a court order or revealing conversations the spouse has had about work.

Spouse or partner shows up at the workplace. He may ask to see the woman or just hang around the workplace to menace her or conduct surveillance.

Spouse used to work at the same location. A particularly tricky situation occurs when the two partners had been working at the same company–perhaps one even helped the other get their job, or they were coworkers who fell in love and got hitched–and then the husband is fired, often for the same kind of obnoxious behavior toward coworkers as he inflicts on his wife at home. Now, he has all the more reason to resent his wife's supposed betrayal of him because, "how can you keep on working for those assholes that fired me?" She may be afraid to tell him directly that they were probably right to can him for his obnoxious behavior, and besides, somebody's got to pay the bills, so she can't just pick up and quit without another job offer. So now the abusive spouse has one more major reason to hate his former workplace and to resent his wife for "taking their side" by continuing to work for them. The other problem is that the now-terminated spouse may still have access to the workplace, knows the personnel, and may be familiar enough with the organization to cause major trouble.

Spouse believes the victim's job caused or contributed to problems in their relationship. Whether or not he used to work there, the man may displace all his dissatisfactions and anger onto the woman's job as the primary cause of their difficulties: "You have plenty of time for those strangers, but you don't spend any time with me [that is, doing the things I want you to do]." She's probably too scared to reveal that, compared to being with him, going to work is a relief because at least the people there treat her with civility. A common problem is seen in marriages where the wife is better educated and has a higher-status job than the husband, which eats at his narcissistic pride: "Who does she think she is, getting on her high horse about her fancy job? Maybe I need to take her down a peg and teach her who her real boss is." This dynamic also occurs when the wife goes back to school or does anything that the husband believes will put him further out of her league.

Employee is persistently late, frequently asks for schedule changes, or has other attendance problems. Of course, this could be for any number of reasons, from a secret second job, to a personality disorder or psychopathology, to drug abuse (Miller, 2003c, 2008c). But managers and coworkers who are familiar with this employee should be able to tell that these behaviors are uncharacteristic of her and take the concerned step of respectfully inquiring into what's wrong. In such cases, the real reason may turn out to be continual interference with the woman's work schedule and/or sabotage of work products (necessitating last-minute catch-ups) by her resentful mate.

Employee's work quality has deteriorated, e.g., increase in mistakes, missed deadlines, with shallow excuses. This is related to the above. Again, using the employee's past work record as a baseline, employers should be able to determine if the poor work output is a situationally-based problem that can be corrected with the right type of intervention.

Obvious signs of physical injury. A prominent black eye or a cast on a fractured limb will be a rather unambiguous sign of injury. But many battered spouses will strain the bounds of credulity in denying that this was anything other than a freak accident ("I ran into a wall." "I was playing with the dog and tripped"). In some cases, the woman is simply not ready to acknowledge to herself that her mate is beating her; in other cases, she fears that letting her job know the truth will get her fired. Often, she's simply embarrassed.

Obvious signs of psychological distress. Some women will be observed or overheard to be crying at their desk, in the ladies' room, or in their car when leaving or arriving at work. Less blatant signs that managers and coworkers can look for include increased isolativeness (probably so others won't see her distress or overhear embarrassing calls), hypervigilance and jumpiness, or overall changes in mood and behavior.

What Employers Can Do

Mental health clinicians are in unique position to advise corporate managers in designing programs to respond forthrightly to domestic violence in the workplace, usually in conjunction with corporate legal counsel (Flannery, 1995; Kinney, 1995; Logan et al., 2007; Meloy, 1997a; Miller, 2008c; Pierce & Aguinis, 1997; Randel & Wells, 2003; Swanberg et al., 2005, 2006a, 2006b). The guiding principle for managers is: ***When you hire people, you hire their lives***. Appropriate company response includes several measures.

Encourage disclosure. Employers should strive to create the kind of workplace climate where employees will feel free to come forward with problems that affect their work, even if these are personal (Allen, 2001; Swanberg et al., 2006b). However, for all of the reasons just mentioned (embarrassment, fear, etc.), battered spouses may be reluctant to disclose this aspect of their personal lives. Then, the manager may have to frame this as an employment issue:

> "Susan, an employee's personal life is just that–personal–unless it directly affects their work performance, their health and safety, or the health, safety, or productivity of other employees. For example, I'd be having this same conversation with you if I thought you had a substance abuse problem that was interfering with your work. Don't worry, I know that's not an issue with you, but it's obvious to everyone around here that your work performance has been dropping and that it's due to something that's going on at home. Again, your personal matters are your own business, but I'm advising you to take advantage of our EAP counseling services to get some help for this problem. If there's something you need us to do from a work-related legal standpoint, let's discuss it in confidence and we'll see if it's something we can accommodate. We'll do our best to keep you working productively here if you give us a chance to help you."

Initiate legal action. There is actually quite a lot that employers can do to keep their workers safe and protect themselves from liability. These include getting court restraining orders against a clearly threatening husband or boyfriend; filing criminal charges if the offending spouse breaks the law by threatening, assaulting, vandalizing, or trespassing; bringing a civil lawsuit if the perpetrator's actions cost the company lost business, increased security and health care costs, and so on.

Develop a domestic violence program for the workplace. This will usually be done in the context of an overall workplace violence program (Chapter 11), and should contain the following key elements: training and policy seminars, including regular training updates and drills; policies and procedures with regard to flexible work schedules and areas, leave-of-absence policies, and off-time; security and alarm systems, along with training in their use; liaison with local law enforcement, including protocol for summoning help when needed; specialized employee assistance and mental health referral services.

Indeed, continued employment and self-sufficiency can be one of the most empowering forces that enable women to make the decision to leave an abusive relationship, which in turn will almost always make them better workers (Browne, 1987; Levendosky et al., 2004; Lloyd, 1997; Lynch & Graham-Bermann, 2004; McCabe & Di Battista, 2004; Strube & Barbour, 1984; Wilson et al., 1989). For example, Rothman et al. (2007) found that having steady employment and a self-sufficient income was a crucial factor in abused women's ability to leave their partners. Moreover, these women reported that being employed made them feel competent, reduced social isolation, afforded a distraction from, and an alternate perspective on, their abusive home lives, provided them with physical security, a sense of emotional safety, and a "place to hear my own thoughts," and gave them a sense of purpose in life. Thus, encouraging and providing *practical* assistance to victims of domestic violence in establishing independent lives can often be the key intervention that pulls the more *psychological* therapeutic efforts together.

SUMMARY AND CONCLUSIONS

Domestic violence (DV), or **intimate partner violence (IPV)**, affects households in virtually every demographic category. Batterers may be generally antisocial men who use violence and intimidation in all aspects of their lives, including their home lives. They may be pathologically dependent or borderline-dysphoric characters who's insecure compulsive control leads to panic and then anger at a threatened separation or perceived lack of allegiance by the spouse. Or they may be more or less regular guys who atypically erupt into aggression at the goading of a particular stress in their lives. In many cases, there is a repeating cycle of domestic violence within families, with injurious outbursts followed by sweet reconciliations, until the pattern begins again. Batterer intervention programs tend to be most effective with the nonpathological occasional perpetrator and least effective with the generally antisocial batterer. IPV sometimes escalates to **IPH** (**intimate partner homicide**), especially when the perpetrator is the generally antisocial or dysphoric-borderline type. IPV and IPH can occur in same-sex couples as well.

Many domestic violence incidents result in a law enforcement response, and victims can be quite forthright in describing what types of police actions tend to make the problem better and what makes it worse. Police families themselves are not immune from domestic violence, and many law enforcement agencies have established programs for dealing with this problem. Finally, having a steady job is often the one island of security and stability that an abused woman has in an otherwise dangerously chaotic life, so employers should make every effort to prevent domestic violence from following employees to work and to take decisive action when it does.

Part V

Other Crimes and Punishments

In Chapters 18–21 we examine the psychological dynamics underlying a variety of common crimes and their punishments. The singleminded obsession and relentless pursuit of a hapless target characterizes the behavior of the stalker. Ubiquitous if unglamorous, theft and robbery may have complex interpersonal motives beyond the mere acquisition of loot. Gang violence may be an expression of a natural human tribalism that characterizes social groups of many types, a trait that achieves its greatest social sophistication in the form of large organized crime cartels. Arsonists may burn things for pleasure, profit, or both, and some crimes of violence are committed out of sheer hatred for a particular class or type of person. Although far more sympathetic when they are the victims, children are not infrequently the perpetrators of criminal behavior, some shockingly violent, and the debate continues on how to treat or adjudicate them. Some term of imprisonment is the usual punishment for most crimes, and the ultimate penalty is death; those so condemned may have unique psychological dynamics and responses of their own.

Chapter 18

Stalking and Harassment

Every breath you take
Every move you make
Every bond you break
Every step you take
I'll be watching you.
— Sting, *Every Move You Make,* 1983

We've all seen that cute little story, the formulaic romantic comedy where some hapless lovesick schlemiel sets his romantic sights on the woman of his dreams, usually someone who is clearly out of reach and way out of his league, and, against the advice of his friends, in the face of rebuff after rebuff, he doggedly persists against all hope and reason, until, many misadventures and zany hijinks later, her resistance is finally worn down and she is ultimately won over by the sheer persistence and intensity of his devoted pursuit, and realizes that, yes, he is the one true man for her, after all. Why, he queries her in breathless ecstatic puzzlement, did it take you this long to realize your love for me, and what made you finally relent? "Because," she says, *"you didn't give up."*

STALKING: DESCRIPTION AND DEMOGRAPHICS

Stalking is generally defined as an intentional pattern of repeated intrusive and intimidating behaviors toward a specific person that causes the target to feel harassed, threatened, and fearful, or that a reasonable person would regard as being so. Stalking is one of the last interpersonally threatening behaviors to have been criminalized; a little over two decades ago, in many places in the United States, stalking was not technically a crime. California was the first state in 1990 to pass an **anti-stalking law**, prompted by several high-profile cases of **celebrity stalking** and murder. By 2000, all 50 U.S. states, the federal government, and many other countries had passed similar legislation, and most of these statues include both physical stalking and electronic stalking, or **cyberstalking** (Dennison, 2007; Dennison &

Thomson, 2000, 2002; Dressing et al., 2006; McAnaney et al., 1993; McEwen et al., 2009; Petrocelli, 2005; Saunders, 1998; Southworth et al., 2007; Spitzberg & Cupach, 2007).

Stalking is not a rare crime. Up to 16 percent of women and 7 percent of men report having been stalked sometime in their life, and this number may approach 20 percent of college undergraduates (Haugaard & Seri, 2003). This translates into more than one million victims stalked annually. The largest number of stalking scenarios develop from pre-existing intimate relationships, followed by work, friendship, or nonromantic family relationships, with stranger stalking being the least common. Eighty percent of stalkers are known to their victims in some way. Across studies, women are far more likely to be the victims, and men the pursuers, in stalking situations. The more intimate the prior relationship, the longer the stalker is likely to persist in his pursuit.

Many studies agree that there appears to be a watershed period of 2–4 weeks, beyond which most stalkers abandon their pursuit and move on, especially in the case of stranger stalkers. However, if the stalking persists for longer than 4 weeks, it is likely to continue for another 6–12 months; this is more common in cases involving a prior relationship of some kind. The intensity and intrusiveness of the stalking is also likely to be greater in these cases of persistent stalking, while in about half of cases, the stalker may desist for a while and then begin stalking again, after a period ranging from 2.5 to 13 years. This type of **recurrent stalking** is especially likely to occur where some circumstance results in a subsequent meeting between the pursuer and the target, such as a child custody exchange or court appearance, although it can occur spontaneously due to changes in the mental state of the stalker. Highly persistent stalkers tend to be over age 30, to have a Cluster-B personality disorder (Chapter 7), to have a female victim, and to be motivated by intimacy seeking or resentful revenge (Finn, 2004; McEwen et al. 2009; Meloy, Mohandie et al., 2006; Mullen et al., 2006; Orion, 1997; Pathe & Mullen, 1997; Pathe et al., 2002; Purcell et al., 2001, 2004; Rosenfeld, 2003; Sheridan et al., 2003; Spitzberg & Cadiz, 2002; Spitzberg & Cupach, 2007; Tjaden & Thoennes, 1998).

STALKER TYPOLOGIES

Over the past several decades, forensic behavioral scientists have developed a number of stalker typologies:

Zona (1993) Stalker Typology

Simple obsessional stalker. This is typically a male stalker with a personality disorder and/or substance abuse problem, who is relentlessly pursuing a former romantic partner ("How dare she reject me!") or is retaliating for a perceived injustice at work or elsewhere ("How dare he fire me!"). This is the largest group of stalkers, comprising more than 50 percent of the total.

Love obsessional stalker. In the next largest group, about 30 percent of stalkers, is the man who is delusionally convinced that he is in love with a woman who either loves him back and can't show it, or just has been denying her love for him to herself for too long, and it is his mission to show her the light. The victim may be someone the stalker knows, but has never had an intimate relationship with, or it may be a stranger he encounters at work or on a college campus. Many cases of **celebrity stalkers** also fall into this category.

Erotomanic stalker. This minority group (10%) of stalkers is where female stalkers predominate, usually pursuing male strangers or casual acquaintances. Several cases of male celebrities having their homes broken into by "star-struck" women (e.g., George Harrison, David Letterman) seem to fit this category.

False victimization syndrome. In a small number of cases (2%), a person claims to be a stalking victim when he or she is not. The motivation may represent a bid for attention, an attempt to create an alibi for a retaliatory action, a delusional preoccupation with the alleged stalker, or for purposes of maintaining a relationship with the alleged perpetrator while retaining the sympathetic role of the victim–a kind of "**reverse stalking**."

Mullen et al. (1999, 2000, 2006) Stalker Typology

Intimacy seeker. This stalker usually has not had a prior relationship with the object of his obsession, but he wants one. He has convinced himself that he and his unwilling (and, in the early stages, probably unaware) paramour are destined to be together. The target, he believes, is secretly in love with him, but external circumstances, such as her profession, social class, or the inconvenience of being mated with another, get in the way of her openly professing her love. Many cases of celebrity stalkers fall in this category, and the pursuer, if sufficiently delusional, often detects "secret messages" directed at him in the words she says on screen, lyrics in the songs she sings, and so forth. Celebrity or not, he will often shower his target with letters, e-mails, and gifts, and he will take the slightest reaction of any kind as proof of her love ("She had the security guard punch me and throw me out because she just can't handle her feelings of intense love for me").

Incompetent suitor. Like the intimacy seeker, this type is infatuated with the object of his affection, but is simply seeking a date or sexual encounter, not an eternal soul-melding. He is typically a socially inept male who is more likely than other stalker types to be deterred by a firm, forthright rejection, and to then turn his attentions to a new target.

Rejected stalker. This person just can't let go and move on from a terminated relationship, and the stalking represents some mixture of the desire for reconciliation and revenge. In the stalker's mind, the relationship can never really be over, and he wants the victim to know that.

Resentful stalker. He wants payback for his rejection or other injury to his ego. The purpose of the stalking is to intimidate and terrorize the victim in order for the spurned stalker to regain a sense of power and control. He is likely to be among the more intrusive and interpersonally destructive of stalkers, harassing friends of the victim, attempting to sabotage her work status, engaging in cyberstalking, vandalizing her home, car, and possessions, kidnapping pets, and so on. While actual physical attacks on the victim are rare, when they occur, they may be characterized by extreme violence.

Predatory stalker. As the term implies, this stalker engages in covert surveillance and pursuit of his victim, usually as preparation for an actual assault, most commonly a sexual assault. He will often remain anonymous to the victim up to the time of the actual attack. This kind of stalking may be a prelude to a more serious act, such as serial rape (Chapter 14) or serial homicide (Chapter 10).

Holmes (2001) Stalker Typology

Sexually driven stalker. He pursues women to have sex with them, sometimes consensual, other times forced.

Unrequited love stalker. He haunts the object of his affections, who stubbornly refuses to return his ardor.

Rejected revenge-seeking stalker. Once having had a relationship with the victim, he is outraged at her rejection and swears vengeance: "How dare she dump *me!* I'll teach her a lesson she'll never forget!"

Celebrity stalker. He targets famous people. In some cases, the stalker believes the celebrity is in love with him (the Madonna stalker); in other cases, he has mentally fused his identity with that of the celebrity to the point that he resents the very existence of his "rival" (Mark David Chapman who gunned down John Lennon).

Political stalker. Anger, not affection, drives this person, who harasses, threatens, and may attack public officials (John Hinckley, who attempted to assassinate President Reagan). This may sometimes be a political subtype of the celebrity stalker, above, if political figures are targeted for their popularity.

Professional contract killer. This is a professional hit man who is motivated strictly by profit, making it questionable whether he belongs in a typology of stalkers at all–any more than a police detective who hunts and tracks a criminal, or a government espionage agent who pursues a terrorist. Yet, there must be a psychological reason (thrills, power) why someone chooses this type of vocation over others.

Sheridan & Boon (2002) Stalker Typology

This typology was developed specifically for use by law enforcement authorities and includes the following categories:

Stalking by a former spouse or partner. This may be characterized by verbal abuse, damage to property, and/or physical violence.

Stalking based on love. Here, the threat potential for violence is lower because the victim, usually a stranger or casual acquaintance, is viewed by the pursuer as an object of love to be won over, not a rejecting partner to be punished.

Stalking based on delusional fixation. This involves the fantasy that a "special relationship" exists between the stalker and his target, and that it is just a matter of time until his persistent efforts bring the two lovers together. Most targets are strangers or casual acquaintances, and celebrity stalkers are most likely to fall into this category.

Sadistic stalkers. These perpetrators derive pleasure from intimidating and terrorizing their victims. These stalkers are on a power trip and carry a high potential for danger.

Stalking Behaviors

A typology, not of stalkers themselves, but of the tactics and strategies used by stalkers in pursuit of their victims, has been proferred by Spitzberg and colleagues (Spitzberg, 2002; Cupach & Spitzberg, 2004; Spitzberg & Cupach, 2007), who identify eight categories of stalking behavior. In some stalkers, these may represent a progression in the seriousness of the stalking, while for others, one or more particular tactics may be utilized throughout the stalking episode.

Hyperintimacy behaviors are extensions of typical romantic courtship behaviors, but are pursued to an extreme level, such as showering the target with cards, emails, flowers, endless phone calls, and so on. Though kind of cute at first, the relentless love barrage begins to take on a creepily desperate and confrontational quality over time.

Mediated contacts are increasingly common and enlist the use of technology, including cell phones, email, instant messaging, text messaging, and so on. In its more extreme forms, this may develop into **cyberstalking** (see below).

Interactional contacts involve efforts at direct interpersonal encounters. This can range from sitting a few tables away at the victim's favorite restaurant, to registering for the same classes the victim takes at college, to getting a job where the victim works, to trying to reach the victim through third parties.

Surveillance tactics are essentially espionage. The stalker follows the victim around, takes photos and videos, breaks into her mailbox, hacks into her Internet account, and so on. Sometimes this is done clandestinely to gather intelligence about the victim; other times the stalker may let the victim know she is a target, but without revealing the pursuer's identity, as a way of further frightening and intimidating the victim.

Invasion tactics up the ante by escalating the intrusiveness of the stalking. The victim's home or workspace may be broken into, computer files may be hacked and infected, and information or physical property may be stolen or vandalized.

Harassment and intimidation is a more severe form of interpersonal intrusiveness. The victim may be verbally insulted, the stalker may attempt to damage the victim's reputation through third parties, friends and relatives of the victim may be harassed, her work status may be jeopardized, and so on.

Coercion and threat behaviors represent an even more serious escalation with a high potential for danger to the victim. The stalker may now directly threaten to harm the victim, her family, friends, or pets, or to damage her car or home. In a desperate bid to influence the victim, the stalker may threaten to kill himself ("See what you've driven me to!").

Physical aggression and violence represents the most severe, and potentially lethal, outcome of stalking. This may include seriously destructive vandalism (e.g., arson; see Chapter 20), physical assault, rape, murder, suicide, murder-suicide, and attacks on friends, workmates, or family members of the victim.

Stalker Typologies: Commonalities

Integrating the previous typologies, a basic categorization can be made into: (1) stalking for the purpose of **acquiring a new relationship**; (2) stalking for the purpose of **intimidation, harassment, coercion, and/or punishment of a prior relationship rejection**; and (3) stalking primarily motivated by **power and control**. Overlaps between categories are probably common. In the first category are the love obsessional and erotomanic stalkers (Zona et al., 1993), the intimacy seeker and incompetent suitor (Mullen et al., 1999, 2000, 2006), the sexual desire, unrequited love, and celebrity stalker, some types of political stalkers (Holmes, 2001), and the love-based and delusional stalker (Sheridan & Boon, 2002). Here, the stalker's first choice is clearly to gain the love, attention, or admiration of the target, but if continually rebuffed, the stalking may change in quality to that of the second, which includes the simple obsessional stalker (Zona et al., 1993), rejected and resentful stalker (Mullen et al., 1999, 2000, 2006), the rejected stalker (Holmes, 2001), and the former intimate partner stalker (Sheridan & Boon, 2002). In the third category can be placed the predatory stalker (Mullen et al., 1999, 2000, 2006) and the sadistic stalker (Sheridan & Boon, 2002). A residual category might include those types of stalkers that are either atypical or don't truly represent the psychological dynamics of stalking per se (see below), such as the false victimization syndrome perpetrator (Zona et al., 1993), the contract killer, and some types of political stalkers (Holmes, 2001), although it could be argued that the latter's fixation on public figure shares certain features with the celebrity stalker.

A type apparently missing from these typologies might be called the **identification stalker**, usually a subspecies of celebrity or political stalker. Some degree of imitative identification with a high-status person is a natural human trait, e.g., wearing a facsimile of a favorite ballplayer's jersey, or forming a tribute band to a beloved musical group. However, the identification stalker so enmeshes himself psychologically with the target that he patterns his entire life after that person's. For example, Mark David Chapman dressed like John Lennon, learned to play guitar, and even married a Japanese woman who resembled Lennon's wife, Yoko Ono. At first the stalker tries to fuse his identity with the target's by such imitation tactics and by making personal contact with the target, visiting his/her home, getting autographs, collecting memorabilia, and so on. Many celebrity stalkers remain at this level, but for some, the desire to *be* the target person begins to foment the delusional idea that by eliminating the target, the imitator will somehow become the real thing. In some cases, the stalker actually comes to believe that *he* is the one who embodies the essence of that celebrity's life even more than the celebrity himself, and that, consequently, he really deserves to *be* that person more than the actual person himself. This leads to a sense of entitled resentment and anger that may propel efforts to eliminate the "imposter."

THE PSYCHOLOGY OF STALKING

Diagnostic Categories of Stalking

Up to half of stalkers studied have some form of diagnosable mental disorder (Mullen et al., 1999; Whyte et al., 2007; Zona et al., 1998). The distinction between stalkers of strangers and stalkers of prior intimates seems to apply to diagnostic distinctions as well, at least according to some estimates. Thus, although there is some overlap, stalkers who pursue strangers, including casual acquaintances or celebrities, tend to more often be characterized by a mood disorder, delusional disorder, or outright psychotic disorder. Stalkers of prior intimates are more likely to be nonpsychotic, but to have narcissistic, borderline, paranoid, or compulsive personality disorders, along with substance abuse problems, mainly involving alcohol and psychostimulant drugs such as cocaine and amphetamines. Thus, the easily bruised egos, the flimsy interpersonal boundaries, the smoldering rage and jealousy, and the relentless tenacity of these personality types, fueled by stimulant drugs, accounts for their ceaseless pursuit of their quarry, either to win her back or to punish her for deserting and betraying them. Having invested their entire identity in the relationship, its rupture threatens to unravel their entire life's purpose, accounting for the white-hot, life-and-death quality of their pursuit (Farnham et al., 2000; Kienlen et al., 1997; Meloy, 1996, 1998, 1999, 2000, 2001; Meloy et al., 2000; Mullen et al., 1999; Segal, 1989).

Interestingly, antisocial personalities make up less than 10 percent of stalker diagnostic categories, compared to their much higher rate in criminal populations generally (Meloy, 2001a, 2001b; Meloy et al., 2000). This is probably because the essence of prior intimate stalking is pathological attachment, and the antisocial personality doesn't become truly attached to anything or anybody. He may be temporarily fuming that his partner would insult him by leaving, and he might even impulsively fly into a murderous rage when confronted by a partner's unaccommodating behavior. But he is far less likely to invest the time and effort needed to make a career of pursuing any particular person, precisely because this cuts into his enjoyment of other exploitive and predatory activities. Any acts of retaliation are likely to occur in the immediate aftermath of the relationship disruption, and the more time passes, the more he is apt to default to a face-saving rationalization: "If she doesn't want me, forget her–it's her loss." Then, he moves on to his next conquest.

Stalker Psychology

But pursuit of romantic targets is hardly itself a pathological phenomenon, otherwise none of us would be here. From an **evolutionary psychology** perspective, a number of stalking researchers see this behavior as an extension of normal interpersonal courtship behavior that thrives on sexual motivational ambivalence (Baumeister & Wotman, 1992; Cupach & Spitzberg, 1998, 2004; Cupach et al., 2000; Spitzberg & Cupach, 2007). In the process of **reciprocal mate selection**, there is typically a certain amount of back-and-forth flirting, withdrawal, pursuit, and pullback that characterizes the fun and foibles that romantic comedies are based on. As with most human traits, people vary with respect to how much they will pursue a desired relationship, with one extreme represented by those who give up at the slightest hint of nonacceptance, and the other tail of the bell curve characterized by those who literally never, ever take no for an answer. When combined with traits of ego-fragility, impulsivity, anger, and/or delusional psychosis, this kind of pursuit behavior crosses the line from amusing romantic infatuation to dangerous criminal stalking.

Attachment theory (Ainsworth et al., 1978; Bowlby, 1969, 1973, 1980; Dutton & Golant, 1995; Hazan & Shaver, 1987; Kienlen, 1998; Lewis et al., 2001; Meloy, 1992, 2003; Morrison, 2008; Spitzberg & Cupach, 2007; Tonin, 2004) has been used to explain dysfunctional relationships in general and stalking behavior in particular. Essentially, the theory posits that one's adult attachment style is strongly influenced by the quality of the parent-child relationship the individual has experienced from infancy onward. Infants who develop a **secure attachment** with parents or other early caregivers develop a feeling of security and confidence in later interpersonal relationships. Insecurely attached infants come to perceive the relational world as a cold, rejecting place, and may develop an **avoidant attachment style**, defensively decoupling themselves emotionally from the caregiver, or an **anxious/ ambivalent attachment style**, in which they simultaneously crave attachment to a caregiver, but then recoil in fear of having that connection ripped away or rejected.

As adults, securely attached individuals view both themselves and other people in a mainly positive light and are able to form mature relationships, with a healthy balance of intimacy and independence. Insecurely attached individuals may develop a **dismissive attachment style**, protecting their fragile egos by maintaining an aloof, standoffish, and sometimes confrontational attitude toward others, as with the antisocial and narcissistic personalities. Individuals with a predominantly **preoccupied attachment style** desperately look to others for approval and reassurance to counteract their inner feelings of unworthiness and self-loathing. Their bottomless need for validation will sooner or later be unfulfilled, resulting in feelings of abandonment and betrayal, and angry blaming of the partner for "ruining" the relationship, as often occurs with borderline personality disorder. Finally, those with a **fearful-avoidant attachment style** try to protect themselves by avoiding interpersonal entanglements altogether (avoidant personality disorder) or by trying to find the one attachment figure that they can totally pin their egos on and trust will take care of them (dependent personality disorder).

According to this model, insecure attachment styles, predominantly the preoccupied style, characterize stalkers who doggedly pursue former intimate partners. The breakup is perceived as a stinging rejection and repudiation of the stalker's whole identity and self-worth, subconsciously tapping into his own self-loathing, and prompting a morbid jealousy expressed in desperate measures to either reclaim the relationship to prove his worthiness, or to punish , humiliate, and ultimately destroy the rejecter who he perceives as holding hostage his very identity by refusing to bend to his will (Cupach et al., 2000; Dutton & Golant, 1995; Dutton et al., 1994; Hazan & Shaver, 1987; Kienlen, 1998; Kingham & Gordon, 2004; Lewis et al., 2001; Meloy, 1989, 1992, 1998, 2003; Morrison, 2001, 2008; Schlesinger, 2002; Spitzberg & Cupach, 2007; Tonin, 2004). As discussed in Chapter 17, a similar dynamic exists in the psyches of intimate partner batterers and, indeed, many of these men become stalkers when their partners try to leave the relationship.

Biological Factors in Stalking

As with many criminal categories, there is no distinctive "biological stalker profile." Rather, different types of underlying personality and psychopathology features may be associated with the biological indices already familiar from the description of other types of offenders. For example, progressive **dementia** or other organic brain syndromes may be associated with delusional jealousy that might fuel intimate-partner stalking. Brain syndromes may be precipitated or aggravated by **alcohol and drug abuse**. These substances can have a disinhibiting effect, as with alcohol, barbiturates or benzodiazepines, or, in the case of stimulant drugs like cocaine or amphetamine, can produce a manic-like psychosis (Chapters 2, 6). Substance abuse is also associated with mood disorders and personality disorders (Chapters 6, 7), all of which are known to have their unique neurobiological correlates (Cobb, 1979; Kingham & Gordon, 2004; Langfeldt, 1961; Michael et al., 1995; Mullen & Maack, 1985; Pillai & Kraya, 2000; Shepherd, 1961; Shrestha et al., 1985).

More specifically, the aggressive and obsessive nature of stalking has been hypothetically linked to abnormally increased dopaminergic activity combined with abnormally low serotonergic activity in the brain (Meloy & Fisher, 2005). Stimulant drugs, as noted above, are one method of exogenously heightening dopaminergic activity, and many stalkers use these substances. Another, far more rare, cause is neurologic disease that affects these brain systems. Recently, a case of stalking associated with **Huntington's disease** has been described (Soliman et al., 2007). This is a genetically transmitted, progressive, degenerative disease of the basal ganglia, specifically, a structure called the **caudate nucleus**, that typically produces progressive impairment in movement and a worsening mood disorder, obsessional symptoms, and delusional psychosis, sometimes accompanied by antisocial behavior (Anouizerate et al., 2004; Aron et al., 2005; Rosenblatt & Leroi, 2000). In the present case, the patient was a woman whose mental symptoms preceded the onset of the motor symptoms, and were characterized by obsessive romantic thoughts about her therapist, followed by stalking of the clinician. The stalking behavior began with multiple gifts and telephone calls to the therapist's home, later escalating to following and making threats toward the therapist. Fortunately, in this case, the symptoms were successfully treated with antipsychotic medication. Thus, Huntington's disease may act as a neurological analogue to more common occurrences of disordered neurophysiology in stalking (Meloy & Fisher, 2005), and obsessional-aggressive behavior more generally.

STALKING AND VIOLENCE

For both safety of the victims (Box 18.1) and decisions with regard to sentencing and parole of the offenders, the question of stalkers' potential for violence is crucial, especially in light of the attention given to high-profile cases in the media where victims have been brutalized and/or killed.

Prevalence and Type of Stalker Violence

The general consensus of research and clinical experience is that most stalkers do not become interpersonally violent. Between 30–60 percent of victims are threatened with violence by their stalkers, and about 25–50 percent of stalkers physically attack their victims. Violence is more likely the longer the stalking persists, and both threats and violence are more common with prior-intimate victims than public-figure victims, with either male or female stalkers. Of those stalkers who commit violence, serious physical injury to the victim is rare, consisting mainly of grabbing, choking, pulling, throwing, shaking, slapping, punching, kicking, or sexually fondling the victim, leaving bruises and abrasions, but seldom severe wounds. A weapon is used in less than a third of assault cases, most commonly consisting of a handgun, knife, or automobile. Interestingly, these weapons are most commonly used to intimidate, terrorize, and control the victim, and are rarely used to seriously injure her. For all the publicity it garners, **stalking-related homicide** appears to be rarer still, occurring in only 2 percent of stalking cases; however, this statistic may underrepresent the lethality of stalking in domestic violence cases (Chapter 17), because these cases are not typically classified as stalking per se, even though stalking may be a component of the abuse. There is some evidence that prior-intimate stalking violence may be more affective, while stranger/public figure stalking veiolence may be more predatory, but combinations of each category probably occur across stalker types (Blaauw et al., 2002; Brewster, 2000; Dietz et al., 1991a, 1991b; Dressing et al., 2006; Hall, 1998; Harmon et al., 1998; McEwen et al. 2007; Meloy, 1989, 1996, 1997b, 2001, 2003; Meloy & Gothard, 1995; Meloy et al., 2000, 2001; Monahan et al., 2001; Morrison, 2001, 2008; Mullen et al., 1999, 2000, 2006; Pathe & Mullen, 1997; Rosenfeld & Harmon, 2002; Zona et al., 1993).

Not just the chosen victim may be in danger, but any others who may try to help her, who may be currently romantically involved with her, or who in any way tries to impede the stalker's access to her. This may include friends, relatives, and workmates of the victim in prior-intimate stalking (see also Chapter 17 and Box 4.1), or law enforcement or private security personnel in public-figure stalking. In some cases, the stalker builds a delusional system placing these third parties in a psychologically triangulated role, making it "necessary" for him to remove this impediment to his noble pursuit (Auchincloss & Weiss, 1992; Meloy, 1996).

Risk Factors for Stalker Violence

Factors that have been found to predict stalking violence are: a prior intimate relationship with the victim; multiple targets pursued concurrently; having been a batterer of the victim; being more highly obsessed with the victim; feeling humiliated by the victim; being angry at the victim; having made more verbal threats to the victim; being less than 30 years of age; having less than a high school education; and general history of antisocial behavior, including past convictions for any kind of violence. This no doubt reflects the behavior of a generally aggressive and unstable subject, with significant psychopathology or personality disorder, who has made a lifestyle out of pursuing and harassing virtually everyone who has rejected or offended him in some way. Personality disorder, especially paranoid, antisocial, borderline, histrionic, or narcissistic types, is associated with greater risk for stalker violence, but psychotic illness actually decreases the risk of violence, perhaps because these individuals' obviously disturbed behavior is more likely to get them noticed and apprehended, or because psychotic disorganization makes it difficult to carry out a goal-directed, protracted campaign of surveillance and pursuit (Burgess et al., 1997, 2001; Douglas et al., 1999; Farnham et al., 2000; Harmon et al., 1998; Kienlen et al., 1997; Kropp et al., 2002; Meloy, 1999; 2001; Menzies et al., 1995; Mullen et al., 1999, 2000, 2006; Palarea et al., 1999; Rosenfeld, 2003, 2004; Rosenfeld & Harmon, 2002; Schwartz-Watts & Morgan, 1998; Sheridan & Davies, 2001; Tjaden & Thoennes, 1998; Zona et al., 1993, 1998).

EFFECT OF STALKING ON VICTIMS

Most serious crimes such as rape, robbery, and assault, are isolated events in the lives of victims, having a beginning, middle, and end. There is an expected emotional aftermath to almost any kind of criminal victimization (Miller, 2008b), but what distinguishes stalking is the added layer of ambiguity, uncertainty, and nonfinality of the ordeal: the victim frequently does not know who is stalking her, how bad it will get, or when it will end. Even when the stalker is known or suspected, the victim often finds that there is very little she can to do to stem the multiple streams of abuse knocking at her door, haunting her phone, or poisoning her email. Thus, the psychological toll of living with a stalking scenario can be a constantly traumatizing nightmare that may persist for months or years. Even when the stalker is apprehended or eventually gives up, the economic, emotional, and social devastation he's wreaked may follow the victim for a long time.

Victim Reactions to Stalking

Clinical syndromes seen in stalking victims can range from anxiety disorders, to depression, to full-blown posttraumatic stress disorder (PTSD), including intrusive recollections, flashbacks, nightmares, and impaired sleep and appetite. Victims may become more cautious and wary even years after the stalking episode has ceased, inhibiting their driving and going to public places, affecting employment options and socializing, and interfering with other activities. Naturally, any pre-existing psychological vulnerabilities will likely be exacerbated by this increased stress. The effects may be equally severe for victims of physical stalking or cyberstalking, and the two often go together (Hall, 1998; Petrocelli, 2005; Meloy, 1996, 2001b; Mullen et al., 2000; Pathe & Mullen, 1997; Sheridan & Grant et al., 2003, 2007).

Spitzberg & Cupach (2007) have identified several categories of effects of stalking victimization based on an analysis of the existing victimology literature on this crime. **General disturbance:** overall effects on the victim's lifestyle and emotional concomitants. **Affective health:** increase in anger, anxiety, depression, fear, jealousy, or paranoia. **Cognitive health:** confusion, distrust, suspiciousness, impaired self-esteem, suicidal ideation. **Physical health:** impaired sleep or appetite, substance abuse, unhealthy lifestyle patterns. **Social health:** impact of the stalking on the victim's relationships with family, friends, workmates, and other people. **Resilience effects:** though less common, this refers to the recognition of inner strengths and social support systems that allows the victim to withstand and transcend the stalking ordeal.

Victim Coping Responses

From a review of the stalking victimology literature, a number of victim coping strategies have been identified (Cupach & Spitzberg, 2004; Spitzberg & Cupach, 2007; Spitzberg, 2002), some with greater or lesser degrees of helpfulness in mitigating the stalking scenario.

Moving-with tactics represent the victim's well-intentioned, if naïve, attempts to reason, implore, or negotiate with the stalker to leave her alone, e.g., "Let's just be friends and go our separate ways." Unfortunately, for the love-obsessional stalker, this keeps the flame of hope alive that, by his persistent contact, he will eventually wear her down and make her realize how much she truly loves him. For the revenge-motivated prior-intimate stalker, this puts additional power in his hands to rebuff the peace offering and continue the campaign of harassment and intimidation.

Moving-against strategies are efforts to quietly or forcefully deter the stalker, often resorted to when the moving-with tactics have proven fruitless. Direct activities include threatening the stalker, actually attempting to injure the stalker (rare), or (more commonly) enlisting the aid of third parties, such as friends, relatives, employer, or law enforcement to intervene. Direct threats and interventions are generally discouraged for several reasons. First, they positively reinforce the stalker's activities because now he knows how important he is in the victim's life and, if he is seeking to intimidate and terrorize the victim, this will usually result in an escalation and expansion of harassment activities. Second, threats are only as good as their back-up, and failure to follow through will only further embolden the stalker who now feels he can get away with anything without repercussions. Finally, some stalkers may become enraged and seek to escalate their abuse from harassment to physical harm.

Moving-away tactics involve attempts to escape from the stalker's orbit, including changing to an unlisted phone number, using a post office box for mail, changing or blocking e-mail addresses, altering travel routes, not going out without other people present, even changing jobs or residences. Unfortunately, through a combination of malevolent persistence and cleverness, and with the aid of ever-expanding Internet databases, many stalkers have little trouble tracking down their victims and reinstating the harassment. Indeed, short of going into the Federal Witness Protection Program, there is little any of us can do to "stay off the grid" in such a way as to be relatively invisible and untraceable, yet still live a semblance of a normal life. Also, where the stalker is an ex-intimate partner or ex-workmate, he will already have access to many details about the victim's life. He may even be a current workmate, boss, or ex-spouse with whom the victim must at least occasionally interact over issues of finances or child custody.

Moving-inward activities refer to attempts by the victim to cope through denial, distraction, redirection, or redefinition. These include ignoring the problem (good if it discourages the stalker, bad if it leads to neglect of safety precautions); restricting one's range of activities; using prescribed medications or unprescribed substances; turning to religion or meditation; seeking psychotherapy; or immersing onself in distracting business matters or hobbies. Some of these activities may temporarily relieve stress and, if safe, are recommended to help the victim cope with the ordeal (e.g., proper medication or psychotherapy). However, they do little to directly address the problem and may even make the victim more vulnerable if she prematurely relaxes her vigilance and softens her resolve to deter the stalker.

Moving-outward activities involve the recruitment of third-party intervention in the form of friends, mental health professionals, law enforcement, or the criminal justice system. Approximately one-half of stalking victims contact the police at some point, and one of the common measures recommended is for the victim to go to court and take out an **order of protection**, or **restraining order**, which places legally enforceable restrictions on the types of contact and proximity the parties may have with one another. These orders can have greater or lesser effect, depending on how rigorously they are enforced and how relentlessly determined the stalker is to circumvent them. In general, restraining orders are effective in about 85 percent of stalking scenarios (Meloy, 2001b), in which the stalker, dedicated though he may be, will not go so far as to risk arrest in pursuit of his quarry. The remaining 15 percent, however, may be so disturbed and relentless in their ardor or thirst for vengeance that they don't care about their own safety and will do anything to get at the victim. In these cases, restraining orders may only further inflame the stalker and reinforce the stalking, which is why the decision to use this recourse is always a careful judgment call. In addition, stalkers are often quick learners when it comes to observing the letter of the law while circumventing its spirit, and exploiting constitutional freedoms of speech and privacy to stay just within the circle of legal behavior, while still finding ingenious ways to make the victim's life miserable.

BOX 18.1. HOW TO DEAL WITH A STALKER

Have you ever been the victim of a stalker? The following represents a consensus of threat management experts in how to deal with this frightening scenario.

Send a clear message and cut off contact. In the case of stranger stalking, it's easy for the stalker to rationalize that, "If she didn't want me to bother her, she'd tell me so." Tell him so. Whatever medium is used—phone, email, or face-to-face—very calmly but very firmly make it crystal clear that you do not want him to contact you again at any time, in any way. Keep a record of your communication and, no matter what his response, do not communicate with him again, ever. Ignore all further messages, but document each one. Don't hang out with his friends, at least some of whom will likely be collecting intelligence for him. If you are forced to make periodic contact with him for work or child care issues, discuss only pertinent practical matters and end each interaction as quickly as possible.

Keep a paper (and/or electronic) trail. Maintain copies or originals of everything the stalker sends you by surface mail, electronically, telephonically, and otherwise. Create and maintain a file, on disk and on paper, and store it in a secure place, but *do not respond* to any of his communications following your unambiguous statement to him to leave you alone. Deliveries of flowers or gifts should be refused and given back to the deliveryman. If they are left for you, remove and discard them immediately, and do not respond, no matter how many pile up. Convey these instructions to neighbors or workmates who may become surrogate recipients of his gifts to you.

Reduce target salience. Get a new phone number and give it to a select few people on a need-to-know basis, but keep the old one connected to an answering system, so the stalker will (at least temporarily) think he's leaving messages on an active line. If you are being harassed at work (see Chapters 11 and 17), see if you can change your phone extension or physical work site. If you're being followed, change routes periodically. If your mailbox is unsecured, consider having your mail delivered to a post office box, to keep the stalker from stealing your mail or putting things in your mailbox. Wherever you go, keep your cell phone handy.

Protect yourself. This involves proper training and practice with self-defense tactics and weapons used for personal protection. Some stalking victims will be more comfortable with these measures than others, so always seek expert advice. Also secure your home and workplace as much as possible with locks, alarm systems, a dog, and so on. Carefully plan out travel routes. It may not be necessary to maintain a total fortress mentality, but use common sense and plan your security system to be commensurate with the level of threat posed by your stalker.

Enlist aid. Report all violations or suspected violations to the police. Some actions by your stalker (vandalism, threats to your safety) may constitute crimes in themselves and lead to the stalker's arrest or at least questioning by the police. Some stalkers may be deterred by law enforcement intervention, but by no means all. Remember, never respond to the stalker directly. Also enlist the aid of mental health counselors, support groups, friends, and family members who can serve as practical and emotional buffers while you're coping with this ordeal.

Use the criminal justice system. Although threat management professionals differ somewhat on the details, most recommend taking out a restraining order or order of protection when the stalking and harassment have escalated to dangerous levels. On the other hand, if the pattern has stabilized to a few calls or emails every month, and you're comfortable just ignoring these, then there is probably little to be gained by stirring up the pot, which will only be interpreted by the stalker as evidence of your increased interest in him. If your stalker is arrested and criminally prosecuted, cooperate with the criminal justice system to the best of your ability, but feel free to enquire as to what type of security you can expect in return for your participation.

No, it's not fair. Why should you have to be the one to contort your whole lifestyle to accommodate one malevolent slimebag who won't leave you alone? But like car crashes, hurricanes, or unexpected illnesses, you-know-what does happen, and you must be prepared to take action to protect yourself. Perhaps the good news is that, in the majority of cases, stalking episodes remain relatively nonviolent and don't persist much longer than a year and a half. If you can maintain your resolve for that long, hopefully you'll be free to get your life back.

CYBERSTALKING

Stalking need not be physically confrontational to shatter a victim's life. Our grandparents may have had to endure anonymous letters, our parents put up with phony-phone calls, and we cope with abusive emails, instant messages, and text messages. With advances in communication technology come more dubious advances in the ability to harass, intimidate, and terrorize other people. The term **cyberstalking** has been used to describe a set of behaviors that involve repeated threats, harassment, or other unwanted contact, by the use of computer or other electronic communication-based technology, that has the effect of making another person feel afraid, intimidated, or concerned for his or her safety. In essence, electronic stalking combines the immediacy of a phone call with a shield of anonymity for the stalker and the depersonalization of the victim, making the harassment all the more relentless and frightening (Bocij & McFarlane, 2003; D'Ovidio & Doyle, 2003; Finn, 2004; Meloy, 1998; Petrocelli, 2005; Southworth et al., 2007).

Forms of cyberstalking include: (1) monitoring the victim's email communication; (2) sending insulting or threatening emails, sometimes anonymously, sometimes not; (3) disrupting the victim's email communications by flooding the victim's inbox; (4) disrupting the victim's email by sending a virus or other malware program; (5) using the victim's email identity to send false messages to others or to purchase goods and services (often pornography) in the victim's name; (6) using information-gathering Internet services to compile personal, financial, and other information about the victim; (7) using spyware software or keystroke hardware (where the stalker has access to the victim's computer, such as with an ex-intimate partner or workmate) to monitor the victim's communications; (8) using social networking sites like Facebook to harass the victim or impersonate the victim to others; (9) sending harassing text messages by cell phone; (10) taking surreptitious photos or videos of the victim, or using previously recorded private intimate images, and sending them to third parties (Burgess & Baker, 2002; Finn, 2004; Finn & Banach, 2000; McGrath & Casey, 2002; Southworth et al., 2007; Spitzberg & Hoobler, 2002). Other diabolically ingenious techniques could no doubt be added to the list.

Cyberstalking is frequently used in conjunction with physical stalking and, in these cases, can be considered an extension of it. In other cases, electronic media may be the preferred means of stalking. In some instances, victims have been horrified to discover that intimate partners or workmates that they had interacted with every day had been the ones secretly stalking and harassing them electronically for months or years. Prior intimate partner stalkers are somewhat less likely to be cyberstalked than physically stalked, probably because the stalker and his victim already know each other; cyberstalking may be more likely used to monitor a victim with whom the stalker desires a relationship. Cyberstalking may also be the preferred pursuit and harassment methodology of women stalkers because of the relative safety and anonymity. Police may not take cyberstalking as seriously as physical stalking, and some victims have been told to just "turn off your computer" (Alexy et al., 2005b; Lee, 1998; Petrocelli, 2005; Sheridan & Grant, 2007).

SUMMARY AND CONCLUSIONS

Romantic pursuit is a natural part of human behavior, but when pressed to an extreme degree, it becomes a form of aggression. Because it can occur so insidiously, **stalking** is a crime that frequently skulks under the radar. A stalker may pursue his victim out of a delusional belief in their common romantic destiny, because they used to be together and he wants her back, out of a sadistic desire to torment the victim, or because of a psychotic overidentification with the (usually famous) victim and the resultant desire to become him by eliminating and replacing him. Stalkers may carry a variety of diagnostic labels, including psychotic disorders, delusional disorders, or cluster-B personality disorders. Risk factors for violence in a stalking scenario include a prior intimate relationship, the stalker's feeling of being rejected or humiliated, and generic risk factors for violence such as low educational level and substance abuse. **Cyberstalking** can be as distressing, if not more so, to victims as physical stalking due to the concealment and anonymity afforded by electronic communication. Victims may adopt varying strategies for dealing with stalkers, such as avoiding him, confronting him, seeking third-party assistance, and accessing the legal system. Although no plan is perfect, threat assessment specialists make certain recommendations that can make it easier for a victim to deter and discourage her stalker.

Chapter **19**

Juvenile Crime

BOX 19.1. BABYSITTER, 11, CHARGED WITH MURDERING 2-YEAR-OLD
AOL News, Sept. 22, 2010

Police in Sandy Springs, Georgia have charged an 11-year-old girl with felony murder and child cruelty for killing a 2-year-old while helping her mother babysit. The toddler's mother left the child with a co-worker and the co-worker's daughter. When she came to pick up her toddler, the child was lying in bed, eyes wide open, her skin turning blue. The younger child was found to suffer severe blunt-force trauma to the head, torso and buttocks, authorities say.

Legal experts are debating whether the 11-year-old can be tried as an adult. In 2004, 8-year-old Amy Yates was strangled to death by a 12-year-old boy. The boy was held for two years, the maximum time then allowed by law. In response to this case, the Georgia General Assembly passed **Amy's Law** in 2006, which lengthened the time a juvenile over age 13 could be held for committing a felony, which is now five years or until the offender turns 21.

JUVENILE CRIME: DESCRIPTION AND DEMOGRAPHICS

The number of juveniles and young adults committing crimes in the United States appears to be rising with each successive generation, with the highest homicide rate consisting of perpetrators in the 15-to-24-year-old age range (Blazei et al., 2006; Malmquist, 1996; Slutske, 1997). Preteens (under age 13) account for 6–7 percent of all juvenile arrests, with crime patterns similar to that of older teens, including isolated acts of murder committed by children as young as 8 (Black, 2009). Seventy percent of preteen crimes occur on a school day, and approximately 30 percent of such crimes occur at or near the school, including simple assault, aggravated assault, sexual assault, and robbery. These crimes appear to be increasing in frequency (see also Chapter 12).

The Age-Crime Curve and the Developmental Trajectory of Criminality

It is a near-universal observation in criminology that crimes of almost all types cluster in frequency around adolescence and early adulthood, historically the prime social role-establishment and reproductive period for humans. In the United States and other industrialized countries, the rate of violent crime increases each successive year from age 12, peaking at age 17, and then dropping from age 18 to 27 (Elliott, 1994; Tremblay, 2001). This **age-crime curve** was first articulated by Quetelet in 1833 and was formally identified and described by Farrington (1987).

Perhaps the most well-known theory of criminal development is the developmental dichotomy proposed by Terrie Moffitt (1993). In this model, **adolescent-limited delinquents** comprise the majority of youths, and their early childhoods are relatively unremarkable. When they reach early adolescence, however, in order to mark their social territory and impress their peers, they begin to display the kind of rebelliously rambunctious behavior that may alienate adults and get these kids in trouble with the law, but rarely do they engage in severe violence or serious antisocial behavior on a sustained basis. If they can survive high school without a significant criminal record, they typically desist in their antisocial behavior by their late teens or early twenties and adjust satisfactorily to the demands of adult life.

Life-course persistent delinquents begin their antisocial behavior earlier in childhood, engage in an unusually high number, severity, and variety of antisocial acts, and persist in this behavior throughout their adolescent and adult lives. For these children, aggressive antisociality is not a developmental stage, but a lifestyle, and they are typically diagnosed as conduct disordered in childhood (Table 19.1) and as antisocial personality disordered adults (Chapter 8). Thus, whereas adolescent-limited delinquency seems to represent a stage of normative, albeit sometimes obnoxious, rule-breaking, life-course persistent delinquency is thought to represent a pathological syndrome tracking conduct disorder and antisocial personality disorder.

While most authorities have endorsed Moffitt's (1993) developmental model, others have attempted to modify it. For example, DiLalla & Gottesman (1989) propose three developmental pathways for antisocial behavior. The first two, the **continuous antisocial** and the **transitory antisocial**, appear to closely track Moffitt's (1993) life-course and adolescent-limited categories, respectively. However, DiLalla & Gottesman's (1989) third category, **late bloomers**, includes a subset of individuals whose relatively peaceful childhood and early teen years are broken by the development of antisocial behavior in late adolescence or early adulthood that persists throughout life.

Some additional research has supported this third subtype, including the finding that most late-bloomers tend to be female (Lyons et al., 1995; Marmorstein & Iacono, 2005).

A four-part developmental antisocial trajectory model has been proposed by Nagin & Tremblay (1999), who followed a group of boys in a poor school district in Montreal from ages 6 to 15. The smallest group of boys (4% of the sample) were rated by teachers as being chronically physically aggressive, consistent with Moffitt's (1993) life-course delinquent. A second group (28%) started out at age 6 showing a high level of aggression, but became less so as they developed. The largest group (53%) started with a moderate aggression level which remained stable or declined over time, while a fourth group (14%) did not show significant aggression at any age. No evidence was found in this study for a delayed-onset (late-bloomer) type of offender, as postulated by DiLalla & Gottesman (1989).

What seems to emerge from this body of literature is that a small group of chronic, persistent, life-course offenders starts their aggressive antisocial behavior in childhood, commit a higher number of offenses of greater severity, and that the earlier the criminal career begins, the worse it becomes. Life-coursers have more family members with histories of antisocial behavior, criminal arrests, domestic violence, and child abuse, than adolescent-limiteds. They also tend to show a higher rate of the known neurodevelopmental and psychosocial risk factors, such as low verbal IQ, poor academic and vocational achievement, hyperactivity, impulsivity, substance abuse, and neuropsychological anomalies. Both of these factors suggest a stronger neurogenetic basis for the more serious life-course delinquent youths. Fortunately, members of the life-course group are relatively rare, about 5 percent of boys and 1 percent of girls, corresponding to the demographically validated finding that 5–6 percent of seriously antisocial individuals commit 50–60 percent of crime in most populations (Bassrath, 2001; Blazei et al., 2006; Dodge et al., 1990; Farrington, 1995; Jacobson et al., 2002; Jaffee et al., 2002; Lahey et al., 1999; Moffitt, 1993; Moffitt & Caspi, 2001; Taylor et al., 2000; Tremblay, 2001). Thus, what we are almost certainly seeing in the life-course persistent delinquent is the conduct-disordered child who becomes the antisocial or psychopathic adult.

In fact, what these developmental antisocial typologies appear to identify in common is a small group of persistent, frequent, severe, and early-onset criminal offenders who seem destined to a life of predatory crime, distinguishable from a larger group of youths who's less frequent and less severe antisocial behavior starts later and fizzles out by early adulthood. As per most of the research described in this text, it is still the minority of offenders at any age who do the most and worst offending.

DIAGNOSTIC CATEGORIES

As emphasized throughout this book, criminality does not equal psychopathology, or vice versa, but as with many of the criminal categories discussed in this text, when a psychological disorder is diagnosed in a juvenile with a criminal history, it tends to fall into one or more of a limited range of syndromes (Table 9.1).

ADHD and Juvenile Crime

Attention deficit hyperactivity disorder (ADHD) is one of the most commonly diagnosed childhood behavioral disorders worldwide. Children with the combined inattention plus hyperactivity syndrome show impaired attention and concentration, hyperactive and impulsive behavior, poor frustration tolerance, dramatic mood swings, and disruptive behavior. They often have one or more learning disabilities, and often have comorbid conduct disorder. They are at heightened risk for substance abuse and antisocial behavior. Children without the hyperactivity component (ADD) seem to be more passively inattentive and inhibited and are more prone to developing internalizing disorders, such as anxiety and depression, later in life. ADD and ADHD are familial disorders with a genetic component, and family members may display a variety of mood and conduct disorders, including substance abuse. The combination of inattentiveness, hyperactivity, impulsivity, low frustration-tolerance, and learning disabilities puts these kids at a serious disadvantage in a standard academic environment, and they typically fall farther and farther behind with each successive year. ADHD's role in delinquent and criminal behavior most probably has to do with its association with conduct disorder (see below), inasmuch as children with an ADHD diagnosis but no conduct disorder diagnosis are not significantly more likely to engage in criminal behavior than age-matched peers (Anderson, 2007; Biederman, 2005; Eyestone & Howell, 1994; Johann et al., 2003; Moffitt, 1990; Molina & Pelham, 2003; Satterfield & Schell, 1997; Sprich et al., 2000; Zagar et al., 1989).

Oppositional Defiant Disorder

Oppositional Defiant Disorder (ODD) is an ongoing pattern of disobedient, hostile and defiant behavior toward authority figures which goes beyond the bounds of normal childhood rebelliousness (APA, 2000). These kids are described by teachers and parents as stubborn, willful, defiant, and "unwilling to take no for an answer." Temper tantrums are the typical re-

TABLE 19.1.
CHILDHOOD MENTAL DISORDERS

Mental Retardation: Subaverage intellectual functioning, usually defined as a psychometrically measured IQ below 70, with associated impairments in adaptive functioning. May be **mild, moderate, severe,** or **profound.** Intellectual limitations may be associated with impaired judgment, poor frustration tolerance, and impaired self-control. May lead to stealing or fighting.

Learning Disorders: Academic functioning substantially below that expected for age, grade level and/or overall intellectual ability. May affect **reading, written expression, mathematics,** and/or other areas of learning.

Communication Disorders: Characterized by impairments in communicative speech and language. May include **expressive language, receptive language, mixed expressive-receptive language, phonological disorder,** and/or **stuttering.**

Autistic Disorder: Severely impaired development of social interaction and social communication, with a markedly restricted range of activities and interests, stereotyped patterns of behavior, obsessive need for order, stability, and routine, and impaired interpersonal communication, sometimes accompanied by bizarre and/or self-injurious behavior. Rarely overtly aggressive, but may become defensively violent if frightened or frustrated.

Asperger's Disorder: Sustained impairment in social interaction and the development of restricted, repetitive patterns of behavior, interests, and activities, usually with preserved, albeit idiosyncratic, communication skills. Impaired empathy, poor understanding of social cues, and need for structure and sameness may result in defensive aggression when personal boundaries are violated. Also may be susceptible to inappropriate behavior, e.g., staring at people, blunt comments, or inappropriate touching.

Attention Deficit Hyperactivity Disorder: Persistent pattern of inattention, impulsivity, and/or hyperactivity that interferes with life tasks, such as schoolwork, family life, and socialization. There are three subdivisions:

> **Primarily Inattentive Type:** Predominance of inattention symptoms over hyperactivity symptoms.

> **Primarily Hyperactive-Impulsive Type:** Predominance of hyperactive and/or impulsive behavior over inattention symptoms. Hyperactivity and impulsivity may lead to risky behavior and emotional outbursts.

> **Combined Type:** Presence of an approximately equal number and severity of both inattentive and hyperactive-impulsive symptoms.

Oppositional Defiant Disorder: Repeated pattern of negativistic, defiant, disobedient, annoying, resentful, and hostile behavior towards authority figures, but without significant interpersonal aggression.

Conduct Disorder: Persistent pattern of violating the rights of others by exploiting, manipulating, intimidating, or aggressing against them. Includes theft, physical fighting, use of weapons, cruelty to people and animals, sexual intimidation or exploitation, and destruction of property.

sponse to not getting their way. Some of these children seem blithely unconcerned about their obnoxious behavior, while others may display a pervasively irritable, dysphoric mood. They rarely take responsibility for their disruptive actions and are quick to externalize blame. Some of these children may act bossy and intimidating, and steal or destroy other kids' property, but serious physical confrontations are rare and, when these occur, are usually signs that the diagnosis has shifted into conduct disorder. In essence, the kid with ODD is the consummate brat, but is rarely the kind of pint-sized predator that defines his conduct-disordered classmate.

Conduct Disorder

Conduct disorder (CD) is a repetitive and persistent pattern of behavior in which the basic rights of others or major age-appropriate societal norms or rules are violated. It can be diagnosed at any age up to 18, beyond which virtually the same diagnostic criteria are used to diagnose antisocial personality disorder (Chapter 8). Conduct disorder is frequently comorbid with ADHD and various learning disorders, and is manifested by the presence of three or more index diagnostic criteria, which include the following:

Physical aggression toward people or animals: bullying or threatening other children; starting fights; using a weapon; physical cruelty to people or animals; confrontational theft (robbery, mugging, chain-snatching, lunch money shakedowns); forced sexual activity.

Destruction of property: smashing furniture or other objects; destroying other people's property; vandalism; arson.

Deceitfulness and theft: breaking into someone else's house, car, or other property; lying, conning, and manipulating people out of their money or possessions; shoplifting and burglary from stores or other locations.

Serious rule violations: frequent school truancy; staying out at night; running away from home—all before the age of 13, indicating a child characterized with precocious rule violation. These children manifest their precocity in other ways as well, often beginning smoking, drinking, drug use, and sexual activity several years earlier than their peers. Generally, the earlier the antisocial behavior starts, the more severe it becomes over time, and it is not unusual to see youths barely past puberty with extensive juvenile criminal and mental health records.

Although conduct disorder is thought to be the precursor of adult antisocial personality disorder, other, albeit related, diagnostic outcomes are not uncommon, for example, borderline personality disorder, paranoid personality disorder or a disorder in the schizophreniform spectrum (Malmquist, 1996). In fact, disorders with a prominent antisocial component, at any age, and covering the diagnostic categories of conduct disorder, oppositional defi-ant disorder, antisocial personality disorder, as well as the more general de-scriptors of delinquency, criminality, aggression, and violence, may really be different phenotypic expressions of a common genetic predisposition to a more generalized externalizing dimention of antisociality (Blazei et al., 2006; Farrington, 1995; Kendler et al., 2007; Krueger et al., 2002; Young et al., 2000). These are probably the classic life-course persistent juvenile delin-quents described by Moffitt (1993).

Animal Cruelty and Delinquency

What do some kids have against animals? In 1987, animal cruelty was added to the *DSM-III-R* as a symptom of conduct disorder and was retained as a diagnostic feature in the 1994 *DSM-IV* and the 2000 *DSM-IV-TR* (Blazei et al., 2006). Cruelty to animals seems to have special significance for later adult violence toward human beings (Hensley & Tallichet, 2009; Merz-Perez et al., 2001; Tallichet & Hensley, 2004). For example, as discussed in Chapter 10, torturing and killing animals is a common historical feature in the early lives of serial murderers who later torture and kill people (Wright & Hensley, 2003). Motivations for animal abuse include peer pressure, sexual gratifica-tion, and projection of the child's own abuse history onto the animal (Ascione, 1997).

The significance of animal abuse among juveniles relates to the implica-tions it has toward risk of violence to humans later in life, in that a propen-sity to aggression toward all living creatures seems to characterize violence-prone individuals. In fact, abuse of pets and companion animals (who are often regarded as members of the family) tends to occur more frequently in households characterized by violence among the human family members, in-cluding heterosexual and homosexual partner abuse, child physical and sex-ual abuse, and sibling abuse (Albert & Bulcroft, 1988; Ascione, 1998; Baldry, 2003; Beirne, 2004; Boat, 1995; Deviney et al., 1983; Flynn, 2000a, 2000b, 2000c; McPhedren, 2006; Munro & Thrusfield, 2001; Siegel, 1993; Wiehe, 1990).

JUVENILE CRIME: TEMPERAMENT AND COGNITIVE STYLE

Across studies, two of the most robust predictors of juvenile aggression and crime are **low capacity for emotional and behavioral self-control** and **association with delinquent peers**, both of which appear to be under control of an interacting array of genetic and psychosocial factors (Akers &

Jensen, 2006; Beaver et al., 2008, 2009; DiLalla, 2002; Morgan & Lilienfeld, 2002; Muris & Ollendick, 2005; Pratt & Cullen, 2000; Lahey & Waldman, 2003; Nigg & Huang-Pollock, 2003; Rhee & Waldman, 2003; Sequin et al., 1999, 2004; Warr, 2002).

As we saw in Chapter 3, Gottfredson & Hirschi's (1990) original **self-control theory** posited this factor as the primary contributing cause of crime and delinquency. These authors argued that parents who supervise their children, recognize the child's misbehavior, and constructively punish and correct the unwanted behavior will inculcate high levels of self-control in their children, whereas parents who shirk these childrearing tasks will raise children low in self-control, who will thereby be at risk for impulsive delinquent behavior. Recall that Gottfredson & Hirschi's (1990) theory is based on a primarily psychosocial premise that emphasizes parental learning effects and downplays the role of innate, genetic factors. However, more recent studies have confirmed that genetic factors account for 50 to 90 percent of the variance in **self-control vs. impulsivity**, the remaining variance attributable to environmental factors. Furthermore, this genetic foundation appears to express itself largely in the structure and function of the **prefrontal cortex of the brain** (Chapters 2 and 8), which forms the substrate for self-monitoring, self-regulation, and self-control (Barkley, 1997; Beaver et al., 2007, 2009; Cauffman et al., 2005; Ishikawa & Raine, 2003; Pfefferbaum et al., 2000; Price et al., 2001; Raine, 2002; Rietveld et al., 2003; Thompson et al., 2001; Toga & Thompson, 2005; Wright & Beaver, 2005).

Self-control may not be a unitary behavioral trait and may instead be composed of several temperamental subcomponents. A number of experts (Calkins & Fox, 2002; Lonigan & Phillips, 2001; Muris & Ollendick, 2005; Murray & Konchanska, 2002) have posited that combination of high neuroticism and low effortful control is the formula for childhood psychopathology that may, in turn be related to delinquent behavior. **Neuroticism** is the term used to describe the trait of unstable and easily excitable emotionality, often seen in individuals with anxiety disorders, mood disorders, and a number of personality disorders (Chapters 6 and 7). **Effortful control** is the ability to focus attention and willpower in order to pursue a goal or solve a problem, and to resist distractions and impulsive responding. Effortful control is highly correlated with what developmental psychologists call maturity and neuropsychologists refer to as **executive functions** that are mediated by the brain's **frontal lobes** (Chapter 2). Effortful control may be composed of two subcomponents: **attentional control**, which describes the ability to focus, shift, and allocate attention as necessary, and **inhibitory control**, which is the ability to restrain and control impulsive responding (Muris & Ollendick, 2005; Murray & Konchanska, 2002).

In this model, children high in effortful control and low in neuroticism will be able to negotiate most challenges adaptively, use their age-appropriate reasoning and communication skills to solve problems, and maintain momentum toward goals, while keeping their emotions from running away with them. Children with the opposite pattern, high neuroticism and low self-control, will show hair-trigger emotional reactions, impulsive behavior, poor reasoning and problem-solving abilities, less flexible and effective coping skills, and difficulty making plans and following through on tasks and goals. Diagnostic expressions of this combination of traits may include many of the children in the ADHD-ODD-CD spectrum, who are at risk for later developing externalizing disorders (e.g., antisocial personality disorder) or internalizing disorders (e.g., anxiety or depression) (Asendorpf et al., 2008; Asendorpf & van Aken, 1999; Barkley, 2004; Block & Block, 1980; Calkins & Fox, 2002; Caspi, 2000; Huesmann et al., 1984; Lengua & Long, 2002; Lonigan & Phillips, 2001; Mangione et al., 2004; Muris & Ollendick, 2005; Mandel, 1997; Moffitt, 1993; Murray & Konchanska, 2002; Nigg et al., 2004; Robins, 1966; Salmon & Pereira, 2002; Thomas & Chess, 1977; Tremblay, 2000). Thus, in this model, gene-environment interaction impacts brain development, which mediates temperament and cognitive style, which comprise the internal influences that direct and control behavior.

An **undercontrolled temperament** appears to be a stable trait from childhood into adulthood. In the now-famous Dunedin Longitudinal Study (Caspi, 2000; Caspi & Silva, 1995; Caspi et al., 1987, 1996, 2003), researchers assessed the developmental trajectory of 1,037 children from age 3 to adulthood. About 10 percent of this sample were classified as undercontrolled and, as young adults, they reported significantly higher levels of emotional distress, particularly feelings of being mistreated, persecuted, and betrayed by others. They were rated as less agreeable, less conscientious, less open to new experiences, and more emotionally labile. They also showed higher rates of antisocial personality disorder, had committed a greater number of criminal offenses, including violent offenses, and had a higher rate of suicide attempts. By middle age, the boys who had been rated as undercontrolled showed a history of marginal and erratic employment and were likely to be divorced. Undercontrolled girls, by middle adulthood, were likely to have been married and divorced from low-status men and to be depressed and irritable mothers.

More recently, Asendorpf et al. (2008) followed two groups of children, one with an **inhibited style** and the other with an **aggressive style**, into adulthood. Whereas the results for the inhibited children were mixed, the aggressive children showed a clear externalizing pattern in adulthood, being rated as more aggressive, less agreeable, less conscientious, less open to experience, more impulsive, and more emotionally labile. Their educational and occupational achievement was lower, and they were more likely to have incurred criminal charges. These findings are strikingly similar to the results of the Dunedin study.

NEUROPSYCHOLOGICAL AND PSYCHOLOGICAL FACTORS

Early accounts of cognitive deficiencies in delinquents focused on intelligence, probably because this was the easiest variable to measure psychometrically. The literature on this subject from 1943 to 1960 was reviewed by Shulman (1951) and Prentice & Kelly (1963). These early studies overwhelmingly found significantly lower Verbal IQs than Performance IQs in delinquent subjects, across age, sex, race, setting, and test forms. This relationship continued to be confirmed by later neuropsychological studies, along with findings that, relative to controls, delinquent youths show impairment in attentional control, sensorimotor and symbol sequencing, speech sounds perception, language skills, spatial localization, verbal and nonverbal conceptual reasoning, and problem solving, especially the ability to comprehend, manipulate, and utilize conceptual material (Berman & Siegal, 1976; Fitzhugh, 1973; Hurwitz et al., 1972).

A later neuropsychological review (Miller, 1988c) concluded that assaultive delinquents tend to be characterized by a greater number of EEG abnormalities, poorer verbal memory, and increased perseveration, as compared with nonassaultive delinquents (Berman & Siegal, 1976; Krynicki, 1978). Adolescent boys incarcerated at a corrections school were found to show severe reading disability, impaired memory, paranoid ideation, and visual hallucinations, associated with a history of violence and abuse (Lewis et al., 1980). Learning disabilities per se have not been found to be associated with higher risk for antisocial behavior (Spreen, 1981), but when combined with deficits in verbal reasoning and poor impulse control, the risk of antisocial acting-out appears to be elevated (Brickman et al., 1984; Eaker et al., 1983; Robbins et al., 1983; Spreen, 1981; Tarter et al., 1983). The significant finding of frontal-like impairment in another series of delinquents led to the hypothesis that antisocial youths have particular problems in planning their actions, perceiving the consequences of those actions, and altering those actions in the face of changing circumstances (Yeudall et al., 1982). These findings seem to implicate areas of the brain associated with left-hemisphere and frontal lobe functioning (Miller, 1987, 1988c).

PEER INFLUENCES

Another robust finding from the literature on juvenile crime is that birds of a delinquent feather do indeed flock together, and **association with delinquent peers** is one of the strongest predictors of a particular youth's own criminal offending (Beaver et al., 2009; Blazei et al., 2006; Cairns & Cairns, 1994; Harris, 1998; Kandel, 1978; Poulin & Boivin, 2000; Warr, 2002). As with other strong correlations, the question is why. A straightforward behavioral genetic explanation is that youths with antisocial tendencies seek out antisocial peer networks in the same way as academically-oriented kids seek out fellow scholars and athletic kids hang out with other jocks (Cleveland et al., 2005; DiLalla, 2002; Lykken, 1995; Scarr, 1992; Scarr & McCartney, 1983; Walsh, 2002)–the concept of **active gene-environment correlation** discussed in Chapter 2. For example, recent findings (Beaver et al., 2009) support the idea that genetic factors account for most of the variance in the association of drug-using youths with drug-using peers, parental influence having very little independent effect.

The pathway to youthful antisocial behavior may not be so simple, however, because both associating with antisocial peers and rejection by the dominant peer group have been shown to be correlated with antisocial behavior in male and female adolescents (Laird et al., 2001). In one case, a crime-supportive delinquent peer group abets antisocial behavior in its members, while in the other, rejected adolescents may act out their pain and anger in violent or destructive acts against the dominant group.

FAMILY FACTORS

Not that families are unimportant–just that modern behavioral research has provided insights into the complex ways nature and nurture interact in influencing behavior, including antisocial behavior.

Genetics, Environment, and Families

One of the most well-established observations in both criminology and psychology is that crime runs in families; any disagreements usually relate to the causal mechanisms involved. Do children learn either prosocial or antisocial behavior patterns from their parents (and later, peers), or do they inherit from their parents the innate predisposition for either prosocial or antisocial behavior, and then these potentialities are further reinforced by the family environment (Herndon & Iacono, 2005; Rowe et al., 1992)? As discussed in Chapter 2, two ways of studying this are through family studies, twin studies, and adoption studies.

As applied to juvenile delinquency and later criminality, this research has found that a diagnosis of antisocial personality disorder (Chapter 8) in either the mother or father is associated with a greater probability of conduct disorder in their children, especially boys, and that the genetic relationship between antisocial behavior and substance abuse may be linked to a single externalizing trait that parents pass on to their offspring (Foley et al., 2001; Hicks et al., 2004). For example, twin studies have generally shown that genetic factors account for about half the variance of transmission of conduct disorder, oppositional defiant disorder, and ADHD, with most of the other half accounted for by nonshared environment, and the remainder by shared environment (Burt et al., 2001; Krueger et al., 2002; Rhee & Waldman, 2002; Young et al., 2000). Biological children of convicted criminals who are adopted and raised in a noncriminal family show a rate of antisocial behavior almost as great as their siblings who stayed with the original family. Conversely, biological offspring of noncriminal parents who find themselves being raised in a criminal household show only a slightly elevated rate of antisociality themselves, although the family effect appears somewhat higher for boys than girls (Cadoret et al., 1987; Mednick et al., 1984). The risk is greatest for biological children of criminal parents raised in the same home.

Parental Discord, Divorce, and Parenting

One of the characteristics of dysfunctional families in general, and criminogenic ones in particular, is the presence of family conflict and/or violence (see also Chapters 16 and 17). Empirical studies confirm what common observation shows, namely that growing up in a single-parent (usually with the mother) household is a strong risk factor for childhood delinquency and later criminal behavior (Blazei, 2006; Demo & Acock, 1988; Henry et al., 1996; Lykken, 2000). Again, the question is why. Do children growing up without fathers lose a vital source of stable socialization that impels them to seek the company of antisocial peers, or are the same traits of impulsivity, irresponsibility, and unstable behavior that characterized the now-absent father genetically transmitted to his offspring (Blazei et al., 2006)?

In many cases, it is not so much the fact of divorce or separation itself that is associated with child delinquency, but the history of parental conflict that precedes it. In some cases, where the child has formed a reasonably healthy, positive attachment to the remaining parent, and especially where drug use by either parent is not a major factor, separation from the more pathological parent, and the resultant lessening of tension and discord within the household, may actually reduce the risk of child antisocial behavior (Amato & Keith, 1991; Blazei et al., 2006; Demo & Acock, 1988; Stanger et al., 2004).

Alternatively, however, bad parenting compounds the detrimental effects of being raised in a single-parent or discordant dual-parent household. A range of bad parenting skills tend to cluster together so that parents who are deficient in, say, proper boundary setting and supervision of school and play activities will also be inept or uninvolved in appropriate discipline for aggressive misbehavior, or they set a bad example themselves by engaging in unhealthy or illegal activities, such as family violence and drug use (Blazei et al., 2006; Patterson & Stouthamer-Lober, 1984).

Antisocial Parents and Antisocial Children

The well-established association between criminal behavior of parents and their biological offspring has given rise to the genetically-based and environmentally-moderated **intergenerational transmission hypothesis** (Caspi et al., 2002; Kim-Cohen et al., 2006; Repo-Tiihonen et al., 2010; Thornberry et al., 2003). As we've noted, one of the things that may be inherited is a predisposition to antisocial behavior or psychopathy, whose traits include impulsivity, shallow emotions, narcissistic egocentricity, lying and deception, lack of empathy or remorse, and the persistent violation of social norms (Cleckley, 1982; Hare, 1993, 2006). A recent study of homicide offenders (Repo-Tiihonen et al., 2010) found that half of the sample had offspring who showed persistent criminal behavior, much of it including violent criminality, especially property destruction and vandalism. Mental disorder or alcoholism in a grandparent increased the risk of violent offending in their grandchildren if that grandchild also had a psychopathic parent.

CHILD ABUSE, NEGLECT, AND VIOLENCE

As discussed in Chapter 16, child abuse and neglect by parents or other caretakers can have a range of adverse effects on the child's physical well-being and mental health (Edwards et al., 2003; Egeland et al., 2002; Miller, 1999a, 1999b, 2008b; Sternberg et al., 2006; Twarzdosz & Lutzker, 2010; Vazsonyi et al., 2001; Wekerle et al., 2001). But can child maltreatment contribute to that child's likelihood of becoming an abuser him- or herself or of committing other types of violent acts—perpetuating the so-called **intergenerational cycle of violence**? As with the case of other family factors, this again invokes the issue of **gene-environment correlations**.

Child Abuse and Maltreatment: Description and Demographics

Between 800,000 and 900,000 children are abused and/or neglected in the United States each year, with girls slightly more likely to be affected. Incidence rates of child maltreatment have been increasing since the 1980s. Sixty percent of these children suffer from neglect and 10 percent are physically abused. About 2000 children die of neglect and abuse every year, most of the victims being under the age of 4. Highest per-capita rates of abuse by ethnicity (in descending order) are African-American, Pacific Islanders and Native Americans, Caucasian and Latino, and Asian-American. As noted in Chapter 16, these statistics may well underrepresent the true rate of child abuse because much abuse goes unreported (U.S. Department of Health and Human Services, 2005, 2006, 2009).

Forms of child abuse and maltreatment include:

Physical abuse: assault or beating of a child that may result in physical injury.

Neglect: failure to properly care for a child by withholding or overlooking sufficient physical, medical, nutritional, educational, and emotional support.

Sexual abuse: sexual assault, molestation, or exploitation of a child.

Psychological abuse: mistreatment of the child, including rejecting, terrorizing, threatening, demeaning, humiliating, inducing excessive guilt, or emotionally isolating the child.

Many children are exposed to multiple forms of abuse, often resulting in diagnosable PTSD and other disorders (Burton et al., 1994; Cauffman et al., 1998; Dixon et al., 2005; Erwin et al., 2000; Greenwald, 2002; Maas et al., 2008; Ruchkin et al., 2002; Steiner et al., 1997; Wood et al., 2002a).

We know that physical child abuse consistently predicts violent behavior in maltreated children, and that this risk is compounded with additional forms of abuse, i.e., sexual, psychological. In turn, such brutalization in the family of origin predicts later partner abuse and child abuse in the victim's later family, males more likely to become perpetrators and females more likely to be victims (Cicchetti & Manly, 2001; Heide, 1999; Heide & Solomon, 2006; Horwitz et al., 2001; Jaffee et al., 2007; Lansford et al., 2002; Lewis et al., 1997, 2001; Maas et al., 2008; Pincus, 2001; Shumaker & Prinz, 2000).

Child Maltreatment and Violence: Developmental Pathways and Outcomes

There are a number of developmental pathways that could account for the association of a child's violent victimization within his or her own family and the later expression of violence by that individual. A genetic predisposition to violence may be passed from parent (usually the father) to child (usually the son). Compounding the neurophysiological problem would be a history of frequent blows to the head sustained during physical abuse that might cumulatively impair brain functions essential for cognitive control and emotional self-regulation. There is evidence that early physical and psychological trauma can cause **sensitization** within the **limbic system**, making the individual prone to a violent reaction upon slight provocation; this might be one mechanism involved in the development of the **limbic psychotic trigger reaction** (**LPTR**) discussed in Chapter 4. Trauma also affects the **hypothalamic-pituitary axis** (Chapter 2), which alters the brain and body's response to cortisol, which plays a role in emotion and memory (Beckman, 2004; Bryan & Freed, 1982; DiLalla & Gottesman, 1991; Else et al., 1993; Felthous, 1980; Giedd, 2004; Goff et al., 1991; Gunnar & Vasquez, 2001; Heide & Solomon, 2006; Heim et al., 2000; Huesman et al., 1984; Lewis et al., 1985; McCord, 1983; Newport & Nemeroff, 2000; Plomin et al., 1985; Pollock et al., 1990; Schmithorst et al., 2005; Sendi & Blomgren, 1975; Solomon & Heide, 2005; van der Kolk, 1996; van der Kolk & Fisler, 1994; Volavka, 1995; Widom, 1989).

Psychosocially, children raised in a violent household would be expected to learn violence as an interpersonal coping strategy and thus come to rely on it themselves when they get older. At the same time, more effective prosocial interpersonal problem solving strategies and emotional self-control would not be learned. Finally, such children are more likely to develop a suspicious, bitter, cynical, and hostile attitude toward other people (Agnew, 1999; Caspi et al., 2002; De Bellis et al., 2000; Dodge et al., 1990, 1995; Egeland et al., 2002; Huesmann, 1994; Maas et al., 2008).

Early Life Experiences of Juvenile Offenders

The life-experience factor was specifically explored in an in-depth, interview-based case study of incarcerated delinquent youths by Paton et al. (2009), which revealed a number of **core themes** in the life experiences and resultant thought processes of these young offenders.

Living in a violent world. Subjects described the everyday experience of living in a rough, violent interpersonal world where only a tough, macho attitude and the wherewithal to back it up allowed one to survive. Aggression and violence were pervasive, experienced in the family, the community, at school, and in custody.

Instability and transitions. The young offenders' lives appeared to be characterized by numerous episodes of instability and transition, characterized by frequent and intense conflicts with parents and other authority figures, that persisted throughout childhood and adolescence.

Depriving environment. This refers to both material deprivation in the form of finances and possessions, and interpersonal deprivation as a consequence of parental absence, either literal absence of at least one parent from the home, and/or emotional distance from the remaining parent. A high number of these youthful offenders grew up without fathers in the home, and many experienced long bouts of virtually no parental care or supervision at all, having to fend for themselves.

Juveniles Offenders' Responses to Life Experiences

As a result of these early experiences, these young offenders developed a variety of cognitive and behavioral responses (Paton et al., 2009).

Thoughts and feelings. Cognitive coping responses included: deliberate thought suppression, lack of memory or alteration of memory, reexperiencing and flashbacks, trying to make sense of violent experiences, minimizing of the impact of violence experiences to oneself ("no big deal"), hypervigilance, desensitization to violence in general, and various defensive reactions. One of these consisted of self-indoctrination with the view that the subject's history of violent and degrading experiences has had a positive effect, either toughening one up or bestowing a kind of warrior wisdom. A number of subjects seemed to reflexively throw up a screen of emotional distance and detachment when describing their traumatic experiences to the examiner.

Behavioral responses. A number of youths reported substance abuse and self-harm as coping responses to painful emotions. All subjects endorsed a causal connection between their youthful tribulations and their later criminal offending, although this could also reflect a self-serving bias (the "abuse excuse").

Changing self and support networks. Although this may have been a rationalization for some subjects ("making lemonade out of lemons"), there was a strong sense for many that incarceration afforded a respite from their violent, unstable lives and an opportunity to reflect on and reevaluate their lives, including whether or not they wanted to continue a criminal lifestyle or pursue more conventional and satisfying life goals. Although many of these youths had sought support from their families or schools at some point, most denied needing any kind of help or support. Many were disappointed with professional counselors who, they felt, did not understand the realities of street life and tended to see all the problems as emanating from the youth's own psychopathology or poor coping abilities. In fact, most of these youths had actually coped rather well with their dangerous and depressing circumstances–that's why they were still alive.

JUVENILE RESILIENCE

Yet, up to 20 percent of children and adolescents, despite equivalent histories of abuse, neglect, and maltreatment, do not follow the downward trajectory of their similarly-buffeted peers and, in some cases, show remarkable levels of competency, stability, and success in adult life (Cicchetti & Rogosch, 1997; Cichetti et al., 1993; Kaufman et al., 1994; McGloin & Widom, 2001; Haskett et al., 2006; Jaffee et al., 2007; Luthar et al., 2000; Masten & Coatsworth, 1998; Masten & Reed, 2002). What distinguishes this lucky minority?

Two of the most important developmental tasks that have been found to influence one's later personality and interaction style are inculcating secure and supportive **attachment relationships** with caregivers and building an adequate degree of cognitive, emotional, and behavioral **self-control**. Thus, it is not surprising that antisocial individuals at any age, who have been raised in households characterized by abuse and neglect, typically show insecure or antagonistic attachment styles along with impulsivity, impaired reflection and self-modulation, and deficient ability to understand and communicate cognitive and emotional states (Appel & Holden, 1998; Cicchetti & Beeghly, 1987; Contreras & Kerns, 2000; Cummings et al., 1994; Eddleson, 1999; Gaensbauer, 1982; Gelles, 1992, Haskett et al., 2006; Jaffee, 2005; Jaffee et al., 2007; Klimes-Dougan & Kistner, 1990; Lynch & Cicchetti, 1998; Morton & Browne, 1998; Parke & Ladd, 1992; Repetti et al., 2002; Rutter, 1979; Sameroff & Chandler, 1975; Sameroff et al., 1998; Shields et al., 2001; Shipman & Zeman, 1999; Whipple & Webster-Stratton, 1991).

Early studies attempted to identify the core features that distinguished a small subset of youths, termed **invulnerable children**, **resilient children**, or "**superkids**." These are children and adolescents who, despite being raised under circumstances that ranged from the dysfunctional to the horrific, nevertheless seem to transcended their seemingly traumatogenic and criminogenic environments and emerge as relatively well-functioning adolescents and adults (Anthony, 1987; Caspi et al., 2002; Cicchetti & Rogosch, 1997; Cicchetti et al., 1993; Cohler, 1987; Dahlin et al., 1990; Davidson-Arad et al., 2003; Dubow et al., 1987; Egeland et al., 1993; Feiring et al., 2002; Foley et al., 2004; Garmezy, 1985; Hart et al., 1996; Heath & Heath, 1991; Heim et al., 2001; Herrenkohl et al., 1994; Jaffee et al., 2005, 2007; Miller, 1988b, 1992a, 1998c, 1998d; Moran & Eckenrode, 1992; Olivan, 2003; Rutter, 1985; Werner & Smith, 1992).

Temperamentally, these resilient children seemed to start life with a certain mental robustness and ability to engage the world constructively, which helped them confront challenges instead of avoiding them or being overwhelmed by them. Helping these children to do this were an array of competencies and coping skills they seemed to naturally possess from an early age and which seemed to grow and mature with age. These youths tended to show a healthy degree of introspection, self-insight, self-esteem, and outer-directed creativity. They were interpersonally skillful, popular with peers and adults, active on their own behalf, and possessed of a strong sense of personal control, personal responsibility, and self-regulation. They seemed to be able to prioritize the particular problems to be dealt with at any given time and then to engage them constructively. Their relationships were soundly based and enduring, yet they seemed to be able to soothe and comfort themselves without becoming overly dependent on other people for emotional support.

Cognitively, these resilient children were characteristically reflective rather than impulsive, and were able to keep a good hold on their emotions, while showing a full range of feelings in appropriate circumstances. They were relatively bright, had especially good verbal reasoning and communications skills, and their natural curiosity, eagerness to learn, and absorption with scholastic subjects (often in the face of ridicule by peers) endeared them to teachers, whom they then accessed as resources and mentors. They used this native intelligence to plan and carry out strategies for overcoming obstacles, which fostered an overall feeling of competence and mastery.

Not all of these children had so rosy an outcome, however. A subgroup, while still considered resilient by the standards of the surrounding community, started life at a relative disadvantage, as frail, weak, and ailing infants and children. Despite this early fragility, they gradually developed a seemingly implacable resolve not to be "broken" and demonstrated an extraordinary degree of persistence in their continuous struggles with adversity. In the service of survival, they often displayed a high degree of creativity, which, however, tended to be inner-directed and agonizingly expressed. They appeared to engage in a lifelong struggle to prove themselves, often absorbing themselves in science and technology projects to the detriment of intimate personal relationships, and rarely finding true satisfaction and happiness, but contributing to society in the form of valuable works and services.

More recently, a number of studies have confirmed the role of cognitive factors and resilience in affecting the relationship of psychosocial adversity to the development of antisocial versus prosocial behavior (Haskett et al., 2006). For example, in one conceptualization, **ego-control** refers to a child's capacity to monitor and moderate one's emotional experiences and behavior, while **ego-resiliency** describes a child's ability to flexibly tune and mod-

ulate those emotional reactions to the demands of different situations (Hartmann, 1958; Luthar, 1991; Miller, 1988b, 1992a, 1998c, 1998d). Research
has shown that both of these related qualities of self-regulatory **ego strength**
appear to cognitively cushion these children from the worst effects of an
adverse upbringing, including various forms of maltreatment. Children with
these ego strengths–reminiscent of Hirschi's (1969) concept of self-control–
enjoy overall better interpersonal relationships and overall better psychological adjustment (Cicchetti & Rogosch, 1997); Cicchetti et al., 1993; Flores et
al., 2005; Rogosch et al., 1995).

Ego strength and autonomy, as conceptualized here, include not only
self-monitoring, self-regulation, and self-control, but also the child's confidence that he or she can control important outside events that affect him or
her, a concept that has been referred to as **self-efficacy** (Bandura, 1977, 1998).
Along with well-developed self-control, a strong sense of self-efficacy, or personal control over events, has been found to be associated with greater resistance to the effects of early maltreatment and other adverse life experiences,
including internalizing disorders such as anxiety and depression, and externalizing disorders such as antisocial behavior (Bolger & Patterson, 2001;
Haskett et al., 2006; Luthar, 1991).

Thus, as in the earlier studies, more recent research has confirmed a connection between a child's resistance to adverse developmental circumstances
and the qualities of good ego autonomy, self-control, self-esteem, self-efficacy, communication skill, and interpersonal problem-solving (Haskett et al.,
2006). In addition, certain features of the early family environment appear
to foster resilient functioning in children, even those who are maltreated by
certain family members. These include affection, sensitivity, and support for
the child's autonomy on the part of at least one parent or caretaker.
Protective factors also include broader features of family functioning such as
overall family coherence and stability. Finally, access to reasonably high-qual-
ity schools with competent and concerned teachers is a valuable resource
that maltreated and other disadvantaged children can potentially utilize to
compensate for deficient support and care at home. Good schools also
enable children with good verbal abilities to develop an area of competence
that is not only important for self-esteem, but has practical implications for
higher education and an overall better life (Catterall, 1998; Gonzales, 1997;
Haskett et al., 2006; Stipek, 1997).

TREATMENT AND INTERVENTION
FOR JUVENILE OFFENDING

Research on resilience may have implications for treatment of delinquent youths in the sense that, if we can identify the factors that help some of these young people avoid the downward spiral, then perhaps we can adapt them into some form of effective intervention strategy. In fact, even youths who do not meet the criteria for resilience as delineated above, may be positively influenced to desist from antisocial trajectories by the proper circumstances (Dodge, 2008). These include being raised in the presence of overall low family stress, especially where family decisions are made in a collaborative and nonpunitive way. In addition, adult subjects who have been maltreated and who have shown antisocial behavior as children and adolescents, may desist in the context of a warm, supportive adult relationship, reminiscent of the adage that "it takes a good woman to straighten a wild man out" (Lansford et al., 2006; Sampson & Laub, 1990; Stouthamer-Loeber et al., 2004).

Before celebrating such a cheerily hopeful prospect of reforming wayward youth, however, we might reasonably ask whether those children with the more favorable outcome would have really met the criteria for serious conduct disorder or life-course persistent delinquency in the first place, or if their antisocial behavior was really more consistent with the adolescent-limited type of delinquency that has a much more favorable outcome overall—in other words, whether intervention works best for those who need it the least. Yet, a few studies that appear to have addressed this question find a sort of contrast effect, whereby children determined to be at high genetic risk for conduct disorder are actually more responsive than less at-risk children to environmental and family effects. That is, nurturing parenting has been found to have an even greater protective effect on at least some high-risk children in terms of inhibiting later antisocial behavior (Caspi et al., 2002; Jaffee et al., 2005).

With regard to formal intervention programs, an air of pessimism has pervaded the field: if the obdurate alloy of juvenile antisocial behavior is genetically forged and psychosocially welded shut at an early age, what kind of interventional dent could any therapeutic program have? And indeed, most short-term, scope-limited programs have failed to have any appreciable effect, as have punitive shock treatment approaches like "scared-straight" and boot camp programs. However, recent work suggests that long-term, consistently applied, and family-based intervention strategies can alter many antisocial trajectories, with success rates approaching 20 to 30 percent. These include such programs as **mutisystemic therapy**, **multidimensional foster care**, and **functional family therapy**. Programs like these provide young offenders with supportive social contexts and targeted training in interpersonal relations, self-control, academic performance, and job skills to assist them in acquiring the capacities necessary to change problem behavior and to attain psychosocial maturity. Some programs focus on teaching and supporting effective parenting skills in caretakers, beginning with home visits by a nurse during the mother's pregnancy and during the first years of the child's life. The problem, as always, is maintaining political and financial commitment to these intervention over the long haul (Alexander & Parsons, 1982; Chamberlain, 2003; Dodge, 2008; Greenwood, 2006; Kazdin, 2003; Lipsey, 1995, 1999; Steinberg, 2009).

YOUNG OFFENDERS, BRAIN DEVELOPMENT, AND THE JUVENILE JUSTICE SYSTEM

In 1993, Christopher Roper, age 17, developed a scheme with two younger accomplices to break into an elderly female neighbor's home, tie her up, burglarize the house, and then dispose of the victim. One accomplice dropped out of the plot, but the remaining two carried out their crime, breaking into the elderly woman's house, binding and blindfolding her, and subsequently murdering her by tossing her off a bridge. Simmons was convicted of first-degree murder and sentenced to death, but his case was appealed to the U.S. Supreme Court.

As of 1990, only a few countries–Congo, Iran, Yemen, Saudi Arabia, Pakistan, and Nigeria–currently allow the execution of juvenile offenders. Specifically, as recently as 2005, twenty-one states in the United States allowed the execution of offenders under the age of 18, and in most of these states, adolescent offenders as young as 16 could be sentenced to death (Bradley, 2002; *Stanford v. Kentucky,* 1989; Scott & Steinberg, 2003; *Thompson v. Oklahoma,* 1998). In the case of *Roper v. Simmons* (2005), the U.S. Supreme Court banned the death penalty for offenders under the age of 18 years, the majority opinion arguing that adolescents do not possess the emotional, intellectual, or biological maturity to be fully culpable for the violent acts that they commit. Adolescents may still be held responsible for their crimes, the Court said, but should not suffer the ultimate penalty for impulses they are developmentally unable to fully control. What was unique about this case is that a key element of Simmons's defense was new brain imaging evidence suggesting that the adolescent brain is not as well developed as that of an adult (Aronson, 2007). Thus, a major decision in United States criminal law was made largely based on neuropsychology. But was this interpretation of neuropsychology correct?

Although the death penalty for juveniles is no longer an issue in this country, questions remain as to what age is required for an individual to be considered fully responsible for his or her actions. Should some juveniles be tried as adults? Should brain evidence be used to argue these cases? And exactly at what age does the brain reach the point of development that allows individuals to control their behavior? And what parts of the brain? And are all brains alike?

The Juvenile Justice System

The first American juvenile court was established in 1899 and, throughout the early part of the twentieth century, its judges had the specific mandate to analyze the moral character and social backgrounds of the juveniles who appeared before them in order to determine the most appropriate disposition of each case which, in most instances, included some form of rehabilitation to turn the young mind from a life of crime. To further protect potentially wayward youth from corrupting influences, courts instituted a set of **status offenses**, i.e., actions that were only criminal based on the age of the offender, such as drinking alcohol or violating curfews. In general, during this period, juvenile offenders were generally considered less blameworthy and more amenable to rehabilitation, in contrast to adult "hardened" criminals (Gerber & Engelhardt-Greer, 1996; Grisso, 1996; Grossberg, 2002; Krisberg & Austin, 1993; Platt, 1977; Shook, 2005; Scott & Steinberg, 2003, 2009).

However, in response to sharp increases in both the frequency and severity of juvenile violence during the 1980s and early 1990s, legislatures adopted a far less rehabilitative and more punitive "get tough" attitude and policy toward youthful offenders, in which juveniles accused of serious crimes were more likely to be charged and prosecuted as adults. This tough approach continues despite a more recent decrease in juvenile crime over the past decade (Beckett, 1997; Bishop, 2000; Feld, 1993; Garland, 2001; Shook, 2005; Snyder, 2002; Snyder & Sickmund, 1995; Steinberg, 2009; Tang & Nunez, 2003; Zimring, 1998).

Currently, almost every state in the United States has adopted some sort of strategy to prosecute some juveniles as adults. The most prevalent strategy is **judicial waiver** which allows a juvenile court judge to waive juvenile court jurisdiction after conducting a hearing. **Prosecutorial waiver** enables the prosecutor to file charges directly against a juvenile defendant in criminal court, while in **automatic legislative transfer**, juveniles who meet a minimum age requirement and are charged with certain (usually more severe) crimes are automatically tried as adults (Feld, 1998; Norman &

Gillespie, 1986; Puzzanchera, 2003; Shook, 2005; Tang & Nunez, 2003; Triplett, 1996). Studies have shown that when charged with violent offenses, juveniles tried as adults are typically judged as harshly or more harshly as adult defendants, presumably on the assumption that "they must be guilty of something really bad," to have been charged as adults in the first place (Eigen, 1981; Griffin et al., 1998; Levine et al., 2001; Rainville & Smith, 2003; Tang & Nunez , 2003).

Cognitive Aspects of Juvenile Crime

Even without invoking neuropsychology, it seems intuitively obvious that one must have reached a certain age to have developed the cognitive capacities necessary for informed decision making and volitional behavior. But what age? And which cognitive capacities? Recently, a number of researchers (Cauffman & Steinberg, 2000; Scott et al., 1995; Scott & Steinberg, 2003, 2009; Steinberg & Cauffman, 1996) have attempted to enumerate a set of cognitive, emotional, and volitional characteristics that comprise adult behavioral self-control, and that they believe most juveniles lack, therefore rendering them less blameworthy for their crimes.

It is well established that reasoning capabilities increase through childhood into early and later adolescence, along with general factual and social knowledge, memory, and other capacities that make adult decision-making possible. In fact, most research shows that adolescents' level of intelligence and ability to reason are generally indistinguishable from adults by the age of 16, as evidenced, for example, by the 16-year-old age cutoff of the **Wechsler Intelligence Scales** for children vs. adults (Conklin et al., 2007; Crone & van der Molen, 2004; Hooper et al., 2004; Luna et al., 2001). However, research also suggests that adolescents are less capable of making sound decisions when under stressful conditions or when peer pressure is strong. However, while many younger teens may show impressive reasoning abilities on formal tests, it is still possible that psychosocial immaturity prevents these youths from utilizing these skills in matters of mature judgment in actual decision-making circumstances, often marked by high stress and emotional arousal, a phenomenon that has been referred to as the **immaturity gap** (Aronson, 2007). This kind of developmental immaturity has been equated with the **diminished capacity** defense invoked in some adults with neurological or psychiatric disorders (Steinberg, 2003). Adolescents are also more responsive to peer influence than adults, which may account for why they are more likely than adults to commit crimes in groups (Steinberg & Monahan, 2007; Zimring, 1998). This may further inhibit autonomous decision making that might otherwise deter them from a criminal act.

Children and adolescents are less **future-oriented** than adults and more likely to discount long-term consequences (Gardner, 1993; Greene, 1986; Nurmi, 1991), rendering decisions about the outcomes of their actions more problematic. This may be abetted by heighted **reward-sensitivity**, making juveniles more likely to be tempted by the thrills of the moment (Galvan et al., 2007; Millstein & Halpern-Felsher, 2002). All of these factors contribute to lower capacities for self-regulation in juveniles relative to adults, and a number of criminologists and behavioral scientists have sought a neuropsychological rationale for this.

The Developing Brain

One immediate problem with using brain-based criteria to make legal determinations is that that neurodevelopmental trajectories are continuous, not to mention highly variable from person to person, whereas determination of legal culpability is binary: the defendant is either tried as an adult or as a juvenile (Aronson, 2007). The other major problem is the cutoff itself: developmental neuropsychology research has demonstrated that the human brain continues to develop well into the third decade of life, so just when does it reach that ideal state of maturation that allows an individual to be designated as an adult instead of a juvenile? And if everybody's brain develops differently, what is the ideal cutoff point that will maximize the number of fair decisions?

These new **neurocriminologists** (my term) point to two main neurophysiological processes associated with brain development, myeliniation and synaptic pruning, and focus on a particular region of the human brain, the frontal lobes. Recall from Chapter 2, that the progressive deposition of **myelin**, the fatty sheath that surrounds and insulates most larger neuronal axons enables brain cells to communicate faster and more efficiently. The process of **myelination** begins in infancy and is still occurring in the brains of many 40-year-olds. Also beginning shortly after birth is the process of **synaptic pruning**, whereby the initial tangle of synaptic connections among neurons is gradually honed and sharpened by experience, thereby reducing signal redundancy and further increasing neuronal speed and efficiency; this latter process is thought to be completed far earlier, usually by middle adolescence (Huttenlocher, 1979; Huttenlocher et al., 1982; Yakovlev & Lecours, 1967).

Anatomical studies demonstrate that the brain regions responsible for basic life functions and sensory-motor processes tend to mature fastest, whereas the regions responsible for behavioral inhibition, impulse control, risk assessment, decision making, risk and reward evaluation, long-term planning, and emotional self-regulation take longer. In fact, it is the brain's

frontal lobes that seem to be the last to finish myelinating well into adulthood and may be responsible for moderating the **limbic system**-mediated emotional expressivity and impulsive sensation-seeking that characterizes early and middle adolescence (Casey et al., 2008; Dahl, 2001; Giedd et al., 1999; Gogtay et al., 2004; Sowell et al., 1999, 2001; Spear, 2000; Scott & Steinberg, 2003, 2009; Yakovlev & Lecours, 1967).

Steinberg (2004, 2007, 2008, 2009) asserts that risky adolescent behavior is the product of activity in two neurobiological systems: (1) a **socioemotional system**, which is mediated by the limbic system and includes the amygdala, ventral striatum, orbitofrontal cortex, medial prefrontal cortex, and superior temporal sulcus; and (2) a **cognitive control system**, which is mainly composed of the parietal cortex, lateral prefrontal cortex, and anterior cingulate cortex. In this model, adolescent risk taking is stimulated by the rapid increase in dopaminergic activity within the socioemotional system during puberty, which leads to a marked increase in reward seeking. This process, however, precedes the maturation of the cognitive control system that would permit more mature self-regulation and impulse control. It is this interval that may comprise the immaturity gap cited by Aronson (2007).

These theories apply to normally developing brains. But, as we've seen in several places throughout this text, adolescent neurodevelopment can be affected by a wide variety of congenital and acquired factors, including anxiety, depression, trauma, intellectual deficiency, learning disabilities, ADHD, or brain injuries (Grisso, 2005; Grisso et al., 2003; McGaha et al., 2001; Viljoen & Grisso, 2007; Viljoen & Roesch, 2005). How do we know how mature a defendant's brain is in these cases?

Legal Aspects of Neurodevelopment

And even if we could come up with a kind of "**brain maturity index**," how do these findings and hypotheses on child and adolescent brain development translate into concrete recommendations for the juvenile justice system? For example, at what age are juveniles competent to stand trial? Similar to the issues associated with trying juveniles as adults, the matter appears to hinge on whether or not the specific defendant in question possesses the cognitive capacities to meet the legal criteria for competency. One large-scale study (Grisso et al., 2003) found that cognitive abilities related to trial competence improve significantly between the ages of 11 and 16, with three age epochs showing weaker (11–13), better (14–15), and best (16 and older) competence-related abilities.

The age issue relates to the **domain specificity** of cognitive abilities and legal competencies and, by implication, the brain mechanisms that underlie them (Steinberg, 2009). For example, where cognitive abilities (reasoning, memory, general knowledge) predominate, such as in competency to stand trial, adolescents older than 15 or 16 could credibly be treated as adults. But in circumstances where socioemotional factors (impulsivity, susceptibility to peer pressure, reward sensitivity, poor future orientation) are of greater importance, such as mental state at the time of the offense, the legal boundaries might be drawn at older ages.

BOX 19.2. MORAL PANIC: TWISTED TEEN BRAINS, SUPERPREDATORS, AND THE END OF CIVILIZATION AS WE KNOW IT—OR NOT

Get tough on crime! But get tough on who? Aside from any scientific rationale, there may be a reason why "get-tough" policies on crime always seem to single out young people and other disenfranchised members of society. A number of scholars (Aronson, 2007; Males, 1996, 1999, 2009; Shook, 2005) have pointed out that society seems to be ever groping to explain the perceived rise in juvenile crime over the past several decades—even though the real juvenile crime spike lasted only from about the early 1980s to mid-1990s. Gang violence, school shootings, drug use, and other behaviors of this modern-day version of "wayward youth," in combination with what many Americans perceive to be a general erosion of political and moral certitude, have fanned the flames of yet another **moral panic**, this time about the fate of our children. Naturally, explanations must be sought and culprits must be blamed. And in our modern era, the brain once again is conscripted into service.

In books, the popular press, television documentaries, magazine features, and Internet blogs, adolescents are increasingly being portrayed as unpredictable, rebellious, risk-taking, thrill-seeking, uncontrollable, and dangerous by their very nature (Bradley, 2003). While earlier generations blamed "raging hormones" (Begley, 2000), modern accounts appeal to the same oversimplified neuropsychological models that are increasingly being evoked in legal decision-making: the dysfunctional juvenile brain. Only this time, the theory is not used for purposes of exoneration or exculpation, but to press the case for more draconian control measures. Indeed, many of the popular commentators on this "new science of the teen brain" are the same experts who have opined prolifically in the legal arena (Steinberg, 2007).

For example, in the early 1990s, legislators, politicians, behavioral scientists, social commentators, and the general public all braced for the onslaught of the **superpredators**—roving gangs of rapacious, ruthless, selfish, bloodthirsty, and remorseless youths, spawned of shiftless, promiscuous, welfare-coddled parents, who would soon swarm from the decaying cities into sedate, tree-lined, suburban neighborhoods to loot and pillage at will, undeterred by conscience or fear of authority (Zimring, 1998). While the threat never materialized, this fearful image

continued

BOX 19.2.—*Continued*

led to legislation at the time that made it easier for states to transfer adolescents from juvenile to adult court, on the rationale that sterner measures had to be prepared to deal with the impending flood of cases involving these hardened child barbarians (Dilulio, 1996; Dodge, 2008; Shook, 2005).

In identifying any group—by age, sex, race, social class, diagnosis, and so on—as potentially dangerous by their very biological nature, society gives itself the justification to take custodial and, if necessary, coercive measures to protect itself on the grounds that the members of this incorrigibly dangerous group are inherently incapable of controlling themselves. It is no coincidence, asserts Males (2009), that these feared and loathed groups almost always turn out to be the most politically powerless and socially disenfranchised members of society. This would explain why racial minorities, immigrant groups, and others perceived as foreign to the dominant culture are often singled out for special opprobrium—a point made by numerous sociologists for over a century. Indeed, the feared super-predators were supposed to come from the poorest, most disenfranchised ghettos of society, and to claim among its members mostly poor, minority youths.

Thus, in the most recent version of the "dangerous other," today's predominantly white, older, working- and middle-class generation is confronting the increasingly minority and economically disadvantaged composition of younger generations, at the same time as they are feeling alienated and out of touch by the rise of new communication technologies that allow these youths increasing freedom of interaction and access to information. According to this view, as the ethnic minority component of America's teenage population has risen from around 15 percent in the 1960s to over 40 percent in the 2000s, fears about young people have periodically coalesced into organized political and public health campaigns to address the variable crises of "teen suicide," "teen pregnancy," "youth violence," "adolescent risk taking," "underage drinking," "kids and guns," "teens and drugs," and similar catastrophes that are putatively threatening to undermine American society (Boyle, 2006; Males, 2007, 2009). In this crusade, neuroscientists have often been pressed into service to bolster the scientific credibility of these social claims.

Perhaps the concerns about heightened youth dangerousness could be taken more seriously if they were even true. However, empirical research seems to suggest the opposite: adolescents do not show inordinately high risks for danger. While teenagers do commit crimes and get in car wrecks at higher rates than adults do, they experience lower rates of other risks. For example, teens aged 15 to 19 have a lower risk of violent deaths from nonvehicular accidents, suicides, homicides, or undetermined causes than for every adult age group. The highest rates of crime and accidents are for ages 20 to 24 years, followed closely by what had been assumed to be the safest ages: 40 to 54 years (Johnston et al., 2007; Males, 2009). Historically, rates of violent juvenile crime peaked in 1994 and have dropped steadily since then, currently reaching levels similar to those of the early 1980s and below those of the 1970s (Bishop, 2000; Shook, 2005).

What risk rates do seem to track, then, are not age per se, but socioeconomic status (Males, 2009). In American society, youth is more likely to be a time of poverty than at any other age, and most of the feared youthful predators are ethnic minorities, children of immigrants, and other unfamiliar groups who are characterized by poor educational attainment that limits their economic prospects. In this view, rather than searching for neuropsychological justifications for alienating and disenfranchising these youths within the criminal justice system and elsewhere, American society should reconsider its priorities in offering educational advantages to all who deserve them before their behavior rises to the level of criminality. This of course will take a level of resource commitment that we have heretofore not been willing to expend.

SUMMARY AND CONCLUSIONS

As stomach-churning as many of the accounts of child physical and sexual abuse may be (Chapters 15 and 16), even greater visceral revulsion is often felt at the idea of children themselves as perpetrators of awful crimes: if the most "innocent" of this planet's human inhabitants can willfully commit such atrocious acts, who among us is safe? Thus, while rates of juvenile crime have declined over the past decade, public fears of "youth predators" remain high, fueling the periodic political paroxysms of "get-tough" legislation. In reality, crime rates peak in late adolescence and early adulthood, and decline steadily thereafter; however, there seems to be a small subset of disproportionately antisocial youths whose criminal careers persist across the life-course, and who appear to be characterized by deficient self-control and low verbal IQ, implicating frontal lobe and left hemisphere systems of the brain. Many of the children in this dangerous subset could be diagnosed with **conduct disorder (CD)**, which is continuous with antisocial personality disorder (Chapter 8) in adults. Other comorbid diagnoses may include **attention deficit hyperactivity disorder (ADHD)**, **oppositional defiant disorder (ODD)**, and one or more types of **learning disability (LD)**.

Aside from neuropsychological influences, peers, family, and the surrounding community can have an impact on the development of juvenile delinquency as a lifestyle. While child abuse or neglect, by itself, will rarely turn a good kid bad, such maltreatment may rob the child of positive role models and inculcate a competitive, confrontational, and predatory mentality that impels the child to claw his way up this dog-eat-dog world. Yet, despite seeming to have all the psychosocial odds stacked against them, a small minority of **resilient "superkids"** appear to defy expectations and emerge relative healthy and successful. Traits that have been identified in these resilient success stories include better verbal reasoning abilities and willingness to seek out appropriate mentorship on their own. Intervention and treatment modalities for childhood antisocial behavior must be comprehensive and long-term to be successful, but rarely is society willing to expend the time and resources for such programs. Debates about juveniles' competency to stand trial and/or culpability for their criminal behavior are often driven by ideology and politics, cloaked in simplistic pseudoscientific theories of brain development and neuropsychological maturity.

Chapter **20**

Other Crimes

S erial murder. Mass homicide. Terrorism. Sex offenses. These are the crimes that make the headlines, that the TV drama scripts get written about, and that we have discussed in previous chapters. But far more people are victimized by the types of "ordinary" crimes that slink, slither, and skulk beneath the media radar, that make you yawn when used as filler on a slow news day, but that suddenly assume earth-shaking proportions when they happen to *you.*

THEFT AND ROBBERY

While not fatal, to steal something from another person is a fundamental violation of that person's dignity and bespeaks a callous disregard for their rights as a human being. That's why we typically react with a burning sting of outrage upon being tricked or strong-armed out of what we believe is rightfully ours.

Demographics of Theft and Robbery

Theft refers to illicit appropriation of resources that rightfully belong to someone else—in other words, taking what isn't yours. Although technically frowned upon in nearly all cultures, and considered a crime in societies with formal legal systems, it is nevertheless a behavioral universal, occurring frequently in all human societies, as well as in many other animal species (Kanazawa, 2008). In every human society studied, more than 90 percent of theft and robbery crimes are committed by men, especially those who are poor, have less education, and are less intelligent (Braithewaite, 1981; Brown, 1991; Clelland & Carter, 1980; Dunaway et al., 2000; Elliott & Huizinga, 1983; Herrnstein & Murray, 1994; Kanazawa, 2004b, 2008; Kanazawa & Still, 2000; Shaw & McKay, 1929; Short & Nye, 1957; Wilson & Herrnstein, 1985).

Burglaries involve breaking into a structure to steal, usually without physical confrontation, although some burglaries can turn violent if the thief is surprised by the occupants. Some criminals also combine burglary with rape (Chapter 14). Burglaries make up 11 percent of all thefts, and burglars are typically young males of low educational and socioeconomic status, with histories of substance abuse and other criminal behavior. The skill level of burglars can range from rank amateurs, such as bored teens breaking into a private residence, to professionals who hit wealthy homes or businesses that contain valuable items or large amounts of cash. Most private dwellings are burglarized during the day, when occupants are likely to be out, whereas businesses are typically hit at night. Some burglars report experiencing a thrill or rush at breaking into a dwelling and stealing items. This thrill may take on a frankly sexual nature in the case of **fetish burglaries** in which intimate items are stolen, or in more violent cases, where rape accompanies the burglary (Chapter 14). Some burglars may urinate, defecate, or masturbate in the burgled dwelling, or otherwise vandalize the premises. Where the criminals force their way into the dwelling by overpowering the occupants, this is referred to as a **home invasion** (Bureau of Justice Statistics, 2003; Conklin, 1992; Palermo & Kocsis, 2005; Pitts, 2001).

Psychodynamics of Theft and Robbery

The ubiquity of theft and robbery in human societies suggests that these crimes are often committed for deeper reasons than just access to needed resources, i.e., that they serve a social, not just an economic function. For example, street robberies are often committed not just against hapless citizens, but often to "send a message" to rival criminals, especially as payback for a perceived wrong. Lacking a formal justice system within their subculture, gangs of street criminals typically resort to revenge and retaliation to even the score (Anderson, 1999; Rosenfeld et al., 2002; Wright & Decker, 1997; Wright et al., 2006), including what Jacobs & Wright (2008) call **moralistic street robbery**.

In this view, predatory robbery serves a number of practical, social, and symbolic functions within the hierarchical power struggle of neighborhood criminal subcultures. Most obviously, it provides access to resources (cash, drugs, weapons) that might not be available otherwise. In so doing, it deals a punishing financial blow to the victim, the impact of which will be felt and remembered for some time. It establishes the raider group as a force to be reckoned with, conferring street respect–really fear–and heightening their position in the criminal hierarchy, while humiliating the victim for being "taken." Street robbery against rivals often provides a thrilling rush of domination and supremacy to the members of this modern-day tribal raiding party, enhanced still further by the sense of righteous payback against victims who "have it coming" in retaliation for a perceived past offense, thus providing a self-justifying convergence of material and moralistic motives for the raid (Jacobs, 2000; Jacobs & Wright, 2008; Katz, 1988).

Types of Street Robbery

The offenses that typically prompt this type of moralistic street robbery can be divided into three main categories (Jacobs & Wright, 2008).

Market-based violations. These comprise the most economically straightforward types of tit-for-tat robberies, in which one criminal group robs another in retaliation for having been robbed or cheated by them in the past.

Status-based violations. Here, the offending party has dealt a blow to the other person's or group's respect, pride, or social status, and the retaliatory robbery is intended to "take them down a peg" and thereby elevate the perpetrator's reputation as a tough character not to be messed with.

Personalistic violations. The offenses in this category may have little to do with money or resources per se; rather the robbery is purely punishment for another type of offense, such as sexual assaults on one party's woman, or in some cases, on behalf of the woman herself (Kim et al., 1998; Jacobs, 2000; Jacobs & Wright, 2008; Wright et al., 2006).

Not surprisingly, these kinds of self-justified retaliations lead to counter-retaliations and counter-counter-retaliations, perpetuating the oft-heard **"cycle of violence"** within criminal subcultures (Bies & Tripp, 2001)–not unlike the same vicious cycle that occurs between rival political groups and even whole nations (Chapter 13).

Evolutionary Psychology of Theft and Robbery

According to the basic evolutionary model, in most societies, males provide the bulk of the external resources needed to keep their families and their communities viable. Across cultures, not only do men commit more thefts and robberies than women, they also make more money through whatever legitimate means are sanctioned by that society (Kanazawa, 2005a, 2008). In this model, it makes adaptive sense that young men commit more robberies than older men, since the younger ones have yet to establish and solidify their hierarchical roles within their communities, and they are usually still searching for mates, which requires the possession of sufficient material resources to attract and hold a reproductive partner (Daly & Wilson, 1988, 1990; Thornhill & Palmer, 2000). At the same time, it requires the establishment of one's feared reputation to discourage rivals from poaching mates or other resources. Thus, for many of the same reasons cited by Jacobs & Wright (2008) for moralistic street robbery in modern criminal subcultures, ancestral humans utilized a combination of mutual cooperation and predatory exploitation to get the things that were necessary for their physical, social, and procreative survival. Even in preindustrial times, selfish group members who relied disproportionately on predation and exploitation would probably have been regarded as that culture's version of a "criminal."

In every society, older males, who have securely mated, built themselves and their families a secure resource base, and are now invested in raising children, become less aggressive as they shift their reproductive efforts from mating effort to parenting effort, i.e., they just feel like "settling down" (Kanazawa, 2008). Studies show that testosterone levels in men (Chapter 2) fall with marriage and the birth of their children, rise again upon divorce, or stay higher in men who are cheaters. The often-cited sociological association of more successful marriages with lower rates of criminality may likewise reflect the psychobiologically palliative effect of stable pair-bonding and child-rearing on interpersonally and sexually aggressive behavior, i.e., family-raising displaces hell-raising as an adaptive reproductive strategy (Blum, 1997; Kanazawa et al., 2003c; 2008; Laub et al., 1998; McIntyre et al., 2006).

Another stable finding across studies and cultures is that higher crime rates, especially for property crimes, are associated with lower socioeconomic status which, in turn is associated with lower intelligence and educational level. It would therefore make adaptive sense for relatively unskilled and resource-poor males to cheat their way to acquiring the goods needed to attract mates and attain social status—if they can get away with it (Braithewaite, 1981; Brown, 1991; Clelland & Carter, 1980; Dunaway et al., 2000; Elliott & Huizinga, 1983; Herrnstein & Murray, 1994; Hirschi & Hindelang, 1977; Kanazawa, 2003c, 2004b, 2008; Kanazawa & Still, 2000; Lynam et al., 1993; Moffitt, 1990; Moffitt et al., 1991; Perusse, 1993; Shaw & McKay, 1929; Short & Nye, 1957; Stark, 1979; Thornberry & Farnsworth, 1982; Wilson & Herrnstein, 1985).

URBAN STREET GANGS

Gang violence has always been big news and big box office, from the Prohibition-era gangster movies of the 1930s, to the *Godfather* franchise and its progeny, to the urban "gangsta" chic of today. Youth gang homicides have actually declined since the 1990s (Flowers, 2002), yet the public remains fascinated by romanticized accounts of street life, blithely unmindful of the cruel and dangerous existence that such a life actually entails.

BOX 20.1. HOW EVOLUTIONARY PSYCHOLOGY
MADE A MONKEY OUT OF A PROFESSOR

In February 1992, psychiatrist Frederick Goodwin, Director the United States Alcohol, Drug Abuse, and Mental Health Administration, was addressing a meeting of the Mental Health Advisory Council convened to study the issue of violence, especially urban youth violence, as a public health concern. Seeking to place the problem in a broader evolutionary context, Dr. Goodwin drew an analogy between the behavior of male monkeys in the wild and violent young men in tough city neighborhoods. It was no coincidence, he said, that certain inner city areas are referred to as urban "jungles," because "the loss of social structure in this society has removed some of the civilizing evolutionary things that we have built up."

For example, Goodwin noted, only about half of male monkeys in the wild survive to adulthood, the remainder knocked off by their hyperaggressive and hypersexual rivals. An equivalent phenomenon could be seen, Goodwin seemed to imply, in modern urban ghettos, wherein dwell a large proportion of disadvantaged minority citizens. Perhaps by studying the biobehavioral commonalities between ourselves and our primate cousins, the doctor mused, we might develop the tools to combat inner-city violence. Laudable enough, right?

"U.S. Government Scientist Compares Poor Minorities to Monkeys!" screamed the headlines, coast to coast. Of course, that wasn't what Dr. Goodwin was saying, just as readers of this text understand that phylogenetic behavioral continuity across species doesn't mean that we actually *are* those species. But the story was too good for the media—and Dr. Goodwin's critics—to pass up. Political activists with axes to grind pressed the case against Dr. Goodwin for incorrigible racism, and he was forced to resign his position from an organization that, remember, was supposed to be dedicated to the dispassionate scientific study of human behavior.

Gang-Related Crime: Description and Demographics

Although gang violence dipped somewhat in the period between the twentieth and twenty-first centuries, youth gang members are still disproportionately involved in a high percentage of property, drug, and violent crimes, including homicides, compared to the rest of the population. Gang-related homicides are more likely to occur in public settings, to involve strangers, to have multiple perpetrators, to utilize firearms and automobiles (e.g., **drive-by shootings**), and to involve the risk of reprisal. In many of these drive-by shootings, killing of any one particular rival gang member is often less important than intimidating the rival gang to gain dominance. Gang-related homicide is more likely to be committed by younger perpetrators and members of ethnic minorities. Like most crimes, the majority of gang homicides are intraracial. Gang homicides are commonly associated with drug trafficking and firearms (Bailey & Unnithan, 1994; Battin et al., 1998; Decker & Van Winkle, 1996; Flowers, 2002b, c; Klein et al., 1991; Maxson & Klein, 1996; Rogers, 1993; Spergel, 1995; US Dept. of Justice, 1998).

Gang Member Characteristics

The average age of an urban gang member is 18, with typical age ranges from 8 to 24. Gang members commit their first criminal offense early, usually before age 10, which usually consists of a minor initiatory crime such as shoplifting or vandalism, but these criminal acts soon escalate to burglary, armed robbery, and sometimes murder. Some kind of criminal activity is usually a prerequisite for joining a gang, and the average age of official initiation into gang membership is 13. Most gang members have limited formal education, and very few hold conventional jobs. Gang members typically come from families characterized by verbal and physical abuse. Outside the family, they have been subject to at least one, possibly many, assaults and beatings; in fact, the **beat-down**, or **jump-in**, is a common gang initiation ritual in which the candidate demonstrates how well he can "take it" from his fellow members. Prospective members typically grow up in neighborhoods controlled by the gangs they eventually join and, prior to their membership, they may have been the victim of assaults and/or robberies by rival gang members (Curry & Decker, 1998; Flowers, 2002; Pinizzotto et al., 2007).

Gang Social Structure

For all their reputation as anarchic rebels, urban street gangs, like virtually all human societies and subcultures, are composed of a variety of hierarchical levels, and all gang members have a set of general and specific roles to play (Pinizzotto et al., 2007), an observation consistent with the **subcultures of violence theory** (Wolfgang & Ferracuti, 1967) discussed in Chapters 3 and 9. Typically, all or most gang members participate in a variety of crimes, such as burglary, robbery, and drug sales. **Original gangsters** are usually the founding members of the gang or their direct descendants, and serve as the leaders or authority figures of the gang, giving the broad orders that are carried out by those below. They also do the major negotiating between their group and rival gangs and determine overall gang rules and policies. **Lieutenants** and **bosses** oversee the daily criminal and maintenance operations of the gang, carry out the directives from above, and resolve disputes among gang members, as well as negotiate more mundane deals and treaties with rival gangs. **Gang enforcers** are always armed and serve to protect the other gang members, especially the drug sellers, from rival gangs, and also enforce the gang's rules among its own members. **Mules** and **transporters** carry and distribute wholesale amounts of drugs, weapons, or other contraband from outside sources into the gang territory. **Burglars** steal cash or other valuables from commercial establishments, office buildings, and private residences to fund gang activities. **Creepers** specialize in procuring weapons for the gang, often stealing them from private residences or vehicles. **Specialists** are generally older and more experienced members with skill in conducting specific types of criminal activities, such as financial and computer fraud, bank robberies, or raids on rival gang member territory. **Lookouts** monitor the perimeter of the gang territory to watch for law enforcement or rival gang activity. **Taggers** are the gang's "advertising department," responsible for artistically marking the gang's territory with graffiti. Gang members who are good at their particular jobs come to be respected and take pride in the roles they play within the social hierarchy.

As a way of further cementing group identity and loyalty, members are given specific **gang names**, sometimes chosen to memorialize a specific heroic gang-related action ("Smoker," "3-Nine") or an adaptation of a celebrity name. Gangs typically show fierce devotion to their territorial neighborhood, which is usually where they have grown up and which comprises the world they know and the place they feel the most safe. In exchange for their loyalty to the gang, the members can count on the gang to protect them from rival gangs and from law enforcement. Indigenous neighborhood youngsters are often recruited into their local gang by the offer of such protection and by the allure of learning more efficient ways to steal money or break into cars, as well as the vicarious reputation for toughness that gang membership confers.

Periodic conflicts among gangs often occur when members of one gang make a foray into a rival gang's territory, often for purposes of robbery, graffiti infringement, or just a petty action to show they can get away with it. This slap of disrespect, of course, warrants swift and severe retaliation by the offended group so as not to appear as punks. More pragmatically, full-scale gang wars are often waged over potentially profitable drug-sale territories and markets, or to avenge more serious offenses. Being ready to commit extreme violence against rival gang members, or even law enforcement officers, confers respect and status on gang members that reflects positively on the gang as a whole (Pinizzotto et al., 2007).

BOX 20.2. EXPLODING THE "BIG GANG THEORY"

Through television, movies, and sensationalistic news reporting, the public may have been given a distortedly pessimistic vision of the danger of gangs and gang violence in American society, at least since the 1980's when we were warned to expect an onslaught of gang violence that would overwhelm law enforcement within a decade. While not to be neglected as a serious crime issue, several criminal justice researchers have recently pointed out that the danger of huge, multiregional gangs as a growing threat to civilization as we know it—the **Big Gang Theory**—may be unnecessarily overblown. Indeed, petty local gang members themselves may relish the undeserved attention they get from popular portrayals of themselves as entwined with feared giant monolithic criminal enterprises (Esbensen & Tusinski, 2007; Felson, 2006). Recently, a number of common perceptions about gangs have been subjected to empirical scrutiny to weed out the myths from the facts (Howell, 2007).

Myth: Gangs are becoming huge, powerful criminal organizations with a tightly organized web of operations, sending emissaries from the big cities to establish satellite networks in every hamlet and township (a variant of the **super-predator** myth; see Box 19.2), all linked to, and controlled by, the gang's powerful but shadowy hub of operations.
Fact: While a few street gangs have evolved, often over several generations, into highly organized, entrepreneurial criminal organizations, the vast majority remain loosely structured local groupings, with transient leadership and membership, and continual splintering and reorganizing into factions and hybrid gangs. Larger, more organized gangs usually only exist within major urban areas that can support their activities, but hybrid gangs or gang wannabes in more provincial locales often adopt or mimic the gang names or symbols of the larger group, despite having no real connection to them, thereby creating the popular impression that a major gang outpost has moved onto Your Street, USA (Esbensen et al., 2001; Klein, 1995; Howell, 2007; Howell et al., 2001; Valdez, 2007; Weisel, 2002; Zatz & Portillos, 2000.

Myth: Violent, predatory street gangs are ruthlessly wiping out local drug dealers and traditional organized crime cartels and seizing the drug trade for themselves.
Fact: They wish. Large-scale organized crime syndicates have been running the illegal drug trade for generations, and they're not about to give it up to a bunch of young street punks. Of course, these traditional crime organizations often rely on local gang dealers for retail marketing of their wares, but most gang homicides revolve around cycles of rivalry, respect, retaliation, and revenge, and have much less to do with turf battles over market control of narcotics, although individual disputes about reneged-on payments or substandard-quality product may fuel a vio-

lent reaction (Braga et al., 2002; Cohen & Tita, 1999; Decker & Curry, 2003; Gugliotta & Leen, 1989; Howell, 1999, 2007; McGarrell & Chermak, 2003).

Myth: All gangs are dominated by black males.

Fact: In black communities, they are, inasmuch as people who share physical and cultural commonalities are more likely to grow up together and feel more comfortable with people like themselves. But gang membership in other areas reflects the ethnic makeup of those locales, accounting for the presence of Irish gangs, Italian gangs, Asian gangs, Russian gangs, Hispanic gangs, and even subgroups within these ethnic categories (Vietnamese gangs, Ukrainian gangs, Guatemalan gangs). The number of female gang members has also been growing, with many of these girls and women either full-fledged gang members with defined roles in the group, or members of a kind of gang "ladies auxiliary" which supports the male gang contingent (Esbensen & Lynskey, 2001).

Myth: Once a gang member, always a gang member. Gangs use brutally coercive tactics to force unwilling youths to join their ranks and to conduct illegal activities, and once someone's in a gang, the only way out is in a box.

Fact: The idea that gangs force people to join comes largely from prison populations, where a gang having sufficient members to defend itself may literally be a matter of life or death, so strength in numbers necessitates conscription. But most ordinary street gangs take a more laid-back attitude, viewing membership in their gang as a privilege to be earned. In most urban areas, there may be many more applicants for gang membership than there are positions to fill precisely because of the protection and sense of tough identity that comes with being the member of a feared and respected gang. In many cases, gang membership is a gradual process, with aspiring youngsters as young as 10 to 12 beginning to hang out with some gang members, eventually earning their trust, or at least familiarity, and being formally initiated into the gang in early- to mid-adolescence. While the popular conception is that gangs use minor members to carry out drug transports or other crimes because of the relative leniency of juvenile sentences if caught, it may be more common that gangs actually protect their youngest members from operations that may be particularly dangerous.

The "life-membership" theory of gang lore also seems to be more an artifact of Hollywood than a fact of reality. Studies reveal that over half of urban street gang members leave their gang within a year, usually through a gradual process that mirrors the process of joining in the first place, that is, the member comes to spend less and less time with the gang, and eventually drifts away. In fact, some short tenure of gang membership seems to be a rite of passage for many adolescents, who later either move on to solo criminal careers or develop adaptive ties to the straight world through education and employment. Only in rare cases, where a gang member has very sensitive and dangerous information that he reveals or threatens to reveal to law enforcement or a rival gang, will it be worth the gang's while to grease the traitor. Indeed, all this may represent an antidote

continued

BOX 20.2.—*Continued*

to the sense of hopelessness that many feel about rehabilitating former gang members. If these youths can be caught young and provided with a credible and safer alternative to a decent life and a fulfilling identity, then getting at least some of them to hang up their gang colors before they are irretrievably lost may not be as daunting as it seems (Best & Hutchinson, 1996; Decker & Van Winkle, 1996; Decker et al., 1998; Esbensen & Huizinga, 1993; Fleisher & Decker, 2001; Hagedorn, 1994; Howell, 2007).

OUTLAW MOTORCYCLE GANGS

As with urban street gangs, it may be difficult to tease apart the Hollywood "Easy Rider/Outlaw-Rebel" mythology from the reality of motorcycle gangs. Biker iconography has become part of American pop culture, with an entire genre of biker movies, biker music, biker fashion, and so on. After decades of sensationalistic journalism on this subject, recent research has provided some important insights.

Motorcycle Gangs: Description and Demographics

To begin with, no self-respecting biker considers himself part of a "gang"; almost invariably, they refer to their organization as "clubs." Most motorcycle enthusiasts are not criminals, and motorcycle clubs have been divided into conventional and deviant clubs (Barker, 2007). **Conventional motorcycle clubs** contain members of both sexes and all ethnicities, who ride bikes of all makes and models, and who are typically law-abiding citizens from all walks of life who share an interest in motorcycle riding for recreation and comradeship. They are often members of traditional bike organizations, such as the American Motorcycle Association (AMA), and have yearly rallies or conferences, similar to those of other special-interest organizations.

Deviant motorcycle clubs, or **one-percenters**, as they like to call themselves, or **outlaw motorcycle gangs** (**OMGs**), as they are commonly labeled by law enforcement agencies and media, are usually racially homogeneous, form clubs and organizations not sanctioned by the AMA, typically ride Harleys or Harley facsimiles with large, powerful engines, wear 3-piece patches signifying club membership and territory, are likely to have a geographically wider range than urban street gangs, as well as an older, sometimes multigenerational membership, engage in illegal drug use, drug trafficking, and other criminal behavior, including organized criminal activity, and generally make the club's life their own; the club becomes their tribal family group, commanding loyalty and respect. Currently, the **Big Four OMGs** in the United States, identified by law enforcement, are the **Hells Angels**, **Outlaws**, **Bandidos**, and **Pagans** (Barker, 2007; Barker & Human, 2009; Quinn, 2001).

Biker Crime Typology

Recently, a typology of OMG crime typology has been proposed (Quinn & Koch, 2003), which divides biker crime into four categories, across two dimensions.

Spontaneous expressive acts are typically one-on-one violent confrontations that erupt between two bikers from the same club, bikers from rival clubs, or a biker and a civilian, such as in the context of a road-rage altercation or bar fight.

Planned aggressive acts are more organized raids, economic turf campaigns, or acts of vengeance usually directed against rival gangs, involving multiple gang members.

Short-term instrumental acts involve one or a few members in isolated robberies, drug sales, or other crimes, varying along a continuum from spontaneous to planned.

Ongoing instrumental enterprises are typically what attract the attention of law enforcement, and involve large-scale, well-planned, organized criminal activity, such as drug trafficking, weapons or vehicle theft and sales, prostitution, and so on. Beginning in the late 1980s, OMGs, along with some better-organized urban street gangs, began to be recognized as one of the new faces of organized crime, although, as with urban street gangs, they have hardly replaced more traditional groups, and sometimes collaborate with them. Like urban gangs, OMGs are extremely territorial, and will violently resist incursions into their territory. The clubs' involvement in organized criminal activity is not monolithic, however, and various factions of the same club in different geographic areas may be more or less involved in criminal behavior, depending on membership characteristics (Barker, 2007; Barker & Human, 2009; Delattre, 1990).

Research (Barker, 2007; Barker & Human, 2009; Quinn & Koch, 2003; Wolf, 1991) has shown that the Big Four OMGs typically operate much as other profit-oriented organized crime syndicates, the most common kind of criminal act being the planned aggressive act of the Quinn & Koch (2003) typology, which involves multiple-member violent campaigns against rival clubs. Like most criminal organizations, OMGs utilize particular membership selection and initiation rites and strictly enforce their own rules and protocols. Much of their activity revolves around the saloon culture, with the liberal use of alcohol and drugs like methamphetamine leading to frequent brawls and fights, the scars of which are typically viewed as badges of honor (hence the door sticker on many biker bars: "Four-Tooth Minimum"). Interestingly, one of the most common forms of OMG criminal activity is motorcycle theft, whose symbolically emasculating nature, aside from the economic impact, is reminiscent of the activities of the horse thieves of the Old West.

ORGANIZED CRIME

As much as urban gangbangers and outlaw bikers may coalesce themselves into formidable criminal enterprises, for most people, the term **organized crime** summons images of the fictional Don Corleone or real-life John Gotti sitting around a table, planning whacks or making offers we can't refuse. Although there is some truth to these stereotypes, the scope of organized crime is much wider.

Characteristics of Organized Crime

According to one conceptualization (Herbert & Tritt, 1984), **organized crime** possesses six major attributes: (1) a conspiracy of two or more persons; (2) an engagement in illegal activities or the infiltration of legitimate business by illegitimate means; (3) organization formed for the acquisition of profit; (4) corruption of government officials; (5) use of risk-averse methodologies; (6) group constructed on a self-perpetuating basis. Two examples are used to illustrate these points (Clark, 2005).

The Mafia

The **Mafia** had its origin in the economic repression of Sicily over the centuries by the northern Italian mainland, spurring distrust of the government, and reliance on the **familiglia** for structure, support, and enforcement of social rules. Extended family groups and family alliances became the foundation of daily life, and criminal activity, along with more legitimate enterprises, became a mainstay of economic self-support. As a self-identified entity, the Mafia began accepting non-family members into the organization in the late 1800s, by means of careful vetting and the use of various rituals and initiation ceremonies. As with many such organizations, the group was characterized by strong charismatic leadership, a hierarchical family or family-like structure, and the assignment of specific roles within the group to various members. Eventually, the Mafia began to influence Sicilian politics and eventually became a force to be reckoned with throughout Italy, so entrenched that not even Mussolini's Fascist regime could uproot it. The Mafia also set up strong presences in other countries of immigration, most prominently in the United States (Clark, 2005; Gambino, 1974; Hobsbawm, 1976; Mann, 1969).

The Yakusa

Half a world away, the **Yakusa** also had its roots in the economic and political turmoil of nineteenth century Japan. Like many other criminal organizations, the Yakusa is organized along family structures, or **gumis**, and originally recruited its extra-familial members from the economically dispossessed and socially disenfranchised populations of Japanese society, using highly ritualized ceremonies to cement group loyalty and adherence to its rules and policies. Like the Mafia, the Yakusa survived changing political regimes in Japan, including the devastation of World War II, and was able to forge connections with the post-war government. To a lesser extent than the Mafia, the Yakusa have also exported their activities in countries where Japanese populations have emigrated and settled (Ames, 1976; Kaplan & Dubro, 1986; Lamont-Brown, 1982; Yokoo, 1986).

Organized Crime Commonalities

Both the Mafia and the Yakusa—and many organized crime groups like them—have their origins in a suppressed, dispossessed, or disenfranchised community who have come to distrust the dominant political and social structure, and so form a self-supporting social structure of their own, based along family, clan, and tribal lines. They are held together by a strong, charismatic leadership class, and the rules are enforced through a combination of loyalty rituals and, if necessary, strong-arm tactics by special "police" or "soldier" members, who also carry out most of the more aggressive criminal activities of the organization. Loyalty is typically reinforced in a positive way as well, by providing practical goods and services, as well as emotional belongingness and social stability to their members, and often to the surrounding community, that the regular government cannot provide. As discussed in Chapter 13, similar group dynamics characterize many terrorist organizations.

Although clearly maintaining their autonomy from the dominant political structure, these groups have no qualms about infiltrating and influencing the prevailing government by using their connections and muscle to steer political power. Depending on the social climate and economic conditions, as well as the groups' direct impact on the lives of ordinary citizens, the general public alternately abhors, glorifies, or indifferently tolerates these criminal organizations (Abadinsky, 1990; Clark, 2005; Cressey, 1969; Sharp, 1984). As with serial killers and outlaw bikers, many people are fascinated by the aura of conscienceless power often portrayed in fictionalized stories of Mafiosi who "do what's necessary" to protect and provide for their family group.

BOUNCING AND BRAWLING

While most citizens are unlikely to be confronted by an urban gang-banger, Hells Angel, or mob goodfella, anyone who frequents places where large numbers of young males gather, especially in the presence of liberal amounts of alcohol and other drugs, faces the chance of getting into some kind of altercation that could end violently. Two venues where this is common are bars and sports events.

Barroom Aggression

From the swinging-door saloons of the Old West, to the pool-table gin joints dotting the gritty downtowns of contemporary America, bars have always played a prominent role in the popular imagination as places for alcohol-fueled contests of fists and wills. Bars and saloons may therefore seem unlikely venues for clipboard-toting social science researchers, but several academic studies over the years of watering holes in Canada, Europe, Australia, and the United States, have tried to identify the features of bar locale, décor, and patron population that contribute to a greater or lesser potential for violent confrontations (Graham et al., 1980; 1996, 1997, 1998; Homel & Clark, 1994; Homel et al., 1992; Pernanen, 1998; Roberts, 2009; Quigley et al., 2003).

Physical establishment characteristics associated with greater likelihood of fighting include cheap and unclean physical surroundings, poor ventilation, and shabby décor. This, of course, may be an artifact of the location of these bars in the poorest areas, populated by the highest number of low SES males, who are demographically most prone to violence (Chapter 3). This is supported by the identification of customer characteristics most predictive of barroom brawling, which include unkempt patrons, patrons drinking rapidly and becoming intoxicated quickly ("We soive hard drinks for men who want to get drunk fast," barks the alternate-reality bartender in the 1946 movie, *It's A Wonderful Life*). A high proportion of male strangers, as opposed to regular customers, as well as a sense of boredom, with little external stimulation, are further risk factors for barroom brawling. Bar staff that are unfriendly and discourteous also heighten the risk of arguments escalating to fights.

One of the most important factors in predicting saloon violence may well be the behavior of those individuals tasked with averting and quelling it: the **bouncers**. When doing their jobs well, these physically imposing employees know, either by instinct or training, how to act professionally by maintaining a firm but friendly demeanor, how to verbally defuse a potentially inflammatory confrontation between patrons and, if a fight has broken out, how to end it with the minimum of injury to keep all patrons safe. Unfortunately, potentially violent confrontations are most likely to explode out of control when bouncers are either not proactive enough or too aggressive in their approach, that is, either ignoring or inflaming a volatile situation (Fox & Sobol, 2000; Graham & Wells, 2001; Graham et al., 1980, 2005; Hobbs et al., 2002, 2005a, 2005b; Homel & Clark, 1994; Homel et al., 1992; Leather & Lawrence, 1995; Lister et al., 2000; Monaghan, 2002, 2003, 2004; Quigley et al., 2003; Roberts, 2007, 2009; Tomsen, 2005; Van Brunschot, 2003; Winlow et al., 2001).

Sins of omission include overlooking or ignoring unruly customer behavior, such as verbal confrontations that are escalating. A common scenario is for a bouncer to downplay or entirely ignore the complaint by a female customer of being sexually harassed, which either encourages the toad to continue his slimy behavior, or compels the woman's male companion, or other nearby male vigilantes, to come to her aid by pounding down the offender. Sins of commission include bouncers taking obnoxious customer behavior personally, overreacting to minor infractions, overuse of physical interventions instead of verbal defusing, or even going out of their way to pick fights with patrons.

Most patron-bouncer altercations begin when the customer violates some stated or unspoken establishment rule, such as harassing another customer or staff member (more common where there are female bartenders or dancers), breaking a bottle or other object, or simply getting too drunk and being too loud. The bouncer may attempt to talk the subject down and may encourage him to step outside to cool off, perhaps reinforcing this with a firm but friendly hand on the shoulder. In many cases, this suffices to end the problem, but where the patron resists, the bouncer may have to become more forceful. Like trained police officers, some bouncers know how to gradually ratchet up the intensity level of their intervention to use the minimum amount of physical force necessary to peacefully resolve the encounter. However, many bouncers propel the situation from bad to worse by becoming unnecessarily aggressive, insulting, and demeaning, thereby "forcing" the customer to defend his honor. Another mistake involves throwing two fighting patrons out the door, with no attempt to resolve the dispute, which usually only transfers the melee to the sidewalk or parking lot, and may result in one or both disputants reentering the bar moments later, swinging or shooting. As in many such instances, bouncers who understand the difference between an **authoritative** presence and an **authoritarian** pretense (Miller, 2006f) will be most effective in ending fights rather that causing them.

Violence at Sporting Events

Alcohol-fueled aggression is hardly confined to bars and saloons, however, and sporting events often cook up the perfect formula of ethanol, testosterone, and adrenalin, distilled in the emotionally-charged atmosphere of symbolic clan warfare, epitomized by the battle between two opposing armies (only, we call them "teams"), each representing their own tribal territory, replete with totemic names and symbols ("Tigers," "Bulls," "Hurricanes," "Vikings"), whose warriors ("players") are lauded as heroes and recompensed accordingly, urged on, in some sports, with the implicit promise of reproductive dominance for the victors, objectified by scantily-clad cheerleaders gyrating at halftime.

While the United States leads the industrialized world in several types of violence, **sports hooliganism**, as it is sometimes called, is far more common in Canada, Europe, and Asia. In some cases, full-scale riots have broken out at sporting events, leading to multiple trampling deaths and injuries. In other cases, destructive mobs of either aggrieved sore losers or reveling sore winners have taken to the streets, smashing and ransacking everything in their path. In other cases, more common in the United States, individual disputes during nonprofessional games, such as Little League, have resulted in one player's parent assaulting and even killing another. Referees or even players themselves may be attacked on occasion. Interestingly, fights among fans appear to be more common in sports characterized by little direct aggression between players, such as baseball games or soccer matches, and are rare during sporting matches where the players themselves beat each other up, as in hockey or boxing (Fields et al., 2007; Kerr, 2005; Lance & Ross, 2000; Tenser, 2005).

HATE CRIMES

If I hate you and attack you because of something you've done to me (or I think you did), it's personal—it may be unjustified, delusional, or criminal, but it's still basically between you and I. But if at least part of the reason for my aggression is because of some identifiable class you belong to, then it may fall in the realm of a **bias crime** or **hate crime**, defined by the U.S. Dept. of Justice (2000) as a criminal offense which is motivated in whole or part by the offender's bias against a race, religion, disability, sexual orientation, or ethnicity. Many jurisdictions impose special penalties for crimes that are proven to have a bias component (Adams & Toth, 2006; Flowers, 2002).

Types of Hate Crimes and Hate Crime Offenders

Race appears to comprise the greatest proportion of hate crime factors, followed by religious bias, sexual orientation bias, and disability bias. About a third of hate crimes involve property crimes such as vandalism or arson, while the majority two-thirds consist of crimes against persons. Most of these involve intimidation and simple assault, but may sometimes include murder, manslaughter, rape, or sexual assault (Uniform Crime Reports, 1999).

The majority of hate crimes are committed by young males, acting alone, in pairs, or in small groups, although some perpetrators may have either formal or loose connections with well-known hate groups like the neo-Nazis or Ku Klux Klan. There may be over 2000 such groups in the United States alone, based on a survey of Internet websites (Flowers, 2002; Lin, 1997). Racially-motivated hate crimes are equally likely or even more likely to be committed by racial minorities as by whites (Adams & Toth, 2006). Although economic deprivation and disorienting cultural change may partly explain the origin of many types of prejudice, the proportion of these individuals willing to commit actual violence is still the exception, as it is for violence generally. Flowers (2002c) provides the following typology of hate crime offenders:

Ideologically-motivated offenders act out a bias-oriented belief system, supported directly or implicitly by others who share their views against a particular group. In essence, they attack the targeted groups because they feel it is the right or necessary thing to do.

Thrill seekers are typically adolescent or young adult males who carry out hate crimes as a way of relieving boredom, and of feeling excited and powerful. They may target minorities and other out-groups (gays, immigrants, the homeless) because members of these groups have less recourse for retaliation or redress, and are thus targets of convenience.

Peer-motivated hate crimes, usually most common among adolescents, occur at the egging-on of one's peers or in the context of a mob mentality that diffuses responsibility within the group. Some hate groups or gangs (see above) may even make such an assault an initiation rite to gain acceptance into the group.

Self-defense hate crimes are typically justified by the perpetrators as being necessary to fend off some dire consequence that would result by leaving the reviled group to their own devices, such as the belief that gays are corrupting the morals of straight youth or that immigrants are stealing jobs from "real" Americans.

There is probably a comingling of motives for any given hate crime. For example, a young man with a pre-existing prejudice toward, or previous bad experience with, a particular racial, religious, or cultural group finds that he can "be a man" and get respect by joining a "resistance movement" against the insidious out-group members. This gives him something exciting to do which, even better, garners the respect of his peers and provides a ready-made rationalization for his aggressive actions ("I'm defending our freedom;" "I'm fighting against evil"). Thus, those with a penchant for violence can find easy justification for their acts (see also Chapter 13).

ARSON AND PYROMANIA

There is something elemental yet novel about fire in the human consciousness. The evolutionary origins of most criminal motives–sex, power, rivalry, revenge–have their primeval origins in the behavior of ancestral humans, our primate forebears, their mammalian ancestors, and indeed within the broader animal kingdom, from insects to fish, to lizards, to birds. But, like language, the control of fire is a strictly human innovation, one which has unalterably shaped our evolution and culture–after all, what would the Fourth of July be without fireworks? Thus, arson may be the only major crime category with so recent a phylogenetic history.

Arson and Pyromania: Description, Demographics, and Diagnostics

Arson is the illegal destruction of property by malicious firesetting. Like most crimes, it is chiefly the province of young males, with boys under 18 committing up to 80 percent of arson crimes, although with a substantial number of young girls in the 13–17 range also setting fires. Firesetting is associated with increased aggression, hostility, impulsivity, running away from home, alcohol abuse, other property crimes, and general antisocial behavior (Kolko, 2002; Palermo & Kocsis, 2005; Stadolnik, 2000).

Diagnostically and conceptually (Grant & Kim, 2007), the distinction needs to be drawn between **arson** as the crime of illegal firesetting, and **pyromania** as a psychopathological syndrome involving compulsive firesetting to satisfy a psychological need (a similar distinction is made between the crime of **shoplifting** and the clinical syndrome of **kleptomania**). In *DSM-IV-TR* (APA, 2000), pyromania is defined as intentional firesetting on more than one occasion, characterized by attraction to and fascination with fire and its effects, emotional arousal or tension before the act, gratification and relief when setting and/or observing fires, absence of a primary motive of monetary gain, anger, or revenge, and not due to another mental disorder (e.g., mania, paranoia). Thus, a store owner who burns down his establishment to perpetrate insurance fraud, or a disgruntled spouse who torches her ex-mate's car to teach him a lesson is committing the crime of arson without necessarily being a pyromaniac, while a high school student who experiences an intoxicating thrill from the campfire his Boy Scout troop sets on their weekend camping trip is committing no crime, yet may have an unnatural fascination with things that burn.

In *DSM-IV,* pyromania is classified as an **Impulse Control Disorder**, along with such diverse syndromes as intermittent explosive disorder, kleptomania, compulsive gambling, and trichotillomania (compulsive hairpulling). What seems to tie these seemingly diverse syndromes together is the cycle of tension and craving building up to the act, the almost orgasmic excitement and relief experienced at the commission of the act, and the sense of satisfaction and quiescence following it, a psychophysiological cascade that seems to characterize almost all life-sustaining functions, such as hunger, thirst, elimination, aggression, and sex.

Thus, while arson, as a crime, seems to have an association with other criminal and antisocial behavior, pyromania as a syndrome may not, as most fires set by pyromaniacs are on their own property and do not appear to harm anyone else or break any laws. However, pyromania is frequently comorbid with mood disorders, substance abuse disorders, self-injury, and impaired impulse control over a variety of activities. It can also be seen in schizophrenia, some types of dementia (where it has to be distinguished from impaired judgment, e.g., a cooking mishap), and as a feature of some cases of temporal lobe epilepsy. In addition, even with legal and initially harmless firesetting, accidents do happen, causing hundreds of tragic, if unintentional, deaths and injuries, and millions of dollars of property damage every year (Coid et al., 1999; Grant & Kim, 2002, 2007; Grant & Potenza, 2005; McElroy et al., 1994; Palermo & Kocsis, 2005; Ritchie & Huff, 1999; Tavares et al., 2005; Wheaton, 2001).

The Psychology of Pyromania and Arson

The association with disorders of impulse control may also yield clues to the psychodynamics of pyromania that connect it to such seemingly diverse criminal phenomena as compulsive sexual assault and serial killing (Chapters 10 and 14). In fact, as noted in Chapter 10, the childhood triad of enuresis, firesetting, and cruelty to animals has been identified as a common feature in the developmental history of many sadistic serial killers, although it may not be specific to it. In clinical studies, many subjects with pyromania describe the thrill they get from anticipating, fantasizing about, watching TV shows and movies about, and even reading about fires. Observing a fire, especially one that he's started himself, provides a state of near-orgasmic pleasure, sometimes within a dissociated state of reverie, as the pyromaniac watches transfixed by the flames dancing and consuming the burning structure. These feelings are sometimes accompanied by a jolt of power, as he observes the frantic efforts of all the desperate little people trying to extinguish his mighty conflagration.

Early psychodynamic theorists made the connection with sexuality explicit, positing that compulsive firesetting is a sublimated form of sexual gratification, although empirical research has not necessarily supported this. Like serial killers, many compulsive firesetters heighten their sense of pleasureable manipulation and control by intruding themselves into the response and rescue efforts of the very fires they have set, sometimes going so far as to join volunteer fire brigades or municipal fire departments, which, of course, has the added benefit of putting them right where the action is when any conflagration breaks out (Grant & Kim, 2007; MacDonald, 1961; Palermo & Kocsis, 2005; Quinsey et al., 1989).

Arson Typologies

Sometimes conflating the categories of criminal arson and syndromic pyromania, several researchers have offered varying typologies of firesetters.

Rider (1980a, 1980b) described four types of arsonists. The **jealousy-motivated adult male arsonist** sets fires to compensate for slights to his vanity and masculinity. The **would-be hero** creates the very fire scenarios that he then rushes into to save the day. The **excitement fire-setter** derives a thrill from watching things burn. Relatedly but more specifically, the **pyromaniac** engages in compulsive fire-setting to achieve a sense of sexual gratification and tension-reduction.

Douglas et al. (1992) actually offers two overlapping typologies. The first dimension relates to the actual carrying out of the act, applying the FBI's organized-disorganized dichotomy developed with serial killers (Chapter 10) to firesetters. **Organized arsonists** are likely to carefully plan out the fire scene, to utilize complex incendiary devices, often with sophisticated accelerants and timing devices, and to take elaborate measures to evade detection. **Disorganized arsonists** usually use whatever incendiary devices and fuels that are available, are sloppier about the arson scene, and leave more physical evidence.

The second Douglas et al. (1992) typology consists of five categories of firesetter motivation, derived from the FBI's Behavioral Science Unit, in collaboration with the Prince George County Fire Department (Douglas et al., 1992; Icove & Estepp, 1987; Palermo & Kocsis, 2005):

Arson for revenge. This act of firesetting has a clear retaliatory motive and is carried out in response to some real or imagined slight or injustice. These arsonists are typically adult males, from a lower socioeconomic background, who are acting alone, although between a quarter and a third of revenge arsonists may be women. The perpetrators frequently use alcohol to bolster their resolve to commit the crime, and set their fires close to home and on weekends when they are less likely to be caught. This crime tends to be relatively well planned, and the arsonist may utilize materials found at the scene and/or bring along accelerants and ignition devices. After setting the fire and assuring it is burning to his satisfaction, the offender typically does not stick around to watch, but flees the scene to avoid capture.

Arson for excitement. There is typically no utilitarian motive (revenge, money) for this arsonist, who sets his fires for the thrill of it. He chooses relatively remote and isolated locations, such as empty lots, construction sites, garbage dumps, or wooded areas, sets the fire, and then observes from a secure distance. He usually acts alone or with a few chosen accomplices, is likely to be a repeat offender, and to have a criminal record. He uses available materials to ignite the fire. Alcohol or drug use is typically not involved.

Arson for vandalism. The motive here is malicious destruction for its own sake. The offenders are typically lower-to-middle-class juveniles living at home, who set their fires on weekdays while playing hookey from school, or may even target their own school during off-hours. The crimes are committed close to home, involving groups of youths, and are often done impulsively, using materials that are readily available at the scene. After setting the fires, some perpetrators flee the area, while others stay behind to watch at a safe distance. In addition to firesetting, these youths typically commit other types of disruptive and destructive pranks, such as smashing property, triggering false alarms, and/or using illegal fireworks. Drug use is not typically associated with these arsons, but about a third of the perpetrators have prior criminal histories.

Arson for crime concealment. The goal here is to destroy the incriminating features of a crime by burning up the evidence. The crime may involve anything from burglary to murder, and the fires are set at times when the arsonist is least likely to be caught. This offender often uses accelerants and flees the scene once the fire is ignited. There is typically a history of alcohol and drug abuse and prior criminal acts.

Arson for profit. This arsonist burns for money, as part of his more general criminal career. He may be paid to set a fire by a third party for purposes of retaliation, intimidation, or insurance fraud, or he may set it himself to illegally collect on an insurance policy or other illicit activity. He tends to be somewhat older and to have a prior criminal history, although juveniles may be used as proxies to commit the crime. These fires are the most carefully planned and carried out, most commonly with the aid of accomplices, often utilizing some sort of kindling and accelerant, and setting up the scene both for maximal burn damage and minimal evidence that could lead to detection and capture. The fires are usually set far from the offender's home territory, and he typically leaves the area to avoid capture.

Extremist-motivated arson. This is basically a fire-related hate crime to carry out some social, religious, or political agenda. It may be used for intimidation or revenge. The crime is usually carried out with like-minded accomplices, and is relatively well-planned, using accelerants, and often leaving behind political messages to heighten the intimidation factor. It may be combined with other types of vandalism and assault.

Common Features of Arson Typologies

The major common categories that emerge seem to involve:

Arson for some utilitarian purpose. This is for profit, revenge, or political violence. Here, the object is not the fire itself, but its use as an instrument to further some other goal.

Arson for wanton thrill-seeking. The goal here is to impress one's peers and achieve a sense of power and control.

Arson for psychosexual gratification. This may coincide with the diagnostic category of pyromania, in which both setting and watching the fire fill a fundamental need in the firesetter.

Of course, these categories may overlap: who better to pick to burn down your rival's store than that kid who always loved setting fires? The downside is that the pyromanic may so cherish his work that he may stick around long enough to be caught and rat out the person who hired him.

SUMMARY AND CONCLUSIONS

Human beings steal and rob for reasons ranging from acquisition of material goods to sending a social message of dominance and control. Criminal gangs–whether they be urban street gangs, outlaw motorcycle clubs, or multinational organized crime cartels–represent tribal subcultures that contain virtually all the features of other human societies that are focused on the survival and procreation of its members. Hate crimes, arson, street brawls, and sporting event violence may be committed for a variety of separate, but frequently overlapping motives, including thrills, revenge, profit, or ideology. Although these types of crimes garner less media attention than more spectacular offenses such as serial killing or terrorism, on a daily basis they affect far more lives and keep law enforcement and the criminal justice system busy.

Chapter **21**

Corrections, the Death
Penalty, and Crime Victims

O f the approximately 9 million people incarcerated worldwide, more than 2 million of these inmates are residing in U.S. jails and prisons. Even though crime rates have been declining since the 1990s, incarceration rates in the United State have increased 700 percent from 1970 to the present, and this country now has approximately 20 percent of the world's prison population. High incarceration rates, prison overcrowding, unmet treatment needs, and inadequate community-transition services contribute to the early release of disturbed offenders, increased recidivism, and more frequent reincarceration, all feeding the vicious cycle of what has been termed the **prison-industrial complex** (Andrews & Bonta, 2010; Clements et al., 2007; Dyer, 2000; Harrison & Beck, 2005; Public Safety Performance Project, 2007; Schlosser, 1998; Shivy et al., 2007).

MENTALLY ILL OFFENDERS

Estimates of the proportion of U.S. jail and prison inmates with some form of diagnosed mental illness range from 7–16 percent, including 16 percent of offenders on parole or probation status; when personality disorders are included, the percentage rises to 35 percent. Up to 68 percent of inmates have a history of drug and alcohol problems. Such dual- or multi-diagnosed inmates may have especially poor outcomes. The number of mentally disordered offenders in jails and prisons appears to be increasing (Beck & Maruschak, 2001; Brems & Johnson, 1997; Clements et al., 2007; Diamond et al., 2001; Ditton, 1999; Fisher et al., 2002; Jemelka et al., 1989; Lamberti et al., 2001; Newman et al., 1998; Reis et al., 1994; Rotter et al., 2002; Torrey, 1995; Ventura et al., 1998; Way et al., 2008).

Inmate Suicide

Of special concern is **inmate suicide**, which is the second leading cause of death in jails and the third leading cause of death in prisons, although for male prison inmates, the suicide rate has been declining since the 1980s, and the inmate suicide rate is now somewhat lower than for males in the general community (Clements et al., 2007; Hayes, 1995; Hayes & Rowan, 1988; Lester, 1987; Mumola, 2005; White & Schimmel, 1995; White et al., 2002). Part of this may relate to the fact that jail and prison inmates are monitored far more closely than ordinary citizens and even most psychiatric patients; nevertheless, a number of these inmates find a way to end their own lives. Rates of suicide are more than three times higher in jails than in prisons (Clements et al., 2007; Mumola, 2005), and this may be because, as the first stop in criminal justice confinement, jails contain a more mentally disturbed population overall, especially considering that those least likely to make bail are those from lower socioeconomic strata, which is itself correlated with psychopathology (Chapter 3), and some of the more disturbed jail inmates will subsequently be diverted to the mental health system rather than sentenced to prison.

In fact, those prisoners who commit suicide seem to have some unique features that distinguish them from suicidal persons in community samples. Whereas suicide is most highly correlated with mood disorders among the general population, delusional paranoia seems to most commonly characterize suicidal inmates. Longer-term inmates (over 5 years) are more likely to kill themselves than those with shorter sentences, and violent inmates are more likely to commit suicide than nonviolent ones (Clements et al., 2007; Mumola, 2005; White et al., 2002).

Mentally Disordered Incarcerated Juvenile Offenders

About 5 percent of those incarcerated in the U.S. consist of offenders under 19 years of age, usually detained in separate facilities from adults (see Chapters 1, 19). Compared to adult inmates, the prevalence of mental disorders in the juvenile offender population appears to be much higher, comprising 40–70 percent of youths who come in contact with the criminal justice system, and often including deliberate self-harm, repeat offending, ADHD, conduct disorder, and substance abuse (AAPCA, 2001; Cottle et al., 2001; Kessler, 2002; Langan et al., 2003; Snyder & Sickmund, 1995).

Recent research (Arseneault et al., 2000; Costello et al., 2003, 2005, 2006; Fazel et al., 2008; Kassen et al., 2001; Kirkbride et al., 2006; Loeber et al., 2000; Polanczyk et al., 2007; van Lier et al., 2007) has disclosed that incarcerated juvenile offenders show 10 times the rate of psychosis as compared to the community population of youths, 10 times the rate of conduct disorder for boys and up to 20 times the rate of conduct disorder for girls (because courts tend to be somewhat more lenient with girls than boys, perhaps girls need to have a higher "dose" of conduct disorder to be prosecuted and convicted), 2–4 times the rate of ADHD (somewhat lower numbers than the previous categories, perhaps because this syndrome is more evenly distrib- uted in the general youth population), twice the rate of major depression for boys and 4–5 times the rate for girls (probably because mood disorders are more commonly diagnosed in females generally).

INMATE THINKING

For all the research on the demographics and outcome of criminal of- fenders, mentally disordered or not, until recently, there has been surpris- ingly little study of what actually goes on in the minds of offenders who are arrested, convicted, and incarcerated, an aspect of criminal psychology that should be of interest to psychologists and criminologists alike (see also Chapter 3).

One common misconception, often gleaned from movies and TV shows, is that everybody in prison insists that they're innocent. Wrong. Most in- mates concede that they committed some kind of offense and some even brag about it. What they can't accept is the fact that they got caught and convict- ed, the idea that other people have done the same things they've done and have gotten off free, or that they would have gotten away this time too, if not for someone else's deception, betrayal, stupidity, or just bad luck. If there is any complaint, it is usually that the criminal justice system has used tricks and traps to ensnare them, saddled them with incompetent defense counsel, and otherwise unfairly violated their constitutional rights and the rules of evi- dence to secure a conviction. They are apparently blind to the irony that they have spent their entire lives flouting the rules and breaking the laws of society, and are now carping that the law didn't follow its own rules in adju- dicating them. Some inmates express a sense of narcissistic outrage at the cosmic unfairness of it all: "How *dare* I get caught! I deserve to be free to do whatever the hell I want." It is this extreme egocentrism, impulsive self-grat- ification, lack of empathy, and disregard for the rights of others that charac- terizes the thinking of most convicted felons (Correia, 2009), the kind of nar- cissistic-antisocial personality complex discussed in Chapter 7.

More systematic study of inmate psychology has led to the identification of a core set of **criminogenic beliefs** (Tangney et al., 2007), by which many convicted felons have rationalized, justified, and allowed themselves to per- petuate their criminal behavior until they got caught.

External attribution. "The only reason I'm in jail is because that cop had it in for me," or "because I had a lousy lawyer," or "because my partner ratted on me," or, "because I couldn't get a job and I had to make money some damn way."

Failure to accept responsibility. "What do you expect with the way I was raised; my family made me a criminal." "Everybody else was doing it and I couldn't look like a punk." "If she didn't want her chain snatched, she shouldn't have been wearing it out like that."

Narcissistic entitlement. "What do you mean, 'why did I take that chain?' I wanted it, that's why." "I deserve things because I'm special." "If I tell you I'm gonna do something, you better not be standing in my way."

Negative attitudes toward authority. "The cops, the politicians, they're all dirty and helping themselves, so why shouldn't I take what I want." "Those goody-two-shoes 'normal' people think they're better than me, so I'll spit in their face every chance I get."

Short-term orientation. "Hey, life is short, you gotta have fun while you can."

Victimless crime. "That store can always make more money." "That woman is just bitching and moaning–I didn't really hurt her."

What is common among these criminogenic beliefs is the utter lack of self-evaluative reflection and the facile use of defensive rationalizations to completely self-justify any act the offender has committed, including self-identification as a "special person" who is exempt from the requirements of ordinary citizens by virtue of having both rejected, and been rejected by, that society. In fact, inmates who see themselves still psychologically connected with their communities, despite their involvement in crimes within those communities, show a higher level of distress and self-doubt than those who have totally repudiated, and show utter contempt for, the rules of society (Mashek et al., 2006; Tangney et al., 2007).

DEATH ROW INMATES: FINAL THOUGHTS, FINAL WORDS

Death row is the ultimate imprisonment. It is distinguished from most other long-term incarcerations in that it does not constitute the punishment itself, but is the indefinite and seemingly interminable holding area in which the inmate is kept while the decision is weighed, commonly through a lengthy appeals process, as to whether to carry out the ultimate sentence. In many cases, the long wait is followed by the grim news that the prisoner will be executed after all. How do these doomed men (and a few women) deal with this sentence, what do they think and say? With the minimal attention paid to the thinking styles of incarcerated offenders (see above) and criminals in general (Chapters 3, 8), even less attention in the forensic psychological literature has been paid to mental state of this special class of incarcerees (Heflick, 2005; Lynch, 2002).

Recently, Vollum & Longmire (2009) used a content analysis of the pre-death statements of 321 inmates executed over a two-decade period, in order to identify the major themes found among their final communications. Their research yielded the following typology of the **last words of the condemned**, presented in descending order of frequency. In many cases, more than one theme was expressed by an inmate and (as with all typologies) some of the categories may overlap.

Well-wishes. The most common theme in these final statements involved expressions of well-wishes, encouragement, and love directed to the condemned inmate's family or friends in the form of a simple "goodbye" or as a more complex consolation to loved ones. In doing this, the inmate appeared to be trying to transform a situation of powerlessness and helplessness into one in which he could feel some level of control and thereby achieve some measure of transcendence to give his death a sense of meaning, even righteous martyrdom, by going to the slaughter with head held high.

Religion. Righteousness and martyrdom accrue an explicitly religious tone in the second most commonly stated theme, in which the condemned inmate made some form of overtly religious reference, ranging from simple prayer rituals from his own religious tradition, to asking God's forgiveness, to describing one's future status in the afterlife, however that may be conceived. Again, this is quite obviously an attempt to give the condemned inmate's life some transcendent meaning, in this case, by making peace with God and hoping for some resolution in Heaven. In a few cases, this appeared as an actual positive statement to the effect that the ordeal was over and the inmate was now going to a "better place."

Contrition. Despite prominent themes of existential transcendence and divine absolution, less common were final statements that explicitly asked forgiveness of those directly harmed by the crime, i.e., the loved ones of the murder victim him/herself. About a third of the statements consisted of a direct apology to the co-victims, and a smaller number of apologies were directed to the condemned inmate's own family and friends for "putting them through" this ordeal. For all the attention to Heavenly matters seen in many final statements, even God gets short shrift in the direct apology department, only a minority of inmates having entreated Him directly for forgiveness. Perhaps they felt this kind of direct request was too forward an approach after having committed the ultimate sin.

Gratitude. It might be hard to imagine what someone condemned to die might feel grateful about, but some inmates expressed thanks to their family and friends for their support and commitment. A smaller number thanked

God or His representative in the form of the prison chaplain or other spiritual advisor, or expressed gratitude toward their lawyer for going the distance for them. Even some prison staff might be singled out for gratitude because of their decent treatment of the inmate during his tenure on death row, as occasionally were the law enforcement officers and prosecutors responsible for his current circumstances ("Thanks for stopping me from doing worse"). Perhaps this was a way of achieving cognitive control of the situation by embracing and making peace with it, even trying to turn it into a transformative experience, a theme that is noted repeatedly throughout these narratives.

Personal reconciliation. In some final statements, the condemned inmate appeared to turn the tables and offer his own forgiveness to others, a kind of "no hard feelings" pronouncement. Sometimes associated with this were statements indicating that he had made his peace with his fate and with his actions and their punishment, again, another form of meaning-making for his upcoming demise, a way of tying up his existential loose ends before leaving this world.

Denial of responsibility. However, some condemned inmates did not go so quietly or humbly. In about a fifth of cases, the inmate used his final statement to deny or dilute personal responsibility for the capital criminal act, ranging from outright protestation of innocence to the recitation of extenuating circumstances. In either case, he asserted that he was wrongfully convicted and was being wrongfully executed. This was often generalized and justified in the quasi-political context of standing up for the rights of all wrongfully accused and condemned citizens, as well as similar diatribes against the death penalty in general, for which he claimed to a martyr for the cause of its abolition. Part of this may have represented abject denial and repudiation of the shame associated with the act, and part may have tied in with the theme of giving his death greater meaning by using it to teach the world a moral lesson. Then, of course, there's always the possibility that he was really innocent.

Anger and resentment. A minority of condemned inmates carried their defiance further by turning their final statements into manifestos of rage against the criminal justice system in general and their own case's law enforcement, judicial, and correctional personnel in particular, sometimes even including their victims in this roster of enmity. In most cases this reaction was coupled with denial of guilt and represented another layer of denial of responsibility and repudiation of their own shame. It might also have afforded them a sense of cognitive control by "condemning the condemners" (Sykes & Matza, 1964).

Resignation. Resignation is not the same as acceptance or reconciliation described above. The final statements of a small number of condemned inmates indicated that they seemed to passively resign themselves to their impending deaths, expressing a reluctant readiness to be released from the travails of this life.

Accountability. As noted above, many inmates show a surprising disconnect between acceptance of a causal relationship between their actions and the crime, and any sense of actual responsibility and accountability for the outcome (Tangney et al., 2007). The same appears to apply to a small number of condemned inmates in Vollum & Longmire's (2009) sample. Even death row inmates who said they're sorry for the victim's death didn't necessarily accept full accountability for this crime. Less than 5% of these inmates explicitly acknowledged their responsibility for the capital murder for which they were about to be executed. Yet, an even smaller proportion actually accepted responsibility for other crimes, sometimes even confessing to murders previously unsolved. Most attempted to mitigate or justify the act: "It wasn't personal–I killed the old lady when she wouldn't hand over her purse because I needed the money for my drug addiction."

In summary, inmates condemned to die may show a variety of overlapping reactions, ranging from transcendent acceptance and humble contrition to in-your-face denial and defiance of their penalty, the criminal justice system, and society at large. Some of these reactions of Vollum and Longmire's (2009) death row inmates seem to represent extensions of the criminogenic thinking patterns identified by Tangney et al. (2007), while others appear to reflect attempts to cobble together some temporary structure of meaning from the last desperate fragments of their lives.

MENTAL HEALTH TREATMENT
OF CORRECTIONAL INMATES

"Treat criminals in prison? Are you kidding me? Just lock 'em up and throw away the key," is the response one often gets to the idea of mental health services for correctional inmates. Indeed, over the past several decades, the judicial and political philosophy on the purposes of corrections has swung back and forth from emphases on inmate rehabilitation to a variety of "get tough" policies emphasizing punishment and deterrence (Andrews & Bonta, 2010).

Yet, there are two separate but overlapping reasons for providing mental health services to prison inmates (Correia, 2009). First, prison is clearly punishment but nothing says it's supposed to be more torturous than necessary.

Typically portrayed in the media as hard-boiled thugs, it surprises many people to learn that prisoners get depressed, they experience panic attacks, they may suffer from PTSD, and they often have difficulties coping with the strictures and demands of institutional life. The purpose of counseling and psychotherapy in these cases is not to "cure" anything, but to give those inmates who request it a helping hand in enduring their tenure in the joint as untraumatically as possible. The practical side is that less-stressed inmates make for an overall less risky and volatile environment for everyone concerned.

The second reason is even more broadly utilitarian: Effective treatment reduces future offending. When properly conducted, and when treatment modalities are matched to inmate needs, mental health treatment programs in prisons have been found to reduce **recidivism rates** (rates of reoffending) of even difficult cases. The singular exception concerns inmates high in traits of psychopathy (Chapter 8), in which case treatment has generally proven ineffective or even resulted in increased recidivism rates, especially for violent crimes. This may be because psychotherapeutic modalities, particularly those that occur in groups, actually arm the psychopath with additional psychological knowledge that he can later use to manipulate, exploit, and prey on people; or it may simply be a matter of reinforcing the view that by "playing sick," one is relieved of the more onerous consequences of one's actions (Andrews et al., 1990; Correia, 2009; Harris et al., 1991; Hart et al., 1988; Rice, 1997; Rice et al., 1992).

With limited resources, it also is important to allocate mental health services efficiently and effectively, and research seems to suggest a **dose-effect relationship** between treatment level and recidivism risk. That is, the more intensive the treatment received by high-risk inmates, the greater the reduction of reoffending, while low-risk inmates require far less intensive intervention, often doing well even without formal intervention.

Correctional Inmate Mental Health Treatment Programs

But what kind of treatment? And what are we treating these inmates for?

The Federal Bureau of Prisons has recently launched new treatment initiatives designed to train inmates to accept greater personal responsibility for their behavior and develop more adaptive interpersonal skills. **The Beckley Responsibility and Values Enhancement (BRAVE) Program** was developed primarily for younger inmates beginning relatively long sentences and most at risk for being institutional disciplinary problems. The approximately 9-month program targets criminogenic beliefs and includes treatment components focused on identification of maladaptive cognitive processes and on instilling prosocial values, communication skills, anger management, responding to peer pressure, drug awareness, and enhancing general physical and spiritual health. Completion requires participation in a "service project" to make amends to the community through a positive social contribution. A similar program, called **Challenge, Opportunity, Discipline and Ethics (CODE)**, is currently being implemented in U.S. and is similarly intended to reduce inmate misbehavior and encourage more prosocial attitudes and skills (Correia, 2009).

But how do we know that inmates can learn these skills? Recall from Chapter 2 that many criminals show deficits in the type of **executive functions** necessary for reasoning, judgment, reflective thinking, empathic relating, flexible responding, consideration of future consequences, planning, self-control, and goal maintenance. Deficiencies in this diverse cognitive skillset, mediated by the brain's **frontal lobes**, might naturally interfere with learning and the kind of adaptive prosocial behaviors promulgated by offender rehabilitation programs. Ross & Hoaken (2010) suggest that correctional psychologists take a cue from their neuropsychological colleagues in the brain injury and schizophrenia treatment fields by utilizing the clinical concepts and technology of **cognitive rehabilitation** to target these deficits (although in the case of both schizophrenics and developmentally cognitively stunted offender, it would actually be **habilitation**). This is typically accomplished either by: (1) retraining the impaired cognitive function, usually the less successful strategy; or (2) training in compensatory strategies to work around the area of impairment. In this process, Ross & Hoaken (2010) make two key recommendations:

Individualize assessment and treatment of executive function deficits. As with any treatment, optimum results usually involve individualized and customized applications of more generally established principles. The trend should be away from one-size-fits-all programs to allow focus on individual characteristics and needs.

Provide opportunities for relevant application and transfer of skills. One problem that has plagued psychological and behavioral treatments from psychoanalysis, to behavior modification, to biofeedback, to cognitive rehabilitation, is **generalizability**: to what extent do the gains made in the clinic or lab help the person in the real world? To this end, offender (re)habilitation programs should learn the lessons from their cognitive rehabilitation cousins and include role plays of graded complexity and, where possible, opportunities to practice these skills in real-world settings.

BOX 21.1. CAN YOU DO PSYCHOTHERAPY WITH CRIMINALS?

As a group, criminal offenders generally shun mental health services, often because their only prior experience with them has been in the context of some forced evaluation or placement decision that they didn't like. In general, the idea of needing "mental help" is often seen as signaling weakness, cowardice, and lack of manhood. Nevertheless, mental health clinicians who consult to, or work within, the criminal justice system will sometimes receive referrals of offenders who have been coerced into treatment as a diversion from harsher adjudication; i.e., they're only there because they have to be. Additionally, not all offenders are steely psychopaths: many suffer from the full range of mental disorders that one sees in any clinical practice—in fact, there is probably a higher rate of psychopathology in this population than in the community at large, especially in the juvenile justice system.

While a full exposition on offender therapy is beyond the scope of this text, the following are a few recommendations for clinicians who do psychotherapy with criminal offenders, gleaned from the sparse literature on this subject, as well as extrapolated from the clinical experience acquired in working with other "tough-guy" types, such as law enforcement officers or military service members, or with intellectually limited or emotionally restricted patients, such as those with brain injuries or developmental disorders, or in residential psychiatric facilities (Ball & Peake, 2006; Brodsky, 2010; Correia, 2009; Miller, 1993a, 1993d, 1998c, 2006f; Werman, 1984).

Keep the goals simple. The purpose of offender therapy is typically not to effect a personality overhaul ("I want to be a more secure person"), but to help the patient deal with particular symptoms ("I feel nervous all the time") or particular problems ("I can't get people to stop picking on me").

Keep communications clear. Modulate your language so that your patient understands you. Be as clear as possible to avoid misunderstandings and misinterpretations that can stall the treatment process. At the same time, don't talk down to your patient, which will only serve to irritate and alienate him.

Maintain "neutral empathy" and "provisional respect." The first refers to a nonjudgmental attitude with regard to your willingness to understand where your patient is coming from and to help him with his problems. The second means treating the patient with basic human dignity, but not tolerating him abusing your efforts, wasting your time, or generally acting like an ass: "I treat you with respect until you give me a reason not to. But if you insist on giving me that reason, I really can't help you." By maintaining your own dignity, you also model self-respect for the patient.

Minimize questions. Sometimes a direct question is unavoidable ("Have you ever taken medication for your mood?" "How'd you get that scar on your arm?"), but try to steer clear of questions that sound like interrogations ("Do you like beating up those guys?") or those that seem to ask for self-reflective insight the patient just doesn't have ("Why do you think you keep getting into trouble with authorit-

continued

BOX 21.1.—*Continued*

ies?"). An alternative strategy is to use **reflective statements**: "Seems like every time you turn around, you find yourself in some kind of jam. I wonder why that is."

Minimize interpretations. With these populations, interpretations of complex psychodynamics will usually amount to so much gobbledygook; however, identification and explanation of concrete cause-and-effect relationships can often be illuminating and lead to adaptive behavior change: "So what I'm getting is that you want to protect yourself by not acting like a punk, so you put on this f— you attitude from the moment you meet someone, but sometimes it sounds like they just pick this up from the get-go and then they're like, 'okay I was going to give you the benefit of the doubt, but if that's your attitude, then f— you, too,' so you end up with the same nastiness you were trying to avoid."

Be prepared to do most of the talking. In traditional forms of psychotherapy, the therapist sits back and lets the patient free-associate, but with inmate patients, this is apt to lead to long uncomfortable silences because these individuals either don't know what to say, are afraid to say anything, are being oppositionally silent, or might actually want to get something off their chest, but lack the vocabulary and articulation skills to express it. Don't be afraid to fill in the gaps, which sometimes may take some creativity on your part. Talk about neutral subjects, if you have to ("You just came from lunch? With the food they serve here, I'm surprised you could walk over." "A lot of guys are going to watch the game Friday night—you follow the Colts?") to get the communication flow started.

But know when to shut up and listen. Ideally, familiarity with talking rather than impulsively acting will gradually develop in your patient, and his expressive ability will slowly progress to the point where you actually find yourself in a dialog from time to time. But occasionally, some combination of trust and a burning desire to unburden himself will result in the eruption of verbiage, in which case, sit back and soak it in. Later you may be able to utilize some of this material to help him to gain some insight and to develop more adaptive problem solving strategies.

Offer practical advice. Another principle of traditional psychotherapy is that the only answers or solutions that are valuable are the ones that the patient discovers for himself. That may be fine with bright, motivated patients with limitless sessions to engage in the process of self-discovery. But your typical inmate patient will require you to be far more directive, to give him something he can use right away, and a therapist who "tells it straight" and offers practical suggestions that actually work will be afforded tremendous credibility. In the best of cases, a few patients may actually begin to internalize the process of thinking through solutions to problems before they act on them.

Encourage reflective feedback. On the latter note, one way of encouraging patients to apply cognitive skills to their daily lives is to inquire about what they did, how it worked, and why it worked—or didn't. Here, the therapist acts more like a coach than a doctor, providing the structure and scaffolding of adaptive behavior while encouraging patients to fill in the details as they proceed.

Use humor appropriately. Be careful about joking around too much with offenders or psychiatric patients who may be concrete and/or paranoid and may not appreciate your crackling irony, or may be insulted that you're "making a joke" out of their predicament. On the other hand, you don't want to always talk and act like you have a stick up your butt. So get to know the thinking style of each patient and tailor your humor-meter accordingly. In the best circumstance, sharing a joke can be a rapport-building and bonding experience and can sometimes lead to a fresh perspective on a problem, using the humorous to highlight the serious. "Show me a man who knows what's funny," said Mark Twain, "and I'll show you a man who knows what's not."

Be attentive to malingering and manipulation. Just when you're patting yourself on the back for making a breakthrough in your patient's evolving sense of responsibility, here comes the question: "Oh, and *by the way,* Doc, can you speak to the Medical Department about getting me some Xanax for my anxiety?" So it was all a ploy and you're the biggest chump in the joint! Get used to it. In institutional settings, inmates (prisoners or psychiatric patients) will test you, play you, goof on you, and try to manipulate you to wheedle drugs or special privileges, or just because sitting and bullshitting with you is a more enjoyable diversion than the card game back on the unit. If you discover or strongly suspect you're being greased, approach it forthrightly and deal with it assertively. You don't have to dump the patient; in fact, maintaining the clinical connection proves that: (1) there are such things as second chances (but not too many), and (2) as a professional, you can take it; you're not going to grab the bait and overreact to being dissed. Remember, the one thing you can always maintain is your own dignity.

CRIME VICTIMS

Each year, more than 25 million Americans are victimized by some form of crime (Herman, 2002). More than most traumas–medical illness, traffic accidents, technological accidents, natural disasters–violence deliberately and maliciously perpetrated by other people robs us of our sense of safety and security in the human world–which is probably why there are far more TV shows and movies about victims of crimes than about victims of car crashes or avalanches (Miller, 2008b).

The U.S. Department of Justice estimates that rapes, robberies, and assaults account for 2.2 million injuries and more than 700,000 hospital stays annually. Annual costs due to medical bills, mental health costs, and lost productivity are estimated to exceed 6.1 billion dollars. Indeed, even in this age of terrorism (Chapter 13), local violent crime is the overriding social and political issue for most Americans. In some populations, as many as 40 to 70 percent of individuals have been exposed to crime-related traumas sufficient to meet diagnostic criteria for posttraumatic stress disorder (PTSD) and other traumatic disability syndromes, and many individuals have endured multiple exposures to such extreme stressors (Bidinotto, 1996; Breslau & Davis, 1992; Breslau et al., 1991, 1998; Davis & Breslau, 1994; Kirwin, 1997; Norris, 1992; Resnick et al., 1993, 1997; Saunders et al., 1989).

In general, women are more likely to be victims of sexual assault, often by people they know, such as husbands, ex-husbands, boyfriends, or relatives (Chapter 14), while men are more likely to be physically assaulted by strangers. The risk of sexual assault diminishes with age, while risk of physical assault increases with age earlier in life, but then declines as men get older. Having been victimized in the past appears to be a risk factor for future victimization, probably because most people cannot easily escape the sociodemographic factors that put them at risk in the first place. Women are likely to develop PTSD at about the same rate to both physical and sexual assault, while the rate of PTSD for men is lower for physical assault, but very high for sexual assault, which is a rarer and more humiliating event for most men (Kilpatrick & Acierno, 2003).

PSYCHOLOGICAL EFFECTS OF CRIME VICTIMIZATION

A number of diagnosable psychiatric syndromes may be seen following criminal assault. Depression, anxiety, panic attacks, posttraumatic stress disorder (PTSD) and substance abuse are common psychological disorders are found in victims of robbery, rape, and burglary, and these reactions may be transient or long-lasting (Falsetti & Resnick, 1995; Frank & Stewart, 1984; Hough, 1985; Rothbaum et al., 1992; Uhde et al., 1985).

Russell & Beigel (1990) conceive of crime victimization as comprising several layers in relation to a person's core self:

Property crimes like burglary generally hurt victims only at the outermost self-layer, i.e., their belongings, although the theft of certain meaning-laden family heirlooms can have a much greater emotional impact.

Armed robbery, which involves personal contact with the criminal and threat to the physical self of the victim, invades a deeper psychological layer.

Assault and battery penetrates still deeper, injuring the victim both physically and psychologically.

Rape goes to the very core of the self, perverts the sense of safety and intimacy that sexual contact is supposed to have, and affects the victim's basic beliefs, values, emotions, and sense of safety in the world (Chapter 14).

Society's response to crime also plays a role in how supported or abandoned victims feel (Russell & Beigel, 1990). For example, when a child comes home from school and tells his parents that the teacher was mean and made him sit in the corner, a common parental response is to inquire, "What did you do to make the teacher punish you?" From experiences such as this, many people grow up thinking that if something bad happens to them, they somehow deserved it. Also, taking the blame for something, even if you logically know it's not your own fault, is often a more existentially reassuring stance than having to believe that something this terrible can just happen for no reason–because, if there's nothing you did to contribute to it, then there's nothing you can do that will prevent it from happening again, or from something even worse happening, anytime, anywhere (Miller, 1998b, 1998c, 1999d, 1999e, 2008b).

Society often regards victimization as contagious. In modern American culture, with its emphasis on tough individualism and fierce competition, victims are often equated with losers. The victim must have done something to bring it on him or herself, otherwise, I'm just as vulnerable too, and who wants to believe that? This often leads to a reluctance to identify or associate with crime victims for fear that their bad luck will "rub off." All of these beliefs and reactions further contribute to the feelings of blame and shame that many crime victims experience (Miller, 1998c, 2008b; Spungen, 1998).

A criminal act can affect those not directly assaulted or killed. When a family member has been murdered, surviving family members may be plagued by intrusive images of what they imagine the scene of their loved one's death to have been (Falsetti & Resnick, 1995; Schlosser, 1997). As noted above, not just direct victims but friends and relatives of crime victims may be ostracized and avoided by those seeking to distance themselves from the contagious taint of vulnerability that crime victims are all too often imbued with.

Fear of crime may even be hazardous to your health. Increasingly, social scientists are finding that the sheer overload of crime and disaster stories in the media, especially on local television newscasts (and now including the Internet), is giving the public a warped view of reality and contributing to a type of media-induced trauma known as **mean world syndrome** (Budiansky et al., 1994). Since most of the general public have little direct experience with crime, our beliefs about crime and the criminal justice system are largely based on what we see on TV, read in the newspapers, or scroll on the Web, where sensational and violent crimes are often overrepresented. This may have the paradoxical effect of oversensitizing people to nonexistent or insignificant threats, while at the same time numbing the public's understanding of the true impact of crime victimization when it does occur. The mean world syndrome makes us paranoid about our neighbors and cynical about society and human nature in general (Budiansky et al., 1996; Miller, 1998c, 2008b).

RESTORATIVE JUSTICE

Victims of crime often feel disenfranchised from the legal system in another way, as well. As noted in Chapter 1, the civil and criminal justice systems differ in that civil cases involve one citizen bringing a lawsuit against another, while in criminal cases, it is the state or federal government which brings the charge. In essence, society prosecutes the offender not necessarily or primarily because of the harm he has done to the victim, but because he has *broken the law*. The actual crime has been committed against the state or federal government, not against the victim. Crime victims often quickly discover that the prosecution's interest in them is chiefly as a witness to secure the defendant's conviction–the DA is not "their" attorney. One of the ironies of the criminal justice system, then, is that those who have been most affected by crime often have the least say as to how it is prosecuted or adjudicated (Miller, 2001c, 2008b).

One way crime victims attempt to personalize the injury done to them is through the filing of an addtional civil lawsuit, seeking damages from the offender for the injuries, losses, and suffering they've endured (Barton, 1990; National Crime Victims Bar Association, 2005), a recourse made famous in the O.J. Simpson case. Yet, even if successful in obtaining money, this only partially achieves the purpose of allowing the victim to make some kind of sense or achieve some kind of resolution in the face of a cruel and malicious act perpetrated on him or her by another human being.

The **restorative justice movement** (Bazemore, 1996, 1998; Braithwaite, 1999, 2002; Braithwaite & Strang, 2001; McCold, 2000; Strang, 2002; Wenzel et al., 2008; Zehr, 1990; Retzinger & Scheff, 1996; Zernova, 2009) seeks to bring offenders and victims together to effect a quintessentially human reconciliation where: (1) particular offenders are carefully vetted for sincerity in wanting to offer an apology to the victim or co-victims (e.g., relatives of a deceased victim) they have harmed; (2) victims are willing and prepared for this encounter; (3) there is no evidence that the encounter will prove harmful to the victim or co-victims and every precaution is made to prevent this; and (4) there is no expectation of any special privilege or effect on the offender's sentence or status as a consequence of participating. At the fundamental core of restorative justice is the offender's willingness to accept not just *responsibility*, which connotes a causal connection between the offender's actions and the injurious event without endorsing one's deliberate intention to cause the harm, but *accountability*, which is one step further in the volitional internalization process, a matter of accepting fault and acknowledging guilt, which is a prerequisite for true atonement.

In the most successful encounters of this type, the offender says something along the lines of: "I hurt you, I deliberately intended to hurt you, there may have been all kinds of reasons leading up to it, but it was my choice to do it. Now, I'm truly sorry and here's why (reflection, religious beliefs, empathy with the victim or co-victim, etc.). I don't expect my apology to change anything and I don't expect your forgiveness, but it's important to me that I tell you this and I thank you for hearing me."

But does it help? Participation in restorative justice programs is reported to be associated with reduced recidivism, perhaps because it helps offenders achieve a psychological reintegration into the human community (Bazemore & Walgrave, 1999; Braithwaite, 2002; Johnstone, 2002; Latimer et al., 2005; Van Ness & Strong, 2002; Walgrave, 2000; Zehr, 1990; Zehr & Mika, 1998), but there would also appear to be an obvious self-selection factor here: prisoners willing to participate in this kind of humbling, accountability-accepting process are the least likely to resemble the modal criminal in terms of egocentric thinking style and defensive behavioral reaction pattern; that is, participants are likely to be among the few inmates who possess a *conscience* (although there is always the danger that a crafty psychopath may choose to feign the role precisely to get off on his manipulation of everyone concerned–prison life is boring, and inmates seek all kinds of diversions they can get away with).

More importantly, most (but certainly not all) victims and co-victims who participate report more personal satisfaction with this process than with the usual criminal justice channels for adjudicating the crime, because this affords them a direct, personal, intimate reckoning with the person who has harmed them (Beven et al., 2005; Latimer et al., 2005; Sherman et al., 2005; Strang, 2002; Wenzel et al., 2008). Here, there is likely to be a selection factor in the other direction: only those victims and co-victims with the stamina, resilience, and broadness of heart to be willing to put themselves through such a wrenching emotional experience will be likely to benefit from it. In all cases, it is emphasized that the encounter is primarily for the victim's benefit, not the offender's, but again, those offenders willing to participate are most likely to accept the fact that their own existential resolution will be a side-benefit of the primary task of helping the victims and co-victims find some meaning and peace.

Restorative justice will not be an option for the majority of offenders who are not disposed to accept responsibility and accountability for their actions, much less apologize for them, nor for the great number of victims and co-victims who are not prepared to hear anything that monster has to say, even if he were willing to say it. Further unintended consequences include access to restorative justice programs being seen as an "entitlement" by either offenders or victims, or that, by being increasingly successful and expanding its range, the standards for inclusion in the program may become watered down, resulting in some painful and harmful encounters that could derail the program as a whole. At the present time, as long as the emphasis remains on restorative justice as primarily a resource for the *victim,* intentional or accidental misuses of the process will hopefully be minimized.

SUMMARY AND CONCLUSIONS

Correctional psychology concerns itself with the evaluation and treatment of prisoners. Mental health services may be offered to incarcerated offenders either for their own benefit in coping with prison life or as part of a variety of **offender rehabilitation programs** designed to reduce reoffending, or **recidivism**. A significant proportion of incarcerees suffer some form of mental disorder, and this ratio is higher in jails than prisons, and higher in juvenile than adult corrections. **Inmate suicide** is a growing problem. Studies of **inmate thinking styles** generally replicate the results from such studies of criminals in general, i.e., that they tend to be egocentric, nonreflective, short-term oriented, and denying of personal responsibility. Analysis of **final statements of condemned death row prisoners** yields a range of responses, from acceptance, to contrition, to apathy, to rebellion; a common theme is making some kind of meaning out of their impending demise. Finally, attention must be paid to **crime victims**, who often face neglect or ostracism by both the legal system and their families and communities. Giving victims a greater role in the adjudication of crimes might well put a little more "justice" into the criminal justice system.

Bibliography

Abadinsky, H. (1990). *Organized crime* (3rd ed.). Chicago: Nelson-Hall.

Abel, E.M. (2001). Comparing the social service utilization, exposure to violence, and trauma symptomatology of domestic violence female "victims" and female "batterers." *Journal of Family Violence, 16,* 401–420.

Abbey, A., Clinton-Sherrod, A.M., McAuslan, P., Zawacki, T., & Buck, P.O. (2003). The relationship between the quantity of alcohol consumed and the severity of sexual assaults committed by college men. *Journal of Interpersonal Violence, 18,* 813–833.

Abbey, A., Ross, L.T., McDuffie, D., & McAuslan, P. (1996). Alcohol and dating risk factors for sexual assault among college women. *Psychology of Women Quarterly, 20,* 147–169.

AbdelMalik, P., Husted, J., Chow, E.W.C., & Bassett, A.S. (2003). Childhood head injuries and expression of schizophrenia in multiply affected families. *Archives of General Psychiatry, 60,* 231–236.

Abel, E.M. (2001). Comparing the social service utilization, exposure to violence, and trauma symptomatology of domestic violence female "victims" and female "batterers." *Journal of Family Violence, 16,* 401–420.

Abel, G.G., Barlow, D.H., Blanchard, E.B., & Guild, D. (1977). The component of rapists' sexual arousal. *Archives of General Psychiatry, 34,* 895–903.

Abel, G.G., Becker, J.V., Cunningham-Rather, J., Mittelman, M., & Rouleau, J.L. (1988). Multiple paraphilic diagnoses among sex offenders. *Bulletin of the American Academy of Psychiatry and the Law, 16,* 153–168.

Abracen, J., & Looman, J. (2006). Evaluation of civil commitment criteria in a high risk sample of sexual offenders. *Journal of Sexual Offender Civil Commitment: Science and the Law, 1,* 124–140.

Abracen, J., Looman, J., Di Fazio, R., Kelly, T., & Stirpe, T. (2006). Patterns of attachment and alcohol abuse in sexual and violent nonsexual offenders. *Journal of Sexual Aggression, 12,* 19–30.

Abrahams, N., Jewkes, Hoffman, M., & Laubscher, R. (2004). Sexual violence against intimate partners in Cape Town: Prevalence and risk factors reported by men. *Bulletin of the World Health Organization, 82,* 330–337.

Abrahamsen, D. (1952). *Who are the guilty?* New York: Rinehart & Co.

Abramson, J. (2009). *Minerva's owl: The tradition of Western political thought.* Cambridge, MA: Harvard University Press.

Absher, J.R., Vogt, B.A., Clark, D.G., Flowers, D.L., Gorman, D.G., & Keyes, J.W. (2000). Hypersexuality and hemiballism due to subthalamic lesion infarction. *Neuropsychiatry, Neuropsychology and Behavioral Neurology, 13,* 220–229.

Abueg, F.R., Drescher, K.D., & Kubany, E.S. (1994). Natural disasters. In F.M. Dattilio & A. Freeman (Eds.), *Cognitive-behavioral strategies in crisis intervention* (pp. 238–257). New York: Guilford.

Adair, T.W., & Doberson, M.J. (1999). A case of suicidal hanging staged as homicide. *Journal of Forensic Science, 44,* 1307–1309.

Adamec, R.E. (1990). Does kindling model anything clinically relevant? *Biological Psychiatry, 27,* 249–279.

Adamec, R.E., & Stark-Adamec, A.C. (1983). Limbic kindling and animal behavior: Implications for human psychopathology associated with complex partial seizures. *Biological Psychiatry, 20,* 269–293.

Adams, M.S., & Toth, R.C. (2006). The unanticipated consequences of the crome legislation. *Judicature, 90,* 129–134.

Adinkrah, M. (2001). When parents kill: An analysis of filicides in Fiji. *International Journal of Offender Therapy and Comparative Criminology, 45,* 144–158.

Adinkrah, M. (2002). Men who kill their own children: Paternal filicide incidents in contemporary Fiji. *Child Abuse and Neglect, 27,* 557–568.

Adler, N.A., & Schutz, J. (1995). Sibling incest offenders. *Child Abuse and Neglect, 19,* 811–819.

Adler, P.A., & Adler, P. (1996). Preadolescent clique stratification and the hierarchy of identity. *Sociological Inquiry, 66,* 111–142.

Adler, A. (1917). *The neurotic constitution* (transl. B. Gluek, J.E. Lind). London: Moffat, Yard.

Adolphs, R., Gosselin, F., Buchanan, T.W., Tranel, D., & Schyns, P. (2005). A mechanism for impaired fear recognition after amygdala damage. *Nature, 433,* 68–72.

Agarwal, D., & Goedde, H.W. (1992). Pharmacogenetics of alcohol metabolism and alcoholism. *Pharmacogenetics, 2,* 48–62.

Aggrawal, A. (2009a). References to the paraphilias and sexual crimes in the Bible. *Journal of Forensic and Legal Medicine, 16,* 109–114.

Aggrawal, A. (2009b). *Forensic and medico-legal aspects of of sexual crimes and unusual sexual practices.* Boca Raton: CRC Press.

Agnew, R. (1992). Foundation for a general theory of crime and delinquency. *Criminology, 30,* 47–87.

Agnew, R. (1999). A general strain theory of community differences in crime rates. *Journal of Research in Crime and Delinquency, 36,* 123–155.

Agnew, R. (2004). A general strain theory approach to violence. In M. Zahn, H. Brownstein, & S. Jackson (Eds.), *Violence: From theory to research* (pp. 37–50). Dayton, OH: Anderson.

Agnew, R. (2005). *Why do criminals offend? A general theory of crime and delinquency.* Los Angeles: Roxbury.

Agnew, R., & Huguley, S. (1989). Adolescent violence toward parents. *Journal of Marriage and the Family, 51,* 699–711.

Ahlmeyer, S.A., Kleinsasser, D., Stoner, J., & Retzlaff, P. (2003). Psychopathology of incarcerated sex offenders. *Journal of Personality Disorders, 17,* 306–318.

Ahrens, W., Hart, R., & Maruyama, N. (1997). Pediatric death: Managing the aftermath in the emergency department. *Journal of Emergency Medicine, 15,* 601–603.

Aigner, M., Eher, R., Fruehwald, S., Frottier, P., Guttierez-Lobos, K., & Dwyer, S.M. (2000). Brain abnormalities and violent behavior. *Journal of Psychology and Human Sexuality, 11,* 57–64.

Ainsworth, M.D.S. (1989). Attachments beyond infancy. *American Psychologist, 44,* 709–716.

Ainsworth, M.D.S., Blehar, M.C., Waters, E., & Wall, S. (1978). *Patterns of attachment: A psychological study of the strange situation.* Hillsdale, NJ: Erlbaum.

Ainsworth, P.B. (2001). *Offender profiling and crime analysis.* Devon: Willan Publishing.

Akers, R.L. (1985). *Deviant behavior: A social learning approach* (3rd ed.). Belmont, CA: Wadsworth.

Akers, R.L. (2003). *Social learning theory and the explanation of crime.* New Brunswick, NJ: Transaction Press.

Akers, R.L., & Jensen, G.F. (2006). The empirical status of social learning theory of crime and deviance: The past, present, and future. In F.T. Cullen, J.P. Wright & K.R. Blevins (Eds.), *Taking stock: The status of criminological theory* (pp. 37–76). New Brunswick, NJ: Transaction Publishers.

Akhtar, S. (1999). The psychodynamic dimension of terrorism. *Psychiatric Annals, 29,* 350–355.

Albert, A., & Bulcroft, K. (1988). Pets, families, and the life course. *Journal of Marriage and the Family, 50,* 543–552.

Alberto-Tassinari, C, Tassi, L., & Calandra-Buonara, G. (2005). Biting behavior, aggression, and seizures. *Epilepsia, 45,* 55–66.

Albrecht, S. (1996). *Crisis management for corporate self-defense.* New York: Amacom.

Albrecht, S. (1997). *Fear and violence on the job: Prevention solutions for the dangerous workplace.* Durham: Carolina Academic Press.

Aldarondo, E., & Straus, M.A. (1994). Screening for physical violence in couple therapy: Methodological, practical, and ethical considerations. *Family Process, 33,* 425–439.

Aldarondo, E., & Sugarman, D.B. (1996). Risk marker analysis of the cessation and persistence of wife assault. *Journal of Consulting and Clinical Psychology, 64,* 1010–1019.

Aldwin, C.M. (1994). *Stress, coping, and development.* New York: Guilford.

Alexander, J.F., & Parsons, B.V. (1982). *Functional family therapy.* Monterey, CA: Brooks-Cole.

Alexander, M.A. (1999). Sexual offender treatment efficacy revisited. *Sexual Abuse: A Journal of Research and Treatment, 11,* 101–116.

Alexy, E.M., Burgess, A.W., & Baker, T. (2005a). Internet offenders: Traders, travelers, and combination trader-travelers. *Journal of Interpersonal Violence, 20,* 804–812.

Alexy, E.M., Burgess, A.W., Baker, T., & Smoyak, S.A. (2005b). Perceptions of cyberstalking among college students. *Brief Treatment and Crisis Intervention, 5,* 279–289.

Allebeck, P., Adamsson, C., Engstrom, A., & Rydberg, U. (1993). Cannabis and schizophrenia: A longitudinal study of cases treated in Stockholm county. *Acta Psychiatrica Scandinavica, 88,* 21–24.

Allen, S.W. (2004). Dynamics in repsonding to departmental personnel. In V. Lord (Ed), *Suicide by cop: Inducing officers to shoot* (pp. 245–257). Flushing: Looseleaf Law Publications.

Allen, D.M., & Farmer, R. G. (1996). Family relationships of adults with borderline personality disorder. *Comprehensive Psychiatry, 37,* 43–51.

Allen, N.E., Bybee, D.I., & Sullivan, C.M. (2004). Battered women's multitude of needs: Evidence supporting the need for comprehensive advocacy. *Violence Against Women, 10,* 1015–1035.

Allen, R., & Lucero, M. (1998). Subordinate aggression against managers: Empirical analyses of published arbitration abstracts. *International Journal of Conflict Management, 9,* 234–257.

Allen, T.D. (2001). Family-supportive work environments: The role of organizational perceptions. *Journal of Vocational Behavior, 58,* 414–435.

Allied Control Council. (1945). Law No. 10: Punishment of personal guilty of war crimes, crimes against peace and against humanity, Art. II, Sect. 1(c). *Official Gazette Control Council for Germany, 1946,* pp. 50–55.

Alm. B., af Klintenberg, B., Humble, K., Leppert, J., Sorenson, S., Tegelman, R., Thorell, L.H., & Lidberg, L. (1996). Criminality and psychopathy as related to thyroid activity in former juvenile delinquents. *Acta Psychiatrica Scandinavica, 94,* 112–117.

Alpert, E.J., Cohen, S., & Sege, R.D. (1997). Family violence: An overview. *Academic Medicine, 72,* S3–S6.

Alvarez, A., & Bachman, R. (2002). *Murder American style.* Belmont, CA: Wadsworth.

Amato, P.R., & Keith, B. (1991). Parental divorce and the well-being of children: A meta-analysis. *Psychological Bulletin, 110,* 25–46.

Ambert, A. (1994). A qualitative study of peer abuse and its effects: Theoretical and epirical implications. *Journal of Marriage and Family, 56,* 119–130.

American Academy of Pediatrics Committee on Adolescence. (2001). Health care for children and adolescents in the juvenile correctional care system. *Pediatrics, 107,* 799–803.

American Law Institute. (1962). *Model penal code,* Sec. 4.01(2).

American Law Institute. (1962). *Model penal code.* Philadelphia: Author.

American Psychiatric Association. (1987). *Diagnostic and statistical manual of mental disorders* (3rd ed., revised). Washington, DC: Author.

American Psychiatric Association. (1994). *Diagnostic and statistical manual of mental disorders* (4th ed.). Washington, DC: Author.

American Psychiatric Association. (2000). *Diagnostic and statistical manual of mental disorders* (4th ed., text revision). Washington, DC: Author.

American Psychological Association Zero Tolerance Task Force. (2008). Are zero tolerance policies effective in the schools? An evidentiary review and recommendations. *American Psychologist, 63,* 852–862.

Ames, W. (1976). *Police and the community in Japan.* Ann Arbor, MI: University of Michigan.

Amir, M. (1971). *Patterns of forcible rape.* Chicago: University of Chicago Press.

Anderson, C. (2002). Report: Police slayings increase. *South Florida Sun-Sentinel,* December 3, p. 3A.

Anderson, C., & Dill, K. (2000). Video games and aggressive thoughts, feelings and behavior in the laboratory and in life. *Journal of Personality and Social Psychology, 78,* 772–790.

Anderson, C.A., & Bushman, B.J. (2002). Human aggression. *Annual Review of Psychology, 53,* 27–51.

Anderson, D.A. (1999). The aggregate burden of crime. *Journal of Law and Economics, 42,* 611–642.

Anderson, E. (1999). *Code of the street: Decency, violence, and the moral life.* New York: Norton.

Anderson, G.S. (2007). *Biological influences on criminal behavior.* Boca Raton, FL: CRC Press.

Anderson, L., & Pearson, C. (1999). Tit for tat? The spiraling effect of incivility in the workplace. *Academy of Management Review, 24,* 452–471.

Anderson, R., Ambosino, R., & Valentine, D. (1983). Child deaths attributed to abuse and neglect: An empirical study. *Child Youth Services Review, 5,* 75–89.

Anderson, R.R. (2006). Commentary: Tattoos and body piercings. *Journal of the American Academy of Dermatology, 55,* 422.

Anderson, W., Swenson, D., & Clay, D. (1995). *Stress management for law enforcement officers.* Englewood Cliffs, NJ: Prentice-Hall.

Andrews, D.A., & Bonta, J. (1994). *The psychology of criminal conduct.* Cincinnati, OH: Anderson.

Andrews, D.A., & Bonta, J. (1998). *The psychology of criminal conduct* (2nd ed.). Cincinnati, OH: Anderson.

Andrews, D.A., & Bonta, J. (2006). *The psychology of criminal conduct* (4th ed.). Cincinnati, OH: Anderson.

Andrews, D.A., & Bonta, J. (2010). Rehabilitating criminal justice policy and practice. *Psychology, Public Policy, and Law, 16,* 39–55.

Andrews, D.A., Bonta, J., & Hoge, R.D. (1990). Classification of effective rehabilitation: Rediscovering psychology. *Criminal Justice and Behavior, 17,* 19–52.

Aneshensel, C.S. (1992). Social stress: Theory and research. *Annual Review of Sociology, 18,* 15–38.

Annon, J.S. (1995). Investigative profiling: A behavioral analysis of the crime scene. *American Journal of Forensic Psychology, 13,* 67–75.

Anouizerate, B., Guehl, D., Cuny, E., Rogier, A., Bioulac, B., & Tignol, J. (2004). Pathophysiology of obsessive-compulsive disorder: A necessary link between phenomenology, neuropsychology, imagery, and physiology. *Progress in Neurobiology, 72,* 195–221.

Anthony, E.J. (1987). Risk, vulnerability, and resilience: An overview. In E.J. Anthony & B.J. Cohler (Eds.), *The invulnerable child* (pp. 3–48). New York: Guilford.

Appel, A.E., & Holden, G.W. (1998). The co-occurrence of spouse and physical child abuse: A review and appraisal. *Journal of Family Psychology, 12,* 578–599.

Appelbaum, P.S., Jick, R.Z., Grisso, T., Givelber, D., Silver, E., & Steadman, H.J. (1993). Use of posttraumatic stress disorder to support an insanity defense. *American Journal of Psychiatry, 150,* 229–234.

Appelbaum, P.S., Robbins, P.C., & Monahan, J. (2000). Violence and delusions: Data from the MacArthur Violence Risk Assessment Study. *American Journal of Psychiatry, 157,* 566–572.

Appelbaum, P.S., Robbins, P.C., & Roth, L.H. (1999). Dimensional approach to delusions: Comparison across types and diagnoses. *American Journal of Psychiatry, 156,* 1938–1943.

Arata, C.M. (2002). Child sexual abuse and sexual revictimization. *Clinical Psychology: Science and Practice, 9,* 135–164.

Arboleda-Florez, J., Holley, H., & Crisanti, A. (1998). Understanding causal paths between mental illness and violence. *Social Psychiatry and Psychiatric Epidemiology, 33,* 32–46.

Archer, J. (1991). The influence of testosterone on human aggression. *British Journal of Psychology, 82,* 1–28.

Archer, J. (1994). Testosterone and aggression. In M. Hillbrand & N.J. Pallone (Eds.), *The psychobiology of aggression: Engines, measurement, control* (pp. 3–35). New York: Haworth.

Ardis, C. (2004). School violence from the classroom teacher's perspective. In W.L. Turk (Ed.), *School crime and policing* (pp. 131–150). Upper Saddle River, NJ: Pearson Education.

Arendt, H. (1963). *Eichmann in Jerusalem: A report on the banality of evil.* New York: Viking.

Arias, I., & Pape, K.T. (1999). Psychological abuse: Implications for adjustment and commitment to leave violent partners. *Violence and Victims, 14,* 55–67.

Arndt, S., Tyrell, G., Flaum, M., & Andreasen, N.C. (1992). Comorbidity of substance abuse and schizophrenia: The role of pre-morbid adjustment. *Psychological Medicine, 22,* 379–388.

Arneklev, B.J., Grasmick, H.G., & Bursick, R.J. (1999). Evaluating the dimensionality and invariance of "low self-control." *Journal of Quantitative Criminology, 15,* 307–331.

Aron, A.R., Fisher, H., Mashek, D.J., Strong, G., Li, H., & Brown, L.L. (2005). Reward, motivation and emotion systems associated with early-stage intense romantic love. *Journal of Neurophysiology, 94,* 327–337.

Aronson, J.D. (2007). Brain imaging, culpability, and the juvenile death penalty. *Psychology, Public Policy, and Law, 13,* 115–142.

Arrigo, B.T. (2006). *Criminal behavior: A systems approach.* Upper Saddle River, NJ: Pearson.

Arrigo, B.A., & Purcell, C.E. (2001). Explaining paraphilias and lust murder: Toward an integrated model. *International Journal of Offender Therapy and Comparative Criminology, 45,* 6–31.

Arrigo, B.A., & Shipley, S. (2001). The confusion over psychopathy: I. Historical considerations. *International Journal of Offender Therapy and Comparative Criminology, 45,* 325–344.

Arsenault, L., Moffitt, T.E., Caspi, A., Taylor, P.J., & Silva, P.A. (2000a). Mental disorders and violence in a total birth cohort: Results from the Dunedin Study. *Archives of General Psychiatry, 57,* 979–986.

Arsenault, L., Tremblay, R.E., Billerica, B., Sequin, J.R., & Saucier, J.F. (2000b). Minor physical anomalies and family adversity as risk factors for violent delinquency in adolescence. *American Journal of Psychiatry, 157,* 917–923.

Ascione, F.R. (1997). Humane education research: Evaluating efforts to encourage children's kindness and caring toward animals. *Genetic, Social, and General Psychology, 123,* 57–78.

Ascione, F.R. (1998). Battered women's reports of their partner's and their children's cruelty to animals. *Journal of Emotional Abuse, 1,* 119–133.

Ascione, F.R., Weber, C.V., & Wood, D.S. (1997). The abuse of animals and domestic violence: A national survey of shelters for women who are battered. *Society and Animals, 5,* 205–218.

Asendorpf, J.B., Denissen, J.A.A., & van Aken, M.A.G. (2008). Inhibited and aggressive preschool children at 23 years of age: Personality and social transitions into adulthood. *Developmental Psychology, 44,* 997–1011.

Asendorpf, J.B., & van Aken, M.A.G. (1999). Resilient, over-controlled, and under-controlled personality prototypes in childhood: Replicability, predictive power, and the trait-type issue. *Journal of Personality and Social Psychology, 77,* 815–832.

Asnis, G.M, Kaplan, M.L., Hundorfean, G., & Saeed, W. (1997). Violence and homicidal behaviors in psychiatric disorders. *Psychiatric Clinics of North America, 20,* 405–425.

Asperger, H. (1944). Autistic psychopathy in childhood. *Archiv fur Psychiatrie und Nervenkrankheiten, 117,* 76–136.

Atran, S. (2004). Combatting Al Qaeda's splinters: Mishandling suicide terrorism. *Washington Quarterly, 27,* 67–90.

Auchincloss, E., & Weiss, R. (1992). Paranoid character and the intolerance of indifference. *Journal of the American Psychoanalytic Association, 40,* 1013–1048.

Ault, R.L., & Reese, J.T. (1980). A psychological assessment of crime profiling. *FBI Law Enforcement Bulletin, 49,* 22–25.

Awadallah, N., Vaughan, A., Franco, C., Munir, F., Aharaby, N., & Goldfarb, J. (2005). Munchausen by proxy: A case, chart series, and literature review of older victims. *Child Abuse and Neglect, 29,* 931–941.

Azam, J.-P. (2005). Suicide bombing as inter-generational investment. *Public Choice, 122,* 177–198.

Babcock, J.C., Miller, S.A., & Siard, C. (2003). Toward a typology of abusive women: Differences between partner-only and generally violent women in the use of violence. *Psychology of Women Quarterly, 27,* 153–161.

Babiak, P. (1995). When psychopaths go to work: A case study of an industrial psychopath. *Applied Psychology: An International Review, 44,* 171–188.

Babiak, P. (2000). Psychopathic manipulation at work. In C.B. Gacono (Ed.), *The clinical and forensic assessment of psychopathy: A practitioner's guide* (pp. 287–311). Mahwah, NJ: Erlbaum.

Babiak, P., & Hare, R.D. (2007). *Snakes in suits: When psychopaths go to work.* New York: Harper.

Bachman, R., & Saltzman, L.E. (1995). *Estimates from the redesigned survey.* Bureau of Justice Statistics, US Department of Justice.

Bach-y-Rita, G., Lion, J.R., & Climent, C.E. (1971). Episodic dyscontrol: A study of 130 violent patients. *American Journal of Psychiatry, 127,* 1473–1478.

Bach-y-Rita, G., Lion, J.R., & Ervin, F.R. (1970). Pathological intoxication: Clinical and electroencephalographic studies. *American Journal of Psychiatry, 127,* 698–703.

Bach-y-Rita, G., & Veno, A. (1974). Habitual violence: A profile of 62 men. *American Journal of Psychiatry, 131,* 1015–1017.

Baechler, J. (1979). *Suicides.* New York: Basic Books.

Bailey, G.W., & Unnithan, N.P. (1994). Gang homicides in California: A discriminant analysis. *Journal of Criminal Justice, 22,* 199–226.

Bailey, J.E., Kellerman, A.L., Somes, G.W., Banton, J.G., Rivara, F.P., & Rushford, N.P. (1997). Risk factors for violent death of women in the home. *Archives of Internal Medicine, 157,* 777–782.

Baker, R.R., & Bellis, M.A. (1989). Number of sperm in human ejaculates varies in accordance with sperm competition theory. *Animal Behaviour, 37,* 867–869.

Baker, R.R., & Bellis, M.A. (1993). Human sperm competition: Ejaculate adjustment by males and the function of masturbation. *Animal Behaviour, 46,* 861–885.

Baker, S.C., Frith, C.D., & Dolan, R.J. (1997). The interaction between mood and cognitive function studied with PET. *Psychological Medicine, 27,* 565–578.

Baldry, A.C. (2003a). Animal abuse and exposure to interpersonal violence in Italian youth. *Journal of Interpersonal Violence, 18,* 258–281.

Baldry, A.C. (2003b). Bullying in schools and exposure to domestic violence. *Child Abuse and Neglect, 27,* 713–732.

Balenovich, J., Grossi, E., & Hughes, T. (2008). Toward a balanced approach: Defining police roles in responding to domestic violence. *American Journal of Criminal Justice, 33,* 19–31.

Ball, J.D., & Peake, T.H. (2006). Military psychology: Clinical and operational applications. In T.H. Peake, C.M. Bordiun, & R.P. Archer (Eds.), *Brief psychotherapy in the U.S. military: Principles and applications* (pp. 6-73). New York: Guilford Press.

Bandura, A. (1973). *Aggression: A social learning analysis.* Englewood Cliffs, NJ: Prentice-Hall.

Bandura, A. (1977). *Social learning theory.* Englewood Cliffs, NJ: Prentice-Hall.

Bandura, A. (1998). Mechanisms of moral disengagement. In W. Reich (Ed.), *Origins of terrorism: Psychologies, ideologies, theologies, states of mind* (pp. 161–192). Washington, DC: Woodrow Wilson Center Press.

Bankier, B.Lenz, G., Gutierrez, K., Bach, M., & Katcching, H. (1999). A case of Asperger's syndrome first diagnosed in adulthood. *Psychopathology, 32,* 43–46.

Bard, L.A., Carter, D.L., Cerce, D.D., Knight, R.A., Rosenberg, R., & Schneider, B. (1987). A descriptive study of rapists and child molesters: Developmental, clinical, and criminal characteristics. *Behavioral Sciences and the Law, 5,* 203–220.

Bardone, A., Moffitt, T., Caspi, A., Dickson, N., & Silva, P. (1996). Adult mental health and social outcomes of adolescent girls with depression and conduct disorder. *Development and Psychopathy, 8,* 811–829.

Bardone, A., Moffitt, T., Caspi, A., Dickson, N., Stanton, W.R., & Silva, P. (1998). Adult physical health outcomes of adolescent girls with conduct disorder, depression, and anxiety. *Journal of the American Academy of Child and Adolescent Psychiatry, 37,* 594–601.

Barker, E.D., Seguin, J.R., White, H.R., Bates, M.E., Lacourse, E., & Carbonneau, R. (2007). Developmental trajectories of male physical violence and theft: Relations to neurocognitive performance. *Archives of General Psychiatry, 64,* 592–599.

Barker, T. (2007). *Biker gangs as organized crime.* Cincinnati, OH: Anderson.

Barker, T., & Human, K.M. (2009). Crimes of the Big Four motorcycle gangs. *Journal of Criminal Justice, 37,* 174–179.

Barkley, R.A. (1997a). Behavioral inhibition, sustained attention, and executive functions: Constructing a unifying theory of ADHD. *Psychological Bulletin, 121,* 65–94.

Barkley, R.A. (1997b). *ADHD and the nature of self-control.* New York: Guilford.

Barkley, R.A. (2004). Attention-deficit/hyperactivity disorder and self-regulation: Taking an evolutionary perspective on executive functioning. In R.F. Baumeister & K.D. Vohs (Eds.), *Handbook of self-regulation: Research, theory, and applications* (pp. 301–323). New York: Guilford.

Barling, J., Dupre, K.E., & Kelloway, E.K. (2009). Predicting workplace aggression and violence. *Annual Review of Psychology, 60,* 671–692.

Baron, L., & Straus, M.A. (1987). Four theories of rape: A macrosociological analysis. *Social Problems, 34,* 467–489.

Baron, R.A., & Neuman, J.H. (1996). Workplace violence and workplace aggression: Evidence on their relative frequency and potential causes. *Aggressive Behavior, 22,* 161–173.

Baron, R.A., Neuman, J.H., & Geddes, D. (1999). Social and personal determinants of workplace aggression: Evidence for the impact of perceived injustice and the type A behavior pattern. *Aggressive Behavior, 25,* 281–296.

Baron-Cohen, S. (1988). An assessment of violence in a young man with Asperger's syndrome. *Journal of Child Psychiatry and Psychology, 29,* 351–360.

Barr, K.N., & Quinsey, V.L. (2004). Is psychopathy a pathology or a life strategy? Implications for social policy. In C. Crawford & C. Salmon (Eds.), *Evolutionary psychology, public policy, and personal decisions* (pp. 293–317). Hillsdale, NJ: Erlbaum.

Barratt, E.S. (1994). Impulsiveness and aggression. In J. Monahan & H.J. Steadman (Eds.), *Violence and mental disorder: Developments in risk assessment* (pp. 61–79). Chicago: University of Chicago Press.

Barratt, E.S., Kent, T., & Stanford, M.S. (1995). The role of biological variables in defining and measuring personality. In J.J. Ratey (Ed.), *Neuropsychiatry of personality disorders* (pp. 35–49). Cambridge, MA: Blackwell Science.

Barratt, E.S., Stanford, M.S., Dowdy, L., Liebman, M.J., & Kent, T.A. (1999). Impulsive and premeditated aggression: A factor analysis of self-reported acts. *Psychiatry Research, 86,* 163–173.

Barratt, E.S., Stanford, M.S. Kent, T.A., & Felthous, A. (1997). Neuropsychological and cognitive psychophysiological substrates of impulsive aggression. *Biological Psychiatry, 41,* 1045–1047.

Barrowcliff, A.L., & Haddock, G. (2006). The relationship between command hallucinations and factors of compliance: A critical review of the literature. *Journal of Forensic Psychiatry and Psychology, 17,* 266–298.

Barry-Walsh, J.B., & Mullen, P.E. (2004). Forensic aspects of Asperger's syndrome. *Journal of Forensic Psychiatry and Psychology, 148,* 21–27.

Barter, C., Renold, E., Berridge, D., & Cawson, P. (2004). *Peer violence in children's residential care.* Hampshire, UK: Palgrave.

Bartholemew, A.A. (1981). Criminal intent and the psychologist. *Australian Psychologist, 16,* 413–421.

Bartol, C.R. (1996). Police psychology: Then, now, and beyond. *Criminal Justice and Behavior, 23,* 70–89.

Barton, W.A. (1990). *Recovering for psychological injuries* (2nd ed.). Washington, DC: Association of Trial Lawyers of America.

Barzman, D.H., DelBello, M.P., Fleck, D.E., Lehmkuhl, H., & Strakowski, S.M. (2007). Rates, types, and psychosocial correlates of legal charges in adolescents with newly diagnosed bipolar disorder. *Bipolar Disorders, 9,* 339–344.

Basile, K.C., Espalage, D.L., Rivers, I., McMahon, P.M., & Simon, T.R. (2009). The theoretical and empirical links between bullying behavior and male sexual violence perpetration. *Aggression and Violent Behavior, 14,* 336–347.

Basoglu, M., Mineka, S., Paker, M., Aker, T., Livanou, M., & Gok, S. (1997). Psychological preparedness for trauma as a protective factor in survivors of torture. *Psychological Medicine, 27,* 1421–1433.

Bassarath, L. (2001). Conduct disorder: A biopsychosocial review. *Canadian Journal of Psychiatry, 46,* 609–616.

Batsche, G.M., & Knoff, H. (1994). Bullies and their victims: Understanding a pervasive problem in the schools. *School Psychology Review, 23,* 165–174.

Battin, S.R., Hill, K.G., Abbott, R.D., Catalano, R.F., & Hawkins, J.D. (1998). The contribution of gang membership to delinquency beyond delinquent friends. *Criminology, 36,* 93–115.

Batton, C. (2004). Gender differences in lethal violence: Historical trends in the relationship between homicide and suicide rates, 1960–2000. *Justice Quarterly, 21,* 423–461.

Baumeister, R.F., Smart, L., & Boden, J.M. (1996). Relation of threatened egotism to violence and aggression: The dark side of high self-esteem. *Psychological Review, 103,* 5–33.

Baumeister, R.F., & Wotman, S.R. (1992). *Breaking hearts: The two sides of unrequited love.* New York: Guilford.

Baumeister, R.F. (1991). *Escaping the self: Alcoholism, spirituality, masochism, and other flights from the burden of selfhood.* New York: Basic Books.

Bazemore, G. (1996). Three paradigms for juvenile justice. In B. Galaway & J. Hudson (Eds.), *Restorative justice: International perspectives* (pp. 37–67). Monsey, NY: Criminal Justice Press.

Bazemore, G. (1998). Restorative justice and earned redemption: Communities, victims, and offender reintegration. *American Behavioral Scientist, 41,* 768–813.

Bazemore, G., & Walgrave, L. (1999). Restorative juvenile justice: In search of fundamentals and outline for systematic reform. In G. Bazemore & L. Walgrave (Eds.), *Restorative justice: Repairing the harm of youth crime* (pp. 45–74). Monsey, NY: Criminal Justice Press.

Beauregard, E., & Proulx, J. (2007). A classification of sexual homicide against men. International *Journal of Offender Therapy and Comparative Criminology, 51,* 420–432.

Beaver, K.M., Shutt, J.E., Boutwell, B.B., Ratchford, M., Roberts, K., & Barnes, J.C. (2009). Genetic and environmental influences on levels of self-control and delinquent peer affiliation: Results from a longitudinal sample of adolescent twins. *Criminal Justice and Behavior, 36,* 41–60.

Beaver, K.M., Wright, J.P., & DeLisi, M. (2007). Self-control as an executive function: Reformulating Gottredson & Hirshi's parental socialization thesis. *Criminal Justice and Behavior, 34,* 1345–1361.

Beaver, K.M., Wright, J.P., & DeLisi, M. (2008). Delinquent peer group formation: Evidence of a gene x environment correlation. *Journal of Genetic Psychology, 169,* 227–244.

Beaver, K.M., Wright, J.P., & Maume, M.O. (2008). The effect of school classroom characteristics on low self-control: a multilevel analysis. *Journal of Criminal Justice, 36,* 174–181.

Bechara, A., Damasio, H., & Damasio, A.R. (2000). Emotion, decision making and the orbitofrontal cortex. *Cerebral Cortex, 10,* 295–307.

Beck, A.J., & Maruschak, L.M. (2001). *Mental health treatment in state prisons, 2000.* Washington, DC: National Criminal Justice Reference Service.

Beck, A.T., & Freeman, A. (1990). *Cognitive therapy of personality disorders.* New York: Guilford.

Becker, E. (1973). *The denial of death.* New York: Free Press.

Becker, E. (1975). *Escape from evil.* New York: Free Press.

Becker, J.V. (1998). What we know about the characteristics and treatment of adolescents who have committed sexual offenses. *Child Maltreatment, 3,* 317–329.

Becker, J.V., Kaplan, M.S., Cunningham-Rathner, B.A., & Kavoussi, R. (1986). Characteristics of adolescent incest sexual perpetrators. *Journal of Family Violence, 1,* 85–87.

Becker, J.V., Stinson, J., Tromp, S., & Messer, G. (2003). Characteristics of individuals petitioned for civil commitment. *International Journal of Offender Therapy and Comparative Criminology, 47,* 185–195.

Beckett, K. (1997). *Making crime pay: Law and order in contemporary American politics.* New York: Oxford University Press.

Beckman, M. (2004). Crime, culpability, and the adolescent brain. *Science, 305,* 596–599.

Beck-Sander, A., Birchwood, M., & Chadwick, P. (1997). Acting on command hallucinations: A cognitive approach. *British Journal of Clinical Psychology, 36,* 139–148.

Beech, A.R., Elliott, I.A., Birgden, A., & Findlater, D. (2008). The internet and child sexual offending: A criminological review. *Aggression and Violent Behavior, 13,* 216–228.

Beech, A.R., & Mitchell, I.J. (2005). A neurobiological perspective on attachment problems in sexual offenders and the role of selective serotonin reuptake inhibitors in the treatment of such problems. *Clinical Psychology Review, 25,* 153–182.

Beech, B., & Leather, P. (2006). Workplace violence in the health care sector: A review of staff training and integration of training evaluation models. *Aggression and Violent Behavior, 11,* 27–43.

Begg, P., Fido, M., & Skinner, K. (1991). *Jack the Ripper, A-Z.* London: Headline.

Begley, S. (2000). Getting inside the teen brain. *Newsweek,* February, p. 58.

Begun, J.H. (1976). The sociopathic or psychopathic personality. *International Journal of Social Psychiatry, 14,* 965–975.

Beirne, P. (2004). From animal abuse to interhuman violence? A critical review of the progression thesis. *Society and Animals, 12,* 39–65.

Belfrage, H. (1998). New evidence for a relation between mental disorder and crime. *British Journal of Criminology, 38,* 145–154.

Bell, M.D., & Vila, R.I. (1996). Homicide in homosexual victims: A study of 67 cases from the Broward County, Florida, Medical Examiner's office, 1982–1992, with special emphasis on "overkill." *American Journal of Forensic Medicine and Pathology, 17,* 65–69.

Bender, L., & Blau, A. (1937). The reaction of children to sexual relations with adults. *American Journal of Orthopsychiatry, 7,* 500–518.

Bender, L., & Curran, F.J. (1940). Children and adolescents who kill. *Journal of Criminal Psychopathology, 1,* 297.

Bender, L.G., Jurkanin, T.J., Sergevnin, V.A., & Dowling, J.L. (2005). *Critical issues in police discipline: Case studies.* Springfield, IL Charles C Thomas.

Bender, W.N., & McLaughlin, P.J. (1997). Weapons violence in schools: Strategies for teachers confronting violence and hostage situations. *Intervention in School and Clinic, 32,* 211–216.

Benedek, E.P., & Cornell, D.G. (1989). *Juvenile homicide.* Washington, DC: American Psychiatric Association Press.

Benedetti, J. (1972). *Gilles de Rais.* New York: Stein & Day.

Bennell, C., Jones, N.J., Taylor, P.J., & Snook, B. (2006). Validities and abilities in criminal profiling: A critique of the studies conducted by Richard Kocsis and his colleagues. *International Journal of Offender Therapy and Comparative Criminology, 50,* 344–360.

Bensley, L., Eenwyk, J.V., & Simmons, K.W. (2003). Childhood family violence history and women's risk for intimate partner violence and poor health. *American Journal of Preventive Medicine, 25,* 38–44.

Benson, M.L., & Moore, E. (1992). Are white-collar and common offenders the same? An empirical and theoretical critique of a recently proposed general theory of crime. *Journal of Research in Crime and Delinquency, 29,* 251–272.

Bentall, R.P., & Taylor, J.L. (2006). Psychological processes and paranoia: Implications for forensic behavioural science. *Behavioral Sciences and the Law, 24,* 277–294.

Berdahl, J.L., & Aquino, K. (2009). Sexual behavior at work: Fun or folly? *Journal of Applied Psychology, 94,* 34–47.

Beresford, H.R. (1988). Legal implications of epilepsy. *Epilepsia, 29,* S114–S121.

Bergen, P., & Pandey, S. (2006). The Madrassa scapegoat. *Washington Quarterly, 29,* 117–125.

Berkowitz, A. (1992). College men as perpetrators of acquaintance rape and sexual assault: A review of recent research. *College Health, 40,* 175–181.

Berkowitz, L. (1993). *Aggression: Its causes, consequences, and control.* Philadelphia: Temple University Press.

Berman, A., & Siegal, A.M. (1976). Adaptive and learning skills in juvenile delinquents: A neuropsychological analysis. *Journal of Learning Disabilities, 9,* 583–590.

Bernard, T.J. (1990). Angry aggression among the "truly disadvantaged." *Criminology, 28,* 73–96.

Bernard, T.J, Snipes, J.B., & Gerould, A.L. (2010). *Vold's theoretical criminology* (6th ed.). New York: Oxford University Press.

Berner, W., Berger, P., & Hill, A. (2003). Sexual sadism. *International Journal of Offender Therapy and Comparative Criminology, 47,* 383–395.

Bernet, W., Vnencak-Jones, C.L., Faraheny, N., & Montgomery, S.A. (2006). Bad nature, bad nurture, and testimony regarding MAOA and SLC6A4 genotyping at murder trials. *Journal of Forensic Science, 52,* 1362–1371.

Bernhardt, P.C. (1997). Influences of serotonin and testosterone on aggression and dominance: Convergence with social psychology. *Current Directions in Psychological Science, 6,* 44–48.

Bernstein, I.S. (1970). Primate status hierarchies. In L.A. Rosenblum (Ed.), *Primate Behavior* (Vol. I, pp. 71–109). New York: Academic Press.

Berry, C.M., Ones, D.S., & Sackett, P.R. (2007). Interpersonal deviance, organizational deviance, and their common correlates. *Journal of Applied Psychology, 92,* 410–424.

Best, J., & Hutchinson, M.M. (1996). The gang initiation rite as a motif in contemporary crime discourse. *Justice Quarterly, 13,* 383–404.

Beven, J.P., Hall, G., Froyland, I., Steels, B., & Golding, D. (2005). Restoration or renovation? Evaluating restorative justice outcomes. *Psychiatry, Psychology, and Law, 12,* 194–206.

Beyer, K., Mack, S.M., & Shelton, J.L. (2008). Investigative analysis of neonaticide: An exploratory study. *Criminal Justice and Behavior, 35,* 522–535.

Beyers, J.M., & Loeber, R. (2003). Untangling developmental relations between depressed mood and delinquency in male adolescents. *Journal of Abnormal Child Psychology, 31,* 247–266.

Bidinotto, R.J. (Ed.) (1996). *Criminal justice? The legal system vs. individual responsibility.* New York: Foundation for Economic Education.

Biederman, J. (2005). Attention-deficit hyperactivity disorder: A selective overview. *Biological Psychiatry, 59,* 829–835.

Biederman, J., Faraone, S., Keenan, K., Benjamin, J., Krifcher, B., Moore, C., Sprich-Buckminster, S., Ugaglia, K., Jellineck, M., Steingard, R., Spencer, T., Norman, D., Kolodny, R., Kraus, I., Perrin, J., Keller, M., & Tsaung, M. (1992). Further evidence for family-genetic risk factors in attention deficit hyperactivity disorder. *Archives of General Psychiatry, 49,* 728–738.

Bies, R.J., & Tripp, T.M. (2001). A passion for justice: The rationality and morality of revenge. In R. Copanzano (Ed.), *Justice in the workplace: From theory to practice* (pp. 197–208). Mahwah, NJ: Lawrence Erlbaum.

Binder, R.L., & McNeil, D.E. (1990). The relationship of gender to violent behavior in acutely disturbed psychiatric patients. *Journal of Clinical Psychiatry, 51,* 110–114.

Binder, R.L. (1995). Women clinicians and patient assaults. In B.S. Eichelman & A.C. Hartwig (Eds.), *Patient violence and the clinician* (pp. 21-32). Washington, DC: American Psychiatric Association.

Birbaumer, N., Veit, R., Lotze, M., Erb, M., & Hermann, C. (2005). Deficient fear conditioning in psychopathy: A functional magnetic resonance imaging study. *Archives of General Psychiatry, 62,* 799–805.

Birger, M., Swartz, M., & Cohen, D. (2003). Aggression: the testosterone-serotonin link. *Israel Medical Association Journal, 5,* 653–658.

Bishop, D.M. (2000). Juvenile offenders in the adult criminal justice system. In M. Tonry (Ed.), *Crime and justice: A review of research* (pp. 81–167). Chicago: University of Chicago Press.

Bjorkly, S. (1999). A ten-year prospective study of aggression in a secure unit for dangerous patients. *Scandinavian Journal of Psychology, 40,* 57–73.

Bjorkly, S. (2002a). Psychotic symptoms and violence toward others: A literature review of some preliminary findings. 1. *Delusions. Aggression and Violent Behavior, 7,* 605–615.

Bjorkly, S. (2002b). Psychotic symptoms and violence toward others: A literature review of some preliminary findings. 2. Hallucinations. *Aggression and Violent Behavior, 7,* 617–631.

Bjorkly, S. (2009). Risk and dynamics of violence in Asperger's syndrome: A systematic review of the literature. *Aggression and Violent Behavior, 14,* 306–312.

Bjorkqvist, K. (1994). Sex differences in physical, verbal, and indirect aggression: A review of recent research. *Sex Roles, 30,* 177–188.

Blaauw, E., Sheridan, L., & Winkel, F.W. (2002a). Designing antistalking legislation on the basis of victims' experiences and psychopathology. *Psychiatry, Psychology, and Law, 9,* 136–145.

Blaauw, E., Winkel, F.W., Arensman, E., Sheridan, L., & Freeve, A. (2002b). The toll of stalking: The relationship between features of stalking and psychopathology of victims. *Journal of Interpersonal Violence, 17,* 50–63.

Black, D. (1983). Crime as social control. *American Sociological Review, 48,* 34–45.

Black, D.W., Baumgard, C.H., & Bell, S.E. (1995). A 16- to 45-year follow-up of 71 men with antisocial personality disorder. *Comprehensive Psychiatry, 36,* 130–140.

Black, D.W., Gunter, T., Allen, J., Blum, N., Arndt, S., Wenman, G., & Sieleni, B. (2007). Borderline personality disorder in male and female offenders newly committed to prison. *Comprehensive Psychiatry, 48,* 400–405.

Black, S. (2009). Preteens and crime. *American School Board Journal,* March, pp. 36-37.

Blackburn, R., & Coid, J.W. (1999). Empirical clusters of DSM-III personality disorder in violent offenders. *Journal of Personality Disorders, 13,* 18–34.

Blair, D.T. (1991). Assaultive behavior: Does provocation begin in the front office? *Journal of Psychosocial Nursing, 29,* 21–26.

Blair, J. Mitchell, D., & Blair, K. (2005). *The psychopath: Emotion and the brain.* Malden, MA: Blackwell.

Blair, R.J.R. (2001). Neurocognitive models of aggression: The antisocial personality disorders and psychopathy. *Journal of Neurology, Neurosurgery, and Psychiatry, 71,* 727–731.

Blair, R.J.R. (2003). Neurobiological basis of psychopathy. *British Journal of Psychiatry, 182,* 5–7.

Blair, R.J.R. (2006). The emergence of psychopathy: Implications for the neuropsychological approach to developmental disorders. *Cognition, 101,* 414–442.

Blake, P.Y., Pincus, J.H., & Buckner, C. (1995). Neurologic abnormalities in murderers. *Neurology, 45,* 1641–1647.

Blanchard, G.T. (1991). Sexually abusive clergymen: A conceptual framework for intervention and recovery. *Pastoral Psychology, 39,* 237–245.

Blanchard, J.J., Brown, S.A., Horan, W.P., & Sherwood, A.R. (2000). Substance use disorders in schizophrenia: Review, integration, and a proposed model. *Clinical Psychology Review, 20,* 207–234.

Blanchard, R., Christensen, B.K., Strong, S.M., Cantor, J.M., Kuban, M.E., Klassen, P., & Dickey, R. (2002). Retrospective self-reports of childhood accidents causing unconsciousness in phallometrically diagnosed pedophiles. *Archives of Sexual Behavior, 31,* 511–526.

Blanchard, R., Klassen, P., Dickey, R., Kuban, M.E., & Blak, T. (2001). Sensitivity and specificity of the phallometric test for pedophilia in nonadmitting sex offenders. *Psychological Assessment, 13,* 118–126.

Blau, T.H. (1994). *Psychological services for law enforcement.* New York: Wiley.

Blazei, R.W., Iacono, W.G., & Krueger, R.F. (2006). Intergenerational transmission of antisocial behavior: How do kids become antisocial adults? *Applied and Preventive Psychology, 11,* 230–253.

Bloch, M., Rosenberg, N., & Koren, D. (2005). Risk factors associated with the development of postpartum mood disorders. *Journal of Affective Disorders, 88,* 9–18.

Block, J.H., & Block, J. (1980). The role of ego-control and ego-resiliency in the organization of behavior. In W.A. Collins (Ed.), *Minnesota symposia on child psychology* (Vol. 13, pp. 39–101). Hillsdale, NJ: Erlbaum.

Blount, E.C. (2003). *Occupational crime: Deterrence, investigation, and reporting in compliance with federal guidelines.* Boca Raton, FL: CRC Press.

Blount, W.R., Silverman, I.J., Sellers, C.S., & Seese, R.A. (1994). Alcohol and drug use among abused women who kill, abused women who don't, and their abusers. *Journal of Drug Issues, 24,* 165–177.

Bluestein, J. (2001). *Creating emotionally safe schools: A guide for educators and parents.* Deerfield Beach, FL: Health Communications, Inc.

Bluglass, R. (1979). The psychiatric assessment of homicide. *British Journal of Hospital Medicine, 22,* 366–367.

Blum, D. (1997). *Sex on the brain: The biological differences between men and women.* New York: Penguin.

Blum, L.N. (2000). *Force under pressure: How cops live and why they die.* New York: Lantern Books.

Blum, K., Braverman, E.R., Holder, J.M., Lubar, J.F., Monastra, V.J., Miller, D., Lubar, J.O., Chen, T.J., & Comings, D.E. (2000). Reward deficiency syndrome: A biogenetic model for the diagnosis and treatment of impulsive, addictive and compulsive behaviors. *Journal of Psychoactive Drugs, 32,* 1–112.

Blum, K., Sheridan, P.J., Wood, R.C., Braverman, E.R., Chen, T.J. and Comings, D.E. (1995). Dopamine D2 receptor gene variants: Association and linkage studies in impulsive-addictive-compulsive behavior. *Pharmacogenetics, 5,* 121–141.

Boat, B.W. (1995). The relationship between violence to children and violence to animals: An ignored link. *Journal of Interpersonal Violence, 10,* 229–235.

Bocij, P., & McFarlane, L. (2003). Cyberstalking: The technology of hate. *Police Journal, 76,* 204–221.

Bohm, J., & Alison, L. (2001). An exploratory study in methods of distinguishing destructive cults. *Psychology, Crime, and Law, 7,* 133–165.

Bohman, M. (1996). Predisposition to criminality: Swedish adoption studies in retrospect. *Ciba Foundation Symposium, 194,* 99–109.

Bolger, K.E., & Patterson, C.J. (2001). Pathways from child maltreatment to internalizing problems: Perceptions of control as mediators and moderators. *Development and Psychopathology, 13,* 913–940.

Bollmer, J.M., Harris, M.J., & Milich, R. (2006). Reactions to bullying and peer victimization: Narratives, physiological arousal, and personality. *Journal of Research in Personality, 40,* 803–828.

Bolz, F., Dudonis, K.J., & Schultz, D.P. (1996). *The counter-terrorism handbook: Tactics, procedures, and techniques.* Boca Raton: CRC Press.

Bond, M.R. (1984). The psychiatry of closed head injury. In N. Brooks (Ed.), *Closed head injury: Psychological, social, and family aspects* (pp. 148–178). New York: Oxford University Press.

Bongar, B. (2002). *The suicidal patient: Clinical and legal standards of care.* Washington DC: American Psychological Association.

Bonwick, R.L., & Morris, P.L.P. (1996). Posttraumatic stress disorder in elderly war veterans. *International Journal of Geriatric Psychiatry, 11,* 1071–1076.

Bools, C.N. (1996). Factitious illness by proxy: Munchausen syndrome by proxy. *British Journal of Psychiatry, 169,* 268–275.

Bools, C.N., Neale, B.A., & Meadow, S.R. (1994). Munchausen syndrome by proxy: A study of psychopathology. *Child Abuse and Neglect, 18,* 773–788.

Booth, A., Shelley, G., Mazur, A., Tharp, G., & Kittock, R. (1989). Testosterone and winning and losing in human competition. *Hormones and Behavior, 23,* 556–571.

Borum, R. (2003). Understanding the terrorist mindset. *FBI Law Enforcement Bulletin,* July, pp. 7–10.

Borum, R., Fein, R., Vossekuil, B., & Berglund, J. (1999). Threat assessment: Defining an approach for evaluating risk of targeted violence. *Behavioral Sciences and the Law, 17,* 323–337.

Boss, P. (1999). *Ambiguous loss: Learning to live with unresolved grief.* Cambridge, MA: Harvard University Press.

Boss, P.G. (2002). Ambiguous loss: Working with families of the missing. *Family Process, 41,* 14–17.

Bourget, D., & Bradford, J.M.W. (1990). Homicidal parents. *Canadian Journal of Psychiatry, 35,* 233–238.

Bourget, D., & Gagne, P. (2002). Maternal filicide in Quebec. *Journal of the American Academy of Psychiatry and the Law, 30,* 345–351.

Bourget, D., & Gagne, P. (2005). Paternal filicide in Quebec. *Journal of the American Academy of Psychiatry and the Law, 33,* 354–360.

Bourget, D., & Gagne, P. (2006). Fratricide: A forensic psychiatric perspective. *Journal of the American Academy of Psychiatry and the Law, 34,* 29–33.

Bourget, D., Gagne, P., & Labelle, M.E. (2007a). Parricide: A comparative study of matricide versus patricide. *Journal of the American Academy of Psychiatry and the Law, 35,* 306–312.

Bourget, D., Gagne, P., & Moami, J. (2000). Spousal homicide and suicide in Quebec. *Journal of the American Academy of Psychiatry and the Law, 28,* 179–182.

Bourget, D., Grace, J., & Whitehurst, L. (2007b). A review of maternal and paternal filicide. *Journal of the American Academy of Psychiatry and the Law, 35,* 74–82.

Bourget, D., & Labelle, A. (1992). Homicide, infanticide, and filicide. *Psychiatric Clinics of North America, 15,* 661–673.

Bourget, D., & Whitehurst, L. (2004). Capgras syndrome: A review of the neuro physiological correlates and presenting clinical features in cases involving physical violence. *Canadian Journal of Psychiatry, 49,* 719–725.

Bowker, A.L. (1994). Handle with care: Dealing with offenders who are mentally retarded. *FBI Law Enforcement Bulletin,* July, pp. 12–16.

Bowlby, J. (1969). *Attachment and loss. Vol. 1: Attachment.* New York: Basic Books.

Bowlby, J. (1973). *Attachment and loss. Vol. 2: Separation: Anxiety and anger.* New York: Basic Books.

Bowlby, J. (1980). *Attachment and loss. Vol. 3: Separation: Sadness and depression.* New York: Basic Books.

Bowlby, J. (1988). *A secure base: Clinical applications of attachment theory.* London: Routledge.

Bowling, N.A., & Beehr, T.A. (2006). Workplace harassment from the victim's perspective: A theoretical model and meta-analysis. *Journal of Applied Psychology, 91,* 998–1012.

Boxer, P.A. (1993). Assessment of potential violence in the paranoid worker. *Journal of Occupational Medicine, 35,* 122–131.

Boyd, N. (2000). *The beast within: Why men are violent.* Vancouver, BC: Greystone Books.

Boyle, P. (2006). Curfews and crime. *Youth Today, 15,* 1–36.

Bradley, C.A. (2002). The juvenile death penalty and international law. *Duke Law Journal, 52,* 485.

Bradley, D. (2003). Perspectives on newborn abandonment. *Pediatric Emergency Care, 19,* 108–111.

Braga, A.A., Kennedy, D.M., & Tita, G.E. (2002). New approaches to the strategic prevention of gang and group-involved violence. In C.R. Huff (Ed.), *Gangs in America III* (pp. 271–285). Thousand Oaks, CA: Sage.

Brain, P. (1993). Hormonal aspects of aggression and violence. In A. Reiss & J. Roth (Eds.), *Understanding and preventing violence* (pp. 173–244). Washington, DC: National Academy Press.

Braithwaite, J. (1981). The myth of social class and criminality reconsidered. *American Sociological Review, 46,* 36–57.

Braithwaite, J. (1999). Restorative justice: Assessing optimistic and pessimistic accounts. In M. Tonry (Ed.), *Crime and justice: A review of research* (Vol. 25, pp. 1–127). Chicago: University of Chicago Press.

Braithwaite, J. (2002). *Restorative justice and responsive regulation.* New York: Oxford University Press.

Braithwaite, J., & Strang, H. (2001). Introduction: Restorative justice and civil society. In H. Strang & J. Braithwaite (Eds.), *Restorative justice and civil society* (pp. 1–13). Cambridge: Cambridge University Press.

Brand, S., Felner, R., Shim, M., Seitsinger, A., & Dumas, T. (2003). Middle school improvement and reform: Development and validation of a school-level assessment of climate, cultural pluralism, and school safety. *Journal of Educational Psychology, 95,* 570–588.

Brannigan, A. (1998). Criminology and the Holocaust: Xenophobia, evolution, and genocide. *Crime and Delinquency, 44,* 257–276.

Brannigan, A., & Hardwick, K.H. (2003). Genocide and general theory. In C.L. Britt & M.R. Gottfredson (Eds.), *Control theories of crime and delinquency* (pp. 109–131). New Brunswick, NJ: Transaction Press.

Braverman, M. (1999). *Preventing workplace violence: A guide for employers and practitioners.* Thousand Oaks, CA: Sage.

Bray, A. (2003). Moral responsibility and borderline personality disorder. *Australian and New Zealand Journal of Psychiatry, 37,* 270–276.

Breier, A., & Astrachan, B.M. (1984). Characteristics of schizophrenic patients who commit suicide. *American Journal of Psychiatry, 141,* 206–209.

Breitenbecher, K.H. (2001). Sexual revictimization among women: A review of the literature focusing on empirical investigations. *Aggression and Violent Behavior, 6,* 415–432.

Bremner, J.D. (1999). Does stress damage the brain? *Biological Psychiatry, 45,* 797–805.

Bremner, J.D. (2005a). Effects of traumatic stress on brain structure and function: Relevance to early responses to trauma. *Journal of Trauma and Dissociation, 6,* 51–68.

Bremner, J.D. (2005b). *Does stress damage the brain? Understanding trauma-related disorders from a mind-body perspective.* New York: Norton.

Brems, C., & Johnson, M.E. (1997). Clinical implications of the co-occurrence of substance use and other psychiatric disorders. *Professional Psychology: Research and Practice, 28,* 437–447.

Brennan, J., Andrews, G., Morris-Yates, A., & Pollock, C. (1990). An examination of defense style in parents who abuse children. *Journal of Nervous and Mental Disease, 178,* 592–595.

Brennan, P.A., Grecian, E.L., Mortensen, E.L., & Mednick, S.A. (2002). Relationship of maternal smoking during pregnancy with criminal arrest and hospitalization for substance abuse in male and female offspring. *American Journal of Psychiatry, 159,* 48–54.

Brennan, P.A., Mednick, S.A., & Hodgins, S. (2000). Major mental disorders and criminal violence in a Danish birth cohort. *Archives of General Psychiatry, 57,* 494–500.

Brennan, P.A., Mednick, S.A., & Jacobsen, B. (1996). Assessing the role of genetics in crime using adoption cohorts. *Ciba Foundation Symposium, 194,* 115–123.

Breslau, N., & Davis, G.C. (1992). Posttraumatic stress disorder in an urban population of young adults. *Archives of General Psychiatry, 149,* 671–675.

Breslau, N., Davis, G.C., Andreski, P., & Peterson, E. (1991). Traumatic events and posttraumatic stress disorder in an urban population of young adults. *Archives of General Psychiatry, 48,* 216–222.

Breslau, N., Kessler, R.C., Chilcoat, H.D., Schultz, L.R., Davis, G.C., & Andreski, P. (1998). Trauma and posttraumatic stress disorder in the community: The 1996 Detroit Area Survey of Trauma. *Archives of General Psychiatry, 55,* 626–632.

Brewster, A., Scalora, M.J., Elbogen, E.B., & Moore, Y.S. (2003). Attempted suicide by cop: A case study of traumatic brain injury and the insanity defense. *Journal of Forensic Science, 48,* 190–194.

Brewster, A.L., Nelson, J.P., & Hymel, K.P. (1998). Victim, perpetrator, family, and incident characteristics of 32 infant maltreatment deaths in the United States Air Force. *Child Abuse and Neglect, 22,* 91–101.

Brewster, M.P. (2000). Stalking by former intimates: Verbal threats and other predictors of physical violence. *Violence and Victims, 15,* 41–54.

Brewster, M.P. (2003). Power and control dynamics in prestalking and stalking situations. *Journal of Family Violence, 18,* 207–217.

Brezina, T. (1999). Teenage violence toward parents as an adaptation of family strain. *Youth and Society, 30,* 416–444.

Brickman, A.S., McManus, M., Grapentine, W.L., & Alessi, N. (1984). Neuropsychological assessment of seriously delinquent adolescents. *Journal of the American Academy of Child Psychiatry, 23,* 453–457.

Bridges-Parlet, S., Knopman, D., & Thompson, T. (1994). A descriptive study of physically aggressive behavior in dementia by direct observation. *Journal of the American Geriatrics Society, 42,* 192–197.

Briggs, F., & Hawkins, R. (1995). Protecting boys from the risk of sexual abuse. *Early Child Development and Care, 110,* 19–32.

Bright, D.A. (1994). Postpartum mental disorders. *American Family Physician, 50,* 595–598.

Briken, P., Haberman, N., Kafka, M.P., Berner, W., & Hill, A. (2006). The paraphilia-related disorders: An investigation of the relevance of the concept in sexual murderers. *Journal of Forensic Sciences, 51,* 683–688.

Brinded, M.J., Stevens, I., & Mulder, R.T. (1999). The Christchurch prisons psychiatric epidemiology study: Methodology and prevalence rates for psychiatric disorders. *Criminal Behavior and Mental Health, 9,* 131–143.

Brink, J.H., Doherty, D., & Boer, A. (2001). Mental disorder in federal offenders: A Canadian prevalence study. *International Journal of Law and Psychiatry, 24,* 339–356.

Britt, C.L., & Gottfredson, M.R. (2003). *Advances in criminological theory: Control theories of crime and delinquency.* New Brunswick, NJ: Transaction Press.

Brittain, R. (1970). The sadistic murderer. *Medicine, Science and the Law, 10,* 198–207.

Brocker, J., & Rubin, J.Z. (1985). *Entrapment in escalating conflicts.* New York: Springer-Verlag.

Brockington, I. F. (1996). *Motherhood and mental health.* Oxford: Oxford University Press.

Brodsky, S.L. (2010). *Psychotherapy with coerced and reluctant clients.* Washington, DC: American Psychological Association.

Brooks, N., Campsie, L., Symington, C., Beattie, A., & McKinlay, W. (1986). The five year outcome of severe blunt head injury: A relative's view. *Journal of Neurology, Neurosurgery, and Psychiatry, 49,* 764–770.

Brophy-Baermann, B., & Conybeare, J.A.C. (1994). Retaliating against terrorism: Rational expectations and the optimality of rules versus discretion. *American Journal of Political Science, 38,* 196–210.

Broude, G.J., & Greene, S.J. (1978). Cross-cultural codes on 20 sexual attitudes and practices. *Ethnology, 15,* 409–340.

Brower, M.C., & Price, B.H. (2001a). Neuropsychological correlates of self-reported impulsive aggression in a college sample. *Personality and Individual Differences, 23,* 961–965.

Brower, M.C., & Price, B.H. (2001b). Neuropsychiatry of frontal lobe dysfunction in violent and criminal behavior: Critical review. *Journal of Neurology, Neurosurgery, and Psychiatry, 71,* 720–726.

Brown, D.E. (1991). *Human universals.* New York: McGraw-Hill.

Browne, A. (1987). *When battered women kill.* New York: Free Press.

Browne, A., & Williams, K.R. (1989). Exploring the effect of resource availability and the likelihood of female-perpetrated homicides. *Law and Society Review, 23,* 75–94.

Browne, K.D., & Hamilton, C.E. (1998). Physical violence between young adults and their parents: Associations with a history of child maltreatment. *Journal of Family Violence, 13,* 59–79.

Browne, K.D., & Lynch, M. (1995). The nature and extent of child homicide and fatal abuse. *Child Abuse Review, 4,* 309–316.

Brownell, P. (1996). Domestic violence in the workplace: An emergent issue. *Crisis Intervention, 3,* 335–351.

Browning, C. (1992). *Ordinary men: Reserve Police Battalion 101 and the Final Solution in Poland.* New York: HarperCollins.

Brownmiller, S. (1975). *Against our will: Men, women, and rape.* New York: Simon & Schuster.

Brunner, H.G. (1996). MAOA deficiency and abnormal behavior: Perspectives on an association. *Cibo Foundation Symposium, 194,* 155–164.

Brozovsky, M., & Falit, H. (1971). Neonaticide: Clinical and psychodynamic considerations. *Journal of the American Academy of Child Psychiatry, 10,* 673–683.

Brush, L. (2003). Effects of work on hitting and hurting. *Violence Against Women, 9,* 1213–1230.

Bryan, J.W., Freed, F.W. (1982). Corporal punishment: Normative data and sociological and psychological correlates in a community college population. *Journal of Youth and Adolescence, 11,* 77–87.

Bryant, E.T., Scott, M.L., Golden, C.J., & Tori, C.D. (1984). Neuropsychological deficits, learning disability, and violent behavior. *Journal of Consulting and Clinical Psychology, 57,* 323–324.

Buchanan, A., & Leese, M. (2001). Detention of people with dangerous severe personality disorders: A systematic review. *Lancet, 358,* 1955–1959.

Buchanan, A., Reed, A., Wessely, S., Garety, P., Taylor, P., Grubin, D., & Dunn, G. (1993). Acting on delusions II: The phenomenological correlates of acting on delusions. *British Journal of Psychiatry, 163,* 77–81.

Bucy, P.C., & Kluver, H. (1955). An anatomical investigation of the temporal lobe in the monkey (Maccaca mulatta). *Journal of Comparative Neurology, 103,* 151–251.

Budiansky, S., Gregory, S., Schmidt, K.F., & Bierk, R. (1994). Local TV: Mayhem central. *U.S. News and World Report* (March 4), pp. 63–64.

Bulatao, E.Q., & VandenBos, G.R. (1996). Workplace violence: Its scope and the issues. In G.R. VandenBos & E.Q. Bulatao (Eds.), *Violence on the job: Identifying risks and developing solutions* (pp. 1–23). Washington, DC: American Psychological Association.

Bullock, C.F., & Cubert, J. (2002). Coverage of domestic violence fatalities by newspapers in Washington State. *Journal of Interpersonal Violence, 17,* 475–499.

Bureau of Justice Statistics. (1998). *Violence between intimates: Analysis of data on crimes by current or former spouses, boyfriends, and girlfriends.* Washington, DC: National Institute of Justice.

Bureau of Justice Statistics. (2003). *Crime in the United States, 1976–2000.* Washington, DC: National Institute of Justice.

Burgess, A.W., & Baker, T. (2002). Cyberstalking. In J.C.W. Boon & L. Sheridan (Eds.), *Stalking and psychosexual obsession: Psychological perspectives for prevention, policing, and treatment* (pp. 201–219). Chichester, UK: Wiley.

Burgess, A.W., Baker, T., Greening, D., Hartman, C., Burgess, A.G., & Douglas, J.E. (1997). Stalking behaviors within domestic violence. *Journal of Family Violence, 12,* 389–403.

Burgess, A.W., Groth, A.N., Holstrom, L.L., & Sgroi, S.M. (1978). *Sexual assault of children and adolescents.* Lexington, MA: D.C. Heath.

Burgess, A.W., Harner, H., Baker, T., Hartman, C.R., & Lole, C. (2001). Batterers' stalking patterns. *Journal of Family Violence, 16,* 309–321.

Burgess, A.W., Hartman, C.R., Ressler, R.K., Douglas, J.E., & McCormack, A. (1986). Sexual homicide: A motivational model. *Journal of Interpersonal Violence, 1,* 251–272.

Burke, A.S. (2007). Domestic violence as a crime of pattern and intent: An alternative reconceptualization. *George Washington Law Review, 75,* 552–612.

Burleigh, M. (2009). *Blood and rage: A cultural history of terrorism.* New York: Harper/HarperCollins.

Burns, J.M., & Swerdlow, R.H. (2003). Right orbitofrontal tumor with pedophilia symptom and constructional apraxia sign. *Archives of Neurology, 60,* 437–440.

Burns, R., & Crawford, C. (1999). School shootings, the media, and public fear: Ingredients for a moral panic. *Crime, Law and Social Change, 32,* 147–168.

Bursik, R., & Grasmick, H. (1993). *Neighborhoods and crime: The dimensions of effective community control.* Lexington, KY: Lexington Books.

Burt, M.R. (1980). Cultural myths and supports for rape. *Journal of Personality and Social Psychology, 38,* 217–130.

Burt, M.R. (1984). Justifying personal violence: A comparison of rapist and the general public. *Victimology: An International Journal, 8,* 131–150.

Burt, S.A. (2009). Are there meaningful etiological differences within antisocial behavior? Results of a meta-analysis. *Clinical Psychology Review, 29,* 163–178.

Burt, S.A., & Donnellan, M.B. (2008). Personality correlates of aggressive and non-aggressive antisocial behavior. *Personality and Individual Differences, 44,* 53–63.

Burt, S.A., Krueger, R.F., McGue, M., & Iacono, W.G. (2001). Sources of covariation among attention-deficit/hyperactivity disorder, oppositional defiant disorder, and conduct disorder: The importance of shared environment. *Journal of Abnormal Psychology, 11,* 516–525.

Burt, S.A., & Larson, C.L. (2007). Differential affective responses in those with aggressive versus non-aggressive antisocial behaviors. *Personality and Individual Differences, 43,* 1481–1492.

Burton, D., Foy, D., Bwanausi, C., Johnson, J., & Moore, L. (1994). The relationship between traumatic exposure, family dysfunction, and posttraumatic stress symptoms in male juvenile offenders. *Journal of Traumatic Stress, 7,* 83–92.

Busby, D.M. (2005). *The impact of violence on the family: Treatment approaches for therapists and other professionals.* Boston: Allyn & Bacon.

Busch, A.B., & Shore, M.F. (2000). Seclusion and restraint: A review of the literature. *Harvard Review of Psychiatry, 8,* 261–270.

Bush, D.E., & O'Shea, P.G. (1996). Workplace violence: Comparative use of prevention practices and policies. In G.R. Vandenbos & E.Q. Bulatao (Eds.), *Violence on the job: Identifying risks and developing solutions* (pp. 283–297). Washington DC: American Psychological Association.

Buss, D.M. (1994a). The strategies of human mating. *American Scientist, 82,* 238–249.

Buss, D.M. (1994b). *The evolution of desire: Strategies of human mating.* New York: Basic Books.

Buss, D.M. (2000). *The dangerous passion: Why jealousy is as necessary as love and sex.* New York: Free Press.

Buss, D.M. (2003). *The evolution of desire: Strategies of human mating* (rev. ed.). New York: Free Press.

Buss, D.M. (2004). *Evolutionary psychology: The new science of the mind* (2nd ed.). New York: Allyn & Bacon.

Buss, D.M. (2008). *Evolutionary psychology: The new science of the mind* (3rd ed.). Boston: Allyn & Bacon.

Buss, D.M., & Duntley, J.D. (2003). Homicide: an evolutionary perspective and implications for public policy. In N. Dess (Ed.), *Violence and public policy* (pp. 233–257). Westport, CT: Greenwood.

Buss, D.M., & Duntley, J.D. (2004). The evolution of gender differences in aggression. In S. Fein (Ed.), *Gender and aggression* (pp. 66–84). New York: Guilford.

Buss, D.M., & Malamuth, N.M. (1996). *Sex, power, conflict: Evolutionary and feminist perspectives.* New York: Oxford University Press.

Buteau, J., Lesage, A.D., & Kiely, M.C. (1993). Homicide followed by suicide: A Quebec case series, 1988–1990. *Canadian Journal of Psychiatry, 38,* 552–556.

Butler, P. (2002). Terrorism and utilitarianism: Lessons from, and for, criminal law. *Journal of Criminal Law and Criminology, 93,* 1–22.

Byrne, M.K. (2003). Trauma reactions in the offender. *International Journal of Forensic Psychology, 1,* 59–70.

Cadoret, R.J., Troughton, E., & O'Gorman, T.W. (1987). Genetic and environmental factors in alcohol abuse and antisocial personality. *Journal of Studies on Alcohol, 48,* 1–8.

Caetano, R., McGrath, C., Ramisetty-Mickle, S., & Field, C.A. (2005). Drinking, alcohol problems and the five year recurrence and incidence of male to female and female to male partner violence. *Alcoholism: Clinical and Experimental Research, 29,* 98–106.

Cairns, R.B., & Cairns, B.D. (1994). *Lifelines and risks: Pathways of youth in our time.* Cambridge, UK: Cambridge University Press.

Calabrese, J.R., Hirschfield, M.A., & Reed, M. (2003). Impact of bipolar disorder on a US community sample. *Journal of Clinical Psychiatry, 64,* 425–432.

Calder, M.C. (2004). The Internet: Potential problems and pathways to hands-on sexual offending. In M.C. Calder (Ed.), *Child sexual abuse and the Internet: Tackling the new frontier* (pp. 1–24). Lyme Regis, UK: Russell House.

Caldwell, C.B., & Gottesmann, I.I. (1990). Schizophrenics kill themselves too: A review of risk factors for suicide. *Schizophrenia Bulletin, 16,* 571–589.

Caldwell, M.F. (2002). What we do not know about juvenile sexual reoffense risk. *Child Maltreatment, 7,* 291–302.

Caldwell, M.F. (2007). Sexual offense adjudication and sexual recidivism among juvenile offenders. *Sexual Abuse: A Journal of Research and Treatment, 19,* 107–113.

Calkins, S.D., & Fox, N.A. (2002). Self-regulatory processes in early personality development: A multilevel approach to the study of childhood social withdrawal and aggression. *Development and Psychopathology, 14,* 477–498.

Campbell, A. (1995). A few good men: Evolutionary psychology and female adolescent aggression. *Ethology and Sociobiology, 16,* 99–123.

Campbell, J.C. (1992a). A review of nursing research on battering. In C. Sampselle (Ed.), *Violence against women: Nursing research, education, and practice issues* (pp. 69–89). London: Taylor & Francis.

Campbell, J.C. (1992b). If I can't have you, no one can: Power and control in homicide of female partners. In J. Radford & D.E. Russell (Eds.), *Femicide: The politics of woman killing* (pp. 99–113). New York: Twayne.

Campbell, J.C. (1995). Prediction of homicide of and by battered women. In J.C. Campbell (Ed.), *Assessing dangerousness: Potential for further violence of sexual offenders, batterers, and child abusers* (pp. 93–113). Thousand Oaks, CA: Sage.

Campbell, J.C. (2002). Health consequences of intimate partner violence. *Lancet, 359,* 1331–1336.

Campbell, J.C., Sharps, P., & Glass, N. (2001). Risk assessment for intimate partner homicide. In G-F. Pinard & L. Pagani (Eds.), *Clinical assessment of dangerousness: Empirical contributions* (pp. 136–157). New York: Cambridge University Press.

Campbell, J.C., & Soeken, K. (1999). Forced sex and intimate partner violence: Effects on women's risk and women's health. *Violence Against Women, 5,* 1017–1035.

Campbell, J.C., Webster, D., Koziol-McLain, J., Block, C.R., Campbell, D., & Curry, M.A. (2003a). Assessing risk factors for intimate partner homicide. *National Institute of Justice Journal, 250,* 14–19.

Campbell, J.C., Webster, D., Koziol-McLain, J., Block, C.R., Campbell, D., & Curry, M.A. (2003b). Risk factors for femicide in abusive relationships: Results from a multi-site case control study. *American Journal of Public Health, 93,* 1089–1097.

Campbell, N.A. (1996). *Biology* (4th ed.). Palo Alto, CA: Benjamin Cummings.

Campion, J.F., Cravens, J.M., & Coven, F. (1988). A study of filicidal men. *American Journal of Psychiatry, 145,* 1141–1144.

Campion, J.F., Cravens, J.M., & Rotholc, A. (1985). A study of 15 matricidal men. *American Journal of Psychiatry, 142,* 312–317.

Campsie, R.L., Geller, S.K., & Campsie, M.E. (2006). Combat stress. In C.H. Kennedy & E.A. Zillmer (Eds.), *Military psychology: Clinical and operational applications* (pp. 215–240). New York: Guilford.

Canter, D.V. (1994). *Criminal shadows: Inside the mind of the serial killer.* London: Harper Collins.

Canter, D.V. (2004). Offender profiling and investigative psychology. *Journal of Investigative Psychology and Offender profiling, 1,* 1–15.

Canter, D.V., Bennell, C., Alison, L.J., & Reddy, S. (2003). Differentiating sex offenses: A behaviorally based thematic classification of stranger rapes. *Behavioral Sciences and the Law, 21,* 157–174.

Canter, D.V., Missen, C., & Hodge, S. (1996). Are serial killers special? *Policing Today, 2,* 1–12.

Canter, D.V., & Wentink, N. (2004). An empirical test of Holmes & Holmes's serial murder typology. *Criminal Justice and Behavior, 31,* 489–515.

Cantor, C.H., Mullen, P.E., & Alpers, P.A. (2000). Mass homicide: The civil massacre. *Journal of the American Academy of Psychiatry and the Law, 28,* 55–63.

Cantor, J.M., Kabani, N., Christensen, B.K., Zipursky, R.B., & Barbaree, H.E. (2008). Cerebral white matter deficiencies in pedophilic men. *Journal of Psychiatric Research, 42,* 167–183.

Capaldi, D.M., & Kim, H.K. (2007). Typological approaches to violence in couples: A critique and alternative conceptual approach. *Clinical Psychology Review, 27,* 253–265.

Capgras, J., & Reboul-Lachaux, J. (1923/1994). L'illusion des 'sosies' dans un delire systematize chronique. *History of Psychiatry, 5,* 117–130.

Caponigro, J.R. (1999). *The crisis counselor: A step-by-step guide to managing a business crisis.* Chicago: Contemporary Books.

Caprara, G.V., Barbaranelli, C., & Zimbardo, P.G. (1996). Understanding the complexity of human aggression: Affective, cognitive, and social dimensions of individual differences in propensity toward aggression. *European Journal of Personality, 10,* 133–155.

Caraulia, A.P., & Steiger, L.K. (1997). *Nonviolent crisis intervention: Learning to defuse explosive behavior.* Brookfield: CPI Publishing.

Carcara, W.S. (2009). Advising houses of worship on a comprehensive and balanced security plan. *The Police Chief,* July, pp. 54–57.

Cardasis, W., Huth-Bocks, A., & Silk, K.R. (2008). Tattoos and antisocial personality disorder. *Personality and Mental Health, 2,* 171–182.

Carlo, G., Fabes, R.A., Laible, D., & Kupanoff, K. (1999). Early adolescence and prosocial/moral behavior II: The role of social and contextual influences. *Journal of Early Adolescence, 19,* 133–147.

Carney, A.G., & Merrell, K.W. (2001). Bullying in schools: Perspectives on understanding and preventing an international problem. *School Psychology International, 22,* 364–382.

Carpentier, M., Silvosky, J.F., & Chaffin, M. (2006). Randomized trial of treatment for children with sexual behavior problems: Ten-year follow-up. *Journal of Consulting and Clinical Psychology, 74,* 482–488.

Carter, R.T., & Forsyth, J.M. (2009). A guide to the forensic assessment of race-based traumatic stress reactions. *Journal of the American Academy of Psychiatry and the Law, 37,* 28–40.

Cartwright, R. (2004). Sleepwalking violence: A sleep disorder, a legal dilemma, and a psychological challenge. *American Journal of Psychiatry, 161,* 1149–1158.

Cascardi, M., O'Leary, K.D., & Schlee, K.A. (1999). Co-occurrence and correlates of posttraumatic stress disorder and major depression in physically abused women. *Journal of Family Violence, 14,* 227–249.

Casey, B.J., Getz, S., Galvan, A. (2008). The adolescent brain. *Developmental Review, 28,* 62–77.

Casey, E.A., & Nurius, P.S. (2005). Trauma exposure and sexual revictimization risk comparisons across single, multiple incident, and multiple perpetrator victimizations. *Violence Against Women, 11,* 505–530.

Cashdan, E. (1993). Attracting mates: Effects of paternal investment on mate attraction strategies. *Ethology and Sociobiology, 14,* 1–23.

Caspi, A. (2000). The child is father of the man: Personality continuities from childhood to adulthood. *Journal of Personality and Social Psychology, 78,* 158–172.

Caspi, A., Harrington, H., Milne, B., Amell, J.W., Theodore, R.F., & Moffitt, T.E. (2003). Children's behavioral styles at age 3 are linked to their adult personality traits at age 26. *Journal of Personality, 71,* 495–513.

Caspi, A., McClay, J., Moffitt, T.E., Mill, J., Martin, J., Craig, I.W., Taylor, A., & Poulton, R. (2002). Role of genotype in the cycle of violence in maltreated children. *Science, 297,* 851–854.

Caspi, A., & Moffitt, T.E. (2006). Gene-environment interactions in psychiatry: Joining forces with neuroscience. *Nature Reviews Neuroscience, 7,* 583–590.

Caspi, A., Moffitt, T.E., Newman, D.L., & Silva, P.A. (1996). Behavioral observations at age 3 years predict adult psychiatric disorders. *Archives of General Psychiatry, 53,* 1033–1039.

Caspi, A., & Silva, P.A. (1995). Temperamental qualities at age three predict personality traits in young adulthood: Longitudinal evidence from a birth cohort. *Child Development, 66,* 486–498.

Caspi, A., Sugden, K., Moffitt, T.E., Taylor, A., Craig, A.W., Harrington, H., McClay, J., Mill, J., Martin, J., Braithwaite, A., & Poulton, R. (2003). Influence of life stress on depression: Moderation by a polymorphism in the 5-HTT gene. *Science, 301,* 386–389.

Cassidy, F., Ahearn, E.P., & Carrol, B.J. (2001). Substance abuse in bipolar disorder. *Bipolar Disorders, 3,* 181–188.

Casu, G., Cascella, N., & Maggini, C. (1994). Homicides in Capgras's syndrome. *Psychopathology, 27,* 281–284.

Catterall, J.S. (1998). Risk and resilience in student transitions to high school. *American Journal of Education, 106,* 302–333.

Cauffman, E., Feldman, S.S., Waterman, J., & Steiner, H. (1998). Posttraumatic stress disorder among female juvenile offenders. *Journal of the American Academy of Child and Adolescent Psychiatry, 37,* 1209–1216.

Cauffman, E., & Steinberg, L. (2000). (Im)maturity of judgment in adolescence: Why adolescents may be less culpable than adults. *Behavioral Sciences and the Law, 18,* 1–21.

Cauffman, E., Steinberg, L., & Piquero, A.R. (2005). Psychological, neuropsychological and physiological correlates of serious antisocial behavior in adolescents: The role of self-control. *Criminology, 43,* 133–176.

Cavanaugh, K., & Dobash, R.P. (2007). The murder of children by fathers in the context of child abuse. *Child Abuse and Neglect, 31,* 747–755.

Chadwick, P., & Birchwood, M. (1994). The omnipotence of voices: A cognitive approach to auditory hallucinations. *British Journal of Psychiatry, 164,* 190–201.

Chaffin, M. (2008). Our minds are made up–don't confuse us with the facts: Commentary on policies concerning children with sexual behavior problems and juvenile sex offenders. *Child Maltreatment, 13,* 110–121.

Chagnon, N. (1988). Life histories, blood revenge, and warfare in a tribal population. *Science, 239,* 985–992.

Chaiken, J.M., Chaiken, M.R., & Rhodes, W. (1994). Predicting violent behavior and classifying violent offenders. In A.J. Reiss & J.A. Roth (Eds.), *Understanding and preventing violence. Volume 4: Consequences and control* (pp. 217–295). Washington, DC: National Academy Press.

Chalk, F., & Jonassohn, K. (1990). *The history and sociology of genocide: Analyses and case studies.* New Haven, CT: Yale University Press.

Chamberlain, P. (2003). *Treating chronic juvenile offenders: Advances made through the Oregon Multidimensional Treatment Foster Care model.* Washington, DC: American Psychological Association.

Chamberlain, T.J. (1986). The dynamics of parricide. *American Journal of Forensic Psychiatry, 7,* 11–23.

Chan, H.C.O., & Heide, K.M. (2009). Sexual homicide: A synthesis of the literature. *Trauma, Violence, and Abuse, 10,* 31–54.

Chang, J., Berg, C.J., Saltzman, L.E., & Herndon, J. (2005). Homicide: A leading cause of injury deaths among pregnant and postpartum women in the United States, 1991–1999. *American Journal of Public Health, 95,* 471–477.

Charles, A.V. (1986). Physically abused parents. *Journal of Family Violence, 1,* 343–355.

Charles, S.T., Reynolds, C.A., & Gatz, M. (2001). Age-related differences and change in positive and negative affect over 23 years. *Journal of Personality and Social Psychology, 80,* 136–151.

Chemtob, C.M., Hamada, R.S., Roitblat, H.L., & Muraoka, M. (1994). Anger, impulsivity and anger control in combat related posttraumatic stress disorder. *Journal of Consulting and Clinical Psychology, 62,* 827–832.

Chen, P., & Spector, P. (1992). Relationships of work stressors with aggression, withdrawal, theft, and substance use: An exploratory study. *Journal of Occupational and Organizational Psychology, 65,* 177–184.

Chen, P.S., Chen, S.J., Yang, Y.K., Yeh, T.L., Chen, C.C., & Lo, H.Y. (2003). Asperger's disorder: A case report of repeated stealing and the collecting behaviors of an adolescent patient. *Acta Psychiatrica Scandinavica, 107,* 73–76.

Chen, W.J.A., & West, J.R. (1999). Alcohol-induced brain damage during development: Potential risk factors. In J.H. Hannigan, L.P. Spear, N.E. Spear & C.R. Goodlet (Eds.), *Alcohol and alcoholism: Effects on brain and development* (pp. 17–37). Mahwah, NJ: Erlbaum.

Chesterman, P., & Rutter, S.C. (1994). A case report: Asperger's syndrome and sexual offending. *Journal of Forensic Psychiatry, 4,* 555–562.

Chertwood, D. (1988). Is there a season for homicide? *Criminology, 26,* 287–306.

Cicchetti, D., & Beeghly, M. (1987). Symbolic development in maltreated young-sters: An organizational perspective. *New Directions for Child Development, 36,* 5–29.

Cicchetti, D., & Manly, J.T. (2001). Operationalizing child maltreatment: Developmental processes and outcomes. *Development and Psychopathology, 4,* 123–140.

Cicchetti, D., & Rogosch, F.A. (1997). The role of self-organization in the promotion of resilience in maltreated children. *Development and Psychopathology, 9,* 797–815.

Cicchetti, D., Rogosch, F.A., Lynch, M., & Holt, K.D. (1993). Resilience in maltreat-ed children: Processes leading to adaptive outcome. *Development and Psychopathology, 5,* 629–647.

Cillissen, A.H.N., & Mayeux, L. (2007). Variations in tha association between aggres-sion and social status: Theoretical and empirical perspectives. In P.H. Hawley, T.D. Little & P.C. Rodkin (Eds.), *Aggression and adaptation: The bright side to bad behavior* (pp. 135–156). Mahwah, NJ: Lawrence Erlbaum.

Clagett, R. (2004). After the echo. *Police,* March, pp. 42–49.

Clare, I.C.H., & Gudjonsson, G.H. (1993). Interrogative suggestibility, confabulation and acquiescence in people with mild learning disabilities (mental handicap): Implications for reliability during police interview. *British Journal of Clinical Psychology, 32,* 295–301.

Clare, I.C.H., Gudjonsson, G.H., & Harari, P.M. (1998). Understanding of the cur-rent police caution. *Journal of Community and Social Psychology, 8,* 323–329.

Clark, L.A., & Watson, D. (1999). Temperament: A new paradigm for trait psychol-ogy. In L.A. Pervin & O.P. Johns (Eds.), *Handbook of personality: Theory and research* (2nd ed., pp. 399–423). New York: Guilford.

Clark, M. (2005). Organised crime: Redefined for social policy. *International Journal of Police Science and Management, 7,* 98–109.

Clark, S.A. (1993). Matricide: The schizophrenic crime? *Medicine, Science and the Law, 33,* 325–328.

Classen, C.C., Palesh, O.G., & Aggarwal, R. (2005). Sexual revictimization: A review of the empirical literature. *Trauma, Violence, and Abuse, 6,* 103–129.

Cleary, M.F. (1988). Rape offenders' perceptions of victim attitudes. *American Journal of Forensic Psychology, 6,* 57–66.

Cleckley, H. (1941). *The mask of sanity.* St. Louis, MO: Mosby.

Cleckley, H. (1955). *The mask of sanity* (3rd ed.). St. Louis, MO: Mosby.

Cleckley, H. (1976). *The mask of sanity* (4th ed.). St. Louis, MO: Mosby.

Cleckley, H. (1982). *The mask of sanity* (rev. ed.). St. Louis, MO: Mosby.

Cleckley, H. (1988). *The mask of sanity* (5th ed.). St. Louis, MO: Mosby.

Clelland, D., & Carter, T.J. (1980). The new myth of class and crime. *Criminology, 18,* 319–336.

Clements, C.B., Althouse, R., Ax, R.K., Magaletta, P.R., Fagan, T.J., & Wormith, J.S. (2007). Systemic issues and correctional outcomes: Expanding the scope of cor-rectional psychology. *Criminal Justice and Behavior, 34,* 919–932.

Clements, C.B., & Ogle, R.L. (2007). A comparison study of coping, family problem-solving, and emotional status in victims of domestic violence, *Journal of Psychological Trauma, 6*, 29–37.

Cleveland, H.H., Wiebe, R.P., & Rowe, D.C. (2005). Source of exposure to smoking and drinking friends among adolescents: A behavioral-genetic evaluation. *Journal of Genetic Psychology, 166*, 153–169.

Climent, C.E., Rollins, A., Ervin, F.R., & Plutchik, R. (1973). Epidemiological studies of female prisoners I: Medical and psychiatric variables related to violent behavior. *American Journal of Psychiatry, 130*(9), 985–990.

Cloninger, C.R. (1987). A systematic method for clinical description and classification of personality disorders. *Archives of General Psychiatry, 44*, 573–588.

Cloninger, C.R., Bohman, M., & Sigvardsson, S. (1981). Inheritance of alcohol abuse: Cross-fostering analysis of adopted men. *Archives of General Psychiatry, 38*, 861–868.

Cloninger, C.R., Svrakic, D.M., & Przybeck, T.R. (1993). A psychobiological model of temperament and character. *Archives of General Psychiatry, 50*, 975–990.

Cobb, J.P. (1979). Morbid jealousy. *British Journal of Hospital Medicine, 21*, 511–518.

Coccaro, E.F. (1989). Central serotonin and impulsive aggression. *British Journal of Psychiatry, 155*, 52–62.

Coccaro, E.F., & Kavoussi, R.J. (1996). Neurotransmitter correlates of impulsive aggression. In D.M. Stoff & R.B. Cairns (Eds.), *Aggression and violence: Genetic, neurobiological and biosocial perspectives* (pp. 67–85). Mahwah, NJ: Erlbaum.

Cochran, G., & Harpending, H. (2009). *The 10,000 year explosion: How civilization accelerated human evolution.* New York: Basic Books.

Cohen, A. (1980). "I've killed that man 10,000 times." *Police, 3*, 4.

Cohen, D., & Leo, J. (2004). An update on ADHD neuroimaging research. *Journal of Mind and Behavior, 25*, 161–166.

Cohen, D., Nisbett, R.E., Bowdle, B.F., & Schwarz, N. (1996). Insult, aggression, and the southern culture of honor: An "experimental ethnography." *Journal of Personality and Social Psychology, 70*, 945–960.

Cohen, D., & Strayer, J. (1996). Empathy in conduct-disordered and comparison youth. *Developmental Psychology, 32*, 988–998.

Cohen, J., Cohen, P., West, S.G., & Aiken, L.S. (2003). *Applied multiple regression/correlation analysis for the behavioral sciences* (3rd ed.). Mahwah, NJ: Erlbaum.

Cohen, J., & Tita, G. (1999). Spatial diffusion in homicide: Exploring a general method of detecting spatial diffusion processes. *Journal of Quantitative Criminology, 15*, 451–493.

Cohen, J.D., Braver, T.S., & Brown, J.W. (2002). Computational perspectives on dopamine function in the prefrontal cortex. *Current Opinion in Neurobiology, 12*, 223–229.

Cohen, L.E., & Felson, M. (1979). Social change and crime rate trends: A routine activity approach. *American Sociological Review, 44*, 588–608.

Cohen, M.L., Garofolo, R., Boucher, R., & Seghorn, T. (1971). The psychology of rapists. *Seminars in Psychiatry, 3*, 307–323.

Cohen, R.A., Brumm, V., & Zawacki, T.M. (2003). Impulsivity and verbal deficits associated with domestic violence. *Journal of the International Neuropsychological Society, 9,* 760–770.

Cohen, R.A., Rosenbaum, A., & Kane, R.I. (1999). Neuropsychological correlates of domestic violence. *Violence and Victims, 4,* 397–411.

Cohen, S. (2002). *Folk devils and moral panics* (3rd ed.). London: Routledge.

Cohler, B.J. (1987). Adversity, resilience, and the study of lives. In E.J. Anthony & B.J. Cohler (Eds.), *The invulnerable child* (pp. 363–424). New York: Guilford.

Coid, J.W. (1992). DSM-III diagnosis in criminal psychopaths: A way forward. *Criminal Behavior and Mental Health, 2,* 78–94.

Coid, J.W., Wilkins, J., & Coid, B. (1999). Firesetting, pyromania, and self-mutilation in female remanded prisoners. *Journal of Forensic Psychiatry, 10,* 119–130.

Coker, A.L., Davis, K.E., Arias, I., Desai, S., Sanderson, M., & Brandt, H.M. et al (2002). Physical and mental health effects of intimate partner violence for men and women. *American Journal of Preventative Medicine, 23,* 260–268.

Colledge, E., & Blair, R.J.R. (2001). The relationship in children between the inattention and impulsivity components of attention deficit hyperactivity disorder and psychopathic tendencies. *Personality and Individual Differences, 30,* 1175–1187.

Collings, S.J. (1994). Sexual aggression: A discriminant analysis of predictors in a non-forensic sample. *South African Journal of Psychology, 24,* 35–38.

Collins, J.J., & Bailey, S.L. (1990). Traumatic stress disorder and violent behavior. *Journal of Traumatic Stress, 3,* 203–220.

Collins, R. (2004). Onset and desistence in criminal careers: Neurobiology and the age-crime relationship. *Journal of Offender Rehabilitation, 39,* 1–19.

Collins, S. (1989). Sudden death counseling protocol. *Dimensions of Critical Care Nursing, 8,* 375–382.

Coloroso, B. (2003). *The bully, the bullied, and the bystander: From preschool to high school–how parents and teachers can help break the cycle of violence.* New York: HarperResource.

Colton, M., & Vanstone, M. (1998). Sexual abuse by men who work with children: An exploratory study. *British Journal of Social Work, 28,* 511–523.

Comings, D.E., & Blum, K. (2000). Reward deficiency syndrome: Genetic aspects of behavioral disorders. *Progress in Brain Research, 126,* 325–341.

Condron, M.K., & Nutter, D.E. (1988). A preliminary examination of the pornography experience of sex offenders, paraphiliacs, sexual dysfunction patients, and controls based on Meese Commission recommendations. *Journal of Sex and Marital Therapy, 14,* 285–298.

Conklin, H., Luciana, M., Hooper, C., & Yarger, R. (2007). Working memory performance in typically developing children and adolescents: Behavioral evidence of protracted frontal lobe development. *Developmental Neuropsychology, 31,* 103–128.

Conklin, J.E. (1992). *Criminology* (4th ed.). New York: Macmillan.

Connell, M. (2002). The postpartum psychosis defense and feminism: More or less justice for women? *Case Western Reserve Law Review, 53,* 143–169.

Contreras, J.M., & Kerns, K.A. (2000). Emotional regulation processes: Explaining links between parent-child attachment and peer relationships. In K.A. Kerns, J.M. Contreras & A.M. Neal Barnett (Eds.), *Family and peers: Linking two social worlds* (pp. 137–168). Westport, CT: Praeger.

Coolidge, F.L., & Anderson, L.W. (2002). Personality profiles of women in multiple abusive relationships. *Journal of Interpersonal Violence, 16,* 1223–1238.

Coolidge, F.L., Thede, L.L., & Jang, K.L. (2001). Heritability of personality disorders in childhood. *Journal of Personality Disorders, 15,* 33–40.

Cooper, M., & Eaves, D. (1996). Suicide following homicide in the family. *Violence and Victims, 11,* 99–112.

Copeland, A.R. (1985). Homicide in childhood: The Metro-Dade County experience from 1956–1982. *American Journal of Forensic Medicine and Pathology, 6,* 21–24.

Coricelli, G., Critchley, H.D., Joffily, M., O'Doherty, J.P., & Sirigu, A. (2005). Regret and its avoidance: A neuroimaging study of choice behavior. *Nature Neuroscience, 8,* 1255–1262.

Cornell, C.P., & Gelles, R.J. (1982). Adolescent-to-parent violence. *Urban and Social Change Review, 15,* 8–14.

Cornell, D.G. (2006). *School violence: Fears versus facts.* Mahwah, NJ: Erlbaum.

Cornell, D.G., Sheras, P.L., Kaplan, S., McConville, D., Douglass, J., Elkon, A., McKnight, L., Branson, C., & Cole, J. (2004). Guidelines for student threat assessment: Field-test findings. *School Psychology Review, 33,* 527–546.

Correia, K.M. (2009). *A handbook for correctional psychologists: Guidance for the prison practitioner.* Springfield, IL: Charles C Thomas.

Corrigan, P.W., & Watson, A.C. (2005). Findings from the National Comorbidity Survey on the frequency of violent behavior in individuals with psychiatric disorders. *Psychiatry Research, 136,* 153–162.

Coryell, W., & Zimmerman, M. (1986). Demographic, historical, and symptomatic features of the nonmanic psychoses. *Journal of Nervous and Mental Disease, 174,* 585–592.

Costello, E., Egger, H., & Angold, A. (2005). 10-year research update review: The epidemiology of child and adolescent psychiatric disorders: I. Methods and public health burden. *Journal of the American Academy of Child and Adolescent Psychiatry, 44,* 972–986.

Costello, E., Erkanli, A., & Angold, A. (2006). Is there an epidemic of child or adolescent depression? *Journal of the American Academy of Child and Adolescent Psychiatry, 47,* 1263–1271.

Costello, E., Mustillo, S., Erkanli, A., Keeler, G., & Angold, A. (2003). Prevalence and development of psychiatric disorders in childhood and adolescence. *Archives of General Psychiatry, 60,* 837–844.

Cottle, C., Lee, R., & Heilbrun, K. (2001). The prediction of criminal recidivism in juveniles: A meta-analysis. *Criminal Justice and Behavior, 28,* 367–394.

Cottrell, B. (2001). *Parent abuse: The abuse of parents by their teenage children.* Heath, Canada: Family Violence Prevention Unit.

Cottrell, B., & Monk, P. (2004). Adolescent to parent abuse: A qualitative overview of common themes. *Journal of Family Issues, 25,* 1072–1095.

Cozzens, D. (2002). *Sacred silence: Denial and the crisis in the Church.* Collegeville, MN: Liturgical Press.

Craig, M.E. (1990). Coercive sexuality in dating relationships: A situational model. *Clinical Psychology Review, 10,* 395–423.

Craig, T.J. (1982). The epidemiological study of problems associated with violence among psychiatric patients. *American Journal of Psychiatry, 139,* 1262–1266.

Craissati, J. (2005). Sexual violence against women: A psychological approach to the assessment and management of rapists in the community. *Probation Journal: The Journal of Community and Criminal Justice, 52,* 401–422.

Cravens, J.M., Campion, J., & Rotholc, A. (1985). A study of 10 men charged with patricide. *American Journal of Psychiatry, 142,* 1089–1092.

Crawley, J. (1992). *Constructive conflict management: Managing to make a difference.* London: Nicholas Brealey.

Crayton, J.W. (1983). Terrorism and the psychology of the self. In L.Z. Freedman & Y. Alexander (Eds.), *Perspectives on terrorism* (pp. 33–41). Wilmington, DE: Scholarly Resources, Inc.

Crenshaw, M. (1986). The psychology of political terrorism. In M.G. Hermann (Ed.), *Political psychology* (pp. 379–413). San Francisco: Jossey-Bass.

Crenshaw, M. (1992). How terrorists think: What psychology can contribute to understanding terrorism. In L. Howard (Ed.), *Terrorism: Roots, impact, responses* (pp. 71–80). New York: Praeger.

Crenshaw, M. (2000). The psychology of terrorism: An agenda for the 21st century. *Political Psychology, 21,* 405–420..

Crenshaw, M. (2009). Intimations of mortality or production lines? The puzzle of "suicide terrorism." *Political Psychology, 30,* 369–364.

Crepault, C., & Couture, M. (1980). Men's erotic fantasies. *Archives of Sexual Behavior, 9,* 565–581.

Cressey, D. (1969). *The theft of nations.* London: Harper & Row.

Cretacci, M.A. (2008). A general test of self-control theory: Has its importance been exaggerated? *International Journal of Offender Therapy and Comparative Criminology, 52,* 538–553.

Crick, N.R., & Dodge, K.A. (1994). A review and reformulation of social-information processing mechanisms in children's social adjustment. *Psychological Bulletin, 115,* 225–236.

Crick, N.R., & Dodge, K.A. (1999). "Superiority" is in the eye of the beholder: A comment on Sutton, Smith and Swettenham. *Social Development, 8,* 128–131.

Crick, N.R., Werner, N.E., Casas, J.F., O'Brien, K.M., Nelson, D.A., & Grotpeter, J.K. (1999). Childhood aggression and gender: A look at an old problem. In D. Bernstein (Ed.), *Nebraska Symposium on Motivation* (pp. 73–101). Lincoln, NE: University of Nebraska Press.

Crittenden, P.M., & Craig, S.E. (1990). Developmental trends in the nature of child homicide. *Journal of Interpersonal Violence, 5,* 202–216.

Crockett, C.M., & Sekulic, R. (1984). Infanticide in red howler monkeys. In G. Hausfater & S.B. Hrdy (Eds.), *Infanticide: Comparative and evolutionary perspectives* (pp. 173–192). New York: Adline.

Crofford, L.J. (2007). Violence, stress, and somatic syndromes. *Trauma, Violence, and Abuse, 8,* 299–313.

Cromartie, R.S., & Duma, R.J. (2009). *High-tech terror: Recognition, management, and prevention of biological, chemical, and nuclear injuries secondary to acts of terrorism.* Springfield, IL: Charles C Thomas.

Crone, E.A., & Van Der Molen, M.W. (2004). Developmental changes in real life decision making: Performance on a gambling task previously shown to depend on the ventromedial prefrontal cortex. *Developmental Neuropsychology, 25,* 251–279.

Crowell, N.A., & Burgess, A.W. (1996). *Understanding violence against women.* Washington, DC: National Academy Press.

Crozier, B. (1960). *The rebels: A study of post-war insurrections.* London: Chatto & Windus.

Cuffel, B.J., Shumway, M., Chouljian, T.L., & MacDonald, T. (1994). A longitudinal study of substance use and community violence in schizophrenia. *Journal of Nervous and Mental Disease, 182,* 704–708.

Cullen, D. (2009). *Columbine.* New York: Hachette.

Cummings, E.M., Hennessy, K.D., Rabideau, G., & Cicchetti, J. (1994). Responses of physically abused boys to interadult anger. *Development and Psychopathology, 6,* 31–41.

Cummings, J.L., & Mendez, M.F. (1984). Secondary mania with focal cerebrovacular lesions. *American Journal of Psychiatry, 141,* 1084–1087.

Cummings, P., & Mueller, B.A. (1994). Infant injury death in Washington State, 1981–1990. *Archives of Pediatric and Adolescent Medicine, 148,* 1021–1026.

Cupach, W.R., & Spitzberg, B.H. (1998). Obsessive relational intrusion and stalking. In B.H. Spitzberg & W.R. Cupach (Eds.), *The dark side of close relationships* (pp. 233–263). Hillsdale, NJ: Erlbaum.

Cupach, W.R., & Spitzberg, B.H. (2000). Obsessive relational intrusion: Incidence, perceived severity, and coping. *Violence and Victims, 15,* 357–372.

Cupach, W.R., & Spitzberg, B.H. (2004). *The dark side of relationship pursuit: From attraction to obsession and stalking.* Mahwah, NJ: Erlbaum.

Cupach, W.R., Spitzberg, B.H., & Carson, C.L. (2000). Toward a theory of obsessive relational intrusion and stalking. In K. Dindia & S. Duck (Eds.), *Communication and personal relationships* (pp. 131–146). New York: Wiley.

Curry, G.D., & Decker, S.H. (1998). *Confronting gangs: Crime and community.* Los Angeles: Roxbury.

Dabbs, J.M., Frady, R.L., Carr, T.S., & Besch, N.F. (1987). Saliva testosterone and criminal violence in young adult prison inmates. *Psychosomatic Medicine, 49,* 174–182.

Dabbs, J.M., Jurkovic, G.J., & Frady, R.L. (1991). Salivary testosterone and cortisol among late adolescent male offenders. *Journal of Abnormal Child Psychology, 19,* 469–478.

Dabbs, J.M., & Morris, R. (1990). Testosterone, social class and antisocial behavior in a sample of 4,462 men. *Psychological Science, 1,* 209–211.

Dabbs, J.M., Ruback, G.J., Frady, R.L., Hopper, C.H., & Sgoutas, D.S. (1988). Saliva testosterone and criminal violence among women. *Personality and Individual Differences, 9,* 269–275.

Dabbs, J.M., & Hargrove, M.F. (1997). Age, testosterone, and behavior among female prison inmates. *Psychosomatic Medicine, 59,* 477–480.

Daffern, M., & Howells, K. (2002). Psychiatric inpatient aggression: A review of structural and functional assessment approaches. *Aggression and Violent Behavior, 7,* 477–497.

Dahl, R.E. (2001). Affect regulation, brain development, and behavioral/emotional health in adolescence. *CNS Spectrums, 6,* 1–12.

Dahl, R.E. (2004). Adolescent brain development: A period of vulnerabilities and opportunities. *Annals of the New York Academy of Sciences, 1021,* 1–22.

Dahlin, L., Cederblad, M., Antonovsky, A., & Hagnell, O. (1990). Childhood vulnerability and adult invincibility. *Acta Psychiatrica Scandinavica, 82,* 228–232.

Daly, M., & Wilson, M. (1988). *Homicide.* Hawthorne, NY: Adline.

Daly, M., & Wilson, M. (1989). Homicide and cultural evolution. *Ethology and Sociobiology, 10,* 99–100.

Daly, M., & Wilson, M. (1990). Killing the competition: Female/female and male/male homicide. *Human Nature, 1,* 83–109.

Daly, M., Wilson, M., & Salmon, C.A. (2001). Siblicide and seniority. *Homicide Studies, 5,* 30–45.

Daly, M., Wilson, M., & Weghorst, J. (1982). Male sexual jealousy. *Ethology and Sociobiology, 3,* 11–27.

Daniels, J.A., Bradley, M.C., & Hays, M. (2007). The impact of school violence on school personnel: Implications for psychologists. *Professional Psychology: Research and Practice, 38,* 652–659.

Darke, J.L. (1990). Sexual aggression: Achieving power through humiliation. In W.L. Marshall, D.R. Laws & H.E. Barbaree (Eds.), *Handbook of sexual assault: Issues, theories, and treatment of the offenders* (pp. 55–72). New York: Plenum.

Darwin, C. (1871). *The descent of man in relation to sex.* London: John Murray.

Darwsin, C. (1959). *On the origin of species by means of natural selection, or the preservation of favoured races in the struggle for life.* London: John Murrary.

Dattilio, F.M., & Freeman, A. (Eds.). (2000). *Cognitive-behavioral strategies in crisis intervention* (2nd ed.). New York: Guilford.

Davidson-Arad, B., Englechin-Segal, D., & Wozner, Y. (2003). Short-term follow-up of children at risk: Comparison of the quality of life of children removed from home and children remaining at home. *Child Abuse and Neglect, 27,* 733–750.

Davies, B.M., & Morgenstern, F.S. (1960). A case of cysticerosis, temporal lobe epilepsy, and transvestism. *Journal of Neurology, Neurosurgery and Psychiatry, 23,* 247–249.

Davis, G.C., & Breslau, N. (1994). Post-traumatic stress disorder in victims of civilian and criminal violence. *Psychiatric Clinics of North America, 17,* 289–299.

Davis, G.E., & Leitenberg, H. (1987). Adolescent sexual offenders. *Psychological Bulletin, 101,* 417–427.

Davis, J.A., Bradley, M.C., Cramer, D.P., Winkler, A.J., Kinebrew, K., & Crockett, D. (2007). The successful resolution of armed hostage/barricade events in schools: A qualitative analysis. *Psychology in the Schools, 44,* 601–613.

Dawkins, J.L. (1995). Bullying in school: Doctors' responsibilities. *British Medical Journal, 310,* 274–275.

Day, K. (1988). A hospital-based treatment programme for male mentally handicapped offenders. *British Journal of Psychiatry, 153,* 635–644.

Day, R., Neilsen, J.A., Korten, A., Ernberg, G., Dube, K.C., Gebhart, J., Jablensky, A., Leon, C, Marsella, A., Olatawara, M., Sartorius, N., Stromgren, E., Takahashi, R., Wig, N., & Wynne, L.C. (1987). Stressful life events preceding the onset of acute schizophrenia: A cross-national study from the World Health Organization. *Culture, Medicine and Psychiatry, 11,* 123–206.

Deadman, W.J. (1964). Medico-legal: Infanticide. *Canadian Medical Association Journal, 91,* 558–560.

Dean, K., Walsh,E., Morgan, C., Demjaha, A., Dazzan, P., Morgan, K., Lloyd, T., Fearon, P., Jones, P.B., & Murray, R.M. (2007).

de Barros, D.M., & de Padua-Scrafim, A. (2008). Association between personality disorder and violent behavior pattern. *Forensic Science International, 179,* 19–22.

Deater-Deckard, K., & Plomin, R. (1999). An adoption study of the etiology of teacher and parent reports of externalizing behavior problems in middle childhood. *Child Development, 70,* 144–154.

De Bellis, M.D., Keshavan, M.S., & Spencer, S.H.J. (2000). N-acetylaspartate concentration in the anterior cingulated of maltreated children and adolescents with PTSD. *American Journal of Psychiatry, 157,* 1175–1177.

Decker, M.R., Martin, S.L., & Moracco, K.E. (2005). Homicide risk factors among pregnant women abused by their partners. *Violence Against Women, 10,* 498–513.

Decker, S.H., Bynum, T., & Weisel, D. (1998). A tale of two cities: Gangs as organized crime groups. *Justice Quarterly, 15,* 395–423.

Decker, S.H., & Curry, G.D. (2003). Suppression without prevention, prevention without suppression. In S.H. Decker (Ed.), *Policing gangs and youth violence* (pp. 191–213). Belmont, CA: Wadsworth/Thompson Learning.

Decker, S.H., & Van Winkle, B. (1996). *Life in the gang: Family, friends, and violence.* New York: Cambridge University Press.

DeFronzo, J., Ditta, A., Hannon, L., & Prochnow, J. (2007). Male serial homicide: the influence of cultural and structural variables. *Homicide Studies, 11,* 3–14.

DeHart-Davis, L. (2007). The unbureaucratic personality. *Public Administration Review, 67,* 892–903.

De Jong, A.R. (1989). Sexual interactions among siblings and cousins: Experimentation or exploitation? *Child Abuse and Neglect, 13,* 271–279.

Delattre, E.J. (1990). New faces of organized crime. *American Enterprise,* May/June, pp. 38–45.

Delgado-Escueta, A.V., Mattson, R.H., King, L., Goldensohn, E.S., Spiegel, H., & Madsen, J. (1981). The nature of aggression during epileptic seizures. *New England Journal of Medicine, 305,* 711–716.

DeLisi, M. (2001). Extreme career criminals. *American Journal of Criminal Justice, 25,* 239–252.

DeLisi, M. (2003). Criminal careers behind bars. *Behavioral Sciences and the Law, 21,* 653–669.

DeLisi, M. (2005). *Career criminals in society.* Thousand Oaks, CA: Sage.

DeLisi, M., Conis, P.J., & Beaver, K.M. (2008). The importance of violent offenders to criminology. In M. DeLisi & P.J. Conis (Eds.), *Violent offenders: Theory, research, public policy, and practice* (pp. 1–14). Sudbury, MA: Jones & Bartlett.

DeLisi, M., Hochstetler, A., & Murphy, D.S. (2003). Self-control behind bars: A validation study of the Grasmick scale. *Justice Quarterly, 20,* 241–263.

DeLisi, M., & Scherer, A.M. (2006). Multiple homicide offenders: Offense characteristics, social correlates, and criminal careers. *Criminal Justice and Behavior, 33,* 367–391.

Delosi, C., & Margolin, G. (2004). The role of family-of-origin violence in men's marital violence perpetration. *Clinical Psychology Review, 24,* 99–122.

Demello, M. (1993). The convict body: Tatooing among male American prisoners. *Anthropology Today, 9,* 10–13.

Demo, D.H., & Acock, A.C. (1988). The impact of divorce on children. *Journal of Marriage and Family, 50,* 619–648.

Denenberg, R.V., & Braverman, M. (1999). *The violence-prone workplace: A new approach to dealing with hostile, threatening, and uncivil behavior.* Ithaca, NY: Cornell University Press.

Dennison, S.M. (2007). Interpersonal relationships and stalking: Identifying when to intervene. *Law and Human Behavior, 31,* 353–367.

Dennison, S.M., & Thomson, D.M. (2000). Community perceptions of stalking: What are the fundamental concerns? *Psychiatry, Psychology and Law, 7,* 159–169.

Dennison, S.M., & Thomson, D.M. (2002). Identifying stalking: The relevance of intent in commonsense reasoning. *Law and Human Behavior, 26,* 543–561.

Denno, D.W. (1988). Human biology and criminal responsibility: Free will or free ride? *University of Pennsylvania Law Review, 137,* 615–671.

Denno, D.W. (1990). *Biology and violence: From birth to adulthood.* Cambridge: Cambridge University Press.

Denov, M.S. (2001). A culture of denial: Exploring professional perspectives on female sex offending. *Canadian Journal of Criminology, 43,* 303–329.

Denov, M.S. (2003). The myth of innocence: Sexual scripts and the recognition of child sexual abuse by female perpetrators. *Journal of Sex Research, 40,* 303–314.

Desai, S., Arias, I., Thompson, M.P., & Basile, K.C. (2002). Childhood victimization and subsequent adult revictimization assessed in a nationally representative sample of women and men. *Violence and Victims, 17,* 639–653.

Deviney, E., Dickert, J., & Lockwood, R. (1983). The care of pets within child abusing families. *International Journal for the Study of Animal Problems, 4,* 321–329.

DeVoe, E., Dean, K., Traube, D., & McKay, M. (2005). The SURVIVE community project: A family-based intervention to reduce the impact of violence exposures in urban youth. *Journal of Aggression, Maltreatment, and Trauma, 11,* 95–116.

Dewan, S. (2008). From hate to murder? Church shooting suspect loathed liberals, police say. *South Florida Sun-Sentinel,* July 29, p. 3A.

Dewhurst, K., Oliver, J.E., & McKnight, A.L. (1970). Socio-psychiatric consequence of Huntington's disease. *British Journal of Psychiatry, 111,* 255–258.

deWit, H., Flory, J.D., Acheson, A., McCloskey, M., & Manuck, S.B. (2007). IQ and nonplanning impulsivity are independently associated with delay discounting in middle-aged adults. *Personality and Individual Differences, 42,* 111–121.

Dhawan, S., & Marshall, W.L. (1996). Sexual abuse histories of sexual offenders. *Sexual Abuse: A Journal of Research and Treatment, 8,* 7–15.

Diamond, P.M., Wang, E.W., Holzer, C.E., Thomas, C., de Anges, C., & Cruser, D.A. (2001). The prevalence of mental illness in prison. *Administration and Policy in Mental Health, 29,* 21–40.

Dias, L., Chabner, B.A., Lynch, T.J., & Penson, R.T. (2003). Breaking bad news: A patient's perspective. *The Oncologist, 8,* 587–596.

Dickman, S.J. (1990). Functional and dysfunctional impulsivity: Personality and cognitive correlates. *Journal of Personality and Social Psychology, 58,* 95–102.

Dickey, R., Nussbaum, D., Chevolleau, K., & Davidson, H. (2002). Age as a differential characteristic of rapists, pedophiles, and sexual sadists. *Journal of Sex and Marital Therapy, 28,* 211–218.

Dietrich, K.N., Douglas, R.M., Succop, P.A., Berger, O.G., & Bornschein, R.L. (2001). Early exposure to lead and juvenile delinquency. *Neurotoxicology and Teratology, 23,* 511–518.

Dietz, P.E. (1986). Mass, serial, and sensational homicides. *Bulletin of the New York Academy of Medicine, 62,* 477–491.

Dietz, P.E. (1987). Patterns in human violence. *Psychiatric Update: American Psychiatric Association Annual Review, 6,* 465–490.

Dietz, P.E., Hazelwood, M.S., & Warren, D.S.W. (1990). The sexually sadistic criminal and his offenses. *Bulletin of the American Academy of Psychiatry and the Law, 16,* 163–178.

Dietz, P.E., Matthews, D., Martell, D., Stewart, T., Hrouda, D., & Warren, J. (1991a). Threatening and otherwise inappropriate letters to members of the United States Congress. *Journal of Forensic Sciences, 36,* 1445–1468.

Dietz, P.E., Matthews, D., Van Duyne, C, Martell, D., Parry, C., Stewart, T., Warren, J., & Crowder, J.D. (1991b). Threatening and otherwise inappropriate letters to Hollywood celebrities. *Journal of Forensic Sciences, 36,* 185–209.

DiLalla, L.F. (2002). Behavior genetics of aggression in children: Review and future directions. *Developmental Review, 22,* 593–622.

DiLalla, L.F., & Gottesman, I.I. (1989). Heterogeneity of causes for delinquency and criminality: Lifespan perspectives. *Development and Psychopathology, 1,* 339–349.

DiLalla, L.F., & Gottesman, I.I. (1991). Biological and genetic contributors to violence–Widom's untold tale. *Psychological Bulletin, 109,* 125–129.

Dill, K.E., Anderson, C.A., Anderson, K.B., & Deuser, W.E. (1997). Effects of aggressive personality on social expectations and social perceptions. *Journal of Personality and Social Psychology, 31,* 272–292.

Dilullio, J.J. (1995). The coming of the superpredators. *The Weekly Standard,* November 27, pp. 23–30.

Dilullio, J.J. (1996). How to deal with the youth crime wave. *The Weekly Standard,* September 16, pp. 30–35.

DiMaio, V.J.M., & Bernstein, J.D. (1974). A case of infanticide. *Journal of Forensic Sciences, 19,* 744–754.

Dinn, W.M., Gansler, D.A., Mosczynski, N., & Fulwiler, C. (2009). Brain dysfunction and community violence in patients with mental illness. *Criminal Justice and Behavior, 36,* 117–136.

Disch, E., & Avery, N. (2001). Sex in the consulting room, the examining room, and the sacristy: Survivors of sexual abuse by professionals. *American Journal of Orthopsychiatry, 71,* 204–217.

Ditton, P.M. (1999). *Mental health and treatment of inmates and probationers.* Washington, DC: Department of Justice, Bureau of Justice Statistics.

Divine, P.E., & Rafalko, R.J. (2005). The mind of the terrorist: A review and critique of psychological approaches. *Journal of Conflict Resolution, 49,* 3–42.

Dixon, A., Howie, P., & Franzep, J.S. (2005). Trauma exposure, posttraumatic stress, and psychiatric comorbidity in female juvenile offenders. *Journal of the American Academy of Child and Adolescent Psychiatry, 44,* 798–806.

Dixon, L., Hamilton-Giachristis, C., & Browne, K. (2008). Classifying partner femicide. *Journal of Interpersonal Violence, 23,* 74–93.

Dobash, R.E., & Dobash, R.P. (1979). *Violence against wives.* New York: Free Press.

Dobash, R.E., Dobash, R, Wilson, M., & Daly, M. (1992). The myth of sexual symmetry in marital violence. *Social Problems, 39,* 81.

Dobson, A. (2003). Caught in the net. *Care and Health, 11,* 6–9.

Dobson, V., & Sales, B. (2000). The science of infanticide and mental illness. *Psychology, Public Policy, and Law, 6,* 1098–1112.

Dodge, K.A. (2008). Framing public policy and prevention of chronic violence in American youths. *American Psychologist, 63,* 573–590.

Dodge, K.A., Bates, J.E., & Pettit, G.S. (1990). Mechanisms in the cycle of violence. *Science, 250,* 1678–1683.

Dodge, K.A., Lochman, J.E., Harnish, J.D., & Bates, J.E. (1997). Reactive and proactive aggression in school children and psychiatrically impaired chronically assaultive youth. *Journal of Abnormal Psychology, 106,* 37–51.

Dodge, K.A., Pettit, G.S., Bates, J.E., & Valente, E. (1995). Social information-processing patterns partially mediate the effect of early physical abuse on later conduct problems. *Journal of Abnormal Psychology, 104,* 632–643.

Dodge, K.A., Price, J.M., Bachorowski, J., & Newman, J.P. (1990). Hostile attributional bias in severely aggressive adolescents. *Journal of Abnormal Psychology, 99,* 385–392.

Dolan, R.J. (2002). Emotion, cognition, and behavior. *Science, 298,* 1191–1194.

D'Orban, P.T. (1979). Women who kill their children. *British Journal of Psychiatry, 134,* 560–571.

Doss, W. (2007). *Condition to win: Dynamic techniques for performance oriented mental conditioning.* Flushing, NY: Looseleaf Law Press.

Douard, J. (2007). Loathing the sinner, medicalizing the sin: Why sexually violent predator statutes are unjust. *International Journal of Law and Psychiatry, 30,* 36–48.

Douglas, J.E., & Burgess, A.W. (1986). Criminal profiling: A viable investigative tool against violent crime. *FBI Law Enforcement Bulletin, 55,* 9–13.

Douglas, J.E., Burgess, A.G., Burgess, A.W., & Ressler, R.K. (1992). *Crime classification manual: A standard system for investigating and classifying violent crimes.* New York: Simon & Schuster.

Douglas, J.E., & Olshaker, M. (1995). *Mindhunter: Inside the FBI's elite serial crime unit.* New York: Scribner.

Douglas, J.E., & Olshaker, M. (1997). *Journey into darkness: The FBI's elite serial crime unit.* New York: Simon & Schuster.

Douglas, J.E., & Olshaker, M. (1998). *Obsession: The FBI's legendary profiler probes the psyches of killers, rapists, and stalkers.* New York: Scribner.

Douglas, J.E., & Olshaker, M. (1999). *The anatomy of motive: The FBI's legendary mindhunter explores the key to understanding and catching violent criminals.* New York: Scribner.

Douglas, J.E., Ressler, R.K., Burgess, A.W., & Hartman, C.R. (1986). Criminal profiling from crime scene analysis. *Behavioral Sciences and the Law, 4,* 401–421.

Douglas, K.S., Cox, D.N., & Webster, C.D. (1999). Violence risk assessment: Science and practice. *Legal and Criminological Psychology, 4,* 149–184.

Douglas, K.S., & Kropp, P.R. (2002). A prevention-based paradigm for violence risk assessment: Clinical and research applications. *Criminal Justice and Behavior, 29,* 617–658.

Douglas, K.S., & Skeem, J.L. (2005). Violence risk assessment: Getting specific about being dynamic. *Psychology, Public Policy and Law, 11,* 347–383.

Douglas, K.S., & Webster, C.D. (1999). Predicting violence in mentally and personality disordered individuals. In R. Roesch, S.D. Hart & J.R.P. Ogloff (Eds.), *Psychology and law: The state of the discipline* (pp. 175–239). New York: Plenum.

Douglas, S.C., & Martinko, M.J. (2001). Exploring the role of individual differences in the prediction of workplace aggression. *Journal of Applied Psychology, 86,* 547–559.

D'Ovidio, R., & Doyle, J. (2003). A study on cyberstalking: Understanding investigative hurdles. *FBI Law Enforcement Bulletin, 72,* 10–17.

Dowden, C., Bennell, C., & Bloomfield, S. (2007). Advances in offender profiling: A systematic review of the profiling literature published over the past three decades. *Journal of Police and Criminal Psychology, 22,* 44–56.

Drapeau, M., Beretta, V., de Roten, Y., Koerner, A., & Despland, J.N. (2008). Defense styles of pedophilic offenders. *International Journal of Offender Therapy and Comparative Criminology, 52,* 185–195.

Drapeau, M., de Roten, Y., & Korner, A.C. (2004a). An exploratory study of child molesters' relationship patterns using the core conflictual relationship themes method. *Journal of Interpersonal Violence, 19,* 264–275.

Drapeau, M., Korner, A.C., & Brunet, L. (2004b). When the goals of therapists and patients clash: A study of pedophiles in treatment. *Journal of Offender Rehabilitation, 38,* 69–80.

Drescher-Burke, K., Krall, J., & Penick, A. (2004). *Discarded infants and neonaticide: A review of the literature.* Berkely, CA: National Abandoned Infants Assistance Resource Center, Univeristy of California at Berkely.

Dressing, H., Kuehner, C., & Gass, P. (2006). The epidemiology and characteristics of stalking. *Current Opinion in Psychiatry, 19,* 395–399.

Driver, M.V., West, L.R., & Faulk, M. (1974). Clinical and EEG studies of prisoners charged with murder. *British Journal of Psychiatry, 125,* 583–587.

Dubin, W.R. (1995). Assaults with weapons. In B.S. Eichelman & A.C. Hartwig (Eds.), *Patient violence and the clinician* (pp. 139–154). Washington DC: American Psychiatric Press.

Dubow, E.F., Huesmann, L.R., & Eron, L.D. (1987). Childhood correlates of adult ego development. *Child Development, 85,* 859–869.

Duhart, D. (2001). *Violence in the workplace, 1993–99.* Washington, DC: U.S. Department of Justice.

Dunaway, R.G., Cullen, F.T., Burton, V.S., & Evans, T.D. (2000). The myth of social class and crime revisited: An examination of class and adult criminality. *Criminology, 38,* 589–632.

Dunsieth, N.W., Nelson, E.B., Brusman-Lovins, L.A., Holcomb, J.L., Beckman, D., & Welge, J.A. (2004). Psychiatric and legal features of 113 men convicted on sexual offenses. *Journal of Clinical Psychiatry, 65,* 293–300.

Duntley, J.D., & Shackelford, T.K. (2008). Victim adaptations. In J.D. Duntley & T.K. Shackelford (Eds.), *Evolutionary forensic psychiatry: Darwinian foundations of crime and law* (pp. 201–229). New York: Oxford University Press.

Duntley, J.D., & Buss, D.M. (2008). The origins of homicide. In J.D. Duntley & T.K. Shackelford (Eds.), *Evolutionary forensic psychiatry: Darwinian foundations of crime and law* (pp. 41–64). New York: Oxford University Press.

Dupre, K.E., & Barling, J. (2006). Predicting and preventing supervisory workplace aggression. *Journal of Occupational Health Psychology, 11,* 13–26.

Duran, P.L. (1999). *Developing the survival attitude.* Flushing, NY: Looseleaf Law Publications.

Duran, P.L., & Nasci, D. (2000). *Tactical attitude.* Flushing, NY: Looseleaf Law Publications.

Durkheim, E. (1897/1951). *Suicide: A study in sociology.* New York: The Free Press.

Durkin, K.F. (1997). Misuse of the Internet by pedophiles: Implications for law enforcement and probation practice. *Federal Probation, 61,* 14–18.

Dusky v. United States, 362 U.S. 402 (1960).

Dutton, D.G. (1995). Trauma symptoms and PTSD-like profiles in perpetrators of intimate abuse. *Journal of Traumatic Stress, 8,* 299–316.

Dutton, D.G., & Golant, S.K. (1995). *The batterer: A psychological profile.* New York: Basic Books.

Dutton, D.G., Saunders, K., & Starsomski, S. (1994). Intimacy-anger and insecure attachment as precursors of abuse in intimate relationships. *Journal of Applied Social Psychology, 24,* 1367–1386.

Dworkin, A.G., Haney, C.A., & Teschow, R.L. (1988). Fear, victimization, and stress among urban public school teachers. *Journal of Organizational Behavior, 9,* 159–171.

Dyer, J. (2000). *The perpetual prison machine.* Boulder, CO: Westview.

Eaker, H.A., Allen, S.S., & Gray, J. (1983). A factor analytic study of personality and intellectual variables in incarcerated delinquent males and females. *Journal of Clinical Psychology, 39,* 614–616.

Eagly, A.H. (1995). The science and politics of comparing women and men. *American Psychologist, 50,* 145–158.

Eberwein, K.E. (2006). A mental health clinician's guide to death notification. *International Journal of Emergency Mental Health, 8,* 117–126.

Eby, K., Campbell, J., Sullivan, C., & Davidson, W. (1995). Health effects of experiences of sexual violence for women with abusive partners. *Health Care for Women International, 16,* 563–576.

Edenborough, M., Jackson, D., Mannix, J., & Wilkes, L.M. (2008). Living in the red zone: The experience of child-to-mother violence. *Child and Family Social Work, 13,* 464–473.

Edin, K.E., Lalos, A., Hogberg, U., & Dahlgren, L. (2008). Violent men: Ordinary and deviant. *Journal of Interpersonal Violence, 23,* 225–244.

Edleson, J.L. (1999). The overlap between child maltreatment and woman battering. *Violence Against Women, 5,* 134–154.

Edwards, D.W., Scott, C.L., Yarvis, R.M., Paizis, C.L., & Panizzon, M.S. (2003). Impulsiveness, impulsive aggression, personality disorder, and spousal violence. *Violence and Victims, 18,* 3–14.

Egeland, B., Carlson, E.A., & Sroufe, L.A. (1993). Resilience as process. *Development and Psychopathology, 5,* 517–528.

Egeland, B., Yates, T., Appleyard, K., & van Dulmen, M. (2002). The long-term consequences of maltreatment in the early years: A developmental pathway model to antisocial behavior. *Children's Services: Social Policy, Research, and Practice, 5,* 249–260.

Egger, S.A. (2002). *The killers among us: An examination of serial murder and its investigation* (2nd ed.). Upper Saddle River, NJ: Prentice-Hall.

Eibl-Eibelsfeldt, I. (1971). *Love and hate: The natural history of behavior patterns.* New York: Holt, Rinehart & Winston.

Eichelman, B.S. (1992). Aggressive behavior: From laboratory to clinic. *Archives of General Psychiatry, 49,* 488–492.

Eichelman, B.S., & Hartwig, A. (1993). The clinical psychopharmacology of violence. *Psychopharmacology Bulletin, 29,* 57–63.

Eigen, J.P. (1981). Punishing youth homicide offenders in Philadelphia. *Journal of Criminal Law and Criminology, 72,* 1072–1073.

Elbogen, E., Swanson, J., Swartz, M., & Van Dorn, R. (2005). Family representative payeeship and violence risk in severe mental illness. *Law and Human Behavior, 29,* 563–564.

Eley, T.C., Lichtenstein, P., & Stevenson, J. (1999). Sex differences in the etiology of aggressive and nonaggressive antisocial behavior: Results from two twin studies. *Child Development, 70,* 155–168.

Eley, T.C., Lichtenstein, T., & Moffitt, T.E. (2003). A longitudinal behavioral genetic analysis of the etiology of aggressive and nonaggressive antisocial behavior. *Development and Psychopathology, 15,* 383–402.

Elias, M. (1981). Serum cholesterol, testosterone, and testosterone binding globulin responses to competitive fighting in human males. *Aggressive Behavior, 7,* 215–224.

Elliott, C. (1996). Key concepts: Criminal responsibility. *Philosophy, Psychiatry, and Psychology, 3,* 305–307.

Elliott, D.M., & Briere, J. (1995). Posttraumatic stress associated with delayed recall of sexual abuse: A general population study. *Journal of Traumatic Stress, 3,* 629–648.

Elliott, D.M., Mok, D.S., & Briere, J. (2004). Adult sexual assault: Prevalence, symptomatology, and sex differences in the general population. *Journal of Traumatic Stress, 17,* 20-211.

3Elliott, D.S. (1994). Serious violent offenders: Onset, developmental course and termination. *Criminology, 32,* 1–21.

Elliott, D.S., & Huizinga, D. (1983). Social class and delinquent behavior in a national youth panel 1976–1980. *Criminology, 21,* 149–177.

Elliott, F.A. (1982). Neurological finding in adult minimal brain dysfunction and the dyscontrol syndrome. *Journal of Nervous of Mental Disease, 170,* 680–687.

Elliott, F.A. (1984). The episodic dyscontrol syndrome and aggression. *Neurologic Clinics of North America, 2,* 113–125.

Elliott, F.A. (1990). Neurology of aggression and episodic dyscontrol. *Seminars in Neurology,* 303–312.

Elliott, F.A. (1992). Violence: The neurologic contribution. An overview. *Archives of Neurology, 49,* 595–603.

Ellis, H. (1907). *The criminal: The contemporary science series* (3rd ed.). London: Walter Scott Publishing Company/Charles Scribner.

Ellis, L. (1989). *Theories of rape: Inquiries into the causes of sexual aggression.* New York: Hemisphere.

Ellis, L. (1991). A synthesized (biosocial) theory of rape. *Journal of Consulting and Clincial Psychology, 59,* 631–642.

Ellis, L. (1993). Rape as a biosocial phenomenon. In G.C.N. Hall, R. Hirschman, J.R. Graham & M.S. Zaragoza (Eds.), *Sexual aggression: Issues in etiology, assessment, and treatment* (pp. 17–41). Washington, DC: Taylor & Francis.

Ellis, L. (2001). The biosocial female choice theory of social stratification. *Social Biology, 48,* 297–319.

Ellis, L. (2005). Theoretically explaining biological correlates of criminal behavior. *European Journal of Criminology, 2,* 287–315.

Ellis, L. (2008). Reducing crime evolutionarily. In J.D. Duntley & T.K. Shackelford (Eds.), *Evolutionary forensic psychiatry: Darwinian foundations of crime and law* (pp. 249–267). New York: Oxford University Press.

Else, L.T., Wonderlich, S.A., & Beatty, W.W. (1993). Personality characteristics of men who physically abuse women. *Hospital and Community Psychiatry, 44,* 54–58.

Elsohly, M.A., & Salamone, S.J. (1999). Prevalence of drugs in cases of alleged sexual assault. *Journal of Analytic Toxicology, 23,* 141–146.

Engel, C.C., Engel, A.L., Campbell, S.J., McFall, M.E., Russo, J., & Katon, W. (1993). Posttraumatic stress disorder symptoms and precombat sexual and physical abuse in Desert Storm veterans. *Journal of Nervous and Mental Disease, 181,* 683–688.

Epstein, A.W. (1961). Relationship of fetishism and transvestism to brain and particularly to temporal lobe dysfunction. *Journal of Nervous and Mental Disease, 133,* 247–253.

Erb, M., Hodgins, S., Freese, R., Muller-Isberner, R & Jockel, D. (2001). Homicide and schizophrenia: Maybe treatment does have a preventative effect. *Criminal Behavior and Mental Health, 11,* 6–26.

Eron, L.D., & Huesmann, L.R. (1984). The relation of prosocial behavior to the development of aggression and psychopathology. *Aggressive Behavior, 10,* 201–212.

Eron, L.D., & Huesmann, L.R. (1990). The stability of aggressive behavior–even unto the third generation. In M. Lewis & S.M. Miller (Eds.), *Handbook of developmental psychopathology* (pp. 147–156). New York: Plenum.

Eronen, M., Hakola, P., & Tiihonen, J. (1996). Mental disorders and homicidal behavior in Finland. *Archives of General Psychiatry, 53,* 497–504.

Eronen, M., Tiihonen, J., & Hakola, P. (1996). Schizophrenia and homicidal behavior. *Schizophrenia Bulletin, 22,* 83–89.

Erschul, W.P. (2001). School psychologists' perceptions of social power bases in teacher consultation. *Journal of Educational and Psychological Consultation, 12,* 483–497.

Erwin, B., Newman, E., McMackin, R, Morrissey, C., & Kaloupek, D. (2000). PTSD, malevolent environment, and criminality among criminally involved male adolescents. *Criminal Justice and Behavior, 27,* 196–215.

Esbensen, E., & Huizinga, D. (1993). Gangs, drugs, and delinquency in a survey of urban youth. *Criminology, 31,* 565–589.

Esbensen, F., & Lunskey, D.P. (2001). Youth gang members in a school survey. In M.W. Klein, H. Kerner, C.L. Maxson, & E. Weitekampf (Eds.), *The Eurogang paradox: Street gangs and youth groups in the U.S. and Europe* (pp. 145–177). Amsterdam: Kluwer Academic Publishers.

Esbensen, E., & Tusinski, K. (2007). Youth gangs in the print media. *Journal of Criminal Justice and Popular Culture, 14,* 21–28.

Esbensen, E., Winfree, L.T., He, N., & Taylor, T.J. (2001). Youth gangs and definitional issues: When is a gang a gang, and why does it matter? *Crime and Delinquency, 47,* 105–130.

Eslinger, P.J. (1998). Neurological and neuropsychological bases of empathy. *European Neurology, 39,* 193–199.

Eslinger, P.J., Grattan, L.M., & Geder, L. (1995). Impact of frontal lobe lesions on rehabilitation and recovery from acute brain injury. *Neurorehabilitation, 5,* 161–185.

Estroff, S.E., Zimmer, C., Lachiotte, W., & Benoit, J. (1991). The influence of social networks and social support on violence by persons with serious mental illness. *Hospital and Community Psychiatry, 45,* 669–678.

Evans, E.D., & Warren-Sohlberg, L. (1988). A pattern of analysis of adolescent abusive behavior toward parents. *Journal of Adolescent Research, 3,* 201–216.

Evans, R.W. (1992). The postconcussion syndrome and sequelae of mild head injury. *Neurologic Clinics, 10,* 815–847.

Evans, R.W. (1994). The postconcussion syndrome: 130 years of controversy. *Seminars in Neurology, 14,* 32–39.

Evans, T.D., Cullen, F.T., Burton, V.S., Dunaway, R.G., & Benson, M.L. (1997). The social consequences of self-control: Testing the general theory of crime. *Criminology, 35,* 475–504.

Everall, I.P., & LeCouteur, A. (1990). Firesetting in an adolescent boy with Asperger's syndrome. *British Journal of Psychiatry, 157,* 284–287.

Everitt, B.J., Cardinal, R.N., Parkinson, J.A., & Robbins, T.W. (2003). Appetitive behavior: Impact of amygdala-dependent mechanisms of emotional learning. *Annals of the New York Academy of Sciences, 985,* 233–250.

Everitt, D. (1999). *Human monsters: An illustrated encyclopedia of the world's most vicious murderers.* Chicago: Contemporary Books.

Everstine, D.S., & Everstine, L. (1993). *The trauma response: Treatment for emotional injury.* New York: Norton.

Ewing, C.P. (1990a). *When children kill: The dynamics of juvenile homicide.* Thousand Oaks, CA: Sage.

Ewing, C.P. (1997). *Fatal families: The dynamics of intrafamilial homicide.* Thousand Oaks, CA: Sage.

Ewing, C.P. (2001). Parricide. In G-F. Pinard & L. Pagani (Eds.), *Clinical assessment of dangerousness: Empirical contributions* (pp. 181–194). New York: Cambridge University Press.

Eyestone, L., & Howell, R. (1994). An epidemiological study of attention-deficit hyperactivity disorder and major depression in a male prison population. *Bulletin of the American Academy of Psychiatry and the Law, 22,* 155–168.

Ezekiel, R.S. (1995). *The racist mind.* New York: Penguin.

Fagan, J. (1990). Intoxication and aggression. In M. Tonry & J.Q. Wilson (Eds.), *Drugs and crime* (pp. 241–320). Chicago: University of Chicago Press.

Fagan, J., Stewart, D., & Hanson, K. (1983). Violent men or violent husbands: Background factors and situational correlates of domestic and extra-domestic violence. In D. Finkelhor, R. Gelles, G. Hotaling & M. Straus (Eds.), *The dark side of families* (pp. 34–55). Thousand Oaks, CA: Sage.

Fagot, B.I., Pears, K.C., Capaldi, D.M., Crosby, L., & Leve, C.S. (1998). Becoming an adolescent father: Precursors and parenting. *Developmental Psychology, 34,* 1209–1219.

Fahey, T.A. (1993). The diagnosis of multiple personality disorder. *British Journal of Psychiatry, 153,* 597–606.

Faller, K.C. (1987). Women who sexually abuse children. *Violence and Victims, 2,* 263–276.

Faller, K.C. (1995). A clinical sample of women who have sexually abused children. *Journal of Child Sexual Abuse, 1,* 13–30.

Falsetti, S.A., & Resnick, H.S. (1995). Helping the victims of violent crime. In J.R. Freedy & S.E. Hobfoll (Eds.), *Traumatic stress: From theory to practice* (pp. 263–285). New York: Plenum.

Fanon, F. (1965). *The wretched of the earth.* New York: Pelican.

Farmer, A., & Tiefenthaler, J. (2003). Explaining the recent decline in domestic violence. *Contemporary Economic Policy, 21,* 158–172.

Farmer, E., & Pollock, S. (1998). *Sexually abused and abusing children in substitute care.* Chichester, UK: Wiley.

Farmer, T.W., & Cadwallader, T.W. (2000). Social interactions and peer support for problem behavior. *Preventing School Failure, 44,* 105–117.

Farmer, T.W., Xie, H., Cairns, B.D., & Hutchins, B.C. (2007). Social synchrony, peer networks, and aggression in school. In P.H. Hawley, T.D. Little & P.C. Rodkin (Eds.), *Aggression and adaptation: The bright side to bad behavior* (pp. 209–234). Mahwah, NJ: Lawrence Erlbaum.

Farnham, F.R., James, D.V., & Cantrell, P. (2000). Association between violence, psychosis, and relationship to victim in stalkers. *Lancet, 355,* 199.

Farr, K.A. (2002). Battered women who were "being killed and survived it": Straight talk from survivors. *Violence and Victims, 17,* 267–281.

Farrell, A., Meyer, A., Kung, E., & Sullivan, T. (2001). Development and evaluation of school-based violence prevention programs. *Journal of Clinical Child Psychology, 30,* 207–220.

Farrington, D.P. (1986a). Age and crime. In M. Tonry & N. Morris (Eds.), *Crime and justice: An annual review of research* (pp. 189–217). Chicago: University of Chicago Press.

Farrington, D.P. (1986b). Stepping stones to adult criminal careers. In D. Olweus, J. Block, & M. Radke-Yarrow (Eds.), *Development of antisocial and prosocial behavior: Research, theories and issues* (pp. 359–384). New York: Academic Press.

Farrington, D.P. (1987). Epidemiology. In H.C. Quay (Ed.), *Handbook of juvenile delinquency* (pp. 33–61). New York: Wiley.

Farrington, D.P. (1991). Childhood aggression and adult violence: Early precursors and later-life outcomes. In D.J. Pepler & F.H. Rubin (Eds.), *The development and treatment of childhood aggression* (pp. 5–29). Hillsdale, NJ: Erlbaum.

Farrington, D.P. (1993). Understanding and preventing bullying. In M. Tonry (Ed.), *Crime and justice: A review of research* (pp. 381–458). Chicago: University of Chicago Press.

Farrington, D.P. (1995). The development of offending and antisocial behaviour from childhood: Key findings from the Cambridge Study in Delinquent Development. *Journal of Child Psychiatry and Psychology, 360,* 929–962.

Farrington, D.P. (2000). Explaining and preventing crime: The globalization of knowledge. *Criminology, 38,* 1–24.

Fazel, S., Doli, H., & Lnagstrom, N. (2008). Mental disorders among adolescents in juvenile detention and correctional facilities: A systematic review and metaregression analysis of 25 surveys. *Journal of the American Academy of Child and Adolescent Psychiatry, 47,* 1010–1019.

Fazel, S., & Grann, M. (2002). Older criminals: A descriptive study of psychiatrically examined offenders in Sweden. *International Journal of Geriatric Psychiatry, 17,* 907–913.

Fazel, S., & Grann, M. (2004). Psychiatric morbidity among homicide offenders: A Swedish population study. *American Journal of Psychiatry, 161,* 2129–2131.

Federal Bureau of Investigation (1995). *Crime in America: Uniform crime reports.* Washington, DC: US Government Printing Office.

Federal Bureau of Investigation (2004). *Crime in the United States, 2003.* Washington, DC: Federal Bureau of Investigation.

Fehrenbach, P.A., Smith, W., Monastersky, C., & Deisher, R.W. (1986) Adolescent sexual offenders: Offenders and offense characteristics. *American Journal of Orthopsychiatry, 56,* 225–233.

Fein, R.A., & Vosskuil, B. (1998). Preventing attacks on public officials and public figures: A Secret Service perspective. In J.R. Meloy (Ed.), *The psychology of stalking: Clinical and forensic perspectives* (pp. 175–191). San Diego, CA: Academic Press.

Feiring, C., Taska, L., & Lewis, M. (2002). Adjustment following sexual abuse discovery: The role of shame and attributional style. *Developmental Psychology, 38,* 79–92.

Feld, B.C. (1993). Criminalizing the American juvenile court. *Criminal Justice, 17,* 197–280.

Feld, B.C. (1998). The juvenile court. In M. Tonry (Ed.), *Handbook of crime and punishment* (pp. 509–541). New York, NY: Oxford University Press.

Feldman, M.D. (2004). *Playing sick? Untangling the web of Munchausen Syndrome, Munchausen by Proxy, Malingering, and Factitious Disorder.* New York: Brunner-Routledge.

Felson, M. (2006). The street gang strategy. In M. Felson (Ed.), *Crime and nature* (pp. 305–324). Thousand Oaks, CA: Sage.

Felson, R.B. (1992). Kick 'em when they're down: Explanations of the relationship between stress and interpersonal aggression and violence. *The Sociological Quarterly, 33,* 1–16.

Felson, R.B. (2004). A rational choice approach to violence. In M. Zahn, H. Brownstein, & S. Jackson (Eds.), *Violence: From theory to research* (pp. 71–90). Dayton, OH: Anderson.

Felson, R.B., & Steadman, H. (2004). Situational factors in disputes leading to criminal violence. *Criminology, 21,* 59–74.

Felthous, A.R. (1980a). Childhood antecedents of aggressive behaviors in male psychiatric patients. *Bulletin of the American Academy of Psychiatry and the Law, 8,* 104–110.

Felthous, A.R. (1980b). Aggression against cats, dogs, and people. *Child Psychiatry and Human Development, 10,* 169–177.

Felthous, A.R., & Hempel, A. (1995). Combined homicide-suicide: A review. *Journal of Forensic Science, 40,* 846–857.

Felthouse, A.R., & Kellert, S.R. (1987a). Childhood cruelty to animals and later aggression against people. *American Journal of Psychiatry, 144,* 710–717.

Felthous, A.R., & Kellert, S.R. (1987b). Psychosocial aspects of selecting animal species for physical abuse. *Journal of Forensic Sciences, 32,* 1713–1723.

Fenton, G.W., Tennent, T.G., & Fenwick, P.B. (1974). The EEG in antisocial behaviour: A study of posterior temporal slow activity in special hospital patients. *Psychological Medicine, 4,* 181–186.

Ferguson, C.J. (2007a). The good, the bad and the ugly: A meta-analytic review of positive and negative effects of violent video games. *Psychiatric Quarterly, 78,* 309–316.

Ferguson, C.J. (2007b). Evidence for publication bias in video game violence effects literature: A meta-analytic review. *Aggression and Violent Behavior, 12,* 470–482.

Ferguson, C.J. (2008). The school shooting/violent video game link: Causal link or moral panic? *Journal of Investigative Psychology and Offender Profiling, 5,* 25–37.

Ferguson, C.J., Rueda, S., Cruz, A., Ferguson, A., Fritz, D., & Smith, S. (2008). Violent video games and aggression: Causal relationship or byproduct of family violence and intrinsic violence motivation? *Criminal Justice and Behavior, 35,* 311–332.

Ferguson, C.J., San Miguel, C., Kilburn, J.C., & Sanchez, P. (2007). The effectiveness of school-based anti-bullying programs: A metanalytic review. *Criminal Justice Review, 32,* 401–414.

Ferguson, C.J., White, D.E., Cherry, S., Lorenz, M., & Bhimani, Z. (2003). Defining and classifying serial murder in the context of perpetrator motivation. *Journal of Criminal Justice, 31,* 287–292.

Fergusson, D.M., & Lynskey, M.T. (1996). Adolescent resiliency to family adversity. *Journal of Child Psychology and Psychiatry, 37,* 281–292.

Fergusson, D.M., Woodward, L., & Horwood, L.J. (1998). Maternal smoking during pregnancy and psychiatric adjustment in late adolescence. *Archives of General Psychiatry, 55,* 721–727.

Feuer, A. (1998). Drawing a bead on a baffling end game: Suicide by cop. *New York Times,* June 21, p. wk-3.

Fields, S.K., Collins, C.L., & Comstock, R.D. (2007). Conflict on the courts: A review of the sports-related violence literature. *Trauma, Violence, and Abuse, 8,* 359–369.

Figueredo, A.J., & McClosky, L.A. (1993). Sex, money, and paternity: The evolution of domestic violence. *Ethology and Sociobiology, 14,* 353–379.

Fink, D. (1995). Violence and psychiatric residency. In B.S. Eichelman & A.C. Hartwig (Eds.), *Patient violence and the clinician* (pp. 33–42). Washington, DC: American Psychiatric Association.

Finkelhor, D. (1994). Current information on the scope and nature of child abuse. *The Future of Children, 4,* 31–53.

Finkelhor, D., Hotaling, G.T., Lewis, I.A., & Smith, C. (1990). Sexual abuse in a national sample of adult men and women: Prevalence, characteristics, and risk factors. *Child Abuse and Neglect, 14,* 19–28.

Finkelhor, D., & Russell, D. (1984). Women as perpetrators: In D. Finkelhor (Ed.), *Child sexual abuse: New theory and research* (pp. 171–185). New York: Free Press.

Finkelhor, D., & Williams, L. (1988). *Nursery crimes: Sexual abuse in day care.* Newbury Park, CA: Sage.

Finkelhor, D., & Yllo, K. (1985). *License to rape: Sexual abuse of wives.* New York: Holt, Rinehart & Winston.

Finn, J. (2004). A survey of online harassment at a university campus. *Journal of Interpersonal Violence, 19,* 468–483.

Finn, J., & Banach, M. (2000). Victimization online: The downside of seeking services for women on the Internet. *Cyberpsychology and Behavior, 3,* 776–785.

Firestone, P., Bradford, J.M., Greenberg, D.M., & Serran, G.A. (2000). The relationship of deviant sexual arousal and psychopathy in incest offenders, extrafamilial child molesters, and rapists. *Journal of the American Academy of Psychiatry and the Law, 28,* 303–308.

Fishbein, D.H. (1992). The psychobiology of female aggression. *Criminal Justice and Behavior, 19,* 99–126.

Fisher, S. (1963). A further appraisal of the body boundary concept. *Journal of Consulting Psychology, 27,* 62–74.

Fisher, W.H., Packer, I., Banks, S., Smith, D., Simon, L., & Roy-Bujnowksi, K. (2002). Self-reported lifetime psychiatric hospitalization histories of jail detainees with mental disorders: Comparison with a non-incarcerated national sample. *Journal of Behavioral Health Services and Research, 29,* 458–465.

Fitzhugh, K.B. (1973). Some neuropsychological features of delinquent subjects. *Perceptual and Motor Skills, 36,* 494.

Flaherty, L.T. (2001). School violence and the school environment. In M. Shafii & S.L. Shafii (Eds.), *School violence: Assessment, management, prevention* (pp. 25–51). Washington, DC: American Psychiatric Publishing.

Flannery, R.B. (1995). *Violence in the workpace.* New York: Crossroad.

Flannery, R.B., Fulton, P., Tausch, J., & DeLoffi, A. (1991). A program to help staff cope with psychological sequelae of assaults by patients. *Hospital and Community Psychiatry, 42,* 935-942.

Flannery, R.B., Penk, W.E., Hanson, M.A., & Flannery, G.J. (1996). The Assaulted Staff Action Program Guidelines for fielding a team. In G.R. VandenBos & E.Q. Bulatao (Eds.), *Violence on the job: Identifying risks and developing solutions* (pp. 327–341). Washington DC: American Psychological Association.

Flannery, R.B., Hanson, M.A., Penk, W.E., Goldfinger, S., Pastva, G.J., & Navon, M.A. (1998). Replicated declines in assault rates after implementation of the Assaulted Staff Action Program. *Psychiatric Services, 49,* 241–243.

Flannery, R.B. (2005). Precipitants to psychiatric patient assaults on staff: Review of empirical findings, 1990–2003, and risk management implications. *Psychiatric Quarterly, 76,* 317–326.

Flannery, R.B., Hanson, M.A., Corrigan, M., & Walker, A.P. (2006). Past violence, substance use, and precipitants to psychiatric patient assaults: Eleven-year analysis of the Assaulted Staff Action Program (ASAP). *International Journal of Emergency Mental Health, 8,* 157–163.

Flannery, R.B., Stevens, V., Juliano, J., & Walker, A.P. (2000). Past violence and substance use disorder and subsequent violence toward others: Six-year analysis of the Assaulted Staff Action Program (ASAP). *International Journal of Emergency Mental Health, 2,* 241–247.

Fleisher, M.S., & Decker, S. (2001). An overview of the challege of prison gangs. *Corrections Management Quarterly, 5,* 1–9.

Flores, E., Cicchetti, D., & Rogosch, F. (2005). Predictors of resilience in maltreated and nonmaltreated Latino children. *Developmental Psychology, 41,* 338–351.

Flor-Henry, P. (1976). Lateralized temporal-limbic dysfunction and psychopathology. *Annals of the New York Academy of Sciences, 280,* 777–797.

Flor-Henry, P. (1987). Cerebral aspects of sexual deviation. In G.D. Wilson (Eds.), *Variant sexuality: Research and theory* (pp. 125–166). Baltimore: Johns Hopkins University Press.

Flowers, B.R. (1986). *Children and criminality: The child as victim and perpetrator.* Westport, CT: Greenwood.

Flowers, B.R. (2000). *Domestic crimes, family violence, and child abuse: A study of contemporary American society.* Jefferson, MO: McFarland.

Flowers, B.R. (2001). *Sex crimes: Predators, perpetrators, prostitutes, and victims: an examination of sexual criminality and victimization.* Springfield, IL: Charles C Thomas.

Flowers, B.R. (2002a). *Kids who commit adult crimes: A study of serious juvenile criminality and delinquency.* Binghamton, NY: Haworth.

Flowers, B.R. (2002b). *Male crime and violence: Exploring the dynamics, nature, and causes.* Westport, CT: Greenwood.

Flowers, B.R. (2002c) *Murder, at the end of the day and night: A study of criminal homicide offenders, victims, and circumstances.* Springfield, IL: Charles C Thomas.

Flowers, B.R. (2006). *Sex crimes: Perpetrators, predators, prostitutes, and victims* (2nd ed.). Springfield, IL: Charles C Thomas.

Flowers, B.R., & Flowers, H.L. (2001). *Murders in the United States: Crimes, killers, and victims of the twentieth century.* Jefferson, MO: McFarland.

Flynn, C.P. (2000a). Why family professionals can no longer ignore violence toward animals. *Family Relations, 49,* 87–95.

Flynn, C.P. (2000b). Battered women and their animal companions: Symbolic interaction between human and nonhuman animals. *Society and Animals, 8,* 99–127.

Flynn, C.P. (2000c). Women's best friend: Pet abuse and the role of companion animals in the lives of battered women. *Violence Against Women, 6,* 162–177.

Fogler, J.M., Shipherd, J.C., Rowe, E., Jensen, J., Clarke, S. (2008). A theoretical foundation for understanding clergy-perpetrated sexual abuse. *Journal of Child Sexual Abuse, 17,* 301–328.

Foley, D.L., Eaves, L.J., Wormley, B.S., Silberg, J.L., Maes, H.H., & Kuhn, J. (2004). Childhood adversity, monoamine oxidase A genotype, and risk for conduct disorder. *Archives of General Psychiatry, 61,* 738–744.

Foley, D.L., Pickles, A., Simonoff, E., Maes, H.H., Silberg, J.L., & Hewitt, J.K. (2001). Parental concordance and comorbidity for psychiatric disorder and associate risks for current psychiatric symptoms and disorders in a community sample of juvenile twins. *Journal of Child Psychology and Psychiatry, 42,* 381–394.

Foley, S.R., Kelly, B.D., & Clarke, M. (2005). Incidence and clinical correlates of aggression and violence at presentation in patients with first episode psychosis. *Schizophrenia Research, 72,* 161–178.

Folino, J.O. (2000). Sexual homicides and their classification according to motivation: A report from Argentina. *International Journal of Offender Therapy and Comparative Criminology, 44,* 740–750.

Follingstad, D.R., Wright, S., Lloyd, S., & Sebastian, J.A. (1991). Sex differences in motivations and effects in dating violence. *Family Relations, 40,* 51–57.

Ford, H. (2006). *Women who sexually abuse children.* Chichester, UK: Wiley.

Forssman, H., & Frey, T.S. (1953). Electroencephalograms of boys with behavior disorders. *Acta Psychiatrica Neurologica Scandinavica, 28,* 61–73.

Fossey, D. (1984). *Gorillas in the mist.* Boston: Houghton Mifflin.

Foucha v. Lousiana, 504, U.S. 71 (1992).

Fowles, D.C., & Dindo, L. (2006). A dual-deficit model of psychopathy. In C.J. Patrick (Ed.), *Handbook of psychopathy* (pp. 14–34). New York: Guilford.

Fowles, D.C., & Kochanska, G. (2000). Temperament as a moderator of pathways to conscience in children: The contribution of electrodermal activity. *Psychophysiology, 37,* 788–795.

Fox, J.A. (1996). *Uniform crime reports: Supplementary homicide reports, 1976–1994.* Boston: Northeastern University College of Criminal Justice.

Fox, J.A., & Levin, J. (1994). *Overkill: Mass murder and serial killing exposed.* New York: Plenum.

Fox, J.A., & Levin, J. (1998). Multiple homicide: Patterns of serial and mass murder. *Crime and Justice, 23,* 407–455.

Fox, J.A., & Levin, J. (2003). Mass murder: An analysis of extreme violence. *Journal of Applied Psychoanalytic Studies, 5,* 47–64.

Fox, J.A., & Zawitz, M.W. (2003). *Crime date brief: Homicide trends in the United States: 2000 update.* Washington, DC: US Department of Justice.

Fox, J.A., & Zawitz, M.W. (2006). *Homicide trends in the United States.* Washington, DC: U.S. Government Printing Office.

Fox, J.G., & Sobol, J.J. (2000). Drinking patterns, social interaction, and barroom behavior: A routine activities approach. *Deviant Behavior, 21,* 429–450.

Francis, P.C., & Turner, N.R. (1995). Sexual misconduct within the Christian church: Who are the perpetrators and who do they victimize? *Counseling and Values, 39,* 218–227.

Frank, E., & Stewart, B.D. (1984). Depressive symptoms in rape victims: A revisit. *Journal of Affective Disorders, 7,* 77–85.

Freckelton, I. (1988). Querulent paranoia and the vexatious complainant. *International Journal of Law and Psychiatry, 11,* 127–143.

Freckelton, I., & List, D. (2009). Asperger's disorder, criminal responsibility, and criminal culpability. *Psychiatry, Psychology and Law, 16,* 16–40.

Freeman, T.W., & Roca, V. (2001). Gun use, attitudes toward violence, and aggression among combat veterans with chronic posttraumatic stress disorder. *Journal of Nervous and Mental Disease, 189,* 317–320.

French, J.R.P., & Raven, B.H. (1959). The bases of social power. In D. Cartwright (Eds.), *Studies in social power* (pp. 150–167). Ann Arbor, MI: Institute for Social Research.

French, L.M., Spector, J., Stiers, W., & Kane, R.L. (2010). Blast injury and traumatic brain injury. In C.H. Kennedy & J.L. Moore (Eds.), *Military neuropsychology* (pp. 101–125). New York: Springer.

Freud, A. (1948). The ego and the mechanisms of defense. London: Hogarth Press.

Freud, S. (1905/1953). Three essays on the theory of sexuality. In J. Strachey (Ed. & Transl.), *The standard edition of the complete psychological works of Sigmund Freud* (Vol. 7, pp. 57–145). London: Hogarth Press.

Freud, S. (1930/1961). Civilization and its discontents. In J. Strachey (Ed. & Transl.), *The standard edition of the complete psychological works of Sigmund Freud* (Vol. 21, pp. 57–145). London: Hogarth Press.

Freud, S. (1933/1964). New introductory lectures on psycho-analysis. In J. Strachey (Ed. & Transl.), *The standard edition of the complete psychological works of Sigmund Freud* (Vol. 22, pp. 1–182). London: Hogarth Press.

Freundlich, M., Avery, R., & Padgett, D. (2007). Care or scare: The safety of youth in congregate care in New York City. *Child Abuse and Neglect, 31,* 173–186.

Frick, P.J. (1995). Callous-unemotional traits and conduct problems: A two-factor model of psychopathy in children. *Issues in Criminological and Legal Psychology, 24,* 47–51.

Frick, P.J., Lahey, B.B., Loeber, R., Tannenbaum, L., Van Horn, Y., & Christ, M.A.G. (1993). Oppositional defiant disorder and conduct disorder: A meta-analytic review of factor analyses and cross-validation in a clinic sample. *Clinical Psychology Review, 13,* 319–340.

Frick, P.J., & Marsee, M.A. (2006). Psychopathy and developmental pathways to antisocial behavior in youth. In C.J. Patrick (Ed.), *Handbook of psychopathy* (pp. 353–374). New York: Guilford.

Frick, P.J., O'Brien, B.S., & Wooton, J.M. (1994). Psychopathy and conduct problems in children. *Journal of Abnormal Psychology, 103,* 700–707.

Fried, P., Watkinson, B., & Gray, R. (1998). Differential effects on cognitive functioning in 9- to 12-year-olds prenatally exposed to cigarettes and marijuana. *Neurotoxicology and Teratology, 20,* 293–306.

Freidman, L.N., Tucker, S.B., Neville, P.R., & Imperial, M. (1996). The impact of domestic violence on the workplace. In G.R. Vandenbos & E.Q. Bulatao (Eds.), *Violence on the job: Identifying risks and developing solutions* (pp. 153-161). Washington, DC: American Psychological Association.

Friedman, M. (2009). Crossing the line: What makes a rabbi violate sexual bound-aries–and what can be done about it? In A. Neustein (Ed.), *Tempest in the temple: Jewish communities and child sex scandals* (pp. 43–59). Waltham, MA: Brandeis University Press.

Friedman, S.H., Horwitz, S.M., & Resnick, P.J. (2005). Child murder by mothers: A critical analysis of the current state of knowledge and a research agenda. *American Journal of Psychiatry, 162,* 1578–1587.

Friedman, S.H., Hrouda, D.R., Holden, C.E., Nofsinger, S.G., & Resnick, P.J. (2005a). Filicide-suicide: Common factors in parents who kill their children and themselves. *Journal of the American Academy of Psychiatry and the Law, 33,* 496–504.

Friedman, S.H., Hrouda, D.R., Holden, C.E., Nofsinger, S.G., & Resnick, P.J. (2005b). Child murder committed by severely mentally ill mothers: An exami-nation of mothers found not guilty by reason of insanity. *Journal of Forensic Sciences, 50,* 1466–1471.

Friedman, S.H., Shelton, M.D., Elhaj, O., Youngstrom, E.A., Rapport, D.J., Packer, K.A., Bilali, S.R., Jackson, K.S., Sakai, H.E., Resnick, P.J., Findling, R.L., & Calabrese, J.R. (2005). Gender differences in criminality: Bipolar disorder with co-occurring substance abuse. *Journal of the American Academy of Psychiatry and the Law, 33,* 188–195.

Friedman, T.L. (2002). The two domes of Belgium. *New York Times,* January 27, p. 13.

Friel, A., White, T., & Hull, A. (2008). Posttraumatic stress disorder and criminal responsibility. *Journal of Forensic Psychiatry and Psychology, 19,* 64–85.

Frierson, R.L. et al. (2002). Competence-to-stand-trial evaluations of geriatric defen-dants. *Journal of the American Academy of Psychiatry and the Law, 30,* 252–256.

Frieze, I.H. (1983). Investigating the causes of marital rape. *Signs: Journal of Women in Culture and Society, 8,* 532–553.

Fromuth, M.E., & Conn, V.E. (1997). Hidden perpetrators: Sexual molestation in a nonclinical sample of college women. *Journal of Interpersonal Violence, 12,* 456–465.

Frye, V. (2001). Examining homicide's contribution to pregnancy-associated deaths. *Journal of the American Medical Association, 285,* 1510–1511.

Fulton, M., Thomson, G., Hunter, R., Raab, G., Laxen, D., & Hepburn, W. (1987). Influence of blood lead on the ability and attainment of children in Edinburgh. *Lancet, i,* 1221–1226.

Fulwiler, C., Eckstine, J., & Kalsy, S. (2005). Impulsive-aggressive traits, serotonin function, and alcohol-enhanced aggression. *Journal of Clinical Pharmacology, 45,* 94–100.

Fulwiler, C., Grossman, H., Forbes, C., & Ruthazer, R. (1997). Early-onset substance abuse and community violence by outpatients with chronic mental illness. *Psychiatric Services, 48,* 1181–1185.

Fulwiler, C., & Ruthazer, R. (1999). Premorbid risk factors for violence in adult men-tal illness. *Comprehensive Psychiatry, 40,* 96–100.

Gabrielli, W.F., & Mednick, S.A. (1980). Sinistrality and delinquency. *Journal of Abnormal Psychology, 89,* 654–661.

Gaensbauer, T.J. (1982). Regulation of emotional expression in infants from two contrasting caregiving environments. *Journal of the American Academy of Child Psychiatry, 21,* 163–171.

Gage, A.J., & Hutchinson, P.L. (2006). Power, control, and intimate partner sexual violence in Haiti. *Archives of Sexual Behavior, 35,* 11–24.

Galdikas, B.M.F. (2005). Subadult male orangutan sociality and reproductive behavior at Tanjung Putting. *American Journal of Primatology, 8,* 87–99.

Gallagher, B. (1999). The abuse of children in public care. *Child Abuse Review, 8,* 357–365.

Gallo, G. (2005). A family affair: Domestic violence in police families. *Police,* February, pp. 36–40.

Galloway, D., & Roland, E. (2004). Is the direct approach to bullying always the best? In P.K. Smith, D. Pepler & K. Rigby (Eds.), *Bullying in schools: How successful can interventions be?* (pp. 37–53). Cambridge, UK: Cambridge University Press.

Gallup-Black, A. (2005). *Rural and urban trends in family and intimate partner homicide: 1980–1999.* Washington, DC: National Institute of Justice.

Galski, T., Thornton, K.E., & Shumsky, D. (1990). Brain dysfunction in sex offenders. *Journal of Offender Rehabilitaton, 16,* 65–80.

Galvan, A., Hare, T., Voss, H., Glover, G., & Casey, B.J. (2007). Risk-taking and the adolescent brain: Who is at risk? *Developmental Science, 10,* 8–14.

Gambino, R. (1974). *Blood of my blood: The dilemma of the Italian-American.* Garden City, NY: Doubleday.

Gannon, T.A., Collie, R.M., Ward, T., & Thakker, J. (2008). Rape: Psychopathology, theory, and treatment. *Clinical Psychology Review, 28,* 982–1008.

Gannon, T.A., & Polaschek, D.L.L. (2006). Cognitive distortions in child molesters: A re-examination of key theories and research. *Clinical Psychology Review, 26,* 1000–1019.

Gannon, T.A., & Rose, M.R. (2008). Female child sexual offenders: Towards integrating theory and practice. *Aggression and Violent Behavior, 13,* 442–461.

Ganor, B. (2000). *Countering sucide terrorism.* Herzliya, Israel: International Institute for Counter-Terrorism.

Garbarino, J. (1997). *Raising children in a socially toxic environment.* San Francisco: Jossey-Bass.

Garcia, L., Soria, C., & Hurwitz, E.L. (2007). Homicides and intimate partner violence: A literature review. *Trauma, Violence, and Abuse, 8,* 370–383.

Gardner, R.W., Holzman, P.S., Klein, G.S., Linton, H.B., & Spence, D.P. (1959). Cognitive control: A study of individual consistencies in cognitive behavior. *Psychological Issues, 1,* 1–185.

Gardner, W. (1993). A life-span rational choice theory of risk taking. In N. Bell & R. Bell (Eds.), *Adolescent risk taking* (pp. 66–83). Newbury Park, CA: Sage.

Garland, D. (2001). *The culture of control: Crime and social order in contemporary society.* Oxford: Oxford University Press.

Garmezy, N. (1985). Stress-resistant children: The search for protective factors. In J.E. Stevenson (Ed.), *Recent research in developmental psychopathology* (pp. 213–233). Oxford: Pergamon Press.

Gaulin, S.J.C., & McBurnery, D. (2004). *Evolutionary psychology.* Upper Saddle River, NJ: Prentice Hall.

Gauthier, D.K., & Brankston, W.B. (2004). "Who kills whom" revisited: A sociological study of variation in the sex ratio of spouse killings. *Homicide Studies, 8,* 96–102.

Gauthier, D.K., Chaudoir, N.K., & Forsyth, C.J. (2003). A sociological analysis of maternal infanticide in the United States, 1984–1996. *Deviant Behavior, 24,* 393–404.

Gavey, N. (1991). Sexual victimization prevalence among New Zealand university students. *Journal of Consulting and Clinical Psychology, 59,* 464–466.

Gazmararian, J.A., Adams, M.M., Saltzman, L.E., Johnson, C.H., Bruce, F.C., & Marks, J.S. (1995). The relationship between pregnancy intendedness and physical violence in mothers of newborns. *Obstetrics and Gynecology, 85,* 1031–1038.

Gazmararian, J.A., Lazorick, S., Spitz, A.M., Ballard, T.H., Saltzman, L.E., & Marks, J.S. (1996). Prevalence of violence against pregnant women. *Journal of the American Medical Association, 275,* 1915–1920.

Gazmararian, J.A., Petersen, R., Spitz, A.M., Goodwin, M.M., Saltzman, L.E., & Marks, J.S. (2000). Violence and reproductive health: Current knowledge and future research directions. *Maternal and Child Health Journal, 4,* 79–84.

Geberth, V.J. (1981). Psychological profiling. *Law and Order, 29,* 401–421.

Geberth, V.J. (1990). *Practical homicide investigation: Tactics, procedures, and forensic techniques* (2nd ed.). Boca Raton: CRC Press.

Geberth, V.J. (1995). Criminal personality profiling. *Law and Order, 43,* 45–49.

Geberth, V.J. (1996a). The staged crime scene. *Law and Order, 44,* 89–91.

Geberth, V.J. (1996b). *Practical homicide investigation. Tactics, procedures, and forensic techniques* (3rd ed.). Boca Raton, FL: CRC Press.

Geberth, V.J. (2003). *Sex-related homicide and death investigation: Practical and clinical perspectives.* Boca Raton, FL: CRC Press.

Geberth, V.J. (2006). Preliminary death investigation. *FBI Law Enforcement Bulletin,* September, pp. 131–140.

Geberth, V.J., & Turco, R.N. (1997). Antisocial personality disorder, sexual sadism, malignant narcissism, and serial murder. *Journal of Forensic Science, 42,* 45–49.

Gebo, E. (2002). A contextual exploration of siblicide. *Violence and Victims, 17,* 157–168.

Gee, D.J., Ward, T., & Eccleston, L. (2003). The function of sexual fantasies for sexual offenders: A preliminary model. *Behaviour Change, 20,* 44–60.

Gelinas, J.D. (1983). The persisting negative effects of incest. *Psychiatry, 46,* 312–332.

Gellately, R., & Kiernan, B. (2003). *The specter of genocide: Mass murder in historical perspective.* Cambridge, UK: Cambridge University Press.

Geller, W.A. (1982). Deadly force: What we know. *Journal of Police Science and Administration, 10,* 151–177.

Geller, W.A. (1993). Put friendly-fire shooting in perspective. *Law Enforcement News, 18,* 9.

Gelles, R.J. (1992). Poverty and violence toward children. *American Behavioral Scientist, 35,* 258–274.

George, L.K., Winfield, I., & Blazier, D.G. (1992). Sociocultural factors in sexual assault: Comparison of two representative samples of women. *Journal of Social Issues, 48,* 105–125.

Gerard, M.E., Spitz, M.C., Towbin, J.A., & Shantz, D. (1998). Subacute postictal aggression. *Neurology, 50,* 384–388.

Gerber, J., & Engelhardt-Greer, S. (1996). Just and painful: Attitudes toward sentencing criminals. In T.J. Flanagan & D.R. Longmire (Eds.), *Americans view crime and justice: A national public opinion survey* (pp. 62–74). Thousand Oaks, CA: Sage.

Gershoff, E.T. (2002). Corporal punishment by parents and associated child behaviors and experiences: A meta-analytic and theoretical review. *Psychological Bulletin, 128,* 539–579.

Geschwind, N., & Galaburda, A.M. (1985). Cerebral lateralization: Biological mechanisms, associations and pathology. A hypothesis and a program for research. *Archives of Neurology, 42,* 428–459, 521–552, 634–654.

Ghaziuddin, M., Tsai, L., & Ghaziuddin, N. (1991). Violence in Asperger's syndrome: A critique. *Journal of Autism and Developmental Disorder, 21,* 349–354.

Ghiglieri, M.P. (1999). *The dark side of man: Tracing the origins of violence.* Reading, MA: Perseus Books.

Ghika-Scmidt, F., Assai, G., De Tribolet, N., & Regli, F. (1995). Kluver-Bucy syndrome after left anterior temporal resection. *Neuropsychologia, 33,* 101–113.

Gibbons, D.C. (1997). Race, ethnicity, crime, and social policy. *Crime and Delinquency, 43,* 358–380.

Gibbs, S. (2005). Islam and Islamic extremism: An existential analysis. *Journal of Humanistic Psychology, 45,* 156–203.

Gibson, C. & Wright, J. (2001). Low self-control and coworker delinquency: A research note. *Journal of Criminal Justice, 29,* 483–492.

Giedd, J.N. (2004). Structural magnetic resonance imaging of the adolescent brain. *Annals of the New York Academy of Sciences, 1021,* 105–109.

Giedd, J.N., Blumenthal, J., Jeffries, N.O., Castellanos, F.X., Liu, H., & Zijenbos, A. (1999). Brain development during childhood and adolescence: A longitudinal MRI study. *Nature Neuroscience, 2,* 861–863.

Gilbert, C.M. (1992). Sibling incest: A descriptive study of family dynamics. *Journal of Child and Adolescent Psychiatric and Mental Health Nursing, 5,* 5–9.

Gillies, H. (1965). Murder in the west of Scotland. *British Journal of Psychiatry, 111,* 1087–1094.

Gilligan, J. (1997). *Violence: Reflections on a national epidemic.* New York: Vintage.

Gilligan, J. (2000). The last mental hospital. *Psychiatric Quarterly, 72,* 45–61.

Gilliland, B.E., & James, R.K. (1993). *Crisis intervention strategies* (2nd ed.). Pacific Grove, CA: Brooks/Cole.

Gini, G. (2006). Social cognition and moral cognition in bullying: What's wrong? *Aggressive Behavior, 32,* 528–539.

Giotakos, O., Markianos, M., Vaidakis, N., & Christodoulou, G.N. (2003). Aggression, impulsivity, plasma sex hormones and biogenic amine turnover in a forensic population of rapists. *Journal of Sex and Marital Therapy, 29,* 215–225.

Gladue, B.A., Boechler, M., & McCaul, K. (1989). Hormonal responses to competition in human males. *Aggressive Behavior, 15,* 409–422.

Glass, N., Koziol-McLain, J., Campbell, J.C., & Block, C.R. (2004). Female-perpetrated femicide and attempted femicide: A case study. *Violence Against Women, 10,* 606–625.

Gleason, W.J. (1993). Mental disorders in battered women: An empirical study. *Violence and Victims, 8,* 53–68.

Glenn, A.L., & Raine, A. (2008). The neurobiology of psychopathy. *Psychiatric Clinics of North America, 31,* 463–475.

Glenn, A.L., Raine, A., & Venables, P.H. (2007). Early temperamental and psychophysiological precursors of adult psychopathic personality. *Journal of Abnormal Psychology, 116,* 508–518.

Glomb, T.M., & Liao, H. (2003). Interpersonal aggression in work groups: Social influence, reciprocal and individual effects. *Academy of Management Journal, 46,* 486–496.

Glover, J. (1999). *Humanity: A moral history of the twentieth century.* New Haven, CT; Yale University Press.

Glueck, S., & Glueck, E. (1950). *Unraveling juvenile delinquency.* Cambridge, MA: Harvard University Press.

Goddard, G.V. (1967). Development of epileptic seizures through brain stimulation at low intensity. *Nature, 214,* 1020-1021.

Godinez v. Moran, 509 U.S. 389 (1993).

Goenjian, A. (1993). A mental health relief programme in Armenia after the 1988 earthquake: Implementation and clinical observations. *British Journal of Psychiatry, 63,* 230–239.

Goetting, A. (1988). When parents kill young children: Detroit 1982–1986. *Journal of Family Violence, 3,* 339–346.

Goetz, A.T., & Shackelford, T.K. (2006). Sexual coercion and forced in-pair copulation as sperm competition tactics in humans. *Human Nature, 17,* 265–282.

Goetz, A.T., Shackelford, T.K., Starratt, V.G., & McKibbin, W.F. (2008). Intimate partner violence. In J.D. Duntley & T.K. Shackelford (Eds.), *Evolutionary forensic psychiatry: Darwinian foundations of crime and law* (pp. 65–78). New York: Oxford University Press.

Goff, D.C., Brotman, A.W., & Kindlon, D. (1991). Self-reports of childhood abuse in chronically psychotic patients. *Psychiatry Research, 37,* 73–80.

Gogtay, N., Giedd, J.N., Lusk, L., Hayashi, K.M., Greenstein, D., & Vaituzi, A.C. (2004). Dynamic mapping of human cortical development during childhood through early adulthood. *Proceedings of the National Academy of Sciences, 101,* 8147–8179.

Golden, C.J., Jackson, M.L., & Peterson, R.A. (1996). Neuropsychological correlates of violence and aggression: A review of the clinical literature. *Aggression and Violent Behavior, 1,* 3–25.

Goldhagen, D.J. (1997). *Hitler's willing executioners: Ordinary Germans and the Holocaust.* New York: Random House.

Golding, J.M. (1994). Sexual assault history and physical health in randomly selected Los Angeles women. *Health Psychology, 13,* 130–138.

Golding, J.M. (1999). Intimate partner violence as a risk factor for mental disorders: A metaanalysis. *Journal of Family Violence, 14,* 99–132.

Golding, J.M., Siegel, J.M., Sorenson, S.B., Burnam, M.A., & Stein, J.A. (1989). Social support sources following sexual assault. *Journal of Community Psychology, 17,* 92–107.

Goldstein, R.L. (1995). Paranoids in the legal system: The litigious paranoid and the paranoid criminal. *Psychiatric Clinics of North America, 18,* 303–315.

Gondolf, E.W., & White, R.J. (2001). Batterer participants who repeatedly reassault: Psychopathic tendencies and other disorders. *Journal of Interpersonal Violence, 16,* 361–380.

Gonzales, R. (1997). The academic resilience of Mexican American high school students. *Hispanic Journal of Behavioral Sciences, 19,* 301–317.

Goodman, M., Triebwasser, J., Shah, S., & New, A.S. (2007). Neuroimaging in personality disorders: Current concepts, findings, and implications. *Psychiatric Annals, 37,* 100–108.

Goodwill, A., Alison, L., & Humann, M. (2009). Multidimensional scaling and the analysis of sexual offence behavior. *Psychology, Crime and Law, 15,* 517–524.

Goodwin, D.W., Alderson, P., & Rosenthal, R. (1971). Clinical significance of hallucinations in psychiatric disorders. *Archives of General Psychiatry, 24,* 76–80.

Gordon, H.L., Baird, A.A., End, A.E. (2004). Functional differences among those high and low on a trait measure of psychopathy. *Biological Psychiatry, 56,* 516–521.

Gore-Felton, C., Gill, M., Koopman, C., & Spiegel, D. (1999). A review of acute stress reactions among victims of violence: Implications for early intervention. *Aggression and Violent Behavior, 4,* 293–306.

Gorenstein, E.E., & Newman, J.P. (1990). Disinhibitory psychopathology: A new perspective and a model for research. *Psychological Review, 87,* 301–315.

Gorman, D.G., & Cummings, J.L. (1992). Hypersexuality following septal injury. *Archives of Neurology, 49,* 308–310.

Gottesman, I.I., & Goldsmith, H.H. (1994). Developmental psychopathology of antisocial behavior: Inserting genes into its ontogenesis and epigenesis. In C. Nelson (Ed.), *Threats to optimum development: Biological, psychological, and social risk factors* (pp. 69–104). Hillsdale, NJ: Erlbaum.

Gottfredson, M.R., & Hirschi, T. (1990). *A general theory of crime.* Stanford, CA: Stanford University Press.

Gottlieb, C.B. (1996). Filicide: A strategic approach. *Psychology, 33,* 40–42.

Gottman, J.M., Jacobson, N.S., Rushe, R.H., Shortt, J.W., Babcock, J., & LaTaillade, J.J. (1995). The relationship between heart rate reactivity, emotionally aggressive behavior, and general violence in batterers. *Journal of Family Psychology, 9,* 227–248.

Gottschall, J. (2004). Explaining wartime rape. *The Journal of Sex Research, 41,* 129–136.

Gottschall, J.A., & Gottschall, T.A. (2003). Are per-incident rape pregnancy rates higher than per-incident consensual pregnancy rates? *Human Nature, 14,* 1–20.

Grafman, J., Schwab, K., Warden, D., Pridgen, A., Brown, H.R., & Salazar, A.M. (1996). Frontal lobe injuries, violence, and aggression: A report of the Vietnam head injury study. *Neurology, 46,* 1231–1238.

Graham, K., Bernards, S., Osgood, D.W., Homel, R., & Purcell, J. (2005). Guardians and handlers: The role of bar staff in preventing and managing aggression. *Addiction, 100,* 755–766.

Graham, K., Bernards, S., Osgood, D.W., & Wells, S. (2006). Bad nights or bad bars? Multi-level analysis of environmental predictors of aggression in late-night large-capacity bars and clubs. *Addiction, 101,* 1569–1580.

Graham, K., La Rocque, L., Yetman, R., Ross, T.J., & Guistra, E. (1980). Aggression and barroom environments. *Journal of Studies on Alcohol, 41,* 277–292.

Graham, K., Leonard, K.E., Room, R., Wild, T.C., Pihl, R.O., & Bois, C. (1998). Current directions in research on understanding and preventing intoxicated aggression. *Addiction, 93,* 659–676.

Graham, K., Schmidt, G., & Gillis, K. (1996). Circumstances when drinking leads to aggression: An overview of research findings. *Contemporary Drug Problems, 23,* 493–557.

Graham, K., & Wells, S. (2001). Aggression among young adults in the social context of the bar. *Addiction Research and Theory, 9,* 193–219.

Graham, K., & Wells, S. (2003). "Somebody's gonna get their head kicked in tonight!": Aggression among young males in bars–A question of values? *British Journal of Criminology, 43,* 546–644.

Graham, K., Wells, S., & West, P. (1997). A framework for applying explanations of alcohol-related aggression to naturally occurring aggressive behavior. *Contemporary Drug Problems, 24,* 625–666.

Graham, S., & Hudley, C. (1994). Attributions of aggressive and nonaggressive African-American male early adolescents: A study of construct accessibility. *Developmental Psychology, 30,* 365–373.

Graney, D.A., & Arrigo, B.A. (2002). *The power-serial rapist: A criminology-victimology of female victim selection.* Springfield, IL: Charles C Thomas.

Grant, J.E. (2005). Clinical characteristics and psychiatric comorbidity in males with exhibitionism. *Journal of Clinical Psychiatry, 66,* 1367–1371.

Grant, J.E., & Kim, S.W. (2002a). Temperament and early environmental influences in kleptomania. *Comprehensive Psychiatry, 43,* 223–228.

Grant, J.E., & Kim, S.W. (2002b). Clinical characteristics and associated psychopathology in 22 patients with kleptomania. *Comprehensive Psychiatry, 43,* 378–384.

Grant, J.E., & Kim, S.W. (2002c). An open-label study of naltrexone in the treatment of kleptomania. *Journal of Clinical Psychiatry, 63,* 349–355.

Grant, J.E., & Kim, S.W. (2007). Clinical characteristics and psychiatric comorbidity of pyromania. *Journal of Clinical Psychiatry, 68,* 1717–1722.

Grant, J.E., & Potenza, M.N. (2005). Pathological gambling and other "behavioral addictions." In R.J. Frances, S.I. Miller & A.H. Mack (Eds.), *Clinical textbook of addictive disorders* (pp. 303–320). New York: Guilford Press.

Graves, K.N., Kaslow, N.J., & Frabutt, J.M. (2010). A culturally-informed approach to trauma, suicidal behavior, and overt aggression in African American adolescents. *Aggression and Violent Behavior, 15,* 36–41.

Gray, J., & Bentovim, A. (1996). Illness induction syndrome: I. A series of 41 children from 37 families identified at Great Ormond Street Hospital for Children NHS Trust. *Child Abuse and Neglect, 20,* 655–673.

Gray, P.B., Kahlenberg, S.M., Barrett, E.S., Lipson, S.F., & Ellison, P.T. (2002). Marriage and fatherhood are associated with lower testosterone in males. *Evolution and Human Behavior, 23,* 193–201.

Grayston, A.D., & De Luca, R.V. (1999). Female perpetrators of child sexual abuse: A review of the clinical and empirical literature. *Aggression and Violent Behavior, 4,* 93–106.

Graz, C., Etschel, E., Schoech, H., & Soyka, M. (2009). Criminal behavior and violent crimes in former inpatients with affective disorder. *Journal of Affective Disorders, 117,* 98–103

Green, A.H., & Kaplan, M.S. (1994). Psychiatric impairment and childhood victimization experiences in female child molesters. *Journal of the American Academy of Child and Adolescent Psychiatry, 33,* 954–961.

Green, C.M. (1981). Matricide by sons. *Medicine, Science and the Law, 21,* 207–214.

Green, C.M., & Manohar, S.V. (1990). Neonaticide and hysterical denial of pregnancy. *British Journal of Psychiatry, 156,* 121–123.

Greenebaum, J.V., & Lurie, L.A. (1948). Encephalitis as a causative factor in behavior disorders in children. *Journal of the American Medical Association, 136,* 923–930.

Greenberg, J. (2010). What is insidious workplace behavior? In J. Greenberg (Ed.), *Insidious workplace behavior* (pp. 3–28). New York: Routledge.

Greenberg, L., & Barling, J. (1999). Predicting employee aggression against coworkers, subordinates, and supervisors: The roles of person behaviors and perceived workplace factors. *Journal of Organizational Behavior, 20,* 897–913.

Greene, A. (1986). Future time perspective in adolescence: The present of things future revisited. *Journal of Youth and Adolescence, 15,* 99–113.

Greenfield, L. (1997). *Sex offenses and offenders.* Washington, DC: Bureau of Justice Statistics, US Department of Justice.

Greenwald, R. (2002). *Trauma and juvenile delinquency: Theory, research and interventions.* New York: Haworth.

Greenwood, P. (2006). *Changing lives: Delinquency prevention as crime control policy.* Chicago: University of Chicago Press.

Greighton, S.J. (1995). Fatal child abuse: How preventable is it? *Child Abuse Review, 4,* 318–328.

Greve, K.W., Sherwin, E., & Stanford, M.S. (2001). Personality and neurocognitive correlates of impulsive aggression in long-term survivors of severe traumatic brain injury. *Brain Injury, 15,* 255–262.

Grey, N.S., Carmen, N.G., Rogers, P., MacCulloch, M.J., Hayward, P., & Snowden, R.J. (2003). Post-traumatic stress disorder in mentally disordered offenders by the committing of serious violent or sexual offense. *Journal of Forensic Psychiatry, 14,* 27–43.

Griffin, P., Torbet, P., Syzmanski, L., & Bilchik, S. (1998). *Trying juveniles as adults in criminal court: An analysis of state transfer provisions.* Washington, DC: US Department of Justice.

Griffin, S., & Bernard, T.J. (2003). Angry aggression among police officers. *Police Quarterly, 6,* 1–21.

Griffiths, M., & Hunt, N. (1995). Computer game playing in adolescence: Prevalence and demographic indicators. *Journal of Community and Applied Social Psychology, 5,* 189–193.

Grimmins, S., Langley, S., & Brownstein, H.H. (1997). Convicted women who have killed children: A self-psychology perspective. *Journal of Interpersonal Violence, 12,* 49–69.

Grinker, R.R., Werble, B., & Drye, R.C. (1968). *The borderline syndrome.* New York: Basic Books.

Grisso, T. (1996). Society's retributive response to juvenile violence: A developmental perspective. *Law and Human Behavior, 20,* 229–247.

Grisso, T. (2005). *Evaluating juveniles' adjudicative competence: A guide for clinical practice.* Sarasota, FL: Professional Resource Exchange.

Grisso, T., Steinberg, L., Woolard, J., Cauffman, E., & Scott, E. (2003). Juveniles' competence to stand trial: A comparison of adolescents' and adults' capacities as trial defendents. *Law and Human Behavior, 27,* 333–363.

Grossberg, M. (2002). Changing conceptions of child welfare in the United States, 1820–1935. In M.K. Rosenheim, F.E. Zimring, D.S. Tanenhaus & B. Dohrn (Eds.), *A century of juvenile justice* (pp. 3–41). Chicago: University of Chicago Press.

Grossman, D. (1996). *On killing: The psychology cost of learning to kill in war and society.* New York: Back Bay Books.

Grossman, D., & Christensen, L.W. (2007). *On combat: The psychology and physiology of deadly conflict in war and in peace* (2nd ed.). Portland, OR: LWC Books.

Grote, D. (1995). Discipline without punishment: The proven strategy that turns *problem employees into superior performers.* New York: Amacom.

Grote, D., & Harvey, E.L. (1983). *Discipline without punishment.* New York: McGraw-Hill.

Groth, A.N., & Birnbaum, A.H. (1979). *Men who rape: The psychology of the offender.* New York: Plenum.

Groth, A.N., & Burgess, A.W. (1970). Rape: A sexual deviation. *American Journal of Orthopsychiatry, 47,* 400–406.

Groth, A.N., & Burgess, A.W. (1978). Rape: A pseudosexual act. *International Journal of Women's Studies, 1,* 207–210.

Groth, A.N., Burgess, A.W., & Holmstrom, L.L. (1977). Rape: Power, anger, and sexuality. *American Journal of Psychiatry, 134,* 1239–1243.

Groth, A.N., & Oliveri, F. (1989). Understanding sexual abuse behavior and differentiating among sexual abusers. In S. Sgroi (Ed.), *Vulnerable populations* (Vol. 2, pp. 309–327). Lexington, MA: Lexington Books.

Grubin, D. (1994a). Sexual murder. *British Journal of Psychiatry, 165,* 624–629.

Grubin, D. (1994b). Sexual sadism. *Criminal Behaviour and Mental Health, 4,* 3–9.

Grubin, D., & Gunn, J. (1990). *The imprisoned rapist and rape.* London: Institute of Psychiatry.

Grumet, G.W. (1983). Psychodynamic implications of tattoos. *American Journal of Orthopsychiatry, 53,* 482–492.

Gugliotta, G., & Leen, J. (1989). *Kings of cocaine: An astonishing true story of murder, money, and corruption.* New York: Simon & Schuster.

Guilleminault, C., Moscovitch, A., & Leger, D. (1995). Forensic sleep medicine: Nocturnal wandering and violence. *Sleep, 18,* 740–748.

Gunderson, J.G. (2001). *Borderline personality disorder* (2nd ed.). Washington, DC: American Psychiatric Press.

Gunderson, J.G., & Singer, M. (1975). Defining borderline patients: An overview. *American Journal of Psychiatry, 132,* 1–10.

Gunn, J. (1978). Epileptic homicide: A case report. *British Journal of Psychiatry, 132,* 510–513.

Gunn, J. (2000). Future directions for treatment in forensic psychiatry. *British Journal of Psychiatry, 176,* 332–338.

Gunn, J., & Fenton, G.W. (1971). Epilepsy, automatism, an crime. *Lancet, 1,* 1173–1176.

Gunnar, M.R., & Vasquez, D.M. (2001). Low cortisol and a flattening of expected daytime rhythm: Potential indices of risk in human development. *Development and Psychopathology, 13,* 515–538.

Gupta, M. (2005). Explaining Asia's "missing women": A new look at the data. *Population and Development Review, 31,* 529–535.

Gurr, T. (1970). *Why men rebel.* Princeton, NJ: Princeton University Press.

Guttmacher, M.S. (1972). The psychiatric approach to crime and correction. In D. Dressler (Ed.), *Readings in criminology and penology* (pp. 294–300). Glencoe, IL: Free Press.

Gyimah-Brempong, K., & Racine, J. (2006). Alcohol availability and crime: A robust approach. *Applied Economics, 38,* 1293–1307.

Haapasalo, J., & Kankkonen, M. (1997). Self-reported abuse among sex and violent offenders. *Archives of Sexual Behavior, 26,* 421–431.

Haapasalo, J., & Petaja, S. (1999). Mothers who killed or attempted to kill their child: Life circumstances, childhood abuse, and types of killing. *Violence and Victims, 14,* 219–239.

Hacker, F.J. (1976). *Crusaders, criminals, and crazies: Terror and terrorism in our time.* New York: Norton.

Haddix, R.C. (1999). Responding to line-of-duty deaths. In L. Territo & J.D. Sewell (Eds.), *Stress management in law enforcement* (pp. 287–296). Durham, NC: Carolina Academic Press.

Hadi, A. (2000). Prevalence and correlates of the risk of marital sexual violence in Bangladesh. *Journal of Interpersonal Violence, 15,* 787–805.

Hafenback, J., & Nasiripour, S. (2005). Ex-NYPD officer killed in standoff. *South Florida Sun-Sentinel,* May 28, pp. 1A, 6A.

Hagedorn, J.M. (1994). Homeboys, dope fiends, legits, and new jacks. *Criminology, 32,* 197–217.

Hahn, S., Zeller, A., Needham, I., Kok, G., Dassen, T., & Halfens, R.J.G. (2008). Patient and visitor violence in general hospitals: A systematic review of the literature. *Aggression and Violent Behavior, 13,* 431–441.

Haines, V.Y., Marchand, A., & Harvey, S. (2006). Crossover of workplace aggression experiences in dual-earner couples. *Journal of Occupational Health Psychology, 11,* 305–314.

Hall, D.C., Lawson, B.Z., & Wilson, L.G. (1981). Command hallucinations and self-amputation of the penis and hand during a first psychotic breakdown. *Journal of Clinical Psychiatry, 42,* 322–324.

Hall, G.C.N., & Hirschman, R. (1991). Towards a theory of sexual aggression: A quadripartite model. *Journal of Consulting and Clinical Psychology, 59,* 662–669.

Hall, H.V. (1993). Criminal-forensic neuropsychology of disorders of executive functions. In H.V. Hall & R.J. Sbordone (Eds.), *Disorders of executive functions: Civil and criminal law applications* (pp. 37–77). Winter Park: PMD Publishers.

Hall, J.A., & Moore, C.B.T. (2008). Drug facilitated sexual assault: A review. *Journal of Forensic and Legal Medicine, 15,* 291–297.

Hall, L., & Bernall, J. (1995). Asperger's syndrome and violence. *British Journal of Psychiatry, 166,* 262–268.

Hall, J.R., & Benning, S.D. (2005). The "successful" psychopath: Adaptive and subclinical manifestations of psychopathy in the general population. In C.J. Patrick (Ed.), *Handbook of psychopathy* (pp. 459–478). New York: Guilford.

Hall, R.L. (1998). The victims of stalking. In J.R. Meloy (Ed.), *The psychology of stalking: Clinical and forensic perspectives* (pp. 113–137). San Diego, CA: Academic Press.

Halleck, S.L. (1967). *Psychiatry and the dilemma of crime.* New York: Harper & Row.

Hall-Smith, P., Moracco, K.E., & Butts, J. (1998). Partner homicide in context. *Homicide Studies, 2,* 400–421.

Hamberger, L.K., & Holtzworth-Munroe, A. (1994). Partner violence. In F.M. Dattilio & A. Freeman (Eds.), *Cognitive-behavioral strategies in crisis intervention* (pp. 302–324). New York: Guilford.

Hamburger, L.K., Lohr, J.M., Bonge, D., & Tolin, D.F. (1996). A large-sample empirical typology of male spouse abusers and its relationship to dimensions of abuse. *Violence and Victims, 11,* 277–301.

Hamilton, W.D. (1964). The genetic evolution of social behavior. *Journal of Theoretical Biology, 7,* 1–52.

Haney, C.W., Banks, C., & Zimbardo, P.G. (1973). Interpersonal dynamics in a simulated prison. *International Journal of Criminology and Penology, 1,* 69–97.

Hansen, W. (1996). Workplace violence in the hospital psychiatric setting: An occupational health perspective. *American Association of Hospital Nurses Journal, 44,* 575–590.

Hanson, R.K., & Bussiere, M.T. (1998). Predicting relapse: A meta-analysis of sexual offender recidivism studies. *Journal of Consulting and Clinical Psychology,* 66, 348–362.

Hanson, R.K., & Morton-Bourgon, K.E. (2005). The characteristics of persistent sexual offenders: A meta-analysis of recidivism studies. *Journal of Consulting and Clinical Psychology, 73,* 1154–1163.

Harbin, H., & Madden, D. (1979). Battered parents: A new syndrome. *American Journal of Psychiatry, 136,* 1288–1291.

Harbort, S., & Mokros, A. (2001). Serial murderers in Germany from 1945 to 1995: A descriptive study. *Homicide Studies, 5,* 311–334.

Harder, T. (1967). The psychopathology of infanticide. *Acta Psychiatrica Scandinavica, 43,* 196–245.

Hare, R.D. (1970). *Psychopathy: Theory and research.* New York: Wiley.

Hare, R.D. (1984). Performance of psychopaths on cognitive tasks related to frontal lobe function. *Journal of Abnormal Psychology, 93,* 133–140.

Hare, R.D., & Jutai, J.W. (1986). Psychopathy, stimulation-seeking and stress. In J. Strelau, F.H. Farley, & A. Gale (Eds.), *The biological bases of personality and behavior* (Vol. 2, pp. 175–184). New York: Hemisphere.

Hare, R.D. (1991). *The Hare Psychopathy Checklist-Revised.* Toronto: Multi-Health Systems.

Hare, R.D. (1993). *Without conscience: The disturbing world of the psychopaths among us.* New York: Guilford Press.

Hare, R.D. (1996). Psychopathy: A clinical construct whose time has come. *Criminal Justice and Behavior, 231,* 25–54.

Hare, R.D. (1999). Psychopathy as a risk factor for violence. *Psychiatric Quarterly, 70,* 181–197.

Hare, R.D. (2003). *Hare Psychopathy Checklist-Revised* (2nd ed.). Toronto: Multi-Health Systems.

Hare, R.D. (2006). Psychopathy: A clinical and forensic overview. *Psychiatric Clinics of North America, 29,* 709–724.

Harmon, R.B., Rosner, R., & Owens, H. (1998). Sex and violence in a forensic population of obsessional harassers. *Psychology, Public Policy, and Law, 4,* 236–249.

Harmon-Jones, E. (2000). Cognitive dissonance and experienced negative affect: Evidence that dissonance increases experienced negative affect even in the absence of aversive consequences. *Personality and Social Psychology Bulletin, 26,* 1490–1501.

Harper, D. (1994). Histories of suspicion in a time of conspiracy: A reflection on Aubrey Lewis' history of paranoia. *History of the Human Sciences, 7,* 89–109.

Harpur, T.J., Hakstian, A.R., & Hare, R.D. (1988). Factor structure of the Psychopathy Checklist. *Journal of Consulting and Clinical Psychology, 56,* 741–747.

Harris, A.R., Thomas, S.H., Fisher, G.A., & Hirsch, D.J. (2002). Murder and medicine. *Homicide Studies, 6,* 128–166.

Harris, G.T., & Rice, M.E. (1984). Mentally disordered firesetters: Psychodynamic versus empirical approaches. *International Journal of Law and Psychiatry, 7,* 19–34.

Harris, G.T., Rice, M.E., & Cormier, C.A. (1991). Psychopathy and violent recidivism. *Law and Human Behavior, 15,* 625–637.

Harris, G.T., Rice, M.E., & Lalumiere, M.L. (2001). Criminal violence: The roles of psychopathy, neurodevelopmental insults, and antisocial parenting. *Criminal Justice and Behavior, 28,* 402–426.

Harris, G.T., Rice, M.E., Quinsey, V.L., Lalumiere, M.L., Boer, D., & Lang, C. (2003). A multi-site comparison of actuarial risk instruments for sex offenders. *Psychological Assessment, 15,* 413–425.

Harris, J.R. (1998). *The nurture assumption: Why children turn out the way they do.* New York: Free Press.

Harris, S. (2010). *The moral landscape: How science can determine human values.* New York: Free Press.

Harrison, P.M & Beck, A.J. (2005). *Prisons in 2004.* Washington, DC: Department of Justice, Bureau of Justice Statistics.

Harry, B., & Resnick, P.J. (1986). Posttraumatic stress disorder in murderers. *Journal of Forensic Sciences, 31,* 609–613.

Hart, J., Gunnar, M., & Cicchetti, D. (1996). Altered neuroendocrine activity in maltreated children related to symptoms of depression. *Development and Psychopathology, 8,* 201–214.

Hart, S.D. (1998). The role of psychopathy in assessing risk for violence: Conceptual and methodological issues. *Legal and Criminological Psychology, 3,* 121–137.

Hart, S.D., & Hare, RD. (1996). Psychopathy and antisocial personality disorder. *Current Opinion in Psychiatry, 9,* 129–132.

Hart, S.D., Kropp, P.R., & Hare, R.D. (1988). Peformance of male psychopaths following conditional release from prison. *Journal of Consulting and Clinical Psychology, 56,* 237–252.

Harter, K. (1990). *Winter of frozen dreams: A true story of passion, greed, and murder.* Chicago: Contemporary Books.

Hartman, C.R., Burgess, A.W., & Lanning, K.V. (1984). Typology of collectors. In A.W. Burgess & M.L. Clark (Eds.), *Child pornography and sex rings* (pp. 93–109). Toronto: Lexington Books.

Hartmann, H. (1939/1958). *Ego psychology and the problem of adaptation.* New York: International Universities Press.

Harvey, S., & Keashly, L. (2003). Predicting the risk for aggression in the workplace: Risk factors, self-esteem and time at work. *Social Behavior and Personality, 31,* 807–814.

Haselton, M.G., & Nettle, D. (2006). The paranoid optimist: An integrative evolutionary model of cognitive biases. *Personality and Social Psychology Review, 10,* 47–66.

Haskett, M.E., Nears, K., Ward, C.S., & McPherson, A.V. (2006). Diversity in adjustment of maltreated children: Factors associated with resilient functioning. *Clinical Psychology Review, 26,* 796–812.

Hassouneh-Phillips, D., & Curry, M.A. (2002). Abuse of women with disabilities: State of the science. *Rehabilitation Counseling Bulletin, 45,* 96–104.

Hastings, P.D., Zahn-Waxler, C., Robinson, J., Usher, B., & Bridges, D. (2000). The development of concern for others in children with behavior problems. *Developmental Psychology, 36,* 531–546.

Hatters, S., Hrouda, D.R., Holden, C.E., Noffsinger, S.G., & Resnick, P.J. (2005). Filicide-suicide: Common factors in parents who kill their children and themselves. *Journal of the American Academy of Psychiatry and the Law, 33,* 496–504.

Haugaard, J.J., & Seri, L.G. (2003). Stalking and other forms of intrusive contact after the dissolution of adolescent dating or romantic relationships. *Violence and Victims, 18,* 279–297.

Hawker, D.S.J., & Boulton, M.J. (2000). Twenty years research on peer victimization and psychosocial maladjustment: A meta-analytic review of cross-sectional studies. *Journal of Child Psychiatry and Psychology, 41,* 441–455.

Hawley, P.H. (2007). Social dominance in childhood and adolescence: Why social competence and aggression may go hand in hand. In P.H. Hawley, T.D. Little & P.C. Rodkin (Eds.), *Aggression and adaptation: The bright side to bad behavior* (pp. 1–29). Mahwah, NJ: Lawrence Erlbaum.

Hayes, L.M. (1995). *Prison suicide: An overview and guide to prevention.* Washington, DC: Department of Justice, National Institute of Corrections.

Hayes, L.M., & Rowan, J.R. (1988). *Prison suicide: An overview and guide to prevention.* Washington, DC: Department of Justice: National Institute of Corrections.

Haynie, D.L., Nansel, T., & Eitel, P. (2001). Bullies, victims, and bully/victims: Distinct groups of at-risk youth. *Journal of Early Adolescence, 21,* 29–49.

Haywood, T.W., Kravitz, H.M., Grossman, L.S., & Wasyliw, O.E. (1996). Psychological aspects of sexual functioning among cleric and noncleric alleged sex offenders. *Child Abuse and Neglect, 20,* 527–536.

Haywood, Y.C., & Haile-Mariam, T. (1999). Violence against women. *Emergency Medicine Clinics of North America, 17,* 603–615.

Hazan, C., & Shaver, P. (1987). Romantic love conceptualized as an attachment process. *Journal of Personality and Social Psychology, 52,* 511–534.

Hazelwood, R.R., & Burgess, A.W. (1987a). An introduction to the serial rapist research by the FBI. *FBI Law Enforcement Bulletin, 56,* 16–24.

Hazelwood, R.R., & Burgess, A.W. (1987b). *Practical aspects of rape investigation: A multidisciplinary approach.* Boca Raton: CRC Press.

Hazelwood, R.R, Dietz, P.E., & Warren, J. (1992). The criminal sexual sadist. *FBI Law Enforcement Bulletin, 61,* 12–20.

Hazelwood, R.R., & Douglas, J.E. (1980). The lust murderer. *FBI Law Enforcement Bulletin, 49,* 18–22.

Hazelwood, R.R., & Michaud, S. (1999). *The evil that men do.* New York: St. Martin Press.

Hazelwood, R.R., & Napier, M.R. (2004). Crime scene staging and its detection. *International Journal of Offender Therapy and Comparative Criminology, 48,* 744–759.

Hazelwood, R.R., & Warren, J. (1993). The criminal behavior of the serial rapist. In *Deviant and criminal sexuality* (2nd ed., pp. 161–166). Quantico, VA: FBI, NCAVC.

Heath, D.H., & Heath, H.E. (1991). *Fulfilling lives: Paths to maturity and success.* San Francisco: Jossey-Bass.

Heck, A.L., & Herrick, S.M. (2007). Geriatric considerations in restoration of competence to stand trial: Two cases of impaired cognition. *Journal of Forensic Psychology Practice, 7,* 73–82.

Heflick, N.A. (2005). Sentenced to die: Last statements and dying on death row. *Omega, 51,* 323–336.

Heide, K.M. (1995). *Why kids kill parents: Child abuse and adolescent homicide.* Thousand Oaks, CA: Sage.

Heide, K.M. (1999). *Young killers: The challenge of juvenile homicide.* Thousand Oaks, CA: Sage.

Heide, K.M., & Solomon, E.P. (2006). Biology, childhood trauma, and murder: Rethinking justice. *International Journal of Law and Psychiatry, 29,* 220–233.

Heilbrun, A.B., & Heilbrun, M.R. (1985). Psychopathy and dangerousness: Comparison, integration, and extension of two psychopathic typologies. *British Journal of Criminal Psychology, 24,* 181–195.

Heilbrun, A.E. (1982). Cognitive models of criminal violence based upon intelligence and psychopathy levels. *Journal of Consulting and Clinical Psychology, 50,* 546–557.

Heim, C., Ehlert, U., & Hellhammer, D.H. (2000). The potential role of hypercortisolism in the pathophysiology of stress-related bodily disorders. *Psychoneuroendocrinology, 25,* 1–35.

Heim, C., Newport, D.J., Bosnall, R., Miller, A.H., & Nemeroff, C.B. (2001). Altered pituitary-adrenal axis responses to provocative challenge tests in adult survivors of childhood abuse. *American Journal of Psychiatry, 158,* 575–581.

Heinrichs, R.W. (1989). Frontal cerebral lesions and violent incidents in chronic neuropsychiatric patients. *Biological Psychiatry, 25,* 174–178.

Hellerstein, D., Frosch, W., & Koenigsberg, H.W. (1987). The clinical significance of command hallucinations. *American Journal of Psychiatry, 144,* 219–221.

Hempel, A.G., Meloy, J.R., & Richards, T.C. (1999). Offender and offense characteristics of a nonrandom sample of mass murderers. *Journal of the American Academy of Psychiatry and the Law, 27,* 213–225.

Hemphill, J.F., Hart, S.D., & Hare, R.D. (1994). Psychopathy and substance use. *Journal of Personality Disorders, 8,* 169–180.

Henry, B., Caspi, A., Moffitt, T.E., & Silva, P.A. (1996). Temperamental and familial predictors of violent and nonviolent criminal convictions: Age 3 to 18. *Developmental Psychology, 32,* 614–623.

Hensing, G., & Alexandron, K. (2000). The relation of adult experience of domestic harassment, violence, and sexual abuse to health and sickness absence. *International Journal of Behavioral Medicine, 7,* 1–18.

Hensley, C., & Tallichet, S.E. (2009). Child and adolescent animal cruelty methods and their possible link to adult violent crimes. *Journal of Interpersonal Violence, 24,* 147–158.

Hepworth, W., & Towler, A. (2004). The effects of individual differences and charismatic leadership on workplace aggression. *Journal of Occupational Health Psychology, 9,* 176–185.

Herbert, D., & Tritt, H. (1984). *Corporations of corruption: A systematic study of organized crime.* Springfield, IL: Charles C Thomas.

Herman, J.L. (1990). Sex offenders: A feminist perspective. In W.L. Marshall, D.r. Laws & H.E. Barbaree (Eds.), *Handbook of sexual assault: Issues, theories, and treatment of the offender* (pp. 177–193). New York: Plenum.

Herman, S. (2002). Law enforcement and victim services: Rebuilding lives together. *The Police Chief,* May, pp. 34–37.

Herndon, R.W., & Iacono, W.G. (2005). Psychiatric disorder in the children of antisocial parents. *Psychological Medicine, 35,* 1815–1824.

Herrenkohl, E.C., Herrenkohl, R.C., & Egolf, M. (1994). Resilient early school-age children from maltreating homes: Outcomes in late adolescence. *American Journal of Orthopsychiatry, 64,* 301–309.

Herrenkohl, T.I., Mason, W.A., Kosterman, R., Lengua, L.J., Hawkins, J.D., & Abbot, R.D. (2004). Pathways from physical childhood abuse to partner violence in young adulthood. *Violence and Victims, 19,* 123–136.

Herrnstein, R.J., & Murray, C. (1994). *The bell curve: Intelligence and class structure in American life.* New York: Free Press.

Hersh, K., & Borum, R. (1998). Command hallucinations, compliance, and risk assessment. *Journal of the American Academy of Psychology and the Law, 26,* 353–359.

Hershcovis, M.S., Turner, N., Barling, J., Arnold, K.A., & Dupre, K.E. (2007). Predicting workplace aggression: A meta-analysis. *Journal of Applied Psychology, 92,* 228–238.

Hetherton, J. (1999). The idealization of women: Its role in the minimization of child sexual abuse by females. *Child Abuse and Neglect, 23,* 161–174.

Heydenberk, R.A., Heydenberk, W.R., & Tzenova, V. (2006). Conflict resolution and bully prevention: Skills for school success. *Conflict Resolution Quarterly, 24,* 55–69.

Hickey, E. (1997). *Serial murderers and their victims* (2nd ed.). Belmont, CA: Wadsworth.

Hickey, E. (2003). *Serial murderers and their victims* (3rd ed.). Belmont, CA: Wadsworth.

Hicks, B.M., Krueger, R.F., Iacono, W.G., McGue, M., & Patrick, C.J. (2004). Family transmission and heritability of externalizing disorders. *Archives of General Psychiatry, 61,* 922–928.

Hicks, S.J., & Sales, B.D. (2006). *Criminal profiling: Developing an effective science and practice.* Washington, DC: American Psychological Association.

Hiday, V.A. (1997). Understanding the connection between mental illness and violence. *International Journal of Law and Psychiatry, 20,* 399–417.

Hiday, V.A. (2006). Putting community risk in perspective: A look at correlations, cause and controls. *International Journal of Law and Psychiatry, 29,* 316–331.

Hiday, V.A., Swanson, J.W., Swartz, M.S., Borum, R., & Wagner, H.R. (2001). Victimization: A link between mental illness and violence? *International Journal of Law and Psychiatry, 24,* 559–572.

Hiday, V.A., Swartz, M.S., Swanson, J.W., Borum, R., & Wagner, H.R. (1999). Criminal victimization of persons with severe mental illnesses. *Psychiatric Services, 50,* 62–68.

Higgins, G.E. (2004). Gender and self-control theory: Are there differences in the measures and the theory's causal model? *Criminal Justice Studies, 17,* 33–55.

Higgins, G.E. (2005). Can low self-control help with the understanding of the software pirating problem? *Deviant Behavior, 26,* 1–24.

Higley, J.D., Mehlman, P.T., Poland, R.E., Taub, D.M., Vickers, J., Suomi, S.J., & Linnoila, M. (1996). CSF testosterone and 5-HIAA correlate with different types of aggressive behaviors. *Biological Psychiatry, 40,* 1067–1082.

Hilberg, R. (1992). *Perpetrators, victims, bystanders: The Jewish catastrophe, 1933–1945.* New York: Harper Collins.

Hill, A., Habermann, M., Berner, W., & Briken, P. (2006). Sexual sadism and sadistic personality disorder in sexual homicide. *Journal of Personality Disorders, 20,* 671–684.

Hill, D., & Pond, D.A. (1952). Reflections on one hundred capital cases submitted to electroencephalography. *Journal of Mental Science, 98,* 23–43.

Hill, M.H., & Chow, K. (2002). Life-history theory and risky driving. *Addiction, 97,* 401–413.

Hillbrand, M. (2001). Homicide-suicide and other forms of co-occurring aggression against self and against others. *Professional Psychology: Research and Practice, 32,* 626–635.

Hillbrand, M., Foster, H., & Hirt, M (1990). Rapists and child molesters: Psychometric comparisons. *Archives of Sexual Behavior, 19,* 65–71.

Hinde, R.A. (1979). The nature of social structure. In D. Hamburger & E. McGowan (Eds.), *The great apes: Perspectives on human evolution* (pp. 295–315). Menlo Park, CA: Benjamin Cummings.

Hindmarch, M., Elsohly, J., Gambles, S., & Salamone, S.J. (2001). Forensic urinalysis of drug use in cases of alleged sexual assault. *Journal of Clinical and Forensic Medicine, 8,* 197–205.

Hinson, J., & Shapiro, M. (2003). Violence in the workplace: Awareness and prevention. *Australian Health Review, 26,* 84–91.

Hiroeh, U., Appleby, L., Mortensen, P.B., & Dunn, G. (2001). Death by homicide, suicide, and other unnatural causes in people wth mental illness: A population-based study. *The Lancet, 358,* 2110–2112.

Hirschel, D., & Buzawa, E. (2002). Understanding the context of dual arrest with directions for future research. *Violence Against Women, 8,* 1449–1473.

Hirschi, T. (1969). *Causes of delinquency.* Berkely: University of California Press.

Hirschi, T., & Hindelang, M.J. (1977). Intelligence and delinquency: A revisionist review. *American Sociological Review, 42,* 571–587.

Hobbs, D., Hadfield, P., Lister, S., & Winlow, S. (2002). "Door lore": The art and economics of intimidation. *British Journal of Criminology, 42,* 352–370.

Hobbs, D., Hadfield, P., Lister, S., & Winlow, S. (2005). Violence and control in the night-time economy. *European Journal of Crime, Criminal Law and Criminal Justice, 13,* 89–102.

Hobsbawn, E. J. (1976). Mafia. In F.E. Ianni & E. Reuss-Ianni (Eds.), *The crime society* (pp. 90–98). New York: New American Library.

Hochstetler, A., & DeLisi, M. (2005). Importation, deprivation, and varieties of serving time: An integrated-lifestyle-exposure model of prison offending. *Journal of Criminal Justice, 33,* 257–266.

Hodelet, N. (2001). Psychosis and offending in British Columbia: Characteristics of a secure hospital population. *Criminal Behaviour and Mental Health, 11,* 163–172.

Hodges, E.V.E., Malone, M.J., & Perry, D.G. (1997). Individual risk and social risk as interacting determinants of victimization in the peer group. *Developmental Psychology, 33,* 1032–1039.

Hodgins, S. (1992). Mental disorder, intellectual deficiency and crime: Evidence from a birth cohort. *Archives of General Psychiatry, 49,* 476–483.

Hodgins, S., Mednick, S.A., Brennan, P.A., Schulsinger, F., & Engberg, M. (1996). Mental disorder and crime: Evidence from a Danish cohort. *Archives of General Psychiatry, 53,* 489–496.

Hoenig, J., & Kenna, J.C. (1979). EEG abnormalities and transexualism. *British Journal of Psychiatry, 134,* 293–300.

Hoffman, B.F. (1977). Two new cases of XYY chromosome complement. *Canadian Psychiatric Association Journal, 22,* 447–455.

Hoffman, S., & Baron, S.A. (2001). Stalkers, stalking, and violence in the workplace. In J.A. Davis (Ed.), *Stalking crimes and victim protection: Prevention, intervention, threat assessment, and case management* (pp. 139–159). Boca Raton: CRC Press.

Holden, C.E., Burland, A.S., & Lemmen, C.A. (1996). Insanity and filicide: Women who murder their children. *New Directions in Mental Health Services, 69,* 25–34.

Holland, A.J., Clare, I.C.H., & Mukhopadhyay, T. (2002). Prevalence of "criminal offending" by men and women with intellectual disability and the characteristics of "offenders": Implications for research and service development. *Journal of Intellectual Disability Research, 46,* 6–20.

Holloway, R.H. (1974). *Primate aggression, territoriality, and xenophobia.* New York: Academic Press.

Holmes, R.M. (1989). *Profiling violent crimes.* Newbury Park, CA: Sage.

Holmes, R.M. (2001). Criminal stalking: An analysis of the various typologies of stalking. In J.A. Davis (Ed.), *Stalking crimes and victim protection* (pp. 132–160). Boca Raton, FL: CRC Press.

Holmes, R.M., & DeBurger, J. (1985). Profiles in terror: The serial murderer. *Federal Probation, 49,* 29–34,

Holmes, R.M., & DeBurger, J. (1988). *Serial murder.* Newbury Park: Sage.

Holmes, R.M., & Holmes, S.T. (1992). Understanding mass murder. *Federal Probation, 56,* 53–61.

Holmes, R.M., & Holmes, S.T. (1994). *Murder in America.* Thousand Oaks, CA: Sage.

Holmes, R.M., & Holmes, S.T. (1996). *Profiling violent crimes: An investigative tool* (2nd ed.). Thousand Oaks, CA: Sage.

Holmes, R.M., & Holmes, S.T. (1998). *Serial murder* (2nd ed.). Thousand Oaks, CA: Sage.

Holmes, R.M., & Holmes, S.T. (2001a). *Mass murder in the United States.* Upper Saddle River, NJ: Prentice-Hall.

Holmes, R.M., & Holmes, S.T. (2001b). *Murder in America* (2nd ed.). Thousand Oaks, CA: Sage.

Holmes, S.T., Tewsbury, R., & Holmes, R.M. (1999). Fractured identity syndrome: A new theory of serial murder. *Journal of Contemporary Criminal Justice, 15,* 262–272.

Holt, M.K., Finkelhor, D., & Kantor, G.K. (2007). Multiple victimization experiences of urban elementary school students: Associations with psychosocial functioning and academic performance. *Child Abuse & Neglect, 31,* 503–515.

Holtzworth-Munroe, A., Meehan, J.C., Herron, K., Rehman, U., & Stuart, G.L. (2000). Testing the Holtzworth-Munroe and Stuart typology. *Journal of Clinical and Consulting Psychology, 68,* 1000–1019.

Holtzworth-Munroe, A., Meehan, J.C., Herron, K., Rehman, U., & Stuart, G.L. (2003). Do subtypes of martially violent men continue to differ over time? *Journal of Clinical and Consulting Psychology, 71,* 728–740.

Holtzworth-Munroe, A., & Stuart, G.L. (1994). Typologies of male batterers: Three subtypes and the differences among them. *Psychological Bulletin, 116,* 476–497.

Homant, R.J., & Kennedy, D.B. (1998). Psychological aspects of crime scene profiling. *Criminal Justice and Behavior, 25,* 319–343.

Homant, R.J., Kennedy, D.B., & Hupp, R.T. (2000). Real and perceived danger in police officer assisted suicide. *Journal of Criminal Justice, 28,* 43–52.

Homel, R., & Clark, J. (1994). The prediction and prevention of violence in pubs and clubs. *Crime Prevention Studies, 3,* 1–46.

Homel, R., Tomsen, S., & Thommeny, J. (1992). Public drinking and violence: Not just an alcohol problem. *Journal of Drug Issues, 22,* 679–697.

Honig, A.L., & Sultan, E. (2004). Reactions and resilience under fire: What an officer can expect. *The Police Chief,* December, pp. 54–60.

Hoobler, J.M., & Swanberg, J. (2006). The enemy is not us: Unexpected workplace violence trends. *Public Personnel Management, 35,* 229–246.

Hooper, C., Luciana, M., Conklin, H., Yarger, R. (2004). Adolescents' performance on the Iowa Gambling Task: Implications for the development of decision making and ventromedial prefrontal cortex. *Developmental Psychology, 40,* 1148–1158.

Hoptman, M.J., Volavka, J., & Johnson, G. (2002). Frontal lobe white matter microstructure, aggression, and impulsivity in men with schizophrenia: A preliminary study. *Biological Psychiatry, 2,* 9–14.

Horgan, J. (1993). Eugenics revisisted. *Scientific American,* June, pp. 122–131.

Horgan, J. (2003a). The search for the terrorist personality. In A. Silke (Ed.), *Terrorists, victims and society: Psychological perspectives on terrorism and its consequences* (pp. 3–27). Chichester: Wiley.

Hogan, J. (2003b). Leaving terrorism beind: An individual perspective. In A. Silke (Ed.), *Terrorists, victims and society: Psychological perspectives on terrorism and its consequences* (pp. 109–130). Chichester: Wiley.

Hogan, J., & Taylor, M. (2001). The making of a terrorist. *Jane's Intelligence Review,* December, pp. 16–18.

Horn, N.R., Dolan, M., Elliott, R. Deakin, J.F., & Woodruff, P.W. (2003). Response inhibition and impulsivity: An fMRI study. *Neuropsychologia, 4,* 1959–1966.

Horvath, M.A.H., & Brown, J. (2006). The role of drugs and alcohol in rape. *Medical Science and Law, 46,* 219–228.

Horwitz, A.V., Widom, C.S., McLaughlin, J., & White, H.R. (2001). The impact of childhood abuse and neglect on adult mental health: A prospective study. *Journal of Health and Social Behavior, 42,* 184–201.

Hough, M. (1985). The impact of victimization: Findings from the British Crime Survey. *Victimology, 10,* 498–511.

Howell, J.C. (1999). Youth gang homicides: A literature review. *Crime and Delinquency, 45,* 208–241.

Howell, J.C. (2007). Menacing or mimicking? Realities of youth gangs. *Juvenile and Family Court Journal, 58,* 39–50.

Howell, J.C., Moore, J.P., & Egley, A. (2001). The changing boundaries of youth gangs. In C.R. Huff (Ed.), *Gangs in America III* (pp. 3–18). Thousand Oaks, CA: Sage.

Howlin, P. (1997). *Autism: Preparing for adulthood.* London: Routledge.

Hoyenga, K.B., & Hoyenga, K.T. (1993). *Gender-related differences: Origins and outcomes.* Boston: Allyn & Bacon.

Hucker, S.J. (1997). Sexual sadism: Psychopathology and theory. In D.R. Laws & W. O'Donohue (Eds.), *Sexual deviance: Theory, assessment, and treatment* (pp. 194–209). New York: Guilford.

Hucker, S.J., Langevin, R., Dickey, R., Handy, L., & Chambers, J. (1988). Cerebral damage and dysfunction in sexually aggressive men. *Annals of Sex Research, 1,* 33–47.

Hudziak, J.J., van Beijsterveldt, C.E.M., Bartels, M., Reitveld, M.J.H., Rettew, D.C., & Derks, E.M. (2003). Individual differences in aggression: Genetic analyses by age, gender, and informant in 3-, 7-, and 10-year-old Dutch twins. *Behavior Genetics, 33,* 575–589.

Huesmann, L.R. (1994). Theories of aggression: From drives to cognitions. In E.L.R. Huesmann (Ed.), *Aggressive behavior: Current perspectives* (pp. 3–9). New York: Plenum.

Huesmann, L.R., Eron, L.D., Lefkowitz, M.M., & Walder, L.O. (1984). Stability of aggression over time and generations. *Developmental Psychology, 20,* 1120–1134.

Hughes, D.T. (1992). *Lullaby and good night.* New York: Pocket Books.

Hughes, F.M., Stuart, G.I., Gordon, K.C., & Moore, T.M. (2007). Predicting the use of aggressive conflict tactics in a sample of women arrested for domestic violence. *Journal of Social and Personal Relationships, 24,* 155–176.

Hunter, J.A., Hazelwood, R.R., & Slesinger, D. (2000). Juvenile-perpetrated sex crimes: Patterns of offending and predictors of violence. *Journal of Family Violence, 15,* 81–93.

Hunter, J.A., Lexier, L.J., Goodwin, D.W., Browne, P.A., & Dennis, C. (1993). Psychosexual, attitudinal, and developmental characteristics of juvenile female perpetrators in a residential treatment setting. *Journal of Child and Family Studies, 2,* 317–326.

Hunter, J.A., & Matthews, R. (1997). Sexual deviance in females. In R.D. Laws & W. O'Donahue (Eds.), *Sexual deviance: Theory, assessment, and treatment* (pp. 465–480). New York: Guilford Press.

Hunter, R., Logue, V., & McMenemy, W.H. (1963). Temporal lobe epilepsy supervening on longstanding transvestism and fetishism. *Epilepsia, 4,* 60–65.

Hurley, M., Parker, H., & Wells, D. (2006). The epidemiology of drug-facilitated sexual assault. *Journal of Clinical Forensic Medicine, 13,* 18-185.

Hurt, S.W., & Clarkin, J.F. (1990). Borderline personality disorder: Prototypic typology and the development of treatment manuals. *Psychiatric Annals, 20,* 13–18.

Hurwitz, I., Bibace, R.M.A., Wolff, P.H., & Rowbotham, B.M. (1972). Neuropsychological function of normal boys and boys with learning problems. *Perceptual and Motor Skills, 35,* 387–394.

Husain, A., & Daniel, A. (1984). A comparative study of filicidal and abusive mothers. *Canadian Journal of Psychiatry, 29,* 596–598.

Huss, M.T., & Ralston, A. (2008). Do batterer subtypes actually matter? Treatment completion, treatment response, and recidivism across a batterer typology. *Criminal Justice and Behavior, 35,* 710–724.

Huttenlocher, P.R. (1979). Synaptic density in human frontal cortex: Developmental changes and effects of aging. *Brain Research, 163,* 195–205.

Huttenlocher, P.R., de Courten, C., Garey, L.J., & Van Der Loos, H. (1982). Synaptogenesis in human visual cortex: Evidence for synapse elimination during normal development. *Neuroscience Letters, 33,* 252–274.

Icove, D.J., & Estepp, M.H. (1987). Motive-based offender profiles of arson and fire-related crimes. *FBI Law Enforcement Bulletin, 56,* 17–23.

Imajo, T. (1983). Suicide by motor vehicle. *Journal of Forensic Science, 28,* 83–89.

Innes, B. (2003). *Profile of a criminal mind.* Leicester: Silverdale Books.

Inness, M., Barling, J., & Turner, N. (2005). Understanding superior-targeted aggression: A within-person, between jobs design. *Journal of Applied Psychology, 90,* 731–739.

Ireland, J.L. (1999). Bullying behaviors amongst male and female prisoners: A study of young offenders and adults. *Aggressive Behavior, 25,* 162–178.

Ireland, J.L., Archer, J., & Power, C.L. (2007). Characteristics of male and female prisoners involved in bullying behavior. *Aggressive Behavior, 33,* 220–229.

Ireland, J.L., & Monaghan, R. (2006). Behaviors indicative of bullying among young and juvenile male offenders: A study of perpetrator and victim characteristics. *Aggressive Behavior, 32,* 172–180.

Ireland, J.L., & Power, C.L. (2004). Attachment, emotional loneliness, and bullying behavior: A study of adult and young offenders. *Aggressive Behavior, 30,* 298–312.

Ishikawa, S.S., & Raine, A. (2003). Prefrontal deficits and antisocial behavior: A causal model. In B.B. Lahey, T.E. Moffitt & A. Caspi (Eds.), *Causes of conduct disorder and juvenile delinquency* (pp. 277–304). New York: Guilford.

Island, I., & Letellier, P.M. (1991). Battered husbands: Domestic violence in gay relationships. *Genre Magazine,* Fall, pp. 36–37.

Ito, M., Okazaki, M., Takahashi, S., Muramatsu, R., Kato, M., & Onuma, T. (2007). Subacute postictal aggression in patients with epilepsy. *Epilepsy and Behavior, 10,* 611–614.

Jackson, D., & Mannix, J. (2004). Giving voice to the burden of blame: A feminist study of mothers' experiences of mother blaming. *International Journal of Nursing Practice, 10,* 150–158.

Jackson, R.L., Rogers, R., & Shuman, D.W. (2004). The adequacy and accuracy of sexually violent predator evaluations: Contextualized risk assessment in clinical practice. *International Journal of Forensic Mental Health, 3,* 115–129.

Jacobs, B.A. (2000). *Robbing drug dealers: Violence beyond the law.* New York: Aldine de Gruyter.

Jacobs, B.A., & Wright, R. (1999). Stick-up, street culture, and offender motivation. *Criminology, 37,* 149–173.

Jacobs, B.A., & Wright, R. (2008). Moralistic street robbery. *Crime and Delinquency, 54,* 511–531.

Jacobsen, A., & Herald, C. (1990). The relevance of childhood sexual abuse to adult psychiatric inpatient care. *Hospital and Community Psychiatry, 147,* 1547–1552.

Jacobson, K.C., Prescott, C.A., & Kendler, K. (2002). Sex differences in the genetic and environmental influences on the development of antisocial behavior. *Development and Psychopathology, 14,* 395–416.

Jaffee, P.G., Johnston, J.R., Crooks, C.V., & Bala, N. (2008). Custody disputes following allegations of domestic violence: Toward a differentiated approach to parenting plans. *Family Court Review, 46,* 500–522.

Jaffee, S.R. (2005). Family violence and parent psychopathology: Implications for chilren's socioemotional development and resilience. In S. Goldstein & R. Brooks (Eds.), *Handbook of resilience in children* (pp. 149–163). New York: Kluwer.

Jaffee, S.R., Caspi, A., Moffitt, T.E., Dodge, K.A., Rutter, M., Taylor, A., & Tully, L.A. (2005). Nature × nurture: Genetic vulnerabilities interact with child maltreatment to promote conduct problems. *Development and Psychopathology, 17,* 67–84.

Jaffee, S.R., Caspi, A., Moffitt, T.E., Polo-Thomas, M., & Taylor, A. (2007). Individual, family, and neighborhood factors distinguish resilient from non-resilient maltreated children: A cumulative stressors model. *Child Abuse and Neglect, 31,* 231–253.

Jaffee, S.R., Caspi, A., Moffitt, T.E., & Taylor, A. (2004). Physical maltreatment victim to antisocial child: Evidence of an environmentally mediated process. *Journal of Abnormal Psychology, 113,* 44–55.

Jaffee, S.R., Moffitt, T.E., Caspi, A., Taylor, A., & Arseneault, L. (2002). Influence of adult domestic violence on children's internalizing and externalizing problems: An environmentally informative twin study. *Journal of the American Academy of Child and Adolescent Psychiatry, 41,* 1095–1103.

Janoff-Bulman, R. (1979). Characterological versus behavioral self-blame: Inquiries into depression and rape. *Journal of Personality and Social Psychology, 37,* 1798–1809.

Janssen, I., Hanssen, M., Bak, M., Bijl, R.V., DeGraaf, R., Vollenberg, W., McKenzie, K., & van Os, J. (2003). Discrimination and delusional ideation. *British Journal of Psychiatry, 182,* 71–76.

Jason, J., Guilliland, J.C., & Tyler, C.W. (1983). Homicide as a cause of pediatric mortality in the United States. *Pediatrics, 72,* 191–197.

Jeffers, H.P. (1992). *Profiles in evil.* London: Warner Bros.

Jemelka, R., Trupin, E., & Chiles, J.A. (1989). The mentally ill in prisons: A review. *Hospital and Community Psychiatry, 40,* 481–491.

Jenkins, M.A., Langlais, P.J., Delis, D., & Cohen, R.A. (2000). Attention dysfunction associated with posttraumatic stress disorder among rape survivors. *The Clinical Neuropsychologist, 14,* 7–12.

Jenkins, P. (1990a). Sharing murder. *Journal of Crime and Justice, 12,* 125–148.

Jensen, V. (2001). *Why women kill: Homicide and gender equality.* Boulder, CO: Lynne Rienner.

Johann, M., Bobbe, G., Putzhammer, A., & Wordaz, N. (2003). Comorbidity of alcohol dependence with attention-deficit hyperactivity disorder: Differences in phenotype with increased severity of the substance disorder but not in genotype (serotonin-transporter and 5-hydroxytryptamine-2c receptor). *Alcoholism: Clinical and Experimental Research, 27,* 1527–1534.

Johansson, P., & Kerr, M. (2005). Psychopathy and intelligence: A second look. *Journal of Personality Disorders, 19,* 357–369.

John Jay College of Criminal Justice. (2004). *The nature and scope of the problem of sexual abuse of minors by Catholic priests and deacons in the United States.* New York: John Jay College of Criminal Justice.

Johnson, B.R., & Becker, J.V. (1997). Natural born killers? The development of the sexually sadistic serial killer. *Journal of the American Academy of Psychiatry and Law, 25,* 335–348.

Johnson, J.G., Cohen, P., Kasen, S., Smailes, E., & Brook, J.S. (2001). Association of maladaptive parental behavior with psychiatric disorder among parents and their offspring. *Archives of General Psychiatry, 58,* 453–460.

Johnson, K. (1989). *Trauma in the lives of children: Crisis and stress management techniques for counselors and other professionals.* Alameda: Hunter House.

Johnson, K. (2000). Crisis response to schools. *International Journal of Emergency Mental Health, 2,* 173–180.

Johnson, M.P. (1995). Patriarchal terrorism and common couple violence: Two forms of violence against women. *Journal of Marriage and the Family, 57,* 283–294.

Johnson, M.P. (2005). Apples and oranges in child custody disputes: Intimate terrorism vs. situational couple violence. *Journal of Child Custody, 2,* 43–52.

Johnson, P.R., & Indvik, J. (2000). Rebels, criticizers, backstabbers, and busybodies: Anger and aggression at work. *Public Personnel Management, 29,* 165–173.

Johnson, S.D., North, C.S., & Smith, E.M. (2002). Psychiatric disorders among victims of a courthouse shooting spree: A three-year follow-up study. *Community Mental Health Journal, 38,* 181–194.

Johnson, T.C. (1988). Child perpetrators–Children who molest other children: Preliminary findings. *Child Abuse and Neglect, 12,* 219–229.

Johnston, F.A., & Johnston, S.A. (1997). A cognitive approach to validation of the fixated-regressed typology of child molesters. *Journal of Clinical Psychology, 53,* 361–368.

Johnston, L.D., O'Malley, P.M., Bachman, J.G., & Schulenberg, J.E. (2007). *Monitoring the future: National survey results on drug use, 1975–2006. Vol. I. Secondary school students.* Bethesda, MD: National Institute on Drug Abuse.

Johnstone, G. (2002). *Restorative justice: Ideas, values, debates.* Cullompton, UK: Willan Publishing.

Jolliffe, D., & Farrington, D.P. (2006). Examining the relationship between low empathy and bullying. *Aggressive Behavior, 32,* 540–550.

Jones v. United States, 463, U.S. 354 (1983).

Jones, G., Huckle, P., & Tanaghow, A. (1992). Command hallucinations, schizophrenia and sexual assaults. *Irish Journal of Psychological Medicine, 9,* 47–49.

Jones, J. (2007). Persons with intellectual disabilities in the criminal justice system. *International Journal of Offender Therapy and Comparative Criminology, 51,* 723–733.

Jones, K.L., Smith, D.W., & Ulleland, C.N. (1973). Pattern of malformation in offspring of chronic alcoholic mothers. *Lancet, 1,* 1267–1271.

Jordan, B.K., Schlenger, W.E., Fairbank, J.A., & Caddell, J.M. (1996). Prevalence of psychiatric disorders among incarcerated women: II. Convicted felons entering prison. *Archives of General Psychiatry, 53,* 513–519.

Joyal, C.C., Black, D.N., & Dassylva, B. (2007). The neuropsychology and neurology of sexual deviance: A review and pilot study. *Sex Abuse, 19,* 155–173.

Joyal, C.C., Halle, P., Lapierre, D., & Hodgins, S. (2003). Drug abuse and/or dependence and better neuropsychological performance in patients with schizophrenia. *Schizophrenia Research, 63,* 297–299.

Joyce, T. (2006). Victimology awareness. *Law and Order,* March, pp. 48–54.

Jozsa, B., & Jozsa, M. (1980). Dirty books, dirty films, and dirty data. In L. Lederer (Ed.), *Take back the night: Women on pornography* (pp. 204–217). New York: Morrow.

Judge, T.A., LePine, J.A., & Rich, B.L. (2006). Loving yourself abundantly: Relationship of the narcissistic personality to self- and other perceptions of workplace deviance, leadership, and task and contextual performance. *Journal of Applied Psychology, 91,* 762–776.

Juergensmeyer, M. (2000). *Terror in the mind of God.* Berkeley, CA: Berkeley University Press.

Junginger, J. (1996). Psychosis and violence: The case for a content analysis of psychotic experience. *Schizophrenia Bulletin, 22,* 91–103.

Jurik, N.C., & Winn, R. (1990). Gender and homicide: A comparison of men and women who kill. *Violence and Victims, 5*, 227–242.

Kaemingk, K., & Paquette, A. (1999). Effects of prenatal alcohol exposure on neuropsychological functioning. *Developmental Neuropsychology, 15*, 111–140.

Kafka, M.P. (2003). Sex offending and sexual desire: The clinical and theoretical relevance of hypersexual desire. *International Journal of Offender Therapy and Comparative Criminology, 47*, 439–451.

Kafka, M.P., & Hennen, J. (2002). A DSM-IV Axis I comorbidity study of males with paraphilia and paraphilia-related disorders. *Sexual Abuse: A Journal of Research and Treatment, 14*, 349–366.

Kafka, M.P., & Prentky, R.A. (1998). Attention deficit/hyperactivity disorder in males with paraphilias and paraphilia-related disorders: A comorbidity study. *Journal of Clinical Psychiatry, 59*, 388–396.

Kagan, J. (1994). *Galen's prophecy: Temperament in human nature.* New York: Basic Books.

Kagan, J. (2010). *The temperamental thread: How genes, culture, time, and luck make us who we are.* New York: Dana Press.

Kagan, J., Reznick, J.S., & Snidman, N. (1988). Biological issues of childhood shyness. *Science, 240*, 167–171.

Kalichman, S.C., Williams, E.A., Cherry, C., Belcher, L., & Nachimson, D. (1998). Sexual coercion, domestic violence, and negotiating condom use among low-income African American women. *Journal of Women's Health, 7*, 371–378.

Kalis, A., Mojzisch, A., Schweizer, T.S., & Kaiser, S. (2008). Weakness of will, akrasia, and the neuropsychiatry of decision making: An interdisciplinary perspective. *Cognitive, Affective, and Behavioral Neuroscience, 8*, 402–417.

Kalmuss, D.S. (1984). The intergenerational transmission of marital aggression. *Journal of Marriage and the Family, 46*, 16–19.

Kanazawa, S. (2003c). Why productivity fades with age: The crime-genius connection. *Journal of Research in Personality, 37*, 257–272.

Kanazawa, S. (2004a). The Savanna Principle. *Managerial and Decision Economics, 25*, 41–54.

Kanazawa, S. (2004b). General intelligence as a domain-specific adaptation. *Psychological Review, 111*, 512–523.

Kanazawa, S. (2005a). Is "discrimination" necessary to explain the sex gap in earnings? *Journal of Economic Psychology, 26*, 269–287.

Kanazawa, S. (2008). Theft. In J.D. Duntley & T.K. Shackelford (Eds.), *Evolutionary forensic psychiatry: Darwinian foundations of crime and law* (pp. 160–175). New York: Oxford University Press.

Kanazawa, S., & Still, M.C (2000). Why men commit crimes (and why they desist). *Sociological Theory, 18*, 434–447.

Kandel, D.B. (1978). Homophily, selection, and socialization in adolescent friendships. *American Journal of Sociology, 84*, 427–436.

Kanemoto, K., Kawasaki, J., & Mori, E. (1999). Violence and epilepsy: A close relation between violence and postictal psychosis. *Epilepsia, 40*, 107–109.

Kanin, E.J. (1985). Rapists: Differential sexual socialization and relative deprivation. *Archives of Sexual Behavior, 14,* 219–231.

Kanner, L. (1943). Autistic disturbances of affective contact. *Nervous Child, 2,* 217–250.

Kansas v. Crane, 534 U.S. 407 (2002).

Kansas v. Hendricks, 521 U.S. 346 (1997).

Kantor, G.K., & Jasinski, J.L. (1998). Dynamics and risk factors in partner violence. In J.L. Jasinski & L.M. Williams (Eds.), *Partner violence: A comprehensive review of 20 years of research* (pp. 20–23). Thousand Oaks, CA: Sage.

Kaplan, D., & Dubro, A. (1986). *Yakusa: The explosive account of Japan's criminal underworld.* Reading, MA: Addison-Wesley.

Kaplan, M.S., & Green, A. (1995). Incarcerated female sex offenders: A comparison of sexual histories with eleven female nonsexual offenders. *Sexual Abuse: A Journal of Research and Treatment, 7,* 287–300.

Karcher, M.J. (2004). Connectedness and school violence: A framework for developmental interventions. In E.R. Gerler (Ed.), *Handbook of school violence* (pp. 7–39). Binghamton, NY: Haworth Press.

Karp, J.G., Whitman, L., & Convit, A. (1991). Intentional injestion of foreign objects by male prison inmates. *Hospital and Community Psychiatry, 42,* 533–535.

Kassen, S., Cohen, P., Skodol, A., Johnson, J., Smalles, E., & Brook, J. (2001). Childhood depression and adult personality disorder: Alternative pathways of continuity. *Archives of General Psychiatry, 58,* 231–236.

Kassim, S.H. (2008). The role of religion in the generation of suicide bombers. *Brief Treatment and Crisis Intervention, 8,* 204–208.

Katz, J. (1988). *Seductions of crime: Moral and sensual attractions of doing evil.* New York: Basic Books.

Katz, N., & Zemishlany, Z. (2006). Criminal responsibility in Asperger's syndrome. *Israel Journal of Psychiatry and Related Sciences, 43,* 166–173.

Katz, N., & Zemishlany, Z. (in press). Criminal responsibility in Asperger's syndrome. *International Journal of Offender Therapy and Comparative Criminology.*

Kaufman, J., Cook, A., Arny, L., Jones, B., & Pittinsky, T. (1994). Problems defining resiliency: Illustrations from the study of maltreated children. *Development and Psychopathology, 6,* 215–229.

Kaufman, K.L., Wallace, A.M., Johnson, C.F., & Reeder, M.L. (1995). Comparing female and male perpetrators' modus operandi: Victims' reports of sexual abuse. *Journal of Interpersonal Violence, 10,* 322–333.

Kavoussi, R.J., Kaplan, M., & Becker, J.V. (1988). Psychiatric diagnosis in adolescent sex offenders. *Journal of the American Academy of Child and Adolescent Psychiatry, 27,* 241–243.

Kay, S.R., Wolkenfeld, F., & Murrill, L.M. (1988). Profiles of aggression among psychiatric patients. *Journal of Nervous and Mental Disease, 176,* 547–557.

Kazdin, A.E. (2003). Psychotherapy for children and adolescents. *Annual Review of Psychology, 54,* 253–276.

Keeney, B.T., & Heide, K.M. (1995). Serial murder: A more accurate and inclusive definition. *International Journal of Offender Therapy and Comparative Criminology, 39,* 299–306.

Kelleher, M.D., & Kelleher, C.L. (1998). *Murder most rare: The female serial killer.* Westport, CT: Praeger.

Keller, B. (2002). Nuclear nightmare. *New York Times Magazine,* May 26, pp. 22–29, 51, 54–55, 57.

Kellerman, A. (1992). Gun ownership as a risk factor for homicide in the home. *New England Journal of Medicine, 329,* 1084–1091.

Kellerman, A.L., & Heron, S. (1999). Firearms and family violence. *Emergency Medicine Clinics of North America, 17,* 699–716.

Kellermann, A.L., & Mercy, J.A. (1992). Men, women, and murder: Gender-specific differences in rates of fatal violence and victimization. *Journal of Trauma, 33,* 1–5.

Kelly, J.B., & Johnson, M.P. (2008). Differentiation among types of partner violence: Research update and implications for interventions. *Family Court Review, 46,* 476–499.

Kemp, D.E., Hirschfeld, R.M.A., Ganocy, S.J., Elhaj, O., Slembarski, R., Bilali, S., Conroy, C., Pontau, J., Findling, R.L., & Calabrese, J.R. (2008). Screening for bipolar disorder in a county jail at the time of criminal arrest. *Journal of Psychiatric Research, 42,* 778–786.

Kemper, T. (1990). *Social structure and testosterone: Explorations of the socio-biosocial chain.* New Brunswick, NJ: Rutgers University Press.

Kendler, K.S., Jacobson, K.C., Gardner, C.O., Gillespie, N., Aggen, S.A., & Prescott, C.A. (2007). Creating a social world: A developmental twin study of peer-group deviance. *Archives of General Psychiatry, 64,* 958–965.

Kennair, N., & Mellor, D. (2007). Parent abuse: A review. *Child Psychiatry and Human Development, 38,* 203–219.

Kennedy, D.B. (2007). A precis of suicide terrorism. *Journal of Homeland Security and Emergency Management, 3,* 1–9.

Kennedy, D.B., & Homant, R.J. (1984). Battered women's evaluation of police response. *Victimology: An International Journal, 9,* 174–179.

Kennedy, D.B., & Homant, R.J. (1997). Problems with the use of criminal profiling in premises security litigation. *Trial Diplomacy Journal, 20,* 223–229.

Kennedy, D.B., Homant, R.J., & Hupp, R.T. (1998). Suicide by cop. *FBI Law Enforcement Bulletin,* August, pp. 21–27.

Keppel, R.D., & Walker, R. (1999). Profiling killers: A revised classification. *International Journal of Offender Therapy and Comparative Criminology, 43,* 417–437.

Kercher, G., & McShane, M. (1984). The prevalence of child sexual abuse victimization in an adult sample of Texas residents. *Child Abuse and Neglect, 8,* 495–502.

Kernberg, O. (1975). *Borderline conditions and pathological narcissism.* New York: Jason Aronson.

Kernberg, O.F. (1976). *Object relations theory and clinical psychoanalysis.* New York: Jason Aronson.

Kernberg, O.F. (1989). The narcissistic personality disorder and the differential diagnosis of antisocial behavior. *Psychiatric Clinics of North America, 12,* 553–570.

Kernberg, O.F. (1992). *Aggression in personality disorders and perversions.* New Haven, CT: Yale University Press.

Kerr, J.H. (2005). *Rethinking aggression and violence in sport.* New York: Routledge.

Kessler, C. (2002). Need for attention to mental health of young offenders. *Lancet, 359,* 1956–1957.

Kessler, R.C., Sonnega, A., Bromet, E., Hughes, M., & Nelson, C.B. (1995). Posttraumatic stress disorder in the National Comorbidity Survey. *Archives of General Psychiatry, 52,* 1048–1060.

Keverne, E.B. (1979). Sexual and aggressive behavior in social groups of Talapin monkeys. In *Symposium on sex, hormones, and behavior* (pp. 271–297). London: Blackwell.

Kiehl, K.A. (2006). A cognitive neuroscience perspective on psychopathy: Evidence for paralimbic system dysfunction. *Psychiatry Research, 142,* 107–128.

Kiehl, K.A., Smith, A.M., Hare, R.D., Mendrek, A., & Forster, B.B. (2001). Limbic abnormalities in affective processing by criminal psychopaths as revealed by functional magnetic resonance imaging. *Biological Psychiatry, 50,* 677–684.

Kienlen, K.K. (1998). Developmental and social antecedents of stalking. In J.R. Meloy (Ed.), *The psychology of stalking: Clinical and forensic perspectives* (pp. 51–67). San Diego, CA: Academic Press.

Kienlen, KK.., Birmingham, D., Solberg, K., O'Regan, J., & Meloy, J.R. (1997). A comparative study of psychotic and nonpsychotic stalking. *Journal of the American Academy of Psychiatry and the Law, 25,* 317–334.

Kilpatrick, D., Edmunds, C., & Seymour, A. (1992). *Rape in America.* Arlington, VA: National Victim Center.

Kilpatrick, D.G., & Acierno, R. (2003). Mental health needs of crime victims: Epidemiology and outcomes. *Journal of Traumatic Stress, 16,* 119–132.

Kim, S.H., Smith, R.H., & Brigham, N.L. (1998). Effects of power imbalance and the presence of third parties on reactions to harm: Upward and downward revenge. *Personality and Social Psychology Bulletin, 24,* 353–361.

Kim-Cohen, J., Caspi, A., Taylor, A., Williams, B., Newcombe, R., & Craig, I.W. (2006). MAOA, maltreatment, and gene-environment interactions predicting children's mental health: New evidence and a meta-analysis. *Molecular Psychiatry, 11,* 903–913.

Kim-Cohen, J., Moffitt, T.E., Caspi, A., & Taylor, A. (2004). Genetic and environmental processes in young children's resilience and vulnerability to socioeconomic deprivation. *Child Development, 75,* 651–668.

Kimmel, M. (1996). *Manhood in America.* New York: Free Press.

King, D.W., & Ajmone, M.C. (1977). Clinical features and ictal patterns in epileptic patients with EEG temporal lobe foci. *Annals of Neurology, 2,* 138–147.

King, R.J., Jones, J., Scheuer, J.W., Curtis, D., & Zarcone, V.P. (1990). Plasma cortisol correlates of impulsivity and substance abuse. *Personality and Individual Differences, 11,* 287–291.

Kingham, M., & Gordon, H. (2004). Aspects of morbid jealousy. *Advances in Psychiatric Treatment, 10,* 207–215.

Kinney, J.A. (1995). *Violence at work: How to make your company safer for employees and customers.* Englewood Cliffs, NJ: Prentice-Hall.

Kirkbride, J., Fearon, P., & Morgan, C. (2006). Heterogeneity in incidence rates of schizophrenia and other psychotic syndromes: Findings from the 3-year center AeSOP study. *Archives of General Psychiatry, 63,* 250–258.

Kirwin, B.R. (1997). *The mad, the bad, and the innocent: The criminal mind on trial–Tales of a forensic psychologist.* Boston: Little Brown.

Kitaeff, J. (2011). *Forensic psychology.* New York: Prentice-Hall.

Klein, G.A. (1998). *Sources of power: How people make decisions.* Cambridge: MIT Press.

Klein, G.S. (1954). Need and regulation. In M.R. Jones (Ed.), *Nebraska symposium on motivation.* Lincoln, NE: University of Nebraska Press.

Klein, M.W. (1995). *The American street gang.* New York: Oxford University Press.

Klein, M.W., Maxson, C.L., & Cunningham, L.C. (1991). Crack, street gangs, and violence. *Criminology, 29,* 623–650.

Klimes-Dougan, B., & Kistner, J. (1990). Physically abused preschoolers' responses to peers's distress. *Developmental Psychology, 26,* 599–602.

Knight, R.A. (1999). Validation of a typology of rapists. *Journal of Interpersonal Violence, 14,* 303–330.

Knight, R.A., & Prentky, R.A. (1987). The developmental antecedents and adult adaptations of rapist subtypes. *Criminal Justice and Behavior, 14,* 403–426.

Knight, R.A., & Prentky, R.A. (1990). Classifying sexual offenders: The development and corroboration of taxonomic models. In W.L. Marshall, D.R. Laws & H.E. Barbaree (Eds.), *Handbook of sexual assault: Issues, theories, and treatment of the offender* (pp. 23–52). New York: Plenum.

Knoll, J.L. (2009). Becoming the victim: Beyond sadism in serial sexual murderers. *Aggression and Violent Behavior, 14,* 106–114.

Koch, J.L. (1891). *Die psychopathischen mindwertigkeite.* Ravensburg, Germany: Heiser.

Koch, W.J., Douglas, K.S., Nicholls, T.L., & O'Neill, M.L. (2006). *Psychological injuries: Forensic assessment, treatment, and law.* New York: Oxford University Press.

Kochanska, G. (1997). Mutually responsive orientation between mothers and their young children: Implications for early socialization. *Child Development, 68,* 94–112.

Kochanska, G., & Aksan, N. (2006). Children's conscience and self-regulation. *Journal of Personality, 74,* 1587–1617.

Kochanska, G., & Murray, K.T. (2000). Mother-child mutually responsive orientations and conscience development: From toddler to early school age. *Child Development, 71,* 417–431.

Kochanska, G., Murray, K.T., Jacques, T.Y., Koenig, A.L., & Vandegeest, K.A. (1996). Inhibitory control in young children and its role in emerging internalization. *Child Development, 68,* 151–158.

Kochenderfer, B.J., & Ladd, G.W. (1997). Victimized children's responses to peers' aggression: Behaviors associated with reduced versus continued victimization. *Development and Psychopathology, 9,* 59–73.

Kocsis, R.N. (2003a). Criminal psychological profiling: Validities and abilities? *International Journal of Offender Therapy and Comparative Criminology, 47,* 1–18.

Kocsis, R.N. (2003b). Criminal psychological profiling: Validities and absurdities. *International Journal of Offender Therapy and Comparative Criminology, 47,* 126–144.

Kocsis, R.N., Irwin, H.J., Hayes, A.F., & Nunn, R. (2000). Expertise in psychological profiling: A comparative assessment. *Journal of Interpersonal Violence, 15,* 311–331.

Koechlin, E., Basso, G., Pietrini, P., Panzer, S., & Grafman, J. (1999). The role of the anterior prefrontal cortex in cognition. *Nature, 399,* 148–151.

Kohn, Y., Fahum, T., Ratzoni, G., & Apter, A. (1998). Aggression and sexual offense in Asperger's syndrome. *Israel Journal of Psychiatry and Related Sciences, 35,* 293–299.

Kohut, H. (1971). *The psychoanalytic study of the child.* New York: International Universities Press.

Kohut, H. (1972). Thoughts on narcissism and narcissistic rage. *Psychoanalytic Study of the Child, 27,* 360–400.

Kohut, H. (1978). *The search for the self.* International Universities Press.

Kolarski, A., Fruend, K., Machek, J., & Polak, O. (1967). Male sexual deviation: Association with early temporal lobe damage. *Archives of General Psychiatry, 17,* 735–743.

Kolbert, J.B., & Crothers, L.M. (2003). Bullying and evolutionary psychology: The dominance hierarchy among students and implications for school personnel. *Journal of School Violence, 2,* 73–91.

Kolko, D.J. (2002). *Handbook on firesetting in children and youth.* San Diego: Academic Press.

Koniak-Griffin, D., Logsdon, M., Hines-Martin, V., & Turner-Carmen, C. (2006). Contemporary mothering in a diverse society. *Journal of Obstetric, Gynecological, and Neonatal Nursing, 35,* 671–678.

Koonz, C. (2003). *The Nazi conscience.* Cambridge, UK: Harvard University Press.

Korbin, J.E. (1989). Fatal maltreatment by mothers: A proposed framework. *Child Abuse and Neglect, 13,* 481–489.

Koss, M.P. (1992). The underdetection of rape: Methodological choices influence incidence estimates. *Journal of Social Issues, 48,* 61–75.

Koss, M.P., Gidycz, C.A., & Wisniewski, N. (1987). The scope of rape: Incidence and prevalence of sexual aggression and victimization in a national sample of higher education students. *Journal of Consulting and Clinical Psychology, 55,* 162–170.

Koss, M.P., Leonard, K., Beezley, D., & Oros, C.J. (1985). Nonstranger sexual aggression: A discriminant analysis of the psychological characteristics of undetected offenders. *Sex Roles, 12,* 981–992.

Koss, M.P., & Oros, C.J. (1982). Sexual experiences survey: A research instrument investigating sexual aggression and victimization. *Journal of Consulting and Clinical Psychology, 50,* 455–457.

Kovacs, M., & Pollock, M. (1995). Bipolar disorder and comorbid conduct disorder in childhood and adolescence. *Journal of the American Academy of Child and Adolescent Psychiatry, 34,* 715–723.

Koziol-McLain, J., Coates, C.J., & Lowenstein, S.R. (2001). Predictive validity of a screen for partner violence against women. *American Journal of Preventative Medicine, 21,* 93–100.

Koziol-McLain, J., Webster, D., McFarlane, J., Block, C.R., Ulrich, Y., & Glass, N. (2006). Risk factors for femicide-suicide in abusive relationships: Results for a multistudy. *Violence and Victims, 21,* 3–12.

Kraemer, H.C., Kazdin, A.E., Offord, D.r., Kessler, R.C., Jensen, P.S., & Kupfer, D.J. (1997). Coming to terms with the terms of risk. *Archives of General Psychiatry, 54,* 337–343.

Kraemer, H.C., Stice, E., Kazdin, A.E., Offord, D.R., & Kupfer, D.J. (2001). How do risk factors work together? Mediators, moderators, and independent, overlapping, and proxy risk factors. *American Journal of Psychiatry, 158,* 848–856.

Kraepelin, E. (1915). *Psychiatrie: Ein lehrbuch* (8th ed.). Leipzig, Germany: Barth.

Krakowski, M., Convit, A., Jaeger, J., Lin, S., & Volavka, J. (1989). Neurological impairment in violent schizophrenic inpatients. *American Journal of Psychiatry, 146,* 849–853.

Krakowski, M., & Czbor, P. (2004). Gender difference in violent behavior: Relationship to clinical symptoms and psychosocial factors. *American Journal of Psychiatry, 161,* 459–465.

Krener, P., & Adelman, R. (1988). Parent salvage and parent sabotage in the care of chronically ill children. *American Journal of Diseases of the Child, 142,* 945–951.

Kressel, Niel J. (1996). *Mass hate: The global rise of genocide and terror.* New York: Plenum.

Kreutzer, J.S., Marwitz, J.H., & Witol, A.D. (1995). Interrelationships between crime, substance abuse, and aggressive behaviors among persons with traumatic brain injury. *Brain Injury, 9,* 757–768.

Krisberg, B., & Austin, J. (1993). *Reinventing juvenile justice.* Newbury Park, CA: Sage.

Krischer, M.K., Stone, M.H., Sevecke, K., & Steinmeyer, E.M. (2007). Motives for maternal filicide: Results from a study with female forensic patients. *International Journal of Law and Psychiatry, 30,* 191–200.

Kropp, P.R., Hart, S.D., & Lyon, D.R. (2002). Risk assessment of stalkers: Some problems and possible solutions. *Criminal Justice and Behavior, 29,* 590–616.

Krueger, R.F., Hicks, B.M., Patrick, C.J., Carlson, S.R., Iacono, W.G., & McGue, M. (2002). Etiologic connections among substance dependence, antisocial behavior, and personality: Modeling the externalizing spectrum. *Journal of Abnormal Psychology, 11,* 411–424.

Krueger, R.F., Markon, K.E., Patrick, C.J., Benning, S.D., & Kramer, M.D. (2007). Linking antisocial behavior, substance abuse, and personality: An integrative quantitative model of the adult externalizing spectrum. *Journal of Abnormal Psychology, 116,* 645–666.

Krueger, T.H.C., Schedlowski, M., & Meyer, G. (2005). Cortisol and heart rate measures during casino gambling in relation to impulsivity. *Neuropsychobiology, 52,* 206–211.

Kruger, K.J., & Valltos, N.G. (2002). Dealing with domestic violence in law enforcement relationships. *FBI Law Enforcement Bulletin,* July, pp. 1–7.

Kruglanski, A.W., Chen, X., Dechesne, M., Fishman, S., & Orehek, E.. (2009). Fully committed: Suicide bombers' motivation and the quest for personal significance. *Political Psychology, 30,* 331–357.

Krugman, R.D. (1985). Fatal child abuse: Analysis of 24 cases. *Pediatrician, 12,* 68–72.

Krulewitch, C.J., Roberts, D.W., & Thompson, L.S. (2003). Adolescent pregnancy and homicide: Findings from the Maryland Office of the Chief Medical Examiner, 1994–1998. *Child Maltreatment, 8,* 122–128.

Krynicki, V.E. (1978). Cerebral dysfunction in repetitively assaultive adolescents. *Journal of Nervous and Mental Disease, 166,* 59–67.

Kubik, E.K., Hecker, J.E., & Righthand, S. (2002). Adolescent females who have sexually offended: Comparisons with delinquent adolescent female offenders and adolescent males who have sexually offended. *Journal of Child Sexual Abuse, 11,* 63–83.

Kubrin, C., & Weitzer, R. (2003). New directions in social disorganization theory. *Journal of Research in Crime and Delinquency, 40,* 374–402.

Kulka, R.A., Schlenger, W.E., Fairbank, J.A., Hough, R.L., Jordan, B.K., & Marmar, C.R. (1990b). *Trauma and the Vietnam War generation: Report of findings from the National Vietnam Veterans Readjustment Study.* New York: Brunner/Mazel.

Kumagai, F. (1981). Filial violence: A peculiar parent-child relationship in the Japanese family today. *Journal of Comparative Family Studies, 12,* 337–349.

Kung, H.-C., Liu, X., & Juon, H.-S. (1998). Risk factors for suicide in Caucasians and in African-Americans: A matched case-control study. *Social Psychiatry and Psychiatric Epidemiology, 33,* 155–161.

Kunz, J., & Bahr, S. (1996). A profile of parental homicide against children. *Journal of Family Violence, 11,* 347–362.

Kushner, M.G., Riggs, D.S., Foa, E.B., & Miller, S.M. (1993). Perceived controllability and the development of posttraumatic stress disorder (PTSD) in crime victims. *Behavior Research and Therapy, 31,* 105–110.

Kutcher, S.P., Marton, P., & Korenblum, M. (1989). Relationship between psychiatric illness and conduct disorder in adolescents. *Canadian Journal of Psychiatry, 34,* 526–529.

Kutner, L., & Olson, C. (2008). *Grand theft childhood: The surprising truth about violent video games and what parents can do.* New York: Simon & Schuster.

Labelle, A., Bradford, J.M., & Bourget, D. (1991). Adolescent murderers. *Canadian Journal of Psychiatry, 36,* 583–587.

Labig, C.E. (1995). *Preventing violence in the workplace.* New York: Amacom.

Labich, K. (1996). How to fire people and still sleep at night. *Fortune,* June, pp. 65–72

LaBrode, R.T. (2007). Etiology of the psychopathic serial killer: an analysis of anti-social personality disorder, psychopathy, and serial killer personality and crime scene characteristics. *Brief Treatment and Crisis Intervention, 7,* 151–160.

Lachs, M.S, Bachman, R., Williams, C.S., & O'Leary, J.R. (2007). Resident-to-resident elder mistreatment and police contact in nursing homes: Findings from a population-based cohort. *Journal of the American Geriatrics Society, 55,* 840–845.

Lachs, M.S., & Pillemer, K. (1995). Abuse and neglect of elderly persons. *New England Journal of Medicine, 332,* 437–443.

Lachs, M.S., Williams, C., O'Brien, S., Hurst, L., & Horwitz, R. (1997). Risk factors for reported elder abuse and neglect: A nine-year observational cohort study. *Gerontologist, 37,* 469–474.

Lafayette, J.M., Frankle, W.G., & Pollock, A. (2003). Clinical characteristics, cognitive functioning, and criminal histories of outpatients with schizophrenia. *Psychiatric Services, 54,* 1635–1640.

Lagerspetz, K.M.J., Bjorkqvist, K., Berts, M., & King, E. (1982). Group aggression among school children in three schools. *Scandinavian Journal of Psychology, 23,* 45–52.

Lagerspetz, K.M.J., Bjorkqvist, K., & Peltonen, T. (1988). Is indirect aggression more typical of females? Gender differences in aggressiveness in 11- to 12-year old children. *Aggressive Behavior, 14,* 403–414.

Lahey, B.B., Goodman, S.H., Waldman, I.D., Bird, H., Canino, G., & Jensen, P. (1999). Relation of age of onset to the type and severity of child and adolescent conduct problems. *Journal of Abnormal Child Psychology, 27,* 247–260.

Lahey, B.B., Loeber, R., Stouthamer-Loeber, M., Christ, M.A.G., Green, S., Russo, M.F., Frick, P.J., & Duncan, M. (1990). Comparison of DSM-III and DSM-IIIR diagnoses for prepubertal children: Changes in prevalence and validity. *Journal of the American Academy of Child Psychology and Psychiatry, 29,* 620–626.

Lahey, B.B., & Waldman, I.D. (2003). A developmental propensity model of the origins of conduct problems during childhood and adolescence. In B.B. Lahey, T.E. Moffitt & A. Caspi (Eds.), *Causes of conduct disorder and juvenile delinquency* (pp. 76–117). New York: Guilford.

Laible, D.J., & Thompson, R.A. (2002). Mother-child conflict in the toddler years: Lessons in emotion, morality, and relationships. *Child Development, 73,* 1187–1203.

Laird, R.D., Jordan, K.Y., Dodge, K.A., Pettit, G.S., & Bates, J.E. (2001). Peer rejection in childhood, involvement with antisocial peers in early adolescence, and the development of externalizing behavior problems. *Development and Psychopathology, 13,* 337–354.

Lakoff, G. (2008). *The political mind.* New York: Viking.

Lalumiere, M.L., Chambers, L.J., Quinsey, V.L., & Seto, M.C. (1996). A test of the mate deprivation hypothesis of sexual coercion. *Ethology and Sociobiology, 17,* 299–318.

Lalumiere, M.L., Harris, G.T., Quinsey, V.L., & Rice, M.E. (2005). *The causes of rape: Understanding individual differences in male propensity for sexual aggression.* Washington, DC: American Psychological Association.

Lalumiere, M.L., Mishra, S., & Harris, G.T. (2008). In cold blood: The evolution of psychopathy. In J.D. Duntley & T.K. Shackelford (Eds.), *Evolutionary forensic psychiatry: Darwinian foundations of crime and law* (pp. 176–197). New York: Oxford University Press.

Lalumiere, M.L., & Quinsey, V.L. (1996). Sexual deviance, antisociality, mating effort, and the use of sexually coercive behaviors. *Personality and Individual Differences, 21,* 33–48.

Lalumiere, M.L., & Quinsey, V.L. (2000). Good genes, mating effort, and delinquency. *Behavioral and Brain Sciences, 23,* 608.

Lamb, H.R. (1984). *The homeless mentally ill.* Washington DC: American Psychiatric Press.

Lamberti, J.S., Weisman, R.L., Schwartzkopf, S.B., Price, N., Ashton, R.M., & Trompeter, J. (2001). The mentally ill in jails and prisons: Toward an integrated model of prevention. *Psychiatric Quarterly, 72,* 63–77.

Lamont-Brown, R. (1982). Yakusa: The international expansion of Japan's criminal brotherhood. *Police Journal, 55,* 355–359.

Lance, L.M., & Ross, C.E. (2000). Views of violence in American sports: A study of college students. *College Student Journal, 34,* 191–200.

Lang, R.A. (1993). Neuropsychological deficits in sexual offenders: Implications for treatment. *Sexual and Marital Therapy, 8,* 181–200.

Lang, R.A., Langevin, R., Van Santen, V., Billingsley, D., & Wright, P. (1990). Marital relations in incest offenders. *Journal of Sex and Marital Therapy, 16,* 214–229.

Langan, P.A. Schmitt, E., & Durose, M. (2003). *Recidivism of sex offenders released from prison in 1994.* Washington, DC: U.S. Department of Justice.

Langevin, R. (2003). A study of the psychosexual characteristics of sex killers: Can we identify them before it is too late? *International Journal of Offender Therapy and Comparative Criminology, 47,* 366–382.

Langevin, R., Ben-Aron, M.H., Wortzman, G., Dickey, R., & Handy, L. (1987). Brain damage, diagnosis, and substance abuse among violent offenders. *Behavioral Sciences and the Law, 5,* 77–94.

Langevin, R., Ben-Aron, M.H., Wright, P., Marchese, V., & Handy, L. (1988). The sex killer. *Annals of Sex Research, 1,* 263–301.

Langevin, R., Lang, R.A., Wortzman, G., Frentzel, R.R., & Wright, P. (1989). An examination of brain damage and dysfunction in genital exhibitionists. *Annals of Sex Research, 2,* 77–87.

Langfeldt, G. (1961). The erotic jealousy syndrome: A clinical study. *Acta Psychiatrica Scandinavica, 36,* 7–68.

Langhinrichsen-Rohling, J., Huss, M.T., & Ramsey, S. (2000). The clinical utility of batterer typologies. *Journal of Family Violence, 15,* 37–54.

Langman, P. (2009a). Rampage school shooters: A typology. *Aggression and Violent Behavior, 14,* 79–86.

Langman, P. (2009b). *Why kids kill: Inside the minds of school shooters.* New York: Palgrave Macmillan.

Langstrom, N., Sjostedt, G., & Grann, M. (2004). Psychiatric disorders and recidivism in sexual offenders. *Sexual Abuse: A Journal of Research and Treatment, 16,* 139–150.

Lanning, K.V. (2001). *Child molesters: A behavioral analysis for law-enforcement officers investigating the sexual exploitation of children by aquaintance molesters.* Alexandria, VA: National Center for Missing and Exploited Children.

Lansford, J.E., Dodge, K.A., Pettit, G.S., Bates, J.E., Crozier, J., & Kaplow, J. (2002). Long-term effects of early childhood physical maltreatment on psychological, behavioral, and academic problems in adolescence: A 12-year prospective study. *Archives of Pediatric and Adolescent Medicine, 156,* 824–830.

Lansford, J.E., Malone, P.S., Stevens, K.I., Dodge, K.A., Bates, J.E., & Pettit, G.S. (2006). Developmental trajectories of externalizing and internalizing behaviors: Factors underlying resilience in physically abused children. *Development and Psychopathology, 18,* 35–55.

Lapierre, D., Braun, C.M., & Hodgins, S. (1995). Neuropsychological correlates of violence in schizophrenia. *Schizophrenia Bulletin, 21,* 253–262.

Laqueur, W. (1987). *The age of terrorism.* Boston: Little, Brown.

Larsson, H., Andershed, A., & Lichtenstein, P. (2006). A genetic factor explains most of the variation in the psychopathic personality. *Journal of Abnormal Psychology, 115,* 221–230.

Lasko, N.B., Guruits, T.V., Kuhne, A.A., Orr, S.P., & Pitman, R.K. (1994). Aggression and its correlates in Vietnam veterans with and without chronic posttraumatic stress disorder. *Comprehensive Psychiatry, 35,* 373–381.

Latimer, J., Dowden, C., & Muise, D. (2005). The effectiveness of restorative justice practices: A meta-analysis. *Prison Journal, 85,* 127–144.

Laub, J.H., Nagin, D.S., & Sampson, R.J. (1998). Trajectories of change in criminal offending: Good marriages and the desistance process. *American Sociological Review, 63,* 225–238.

Laumann, E.O., Paik, A., & Rosen, R. (1999). Sexual dysfunction in the United States: Prevalence and predictors. *Journal of the American Medical Association, 281,* 537–544.

Laviola, M. (1992). Effects of older brother-younger sister incest: A study of the dynamics of 17 cases. *Child Abuse and Neglect, 16,* 406–421.

Lawrence, R., & Mueller, D. (2003). School shootings and the man-bites-dog criterion for news worthiness. *Youth Violence and Juvenile Justice, 1,* 330–345.

Leap, T.L. (2007). *Dishonest dollars: The dynamics of white-collar crime.* Ithaca, NY: IRL Press.

Leary, M., Kowalski, R., Smith, L., & Phillips, S. (2003). Teasing, rejection, and violence: Case studies of the school shootings. *Aggressive Behavior, 29,* 202–214.

LeBeau, M., & Moyazani, A. (2001). *Drug-facilitated sexual assault: A forensic handbook.* New York: Academic Press.

LeBlanc, M.M., & Barling, J. (2005). Understanding the many faces of workplace violence. In S. Fox & P.E. Spector (Eds.), *Counterproductive work behavior: Investigations of actors and targets* (pp. 41–63). Washington, DC: American Psychological Association.

Le Blanc, M.M., & Kelloway, E.K. (2002). Predictors and outcomes of workplace violence and aggression. *Journal of Applied Psychology, 87,* 444–453.

LeDoux, J.E. (1996). *The emotional brain: The mysterious underpinnings of emotional life.* New York: Simon & Schuster.

Lee, M.Y., Uken, A., & Sebold, J. (2004). Accountability for change: Solution-focused treatment with domestic violence offenders. *Families in Society, 85,* 463–476.

Lee, R.K. (1998). Romantic and electronic stalking in a college context. *William and Mary Journal of Women and the Law, 4,* 373–409.

Lee, R.K., Thompson, V.L., & Mechanic, M.B. (2002). Intimate partner violence and women of color: A call for innovations. *American Journal of Public Health, 92,* 530–534.

Lengua, L.J., & Long, A.C. (2002). The role of emotionality and self-regulation in the appraisal-coping process: Tests of direct and moderating effects. *Journal of Applied Developmental Psychology, 23,* 471–493.

Leo, J., & Cohen, D. (2003). Broken brain or flawed studies? A critical review of ADHD neuroimaging research. *Journal of Mind and Behavior, 24,* 29–56.

Leon-Carrion, J., & Ramos, F.J.C. (2003). Blows to the head during development can predispose to violent criminal behavior. *Brain Injury, 17,* 207–216.

Leone, J., Johnson, M., Cohan, C., & Lloyd, S. (2004). Consequences of male partner violence on low-income minority women. *Journal of Marriage and Family, 66,* 472–490.

Lesnick-Oberstein, M., Koers, A.J., & Cohen, L. (1995). Parental hostility and its sources in psychologically abusive mothers: A test of the three-factor theory. *Child Abuse and Neglect, 19,* 33–49.

Lesserman, J., & Drossman, D.A. (2007). Relationship of abuse history to functional gastrointestinal disorders and symptoms: Some possible mediating mechanisms. *Trauma, Violence, and Abuse, 8,* 331–343.

Lester, D. (1995). *Serial killers: The insatiable passion.* Philadelphia: Charles Press Publishers.

Lester, D. (1987). Suicide and homicide in USA prisons. *Psychological Reports, 61,* 126.

Lester, D. (2002). Trends in mass murder. *Psychological Reports, 90,* 1122.

Lester, D., Stack, S., Schmidtke, A., Schaller, S., & Muller, I. (2005). Mass homicide and suicide: Deadliness and outcome. *Crisis, 26,* 184–187.

Lester, D., Yang, B., & Lindsay, M. (2004). Suicide bombers: Are psychological profiles possible? *Studies in Conflict and Terrorism, 27,* 283–295.

Levondosky, A.A., Bogat, G.A., Theran, S.A., Trotter, J.S., von Eye, A., & Davidson, W.S. (2004). The social networks of women experiencing domestic violence. *American Journal of Community Psychology, 34,* 95–109.

Levenson, J.S. (2004). Sexual predator civil commitment: A comparison of selected and released offenders. *International Journal of Offender Therapy and Comparative Criminology, 48,* 638–648.

Levenson, M.R., Kiehl, K.A., & Fitzpatrick, C.M. (1995). Assessing psychopathic attributes in a noninstitutionalized population. *Journal of Personality and Social Psychology, 68,* 151–168.

Levin, H.S. (1990). Pioneers in research on the behavioral sequelae of head injury. *Journal of Clinical and Experimental Neuropsychology, 13,* 1–22.

Levine, M., Williams, A., Sixt, A., & Valenti, R. (2001). Is it inherently prejudicial to try a juvenile as an adult? *Behavioral Sciences and the the Law, 19,* 23–31.

Levy, S. (1959). Post-encephalitic behavior disorder–a forgotten entity: A report of 100 cases. *American Journal of Psychiatry, 115,* 1062–1067.

Lewandowski, L.A., McFarlane, J., Campbell, J.C., Gary, F., & Barenski, C. (2004). "He killed my mommy!" Murder or attempted murder of a child's mother. *Journal of Family Violence, 19,* 211–220.

Lewinsohn, P.M., Klein, D.N., & Seeley, J.R. (1995). Bipolar disorder in a community sample of older adolescents: Prevalence, phenomenology, comorbidity, and course. *Journal of the American Academy of Child and Adolescent Psychiatry, 34,* 454–463.

Lewis, C.F., Baranski, M.V., & Buchanan, J.A. (1998). Factors associated with weapon use in maternal filicide. *Journal of Forensic Science, 43,* 613–618.

Lewis, C.F., & Bunce, S.C. (2003). Filicidal mothers and the impact of psychosis on maternal filicide. *Journal of the American Academy of Psychiatry and the Law, 31,* 459–470.

Lewis, C.F., & Stanley, C.R. (2000). Women accused of sexual offenses. *Behavioral Sciences and the Law, 18,* 73–81.

Lewis, D.O., Moy, E., Jackson, L., Aaronson, R., Restifo, N., & Serra, S. (1985). Biosocial characteristics of children who later murder: A prospective study. *American Journal of Psychiatry, 142,* 1161–1167.

Lewis, D.O., Pincus, J.H. Bard, B., Richardson, E., Feldman, M., & Prichep, L.S. (1988). Neuropsychiatric, psychoeducational, and family characteristics of 14 juveniles condemned to death in the United States. *American Journal of Psychiatry, 145,* 584–589.

Lewis, D.O., Pincus, J.H., Feldman, M., Jackson, L., & Bard, B. (1986). Psychiatric, neurologic, and psychoeducational characteristics of 15 death row inmates in the U.S. *American Journal of Psychiatry, 143,* 838–845.

Lewis, D.O., Pincus, J.H., & Shanok, S.S. (1982). Psychomotor epilepsy and violence in a group of incarcerated adolescent boys. *American Journal of Psychiatry, 139,* 882–887.

Lewis, D.O., Shanok, S.S., Balla, D.A., & Bond, B. (1980). Psychiatric correlates of severe reading disabilities in an incarcerated delinquent population. *Journal of the American Academy of Child Psychiatry, 19,* 611–622.

Lewis, D.O., Yeager, C.A., Cobham-Portorreal, C.S., Klein, N., Showalter, C., & Anthony, A. (1991). A follow-up of female delinquents: Maternal contributions to the perpetuation of deviance. *Journal of the American Academy of Child and Adolescent Psychiatry, 30,* 197–201.

Lewis, D.O., Yeager, C.A., Gidlow, B., & Lewis, M. (2001). Six adoptees who murdered: Neuropsychiatric vulnerabilities and characteristics of biological and adoptive parents. *Journal of the American Academy of Psychiatry and the Law, 29,* 390–397.

Lewis, D.O., Yeager, C.A., Swica, Y., Pincus, J.H., & Lewis, M. (1997). Objective documentation of child abuse and dissociation in 12 murderers with dissociative identity disorder. *American Journal of Psychiatry, 154,* 1703–1710.

Lewis, D.O., & Shanok, S.S. (1977). Medical histories of delinquent and nondelinquent children: An epidemiological study. *American Journal of Psychiatry, 134,* 1020–1025.

Lewis, S.F., Fremouw, W.J., Del Ben, K., & Farr, C. (2001). An investigation of the psychological characteristics of stalkers: Empathy, problem-solving, attachment, and borderline personality features. *Journal of Forensic Sciences, 46,* 80–84.

Leyman, H. (1996). The content and development of mobbing at work. *European Journal of Work and Organizational Psychology, 5,* 165–184.

Lezak, M.D., Howieson, D.B., & Loring, D.W. (2004). *Neuropsychological assessment* (4th ed.). New York: Oxford University Press.

Lieber, A.L. (1978). *The lunar effect.* Garden City, NJ: Anchor Press/Doubleday.

Liebschutz, J., Savetsky, J.B., Saitz, R., Horton, N.J., Lloyd-Travaglini, C., & Samet, J.H. (2002). The relationship between sexual and physical abuse and substance abuse consequences. *Journal of Substance Abuse Treatment, 22,* 121–128.

Lifton, R.J. (2000). *Destroying the world to save it: Aum Shinrikyo and the new global terrorism.* New York: Holt.

Lin, W. (1997). Perpetrators of hate. *Yale Political Quarterly, 19,* 12.

Lindqvist, P. (1986). Criminal homicide in Northern Sweden 1970–1981: Alcohol intoxication, alcohol abuse and mental illness. *International Journal of Law and Psychiatry, 8,* 19–37.

Lindqvist, P., & Allebeck, P. (1990). Schizophrenia and crime: A longitudinal follow-up of 644 schizophrenics in Stockholm. *British Journal of Psychiatry, 157,* 345–350.

Lindsay, M.S., & Dickson, D. (2004). Negotiating with the suicide-by-cop subject. In V. Lord (Ed.), *Suicide by cop: Inducing officers to shoot* (pp. 153–162). Flushing, NY: Looseleaf Law Publications.

Link, B.G., Andrews, H., & Cullen, F.T. (1992). The violent and illegal behavior of mental patients reconsidered. *American Sociological Review, 57,* 275–292.

Link, B.G., Cullen, F.T., & Andrews, H. (1992). The violent and illegal behavior of mental patients reconsidered. *American Sociological Review, 57,* 275–272.

Link, B.G., Monahan, J., Stueve, A., & Cullen, F.T. (1999). Real in their consequences: A sociological approach to understanding the association between psychotic symptoms and violence. *American Sociological Review, 64,* 316–332.

Link, B.G., Phelan, J., Bresnahan, M., Stueve, A., & Pescosolido, B. (1999). Public conceptions of mental illness: Labels, causes, dangerousness, and social distance. *American Journal of Public Health, 89,* 1328–1333.

Link, B.G., & Stueve, A. (1994). Psychotic symptoms and the violent/illegal behavior of mental patients compared to community controls. In J. Monahan & H. Steadman (Eds.), *Violence and mental disorder: Developments in risk assessment* (pp. 137–159). Chicago: University of Chicago Press.

Link, B.G., & Stueve, A. (1995). Evidence bearing on mental illness as a possible cause of violent behavior. *Epidemiologic Reviews, 17,* 172–181.

Link, B.G., Stueve, A., & Phelan, J. (1998). Psychotic symptoms and violent behaviours: Probing the components of "threat/control override" symptoms. *Social Psychology and Psychiatric Epidemiology, 33*, 495–560.

Linnoila, M., Virkkunen, M., Scheinin, M., Nuutila, A., Rimon, R., & Goodwin, F.K. (1983). Low cerebrospinal fluid 5-hydroxy indoleacetic acid concentration differentiates impulsive from nonimpulsive violent behavior. *Life Sciences, 33,* 2609–2614.

Lipsey, M. (1995). What do we learn from 400 research studies on the effectiveness of treatment with juvenile delinquents? In J. McGuire (Ed.), *What works? Reducing reoffending* (pp. 63–78). New York: Wiley.

Lipsey, M. (1999). Can rehabilitative programs reduce the recidivism of young offenders? An inquiry into the effectiveness of practical programs. *Virginia Journal of Social Policy and Law, 6,* 611–641.

Lipsey, M.W., Wilson, D.B., Cohen, M.A., & Derzon, J.H. (1997a). Is there a causal relationship between alcohol use and violence? A synthesis of evidence. *Recent Developments in Alcoholism, 13,* 245–282.

Lipsey, M.W., Wilson, D.B., Cohen, M.A., & Derzon, J.H. (1997b). Is there a causal relationship between alcohol use and violence? In M. Galanter (Ed.), *Recent developments in alcoholism: Alcohol and violence: Epidemiology, neurobiology, psychology, family issues* (Vol. 13, pp. 245–282). New York: Plenum.

Lipton, D.N., McDonel, E.C., & McFall, R.M. (1987). Heterosocial perception in rapists. *Journal of Consulting and Clinical Psychology, 55,* 17–21.

Lipton, M.I., & Schaffer, W.R. (1986). Posttraumatic stress disorder in the older veteran. *Military Medicine, 151,* 522–524.

Lisak, D., & Roth, S. (1990). Motives and psychodynamics of self-reported unincarcerated rapists. *American Journal of Orthopsychiatry, 60,* 268–280.

Lishman, W.A. (1978). *Organic psychiatry: The psychological consequences of cerebral disorder.* London: Blackwell.

Lister, S., Hobbs, D., Hall, S., & Winlow, S. (2000). Violence in the night-time economy; bouncers: The reporting, recording and prosecution of assaults. *Policing and Society, 10,* 383–402.

Livingston, L. (1986). Children's violence to single mothers. *Journal of Sociology and Social Welfare, 13,* 920–933.

Lloyd, S. (1997). The effects of domestic violence on women's employment. *Law and Policy, 19,* 139–167.

Loeber, R., Burke, J.D., & Lahey, B.B. (2002). What are the antecedents of antisocial personality disorder? *Criminal Behavior and Mental Health, 12,* 24–36.

Loeber, R., Burke, J.D., Lahey, B., Winters, A., & Zera, M. (2000). Oppositional defiant and conduct disorder: A review of the past 10 years. Part I. *Journal of the American Academy of Child and Adolescent Psychiaty, 39,* 1484–1486.

Loeber, R., & Schmaling, K.B. (1985). Empirical evidence for overt and covert patterns of antisocial conduct problems: A meta-analysis. *Journal of Abnormal Child Psychology, 13,* 337–352.

Logan, T.K., Shannon, L., Cole, J., & Swanberg, J. (2007). Partner stalking and implications for women's employment. *Journal of Interpersonal Violence, 22,* 268–291.

Logan, T.K., Walker, R., Jordan, C., & Campbell, J. (2004). An integrative review of separation in the context of victimization. *Trauma, Violence, and Abuse, 5,* 143–193.

Logan, T.K., Walker, R., Cole, J., & Leukefeld, C. (2002). Victimization and substance use among women: Contributing factors interventions, and implications. *Review of General Psychology, 6,* 325–397.

Logsdail, S.J., & Toone, B.K. (1988). Post-ictal psychoses: A clinical and phenomenological description. *British Journal of Psychiatry, 152,* 246–252.

Lombroso, C. (1876). *L'uomo delinquente.* Milan, Italy: Hoepli.

Lombroso, C. (1889). *L'uomo delinquente* (4th ed.). Torino, Italy: Bocca.

Loney, B.R., Frick, P.J., & Clements, C.B. (2003). Emotional reactivity and callous unemotional traits in adolescents. *Journal of Clinical Child and Adolescent Psychology, 32,* 66–80.

Longshore, D., Chang, E., Hsieh, S.C., & Messina, N. (2004). Self-control and social bonds: A combined control perspective on deviance. *Crime and Deliquency, 50,* 542–564.

Lonigan, C.J., & Phillips, B.M. (2001). Temperamental influences on the development of anxiety disorders. In M.W. Vasey & M.R. Dadds (Eds.), *The developmental psychopathology of anxiety* (pp. 60–91). New York: Oxford University Press.

Looman, J., Abracen, J., DiFazio, R., & Maillet, G. (2004). Alcohol and drug use among sexual and nonsexual offenders: Relationship to intimacy deficits and coping strategy. *Sexual Abuse: A Journal of Research and Treatment, 16,* 177–189.

Lord, V.B. (2000). Law enforcement-assisted suicide. *Criminal Justice and Behavior, 27,* 401–419.

Los Angeles Board of Police Commissioners. (1997). *Domestic violence in the Los Angeles Police Department: How well does the Los Angeles Police Department police its own? Report on the Domestic Violence Task Force.* Office of Inspector General, Los Angeles, CA.

Lothstein, L. (1999). Neuropsychological findings in clergy who sexually abuse. In T.G. Plante (Ed.), *Bless me father for I have sinned: Perspectives on sexual abuse committed by Roman Catholic priests* (pp. 87–110). Westport, CT: Greenwood.

Lott, L.D. (1999). Deadly secrets: Violence in the police family. In L. Territo & J.D. Sewell (Eds.), *Stress management in law enforcement* (pp. 149–155). Durham: Carolina Academic Press.

Lowman, R.L. (1993). *Counseling and psychotherapy of work dysfunctions.* Washington DC: American Psychological Association.

Loza, W. (2007). The psychology of extremism and terrorism: A Middle-Eastern perspective. *Aggression and Violent Behavior, 12,* 141–155.

Loza, W., & Hanna, S. (2006). Is schizoid personality a forerunner of homicidal or suicidal behavior? A case study. *International Journal of Offender Therapy and Comparative Criminology, 50,* 338–343.

Lubit, R.H. (2004). *Coping with toxic managers, subordinates . . . and other difficult people.* Upper Saddle River, NJ: Prentice-Hall.

Lucas, D.R., Wezner, K.C., & Milner, J.S. (2002). Victim, perpetrator, family, and incident characteristics of infant and child homicide in the United States Air Force. *Child Abuse and Neglect, 26,* 167–186.

Luna, B., Thulborn, K., Munoz, D., Merriam, E., & Garver, K. (2001). Maturation of widely distributed brain function subserves cognitive development. *Neuroimage, 13,* 786–793.

Luria, A.R. (1980). *Higher cortical functions in man* (2nd ed.). New York: Basic Books.

Luthar, S.S. (1991). Vulnerability and resilience: A study of high-risk adolescents. *Child Development, 62,* 600–616.

Luthar, S.S., Cicchetti, D., & Becker, B. (2000). The construct of resilience: A critical evaluation and guidelines for future work. *Child Development, 71,* 543–562.

Lykken, D.T. (1995). *The antisocial personalities.* Hillsdale, NJ: Erlbaum.

Lykken, D.T. (2000). The causes and costs of crime and a controversial cure. *Journal of Personality, 68,* 559–605.

Lynam, D.R., & Gudonis, L. (2005). The development of psychopathy. *Annual Review of Clinical Psychology, 1,* 381–407.

Lynam, D.R., Loeber, R., & Stouthamer-Loeber, M. (2008). The stability of psychopathy from adolescence into adulthood: The search for moderators. *Criminal Justice and Behavior, 35,* 228–243.

Lynam, D.R., Moffitt, T.E., & Stouthamer-Loeber, M. (1993). Explaining the relation between IQ and delinquency: Class, race, test motivation, school failure, or self-control? *Journal of Abnormal Psychology, 102,* 187–196.

Lynam, D.R., Whiteside, S., & Jones, S. (1999). Self-reported psychopathy: A validation study. *Journal of Personality Assessment, 73,* 110–132.

Lynch, M. (2002). Capital punishment as moral imperative: Pro-death penalty discourse on the internet. *Punishment and Society, 4,* 213–236.

Lynch, M., & Cicchetti, D. (1998). An ecological-transactional analysis of children and contexts: The longitudinal interplay among child maltreatment, community violence, and children's symptomatology. *Development and Psychopathology, 10,* 235–257.

Lynch, S., & Graham-Bermann, S. (2004). Exploring the relationship between positive work experiences and women's sense of self in the context of partner abuse. *Psychology of Women Quarterly, 28,* 159–167.

Lyons, H.A., & Harbinson, H.J. (1986). A comparison of political and non-political murderers in Northern Ireland, 1974–1984. *Medicine, Science and the Law, 26,* 193–198.

Lyons, M.J., True, W.R., Eisen, S.A., Goldberg, J., Meyer, J.M., Faraone, S.V., Eaves, L.J., & Tsuang, M.T. (1995). Differential heritability of adult and juvenile antisocial traits. *Archives of General Psychiatry, 52,* 906–915.

Lytton, H. (1990). Child and parent effects in boys' conduct disorder: A reinterpretation. *Developmental Psychology, 26,* 683–697.

Lyukouras, E., Christodoulou, G.N., & Malliaras, D. (1987). Type and content of delusions in unipolar psychotic depression. *Journal of Affective Disorders, 9,* 249–252.

Maas, C., Herrenkohl, T.I., & Sousa, C. (2008). Review of research on child maltreatment and violence in youth. *Trauma, Violence, and Abuse, 9,* 56–67.

Maas, R.L., Prakash, R., & Hollender, M.H. (1984). Double parricide: Matricide and parricide–a comparison with other schizophrenic murders. *Psychiatric Quarterly, 56,* 286–290.

MacCulloch, M.J., Bailey, J., Jones, C., & Hunter, C. (1993). Nineteen male serious reoffenders who were discharged direct to the community from a Special Hospital: I. General characteristics. *Journal of Forensic Psychiatry, 4,* 237–248.

MacCulloch, M.J., Snowden, P.R., Wood, P.J.W., & Mills, H.E. (1983). Sadistic fantasy, sadistic behavior, and offending. *British Journal of Psychiatry, 143,* 20–29.

MacDonald, A., Cohen, J.D., Stenger V.A., & Carter, C.S. (2000). Dissociating the role of the dorsolateral prefrontal and anterior cingulated cortex in cognitive control. *Science, 288,* 1835–1888.

MacDonald, J.M. (1961). *The murderer and his victim.* Springfield, IL: Charles C Thomas.

MacDonald, J.M. (1963). The threat to kill. *American Journal of Psychiatry, 120,* 120–130.

Macgregor, J.R. (1991). Identification with the victim. *Psychoanalytic Quarterly, 60,* 53–68.

Mack, D.A., Shannon, C., Quick, J.D., & Quick, J.C. (1998). Stress and the preventive management of workplace violence. In R.W. Griffith, A. O'Leary-Kelly & J.M. Collins (Eds.), *Dysfunctional behavior in organizations: Violent and deviant behavior* (pp. 119–141). Stanford: JAI Press.

Mackay, R.D., & Kearns, G. (1999). More facts about the insanity defense. *Criminal Law Review, 10,* 714–725.

Macy, R.J. (2007). A coping theory framework towad preventing sexual revictimization. *Aggression and Violent Behavior, 12,* 177–192, 123–132.

Magdol, L., Moffitt, T.E., Caspi, A., & Silva, P.A. (1998). Developmental antecedents of partner abuse: A prospective-longitudinal study. *Journal of Abnormal Psychology, 107,* 375–389.

Maier-Katin, D., Mears, D.P., & Bernard, T.J. (2009). Towards a criminology of crimes against humanity. *Theoretical Criminology, 13,* 227–255.

Maker, A.H., Kemmelmeier, M., & Peterson, C. (2001). Child sexual abuse, peer sexual abuve, and sexual assault in adulthood: A multi-risk model of revictimization. *Journal of Traumatic Stress, 14,* 351–365.

Malamuth, N.M. (1986). Predictors of naturalistic sexual aggression. *Journal of Personality and Social Psychology, 50,* 953–962.

Malamuth, N.M., & Brown, L.M. (1994). Sexually aggressive men's perceptions of women's communications: Testing three explanations. *Journal of Personality and Social Psychology, 67,* 699–712.

Malamuth, N.M., & Heilman, M.F. (1998). Evolutionary psychology and sexual aggression. In C.B. Crawford & D.L. Krebs (Eds.), *Handbook of evolutionary psychology: Ideas, issues and applications* (pp. 515–542). Mahwah, NJ: Erlbaum.

Malamuth, N.M. Huppin, M., & Paul, B. (2005). Sexual coercion. In D.M. Buss (Ed.), *Handbook of evolutionary psychology* (pp. 394–418). New York: Wiley.

Males, M.A. (1996). *The scapegoat generation: America's war on adolescents.* Monroe, ME: Common Courage Press.

Males, M.A. (1999). *Framing youth: 10 myths about the next generation.* Monroe, ME: Common Courage Press.

Males, M.A. (2007). The new Bull Connors. *Youth Today,* February 15, p. 16.

Males, M.A. (2009). Does the adolescent brain make risk taking inevitable? A skeptical appraisal. *Journal of Adolescent Research, 24,* 3–20.

Malmquist, C.P. (1981). Psychiatric aspects of familicide. *Bulletin of the American Academy of Psychiatry and Law, 8,* 298–304.

Malmquist, C.P. (1996). *Homicide: A psychiatric perspective.* Washington, DC: American Psychiatric Press.

Malmquist, C.P. (2006). Combined murder-suicide. In R.I. Simon & R.E. Hales (Ed.), *Textbook of suicide assessment and management* (pp. 495–509). Washington, DC: American Psychiatric Publishing.

Maloney, M. (1994). Children who kill their parents. *Prosecutor's Brief: California District Attorney's Association Journal, 16,* 20.

Maltz, W. (2003). Treating the sexual intimacy concerns of sexual abuse survivors. *Contemporary Sexuality, 37,* 1–8.

Mamdani, M. (2001). *When victims become killers: Colonialism, nativism and genocide in Rwanda.* Princeton, NJ: Princeton University Press.

Mandel, H.P. (1997). *Conduct disorder and underachievement: Risk factors, assessment, treatment, and prevention.* New York: Wiley.

Mandracchia, J.T., Morgan, R.D., Garos, S., & Garland, J.T. (2007). Inmate thinking patterns: An empirical investigation. *Criminal Justice and Behavior, 34,* 1029–1043.

Mangione-Walcott, C., & Landau, S. (2004). The relation between disinhibition and emotion regulation in boys with attention deficit hyperactivity disorder. *Journal of Clinical Child and Adolescent Psychology, 33,* 772–782.

Mann, L. (1969). *Social psychology.* New York: Wiley.

Mantell, M., & Albrecht, S. (1994). *Ticking bombs: Defusing violence in the workplace.* New York: Irwin.

Manuel, L., & Retzlaff, P.D. (2002). Psychopathology and tattooing among prisoners. *International Journal of Offender Therapy and Comparative Criminology, 46,* 522–531.

Margolin, L. (1991). Child sexual abuse by nonrelated caregivers. *Child Abuse and Neglect, 15,* 213–221.

Margolin, L., & Craft, J.L. (1989). Child sexual abuse by caretakers. *Family Relations, 38,* 450–455.

Margolin, L., & Craft, J.L. (1990). Child abuse by adolescent caregivers. *Child Abuse and Neglect, 14,* 365–373.

Mark, V.H., & Ervin, F.R. (1970). *Violence and the brain.* New York: Harper & Row.

Marks, M.N. (2001). Parents at risk of filicide. In G-F. Pinard & L. Pagani (Eds.), *Clinical assessment of dangerousness: Empirical contributions* (pp. 158–180). New York: Cambridge University Press.

Marks, M.N., & Kumar, R. (1993). Infanticide in England and Wales. *Medicine, Science and the Law, 33,* 329–339.

Marks, M.N., & Kumar, R. (1995). Parents who kill their infants. *British Journal of Midwifery, 3,* 249–253.

Marks, M.N., & Kumar, R. (1996). Infanticide in Scotland. *Medicine, Science and the Law, 36,* 299–305.

Marleau, J.D., Poulin, B., Webanck, T., Roy, R., & Laporte, L. (1999). Paternal filicide: A study of 10 men. *Canadian Journal of Psychiatry, 44,* 57–63.

Marleau, J.D., & Saucier, J.F. (1998). Birth order and fratricidal behavior in Canada. *Psychological Reports, 82,* 817–818.

Marlowe, M., & Bliss, L. (1993). Hair element concentrations and young children's behavior at school and home. *Journal of Orthomolecular Medicine, 9,* 1–12.

Marlowe, M., Stellen, J., & Moon, C. (1985). Main and interaction effects of metallic toxins on aggressive classroom behavior. *Aggressive Behavior, 11,* 41–48.

Marlowe, W.B., Mancall, E.L., & Thomas, J.J. (1975). Complete Kluver-Bucy syndrome in man. *Cortex, 11,* 53–59.

Marmorstein, N.R., & Iacono, W.G. (2005). Longitudinal follow-up of adolescents with late-onset antisocial behavior: A pathological yet overlooked group. *Journal of the American Academy of Child and Adolescent Psychiatry, 44,* 1284–1291.

Marsh, N.V., & Martinovich, W.M. (2006). Executive function and domestic violence. *Brain Injury, 20,* 61–66.

March, L., & Krauss, G.L. (2000). Aggression and violence in patients with epilepsy. *Epilepsy and Behavior, 1,* 160–168.

Marshall, W.L., & Barbaree, H.E. (1989). Sexual violence. In K. Howells & C.R. Hollin (Eds.), *Clinical approaches to violence* (pp. 205–246). Chichester, UK: Wiley.

Marshall, W.L., & Barbaree, H.E. (1990). An integrated theory of the etiology of sexual offending. In W.L. Marshall, D.R. Laws & H.E. Barbaree (Eds.), *Handbook of sexual assault: Issues, theories, and treatment of the offender* (pp. 257–275). New York: Plenum.

Marshall, W.L., Ward, T., Mann, R.E., Moulden, H., Fernandez, Y.M., & Serran, G. (2005). Working positively with sexual offenders: Maximizing the effectiveness of treatment. *Journal of Interpersonal Violence, 20,* 1096–1114.

Martell, D.A. (1996). Organic brain dysfunctions and criminality. In L.B. Schlesinger (Ed.), *Explorations in criminal psychopathology: Clinical syndromes with forensic implications* (pp. 170–186). Springfield, IL: Charles C Thomas.

Martens, W.H.J. (2000). Antisocial and psychopathic personality disorders: Causes, curse, and remission: A review. *International Journal of Offender Therapy and Comparative Criminology, 44,* 406–430.

Martens, W.H.J. (2004). The terrorist with Antisocial Personality Disorder. *Journal of Forensic Psychology Practice, 4*(1), 45–56.

Martin, E.K. (2007). A review of marital rape. *Aggression and Violent Behavior, 12,* 329–347.

Martin, M.E. (1997). Double your trouble: Dual arrest in family violence. *Journal of Family Violence, 12,* 139–157.

Marzuk, P.M., Tardiff, K., & Hirsch, C. (1992). The epidemiology of murder-suicide. *Journal of the American Medical Association, 267,* 3179–3183.

Mashek, D., Stuewig, J., Furukawa, E., & Tangney, J. (2006). Psychological and behavioral implications of connectedness to communities with opposing beliefs and values. *Journal of Social and Clinical Psychology, 25,* 382–407.

Masten, A.S., & Coatesworth, J.D. (1998). The development of competence in favorable and unfavorable environments. *American Psychologist, 53,* 205–220.

Masten, A.S., & Reed, M.J. (2002). Resilience in development. In R. Snyder & S.J. Lopez (Eds.), *Handbook of positive psychology* (pp. 74–88). New York: Oxford University Press.

Masters, R.D., Hone, B., & Doshi, A. (1998). Environmental pollution, neurotoxicity, and criminal violence. In J. Rose (Ed.), *Environmental toxicology* (pp. 235–261). Amsterdam: Gordon & Breach.

Matsakis, A. (1994). *Post-traumatic stress disorder: A complete treatment guide.* Oakland, CA: New Harbinger.

Matsueda, R.L. (1988). The current state of differential association theory. *Crime and Delinquency, 34,* 277–306.

Matthews, B.A., & Norris, F.H. (2002). When is believing "seeing"? Hostile attribution bias as a function of self-reported aggression. *Journal of Applied Social Psychology, 32,* 1–32.

Matthews, J.K. (1993). Working with female sexual abusers. In M. Elliott (Ed.), *Female sexual abuse of children* (pp. 57–73). New York: Guilford Press.

Matthews, J.K., Mathews, R., & Speltz, K. (1991). Female sexual offenders: A typology. In M.Q. Patton (Ed.), *Family sexual abuse: Frontline research and evolution* (pp. 199–219). London: Sage.

Mattson, A.J., & Levin, H.S. (1990). Frontal lobe dysfunction following closed head injury. *Journal of Nervous and Mental Disease, 178,* 282–291.

Mattson, S.N., & Riley, E.P. (1998). A review of the neurobehavioral deficits in children with fetal alcohol syndrome or prenatal exposure to alcohol. *Alcoholism: Clinical and Experimental Research, 22,* 279–294.

Maudsley, H. (1898). *Responsibility in mental disease.* New York: Appleton & Company.

Maume, D. (1989). Inequality and metropolitan rape rates: A routine activities approach. *Justice Quarterly, 6,* 513–527.

Mawson, D., Grounds, A., & Tantam, D. (1985). Violence and Asperger's syndrome: A case study. *British Journal of Psychiatry, 147,* 566–569.

Max, J., Robertson, B., & Lansing, A. (2001). The phenomenology of personality change due to traumatic brain injury in children and adolescents. *Journal of Neuropsychiatry and Clinical Neurosciences, 13,* 161–170.

Maxson, C.L., & Klein, M.W. (1996). Defining gang homicide: An updated look at member and motive approaches. In C.R. Huff (Ed.), *Gangs in America* (2nd ed., pp. 3–20). Thousand Oaks, CA: Sage.

Mazur, A. (1985). A biosocial model of status in face-to-face primate groups. *Social Forces, 64,* 377–402.

Mazur, A. (1994). A neurohormonal model of social stratification among humans: A microsocial perspective. In L. Ellis (Ed.), *Social stratification and socioeconomic inequality: Vol. 2. Reproductive and interpersonal aspects of dominance and status* (pp. 37–45). Westport, CT: Praeger.

Mazur, A., & Booth, A. (1998). Testosterone and dominance in men. *Behavioral and Brain Sciences, 21,* 353–397.

Mazur, A., Booth, A., & Dabbs, J.M. (1992). Testosterone and chess competition. *Social Psychology Quarterly, 55,* 70–77.

Mazur, A., & Lamb, T.A. (1980). Testosterone, status, and mood in human males. *Hormones and Behavior, 14,* 236–246.

Mbilinyi, L.F., Edleson, J.L., Hagemeister, A.K., & Beeman, S.K. (2007). What happens to children when their mothers are battered? Results from a four city anonymous telephone survey. *Journal of Family Violence, 22,* 309–317.

McAllister, T.W. (1992). Neuropsychiatric sequelae of head injuries. *Psychiatric Clinics of North America, 15,* 395–413.

McAnaney, K.G., Curliss, L.A., & Abeyta-Price, C.E. (1993). From imprudence to crime: Antistalking laws. *Notre Dame Law Review, 68,* 819–909.

McBurnett, L., Lahey, B.B., Capasso, L., & Loeber, R. (1996). Aggressive symptoms and salivary cortisol in clinic-referred boys with conduct disorder. *Annals of the New York Academy of Sciences, 794,* 169–178.

McBurnett, L., Lahey, B.B., Rathouz, P.J., & Loeber, R. (2000). Low salivary cortisol and persistent aggression in boys referred for disruptive behavior. *Archives of General Psychiatry, 57,* 38–43.

McCabe, M.P., & Di Battista, J. (2004). Role of health, relationships, work and coping on adjustment among people with multiple sclerosis: A longitudinal investigation. *Psychology Health and Medicine, 9,* 431–439.

McCann, I.L., & Pearlman, L.A. (1990). *Psychological trauma and the adult survivor: Theory, therapy, and transformation.* New York: Brunner/Mazel.

McCann, J.T. (1992). Criminal personality profiling in the investigation of violent crime: Recent advances and future directions. *Behavioral Sciences and the Law, 10,* 475–481.

McCarthy, E., Tarrier, N., & Gregg, L. (2002). The nature and timing of seasonal affective symptoms and the influence of self-esteem and social support: A longitudinal prospective study. *Psychological Medicine, 32,* 1425–1434.

McCarty, L.M. (1986) Mother-child incest; Characteristics of the offender. *Child Welfare, 65,* 447–458.

McCaul, K.D., Gladue, B.A., & Joppa, M. (1992). Winning, losing, mood, and testosterone. *Hormones and Behavior, 26,* 486–504.

McCauley, C. (2007). Psychological issues in understanding terrorism and the response to terrorism. In B. Bongar, L.M. Brown, L.E. Beutler, J.N. Breckenridge & P.G. Zimbardo (Eds.), *Psychology of terrorism* (pp. 13–31). New York: Oxford University Press.

McCold, P. (2000). Toward a holistic vision of restorative juvenile justice: A reply to the maximalist model. *Contemporary Justice Review, 3,* 357–414.

McCord, J. (1983). A longitudinal study of aggression and antisocial behavior. In K.T. Van Dusen & S.A. Mednick (Eds.), *Prospective studies of crime and delinquency* (pp. 269–275). Boston: Kluwer-Nijhoff.

McCrary, G., & Ramsland, K. (2003). *The unknown darkness.* New York: Morrow.

McElroy, S.L., Keck, P.E., & Pope, H.G. (1994). Compulsive buying: A report of 20 cases. *Journal of Clinical Psychiatry, 55,* 242–248.

McElroy, S.L., Pope, H.G., Hudson, J.I., Keck, P.E., & White, K.L. (1991). Kleptomania: A report of 20 cases. *American Journal of Psychiatry, 148,* 652–657.

McEwen, T., Mullen, P.E., & MacKenzie, R. (2009). A study of the predictors of persistence in stalking situations. *Law and Human Behavior, 33,* 149–158.

McEwen, T., Mullen, P.E., & Purcell, R. (2007). Identifying risk factors in stalking: A review of current research. *International Journal of Law and Psychiatry, 30,* 1–9.

McFarlane, J., Campbell, J., & Watson, K. (2002). Intimate partner stalking and femicide: Urgent implications for women's safety. *Behavioral Sciences and the Law, 20,* 51–68.

McFarlane, J.M., Campbell, J.C., Wilt, S., Sachs, C.J. Ulrich, Y., & Xu, X. (1999). Stalking and intimate partner femicide. *Homicide Studies, 3,* 300–316.

McFarlane, J., Malecha, A., Watson, K., Gist, J., Batten, E., & Hall, I. (2005). Intimate partner sexual assault against women: Frequency, health consequences, and treatment coutcomes. *Obstetrics & Gynecology, 105,* 99–108.

McFarlane, J.M., Parker, B., & Soeken, K. (1996). Abuse during pregnancy: Associations with maternal health and infant birth weight. *Nursing Research, 45,* 37–42.

McFarlane, J.M., Parker, B., Soeken, K., Silva, C., & Reed, S. (1999). Research exchange: Severity of abuse before and during pregnancy for African American, Hispanic, and Anglo women. *Journal of Nurse-Midwifery, 44,* 139–144.

McFarlin, S.K., Fals-Stewart, W., Major, D.A., & Justice, E.M. (2001). Alcohol use and workplace aggression: An examination of perpetuation and victimization. *Journal of Substance Abuse, 13,* 303–321.

McFie, J. (1975). *Assessment of organic intellectual impairment.* New York: Academic Press.

McGaha, A., Otto, R.K., McClaren, M.D., & Petrila, J. (2001). Juveniles adjudicated incompetent to proceed: A descriptive study of Florida's competence restoration program. *Journal of the American Academy of Psychiatry and the Law, 29,* 427–437.

McGarrell, E.E., & Chermak, S. (2003). Problem solving to reduce gangs and drug-related violence in Indianapolis. In S.H. Decker (Ed.), *Policing gangs and youth violence* (pp. 77–101). Belmont, CA: Wadsworth/Thompson Learning.

McGee, J., & DeBernardo, C. (1999). The classroom avenger: A behavioral profile of school based shootings. *The Forensic Examiner, 8,* 16–18.

McGloin, J.M., Pratt, T.C., & Maahs, J. (2004). Rethinking the IQ-delinquency relationship: A longitudinal analysis of multiple theoretical models. *Justice Quarterly, 21,* 603–631.

McGloin, J.M., & Widom, C.S. (2001). Resilience among abused and neglected children grown up. *Development and Psychopathology, 13,* 1021–1038.

McGrath, M.G., & Casey, E. (2002). Forensic psychiatry and the internet: Practical perspectives on sexual predators and obsessional harassers in cyberspace. *Journal of the American Academy of Psychiatry and the Law, 30,* 81–94.

McKee, G.R., & Shea, S.J. (1998). Maternal filicide: A cross-national comparison. *Journal of Clinical Psychology, 54,* 679–687.

McKenzie, C. (1995). A study of serial murder. *International Journal of Offender Therapy and Comparative Criminology, 39,* 3–10.

McKibbin, W.F., Shackelford, T.K., Goetz, A.T., & Starratt, V.G. (2008). Evolutionary psychological perspectives on rape. In J.D. Duntley & T.K. Shackelford (Eds.), *Evolutionary forensic psychiatry: Darwinian foundations of crime and law* (pp. 101–120). New York: Oxford University Press.

McKinlay, W.W., Brooks, D.N., Bond, M.R., Martinage, D.P., & Marshall, M.M. (1981). The short-term outcome of severe blunt head injury as reported by relatives of the injured persons. *Journal of Neurology, Neurosurgery, and Psychiatry, 44,* 527–533.

McKinney, F., Cheng, K.M., & Bruggers, D.J. (1984). Sperm competition in apparently monogamous birds. In R.L. Smith (Ed.), *Sperm competition and evolution of animal mating systems* (pp. 523–545). New York: Academic Press.

McMains, M.J., & Mullins, W.C. (1996). *Crisis negotiations: Managing critical incidents and hostage situations in law enforcement and corrections.* Cincinnati: Anderson.

McMains, M.J. (2002). Active listening: The aspirin of negotiations. *Journal of Police Crisis Negotiations, 2,* 69–74.

McNiel, D.E., Eisner, J.P., & Binder, R.L. (2003). The relationship between aggressive attributional style and violence by psychiatric patients. *Journal of Consulting and Clinical Psychology, 71,* 399–403.

McPhedren, S. (2006). Animal abuse, family violence, and child wellbeing: A review. *Journal of Family Violence, 24,* 41–52.

Meadow, R. (1977). Munchausen syndrome by proxy: The hinterland of child abuse. *Lancet, 2,* 343–345.

Meadow, R. (1980). Munchausen syndrome by proxy. *Archives of Diseases in Childhood, 55,* 731–732.

Meadow, R. (1995). What is, and what is not, "Munchausen syndrome by proxy?" *Archives of Diseases in Childhood, 72,* 534–538.

Mears, D.P., Carlson, M.J., Holden, G.W., & Harris, S.D. (2001). Reducing domestic violence revictimization: The effects of individual and contextual factors and type of legal intervention. *Journal of Interpersonal Violence, 16,* 1260–1283.

Mednick, S.A., Gabrielli, W.F.J., & Hutchings, B. (1984). Genetic influences in criminal convictions: Evidence from an adoption cohort. *Science, 224,* 891–894.

Mednick, S.A., Gabrielli, W.F.J., & Hutchings, B. (1987). Genetic factors in the etiology of criminal behavior. In S.A. Mednick, T.E. Moffitt & S.A. Stack (Eds.), *The causes of crime: New biological approaches* (pp. 74–91). Cambridge: Cambridge University Press.

Mednick, S.A., & Kandel, E. (1988). Genetic and perinatal factors in violence. In S.A. Mednick & T.E. Moffitt (Eds.), *Biological contributions to crime causation* (pp. 121–131). Dordrecht, Holland: Martinus Nijhoff.

Mednick, S.A., Volavka, J., & Gabrielli, W.F.J. (1981). EEG as predictor of antisocial behavior. *Criminology, 19,* 219–229.

Meek, C.L. (1990). Evaluation and assessment of post-traumatic and other stress-related disorders. In C.L. Meek (Ed.), *Post-traumatic stress disorder: Assessment, differential diagnosis, and forensic evaluation* (pp. 9–61). Sarasota: Professional Resource Exchange.

Mega, M.S., & Cummings, J.L. (1994). Frontal-subcortical circuits and neuropsychiatric disorders. *Journal of Neuropsychiatry and Clinical Neurosciences, 6,* 358–370.

Mellesdal, L. (2003). Aggression on a psychiatric acute ward: A three-year prospective study. *Psychological Reports, 92,* 1229–1248.

Meloy, J.R. (1989). Unrequited love and the wish to kill: Diagnosis and treatment of borderline erotomania. *Bulletin of the Menninger Clinic, 53,* 477–492.

Meloy, J.R. (1992). *Violent attachments.* Northvale, NJ: Aronson.

Meloy, J.R. (1995). *The psychopathic mind: Origins, dynamics, and treatment.* Northvale, NJ: Jason Aronson.

Meloy, J.R. (1996). Stalking (obsessional following): A review of some preliminary studies. *Aggression and Violent Behavior, 1,* 147–162.

Meloy, J.R. (1997a). The clinical risk management of stalking: "Someone is watching over me. . . ." *American Journal of Psychotherapy, 51,* 174–184.

Meloy, J.R. (1997b). Predatory violence during mass murder. *Journal of Forensic Sciences, 42,* 326–329.

Meloy, J.R. (1998). The psychology of stalking. In J.R. Meloy (Ed.), *The psychology of stalking: Clinical and forensic perspectives* (pp. 1–23). San Diego: Academic Press.

Meloy, J.R., & McEllistrem, J.E. (1998). Bombing and psychopathy: An integrative review. *Journal of Forensic Science, 43,* 556–562.

Meloy, J.R. (1999). Stalking: An old behavior, a new crime. *Psychiatric Clinics of North America, 22,* 85–99.

Meloy, J.R. (2000). The nature and dynamics of sexual homicide: An integrative review. *Aggression and Violent Behavior, 5,* 1–22.

Meloy, J.R. (2001a). Communicated threats and violence toward public and private targets: Discerning differences among those who stalk and attack. *Journal of Forensic Sciences, 46,* 1211–1213.

Meloy, J.R. (2001b). Threats, stalking, and criminal harassment. In G-F. Pinard & L. Pagani (Eds.), *Clinical assessment of dangerousness: Empirical contributions* (pp. 238–257). New York: Cambridge University Press.

Meloy, J.R. (2002). Stalking and violence. In J. Boon & L. Sheridan (Eds.), *Stalking and psychosexual obsession* (pp. 105–124). London: Wiley.

Meloy, J.R. (2003a). When stalkers become violent: The threat to public figures and private lives. *Psychiatric Annals, 33,* 659–665.

Meloy, J.R. (2003b). Pathologies of attachment, violence and criminality. In A. Goldman (Ed.), *Handbook of psychology: Vol. II. Forensic psychology* (pp. 509–526). New York: Wiley.

Meloy, J.R., & Boyd, C. (2003). Female stalkers and their victims. *Journal of the American Academy of Psychiatry and the Law, 31,* 211–219.

Meloy, J.R., Cowett, P.Y., Parker, S., Hofland, B., & Friedland, A. (1997). Domestic protection orders and the prediction of subsequent criminality and violence toward protectees. *Psychotherapy, 34,* 447–458.

Meloy, J.R., Davis, B., & Lovette, J. (2001). Risk factors for violence among stalkers. *Journal of Threat Assessment, 1,* 3–16.

Meloy, J.R., & Fisher, H. (2005). Some thoughts on the neurobiology of stalking. *Journal of Forensic Sciences, 50,* 1472–1480.

Meloy, J.R., Gacono, C.B., & Kenney, L. (1994). A Rorschach investigation of sexual homicide. *Journal of Personality Assessment, 62,* 58–67.

Meloy, J.R., & Gothard, S. (1995). Demographic and clinical comparison of obsessional followers and offenders with mental disorders. *American Journal of Psychiatry, 152,* 258–263.

Meloy, J.R., Hempel, A.G., Mohandie, K., Shiva, A.A., & Gray, B.T. (2001). Offenders and offense characteristics of a nonrandom sample of adolescent mass murderers. *Journal of the American Academy of Child and Adolescent Psychiatry, 40,* 719–728.

Meloy, J.R., James, D.V., & Farnham, F.R. (2004). A research review of public figure threats, approaches, attacks, and assassinations in the United States. *Journal of Forensic Science, 49,* 1086–1093.

Meloy, J.R., Reid, J., Kris, M., Anthony, H., & Shiva, A. (2001). The violent true believer: Homicidal and suicidal states of mind. *Journal of Threat Assessment, 1,* 1–14.

Meloy, J.R., Rivers, L., Siegel, L., Gothard, S., Naimark, D., & Nicolini, R. (2000). A replication study of obsessional followers and offenders with mental disorders. *Journal of Forensic Sciences, 45,* 147–152.

Melton, G.B., Petrila, J., Poythress, N.G., & Slobogin, C. (1997). *Psychological evaluations for the courts* (2nd ed.). New York: Guilford Press.

Mendez, M.F., Chow, T., Ringman, J., Twitchell, G., & Hinken, C.H. (2000). Pedophilia and temporal lobe disturbances. *Journal of Neuropsychiatry and Clinical Neurosciences, 12,* 71–76.

Mendez, M.F., O'Connor, S.M., & Lim, G.T. (2004). Hypersexuality after right pallidotomy for Parkinson's disease. *Journal of Neuropsychiatry and Clinical Neurosciences, 16,* 37–40.

Menninger, K.A., Mayman, M., & Pruyser, P. (1963). *The vital balance: The life process in mental health and illness.* New York: Viking.

Menninger, K.A. (1938). *Man against himself.* New York: Harcourt Brace.

Menninger, W.W. (1984). Guns and violence: An American phenomenon. *American Journal of Social Psychiatry, 4,* 37–40.

Menninger, W.W. (2007). Uncontained rage: A psychoanalytic perspective on violence. *Bulletin of the Menninger Clinic, 71,* 115–131.

Menzies, R.J., Federoff, J., Green, C., & Isaacson, K. (1995). Prediction of dangerous behavior in male erotomania. *British Journal of Psychiatry, 166,* 529–536.

Merari, A. (1990). The readiness to kill and die: Suicidal terrorism in the Middle East. In W. Reich (Ed.), *Origins of terrorism: Psychologies, ideologies, theologies, states of mind* (pp. 192–207). New York: Cambridge University Press.

Merari, A. (2007). Psychological aspects of suicide terrorism. In B. Bongar, L.M. Brown, L.E. Beutler, J.N. Breckenridge & P.G. Zimbardo (Eds.), *Psychology of terrorism* (pp. 101–115). New York: Oxford University Press.

Mercy, J.A., & Saltzman, L.E. (1989). Fatal violence among spouses in the United States 1976–85. *American Journal of Public Health, 79,* 595–599.

Merskey, H. (1992). Psychiatric aspects of the neurology of trauma. *Neurologic Clinics, 10,* 895–905.

Merton, R.K. (1938). Social structure and anomie. *American Sociological Review, 3,* 672–682.

Merton, R.K. (1957). *Social theory and social structure.* New York: Free Press.

Merz-Perez, L., Heide, K.M., & Silverman, I.J. (2001). Childhood cruelty to animals and subsequent violence against humans. *International Journal of Offender Therapy and Comparative Criminology, 45,* 556–573.

Messman, T.L., & Long, P.J. (1996). Child sexual abuse and its relationship to revictimization in adult women: A review. *Clinical Psychology Review, 16,* 397–420.

Mester, R., Birger, M., & Margolin, J. (2006). Stalking. *Israel Journal of Psychiatry and Related Sciences, 43,* 102–111.

Meyer, C.B., & Taylor, S.E. (1986). Adjustment to rape. *Journal of Personality and Social Psychology, 50,* 1226–1234.

Meyer, C.L., & Oberman, M. (2001). *Mothers who kill their children: Understanding the acts of moms from Susan Smith to the "prom mom."* New York: University Press.

Meyer-Lindenberg, A., Buckholtz, J.W., Kolachana, B., Hariri, A.R., & Pezawas, L. (2006). Neural mechanisms of genetic risk for impulsivity and violence in humans. *Proceedings of the National Academy of Sciences, 103,* 6269–6274.

Miccio-Fonseca, L.C. (2000). Adult and adolescent female sex offenders: Experiences compared to other female and male sex offenders. *Journal of Psychology and Human Sexuality, 11,* 75–88.

Michael, A., Mirza, S., & Mirza, K.A.H. (1995). Morbid jealousy in alcoholism. *British Journal of Psychiatry, 167,* 668–672.

Michaud, S.G., & Hazelwood, R.R. (1999). *The evil that men do.* New York: St. Martin's Press.

Micucci, J.A. (1995). Adolescents who assault their parents: A family systems approach to treatment. *Psychotherapy: Theory, Research, Practice, Training, 32,* 154–161.

Midgley, M. (1984). *Wickedness.* London: Routledge.

Milgram, S. (1974). *Obediance to authority: An experimental view.* New York: Harper & Row.

Millaud, F., Auclair, N., & Meunier, D. (1996). Parricide and mental illness: A study of 12 cases. *International Journal of Law and Psychiatry, 19,* 173–182.

Miller, B.L., Cummings, J.L., McIntyre, H., Ebers, G., & Grode, M. (1986). Hypersexuality or altered sexual preference following brain injury. *Journal of Neurology, Neurosurgery and Psychiatry, 49,* 867–873.

Miller, E. (2002). Brain injury as a contributing factor in offending. In J. Glickson (Ed.), *The neurobiology of criminal behavior* (pp. 134–156). Dordrecht, Netherlands: Kluwer.

Miller, H.B., Miller, L., & Bjorklund, D. (2010). Helping military parents cope with parental deployment: Role of attachment theory and recommendations for mental health clinicians and counselors. *International Journal of Emergency Mental Health, 12,* 231–235.

Miller, L. (1984a). Neuropsychological concepts of somatoform disorders. *International Journal of Psychiatry in Medicine, 14,* 31–46.

Miller, L. (1984b). Hemispheric asymmetry of cognitive processing in schizophrenics. *Psychological Reports, 55,* 932–934.

Miller, L. (1985a). Tourette syndrome and drug addiction. *British Journal of Psychiatry, 147,* 584–585.

Miller, L. (1985b). Neuropsychological assessment of substance abusers: Review and recommendations. *Journal of Substance Abuse Treatment, 2,* 5–17.

Miller, L. (1986a). Binge drinking and strokes in young adults. *Alcoholism and Addiction,* February, p. 48.

Miller, L. (1986b). Conversion, paranoia, and brain dysfunction. *British Journal of Psychiatry, 148,* 481.

Miller, L. (1986c). Some comments on cerebral hemispheric models of consciousness. *Psychoanalytic Review, 73,* 129–144.

Miller, L. (1986d). The subcortex, frontal lobes, and psychosis. *Schizophrenia Bulletin, 12,* 340–341.

Miller, L. (1986e). "Narrow localizationism" in psychiatric neuropsychology. *Psychological Medicine, 16,* 729–734.

Miller, L. (1986f). In search of the unconscious: Psychoanalysis and brain research come of age. *Psychology Today,* December, pp. 60–64.

Miller, L. (1987). Neuropsychology of the aggressive psychopath: An integrative review. *Aggresssive Behavior, 13,* 119–140.

Miller, L. (1988a). The emotional brain. *Psychology Today,* February, pp. 34–42.

Miller, L. (1988b). Ego autonomy, creativity, and cognitive style: A neuropsychodynamic approach. In K.D. Hoppe (Ed.), *Hemispheric specialization* (pp. 383–397). Philadelpha: Saunders.

Miller, L. (1988c). Neuropsychological perspectives on delinquency. *Behavioral Sciences and the Law, 6,* 409–428.

Miller, L. (1989a). Neuropsychology, personality, and substance abuse: Implications for head injury rehabilitation. *Cognitive Rehabilitation, 7*(5), 26–31.

Miller, L. (1989b). Neurocognitive aspects of remorse: Impulsivity compulsivity reflectivity. In E.M. Stern (Ed.), *Psychotherapy and the remorseful patient* (pp. 63–76). New York: Haworth.

Miller, L. (1989c). On the neuropsychology of dreams. *Psychoanalytic Review, 76,* 375–401.

Miller, L. (1990a). Neuropsychodynamics of alcoholism and addiction: Personality, psychopathology, and cognitive style. *Journal of Substance Abuse Treatment, 7,* 31–49.

Miller, L. (1990b). Major syndromes of aggressive behavior following head injury. *Cognitive Rehabilitation, 8*(6), 14–19.

Miller, L. (1990c). *Inner natures: Brain, self, and personality.* New York: St. Martin's Press.

Miller, L. (1991a). Psychotherapy of the brain-injured patient: Principles and practices. *Journal of Cognitive Rehabilitation, 9*(2), 24–30.

Miller, L. (1991b). Predicting relapse and recovery in alcoholism and addiction: Neuropsychology, personality, and cognitive style. *Journal of Substance Abuse Treatment, 8,* 277–291.

Miller, L. (1991c). Brain and self: Toward a neuropsychodynamic model of ego autonomy and personality. *Journal of the American Academy of Psychoanalysis, 19,* 213–234.

Miller, L. (1991d). *Freud's brain: Neuropsychodynamic foundations of psychoanalysis.* New York: Guilford.

Miller, L. (1992a). The primitive personality and the organic personality: A neuropsychodynamic model for evaluation and treatment. *Psychoanalytic Psychology, 9,* 93–109.

Miller, L. (1992b). Neuropsychology, personality, and substance abuse in the head injury case: Clinical and forensic issues. *International Journal of Law and Psychiatry, 15,* 303–316.

Miller, L. (1993a). Who are the best psychotherapists? Qualities of the effective practitioner. *Psychotherapy in Private Practice, 12*(1), 1–18.

Miller, L. (1993b). Freud's brain: Toward a unified neuropsychodynamic model of personality and psychotherapy. *Journal of the American Academy of Psychoanalysis, 21,* 183–212.

Miller, L. (1993c). The "trauma" of head trauma: Clinical, neuropsychological, and forensic aspects of posttraumatic stress syndromes in brain injury. *Journal of Cognitive Rehabilitation, 11*(4), 18–29.

Miller, L. (1993d). *Psychotherapy of the brain-injured patient: Reclaiming the shattered self.* New York: Norton.

Miller, L. (1994a). Unusual head injury syndromes: Clinical, neuropsychological, and forensic considerations. *Journal of Cognitive Rehabilitation, 12*(6), 12–22.

Miller, L. (1994b). Traumatic brain injury and aggression. In M. Hillbrand & N.J. Pallone, (Eds.), *The psychobiology of aggression: Engines, measurement, control* (pp. 91–103). New York: Haworth.

Miller, L. (1994c). Civilian posttraumatic stress disorder: Clinical syndromes and psychotherapeutic strategies. *Psychotherapy, 31,* 655–664.

Miller, L. (1994d). Psychotherapy of epilepsy: Seizure control and psychosocial adjustment. *Journal of Cognitive Rehabilitation, 12*(1), 14–30.

Miller, L. (1994e). The epilepsy patient: Personality, psychodynamics, and psychotherapy. *Psychotherapy, 31,* 735–743.

Miller, L. (1994f). Sex and the brain-injured patient: Regaining love, pleasure, and intimacy. *Journal of Cognitive Rehabilitation, 12*(3), 12–20.

Miller, L. (1996). Neuropsychology and pathophysiology of mild head injury and the postconcussion syndrome: Clinical and forensic considerations. *Journal of Cognitive Rehabilitation, 14*(1), 8–23.

Miller, L. (1997a). Freud and consciousness: The first 100 years of neuropsychodynamics in theory and clinical practice. *Seminars in Neurology, 17,* 171–177.

Miller, L. (1997b). Workplace violence in the rehabilitation setting: How to prepare, respond, and survive. *Florida State Association of Rehabilitation Nurses Newsletter, 7,* 4–8.

Miller, L. (1997c). Neurosensitization: A pathophysiological model for traumatic disability syndromes. *Journal of Cognitive Rehabilitation, 15*(6), 12–23.

Miller, L. (1998a). Brain injury and violent crime: Clinical, neuropsychological, and forensic considerations. *Journal of Cognitive Rehabilitation, 16*(6), 2–17.

Miller, L. (1998b). Psychotherapy of crime victims: Treating the aftermath of interpersonal violence. *Psychotherapy, 35,* 336–345.

Miller, L. (1998c). *Shocks to the system: Psychotherapy of traumatic disability syndromes.* New York: Norton.

Miller, L. (1998d). Ego autonomy and the healthy personality: Psychodynamics, cognitive style, and clinicial applications. *Psychoanalytic Review, 85,* 423–448.

Miller, L. (1998e). Our own medicine: Traumatized psychotherapists and the stresses of doing therapy. *Psychotherapy, 35,* 137–146.

Miller, L. (1999a). Pediatric brain injury: Current and future disabilities. *Neurolaw Letter, 8,* 65–71.

Miller, L. (1999b). Child abuse brain injury: Clinical, neuropsychological, and forensic considerations. *Journal of Cognitive Rehabilitation, 17*(2), 10–19.

Miller, L. (1999c). Atypical psychological responses to traumatic brain injury: PTSD and beyond. *Neurorehabilitation, 13,* 13–24.

Miller, L. (1999d). Posttraumatic stress disorder in child victims of violent crime: Making the case for psychological injury. *Victim Advocate, 1*(1), 6–10.

Miller, L. (1999e). Posttraumatic stress disorder in elderly victims of violent crime: Making the case for psychological injury. *Victim Advocate, 1*(2), 7–10.

Miller, L. (1999f). Treating posttraumatic stress disorder in children and families: Basic principles and clinical applications. *American Journal of Family Therapy, 27,* 21–34.

Miller, L. (1999g). Workplace violence: Prevention, response, and recovery. *Psychotherapy, 36,* 160–169.

Miller, L. (2000a). Law enforcement traumatic stress: Clinical syndromes and intervention strategies. *Trauma Response, 6*(1), 15–20.

Miller, L. (2000b). Neurosensitization: A model for persistent disability in chronic pain, depression, and posttraumatic stress disorder following injury. *Neurorehabilitation, 14,* 25–32.

Miller, L. (2000c). The predator's brain: Neuropsychodynamics of serial killers. In L.B. Schlesinger (Ed.), *Serial offenders: Current thought, recent findings, unusual syndromes* (pp. 135–166). Boca Raton: CRC Press.

Miller, L. (2001a). Workplace violence and psychological trauma: Clinical disability, legal liability, and corporate policy. Part I. *Neurolaw Letter, 11,* 1–5.

Miller, L. (2001b). Workplace violence and psychological trauma: Clinical disability, legal liability, and corporate policy. Part II. *Neurolaw Letter, 11,* 7–13.

Miller, L. (2001c). Crime victim trauma and psychological injury: Clinical and forensic guidelines. In E. Pierson (Ed.), *2001 Wiley expert witness update: New developments in personal injury litigation* (pp. 171–205). New York: Aspen.

Miller, L. (2002a). How safe is your job? The threat of workplace violence. *USA
Today Magazine,* March, pp. 52–54.

Miller, L. (2002b). Posttraumatic stress disorder in school violence: Risk management lessons from the workplace. *Neurolaw Letter, 11,* 33, 36–40.

Miller, L. (2002c). What is the true spectrum of functional disorders in rehabilitation? In N.D. Zasler & M.F. Martelli (Eds.), *Functional disorders* (pp. 1–20).
Philadelphia: Hanley & Belfus.

Miller, L. (2003a). Psychological interventions for terroristic trauma: Symptoms, syndromes, and treatment strategies. *Psychotherapy, 39,* 283–296.

Miller, L. (2003b). Family therapy of terroristic trauma: Psychological syndromes
and treatment strategies. *American Journal of Family Therapy, 31,* 257–280.

Miller, L. (2003c). Personalities at work: Understanding and managing human
nature on the job. *Public Personnel Management, 32,* 419–433.

Miller, L. (2003d). Police personalities: Understanding and managing the problem
officer. *The Police Chief,* May, pp. 53–60.

Miller, L. (2004). Psychotherapeutic interventions for survivors of terrorism.
American Journal of Psychotherapy, 58, 1–16.

Miller, L. (2005). Psychotherapy for terrorism survivors: New directions in evaluation and treatment. *Directions in Clinical and Counseling Psychology, 17,* 59–74.

Miller, L. (2006a). The terrorist mind: I. A psychological and political analysis.
International Journal of Offender Rehabilitation and Comparative Criminology, 50,
121–138.

Miller, L. (2006b). The terrorist mind: II. Typologies, psychopathologies, and practical guidelines for investigation. *International Journal of Offender Rehabilitation and
Comparative Criminology, 50,* 255–268.

Miller, L. (2006c). Suicide by cop: Causes, reactions, and practical intervention
strategies. *International Journal of Emergency Mental Health, 8,* 165–174.

Miller, L. (2006d). Officer-involved shooting: Reaction patterns, response protocols,
and psychological intervention strategies. *International Journal of Emergency Mental
Health, 8,* 239–254.

Miller, L. (2006e). On the spot: Testifying in court for law enforcement officers. *FBI
Law Enforcement Bulletin,* October, pp. 1–6.

Miller, L. (2006f). *Practical police psychology: Stress management and crisis intervention for
law enforcement.* Springfield, IL: Charles C Thomas.

Miller, L. (2007a). School violence: Effective response protocols for maximum safety and minimum liability. *International Journal of Emergency Mental Health, 9,*
105–110.

Miller, L. (2007b). Workplace violence: Practical policies and strategies for prevention, response, and recovery. *International Journal of Emergency Mental Health, 9,*
259–279.

Miller, L. (2007c). Traumatic stress disorders. In F.M. Dattilio & A. Freeman (Eds.), *Cognitive-behavioral strategies in crisis intervention* (3rd ed., pp. 494–527). New York: Guilford.

Miller, L. (2007d). Stress, traumatic stress, and posttraumatic stress syndromes. In L. Territo & J.D. Sewell (Eds.), *Stress management in law enforcement* (2nd ed., pp. 15–39). Durham, NC: Carolina Academic Press.

Miller, L. (2007e). The psychological fitness-for-duty evaluation. *FBI Law Enforcement Bulletin*, August, pp. 10–16.

Miller, L. (2007f). Line-of-duty death: Psychological treatment of traumatic bereavement in law enforcement. *International Journal of Emergency Mental Health, 9*, 13–23.

Miller, L. (2008a). Death notification for families of murder victims: Healing dimensions of a complex process. *Omega: Journal of Death and Dying, 57*, 367–380.

Miller, L. (2008b). *Counseling crime victims: Practical strategies for mental health professionals.* New York: Springer.

Miller, L. (2008c). *From difficult to disturbed: Understanding and managing dysfunctional employees.* New York: Amacom.

Miller, L. (2008d). Military psychology and police psychology: Mutual contributions to crisis intervention and stress management. *International Journal of Emergency Mental Health, 10*, 9–26.

Miller, L. (2009a). Family survivors of homicide: I. Symptoms, syndromes, and reaction patterns. *American Journal of Family Therapy, 37*, 67–79.

Miller, L. (2009b). Family survivors of homicide: II. Practical therapeutic strategies. *American Journal of Family Therapy, 37*, 85–98.

Miller, L. (2009c). Criminal investigator stress: Symptoms, syndromes, and practical coping strategies. *International Journal of Emergency Mental Health, 11*, 87–92.

Miller, L. (2009d). Testifying in court: Practical strategies for public safety, emergency services, and mental health professionals. *International Journal of Emergency Mental Health, 11*, 263–269.

Miller, L. (2010). On-scene crisis intervention: Psychological guidelines and communication strategies. *International Journal of Emergency Mental Health, 12*, 11–19.

Miller, L., & Schlesinger, L.B. (2000). Survivors, families, and co-victims of serial offenders. In L.B. Schlesinger (Ed.), *Serial offenders: Current thought, recent findings, unusual syndromes* (pp. 309–334). Boca Raton: CRC Press.

Miller, L.J. (2003). Denial of pregnancy. In M.G. Spinelli (Ed.), *Infanticide: Psychosocial and legal perspectives on mothers who kill* (pp. 81–104). Washington, DC: American Psychiatric Publishing.

Miller, R.D. (2003). Hospitalization of criminal defendants for evaluation of competence to stand trial or for restoration of competence: Clinical and legal issues. *Behavioral Sciences and the Law, 21*, 369–391.

Millis, J.B., & Kornblith, P.R. (1992). Fragile beginnings: Identification and treatment of postpartum disorders. *Health and Social Work, 17*, 192–199.

Millon, T., & Davis, R. (2000). *Personality disorders in modern life.* New York: Wiley.

Millon, T. (1981). *Disorders of personality: DSM-III, Axis 2.* New York: Wiley.

Mills, J.F. (2005). Advances in the assessment and prediction of interpersonal violence. *Journal of Interpersonal Violence, 20,* 236–241.

Mills, S., & Raine, A. (1994). Neuroimaging and aggression. *Journal of Offender Rehabilitation, 21,* 145–158.

Millstein, S.G., & Halpern-Feisher, B.L. (2002). Perceptions of risk and vulnerability. *Journal of Adolescent Health, 315,* 10–27.

Milroy, C.M. (1995). The epidemiology of homicide-suicide (dyadic death). *Forensic Science International, 71,* 117–122.

Milton, J., Duggan, C., Latham, A., Egan, V., & Tantam, D. (2002). Case history of co-morbid Asperger's syndrome and paraphilic behavior. *Medical Science of Law, 42,* 237–244.

Mishna, F. (2003). Learning disabilities and bullying: Double jeopardy. *Journal of Learning Disabilities, 36,* 336–347.

Mishna, F. (2008). An overview of the evidence on bullying prevention and intervention programs. *Brief Treatment and Crisis Intervention, 8,* 327–341.

Mishra, S., & Lalumiere, M.L. (2008). Risk-taking, antisocial behavior, and life histories. In J.D. Duntley & T.K. Shackelford (Eds.), *Evolutionary forensic psychiatry: Darwinian foundations of crime and law* (pp. 139–159). New York: Oxford University Press.

Mitchell, J.T., & Everly, G.S. (1996). *Critical incident stress debriefing: Operations manual* (rev. ed.). Ellicott City: Chevron.

Mitchell, W., Falconer, M.A., & Hill, D. (1954). Epilepsy with fetishism relieved by temporal lobectomy. *Lancet, 267,* 626–630.

Mitroff, I.I. (2001). *Managing crises before they happen: What every executive manager needs to know about crisis management.* New York: Amacom.

Mobbs, D., Lau, H.C., Jones, O.D., & Frith, C.D. (2007). Law, responsibility, and the brain. *PLoS Biology, 5,* 693–700.

Model Penal Code, Section 2.01. Philadelphia: American Law Institute.

Modestin, J., & Ammann, R. (1995). Mental disorder and criminal behaviour. *British Journal of Psychiatry, 166,* 667–675.

Modestin, J., Hug, A., & Ammann, R. (1997). Criminal behaviors in males with affective disorders. *Journal of Affective Disorders, 42,* 29–38.

Modlin, H.C. (1983). Traumatic neurosis and other injuries. *Psychiatric Clinics of North America, 6,* 661–682.

Modlin, H.C. (1990). Post-traumatic stress disorder: Differential diagnosis. In C.L. Meek (Ed.), *Post-traumatic stress disorder: Assessment, differential diagnosis, and forensic evaluation* (pp. 63–89). Sarasota: Professional Resource Exchange.

Moffitt, T.E. (1990a). The neuropsychology of delinquency: A critical review of theory and research. *Crime and Justice: An Annual Review of Research, 12,* 99–169.

Moffitt, T.E. (1990b). Juvenile delinquency and attention deficit disorder: Boys' developmental trajectories from age 3 to age 15. *Child Development, 61,* 893–910.

Moffitt, T.E. (1993). Adolescence-limited and life-course persistent antisocial behavior: A developmental taxonomy. *Psychological Review, 100,* 674–701.

Moffitt, T.E. (1997). Adolescence-limited and life-course persistent antisocial behavior: A complimentary pair of developmental theories. In T. Thornberry (Ed.), *Advances in criminological theory: Developmental theories of crime and delinquency* (pp. 11–54). London: Transaction Press.

Moffitt, T.E. (2003). Life-course persistent and adolescent-limited antisocial behavior: A research review and research agenda. In B. Lahey, T.E. Moffitt & A. Caspi (Eds.), *The causes of conduct disorder and serious juvenile delinquency* (pp. 97–125). New York: Guilford.

Moffitt, T.E. (2005). The new look of behavioral genetics in developmental psychopathology: Gene-envrionment interplay in antisocial behavior. *Psychological Bulletin, 131,* 533–554.

Moffitt, T.E., & Caspi, A. (2001). Childhood predictors differentiate life-course persistent and adolescent-limited antisocial pathways among males and females. *Development and Psychopathology, 13,* 355–375.

Moffitt, T.E., Caspi, A., Harrington, H., & Milne, B.J. (2002). Males on the life-course-persistent and adolescent-limited antisocial pathways: Follow-up at age 26 years. *Developmental Psychopathology, 14,* 179–207.

Moffitt, T.E., & Henry, B. (1989). Neuropsychological assessment of executive function in self-reported delinquents. *Development and Psychopathology, 1,* 105–118.

Moffitt, T.E., & Henry, B. (1991). Neuropsychological studies of juvenile delinquency and juvenile violence. In J.S. Milner (Ed.), *Neuropsychology of aggression* (pp. 67–91). Boston: Kluwer.

Moffitt, T.E., Mednick, S.A., & Gabrielli, W.F. (1989). Predicting careers of criminal violence: Descriptive data and dispositional factors. In D.A. Brizer & M. Crowner (Eds.), *Current approaches to the prediction of violence* (pp. 13–34). Washington, DC: American Psychiatric Press.

Moghaddam, F.M. (2007). The staircase to terrorism: A psychological exploration. In B. Bongar, L.M. Brown, L.E. Beutler, J.N. Breckenridge & P.G. Zimbardo (Eds.), *Psychology of terrorism* (pp. 69–80). New York: Oxford University Press.

Moghaddam, F.M. (2009). The new global American dilemma and terrorism. *Political Psychology, 30,* 373–380.

Mogil, M. (1989). Maximizing your courtroom testimony. *FBI Law Enforcement Bulletin,* May, pp. 7–9.

Mohandle, K., & Duffy, J.E. (1999). Understanding subjects with paranoid schizophrenia. *FBI Law Enforcement Bulletin,* December, pp. 8–16.

Mohandie, K., & Meloy, J.R. (2000). Clinical and forensic indicators of "suicide by cop." *Journal of Forensic Science, 45,* 384–389.

Mohandie, K., Meloy, J.R., McGowan, M.G., & Williams, J. (2006). The RECON typology of stalking: Reliability and validity based upon a large sample of North American Stalkers. *Journal of Forensic Sciences, 51,* 147–155.

Molina, B.S., & Pelham, W.E.J. (2003). Childhood predictors of adolescent substance use in a longitudinal study of children with ADHD. *Journal of Abnormal Psychology, 112,* 497–507.

Monaghan, L.F. (2002). Hard men, shop boys, and others: Embodying competence in a masculinist occupation. *Sociological Review, 50,* 332–353.

Monaghan, L.F. (2003). Danger on the doors: Bodily risk in a demonized occupation. *Health, Risk and Society, 5*, 11–31.

Monaghan, L.F. (2004). Doorwork and legal risk: Observations from an embodied enthnography. *Social and Legal Studies, 13*, 453–480.

Monahan, J. (1992). Mental disorder and violent behavior: Perceptions and evidence. *American Psychologist, 47*, 511–521.

Monahan, J. (1996). Violence prediction: The past twenty and the next twenty years. *Criminal Justice and Behavior, 23*, 107–120.

Monahan, J. (2001). Major mental disorder and violence: Epidemiology and risk assessment. In G-F. Pinard & L. Pagani (Eds.), *Clinical assessment of dangerousness: Empirical contributions* (pp. 89–102). New York: Cambridge University Press.

Monahan, J. (2002). The scientific status of research on clinical and actuarial predictions of violence. In D. Faigman, D. Kaye, M. Saks & J. Sanders (Eds.), *Modern scientific evidence: The law and science of expert testimony* (pp. 423–445). St. Paul, MN: West Publishing.

Monahan, J., Bonnie, R., Appelbaum, P.S., Hyde, P.S., Steadman, H.J., & Swartz, M.S. (2001). Mandated community treatment: Beyond outpatient commitment. *Psychiatric Services, 52*, 1198–1205.

Monahan, J., & Steadman, H.J. (1983). Crime and mental disorder: An epidemiological approach. In M. Tonry & N. Morris (Eds.), *Crime and justice: An annual review of research* (Vol. 4, pp. 145–189). Chicago: University of Chicago Press.

Monahan, J., Steadman, H.J., Appelbaum, P.S., Robbins, P.C., Mulvey, E.P., & Silver, E. (2000). Developing a clinically useful actuarial tool for assessing violence risk. *British Journal of Psychiatry, 176*, 312–319.

Monahan, J., Steadman, H.J., Silver, E., Appelbaum, P.S., Robbins, P.C., & Mulvery, E.P. (2001). *Rethinking risk assessment: The MacArthur study of mental disorder and violence.* New York: Oxford University Press.

Mones, P.A. (1991). *When a child kills: Abused children who kill their parents.* New York: Pocket Books.

Money, J. (1990). Forensic sexology: Paraphilic serial rape (brastophilia) and lust murder (erotophenophilia). *American Journal of Psychotherapy, 64*, 26–36.

Monks, C.P., Smith, P.K., & Swettenham, J. (2003). The psychological correlates of peer victimization in preschool: Social cognitive skills, executive function and attachment profiles. *Aggressive Behavior, 31*, 571–588.

Monks, C.P., Ortega-Ruiz, R., & Rodriguez-Hidalgo, A.J. (2008). Peer victimization in multi-cultural schools in Spain and England. *European Journal of Developmental Psychology, 5*, 507–535.

Monks, C.P., Smith, P.K., Naylor, P., Barter, C., Ireland, J.L., & Coyne, I. (2009). Bullying in different contexts: Commonalities, differences, and the role of theory. *Aggression and Violent Behavior, 14*, 146–156.

Monks, C.P., Smith, P.K., & Swettenham, J. (2003). The psychological correlates of peer victimization in preschool: Social cognitive skills, executive function and attachment profiles. *Aggressive Behavior, 31*, 571–588.

Monroe, R.R. (1978). *Brain dysfunction in aggressive criminals.* Lexington, MA: Lexington Books.

Monroe, R.R. (1982). DSM-III style diagnoses of episodic disorders. *Journal of Nervous & Mental Disease, 170,* 664–669.

Monroe, S.M., & Simons, A.D. (1991). Diathesis-stress theories in the context of life stress research: Implications for the depressive disorders. *Psychological Bulletin, 110,* 406–425.

Montag, B.A., & Montag, T.W. (1979). Infanticide: A historical perspective. *Minnesota Medicine, 62,* 368–372.

Moracco, K.E., Runyan, C.W., & Butts, J. (1998). Femicide in North Carolina. *Homicide Studies, 2,* 422–446.

Moran, P.B., & Eckenrode, J. (1992). Protective personality characteristics among adolescent victims of maltreatment. *Child Abuse and Neglect, 16,* 743–754.

Morf, G. (1970). *Terror in Quebec: Case studies of the FLQ.* Toronto, Canada: Clarke Irwin.

Morgan, A.P., & Lilienfeld, S.O. (2000). A meta-analytic review of the relation between antisocial behavior and neuropsychological measures of executive function. *Clinical Psychology Review, 20,* 113–136.

Morgan, D.G., & Stewart, N.J. (1998). High versus low density special care units: Impact on the behavior of elderly residents with dementia. *Canadian Journal on Aging, 17,* 143–165.

Morley, C.J. (1995). Practical concerns about the diagnosis of Munchausen syndrome by proxy. *Archives of Diseases in Childhood, 72,* 528–539.

Morris, D. (1977). *Manwatching: A field guide to human behavior.* New York: Harry N. Abrams.

Morris, D.R., & Parker, G.F. (2009). Effects of advanced age and dementia on restoration of competence to stand trial. *International Journal of Law and Psychiatry, 32,* 156–160.

Morris, N.M., & Udry, J.R. (1982). Epidemiological patterns of sexual behavior in the menstrual cycle. In R.C. Friedman (Ed.), *Behavior and the menstrual cycle* (pp. 129–153). New York: Marcel Dekker.

Morrison, K.A. (2001). Predicting violent behavior in stalkers: A preliminary investigation of Canadian cases in criminal harassment. *Journal of Forensic Science, 46,* 1403–1410.

Morrison, K.A. (2008). Differentiating between physically violent and nonviolent stalkers: An examination of Canadian cases. *Journal of Forensic Sciences, 53,* 742–751.

Morse, S.J. (2004). New neuroscience, old problems. In B. Garland (Ed.), *Neuroscience and the law: Brain, mind and the scales of justice* (pp. 157–198). New York: Dana Press.

Morse, S.J. (2006). Brain overclaim syndrome and criminal responsibility: A diagnostic note. *Ohio State Journal of Criminal Law, 3,* 397–412.

Morse, S.J. (2008). Psychopathy and criminal responsibility. *Neuroethics, 1,* 205–212.

Morton, N., & Browne, K.D. (1998). Theory and observation of attachment and its relation to child maltreatment: A review. *Child Abuse and Neglect, 22,* 1093–1104.

Moseley, K.L. (1986). The history of infanticide in Western society. *Issues in Law and Medicine, 1,* 345–361.

Mosher, D.L., & Anderson, R. (1986). Macho personality, sexual aggression, and reactions to guided imagery of realistic rape. *Journal of Research in Personality, 20,* 77–94.

Moskowitz, A. (2004). Dissociation and violence. *Trauma, Violence and Abuse, 5,* 21–46.

Moulden, H.M., Firestone, P., & Wexler, A.F. (2007). Child care providers who commit sexual offenses: A description of offender, offense, and victim characteristics. *International Journal of Offender Therapy and Comparative Criminology, 51,* 384–406.

Mouridsen, S.E., Rich, B., Isager, T., & Nedergaard, N.J. (2008). Pervasive developmental disorder and criminal behaviour: A case control study. *International Journal of Offender Therapy and Comparative Criminology, 52,* 196–205.

Muehlenhard, C.L., & Linton, M.A. (1987). Date rape and sexual aggression in dating situations: Incidence and risk factors. *Journal of Counseling Psychology, 34,* 186–196.

Muehlenhard, C.L., Powch, I.G., Phelps, J.L., & Giusti, L.M. (1992). Definitions of rape: Scientific and political implications. *Journal of Social Issues, 48,* 23–44.

Mueser, K.T., Drake, R.E., Ackerson, T.H., Alterman, A.L., Miles, K.M., & Noordsy, D.L. (1997). Antisocial personality disorder, conduct disorder, and substance abuse in schizophrenia. *Journal of Abnormal Psychology, 106,* 473–477.

Mueser, K.T., Drake, R.E., & Wallace, M.A. (1998). Dual diagnosis: A review of etiological theories. *Addictive Behaviors, 23,* 717–734.

Mueser, K.T., Goodman, L.B., Trumbetta, S.L., Rosenberg, S.D., Osher, C., & Vidaver, R. (1998). Trauma and posttraumatic stress disorder in severe mental illness. *Journal of Consulting and Clinical Psychology, 66,* 493–499.

Mullen, P.E. (2004). The autogenic (self-generated) massacre. *Behavioral Sciences and the Law, 22,* 311–323.

Mullen, P.E., Burgess, P., & Wallace, C. (2000). Community care and criminal offending in schizophrenia. *Lancet, 355,* 614–617.

Mullen, P.E., & Lester, G. (2006). Vexatious litigants and unusually persistent complainants and petitioners: From querulous paranoia to querulous behavior. *Behavioral Sciences and the Law, 24,* 333–349.

Mullen, P.E., & Maack, L.H. (1985). Jealousy, pathological jealousy and aggression. In D.P. Farrington & J. Gunn (Eds.), *Aggression and dangerousness* (pp. 103–126). London: Wiley.

Mullen, P.E., Mackenzie, R., Ogloff, J.R.P., Pathe, M., McEwan, T., & Purcell, R. (2006). Assessing and managing the risks in the stalking situation. *Journal of the American Academy of Psychiatry and the Law, 34,* 439–450.

Mullen, P.E., Pathe, M., & Purcell, R. (1999). Study of stalkers. *American Journal of Psychiatry, 156,* 1244–1249.

Mullen, P.E., Pathe, M., & Purcell, R. (2000). *Stalkers and their victims.* Cambridge, UK: Cambridge University Press.

Mullen, P.E., Pathe, M., & Purcell, R. (2001). The management of stalkers. *Advances in Psychiatric Treatment, 7,* 335–342.

Mullen, P.E., Pathe, M., Purcell, R., & Stuart, G.W. (2001). A study of stalkers. *American Journal of Psychiatry, 156,* 1244–1249.

Muller, D.A. (2000). Criminal profiling: Real science or just wishful thinking? *Homicide Studies, 4,* 234–264.

Mulvey, E., & Cauffman, E. (2001). The inherent limits of predicting school violence. *American Psychologist, 56,* 797–802.

Mulvey, E.P. (1994). Assessing the evidence of a link between mental illness and violence. *Hospital and Community Psychiatry, 45,* 663–668.

Mulvey, E.P., Lidz, C., Gardner, W., & Shaw, E. (1996). Clinical versus actuarial predictions of violence in patients with mental illnesses. *Journal of Consulting and Clinical Psychology, 64,* 602–609.

Mumola, C. (2005). *Suicide and homicide in state prisons and local jails.* Washington, DC: Department of Justice: Office of Justice Programs.

Mungas, D. (1983). An empirical analysis of specific syndromes of violent behavior. *Journal of Nervous and Mental Disease, 171,* 354–361.

Mungas, D. (1988). Psychometric correlates of episodic violent behavior: A multidimensional neuropsychological approach. *British Journal of Psychiatry, 152,* 180–187.

Munro, H.M.C., & Thrusfield, M.V. (2001). Battered pets: Features that raise suspicion of non-accidental injury. *Journal of Small Animal Practice, 42,* 218–226.

Murakami, S., Rappaport, N., & Penn, J.V. (2006). An overview of juveniles and school violence. *Psychiatric Clinics of North America, 29,* 725–741.

Muran, E., & DiGiuseppe, R. (2000). Rape trauma. In F.M. Dattilio & A. Freeman (Eds.), *Cognitive-behavioral strategies in crisis intervention* (2nd ed., pp. 150–165). New York: Guilford.

Muris, P., & Ollendick, T.H. (2005). The role of temperaent in the etiology of child psychopathology. *Clinical Child and Family Psychology Review, 8,* 271–289.

Murnen, S.K., Wright, C., & Kaluzny, G. (2002). If "boys will be boys," then girls will be victims? A meta-analytic review of the research that relates masculine ideology to sexual aggression. *Sex Roles, 46,* 359–375.

Murphy, G.H., Harnett, H., & Holland, A.J. (1995). A survey of intellectual disabilities amongst men on remand in prison. *Mental Handicap Research, 8,* 81–98.

Murphy, J.G. (1972). Moral death: A Kantian essay on psychopathy. *Ethics, 82,* 284–298.

Murphy, N., & Brown, W.S. (2007). *Did my neurons make me do it? Philosophical and neurobiological perspectives on moral responsibility and free will.* New York: Oxford University Press.

Murray, K.T., & Kochanska, G. (2002). Effortful control: Factor structure and relation to externalizing and internalizing behaviors. *Journal of Abnormal Child Psychology, 30,* 503–514.

Murrie, D.C., Warren, J.I., Kristiansson, M., & Dietz, P.E. (2002). Asperger's syndrome in forensic settings. *International Journal of Forensic Mental Health, 1,* 59–70.

Myers, S.A. (1970). Maternal filicide. *American Journal of Diseases in Childhood, 120,* 534–536.

Myers, W.C. (2004). Serial murder by children and adolescents. *Behavioral Sciences and the Law, 22,* 357–374.

Myers, W.C., Bukhanovskiy, A., Justen, E., Morton, R.J., Tilley, J., & Adams, K. (2008). The relationship between serial sexual murder and autonomic asphyxiation. *Forensic Science International, 176,* 187–195.

Myers, W.C., Burgess, A.W., & Nelson, J.A. (1998). Criminal and behavioral aspects of juvenile sexual homicide. *Journal of Forensic Sciences, 43,* 340–347.

Myers, W.C., Eggleston, C.F., & Smoak, P. (2003). A media violence-inspired juvenile sexual homicide offender 13 years later. *Journal of Forensic Sciences, 48,* 1–5.

Myers, W.C., Husted, D.S., Safarik, M.E., & O'Toole, M.E. (2006). The motivation behind serial sexual homicide: Is it sex, power, and control, or anger? *Journal of Forensic Science, 51,* 900–907.

Nachshon, I. (1988). Hemisphere function in violent offenders. In T.E. Moffitt & S.A. Mednick (Eds.), *Biological contributions to crime causation* (pp. 55–67). Dordrecht, Netherlands: Martinus Nijhoff.

Nachshon, I. (1991). Violence and cerebral lateralization. *Crime and Social Deviance, 18,* 514.

Nacos, B.L. (2003). The terrorist calculus behind 9-11: A model for future terrorism? *Studies in Conflict and Terrorism, 26,* 1–16.

Nagin, D.S., & Farrington, D.P. (1992). The onset and persistence of offending. *Criminology, 30,* 501–523.

Nagin, D., & Tremblay, R.E. (1999). Trajectories of boys' physical aggression, opposition, and hyperactivity on the path to physically violent and non-violent juvenile delinquency. *Child Development, 70,* 1181–1196.

Namie, G., & Namie, R. (2000). *The bully at work: What you can do to stop the hurt and reclaim your dignity on the job.* Naperville, IL: Sourcebooks.

Nansel, T.R., Overpeck, M.D., & Haynie, D.L. (2003). Relationships between bullying and violence among U.S. youth. *Archives of Pediatric and Adolescent Medicine, 157,* 348–353.

Nansel, T.R., Overpeck, M., Pilla, R.S., Ruan, W.J., Simons-Morton, B., & Scheidt, P. (2001). Bullying behavior among U.S. youth: Prevalence and association with psychosocial adjustment. *Journal of the American Medical Association, 285,* 2094–2100.

Napier, M.R., & Baker, K.P. (2002). Criminal personality profiling. In S.H. James & J.J. Nordby (Eds.), *Forensic science: An introduction to scientific and investigative techniques* (pp. 531–550). Boca Raton: CRC Press.

Napier, M.R., & Hazelwood, R.R. (2003). Homicide investigation: The significance of victimology. *National Academy Associate, 5,* 14–15, 21–22, 30–32.

Nardi, T.J., & Keefe-Cooperman, K. (2006). Communicating bad news: A model for emergency mental health helpers. *International Journal of Emergency Mental Health, 8,* 203–207.

Nasby, W., Hayden, B., & DePaulo, B.M. (1980). Attributional bias among aggressive boys to interpret unambiguous social stimuli as displays of hostility. *Journal of Abnormal Psychology, 89,* 459–468.

Nash, W.P. (2007). Combat/operational stress adaptations and injuries. In C.R. Figley & W.P. Nash (Eds.), *Combat stress injury: Theory, research, and management* (pp. 33–63). New York: Routledge.

Nathan, P., & Ward, T. (2001). Females who sexually abuse children: Assessment and treatment issues. *Psychiatry, Psychology and Law, 8,* 44–45.

Nathan, P., & Ward, T. (2002). Female sex offenders: Clinical and demographic features. *The Journal of Sexual Aggression, 8,* 5–21.

National Crime Victim Bar Association. (2005). *Civil justice for victims of crime in Florida.* Washington, DC: National Crime Victim Bar Association.

National Institute of Justice. (1997). *A study of homicide in eight US cities: An NIJ intramural research project.* Washington, DC: US Department of Justice.

Naudts, K., & Hodgins, S. (2006a). Neurobiological correlates of violent behavior among persons with schizophrenia. *Schizophrenia Bulletin, 32,* 562–572.

Naudts, K., & Hodgins, S. (2006b). Schizophrenia and violence: A search for neurobiological correlates. *Current Opinion in Psychiatry, 19,* 533–538.

Nauta, W. (1971). The problem of the frontal lobe: A reinterpretation. *Journal of Psychiatric Research, 17,* 367–370.

Naylor, P., Cowie, H., & del Rey, R. (2001). Coping strategies of secondary school children in response to being bullied. *Child Psychology and Psychiatry Review, 6,* 114–120.

Neal, A., & Griffin, M.A. (2004). Safety climate and safety at work. In J. Barling & M.R. Frone (Eds.), *The psychology of workplace safety* (pp. 15–34). Washington, DC: American Psychological Association.

Neidig, P.H., Russell, H.E., & Senig, A.F. (1992). Interpersonal aggression in law enforcement families: A preliminary investigation. *Police Studies, 15,* 30–38.

Nestor, P.G., Daggett, D., Haycock, J., & Price, M. (1999). Competence to stand trial: A neuropsychological inquiry. *Law and Human Behavior, 23,* 397–412.

Nestor, P.G., & Haycock, J. (1997). Not guilty by reason of insanity of murder: Clinical and neuropsychological characteristics. *Journal of the American Academy of Psychiatry and the Law, 25,* 161–171.

Neuman, J.H., & Baron, R.A. (2005). Aggression in the workplace: A social-psychological perspective. In S. Fox & P.E. Spector (Eds.), *Counterproductive work behavior: Investigations of actors and targets* (pp. 13–40). Washington, DC: American Psychological Association.

Neuman, J.H., & Baron, R.A. (1998). Workplace violence and workplace aggression. Evidence concerning specific forms, potential causes, and preferred targets. *Journal of Management, 24,* 391–419.

Neuman, J.H., & Baron, R.A. (1997). Aggression in the workplace. In R. Giacalone & J. Greenberg (Eds.), *Antisocial behavior in organizations* (pp. 37–67). Thousand Oaks, CA: Sage.

Neustein, A. (2009). *Tempest in the temple: Jewish communities and child sex scandals.* New York: Brandeis.

Neuwirth, W., & Eher, R. (2003). What differentiates anal rapists from vaginal rapists? *International Journal of Offender Therapy and Comparative Criminology, 47,* 482–488.

Newhill, C.E. (1991). Parricide. *Journal of Family Violence, 64,* 375–394.

Newman, D.L., Moffitt, T.E., Caspi, A., & Silva, P.A. (1998). Comorbid mental disorders: Implications for treatment and sample selection. *Journal of Abnormal Psychology, 107,* 305–311.

Newman, K.S., Fox, C. Harding, D.J., Mehta, J., & Roth, W. (2004). *Rampage: The social roots of school shootings.* New York: Basic Books.

Newport, D.J., & Nemeroff, C.B. (2000). Neurobiology of posttraumatic stress disorder. *Current Opinion in Neurobiology, 10,* 211–218.

Newton, M. (1990). *Hunting humans: An encyclopedia of modern serial killers.* Port Townsend, WA: Loompanics Unlimited.

Ng, B., Kumar, S., Ranclaud, M., & Robinson, E. (2001). Ward crowding and incidents of violence on an acute psychiatric inpatient unit. *Psychiatric Services, 52,* 521–525.

Nicastro, A., Cousins, A., & Spitzberg, B. (2000). The tactical face of stalking. *Journal of Criminal Justice, 28,* 69–82.

Nichols, B.L., & Czirr, D.K. (1986). Posttraumatic stress disorder: Hidden syndrome in elders. *Clinical Gerontologist, 5,* 417–433.

Niehoff, D. (1999). *The biology of violence.* New York: Free Press.

Nielsen, E. (1991). Traumatic incident corps: Lessons learned. In J. Reese, J. Horn, & C. Dunning (Eds.), *Critical incidents in policing* (pp. 221–226). Washington, DC: US Government Printing Office.

Nigg, J.T., Goldsmith, H.H., & Sachek, J. (2004). Temperament and attention deficit hyperactivity disorder: The development of a multiple pathway model. *Journal of Clinical Child and Adolescent Psychology, 33,* 42–53.

Nigg, J.T., & Huang-Pollock, C.L. (2003). An early-onset model of the role of executive functions and intelligence in conduct disorder/delinquency. In B.B. Lahey, T.E. Moffitt & A. Caspi (Eds.), *Causes of conduct disorder and juvenile delinquency* (pp. 227–253). New York: Guilford.

Nihei, M.K., Desmond, J.L, McGlothan, J.L., Kuhlmann, A.C., & Guilarte, T.R. (2000). N-methyl-D-aspartate receptor subunit changes are associated with lead-induced deficits of long-term potentiation and spatial learning. *Neuroscience, 99,* 233–244.

Nijman, H.L., & Rector, G. (1999). Crowding and aggression on inpatient psychiatric wards. *Psychiatric Services, 50,* 830–831.

Nims, D.R. (2000). Violence in the schools: A national crisis. In D.S. Sandhu & C.B. Aspy (Eds.), *Violence in American schools: A practical guide for counselors* (pp. 3–20). Alexandria, VA: American Counseling Association.

Nisbett, R.E. (1993). Violence and U.S. regional culture. *American Psychologist, 48,* 441–449.

Nitschke, J., Blendl, V., Otterman, B., Osterheider, M., & Mokros, A. (2009). Severe sexual sadism–an undiagnosed disorder? Evidence from a sample of forensic inpatients. *Journal of Forensic Sciences, 54,* 685–691.

Noble, J.H., & Conley, R.W. (1992). Toward an epidemiology of relevant attributes. In R.W. Conley, R. Luckasson & G.N. Bouthilet (Eds.), *The criminal justice system and mental retardation* (pp. 17–53). Baltimore: Paul Brookes.

Nock, M.K., & Kazdin, A.E. (2002). Parent-directed physical aggression by clinic-referred youths. *Journal of Clinical Child Psychology, 31,* 193–205.

Noesner, G.W., & Webster, M. (1997). Crisis intervention: Using active listening skills in negotiations. *FBI Law Enforcement Bulletin,* August, pp. 13–19.

Norman, M., & Gillespie, L.K. (1986). Changing horses: Utah's shift in adjudicating serious juvenile offenders. *Journal of Contemporary Law, 12,* 85–98.

Norris, F.H. (1992). Epidemiology of trauma: Frequency and impact of different potentially traumatic events on different demographic groups. *Journal of Consulting and Clinical Psychology, 60,* 409–418.

North, C.S., Smith, E.M., & Spitznagel, E.L. (1994). Posttraumatic stress disorder in survivors of a mass shooting. *American Journal of Psychiatry, 151,* 82–88.

North, C.S., Smith, E.M., & Spitznagel, E.L. (1997). One-year follow-up of survivors of a mass shooting. *American Journal of Psychiatry, 154,* 1696–1702.

Northoff, G., Richter, A., Gessner, M., Schlagenhauf, F., Fell, J., & Baumgart, F. (2000). Functional dissociation between medial and lateral prefrontal cortical spatiotemporal activation in negative and positive emotions: A combined fMRI/MEG study. *Cerebral Cortex, 10,* 93–107.

Novaco, R.W. (1994). Anger as a risk factor for violence among the mentally disordered. In J. Monahan & H.J. Steadman (Eds.), *Violence and mental disorder: Developments in risk assessment* (pp. 21–59). Chicago: University of Chicago Press.

Nurmi, J. (1991). How do adolescents see their future? A review of the development of future orientation and planning. *Developmental Review, 11,* 1–59.

Nutter, D., & Kearns, M. (1993). Patterns of exposure to sexually explicit material among sex offenders, child molesters, and controls. *Journal of Sex and Marital Therapy, 19,* 77–85.

Oberman, M. (1996). Mothers who kill: Coming to terms with modern American infanticide. *American Criminal Law Review, 4,* 1–110.

O'Brien, M., & Bera, W. (1986). Adolescent sex offenders: A descriptive typology. *Preventing Sexual Abuse, 1,* 1–4.

O'Brien, P. (1992). *Positive management: Assertiveness for managers.* London: Nicholas Brealey.

O'Connell, B. (1963). Matricide. *Lancet, 1,* 1083–1084.

O'Connell, R. (2001). Pedophiles networking on the internet. In C. Arnaldo (Ed.), *Child abuse on the internet: Ending the silence* (pp. 134–155). New York: Berghahn Books.

O'Connor, A.A. (1987). Female sex offenders. *British Journal of Psychiatry, 150,* 615–620.

O'Connor, P., Deater-Deckard, K., Fulker, D., Rutter, M., & Plomin, R. (1998). Genotype-environment correlations in late childhood and early adolescence: Antisocial behavioral problems and coercive parenting. *Developmental Psychology, 34,* 970–981.

O'Connor, T.G., McGuire, S., Reiss, D., Hetherington, E.M., & Plomin, R. (1998). Co-occurrence of depressive symptoms and antisocial behavior in adolescence: A common genetic liability. *Journal of Abnormal Psychology, 107,* 27–37.

O'Doherty, J., Kringelbach, M.L., Rolls, E.T., Hornak, J., & Andrews, C. (2001). Abstract reward and punishment representations in the human orbitofrontal cortex. *Nature-Neuroscience, 4,* 95–102.

O'Donohue, W., Regev, L.G., & Hagstrom, A. (2000). Problems with the DSM-IV diagnosis of pedophilia. *Sexual Abuse: A Journal of Research and Treatment, 12,* 95–105.

Ogilvie, B., & Daniluk, J. (1995). Common themes in the experiences of mother-daughter incest survivors: Impications for counseling. *Journal of Counseling and Development, 73,* 598–602.

Ogle, R., Maier-Katkin, D., & Bernard, T.J. (1995). A theory of homicidal behavior among women. *Criminology, 33,* 173–193.

O'Hara, M.W. (1995). *Postpartum depression: Causes and consequences.* New York: Springer-Verlag.

O'Hara, M.W., Swain, A.M. (1996). Rates and risk of postpartum depression: A meta-analysis. *International Review of Psychiatry, 8,* 37–54.

Ohayon, M.M. (2000). Violence and sleep. *Sleep and Hypnosis, 2,* 1–7.

Okasha, A., Sadek, A.O., & Moneim, S.A. (1975). Psychosocial and electroencephalographic studies of Egyptian murderers. *British Journal of Psychiatry, 126,* 34–40.

O'Leary, K.D., & Schumacher, J.A. (2003). The association between alcohol use and intimate partner violence: Linear effect, threshold effect, or both? *Addictive Behaviors, 28,* 1575–1585.

Olivan, G. (2003). Catch-up growth assessment in long-term physically neglected and emotionally abused preschool age male children. *Child Abuse and Neglect, 27,* 103–108.

Oliver, C.J., Beech, A.R., Fisher, D., & Beckett, R. (2007). A comparison of rapists and sexual murderers on demographic and selected psychometric measures. *International Journal of Offender Therapy and Comparative Criminology, 51,* 298–312.

Olshaker, J.S., Jackson, M.C., & Smock, W.S. (2001). *Forensic emergency medicine.* Philadelphia: Lippincott Williams & Wilkins.

Olson, C., Kutner, L., Warner, D., Almerigi, J., Baer, L., Nicholi, A., & Beresin, E. (2007). Factors correlated with violent video game use by adolescent boys and girls. *Journal of Adolescent Health, 41,* 77–83.

Olsson, P.A. (1988). The terrorist and the terrorized: Some psychoanalytic considerations. *Journal of Psychohistory, 16,* 47–60.

Olweus, D. (1979). Stability of aggressive reaction patterns in males: A review. *Psychological Bulletin, 86,* 852–875.

Olweus, D. (1988). Circulating testosterone levels and aggression in adolescent males: A causal analysis. *Psychosomatic Medicine, 50,* 261–272.

Olweus, D. (1993a). *Bullying at school: What we know and what we can do.* Oxford, UK: Blackwell.

Olweus, D. (1993b). Bully/victim problems among schoolchildren: Long-term consequences and an effective intervention program. In S. Hodgins (Ed.), *Mental disorder and crime* (pp. 317–349). Newbury Park, CA: Sage.

Olweus, D. (1993c). Victimization by peers: Antecedents and long-term consequences. In K.H. Rubin & J.B. Asendorpf (Eds.), *Social withdrawal, inhibition, and shyness in childhood* (pp. 315–341). Hillsdale, NJ: Erlbaum.

Olweus, D. (1995). Bullying or peer abuse at school: Facts and interventions. *Current Directions in Psychology, 4,* 196–200.

Olweus, D., Mattson, A., Schalling, D., & Low, H. (1980). Testosterone, aggression, and physical and personality dimensions in normal adolescent males. *Psychosomatic Medicine, 42,* 253–269.

Ommaya, A.K., Salazar, A.M., Dannenberg, A.L., Chervinsky, A.B., & Schwab, K. (1996). Outcome after traumatic brain injury in the US military medical system. *Journal of Trauma, 41,* 972–975.

O'Moore, M. (2000). Critical issues for teacher training to counter bullying and victimization in Ireland. *Aggressive Behavior, 26,* 96–111.

Ones, D.S. (2002). Introduction to the special issue on counterproductive behaviors at work. *International Journal of Selection and Assessment, 10,* 1–4.

Orecklin, M. (2000). Beware of the in crowd. *Time,* August 21, p. 69.

Orion, D. (1997). *I know you really love me: A psychiatrist's journal of erotomania, stalking, and obsessive love.* New York: Macmillan.

Orlebeke, J.F., Knol, D.L., & Verhulst, F.C. (1997). Increase in child behavior problems resulting from maternal smoking during pregnancy. *Archives of Environmental Health, 52,* 317–321.

O'Toole, M. (2000). *The school shooter: A threat assessment perspective.* Quantico, VA: National Center for the Analysis of Violent Crime: Federal Bureau of Investigation.

Overpeck, M.D., Brenner, R.A., Trumble, A.C., Trifiletti, L.B., & Berendes, H.W. (2002). Risk factors for infant homicide in the United States. *New England Journal of Medicine, 339,* 1211–1216.

Owen, D. (2004). *Criminal minds: The science and psychology of profiling.* New York: Barnes & Noble Books.

Owen, D.R. (1972). The 47,XYY male: A review. *Psychological Bulletin, 78,* 209–233.

Packer, I.K. (1983). Post-traumatic stress disorder and the insanity defense: A critical analysis. *Journal of Psychiatry and the Law, 11,* 125–136.

Pagani, L., & Pinard, G-F. (2001). Clinical assessment of dangerousness: An overview of the literature. In G-F. Pinard & L. Pagani (Eds.), *Clinical assessment of dangerousness: Empirical contributions* (pp. 1–22). New York: Cambridge University Press.

Pajer, K. (1998). What happens to "bad" girls? A review of the adult outcomes of antisocial adolescent girls. *American Journal of Psychiatry, 155,* 862–870.

Pajer, K., Stouthamer-Loeber, M., Gardner, W., & Loeber, R. (2006). Women with antisocial behavior: Long-term health disability and help-seeking for emotional problems. *Criminal Behavior and Mental Health, 16,* 29–42.

Palarea, R.E., Zona, M.A., Lane, J.C., & Langhinrischin-Rohling, J. (1999). The dangerous nature of intimate relationship stalking: Threats, violence, and associated risk factors. *Behavioral Sciences and the Law, 17,* 269–283.

Palermo, G.B. (1997). The berserk syndrome. *Aggression and Violent Behavior, 2,* 1–8.

Palermo, G.B. (2002). Murderous parents. *International Journal of Offender Therapy and Comparative Criminology, 46,* 123–143.

Palermo, G.B. (2004). *The faces of violence* (2nd ed.). Springfield, IL: Charles C Thomas.

Palermo, G.B. (2007a). New vistas on personality disorders and criminal responsibility. *International Journal of Offender Therapy and Comparative Criminology, 51,* 127–129.

Palermo, G.B. (2007b). The mind of the sexual predator. *Current Opinion in Psychiatry, 20,* 497–500.

Palermo, G.B. (2009). Antisocial behaviors and personality disorders. In R.N. Kocsis (Ed.), *Applied criminal psychology: A guide to forensic behavioral sciences* (pp. 21–43). Springfield, IL: Charles C Thomas.

Palermo, G.B., Farkas, M.A. (2001). *The dilemma of the sexual offender.* Springfield, IL: Charles C Thomas.

Palermo, G.B., & Kocsis, R.N. (2005). *Offender profiling: An introduction to the sociopsychological analysis of violent crime.* Springfield, IL: Charles C Thomas.

Palermo, G.B., Smith, M.B., Jentzen, J.M., Henry, T.E., Konicek, P.J., & Peterson, G.F. (1997). Murder-suicide of the jealous paranoia type: A multicenter statistical pilot study. *American Journal of Forensic Medicine and Pathology, 18,* 374–383.

Pallone, N.J., & Hennessy, J.J. (1996). *Tinder-box criminal aggression: Neuropsychology, demography, phenomenology.* New Brunswick, NJ: Transaction.

Palmer, C.T. (1989). Is rape a cultural universal? A re-examination of the ethnographic evidence. *Ethnology, 28,* 1–16.

Palmer, C.T. (1991). Human rape: Adaptation or by-product? *Journal of Sex Research, 28,* 365–386.

Pam, E. (2001). Police homicide-suicide in relation to domestic violence. In D.C. Sheehan & J.I. Warren (Eds.), *Suicide and law enforcement.* Washington, DC: US Government Printing Office.

Pankratz, L. (2006). Persistent problems with the Munchausen syndrome by proxy label. *Journal of the American Academy of Psychiatry and the Law, 34,* 90–95.

Papanastassiou, M., Waldron, G., Boyle, J., & Chesterman, L.P. (2004). Posttraumatic stress disorder in mentally ill perpetrators of homicide. *Journal of Forensic Psychiatry, 15,* 66–75.

Pape, R.A. (2003). The strategic logic of suicide terrorism. *American Political Science Review, 97,* 20–32.

Pape, R.A. (2005). *Dying to win: The strategic logic of suicide terrorism.* New York: Random House.

Pardini, D.A., Lochman, J.E., & Frick, P.J. (2003). Callous/unemotional traits and social cognitive processes in adjudicated youth. *Journal of the American Academy of Child and Adolescent Psychiatry, 42,* 364–371.

Pardini, D.A., & Loeber, R. (2007). Interpersonal and affective features of psychopathy in children and adolescents: Advancing a developmental perspective. *Journal of Clinical Child and Adolescent Psychology, 36,* 269–275.

Parke, R.D., & Ladd, G.W. (1992). *Family-peer relationships: Modes of linkage.* Hillsdale, NJ: Erlbaum.

Parker, R.S. (1990). *Traumatic brain injury and neuropsychological impairment: Sensorimotor, cognitive, emotional, and adaptive problems in children and adults.* New York: Springer-Verlag.

Parker, R.S. (2001). *Concussive brain trauma: Neurobehavioral impairment and maladaptation.* Boca Raton: CRC Press.

Parkins, I.S., Fishbein, H.D., & Ritchey, P.N. (2006). The influence of personality on workplace bullying and discrimination. *Journal of Applied Social Psychology, 36,* 2554–2577.

Parrish, G.A., Holdren, K.S., Skiendzielewski, J.J., & Lumpkin, O.A. (1987). Emergency department experience with sudden death: A survey of survivors. *Annals of Emergency Medicine, 16,* 792–796.

Partridge, G.E. (1930). Current conceptions of psychopathic personality. *American Journal of Psychiatry, 10,* 53–99.

Paschall, M.J., & Fishbein, D.H. (2002). Executive cognitive functioning and aggression: A public health perspective. *Aggression and Violent Behavior, 17,* 215–235.

Paternoster, R., & Brame, R. (1997). Multiple routes to delinquency? A test of developmental and general theories of crime. *Criminology, 35,* 49 84.

Paternoster, R., & Brame, R. (2000). On the association among self-control, crime, and analogous behaviors. *Criminology, 38,* 971–982.

Paterson, R., Luntz, H., Perlesz, A., & Cotton, S. (2002). Adolescent violence towards parents: Maintaining family connections when the going gets tough. *Autralian and New Zealand Journal of Family Therapy, 23,* 90–100.

Pathe, M. (2002). *Surviving stalking.* Cambridge, UK: Cambridge University Press.

Pathe, M., & Mullen, P. (1997). The impact of stalkers on their victims. *British Journal of Psychiatry, 170,* 12–19.

Pathe, M., Mullen, P., & Purcell, R. (2002). Patients who stalk doctors: their motives and management. *Medical Journal of Australia, 176,* 335–338.

Paton, J., Crouch, W., & Camic, P. (2009). Young offenders' experiences of traumatic life events: A qualitative investigation. *Clinical Child Psychology and Psychiatry, 14,* 43–62.

Patterson, G.R., & Stouthamer-Lober, M. (1984). The correlation of family management practices and delinquency. *Child Development, 55,* 1299–1307.

Paulozzi, L.J., Saltzman, L.E., Thompson, M.P., & Holmgrecn, P. (2001). Surveillance for homicide among intimate partners: United States, 1981–1998. *Mortality and Morbidity Weekly Reports, 50,* 1–15.

Paulson, M.J., Coombs, R.H., & Landsverk, J. (1990). Youth who physically assault their parents. *Journal of Family Violence, 5,* 121–133.

Peak, K.J. (2003). *Policing America: Methods, issues, challenges* (4th ed.). Upper Saddle River: Prentice-Hall.

Pearlstein, R.M. (1991). *The mind of the political terrorist.* Wilmington, DE: SR Books.

Pedahzur, A., Perliger, A., & Weinberg, L. (2003). Altruism and fatalism: The characteristics of Palestinian suicide terrorists. *Deviant Behavior, 24,* 405–423.

Peek, C., Fisher, J., & Kidwell, J. (1985). Teenage violence toward parents: A neglected dimension of family violence. *Journal of Marriage and Family, 47,* 1051–1060.

Pellegrini, A.D. (2007). Is aggression adaptive? Yes: some kinds are in some ways. In P.H. Hawley, T.D. Little & P.C. Rodkin (Eds.), *Aggression and adaptation: The bright side to bad behavior* (pp. 85–106). Mahwah, NJ: Lawrence Erlbaum.

Penney, L.M., & Spector, P.E. (2002). Narcissism and counterproductive work behaviour: Do bigger egos mean bigger problems? *International Journal of Selection and Assessment, 10,* 126–134.

Pernanen, K. (1998). Prevention of alcohol-related violence. *Contemporary Drug Problems, 25,* 477–509.

Perri, F.S., & Lictenwald, T.G. (2010). The last frontier: Myths of the female psychopathic killer. *The Forensic Examiner,* Summer, pp. 51–67.

Perrou, B., & Farrell, B. (2004). Officer-involved shootings: Case management and psychosocial investigations. In V. Lord (Ed.), *Suicide by cop: Inducing officers to shoot* (pp. 239–242). Flushing: Looseleaf Law Publications.

Perry, J.C. (1990). *Defense mechanism rating scales* (5th ed.). Boston: Cambridge University Press.

Perry, J.C., & Herman, J. (1993). Trauma and defense in the ideology of borderline personality disorder. In J. Paris (Ed.), *Borderline personality disorder: Etiology and treatment* (pp. 135–139). Washington, DC: American Psychiatric Press.

Perusse, D. (1993). Cultural and reproductive success in industrial societies: Testing the relationship at proximate and ultimate levels. *Behavioral and Brain Sciences, 16,* 267–322.

Petee, T.A., Padgett, K.G., & York, T.S. (1997). Debunking the stereotype: An examination of mass murder in public places. *Homicide Studies, 1,* 317–337.

Peters, J. Shackelford, T.K., & Buss, D.M. (2002). Understanding domestic violence against women: Using evolutionary psychology to extend the feminist functional analysis. *Violence and Victims, 17,* 255–264.

Petersen, K.G.I., Matousek, M., & Mednick, S.A. (1982). EEG antecedents of thievery. *Acta Psychiatric Scandanavica, 65,* 331–338.

Petrides, M. (1995). Functional organization of the human frontal cortex for mnemonic processing: Evidence from neuroimaging studies. *Annals of the New York Academy of Sciences, 15,* 85–96.

Petrocelli, J. (2005). Cyberstalking. *Law and Order,* December, pp. 56–57.

Petty, R.A., & Kosch, L.M. (2001). Workplace violence and unwanted pursuit: From an employer's perspective. In J.A. Davis (Ed.), *Stalking crimes and victim protection: Prevention, intervention, threat assessment, and case management* (pp. 459–485). Boca Raton: CRC Press.

Pfefferbaum, A., Sullivan, E.V., Swan, G.E., & Carmelli, D. (2000). Brain structure in men remains highly heritable in the seventh and eighth decades of life. *Neurobiology of Aging, 21,* 63–74.

Philipse, M.W.G., Koeter, M.W.J., van der Staak, C.P.F., & van den Brink, W. (2006). Static and dynamic patient characteristics as predictors of criminal recidivism: A prospective study in a Dutch forensic psychiatric sample. *Law and Human Behavior, 30,* 309–327.

Phillips, D.A. (2007). Punking and bullying: Strategies in middle school, high school, and beyond. *Journal of Interpersonal Violence, 22,* 158–178.

Pierce, C.A., & Aguinis, H. (1997). The incubator: Bridging the gap between romantic relationships and sexual harassment in organizations. *Journal of Organizational Behavior, 18,* 197–200.

Pierce, C.A., Muslin, I.V., Dudley, C.M., & Aguinis, H. (2008). From charm to harm: A content-analytic review of sexual harassment court cases involving workplace romance. *Management Research, 6,* 27–45.

Pierce, L.H., & Pierce, R.L. (1987). Incestuous victimization by juvenile sex offenders. *Journal of Family Violence, 2,* 351–364.

Pihl, R.O., & Ervin, F. (1990). Lead and cadmium levels in violent criminals. *Psychological Reports, 66,* 839–844.

Pillai, K., & Kraya, N. (2000). Psychostimulants, adult attention deficit and hyperactivity disorder and morbid jealousy. *Australian and New Zealand Journal of Psychiatry, 34,* 160–163.

Pillimer, K., & Moore, D.W. (1989). Abuse of patients in nursing homes: Findings from a survey of staff. *Gerontologist,* 29, 314–320.

Pillemer, K., & Suitor, J.J. (1992). Violence and violent feelings: What causes them among family caregivers? *Journal of Gerontology, 47,* S165–S172.

Pinard, G-F., & Pagani, L. (2001). Discussion and clinical commentary on issues in the assessment and prediction of dangerousness. In G-F. Pinard & L. Pagani (Eds.), *Clinical assessment of dangerousness: Empirical contributions* (pp. 181–194). New York: Cambridge University Press.

Pincus, J.H., & Tucker, G.J. (1978). *Behavioral neurology* (2nd ed.). New York: Oxford University Press.

Pincus, J.H. (2001). *Base instincts: What makes killers kill.* New York: Norton.

Pinel, P. (1801/1977). *A treatise on insanity* (Transl. by D.D. Davis). Washington, DC: University Publication of America.

Pinizzotto, A.J. (1984). Forensic psychology: Criminal personality profiling. *Journal of Police Science and Administration, 12,* 32–40.

Pinizzotto, A.J., Davis, E.F., & Miller, C.E. (2005). Suicide by cop: Defining a devastating dilemma. *FBI Law Enforcement Bulletin,* February, pp. 8–20.

Pinizzotto, A.J., Davis, E.F., & Miller, C.E. (2007). Street-gang mentality: A mosaic of remorseless violence and relentless loyalty. *FBI Law Enforcement Bulletin,* September, pp. 1–7.

Pinizzotto, A.J., & Finkel, N.J. (1990). Criminal personality profiling: An outcome and process study. *Law and Human Behavior, 14,* 215–233.

Piquero, A.R., Farrington, D.P., & Blumstein, A. (2003). The criminal career paradigm: Background and recent developments. *Crime and Justice, 30,* 359–506.

Piquero, A.R., MacDonald, J., Dobrin, A., Daigle, L.E., & Cullen, F.T. (2005). Self-control, violent offending, and homicide victimization: Assessing the general theory of crime. *Journal of Quantitative Criminology, 21,* 55–71.

Pitcavage, M. (2003). Domestic extremism: Still a potent threat. *The Police Chief,* August, pp. 32–35.

Pitcher, G.D., & Poland, S. (1992). *Crisis intervention in the schools.* New York: Guilford.

Pitt, S.E., & Bale, E.M. (1995). Neonaticide, infanticide, and filicide: A review of the literature. *Bulletin of the American Academy of Psychiatry and the Law, 23,* 375–386.

Pitts, J. (2001). The new correctionalism. In R. Matthews & J. Pitts (Eds.), *Crime, disorders, and community safety* (pp. 167–192). New York: Routledge.

Planansky, K., & Johnston, R. (1977). Homicidal aggression in schizophrenic men. *Acta Psychiatrica Scandinavica, 55,* 65–73.

Plante, T.G. (1999). Sexual abuse committed by Roman Catholic priests: Current status, future objectives. In T.G. Plante (Ed.), *Bless me father for I have sinned: Perspectives on sexual abuse committed by Roman Catholic priests* (pp. 171–178). Westport, CT: Greenwood.

Plante, T.G. (2004). *Sin against the innocents: Sexual abuse by priests and the role of the Catholic Church.* Westport, CT: Greenwood.

Plante, T.G., & Aldridge, A. (2005). Psychological patterns among Roman Catholic clergy accused of sexual misconduct. *Pastoral Psychology, 54,* 73–80.

Plante, T.G., & Daniels, C. (2004). The sexual abuse crisis in the Roman Catholic Church: What psychologists and counselors should know. *Pastoral Psychology, 52,* 381–393.

Plante, T.G., Manuel, G.M., & Bryant, C. (1996). Personality and cognitive functioning among sexual offending Roman Catholic priests. *Pastoral Psychology, 45,* 129–139.

Platte, A. (1977). *The child savers: The intervention of delinquency* (2nd ed.). Chicago: University of Chicago Press.

Pliszka, S.R., Sherman, J.O., Barrow, M.V., & Irick, S. (2000). Affective disorder in juvenile offenders: A preliminary study. *American Journal of Psychiatry, 157,* 130–132.

Plomin, R., DeFries, J.C., & Loehlin, J.C. (1977). Genotype environment interaction and correlation in the analysis of human behavior. *Psychological Bulletin, 84,* 309–322.

Plomin, R., Loehlin, J.C., & DeFries, J.C. (1985). Genetic and environmental components of "environmental" influences. *Developmental Psychology, 21,* 391–402.

Polanczyk, G., de Lima, M.S., Horta, B.L., Biederman, J., & Rohde, L.A. (2007). The worldwide prevalence of ADHD: A systematic review and metaregression analysis. *American Journal of Psychiatry, 164,* 942–948.

Polaschek, D.L.L., Calvert, S.W., & Gannon, T.A. (2009). Linking violent thinking: Implicit theory-based research with violent offenders. *Journal of Interpersonal Violence, 24,* 75–96.

Polaschek, D.L.L., & Collie, R.M. (2004). Rehabilitating serious violent adult offenders: An empirical and theoretical stocktake. *Psychology, Crime and Law, 10,* 321–333.

Polaschek, D.L.L., & Gannon, T. (2004). The implicit theories of rapists: What convicted offenders tell us. *Sexual Abuse: A Journal of Research and Treatment, 16,* 299–315.

Polaschek, D.L.L., & Ward, T. (2002). The implicit theories of potential rapists: What our questionnaires tell us. *Aggression and Violent Behavior, 7,* 385–406.

Polaschek, D.L.L., Ward, T., & Hudson, S.M. (1997). Rape and rapists: Theory and treatment. *Clinical Psychology Review, 17,* 117–144.

Polk, K., & Ransom, D. (1991). The role of gender in intimate homicide. *Australian and New Zealand Journal of Criminology, 24,* 20.

Pollack, R. (1984). The epilepsy defense. *Atlantic Monthly,* May, pp. 20–28.

Pollack, V.E., Briere, J., & Schneider, L. (1990). Childhood antecedents of antisocial behavior: Parental alcoholism and physical abusiveness. *American Journal of Psychiatry, 147,* 1290–1293.

Pollock, P.H. (1999). When the killer suffers: Post-traumatic stress reactions following homicide. *Legal and Criminological Psychology, 4,* 185–202.

Pontius, A.A., & Yudowitz, B.S. (1980). Frontal lobe dysfunction in some criminal actions shown in the narratives test. *Journal of Nervous and Mental Disease, 168,* 111–117.

Pontius, A.A. (1981). Stimuli triggering violence in psychoses. *Journal of Forensic Sciences, 26,* 123–128.

Pontius, A.A. (1984). Specific stimulus-evoked violent action in psychotic trigger reaction: A seizure-like imbalance between frontal lobe and limbic systems? *Perceptual and Motor Skills, 59,* 299–333.

Pontius, A.A. (1987). Psychotic trigger reaction: Neuro-psychiatric and neuro-biological (limbic?) aspects of homicide, reflecting on normal action. *Integrative Psychiatry, 5,* 116–139.

Pontius, A.A. (1996). Forensic significance of the limbic psychotic trigger reaction. *Bulletin of the American Academy of Psychiatry and the Law, 24,* 125–134.

Pontius, A.A. (1997). Homicide linked to moderate repetitive stresses kindling limbic seizures in 14 cases of limbic psychotic trigger reaction. *Aggression and Violent Behaviour, 2,* 125–141.

Pope, G.H., Jonas, J.M., & Hudson, J.I. (1983). The validity of DSM-III borderline personality disorder. *Archives of General Psychiatry, 40,* 23–30.

Popplestone, J. (1963). A syllabus of the exoskeletal defenses. *Psychological Record, 13,* 15–25.

Porter, S., Fairweather, D., Drugge, J., Herve, H., Birt, A., & Boer, D.P. (2000). Profiles of psychopathy in incarcerated sexual offenders. *Criminal Justice and Behavior, 27,* 216–233.

Posey, A.J., & Wrightsman, L.S. (2005). *Trial consulting.* New York: Oxford University Press.

Post, J.M. (1986). Hostilite, conformite, fraternite: The group dynamics of terrorist behavior. *International Journal of Group Psychotherapy, 36,* 211–224.

Post, J.M. (1998). Terrorist psycho-logic: Terrorist behavior as a product of psychological forces. In W. Reich (Ed.), *Origins of terrorism: Psychologies, ideologies, theologies, states of mind* (pp. 25–40). Washington, DC: Woodrow Wilson Center Press.

Post, J.M. (2004). *Leaders and their followers in a dangerous world: The psychology of political behavior.* Ithaca, NY: Cornell University Press.

Post, J.M. (2009). Reframing martyrdom and jihad and the socialization of suicide terrorists. *Political Psychology, 30,* 381–385.

Post, J.M., Sprinzak, E., & Denny, M. (2003). The terrorists in their own words: Interviews with thirty-five incarcerated Middle Eastern terrorists. *Terrorism and Political Violence, 15,* 171–184.

Post, R.M. (1980). Intermittent versus continuous stimulation: Effect of time interval on the development of sensitization or tolerance. *Life Sciences, 26,* 1275–1282.

Potter-Efron, R.T. (1998). *Work rage: Preventing anger and resolving conflict on the job.* New York: Barnes & Noble.

Potts, M.K. (1994). Long-term effects of trauma: Posttraumatic stress among civilian internees of the Japanese during World War II. *Journal of Clinical Psychiatry, 50,* 681–698.

Poulin, F., & Boivin, M. (2000). The role of proactive and reactive aggression in the formation and development of boys' friendships. *Developmental Psychopathology, 36,* 233–240.

Praet, B.D. (2002). Suicide by cop or death by indifference? *The Police Chief,* July, pp. 14.

Pratt, T.C., & Cullen, F.T. (2000). The empirical status of Gottfredson and Hirschi's general theory of crime: A meta-analysis. *Criminology, 38,* 931–964.

Prentice, N.M., & Kelly, F.J. (1963). Intelligence and delinquency: A reconsideration. *Journal of Social Psychology, 60,* 327–337.

Prentky, R.A., Burgess, A.W., Rokous, F., Lee, A., Hartman, C., Ressler, R., & Douglas, J. (1989). The presumptive role of fantasy in serial sexual homicide. *American Journal of Psychiatry, 146,* 887–891.

Prentky, R.A., Janus, E., Barbaree, H., Schwartz, B.K., & Kafka, M.P. (2006). Sexually violent predators in the courtroom: Science on trial. *Psychology, Public Policy, and Law, 12,* 357–393.

Pressman, M.R. (2007a). Factors that predispose, prime and precipitate NREM parasomnias in adults: *Clinical and Forensic Implications, 11,* 5–30.

Pressman, M.R. (2007b). Disorders of arousal from sleep and violent behavior: The role of physical contact and proximity. *Sleep, 30,* 1039–1047.

Price, J. (1988). Alternative channels for negotiating asymmetry in social relationships. In M.R. Chance (Ed.), *Social fabrics of the mind* (pp. 157–196). Hillsdale, NJ: Erlbaum.

Price, T.S., Simonoff, E., Waldman, I., Asherson, P., & Plomin, R. (2001). Hyperactivity in preschool children is highly heritable. *Journal of the American Academy of Child and Adolescent Psychiatry, 12,* 1362–1364.

Pritchard, J.C. (1835/1973). *A treatise on insanity and other disorders affecting the mind.* New York: Arno Press.

Prodgers, A. (1984). Psychopathology of the physically abusing parent: A comparison with the borderline syndrome. *Journal of Child Abuse and Neglect, 8,* 411–424.

Proulx, J., Beauregard, E, Cusson, M., & Nicole, A. (2007). *Sexual murderers: A comparative analysis and new perspectives.* Hoboken, NJ: Wiley.

Proulx, J., McKibben, A., & Lusignan, R. (1996). Relationships between affective components and sexual behaviors in sexual aggressors. *Sexual Abuse: Journal of Research and Treatment, 8,* 279–289.

Ptacek, J.T., & Eberhardt, T.L. (1996). Breaking bad news: A review of the literature. *Journal of the American Medical Association, 276,* 496–502.

Public Safety Performance Project. (2007). *Public safety, public spending: Forecasting America's prison population, 2007–2011.* Washington, DC: Pew Charitable Trusts.

Purcell, C.E., & Arrigo, B.A. (2006). *The psychology of lust murder: Paraphilia, sexual killing, and serial homicide.* Burlington, MA: Academic Press.

Purcell, R., Pathe, M., & Mullen, P.E. (2001). A study of women who stalk. *American Journal of Psychiatry, 158,* 2056–2060.

Purcell, R., Pathe, M., & Mullen, P.E. (2004a). Stalking: Defining and prosecuting a new category of offending. *International Journal of Law and Psychiatry, 27,* 157–169.

Purcell, R., Pathe, M., & Mullen, P.E. (2004b). When do repeated intrusions become stalking? *Journal of Forensic Psychiatry and Psychology, 15,* 571–583.

Puzzanchera, C.M. (2003). *Delinquency cases waived to criminal court, 1990–1999.* Washington, DC: US Department of Justice.

Pynoos, R.S., Frederick, C., Nader, K., Arroyo, W., Steinberg, A., Eth, S., Nunez, F., & Fairbanks, L. (1987). Life threat and posttraumatic stress in school-age children. *Archives of General Psychiatry, 44,* 1057–1063.

Quanbeck, C.D., McDermott, B.E., & Frye, M.A. (2005). Clinical and legal characteristics of inmates with bipolar disorder. *Current Psychiatry Reports, 7,* 478–484.

Quanbeck, C.D., Stone, D.C., & McDermott, B.E. (2005). Relationship among criminal arrest and and community treatment history among patients with bipolar disorder. *Psychiatric Services, 56,* 847–852.

Quanbeck, C.D., Stone, D.C., Scott, C.L., McDermott, B.E., Altshuler, L.L., & Frye, M.A. (2004). Clincal and legal correlates of inmates with bipolar disorder at time of criminal arrest. *Journal of Clinical Psychiatry, 65,* 198–203.

Quetelet, A. (1833). *Research on the propensity for crime at different ages.* Brussels: M. Hayez.

Quiggle, N.L., Garber, J., Panak, W.F., & Dodge, K.A. (1992). Social information processing in aggressive and depressed children. *Child Development, 63,* 1305–1320.

Quigley, B.M., Leonard, K.E., & Collins, R.L. (2003). Characteristics of violent bars and bar patrons. *Journal of Studies on Alcohol, 64,* 765–772.

Quinn, J.F. (2001). Angels, Bandidos, Outlaws, and Pagans: The evolution of organized crime among the Big Four 1% motorcycle clubs. *Deviant Behavior, 24,* 281–305.

Quinn, J.F., & Koch, D.S. (2003). The nature of criminality within one-percent motorcycle clubs. *Deviant Behavior, 24,* 281–305.

Quinsey, V.L., Book, A., & Lalumiere, M.L. (2001). A factor analysis of traits related to individual differences in antisocial behavior. *Criminal Justice and Behavior, 28,* 522–536.

Quinsey, V.L., Chaplain, T.C., & Upfold, D. (1984). Sexual arousal to non-sexual violence and sadomasochistic themes among rapists and non-sex-offenders. *Journal of Consulting and Clinical Psychology, 52,* 651–657.

Quinsey, V.L., Chaplain, T.C., & Upfold, D. (1989). Arsonists and sexual arousal to firesetting: Correlation unsupported. *Journal of Behavior Therapy and Experimental Psychiatry, 20,* 203–209.

Quinsey, V.L., Skilling, T.A., LaLumiere, M.L., & Craig, W.M. (2004). *Juvenile delinquency: Understanding the origins of individual differences.* Washington, DC: American Psychological Association.

Quinsey, V.L., Chaplin, T.C., & Varney, G. (1981). A comparison of rapists' and non-sex offenders' sexual preferences for mutually consenting sex, rape, and sadistic acts. *Behavioral Assessment, 3,* 127–135.

Quinsey, V.L., Harris, G.T., Rice, M.E., & Cormier, C.A. (2005). *Violent offenders: Appraising and managing risk* (2nd ed.). Washington, DC: American Psychological Association.

Quinsey, V.L., & Lalumiere, M.L. (1995). Evolutionary perspectives on sexual offending. *Sexual Abuse: A Journal of Research and Treatment, 7,* 301–315.

Quinsey, V.L., Lalumiere, M.L., Rice, M.E., & Harris, G.T. (1995). Predicting sexual offenses. In J.C. Campbell (Ed.), *Assessing dangerousness: Violence by sexual offenders, batterers, child abusers* (pp. 114–137). Thousand Oaks, CA: Sage.

Quinsey, V.L., Rice, M.E., & Harris, G.T. (1995). Actuarial prediction of sexual recidivism. *Journal of Interpersonal Violence, 10,* 85–105.

Quinton, D., & Rutter, M. (1988). *Parenting breakdown: The making and breaking of intergenerational links.* Aldershot, UK: Avebury.

Quitkin, F., Rifkin, A., & Klein, D.F. (1976). Neurological soft signs in schizophrenia and character disorders. *Archives of General Psychiatry, 33,* 845–853.

RachBeisel, J., Scott, J., & Dixon, L. (1999). Co-occurring severe mental illness and substance use disorders: A review of recent research. *Psychiatric Services, 50,* 1427–1434.

Racine, R. (1978). Kindling: The first decade. *Neurosurgery, 3,* 234–252.

Radzinowicz, L. (1966). *Ideology and crime.* New York: Columbia University Press.

Rae, G.W. (1967). *Confessions of the Boston strangler.* New York: Pyramid Books.

Raine, A. (1988). Evoked potentials and antisocial behavior. In T.E. Moffitt & S.A. Mednick (Eds.), *Biological contributions to crime causation* (pp. 14–39). Dordrecht: Nijhoff.

Raine, A. (1993). *The psychopathology of crime: Criminal behavior as a clinical disorder.* San Diego, CA: Academic Press.

Raine, A. (2002a). Biosocial studies of antisocial and violent behavior in children and adults: A review. *Journal of Abnormal Child Psychology, 30,* 311–326.

Raine, A. (2002b). Annotation: The role of prefrontal deficits, low autonomic arousal, and early health factors in the development of antisocial and aggressive behavior in children. *Journal of Child Psychology and Psychiatry, 43,* 417–434.

Raine, A., Brennan, P., Farrington, D., & Mednick, S.A. (1997). *Biosocial bases of violence.* New York: Plenum.

Raine, A., Brennan, P., & Mednick, S.A. (1997). Interaction between birth complication and early maternal rejection in predisposing individuals to adult violence:
Specificity to serious, early-onset violence. *American Journal of Psychiatry, 154,*
1265–1271.

Raine, A., Buchsbaum, M.S., & LaCasse, L. (1997). Brain abnormalities in murderers indicated by positron emission tomography. *Biological Psychiatry, 42,*
495–508.

Raine, A., Ishikawa, S.S., Arce, E., Lencz, T., Knuth, K.H., Bihrle, S., LaCasse, L., &
Colletti, P. (2004). Hippocampal structural asymmetry in unsuccessful psychopaths. *Biological Psychiatry, 55,* 185–191.

Raine, A., Lencz, T., Bihrle, S., LaCasse, L., & Colletti, P. (2000). Reduced prefrontal
gray matter volume and reduced autonomic activity in antisocial personality disorder. *Archives of General Psychiatry, 57,* 119–127.

Raine, A., Lencz, T., & Scerbo, A. (1995). Antisocial behavior: Neuroimaging, neuropsychology, neurochemistry, and pathophysiology. In J.J. Ratey (Ed.),
Neuropsychiatry of personality disorders (pp. 50–78). Cambridge: Blackwell Science.

Raine, A., Meloy, J.R., Bihrle, S., Stoddard, J., & La Casse, L. (1998). Reduced prefrontal and increased subcortical brain functioning assessed using positron emission tomography in predatory and affective murderers. *Behavioral Sciences and the
Law, 16,* 319–332.

Raine, A., Reynolds, C., Venables, P., & Mednick, S. (1997). Biosocial bases of
aggressive behavior in childhood: Resting heart rate, skin conductance orienting
and physique. In A. Raine, P. Brennan, D. Farrington & S. Mednick (Eds.),
Biosocial bases of violence (pp. 107–126). New York: Plenum.

Raine, A., Venables, P.H., & Williams, M. (1990). Relationships between central and
autonomic measures of arousal age 15 years and criminality at age 24 years.
Archives of General Psychiatry, 47, 1003–1007.

Rainville, G.A., & Smith, S.K. (2003). *Survey of 40 counties, 1998: Juvenile felony defendants in criminal courts.* Washington, DC: US Department of Justice.

Raja, M., & Azzoni, A. (2001). Asperger's disorder in the emergency psychiatric setting. *General Hospital Psychiatry, 23,* 285–293.

Ramani, V., & Gummit, R.J. (1981). Intensive monitoring of epileptic patients with a
history of episodic aggression. *Archives of Neurology, 38,* 570–571.

Ramirez, J.M. (2003). Hormones and aggression in childhood and adolescence.
Aggression and Violent Behavior, 8, 621–644.

Rand, D.C., & Feldman, M.D. (2001). An explanatory model for Munchausen by
proxy abuse. *International Journal of Psychiatry in Medicine, 31,* 113–126.

Randel, J., & Wells, K. (2003). Corporate approaches to reducing intimate partner
violence through workplace initiatives. *Occupational and Environmental Medicine,
3,* 821–841.

Rappaport, R.G. (1988). The serial and mass murderer. *American Journal of Forensic
Psychiatry, 9,* 39–48.

Rasanen, P., Tiihonen, J., Isohanni, M., Rantakallio, P., Lehtonen, J., & Moring, J.
(1998). Schizophrenia, alcohol abuse, and violent behavior: A 26-year follow-up
study of an unselected birth cohort. *Schizophrenia Bulletin, 24,* 437–441.

Rasmussen, K., Levander, S., & Sletvold, H. (1995). Aggressive and nonaggressive schizophrenics: Symptom profile and neuropsychological differences. *Psychology, Crime, and Law, 2,* 119–129.

Raymond, N.C., Coleman, E., Ohlerking, E., Christenson, G.A., & Miner, M. (1999). Psychiatric comorbidity in pedophilic sex offenders. *American Journal of Psychiatry, 156,* 786–788.

Reddy, M., Borum, R., Berglund, J., Vossekuil, B., Fein, R., & Modzeleski, W. (2001). Evaluating risk for targeted violence in schools: Comparing risk assessment, threat assessment, and other approaches. *Psychology in the Schools, 38,* 157–172.

Regier, D.A., Farmer, M.E., Rae, D.S., Locke, B.Z., Keith, S.J., & Judd, L.L. (1990). Comorbidity of mental disorders with alcohol and other drug abuse: Results from the Epidemiological Catchment Area (ECA) Study. *Journal of the American Medical Association, 264,* 2511–2518.

Reid-Proctor, G.M., Galin, K., & Cummings, M.A. (2001). Evaluation of legal competency in patients with frontal lobe injury. *Brain Injury, 15,* 377–386.

Reijneveld, S.A., Crone, M.R., Verhulst, F.C., & Verloove-Vanhorick, S.P. (2003). The effect of a severe disaster on the mental health of adolescents: A controlled study. *Lancet, 362,* 691–696.

Reis, R., Mullen, M., & Cox, G. (1994). Symptom severity and utilization of treatment resources among dually diagnosed inpatients. *Hospital and Community Psychiatry, 45,* 562–568.

Reiss, I.L. (1986). *Journey into sexuality: An exploratory voyage.* Englewood Cliffs, NJ: Prentice-Hall.

Reiss, A.J., Jr., & Roth, J.A. (Eds.). (1993). *Understanding and preventing violence.* Washington, DC: National Academy Press.

Reiwald, P. (1950). *Society and its criminals.* New York: International Universities Press.

Rejeski, W.J., Gange, M., Parker, P.E., & Koritnik, D.R. (1989). Acute stress reactivity from contested dominance in dominant and submissive males. *Behavioral Medicine, 15,* 118–124.

Rennison, C.M., & Welchans, S. (2000). *Intimate partner violence.* Washington, DC: US Department of Justice, Bureau of Justice Statistics.

Repetti, R.L., Taylor, S.E., & Seeman, T.E. (2002). Risky families: Family social environments and the mental and physical health of offspring. *Psychological Bulletin, 128,* 330–366.

Repo, E., & Virkkunen, M. (1997). Young arsonists: History of conduct disorder, psychiatric diagnoses, and criminal recidivism. *Journal of Forensic Psychiatry, 8,* 311–320.

Repo-Tiihonen, E., Tiihonen, J., Lindberg, N., Weizmann-Henelius, G., Putkonen, H., & Hakkanen, H. (2010). The intergenerational cycle of criminality: Association with psychopathy. *Journal of Forensic Science, 55,* 116–120.

Resick, P.a. (1993). The psychological impact of rape. *Journal of Interpersonal Violence, 8,* 223–255.

Resnick, H.S., Acierno, R., & Kilpatrick, D.G. (1997). Health impact of interpersonal violence 2: Medical and mental health outcomes. *Behavioral Medicine, 23,* 65–78.

Resnick, H.S., Kilpatrick, D.G., Dansky, B.S., Saunders, B.E., & Best, C.L. (1993). Prevalence of civilian trauma and posttraumatic stress disorder in a representative national sample of women. *Journal of Consulting and Clinical Psychology, 61,* 984–991.

Resnick, P.J. (1969). Child murder by parents: A psychiatric review of filicide. *American Journal of Psychiatry, 126,* 325–334.

Resnick, P.J. (1970). Murder of the newborn: A psychiatric review of neonaticide. *American Journal of Psychiatry, 126,* 1414–1420.

Ressler, R.K., Burgess, A.W., & Douglas, J.E. (1983). Rape and rape-murder: One offender and twelve victims. *American Journal of Psychiatry, 140,* 36–46.

Ressler, R.K., Burgess, A.W., & Douglas, J.E. (1988). *Sexual homicide: Patterns and motives.* New York: Lexington Books.

Ressler, R.K., Burgess, A.W., Douglas, J.E., Hartman, C.R., & D'Agostino, R.B. (1986a). Sexual killers and their victims: Identifying patterns through crime scene analysis. *Journal of Interpersonal Violence, 1,* 288–308.

Ressler, R.K., Burgess, A.W., Hartman, C.R., Douglas, J.E., & McCormack, A. (1986b). Murderers who rape and mutilate. *Journal of Interpersonal Violence, 1,* 273–287.

Ressler, R.K., & Schactman, T. (1992). *Whoever fights monsters: My twenty years tracking serial killers for the FBI.* New York: Simon & Schuster.

Ressler, R.K., & Schactman, T. (1997). *I have lived the monster: Inside the minds of the world's most notorious serial killers.* New York: St. Martin's Press.

Retzinger, S.M., & Scheff, T.J. (1996). Strategy for community conferences: Emotions and social bonds. In B. Galaway & J. Hudson (Eds.), *Restorative justice: International perspectives* (pp. 315–336). Monsey: Criminal Justice Press.

Revitch, E., & Schlesinger, L.B. (1981a). *Psychopathology of homicide.* Springfield, IL: Charles C Thomas.

Revitch, E., & Schlesinger, L.B. (1981b). *Sex murder and sex aggression.* Springfield, IL: Charles C Thomas.

Rhee, S.H., & Waldman, I.D. (2002). Genetic and environmental influences on antisocial behavior: A meta-analysis of twin and adoption studies. *Psychological Bulletin, 128,* 490–529.

Rhee, S.H., & Waldman, I.D. (2003). Testing alternative hypotheses regarding the role of development on genetic and environmental influences underlying antisocial behavior. In B.B. Lahey, T.E. Moffitt & A. Caspi (Eds.), *Causes of conduct disorder and juvenile delinquency* (pp. 305–318). New York: Guilford.

Rice, M.E. (1997). Violent offender research and implications for the criminal justice system. *American Psychologist, 52,* 414–423.

Rice, M.E., & Harris, G.T. (1995). Psychopathy, schizophrenia, alcohol abuse, and violent recidivism. *International Journal of Law and Psychiatry, 18,* 333–342.

Rice, M.E., Harris, G.T., & Cormier, C.A. (1992). Evaluation of a maximum security therapeutic community for psychopaths and other mentally disordered
offenders. *Law and Human Behavior, 16,* 399–412.

Richards, A. F. C. (2004). Sexual misconduct by clergy in the Episcopal Church.
Studies in Gender and Sexuality, 5, 139–165.

Rickert, V.I., & Wiemann, C.M. (1998). Date rape among adolescents and young
adults. *Journal of Pediatric and Adolescent Gynecology, 11,* 167–175.

Ridderinkof, K.R., van den Widenberg, W.P., Segalowitz, S.J., & Carter, C.S. (2004).
Neurocognitive mechanism of cognitive control: The role of prefrontal cortex in
action selection, response inhibition, performance monitoring, and reward-
based learning. *Brain and Congnition, 56,* 129–140.

Rider, A.O. (1980a). The firesetter: A psychological profile. Part I. *FBI Law
Enforcement Bulletin, 49,* 6–11.

Rider, A.O. (1980b). The firesetter: A psychological profile. Part II. *FBI Law
Enforcement Bulletin, 49,* 12–17.

Ridley, M. (1996). *The origins of virtue: Human instincts and the evolution of cooperation.*
New York: Penguin.

Riegel, D.L. (2004). Effects on boy-attracted pedosexual males of viewing boy erotica. *Archives of Sexual Behavior, 33,* 321–323.

Rietveld, M.J.H., Hudziak, J.J., Bartels, M., van Beijsterveldt, C.E.M., & Boomsma,
D.I. (2003). Heritability of attention problems in children: Cross-sectional
results from a study of twins, age 3 to 12 years. *Neuropsychiatric Genetics, 1176,*
102–113.

Rigby, K. (2002). *New perspectives on bullying.* London: Jessica Kingsley.

Rigby, K. (2003). Consequences of bullying in school. *Canadian Journal of Psychiatry,
48,* 583–590.

Riger, S., Ahrens, C., & Bickenstaff, A. (2000). Measuring interference with employment and education reported by women of abusive partners: Preliminary data.
Violence and Victims, 15, 161–172.

Riger, S., Raja, S., & Camacho, J. (2002). The radiating impact of intimate partner
violence. *Journal of Interpersonal Violence, 17,* 184–205.

Riley, T.L. (1979). The electroencephalogram in patients with rage attacks or episodic violent behavior. *Military Medicine, 144,* 515–517.

Ritchie, E.C., & Huff, T.G. (1999). Psychiatric aspects of arsonists. *Journal of Forensic
Science, 44,* 733–740.

Robbins, D.M., Beck, J.C., Pries, R., Cage, D.J., & Smith, C. (1983). Learning disability and neuropsychological impairment in adjudicated, unincarcerated male
delinquents. *Journal of the American Academy of Child Psychiatry, 22,* 40–46.

Robbins, S. (2001). Breaking news of layoffs must be handled kindly. *South Florida
Sun-Sentinel,* June 30, p. 7.

Roberts, B.W., Harms, P.D., Caspi, A., & Moffitt, T.E. (2007). Predicting the counterproductive employee in a child-to-adult prospective study. *Journal of Applied
Psychology, 92,* 1427–1436.

Roberts, D.W. (2009). Intimate partner homicide: Relationships to alcohol and
firearms. *Journal of Contemporary Criminal Justice, 25,* 67–88.

Roberts, J.C. (2007). Barroom aggression in Hoboken, New Jersey: Don't blame the
bouncers! *Journal of Drug Education, 37,* 429–445.

Roberts, J.C. (2009). Bouncers and barroom aggression: A review of the research. *Aggression and Violent Behavior, 14,* 59–68.

Robertson, R., Bankier, R., & Schwartz, L. (1987). The female offender: A Canadian study. *Canadian Journal of Psychiatry, 32,* 749–755.

Robins, L.N. (1966). *Deviant children grown up: A sociological and psychiatric study of sociopathic personaltiy.* Baltimore: Williams & Wilkins.

Robins, L.N. (1978). Sturdy childhood predictors of adult antisocial behavior: Replications from longitudinal studies. *Psychological Medicine, 8,* 611–622.

Robins, L.N., & Price, R.K. (1991). Adult disorders predicted by childhood conduct problems: Results from the NIMH epidemiologic catchment area project. *Psychiatry, 54,* 116–132.

Robinson, S., Rappaport-Bar-Server, M., & Rappaport, J. (1994). The present state of people who survived the Holocaust as children. *Acta Psychiatrica Scandinavica, 89,* 242–245.

Robinson, S.L., & O'Leary-Kelly, A.M. (1998). Monkey see, monkey do: The influence of work groups on the antisocial behavior of employees. *Academy of Management Journal, 41,* 658–672.

Rodenburg, M. (1971). Child murder by depressed parents. *Canadian Psychiatric Association Journal, 16,* 41–49.

Rodgers, B.A. (2006). *Psychological aspects of police work.* Springfield, IL: Charles C Thomas.

Rodin, E.A. (1973). Psychomotor epilepsy and aggressive behavior. *Archives of General Psychiatry, 28,* 210–213.

Rodin, E.A., Katz, M., & Lennox, K. (1976). Differences between patients with temporal lobe seizures and those with other forms of epileptic attacks. *Epilepsia, 17,* 313–320.

Roesch, R., Zapf, P.A., & Hart, S.D. (2010). *Forensic psychology and law.* Hoboken, NJ: Wiley.

Rogan, R.G., & Hammer, M.R. (1995). Assessing message affect in crisis negotiations: An exploratory study. *Human Communication Research, 21,* 553–574.

Rogan, R.G., Hammer, M.R., & Van Zandt, C.R. (1997). *Dynamic processes of crisis negotiation: Theory, research, and practice.* Westport: Praeger.

Rogers, C. (1993). Gang-related homicides in Los Angeles County. *Journal of Forensic Sciences, 38,* 831–834.

Rogers, R., Watt, A., Gray, N.S., MacCulloch, M.J., & Gournay, K. (2002). Content of command hallucinations predicts self-harm but not violence in a medium secure unit. *Journal of Forensic Psychiatry, 13,* 251–262.

Rogers, R., Gillis, J.R., Turner, R.E., & Frise-Smith, T. (1990). The clinical presentation of command hallucinations in a forensic population. *American Journal of Psychiatry, 147,* 1034–1037.

Rogosch, F.A., Cicchetti, D., & Aber, J. (1995). The role of child maltreatment in early deviations in cognitive and affective processing abilities and later peer relationship problems. *Development and Psychopathology, 7,* 591–609.

Roland, E., & Galloway, D. (2002). Classroom influences on bullying. *Educational Research, 44,* 299–312.

Rolls, E.T. (1995). A theory of emotion and consciousness, and its application to understanding the neural basis of emotion. In M.S. Gazzaniga (Ed.), *The cognitive neurosciences* (pp. 325–344). Cambridge, MA: MIT Press.

Rolls, E.T. (1998). The orbitofrontal cortex. In A.C. Roberts, T.W. Robbins & L. Weiskrantz (Eds.), *The prefrontal cortex: Executive and cognitive functions* (pp. 67–86). Oxford: Oxford University Press.

Rome Statute of the International Criminal Court. 2002. 2187 U.N.T.S. 90.

Root, D.A., & Ziska, M.D. (1996). Violence prevention during corporate downsizing: The use of a people team as context for the critical incident team. In G.R. Vandenbos & E.Q. Bulatao (Eds.), *Violence on the job: Identifying risks and Developing Solutions* (pp. 353–365). Washington DC: American Psychological Association.

Roper v. Simmons, 543 US 1040 (2005).

Rose, R.J., Dick, D.M., Vikenand, R.J., & Kaprio, J. (2001). Gene-environment interaction in patterns of adolescent drinking: Regional residency moderates longitudinal influences on alcohol use. *Alcohol: Clinical and Experimental Research, 25,* 637–643.

Rose, R.M., Bernstein, I.S., & Gordon, T.P. (1975). Consequence of social conflict on plasma testosterone levels in rhesus monkeys. *Psychosomatic Medicine, 37,* 50–61.

Rosen, T., Pillemer, K., & Lachs, M. (2008). Resident-to-resident aggression in long-term care facilities: An understudied problem. *Aggression and Violent Behavior, 13,* 77–87.

Rosenbaum, A., & Hoge, S.K. (1989). Head injury and marital aggression. *American Journal of Psychiatry, 146,* 1048–1051.

Rosenbaum, A., Hoge, S.K., Adelman, S.A., Warnken, W.J., Fletcher, K.E., & Kane, R.L. (1994). Head injury in partner-abusive men. *Journal of Consulting and Clinical Psychology, 62,* 1187–1193.

Rosenbaum, M. (1990). The role of depression in couples involved in murder-suicide and homicide. *American Journal of Psychiatry, 147,* 1036–1039.

Rosenberg, D. (1987). Web of deceit: A literature review of Munchausen syndrome by proxy. *Child Abuse and Neglect, 11,* 547–563.

Rosenberg, D. (1995). From lying to homicide: The spectrum of Munchausen syndrome by proxy. *Child Abuse and Neglect, 11,* 547–563.

Rosenblatt, A., & Leroi, I. (2000). Neuropsychiatry of Huntington's Disease and other basal ganglia disorders. *Psychosomatics, 41,* 24–30.

Rosenfeld, B.D. (1992). Court-ordered treatment of spouse abuse. *Clinical Psychology Review, 12,* 205–226.

Rosenfeld, B.D. (2003). Recidivism in stalking and obsessional harassment. *Law and Human Behavior, 27,* 251–265.

Rosenfeld, B.D. (2004). Violence risk factors in stalking and obsessional harassment: A review and preliminary meta-analysis. *Criminal Justice and Behavior, 31,* 9–36.

Rosenfeld, B.D., & Harmon, R. (2002). Factors associated with violence in stalking and obsessional harassment cases. *Criminal Justice and Behavior, 29,* 671–691.

Rosenfeld, R., Jacobs, B.A., & Wright, R. (2003). *Snitching and the code of the streets. British Journal of Criminology, 43,* 291–309.

Rosenthal, M. (1987). Traumatic head injury: Neurobehavioral consequences. In B. Caplan (Ed.), *Rehabilitation psychology desk reference* (pp. 247–280). Rockville: Aspen.

Ross, D.M. (1996). *Childhood bullying and teasing: What school personnel, other professionals, and parents can do.* Alexandria, VA: American Counseling Association.

Ross, E.H., & Hoaken, P.N.S. (2010). Correctional remediation meets neuropsychological rehabilitation: How brain injury and schizophrenia research can improve offender programming. *Criminal Justice and Behavior, 37,* 656–677.

Rossi, D. (1982). Crime scene behavioral analysis: Another tool for the law enforcement investigator. *The Police Chief, 18,* 152–155.

Rossmo, D.K. (2009). *Criminal investigative failures.* Boca Raton: CRC Press.

Rostow, C.D., & Davis, R.D. (2002). Psychological fitness for duty evaluations in law enforcement. *The Police Chief,* September, pp. 58–66.

Rostow, C.D., & Davis, R.D. (2004). *A handbook for psychological fitness-for-duty evaluations in law enforcement.* New York: Haworth.

Rothbart, M.K., Ahadi, S.A., & Evans, D.E. (2000). Temperament and personality: Origins and outcomes. *Journal of Personality and Social Psychology, 78,* 122–135.

Rothbaum, B.O., Foa, E.B., Riggs, D.S., Murdock, T., & Walsh, W. (1992). A prospective examination of posttraumatic stress disorder in rape victims. *Journal of Traumatic Stress, 5,* 455–475.

Rothman, E.F., Hathaway, J., Stidsen, A., & de Vries, H.F. (2007). How employment helps female victims of intimate partner violence: A qualitative study. *Journal of Occupational Health Psychology, 12,* 136–143.

Rotter, M., Way, B., Steinbacher, M., Sawyer, D., & Smith, H. (2002). Personality disorders in prison: Aren't they all antisocial? *Psychiatric Quarterly, 73,* 337–349.

Rowan, A.B., & Malone, R.P. (1997). Tics with Respiridone withdrawal. *Journal of the American Academy of Child and Adolescent Psychiatry, 36,* 162–163.

Rowe, D.C., Rodgers, J.L., & Meseck-Bushey, S. (1992). Sibling delinquency and the family environment: Shared and unshared influences. *Child Development, 63,* 59–67.

Rowlands, M.W. (1988). Psychiatric and legal aspects of persistent litigation. *British Journal of Psychiatry, 153,* 317–323.

Rozee, P.D. (1993). Forbidden or forgiven? Rape in cross-cultural perspective. *Psychology of Women Quarterly, 17,* 499–514.

Ruchkin, V, Schwab-Stone, M., Koposov, R., Vermeiren, R., & Steiner, H. (2002). Violence exposure, posttraumatic stress, and personality in juvenile delinquents. *Journal of the American Academy of Child and Adolescent Psychiatry, 41,* 322–329.

Rudman, D., Bross, D., & Mattson, D.E. (1994). Clinical indicators derived from the patient assessment instrument in the long-stay residents of 69 VA nursing homes. *Journal of General Internal Medicine, 9,* 261–267.

Rudofossi, D.M. (2007). *Working with traumatized police officers: A clinician's guide to complex PTSD syndromes in public safety profssionals.* Amityville, NY: Baywood Publishing.

Rueda, M.R., Posner, M.I., & Rothbart, M.K. (2004). Attentional self-control and self-regulation. In R.F. Baumeister & K.D. Vohs (Eds.), *Handbook of self-regulation: Research, theory, and applications* (pp. 283–300). New York: Guilford.

Ruff, C.C., Knauff, M., & Fangmeier, T. (2003). Reasoning and working memory: Common and distinct neuronal processes. *Neuropsychologia, 41,* 1241–1253.

Rugala, E.A., & Isaacs, A.R. (2004). *Workplace violence: Issues in response.* Quantico, VA: Critical Incident Response Group, National Center for the Analysis of Violent Crime, FBI Academy.

Rumsey, J.M., & Rapoport, J.L. (1983). *Nutrition and the brain.* New York: Raven Press.

Rush, A.J. (2007). The varied clinical presentations of major depressive disorder. *Journal of Clinical Psychiatry, 68,* 4–10.

Rush, B. (1812). *Medical inquiries and observations upon the diseases of the mind.* Philadelphia: Kimber & Richardson.

Rusk, T.N., & Rusk, N. (2007). Not by genes alone: New hope for prevention. *Bulletin of the Menninger Clinic, 71,* 1–21.

Russell, D.E.H. (1982). *Rape in marriage.* New York: Macmillan.

Russell, D.E.H. (1984). *Sexual exploitation: Rape, child sexual abuse, and workplace harassment.* Beverly Hills, CA: Sage.

Russell, D.E.H. (1988). Pornography and rape: A causal model. *Political Psychology, 9,* 41–73.

Russell, D.E.H. (1990). *Rape in marriage* (rev. ed.). Indianapolis: Indiana University Press.

Russell, H.E., & Beigel, A. (1990). *Understanding human behavior for effective police work* (3rd ed.). New York: Basic Books.

Rutter, M.L. (1979). Protective factors in children's responses to stress and disadvantage. In M.W. Kent & J.E. Rolf (Eds.), *Primary prevention of psychopathology: Social competence in children* (pp. 49–74). Hanover, NH: University Press of New England.

Rutter, M.L. (1985). Resilience in the face of adversity: Protective factors and resistance to psychiatric disorder. *British Journal of Psychiatry, 147,* 598–611.

Ruzicjka, M.F. (1997). Predictor variables on clergy pedophiles. *Psychological Reports, 81,* 589–590.

Ryden, M.B., Bossenmaier, M., & McLachlan, C. (1991). Aggressive behavior in cognitively impaired nursing home residents. *Research in Nursing and Health, 14,* 87–95.

Rynearson, E.K. (1984). Bereavement after homicide: A descriptive study. *American Journal of Psychiatry, 141,* 1452–1454.

Rynearson, E.K. (1988). The homicide of a child. In F.M. Ochberg (Ed.), *Post-traumatic therapy and victims of violence* (pp. 213–224). New York: Brunner/Mazel.

Rynearson, E.K. (1994). Psychotherapy of bereavement after homicide. *Journal of Psychotherapy Practice and Research, 3,* 341–347.

Rynearson, E.K. (1996). Psychotherapy of bereavement after homicide: Be offensive. *In Session: Psychotherapy in Practice, 2,* 47–57.

Rynearson, E.K. (2001). *Retelling violent death.* Philadelphia: Brunner-Routledge.

Rynearson, E.K., & McCreery, J.M. (1993). Bereavement after homicide: A synergism of trauma and loss. *American Journal of Psychiatry, 150,* 258–261.

Sadler, A.G., Booth, B.M., Mengeling, M.A., & Doebbeling, B.N. (2004). Life span and repeated violence against women during military service: Effects on health status and outpatient utilization. *Journal of Women's Health, 13,* 799–811.

Sadoff, R.L. (1971). Clinical observation on parricide. *Psychiatric Quarterly, 45,* 65–69.

Sadoff, R.L. (1995). Mothers who kill their children. *Contemporary Psychiatry, 25,* 601–605.

Sagan, C., & Druyan, A. (1992). *Shadows of forgotten ancestors.* New York: Random House.

Sageman, M. (2004). *Understanding terror networks.* Philadelphia: University of Pennsylvania Press.

Sageman, M. (2005). The normality of global Jihadi terrorism. *Journal of International Security Affairs, 8,* 1–10.

Sakheim, G.A., & Osborn, E. (1999). Severe vs. nonsevere firesetters revisited. *Child Welfare, 78,* 411–434.

Salekin, R.T., & Lochman, J.E. (2008). Child and adolescent psychopathy: The search for protective factors. *Criminal Justice and Behavior, 35,* 159–172.

Sallom, I.M., Cornelius, J.R., & Mezzich, J.F. (2002). Impact of concurrent alcohol misuse on symptom presentation of acute mania at initial evaluation. *Bipolar Disorders, 4,* 418–421.

Salmivalli, C., Lagerspetz, K., Bjorkqvist, K., Osterman, K., & Kaukiainen, A. (1996). Bullying as a group process: Participant roles and their relations to social status within the group. *Aggressive Behavior, 22,* 1–15.

Salmon, C. (2008). The world's oldest profession: Evolutionary insights into prostitution. In J.D. Duntley & T.K. Shackelford (Eds.), *Evolutionary forensic psychiatry: Darwinian foundations of crime and law* (pp. 121–135). New York: Oxford University Press.

Salmon, K., & Pereira, J.K. (2002). Predicting children's response to an invasive medical investigation: The influence of effortful control and parent behaviour. *Journal of Pediatric Psychology, 27,* 227–233.

Salvador, A., Simon, V.M., Suay, F & Lorens, L. (1985). Testosterone and cortisol responses to competitive fighting in human males: A pilot study. *Aggressive Behavior, 13,* 9–13.

Salvador, A., Suay, F., Martinez-Sanchis, S., Simon, V.M., & Brain, P.F. (1999). Correlating testosterone and fighting in male participants in judo contests. *Physiology and Behavior, 68,* 205–209.

Salyers, M.P., & Mueser, K.T. (2001). Social functioning, psychopathology, and medication side effects in relation to substance use and abuse in schizophrenia. *Schizophrenia Research, 48,* 109–123.

Samenow, S.E. (1984). *Inside the criminal mind.* New York: Times Books.

Samenow, S.E. (2002). *Straight talk about criminals: Understanding and treating antisocial individuals.* New York: Jason Aronson.

Samenow, S.E. (2004) *Inside the criminal mind* (rev. ed.). New York: Crown.

Samenow, S.E. (2007). *The myth of the out-of-character crime.* Westport, CT: Praeger.

Sameroff, A.J., Bartko, W.T., Baldwin, A., Baldwin, C., & Seifer, R. (1998). Family and social influence on the development of child competence. In M. Lewis & C. Feiring (Eds.), *Families, risk, and competence* (pp. 161–185). Mahwah, NJ: Erlbaum.

Sameroff, A.J., & Chandler, M.J. (1975). Reproductive risk and the continuum of caretaking casualty. In F.D. Horowitz, M. Hetherington, S. Scarr-Salapetek & G. Siegal (Eds.), *Review of child development research* (pp. 187–244). Chicago: University of Chicago Press.

Sampson, R.J., & Laub, J.H. (1990). Crime and deviance over the life course: the salience of adult social bonds. *American Sociology Review, 55,* 609–627.

Sampson, R.J., & Laub, J.H. (1993). *Crime in the making: Pathways and turning points through life.* Cambridge, MA: Harvard University Press.

Sampson, R.J., Raudenbush, S., & Earls, F. (1997). Neighborhoods and violent crime: A multilevel study of collective efficacy. *Science, 277,* 918–924.

Samuels, M.P., McClaughlin, W., Jacobson, R.R., Poets, C., & Southall, D. (1992). Fourteen cases of imposed upper airway obstruction. *Archives of Diseases in Childhood, 67,* 162–170.

Sanchez-Martin, J.R., Fano, E., Ahedo, L., Cardas, J., Brain, P.F., & Azpiroz, A. (2000). Relating testosterone levels and free play social behavior in male and female preschool children. *Psychoneuroendocrinology, 25,* 773–783.

Sanday, P.R. (1981). The socio-cultural context of rape: A cross-cultural study. *Journal of Social Issues, 37,* 5–27.

Sanders, D.L. (1997). Responding to domestic violence. *The Police Chief,* June, p. 6.

Sanders, M.J., & Bursch, B. (2002). Forensic assessment of illness falsification, Munchausen by proxy, and factitious disorder NOS. *Child Maltreatment, 7,* 112–124.

Sapolsky, R.M., & Plotsky, P.M. (1990). Hypercortisolism and its possible neural bases. *Biological Psychiatry, 27,* 937–952.

Sapolsky, R.M., Uno, H., Rebert, C.S., & Finch, C.E. (1990). Hippocampal damage associated with prolonged glucocorticoid exposure. *Journal of Neuroscience, 10,* 2897–2902.

Saradjian, J. (1996). *Women who sexually abuse children: From research to clinical practice.* Chichester, UK: Wiley.

Sartin, M., Hansen, D.J., & Huss, M.T. (2006). Domestic violence treatment response and recidivism: A review and implications for the study of family violence. *Aggression and Violent Behavior, 11,* 425–440.

Satterfield, J.H., & Schell, A. (1997). A prospective study of hyperactive boys with conduct problems and normal boys: Adolescent and adult criminality. *Journal of the American Academy of Child and Adolescent Psychiatry, 36,* 1726–1735.

Saunders, B.E., Kilpatrick, D.G., Resnick, H.S., & Tidwell, R.P. (1989). Brief screening for lifetime history of criminal victimization at mental health intake: A preliminary study. *Journal of Interpersonal Violence, 4,* 267–277.

Saunders, R. (1998). Legal perspectives on stalking. In J.R. Meloy (Ed.), *The psychology of stalking: Clinical and forensic perspectives* (pp. 28–51). San Diego, CA: Academic Press.

Savage, J. (2008). The effects of media violence exposure on criminal aggression: A meta-analysis. *Criminal Justice and Behavior, 35,* 1123–1136.

Savard, G., Andermann, F., Olivier, A., & Remillard, G.M. (1991). Postictal psychosis after partial complex seizures: A multiple case study. *Epilepsia, 32,* 225–231.

Savitch, H.V. (2003). Does 9-11 portend a new paradigm for cities? *Urban Affairs Review, 39,* 103–127.

Sayed, Z.A., Lewis, S.A., & Brittain, R.P. (1969). An electroencephalographic and psychiatric study of thirty-two insane murderers. *British Journal of Psychiatry, 115,* 1115–1124.

Scalora, M.J., Washington, D.O., Casady, T., & Newell, S.P. (2003). Nonfatal workplace violence risk factors: Data from a police contact sample. *Journal of Interpersonal Violence, 18,* 310–327.

Scarpa, A. (2001). Community violence exposure in a young adult sample: Lifetime prevalence and socioemotional effects. *Journal of Interpersonal Violence, 16,* 36–53.

Scarpa, A., Fikretoglu, D., Bowser, F., Hurley, J.D., Pappert, C.A., Romero, N., & Van Voorhees, E. (2002). Community violence exposure in university students: A replication and extension. *Journal of Interpersonal Violence, 17,* 253–272.

Scarpa, A., & Haden, S.C. (2006). Community violence victimization and aggressive behavior: The moderating effects of coping and social support. *Aggressive Behavior, 32,* 502–515.

Scarr, S. (1992). Developmental theories for the 1990s: Development and individual differences. *Child Development, 63,* 1–19.

Scarr, S., & McCartney, K. (1983). How people make their own environments: A theory of genotype-environment effects. *Child Development, 54,* 424–435.

Schaal, B., Tremblay, R.E., Soussignan, R., & Susman, E.J. (1996). Male testosterone linked to high social dominance but low physical aggression in early adolescence. *Journal of the American Academy of Child and Adolescent Psychiatry, 35,* 1322–1330.

Schanda, H., Fodes, P., Topitz, A., Fliedl, R., & Knecht, G. (1992). Premorbid adjustment of schizophrenic criminal offenders. *Acta Psychiatrica Scandinavica, 86,* 121–126.

Schaner, D.J. (1996). Have gun, will carry: Concealed handgun laws, workplace violence, and employer liability. *Employee Relations Law Journal, 22,* 83–100.

Schechter, H. (1990). *Deranged: The shocking true story of America's most fiendish killer.* New York: Pocket Books.

Schenck, C.H., Lee, S.A., Bornemann, M.A.C., & Mahowald, M.W. (2009). Potentially lethal behaviors associated with rapid eye movement sleep behavior disorder: Review of the literature and forensic implications. *Journal of Forensic Sciences, 54,* 1475–1484.

Schenck, C.H., Bundlie, S.R., Eitinger, M.G., & Mahowald, M.W. (1986). Chronic behavioral disorders of human REM sleep: A new category of parasomnia. *Sleep, 9,* 293–308.

Schenck, C.H., & Mahowald, M.W. (1995). A polysomnographically documented case of adult somnambulism with long-distance automobile driving and frequent nocturnal violence: Parasomnia with continuing danger as a noninsane automatism? *Sleep, 18,* 765–772.

Schlesinger, L.B. (2000a). Familicide, depression and the catathymic process. *Journal of Forensic Sciences, 45,* 200–203.

Schlesinger, L.B. (2000b). Serial homicide, sadism, fantasy, and a compulsion to kill. In L.B. Schlesinger (Ed.), *Serial offenders: Current thoughts, recent findings* (pp. 3–22). Boca Raton, FL: CRC Press.

Schlesinger, L.B. (2002). Stalking, homicide, and catathymic process: A case study. International *Journal of Offender Therapy and Comparative Criminology, 46,* 64–74.

Schlesinger, L.B. (2004). *Sexual murder: Catathymic and compulsive homicides.* Boca Raton, FL: CRC Press.

Schlesinger, L.B. (2007). Sexual homicide: Differentiating catathymic and compulsive murders. *Aggression and Violent Behavior, 12,* 242–256.

Schlesinger, L.B., & Miller, L. (2003). Learning to kill: serial, contract, and terrorist murderers. In R.S. Moser & C.E. Franz (Ed.), *Shocking violence II: Violent disaster, war, and terrorism affecting our youth* (pp. 145–164). Springfield, IL: Charles C Thomas.

Schlesinger, L.B., & Revitch, E. (1999). Sexual burglaries and sexual homicide: Clinical, forensic, and investigative considerations. *Journal of the American Academy of Psychiatry and the Law, 27,* 227–238.

Schlesinger, L.B., & Revitch, E. (1980). Stress, violence, and crime. In I.L. Kutash & L.B. Schlesinger (Eds.), *Handbook on stress and anxiety* (p. 4–25). San Francisco: Jossey-Bass.

Schloesser, P., Pierpont, J., & Poertner, J. (1992). Active surveillance of child abuse fatalities. *Child Abuse and Neglect, 16,* 3–10.

Schlosser, E. (1997). A grief like no other. *The Atlantic Monthly,* September, pp. 37–76.

Schlosser, E. (1998). The prison-industrial complex. *The Atlantic Monthly,* December, pp. 51–77.

Schmalleger, F. (2007). *Criminal justice today: An introduction for the 21st century* (9th ed.). Upper Saddle River, NJ: Pearson.

Schmid, A. P. (2000). *Magnitudes of terrorist victimization: Past, present and future.* Paper presented at the Ancillary Meeting on Terrorist Victimization Prevention, Control and Recovery, Tenth United Nations Congress on the Prevention of Crime and the Treatment of Offenders, Vienna, Austria, April 12.

Schmithorst, V.J., Wilke, M., Dardzinski, B.J., Scott, K., & Holland, S.K. (2005). Cognitive functions correlate with white matter architecture in a normal pediatric population: A diffusion tensor MRI study. *Human Brain Mapping, 26,* 139–149.

Schmitt, D.P., & Buss, D.M. (2001). Human mate poaching: Tactics and temptations for infiltrating existing mateships. *Journal of Personality and Social Psychology, 80,* 894–917.

Schneid, T.D. (1999). *Occupational health guide to violence in the workplace.* Boca Raton: CRC Press.

Schoenbaum, G., Chiba, A.A., & Gallagher, M. (1998). Orbitofrontal cortex and basolateral amygdale encode expected outcomes during learning. *Nature Neuroscience, 1,* 155–159.

Schouten, R. (1994). Distorting posttraumatic stress disorder for court. *Harvard Review of Psychiatry, 2,* 171–173.

Schouten, R. (1996). Sexual harassment and the role of psychiatry. *Harvard Review of Psychiatry, 3,* 296–298.

Schouten, R. (2006). Workplace violence: A overview for practicing clinicians. *Psychiatric Annals, 36,* 791–797.

Schreier, H.A. (1997). Factitious presentation of psychiatric disorder: When is it Munchausen by proxy? *Child Psychology and Psychiatry Review, 2,* 108–115.

Schreier, H.A. (2002a). Munchausen by proxy defined. *Pediatrics, 110,* 985–988.

Schreier, H.A. (2002b). On the importance of motivation in Munchausen by proxy: The case of Kathy Bush. *Child Abuse and Neglect, 26,* 537–549.

Schreier, H.A., & Libow, J. (1993). *Hurting for love: Munchausen by proxy syndrome.* New York: Guilford.

Schultz, S. (2004). Problems with the versatility construct of Gottfredson and Hirschi's general theory of crime. *European Journal of Crime, Criminal Law and Criminal Justice, 12,* 61–82.

Schurmann, C.L., & van Hooff, J. (1986). Reproductive strategies of the orang-utan: New data and a reconsideration of existing sociosexual models. International *Journal of Primatology, 7,* 265–287.

Schwartz, D., Dodge, K.A., Coie, J.D., Hubbard, J.A., Cillessen, A.H.N., Lemerise, E.A., & Bateman, H. (1998). Social-cognitive and behavioral correlates of aggression and victimization in boys' play groups. *Journal of Abnormal Child Psychology, 26,* 431–440.

Schwartz, D., Dodge, K.A., Petit, G.S., & Bates, J.E. (1997). The early socialization of aggressive victims of bullying. *Child Development, 68,* 665–675.

Schwartz, E. (2008). Mental health courts: How special courts can serve justice and help mentally ill offenders. *US News and World Report, February 2,* pp. 44–45.

Schwartz, R.H., Milteer, R., & LeBeau, M.A. (2000). Drug-facilitated sexual assault ("date rape"). *Southern Medical Journal, 93,* 558–561.

Schwartz-Watts, D.M. (2005). Asperger's disorder and murder. *Journal of the American Academy of Psychiatry and the Law, 33,* 390–393.

Schwatz-Watts, D.M., & Morgan, D.W. (1998). Violent versus nonviolent stalkers. *Journal of the American Academy of Psychiatry and the Law, 26,* 241–245.

Scott, E.S., Reppucci, N., & Woolard, J. (1995). Evaluating adolescent decision making in legal contexts. *Law and Human Behavior, 19,* 221–244.

Scott, , E.S., & Steinberg, L. (2003). Blaming youth. *Texas Law Review, 81,* 799–840.

Scott, E.S.., & Steinberg, L. (2008). *Rethinking juvenile justice.* Cambridge, MA: Harvard University Press.

Scott, J.L. (1999). Violence as a public health emergency. *Emergency Medicine Clinics of North America, 17,* 567–573.

Scott, P.D. (1973a). Parents who kill their children. *Medicine, Science and the Law, 13,* 120–126.

Scott, P.D. (1973b). Fatal battered baby cases. *Medicine, Science and the Law, 13,* 197–206.

Scoville, D. (2003). The enemies within. *Police Magazine,* September, pp. 44-50.

Scragg, P., & Shah, A. (1994). Prevalence of Asperger's syndrome in a secure hospital. *British Journal of Psychiatry, 165,* 679–682.

Scully, D. (1988). Convicted rapists' perceptions of self and victim: Role taking and emotions. *Gender and Society, 2,* 200–213.

Scully, D. (1990). *Understanding sexual violence: A study of convicted rapists.* New York: Harper Collins.

Scully, D., & Marolla, J. (1984). Convicted rapists' vocabulary of motive: Excuses and justifications. *Social Problems, 31,* 530–544.

Scully, D., & Marolla, J. (1985). "Riding the bull at Gilley's": Convicted rapists describe the rewards of rape. *Social Problems, 32,* 251–263.

Seagrave, K. (1992). *Women serial and mass murderers.* Jefferson, MO: McFarland.

Sears, D. (1991). *To kill again.* Wilmington, DE: Scholarly Resources.

Segal, J. (1989). Erotomania revisted: From Kraepelin to DSM-III-R. *American Journal of Psychiatry, 146,* 1261–1266.

Segal, Z.V., & Marshall, W.L. (1985). Heterosexual social skills in a population of rapists and child offenders. *Journal of Consulting and Clinical Psychology, 53,* 55–63.

Seger, K.A. (2003). Deterring terrorists. In A. Silke (Ed.), *Terrorists, victims and society: Psychological perspectives on terrorism and its consequences* (pp. 257–269). Chichester: Wiley.

Seghorn, T.K., Prentky, R.A., & Boucher, R.J. (1987). Childhood sexual abuse in the lives of sexually aggressive offenders. *Journal of the American Academy of Child and Adolescent Psychiatry, 26,* 262–267.

Seguin, J.R., Boulerice, B., Harden, P.W., Tremblay, R.E., & Pihl, R.O. (1999). Executive functions and physical aggression after controlling for attention deficit hyperactivity disorder, general memory, and IQ. *Journal of Child Psychology and Psychiatry, 40,* 1197–1208.

Seguin, J.R., Nagin, D., Assaad, J.M., & Tremblay, R.E. (2004). Cognitive-neuropsychological function in chronic physical aggression and hyperactivity. *Journal of Abnormal Psychology, 113,* 603–613.

Seidenwurm, D., Pounds, T.R., Globus, A., & Valk, P.E. (1997). Abnormal temporal lobe metabolism in violent subjects: Correlation of imaging and neuropsychiatric findings. *American Journal of Neuroradiology, 18,* 625–631.

Seltzer, J., Conrad, C., & Cassens, G. (1997). Neuropsychological profiles in schizophrenia: Paranoid versus undifferentiated distinctions. *Schizophrenia Research, 23,* 131–138.

Sendi, I.B., & Blomgren, P.G. (1975). A comparative study of predictive criteria in the predisposition of homicidal adolescents. *American Journal of Psychiatry, 132,* 423–427.

Serafetinides, E.A. (1965). Aggressiveness in temporal lobe epileptics and its relation to cerebral dysfunction and environmental factors. *Epilepsia, 6,* 33–42.

Serbin, L.A., Cooperman, J.M., Peters, P.L., Lehoux, P.M., Stack, D.M., & Schwartzman, A.E. (1998). Intergenerational transfer of psychosocial risk in women with childhood histories of aggression, withdrawal, or aggression and withdrawal. *Developmental Psychology, 34,* 1246–1262.

Serin, R. (1991). Psychopathy and violence in criminals. *Journal of Interpersonal Violence, 6,* 423–431.

Serin, R.C., Mailoux, D.L., & Malcolm, P.B. (2001). Psychopathy, deviant sexual arousal and recidivism among sexual offenders. *Journal of Interpersonal Violence, 16,* 234–246.

Serin, R.C., Malcolm, P.B., Khanna, A., & Barbaree, H.E. (1994). Psychopathy and deviant sexual arousal in incarcerated sexual offenders. *Journal of Interpersonal Violence, 9,* 3–11.

Seto, M.C. (2002). Precisely defining pedophilia. *Archives of Sexual Behavior, 31,* 498–499.

Seto, M.C. (2008). *Pedophilia and sexual offending against children: Theory, assessment, and intervention.* Washington, DC: American Psychological Association.

Seto, M.C. (2009). Pedophilia. *Annual Review of Clinical Psychology, 5,* 391–407.

Seto, M.C., Cantor, J.M., & Blanchard, R. (2006). Child pornography offenses are a valid diagnostic indicator of pedophilia. *Journal of Abnormal Psychology, 115,* 610–615.

Seto, M.C., & Eke, A.W. (2005). The future offending of child pornography offenders. *Sex Abuse, 17,* 201–210.

Seto, M.C., Harris, G.T., Rice, M.E., & Barbaree, H.E. (2004). The Screening Scale for Pedophillic Interests and recidivism among adult sex offenders with child victims. *Archives of Sexual Behavior, 33,* 455–466.

Seto, M.C., & Lalumiere, M.L. (2001). A brief screening scale to identify pedophilic interests among child molesters. *Sex Abuse, 13,* 15–25.

Shackelford, T.K., & Buss, D.M. (1997). Cues to infidelity. *Personality and Social Psychology Bulletin, 23,* 1034–1045.

Shackleford, T.K., Buss, D.M., & Peters, J. (2000). Wife killing: Risk to women as a function of age. *Violence and Victims, 15,* 273–282.

Shackelford, T.K., & Duntley, J.D. (2008). Evolutionary forensic psychology. In J.D. Duntley & T.K. Shackelford (Eds.), *Evolutionary forensic psychiatry: Darwinian foundations of crime and law* (pp. 3–19). New York: Oxford University Press.

Shackelford, T.K., & Goetz, A.T. (2004). Men's sexual coercion in intimate relationships: Development and initial validation of the Sexual Coercion in Intimate Relationships Scale. *Violence and Victims, 19,* 21–36.

Shackelford, T.K., LeBlanc, G.J., & Drass, E. (2000). Emotional reactions to infidelity. *Cognition and Emotion, 14,* 643–659.

Shackelford, T.K., LeBlanc, G.J., Weekes-Shackelford, V.A., Bleske-Rechek, A.L., Euler, H.A., & Hoier, S. (2002). Psychological adaptation to human sperm competition. *Evolution and Human Behavior, 23,* 123–138.

Shafii, M., & Shafii, S.L. (Eds.). (2001). *School violence: Assessment, management, prevention.* Washington, DC: American Psychiatric Publishing.

Shallice, T., & Burgess, P.W. (1991). Deficits in strategy application after frontal lobe damage in man. *Brain, 114,* 727–741.

Shapiro, D. (1965). *Neurotic styles.* New York: Basic Books.

Shapiro, R.M., Jankowski, M.A., & Dale, J. (2005). *Bullies, tyrants, and impossible people: How to beat them without joining them.* New York: Crown.

Sharma, V., & Mazmanian, D. (2003). Sleep loss and postpartum psychosis. *Bipolar Disorders, 5,* 98–105.

Sharp, G. (1984). *The politics of nonviolent action: Power and struggle.* Boston: Porter & Sargent.

Shaw, C.R. & McKay, H.D. (1929). *Delinquency areas.* Chicago: University of Chicago Press.

Shaw, C.R. & McKay, H.D. (1942). *Juvenile delinquency and urban areas.* Chicago, IL: University of Chicago Press.

Shaw, D.M., Churchill, C.M., Noyes, R., & Loeffelholz, P.L. (1987). Criminal behavior and post-traumatic stress disorder in Vietnam veterans. *Comprehensive Psychiatry, 28,* 403–411.

Shaywitz, S.E., Cohen, D.J., & Shaywitz, B.A. (1980). Behavior and learning difficulties in children of normal intelligence born to alcoholic mothers. *Journal of Pediatrics, 96,* 978–982.

Shepherd, M. (1961). Morbid jealousy: Some clinical and social aspects of a psychiatric symptom. *Journal of Mental Science, 107,* 688–704.

Sher, L., Oquendo, M.A., Coason, A.H., Brent, D.A., Grunebaum, M.F., Zalsman, G., Burke, A.K., & Mann, J.J. (2005). Clinical features of depressed patients with or without a family history of alcoholism. *Acta Psychiatrica Scandinavica, 112,* 266–271.

Sheridan, D.J., & Nash, K.R. (2007). Acute injury patterns of intimate partner violence victims. *Trauma, Violence, and Abuse, 8,* 281–289.

Sheridan, L.P., Blaauw, E., & Davies, G.M. (2003). Stalking: Knowns and unknowns. *Trauma, Violence and Abuse, 4,* 148–162.

Sheridan, L.P., & Boon, J. (2002). Stalker typologies: Implications for law enforcement. In Boone, J., & Sheridan, L. (Eds.), *Stalking and psychological obsession: Psychological perspectives for prevention, policing, and treatment* (pp. 63–82). Chichester, UK: Wiley.

Sheridan, L.P., & Davies, G.M. (2001). Violence and the prior victim-stalker relationship. *Criminal Behavior and Mental Health, 11,* 102–116.

Sheridan, L.P., Gillett, R., Blauuw, E., Davies, G.M., & Patel, D. (2003). "There's no smoke without fire": Are male ex-partners perceived as more "entitled" to stalk than stranger or acquaintance stalkers? *British Journal of Psychology, 94,* 87–98.

Sheridan, L.P., & Grant, T. (2007). Is cyberstalking different? *Psychology, Crime and Law, 13,* 627–640.

Sheridan, M.S. (2003). The deceit continues: An updated literature review of Munchausen syndrome by proxy. *Child Abuse and Neglect*, 27, 431–451.

Sherman, L.W., Strang, H., Angel, C., Woods, D, Barnes, G.C., Bennett, S., & Inkpen, N. (2005). Effects of face-to-face restorative justice on victims of crime in four randomized, controlled trials. *Journal of Experimental Criminology, 1*, 367–395.

Shermer, M. (2004). *The science of good and evil: Why people cheat, gossip, care, share, and follow the golden rule.* New York: Times Books.

Sherry, J. (2007). Violent video games and aggression: Why can't we find the links? In R. Preiss, B. Gayle, N. Burrell, M. Allen & J. Bryant (Eds.), *Mass media effects research: Advances through meta-analysis* (pp. 231–248). Mahwah, NJ: Erlbaum.

Shields, A., Ryan, R.M., & Cichetti, D. (2001). Narrative representations of care-givers and emotion dysregulation as predictors of maltreated children's rejection by peers. *Developmental Psychology, 37,* 321–337.

Shields, W.M., & Shields, L.M. (1983). Forcible rape: An evolutionary perspective. *Ethology and Sociobiology, 4,* 115–136.

Shilling, C. (2003). *The body and social theory* (2nd ed.). London: Sage.

Shinoda-Tagawa, T., Leonard, R., Pontikas, J., McDonough, J.E., Allen, D., & Dreyer, P.I. (2004). Resident-to-resident violent incidents in nursing homes. *Journal of the American Medical Association, 291,* 591–598.

Shipman, K.L., & Zeman, J. (1999). Emotional understanding: A comparison of mal-treating and nonmaltreating mother-child dyads. *Journal of Clinical Child Psychology, 28,* 407–417.

Shivy, V.A., Wu, J.J., Moon, A.E., Mann, S.C., Holland, J.G., & Eacho, C. (2007). Ex-offenders reentering the workforce. *Journal of Counseling Psychology, 54,* 466–473.

Shook, J.J. (2005). Contesting childhood in the US justice system: The transfer of juveniles to adult criminal court. *Childhood, 12,* 461–478.

Shore, D., Filson, R., Johnson, W., Rae, D., Muehrer, P., & Kelley, D. (1989). Murder and assault arrests of White House cases. *American Journal of Psychiatry, 36,* 162–163.

Shore, D., Filson, C.R., Davis, T.S., Olivos, G., DeLisi, L., & Wyatt R.J. (1985). White House cases: Psychiatric patients and the Secret Service. *American Journal of Psychiatry, 142,* 308-312.

Shore, D., Filson, C.R., & Johnson, W.E. (1988). Violent crime arrests and paranoid schizophrenia: The White House case studies. *Schizophrenia Bulletin, 14,* 279 281.

Short, J.F., & Nye, F.I. (1957). Reported behavior as a criterion of deviant behavior. *Social Problems, 5,* 207–213.

Shrestha, K., Rees, D.W., & Rix, K.J.B. (1985). Sexual jealousy in alcoholics. *Acta Psychiatrica Scandinavica, 72,* 283–290.

Shulman, H.M. (1951). Intelligence and delinquency. *Journal of Criminal Law and Criminology, 41,* 763–781.

Shumaker, D.M., & Prinz, R.J. (2000). Children who murder: A review. *Clinical Child and Family Psychology Review, 3,* 97–115.

Siegal, A., & Pott, C.B. (1988). Neural substrates of aggression and flight in the cat. *Progress in Neurobiology, 31,* 261–283.

Siegel, J.M. (1993). Companion animals: In sickness and in health. *Journal of Social Issues, 49,* 157–167.

Silberg, J., & Dallam, S. (2009). Out of the Jewish closet: Facing the hidden secrets of child sex abuse–and the damage done to victims. In A. Neustein (Ed.), *Tempest in the temple: Jewish communities and child sex scandals* (pp. 77–104). Waltham, MA: Brandeis University Press.

Silke, A.P. (1998). Cheshire-cat logic: The recurring theme of terrorist abnormality in psychological research. *Psychology, Crime, and Law, 4,* 51–69.

Silke, A. (2003a). Becoming a terrorist. In A. Silke (Ed.), *Terrorists, victims and society* (pp. 29–53). Chichester, UK: Wiley.

Silke, A.P. (2003b). The psychology of suicidal terrorism. In A. Silke (Ed.), *Terrorists, victims and society: Psychological perspectives on terrorism and its consequences* (pp. 93–108). Chichester: Wiley.

Silke, A. (2003c) Retaliating against terrorism. In A. Silke (Ed.), *Terrorists, victims and society: Psychological perspectives on terrorism and its consequences* (pp. 93–108). Chichester: Wiley.

Silke, A. (2005) Children, terrorism and counterterrorism: Lessons in policy and practice. *Terrorism and Political Violence, 17,* 201–213.

Silva, J.A., Derecho, D.V., Leong, G.B., Weinstock, R., & Ferrari, M.M. (2001). A classification of psychological factors leading to violent behavior in posttraumatic stress disorder. *Journal of Forensic Sciences, 46,* 309–316.

Silva, J.A., Ferrari, M.M., & Leong, G.B. (1998). The dangerousness of persons with delusional jealousy. *Journal of the American Academy of Psychiatry and the Law, 26,* 607–623.

Silva, J.A., Ferrari, M.M., & Leong, G.B. (2002). The case of Jeffrey Dahmer: Sexual serial homicide from a neuropsychiatric developmental perspective. *Journal of Forensic Science, 47,* 1–13.

Silva, J.A., Leong, G.B., & Weinstock, R. (1989). Capgras syndrome and dangerousness. *Bulletin of the American Academy of Psychiatry and the Law, 17,* 5–14.

Silva, J.A., Leong, G.B., & Weinstock, R. (1992). The dangerousness of persons with misidentification syndromes. *Bulletin of the American Academy of Psychiatry and the Law, 20,* 77–86.

Silver, E. (2000a). Extending social disorganization theory: A multilevel approach to the study of violence among persons with mental illnesses. *Criminology, 38,* 1043–1074.

Silver, E. (2000b). Race, neighborhood disadvantage, and violence among persons with mental disorders: The importance of contextual measurement. *Law and Human Behavior, 24,* 449–456.

Silver, E. (2002). Mental disorder and violent victimization: The mediating role of involvement in conflicted social relationships. *Criminology, 40,* 191–212.

Silver, E. (2006). Understanding the relationship between mental disorder and violence: The need for a criminological perspective. *Law and Human Behavior, 30,* 685–706.

Silver, E., Felson, R.B., & Vaneseltine, M. (2008). The relationship between mental health problems and violence among criminal offenders. *Criminal Justice and Behavior, 35,* 405–426.

Silver, E., Felson, R.B., & Vaneseltine, M. (2008). The relationship between mental health problems and violence among criminal offenders. *Criminal Justice and Behavior, 35,* 405–426.

Silver, E., & Miller, L. (2004). Sources of informal social control in Chicago neighborhoods. *Criminology, 42,* 551–583.

Silver, E., Mulvey, E., & Swanson, F. (2002). Neighborhood structural characteristics and mental disorder: Faris and Dunham revisited. *Social Science and Medicine, 55,* 1457–1470.

Silver, E., & Teasdale, b. (2005). Mental disorder and violence: An examination of stressful life events and impaired social support. *Social Problems, 52,* 62–78.

Silverman, R.A., & Kennedy, L.W. (1987). Relational distance and homicide: The role of the stranger. *Journal of Criminal Law and Criminology, 78,* 272–308.

Simmons, C.A., & Lehman, P. (2007). Exploring the link between pet abuse and controlling behavior in violent relationships. *Journal of Interpersonal Violence, 22,* 1211–1222.

Simon, L.M.J. (2000). An examination of the assumption of specialization, mental disorder, and dangerousness in sex offenders. *Behavioral Sciences and the Law, 18,* 275–308.

Simon, R.I. (1995). Toward the development of guidelines in the forensic evaluation of posttraumatic stress disorder claims. In R.I. Simon (Ed.), *Posttraumatic stress disorder in litigation: Guidelines for forensic assessment* (pp. 31-84). Washington, DC: American Psychiatric Press.

Simon, R.I. (1996). *Bad men do what good men dream: A forensic psychiatrist illuminates the dark side of human behavior.* Washington, DC: American Psychiatric Press.

Simpson, A., & Stanton, J. (2000). Maternal filicide: A reformulation of factors relevant to risk. *Criminal Behavior and Mental Health, 10,* 136-147.

Sinclair, I., & Gibbs, I. (1998). *Children's homes: A study in diversity.* Chichester, UK: Wiley.

Singhal, S., & Dutta, A. (1990). Who commits patricide? *Acta Psychiatrica Scandinavica, 82,* 40-43.

Sipe, A.W.R. (1990). *A secret world: Sexuality and the search for celibacy.* New York: Brunner/Mazel.

Sipe, A.W.R. (1995). *Sex, priests, and power: Anatomy of a crisis.* New York: Brunner/Mazel.

Sipormaa, L., Kristiansson, M., Jonson, C., Nyden, A., & Gillberg, C. (2001). Juvenile and young adult mentally disordered offenders: The role of child neuropsychiatric disorders. *Journal of the American Academy of Psychiatry and the Law, 29,* 420-426.

Skarlicki, D.P., & Folger, R. (1997). Retaliation in the workplace: The roles of distributive, procedural, and interactional justice. *Journal of Applied Psychology, 82,* 434-443.

Skeem, J.L., & Golding, S.L. (1998). Community examiners' evaluations of competence to stand trial: Common problems and suggestions for improvement. *Professional Psychology: Research and Practice, 29,* 357-367.

Skeem, J.L., Miller, J., Mulvey, J., Tiemann, J., & Monahan, J. (2005). Personality traits and violence among psychiatric patients: Using a five-factor lens to explore the relationship. *Journal of Consulting and Clinical Psychology, 73,* 454-465.

Skeem, J.L., & Mulvey, E. (2002). Monitoring the violence potential of mentally disordered offenders being treated in the community. In A. Buchanan (Ed.), *Care of the mentally disordered offender in the community* (pp. 111-142). New York: Oxford University Press.

Skeem, J.L., Mulvey, E., Appelbaum, A., Banks, S., Grisso, T., Silver, E., & Robbins, P. (2004). Identifying subtypes of civil psychiatric patients at high risk for violence. *Criminal Justice and Behavior, 31,* 392–437.

Skeem, J.L., Mulvey, E.P., & Lidz, C.W. (2000). Building mental health professionals' decisional models into tests of predictive validity: The accuracy of contextualized predictions of violence. *Law and Human Behavior, 24,* 607–628.

Skiba, R.J., & Knesting, K. (2002). Zero tolerance, zero evidence: An analysis of school disciplinary practice. In R.J. Skiba & G.G. Noam (Eds.), *Zero tolerance: Can suspension and expulsion keep schools safe?* (pp. 17–43). San Francisco, CA: Jossey-Bass.

Skodol, A.E., Gunderson, J.G., & McGlashan, T.H. (2002). Functional impairment in patients with schizotypal, borderline, avoidant, or obsessive-compulsive personality disorder. *American Journal of Psychiatry, 159,* 276–283.

Slaby, R.G., & Guerra, N.G. (1988). Cognitive mediators of aggression in adolescent offenders: I. Asssessment. *Developmental Psychology, 24,* 580–588.

Slagle, D.A. (1990). Psychiatric disorders following closed head injury: An overview of biopsychosocial factors in their etiology and management. *International Journal of Psychiatry in Medicine, 20,* 1–35.

Slaiku, K.A. (1996). *When push comes to shove: A practical guide to mediating disputes.* San Francisco: Jossey-Bass.

Slaughter, B., Fann, J.R., & Ehde, D. (2003). Traumatic brain injury in a county jail population: Prevalence, neuropsychological functioning and psychiatric disorders. *Brain Injury, 17,* 731–741.

Slaughter, L. (2000). Involvement of drugs in sexual assault. *Journal of Reproductive Medicine, 45,* 425–430.

Sloan, J. (1988). Institutional abuse. *Child Abuse Review, 2,* 7–8.

Slobogin, C. (2007). *Proving the unprovable: The role of law, science, and speculation in adjudicating culpability and dangerousness.* New York: Oxford University Press.

Slutske, W.S., Heath, A.C., Dinwiddie, S.H., Madden, P.A., Bucholz, K.K., Dunne, M.P., Statham, D.J., & Martin, N.G. (1997). Modeling genetic and environmental influences in the etiology of conduct disorder: A study of 2,682 adult twin pairs. *Journal of Abnormal Psychology, 106,* 266–279.

Small, J.G. (1966). The organic dimension of crime. *Archives of General Psychiatry, 15,* 82–89.

Smallbone, S.W., & Dadds, M.R. (1998). Childhood attachment and adult attachment in incarcerated adult male sex offenders. *Journal of Interpersonal Violence, 13,* 555–573.

Smallbone, S.W., Wheaton, J., & Hourigan, D. (2003). Trait empathy and criminal versatility in sexual offenders. *Sexual Abuse: A Journal of Research and Treatment, 15,* 49–60.

Smith, B.L. (1994). *Terorism in America: Pipe bombs and pipe dreams.* Albany: State University of New York Press.

Smith, H., & Israel, E. (1987). Sibling incest: As study of the dynamics of 25 cases. *Child Abuse and Neglect, 11,* 101–108.

Smith, J., & Hucker, S. (1994). Schizophrenia and substance abuse. *British Journal of Psychiatry, 165,* 13–21.

Smith, P.H., Moracco, K.E., & Butts, J. (1998). Partner homicide in context: A population based perspective. *Homicide Studies, 2,* 400–421.

Smith, P.K., Mahdavi, J., Carvalho, M., Fisher, S., Russell, S., & Tippett, N. (2008). Cyberbullying: Its nature and impact on secondary school pupils. *Journal of Child Psychology and Psychiatry, 49,* 376–385.

Smith, P.K., Morita, Y., Junger-Tas, J., Olweus, D., Catalano, R., & Slee, P. (1999). *The nature of school bullying: A cross-national perspective.* London: Routledge.

Smith, P.K., & Sharp, S. (1994). *School bullying: Insights and perspectives.* London: Routledge.

Smith, R.J. (1978). *The psychopath in society.* New York: Academic Press.

Smith, S.S., & Newman, J.P. (1990). Alcohol and drug abuse/dependence disorders in psychopathic and nonpsychopathic criminal offenders. *Journal of Abnormal Psychology, 94,* 430–439.

Smuts, B.B. (1992). Male aggression against women. *Human Nature, 6,* 1–32.

Snook, B., Eastwood, J., Gendreau, P., Goggin, C., & Cullen, R.M. (2007). Taking stock of criminal profiling: A narrative review and meta-analysis. *Criminal Justice and Behavior, 34,* 437–453.

Snyder, H.N. (2002). *Juvenile arrests 2000.* Washington, DC: US Department of Justice.

Snyder, H.N., & Sickmund, M. (1995). *Juvenile offenders and victims: A national report.* Washington, DC: US Department of Justice.

Soderstrom, H., Tullberg, M., Wikkelso, C., Ekholm, S., & Forsman, A. (2000). Reduced regional cerebral blood flow in nonpsychotic violent offenders. *Psychiatry Research, 98,* 29–41.

Soderstrom, H., Blennow, K., Sjodin, A.K., & Forsman, A. (2003). New evidence for an association between the CSF HVA:5-HIAA ratio and psychopathic traits. *Journal of Neurology, Neurosurgery, and Psychiatry, 74,* 918–924.

Soler, H., Vinayak, P., & Quadagno, D. (2000). Biosocial aspects of domestic violence. *Psychoneuroendocrinology, 25,* 721–739.

Soliman, S., Haque, S., & George, E. (2007). Stalking and Huntington's disease: A neurobiological link? *Journal of Forensic Sciences, 52,* 1202–1204.

Solomon, E.P., & Heide, K.M. (2005). The biology of trauma: Implications for treatment. *Journal of Interpersonal Violence, 20,* 51–60.

Solomon, P., & Draine, J. (1999). Explaining lifetime criminal arrests among clients of a psychiatric probation and parole service. *Journal of the American Academy of Psychiatry and the Law, 27,* 239–251.

Solursh, L.P., Meyer, C.A., & Nolan, W.P. (1991). Addiction to violence in the United States Vietnam combat veteran. *Medical Law, 10,* 375–379.

Somander, L.H., & Rammer, L.M. (1991). Intra- and extrafamilial child homicide in Sweden, 1971–1980. *Child Abuse and Neglect, 15,* 45–55.

Sonne, S.C., Brady, K.T., & Morton, W.A. (1994). Substance abuse and bipolar affective disorder. *Journal of Nervous and Mental Disease, 182,* 349–352.

Sorenson, S.B., & Peterson, J.G. (1994). Traumatic child death and documented maltreatment history. *American Journal of Public Health, 84,* 623–627.

Sorenson, S.B., & Wiebe, D.J. (2004). Weapons in the lives of battered women. *American Journal of Public Health, 94,* 1412–1417.

Southwestern Law Enforcement Institute. (1995). *Domestic assault among police: A survey of internal affairs policies.* Richardson, TX: Southwestern Law Enforcement Institute.

Southworth, C., Finn, J., Dawson, S., Fraser, C., & Tucker, S. (2007). Intimate partner violence, technology, and stalking. *Violence Against Women, 13,* 842–856.

Soutullo, C.A., McElroy, S.L., & Goldmith, J. (1998). Cravings and irresistible impulses: Similarities between addictions and impulse control disorders. *Psychiatric Annals, 28,* 592–600.

Sowell, E.R., Thompson, P.M., Holmes, C., Jernigan, T., & Toga, A. (1999). In vivo evidence for post-adolescent brain maturation in frontal and striatal regions. *Nature Neuroscience, 2,* 859–861.

Sowell, E.R., Thompson, P.M., Tessner, K.D., & Toga, A. (2001). Mapping continued brain growth and gray matter density reduction in the dorsal frontal cortex: Inverse relationships during postadolescent brain maturation. *Journal of Neuroscience, 21,* 8819–8829.

Sparr, L.F. (1996). Mental defenses and posttraumatic stress disorder: Assessment of criminal intent. *Journal of Traumatic Stress, 9,* 405–425.

Sparr, L.F., & Atkinson, R.M. (1986). Posttraumatic stress disorder as an insanity defense: Medicolegal quicksand. *American Journal of Psychiatry, 143,* 608–612.

Sparr, L.F., Reaves, M.E., & Atkinson, R.M. (1987). Military combat, post-traumatic stress disorder, and criminal behaviour in Vietnam veterans. *Bulletin of the American Academy of Psychiatry and the Law, 15,* 141–162.

Spear, P. (2000). The adolescent brain and age-related behavioral manifestations. *Neuroscience and Biobehavioral Reviews, 24,* 417–463.

Spector, P.E., Coulter, M.L., Stockwell, H.G., & Matz, M.W. (2007). Perceived violence climate: A new construct and its relationship to workplace physical violence and verbal aggression, and their potential consequences. *Work and Stress, 21,* 117–130.

Spellacy, F. (1978). Neuropsychological differences between violent and nonviolent adolescents. *Journal of Clinical Psychology, 33,* 966–969.

Spergel, I.A. (1995). *The youth gang problem: A community approach.* New York: Oxford University Press.

Sperry, L. (1995). *Handbook of the diagnosis and treatment of the DSM-IV personality disorders.* New York: Brunner/Mazel.

Spinella, M., White, J., Frank, M.L., & Schiraldi, J. (2006). Evidence of orbitofrontal dysfunction in sex offenders. *International Journal of Forensic Psychology, 1,* 62–68.

Spinelli, M.G. (2001). A systematic investigation of 16 cases of neonaticide. *American Journal of Psychiatry, 158,* 811–813.

Spinelli, M.G. (2004). Maternal infanticide associated with mental illness: Prevention and the promise of saved lives. *American Journal of Psychiatry, 161,* 1548–1557.

Spitzberg, B.H. (2002). The tactical topography of stalking victimization and management. *Trauma, Violence, and Abuse, 3,* 261–288.

Spitzberg, B.H., & Cadiz, M. (2002). The media construction of stalking stereotypes. *Journal of Criminal Justice and Popular Culture, 9,* 128–149.

Spitzberg, B.H., & Cupach, W.R. (2007). The state of the art of stalking: Taking stock of the emerging literature. *Aggression and Violent Behavior, 12,* 64–86.

Spitzberg, B.H., & Hoobler, G. (2002). Cyberstalking and the technologies of interpersonal terrorism. *New Media and Society, 4,* 71–92.

Sprang, M.V., McNeil, J.S., & Wright, R. (1989). Psychological changes after the murder of a significant other. *Social Casework, 70,* 159–164.

Spreen, O. (1981). The relationship between learning disability, neurological impairment and delinquency: Results of a follow-up study. *Journal of Nervous and Mental Disease, 169,* 791–799.

Sprinzak, E. (2001). The lone gunmen: The global war on terrorism faces a new brand of enemy. *Foreign Policy 1127,* 72–73.

Spritch, S., Biederman, J., Crawford, M.M., Mundy, E., & Faraone, S.V. (2000). Adoptive and biological families of children and adolescents with ADHD. *Journal of the Academy of Child and Adolescent Psychiatry, 39,* 1432–1437.

Spungen, D. (1998). *Homicide: The hidden victims. A guide for professionals.* Thousand Oaks, CA: Sage.

Stadolnik, R.F. (2000). *Drawn to the flame: Assessment and treatment of juvenile firesetting behavior.* Sarasota, FL: Professional Resource Press.

Stalenheim, E.G., Von Knorring, L., & Wide, L. (1998). Serum levels of thyroid hormones as biological markers in a Swedish forensic psychiatric population. *Biological Psychology, 43,* 745–761.

Stanford v. Kentucky, 492 U.S. 361 (1989).

Stanger, C., Dumeci, L., Kamon, J., & Burstein, M. (2004). Parenting and children's externalizing problems in substance-abusing families. *Journal of Clinical Child and Adolescent Psychology, 33,* 590–600.

Stanton, J., Simpson, A., & Wouldes, T. (2000). A qualitative study of filicide by mentally ill mothers. *Child Abuse and Neglect, 24,* 1451–1460.

Stark, E., & Flitcraft, A. (1996). *Women at risk: Domestic violence and women's health.* Thousand Oaks, CA: Sage.

Stark, R. (1979). Whose status counts? *American Sociological Review, 44,* 668–669.

Starr, K., Hobart, M., & Fawcett, J. (2004). Findings and recommendations from the Washington State Domestic Violence Fatality Review. *Washington State Coalition Against Domestic Violence,* pp. 1–98.

Starr, M., Raine, G., Pedersen, D., Shapiro, D., Cooper, N., Morris, H., King, P., & Harris, J. (1984). The random killers: An epidemic of serial murder sparks growing concern. *Newsweek,* November 26, pp. 100–106.

Starzomski, A., & Nussbaum, D. (2000). The self and the psychology of domestic homicide-suicide. *International Journal of Offender Therapy and Comparative Criminology, 44,* 468–479.

Staub, E. (2003a). Notes on cultures of violence, cultures of caring and peace, and the fulfillment of basic human needs. *Political Psychology, 24,* 1–21.

Staub, E. (2003b). *The psychology of good and evil: Why children, adults and groups help and harm others.* New York: Cambridge University Press.

Steadman, H.J., Davidson, S., & Brown, C. (2001). Mental health courts: Their promise and unanswered questions. *Psychiatric Services, 52,* 457–458.

Steadman, H.J., Redlich, A., Callahan, L., Robbins, P.C., & Vesselinov, R. (2010). Effect of mental health courts on arrest and jail days. *Archives of General Psychiatry, 134,* 1341–1346.

Steele, B.F. (1978). Psychology of infanticide resulting from maltreatment. In M. Kohl (Ed.), *Infanticide and the value of life* (pp. 76–85). New York: Prometheus Books.

Steele, B.F. (1987). Psychodynamic factors. In R.E. Helfer & R.S. Kempe (Eds.), *The battered child* (4th ed., pp. 81–114). Chicago: University of Chicago Press.

Stein, A. (2004). Fantasy, fusion, and sexual homicide. *Contemporary Psychoanalysis, 40,* 495–517.

Stein, D.J., Hollander, E., & Cohen, L. (1993). Neuropsychiatric impairment in impulsive personality disorders. *Psychiatry Research, 48,* 257–266.

Stein, M.A., Weiss, R.E., & Refetoff, S. (1995). Neurocognitive characteristics of individuals with resistance to thyroid hormone: Comparisons with individuals with attention deficit hyperactivity disorder. *Journal of Developmental Behavioral Pediatrics, 16,* 406–411.

Steinberg, L. (2002). *Adolescence* (6th ed.). New York: McGraw-Hill.

Steinberg, L. (2004). Risk-taking in adolescence: What changes and why? *Annals of the New York Academy of Sciences, 1021,* 51–58.

Steinberg, L. (2005). Cognitive and affective development in adolescence. *Trends in Cognitive Sciences, 9,* 69–74.

Steinberg, L. (2007). Risk-taking in adolescence: New perspectives from brain and behavioral science. *Current Directions in Psychological Science, 16,* 55–59.

Steinberg, L. (2008). A social neuroscience perspective on adolescent risk-taking. *Developmental Review, 28,* 78–106.

Steinberg, L. (2009). Adolescent development and juvenile justice. *Annual Review of Clinical Psychology, 5,* 47–73.

Steinberg, L., & Cauffman, E. (1996). Maturity of judgment in adolescence: Psychosocial factors in adolescent decision-making. *Law and Human Behavior, 20,* 249–272.

Steinberg, L., & Monahan, K. (2007). Age differences in resistance to peer influence. *Developmental Psychology, 43,* 1531–1543.

Steiner, H., Garcia, I., & Matthews, Z. (1997). Post-traumatic stress disorder in incarcerated juvenile delinquents. *Journal of the American Academy of Child and Adolescent Psychiatry, 36,* 357–365.

Steinmetz, S.K., & Lucca, J.S. (1988). Husband battering. In Van Hasselt, V.B. (Ed.), *Handbook of family violence* (pp. 233–246). New York: Plenum.

Stephens, R.D. (1997). National trends in school violence: Statistics and prevention strategies. In A.P. Goldstein & J.C. Conoley (Eds.), *School violence intervention: A practical handbook* (pp. 72–90). New York: Guilford Press.

Stermac, L.E., & Quinsey, V.L. (1986). Social competence among rapists. *Behavioral Assessment, 8,* 171–185.

Stermac, L.E., & Segal, S.V. (1989). Adult sexual contact with children: An examination of cognitive factors. *Behavior Therapy, 20,* 573–584.

Stern, J. (1999). *The ultimate terrorists.* Cambridge, MA: Harvard University Press.

Stern, J. (2003). *Terror in the name of God: Why religious militants kill.* New York: Ecco.

Sternberg, K.J., Lamb, M.E., Guterman, E., & Abbott, C.B. (2006). Effects of early and later family violence on children's behavior problems and depression: A longitudinal, multi-informant perspective. *Child Abuse and Neglect, 30,* 283–306.

Sternheimer, K. (2007). Do video games kill? *Contexts, 6,* 13–17.

Steuve, A., & Link, B.G. (1997). Violence and psychiatric disorders: Results from an epidemiological study of young adults in Israel. *Psychiatric Quarterly, 68,* 327–342.

Stewart, A.E. (1999). Complicated bereavement and posttraumatic stress disorder following fatal car crashes: Recommendations for death notification practice. *Death Studies, 23,* 289–321.

Stewart, E.A., Elifson, K.W., & Sterk, C.E. (2004). Integrating the general theory of crime into an explanation of violent victimization among female offenders. *Justice Quarterly, 21,* 159–181.

Stipek, D. (1997). Success in school—for a head start in life. In S.S. Luthar, J.A. Burack, D. Cicchetti & J.R. Weisz (Eds.), *Developmental psychopathology: Perpsectives on adjustment, risk, and disorder* (pp. 75–92). New York: Cambridge University Press.

Stirling, J., Lewis, S., Hopkins, R., & White, C. (2005). Cannabis use prior to first onset psychosis predicts spared neurocognition at 10-year follow-up. *Schizophrenia Research, 75,* 135–137.

Stompe, T., Friedman, A., Ortwein, G., Strobl, R., Chaudhry, H.R., Najam, N., & Chaudhdry, M.R. (1999). Comparisons of delusions among schizophrenics in Austria and Pakistan. *Psychopathology, 32,* 225–234.

Stone, A.V. (1995). Law enforcement psychological fitness for duty: Clinical issues. In M.I. Kurke & E.M. Scrivner (Eds.), *Police psychology into the 21st century* (pp. 109–131).

Stone, A.V. (2000). *Fitness for duty: Principles, methods, and legal issues.* Boca Raton: CRC Press.

Stone, M.H. (1989a). Long-term outcome in personality disorders. *British Journal of Psychiatry, 162,* 299–313.

Stone, M.H. (1989b). Murder in the narcissistic personality disorder. *Psychiatric Clinics of North America, 12,* 643–651.

Stone, M.H. (2001). Serial sexual homicide: Biological, psychological, and sociological aspects. *Journal of Personality Disorders, 15,* 1–18.

Stone, M.H. (2007). Violent crimes and their relationship to personality disorders. *Personality and Mental Health, 1,* 138–153.

Storm-Mathiesen, A., & Vaughn, P. (1994). Conduct disorder patients 20 years later: A personal follow-up study. *Acta Psychiatrica Scandinavica, 89,* 416–420.

Stoudemire, A. (1994). *Clinical psychiatry for medical students.* New York: Lippincott.

Stout, M. (2005). *The sociopath next door.* New York: Broadway Books.

Stouthamer-Loeber, M., & Wei, E.H. (1998). The precursors of young fatherhood and its effect on delinquency of teenage males. *Journal of Adolescent Health, 22,* 56–65.

Stouthamer-Loeber, M., & Wei, E.H., Loeber, R., & Masten, A.F. (2004). Desistance from persistent serious delinquency in the transition to adulthood. *Development and Psychopathology, 16,* 897–918.

Stover, C.S. (2005). Domestic violence research: What have we learned and where do we go from here? *Journal of Interpersonal Violence, 20,* 448–454.

Strang, H. (2002). *Repair or revenge: Victims and restorative justice.* London: Oxford University Press.

Strauss, I., & Savitsky, N. (1934). Head injury: Neurologic and psychiatric aspects. *Archives of Neurology and Psychiatry, 31,* 893–955.

Streissguth, A.P., Randels, S.P., & Smith, D.F. (1991). A test-retest study of intelligence in patients with fetal alcohol syndrome: Implications for care. *Journal of the American Academy of Child and Adolescent Psychiatry, 30,* 584–587.

Strentz, T. (1988). A terrorist psychological profile. *FBI Law Enforcement Bulletin, 57*(4), 13–19.

Stretesky, P.B., & Lynch, M.J. (2001). The relationship between lead exposure and homicide. *Archives of Pediatrics and Adolescent Medicine, 155,* 579–582.

Strickland, S.M. (2008). Female sex offenders: Exploring issues of personality, trauma, and cognitive distortions. *Journal of Interpersonal Violence, 23,* 474–489.

Strube, M., & Barbour, L. (1984). Factors related to the decision to leave an abusive relationship. *Journal of Marriage and the Family, 46,* 837–844.

Stuart, G.L., Moore, T.M., Ramsey, S.E., & Kahler, C.W. (2004). Hazardous drinking and relationship violence perpetration and victimization in women arrested for domestic violence. *Journal of Studies on Alcohol, 65,* 46–53.

Stuss, D.T., & Benson, D.F. (1984). Neuropsychological studies of the frontal lobes. *Psychological Bulletin, 95,* 3–28.

Stuss, D.T., Benson, D.F., & Kaplan, E.F. (1983). The involvement of orbitofrontal cerebrum in cognitive tasks. *Neuropsychologia, 21,* 235–248.

Stuss, D., Gow, C., & Hetherington, R. (1992). "No longer Gage." Frontal lobe dysfunction and emotion changes. *Journal of Consulting and Clinical Psychology, 60,* 349–359.

Stuss, D.T., & Knight, R.T. (2002). *Principles of frontal lobe function.* New York: Oxford Univesrity Press.

Sullivan, C., Basta, J., Tan, C., & Davidson, W. (1992). After the crisis: A needs assessment of women leaving a domestic violence shelter. *Violence and Victims, 7,* 267–274.

Sullivan, C., Campbell, R., Angelique, H., Eby, K., & Davidson, W. (1994). An advocacy intervention program for women with abusive partners: Six month follow-up. *American Journal of Community Psychology, 11,* 101–122.

Sullivan, J., & Beech, A. (2002). Professional perpetrators: Sex offenders who use their employment to target and sexually abuse the children with whom they work. *Child Abuse Review, 11,* 153–167.

Sullivan, J., & Beech, A. (2004). Assessing Internet sex offenders. In M.C. Calder (Ed.), *Child sexual abuse and the Internet: Tackling the new frontier* (pp. 69–83). Lyme Regis, UK: Russell House.

Sullivan, P.M., & Knutson, J.F. (2003). Maltreatment and disabilities: A population-based epidemiological study. *Journal of Early Intervention, 1,* 2-133.

Sumer, M.M., Atik, L., Unal, A., Emre, U., & Atasoy, H.T. (2007). Frontal lobe epilepsy presented as ictal aggression. *Neurological Science, 28,* 48–51.

Sun, I.Y. (2007). Policing domestic violence: Does officer gender matter? *Journal of Criminal Justice, 35,* 581–595.

Surette, R. (2006). *Media, crime and criminal justice: Images, realities and policies.* Belmont, CA: Wadsworth.

Susman, E.J. (2006). Psychobiology of persistent antisocial behaviour: Stress, early vulnerability and the attenuation hypothesis. *Neuroscience and Biobehavioral Reviews, 30,* 376–389.

Susskind, L., & Field, P. (1996). *Dealing with an angry public: The mutual gains approach to resolving disputes.* New York: Free Press.

Sutherland, E.H. (1929). The person versus the act in criminology. *Cornell Law Quarterly, 14,* 159–167.

Sutherland, E.H. (1932). Social process in behavior problems. *Publications of the American Sociological Society, 26,* 55–61.

Sutherland, E.H. (1934). *Principles of criminology* (2nd ed.). Philadelphia: Lippincott.

Sutherland, E.H., & Cressey, D. (1974). *Principles of criminology* (7th ed.). Philadelphia: Lippincott.

Sutker, P.B., & Allain, A.N. (1987). Cognitive abstraction, shifting, and control: Clinical sample comparisons of psychopaths and nonpsychopaths. *Journal of Abnormal Psychology, 96,* 73–75.

Sutton, J., Smith, P.K., & Swettenham, J. (1999). Social cognition and bullying: Social inadequacy or skilled manipulation? *British Journal of Developmental Psychology, 17,* 435–450.

Swan, S.C., & Snow, D.L. (2002). A typology of women's use of violence in intimate relationships. *Violence Against Women, 57,* 557–583.

Swanberg, J., & Logan, T. (2005). Domestic violence and employment: A qualitative study of rural and urban women. *Journal of Occupational Health Psychology, 10,* 3–17.

Swanberg, J., Logan, T.K., & Macke, C. (2006a). The consequences of partner violence on employment in the workplace. In K. Kelloway, J. Barling, & J. Hurrell (Eds.), *Handbook of workplace violence* (pp. 351–379). Thousand Oaks, CA: Sage.

Swanberg, J., Macke, C., & Logan, T.K. (2007). Working women making it work: Intimate partner violence, employment, and workplace support. *Journal of Interpersonal Violence, 22,* 292–311.

Swanberg, J.E., Logan, T.K., & Marke, C. (2006). The consequences of partner violence on employment and the workplace. In E.K. Kelloway, J. Barling & J.J. Hurrell (Eds.), *Handbook of workplace violence* (pp. 351–380). Thousand Oaks, CA: Sage.

Swann, A.C., Dougherty, D.M., & Pazzaglia, P.J. (2004). Impulsivity: A link between bipolar disorder and substance abuse. *Bipolar Disorders, 6,* 204–212.

Swanson, J.W. (1993). Alcohol abuse, mental disorder, and violent behavior: An epidemiologic inquiry. *Alcohol Health and Research World, 17,* 123–132.

Swanson, J.W., Borum, R., Swartz, M., & Monahan, J. (1996). Psychotic symptoms and disorders and the risk of violent behavior in the community. *Criminal Behavior and Mental Health, 6,* 317–332.

Swanson, J.W., Holzer, C.E., Ganju, V.K., & Jono, R.T. (1990). Violence and psychiatric disorder in the community: Evidence from the epidemiologic catchment area surveys. *Hospital and Community Psychiatry, 41,* 761–770.

Swanson, J.W., Swartz, M.S., Van Dorn, R.A., Ellenbogen, E.B., Wagner, H.R., & Rosenheck, R.A. (2006). A national study of violent behavior in persons with schizophrenia. *Archives of General Psychiatry, 63,* 490–499.

Swerdlow, R., & Burns, J. (2002). Brain tumor causes uncontrolled pedophilia. *New Scientist,* October, pp. 14–17.

Sykes, G., & Matza, D. (1957). Techniques of neutralization: A theory of delinquency. *American Journal of Sociology, 22,* 664–670.

Symblett, G.J., & Wilson, D.N. (1993). Asperger's syndrome: Three cases and a discussion. *Journal of Intellectual Disability Research, 37,* 85–94.

Symons, D. (1979). *The evolution of human sexuality.* New York: Oxford University Press.

Tackett, J.L., Krueger, R.F., Iacono, W.G., & McGue, M. (2005). Symptom-based subfactors of DSM-defined conduct disorder: Evidence for etiological distinctions. *Journal of Abnormal Psychology, 114,* 483–487.

Taff, M.L., & Boglioli, L.R. (1997). Gay homicides and "overkill." *American Journal of Forensic Medicine and Pathology, 18,* 411–413.

Takahashi, H., Yahata, N., Koeda, M., Matsuda, T., & Asai, K. (2004). Brain activation associated with evaluative processes of guilt and embarrassment: An fMRI study. *Neuroimage, 23,* 967–974.

Tallichet, S.E., & Hensley, C. (2004). Exploring the link between recurrent acts of childhood and adolescent animal cruelty and subsequent violent crime. *Criminal Justice Review, 29,* 304–316.

Tanay, E. (1976). Reactive homicide. *Journal of Forensic Sciences, 21,* 76.

Tancredi, L. (2005). *Hardwired behavior: What neuroscience reveals about morality.* New York: Cambridge University Press.

Tang, C.M., & Nunez, N. (2003). Effects of defendant age and juror bias on judgment of culpability: What happens when a juvenile is tried as an adult? *American Journal of Criminal Justice, 28,* 37–52.

Tangney, J.P., Mashek, D., & Stuewig, J. (2007). Working at the social-clinical-community-criminology interface: The George Mason University Inmate Study. *Journal of Social and Clinical Psychology, 26,* 1–21.

Tardiff, K. (1984). Characteristics of assaultive patients in private hospitals. *American Journal of Psychiatry, 141,* 1232–1235.

Tardiff, K. (1997). Evaluation and treatment of violent patients. In D.M. Stoff, J. Breiling & J.D. Maser (Eds.), *Handbook of antisocial behavior* (pp. 445–453). New York: Wiley.

Tardiff, K. (1995). The risk of being attacked by patients: Who, how often, and where? In B.S. Eichelman & A.C. Hartwig (Eds.), *Patient violence and the clinician* (pp. 13–20). Washington, DC: American Psychiatric Association.

Tardiff, K. (1998). Unusual diagnoses among violent patients. *Psychiatric Clinics of North America, 21,* 567–576.

Tardiff, K. (2001). Axis II disorders and dangerousness. In G-F. Pinard & L. Pagani (Eds.), *Clinical assessment of dangerousness: Empirical contributions* (pp. 103–120). New York: Cambridge University Press.

Tardiff, K., & Koenigsberg, H.W. (1985). Assaultive behavior among psychiatric outpatients. *American Journal of Psychiatry, 142,* 960–963.

Tarter, R.E., Hegedus, A.M., Alterman, A.I., & Katz-Garris, L. (1983). Cognitive capacities of juvenile violent, nonviolent and sexual offenders. *Journal of Nervous and Mental Disease, 171,* 564–567.

Tarter, R.E., Hegedus, A.M., Winston, M.E., & Alterman, A.I. (1984). Neuropsychological, personality, and family characteristics of physically abused children. *Journal of the American Academy of Child Psychiatry, 23,* 668–674.

Tateno, A., Jorge, R., & Robinson, R. (2003). Clinical correlates of aggressive behavior after traumatic brain injury. *Journal of Neuropsychiatry and Clinical Neurosciences, 15,* 155–160.

Taveras, H., Zilberman, M.L., Hodgins, D.C. (2005). Comparison of craving between pathological gamblers and alcoholics. *Alcohol: Clinical and Experimental Research, 29,* 1427–1431.

Taylor, J., Iacono, W.G., & McGue, M. (2000). Evidence for a genetic etiology of early-onset delinquency. *Journal of Abnormal Psychology, 109,* 634–643.

Taylor, J.S. (1997). *Neurolaw: Brain and spinal cord.* Washington DC: ATLA Press.

Taylor, M., & Quayle, E. (1994). *Terrorist lives.* London: Brassey's.

Taylor, M., & Quayle, E. (2003). *Child pornography: An internet crime.* London: Brunner-Routledge.

Taylor, M., & Ryan, H. (1988). Fanaticism, political suicide and terrorism. *Terrorism, 11,* 91–111.

Taylor, P.J., & Gunn, J. (1999). Homicides by people with mental illness: Myth and reality. *British Journal of Psychiatry, 174,* 9–14.

Tedeschi, J., & Felson, R. (1994). *Violence, aggression, and coercive actions.* Washington, DC: American Psychological Association.

Tellegen, A. (1985). Structure of mood and personality and their relevance to assessing anxiety, with an emphasis on self-report. In A.H. Tuma & J.D. Maser (Eds.), *Anxiety and the anxiety disorders* (pp. 681–706). Hillsdale, NJ: Erlbaum.

Tengstrom, A., Grann, M., Langstrom, N., & Kullgren, G. (2000). Psychopathy (PCL-R) as a predictor of violent recidivism among criminal offenders with schizophrenia. *Law and Human Behavior, 24,* 45–58.

Tengstrom, A., Hodgins, S., Grann, M., Langstrom, N., & Kullgren, G. (2004). Schizophrenia and criminal offending: The role of psychopathy and substance use disorders. *Criminal Justice and Behavior, 31,* 367–391.

Tengstrom, A., Hodgins, S., & Kullgren, G. (2001). Men with schizophrenia who behave violently: The usefulness of an early- versus late-start offender typology. *Schizophrenia Bulletin, 27,* 205–218.

Tennes, K., & Krey, M. (1985). Children's adrenocortical response to classroom activities in elementary school. *Psychosomatic Medicine, 47,* 451–460.

Tenser, J. (2005). Fans take violence in stride. *Advertising Age, 76,* 5–9.

Teplin, L.A., Abram, K., & McClelland, G. (1996). Prevalence of psychiatric disorders among incarcerated women I: Pretrial jail detainees. *Archives of General Psychiatry, 53,* 505–512.

Testa, M., Vanzile-Tamsen, C., & Livingston, J.A. (2004). The role of victim and perpetrator intoxication on sexual assault outcomes. *Journal of Studies on Alcohol, 65,* 320–329.

Thackrah, J.R. (2004). *Dictionary of terrorism* (2nd ed.). London: Routledge.

Thanos, P.K., Taintor, N.B., Rivera, S.N., Umegaki, H., Ikari, H., Roth, G., Ingram, D.K., Hitzemann, J.S., Fowler, J.S., Gatley, S.J., Wang, G.J., & Volkow, N.D. (2004). DRD2 gene transfer into the nucleus accumbens core of the alcohol preferring and nonpreferring rats attenuates alcohol drinking. *Alcoholism: Clinical and Experimental Research, 28,* 720–728.

Thilmany, J. (2007). In case of emergency: Training managers can reduce workplace violence and prepare organizations to cope in a crisis. *HR Magazine,* November, pp. 79–83.

Thomas, A., & Chess, S. (1977). *Temperament and development.* New York: Brunner/Mazel.

Thompson, D., & Brown, H. (1997). Men with intellectual abilities who sexually abuse: A review of the literature. *Journal of Applied Research in Intellectual Disabilities, 46,* 57–73.

Thompson, G.N. (1970). Cerebral lesions simulating schizophrenia: Three case reports. *Biological Psychiatry, 2,* 59–64.

Thompson, J.S., Stuart, G.L., & Holden, C.E. (1992). Command hallucinations and legal insanity. *Forensic Reports, 5,* 29–43.

Thompson, P.M., Cannon, T.D., Narr, K.L., van Erp, T., Poutanen, V.-P., & Huttunen, M. (2001). Genetic influences on brain structure. *Nature Neuroscience, 4,* 1253–1258.

Thompson v. Oklahoma, 487 U.S. 815 (1998).

Thornberry, T.P., & Farnsworth, M. (1982). Social correlates of criminal involvement: Further evidence on the relationship between social status and criminal behavior. *American Sociological Review, 47,* 505–518.

Thornberry, T.P., Freeman-Gallant, A., & Lizotte, A.J. (2003). Linked lives: The intergenerational transmission of antisocial behavior. *Journal of Abnormal Child Psychology, 31,* 171–184.

Thornhill, N.W., & Thornhill, R. (1990a). Evolutionary analysis of the psychological pain of rape victims I: The effects of victim's age and marital status. *Ethology and Sociobiology, 11,* 155–176.

Thornhill, N.W., & Thornhill, R. (1990b). Evolutionary analysis of the psychological pain of rape victims II: The effects of stranger, friend, and family member offenders. *Ethology and Sociobiology, 11,* 177–193.

Thornhill, R. (1980). Rape in panorpa scorpionflies and a general rape hypothesis. *Animal Behavior, 28,* 52–59.

Thornhill, R., & Palmer, C. (2000). *A natural history of rape: Biological bases of sexual coercion.* Cambridge, MA: MIT Press.

Thornhill, R., & Thornhill, N.W. (1983). Human rape: An evolutionary analysis. *Ethology and Sociobiology, 4,* 137–173.

Thornhill, R., & Thornhill, N.W. (1992). The evolutionary psychology of men's coercive sexuality. *Behavioral and Brain Sciences, 15,* 363–421.

Tibbetts, S.G. (2003). Selfishness, social control, and emotions: An integrated perspective on criminality. In A. Walsh & L. Ellis (Eds.), *Biosocial criminology: Challenging environmentalism's supremacy* (pp. 83–101). Happauge, NY: Nova Science.

Tiedens, L.Z. (2001). The effect of anger on the hostile inferences of aggressive and nonaggressive people: Specific emotions, cognitive processing, and chronic aceessibility. *Motivation and Emotion, 25,* 233–251.

Tiihonen, J. (2001). Recidivistic violent behavior and Axis I and Axis II disorders. In G-F. Pinard & L. Pagani (Eds.), *Clinical assessment of dangerousness: Empirical contributions* (pp. 121–135). New York: Cambridge University Press.

Tiihonen, J., Hakola, P., Eronen, M, Vartiainen, H., & Ryynanen, O-P. (1996). Risk of homicidal behavior among discharged forensic psychiatric patients. *Forensic Science International, 79,* 123–129.

Tiihonen, J., Isohanni, M., Rasanen, P., Koiranen, M., & Moring, J. (1997). Specific major mental disorders and criminalilty: A 26-year prospective study of the 1966 Northern Finland birth cohort. *American Journal of Psychiatry, 154,* 840–845.

Tiihonen, J., Kuikka, J.T., Bergstrom, K.A., Karhu, J., Viinamaki, H., Lehtonen, J., Hallikainen, T., Yang, J., & Hakola, P. (1997). Single photon emission tomography imaging of monoamine transporters in impulsive violent behaviour. *European Journal of Nuclear Medicine, 24,* 1253–1260.

Tjaden, P., & Thoennes, N. (1998). *Stalking in America: Findings from the National Violence Against Women survey.* Washington, DC: National Intitute of Justice and Centers for Disease Control and Prevention.

Tjaden, P., & Thoennes, N. (2000a). *Extent, nature and consequences of intimate partner violence: Findings from the National Violence Against Women survey.* Washington, DC: National Intitute of Justice and Centers for Disease Control and Prevention.

Tjaden, P., & Thoennes, N. (2000b). *Full report of the prevalence, incidence, and consequences of violence against women.* Washington, DC: National Intitute of Justice and Centers for Disease Control and Prevention.

Tjaden, P., & Thoennes, N. (2000c). Prevalence and consequences of male-to-female and female-to-male intimate partner violence as measured by the National Violence Against Women Survey. *Violence Against Women, 6,* 142–161.

Toch, H. (1980). *Violent men* (rev. ed.). Cambridge, MA: Schnekman.

Toch, H., & Grant, J.D. (2005). *Police as problem solvers: How frontline workers can promote organizational and community change.* Washington, DC: American Psychological Association.

Toch, H.H. (1992). *Violent men: An inquiry into the psychology of violence* (2nd ed.). Washington DC: American Psychological Association.

Todd, J., & Dewhurst, K. (1955). The Othello syndrome: A study in the psychopathology of sexual jealousy. *Journal of Nervous and Mental Disease, 122* (4), 367-374.

Toga, A.W., & Thompson, P.M. (2005). Genetics of brain structure and intelligence. *Annual Review of Neuroscience, 28,* 1–23.

Tolman, R.M., & Raphael, J. (2000). A review of research on welfare and domestic violence. *Journal of Social Issues, 56,* 655–682.

Tolman, R.M., & Rosen, D. (2001). Domestic violence in the lives of women receiving welfare: Mental health, substance dependence, and economic well-being. *Violence Against Women, 7,* 141–158.

Tolnay, S.E., & Beck, E.M. (1992). *A festival of violence: An analysis of southern lynchings, 1882–1930.* Urbana, IL: University of Illinois Press.

Tomsen, S. (2005). "Boozers and bouncers": Masculine conflict, disengagement and the contemporary governance of drinking-related violence and disorder. *Australian and New Zealand Journal of Criminology, 38,* 283–297.

Tonin, E. (2004). The attachment styles of stalkers. *Journal of Forensic Psychiatry and Psychology, 15,* 584–590.

Tonkonogy, J.M. (1991). Violence and temporal lobe lesion: Head CT and MRI data. *Journal of Neuropsychiatry and Clinical Neurosciences, 3,* 189–196.

Toone, B.K., Edeh, J., Nanjee, M.N., & Wheeler, M. (1989). Hyposexuality and epilepsy: A community survey of hormonal and behavioural changes in male epileptics. *Psychological Medicine, 19,* 937–943.

Torrey, E.F. (1995). Jails and prisons: America's new mental hospitals. *American Journal of Public Health, 85,* 1611–1613.

Tran, T.T., Chowanadisai, W., Lonnendal, B., Le, L., Parker, M., Chicz-Demet, A., & Crinella, F.M. (2002). Effects of neonatal dietary manganese exposure on brain dopamine levels and neurocognitive functions. *Neurotoxicology, 145,* 1–7.

Travin, S., Cullen, K., & Proctor, B. (1990). Female sex offenders: Severe victims and victimizers. *Journal of Forensic Sciences, 35,* 140–150.

Tremblay, P., & Pare, P.O. (2003). Crime and destiny: Patterns in serious offenders' mortality rates. *Canadian Journal of Criminology and Criminal Justice, 45,* 299–326.

Tremblay, R.E. (2000). The development of aggressive behavior during childhood: What have we learned in the past century? *International Journal of Behavioral Development, 24,* 129–141.

Tremblay, R.E. (2001). The development of physical aggression during childhood and the prediction of later dangerousness. In G-F. Pinard & L. Pagani (Eds.), *Clinical assessment of dangerousness: Empirical contributions* (pp. 47–65). New York: Cambridge University Press.

Tremblay, R.E. (2003). Why socialization fails: The case of chronic physical aggression. In B.B. Lahey, T.E. Moffitt & A. Caspi (Eds.), *Causes of conduct disorder and juvenile delinquency* (pp. 182–224). New York: Guilford.

Trend, D. (2007). *The myth of media violence: A critical introduction.* Malden, MA: Blackwell.

Trimble, M. (2004). *Somatoform disorders: A medicolegal guide.* Cambridge, UK: Cambridge University Press.

Triplett, R. (1996). The growing threat: Gangs and juvenile offenders. In T.J. Flanagan & D.R. Longmire (Eds.), *Americans view crime and justice: A national public opinion survey* (pp. 137–150). Thousand Oaks, CA: Sage.

Trower, P., & Chadwick, P. (1995). Pathways to defense of the self: A theory of two types of paranoia. *Clinical Psychology: Science and Practice, 2,* 263–278.

Troy, M., & Sroufe, L.A. (1987). Victimization among preschoolers: Role of attachment relationship history. *Journal of the American Academy of Child and Adolescent Psychiatry, 26,* 166–172.

Turvey, B.E. (1999). *Criminal profiling: An introduction to behavioral evidence analysis.* New York: Academic Press.

Tuteur, W., & Gloptzer, J. (1959). Murdering mothers. *American Journal of Psychiatry, 116,* 447–452.

Twardosz, S., & Lutzker, J.R. (2010). Child maltreatment and the developing brain: A review of neuroscience perspectives. *Aggression and Violent Behavior, 15,* 59–68.

Tweed, R.G., & Dutton, D.G. (1998). A comparison of impulsive and instrumental subgroups of batterers. *Violence and Victims, 13,* 217–230.

Twemlow, S.W., & Fonagy, P. (2005). The prevalence of teachers who bully students in schools with differing levels of behavioral problems. *American Journal of Psychiatry, 162,* 2387–2389.

Uhde, T.W., Boulenger, J.P., Roy-Byrne, P.P., Geraci, M.P., Vittone, B.J., & Post, R.M. (1985). Longitudinal course of panic disorder. Clinical and biological considerations. *Progress in Neuropharmacology and Biological Psychiatry, 9,* 39–51.

Ullman, S.E. (2007). Mental health services seeking in sexual assault victims. *Women and Therapy, 30,* 61–84.

Ullman, S.E., Karabatsos, G., & Koss, M. P. (1999a). Alcohol and sexual assault in a national sample of college men. *Psychology of Women Quarterly, 23,* 673–689.

Ullman, S.E., Karabatsos, G., & Koss, M.P. (1999b). Alcohol and sexual assault in a national sample of college women. *Journal of Interpersonal Violence, 14,* 603–625.

Ullman, S.E., & Brecklin, L.R. (2000). Alcohol and adult sexual assault in a national sample of women. *Journal of Substance Abuse, 11,* 405–420.

Underwood, R.C., & Patch, P.C. (1999). Siblicide: A descriptive analysis of sibling homicide. *Homicide Studies, 3,* 333–348.

Uniform Crime Reports. (1999). *Crime in the United States 1999.* Washington, DC: U.S. Department of Justice.

United Nations. (1998). *United Nations 1996 demographic yearbook.* New York: United Nations.

Unnever, J.D., Cullen, F.T., & Pratt, T.C. (2003). Parental management, ADHD, and delinquent involvement: Reassessing Gottfredson and Hirschi's general theory. *Justice Quarterly, 20,* 471–500.

U.S. Department of Health and Human Services. (2005). *Child maltreatment 2003.* Washington, DC: U.S. Government Printing Office.

U.S. Department of Health and Human Services. (2006). *Child maltreatment 2004.* Washington, DC: US Government Printing Office.

U.S. Department of Health and Human Services. (2009). *Child maltreatment 2007.* Washington, DC: US Government Printing Office.

U.S. Department of Justice. (1994). *Domestic violence: Violence between intimates.* Washington, DC: Bureau of Justice Statistics.

U.S. Department of Justice. (1998a). *Violence by intimates: Analysis of data on crimes by current or former spouses, boyfriends, and girlfriends.* Washington, DC: US Department of Justice.

U.S. Department of Justice. (1998b). *Youth gangs: An overview.* Washington, DC: Office of Juvenile Justice and Delinquency Prevention.

U.S. Department of Justice. (2006). *Criminal offender statistics.* Washington, DC: Bureau of Justice Statistics.

U.S. Department of Justice, Bureau of Justice Statistics. (1994). *Murder in families.* Washington, DC: US Government Printing Office.

U.S. Department of Justice, Bureau of Justice Statistics. (1997a). *Sex offenses and offenders: An analysis of data on rape and sexual assault.* Washington, DC: US Government Printing Office.

U.S. Department of Justice, Bureau of Justice Statistics. (1997b). *Sex offenses and offenders: Executive summary.* Washington, DC: US Government Printing Office.

U.S. Department of Justice, Bureau of Justice Statistics Crime Data Brief. (2000). *Homicide trends in the United States: 1998 update.* Washington, DC: Office of Justice Programs.

U.S. Department of Justice, Bureau of Justice Statistics Special Report. (1998). *Workplace violence, 1992–1996.* Washington, DC: Office of Justice Programs.

U.S. Department of Justice, Federal Bureau of Investigations. (2000). *Crime in the United States: Uniform crime reports 1999.* Washington, DC: US Government Printing Office.

U.S. Department of Justice, Federal Bureau of Investigations. (2007). *Crime in the United States: Uniform crime reports 2006.* Washington, DC: US Government Printing Office.

Vaillant, G.E. (1977). *Adaptation to life.* Boston: Little, Brown.

Vaillant, G.E. (1993). *The wisdom of the ego.* Cambridge: Harvard University Press.

Valdez, A. (2007). *Gangs: A guide to understanding street gangs* (5th ed.). San Clemente, CA: LawTech Publishing.

Vallone, D.C., & Hoffman, L.M. (2003). Preventing the tragedy of neonaticide. *Holistic Nursing Practice, 17,* 223–228.

van Alphen, S.P.J., Nijhuis, P.E.P., & Oei, T.I. (2007). Antisocial personality disorder in older adults: A qualitative study of Dutch forensic psychiatrists and forensic psychologists. *International Journal of Geriatric Psychiatry, 22,* 813–815.

Van Brunschot, E.G. (2003). Freedom and integrity: Relationships and assaults. *British Journal of Criminology, 43,* 122–140.

van der Kolk, B.A. (1996). The body keeps the score: Approaches to the psychobiology of posttraumatic stress disorder. In B.A. van der Kolk, A.C. McFarlane & L. Weisaeth (Eds.), *Traumatic stress: The effects of overwhelming experience on mind, body, and society* (pp. 214–241). New York: Guilford.

van der Kolk, B.A., & Fisler, R.E. (1994). Childhood abuse and neglect and loss of self-regulation. *Bulletin of the Menninger Clinic, 58,* 145–168.

van der Valk, J.C., Verhulst, F.C., Neale, M.C., & Boomsma, D.I. (1998). Longitudinal genetic analysis of problem behaviors in biologically related and unrelated adoptees. *Behavior Genetics, 28,* 365–380.

Vandiver, D.M. (2006). Female sex offenders: A comparison of solo offenders and co-offenders. *Violence and Victims, 21,* 339–354.

Vandiver, D.M., & Kercher, G. (2004). Offender and victim characteristics of registered female sexual offenders in Texas: A proposed typology of female sexual offenders. *Sexual Abuse: A Journal of Research and Treatment, 16,* 121–137.

Vandiver, D.M., & Walker, J.T. (2002). Female sex offenders: An overview and analysis of 40 cases. *Criminal Justice Review, 27,* 284–300.

Van Honk, J., & Schutter, D.J. (2006). Unmasking feigned sanity: A neurobiological model of emotion processing in primary psychopathy. *Cognitive Neuropsychiatry, 11,* 285–306.

van Lier, P., der Ende, J., Koot, H., & Verhulst, F. (2007). Which better predicts conduct problems? The relationship trajectories of conduct problems with ODD and ADHD symptoms from childhood to adolescence. *Journal of Child Psychology and Psychiatry, 48,* 601–608.

van Marle, H. (2009). Mental disorders and criminal behavior. In R.N. Kocsis (Ed.), *Applied criminal psychology: A guide to forensic behavioral sciences* (pp. 5–19). Springfield, IL: Charles C Thomas.

Van Natta, D. (2003). Terror's ultimate weapon. *New York Times,* August 24, pp. 1, 7.

Van Ness, D., & Strong, K.H. (2002). *Restoring justice* (2nd ed.). Cincinnati, OH: Anderson.

Van Praag, H.M. (1996). Faulty cortisol/serotonin interplay. *Psychiatry Research, 65,* 143–157.

Van Zandt, C.R. (1993). Suicide by cop. *The Police Chief, 60,* 24–30.

Vartiainen, H.T., & Hakola, H.P.A. (1992). How changes in mental health law adversely affect offenders discharged from security hospital. *Journal of Forensic Psychiatry, 3,* 563–570.

Vasterling, J.J., MacDonald, H.Z., Ulloa, E.W., & Rodier, N. (2010). Neuropsychological correlates of PTSD: A military perspective. In C.H. Kennedy & J.L. Moore (Eds.), *Military psychology* (pp. 321–359). New York: Springer.

Vaughn, B.E., & Santos, A.J. (2007). An evolutionary/ecological account of aggressive behavior and trait aggression in human children and adolescents. In P.H. Hawley, T.D. Little & P.C. Rodkin (Eds.), *Aggression and adaptation: The bright side to bad behavior* (pp. 31–64). Mahwah, NJ: Lawrence Erlbaum.

Vazsonyi, A.T., Pickering, L.E., & Bolland, J.M. (2006). Growing up in a dangerous developmental milieu: The effects of parenting processes on adjustment in inner-city African American adolescents. *Journal of Community Psychology, 34,* 47–73.

Vazsonyi, A.T., Wittekind, J.E.C., Belliston, L.M., & Van Loh, T.D. (2004). Extending the general theory of crime to "the East": Low self-control in Japanese late adolescents. *Journal of Quantitative Criminology, 20,* 189–216.

Vega, G., & Comer, D.R. (2005). Bullying and harassment in the workplace. In R.E. Kidwell & C.L. Martin (Eds.), *Managing organizational deviance* (pp. 183–209). Thousand Oaks, CA: Sage.

Ventura, L., Cassel, C., Jacoby, J., & Huang, B. (1998). Case management and recidivism of mentally ill persons released from jail. *Psychiatric Services, 49,* 1330–1337.

Verduin, M.L., Carter, R.E., Brady, K.T., Myrick, H., & Timmerman, M.A. (2005). Health service use among persons with comorbid bipolar and substance use disorders. *Psychiatric Services, 56,* 475–480.

Verlinden, S., Hersen, M., & Thomas, J. (2000). Risk factors in school shootings. *Clinical Psychology Review, 20,* 3–56.

Vess, J., Murphy, C., & Arkowitz, S. (2004). Clinical and demographic differences between sexually violent predators and other concomitant types in a state forensic hospital. *Journal of Forensic Psychiatry and Psychology, 15,* 669–681.

Vickerman, K.A., & Margolin, G. (2009). Rape treatment outcome research: Empirical findings and state of the literature. *Clinical Psychology Review, 29,* 431–448.

Victoroff, J. (2005). The mind of the terrorist: A review and critique of psychological approaches. *Journal of Conflict Resolution, 49,* 3–42.

Vien, A., & Beech, A.R. (2006). Psychopathy: Theory, measurement, and treatment. *Trauma, Violence, and Abuse, 7,* 1–21.

Vigil, J.D. (2003). Urban violence and street gangs. *Annual Review of Anthropology, 32,* 225–242.

Viljoen, J.L., & Grisso, T. (2007). Prospects for remediating juveniles' adjudicative incompetence. *Psychology, Public Policy, and Law, 13,* 87–114.

Viljoen, J.L., & Roesch, R. (2005). Competence to waive interrogation rights and adjudicative competence in adolescent defendants: Cognitive development, attorney contact, and psychological symptoms. *Law and Human Behavior, 29,* 723–742.

Vinson, D.E., & Davis, D.S. (1993). *Jury persuasion: Psychological strategies and trial techniques.* Little Falls, NJ: Glasser Legalworks.

Violanti, J.M. (1999). Death on duty: Police survivor trauma. In J.M. Violanti & D. Paton (Eds.), *Police trauma: Psychologial aftermath of civilian combat* (pp. 139–158). Springfield, IL: Charles C Thomas.

Violanti, J.M. (2007). Homicide-suicide in police families: Aggression full circle. *International Journal of Emergency Mental Health, 9,* 97–104.

Virkkunen, M. (1974). Observations on violence in schizophrenia. *Acta Psychiatrica Scandinavica, 50,* 145–151.

Virkkunen, M. (1985). Urinary free cortisol secretion in habitually violent offenders. *Acta Psychiatrica Scandinavica, 72,* 40–44.

Virkkunen, M., Eggert, M., Rawlings, R., & Linnoila, M. (1996a). A prospective follow-up study of alcoholic violent offenders and fire setters. *Archives of General Psychiatry, 53,* 523–529.

Virkkunen, M., Goldman, D., & Linnoila, M. (1996b). Serotonin in alcoholic violent offenders: Genetics of criminal and antisocial behavior. *Ciba Foundation Symposium, 194,* 168–177.

Virkkunen, M., Goldman, D., Nielsen, D.A., & Linnoila, M. (1995). Low brain serotonin turnover rate (low CSF 5-HIAA) and impulsive violence. *Journal of Psychiatry and Neuroscience, 20,* 271–275.

Vitacco, M.J., Neumann, C.S., & Wodushek, T. (2008). Differential relationships between the dimensions of psychopathy and intelligence: Replication with adult jail inmates. *Criminal Justice and Behavior, 35,* 48–55.

Vitanza, S., Vogel, L.C.M., & Marshall, L.L. (1995). Distress and symptoms of post-traumatic stress disorder in abused women. *Violence and Victims, 10,* 23–34.

Volavka, J. (1995). *Neurobiology of violence.* Washington, DC: American Psychiatric Press.

Volavka, J. (1999). The neurobiology of violence: An update. *Journal of Neuropsychiatry and Clinical Neuroscience, 11,* 307–314.

Volavka, J. (2002). *Neurobiology of violence* (2nd ed.). Washington, DC: American Psychiatric Publishing.

Volkan, V.D. (1997). *Blood lines: From ethnic pride to ethnic terrorism.* New York: Farrar, Straus & Giroux.

Volkow, N.D., Fowler, J.S., & Wang, G.-J. (2003). Positron emission tomography and single-photon emission computed tomography in substance abuse research. *Seminars in Nuclear Medicine, 33,* 114–128.

Volkow, N.D., Gillespie, H., Tancredi, L., & Hollister, L. (1995). The effects of marijuana in the human brain measured with regional brain glucose metabolism. In A. Biegon & N.D. Volkow (Eds.), *Sites of drug action in the human brain* (pp. 75–86). Boca Raton, FL: CRC Press.

Volkow, N.D., & Tancredi, L. (1987). Neural substrates of violent behaviour: A preliminary study with positron emission tomography. *British Journal of Psychiatry, 151,* 668–673.

Vollum, S., & Longmire, D.R. (2009). Giving voice to the dead: Last statements of the condemned. *Contemporary Justice Review, 12,* 5–26.

Von Bloch, L. (1996). Breaking the bad news when sudden death occurs. *Social Work in Health Care, 24,* 91–97.

von Krafft-Ebing, R. (1922/1972). *Psychopathia sexualis, with special reference to the antipathetic sexual instinct: A medico-forensic study* (rev ed. transl. F.J. Rebman). New York: Medical Art Agency.

Vorpagel, R.E. (1982). Painting psychological profiles: Charlatanism, coincidence, charisma or new science? *The Police Chief, 3,* 156–159.

Vorpagel, R.E., & Harrington, J. (1998). *Profiles in murder.* New York: Plenum.

Vossekuil, B., Reddy, M., & Fein, R. (2002). *The final report and findings of the Safe Schools Initiative: Implications for the prevention of school attacks in the United States.* Washington, DC: US Department of Education, Office of Elementary and Secondary Education, Safe and Drug-Free Schools Program, and US Secret Service, National Threat Assessment Center.

Wacholtz, S., & Mullaly, R. (1993). Policing the deinstitutionalized mentally ill: Toward an understanding of its function. *Crime, Law, and Social Change, 19,* 281–300.

Wainscot, J., Naylor, P., Sutcliffe, P., Tantam, D., & Williams, J. (2008). Relationships with peers and use of the school environment of mainstream secondary school pupils with Asperger Syndrome (High-Functioning Autism): A case-control study. *International Journal of Psychology and Psychological Therapy, 8,* 25–38.

Walgrave, L. (2000). How pure can a maximalist approach to restorative justice remain? Or can a purist model of restorative justice become maximalist? *Contemporary Justice Review, 3,* 415–432.

Walinder, J. (1965). Transvestism: Definition and evidence of occasional deviation from cerebral dysfunction. *International Journal of Neuropsychiatry, 1,* 567–573.

Walker, L.E. (1984). *The battered woman syndrome.* New York: Springer.

Walker, L.E. (1994). *Abused women and survivor therapy: A practical guide for the psychotherapist.* Washington, DC: American Psychological Association.

Wallace, C., Mullen, P.E., & Burgess, P. (2004). Criminal offending in schizophrenia over a 25-year period marked by deinstitutionalization and increasing prevalence of co-morbid substance use disorders. *American Journal of Psychiatry, 161,* 716–727.

Walsh, A. (2002a). *Biosocial criminology: Introduction and integration.* Cincinnati, OH: Anderson.

Walsh, A. (2002b). Essay review: Companions in crime: A biosocial perspective. *Human Nature Review, 2,* 169–178.

Walsh, A. & Beaver, K.M. (2008). The promise of evolutionary psychology in criminology: The examples of gender and age. In J.D. Duntley & T.K. Shackelford (Eds.), *Evolutionary forensic psychiatry: Darwinian foundations of crime and law* (pp. 20–37). New York: Oxford University Press.

Walsh, E., Buchanan, A., & Fahy, T. (2001). Violence and schizophrenia: Examining the evidence. *British Journal of Psychiatry, 180,* 490–495.

Walsh, K., Fortier, M.A., & Dilillo, D. (2010). Adult coping with childhood sexual abuse: A theoretical and empirical review. *Aggression and Violent Behavior, 15,* 1–13.

Walsh, S., & Hemenway, D. (2005). Intimate partner violence: Homicides followed by suicides in Kentucky. *Journal of the Kentucky Medical Association, 103,* 10–13.

Walsh, Z., Swogger, M.T., & Kosson, D.S. (2004). Psychopathy, IQ, and violence in European American and African American county jail inmates. *Journal of Consulting and Clinical Psychology, 72,* 1165–1169.

Walters, G.D. (1987). Child sex offenders and rapists in a military setting. *International Journal of Offender Therapy and Comparative Criminology, 31,* 261–269.

Walters, G.D. (1990). *The criminal lifestyle: Patterns of serious criminal conduct.* Newbury Park, CA: Sage.

Walters, G.D. (1995). The Psychological Inventory of Criminal Thinking Styles, Part I: Reliability and preliminary validity. *Criminal Justice and Behavior, 22,* 307–325.

Walters, G.D. (2002). The Psychological Inventory of Criminal Thinking Styles (PICTS): A review and meta-analysis. *Assessment, 9,* 278–291.

Waltz, J., Babcock, J.C., Jacobson, N.S., & Gottman, J.M. (2000). Testing a typology of batterers. *Journal of Consulting and Clinical Psychology, 68,* 658–669.

Wang, R., Bianchi, S., & Raley, S. (2005). Teenagers' internet use and family rules: A research note. *Journal of Marriage and Family, 67,* 1249–1258.

Ward, C. (1995). *Attitudes toward rape: Feminist and social psychological perspectives.* London: Sage.

Ward, T. (2000a). Sexual offenders' cognitive distortions as implicit theories. *Aggression and Violent Behavior, 5,* 491–507.

Ward, T. (2000b). Relapse prevention: Critique and reformulation. *Journal of Sexual Aggression, 5,* 118–133.

Ward, T., Hudson, S.M., & Keenan, T. (1998). A self-regulation model of the sexual offense process. *Sexual Abuse: A Journal of Research and Treatment, 10,* 141–157.

Ward, T., Hudson, S.M., & Marshall, W.L. (1996). Attachment style in sex offenders: A preliminary study. *Journal of Sex Research, 33,* 17–36.

Ward, T., & Keenan, T. (1999). Child molesters' implicit theories. *Journal of Interpersonal Violence, 14,* 821–838.

Warr, M. (2002). *Companions in crime: The social aspects of criminal conduct.* New York: Cambridge University Press.

Warren, J.I., & Hazelwood, R.R. (2002). Relational patterns associated with sexual sadism: A study of 20 wives and girlfriends. *Journal of Family Violence, 17,* 75–89.

Warren, J.I., Hazelwood, R.R., & Dietz, P.E. (1996). The sexually sadistic serial killer. *Journal of Forensic Sciences, 41,* 970–974.

Wasserman, J., Kappel, S., Coffin, R., Aronson, R., & Walton, A.J. (1986). Adolescent sex offenders. *Journal of the American Medical Association, 255,* 181–182.

Watts, C. Keogh, E., Ndlovu, M., & Kwaramba, R. (1998). Withholding of sex and forced sex: Dimensions of violence against Zimbabwean women. *Reproductive Health Matters, 6,* 57–65.

Way B.B., Sawyer, D.A., Lilly, S.N., Moffitt, C., & Stapholz, B.J. (2008). Characteristics of inmates who received a diagnosis of serious mental illness upon entry to New York State Prison. *Psychiatric Services, 59,* 1335–1337.

Weaver, T.L., & Clum, G.A. (1993). Early family environments and traumatic experiences associated with borderline personality disorder. *Journal of Consulting and Clinical Psychology, 61,* 1068–1075.

Websdale, N. (1999). *Understanding domestic homicide.* Boston: Northeastern University Press.

Webster, C.D., Douglas, K.S., Belfrage, H., & Link, B. (2000). Capturing change: An approach to managing violence and improving mental health. In S. Hodgins & R. Miller-Isberner (Eds.), *Violence among the mentally ill* (pp. 119–144). Dordrecht, Netherlands: Kluwer/Academic.

Webster, C.D., Douglas, K.S., Eaves, D., & Hart, S.D. (1997). *HCR-20: Assessing risk for violence* (Version 2). Vancouver, BC: Mental Health Law & Policy Institute: Simon Fraser University.

Webster, C.D., & Jackson, M.A. (Eds.) (1997). *Impulsivity: Theory, assessment, and treatment.* New York: Guilford.

Weekes-Shackelford, V.A., & Shackelford, T.K. (2004). Methods of filicide: Stepparents and genetic parents kill differently. *Violence and Victims, 19,* 75–81.

Weinberg, L., & Eubank, W.L. (1987). Italian women terrorists. *Terrorism: An International Journal, 9,* 241–262.

Weiner, H. (1992). *Perturbing the organism: The biology of stressful experience.* Chicago: University of Chicago Press.

Weinscheimer, R.L., Schermer, C.R., Malcoe, L.H., Balduf, L.M., & Bloomfield, L.A. (2005). Severe intimate partner violence and alcohol use among female trauma patients. *Journal of Trauma, Injury, Infection, and Critical Care, 58,* 22–29.

Weis, K., & Borges, S.S. (1973). Victimology and rape: The case of the legitimate victim. *Issues in Criminology, 8,* 71–115.

Weisel, D.L. (2002). The evolution of street gangs: An examination of form and variation. In W. Reed & S. Decker (Eds.), *Responding to gangs: Evaluation and research* (pp. 25–65). Washington, DC: US Department of Justice, National Institute of Justice.

Weisman, A.M., Ehrenclou, M., & Sharma, K.K. (2002). Double parricide: Forensic analysis and psycholegal implications. *Journal of Forensic Sciences, 47,* 313–317.

Weisman, A.M., & Sharma, K.K. (1997). Forensic analysis and psychological implications of parricide and attempted parricide. *Journal of Forensic Sciences, 42,* 1107–1113.

Weiss, E.M., Kohler, C.G., Nolan, K.A., Czobor, P., & Volavka, J. (2006). The relationship between history of violent and criminal behavior and recognition of facial expression of emotions in men with schizophrenia and schizoaffective disorder. *Aggressive Behavior, 32,* 1–8.

Wekerle, C., Wolfe, D.A., Hawkins, D.L., Pittman, A.L., Glickman, A., & Lovald, B.E. (2001). Childhood maltreatment, posttraumatic stress symptomatology, and adolescent dating violence: Considering the value of adolescent perceptions of abuse and a trauma mediational model. *Development and Psychopathology, 13,* 847–871.

Wellard, S. (2001). Cause and effect. *Community Care,* March, pp. 26–27.

Wellman, H.M. (1990). *The child's theory of the mind.* Cambridge, MA: MIT Press.

Wells, J., & Bowers, L. (2002). How prevalent is violence towards nurses working in general hospitals in the UK? *Journal of Advanced Nursing, 24,* 326–333.

Wells, M.G. (1987). Adolescent violence against parents: An assessment. *Family Therapy, 14,* 125–133.

Sells, P.J. (1993). Preparing for sudden death: Social work in the emergency room. *Social Work, 38,* 339–342.

Welte, J.W., & Abel, E.L. (1989). Homicide: drinking by the victim. *Journal of Studies on Alcohol, 50,* 197–201.

Wenzel, M., Okimoto, T.G., Feather, N.T., & Platow, M.J. (2008). Retributive and restorative justice. *Law and Human Behavior, 32,* 375–389.

Werman, D.S. (1984). *The practice of supportive psychotherapy.* New York: Brunner/Mazel.

Werner, E.E., & Smith, R.S. (1992). *Overcoming the odds: High risk children from birth to adulthood.* Ithaca, NY: Cornell University Press.

Wessely, S.C., Buchanan, A., Reed, A., Cutting, J., Garety, P., & Taylor, P. (1993). Acting on delusions I: Prevalence. *British Journal of Psychiatry, 163,* 69–76.

Wessely, S.C., Castle, D., Douglas, A.J., & Taylor, P.J. (1994). The criminal careers of incident cases of schizophrenia. *Psychological Medicine, 24,* 483–502.

Wessely, S.C., & Taylor, P.J. (1991). Madness and crime: Criminology versus psychology. *Criminal Behaviour and Mental Health, 1,* 193–228.

West, D.A., & Lichtenstein, B. (2006). Andrea Yates and the criminalization of the filicidal maternal body. *Feminist Criminology, 1,* 173–187.

West, S.G., Friedman, S.H., & Resnick, P.J. (2009). Fathers who kill their children: An analysis of the literature. *Journal of Forensic Sciences, 54,* 463–468.

Wettersten, K., Rudolf, S., Faul, K., Gallagher, K., Transgrud, H., & Adams, K. (2004). Freedom through self-sufficiency: A qualitative examination of the impact of domestic violence on the working lives of women in shelter. *Journal of Counseling Psychology, 5,* 447–462.

Wheaton, S. (2001). Personal accounts: Memoirs of a compulsive firesetter. *Psychiatric Services, 52,* 1035–1036.

Whipple, E.E., & Webster-Stratton, C. (1991). The role of parental stress in physically abusive families. *Child Abuse and Neglect, 15,* 279–291.

Whitaker, R. (2002). *Mad in America: Bad science, bad medicine, and the enduring mistreatment of the mentally ill.* Cambridge, MA: Perseus.

White, H.R., & Widom, C.S. (2003). Intimate partner violence among abused and neglected children in young adulthood: The mediating effects of early aggression, antisocial personality, hostility, and alcohol problems. *Aggressive Behavior, 29,* 332–345.

White, S.G., & Cawood, J.S. (1998). Threat management of stalking cases. In J.R. Meloy (Ed.), *The psychology of stalking* (pp. 296–315). San Diego, CA: Academic Press.

White, M.D., & Terry, K.J. (2008). Child sexual abuse in the Catholic Church: Revisiting the rotten apples explanation. *Criminal Justice and Behavior, 35,* 658–678.

White, R.E., Thornhill, S., & Hampson, E. (2006). Entrepreneurs and evolutionary biology: The relationship between testosterone and new venture creation. *Organizational Behavior and Human Decision Processes, 100,* 21–34.

White, T.W., & Schimmel, D.J. (1995). Suicide prevention: A successful 5-step program. In L.M. Hayes (Ed.), *Prison suicide: An overview and guide to prevention* (pp. 46–57). Washington, DC: Department of Justice, National Institute of Corrections.

White, T.W., Schimmel, D.J., & Frickey, R. (2002). A comprehensive analysis of suicide in federal prisons: A fifteen-year review. *Journal of Correctional Health Care, 9,* 321–343.

Whiteside, S.P., & Lynam, D.R. (2001). The five-factor model and impulsivity: Using a structural model of personality to understand impulsivity. *Personality and Individual Differences, 30,* 669–689.

Whitfield, C.L., Anda, R.F., Dube, S.R., & Felitti, V.J. (2003). Violent childhood experiences and the risk of intimate partner violence in adults: Assessment in a large health maintenance organization. *Journal of Interpersonal Violence, 18,* 166–185.

Whyte, S., Petch, E., Penny, C., & Reiss, D. (2007). Factors associated with stalking behaviour in patients admitted to a high security hospital. *Journal of Forensic Psychiatry and Psychology, 18,* 16–22.

Widom, C.S. (1977). A methodology for studying noninstitutionalized psychopaths. *Journal of Consulting and Clinical Psychology, 45,* 674–683.

Widom, C.S. (1989a). Child abuse, neglect, and adult behavior: Research design and findings on criminality, violence, and child abuse. *American Journal of Orthopsychiatry, 59,* 355–367.

Widom, C.S. (1989b). The cycle of violence. *Science, 244,* 160–166.

Wiebe, R.P. (2003). Reconciling psychopathy and low self-control. *Justice Quarterly, 20,* 297–336.

Wiehe, V.R. (1990). *Sibling abuse.* New York: Lexington Books.

Wikin, G. (1996). How the FBI paints portraits of the nation's most wanted. *U.S. News and World Report,* April 22, p. 32.

Wilczynski, A. (1995). Child killing by parents: A motivational model. *Child Abuse Review, 4,* 365–370.

Wildgruber, D., Hertrich, I., Riecker, A., Erb, M., Anders, S., & Grodd, W. (2004). Distinct frontal regions subserve evaluation of linguistic and emotional aspects of speech intonation. *Cerebral Cortex, 14,* 1384–1389.

Wilkey, I., Pearn, J., Petrie, G., & Nixon, J. (1982). Neonaticide, infanticide and child homicide. *Medicne, Science and the Law, 22,* 31–34.

Wilkowski, B.M., & Robinson, M.D. (2008). Putting the brakes on antisocial behavior: Secondary psychopathy and post-error adjustments in reaction time. *Personality and Individual Differences, 44,* 1807–1818.

Williams, D. (1969). Neural factors related to habitual aggression: Consideration of difference between those habitually aggressive and others who have committed crimes of violence. *Brain, 92,* 503–520.

Williams, G.J. (1976). Origins of filicidal impulses in the American way of life. *Journal of Clinical Child Psychology, 5,* 2–11.

Williams, M.B. (1999). Impact of duty-related death on officers' children: Concepts of death, trauma reactions, and treatment. In J.M. Violanti & D. Paton (Eds.), *Police trauma: Psychological aftermath of civilian combat* (pp. 159–174). Springfield, IL: Charles C Thomas.

Williamson, S., Hare, R., & Wong, S. (1987). Violence: Criminal psychopaths and their victims. *Canadian Journal of Behavioral Sciences, 19*, 454–462.

Wills, G. (2000). *Papal sin.* New York: Doubleday.

Wilson, A.E., Smith, M.D., Ross, H.S., & Ross, M. (2003). Young children's personal accounts of their sibling disputes. *Merrill-Palmer Quarterly, 50,* 39–60.

Wilson, D., McBride-Henry, K., & Huntington, A. (2004). Family violence: Walking the tightrope between maternal alienation and child safety. *Contemporary Nurse, 18,* 85–96.

Wilson, J.Q., & Herrnstein, R.J. (1985). *Crime and human nature: The definitive study of the causes of crime.* New York: Simon and Schuster.

Wilson, M., Bagliono, A., & Downing, D. (1989). Analyzing factors influencing readmission to a battered women's shelter. *Journal of Family Violence, 4,* 275–284.

Wilson, M., & Daly, M. (1985). Competitiveness, risk taking, and violence: The young male syndrome. *Ethology and Sociobiology, 6,* 59–73.

Wilson, M., & Daly, M. (1993a). The man who mistook his wife for a chattel. In J.H. Barkow, L. Cosmides & J. Tooby (Eds.), *The adapted mind: Evolutionary psychology and the generation of culture.* (pp. 289–322). New York: Oxford University Press.

Wilson, M., & Daly, M. (1993b). Spousal homicide risk and estrangement. *Violence and Victims, 8,* 3–15.

Wilson, M., & Daly, M. (1993c). Male sexual proprietariness and violence against women. *Current Directions in Psychological Science, 5,* 2–7.

Wilson, M., & Mesnick, S.L. (1997). An empirical test of the bodyguard hypothesis. In P.A. Gowaty (Ed.), *Feminism and evolutionary biology* (pp. 505–511). New York: Chapman & Hall.

Wilson, M.A. (2000). Toward a model of terrorist behavior in hostage-taking incidents. *Journal of Conflict Resolution, 44,* 403–24.

Wilson, M.I., & Daly, M. (1996). Male sexual proprietariness and violence against wives. *Current Directions in Psychological Science, 5,* 2–7.

Wilson, P., & Soothill, K. (1996). Psychological profiling: Red, green or amber? *The Police Journal,* January, pp. 12–20.

Windle, M. (1999). Psychopathy and antisocial personality disorder among alcoholic inpatients. *Journal of Studies on Alcohol, 60,* 330–336.

Winfree, L.T., Taylor, T.J, He, N., & Esbensen, F. (2006). Self-control and variability over time: Multivariate results using a 5-year, multisite panel of youths. *Crime and Delinquency, 52,* 253–286.

Wing, L. (1977). Asperger's syndrome: Management requires diagnosis. *Journal of Forensic Psychiatry, 8,* 253–257.

Wing, L. (1981). Asperger's syndrome: A clinical account. *Psychological Medicine, 11,* 115–129.

Wing, L. (1986). Clarification of Asperger's syndrome. *Journal of Autism and Developmental Disorders, 16,* 513–515.

Winlow, S., Hobbs, D., Lister, S., & Hadfield, P. (2001). Get ready to duck: Bouncers and the realities of ethnographic research on violent groups. *British Journal of Criminology, 41,* 536–548.

Winstanley, S. (2005). Cognitive model of patient aggression towards health care staff: The patient's perspective. *Work and Stress, 19,* 340–350.

Winter, C.D., Pringle, A.K., Clough, G.F., & Church, M.K. (2004). Raised parenchymal interleukin-6 levels correlate with improved outcome after traumatic brain injury. *Brain, 127,* 315–320.

Witkin, H.A., Mednick, S.A., & Schulsinger, F. (1976). Criminality, aggression, and intelligence among XYY and XXY men. *Science, 193,* 547–555.

Witkin, H.A., Mednick, S.A., & Schulsinger, F. (1977). Criminality, aggression, and intelligence among XYY and XXY men. In S.A. Mednick & K.O. Christiansen (Eds.), *Biosocial bases of criminal behavior* (pp. 165–188). New York: Gardner Press.

Witkin, H.A., Mednick, S.A., & Schulsinger, F., Bakkestrom, E., Christiansen, K.O., Goodenough, D.R., Hirschhorn, K., Lundsteen, C., Owen, D.R., Philip, J., Rubin, D.B., & Stocking, M. (1976). XYY and XXY men: Criminality and aggression. *Science, 193,* 547–555.

Wohlrab, S., Stahl, J., & Kappeler, P.M. (2007). Modifying the body: Motivation for getting tattooed and pierced. *Body Image, 4,* 87–95.

Wolak, J., Finkelhor, D., & Mitchell, K.J. (2004). Internet-initiated sex crimes against minors: Implications for prevention based on findings from a national study. *Journal of Adolescent Health, 35,* 11–20.

Wolak, J., Finkelhor, D., Mitchell, K.J., & Ybarra, M.L. (2008). Online "predators" and their victims: Myths, realities, and implications for prevention and treatment. *American Psychologist, 63,* 111–128.

Wolf, D.R. (1991). *The rebels: A brotherhood of outlaw bikers.* Toronto, Canada: University of Toronto Press.

Wolfgang, M.E. (1967). Criminal homicide and the subculture of violence. In M.E. Wolfgang (Ed.), *Studies in homicide* (pp. 3–14). New York: Harper & Row.

Wolfgang, M.E., & Ferracuti, F. (1967). *The subculture of violence.* London: Tavistock.

Wolfgang, M.E., Figlio, R.M., & Sellin, T. (1972). *Delinquency in a birth cohort.* Chicago: University of Chicago Press.

Wong, M.T., Lumsden, J., Fenton, G.W., & Fenwick, P.B. (1994). Electro-encephalograpy, computed tomography and violence ratings of male patients in a maximum-security mental hospital. *Acta Psychiatrica Scandinavica, 90,* 97–101.

Wood, J., Foy, D., Goguen, C., Pynoos, R., & James, B. (2002a). Violence exposure and PTSD among delinquent girls. *Journal of Aggression, Maltreatment and Trauma, 6,* 109–126.

Wood, J., Foy, D., Layne, C., Pynoos, R., & James, B. (2002b). An examination of the relationships between violence exposure, posttraumatic stress symptomatology, and delinquent activity. *Journal of Aggression, Maltreatment and Trauma, 6,* 127–145.

Wood, R.L. (1987). *Brain injury rehabilitation: A neurobehavioral approach.* Rockville, MD: Aspen.

Wood, R.L., & Liossi, C. (2006). Neuropsychological and neurobehavioral correlates of aggression following traumatic brain injury. *Journal of Neuropsychiatry and Clinical Neuroscience, 18,* 333–341.

Wood, R.L., Liossi, C., & Wood, L. (2005). The impact of head injury: Neurobehavioral sequelae on personal relationships: Preliminary findings. *Brain Injury, 19,* 845–853.

Wood, R.L., & Rutherford, N. (2004). Relationships between measured cognitive ability and reported psychosocial activity after bilateral frontal lobe injury: An 18 year follow-up. *Neuropsychological Rehabilitation, 14,* 329–350.

Wootton, J.M., Frick, P.J., Shelton, K.K., & Silverthorn, P. (1997). Ineffective parenting and childhood conduct problems: The moderating role of callous-unemotional traits. *Journal of Consulting and Clinical Psychology, 65,* 292–300.

Wozniak, J., Biederman, J., & Kiely, K. (1995). Mania-like symptoms suggestive of childhood onset bipolar disorder in clinically referred children. *Journal of the American Academy of Child and Adolescent Psychiatry, 34,* 867–876.

Wrangham, R., & Peterson, D. (1996). *Demonic males.* Boston: Houghton Mifflin.

Wright, J., Burgess, A., Laszlo, A., McCrary, G., & Douglas, J. (1996). A typology of interpersonal stalking. *Journal of Interpersonal Violence, 11,* 487–502.

Wright, J., & Hensley, C. (2003). From animal cruelty to serial murder: Applying the graduation hypothesis. *International Journal of Offender Therapy and Comparative Criminology, 47,* 71–88.

Wright, J.P., & Beaver, K.M. (2005). Do parents matter in creating self-control in their children? A genetically informed test of Gottfredson and Hirschi's theory of low self-control. *Criminology, 43,* 1169–1202.

Wright, P., Nobrega, J., Langevin, R., & Wortzman, G. (1990). Brain density and symmetry in pedophilic and sexually aggressive offenders. *Annals of Sex Research, 3,* 319–328.

Wright, R.T., Brookman, F., & Bennett, T. (2006). The foreground dynamics of street robbery in Britain. *British Journal of Criminology, 46,* 1–15.

Wright, R.T., & Decker, S.H. (1997). *Armed robbers in action.* Boston: Northeastern University Press.

Wrightsman, L.S. (2001). *Forensic psychology.* Stamford, CT: Wadsworth.

Wulach, J.S. (1983). Mania and crime: A study of 100 manic defendants. *Bulletin of the American Academy of Psychiatry and the Law, 11,* 69–75.

Yagil, D. (2008). When the customer is wrong: A review of research on aggression and sexual harassment in service encounters. *Aggression and Violent Behavior, 13,* 141–152.

Yakovlev, P., & Lecours, A.R. (1967). The myelination cycles of regional maturation of the brain. In A. Minkowski (Ed.), *Regional brain development in early life* (pp. 3–70). Oxford, UK: Blackwell Science.

Yalom, I. *Existential psychotherapy.* New York: Basic Books.

Yandrick, R.M. (1996). *Behavioral risk management: How to avoid preventable losses from mental health problems in the workplace.* San Francisco, CA: Jossey-Bass.

Ybarra, M.L., & Mitchell, K.J. (2004). Online aggressor/targets, aggressors, and targets: A comparison of associated youth characteristics. *Journal of Child Psychology and Psychiatry, 45,* 1308–1316.

Yesavage, J.A. (1983). Inpatient violence and the schizophrenic patient. *Acta Psychiatrica Scandinavica, 67,* 353–357.

Yesavage, J.A., & Zarcone, V. (1983). History of drug abuse and dangerous behavior in inpatient schizophrenics. *Journal of Clinical Psychiatry, 44,* 259–261.

Yeudall, L.T. (1977). Neuropsychological assessment of forensic disorder. *Canada's Mental Health, 25,* 7–15.

Yeudall, L.T., & Fromm-Auch, D. (1979). Neuropsychological impairments in various psychopathological populations. In J. Gruzelier & P. Flor-Henry (Eds.), *Hemisphere asymmetries of function in psychopathology* (pp. 401–428). New York: Elsevier.

Yeudall, L.T., Fromm-Auch, D., & Davies, P. (1982). Neuropsychological impairment of persistent delinquency. *Journal of Nervous and Mental Disease, 170,* 257–265.

Yochelson, S., & Samenow, S.E. (1976a). *The criminal personality, Vol. 1: A profile for change.* New York: Jason Aronson.

Yochelson, S., & Samenow, S.E. (1976b). *The criminal personality, Vol. 2: The change process.* New York: Jason Aronson.

Yokoo, J. (1986). The Japanese police campaign against the Boryokudan. *International Criminal Police Review, 395,* 38–45.

Young, J.L., & Griffith, E.E.H. (1995). Regulating pastoral counseling practice: The problem of sexual misconduct. *Bulletin of the American Academy of Psychiatry and the Law, 23,* 421–432.

Young, N.K. (1997). Effects of alcohol and other drugs on children. *Journal of Psychoactive Drugs, 29,* 23–42.

Young, S.E., Smolen, A., Corley, R.P., Krauter, K.S., DeFries, J.C., Crowley, T.J., & Hewitt, J.K. (2002). Dopamine transporter polymorphism associated with externalizing behavior problems in children. *American Journal of Medical Genetics, 114,* 144–149.

Young, S.E., Stallings, M.C., Corley, R.P., Krauter, K.S., & Hewitt, J.K. (2000). Genetic and environmental influences on behavioral disinhibition. *American Journal of Medical Genetics, 96,* 684–694.

Zagar, R., Arbit, J., Hughes, J., Buscell, R., & Busch, K. (1989). Developmental and disruptive behavior disorders among delinquents. *Journal of the American Academy of Child and Adolescent Psychiatry, 28,* 437–440.

Zahn, M.A., & Sagi, P.C. (1987). Stranger homicides in nine American cities. *Journal of Criminal Law and Criminology, 78,* 377–397.

Zakaria, F. (2003). Suicide bombers can be stopped. *Newsweek,* August 25, p. 57.

Zammit, S., Allebeck, P., Andreasson, S., Lundberg, I., & Lewis, G. (2002). Self-reported cannabis use as a risk factor for schizophrenia in Swedish conscripts of 1969: Historical cohort study. *British Medical Journal, 325,* 1199–1201.

Zanarini, M.C., Frankenburg, F.R., & Dubo, E.D. (1998). Axis I co-morbidity of borderline personality disorder. *American Journal of Psychiatry, 155,* 1733–1739.

Zander, T.K. (2005). Civil commitment without psychosis: The law's reliance on the weakest link in psychodiagnosis. *Journal of Sexual Offender Commitment: Science and the Law, 1,* 17–82.

Zasler, N.D. (1994). Sexual dysfunction. In J.M. Silver, S.C. Yudofsy & R.E. Hales (Eds.), *Neuropsychiatry of traumatic brain injury* (pp. 274–312). Washington DC: American Psychiatric Press.

Zatz, M.S., & Portillos, E.L. (2000). Voices from the barrio: Chicano/a gangs, families, and communities. *Criminology, 38,* 369–401.

Zavaliy, A.G. (2008). Absent, full and partial responsibility of the psychopaths. *Journal for the Theory of Social Behavior, 38,* 87–103.

Zawitz, M.W. (1994). *Violence between intimates.* Washington, DC: Bureau of Justice Statistics.

Zeglin, R. (1996). Now for the bad news: A teenage time bomb. *Time,* January 15, 48–55.

Zehr, H. (1990). *Changing lenses: A new focus for crime and justice.* Scottsdale, PA: Herald Press.

Zehr, H., & Mika, H. (1998). Fundamental concepts of restorative justice. *Contemporary Justice Review, 1,* 47–55.

Zelli, A., Huesman, L.R., & Cervone, D. (1995). Social inference and individual differences in aggression: Evidence for spontaneous judgments of hostility. *Aggressive Behavior, 21,* 405–417.

Zepp, J. (1996). *Domestic and sexual violence data collection: A report to Congress under the Violence Against Women Act.* Washington, DC: National Institute of Justice.

Zernova, M. (2009). Integrating the restorative and rehabilitative models: Lessons from one family group conferencing project. *Contemporary Justice Review, 12,* 59–75.

Zimbardo, P.G. (2007). *The Lucifer effect: Understanding how good people turn evil.* New York: Random House.

Zimbardo, P.G., Haney, C., Banks, W.C., & Jaffe, D. (1973). The mind is a formidable jailer: A Pirandellian prison. *New York Times Magazine,* April 8, p. 38.

Zimbardo, P.G., Maslach, C., & Haney, C. (2000). Reflections on the Stanford prison experiment: Genesis, transformations, consequences. In T. Blass (Ed.), *Obedience to authority: Current perspectives on the Milgram paradigm* (pp. 193–237). Mahwah, NJ: Erlbaum.

Zimmerman, M., & Coryell, W. (1989). DSM-III personality disorder diagnoses in a non-patient sample: Demographic correlates and co-morbidity. *Archives of General Psychiatry, 46,* 682–689.

Zimring, F.E. (1998). *American youth violence.* New York: Oxford University Press.

Zinzow, H.M., Grubaugh, A.L., Monnier, J., Suffoletta-Maierie, S., & Frueh, B.C. (2007). Trauma among female veterans: A critical review. *Trauma, Violence, and Abuse, 8,* 384–400.

Zisook, S., Byrd, D., Kuck, J., & Jeste, D.V. (1995). Command hallucinations in outpatients with schizophrenia. *Journal of Clinical Psychology, 56,* 462–465.

Zoccolillo, M., & Rogers, K. (1991). Characteristics and outcomes of hospitalized adolescent girls with conduct disorder. *Journal of the American Academy of Child and Adolescent Psychiatry, 30,* 973–981.

Zona, M.A., Palarea, R.E., & Lane, J.C. (1998). Psychiatric diagnosis and the offender-victim typology of stalking. In J.R. Meloy (Ed.), *The psychology of stalking: Clinical and forensic perspectives* (pp. 69–84). San Diego, CA: Academic Press.

Zona, M.A., Sharma, K.K., & Lane, J.C. (1993). A comparative study of ertotomanic and obsessional subjects in a forensic sample. *Journal of Forensic Sciences, 38,* 894–903.

Zubin, J., & Spring, B. (1977). Vulnerability: A new view of schizophrenia. *Journal of Abnormal Psychology, 86,* 103–126.

Zuckerman, M. (1979). *Sensation seeking: Beyond the optimum level of arousal.* Hillsdale: Erlbaum.

Zuckerman, M. (1990). The psychophysiology of sensation seeking. *Journal of Personality, 58,* 313–345.

Zuckerman, M. (1991). *Psychobiology of personality.* Cambridge: Cambridge University Press.

Zuckerman, M. (2002). Genetics of sensation seeking. In J. Benjamin, R.P. Ebstein & R.H. Belmaker (Eds.), *Molecular genetics and human personality* (pp. 177–209). Washington, DC: American Psychiatric Publishing.

Zuckerman, M., & Kuhlman, D.M. (2000). Personality and risk-taking: Common biosocial factors. *Journal of Personality, 68,* 999–1029.

Index

Criminal Psychology

Pathological gambling, 270
Pathological intoxication, 102
    and workplace violence, 294
Patricide, 217
Pavlov, Ivan, 67
Pediatric condition falsification syndrome,
    457
Pedophile typologies, 422–424
    fixated molester, 423
    morally indiscriminate pedophile, 423
    naïve/inadequate child molester, 423
    preferential child molester, 423
    regressed pedophile, 423,
    sadistic pedophile, 423–424
    seductive molester, 423
    sexually indiscriminate molester, 423
    situational child molester, 422–423
Pedophilia, 415, 418–424
    and child sexual abuse, 418–424
    evolutionary psychology of, 422
Peer victimization, 310
People v. Uncapher (2004), 43
Peptides, 36
Perjury, 23
Personality disorder clusters, 161
Personality disorders, 160–199 (*see* individual subtypes)
Petit jury, 13
Phenotype, 36
Phobias, 137
Pinel, Philipe, 181
Piquerism, 245
Pituitary gland, 44
Plaintiff, 5
Plea, 13
    guilty, 13
    no contest, 13
    nolo contendere, 13
    not guilty, 13
Plea bargaining, 13
PoliceOne.com, ix
Police Psychology, 6
Police response
    to citizens with antisocial personality disorder, 195–196
    to citizens with mood disorders, 156
    to citizens with personality disorders, 177–179

to domestic violence calls, 480–483
    to mentally retarded citizens, 111–112
    to severely mentally ill citizens, 129–130
Police stop, what to do, 9–11
Pontius, Anneliese, 104
Positron emission tomography (PET), 202
Postconcussion syndrome, 105–106
Postpartum depression, 153–154
Postpartum psychosis, 154
Postsynaptic membrane, 40
Posttraumatic stress disorder (PTSD),
    137–149
    and acute stress disorder, (ASD),
        138–139
    and battered woman syndrome, 79
    and combat addiction, 144
    and diminished capacity, 147–149
    and homicide, 230
    and military combat, 143
    and perpetrators of violence, 145–147
    and the insanity defense, 147–149
    and Vietnam veterans, 148
    and violent crime, 143–144
    criminal forensic aspects of, 147–149
    development and persistence of, 141–143
    diagnostic criteria for, 138
    dissociative flashbacks in, 143
    mood disorders in, 144
    sleep disorders in, 144
    symptoms of, 139–141
Practical Police Psychology
    book, vi
    web column, ix
Predatory murderers, 202
Preliminary hearing, 12
Premenstrual syndrome, 46
Preponderance of the evidence, 5
Prison, 14, 15
Prisonerization study, 376–377
Pritchard, James C., 182
Probable cause, 10
Probation officer, 14
Progesterone, 46
Projection, 65,
    in paranoia, 172
Projective identification, 165
Pro se, 87
Prosecutor, 12